D1637127

Linux Core Kernel
Commentary
2nd Edition

Scott Andrew Maxwell

Publisher

Steve Sayre

Acquisitions Editor

Jawahara Saidullah

Product Marketing Manager

Tracy Rooney

Project Editor

Toni Zuccarini Ackley

Technical Reviewer

Ivan McDonagh

Production Coordinator

Thomas Riker

Cover Designer

Jody Winkler

Layout Designer

April E. Nielsen

CD-ROM Developer

Chris Nusbaum

The Coriolis Group, LLC
14455 N. Hayden Road, Suite 220
Scottsdale, Arizona 85260

480/483-0192
FAX 480/483-0193
http://www.coriolis.com

Library of Congress Cataloging-in-Publication Data
Maxwell, Scott, 1971-
        Linux Core Kernel commentary / by Scott Maxwell.– 2nd ed.
            p.   cm.
        Includes index.
        ISBN 1-58880-149-7
        1. Linux.   2. Operating systems (Computers).   I. Title.
QA76.76.O63 M373337 2001
005.4'469–dc21

2001042333

Printed in the United States of America
10 9 8 7 6 5 4 3 2 1

CORIOLIS

The Coriolis Group, LLC • 14455 North Hayden Road, Suite 220 • Scottsdale, Arizona 85260

A Note from Coriolis

The Coriolis Technology Press was founded to create a very elite group of books: the ones you keep closest to your machine. In the real world, you have to choose the books you rely on every day *very* carefully, and we understand that.

To win a place for our books on that coveted shelf beside your PC, we guarantee several important qualities in every book we publish. These qualities are:

- *Technical accuracy*—It's no good if it doesn't work. Every Coriolis Technology Press book is reviewed by technical experts in the topic field, and is sent through several editing and proofreading passes in order to create the piece of work you now hold in your hands.

- *Innovative editorial design*—We've put years of research and refinement into the ways we present information in our books. Our books' editorial approach is uniquely designed to reflect the way people learn new technologies and search for solutions to technology problems.

- *Practical focus*—We put only pertinent information into our books and avoid any fluff. Every fact included between these two covers must serve the mission of the book as a whole.

- *Accessibility*—The information in a book is worthless unless you can find it quickly when you need it. We put a lot of effort into our indexes, and heavily cross-reference our chapters, to make it easy for you to move right to the information you need.

Here at The Coriolis Group we have been publishing and packaging books, technical journals, and training materials since 1989. We have put a lot of thought into our books; please write to us at **ctp@coriolis.com** and let us know what you think. We hope that you're happy with the book in your hands, and that in the future, when you reach for software development and networking information, you'll turn to one of our books first.

The Coriolis Group
14455 N. Hayden Road, Suite 220
Scottsdale, Arizona
85260

Email: ctp@coriolis.com
Phone: (480) 483-0192
Toll free: (800) 410-0192

Look for these related books from The Coriolis Group:

Kylix Power Solutions
by Don Taylor, Jim Mischel, and Tim Gentry

Open Source Development with CVS, 2nd Edition
by Karl Fogel and Moshe Bar

Linux Install and Configuration Little Black Book, 2nd Edition
by Dee-Ann LeBlanc

Linux Graphics Programming with SVGAlib
by Jay Link

Linux System Administration Black Book
by Dee-Ann LeBlanc

Also published by Coriolis Technology Press:

Perl Black Book, 2nd Edition
by Steven Holzner

PHP Black Book
by Peter Moulding

Java 2 Black Book
by Steven Holzner

Java 2 Network Protocols Black Book
by Al Williams

Samba Black Book
by Dominic Baines

For Candace.

❧

About the Author

Scott Andrew Maxwell got hooked on programming circa 1980 with a TRS-80 Model I Level 1. Subsequent computers included a Timex/Sinclair 1000, a Timex/Sinclair 1500, two Commodore VIC-20s, too many Commodore 64s to count, a Commodore 128, three Amigas, three Ataris, and other wonderful machines. Many of these still reside in his closet.

This obsession later led to a master's degree in Computer Science from the University of Illinois at Urbana-Champaign, as well as bachelor's degrees in Computer Science and English from East Carolina University.

Since graduating from the University of Illinois in 1994, he has been a Unix software developer at the Jet Propulsion Laboratory in Pasadena, CA, where he currently writes software that will be used to drive the next group of Mars rovers.

Acknowledgments

First, thanks to everyone at Coriolis—especially Toni Zuccarini Ackley, project editor, and Kevin Weeks, acquisitions editor, who suggested the second edition. Also thanks to Louise Kohl Leahy, copy editor, who had to change practically every occurrence of "may," "might," and "can" to one of the other two. Ivan McDonagh did double duty, serving as technical reviewer and helping with the grunt work of updating the second edition so that my wrists and I could have an easier time of it. Thank you, Ivan. This book is the stronger for their involvement. Anything that's still wrong with it is, of course, entirely my fault.

I'd also like to thank the other people who worked behind the scenes at Coriolis: Thomas Riker, Production Coordinator; April Nielsen, Layout Designer, Laura Wellander, Cover Designer; and Chris Nusbaum, CD-ROM Developer.

Thanks to everyone who reported an erratum in the first edition. In alphabetical order, thanks to Jonathan Corbet (whose own Linux book is due out soon), George Voon Hian Hee, Dan Kegel, Nate E. Kidwell, Ross Patterson, Rodrigo Real, Chris Sears, and one correspondent who asked to remain anonymous. Chris Sears also kindly allowed me to use the code cross-reference included on the CD-ROM, which was generated by a Perl script he wrote. Thanks twice, Chris.

Thanks to Mark Hahn, who let me know that an optimization I suggest in Chapter 9 won't be a win in future gcc releases, and Manfred Spraul, the source of an observation I refer to in Chapter 10.

If there were any justice in the world, there would be a special Congressional Medal of Honor reserved just for people who have to put up with me while I'm writing a book. Its first recipient would be my wife, Candace, who is much better than I deserve and who makes my life worth living. Anyone who can put up with me at times like this while earning her own master's degree, and still display more grace and good humor than anyone I know, was definitely the right woman to marry. Thanks, Sweetie.

The medal's second recipient would be my typist, who prefers to remain anonymous and who now knows more about Emacs (and the Linux kernel) than anyone should have to. Not only did she handle a difficult job with humor and aplomb, she also gave my wrists a much-needed chance to heal from a repetitive stress injury. As a bonus, she drew most of the figures, and she made them look a lot better than I would have. Thanks, nice lady.

Thanks to everyone who helped with the first edition and didn't return this time: Andrea Arcangeli, Robert Clarfield, Jon Gabriel, Bill McManus, Bryan James Phillippe, Joe Pranevich, Stephanie Wall, and Jody Winkler.

And finally, thanks to Richard Stallman, Linus Torvalds, and the thousands upon thousands of others whose work resulted in the Linux kernel and the GNU software that surrounds it. I said it in the first edition, and I'll say it again: The best is yet to come.

Table of Contents

Part II   Linux Core Kernel Commentary

Introduction

Thanks for buying *Linux Core Kernel Commentary, 2nd Edition*. This book is intended to provide programmers and students with more detailed and comprehensive comments on the Linux kernel code than have ever been provided before. I have examined the core code, and provided extensive comments on the most important functions, system calls, and data structures.

Linux Core Kernel Commentary, 2nd Edition is also intended to be an inside look at the structure and functioning of a popular and powerful operating system. The primary goals of this book are the following:

- To provide a printed version of the source for the core of a recent version of the kernel. (Version 2.4.1, which is examined in this book, was the most recent release as the book was written.)
- To provide a general overview of how each subsystem functions.
- To explore the principal functions and data structures in each subsystem.
- To suggest ways in which developers can improve and extend the kernel by modifying its code.

The last item in this list—customization—is one of the best reasons to study the kernel code. By understanding how the kernel works, you can write your own code to make it function the way you want. If you share your improvements with others, your code may even end up in the official kernel distribution, to be used by millions of people around the world.

Letting developers work on the code and extend its functionality is what free and open source software are all about. It's one of the primary reasons that Linux is the fastest-growing operating system in the world. From playing games, to surfing the Web, to providing large and small ISPs with a stable Web server platform, to tackling the largest scientific problems, Linux can do it all. And it got there because of people like you—developers motivated to study, learn from, and extend the system.

Is This Book for You?

Linux Core Kernel Commentary, 2nd Edition was written with the intermediate or advanced user in mind. This book assumes that you can read C code, that you aren't afraid to occasionally delve into a little assembler code, and that you want to understand how a fast, solid, reliable, robust, modern, real-world operating system works. Some readers may be programmers who want to contribute their own improvements and additions to the ongoing Linux kernel development effort. Among the topics that are covered, are:

- Process creation and scheduling
- System calls
- How signals are generated and delivered
- Kernel initialization
- General tradeoffs between simplicity, speed, and other Linux design goals
- How the kernel handles hardware interrupts
- Memory management
- System V Interprocess Communication (IPC)
- Symmetric Multiprocessing (SMP)
- Tunable kernel parameters

How to Use This Book

Feel free to navigate this book in the way that best suits your needs. Because this book is designed to be a reference resource, it isn't necessarily intended to be read from start to finish. Because lines of source code point to commentary about them, and lines of commentary point back to the source code, you can approach the kernel from either direction.

The *Commentary* Philosophy

Written by experienced professionals, books in the Coriolis *Commentary* series examine the code and present extensive comments on it, highlighting the most important features and functions. The key to this series is its unique two-part format: In Part I, you'll find all the code discussed in the book; Part II is a cross-referenced discussion of the code presented in Part I. The inspiration for the *Commentary* series was the vastly popular *Lions' Commentary on Unix* by John Lions, which gives an inside look at the workings of an early version of AT&T's Unix operating system.

Following the main body of the book, you'll find an appendix containing the complete GNU General Public License (GPL), which is the software license used by the kernel. Finally, the book concludes with an index that you can use to search for specific terms or topics, which will make using this book as a reference tool even quicker and more effective.

My wife likens this book to the best travel books—the ones that go beyond a breezy overview of the major sights and encourage you to get the feel of the place, to hang out in the bars and learn to speak the language. This isn't the only Linux kernel book that can give you an overview of the major subsystems, but as a programmer, you know that what really matters is the code itself. This book brings you that code and guides you through it better than any other. I don't pretend to teach you everything there is to know about the Linux kernel; like most people who hack the kernel, I don't know everything about it myself. Rather, my goal is to give you the feel of the place, to demystify the code for you so that you'll have the confidence to strike out on your own. If this book achieves that, then I've done my job.

I welcome your feedback on this book. You can either email The Coriolis Group at **ctp@coriolis.com** or email me directly at **lckc@ScottMaxwell.org**. Errata, updates, and more are available at **www.ScottMaxwell.org/lckc/** and **www.coriolis.com**.

Part I

Linux Core Kernel Code

arch/i386/kernel/apic.c

```
1 /*
2 *        Local APIC handling, local APIC timers
3 *
4 *        (c) 1999, 2000 Ingo Molnar <mingo@redhat.com>
5 *
6 * Fixes
7 * Maciej W. Rozycki: Bits for genuine 82489DX APICs;
8 *                       thanks to Eric Gilmore
9 *                       and Rolf G. Tews
10 *                       for testing these extensively.
11 * Maciej W. Rozycki: Various updates and fixes.
12 */
13
14 #include <linux/config.h>
15 #include <linux/init.h>
16
17 #include <linux/mm.h>
18 #include <linux/irq.h>
19 #include <linux/delay.h>
20 #include <linux/bootmem.h>
21 #include <linux/smp_lock.h>
22 #include <linux/interrupt.h>
23 #include <linux/mc146818rtc.h>
24 #include <linux/kernel_stat.h>
25
26 #include <asm/smp.h>
27 #include <asm/mtrr.h>
28 #include <asm/mpspec.h>
29 #include <asm/pgalloc.h>
30
31 int prof_multiplier[NR_CPUS] = { 1, };
32 int prof_old_multiplier[NR_CPUS] = { 1, };
33 int prof_counter[NR_CPUS] = { 1, };
34
35 int get_maxlvt(void)
36 {
37   unsigned int v, ver, maxlvt;
38
39   v = apic_read(APIC_LVR);
40   ver = GET_APIC_VERSION(v);
41   /* 82489DXs do not report # of LVT entries. */
42   maxlvt = APIC_INTEGRATED(ver) ? GET_APIC_MAXLVT(v) : 2;
43   return maxlvt;
44 }
45
46 static void clear_local_APIC(void)
47 {
48   int maxlvt;
49   unsigned long v;
50
51   maxlvt = get_maxlvt();
52
53   /* Careful: we have to set masks only first to deassert
54    * any level-triggered sources.  */
55   v = apic_read(APIC_LVTT);
56   apic_write_around(APIC_LVTT, v | APIC_LVT_MASKED);
57   v = apic_read(APIC_LVT0);
58   apic_write_around(APIC_LVT0, v | APIC_LVT_MASKED);
59   v = apic_read(APIC_LVT1);
60   apic_write_around(APIC_LVT1, v | APIC_LVT_MASKED);
61   if (maxlvt >= 3) {
62     v = apic_read(APIC_LVTERR);
63     apic_write_around(APIC_LVTERR, v | APIC_LVT_MASKED);
64   }
65   if (maxlvt >= 4) {
66     v = apic_read(APIC_LVTPC);
67     apic_write_around(APIC_LVTPC, v | APIC_LVT_MASKED);
68   }
69
70   /* Clean APIC state for other OSs: */
71   apic_write_around(APIC_LVTT, APIC_LVT_MASKED);
72   apic_write_around(APIC_LVT0, APIC_LVT_MASKED);
73   apic_write_around(APIC_LVT1, APIC_LVT_MASKED);
74   if (maxlvt >= 3)
75     apic_write_around(APIC_LVTERR, APIC_LVT_MASKED);
76   if (maxlvt >= 4)
77     apic_write_around(APIC_LVTPC, APIC_LVT_MASKED);
78 }
79
80 void __init connect_bsp_APIC(void)
81 {
82   if (pic_mode) {
83     /* Do not trust the local APIC being empty at bootup.
84      */
85     clear_local_APIC();
86     /* PIC mode, enable symmetric IO mode in the IMCR,
87      * i.e. connect BSP's local APIC to INT and NMI
88      * lines.  */
89     printk("leaving PIC mode,"
90            " enabling symmetric IO mode.\n");
91     outb(0x70, 0x22);
92     outb(0x01, 0x23);
93   }
94 }
```

```
95
96 void disconnect_bsp_APIC(void)
97 {
98   if (pic_mode) {
99     /* Put the board back into PIC mode (has an effect
100       * only on certain older boards).  Note that APIC
101       * interrupts, including IPIs, won't work beyond this
102       * point!  The only exception are INIT IPIs.  */
103     printk("disabling symmetric IO mode,"
104            " entering PIC mode.\n");
105     outb(0x70, 0x22);
106     outb(0x00, 0x23);
107   }
108 }
109
110 void disable_local_APIC(void)
111 {
112   unsigned long value;
113
114   clear_local_APIC();
115
116   /* Disable APIC (implies clearing of registers for
117    * 82489DX!).  */
118   value = apic_read(APIC_SPIV);
119   value &= ~(1 << 8);
120   apic_write_around(APIC_SPIV, value);
121 }
122
123 /* This is to verify that we're looking at a real local
124  * APIC.  Check these against your board if the CPUs
125  * aren't getting started for no apparent reason. */
126 int __init verify_local_APIC(void)
127 {
128   unsigned int reg0, reg1;
129
130   /* The version register is read-only in a real APIC. */
131   reg0 = apic_read(APIC_LVR);
132   Dprintk("Getting VERSION: %x\n", reg0);
133   apic_write(APIC_LVR, reg0 ^ APIC_LVR_MASK);
134   reg1 = apic_read(APIC_LVR);
135   Dprintk("Getting VERSION: %x\n", reg1);
136
137   /* The two version reads above should print the same
138    * numbers.  If the second one is different, then we
139    * poke at a non-APIC.  */
140   if (reg1 != reg0)
141     return 0;
142
143   /* Check if the version looks reasonably.  */
144   reg1 = GET_APIC_VERSION(reg0);
145   if (reg1 == 0x00 || reg1 == 0xff)
146     return 0;
147   reg1 = get_maxlvt();
148   if (reg1 < 0x02 || reg1 == 0xff)
149     return 0;
150
151   /* The ID register is read/write in a real APIC.  */
152   reg0 = apic_read(APIC_ID);
153   Dprintk("Getting ID: %x\n", reg0);
154   apic_write(APIC_ID, reg0 ^ APIC_ID_MASK);
155   reg1 = apic_read(APIC_ID);
156   Dprintk("Getting ID: %x\n", reg1);
157   apic_write(APIC_ID, reg0);
158   if (reg1 != (reg0 ^ APIC_ID_MASK))
159     return 0;
160
161   /* The next two are just to see if we have sane values.
162    * They're only really relevant if we're in Virtual
163    * Wire compatibility mode, but most boxes are anymore.
164    */
165   reg0 = apic_read(APIC_LVT0);
166   Dprintk("Getting LVT0: %x\n", reg0);
167   reg1 = apic_read(APIC_LVT1);
168   Dprintk("Getting LVT1: %x\n", reg1);
169
170   return 1;
171 }
172
173 void __init sync_Arb_IDs(void)
174 {
175   /* Wait for idle.  */
176   apic_wait_icr_idle();
177
178   Dprintk("Synchronizing Arb IDs.\n");
179   apic_write_around(APIC_ICR,
180       APIC_DEST_ALLINC | APIC_INT_LEVELTRIG |
181       APIC_DM_INIT);
182 }
183
184 extern void __error_in_apic_c(void);
185
186 void __init setup_local_APIC(void)
187 {
188   unsigned long value, ver, maxlvt;
189
190   value = apic_read(APIC_LVR);
```

```
191    ver = GET_APIC_VERSION(value);
192
193    if ((SPURIOUS_APIC_VECTOR & 0x0f) != 0x0f)
194      __error_in_apic_c();
195
196    /* Double-check wether this APIC is really registered.
197     */
198    if (!test_bit(GET_APIC_ID(apic_read(APIC_ID)),
199          &phys_cpu_present_map)) BUG();
200
201    /* Intel recommends to set DFR, LDR and TPR before
202     * enabling an APIC.  See e.g. "AP-388 82489DX User's
203     * Manual" (Intel document number 292116).  So here it
204     * goes...  */
205
206    /* Put the APIC into flat delivery mode.  Must be "all
207     * ones" explicitly for 82489DX.  */
208    apic_write_around(APIC_DFR, 0xffffffff);
209
210    /* Set up the logical destination ID.  */
211    value = apic_read(APIC_LDR);
212    value &= ~APIC_LDR_MASK;
213    value |= (1 << (smp_processor_id() + 24));
214    apic_write_around(APIC_LDR, value);
215
216    /* Set Task Priority to 'accept all'. We never change
217     * this later on.  */
218    value = apic_read(APIC_TASKPRI);
219    value &= ~APIC_TPRI_MASK;
220    apic_write_around(APIC_TASKPRI, value);
221
222    /* Now that we are all set up, enable the APIC */
223    value = apic_read(APIC_SPIV);
224    value &= ~APIC_VECTOR_MASK;
225    /* Enable APIC */
226    value |= (1 << 8);
227
228    /* Some unknown Intel IO/APIC (or APIC) errata is
229     * biting us with certain networking cards. If high
230     * frequency interrupts are happening on a particular
231     * IOAPIC pin, plus the IOAPIC routing entry is
232     * masked/unmasked at a high rate as well then sooner
233     * or later IOAPIC line gets 'stuck', no more
234     * interrupts are received from the device. If focus
235     * CPU is disabled then the hang goes away, oh well :-(
236     *
237     * [ This bug can be reproduced easily with a
238     * level-triggered PCI Ne2000 networking cards and
```

```
239     * PII/PIII processors, dual BX chipset. ] */
240 #if 0
241    /* Enable focus processor (bit==0) */
242    value &= ~(1 << 9);
243 #else
244    /* Disable focus processor (bit==1) */
245    value |= (1 << 9);
246 #endif
247    /* Set spurious IRQ vector */
248    value |= SPURIOUS_APIC_VECTOR;
249    apic_write_around(APIC_SPIV, value);
250
251    /* Set up LVT0, LVT1:
252     *
253     * set up through-local-APIC on the BP's LINT0. This is
254     * not strictly necessery in pure symmetric-IO mode,
255     * but sometimes we delegate interrupts to the 8259A.
256     */
257    /* TODO: set up through-local-APIC from
258     * through-I/O-APIC? —macro */
259    value = apic_read(APIC_LVT0) & APIC_LVT_MASKED;
260    if (!smp_processor_id() && (pic_mode || !value)) {
261      value = APIC_DM_EXTINT;
262      printk("enabled ExtINT on CPU#%d\n",
263          smp_processor_id());
264    } else {
265      value = APIC_DM_EXTINT | APIC_LVT_MASKED;
266      printk("masked ExtINT on CPU#%d\n",
267          smp_processor_id());
268    }
269    apic_write_around(APIC_LVT0, value);
270
271    /* only the BP should see the LINT1 NMI signal,
272     * obviously.  */
273    if (!smp_processor_id())
274      value = APIC_DM_NMI;
275    else
276      value = APIC_DM_NMI | APIC_LVT_MASKED;
277    if (!APIC_INTEGRATED(ver))    /* 82489DX */
278      value |= APIC_LVT_LEVEL_TRIGGER;
279    apic_write_around(APIC_LVT1, value);
280
281    if (APIC_INTEGRATED(ver)) {    /* !82489DX */
282      maxlvt = get_maxlvt();
283      if (maxlvt > 3)              /* Due to the Pentium
284                                   * erratum 3AP. */
285        apic_write(APIC_ESR, 0);
286      value = apic_read(APIC_ESR);
```

```
287      printk("ESR value before enabling vector: %081x\n",
288          value);
289
290      value = ERROR_APIC_VECTOR;   // enables sending
291                                   // errors
292      apic_write_around(APIC_LVTERR, value);
293      /* spec says clear errors after enabling vector. */
294      if (maxlvt > 3)
295          apic_write(APIC_ESR, 0);
296      value = apic_read(APIC_ESR);
297      printk("ESR value after enabling vector: %081x\n",
298          value);
299  } else
300      printk("No ESR for 82489DX.\n");
301 }
302
303 void __init init_apic_mappings(void)
304 {
305   unsigned long apic_phys;
306
307   if (smp_found_config) {
308      apic_phys = mp_lapic_addr;
309   } else {
310      /* set up a fake all zeroes page to simulate the
311       * local APIC and another one for the IO-APIC. We
312       * could use the real zero-page, but it's safer this
313       * way if some buggy code writes to this page ... */
314      apic_phys =
315          (unsigned long) alloc_bootmem_pages(PAGE_SIZE);
316      apic_phys = __pa(apic_phys);
317   }
318   set_fixmap_nocache(FIX_APIC_BASE, apic_phys);
319   Dprintk("mapped APIC to %081x (%081x)\n", APIC_BASE,
320      apic_phys);
321
322   /* Fetch the APIC ID of the BSP in case we have a
323    * default configuration (or the MP table is broken).
324    */
325   if (boot_cpu_id == -1U)
326      boot_cpu_id = GET_APIC_ID(apic_read(APIC_ID));
327
328 #ifdef CONFIG_X86_IO_APIC
329   {
330     unsigned long ioapic_phys, idx = FIX_IO_APIC_BASE_0;
331     int i;
332
333     for (i = 0; i < nr_ioapics; i++) {
334         if (smp_found_config) {
335             ioapic_phys = mp_ioapics[i].mpc_apicaddr;
336         } else {
337             ioapic_phys = (unsigned long)
338                 alloc_bootmem_pages(PAGE_SIZE);
339             ioapic_phys = __pa(ioapic_phys);
340         }
341         set_fixmap_nocache(idx, ioapic_phys);
342         Dprintk("mapped IOAPIC to %081x (%081x)\n",
343             __fix_to_virt(idx), ioapic_phys);
344         idx++;
345     }
346   }
347 #endif
348 }
349
350 /* This part sets up the APIC 32 bit clock in LVTT1, with
351  * HZ interrupts per second. We assume that the caller
352  * has already set up the local APIC.
353  *
354  * The APIC timer is not exactly sync with the external
355  * timer chip, it closely follows bus clocks.  */
356 /* The timer chip is already set up at HZ interrupts per
357  * second here, but we do not accept timer interrupts
358  * yet. We only allow the BP to calibrate.  */
359 static unsigned int __init get_8254_timer_count(void)
360 {
361   extern spinlock_t i8253_lock;
362   unsigned long flags;
363
364   unsigned int count;
365
366   spin_lock_irqsave(&i8253_lock, flags);
367
368   outb_p(0x00, 0x43);
369   count = inb_p(0x40);
370   count |= inb_p(0x40) << 8;
371
372   spin_unlock_irqrestore(&i8253_lock, flags);
373
374   return count;
375 }
376
377 void __init wait_8254_wraparound(void)
378 {
379   unsigned int curr_count, prev_count = ~0;
380   int delta;
381
382   curr_count = get_8254_timer_count();
```

```
383
384   do {
385     prev_count = curr_count;
386     curr_count = get_8254_timer_count();
387     delta = curr_count - prev_count;
388
389     /* This limit for delta seems arbitrary, but it
390      * isn't, it's slightly above the level of error a
391      * buggy Mercury/Neptune chipset timer can cause. */
392   } while (delta < 300);
393 }
394
395 /* This function sets up the local APIC timer, with a
396  * timeout of 'clocks' APIC bus clock. During calibration
397  * we actually call this function twice on the boot CPU,
398  * once with a bogus timeout value, second time for
399  * real. The other (noncalibrating) CPUs call this
400  * function only once, with the real, calibrated value.
401  *
402  * We do reads before writes even if unnecessary, to get
403  * around the P5 APIC double write bug. */
404 #define APIC_DIVISOR 16
405
406 void __setup_APIC_LVTT(unsigned int clocks)
407 {
408   unsigned int lvtt1_value, tmp_value;
409
410   lvtt1_value =
411       SET_APIC_TIMER_BASE(APIC_TIMER_BASE_DIV) |
412       APIC_LVT_TIMER_PERIODIC | LOCAL_TIMER_VECTOR;
413   apic_write_around(APIC_LVTT, lvtt1_value);
414
415   /* Divide PICLK by 16 */
416   tmp_value = apic_read(APIC_TDCR);
417   apic_write_around(APIC_TDCR, (tmp_value
418                                 & ~(APIC_TDR_DIV_1 |
419                                     APIC_TDR_DIV_TMBASE))
420                                 | APIC_TDR_DIV_16);
421
422   apic_write_around(APIC_TMICT, clocks / APIC_DIVISOR);
423 }
424
425 void setup_APIC_timer(void *data)
426 {
427   unsigned int clocks =
428       (unsigned int) data, slice, t0, t1;
429   unsigned long flags;
430   int delta;
431
432   __save_flags(flags);
433   __sti();
434   /* ok, Intel has some smart code in their APIC that
435    * knows if a CPU was in 'hlt' lowpower mode, and this
436    * increases its APIC arbitration priority. To avoid
437    * the external timer IRQ APIC event being in synchron
438    * with the APIC clock we introduce an interrupt skew
439    * to spread out timer events.
440    *
441    * The number of slices within a 'big' timeslice is
442    * smp_num_cpus+1 */
443   slice = clocks / (smp_num_cpus + 1);
444   printk("cpu: %d, clocks: %d, slice: %d\n",
445       smp_processor_id(), clocks, slice);
446
447   /* Wait for IRQ0's slice: */
448   wait_8254_wraparound();
449
450   __setup_APIC_LVTT(clocks);
451
452   t0 = apic_read(APIC_TMICT) * APIC_DIVISOR;
453   /* Wait till TMCCT gets reloaded from TMICT... */
454   do {
455     t1 = apic_read(APIC_TMCCT) * APIC_DIVISOR;
456     delta = (int)
457       (t0 - t1 - slice * (smp_processor_id() + 1));
458   } while (delta >= 0);
459   /* Now wait for our slice for real. */
460   do {
461     t1 = apic_read(APIC_TMCCT) * APIC_DIVISOR;
462     delta = (int)
463       (t0 - t1 - slice * (smp_processor_id() + 1));
464   } while (delta < 0);
465
466   __setup_APIC_LVTT(clocks);
467
468   printk("CPU%d<T0:%d,T1:%d,D:%d,S:%d,C:%d>\n",
469       smp_processor_id(), t0, t1, delta, slice, clocks);
470
471   __restore_flags(flags);
472 }
473
474 /* In this function we calibrate APIC bus clocks to the
475  * external timer. Unfortunately we cannot use jiffies
476  * and the timer irq to calibrate, since some later
477  * bootup code depends on getting the first irq? Ugh.
478  *
```

```
479    * We want to do the calibration only once since we
480    * want to have local timer irqs syncron. CPUs connected
481    * by the same APIC bus have the very same bus frequency.
482    * And we want to have irqs off anyways, no accidental
483    * APIC irq that way.  */
484  int __init calibrate_APIC_clock(void)
485  {
486    unsigned long long t1 = 0, t2 = 0;
487    long tt1, tt2;
488    long result;
489    int i;
490    const int LOOPS = HZ / 10;
491
492    printk("calibrating APIC timer ...\n");
493
494    /* Put whatever arbitrary (but long enough) timeout
495     * value into the APIC clock, we just want to get the
496     * counter running for calibration.  */
497    __setup_APIC_LVTT(1000000000);
498
499    /* The timer chip counts down to zero. Let's wait for a
500     * wraparound to start exact measurement: (the current
501     * tick might have been already half done) */
502    wait_8254_wraparound();
503
504    /* We wrapped around just now. Let's start: */
505    if (cpu_has_tsc)
506      rdtscll(t1);
507    tt1 = apic_read(APIC_TMCCT);
508
509    /* Let's wait LOOPS wraprounds: */
510    for (i = 0; i < LOOPS; i++)
511      wait_8254_wraparound();
512
513    tt2 = apic_read(APIC_TMCCT);
514    if (cpu_has_tsc)
515      rdtscll(t2);
516
517    /* The APIC bus clock counter is 32 bits only, it might
518     * have overflown, but note that we use signed longs,
519     * thus no extra care needed.
520     *
521     * underflown to be exact, as the timer counts down ;)
522     */
523    result = (tt1 - tt2) * APIC_DIVISOR / LOOPS;
524
525    if (cpu_has_tsc)
```

```
526      printk("..... CPU clock speed is %ld.%04ld MHz.\n",
527          ((long) (t2 - t1) / LOOPS) / (1000000 / HZ),
528          ((long) (t2 - t1) / LOOPS) % (1000000 / HZ));
529
530    printk
531        ("..... host bus clock speed is %ld.%04ld MHz.\n",
532        result / (1000000 / HZ), result % (1000000 / HZ));
533
534    return result;
535  }
536
537  static unsigned int calibration_result;
538
539  void __init setup_APIC_clocks(void)
540  {
541    __cli();
542
543    calibration_result = calibrate_APIC_clock();
544    /* Now set up the timer for real.  */
545    setup_APIC_timer((void *) calibration_result);
546
547    __sti();
548
549    /* and update all other cpus */
550    smp_call_function(setup_APIC_timer,
551        (void *) calibration_result, 1, 1);
552  }
553
554  /* the frequency of the profiling timer can be changed by
555   * writing a multiplier value into /proc/profile.  */
556  int setup_profiling_timer(unsigned int multiplier)
557  {
558    int i;
559
560    /* Sanity check. [at least 500 APIC cycles should be
561     * between APIC interrupts as a rule of thumb, to avoid
562     * irqs flooding us] */
563    if ((!multiplier) ||
564        (calibration_result / multiplier < 500))
565      return -EINVAL;
566
567    /* Set the new multiplier for each CPU. CPUs don't
568     * start using the new values until the next timer
569     * interrupt in which they do process accounting. At
570     * that time they also adjust their APIC timers
571     * accordingly.  */
572    for (i = 0; i < NR_CPUS; ++i)
573      prof_multiplier[i] = multiplier;
```

```
574
575   return 0;
576 }
577
578 #undef APIC_DIVISOR
579
580 /* Local timer interrupt handler. It does both profiling
581  * and process statistics/rescheduling.
582  *
583  * We do profiling in every local tick,
584  * statistics/rescheduling happen only every 'profiling
585  * multiplier' ticks. The default multiplier is 1 and it
586  * can be changed by writing the new multiplier value
587  * into /proc/profile.  */
588 inline void smp_local_timer_interrupt(struct pt_regs
589     *regs)
590 {
591   int user = user_mode(regs);
592   int cpu = smp_processor_id();
593
594   /* The profiling function is SMP safe. (nothing can
595    * mess around with "current", and the profiling
596    * counters are updated with atomic operations). This
597    * is especially useful with a profiling multiplier !=
598    * 1 */
599   if (!user)
600     x86_do_profile(regs->eip);
601
602   if (—prof_counter[cpu] <= 0) {
603     /* The multiplier may have changed since the last
604      * time we got to this point as a result of the user
605      * writing to /proc/profile. In this case we need to
606      * adjust the APIC timer accordingly.
607      *
608      * Interrupts are already masked off at this point.*/
609     prof_counter[cpu] = prof_multiplier[cpu];
610     if (prof_counter[cpu] != prof_old_multiplier[cpu]) {
611       __setup_APIC_LVTT(calibration_result /
612           prof_counter[cpu]);
613       prof_old_multiplier[cpu] = prof_counter[cpu];
614     }
615 #ifdef CONFIG_SMP
616     update_process_times(user);
617 #endif
618   }
619
620   /* We take the 'long' return path, and there every
621    * subsystem grabs the apropriate locks (kernel lock/
```

p 691 (marker at line 588)

```
622    * irq lock).
623    *
624    * we might want to decouple profiling from the 'long
625    * path', and do the profiling totally in assembly.
626    *
627    * Currently this isn't too much of an issue
628    * (performance wise), we can take more than 100K local
629    * irqs per second on a 100 MHz P5.  */
630 }
631
632 /* Local APIC timer interrupt. This is the most natural
633  * way for doing local interrupts, but local timer
634  * interrupts can be emulated by broadcast interrupts
635  * too. [in case the hw doesnt support APIC timers]
636  *
637  * [ if a single-CPU system runs an SMP kernel then we
638  * call the local interrupt as well. Thus we cannot
639  * inline the local irq ... ] */
640 unsigned int apic_timer_irqs[NR_CPUS];
641
642 void smp_apic_timer_interrupt(struct pt_regs *regs)
643 {
644   int cpu = smp_processor_id();
645
646   /* the NMI deadlock-detector uses this.  */
647   apic_timer_irqs[cpu]++;
648
649   /* NOTE! We'd better ACK the irq immediately, because
650    * timer handling can be slow.  */
651   ack_APIC_irq();
652   /* update_process_times() expects us to have done
653    * irq_enter().  Besides, if we don't timer interrupts
654    * ignore the global interrupt lock, which is the
655    * WrongThing (tm) to do.  */
656   irq_enter(cpu, 0);
657   smp_local_timer_interrupt(regs);
658   irq_exit(cpu, 0);
659 }
660
661 /* This interrupt should _never_ happen with our APIC/SMP
662  * architecture */
663 asmlinkage void smp_spurious_interrupt(void)
664 {
665   unsigned long v;
666
667   /* Check if this really is a spurious interrupt and ACK
668    * it if it is a vectored one.  Just in case...
669    * Spurious interrupts should not be ACKed.  */
```

```
670    v = apic_read(APIC_ISR +
671                    ((SPURIOUS_APIC_VECTOR & ~0x1f) >> 1));
672    if (v & (1 << (SPURIOUS_APIC_VECTOR & 0x1f)))
673      ack_APIC_irq();
674
675    /* see sw-dev-man vol 3, chapter 7.4.13.5 */
676    printk(KERN_INFO "spurious APIC interrupt on CPU#%d,"
677            " should never happen.\n", smp_processor_id());
678  }
679
680  /* This interrupt should never happen with our APIC/SMP
681   * architecture */
682  asmlinkage void smp_error_interrupt(void)
683  {
684    unsigned long v, v1;
685
686    /* First tickle the hardware, only then report what
687     * went on. — REW */
688    v = apic_read(APIC_ESR);
689    apic_write(APIC_ESR, 0);
690    v1 = apic_read(APIC_ESR);
691    ack_APIC_irq();
692    irq_err_count++;
693
694    /* Here is what the APIC error bits mean: 0: Send CS
695     * error 1: Receive CS error 2: Send accept error 3:
696     * Receive accept error 4: Reserved 5: Send illegal
697     * vector 6: Received illegal vector 7: Illegal
698     * register address */
699    printk(KERN_ERR "APIC error on CPU%d: %02lx(%02lx)\n",
700          smp_processor_id(), v, v1);
701  }
```

arch/i386/kernel/entry.S

```
702  /*
703   *  linux/arch/i386/entry.S
704   *
705   *  Copyright (C) 1991, 1992  Linus Torvalds
706   */
707
708  /*
709   * entry.S contains the system-call and fault low-level
710   * handling routines.  This also contains the
711   * timer-interrupt handler, as well as all interrupts and
712   * faults that can result in a task-switch.
713   *
714   * NOTE: This code handles signal-recognition, which
715   * happens every time after a timer-interrupt and after
716   * each system call.
717   *
718   * I changed all the .align"'s to 4 (16 byte alignment),
719   * as that's faster on a 486.
720   *
721   * Stack layout in 'ret_from_system_call':
722   *    ptrace needs to have all regs on the stack.
723   *    if the order here is changed, it needs to be
724   *    updated in fork.c:copy_process, signal.c:do_signal,
725   *    ptrace.c and ptrace.h
726   *
727   *       0(%esp) - %ebx
728   *       4(%esp) - %ecx
729   *       8(%esp) - %edx
730   *       C(%esp) - %esi
731   *      10(%esp) - %edi
732   *      14(%esp) - %ebp
733   *      18(%esp) - %eax
734   *      1C(%esp) - %ds
735   *      20(%esp) - %es
736   *      24(%esp) - orig_eax
737   *      28(%esp) - %eip
738   *      2C(%esp) - %cs
739   *      30(%esp) - %eflags
740   *      34(%esp) - %oldesp
741   *      38(%esp) - %oldss
742   *
743   * "current" is in register %ebx during any slow entries.
744   */
745
746  #include <linux/config.h>
747  #include <linux/sys.h>
748  #include <linux/linkage.h>
749  #include <asm/segment.h>
750  #define ASSEMBLY
751  #include <asm/smp.h>
752
753  EBX          = 0x00
754  ECX          = 0x04
755  EDX          = 0x08
756  ESI          = 0x0C
757  EDI          = 0x10
758  EBP          = 0x14
759  EAX          = 0x18
760  DS           = 0x1C
761  ES           = 0x20
762  ORIG_EAX     = 0x24
```

```
763 EIP              = 0x28
764 CS               = 0x2C
765 EFLAGS           = 0x30
766 OLDESP           = 0x34
767 OLDSS            = 0x38
768
769 CF_MASK          = 0x00000001
770 IF_MASK          = 0x00000200
771 NT_MASK          = 0x00004000
772 VM_MASK          = 0x00020000
773
774 /*
775  * these are offsets into the task-struct.
776  */
777 state            = 0
778 flags            = 4
779 sigpending       = 8
780 addr_limit       = 12
781 exec_domain      = 16
782 need_resched     = 20
783 tsk_ptrace       = 24
784 processor        = 52
785
786 ENOSYS = 38
787
788
789 #define SAVE_ALL                             \
790   cld;                                       \
791   pushl %es;                                 \
792   pushl %ds;                                 \
793   pushl %eax;                                \
794   pushl %ebp;                                \
795   pushl %edi;                                \
796   pushl %esi;                                \
797   pushl %edx;                                \
798   pushl %ecx;                                \
799   pushl %ebx;                                \
800   movl $(__KERNEL_DS),%edx;                  \
801   movl %edx,%ds;                             \
802   movl %edx,%es;
803
804 #define RESTORE_ALL                          \
805   popl %ebx;                                 \
806   popl %ecx;                                 \
807   popl %edx;                                 \
808   popl %esi;                                 \
809   popl %edi;                                 \
810   popl %ebp;                                 \
```

```
811   popl %eax;                                           \
812 1:    popl %ds;                                        \
813 2:    popl %es;                                        \
814   addl $4,%esp;                                         \
815 3:    iret;                                            \
816 .section .fixup,"ax";                                  \
817 4:    movl $0,(%esp);                                  \
818   jmp 1b;                                               \
819 5:    movl $0,(%esp);                                  \
820   jmp 2b;                                               \
821 6:    pushl %ss;                                       \
822   popl %ds;                                             \
823   pushl %ss;                                            \
824   popl %es;                                             \
825   pushl $11;                                            \
826   call do_exit;                                         \
827 .previous;                                              \
828 .section __ex_table,"a";                               \
829   .align 4;                                             \
830   .long 1b,4b;                                          \
831   .long 2b,5b;                                          \
832   .long 3b,6b;                                          \
833 .previous
834
835 #define GET_CURRENT(reg)                     \
836   movl $-8192, reg;                          \
837   andl %esp, reg
838
839 ENTRY(lcall7)
840   pushfl     # We get a different stack layout with call
841   pushl %eax # gates, which has to be cleaned up later..
842   SAVE_ALL              # due to call gates,
843   movl EIP(%esp),%eax   # this is eflags, not eip..
844   movl CS(%esp),%edx    # this is eip..
845   movl EFLAGS(%esp),%ecx # and this is cs..
846   movl %eax,EFLAGS(%esp) #
847   movl %edx,EIP(%esp)   # Now we move them to their
848   movl %ecx,CS(%esp)    # "normal" places
849   movl %esp,%ebx
850   pushl %ebx
851   andl $-8192,%ebx      # GET_CURRENT
852   movl exec_domain(%ebx),%edx  # Get the execution domain
853   movl 4(%edx),%edx     # Get lcall7 handler for domain
854   pushl $0x7
855   call *%edx
856   addl $4, %esp
857   popl %eax
858   jmp ret_from_sys_call
```

p 567 → 839

```
859
860 ENTRY(lcall27)
861   pushfl      # We get a different stack layout with call
862   pushl %eax  # gates, which has to be cleaned up later..
863   SAVE_ALL            # due to call gates,
864   movl EIP(%esp),%eax    # this is eflags, not eip..
865   movl CS(%esp),%edx     # this is eip..
866   movl EFLAGS(%esp),%ecx # and this is cs..
867   movl %eax,EFLAGS(%esp) #
868   movl %edx,EIP(%esp)    # Now we move them to their
869   movl %ecx,CS(%esp)     # "normal" places
870   movl %esp,%ebx
871   pushl %ebx
872   andl $-8192,%ebx       # GET_CURRENT
873   movl exec_domain(%ebx),%edx # Get the execution domain
874   movl 4(%edx),%edx      # Get lcall7 handler for domain
875   pushl $0x27
876   call *%edx
877   addl $4, %esp
878   popl %eax
879   jmp ret_from_sys_call
880
881
882 ENTRY(ret_from_fork)
883   pushl %ebx
884   call SYMBOL_NAME(schedule_tail)
885   addl $4, %esp
886   GET_CURRENT(%ebx)
887   testb $0x02,tsk_ptrace(%ebx)    # PT_TRACESYS
888   jne tracesys_exit
889   jmp     ret_from_sys_call
890
891 /*
892  * Return to user mode is not as complex as all this
893  * looks, but we want the default path for a system call
894  * return to go as quickly as possible which is why some
895  * of this is less clear than it otherwise should be.
896  */
897
898 ENTRY(system_call)
899   pushl %eax                 # save orig_eax
900   SAVE_ALL
901   GET_CURRENT(%ebx)
902   cmpl $(NR_syscalls),%eax
903   jae badsys
904   testb $0x02,tsk_ptrace(%ebx)    # PT_TRACESYS
905   jne tracesys
906   call *SYMBOL_NAME(sys_call_table)(,%eax,4)
```

p 564

```
907   movl %eax,EAX(%esp)              # save the return value
908 ENTRY(ret_from_sys_call)
909 #ifdef CONFIG_SMP
910   movl processor(%ebx),%eax
911   shll $CONFIG_X86_L1_CACHE_SHIFT,%eax
912   movl SYMBOL_NAME(irq_stat)(,%eax),%ecx # softirq_active
913   testl SYMBOL_NAME(irq_stat)+4(,%eax),%ecx #softirq_mask
914 #else
915   movl SYMBOL_NAME(irq_stat),%ecx         # softirq_active
916   testl SYMBOL_NAME(irq_stat)+4,%ecx      # softirq_mask
917 #endif
918   jne    handle_softirq
919
920 ret_with_reschedule:
921   cmpl $0,need_resched(%ebx)
922   jne reschedule
923   cmpl $0,sigpending(%ebx)
924   jne signal_return
925 restore_all:
926   RESTORE_ALL
927
928   ALIGN
929 signal_return:
930   sti          # we can get here from an interrupt handler
931   testl $(VM_MASK),EFLAGS(%esp)
932   movl %esp,%eax
933   jne v86_signal_return
934   xorl %edx,%edx
935   call SYMBOL_NAME(do_signal)
936   jmp restore_all
937
938   ALIGN
939 v86_signal_return:
940   call SYMBOL_NAME(save_v86_state)
941   movl %eax,%esp
942   xorl %edx,%edx
943   call SYMBOL_NAME(do_signal)
944   jmp restore_all
945
946   ALIGN
947 tracesys:
948   movl $-ENOSYS,EAX(%esp)
949   call SYMBOL_NAME(syscall_trace)
950   movl ORIG_EAX(%esp),%eax
951   cmpl $(NR_syscalls),%eax
952   jae tracesys_exit
953   call *SYMBOL_NAME(sys_call_table)(,%eax,4)
954   movl %eax,EAX(%esp)              # save the return value
```

```
955 tracesys_exit:
956    call SYMBOL_NAME(syscall_trace)
957    jmp ret_from_sys_call
958 badsys:
959    movl $-ENOSYS,EAX(%esp)
960    jmp ret_from_sys_call
961
962    ALIGN
963 ret_from_exception:
964 #ifdef CONFIG_SMP
965    GET_CURRENT(%ebx)
966    movl processor(%ebx),%eax
967    shll $CONFIG_X86_L1_CACHE_SHIFT,%eax
968    movl SYMBOL_NAME(irq_stat)(,%eax),%ecx # softirq_active
969    testl SYMBOL_NAME(irq_stat)+4(,%eax),%ecx #softirq_mask
970 #else
971    movl SYMBOL_NAME(irq_stat),%ecx        # softirq_active
972    testl SYMBOL_NAME(irq_stat)+4,%ecx      # softirq_mask
973 #endif
974    jne    handle_softirq
975
976 ENTRY(ret_from_intr)
977    GET_CURRENT(%ebx)
978    movl EFLAGS(%esp),%eax         # mix EFLAGS and CS
979    movb CS(%esp),%al
980    testl $(VM_MASK | 3),%eax # rtn to VM86 mode|non-super?
981    jne ret_with_reschedule
982    jmp restore_all
983
984    ALIGN
985 handle_softirq:
986    call SYMBOL_NAME(do_softirq)
987    jmp ret_from_intr
988
989    ALIGN
990 reschedule:
991    call SYMBOL_NAME(schedule)     # test
992    jmp ret_from_sys_call
993
994 ENTRY(divide_error)
995    pushl $0                    # no error code
996    pushl $ SYMBOL_NAME(do_divide_error)
997    ALIGN
998 error_code:
999    pushl %ds
1000   pushl %eax
1001   xorl %eax,%eax
1002   pushl %ebp

1003   pushl %edi
1004   pushl %esi
1005   pushl %edx
1006   decl %eax                       # eax = -1
1007   pushl %ecx
1008   pushl %ebx
1009   cld
1010   movl %es,%ecx
1011   movl ORIG_EAX(%esp), %esi       # get the error code
1012   movl ES(%esp), %edi             # get the function addr
1013   movl %eax, ORIG_EAX(%esp)
1014   movl %ecx, ES(%esp)
1015   movl %esp,%edx
1016   pushl %esi                      # push the error code
1017   pushl %edx                      # push pt_regs pointer
1018   movl $(__KERNEL_DS),%edx
1019   movl %edx,%ds
1020   movl %edx,%es
1021   GET_CURRENT(%ebx)
1022   call *%edi
1023   addl $8,%esp
1024   jmp ret_from_exception
1025
1026 ENTRY(coprocessor_error)
1027   pushl $0
1028   pushl $ SYMBOL_NAME(do_coprocessor_error)
1029   jmp error_code
1030
1031 ENTRY(simd_coprocessor_error)
1032   pushl $0
1033   pushl $ SYMBOL_NAME(do_simd_coprocessor_error)
1034   jmp error_code
1035
1036 ENTRY(device_not_available)
1037   pushl $-1                # mark this as an int
1038   SAVE_ALL
1039   GET_CURRENT(%ebx)
1040   pushl $ret_from_exception
1041   movl %cr0,%eax
1042   testl $0x4,%eax          # EM (math emulation bit)
1043   je SYMBOL_NAME(math_state_restore)
1044   pushl $0                 # temporary storage for ORIG_EIP
1045   call   SYMBOL_NAME(math_emulate)
1046   addl $4,%esp
1047   ret
1048
1049 ENTRY(debug)
1050   pushl $0
```

```
1051    pushl $ SYMBOL_NAME(do_debug)
1052    jmp error_code
1053
1054 ENTRY(nmi)
1055    pushl %eax
1056    SAVE_ALL
1057    movl %esp,%edx
1058    pushl $0
1059    pushl %edx
1060    call SYMBOL_NAME(do_nmi)
1061    addl $8,%esp
1062    RESTORE_ALL
1063
1064 ENTRY(int3)
1065    pushl $0
1066    pushl $ SYMBOL_NAME(do_int3)
1067    jmp error_code
1068
1069 ENTRY(overflow)
1070    pushl $0
1071    pushl $ SYMBOL_NAME(do_overflow)
1072    jmp error_code
1073
1074 ENTRY(bounds)
1075    pushl $0
1076    pushl $ SYMBOL_NAME(do_bounds)
1077    jmp error_code
1078
1079 ENTRY(invalid_op)
1080    pushl $0
1081    pushl $ SYMBOL_NAME(do_invalid_op)
1082    jmp error_code
1083
1084 ENTRY(coprocessor_segment_overrun)
1085    pushl $0
1086    pushl $ SYMBOL_NAME(do_coprocessor_segment_overrun)
1087    jmp error_code
1088
1089 ENTRY(double_fault)
1090    pushl $ SYMBOL_NAME(do_double_fault)
1091    jmp error_code
1092
1093 ENTRY(invalid_TSS)
1094    pushl $ SYMBOL_NAME(do_invalid_TSS)
1095    jmp error_code
1096
1097 ENTRY(segment_not_present)
1098    pushl $ SYMBOL_NAME(do_segment_not_present)
1099    jmp error_code
1100
1101 ENTRY(stack_segment)
1102    pushl $ SYMBOL_NAME(do_stack_segment)
1103    jmp error_code
1104
1105 ENTRY(general_protection)
1106    pushl $ SYMBOL_NAME(do_general_protection)
1107    jmp error_code
1108
1109 ENTRY(alignment_check)
1110    pushl $ SYMBOL_NAME(do_alignment_check)
1111    jmp error_code
1112
1113 ENTRY(page_fault)
1114    pushl $ SYMBOL_NAME(do_page_fault)
1115    jmp error_code
1116
1117 ENTRY(machine_check)
1118    pushl $0
1119    pushl $ SYMBOL_NAME(do_machine_check)
1120    jmp error_code
1121
1122 ENTRY(spurious_interrupt_bug)
1123    pushl $0
1124    pushl $ SYMBOL_NAME(do_spurious_interrupt_bug)
1125    jmp error_code
1126
1127 .data
1128 ENTRY(sys_call_table)
1129    .long SYMBOL_NAME(sys_ni_syscall) /* 0 - old setup() */
1130    .long SYMBOL_NAME(sys_exit)
1131    .long SYMBOL_NAME(sys_fork)
1132    .long SYMBOL_NAME(sys_read)
1133    .long SYMBOL_NAME(sys_write)
1134    .long SYMBOL_NAME(sys_open)           /* 5 */
1135    .long SYMBOL_NAME(sys_close)
1136    .long SYMBOL_NAME(sys_waitpid)
1137    .long SYMBOL_NAME(sys_creat)
1138    .long SYMBOL_NAME(sys_link)
1139    .long SYMBOL_NAME(sys_unlink)         /* 10 */
1140    .long SYMBOL_NAME(sys_execve)
1141    .long SYMBOL_NAME(sys_chdir)
1142    .long SYMBOL_NAME(sys_time)
1143    .long SYMBOL_NAME(sys_mknod)
1144    .long SYMBOL_NAME(sys_chmod)          /* 15 */
1145    .long SYMBOL_NAME(sys_lchown16)
1146    .long SYMBOL_NAME(sys_ni_syscall) /* old break holder*/
```

```
1147    .long SYMBOL_NAME(sys_stat)
1148    .long SYMBOL_NAME(sys_lseek)
1149    .long SYMBOL_NAME(sys_getpid)          /* 20 */
1150    .long SYMBOL_NAME(sys_mount)
1151    .long SYMBOL_NAME(sys_oldumount)
1152    .long SYMBOL_NAME(sys_setuid16)
1153    .long SYMBOL_NAME(sys_getuid16)
1154    .long SYMBOL_NAME(sys_stime)           /* 25 */
1155    .long SYMBOL_NAME(sys_ptrace)
1156    .long SYMBOL_NAME(sys_alarm)
1157    .long SYMBOL_NAME(sys_fstat)
1158    .long SYMBOL_NAME(sys_pause)
1159    .long SYMBOL_NAME(sys_utime)           /* 30 */
1160    .long SYMBOL_NAME(sys_ni_syscall) /* old stty holder */
1161    .long SYMBOL_NAME(sys_ni_syscall) /* old gtty holder */
1162    .long SYMBOL_NAME(sys_access)
1163    .long SYMBOL_NAME(sys_nice) /* next: old ftime holder*/
1164    .long SYMBOL_NAME(sys_ni_syscall)      /* 35 */
1165    .long SYMBOL_NAME(sys_sync)
1166    .long SYMBOL_NAME(sys_kill)
1167    .long SYMBOL_NAME(sys_rename)
1168    .long SYMBOL_NAME(sys_mkdir)
1169    .long SYMBOL_NAME(sys_rmdir)           /* 40 */
1170    .long SYMBOL_NAME(sys_dup)
1171    .long SYMBOL_NAME(sys_pipe)
1172    .long SYMBOL_NAME(sys_times)
1173    .long SYMBOL_NAME(sys_ni_syscall) /* old prof holder */
1174    .long SYMBOL_NAME(sys_brk)             /* 45 */
1175    .long SYMBOL_NAME(sys_setgid16)
1176    .long SYMBOL_NAME(sys_getgid16)
1177    .long SYMBOL_NAME(sys_signal)
1178    .long SYMBOL_NAME(sys_geteuid16)
1179    .long SYMBOL_NAME(sys_getegid16)       /* 50 */
1180    .long SYMBOL_NAME(sys_acct)
1181    .long SYMBOL_NAME(sys_umount) /*recyc never used phys*/
1182    .long SYMBOL_NAME(sys_ni_syscall) /* old lock holder */
1183    .long SYMBOL_NAME(sys_ioctl)
1184    .long SYMBOL_NAME(sys_fcntl)           /* 55 */
1185    .long SYMBOL_NAME(sys_ni_syscall) /* old mpx holder */
1186    .long SYMBOL_NAME(sys_setpgid)
1187    .long SYMBOL_NAME(sys_ni_syscall) /*old ulimit holder*/
1188    .long SYMBOL_NAME(sys_olduname)
1189    .long SYMBOL_NAME(sys_umask)           /* 60 */
1190    .long SYMBOL_NAME(sys_chroot)
1191    .long SYMBOL_NAME(sys_ustat)
1192    .long SYMBOL_NAME(sys_dup2)
1193    .long SYMBOL_NAME(sys_getppid)
1194    .long SYMBOL_NAME(sys_getpgrp)         /* 65 */

1195    .long SYMBOL_NAME(sys_setsid)
1196    .long SYMBOL_NAME(sys_sigaction)
1197    .long SYMBOL_NAME(sys_sgetmask)
1198    .long SYMBOL_NAME(sys_ssetmask)
1199    .long SYMBOL_NAME(sys_setreuid16)      /* 70 */
1200    .long SYMBOL_NAME(sys_setregid16)
1201    .long SYMBOL_NAME(sys_sigsuspend)
1202    .long SYMBOL_NAME(sys_sigpending)
1203    .long SYMBOL_NAME(sys_sethostname)
1204    .long SYMBOL_NAME(sys_setrlimit)       /* 75 */
1205    .long SYMBOL_NAME(sys_old_getrlimit)
1206    .long SYMBOL_NAME(sys_getrusage)
1207    .long SYMBOL_NAME(sys_gettimeofday)
1208    .long SYMBOL_NAME(sys_settimeofday)
1209    .long SYMBOL_NAME(sys_getgroups16)     /* 80 */
1210    .long SYMBOL_NAME(sys_setgroups16)
1211    .long SYMBOL_NAME(old_select)
1212    .long SYMBOL_NAME(sys_symlink)
1213    .long SYMBOL_NAME(sys_lstat)
1214    .long SYMBOL_NAME(sys_readlink)        /* 85 */
1215    .long SYMBOL_NAME(sys_uselib)
1216    .long SYMBOL_NAME(sys_swapon)
1217    .long SYMBOL_NAME(sys_reboot)
1218    .long SYMBOL_NAME(old_readdir)
1219    .long SYMBOL_NAME(old_mmap)            /* 90 */
1220    .long SYMBOL_NAME(sys_munmap)
1221    .long SYMBOL_NAME(sys_truncate)
1222    .long SYMBOL_NAME(sys_ftruncate)
1223    .long SYMBOL_NAME(sys_fchmod)
1224    .long SYMBOL_NAME(sys_fchown16)        /* 95 */
1225    .long SYMBOL_NAME(sys_getpriority)
1226    .long SYMBOL_NAME(sys_setpriority)
1227    .long SYMBOL_NAME(sys_ni_syscall) /*old profil holder*/
1228    .long SYMBOL_NAME(sys_statfs)
1229    .long SYMBOL_NAME(sys_fstatfs)         /* 100 */
1230    .long SYMBOL_NAME(sys_ioperm)
1231    .long SYMBOL_NAME(sys_socketcall)
1232    .long SYMBOL_NAME(sys_syslog)
1233    .long SYMBOL_NAME(sys_setitimer)
1234    .long SYMBOL_NAME(sys_getitimer)       /* 105 */
1235    .long SYMBOL_NAME(sys_newstat)
1236    .long SYMBOL_NAME(sys_newlstat)
1237    .long SYMBOL_NAME(sys_newfstat)
1238    .long SYMBOL_NAME(sys_uname)
1239    .long SYMBOL_NAME(sys_iopl)            /* 110 */
1240    .long SYMBOL_NAME(sys_vhangup)
1241    .long SYMBOL_NAME(sys_ni_syscall) /* old idle syscall*/
1242    .long SYMBOL_NAME(sys_vm86old)
```

```
1243    .long SYMBOL_NAME(sys_wait4)
1244    .long SYMBOL_NAME(sys_swapoff)          /* 115 */
1245    .long SYMBOL_NAME(sys_sysinfo)
1246    .long SYMBOL_NAME(sys_ipc)
1247    .long SYMBOL_NAME(sys_fsync)
1248    .long SYMBOL_NAME(sys_sigreturn)
1249    .long SYMBOL_NAME(sys_clone)           /* 120 */
1250    .long SYMBOL_NAME(sys_setdomainname)
1251    .long SYMBOL_NAME(sys_newuname)
1252    .long SYMBOL_NAME(sys_modify_ldt)
1253    .long SYMBOL_NAME(sys_adjtimex)
1254    .long SYMBOL_NAME(sys_mprotect)        /* 125 */
1255    .long SYMBOL_NAME(sys_sigprocmask)
1256    .long SYMBOL_NAME(sys_create_module)
1257    .long SYMBOL_NAME(sys_init_module)
1258    .long SYMBOL_NAME(sys_delete_module)
1259    .long SYMBOL_NAME(sys_get_kernel_syms) /* 130 */
1260    .long SYMBOL_NAME(sys_quotactl)
1261    .long SYMBOL_NAME(sys_getpgid)
1262    .long SYMBOL_NAME(sys_fchdir)
1263    .long SYMBOL_NAME(sys_bdflush)
1264    .long SYMBOL_NAME(sys_sysfs)           /* 135 */
1265    .long SYMBOL_NAME(sys_personality)
1266    .long SYMBOL_NAME(sys_ni_syscall) /* for afs_syscall */
1267    .long SYMBOL_NAME(sys_setfsuid16)
1268    .long SYMBOL_NAME(sys_setfsgid16)
1269    .long SYMBOL_NAME(sys_llseek)          /* 140 */
1270    .long SYMBOL_NAME(sys_getdents)
1271    .long SYMBOL_NAME(sys_select)
1272    .long SYMBOL_NAME(sys_flock)
1273    .long SYMBOL_NAME(sys_msync)
1274    .long SYMBOL_NAME(sys_readv)           /* 145 */
1275    .long SYMBOL_NAME(sys_writev)
1276    .long SYMBOL_NAME(sys_getsid)
1277    .long SYMBOL_NAME(sys_fdatasync)
1278    .long SYMBOL_NAME(sys_sysctl)
1279    .long SYMBOL_NAME(sys_mlock)           /* 150 */
1280    .long SYMBOL_NAME(sys_munlock)
1281    .long SYMBOL_NAME(sys_mlockall)
1282    .long SYMBOL_NAME(sys_munlockall)
1283    .long SYMBOL_NAME(sys_sched_setparam)
1284    .long SYMBOL_NAME(sys_sched_getparam)  /* 155 */
1285    .long SYMBOL_NAME(sys_sched_setscheduler)
1286    .long SYMBOL_NAME(sys_sched_getscheduler)
1287    .long SYMBOL_NAME(sys_sched_yield)
1288    .long SYMBOL_NAME(sys_sched_get_priority_max)
1289    .long SYMBOL_NAME(sys_sched_get_priority_min) /* 160 */
1290    .long SYMBOL_NAME(sys_sched_rr_get_interval)
1291    .long SYMBOL_NAME(sys_nanosleep)
1292    .long SYMBOL_NAME(sys_mremap)
1293    .long SYMBOL_NAME(sys_setresuid16)
1294    .long SYMBOL_NAME(sys_getresuid16)     /* 165 */
1295    .long SYMBOL_NAME(sys_vm86)
1296    .long SYMBOL_NAME(sys_query_module)
1297    .long SYMBOL_NAME(sys_poll)
1298    .long SYMBOL_NAME(sys_nfsservctl)
1299    .long SYMBOL_NAME(sys_setresgid16)     /* 170 */
1300    .long SYMBOL_NAME(sys_getresgid16)
1301    .long SYMBOL_NAME(sys_prctl)
1302    .long SYMBOL_NAME(sys_rt_sigreturn)
1303    .long SYMBOL_NAME(sys_rt_sigaction)
1304    .long SYMBOL_NAME(sys_rt_sigprocmask)  /* 175 */
1305    .long SYMBOL_NAME(sys_rt_sigpending)
1306    .long SYMBOL_NAME(sys_rt_sigtimedwait)
1307    .long SYMBOL_NAME(sys_rt_sigqueueinfo)
1308    .long SYMBOL_NAME(sys_rt_sigsuspend)
1309    .long SYMBOL_NAME(sys_pread)           /* 180 */
1310    .long SYMBOL_NAME(sys_pwrite)
1311    .long SYMBOL_NAME(sys_chown16)
1312    .long SYMBOL_NAME(sys_getcwd)
1313    .long SYMBOL_NAME(sys_capget)
1314    .long SYMBOL_NAME(sys_capset)          /* 185 */
1315    .long SYMBOL_NAME(sys_sigaltstack)
1316    .long SYMBOL_NAME(sys_sendfile)
1317    .long SYMBOL_NAME(sys_ni_syscall) /* streams1 */
1318    .long SYMBOL_NAME(sys_ni_syscall) /* streams2 */
1319    .long SYMBOL_NAME(sys_vfork)           /* 190 */
1320    .long SYMBOL_NAME(sys_getrlimit)
1321    .long SYMBOL_NAME(sys_mmap2)
1322    .long SYMBOL_NAME(sys_truncate64)
1323    .long SYMBOL_NAME(sys_ftruncate64)
1324    .long SYMBOL_NAME(sys_stat64)          /* 195 */
1325    .long SYMBOL_NAME(sys_lstat64)
1326    .long SYMBOL_NAME(sys_fstat64)
1327    .long SYMBOL_NAME(sys_lchown)
1328    .long SYMBOL_NAME(sys_getuid)
1329    .long SYMBOL_NAME(sys_getgid)          /* 200 */
1330    .long SYMBOL_NAME(sys_geteuid)
1331    .long SYMBOL_NAME(sys_getegid)
1332    .long SYMBOL_NAME(sys_setreuid)
1333    .long SYMBOL_NAME(sys_setregid)
1334    .long SYMBOL_NAME(sys_getgroups)       /* 205 */
1335    .long SYMBOL_NAME(sys_setgroups)
1336    .long SYMBOL_NAME(sys_fchown)
1337    .long SYMBOL_NAME(sys_setresuid)
1338    .long SYMBOL_NAME(sys_getresuid)
```

```
1339    .long SYMBOL_NAME(sys_setresgid)        /* 210 */
1340    .long SYMBOL_NAME(sys_getresgid)
1341    .long SYMBOL_NAME(sys_chown)
1342    .long SYMBOL_NAME(sys_setuid)
1343    .long SYMBOL_NAME(sys_setgid)
1344    .long SYMBOL_NAME(sys_setfsuid)        /* 215 */
1345    .long SYMBOL_NAME(sys_setfsgid)
1346    .long SYMBOL_NAME(sys_pivot_root)
1347    .long SYMBOL_NAME(sys_mincore)
1348    .long SYMBOL_NAME(sys_madvise)
1349    .long SYMBOL_NAME(sys_getdents64)      /* 220 */
1350    .long SYMBOL_NAME(sys_fcntl64)
1351    .long SYMBOL_NAME(sys_ni_syscall) /* reserved for TUX*/
1352
1353    /*
1354     * NOTE!! This doesn't have to be exact - we just have
1355     * to make sure we have _enough_ of the
1356     * "sys_ni_syscall" entries. Don't panic if you notice
1357     * that this hasn't been shrunk every time we add a new
1358     * system call.
1359     */
1360    .rept NR_syscalls-221
1361      .long SYMBOL_NAME(sys_ni_syscall)
1362    .endr
```

arch/i386/kernel/i8259.c

```
1363 #include <linux/config.h>
1364 #include <linux/ptrace.h>
1365 #include <linux/errno.h>
1366 #include <linux/signal.h>
1367 #include <linux/sched.h>
1368 #include <linux/ioport.h>
1369 #include <linux/interrupt.h>
1370 #include <linux/timex.h>
1371 #include <linux/malloc.h>
1372 #include <linux/random.h>
1373 #include <linux/smp_lock.h>
1374 #include <linux/init.h>
1375 #include <linux/kernel_stat.h>
1376
1377 #include <asm/system.h>
1378 #include <asm/io.h>
1379 #include <asm/irq.h>
1380 #include <asm/bitops.h>
1381 #include <asm/pgtable.h>
1382 #include <asm/delay.h>
1383 #include <asm/desc.h>
```

```
1384
1385 #include <linux/irq.h>
1386
1387 /* Common place to define all x86 IRQ vectors
1388  *
1389  * This builds up the IRQ handler stubs using some ugly
1390  * macros in irq.h
1391  *
1392  * These macros create the low-level assembly IRQ
1393  * routines that save register context and call
1394  * do_IRQ(). do_IRQ() then does all the operations that
1395  * are needed to keep the AT (or SMP IOAPIC)
1396  * interrupt-controller happy.  */
1397 BUILD_COMMON_IRQ()
1398 #define BI(x,y)                                        \
1399         BUILD_IRQ(x##y)
1400 #define BUILD_16_IRQS(x)                               \
1401         BI(x,0) BI(x,1) BI(x,2) BI(x,3)                \
1402         BI(x,4) BI(x,5) BI(x,6) BI(x,7)                \
1403         BI(x,8) BI(x,9) BI(x,a) BI(x,b)                \
1404         BI(x,c) BI(x,d) BI(x,e) BI(x,f)
1405 /* ISA PIC or low IO-APIC triggered (INTA-cycle or APIC)
1406  * interrupts: (these are usually mapped to vectors
1407  * 0x20-0x2f) */
1408 BUILD_16_IRQS(0x0)
1409 #ifdef CONFIG_X86_IO_APIC
1410 /* The IO-APIC gives us many more interrupt sources. Most
1411  * of these are unused but an SMP system is supposed to
1412  * have enough memory ...  sometimes (mostly wrt. hw
1413  * bugs) we get corrupted vectors all across the
1414  * spectrum, so we really want to be prepared to get all
1415  * of these. Plus, more powerful systems might have more
1416  * than 64 IO-APIC registers.
1417  *
1418  * (these are usually mapped into the 0x30-0xff vector
1419  * range) */
1420 BUILD_16_IRQS(0x1) BUILD_16_IRQS(0x2) BUILD_16_IRQS(0x3)
1421 BUILD_16_IRQS(0x4) BUILD_16_IRQS(0x5) BUILD_16_IRQS(0x6)
1422 BUILD_16_IRQS(0x7) BUILD_16_IRQS(0x8) BUILD_16_IRQS(0x9)
1423 BUILD_16_IRQS(0xa) BUILD_16_IRQS(0xb) BUILD_16_IRQS(0xc)
1424 BUILD_16_IRQS(0xd)
1425 #endif
1426 #undef BUILD_16_IRQS
1427 #undef BI
1428 /* The following vectors are part of the Linux
1429  * architecture, there is no hardware IRQ pin equivalent
1430  * for them, they are triggered through the ICC by us
1431  * (IPIs) */
```

```
1432 #ifdef CONFIG_SMP
1433 BUILD_SMP_INTERRUPT(reschedule_interrupt,
1434                     RESCHEDULE_VECTOR)
1435 BUILD_SMP_INTERRUPT(invalidate_interrupt,
1436                     INVALIDATE_TLB_VECTOR)
1437 BUILD_SMP_INTERRUPT(call_function_interrupt,
1438                     CALL_FUNCTION_VECTOR)
1439 #endif
1440 /* every pentium local APIC has two 'local interrupts',
1441  * with a soft-definable vector attached to both
1442  * interrupts, one of which is a timer interrupt, the
1443  * other one is error counter overflow. Linux uses the
1444  * local APIC timer interrupt to get a much simpler SMP
1445  * time architecture: */
1446 #ifdef CONFIG_X86_LOCAL_APIC
1447 BUILD_SMP_TIMER_INTERRUPT(apic_timer_interrupt,
1448                           LOCAL_TIMER_VECTOR)
1449 BUILD_SMP_INTERRUPT(error_interrupt, ERROR_APIC_VECTOR)
1450 BUILD_SMP_INTERRUPT(spurious_interrupt,
1451                     SPURIOUS_APIC_VECTOR)
1452 #endif
1453 #define IRQ(x,y)                                        \
1454         IRQ##x##y##_interrupt
1455 #define IRQLIST_16(x)                                   \
1456         IRQ(x,0), IRQ(x,1), IRQ(x,2), IRQ(x,3),         \
1457         IRQ(x,4), IRQ(x,5), IRQ(x,6), IRQ(x,7),         \
1458         IRQ(x,8), IRQ(x,9), IRQ(x,a), IRQ(x,b),         \
1459         IRQ(x,c), IRQ(x,d), IRQ(x,e), IRQ(x,f)
1460 void (*interrupt[NR_IRQS]) (void) =
1461 {
1462    IRQLIST_16(0x0),
1463 #ifdef CONFIG_X86_IO_APIC
1464    IRQLIST_16(0x1), IRQLIST_16(0x2), IRQLIST_16(0x3),
1465    IRQLIST_16(0x4), IRQLIST_16(0x5), IRQLIST_16(0x6),
1466    IRQLIST_16(0x7), IRQLIST_16(0x8), IRQLIST_16(0x9),
1467    IRQLIST_16(0xa), IRQLIST_16(0xb), IRQLIST_16(0xc),
1468    IRQLIST_16(0xd)
1469 #endif
1470 };
1471
1472 #undef IRQ
1473 #undef IRQLIST_16
1474
1475 /* This is the 'legacy' 8259A Programmable Interrupt
1476  * Controller, present in the majority of PC/AT boxes.
1477  * plus some generic x86 specific things if generic
1478  * specifics makes any sense at all.  this file should
1479  * become arch/i386/kernel/irq.c when the old irq.c moves
```

```
1480  * to arch independent land */
1481 spinlock_t i8259A_lock = SPIN_LOCK_UNLOCKED;
1482
1483 static void end_8259A_irq(unsigned int irq)
1484 {
1485   if (!(irq_desc[irq].
1486         status & (IRQ_DISABLED | IRQ_INPROGRESS)))
1487         enable_8259A_irq(irq);
1488 }
1489
1490 #define shutdown_8259A_irq      disable_8259A_irq
1491
1492 void mask_and_ack_8259A(unsigned int);
1493
1494 static unsigned int startup_8259A_irq(unsigned int irq)
1495 {
1496    enable_8259A_irq(irq);
1497    return 0;                     /* never anything pending */
1498 }
1499
1500 static struct hw_interrupt_type i8259A_irq_type = {
1501    "XT-PIC",
1502    startup_8259A_irq,
1503    shutdown_8259A_irq,
1504    enable_8259A_irq,
1505    disable_8259A_irq,
1506    mask_and_ack_8259A,
1507    end_8259A_irq,
1508    NULL
1509 };
1510
1511 /* 8259A PIC functions to handle ISA devices: */
1512 /* This contains the irq mask for both 8259A irq
1513  * controllers. */
1514 static unsigned int cached_irq_mask = 0xffff;
1515
1516 #define __byte(x,y)       (((unsigned char *)&(y))[x])
1517 #define cached_21         (__byte(0,cached_irq_mask))
1518 #define cached_A1         (__byte(1,cached_irq_mask))
1519
1520 /* Not all IRQs can be routed through the IO-APIC, eg. on
1521  * certain (older) boards the timer interrupt is not
1522  * really connected to any IO-APIC pin, it's fed to the
1523  * master 8259A's IRQ line only.
1524  *
1525  * Any '1' bit in this mask means the IRQ is routed
1526  * through the IO-APIC.  this 'mixed mode' IRQ handling
1527  * costs nothing because it's only used at IRQ setup
```

```
1528  * time. */
1529 unsigned long io_apic_irqs;
1530
1531 void disable_8259A_irq(unsigned int irq)
1532 {
1533   unsigned int mask = 1 << irq;
1534   unsigned long flags;
1535
1536   spin_lock_irqsave(&i8259A_lock, flags);
1537   cached_irq_mask |= mask;
1538   if (irq & 8)
1539     outb(cached_A1, 0xA1);
1540   else
1541     outb(cached_21, 0x21);
1542   spin_unlock_irqrestore(&i8259A_lock, flags);
1543 }
1544
1545 void enable_8259A_irq(unsigned int irq)
1546 {
1547   unsigned int mask = ~(1 << irq);
1548   unsigned long flags;
1549
1550   spin_lock_irqsave(&i8259A_lock, flags);
1551   cached_irq_mask &= mask;
1552   if (irq & 8)
1553     outb(cached_A1, 0xA1);
1554   else
1555     outb(cached_21, 0x21);
1556   spin_unlock_irqrestore(&i8259A_lock, flags);
1557 }
1558
1559 int i8259A_irq_pending(unsigned int irq)
1560 {
1561   unsigned int mask = 1 << irq;
1562   unsigned long flags;
1563   int ret;
1564
1565   spin_lock_irqsave(&i8259A_lock, flags);
1566   if (irq < 8)
1567     ret = inb(0x20) & mask;
1568   else
1569     ret = inb(0xA0) & (mask >> 8);
1570   spin_unlock_irqrestore(&i8259A_lock, flags);
1571
1572   return ret;
1573 }
1574
1575 void make_8259A_irq(unsigned int irq)
1576 {
1577   disable_irq_nosync(irq);
1578   io_apic_irqs &= ~(1 << irq);
1579   irq_desc[irq].handler = &i8259A_irq_type;
1580   enable_irq(irq);
1581 }
1582
1583 /* This function assumes to be called rarely. Switching
1584  * between 8259A registers is slow.  This has to be
1585  * protected by the irq controller spinlock before being
1586  * called.  */
1587 static inline int i8259A_irq_real(unsigned int irq)
1588 {
1589   int value;
1590   int irqmask = 1 << irq;
1591
1592   if (irq < 8) {
1593     outb(0x0B, 0x20);        /* ISR register */
1594     value = inb(0x20) & irqmask;
1595     outb(0x0A, 0x20);        /* back to the IRR register */
1596     return value;
1597   }
1598   outb(0x0B, 0xA0);          /* ISR register */
1599   value = inb(0xA0) & (irqmask >> 8);
1600   outb(0x0A, 0xA0);          /* back to the IRR register */
1601   return value;
1602 }
1603
1604 /* Careful! The 8259A is a fragile beast, it pretty much
1605  * _has_ to be done exactly like this (mask it first,
1606  * _then_ send the EOI, and the order of EOI to the two
1607  * 8259s is important!  */
1608 void mask_and_ack_8259A(unsigned int irq)
1609 {
1610   unsigned int irqmask = 1 << irq;
1611   unsigned long flags;
1612
1613   spin_lock_irqsave(&i8259A_lock, flags);
1614   /* Lightweight spurious IRQ detection. We do not want
1615    * to overdo spurious IRQ handling - it's usually a
1616    * sign of hardware problems, so we only do the checks
1617    * we can do without slowing down good hardware
1618    * unnecesserily.
1619    *
1620    * Note that IRQ7 and IRQ15 (the two spurious IRQs
1621    * usually resulting from the 8259A-1|2 PICs) occur
1622    * even if the IRQ is masked in the 8259A. Thus we
1623    * can check spurious 8259A IRQs without doing the
```

```
1624      * quite slow i8259A_irq_real() call for every IRQ.
1625      * This does not cover 100% of spurious interrupts,
1626      * but should be enough to warn the user that there
1627      * is something bad going on ...  */
1628     if (cached_irq_mask & irqmask)
1629       goto spurious_8259A_irq;
1630     cached_irq_mask |= irqmask;
1631
1632 handle_real_irq:
1633     if (irq & 8) {
1634       inb(0xA1);          /* DUMMY - (do we need this?) */
1635       outb(cached_A1, 0xA1);
1636       outb(0x60 + (irq & 7), 0xA0); /* 'Specific EOI' to
1637                             * slave */
1638       outb(0x62, 0x20); /* 'Specific EOI' to master-IRQ2 */
1639     } else {
1640       inb(0x21);          /* DUMMY - (do we need this?) */
1641       outb(cached_21, 0x21);
1642       outb(0x60 + irq, 0x20); /* 'Specific EOI' to master*/
1643     }
1644     spin_unlock_irqrestore(&i8259A_lock, flags);
1645     return;
1646
1647 spurious_8259A_irq:
1648     /* this is the slow path - should happen rarely.  */
1649     if (i8259A_irq_real(irq))
1650       /* oops, the IRQ _is_ in service according to the
1651        * 8259A - not spurious, go handle it.  */
1652       goto handle_real_irq;
1653
1654     {
1655       static int spurious_irq_mask;
1656       /* At this point we can be sure the IRQ is spurious,
1657        * lets ACK and report it. [once per IRQ] */
1658       if (!(spurious_irq_mask & irqmask)) {
1659         printk("spurious 8259A interrupt: IRQ%d.\n", irq);
1660         spurious_irq_mask |= irqmask;
1661       }
1662       irq_err_count++;
1663       /* Theoretically we do not have to handle this IRQ,
1664        * but in Linux this does not cause problems and is
1665        * simpler for us.  */
1666       goto handle_real_irq;
1667     }
1668 }
1669
1670 void __init init_8259A(int auto_eoi)
1671 {
1672   unsigned long flags;
1673
1674   spin_lock_irqsave(&i8259A_lock, flags);
1675
1676   outb(0xff, 0x21);        /* mask all of 8259A-1 */
1677   outb(0xff, 0xA1);        /* mask all of 8259A-2 */
1678
1679   /* outb_p - this has to work on a wide range of PC
1680    * hardware.  */
1681   outb_p(0x11, 0x20);      /* ICW1: select 8259A-1 init */
1682   outb_p(0x20 + 0, 0x21); /* ICW2: 8259A-1 IR0-7
1683                            * mapped to 0x20-0x27 */
1684   outb_p(0x04, 0x21);      /* 8259A-1 (the master)
1685                            * has a slave on IR2 */
1686   if (auto_eoi)
1687     outb_p(0x03, 0x21);    /* master does Auto EOI */
1688   else
1689     outb_p(0x01, 0x21);    /* master expects normal EOI */
1690
1691   outb_p(0x11, 0xA0);      /* ICW1: select 8259A-2 init */
1692   outb_p(0x20 + 8, 0xA1); /* ICW2: 8259A-2 IR0-7
1693                            * mapped to 0x28-0x2f */
1694   outb_p(0x02, 0xA1);      /* 8259A-2 is a slave on
1695                            * master's IR2 */
1696   outb_p(0x01, 0xA1);      /* (slave's support for
1697                            * AEOI in flat mode is
1698                            * to be investigated) */
1699
1700   if (auto_eoi)
1701     /* in AEOI mode we just have to mask the interrupt
1702      * when acking.  */
1703     i8259A_irq_type.ack = disable_8259A_irq;
1704   else
1705     i8259A_irq_type.ack = mask_and_ack_8259A;
1706
1707   udelay(100);             /* wait for 8259A to init */
1708
1709   outb(cached_21, 0x21);  /* restore master IRQ mask */
1710   outb(cached_A1, 0xA1);  /* restore slave IRQ mask */
1711
1712   spin_unlock_irqrestore(&i8259A_lock, flags);
1713 }
1714
1715 /* Note that on a 486, we don't want to do a SIGFPE on an
1716  * irq13 as the irq is unreliable, and exception 16 works
1717  * correctly (ie as explained in the intel
```

```
1718  * literature). On a 386, you can't use exception 16 due
1719  * to bad IBM design, so we have to rely on the less
1720  * exact irq13.
1721  *
1722  * Careful.. Not only is IRQ13 unreliable, but it is also
1723  * leads to races. IBM designers who came up with it
1724  * should be shot. */
1725 static void math_error_irq(int cpl, void *dev_id,
1726     struct pt_regs *regs)
1727 {
1728   extern void math_error(void *);
1729   outb(0, 0xF0);
1730   if (ignore_irq13 || !boot_cpu_data.hard_math)
1731     return;
1732   math_error((void *) regs->eip);
1733 }
1734
1735 /* New motherboards sometimes make IRQ 13 be a PCI
1736  * interrupt, so allow interrupt sharing.  */
1737 static struct irqaction irq13 =
1738     { math_error_irq, 0, 0, "fpu", NULL, NULL };
1739
1740 /* IRQ2 is cascade interrupt to second interrupt
1741  * controller */
1742 #ifndef CONFIG_VISWS
1743 static struct irqaction irq2 =
1744     { no_action, 0, 0, "cascade", NULL, NULL };
1745 #endif
1746
1747
1748 void __init init_ISA_irqs(void)
1749 {
1750   int i;
1751
1752   init_8259A(0);
1753
1754   for (i = 0; i < NR_IRQS; i++) {
1755     irq_desc[i].status = IRQ_DISABLED;
1756     irq_desc[i].action = 0;
1757     irq_desc[i].depth = 1;
1758
1759     if (i < 16) {
1760       /* 16 old-style INTA-cycle interrupts: */
1761       irq_desc[i].handler = &i8259A_irq_type;
1762     } else {
1763       /* 'high' PCI IRQs filled in on demand */
1764       irq_desc[i].handler = &no_irq_type;
```

```
1765     }
1766   }
1767 }
1768
1769 void __init init_IRQ(void)
1770 {
1771   int i;
1772
1773 #ifndef CONFIG_X86_VISWS_APIC
1774   init_ISA_irqs();
1775 #else
1776   init_VISWS_APIC_irqs();
1777 #endif
1778   /* Cover the whole vector space, no vector can escape
1779    * us. (some of these will be overridden and become
1780    * 'special' SMP interrupts) */
1781   for (i = 0; i < NR_IRQS; i++) {
1782     int vector = FIRST_EXTERNAL_VECTOR + i;
1783     if (vector != SYSCALL_VECTOR)
1784       set_intr_gate(vector, interrupt[i]);
1785   }
1786
1787 #ifdef CONFIG_SMP
1788   /* IRQ0 must be given a fixed assignment and
1789    * initialized, because it's used before the IO-APIC is
1790    * set up.  */
1791   set_intr_gate(FIRST_DEVICE_VECTOR, interrupt[0]);
1792
1793   /* The reschedule interrupt is a CPU-to-CPU
1794    * reschedule-helper IPI, driven by wakeup.  */
1795   set_intr_gate(RESCHEDULE_VECTOR, reschedule_interrupt);
1796
1797   /* IPI for invalidation */
1798   set_intr_gate(INVALIDATE_TLB_VECTOR,
1799       invalidate_interrupt);
1800
1801   /* IPI for generic function call */
1802   set_intr_gate(CALL_FUNCTION_VECTOR,
1803       call_function_interrupt);
1804 #endif
1805
1806 #ifdef CONFIG_X86_LOCAL_APIC
1807   /* self generated IPI for local APIC timer */
1808   set_intr_gate(LOCAL_TIMER_VECTOR,
1809       apic_timer_interrupt);
1810
1811   /* IPI vectors for APIC spurious and error interrupts*/
```

```
1812   set_intr_gate(SPURIOUS_APIC_VECTOR,
1813       spurious_interrupt);
1814   set_intr_gate(ERROR_APIC_VECTOR, error_interrupt);
1815 #endif
1816
1817   /* Set the clock to HZ Hz, we already have a valid
1818    * vector now: */
1819   outb_p(0x34, 0x43);          /* binary, mode 2,
1820                                 * LSB/MSB, ch 0 */
1821   outb_p(LATCH & 0xff, 0x40);  /* LSB */
1822   outb(LATCH >> 8, 0x40);      /* MSB */
1823
1824 #ifndef CONFIG_VISWS
1825   setup_irq(2, &irq2);
1826 #endif
1827
1828   /* External FPU? Set up irq13 if so, for original
1829    * braindamaged IBM FERR coupling.  */
1830   if (boot_cpu_data.hard_math && !cpu_has_fpu)
1831     setup_irq(13, &irq13);
1832 }
```

arch/i386/kernel/init_task.c

```
1833 #include <linux/mm.h>
1834 #include <linux/sched.h>
1835 #include <linux/init.h>
1836
1837 #include <asm/uaccess.h>
1838 #include <asm/pgtable.h>
1839 #include <asm/desc.h>
1840
1841 static struct vm_area_struct init_mmap = INIT_MMAP;
1842 static struct fs_struct init_fs = INIT_FS;
1843 static struct files_struct init_files = INIT_FILES;
1844 static struct signal_struct init_signals = INIT_SIGNALS;
1845 struct mm_struct init_mm = INIT_MM(init_mm);
1846
1847 /* Initial task structure.
1848  *
1849  * We need to make sure that this is 8192-byte aligned
1850  * due to the way process stacks are handled. This is
1851  * done by having a special "init_task" linker map
1852  * entry..  */
1853 union task_union init_task_union
1854     __attribute__ ((__section__(".data.init_task"))) = {
1855       INIT_TASK(init_task_union.task)
1856     };
```

```
1857
1858 /* per-CPU TSS segments. Threads are completely 'soft' on
1859  * Linux, no more per-task TSS's. The TSS size is kept
1860  * cacheline-aligned so they are allowed to end up in the
1861  * .data.cacheline_aligned section. Since TSS's are
1862  * completely CPU-local, we want them on exact cacheline
1863  * boundaries, to eliminate cacheline ping-pong.  */
1864 struct tss_struct init_tss[NR_CPUS] __cacheline_aligned =
1865     { [0 ... NR_CPUS - 1] = INIT_TSS };
```

arch/i386/kernel/irq.c

```
1866 /*
1867  *      linux/arch/i386/kernel/irq.c
1868  *
1869  *      Copyright (C) 1992, 1998 Linus Torvalds, Ingo
1870  *      Molnar
1871  *
1872  * This file contains the code used by various IRQ
1873  * handling routines: asking for different IRQ's should
1874  * be done through these routines instead of just
1875  * grabbing them. Thus setups with different IRQ numbers
1876  * shouldn't result in any weird surprises, and
1877  * installing new handlers should be easier.
1878  */
1879 /* (mostly architecture independent, will move to
1880  * kernel/irq.c in 2.5.)
1881  *
1882  * IRQs are in fact implemented a bit like signal
1883  * handlers for the kernel.  Naturally it's not a 1:1
1884  * relation, but there are similarities.  */
1885
1886 #include <linux/config.h>
1887 #include <linux/ptrace.h>
1888 #include <linux/errno.h>
1889 #include <linux/signal.h>
1890 #include <linux/sched.h>
1891 #include <linux/ioport.h>
1892 #include <linux/interrupt.h>
1893 #include <linux/timex.h>
1894 #include <linux/malloc.h>
1895 #include <linux/random.h>
1896 #include <linux/smp_lock.h>
1897 #include <linux/init.h>
1898 #include <linux/kernel_stat.h>
1899 #include <linux/irq.h>
1900 #include <linux/proc_fs.h>
1901
```

```
1902 #include <asm/io.h>
1903 #include <asm/smp.h>
1904 #include <asm/system.h>
1905 #include <asm/bitops.h>
1906 #include <asm/uaccess.h>
1907 #include <asm/pgalloc.h>
1908 #include <asm/delay.h>
1909 #include <asm/desc.h>
1910 #include <asm/irq.h>
1911
1912
1913
1914 /* Linux has a controller-independent x86 interrupt
1915  * architecture. every controller has a
1916  * 'controller-template', that is used by the main code
1917  * to do the right thing. Each driver-visible interrupt
1918  * source is transparently wired to the apropriate
1919  * controller. Thus drivers need not be aware of the
1920  * interrupt-controller.
1921  *
1922  * Various interrupt controllers we handle: 8259 PIC, SMP
1923  * IO-APIC, PIIX4's internal 8259 PIC and SGI's Visual
1924  * Workstation Cobalt (IO-)APIC.  (IO-APICs assumed to be
1925  * messaging to Pentium local-APICs)
1926  *
1927  * the code is designed to be easily extended with
1928  * new/different interrupt controllers, without having to
1929  * do assembly magic. */
1930 /* Controller mappings for all interrupt sources: */
1931 irq_desc_t irq_desc[NR_IRQS] __cacheline_aligned = {
1932   [0 ... NR_IRQS - 1] =
1933   {0, &no_irq_type, NULL, 0, SPIN_LOCK_UNLOCKED}
1934 };
1935
1936 static void register_irq_proc(unsigned int irq);
1937
1938 /* Special irq handlers.  */
1939
1940 void no_action(int cpl, void *dev_id,
1941     struct pt_regs *regs)
1942 {
1943 }
1944
1945 /* Generic no controller code */
1946
1947 static void enable_none(unsigned int irq)
1948 {
1949 }
1950 static unsigned int startup_none(unsigned int irq)
1951 {
1952   return 0;
1953 }
1954 static void disable_none(unsigned int irq)
1955 {
1956 }
1957 static void ack_none(unsigned int irq)
1958 {
1959   /* 'what should we do if we get a hw irq event on an
1960    * illegal vector'.  each architecture has to answer
1961    * this themselves, it doesnt deserve a generic
1962    * callback i think.  */
1963 #if CONFIG_X86
1964   printk("unexpected IRQ trap at vector %02x\n", irq);
1965 #ifdef CONFIG_X86_LOCAL_APIC
1966   /* Currently unexpected vectors happen only on SMP and
1967    * APIC.  We _must_ ack these because every local APIC
1968    * has only N irq slots per priority level, and a
1969    * 'hanging, unacked' IRQ holds up an irq slot - in
1970    * excessive cases (when multiple unexpected vectors
1971    * occur) that might lock up the APIC completely.  */
1972   ack_APIC_irq();
1973 #endif
1974 #endif
1975 }
1976
1977 /* startup is the same as "enable", shutdown is same as
1978  * "disable" */
1979 #define shutdown_none    disable_none
1980 #define end_none         enable_none
1981
1982 struct hw_interrupt_type no_irq_type = {
1983   "none",
1984   startup_none,
1985   shutdown_none,
1986   enable_none,
1987   disable_none,
1988   ack_none,
1989   end_none
1990 };
1991
1992 volatile unsigned long irq_err_count;
1993
1994 /* Generic, controller-independent functions: */
1995
```

```
1996 int get_irq_list(char *buf)
1997 {
1998   int i, j;
1999   struct irqaction *action;
2000   char *p = buf;
2001
2002   p += sprintf(p, "              ");
2003   for (j = 0; j < smp_num_cpus; j++)
2004     p += sprintf(p, "CPU%d        ", j);
2005   *p++ = '\n';
2006
2007   for (i = 0; i < NR_IRQS; i++) {
2008     action = irq_desc[i].action;
2009     if (!action)
2010       continue;
2011     p += sprintf(p, "%3d: ", i);
2012 #ifndef CONFIG_SMP
2013     p += sprintf(p, "%10u ", kstat_irqs(i));
2014 #else
2015     for (j = 0; j < smp_num_cpus; j++)
2016       p += sprintf(p, "%10u ",
2017                 kstat.irqs[cpu_logical_map(j)][i]);
2018 #endif
2019     p += sprintf(p, " %14s",
2020                 irq_desc[i].handler->typename);
2021     p += sprintf(p, "  %s", action->name);
2022
2023     for (action = action->next; action;
2024          action = action->next)
2025       p += sprintf(p, ", %s", action->name);
2026     *p++ = '\n';
2027   }
2028   p += sprintf(p, "NMI: ");
2029   for (j = 0; j < smp_num_cpus; j++)
2030     p += sprintf(p, "%10u ",
2031               nmi_count(cpu_logical_map(j)));
2032   p += sprintf(p, "\n");
2033 #if CONFIG_SMP
2034   p += sprintf(p, "LOC: ");
2035   for (j = 0; j < smp_num_cpus; j++)
2036     p += sprintf(p, "%10u ",
2037               apic_timer_irqs[cpu_logical_map(j)]);
2038   p += sprintf(p, "\n");
2039 #endif
2040   p += sprintf(p, "ERR: %10lu\n", irq_err_count);
2041   return p - buf;
2042 }
2043
2044
2045 /* Global interrupt locks for SMP. Allow interrupts to
2046  * come in on any CPU, yet make cli/sti act globally to
2047  * protect critical regions..  */
2048 #ifdef CONFIG_SMP
2049 unsigned char global_irq_holder = NO_PROC_ID;
2050 /* pendantic: long for set_bit -RR */
2051 unsigned volatile long global_irq_lock;
2052
2053 extern void show_stack(unsigned long *esp);
2054
2055 static void show(char *str)
2056 {
2057   int i;
2058   int cpu = smp_processor_id();
2059
2060   printk("\n%s, CPU %d:\n", str, cpu);
2061   printk("irq:  %d [", irqs_running());
2062   for (i = 0; i < smp_num_cpus; i++)
2063     printk(" %d", local_irq_count(i));
2064   printk(" ]\nbh:   %d [",
2065       spin_is_locked(&global_bh_lock) ? 1 : 0);
2066   for (i = 0; i < smp_num_cpus; i++)
2067     printk(" %d", local_bh_count(i));
2068
2069   printk(" ]\nStack dumps:");
2070   for (i = 0; i < smp_num_cpus; i++) {
2071     unsigned long esp;
2072     if (i == cpu)
2073       continue;
2074     printk("\nCPU %d:", i);
2075     esp = init_tss[i].esp0;
2076     if (!esp) {
2077       /* tss->esp0 is set to NULL in cpu_init(), it's
2078        * initialized when the cpu returns to user
2079        * space. - manfreds */
2080       printk(" <unknown> ");
2081       continue;
2082     }
2083     esp &= ~(THREAD_SIZE - 1);
2084     esp += sizeof(struct task_struct);
2085     show_stack((void *) esp);
2086   }
2087   printk("\nCPU %d:", cpu);
2088   show_stack(NULL);
2089   printk("\n");
```

```
2090 }
2091
2092 #define MAXCOUNT 100000000
2093
2094 /* I had a lockup scenario where a tight loop doing
2095  * spin_unlock()/spin_lock() on CPU#1 was racing with
2096  * spin_lock() on CPU#0. CPU#0 should have noticed
2097  * spin_unlock(), but apparently the spin_unlock()
2098  * information did not make it through to CPU#0
2099  * ... nasty, is this by design, do we have to limit
2100  * 'memory update oscillation frequency' artificially
2101  * like here?
2102  *
2103  * Such 'high frequency update' races can be avoided by
2104  * careful design, but some of our major constructs like
2105  * spinlocks use similar techniques, it would be nice to
2106  * clarify this issue. Set this define to 0 if you want
2107  * to check whether your system freezes.  I suspect the
2108  * delay done by SYNC_OTHER_CORES() is in correlation
2109  * with 'snooping latency', but i thought that such
2110  * things are guaranteed by design, since we use the
2111  * 'LOCK' prefix.  */
2112 #define SUSPECTED_CPU_OR_CHIPSET_BUG_WORKAROUND 0
2113
2114 #if SUSPECTED_CPU_OR_CHIPSET_BUG_WORKAROUND
2115 # define SYNC_OTHER_CORES(x) udelay(x+1)
2116 #else
2117 /* We have to allow irqs to arrive between __sti and
2118  * __cli */
2119 # define SYNC_OTHER_CORES(x) __asm__ __volatile__ ("nop")
2120 #endif
2121
2122 static inline void wait_on_irq(int cpu)
2123 {
2124   int count = MAXCOUNT;
2125
2126   for (;;) {
2127
2128     /* Wait until all interrupts are gone. Wait for
2129      * bottom half handlers unless we're already
2130      * executing in one..  */
2131     if (!irqs_running())
2132       if (local_bh_count(cpu) ||
2133           !spin_is_locked(&global_bh_lock))
2134         break;
2135
2136     /* Duh, we have to loop. Release the lock to avoid
2137      * deadlocks */
2138     clear_bit(0, &global_irq_lock);
2139
2140     for (;;) {
2141       if (!--count) {
2142         show("wait_on_irq");
2143         count = ~0;
2144       }
2145       __sti();
2146       SYNC_OTHER_CORES(cpu);
2147       __cli();
2148       if (irqs_running())
2149         continue;
2150       if (global_irq_lock)
2151         continue;
2152       if (!local_bh_count(cpu) &&
2153           spin_is_locked(&global_bh_lock))
2154         continue;
2155       if (!test_and_set_bit(0, &global_irq_lock))
2156         break;
2157     }
2158   }
2159 }
2160
2161 /* This is called when we want to synchronize with
2162  * interrupts. We may for example tell a device to stop
2163  * sending interrupts: but to make sure there are no
2164  * interrupts that are executing on another CPU we need
2165  * to call this function.  */
2166 void synchronize_irq(void)
2167 {
2168   if (irqs_running()) {
2169     /* Stupid approach */
2170     cli();
2171     sti();
2172   }
2173 }
2174
2175 static inline void get_irqlock(int cpu)
2176 {
2177   if (test_and_set_bit(0, &global_irq_lock)) {
2178     /* do we already hold the lock? */
2179     if ((unsigned char) cpu == global_irq_holder)
2180       return;
2181     /* Uhhuh.. Somebody else got it. Wait.. */
2182     do {
2183       do {} while (test_bit(0, &global_irq_lock));
```

```
2184      } while (test_and_set_bit(0, &global_irq_lock));
2185  }
2186  /* We also to make sure that nobody else is running in
2187   * an interrupt context.  */
2188  wait_on_irq(cpu);
2189
2190  /* Ok, finally..  */
2191  global_irq_holder = cpu;
2192 }
2193
2194 #define EFLAGS_IF_SHIFT 9
2195
2196 /* A global "cli()" while in an interrupt context turns
2197  * into just a local cli(). Interrupts should use
2198  * spinlocks for the (very unlikely) case that they ever
2199  * want to protect against each other.
2200  *
2201  * If we already have local interrupts disabled,
2202  * this will not turn a local disable into a
2203  * global one (problems with spinlocks: this makes
2204  * save_flags+cli+sti usable inside a spinlock).  */
2205 void __global_cli(void)
2206 {
2207   unsigned int flags;
2208
2209   __save_flags(flags);
2210   if (flags & (1 << EFLAGS_IF_SHIFT)) {
2211     int cpu = smp_processor_id();
2212     __cli();
2213     if (!local_irq_count(cpu))
2214       get_irqlock(cpu);
2215   }
2216 }
2217
2218 void __global_sti(void)
2219 {
2220   int cpu = smp_processor_id();
2221
2222   if (!local_irq_count(cpu))
2223     release_irqlock(cpu);
2224   __sti();
2225 }
2226
2227 /* SMP flags value to restore to:
2228  * 0 - global cli
2229  * 1 - global sti
2230  * 2 - local cli
```

```
2231  * 3 - local sti */
2232 unsigned long __global_save_flags(void)
2233 {
2234   int retval;
2235   int local_enabled;
2236   unsigned long flags;
2237   int cpu = smp_processor_id();
2238
2239   __save_flags(flags);
2240   local_enabled = (flags >> EFLAGS_IF_SHIFT) & 1;
2241   /* default to local */
2242   retval = 2 + local_enabled;
2243
2244   /* check for global flags if we're not in an interrupt
2245    */
2246   if (!local_irq_count(cpu)) {
2247     if (local_enabled)
2248       retval = 1;
2249     if (global_irq_holder == cpu)
2250       retval = 0;
2251   }
2252   return retval;
2253 }
2254
2255 void __global_restore_flags(unsigned long flags)
2256 {
2257   switch (flags) {
2258   case 0:
2259     __global_cli();
2260     break;
2261   case 1:
2262     __global_sti();
2263     break;
2264   case 2:
2265     __cli();
2266     break;
2267   case 3:
2268     __sti();
2269     break;
2270   default:
2271     printk("global_restore_flags: %08lx (%08lx)\n",
2272         flags, (&flags)[-1]);
2273   }
2274 }
2275
2276 #endif
2277
```

```
2278 /* This should really return information about whether we
2279  * should do bottom half handling etc. Right now we end
2280  * up _always_ checking the bottom half, which is a waste
2281  * of time and is not what some drivers would prefer.  */
2282 int handle_IRQ_event(unsigned int irq,
2283     struct pt_regs *regs, struct irqaction *action)
2284 {
2285   int status;
2286   int cpu = smp_processor_id();
2287
2288   irq_enter(cpu, irq);
2289
2290   status = 1;       /* Force the "do bottom halves" bit */
2291
2292   if (!(action->flags & SA_INTERRUPT))
2293     __sti();
2294
2295   do {
2296     status |= action->flags;
2297     action->handler(irq, action->dev_id, regs);
2298     action = action->next;
2299   } while (action);
2300   if (status & SA_SAMPLE_RANDOM)
2301     add_interrupt_randomness(irq);
2302   __cli();
2303
2304   irq_exit(cpu, irq);
2305
2306   return status;
2307 }
2308
2309 /* Generic enable/disable code: this just calls down into
2310  * the PIC-specific version for the actual hardware
2311  * disable after having gotten the irq controller lock.
2312  */
2313
2314 /**
2315  * disable_irq_nosync - disable an irq without waiting
2316  * @irq: Interrupt to disable
2317  *
2318  * Disable the selected interrupt line. Disables of an
2319  * interrupt stack. Unlike disable_irq(), this function
2320  * does not ensure existing instances of the IRQ handler
2321  * have completed before returning.
2322  *
2323  * This function may be called from IRQ context.  */
2324 void inline disable_irq_nosync(unsigned int irq)
2325 {
2326   irq_desc_t *desc = irq_desc + irq;
2327   unsigned long flags;
2328
2329   spin_lock_irqsave(&desc->lock, flags);
2330   if (!desc->depth++) {
2331     desc->status |= IRQ_DISABLED;
2332     desc->handler->disable(irq);
2333   }
2334   spin_unlock_irqrestore(&desc->lock, flags);
2335 }
2336
2337 /**
2338  * disable_irq - disable an irq and wait for completion
2339  * @irq: Interrupt to disable
2340  *
2341  * Disable the selected interrupt line. Disables of an
2342  * interrupt stack. That is for two disables you need two
2343  * enables. This function waits for any pending IRQ
2344  * handlers for this interrupt to complete before
2345  * returning. If you use this function while holding a
2346  * resource the IRQ handler may need you will deadlock.
2347  *
2348  * This function may be called - with care - from IRQ
2349  * context.  */
2350 void disable_irq(unsigned int irq)
2351 {
2352   disable_irq_nosync(irq);
2353
2354   if (!local_irq_count(smp_processor_id())) {
2355     do {
2356       barrier();
2357     } while (irq_desc[irq].status & IRQ_INPROGRESS);
2358   }
2359 }
2360
2361 /**
2362  * enable_irq - enable interrupt handling on an irq
2363  * @irq: Interrupt to enable
2364  *
2365  * Re-enables the processing of interrupts on this IRQ
2366  * line providing no disable_irq calls are now in effect.
2367  *
2368  * This function may be called from IRQ context.  */
2369 void enable_irq(unsigned int irq)
2370 {
2371   irq_desc_t *desc = irq_desc + irq;
```

```
2372   unsigned long flags;
2373
2374   spin_lock_irqsave(&desc->lock, flags);
2375   switch (desc->depth) {
2376   case 1:
2377   {
2378     unsigned int status = desc->status & ~IRQ_DISABLED;
2379     desc->status = status;
2380     if ((status & (IRQ_PENDING | IRQ_REPLAY)) ==
2381         IRQ_PENDING) {
2382       desc->status = status | IRQ_REPLAY;
2383       hw_resend_irq(desc->handler, irq);
2384     }
2385     desc->handler->enable(irq);
2386     /* fall-through */
2387   }
2388   default:
2389     desc->depth--;
2390     break;
2391   case 0:
2392     printk("enable_irq(%u) unbalanced from %p\n", irq,
2393           __builtin_return_address(0));
2394   }
2395   spin_unlock_irqrestore(&desc->lock, flags);
2396 }
2397
2398 /* do_IRQ handles all normal device IRQ's (the special
2399  * SMP cross-CPU interrupts have their own specific
2400  * handlers).  */
2401 asmlinkage unsigned int do_IRQ(struct pt_regs regs)
2402 {
2403   /* We ack quickly, we don't want the irq controller
2404    * thinking we're snobs just because some other CPU has
2405    * disabled global interrupts (we have already done the
2406    * INT_ACK cycles, it's too late to try to pretend to
2407    * the controller that we aren't taking the interrupt).
2408    *
2409    * 0 return value means that this irq is already being
2410    * handled by some other CPU. (or is disabled) */
2411   /* high bits used in ret_from_ code */
2412   int irq = regs.orig_eax & 0xff;
2413   int cpu = smp_processor_id();
2414   irq_desc_t *desc = irq_desc + irq;
2415   struct irqaction *action;
2416   unsigned int status;
2417
2418   kstat.irqs[cpu][irq]++;
```

p 588

```
2419   spin_lock(&desc->lock);
2420   desc->handler->ack(irq);
2421   /* REPLAY is when Linux resends an IRQ that was dropped
2422    * earlier WAITING is used by probe to mark irqs that
2423    * are being tested */
2424   status = desc->status & ~(IRQ_REPLAY | IRQ_WAITING);
2425   status |= IRQ_PENDING;    /* we _want_ to handle it */
2426
2427   /* If the IRQ is disabled for whatever reason, we
2428    * cannot use the action we have.  */
2429   action = NULL;
2430   if (!(status & (IRQ_DISABLED | IRQ_INPROGRESS))) {
2431     action = desc->action;
2432     status &= ~IRQ_PENDING;   /* we commit to handling */
2433     status |= IRQ_INPROGRESS; /* we are handling it */
2434   }
2435   desc->status = status;
2436
2437   /* If there is no IRQ handler or it was disabled, exit
2438    * early.  Since we set PENDING, if another processor
2439    * is handling a different instance of this same irq,
2440    * the other processor will take care of it.  */
2441   if (!action)
2442     goto out;
2443
2444   /* Edge triggered interrupts need to remember pending
2445    * events.  This applies to any hw interrupts that
2446    * allow a second instance of the same irq to arrive
2447    * while we are in do_IRQ or in the handler. But the
2448    * code here only handles the _second_ instance of the
2449    * irq, not the third or fourth. So it is mostly useful
2450    * for irq hardware that does not mask cleanly in an
2451    * SMP environment.  */
2452   for (;;) {
2453     spin_unlock(&desc->lock);
2454     handle_IRQ_event(irq, &regs, action);
2455     spin_lock(&desc->lock);
2456
2457     if (!(desc->status & IRQ_PENDING))
2458       break;
2459     desc->status &= ~IRQ_PENDING;
2460   }
2461   desc->status &= ~IRQ_INPROGRESS;
2462 out:
2463   /* The ->end() handler has to deal with interrupts
2464    * which got disabled while the handler was running. */
2465   desc->handler->end(irq);
```

```
2466    spin_unlock(&desc->lock);
2467
2468    if (softirq_active(cpu) & softirq_mask(cpu))
2469      do_softirq();
2470    return 1;
2471 }
2472
2473 /**
2474  * request_irq - allocate an interrupt line
2475  * @irq: Interrupt line to allocate
2476  * @handler: Function to be called when the IRQ occurs
2477  * @irqflags: Interrupt type flags
2478  * @devname: An ascii name for the claiming device
2479  * @dev_id: A cookie passed back to the handler function
2480  *
2481  * This call allocates interrupt resources and enables
2482  * the interrupt line and IRQ handling. From the point
2483  * this call is made your handler function may be
2484  * invoked. Since your handler function must clear any
2485  * interrupt the board raises, you must take care both to
2486  * initialise your hardware and to set up the interrupt
2487  * handler in the right order.
2488  *
2489  * Dev_id must be globally unique. Normally the address
2490  * of the device data structure is used as the
2491  * cookie. Since the handler receives this value it makes
2492  * sense to use it.
2493  *
2494  * If your interrupt is shared you must pass a non NULL
2495  * dev_id as this is required when freeing the interrupt.
2496  *
2497  * Flags:
2498  *
2499  * SA_SHIRQ        Interrupt is shared
2500  *
2501  * SA_INTERRUPT    Disable local interrupts while
2502  *                 processing
2503  *
2504  * SA_SAMPLE_RANDOM The interrupt can be used for entropy
2505  */
2506 int request_irq(unsigned int irq,
2507     void (*handler) (int, void *, struct pt_regs *),
2508     unsigned long irqflags,
2509     const char *devname, void *dev_id)
2510 {
2511   int retval;
2512   struct irqaction *action;
```

```
2513
2514 #if 1
2515    /* Sanity-check: shared interrupts should REALLY pass
2516     * in a real dev-ID, otherwise we'll have trouble later
2517     * trying to figure out which interrupt is which
2518     * (messes up the interrupt freeing logic etc).  */
2519    if (irqflags & SA_SHIRQ) {
2520      if (!dev_id)
2521        printk("Bad boy: %s (at 0x%x) called us without a "
2522               "dev_id!\n", devname, (&irq)[-1]);
2523    }
2524 #endif
2525
2526    if (irq >= NR_IRQS)
2527      return -EINVAL;
2528    if (!handler)
2529      return -EINVAL;
2530
2531    action = (struct irqaction *)
2532        kmalloc(sizeof(struct irqaction), GFP_KERNEL);
2533    if (!action)
2534      return -ENOMEM;
2535
2536    action->handler = handler;
2537    action->flags = irqflags;
2538    action->mask = 0;
2539    action->name = devname;
2540    action->next = NULL;
2541    action->dev_id = dev_id;
2542
2543    retval = setup_irq(irq, action);
2544    if (retval)
2545      kfree(action);
2546    return retval;
2547 }
2548
2549 /**
2550  * free_irq - free an interrupt
2551  * @irq: Interrupt line to free
2552  * @dev_id: Device identity to free
2553  *
2554  * Remove an interrupt handler. The handler is removed
2555  * and if the interrupt line is no longer in use by any
2556  * driver it is disabled.  On a shared IRQ the caller
2557  * must ensure the interrupt is disabled on the card it
2558  * drives before calling this function. The function does
2559  * not return until any executing interrupts for this IRQ
```

p 587

```
2560   * have completed.
2561   *
2562   * This function may be called from interrupt context.
2563   *
2564   * Bugs: Attempting to free an irq in a handler for the
2565   * same irq hangs the machine.  */
2566  void free_irq(unsigned int irq, void *dev_id)
2567  {
2568    irq_desc_t *desc;
2569    struct irqaction **p;
2570    unsigned long flags;
2571
2572    if (irq >= NR_IRQS)
2573      return;
2574
2575    desc = irq_desc + irq;
2576    spin_lock_irqsave(&desc->lock, flags);
2577    p = &desc->action;
2578    for (;;) {
2579      struct irqaction *action = *p;
2580      if (action) {
2581        struct irqaction **pp = p;
2582        p = &action->next;
2583        if (action->dev_id != dev_id)
2584          continue;
2585
2586        /* Found it - now remove it from the list of
2587         * entries */
2588        *pp = action->next;
2589        if (!desc->action) {
2590          desc->status |= IRQ_DISABLED;
2591          desc->handler->shutdown(irq);
2592        }
2593        spin_unlock_irqrestore(&desc->lock, flags);
2594
2595  #ifdef CONFIG_SMP
2596        /* Wait to make sure it's not being used on
2597         * another CPU */
2598        while (desc->status & IRQ_INPROGRESS)
2599          barrier();
2600  #endif
2601        kfree(action);
2602        return;
2603      }
2604      printk("Trying to free free IRQ%d\n", irq);
2605      spin_unlock_irqrestore(&desc->lock, flags);
2606      return;
```

```
2607    }
2608  }
2609
2610  /* IRQ autodetection code..
2611   *
2612   * This depends on the fact that any interrupt that
2613   * comes in on to an unassigned handler will get stuck
2614   * with "IRQ_WAITING" cleared and the interrupt
2615   * disabled.  */
2616
2617  static DECLARE_MUTEX(probe_sem);
2618
2619  /**
2620   * probe_irq_on    - begin an interrupt autodetect
2621   *
2622   * Commence probing for an interrupt. The interrupts are
2623   * scanned and a mask of potential interrupt lines is
2624   * returned.  */
2625  unsigned long probe_irq_on(void)
2626  {
2627    unsigned int i;
2628    irq_desc_t *desc;
2629    unsigned long val;
2630    unsigned long delay;
2631
2632    down(&probe_sem);
2633    /* something may have generated an irq long ago and we
2634     * want to flush such a longstanding irq before
2635     * considering it as spurious.  */
2636    for (i = NR_IRQS - 1; i > 0; i—) {
2637      desc = irq_desc + i;
2638
2639      spin_lock_irq(&desc->lock);
2640      if (!irq_desc[i].action)
2641        irq_desc[i].handler->startup(i);
2642      spin_unlock_irq(&desc->lock);
2643    }
2644
2645    /* Wait for longstanding interrupts to trigger. */
2646    for (delay = jiffies + HZ / 50;
2647        time_after(delay, jiffies);)
2648      /* about 20ms delay */
2649      synchronize_irq();
2650
2651    /* enable any unassigned irqs (we must startup again
2652     * here because if a longstanding irq happened in the
2653     * previous stage, it may have masked itself) */
```

p 587

```
2654    for (i = NR_IRQS - 1; i > 0; i--) {
2655      desc = irq_desc + i;
2656
2657      spin_lock_irq(&desc->lock);
2658      if (!desc->action) {
2659        desc->status |= IRQ_AUTODETECT | IRQ_WAITING;
2660        if (desc->handler->startup(i))
2661          desc->status |= IRQ_PENDING;
2662      }
2663      spin_unlock_irq(&desc->lock);
2664    }
2665
2666    /* Wait for spurious interrupts to trigger */
2667    for (delay = jiffies + HZ / 10;
2668        time_after(delay, jiffies);)
2669      /* about 100ms delay */
2670      synchronize_irq();
2671
2672    /* Now filter out any obviously spurious interrupts */
2673    val = 0;
2674    for (i = 0; i < NR_IRQS; i++) {
2675      irq_desc_t *desc = irq_desc + i;
2676      unsigned int status;
2677
2678      spin_lock_irq(&desc->lock);
2679      status = desc->status;
2680
2681      if (status & IRQ_AUTODETECT) {
2682        /* It triggered already - consider it spurious. */
2683        if (!(status & IRQ_WAITING)) {
2684          desc->status = status & ~IRQ_AUTODETECT;
2685          desc->handler->shutdown(i);
2686        } else if (i < 32)
2687          val |= 1 << i;
2688      }
2689      spin_unlock_irq(&desc->lock);
2690    }
2691
2692    return val;
2693 }
2694
2695 /* Return a mask of triggered interrupts (this can handle
2696  * only legacy ISA interrupts).  */
2697
2698 /**
2699  * probe_irq_mask - scan a bitmap of interrupt lines
2700  * @val:   mask of interrupts to consider
2701  *
2702  * Scan the ISA bus interrupt lines and return a bitmap
2703  * of active interrupts. The interrupt probe logic state
2704  * is then returned to its previous value.
2705  *
2706  * Note: we need to scan all the irq's even though we
2707  * will only return ISA irq numbers - just so that we
2708  * reset them all to a known state.  */
2709 unsigned int probe_irq_mask(unsigned long val)
2710 {
2711    int i;
2712    unsigned int mask;
2713
2714    mask = 0;
2715    for (i = 0; i < NR_IRQS; i++) {
2716      irq_desc_t *desc = irq_desc + i;
2717      unsigned int status;
2718
2719      spin_lock_irq(&desc->lock);
2720      status = desc->status;
2721
2722      if (status & IRQ_AUTODETECT) {
2723        if (i < 16 && !(status & IRQ_WAITING))
2724          mask |= 1 << i;
2725
2726        desc->status = status & ~IRQ_AUTODETECT;
2727        desc->handler->shutdown(i);
2728      }
2729      spin_unlock_irq(&desc->lock);
2730    }
2731    up(&probe_sem);
2732
2733    return mask & val;
2734 }
2735
2736 /* Return the one interrupt that triggered (this can
2737  * handle any interrupt source).  */
2738
2739 /**
2740  * probe_irq_off  - end an interrupt autodetect
2741  * @val: mask of potential interrupts (unused)
2742  *
2743  * Scans the unused interrupt lines and returns the line
2744  * which appears to have triggered the interrupt. If no
2745  * interrupt was found then zero is returned. If more
2746  * than one interrupt is found then minus the first
2747  * candidate is returned to indicate their is doubt.
```

```
2748  *
2749  * The interrupt probe logic state is returned to its
2750  * previous value.
2751  *
2752  * BUGS: When used in a module (which arguably shouldnt
2753  * happen) nothing prevents two IRQ probe callers from
2754  * overlapping. The results of this are non-optimal.  */
2755 int probe_irq_off(unsigned long val)
2756 {
2757    int i, irq_found, nr_irqs;
2758
2759    nr_irqs = 0;
2760    irq_found = 0;
2761    for (i = 0; i < NR_IRQS; i++) {
2762      irq_desc_t *desc = irq_desc + i;
2763      unsigned int status;
2764
2765      spin_lock_irq(&desc->lock);
2766      status = desc->status;
2767
2768      if (status & IRQ_AUTODETECT) {
2769        if (!(status & IRQ_WAITING)) {
2770          if (!nr_irqs)
2771            irq_found = i;
2772          nr_irqs++;
2773        }
2774        desc->status = status & ~IRQ_AUTODETECT;
2775        desc->handler->shutdown(i);
2776      }
2777      spin_unlock_irq(&desc->lock);
2778    }
2779    up(&probe_sem);
2780
2781    if (nr_irqs > 1)
2782      irq_found = -irq_found;
2783    return irq_found;
2784 }
2785
2786 /* this was setup_x86_irq but it seems pretty generic */
2787 int setup_irq(unsigned int irq, struct irqaction *new)
2788 {
2789    int shared = 0;
2790    unsigned long flags;
2791    struct irqaction *old, **p;
2792    irq_desc_t *desc = irq_desc + irq;
2793
2794    /* Some drivers like serial.c use request_irq()
```

```
2795  * heavily, so we have to be careful not to interfere
2796  * with a running system. */
2797 if (new->flags & SA_SAMPLE_RANDOM) {
2798    /* This function might sleep, we want to call it
2799     * first, outside of the atomic block.  Yes, this
2800     * might clear the entropy pool if the wrong driver
2801     * is attempted to be loaded, without actually
2802     * installing a new handler, but is this really a
2803     * problem, only the sysadmin is able to do this.  */
2804    rand_initialize_irq(irq);
2805 }
2806
2807 /* The following block of code has to be executed
2808  * atomically */
2809 spin_lock_irqsave(&desc->lock, flags);
2810 p = &desc->action;
2811 if ((old = *p) != NULL) {
2812    /* Can't share interrupts unless both agree to */
2813    if (!(old->flags & new->flags & SA_SHIRQ)) {
2814      spin_unlock_irqrestore(&desc->lock, flags);
2815      return -EBUSY;
2816    }
2817
2818    /* add new interrupt at end of irq queue */
2819    do {
2820      p = &old->next;
2821      old = *p;
2822    } while (old);
2823    shared = 1;
2824 }
2825
2826 *p = new;
2827
2828 if (!shared) {
2829    desc->depth = 0;
2830    desc->status &=
2831        ~(IRQ_DISABLED | IRQ_AUTODETECT | IRQ_WAITING);
2832    desc->handler->startup(irq);
2833 }
2834 spin_unlock_irqrestore(&desc->lock, flags);
2835
2836 register_irq_proc(irq);
2837 return 0;
2838 }
2839
2840 static struct proc_dir_entry *root_irq_dir;
2841 static struct proc_dir_entry *irq_dir[NR_IRQS];
```

```
2842 static struct proc_dir_entry
2843    *smp_affinity_entry[NR_IRQS];
2844
2845 static unsigned long irq_affinity[NR_IRQS] =
2846    { [0 ... NR_IRQS - 1] = ~0UL };
2847
2848 #define HEX_DIGITS 8
2849
2850 static int irq_affinity_read_proc(char *page,
2851 char **start, off_t off, int count, int *eof, void *data)
2852 {
2853    if (count < HEX_DIGITS + 1)
2854      return -EINVAL;
2855    return sprintf(page, "%08lx\n",
2856                  irq_affinity[(long) data]);
2857 }
2858
2859 static unsigned int
2860 parse_hex_value(const char *buffer, unsigned long count,
2861                  unsigned long *ret)
2862 {
2863    unsigned char hexnum[HEX_DIGITS];
2864    unsigned long value;
2865    int i;
2866
2867    if (!count)
2868      return -EINVAL;
2869    if (count > HEX_DIGITS)
2870      count = HEX_DIGITS;
2871    if (copy_from_user(hexnum, buffer, count))
2872      return -EFAULT;
2873
2874    /* Parse the first 8 characters as a hex string, any
2875     * non-hex char is end-of-string. '00e1', 'e1', '00E1',
2876     * 'E1' are all the same. */
2877    value = 0;
2878
2879    for (i = 0; i < count; i++) {
2880      unsigned int c = hexnum[i];
2881
2882      switch (c) {
2883      case '0'...'9':
2884        c -= '0';
2885        break;
2886      case 'a' ... 'f':
2887        c -= 'a' - 10;
2888        break;
```

```
2889      case 'A' ... 'F':
2890        c -= 'A' - 10;
2891        break;
2892      default:
2893        goto out;
2894      }
2895      value = (value << 4) | c;
2896    }
2897 out:
2898    *ret = value;
2899    return 0;
2900 }
2901
2902 static int irq_affinity_write_proc(struct file *file,
2903    const char *buffer, unsigned long count, void *data)
2904 {
2905    int irq = (long) data, full_count = count, err;
2906    unsigned long new_value;
2907
2908    if (!irq_desc[irq].handler->set_affinity)
2909      return -EIO;
2910
2911    err = parse_hex_value(buffer, count, &new_value);
2912
2913 #if CONFIG_SMP
2914    /* Do not allow disabling IRQs completely - it's a too
2915     * easy way to make the system unusable accidentally
2916     * :-) At least one online CPU still has to be
2917     * targeted.  */
2918    if (!(new_value & cpu_online_map))
2919      return -EINVAL;
2920 #endif
2921
2922    irq_affinity[irq] = new_value;
2923    irq_desc[irq].handler->set_affinity(irq, new_value);
2924
2925    return full_count;
2926 }
2927
2928 static int prof_cpu_mask_read_proc(char *page,
2929 char **start, off_t off, int count, int *eof, void *data)
2930 {
2931    unsigned long *mask = (unsigned long *) data;
2932    if (count < HEX_DIGITS + 1)
2933      return -EINVAL;
2934    return sprintf(page, "%08lx\n", *mask);
2935 }
```

```
2936
2937 static int prof_cpu_mask_write_proc(struct file *file,
2938    const char *buffer, unsigned long count, void *data)
2939 {
2940   unsigned long *mask = (unsigned long *) data,
2941     full_count = count,
2942     err;
2943   unsigned long new_value;
2944
2945   err = parse_hex_value(buffer, count, &new_value);
2946   if (err)
2947     return err;
2948
2949   *mask = new_value;
2950   return full_count;
2951 }
2952
2953 #define MAX_NAMELEN 10
2954
2955 static void register_irq_proc(unsigned int irq)
2956 {
2957   struct proc_dir_entry *entry;
2958   char name[MAX_NAMELEN];
2959
2960   if (!root_irq_dir
2961       || (irq_desc[irq].handler == &no_irq_type)
2962       || irq_dir[irq])
2963     return;
2964
2965   memset(name, 0, MAX_NAMELEN);
2966   sprintf(name, "%d", irq);
2967
2968   /* create /proc/irq/1234 */
2969   irq_dir[irq] = proc_mkdir(name, root_irq_dir);
2970
2971   /* create /proc/irq/1234/smp_affinity */
2972
2973   entry = create_proc_entry("smp_affinity", 0600,
2974                     irq_dir[irq]);
2975
2976   entry->nlink = 1;
2977   entry->data = (void *) (long) irq;
2978   entry->read_proc = irq_affinity_read_proc;
2979   entry->write_proc = irq_affinity_write_proc;
2980
2981   smp_affinity_entry[irq] = entry;
2982 }
2983
2984 unsigned long prof_cpu_mask = -1;
2985
2986 void init_irq_proc(void)
2987 {
2988   struct proc_dir_entry *entry;
2989   int i;
2990
2991   /* create /proc/irq */
2992   root_irq_dir = proc_mkdir("irq", 0);
2993
2994   /* create /proc/irq/prof_cpu_mask */
2995   entry = create_proc_entry("prof_cpu_mask", 0600,
2996                     root_irq_dir);
2997
2998   entry->nlink = 1;
2999   entry->data = (void *) &prof_cpu_mask;
3000   entry->read_proc = prof_cpu_mask_read_proc;
3001   entry->write_proc = prof_cpu_mask_write_proc;
3002
3003   /* Create entries for all existing IRQs.  */
3004   for (i = 0; i < NR_IRQS; i++)
3005     register_irq_proc(i);
3006 }
```

arch/i386/kernel/process.c

```
3007 /*
3008  *  linux/arch/i386/kernel/process.c
3009  *
3010  *  Copyright (C) 1995  Linus Torvalds
3011  *
3012  *  Pentium III FXSR, SSE support
3013  *      Gareth Hughes <gareth@valinux.com>, May 2000
3014  */
3015
3016 /* This file handles the architecture-dependent parts of
3017  * process handling..  */
3018
3019 #define __KERNEL_SYSCALLS__
3020 #include <stdarg.h>
3021
3022 #include <linux/errno.h>
3023 #include <linux/sched.h>
3024 #include <linux/kernel.h>
3025 #include <linux/mm.h>
3026 #include <linux/smp.h>
3027 #include <linux/smp_lock.h>
```

```
3028 #include <linux/stddef.h>
3029 #include <linux/unistd.h>
3030 #include <linux/ptrace.h>
3031 #include <linux/malloc.h>
3032 #include <linux/vmalloc.h>
3033 #include <linux/user.h>
3034 #include <linux/a.out.h>
3035 #include <linux/interrupt.h>
3036 #include <linux/config.h>
3037 #include <linux/delay.h>
3038 #include <linux/reboot.h>
3039 #include <linux/init.h>
3040 #include <linux/mc146818rtc.h>
3041
3042 #include <asm/uaccess.h>
3043 #include <asm/pgtable.h>
3044 #include <asm/system.h>
3045 #include <asm/io.h>
3046 #include <asm/ldt.h>
3047 #include <asm/processor.h>
3048 #include <asm/i387.h>
3049 #include <asm/desc.h>
3050 #include <asm/mmu_context.h>
3051 #ifdef CONFIG_MATH_EMULATION
3052 #include <asm/math_emu.h>
3053 #endif
3054
3055 #include <linux/irq.h>
3056
3057 asmlinkage void ret_from_fork(void)
3058 __asm__("ret_from_fork");
3059
3060 int hlt_counter;
3061
3062 /* Powermanagement idle function, if any.. */
3063 void (*pm_idle) (void);
3064
3065 /* Power off function, if any */
3066 void (*pm_power_off) (void);
3067
3068 void disable_hlt(void)
3069 {
3070   hlt_counter++;
3071 }
3072
3073 void enable_hlt(void)
3074 {
3075   hlt_counter--;
3076 }
3077
3078 /* We use this if we don't have any better idle routine..
3079  */
3080 static void default_idle(void)
3081 {
3082   if (current_cpu_data.hlt_works_ok && !hlt_counter) {
3083     __cli();
3084     if (!current->need_resched)
3085       safe_halt();
3086     else
3087       __sti();
3088   }
3089 }
3090
3091 /* On SMP it's slightly faster (but much more
3092  * power-consuming!)  to poll the ->need_resched flag
3093  * instead of waiting for the cross-CPU IPI to
3094  * arrive. Use this option with caution.  */
3095 static void poll_idle(void)
3096 {
3097   int oldval;
3098
3099   __sti();
3100
3101   /* Deal with another CPU just having chosen a thread to
3102    * run here: */
3103   oldval = xchg(&current->need_resched, -1);
3104
3105   if (!oldval)
3106     asm volatile (
3107       "2:"
3108       "cmpl $-1, %0;"
3109       "rep; nop;"
3110       "je 2b;"::"m" (current->need_resched));
3111 }
3112
3113 /* The idle thread. There's no useful work to be done, so
3114  * just try to conserve power and have a low exit latency
3115  * (ie sit in a loop waiting for somebody to say that
3116  * they'd like to reschedule) */
3117 void cpu_idle(void)
3118 {
3119   /* endless idle loop with no priority at all */
3120   init_idle();
3121   current->nice = 20;
```

```
3122    current->counter = -100;
3123
3124    while (1) {
3125      void (*idle) (void) = pm_idle;
3126      if (!idle)
3127        idle = default_idle;
3128      while (!current->need_resched)
3129        idle();
3130      schedule();
3131      check_pgt_cache();
3132    }
3133  }
3134
3135  static int __init idle_setup(char *str)
3136  {
3137    if (!strncmp(str, "poll", 4)) {
3138      printk("using polling idle threads.\n");
3139      pm_idle = poll_idle;
3140    }
3141
3142    return 1;
3143  }
3144
3145  __setup("idle=", idle_setup);
3146
3147  static long no_idt[2];
3148  static int reboot_mode;
3149  static int reboot_thru_bios;
3150
3151  static int __init reboot_setup(char *str)
3152  {
3153    while (1) {
3154      switch (*str) {
3155      case 'w':  /* "warm" reboot (no memory testing etc)*/
3156        reboot_mode = 0x1234;
3157        break;
3158      case 'c':  /* "cold" reboot (with memory testing etc)
3159                 */
3160        reboot_mode = 0x0;
3161        break;
3162      case 'b':  /* "bios" reboot by jumping through the
3163                  * BIOS */
3164        reboot_thru_bios = 1;
3165        break;
3166      case 'h':  /* "hard" reboot by toggling RESET and/or
3167                  * crashing the CPU */
3168        reboot_thru_bios = 0;
3169        break;
3170      }
3171      if ((str = strchr(str, ',')) != NULL)
3172        str++;
3173      else
3174        break;
3175    }
3176    return 1;
3177  }
3178
3179  __setup("reboot=", reboot_setup);
3180
3181  /* The following code and data reboots the machine by
3182   * switching to real mode and jumping to the BIOS reset
3183   * entry point, as if the CPU has really been reset.
3184   * The previous version asked the keyboard controller to
3185   * pulse the CPU reset line, which is more thorough, but
3186   * doesn't work with at least one type of 486
3187   * motherboard.  It is easy to stop this code working;
3188   * hence the copious comments. */
3189
3190  static unsigned long long
3191  real_mode_gdt_entries[3] = {
3192    0x0000000000000000ULL,        /* Null descriptor */
3193    0x00009a000000ffffULL,        /* 16-bit real-mode 64k
3194                                   * code at 0x00000000 */
3195    0x000092000100ffffULL         /* 16-bit real-mode 64k
3196                                   * data at 0x00000100 */
3197  };
3198
3199  static struct {
3200    unsigned short size __attribute__ ((packed));
3201    unsigned long long *base __attribute__ ((packed));
3202  } real_mode_gdt = {
3203    sizeof(real_mode_gdt_entries) - 1,
3204    real_mode_gdt_entries
3205  }, real_mode_idt = {
3206    0x3ff, 0
3207  };
3208
3209  /* This is 16-bit protected mode code to disable paging
3210   * and the cache, switch to real mode and jump to the
3211   * BIOS reset code.
3212   *
3213   * The instruction that switches to real mode by writing
3214   * to CR0 must be followed immediately by a far jump
3215   * instruction, which set CS to a valid value for real
```

```
3216   * mode, and flushes the prefetch queue to avoid running
3217   * instructions that have already been decoded in
3218   * protected mode.
3219   *
3220   * Clears all the flags except ET, especially PG
3221   * (paging), PE (protected-mode enable) and TS (task
3222   * switch for coprocessor state save).  Flushes the TLB
3223   * after paging has been disabled.  Sets CD and NW, to
3224   * disable the cache on a 486, and invalidates the
3225   * cache.  This is more like the state of a 486 after
3226   * reset.  I don't know if something else should be done
3227   * for other chips.
3228   *
3229   * More could be done here to set up the registers as if
3230   * a CPU reset had occurred; hopefully real BIOSs don't
3231   * assume much. */
3232  static unsigned char real_mode_switch[] = {
3233    0x66, 0x0f, 0x20, 0xc0,          /* movl  %cr0,%eax */
3234    0x66, 0x83, 0xe0, 0x11,          /* andl $0x00000011,
3235                                     * %eax */
3236    0x66, 0x0d, 0x00, 0x00, 0x00, 0x60, /* orl $0x60000000,
3237                                     * %eax */
3238    0x66, 0x0f, 0x22, 0xc0,          /* movl  %eax,%cr0 */
3239    0x66, 0x0f, 0x22, 0xd8,          /* movl  %eax,%cr3 */
3240    0x66, 0x0f, 0x20, 0xc3,          /* movl  %cr0,%ebx */
3241                                     /* andl
3242                                     * $0x60000000,%ebx */
3243    0x66, 0x81, 0xe3, 0x00, 0x00, 0x00, 0x60,
3244    0x74, 0x02,                      /* jz    f */
3245    0x0f, 0x08,                      /* invd */
3246    0x24, 0x10,                      /* f: andb  $0x10,al */
3247    0x66, 0x0f, 0x22, 0xc0           /* movl  %eax,%cr0 */
3248  };
3249  static unsigned char jump_to_bios[] = {
3250    0xea, 0x00, 0x00, 0xff, 0xff  /* ljmp $0xffff,$0x0000*/
3251  };
3252
3253  static inline void kb_wait(void)
3254  {
3255    int i;
3256
3257    for (i = 0; i < 0x10000; i++)
3258      if ((inb_p(0x64) & 0x02) == 0)
3259        break;
3260  }
3261
3262  /* Switch to real mode and then execute the code
3263   * specified by the code and length parameters.  We
3264   * assume that length will aways be less that 100! */
3265  void machine_real_restart(unsigned char *code,
3266      int length)
3267  {
3268    unsigned long flags;
3269
3270    cli();
3271
3272    /* Write zero to CMOS register number 0x0f, which the
3273     * BIOS POST routine will recognize as telling it to
3274     * do a proper reboot.  (Well that's what this book in
3275     * front of me says — it may only apply to the
3276     * Phoenix BIOS though, it's not clear).  At the same
3277     * time, disable NMIs by setting the top bit in the
3278     * CMOS address register, as we're about to do
3279     * peculiar things to the CPU.  I'm not sure if
3280     * 'outb_p' is needed instead of just 'outb'.  Use it
3281     * to be on the safe side.  (Yes, CMOS_WRITE does
3282     * outb_p's. -  Paul G.) */
3283    spin_lock_irqsave(&rtc_lock, flags);
3284    CMOS_WRITE(0x00, 0x8f);
3285    spin_unlock_irqrestore(&rtc_lock, flags);
3286
3287    /* Remap the kernel at virtual address zero, as well
3288     * as offset zero from the kernel segment.  This
3289     * assumes the kernel segment starts at virtual
3290     * address PAGE_OFFSET. */
3291    memcpy(swapper_pg_dir, swapper_pg_dir + USER_PGD_PTRS,
3292        sizeof(swapper_pg_dir[0]) * KERNEL_PGD_PTRS);
3293
3294    /* Make sure the first page is mapped to the start of
3295     * physical memory. It is normally not mapped, to trap
3296     * kernel NULL pointer dereferences. */
3297    pg0[0] = _PAGE_RW | _PAGE_PRESENT;
3298
3299    /* Use 'swapper_pg_dir' as our page directory.  */
3300    asm volatile ("movl %0,%%cr3"
3301                  ::"r" (__pa(swapper_pg_dir)));
3302
3303    /* Write 0x1234 to absolute memory location 0x472.
3304     * The BIOS reads this on booting to tell it to
3305     * "Bypass memory test (also warm boot)".  This seems
3306     * like a fairly standard thing that gets set by
3307     * REBOOT.COM programs, and the previous reset routine
3308     * did this too. */
3309    *((unsigned short *) 0x472) = reboot_mode;
```

```
3310
3311     /* For the switch to real mode, copy some code to low
3312      * memory.  It has to be in the first 64k because it
3313      * is running in 16-bit mode, and it has to have the
3314      * same physical and virtual address, because it turns
3315      * off paging.  Copy it near the end of the first page,
3316      * out of the way of BIOS variables. */
3317     memcpy((void *) (0x1000 - sizeof(real_mode_switch) -
3318                       100),
3319           real_mode_switch, sizeof(real_mode_switch));
3320     memcpy((void *) (0x1000 - 100), code, length);
3321
3322     /* Set up the IDT for real mode. */
3323     __asm__ __volatile__("lidt %0"::"m"(real_mode_idt));
3324
3325     /* Set up a GDT from which we can load segment
3326      * descriptors for real mode.  The GDT is not used in
3327      * real mode; it is just needed here to prepare the
3328      * descriptors. */
3329     __asm__ __volatile__("lgdt %0"::"m"(real_mode_gdt));
3330
3331     /* Load the data segment registers, and thus the
3332      * descriptors ready for real mode.  The base address
3333      * of each segment is 0x100, 16 times the selector
3334      * value being loaded here.  This is so that the
3335      * segment registers don't have to be reloaded after
3336      * switching to real mode: the values are consistent
3337      * for real mode operation already. */
3338     __asm__ __volatile__("movl $0x0010,%%eax\n"
3339                          "\tmovl %%eax,%%ds\n"
3340                          "\tmovl %%eax,%%es\n"
3341                          "\tmovl %%eax,%%fs\n"
3342                          "\tmovl %%eax,%%gs\n"
3343                          "\tmovl %%eax,%%ss"::"eax");
3344
3345     /* Jump to the 16-bit code that we copied earlier.  It
3346      * disables paging and the cache, switches to real
3347      * mode, and jumps to the BIOS reset entry point. */
3348     __asm__ __volatile__("ljmp $0x0008,%0"
3349                          ::"i"((void *) (0x1000 -
3350                                sizeof(real_mode_switch) - 100)));
3351 }
3352
3353 void machine_restart(char *__unused)
3354 {
3355 #if CONFIG_SMP
3356     /* Stop all CPUs and turn off local APICs and the
3357      * IO-APIC, so other OSs see a clean IRQ state.  */
3358     smp_send_stop();
3359     disable_IO_APIC();
3360 #endif
3361
3362     if (!reboot_thru_bios) {
3363         /* rebooting needs to touch the page at absolute
3364          * addr 0 */
3365         *((unsigned short *) __va(0x472)) = reboot_mode;
3366         for (;;) {
3367             int i;
3368             for (i = 0; i < 100; i++) {
3369                 kb_wait();
3370                 udelay(50);
3371                 outb(0xfe, 0x64);         /* pulse reset low */
3372                 udelay(50);
3373             }
3374             /* That didn't work - force a triple fault.. */
3375             __asm__ __volatile__("lidt %0"::"m"(no_idt));
3376             __asm__ __volatile__("int3");
3377         }
3378     }
3379
3380     machine_real_restart(jump_to_bios,
3381             sizeof(jump_to_bios));
3382 }
3383
3384 void machine_halt(void)
3385 {
3386 }
3387
3388 void machine_power_off(void)
3389 {
3390     if (pm_power_off)
3391         pm_power_off();
3392 }
3393
3394 extern void show_trace(unsigned long *esp);
3395
3396 void show_regs(struct pt_regs *regs)
3397 {
3398     unsigned long cr0 = 0L, cr2 = 0L, cr3 = 0L, cr4 = 0L;
3399
3400     printk("\n");
3401     printk("EIP: %04x:[<%08lx>] CPU: %d",
3402         0xffff & regs->xcs, regs->eip, smp_processor_id());
3403     if (regs->xcs & 3)
```

```
3404     printk(" ESP: %04x:%08lx", 0xffff & regs->xss,
3405         regs->esp);
3406   printk(" EFLAGS: %08lx\n", regs->eflags);
3407   printk("EAX: %08lx EBX: %08lx ECX: %08lx EDX: %08lx\n",
3408       regs->eax, regs->ebx, regs->ecx, regs->edx);
3409   printk("ESI: %08lx EDI: %08lx EBP: %08lx",
3410       regs->esi, regs->edi, regs->ebp);
3411   printk(" DS: %04x ES: %04x\n",
3412       0xffff & regs->xds, 0xffff & regs->xes);
3413
3414   __asm__("movl %%cr0, %0":"=r"(cr0));
3415   __asm__("movl %%cr2, %0":"=r"(cr2));
3416   __asm__("movl %%cr3, %0":"=r"(cr3));
3417   /* This could fault if %cr4 does not exist */
3418   __asm__("1: movl %%cr4, %0           \n"
3419       "2:                              \n"
3420       ".section __ex_table,\"a\"       \n"
3421       ".long 1b,2b                     \n"
3422       ".previous                       \n"
3423       : "=r"(cr4):"0"(0));
3424   printk("CR0: %08lx CR2: %08lx CR3: %08lx CR4: %08lx\n",
3425       cr0, cr2, cr3, cr4);
3426   show_trace(&regs->esp);
3427 }
3428
3429 /* No need to lock the MM as we are the last user */
3430 void release_segments(struct mm_struct *mm)
3431 {
3432   void *ldt = mm->context.segments;
3433
3434   /* free the LDT */
3435   if (ldt) {
3436     mm->context.segments = NULL;
3437     clear_LDT();
3438     vfree(ldt);
3439   }
3440 }
3441
3442 /* Create a kernel thread */
3443 int kernel_thread(int (*fn) (void *), void *arg,
3444     unsigned long flags)
3445 {
3446   long retval, d0;
3447
3448   __asm__ __volatile__
3449   ( "movl %%esp,%%esi\n\t"
3450     "int $0x80\n\t"              /* Linux/i386 sys call */
3451     "cmpl %%esp,%%esi\n\t"      /* child or parent? */
3452     "je 1f\n\t"                  /* parent - jump */
3453     /* Load the argument into eax, and push it.  That
3454      * way, it does not matter whether the called
3455      * function is compiled with -mregparm or not.  */
3456     "movl %4,%%eax\n\t"
3457     "pushl %%eax\n\t"
3458     "call *%5\n\t"               /* call fn */
3459     "movl %3,%0\n\t"             /* exit */
3460     "int $0x80\n"
3461     "1:\t"
3462     :"=&a"(retval), "=&S"(d0)
3463     :"0"(__NR_clone), "i"(__NR_exit),
3464     "r"(arg), "r"(fn),
3465     "b"(flags | CLONE_VM)
3466     :"memory");
3467   return retval;
3468 }
3469
3470 /* Free current thread data structures etc.. */
3471 void exit_thread(void)
3472 {
3473   /* nothing to do ... */
3474 }
3475
3476 void flush_thread(void)
3477 {
3478   struct task_struct *tsk = current;
3479
3480   memset(tsk->thread.debugreg, 0,
3481       sizeof(unsigned long) * 8);
3482   /* Forget coprocessor state.. */
3483   clear_fpu(tsk);
3484   tsk->used_math = 0;
3485 }
3486
3487 void release_thread(struct task_struct *dead_task)
3488 {
3489   if (dead_task->mm) {
3490     void *ldt = dead_task->mm->context.segments;
3491
3492     // temporary debugging check
3493     if (ldt) {
3494       printk("WARNING: dead process %8s still has LDT? "
3495           "<%p>\n", dead_task->comm, ldt);
3496       BUG();
3497     }
```

```
3498     }
3499 }
3500
3501 /* we do not have to muck with descriptors here, that is
3502  * done in switch_mm() as needed.  */
3503 void copy_segments(struct task_struct *p,
3504     struct mm_struct *new_mm)
3505 {
3506   struct mm_struct *old_mm;
3507   void *old_ldt, *ldt;
3508
3509   ldt = NULL;
3510   old_mm = current->mm;
3511   if (old_mm
3512       && (old_ldt = old_mm->context.segments) != NULL) {
3513     /* Completely new LDT, we initialize it from the
3514      * parent: */
3515     ldt = vmalloc(LDT_ENTRIES * LDT_ENTRY_SIZE);
3516     if (!ldt)
3517       printk(KERN_WARNING "ldt allocation failed\n");
3518     else
3519       memcpy(ldt, old_ldt, LDT_ENTRIES * LDT_ENTRY_SIZE);
3520   }
3521   new_mm->context.segments = ldt;
3522 }
3523
3524 /* Save a segment.  */
3525 #define savesegment(seg,value)                              \
3526   asm volatile("movl %%" #seg ",%0"                         \
3527                   :"=m" (*(int *)&(value)))
3528
3529 int copy_thread(int nr, unsigned long clone_flags,
3530     unsigned long esp, unsigned long unused,
3531     struct task_struct *p, struct pt_regs *regs)
3532 {
3533   struct pt_regs *childregs;
3534
3535   childregs = ((struct pt_regs *)
3536           (THREAD_SIZE + (unsigned long) p)) - 1;
3537   struct_cpy(childregs, regs);
3538   childregs->eax = 0;
3539   childregs->esp = esp;
3540
3541   p->thread.esp = (unsigned long) childregs;
3542   p->thread.esp0 = (unsigned long) (childregs + 1);
3543
3544   p->thread.eip = (unsigned long) ret_from_fork;
3545
3546   savesegment(fs, p->thread.fs);
3547   savesegment(gs, p->thread.gs);
3548
3549   unlazy_fpu(current);
3550   struct_cpy(&p->thread.i387, &current->thread.i387);
3551
3552   return 0;
3553 }
3554
3555 /* fill in the user structure for a core dump..  */
3556 void dump_thread(struct pt_regs *regs, struct user *dump)
3557 {
3558   int i;
3559
3560   /* changed the size calculations - should hopefully
3561    * work better. lbt */
3562   dump->magic = CMAGIC;
3563   dump->start_code = 0;
3564   dump->start_stack = regs->esp & ~(PAGE_SIZE - 1);
3565   dump->u_tsize = ((unsigned long)
3566             current->mm->end_code) >> PAGE_SHIFT;
3567   dump->u_dsize =
3568     ((unsigned long)(current->mm->brk + (PAGE_SIZE - 1)))
3569       >> PAGE_SHIFT;
3570   dump->u_dsize -= dump->u_tsize;
3571   dump->u_ssize = 0;
3572   for (i = 0; i < 8; i++)
3573     dump->u_debugreg[i] = current->thread.debugreg[i];
3574
3575   if (dump->start_stack < TASK_SIZE)
3576     dump->u_ssize =
3577       ((unsigned long) (TASK_SIZE - dump->start_stack))
3578         >> PAGE_SHIFT;
3579
3580   dump->regs.ebx = regs->ebx;
3581   dump->regs.ecx = regs->ecx;
3582   dump->regs.edx = regs->edx;
3583   dump->regs.esi = regs->esi;
3584   dump->regs.edi = regs->edi;
3585   dump->regs.ebp = regs->ebp;
3586   dump->regs.eax = regs->eax;
3587   dump->regs.ds = regs->xds;
3588   dump->regs.es = regs->xes;
3589   savesegment(fs, dump->regs.fs);
3590   savesegment(gs, dump->regs.gs);
3591   dump->regs.orig_eax = regs->orig_eax;
```

```
3592   dump->regs.eip = regs->eip;
3593   dump->regs.cs = regs->xcs;
3594   dump->regs.eflags = regs->eflags;
3595   dump->regs.esp = regs->esp;
3596   dump->regs.ss = regs->xss;
3597
3598   dump->u_fpvalid = dump_fpu(regs, &dump->i387);
3599 }
3600
3601 /* This special macro can be used to load a debugging
3602  * register */
3603 #define loaddebug(thread,register)                    \
3604             __asm__("movl %0,%%db" #register          \
3605                 : /* no output */                     \
3606                 :"r" (thread->debugreg[register]))
3607
3608 /*      switch_to(x,yn) should switch tasks from x to y.
3609  *
3610  * We fsave/fwait so that an exception goes off at the
3611  * right time (as a call from the fsave or fwait in
3612  * effect) rather than to the wrong process. Lazy FP
3613  * saving no longer makes any sense with modern CPU's,
3614  * and this simplifies a lot of things (SMP and UP become
3615  * the same).
3616  *
3617  * NOTE! We used to use the x86 hardware context
3618  * switching. The reason for not using it any more
3619  * becomes apparent when you try to recover gracefully
3620  * from saved state that is no longer valid (stale
3621  * segment register values in particular). With the
3622  * hardware task-switch, there is no way to fix up bad
3623  * state in a reasonable manner.
3624  *
3625  * The fact that Intel documents the hardware
3626  * task-switching to be slow is a fairly red herring -
3627  * this code is not noticeably faster. However, there
3628  * _is_ some room for improvement here, so the
3629  * performance issues may eventually be a valid point.
3630  * More important, however, is the fact that this allows
3631  * us much more flexibility.  */
3632 void __switch_to(struct task_struct *prev_p,
3633         struct task_struct *next_p)
3634 {
3635   struct thread_struct *prev = &prev_p->thread,
3636         *next = &next_p->thread;
3637   struct tss_struct *tss = init_tss + smp_processor_id();
3638
3639   unlazy_fpu(prev_p);
3640
3641   /* Reload esp0, LDT and the page table pointer: */
3642   tss->esp0 = next->esp0;
3643
3644   /* Save away %fs and %gs. No need to save %es and %ds,
3645    * as those are always kernel segments while inside the
3646    * kernel.  */
3647   asm volatile("movl %%fs,%0":"=m" (*(int *) &prev->fs));
3648   asm volatile("movl %%gs,%0":"=m" (*(int *) &prev->gs));
3649
3650   /* Restore %fs and %gs.  */
3651   loadsegment(fs, next->fs);
3652   loadsegment(gs, next->gs);
3653
3654   /* Now maybe reload the debug registers */
3655   if (next->debugreg[7]) {
3656     loaddebug(next, 0);
3657     loaddebug(next, 1);
3658     loaddebug(next, 2);
3659     loaddebug(next, 3);
3660     /* no 4 and 5 */
3661     loaddebug(next, 6);
3662     loaddebug(next, 7);
3663   }
3664
3665   if (prev->ioperm || next->ioperm) {
3666     if (next->ioperm) {
3667       /* 4 cachelines copy ... not good, but not that bad
3668        * either. Anyone got something better?  This only
3669        * affects processes which use ioperm().  [Putting
3670        * the TSSs into 4k-tlb mapped regions and playing
3671        * VM tricks to switch the IO bitmap is not really
3672        * acceptable.] */
3673       memcpy(tss->io_bitmap, next->io_bitmap,
3674           IO_BITMAP_SIZE * sizeof(unsigned long));
3675       tss->bitmap = IO_BITMAP_OFFSET;
3676     } else
3677       /* a bitmap offset pointing outside of the TSS
3678        * limit causes a nicely controllable SIGSEGV if a
3679        * process tries to use a port IO instruction. The
3680        * first sys_ioperm() call sets up the bitmap
3681        * properly.  */
3682       tss->bitmap = INVALID_IO_BITMAP_OFFSET;
3683   }
3684 }
3685
```

```
3686 asmlinkage int sys_fork(struct pt_regs regs)
3687 {
3688   return do_fork(SIGCHLD, regs.esp, &regs, 0);
3689 }
3690
3691 asmlinkage int sys_clone(struct pt_regs regs)
3692 {
3693   unsigned long clone_flags;
3694   unsigned long newsp;
3695
3696   clone_flags = regs.ebx;
3697   newsp = regs.ecx;
3698   if (!newsp)
3699     newsp = regs.esp;
3700   return do_fork(clone_flags, newsp, &regs, 0);
3701 }
3702
3703 /* This is trivial, and on the face of it looks like it
3704  * could equally well be done in user mode.
3705  *
3706  * Not so, for quite unobvious reasons - register
3707  * pressure.  In user mode vfork() cannot have a stack
3708  * frame, and if done by calling the "clone()" system
3709  * call directly, you do not have enough call-clobbered
3710  * registers to hold all the information you need.  */
3711 asmlinkage int sys_vfork(struct pt_regs regs)
3712 {
3713   return do_fork(CLONE_VFORK | CLONE_VM | SIGCHLD,
3714       regs.esp, &regs, 0);
3715 }
3716
3717 /* sys_execve() executes a new program.  */
3718 asmlinkage int sys_execve(struct pt_regs regs)
3719 {
3720   int error;
3721   char *filename;
3722
3723   filename = getname((char *) regs.ebx);
3724   error = PTR_ERR(filename);
3725   if (IS_ERR(filename))
3726     goto out;
3727   error = do_execve(filename, (char **) regs.ecx,
3728                     (char **) regs.edx, &regs);
3729   if (error == 0)
3730     current->ptrace &= ~PT_DTRACE;
3731   putname(filename);
3732 out:
```

```
3733   return error;
3734 }
3735
3736 /* These bracket the sleeping functions..  */
3737 extern void scheduling_functions_start_here(void);
3738 extern void scheduling_functions_end_here(void);
3739 #define first_sched                                    \
3740     ((unsigned long) scheduling_functions_start_here)
3741 #define last_sched                                     \
3742     ((unsigned long) scheduling_functions_end_here)
3743
3744 unsigned long get_wchan(struct task_struct *p)
3745 {
3746   unsigned long ebp, esp, eip;
3747   unsigned long stack_page;
3748   int count = 0;
3749   if (!p || p == current || p->state == TASK_RUNNING)
3750     return 0;
3751   stack_page = (unsigned long) p;
3752   esp = p->thread.esp;
3753   if (!stack_page ||
3754       esp < stack_page ||
3755       esp > 8188 + stack_page)
3756     return 0;
3757   /* include/asm-i386/system.h:switch_to() pushes ebp
3758    * last. */
3759   ebp = *(unsigned long *) esp;
3760   do {
3761     if (ebp < stack_page || ebp > 8184 + stack_page)
3762       return 0;
3763     eip = *(unsigned long *) (ebp + 4);
3764     if (eip < first_sched || eip >= last_sched)
3765       return eip;
3766     ebp = *(unsigned long *) ebp;
3767   } while (count++ < 16);
3768   return 0;
3769 }
3770 #undef last_sched
3771 #undef first_sched
```

arch/i386/kernel/semaphore.c

```
3772 /*
3773  * i386 semaphore implementation.
3774  *
3775  * (C) Copyright 1999 Linus Torvalds
3776  *
3777  * Portions Copyright 1999 Red Hat, Inc.
```

```
3778  *
3779  *     This program is free software; you can
3780  *     redistribute it and/or modify it under the terms
3781  *     of the GNU General Public License as published by
3782  *     the Free Software Foundation; either version 2 of
3783  *     the License, or (at your option) any later
3784  *     version.
3785  *
3786  * rw semaphores implemented November 1999 by Benjamin
3787  * LaHaise <bcrl@redhat.com> */
3788  #include <linux/config.h>
3789  #include <linux/sched.h>
3790
3791  #include <asm/semaphore.h>
3792
3793  /* Semaphores are implemented using a two-way counter:
3794   * The "count" variable is decremented for each process
3795   * that tries to acquire the semaphore, while the
3796   * "sleeping" variable is a count of such acquires.
3797   *
3798   * Notably, the inline "up()" and "down()" functions can
3799   * efficiently test if they need to do any extra work (up
3800   * needs to do something only if count was negative
3801   * before the increment operation.
3802   *
3803   * "sleeping" and the contention routine ordering is
3804   * protected by the semaphore spinlock.
3805   *
3806   * Note that these functions are only called when there
3807   * is contention on the lock, and as such all this is the
3808   * "non-critical" part of the whole semaphore
3809   * business. The critical part is the inline stuff in
3810   * <asm/semaphore.h> where we want to avoid any extra
3811   * jumps and calls.  */
3812
3813  /* Logic:
3814   * - only on a boundary condition do we need to
3815   *   care. When we go from a negative count to a
3816   *   non-negative, we wake people up.
3817   * - when we go from a non-negative count to a negative
3818   *   do we (a) synchronize with the "sleeper" count and
3819   *   (b) make sure that we're on the wakeup list before
3820   *   we synchronize so that we cannot lose wakeup
3821   *   events.  */
3822
3823  void __up(struct semaphore *sem)
3824  {
```

```
3825    wake_up(&sem->wait);
3826  }
3827
3828  static spinlock_t semaphore_lock = SPIN_LOCK_UNLOCKED;
3829
3830  void __down(struct semaphore * sem)
3831  {
3832    struct task_struct *tsk = current;
3833    DECLARE_WAITQUEUE(wait, tsk);
3834    tsk->state = TASK_UNINTERRUPTIBLE;
3835    add_wait_queue_exclusive(&sem->wait, &wait);
3836
3837    spin_lock_irq(&semaphore_lock);
3838    sem->sleepers++;
3839    for (;;) {
3840      int sleepers = sem->sleepers;
3841
3842      /* Add "everybody else" into it. They aren't playing,
3843       * because we own the spinlock.  */
3844      if (!atomic_add_negative(sleepers - 1,
3845                              &sem->count)) {
3846        sem->sleepers = 0;
3847        break;
3848      }
3849      sem->sleepers = 1;          /* us - see -1 above */
3850      spin_unlock_irq(&semaphore_lock);
3851
3852      schedule();
3853      tsk->state = TASK_UNINTERRUPTIBLE;
3854      spin_lock_irq(&semaphore_lock);
3855    }
3856    spin_unlock_irq(&semaphore_lock);
3857    remove_wait_queue(&sem->wait, &wait);
3858    tsk->state = TASK_RUNNING;
3859    wake_up(&sem->wait);
3860  }
3861
3862  int __down_interruptible(struct semaphore * sem)
3863  {
3864    int retval = 0;
3865    struct task_struct *tsk = current;
3866    DECLARE_WAITQUEUE(wait, tsk);
3867    tsk->state = TASK_INTERRUPTIBLE;
3868    add_wait_queue_exclusive(&sem->wait, &wait);
3869
3870    spin_lock_irq(&semaphore_lock);
3871    sem->sleepers ++;
```

```
3872    for (;;) {
3873      int sleepers = sem->sleepers;
3874
3875      /* With signals pending, this turns into the trylock
3876       * failure case - we won't be sleeping, and we can't
3877       * get the lock as it has contention. Just correct
3878       * the count and exit.  */
3879      if (signal_pending(current)) {
3880        retval = -EINTR;
3881        sem->sleepers = 0;
3882        atomic_add(sleepers, &sem->count);
3883        break;
3884      }
3885
3886      /* Add "everybody else" into it. They aren't playing,
3887       * because we own the spinlock. The "-1" is because
3888       * we're still hoping to get the lock.  */
3889      if (!atomic_add_negative(sleepers - 1,
3890                             &sem->count)) {
3891        sem->sleepers = 0;
3892        break;
3893      }
3894      sem->sleepers = 1;  /* us - see -1 above */
3895      spin_unlock_irq(&semaphore_lock);
3896
3897      schedule();
3898      tsk->state = TASK_INTERRUPTIBLE;
3899      spin_lock_irq(&semaphore_lock);
3900    }
3901    spin_unlock_irq(&semaphore_lock);
3902    tsk->state = TASK_RUNNING;
3903    remove_wait_queue(&sem->wait, &wait);
3904    wake_up(&sem->wait);
3905    return retval;
3906 }
3907
3908 /* Trylock failed - make sure we correct for having
3909  * decremented the count.
3910  *
3911  * We could have done the trylock with a single "cmpxchg"
3912  * without failure cases, but then it wouldn't work on a
3913  * 386.  */
3914 int __down_trylock(struct semaphore * sem)
3915 {
3916    int sleepers;
3917    unsigned long flags;
3918
3919    spin_lock_irqsave(&semaphore_lock, flags);
3920    sleepers = sem->sleepers + 1;
3921    sem->sleepers = 0;
3922
3923    /* Add "everybody else" and us into it. They aren't
3924     * playing, because we own the spinlock.  */
3925    if (!atomic_add_negative(sleepers, &sem->count))
3926      wake_up(&sem->wait);
3927
3928    spin_unlock_irqrestore(&semaphore_lock, flags);
3929    return 1;
3930 }
3931
3932
3933 /* The semaphore operations have a special calling
3934  * sequence that allow us to do a simpler in-line version
3935  * of them. These routines need to convert that sequence
3936  * back into the C sequence when there is contention on
3937  * the semaphore.
3938  *
3939  * %ecx contains the semaphore pointer on entry. Save the
3940  * C-clobbered registers (%eax, %edx and %ecx) except
3941  * %eax when used as a return value..  */
3942 asm(".align 4\n"
3943     ".globl __down_failed\n"
3944     "__down_failed:\n\t"
3945     "pushl %eax\n\t"
3946     "pushl %edx\n\t"
3947     "pushl %ecx\n\t"
3948     "call __down\n\t"
3949     "popl %ecx\n\t"
3950     "popl %edx\n\t"
3951     "popl %eax\n\t"
3952     "ret");
3953
3954 asm(".align 4\n"
3955     ".globl __down_failed_interruptible\n"
3956     "__down_failed_interruptible:\n\t"
3957     "pushl %edx\n\t"
3958     "pushl %ecx\n\t"
3959     "call __down_interruptible\n\t"
3960     "popl %ecx\n\t"
3961     "popl %edx\n\t"
3962     "ret");
3963
3964 asm(".align 4\n"
3965     ".globl __down_failed_trylock\n"
```

```
3966         "__down_failed_trylock:\n\t"
3967         "pushl  %edx\n\t"
3968         "pushl  %ecx\n\t"
3969         "call  __down_trylock\n\t"
3970         "popl   %ecx\n\t"
3971         "popl   %edx\n\t"
3972         "ret");
3973
3974 asm(".align 4\n"
3975         ".globl __up_wakeup\n"
3976         "__up_wakeup:\n\t"
3977         "pushl  %eax\n\t"
3978         "pushl  %edx\n\t"
3979         "pushl  %ecx\n\t"
3980         "call  __up\n\t"
3981         "popl   %ecx\n\t"
3982         "popl   %edx\n\t"
3983         "popl   %eax\n\t"
3984         "ret");
3985
3986 asm(".align 4
3987         .globl __down_read_failed
3988         __down_read_failed:
3989                 pushl  %edx
3990                 pushl  %ecx
3991                 jnc   2f
3992
3993         3:      call  down_read_failed_biased
3994
3995         1:      popl   %ecx
3996                 popl   %edx
3997                 ret
3998
3999         2:      call  down_read_failed
4000                 " LOCK "subl   $1,(%eax)
4001                 jns   1b
4002                 jnc   2b
4003                 jmp   3b");
4004
4005 asm(".align 4
4006         .globl __down_write_failed
4007         __down_write_failed:
4008                 pushl  %edx
4009                 pushl  %ecx
4010                 jnc   2f
4011
4012         3:      call  down_write_failed_biased
```

```
4013
4014         1:      popl   %ecx
4015                 popl   %edx
4016                 ret
4017
4018         2:      call  down_write_failed
4019                 " LOCK "subl      $" RW_LOCK_BIAS_STR ",(%eax)
4020                 jz    1b
4021                 jnc   2b
4022                 jmp   3b");
4023
4024 struct rw_semaphore *
4025 FASTCALL(rwsem_wake_readers(struct rw_semaphore *sem));
4026 struct rw_semaphore *
4027 FASTCALL(rwsem_wake_writer(struct rw_semaphore *sem));
4028
4029 struct rw_semaphore *
4030 FASTCALL(down_read_failed_biased(struct rw_semaphore *
4031                                         sem));
4032 struct rw_semaphore *
4033 FASTCALL(down_write_failed_biased(struct rw_semaphore *
4034                                         sem));
4035 struct rw_semaphore *
4036 FASTCALL(down_read_failed(struct rw_semaphore *sem));
4037 struct rw_semaphore *
4038 FASTCALL(down_write_failed(struct rw_semaphore *sem));
4039
4040 struct rw_semaphore *
4041 down_read_failed_biased(struct rw_semaphore *sem)
4042 {
4043   struct task_struct *tsk = current;
4044   DECLARE_WAITQUEUE(wait, tsk);
4045
4046   /* put ourselves at the head of the list */
4047   add_wait_queue(&sem->wait, &wait);
4048
4049   for (;;) {
4050     if (sem->read_bias_granted &&
4051         xchg(&sem->read_bias_granted, 0))
4052       break;
4053     set_task_state(tsk, TASK_UNINTERRUPTIBLE);
4054     if (!sem->read_bias_granted)
4055       schedule();
4056   }
4057
4058   remove_wait_queue(&sem->wait, &wait);
4059   tsk->state = TASK_RUNNING;
```

```
4060
4061    return sem;
4062 }
4063
4064 struct rw_semaphore *
4065 down_write_failed_biased(struct rw_semaphore *sem)
4066 {
4067    struct task_struct *tsk = current;
4068    DECLARE_WAITQUEUE(wait, tsk);
4069
4070    /* put ourselves at the end of the list */
4071    add_wait_queue_exclusive(&sem->write_bias_wait, &wait);
4072
4073    for (;;) {
4074      if (sem->write_bias_granted &&
4075          xchg(&sem->write_bias_granted, 0))
4076        break;
4077      set_task_state(tsk, TASK_UNINTERRUPTIBLE);
4078      if (!sem->write_bias_granted)
4079        schedule();
4080    }
4081
4082    remove_wait_queue(&sem->write_bias_wait, &wait);
4083    tsk->state = TASK_RUNNING;
4084
4085    /* if the lock is currently unbiased, awaken the
4086     * sleepers FIXME: this wakes up the readers early in a
4087     * bit of a stampede -> bad!  */
4088    if (atomic_read(&sem->count) >= 0)
4089      wake_up(&sem->wait);
4090
4091    return sem;
4092 }
4093
4094 /* Wait for the lock to become unbiased.  Readers are
4095  * non-exclusive. =) */
4096 struct rw_semaphore *
4097 down_read_failed(struct rw_semaphore *sem)
4098 {
4099    struct task_struct *tsk = current;
4100    DECLARE_WAITQUEUE(wait, tsk);
4101
4102    /* this takes care of granting the lock */
4103    __up_read(sem);
4104
4105    add_wait_queue(&sem->wait, &wait);
4106
4107    while (atomic_read(&sem->count) < 0) {
4108      set_task_state(tsk, TASK_UNINTERRUPTIBLE);
4109      if (atomic_read(&sem->count) >= 0)
4110        break;
4111      schedule();
4112    }
4113
4114    remove_wait_queue(&sem->wait, &wait);
4115    tsk->state = TASK_RUNNING;
4116
4117    return sem;
4118 }
4119
4120 /* Wait for the lock to become unbiased. Since we're a
4121  * writer, we'll make ourselves exclusive.  */
4122 struct rw_semaphore *
4123 down_write_failed(struct rw_semaphore *sem)
4124 {
4125    struct task_struct *tsk = current;
4126    DECLARE_WAITQUEUE(wait, tsk);
4127
4128    /* this takes care of granting the lock */
4129    __up_write(sem);
4130
4131    add_wait_queue_exclusive(&sem->wait, &wait);
4132
4133    while (atomic_read(&sem->count) < 0) {
4134      set_task_state(tsk, TASK_UNINTERRUPTIBLE);
4135      if (atomic_read(&sem->count) >= 0)
4136        /* we must attempt to acquire or bias the lock */
4137        break;
4138      schedule();
4139    }
4140
4141    remove_wait_queue(&sem->wait, &wait);
4142    tsk->state = TASK_RUNNING;
4143
4144    return sem;
4145 }
4146
4147 asm(".align 4
4148      .globl __rwsem_wake
4149      __rwsem_wake:
4150              pushl   %edx
4151              pushl   %ecx
4152
4153              jz      1f
```

```
4154                call    rwsem_wake_readers
4155                jmp     2f
4156
4157        1:      call    rwsem_wake_writer
4158
4159        2:      popl    %ecx
4160                popl    %edx
4161                ret");
4162
4163 /* Called when someone has done an up that transitioned
4164  * from negative to non-negative, meaning that the lock
4165  * has been granted to whomever owned the bias.  */
4166 struct rw_semaphore *
4167 rwsem_wake_readers(struct rw_semaphore *sem)
4168 {
4169   if (xchg(&sem->read_bias_granted, 1))
4170     BUG();
4171   wake_up(&sem->wait);
4172   return sem;
4173 }
4174
4175 struct rw_semaphore *
4176 rwsem_wake_writer(struct rw_semaphore *sem)
4177 {
4178   if (xchg(&sem->write_bias_granted, 1))
4179     BUG();
4180   wake_up(&sem->write_bias_wait);
4181   return sem;
4182 }
4183
4184 #if defined(CONFIG_SMP)
4185 asm(".align  4
4186       .globl  __write_lock_failed
4187       __write_lock_failed:
4188             " LOCK "addl    $" RW_LOCK_BIAS_STR ",(%eax)
4189       1:    cmpl    $" RW_LOCK_BIAS_STR ",(%eax)
4190             jne     1b
4191
4192             " LOCK "subl    $" RW_LOCK_BIAS_STR ",(%eax)
4193             jnz     __write_lock_failed
4194             ret
4195
4196
4197       .align  4
4198       .globl  __read_lock_failed
4199       __read_lock_failed:
4200             lock ; incl    (%eax)
```

(p 688) → 4187
(p 688) → 4199

```
4201       1:    cmpl    $1,(%eax)
4202             js      1b
4203
4204             lock ; decl    (%eax)
4205             js      __read_lock_failed
4206             ret");
4207 #endif
4208
```

arch/i386/kernel/signal.c

```
4209 /*
4210  *  linux/arch/i386/kernel/signal.c
4211  *
4212  *  Copyright (C) 1991, 1992  Linus Torvalds
4213  *
4214  *  1997-11-28 Modified for POSIX.1b signals by Richard
4215  *  Henderson
4216  *  2000-06-20 Pentium III FXSR, SSE support by Gareth
4217  *  Hughes
4218  */
4219
4220 #include <linux/sched.h>
4221 #include <linux/mm.h>
4222 #include <linux/smp.h>
4223 #include <linux/smp_lock.h>
4224 #include <linux/kernel.h>
4225 #include <linux/signal.h>
4226 #include <linux/errno.h>
4227 #include <linux/wait.h>
4228 #include <linux/ptrace.h>
4229 #include <linux/unistd.h>
4230 #include <linux/stddef.h>
4231 #include <asm/ucontext.h>
4232 #include <asm/uaccess.h>
4233 #include <asm/i387.h>
4234
4235 #define DEBUG_SIG 0
4236
4237 #define _BLOCKABLE                                            \
4238  (~(sigmask(SIGKILL) | sigmask(SIGSTOP)))
4239
4240 asmlinkage int FASTCALL(do_signal(struct pt_regs *regs,
4241         sigset_t * oldset));
4242
4243 int copy_siginfo_to_user(siginfo_t * to,
4244     siginfo_t * from)
4245 {
```

```
4246    if (!access_ok(VERIFY_WRITE, to, sizeof(siginfo_t)))
4247      return -EFAULT;
4248    if (from->si_code < 0)
4249      return __copy_to_user(to, from, sizeof(siginfo_t));
4250    else {
4251      int err;
4252
4253      /* If you change siginfo_t structure, please be sure
4254       * this code is fixed accordingly. It should never
4255       * copy any pad contained in the structure to avoid
4256       * security leaks, but must copy the generic 3 ints
4257       * plus the relevant union member. */
4258      err = __put_user(from->si_signo, &to->si_signo);
4259      err |= __put_user(from->si_errno, &to->si_errno);
4260      err |= __put_user((short) from->si_code,
4261                          &to->si_code);
4262      /* First 32bits of unions are always present. */
4263      err |= __put_user(from->si_pid, &to->si_pid);
4264      switch (from->si_code >> 16) {
4265      case __SI_FAULT >> 16:
4266        break;
4267      case __SI_CHLD >> 16:
4268        err |= __put_user(from->si_utime, &to->si_utime);
4269        err |= __put_user(from->si_stime, &to->si_stime);
4270        err |= __put_user(from->si_status, &to->si_status);
4271      default:
4272        err |= __put_user(from->si_uid, &to->si_uid);
4273        break;
4274        /* case __SI_RT: This is not generated by the
4275         * kernel as of now. */
4276      }
4277      return err;
4278    }
4279  }
4280
4281  /* Atomically swap in the new signal mask, and wait for a
4282   * signal. */
4283  asmlinkage int
4284  sys_sigsuspend(int history0, int history1,
4285                  old_sigset_t mask)
4286  {
4287    struct pt_regs *regs = (struct pt_regs *) &history0;
4288    sigset_t saveset;
4289
4290    mask &= _BLOCKABLE;
4291    spin_lock_irq(&current->sigmask_lock);
4292    saveset = current->blocked;
4293    siginitset(&current->blocked, mask);
4294    recalc_sigpending(current);
4295    spin_unlock_irq(&current->sigmask_lock);
4296
4297    regs->eax = -EINTR;
4298    while (1) {
4299      current->state = TASK_INTERRUPTIBLE;
4300      schedule();
4301      if (do_signal(regs, &saveset))
4302        return -EINTR;
4303    }
4304  }
4305
4306  asmlinkage int
4307  sys_rt_sigsuspend(sigset_t * unewset, size_t sigsetsize)
4308  {
4309    struct pt_regs *regs = (struct pt_regs *) &unewset;
4310    sigset_t saveset, newset;
4311
4312    /* XXX: Don't preclude handling different sized
4313     * sigset_t's. */
4314    if (sigsetsize != sizeof(sigset_t))
4315      return -EINVAL;
4316
4317    if (copy_from_user(&newset, unewset, sizeof(newset)))
4318      return -EFAULT;
4319    sigdelsetmask(&newset, ~_BLOCKABLE);
4320
4321    spin_lock_irq(&current->sigmask_lock);
4322    saveset = current->blocked;
4323    current->blocked = newset;
4324    recalc_sigpending(current);
4325    spin_unlock_irq(&current->sigmask_lock);
4326
4327    regs->eax = -EINTR;
4328    while (1) {
4329      current->state = TASK_INTERRUPTIBLE;
4330      schedule();
4331      if (do_signal(regs, &saveset))
4332        return -EINTR;
4333    }
4334  }
4335
4336  asmlinkage int
4337  sys_sigaction(int sig, const struct old_sigaction *act,
4338                struct old_sigaction *oact)
4339  {
```

```
4340    struct k_sigaction new_ka, old_ka;
4341    int ret;
4342
4343    if (act) {
4344      old_sigset_t mask;
4345      if (verify_area(VERIFY_READ, act, sizeof(*act))
4346          || __get_user(new_ka.sa.sa_handler,
4347                        &act->sa_handler)
4348          || __get_user(new_ka.sa.sa_restorer,
4349                        &act->sa_restorer))
4350        return -EFAULT;
4351      __get_user(new_ka.sa.sa_flags, &act->sa_flags);
4352      __get_user(mask, &act->sa_mask);
4353      siginitset(&new_ka.sa.sa_mask, mask);
4354    }
4355
4356    ret = do_sigaction(sig,
4357                       act  ? &new_ka : NULL,
4358                       oact ? &old_ka : NULL);
4359
4360    if (!ret && oact) {
4361      if (verify_area(VERIFY_WRITE, oact, sizeof(*oact))
4362          || __put_user(old_ka.sa.sa_handler,
4363                        &oact->sa_handler)
4364          || __put_user(old_ka.sa.sa_restorer,
4365                        &oact->sa_restorer))
4366        return -EFAULT;
4367      __put_user(old_ka.sa.sa_flags, &oact->sa_flags);
4368      __put_user(old_ka.sa.sa_mask.sig[0], &oact->sa_mask);
4369    }
4370
4371    return ret;
4372  }
4373
4374  asmlinkage int
4375  sys_sigaltstack(const stack_t * uss, stack_t * uoss)
4376  {
4377    struct pt_regs *regs = (struct pt_regs *) &uss;
4378    return do_sigaltstack(uss, uoss, regs->esp);
4379  }
4380
4381
4382  /* Do a signal return; undo the signal stack.  */
4383
4384  struct sigframe {
4385    char *pretcode;
4386    int sig;
```

```
4387    struct sigcontext sc;
4388    struct _fpstate fpstate;
4389    unsigned long extramask[_NSIG_WORDS - 1];
4390    char retcode[8];
4391  };
4392
4393  struct rt_sigframe {
4394    char *pretcode;
4395    int sig;
4396    struct siginfo *pinfo;
4397    void *puc;
4398    struct siginfo info;
4399    struct ucontext uc;
4400    struct _fpstate fpstate;
4401    char retcode[8];
4402  };
4403
4404  static int
4405  restore_sigcontext(struct pt_regs *regs,
4406                     struct sigcontext *sc, int *peax)
4407  {
4408    unsigned int err = 0;
4409
4410  #define COPY(x)  err |= __get_user(regs->x, &sc->x)
4411
4412  #define COPY_SEG(seg)                                      \
4413          { unsigned short tmp;                              \
4414            err |= __get_user(tmp, &sc->seg);                \
4415            regs->x##seg = tmp; }
4416
4417  #define COPY_SEG_STRICT(seg)                               \
4418          { unsigned short tmp;                              \
4419            err |= __get_user(tmp, &sc->seg);                \
4420            regs->x##seg = tmp|3; }
4421
4422  #define GET_SEG(seg)                                       \
4423          { unsigned short tmp;                              \
4424            err |= __get_user(tmp, &sc->seg);                \
4425            loadsegment(seg,tmp); }
4426
4427    GET_SEG(gs);
4428    GET_SEG(fs);
4429    COPY_SEG(es);
4430    COPY_SEG(ds);
4431    COPY(edi);
4432    COPY(esi);
4433    COPY(ebp);
```

```
4434    COPY(esp);
4435    COPY(ebx);
4436    COPY(edx);
4437    COPY(ecx);
4438    COPY(eip);
4439    COPY_SEG_STRICT(cs);
4440    COPY_SEG_STRICT(ss);
4441
4442    {
4443        unsigned int tmpflags;
4444        err |= __get_user(tmpflags, &sc->eflags);
4445        regs->eflags =
4446            (regs->eflags & ~0x40DD5) | (tmpflags & 0x40DD5);
4447        regs->orig_eax = -1;      /* disable syscall checks */
4448    }
4449
4450    {
4451        struct _fpstate *buf;
4452        err |= __get_user(buf, &sc->fpstate);
4453        if (buf) {
4454            if (verify_area(VERIFY_READ, buf, sizeof(*buf)))
4455                goto badframe;
4456            err |= restore_i387(buf);
4457        }
4458    }
4459
4460    err |= __get_user(*peax, &sc->eax);
4461    return err;
4462
4463 badframe:
4464    return 1;
4465 }
4466
4467 asmlinkage int sys_sigreturn(unsigned long __unused)
4468 {
4469    struct pt_regs *regs = (struct pt_regs *) &__unused;
4470    struct sigframe *frame =
4471        (struct sigframe *) (regs->esp - 8);
4472    sigset_t set;
4473    int eax;
4474
4475    if (verify_area(VERIFY_READ, frame, sizeof(*frame)))
4476        goto badframe;
4477    if (__get_user(set.sig[0], &frame->sc.oldmask) ||
4478        (_NSIG_WORDS > 1 &&
4479            __copy_from_user(&set.sig[1],
4480                        &frame->extramask,
4481                            sizeof(frame->extramask))))
4482        goto badframe;
4483
4484    sigdelsetmask(&set, ~_BLOCKABLE);
4485    spin_lock_irq(&current->sigmask_lock);
4486    current->blocked = set;
4487    recalc_sigpending(current);
4488    spin_unlock_irq(&current->sigmask_lock);
4489
4490    if (restore_sigcontext(regs, &frame->sc, &eax))
4491        goto badframe;
4492    return eax;
4493
4494 badframe:
4495    force_sig(SIGSEGV, current);
4496    return 0;
4497 }
4498
4499 asmlinkage int sys_rt_sigreturn(unsigned long __unused)
4500 {
4501    struct pt_regs *regs = (struct pt_regs *) &__unused;
4502    struct rt_sigframe *frame =
4503        (struct rt_sigframe *) (regs->esp - 4);
4504    sigset_t set;
4505    stack_t st;
4506    int eax;
4507
4508    if (verify_area(VERIFY_READ, frame, sizeof(*frame)))
4509        goto badframe;
4510    if (__copy_from_user(&set, &frame->uc.uc_sigmask,
4511                    sizeof(set)))
4512        goto badframe;
4513
4514    sigdelsetmask(&set, ~_BLOCKABLE);
4515    spin_lock_irq(&current->sigmask_lock);
4516    current->blocked = set;
4517    recalc_sigpending(current);
4518    spin_unlock_irq(&current->sigmask_lock);
4519
4520    if (restore_sigcontext(regs, &frame->uc.uc_mcontext,
4521                        &eax))
4522        goto badframe;
4523
4524    if (__copy_from_user(&st, &frame->uc.uc_stack,
4525                    sizeof(st)))
4526        goto badframe;
4527    /* It is more difficult to avoid calling this function
```

```
4528    * than to call it and ignore errors.   */
4529    do_sigaltstack(&st, NULL, regs->esp);
4530
4531    return eax;
4532
4533 badframe:
4534    force_sig(SIGSEGV, current);
4535    return 0;
4536 }
4537
4538 /* Set up a signal frame.  */
4539 static int
4540 setup_sigcontext(struct sigcontext *sc,
4541                      struct _fpstate *fpstate,
4542                      struct pt_regs *regs,
4543                      unsigned long mask)
4544 {
4545    int tmp, err = 0;
4546
4547    tmp = 0;
4548    __asm__("movl %%gs,%0": "=r"(tmp):"0"(tmp));
4549    err |= __put_user(tmp, (unsigned int *) &sc->gs);
4550    __asm__("movl %%fs,%0": "=r"(tmp):"0"(tmp));
4551    err |= __put_user(tmp, (unsigned int *) &sc->fs);
4552
4553    err |= __put_user(regs->xes, (unsigned int *) &sc->es);
4554    err |= __put_user(regs->xds, (unsigned int *) &sc->ds);
4555    err |= __put_user(regs->edi, &sc->edi);
4556    err |= __put_user(regs->esi, &sc->esi);
4557    err |= __put_user(regs->ebp, &sc->ebp);
4558    err |= __put_user(regs->esp, &sc->esp);
4559    err |= __put_user(regs->ebx, &sc->ebx);
4560    err |= __put_user(regs->edx, &sc->edx);
4561    err |= __put_user(regs->ecx, &sc->ecx);
4562    err |= __put_user(regs->eax, &sc->eax);
4563    err |= __put_user(current->thread.trap_no,
4564                       &sc->trapno);
4565    err |= __put_user(current->thread.error_code,
4566                       &sc->err);
4567    err |= __put_user(regs->eip, &sc->eip);
4568    err |= __put_user(regs->xcs, (unsigned int *) &sc->cs);
4569    err |= __put_user(regs->eflags, &sc->eflags);
4570    err |= __put_user(regs->esp, &sc->esp_at_signal);
4571    err |= __put_user(regs->xss, (unsigned int *) &sc->ss);
4572
4573    tmp = save_i387(fpstate);
4574    if (tmp < 0)
4575      err = 1;
4576    else
4577      err |= __put_user(tmp ? fpstate : NULL,
4578                         &sc->fpstate);
4579
4580    /* non-iBCS2 extensions.. */
4581    err |= __put_user(mask, &sc->oldmask);
4582    err |= __put_user(current->thread.cr2, &sc->cr2);
4583
4584    return err;
4585 }
4586
4587 /* Determine which stack to use..   */
4588 static inline void *get_sigframe(struct k_sigaction *ka,
4589      struct pt_regs *regs, size_t frame_size)
4590 {
4591    unsigned long esp;
4592
4593    /* Default to using normal stack */
4594    esp = regs->esp;
4595
4596    /* This is the X/Open sanctioned signal stack
4597     * switching.  */
4598    if (ka->sa.sa_flags & SA_ONSTACK) {
4599      if (!on_sig_stack(esp))
4600        esp = current->sas_ss_sp + current->sas_ss_size;
4601    }
4602
4603    /* This is the legacy signal stack switching. */
4604    else if ((regs->xss & 0xffff) != __USER_DS &&
4605        !(ka->sa.sa_flags & SA_RESTORER) &&
4606        ka->sa.sa_restorer) {
4607      esp = (unsigned long) ka->sa.sa_restorer;
4608    }
4609
4610    return (void *) ((esp - frame_size) & -8ul);
4611 }
4612
4613 static void setup_frame(int sig, struct k_sigaction *ka,
4614      sigset_t * set, struct pt_regs *regs)
4615 {
4616    struct sigframe *frame;
4617    int err = 0;
4618
4619    frame = get_sigframe(ka, regs, sizeof(*frame));
4620
4621    if (!access_ok(VERIFY_WRITE, frame, sizeof(*frame)))
```

```
4622      goto give_sigsegv;
4623
4624   err |=
4625    __put_user((current->exec_domain
4626              && current->exec_domain->signal_invmap
4627              && sig < 32
4628              ? current->exec_domain->signal_invmap[sig]
4629              : sig),
4630              &frame->sig);
4631   if (err)
4632     goto give_sigsegv;
4633
4634   err |= setup_sigcontext(&frame->sc, &frame->fpstate,
4635                     regs, set->sig[0]);
4636   if (err)
4637     goto give_sigsegv;
4638
4639   if (_NSIG_WORDS > 1) {
4640     err |= __copy_to_user(frame->extramask, &set->sig[1],
4641                     sizeof(frame->extramask));
4642   }
4643   if (err)
4644     goto give_sigsegv;
4645
4646   /* Set up to return from userspace.  If provided, use
4647    * a stub already in userspace.  */
4648   if (ka->sa.sa_flags & SA_RESTORER) {
4649     err |= __put_user(ka->sa.sa_restorer,
4650                     &frame->pretcode);
4651   } else {
4652     err |= __put_user(frame->retcode, &frame->pretcode);
4653     /* This is popl %eax ; movl $,%eax ; int $0x80 */
4654     err |= __put_user(0xb858,
4655                     (short *) (frame->retcode + 0));
4656     err |= __put_user(__NR_sigreturn,
4657                     (int *) (frame->retcode + 2));
4658     err |= __put_user(0x80cd,
4659                     (short *) (frame->retcode + 6));
4660   }
4661
4662   if (err)
4663     goto give_sigsegv;
4664
4665   /* Set up registers for signal handler */
4666   regs->esp = (unsigned long) frame;
4667   regs->eip = (unsigned long) ka->sa.sa_handler;
4668
4669   set_fs(USER_DS);
4670   regs->xds = __USER_DS;
4671   regs->xes = __USER_DS;
4672   regs->xss = __USER_DS;
4673   regs->xcs = __USER_CS;
4674   regs->eflags &= ~TF_MASK;
4675
4676 #if DEBUG_SIG
4677   printk("SIG deliver (%s:%d): sp=%p pc=%p ra=%p\n",
4678       current->comm, current->pid, frame, regs->eip,
4679       frame->pretcode);
4680 #endif
4681
4682   return;
4683
4684 give_sigsegv:
4685   if (sig == SIGSEGV)
4686     ka->sa.sa_handler = SIG_DFL;
4687   force_sig(SIGSEGV, current);
4688 }
4689
4690 static void setup_rt_frame(int sig,
4691     struct k_sigaction *ka, siginfo_t * info,
4692     sigset_t * set, struct pt_regs *regs)
4693 {
4694   struct rt_sigframe *frame;
4695   int err = 0;
4696
4697   frame = get_sigframe(ka, regs, sizeof(*frame));
4698
4699   if (!access_ok(VERIFY_WRITE, frame, sizeof(*frame)))
4700     goto give_sigsegv;
4701
4702   err |=
4703    __put_user((current->exec_domain
4704              && current->exec_domain->signal_invmap
4705              && sig < 32
4706              ? current->exec_domain->signal_invmap[sig]
4707              : sig), &frame->sig);
4708   err |= __put_user(&frame->info, &frame->pinfo);
4709   err |= __put_user(&frame->uc, &frame->puc);
4710   err |= copy_siginfo_to_user(&frame->info, info);
4711   if (err)
4712     goto give_sigsegv;
4713
4714   /* Create the ucontext.  */
4715   err |= __put_user(0, &frame->uc.uc_flags);
```

```
4716    err |= __put_user(0, &frame->uc.uc_link);
4717    err |= __put_user(current->sas_ss_sp,
4718                    &frame->uc.uc_stack.ss_sp);
4719    err |= __put_user(sas_ss_flags(regs->esp),
4720                    &frame->uc.uc_stack.ss_flags);
4721    err |= __put_user(current->sas_ss_size,
4722                    &frame->uc.uc_stack.ss_size);
4723    err |= setup_sigcontext(&frame->uc.uc_mcontext,
4724                    &frame->fpstate, regs,
4725                    set->sig[0]);
4726    err |= __copy_to_user(&frame->uc.uc_sigmask, set,
4727                    sizeof(*set));
4728    if (err)
4729        goto give_sigsegv;
4730
4731    /* Set up to return from userspace.  If provided, use
4732     * a stub already in userspace.  */
4733    if (ka->sa.sa_flags & SA_RESTORER) {
4734        err |= __put_user(ka->sa.sa_restorer,
4735                    &frame->pretcode);
4736    } else {
4737        err |= __put_user(frame->retcode, &frame->pretcode);
4738        /* This is movl $,%eax ; int $0x80 */
4739        err |= __put_user(0xb8,
4740                    (char *) (frame->retcode + 0));
4741        err |= __put_user(__NR_rt_sigreturn,
4742                    (int *) (frame->retcode + 1));
4743        err |= __put_user(0x80cd,
4744                    (short *) (frame->retcode + 5));
4745    }
4746
4747    if (err)
4748        goto give_sigsegv;
4749
4750    /* Set up registers for signal handler */
4751    regs->esp = (unsigned long) frame;
4752    regs->eip = (unsigned long) ka->sa.sa_handler;
4753
4754    set_fs(USER_DS);
4755    regs->xds = __USER_DS;
4756    regs->xes = __USER_DS;
4757    regs->xss = __USER_DS;
4758    regs->xcs = __USER_CS;
4759    regs->eflags &= ~TF_MASK;
4760
4761 #if DEBUG_SIG
4762    printk("SIG deliver (%s:%d): sp=%p pc=%p ra=%p\n",
4763                    current->comm, current->pid, frame, regs->eip,
4764                    frame->pretcode);
4765 #endif
4766
4767    return;
4768
4769 give_sigsegv:
4770    if (sig == SIGSEGV)
4771        ka->sa.sa_handler = SIG_DFL;
4772    force_sig(SIGSEGV, current);
4773 }
4774
4775 /* OK, we're invoking a handler */
4776 static void handle_signal(unsigned long sig,
4777    struct k_sigaction *ka, siginfo_t * info,
4778    sigset_t * oldset, struct pt_regs *regs)
4779 {
4780    /* Are we from a system call? */
4781    if (regs->orig_eax >= 0) {
4782        /* If so, check system call restarting.. */
4783        switch (regs->eax) {
4784        case -ERESTARTNOHAND:
4785            regs->eax = -EINTR;
4786            break;
4787
4788        case -ERESTARTSYS:
4789            if (!(ka->sa.sa_flags & SA_RESTART)) {
4790                regs->eax = -EINTR;
4791                break;
4792            }
4793            /* fallthrough */
4794        case -ERESTARTNOINTR:
4795            regs->eax = regs->orig_eax;
4796            regs->eip -= 2;
4797        }
4798    }
4799
4800    /* Set up the stack frame */
4801    if (ka->sa.sa_flags & SA_SIGINFO)
4802        setup_rt_frame(sig, ka, info, oldset, regs);
4803    else
4804        setup_frame(sig, ka, oldset, regs);
4805
4806    if (ka->sa.sa_flags & SA_ONESHOT)
4807        ka->sa.sa_handler = SIG_DFL;
4808
4809    if (!(ka->sa.sa_flags & SA_NODEFER)) {
```

p 582

```
4810        spin_lock_irq(&current->sigmask_lock);
4811        sigorsets(&current->blocked, &current->blocked,
4812            &ka->sa.sa_mask);
4813        sigaddset(&current->blocked, sig);
4814        recalc_sigpending(current);
4815        spin_unlock_irq(&current->sigmask_lock);
4816    }
4817 }
4818
4819 /* Note that 'init' is a special process: it doesn't get
4820  * signals it doesn't want to handle. Thus you cannot
4821  * kill init even with a SIGKILL even by mistake.  */
4822 int do_signal(struct pt_regs *regs, sigset_t * oldset)
4823 {
4824   siginfo_t info;
4825   struct k_sigaction *ka;
4826
4827   /* We want the common case to go fast, which is why we
4828    * may in certain cases get here from kernel mode. Just
4829    * return without doing anything if so.  */
4830   if ((regs->xcs & 3) != 3)
4831     return 1;
4832
4833   if (!oldset)
4834     oldset = &current->blocked;
4835
4836   for (;;) {
4837     unsigned long signr;
4838
4839     spin_lock_irq(&current->sigmask_lock);
4840     signr = dequeue_signal(&current->blocked, &info);
4841     spin_unlock_irq(&current->sigmask_lock);
4842
4843     if (!signr)
4844       break;
4845
4846     if ((current->ptrace & PT_PTRACED)
4847         && signr != SIGKILL) {
4848       /* Let the debugger run.  */
4849       current->exit_code = signr;
4850       current->state = TASK_STOPPED;
4851       notify_parent(current, SIGCHLD);
4852       schedule();
4853
4854       /* We're back.  Did the debugger cancel the sig? */
4855       if (!(signr = current->exit_code))
4856         continue;
```

```
4857       current->exit_code = 0;
4858
4859       /* The debugger continued.  Ignore SIGSTOP.  */
4860       if (signr == SIGSTOP)
4861         continue;
4862
4863       /* Update the siginfo structure.  Is this good?  */
4864       if (signr != info.si_signo) {
4865         info.si_signo = signr;
4866         info.si_errno = 0;
4867         info.si_code = SI_USER;
4868         info.si_pid = current->p_pptr->pid;
4869         info.si_uid = current->p_pptr->uid;
4870       }
4871
4872       /* If the (new) signal is now blocked, requeue it.
4873        */
4874       if (sigismember(&current->blocked, signr)) {
4875         send_sig_info(signr, &info, current);
4876         continue;
4877       }
4878     }
4879
4880     ka = &current->sig->action[signr - 1];
4881     if (ka->sa.sa_handler == SIG_IGN) {
4882       if (signr != SIGCHLD)
4883         continue;
4884       /* Check for SIGCHLD: it's special.  */
4885       while (sys_wait4(-1, NULL, WNOHANG, NULL) > 0)
4886         /* nothing */ ;
4887       continue;
4888     }
4889
4890     if (ka->sa.sa_handler == SIG_DFL) {
4891       int exit_code = signr;
4892
4893       /* Init gets no signals it doesn't want.  */
4894       if (current->pid == 1)
4895         continue;
4896
4897       switch (signr) {
4898       case SIGCONT:
4899       case SIGCHLD:
4900       case SIGWINCH:
4901         continue;
4902
4903       case SIGTSTP:
```

p 580

```
4904      case SIGTTIN:
4905      case SIGTTOU:
4906          if (is_orphaned_pgrp(current->pgrp))
4907              continue;
4908          /* FALLTHRU */
4909
4910      case SIGSTOP:
4911          current->state = TASK_STOPPED;
4912          current->exit_code = signr;
4913          if (!(current->p_pptr->sig->
4914                  action[SIGCHLD - 1].sa.sa_flags &
4915                                      SA_NOCLDSTOP))
4916              notify_parent(current, SIGCHLD);
4917          schedule();
4918          continue;
4919
4920      case SIGQUIT:
4921      case SIGILL:
4922      case SIGTRAP:
4923      case SIGABRT:
4924      case SIGFPE:
4925      case SIGSEGV:
4926      case SIGBUS:
4927      case SIGSYS:
4928      case SIGXCPU:
4929      case SIGXFSZ:
4930          if (do_coredump(signr, regs))
4931              exit_code |= 0x80;
4932          /* FALLTHRU */
4933
4934      default:
4935          sigaddset(&current->pending.signal, signr);
4936          recalc_sigpending(current);
4937          current->flags |= PF_SIGNALED;
4938          do_exit(exit_code);
4939          /* NOTREACHED */
4940      }
4941  }
4942
4943  /* Reenable any watchpoints before delivering the
4944   * signal to user space. The processor register will
4945   * have been cleared if the watchpoint triggered
4946   * inside the kernel. */
4947  __asm__("movl %0,%%db7"
4948          : :"r"(current->thread. debugreg[7]));
4949
4950  /* Whee!  Actually deliver the signal.  */
```

```
4951          handle_signal(signr, ka, &info, oldset, regs);
4952          return 1;
4953      }
4954
4955      /* Did we come from a system call? */
4956      if (regs->orig_eax >= 0) {
4957          /* Restart the system call - no handlers present */
4958          if (regs->eax == -ERESTARTNOHAND ||
4959              regs->eax == -ERESTARTSYS ||
4960              regs->eax == -ERESTARTNOINTR) {
4961          regs->eax = regs->orig_eax;
4962          regs->eip -= 2;
4963      }
4964  }
4965  return 0;
4966 }
```

arch/i386/kernel/smp.c

```
4967 /*
4968  *      Intel SMP support routines.
4969  *
4970  *      (c) 1995 Alan Cox, Building #3 <alan@redhat.com>
4971  *      (c) 1998-99, 2000 Ingo Molnar <mingo@redhat.com>
4972  *
4973  *      This code is released under the GNU public
4974  *      license version 2 or later.  */
4975
4976 #include <linux/init.h>
4977
4978 #include <linux/mm.h>
4979 #include <linux/irq.h>
4980 #include <linux/delay.h>
4981 #include <linux/spinlock.h>
4982 #include <linux/smp_lock.h>
4983 #include <linux/kernel_stat.h>
4984 #include <linux/mc146818rtc.h>
4985
4986 #include <asm/mtrr.h>
4987 #include <asm/pgalloc.h>
4988
4989 /* Some notes on x86 processor bugs affecting SMP
4990  * operation:
4991  *
4992  * Pentium, Pentium Pro, II, III (and all CPUs) have
4993  * bugs.  The Linux implications for SMP are handled as
4994  * follows:
4995  *
```

```
4996  * Pentium III / [Xeon]
4997  * None of the E1AP-E3AP erratas are visible to the user.
4998  *
4999  * E1AP.    see PII A1AP
5000  * E2AP.    see PII A2AP
5001  * E3AP.    see PII A3AP
5002  *
5003  * Pentium II / [Xeon]
5004  * None of the A1AP-A3AP erratas are visible to the user.
5005  *
5006  * A1AP.    see PPro 1AP
5007  * A2AP.    see PPro 2AP
5008  * A3AP.    see PPro 7AP
5009  *
5010  * Pentium Pro
5011  * None of 1AP-9AP erratas are visible to the normal
5012  * user, except occasional delivery of 'spurious
5013  * interrupt' as trap #15.  This is very rare and a
5014  * non-problem.
5015  *
5016  * 1AP.    Linux maps APIC as non-cacheable
5017  * 2AP.    worked around in hardware
5018  * 3AP.    fixed in C0 and above steppings microcode
5019  *         update. Linux does not use excessive
5020  *         STARTUP_IPIs.
5021  * 4AP.    worked around in hardware
5022  * 5AP.    symmetric IO mode (normal Linux operation) not
5023  *         affected. 'noapic' mode has vector 0xf filled
5024  *         out properly.
5025  * 6AP.    'noapic' mode might be affected - fixed in
5026  *         later steppings
5027  * 7AP.    We do not assume writes to the LVT deassering
5028  *         IRQs
5029  * 8AP.    We do not enable low power mode (deep sleep)
5030  *         during MP bootup
5031  * 9AP.    We do not use mixed mode
5032  *
5033  * Pentium
5034  * There is a marginal case where REP MOVS on 100MHz SMP
5035  * machines with B stepping processors can fail. XXX
5036  * should provide an L1cache=Writethrough or L1cache=off
5037  * option.
5038  *
5039  * B stepping CPUs may hang. There are hardware work
5040  * arounds for this. We warn about it in case your board
5041  * doesnt have the work arounds. Basically thats so I can
5042  * tell anyone with a B stepping CPU and SMP problems
5043  * "tough".
5044  *
5045  * Specific items [From Pentium Processor Specification
5046  * Update]
5047  *
5048  * 1AP.    Linux doesn't use remote read
5049  * 2AP.    Linux doesn't trust APIC errors
5050  * 3AP.    We work around this
5051  * 4AP.    Linux never generated 3 interrupts of the same
5052  *         priority to cause a lost local interrupt.
5053  * 5AP.    Remote read is never used
5054  * 6AP.    not affected - worked around in hardware
5055  * 7AP.    not affected - worked around in hardware
5056  * 8AP.    worked around in hardware - we get explicit CS
5057  *         errors if not
5058  * 9AP.    only 'noapic' mode affected. Might generate
5059  *         spurious interrupts, we log only the first one
5060  *         and count the rest silently.
5061  * 10AP.   not affected - worked around in hardware
5062  * 11AP.   Linux reads the APIC between writes to avoid
5063  *         this, as per the documentation. Make sure you
5064  *         preserve this as it affects the C stepping
5065  *         chips too.
5066  * 12AP.   not affected - worked around in hardware
5067  * 13AP.   not affected - worked around in hardware
5068  * 14AP.   we always deassert INIT during bootup
5069  * 15AP.   not affected - worked around in hardware
5070  * 16AP.   not affected - worked around in hardware
5071  * 17AP.   not affected - worked around in hardware
5072  * 18AP.   not affected - worked around in hardware
5073  * 19AP.   not affected - worked around in BIOS
5074  *
5075  * If this sounds worrying believe me these bugs are
5076  * either ___RARE___, or are signal timing bugs worked
5077  * around in hardware and there's about nothing of note
5078  * with C stepping upwards.  */
5079
5080  /* The 'big kernel lock' */
5081  spinlock_t kernel_flag = SPIN_LOCK_UNLOCKED;
5082
5083  struct tlb_state cpu_tlbstate[NR_CPUS] =
5084      { [0 ... NR_CPUS - 1] = {&init_mm, 0} };
5085
5086  /* the following functions deal with sending IPIs between
5087   * CPUs.
5088   *
5089   * We use 'broadcast', CPU->CPU IPIs and self-IPIs too.
```

```
5090  */
5091
5092  static inline int __prepare_ICR(unsigned int shortcut,
5093      int vector)
5094  {
5095    return APIC_DM_FIXED | shortcut | vector |
5096        APIC_DEST_LOGICAL;
5097  }
5098
5099  static inline int __prepare_ICR2(unsigned int mask)
5100  {
5101    return SET_APIC_DEST_FIELD(mask);
5102  }
5103
5104  static inline void __send_IPI_shortcut(
5105    unsigned int shortcut, int vector)
5106  {
5107    /* Subtle. In the case of the 'never do double writes'
5108     * workaround we have to lock out interrupts to be
5109     * safe.  As we don't care of the value read we use an
5110     * atomic rmw access to avoid costly cli/sti.
5111     * Otherwise we use an even cheaper single atomic write
5112     * to the APIC.  */
5113    unsigned int cfg;
5114
5115    /* Wait for idle.  */
5116    apic_wait_icr_idle();
5117
5118    /* No need to touch the target chip field */
5119    cfg = __prepare_ICR(shortcut, vector);
5120
5121    /* Send the IPI. The write to APIC_ICR fires this off.
5122     */
5123    apic_write_around(APIC_ICR, cfg);
5124  }
5125
5126  static inline void send_IPI_allbutself(int vector)
5127  {
5128    /* if there are no other CPUs in the system then we get
5129     * an APIC send error if we try to broadcast.  thus we
5130     * have to avoid sending IPIs in this case. */
5131    if (smp_num_cpus > 1)
5132      __send_IPI_shortcut(APIC_DEST_ALLBUT, vector);
5133  }
5134
5135  static inline void send_IPI_all(int vector)
5136  {
```

```
5137      __send_IPI_shortcut(APIC_DEST_ALLINC, vector);
5138  }
5139
5140  void send_IPI_self(int vector)
5141  {
5142    __send_IPI_shortcut(APIC_DEST_SELF, vector);
5143  }
5144
5145  static inline void send_IPI_mask(int mask, int vector)
5146  {
5147    unsigned long cfg;
5148    unsigned long flags;
5149
5150    __save_flags(flags);
5151    __cli();
5152
5153    /* Wait for idle.  */
5154    apic_wait_icr_idle();
5155
5156    /* prepare target chip field */
5157    cfg = __prepare_ICR2(mask);
5158    apic_write_around(APIC_ICR2, cfg);
5159
5160    /* program the ICR */
5161    cfg = __prepare_ICR(0, vector);
5162
5163    /* Send the IPI. The write to APIC_ICR fires this off.
5164     */
5165    apic_write_around(APIC_ICR, cfg);
5166    __restore_flags(flags);
5167  }
5168
5169  /*      Smarter SMP flushing macros.
5170   *            c/o Linus Torvalds.
5171   *
5172   *      These mean you can really definitely utterly
5173   *      forget about writing to user space from
5174   *      interrupts. (Its not allowed anyway).
5175   *
5176   *      Optimizations Manfred Spraul
5177   *      <manfred@colorfullife.com>
5178   */
5179
5180  static volatile unsigned long flush_cpumask;
5181  static struct mm_struct *flush_mm;
5182  static unsigned long flush_va;
5183  static spinlock_t tlbstate_lock = SPIN_LOCK_UNLOCKED;
```

p 689

```
5184 #define FLUSH_ALL        0xffffffff
5185
5186 /* We cannot call mmdrop() because we are in interrupt
5187  * context, instead update mm->cpu_vm_mask. */
5188 static void inline leave_mm(unsigned long cpu)
5189 {
5190   if (cpu_tlbstate[cpu].state == TLBSTATE_OK)
5191     BUG();
5192   clear_bit(cpu,
5193       &cpu_tlbstate[cpu].active_mm->cpu_vm_mask);
5194 }
5195
5196 /* The flush IPI assumes that a thread switch happens in
5197  * this order:
5198  * [cpu0: the cpu that switches]
5199  * 1) switch_mm() either 1a) or 1b)
5200  * 1a) thread switch to a different mm
5201  * 1a1) clear_bit(cpu, &old_mm->cpu_vm_mask);
5202  *       Stop ipi delivery for the old mm. This is not
5203  *       synchronized with the other cpus, but
5204  *       smp_invalidate_interrupt ignore flush ipis for
5205  *       the wrong mm, and in the worst case we perform a
5206  *       superflous tlb flush.
5207  * 1a2) set cpu_tlbstate to TLBSTATE_OK
5208  *       Now the smp_invalidate_interrupt won't call
5209  *       leave_mm if cpu0 was in lazy tlb mode.
5210  * 1a3) update cpu_tlbstate[].active_mm
5211  *       Now cpu0 accepts tlb flushes for the new mm.
5212  * 1a4) set_bit(cpu, &new_mm->cpu_vm_mask);
5213  *       Now the other cpus will send tlb flush ipis.
5214  * 1a4) change cr3.
5215  * 1b) thread switch without mm change
5216  *       cpu_tlbstate[].active_mm is correct, cpu0 already
5217  *       handles flush ipis.
5218  * 1b1) set cpu_tlbstate to TLBSTATE_OK
5219  * 1b2) test_and_set the cpu bit in cpu_vm_mask.
5220  *       Atomically set the bit [other cpus will start
5221  *       sending flush ipis], and test the bit.
5222  * 1b3) if the bit was 0: leave_mm was called, flush the
5223  *       tlb.
5224  * 2) switch %%esp, ie current
5225  *
5226  * The interrupt must handle 2 special cases:
5227  * - cr3 is changed before %%esp, ie. it cannot use
5228  * current->{active_,}mm.
5229  * - the cpu performs speculative tlb reads, i.e. even if
5230  * the cpu only runs in kernel space, the cpu could load
5231  * tlb entries for user space pages.
5232  *
5233  * The good news is that cpu_tlbstate is local to each
5234  * cpu, no write/read ordering problems. */
5235
5236 /* TLB flush IPI:
5237  *
5238  * 1) Flush the tlb entries if the cpu uses the mm that's
5239  *    being flushed.
5240  * 2) Leave the mm if we are in the lazy tlb mode. */
5241 asmlinkage void smp_invalidate_interrupt(void)
5242 {
5243   unsigned long cpu = smp_processor_id();
5244
5245   if (!test_bit(cpu, &flush_cpumask))
5246     return;
5247   /* This was a BUG() but until someone can quote me the
5248    * line from the intel manual that guarantees an IPI to
5249    * multiple CPUs is retried _only_ on the erroring CPUs
5250    * its staying as a return
5251    *
5252    * BUG(); */
5253
5254   if (flush_mm == cpu_tlbstate[cpu].active_mm) {
5255     if (cpu_tlbstate[cpu].state == TLBSTATE_OK) {
5256       if (flush_va == FLUSH_ALL)
5257         local_flush_tlb();
5258       else
5259         __flush_tlb_one(flush_va);
5260     } else
5261       leave_mm(cpu);
5262   }
5263   ack_APIC_irq();
5264   clear_bit(cpu, &flush_cpumask);
5265 }
5266
5267 static void flush_tlb_others(unsigned long cpumask,
5268     struct mm_struct *mm, unsigned long va)
5269 {
5270   /* A couple of (to be removed) sanity checks:
5271    *
5272    * - we do not send IPIs to not-yet booted CPUs.
5273    * - current CPU must not be in mask
5274    * - mask must exist :) */
5275   if (!cpumask)
5276     BUG();
5277   if ((cpumask & cpu_online_map) != cpumask)
```

```
5278     BUG();
5279   if (cpumask & (1 << smp_processor_id()))
5280     BUG();
5281   if (!mm)
5282     BUG();
5283
5284   /* i'm not happy about this global shared spinlock in
5285    * the MM hot path, but we'll see how contended it is.
5286    * Temporarily this turns IRQs off, so that lockups are
5287    * detected by the NMI watchdog.  */
5288   spin_lock(&tlbstate_lock);
5289
5290   flush_mm = mm;
5291   flush_va = va;
5292   atomic_set_mask(cpumask, &flush_cpumask);
5293   /* We have to send the IPI only to CPUs affected.  */
5294   send_IPI_mask(cpumask, INVALIDATE_TLB_VECTOR);
5295
5296   while (flush_cpumask)
5297     /* nothing. lockup detection does not belong here */
5298       ;
5299
5300   flush_mm = NULL;
5301   flush_va = 0;
5302   spin_unlock(&tlbstate_lock);
5303 }
5304
5305 void flush_tlb_current_task(void)
5306 {
5307   struct mm_struct *mm = current->mm;
5308   unsigned long cpu_mask =
5309       mm->cpu_vm_mask & ~(1 << smp_processor_id());
5310
5311   local_flush_tlb();
5312   if (cpu_mask)
5313     flush_tlb_others(cpu_mask, mm, FLUSH_ALL);
5314 }
5315
5316 void flush_tlb_mm(struct mm_struct *mm)
5317 {
5318   unsigned long cpu_mask =
5319       mm->cpu_vm_mask & ~(1 << smp_processor_id());
5320
5321   if (current->active_mm == mm) {
5322     if (current->mm)
5323       local_flush_tlb();
5324     else

5325       leave_mm(smp_processor_id());
5326   }
5327   if (cpu_mask)
5328     flush_tlb_others(cpu_mask, mm, FLUSH_ALL);
5329 }
5330
5331 void flush_tlb_page(struct vm_area_struct *vma,
5332     unsigned long va)
5333 {
5334   struct mm_struct *mm = vma->vm_mm;
5335   unsigned long cpu_mask =
5336       mm->cpu_vm_mask & ~(1 << smp_processor_id());
5337
5338   if (current->active_mm == mm) {
5339     if (current->mm)
5340       __flush_tlb_one(va);
5341     else
5342       leave_mm(smp_processor_id());
5343   }
5344
5345   if (cpu_mask)
5346     flush_tlb_others(cpu_mask, mm, va);
5347 }
5348
5349 static inline void do_flush_tlb_all_local(void)
5350 {
5351   unsigned long cpu = smp_processor_id();
5352
5353   __flush_tlb_all();
5354   if (cpu_tlbstate[cpu].state == TLBSTATE_LAZY)
5355     leave_mm(cpu);
5356 }
5357
5358 static void flush_tlb_all_ipi(void *info)
5359 {
5360   do_flush_tlb_all_local();
5361 }
5362
5363 void flush_tlb_all(void)
5364 {
5365   smp_call_function(flush_tlb_all_ipi, 0, 1, 1);
5366
5367   do_flush_tlb_all_local();
5368 }
5369
5370 /* this function sends a 'reschedule' IPI to another CPU.
5371  * it goes straight through and wastes no time
```

```
5372   * serializing anything. Worst case is that we lose a
5373   * reschedule ... */
5374 void smp_send_reschedule(int cpu)
5375 {
5376     send_IPI_mask(1 << cpu, RESCHEDULE_VECTOR);
5377 }
5378
5379 /* Structure and data for smp_call_function(). This is
5380  * designed to minimise static memory requirements. It
5381  * also looks cleaner.  */
5382 static spinlock_t call_lock = SPIN_LOCK_UNLOCKED;
5383
5384 struct call_data_struct {
5385     void (*func) (void *info);
5386     void *info;
5387     atomic_t started;
5388     atomic_t finished;
5389     int wait;
5390 };
5391
5392 static struct call_data_struct *call_data;
5393
5394 /* this function sends a 'generic call function' IPI to
5395  * all other CPUs in the system.  */
5396 int smp_call_function(void (*func) (void *info),
5397     void *info, int nonatomic, int wait)
5398 /* [SUMMARY] Run a function on all other CPUs.
5399  * <func> The function to run. This must be fast and
5400  * non-blocking.
5401  * <info> An arbitrary pointer to pass to the function.
5402  * <nonatomic> currently unused.
5403  * <wait> If true, wait (atomically) until function has
5404  * completed on other CPUs.
5405  * [RETURNS] 0 on success, else a negative status
5406  * code. Does not return until remote CPUs are nearly
5407  * ready to execute <<func>> or are or have executed.
5408  *
5409  * You must not call this function with disabled
5410  * interrupts or from a hardware interrupt handler, you
5411  * may call it from a bottom half handler.  */
5412 {
5413     struct call_data_struct data;
5414     int cpus = smp_num_cpus - 1;
5415
5416     if (!cpus)
5417         return 0;
5418
5419     data.func = func;
5420     data.info = info;
5421     atomic_set(&data.started, 0);
5422     data.wait = wait;
5423     if (wait)
5424         atomic_set(&data.finished, 0);
5425
5426     spin_lock_bh(&call_lock);
5427     call_data = &data;
5428     /* Send a message to all other CPUs and wait for them
5429      * to respond */
5430     send_IPI_allbutself(CALL_FUNCTION_VECTOR);
5431
5432     /* Wait for response */
5433     while (atomic_read(&data.started) != cpus)
5434         barrier();
5435
5436     if (wait)
5437         while (atomic_read(&data.finished) != cpus)
5438             barrier();
5439     spin_unlock_bh(&call_lock);
5440
5441     return 0;
5442 }
5443
5444 static void stop_this_cpu(void *dummy)
5445 {
5446     /* Remove this CPU: */
5447     clear_bit(smp_processor_id(), &cpu_online_map);
5448     __cli();
5449     disable_local_APIC();
5450     if (cpu_data[smp_processor_id()].hlt_works_ok)
5451         for (;;)
5452             __asm__("hlt");
5453     for (;;) ;
5454 }
5455
5456 /* this function calls the 'stop' function on all other
5457  * CPUs in the system.  */
5458 void smp_send_stop(void)
5459 {
5460     smp_call_function(stop_this_cpu, NULL, 1, 0);
5461     smp_num_cpus = 1;
5462
5463     __cli();
5464     disable_local_APIC();
5465     __sti();
```

p 689 (marker at line 5374)

```
5466 }
5467
5468 /* Reschedule call back. Nothing to do, all the work is
5469  * done automatically when we return from the interrupt.
5470  */
5471 asmlinkage void smp_reschedule_interrupt(void)
5472 {
5473   ack_APIC_irq();
5474 }
5475
5476 asmlinkage void smp_call_function_interrupt(void)
5477 {
5478   void (*func) (void *info) = call_data->func;
5479   void *info = call_data->info;
5480   int wait = call_data->wait;
5481
5482   ack_APIC_irq();
5483   /* Notify initiating CPU that I've grabbed the data and
5484    * am about to execute the function */
5485   atomic_inc(&call_data->started);
5486   /* At this point the info structure may be out of scope
5487    * unless wait==1 */
5488   (*func) (info);
5489   if (wait)
5490     atomic_inc(&call_data->finished);
5491 }
```

arch/i386/kernel/sys_i386.c

```
5492 /*
5493  * linux/arch/i386/kernel/sys_i386.c
5494  *
5495  * This file contains various random system calls that
5496  * have a non-standard calling sequence on the Linux/i386
5497  * platform.
5498  */
5499
5500 #include <linux/errno.h>
5501 #include <linux/sched.h>
5502 #include <linux/mm.h>
5503 #include <linux/smp.h>
5504 #include <linux/smp_lock.h>
5505 #include <linux/sem.h>
5506 #include <linux/msg.h>
5507 #include <linux/shm.h>
5508 #include <linux/stat.h>
5509 #include <linux/mman.h>
5510 #include <linux/file.h>
5511 #include <linux/utsname.h>
5512
5513 #include <asm/uaccess.h>
5514 #include <asm/ipc.h>
5515
5516 /* sys_pipe() is the normal C calling standard for
5517  * creating a pipe. It's not the way Unix traditionally
5518  * does this, though.  */
5519 asmlinkage int sys_pipe(unsigned long *fildes)
5520 {
5521   int fd[2];
5522   int error;
5523
5524   error = do_pipe(fd);
5525   if (!error) {
5526     if (copy_to_user(fildes, fd, 2 * sizeof(int)))
5527       error = -EFAULT;
5528   }
5529   return error;
5530 }
5531
5532 /* common code for old and new mmaps */
5533 static inline long do_mmap2(
5534     unsigned long addr, unsigned long len,
5535     unsigned long prot, unsigned long flags,
5536     unsigned long fd, unsigned long pgoff)
5537 {
5538   int error = -EBADF;
5539   struct file *file = NULL;
5540
5541   flags &= ~(MAP_EXECUTABLE | MAP_DENYWRITE);
5542   if (!(flags & MAP_ANONYMOUS)) {
5543     file = fget(fd);
5544     if (!file)
5545       goto out;
5546   }
5547
5548   down(&current->mm->mmap_sem);
5549   error =
5550       do_mmap_pgoff(file, addr, len, prot, flags, pgoff);
5551   up(&current->mm->mmap_sem);
5552
5553   if (file)
5554     fput(file);
5555 out:
5556   return error;
5557 }
```

```
5558
5559 asmlinkage long sys_mmap2(unsigned long addr,
5560     unsigned long len, unsigned long prot,
5561     unsigned long flags, unsigned long fd,
5562     unsigned long pgoff)
5563 {
5564   return do_mmap2(addr, len, prot, flags, fd, pgoff);
5565 }
5566
5567 /* Perform the select(nd, in, out, ex, tv) and mmap()
5568  * system calls. Linux/i386 didn't use to be able to
5569  * handle more than 4 system call parameters, so these
5570  * system calls used a memory block for parameter
5571  * passing.. */
5572 struct mmap_arg_struct {
5573   unsigned long addr;
5574   unsigned long len;
5575   unsigned long prot;
5576   unsigned long flags;
5577   unsigned long fd;
5578   unsigned long offset;
5579 };
5580
5581 asmlinkage int old_mmap(struct mmap_arg_struct *arg)
5582 {
5583   struct mmap_arg_struct a;
5584   int err = -EFAULT;
5585
5586   if (copy_from_user(&a, arg, sizeof(a)))
5587     goto out;
5588
5589   err = -EINVAL;
5590   if (a.offset & ~PAGE_MASK)
5591     goto out;
5592
5593   err = do_mmap2(a.addr, a.len, a.prot, a.flags, a.fd,
5594                  a.offset >> PAGE_SHIFT);
5595 out:
5596   return err;
5597 }
5598
5599
5600 extern asmlinkage int sys_select(int, fd_set *, fd_set *,
5601     fd_set *, struct timeval *);
5602
5603 struct sel_arg_struct {
5604   unsigned long n;
5605   fd_set *inp, *outp, *exp;
5606   struct timeval *tvp;
5607 };
5608
5609 asmlinkage int old_select(struct sel_arg_struct *arg)
5610 {
5611   struct sel_arg_struct a;
5612
5613   if (copy_from_user(&a, arg, sizeof(a)))
5614     return -EFAULT;
5615   /* sys_select() does the appropriate kernel locking */
5616   return sys_select(a.n, a.inp, a.outp, a.exp, a.tvp);
5617 }
5618
5619 /* sys_ipc() is the de-multiplexer for the SysV IPC
5620  * calls..
5621  *
5622  * This is really horribly ugly.  */
5623 asmlinkage int sys_ipc(uint call, int first, int second,
5624     int third, void *ptr, long fifth)
5625 {
5626   int version, ret;
5627
5628   version = call >> 16;          /* hack for backward
5629                                   * compatibility */
5630   call &= 0xffff;
5631
5632   switch (call) {
5633   case SEMOP:
5634     return sys_semop(first, (struct sembuf *) ptr,
5635                      second);
5636   case SEMGET:
5637     return sys_semget(first, second, third);
5638   case SEMCTL:{
5639     union semun fourth;
5640     if (!ptr)
5641       return -EINVAL;
5642     if (get_user(fourth.__pad, (void **) ptr))
5643       return -EFAULT;
5644     return sys_semctl(first, second, third, fourth);
5645   }
5646
5647   case MSGSND:
5648     return sys_msgsnd(first, (struct msgbuf *) ptr,
5649                       second, third);
5650   case MSGRCV:
5651     switch (version) {
```

```
5652      case 0:
5653      {
5654        struct ipc_kludge tmp;
5655        if (!ptr)
5656          return -EINVAL;
5657
5658        if (copy_from_user(&tmp,
5659                  (struct ipc_kludge *) ptr, sizeof(tmp)))
5660          return -EFAULT;
5661        return sys_msgrcv(first, tmp.msgp, second,
5662                          tmp.msgtyp, third);
5663      }
5664      default:
5665        return sys_msgrcv(first,
5666            (struct msgbuf *) ptr, second, fifth, third);
5667      }
5668    case MSGGET:
5669      return sys_msgget((key_t) first, second);
5670    case MSGCTL:
5671      return sys_msgctl(first, second,
5672                        (struct msqid_ds *) ptr);
5673
5674    case SHMAT:
5675      switch (version) {
5676      default:
5677      {
5678        ulong raddr;
5679        ret = sys_shmat(first, (char *) ptr, second,
5680                        &raddr);
5681        if (ret)
5682          return ret;
5683        return put_user(raddr, (ulong *) third);
5684      }
5685      case 1:            /* iBCS2 emulator entry point */
5686        if (!segment_eq(get_fs(), get_ds()))
5687          return -EINVAL;
5688        return sys_shmat(first, (char *) ptr, second,
5689                        (ulong *) third);
5690      }
5691    case SHMDT:
5692      return sys_shmdt((char *) ptr);
5693    case SHMGET:
5694      return sys_shmget(first, second, third);
5695    case SHMCTL:
5696      return sys_shmctl(first, second,
5697                        (struct shmid_ds *) ptr);
5698    default:
```

```
5699      return -EINVAL;
5700    }
5701 }
5702
5703 /* Old cruft */
5704 asmlinkage int sys_uname(struct old_utsname *name)
5705 {
5706   int err;
5707   if (!name)
5708     return -EFAULT;
5709   down_read(&uts_sem);
5710   err =
5711     copy_to_user(name, &system_utsname, sizeof(*name));
5712   up_read(&uts_sem);
5713   return err ? -EFAULT : 0;
5714 }
5715
5716 asmlinkage int sys_olduname(struct oldold_utsname *name)
5717 {
5718   int error;
5719
5720   if (!name)
5721     return -EFAULT;
5722   if (!access_ok(VERIFY_WRITE, name,
5723                  sizeof(struct oldold_utsname)))
5724     return -EFAULT;
5725
5726   down_read(&uts_sem);
5727
5728   error = __copy_to_user(&name->sysname,
5729                          &system_utsname.sysname,
5730                          __OLD_UTS_LEN);
5731   error |= __put_user(0, name->sysname + __OLD_UTS_LEN);
5732   error |= __copy_to_user(&name->nodename,
5733                          &system_utsname.nodename,
5734                          __OLD_UTS_LEN);
5735   error |= __put_user(0, name->nodename + __OLD_UTS_LEN);
5736   error |= __copy_to_user(&name->release,
5737                          &system_utsname.release,
5738                          __OLD_UTS_LEN);
5739   error |= __put_user(0, name->release + __OLD_UTS_LEN);
5740   error |= __copy_to_user(&name->version,
5741                          &system_utsname.version,
5742                          __OLD_UTS_LEN);
5743   error |= __put_user(0, name->version + __OLD_UTS_LEN);
5744   error |= __copy_to_user(&name->machine,
5745                          &system_utsname.machine,
```

```
5746                          __OLD_UTS_LEN);
5747   error |= __put_user(0, name->machine + __OLD_UTS_LEN);
5748
5749   up_read(&uts_sem);
5750
5751   error = error ? -EFAULT : 0;
5752
5753   return error;
5754 }
5755
5756 asmlinkage int sys_pause(void)
5757 {
5758   current->state = TASK_INTERRUPTIBLE;
5759   schedule();
5760   return -ERESTARTNOHAND;
5761 }
```

arch/i386/kernel/time.c

```
5762 /*
5763  *  linux/arch/i386/kernel/time.c
5764  *
5765  *  Copyright (C) 1991, 1992, 1995  Linus Torvalds
5766  *
5767  * This file contains the PC-specific time handling
5768  * details: reading the RTC at bootup, etc..
5769  * 1994-07-02    Alan Modra
5770  *      fixed set_rtc_mmss, fixed time.year for >= 2000,
5771  *      new mktime
5772  * 1995-03-26    Markus Kuhn
5773  *      fixed 500 ms bug at call to set_rtc_mmss, fixed
5774  *      DS12887 precision CMOS clock update
5775  * 1996-05-03    Ingo Molnar
5776  *      fixed time warps in
5777  *      do_[slow|fast]_gettimeoffset()
5778  * 1997-09-10 Updated NTP code according to technical
5779  *              memorandum Jan '96 "A Kernel Model for
5780  *              Precision Timekeeping" by Dave Mills
5781  * 1998-09-05    (Various)
5782  *      More robust do_fast_gettimeoffset() algorithm
5783  *      implemented (works with APM, Cyrix 6x86MX and
5784  *      Centaur C6), monotonic gettimeofday() with
5785  *      fast_get_timeoffset(), drift-proof precision TSC
5786  *      calibration on boot (C. Scott Ananian
5787  *      <cananian@alumni.princeton.edu>, Andrew D.  Balsa
5788  *      <andrebalsa@altern.org>, Philip Gladstone
5789  *      <philip@raptor.com>; ported from 2.0.35 Jumbo-9
5790  *      by Michael Krause <m.krause@tu-harburg.de>).
5791  * 1998-12-16    Andrea Arcangeli
5792  *      Fixed Jumbo-9 code in 2.1.131: do_gettimeofday
5793  *      was missing 1 jiffy because was not accounting
5794  *      lost_ticks.
5795  * 1998-12-24 Copyright (C) 1998  Andrea Arcangeli
5796  *      Fixed a xtime SMP race (we need the xtime_lock rw
5797  *      spinlock to serialize accesses to
5798  *      xtime/lost_ticks).  */
5799
5800 #include <linux/errno.h>
5801 #include <linux/sched.h>
5802 #include <linux/kernel.h>
5803 #include <linux/param.h>
5804 #include <linux/string.h>
5805 #include <linux/mm.h>
5806 #include <linux/interrupt.h>
5807 #include <linux/time.h>
5808 #include <linux/delay.h>
5809 #include <linux/init.h>
5810 #include <linux/smp.h>
5811
5812 #include <asm/io.h>
5813 #include <asm/smp.h>
5814 #include <asm/irq.h>
5815 #include <asm/msr.h>
5816 #include <asm/delay.h>
5817 #include <asm/mpspec.h>
5818 #include <asm/uaccess.h>
5819 #include <asm/processor.h>
5820
5821 #include <linux/mc146818rtc.h>
5822 #include <linux/timex.h>
5823 #include <linux/config.h>
5824
5825 #include <asm/fixmap.h>
5826 #include <asm/cobalt.h>
5827
5828 /* for x86_do_profile() */
5829 #include <linux/irq.h>
5830
5831
5832 /* Detected as we calibrate the TSC */
5833 unsigned long cpu_khz;
5834
5835 /* Number of usecs that the last interrupt was delayed */
5836 static int delay_at_last_interrupt;
5837
```

```
5838 /* lsb 32 bits of Time Stamp Counter */
5839 static unsigned long last_tsc_low;
5840
5841 /* Cached *multiplier* to convert TSC counts to
5842  * microseconds. (see the equation below).
5843  * Equal to 2^32 * (1 / (clocks per usec) ).
5844  * Initialized in time_init. */
5845 unsigned long fast_gettimeoffset_quotient;
5846
5847 extern rwlock_t xtime_lock;
5848 extern unsigned long wall_jiffies;
5849
5850 spinlock_t rtc_lock = SPIN_LOCK_UNLOCKED;
5851
5852 static inline unsigned long do_fast_gettimeoffset(void)
5853 {
5854   register unsigned long eax, edx;
5855
5856   /* Read the Time Stamp Counter */
5857   rdtsc(eax,edx);
5858
5859   /* .. relative to previous jiffy (32 bits is enough) */
5860   eax -= last_tsc_low;  /* tsc_low delta */
5861
5862   /* Time offset
5863    *      = (tsc_low delta) * fast_gettimeoffset_quotient
5864    *      = (tsc_low delta) * (usecs_per_clock)
5865    *      = (tsc_low delta) * (usecs_per_jiffy /
5866    *                           clocks_per_jiffy)
5867    *
5868    * Using a mull instead of a divl saves up to 31 clock
5869    * cycles in the critical path.  */
5870   __asm__("mull %2"
5871          :"=a" (eax), "=d" (edx)
5872          :"rm" (fast_gettimeoffset_quotient),
5873          "0" (eax));
5874
5875   /* our adjusted time offset in microseconds */
5876   return delay_at_last_interrupt + edx;
5877 }
5878
5879 #define TICK_SIZE tick
5880
5881 spinlock_t i8253_lock = SPIN_LOCK_UNLOCKED;
5882
5883 extern spinlock_t i8259A_lock;
5884
5885 #ifndef CONFIG_X86_TSC
5886
5887 /* This function must be called with interrupts disabled
5888  * It was inspired by Steve McCanne's microtime-i386 for
5889  * BSD.  — jrs
5890  *
5891  * However, the pc-audio speaker driver changes the
5892  * divisor so that it gets interrupted rather more often
5893  * - it loads 64 into the counter rather than 11932! This
5894  * has an adverse impact on do_gettimeoffset() — it
5895  * stops working! What is also not good is that the
5896  * interval that our timer function gets called is no
5897  * longer 10.0002 ms, but 9.9767 ms. To get around this
5898  * would require using a different timing source. Maybe
5899  * someone could use the RTC - I know that this can
5900  * interrupt at frequencies ranging from 8192Hz to
5901  * 2Hz. If I had the energy, I'd somehow fix it so that
5902  * at startup, the timer code in sched.c would select
5903  * using either the RTC or the 8253 timer. The decision
5904  * would be based on whether there was any other device
5905  * around that needed to trample on the 8253. I'd set up
5906  * the RTC to interrupt at 1024 Hz, and then do some
5907  * jiggery to have a version of do_timer that advanced
5908  * the clock by 1/1024 s. Every time that reached over
5909  * 1/100 of a second, then do all the old code. If the
5910  * time was kept correct then do_gettimeoffset could just
5911  * return 0 - there is no low order divider that can be
5912  * accessed.
5913  *
5914  * Ideally, you would be able to use the RTC for the
5915  * speaker driver, but it appears that the speaker driver
5916  * really needs interrupt more often than every 120 us or
5917  * so.
5918  *
5919  * Anyway, this needs more thought.... pjsg (1993-08-28)
5920  *
5921  * If you are really that interested, you should be
5922  * reading comp.protocols.time.ntp! */
5923 static unsigned long do_slow_gettimeoffset(void)
5924 {
5925   int count;
5926
5927   /* for the first call after boot */
5928   static int count_p = LATCH;
5929   static unsigned long jiffies_p = 0;
5930
5931   /* cache volatile jiffies temporarily; we have IRQs
```

```
5932       * turned off.  */
5933      unsigned long jiffies_t;
5934
5935      /* gets recalled with irq locally disabled */
5936      spin_lock(&i8253_lock);
5937      /* timer count may underflow right here */
5938      outb_p(0x00, 0x43);    /* latch the count ASAP */
5939
5940      count = inb_p(0x40);   /* read the latched count */
5941
5942      /* We do this guaranteed double memory access instead
5943       * of a _p postfix in the previous port access. Wheee,
5944       * hackady hack */
5945      jiffies_t = jiffies;
5946
5947      count |= inb_p(0x40) << 8;
5948      spin_unlock(&i8253_lock);
5949
5950      /* avoiding timer inconsistencies (they are rare, but
5951       * they happen)...  there are two kinds of problems
5952       * that must be avoided here:
5953       * 1. the timer counter underflows
5954       * 2. hardware problem with the timer, not giving us
5955       *    continuous time, the counter does small "jumps"
5956       *    upwards on some Pentium systems, (see c't 95/10
5957       *    page 335 for Neptun bug.)  */
5958
5959  /* you can safely undefine this if you don't have the
5960   * Neptune chipset */
5961  #define BUGGY_NEPTUN_TIMER
5962
5963    if( jiffies_t == jiffies_p ) {
5964      if( count > count_p ) {
5965        /* the nutcase */
5966
5967        int i;
5968
5969        spin_lock(&i8259A_lock);
5970        /* This is tricky when I/O APICs are used; see
5971         * do_timer_interrupt().  */
5972        i = inb(0x20);
5973        spin_unlock(&i8259A_lock);
5974
5975        /* assumption about timer being IRQ0 */
5976        if (i & 0x01) {
5977          /* We cannot detect lost timer interrupts ...
5978           * well, that's why we call them lost, don't we?
5979           * :) [hmm, on the Pentium and Alpha we can
5980           * ... sort of] */
5981          count -= LATCH;
5982        } else {
5983  #ifdef BUGGY_NEPTUN_TIMER
5984          /* for the Neptun bug we know that the 'latch'
5985           * command doesnt latch the high and low value of
5986           * the counter atomically. Thus we have to
5987           * substract 256 from the counter ... funny, isnt
5988           * it? :) */
5989          count -= 256;
5990  #else
5991          printk("do_slow_gettimeoffset(): "
5992                 "hardware timer problem?\n");
5993  #endif
5994        }
5995      }
5996    } else
5997      jiffies_p = jiffies_t;
5998
5999    count_p = count;
6000
6001    count = ((LATCH-1) - count) * TICK_SIZE;
6002    count = (count + LATCH/2) / LATCH;
6003
6004    return count;
6005  }
6006
6007  static unsigned long (*do_gettimeoffset)(void) =
6008    do_slow_gettimeoffset;
6009
6010  #else
6011
6012  #define do_gettimeoffset()       do_fast_gettimeoffset()
6013
6014  #endif
6015
6016  /* This version of gettimeofday has microsecond
6017   * resolution and better than microsecond precision on
6018   * fast x86 machines with TSC.  */
6019  void do_gettimeofday(struct timeval *tv)
6020  {
6021    unsigned long flags;
6022    unsigned long usec, sec;
6023
6024    read_lock_irqsave(&xtime_lock, flags);
6025    usec = do_gettimeoffset();
```

```
6026    {
6027      unsigned long lost = jiffies - wall_jiffies;
6028      if (lost)
6029        usec += lost * (1000000 / HZ);
6030    }
6031    sec = xtime.tv_sec;
6032    usec += xtime.tv_usec;
6033    read_unlock_irqrestore(&xtime_lock, flags);
6034
6035    while (usec >= 1000000) {
6036      usec -= 1000000;
6037      sec++;
6038    }
6039
6040    tv->tv_sec = sec;
6041    tv->tv_usec = usec;
6042 }
6043
6044 void do_settimeofday(struct timeval *tv)
6045 {
6046    write_lock_irq(&xtime_lock);
6047    /* This is revolting. We need to set "xtime"
6048     * correctly. However, the value in this location is
6049     * the value at the most recent update of wall time.
6050     * Discover what correction gettimeofday() would have
6051     * made, and then undo it! */
6052    tv->tv_usec -= do_gettimeoffset();
6053    tv->tv_usec -=
6054      (jiffies - wall_jiffies) * (1000000 / HZ);
6055
6056    while (tv->tv_usec < 0) {
6057      tv->tv_usec += 1000000;
6058      tv->tv_sec-;
6059    }
6060
6061    xtime = *tv;
6062    time_adjust = 0;              /* stop active adjtime() */
6063    time_status |= STA_UNSYNC;
6064    time_maxerror = NTP_PHASE_LIMIT;
6065    time_esterror = NTP_PHASE_LIMIT;
6066    write_unlock_irq(&xtime_lock);
6067 }
6068
6069 /* In order to set the CMOS clock precisely, set_rtc_mmss
6070  * has to be called 500 ms after the second nowtime has
6071  * started, because when nowtime is written into the
6072  * registers of the CMOS clock, it will jump to the next
6073  * second precisely 500 ms later. Check the Motorola
6074  * MC146818A or Dallas DS12887 data sheet for details.
6075  *
6076  * BUG: This routine does not handle hour overflow
6077  *      properly; it just sets the minutes. Usually
6078  *      you'll only notice that after reboot!  */
6079 static int set_rtc_mmss(unsigned long nowtime)
6080 {
6081    int retval = 0;
6082    int real_seconds, real_minutes, cmos_minutes;
6083    unsigned char save_control, save_freq_select;
6084
6085    /* gets recalled with irq locally disabled */
6086    spin_lock(&rtc_lock);
6087    /* tell the clock it's being set */
6088    save_control = CMOS_READ(RTC_CONTROL);
6089    CMOS_WRITE((save_control|RTC_SET), RTC_CONTROL);
6090
6091    /* stop and reset prescaler */
6092    save_freq_select = CMOS_READ(RTC_FREQ_SELECT);
6093    CMOS_WRITE((save_freq_select|RTC_DIV_RESET2),
6094            RTC_FREQ_SELECT);
6095
6096    cmos_minutes = CMOS_READ(RTC_MINUTES);
6097    if (!(save_control & RTC_DM_BINARY) || RTC_ALWAYS_BCD)
6098      BCD_TO_BIN(cmos_minutes);
6099
6100    /* since we're only adjusting minutes and seconds,
6101     * don't interfere with hour overflow. This avoids
6102     * messing with unknown time zones but requires your
6103     * RTC not to be off by more than 15 minutes */
6104    real_seconds = nowtime % 60;
6105    real_minutes = nowtime / 60;
6106    if (((abs(real_minutes - cmos_minutes) + 15)/30) & 1)
6107      /* correct for half hour time zone */
6108      real_minutes += 30;
6109    real_minutes %= 60;
6110
6111    if (abs(real_minutes - cmos_minutes) < 30) {
6112      if (!(save_control & RTC_DM_BINARY) ||
6113         RTC_ALWAYS_BCD) {
6114        BIN_TO_BCD(real_seconds);
6115        BIN_TO_BCD(real_minutes);
6116      }
6117      CMOS_WRITE(real_seconds,RTC_SECONDS);
6118      CMOS_WRITE(real_minutes,RTC_MINUTES);
6119    } else {
```

```
6120      printk(KERN_WARNING
6121          "set_rtc_mmss: can't update from %d to %d\n",
6122          cmos_minutes, real_minutes);
6123      retval = -1;
6124    }
6125
6126    /* The following flags have to be released exactly in
6127     * this order, otherwise the DS12887 (popular MC146818A
6128     * clone with integrated battery and quartz) will not
6129     * reset the oscillator and will not update precisely
6130     * 500 ms later. You won't find this mentioned in the
6131     * Dallas Semiconductor data sheets, but who believes
6132     * data sheets anyway ...    - Markus Kuhn */
6133    CMOS_WRITE(save_control, RTC_CONTROL);
6134    CMOS_WRITE(save_freq_select, RTC_FREQ_SELECT);
6135    spin_unlock(&rtc_lock);
6136
6137    return retval;
6138 }
6139
6140 /* last time the cmos clock got updated */
6141 static long last_rtc_update;
6142
6143 int timer_ack;
6144
6145 /* timer_interrupt() needs to keep up the real-time
6146  * clock, as well as call the "do_timer()" routine every
6147  * clocktick */
6148 static inline void do_timer_interrupt(int irq,
6149    void *dev_id, struct pt_regs *regs)
6150 {
6151 #ifdef CONFIG_X86_IO_APIC
6152   if (timer_ack) {
6153     /* Subtle, when I/O APICs are used we have to ack
6154      * timer IRQ manually to reset the IRR bit for
6155      * do_slow_gettimeoffset().  This will also deassert
6156      * NMI lines for the watchdog if run on an
6157      * 82489DX-based system.  */
6158     spin_lock(&i8259A_lock);
6159     outb(0x0c, 0x20);
6160     /* Ack the IRQ; AEOI will end it automatically. */
6161     inb(0x20);
6162     spin_unlock(&i8259A_lock);
6163   }
6164 #endif
6165
6166 #ifdef CONFIG_VISWS
6167   /* Clear the interrupt */
6168   co_cpu_write(CO_CPU_STAT,
6169     co_cpu_read(CO_CPU_STAT) & ~CO_STAT_TIMEINTR);
6170 #endif
6171   do_timer(regs);
6172 /* In the SMP case we use the local APIC timer interrupt
6173  * to do the profiling, except when we simulate SMP mode
6174  * on a uniprocessor system, in that case we have to call
6175  * the local interrupt handler.  */
6176 #ifndef CONFIG_X86_LOCAL_APIC
6177   if (!user_mode(regs))
6178     x86_do_profile(regs->eip);
6179 #else
6180   if (!smp_found_config)
6181     smp_local_timer_interrupt(regs);
6182 #endif
6183
6184   /* If we have an externally synchronized Linux clock,
6185    * then update CMOS clock accordingly every ~11
6186    * minutes. Set_rtc_mmss() has to be called as close as
6187    * possible to 500 ms before the new second starts.  */
6188   if ((time_status & STA_UNSYNC) == 0 &&
6189     xtime.tv_sec > last_rtc_update + 660 &&
6190     xtime.tv_usec >= 500000 - ((unsigned) tick) / 2 &&
6191     xtime.tv_usec <= 500000 + ((unsigned) tick) / 2) {
6192     if (set_rtc_mmss(xtime.tv_sec) == 0)
6193       last_rtc_update = xtime.tv_sec;
6194     else
6195       /* do it again in 60 s */
6196       last_rtc_update = xtime.tv_sec - 600;
6197   }
6198
6199 #ifdef CONFIG_MCA
6200   if( MCA_bus ) {
6201     /* The PS/2 uses level-triggered interrupts.  You
6202      * can't turn them off, nor would you want to (any
6203      * attempt to enable edge-triggered interrupts
6204      * usually gets intercepted by a special hardware
6205      * circuit).  Hence we have to acknowledge the timer
6206      * interrupt.  Through some incredibly stupid design
6207      * idea, the reset for IRQ 0 is done by setting the
6208      * high bit of the PPI port B (0x61).  Note that some
6209      * PS/2s, notably the 55SX, work fine if this is
6210      * removed.  */
6211     irq = inb_p( 0x61 );     /* read the current state */
6212     outb_p( irq|0x80, 0x61 );   /* reset the IRQ */
6213   }
```

```
6214 #endif
6215 }
6216
6217 static int use_tsc;
6218
6219 /* This is the same as the above, except we _also_ save
6220  * the current Time Stamp Counter value at the time of
6221  * the timer interrupt, so that we later on can estimate
6222  * the time of day more exactly.  */
6223 static void timer_interrupt(int irq, void *dev_id,
6224                            struct pt_regs *regs)
6225 {
6226   int count;
6227
6228   /* Here we are in the timer irq handler. We just have
6229    * irqs locally disabled but we don't know if the
6230    * timer_bh is running on the other CPU. We need to
6231    * avoid to SMP race with it. NOTE: we don' t need the
6232    * irq version of write_lock because as just said we
6233    * have irq locally disabled. -arca */
6234   write_lock(&xtime_lock);
6235
6236   if (use_tsc)
6237   {
6238     /* It is important that these two operations happen
6239      * almost at the same time. We do the RDTSC stuff
6240      * first, since it's faster. To avoid any
6241      * inconsistencies, we need interrupts disabled
6242      * locally.  */
6243
6244     /* Interrupts are just disabled locally since the
6245      * timer irq has the SA_INTERRUPT flag set. -arca */
6246
6247     /* read Pentium cycle counter */
6248
6249     rdtscl(last_tsc_low);
6250
6251     spin_lock(&i8253_lock);
6252     outb_p(0x00, 0x43);     /* latch the count ASAP */
6253
6254     count = inb_p(0x40);    /* read the latched count */
6255     count |= inb(0x40) << 8;
6256     spin_unlock(&i8253_lock);
6257
6258     count = ((LATCH-1) - count) * TICK_SIZE;
6259     delay_at_last_interrupt = (count + LATCH/2) / LATCH;
6260   }
6261
6262   do_timer_interrupt(irq, NULL, regs);
6263
6264   write_unlock(&xtime_lock);
6265
6266 }
6267
6268 /* not static: needed by APM */
6269 unsigned long get_cmos_time(void)
6270 {
6271   unsigned int year, mon, day, hour, min, sec;
6272   int i;
6273
6274   /* The Linux interpretation of the CMOS clock register
6275    * contents: When the Update-In-Progress (UIP) flag
6276    * goes from 1 to 0, the RTC registers show the second
6277    * which has precisely just started.  Let's hope other
6278    * operating systems interpret the RTC the same way. */
6279   /* read RTC exactly on falling edge of update flag */
6280   /* may take up to 1 second... */
6281   for (i = 0 ; i < 1000000 ; i++)
6282     if (CMOS_READ(RTC_FREQ_SELECT) & RTC_UIP)
6283       break;
6284   /* must try at least 2.228 ms */
6285   for (i = 0 ; i < 1000000 ; i++)
6286     if (!(CMOS_READ(RTC_FREQ_SELECT) & RTC_UIP))
6287       break;
6288   do {
6289     /* Isn't this overkill ? UIP above should guarantee
6290      * consistency */
6291     sec = CMOS_READ(RTC_SECONDS);
6292     min = CMOS_READ(RTC_MINUTES);
6293     hour = CMOS_READ(RTC_HOURS);
6294     day = CMOS_READ(RTC_DAY_OF_MONTH);
6295     mon = CMOS_READ(RTC_MONTH);
6296     year = CMOS_READ(RTC_YEAR);
6297   } while (sec != CMOS_READ(RTC_SECONDS));
6298   if (!(CMOS_READ(RTC_CONTROL) & RTC_DM_BINARY) ||
6299       RTC_ALWAYS_BCD)
6300   {
6301     BCD_TO_BIN(sec);
6302     BCD_TO_BIN(min);
6303     BCD_TO_BIN(hour);
6304     BCD_TO_BIN(day);
6305     BCD_TO_BIN(mon);
6306     BCD_TO_BIN(year);
6307   }
```

```
6308    if ((year += 1900) < 1970)
6309      year += 100;
6310    return mktime(year, mon, day, hour, min, sec);
6311  }
6312
6313  static struct irqaction irq0 =
6314  { timer_interrupt, SA_INTERRUPT, 0, "timer", NULL, NULL};
6315
6316  /* ── Calibrate the TSC ──
6317   * Return 2^32 * (1 / (TSC clocks per usec)) for
6318   * do_fast_gettimeoffset().  Too much 64-bit arithmetic
6319   * here to do this cleanly in C, and for accuracy's sake
6320   * we want to keep the overhead on the CTC speaker
6321   * (channel 2) output busy loop as low as possible. We
6322   * avoid reading the CTC registers directly because of
6323   * the awkward 8-bit access mechanism of the 82C54
6324   * device. */
6325
6326  #define CALIBRATE_LATCH (5 * LATCH)
6327  #define CALIBRATE_TIME  (5 * 1000020/HZ)
6328
6329  static unsigned long __init calibrate_tsc(void)
6330  {
6331    /* Set the Gate high, disable speaker */
6332    outb((inb(0x61) & ~0x02) | 0x01, 0x61);
6333
6334    /* Now let's take care of CTC channel 2
6335     *
6336     * Set the Gate high, program CTC channel 2 for mode 0,
6337     * (interrupt on terminal count mode), binary count,
6338     * load 5 * LATCH count, (LSB and MSB) to begin
6339     * countdown. */
6340    /* binary, mode 0, LSB/MSB, Ch 2 */
6341    outb(0xb0, 0x43);
6342    /* LSB of count */
6343    outb(CALIBRATE_LATCH & 0xff, 0x42);
6344    /* MSB of count */
6345    outb(CALIBRATE_LATCH >> 8, 0x42);
6346
6347    {
6348      unsigned long startlow, starthigh;
6349      unsigned long endlow, endhigh;
6350      unsigned long count;
6351
6352      rdtsc(startlow,starthigh);
6353      count = 0;
6354      do {
```

```
6355        count++;
6356      } while ((inb(0x61) & 0x20) == 0);
6357      rdtsc(endlow,endhigh);
6358
6359      last_tsc_low = endlow;
6360
6361      /* Error: ECTCNEVERSET */
6362      if (count <= 1)
6363        goto bad_ctc;
6364
6365      /* 64-bit subtract - gcc just messes up with long
6366       * longs */
6367      __asm__("subl %2,%0\n\t"
6368            "sbbl %3,%1"
6369            :"=a" (endlow), "=d" (endhigh)
6370            :"g" (startlow), "g" (starthigh),
6371            "0" (endlow), "1" (endhigh));
6372
6373      /* Error: ECPUTOOFAST */
6374      if (endhigh)
6375        goto bad_ctc;
6376
6377      /* Error: ECPUTOOSLOW */
6378      if (endlow <= CALIBRATE_TIME)
6379        goto bad_ctc;
6380
6381      __asm__("divl %2"
6382            :"=a" (endlow), "=d" (endhigh)
6383            :"r"(endlow), "0" (0), "1" (CALIBRATE_TIME));
6384
6385      return endlow;
6386    }
6387
6388    /* The CTC wasn't reliable: we got a hit on the very
6389     * first read, or the CPU was so fast/slow that the
6390     * quotient wouldn't fit in 32 bits.. */
6391  bad_ctc:
6392    return 0;
6393  }
6394
6395  void __init time_init(void)
6396  {
6397    extern int x86_udelay_tsc;
6398
6399    xtime.tv_sec = get_cmos_time();
6400    xtime.tv_usec = 0;
6401
```

```
6402  /* If we have APM enabled or the CPU clock speed is
6403   * variable (CPU stops clock on HLT or slows clock to
6404   * save power) then the TSC timestamps may diverge by up
6405   * to 1 jiffy from 'real time' but nothing will break.
6406   * The most frequent case is that the CPU is "woken" from
6407   * a halt state by the timer interrupt itself, so we get
6408   * 0 error. In the rare cases where a driver would "wake"
6409   * the CPU and request a timestamp, the maximum error is
6410   * < 1 jiffy. But timestamps are still perfectly ordered.
6411   * Note that the TSC counter will be reset if APM
6412   * suspends to disk; this won't break the kernel, though,
6413   * 'cuz we're smart.  See arch/i386/kernel/apm.c.  */
6414    /* Firstly we have to do a CPU check for chips with a
6415     * potentially buggy TSC. At this point we haven't run
6416     * the ident/bugs checks so we must run this hook as it
6417     * may turn off the TSC flag.
6418     *
6419     * NOTE: this doesnt yet handle SMP 486 machines where
6420     * only some CPU's have a TSC. Thats never worked and
6421     * nobody has moaned if you have the only one in the
6422     * world - you fix it!  */
6423
6424    dodgy_tsc();
6425
6426    if (cpu_has_tsc) {
6427      unsigned long tsc_quotient = calibrate_tsc();
6428      if (tsc_quotient) {
6429        fast_gettimeoffset_quotient = tsc_quotient;
6430        use_tsc = 1;
6431        /* We could be more selective here I suspect and
6432         * just enable this for the next intel chips ?  */
6433        x86_udelay_tsc = 1;
6434  #ifndef do_gettimeoffset
6435        do_gettimeoffset = do_fast_gettimeoffset;
6436  #endif
6437        do_get_fast_time = do_gettimeofday;
6438
6439        /* report CPU clock rate in Hz. The formula is
6440         * (10^6 * 2^32) / (2^32 * 1 / (clocks/us)) =
6441         * clock/second. Our precision is about 100 ppm. */
6442        {
6443          unsigned long eax=0, edx=1000;
6444          __asm__("divl %2"
6445                 :"=a" (cpu_khz), "=d" (edx)
6446                 :"r" (tsc_quotient),
6447                 "0" (eax), "1" (edx));
6448          printk("Detected %lu.%03lu MHz processor.\n",
6449                 cpu_khz / 1000, cpu_khz % 1000);
6450        }
6451      }
6452  }
6453
6454  #ifdef CONFIG_VISWS
6455    printk("Starting Cobalt Timer system clock\n");
6456
6457    /* Set the countdown value */
6458    co_cpu_write(CO_CPU_TIMEVAL, CO_TIME_HZ/HZ);
6459
6460    /* Start the timer */
6461    co_cpu_write(CO_CPU_CTRL,
6462      co_cpu_read(CO_CPU_CTRL) | CO_CTRL_TIMERUN);
6463
6464    /* Enable (unmask) the timer interrupt */
6465    co_cpu_write(CO_CPU_CTRL,
6466      co_cpu_read(CO_CPU_CTRL) & ~CO_CTRL_TIMEMASK);
6467
6468    /* Wire cpu IDT entry to s/w handler (and Cobalt APIC
6469     * to IDT) */
6470    setup_irq(CO_IRQ_TIMER, &irq0);
6471  #else
6472    setup_irq(0, &irq0);
6473  #endif
6474  }
```

arch/i386/kernel/traps.c

```
6475  /*
6476   *  linux/arch/i386/traps.c
6477   *
6478   *  Copyright (C) 1991, 1992  Linus Torvalds
6479   *
6480   *  Pentium III FXSR, SSE support
6481   *      Gareth Hughes <gareth@valinux.com>, May 2000
6482   */
6483
6484  /* 'Traps.c' handles hardware traps and faults after we
6485   * have saved some state in 'asm.s'.  */
6486  #include <linux/config.h>
6487  #include <linux/sched.h>
6488  #include <linux/kernel.h>
6489  #include <linux/string.h>
6490  #include <linux/errno.h>
6491  #include <linux/ptrace.h>
6492  #include <linux/timer.h>
6493  #include <linux/mm.h>
```

```
6494  #include <linux/init.h>
6495  #include <linux/delay.h>
6496  #include <linux/spinlock.h>
6497  #include <linux/interrupt.h>
6498  #include <linux/highmem.h>
6499
6500  #ifdef CONFIG_MCA
6501  #include <linux/mca.h>
6502  #include <asm/processor.h>
6503  #endif
6504
6505  #include <asm/system.h>
6506  #include <asm/uaccess.h>
6507  #include <asm/io.h>
6508  #include <asm/atomic.h>
6509  #include <asm/debugreg.h>
6510  #include <asm/desc.h>
6511  #include <asm/i387.h>
6512
6513  #include <asm/smp.h>
6514  #include <asm/pgalloc.h>
6515
6516  #ifdef CONFIG_X86_VISWS_APIC
6517  #include <asm/fixmap.h>
6518  #include <asm/cobalt.h>
6519  #include <asm/lithium.h>
6520  #endif
6521
6522  #include <linux/irq.h>
6523
6524  asmlinkage int system_call(void);
6525  asmlinkage void lcall7(void);
6526  asmlinkage void lcall27(void);
6527
6528  struct desc_struct default_ldt[] = {
6529    {0, 0}, {0, 0}, {0, 0}, {0, 0}, {0, 0}
6530  };
6531
6532  /* The IDT has to be page-aligned to simplify the Pentium
6533   * F0 0F bug workaround.. We have a special link segment
6534   * for this. */
6535  struct desc_struct idt_table[256]
6536      __attribute__ ((__section__(".data.idt"))) =
6537        { { 0, 0 }, };
6538
6539  extern void bust_spinlocks(void);
6540
6541  asmlinkage void divide_error(void);
6542  asmlinkage void debug(void);
6543  asmlinkage void nmi(void);
6544  asmlinkage void int3(void);
6545  asmlinkage void overflow(void);
6546  asmlinkage void bounds(void);
6547  asmlinkage void invalid_op(void);
6548  asmlinkage void device_not_available(void);
6549  asmlinkage void double_fault(void);
6550  asmlinkage void coprocessor_segment_overrun(void);
6551  asmlinkage void invalid_TSS(void);
6552  asmlinkage void segment_not_present(void);
6553  asmlinkage void stack_segment(void);
6554  asmlinkage void general_protection(void);
6555  asmlinkage void page_fault(void);
6556  asmlinkage void coprocessor_error(void);
6557  asmlinkage void simd_coprocessor_error(void);
6558  asmlinkage void alignment_check(void);
6559  asmlinkage void spurious_interrupt_bug(void);
6560  asmlinkage void machine_check(void);
6561
6562  int kstack_depth_to_print = 24;
6563
6564  /* These constants are for searching for possible module
6565   * text segments. */
6566  void show_trace(unsigned long *stack)
6567  {
6568    int i;
6569    unsigned long addr, module_start, module_end;
6570
6571    if (!stack)
6572      stack = (unsigned long *) &stack;
6573
6574    printk("Call Trace: ");
6575    i = 1;
6576    module_start = VMALLOC_START;
6577    module_end = VMALLOC_END;
6578    while (((long) stack & (THREAD_SIZE - 1)) != 0) {
6579      addr = *stack++;
6580      /* If the address is either in the text segment of
6581       * the kernel, or in the region which contains
6582       * vmalloc'ed memory, it *may* be the address of a
6583       * calling routine; if so, print it so that someone
6584       * tracing down the cause of the crash will be able
6585       * to figure out the call path that was taken. */
6586      if (((addr >= (unsigned long) &_stext) &&
6587          (addr <= (unsigned long) &_etext)) ||
```

```
6588              ((addr >= module_start) &&
6589               (addr <= module_end))) {
6590        if (i && ((i % 8) == 0))
6591          printk("\n        ");
6592        printk("[<%08lx>] ", addr);
6593        i++;
6594      }
6595    }
6596    printk("\n");
6597 }
6598
6599 void show_stack(unsigned long *esp)
6600 {
6601    unsigned long *stack;
6602    int i;
6603
6604    // debugging aid: "show_stack(NULL);" prints the
6605    // back trace for this cpu.
6606
6607    if (esp == NULL)
6608      esp = (unsigned long *) &esp;
6609
6610    stack = esp;
6611    for (i = 0; i < kstack_depth_to_print; i++) {
6612      if (((long) stack & (THREAD_SIZE - 1)) == 0)
6613        break;
6614      if (i && ((i % 8) == 0))
6615        printk("\n       ");
6616      printk("%08lx ", *stack++);
6617    }
6618    printk("\n");
6619    show_trace(esp);
6620 }
6621
6622 static void show_registers(struct pt_regs *regs)
6623 {
6624    int i;
6625    int in_kernel = 1;
6626    unsigned long esp;
6627    unsigned short ss;
6628
6629    esp = (unsigned long) (&regs->esp);
6630    ss = __KERNEL_DS;
6631    if (regs->xcs & 3) {
6632      in_kernel = 0;
6633      esp = regs->esp;
6634      ss = regs->xss & 0xffff;
6635    }
6636    printk("CPU:    %d\nEIP:    %04x:[<%08lx>]\n"
6637         "EFLAGS: %08lx\n", smp_processor_id(),
6638         0xffff & regs->xcs, regs->eip, regs->eflags);
6639    printk("eax: %08lx   ebx: %08lx   "
6640         "ecx: %08lx   edx: %08lx\n",
6641         regs->eax, regs->ebx, regs->ecx, regs->edx);
6642    printk("esi: %08lx   edi: %08lx   "
6643         "ebp: %08lx   esp: %08lx\n",
6644         regs->esi, regs->edi, regs->ebp, esp);
6645    printk("ds: %04x   es: %04x   ss: %04x\n",
6646         regs->xds & 0xffff, regs->xes & 0xffff, ss);
6647    printk("Process %s (pid: %d, stackpage=%08lx)",
6648         current->comm, current->pid,
6649         4096 + (unsigned long) current);
6650    /* When in-kernel, we also print out the stack and code
6651     * at the time of the fault..   */
6652    if (in_kernel) {
6653
6654      printk("\nStack: ");
6655      show_stack((unsigned long *) esp);
6656
6657      printk("\nCode: ");
6658      if (regs->eip < PAGE_OFFSET)
6659        goto bad;
6660
6661      for (i = 0; i < 20; i++) {
6662        unsigned char c;
6663        if (__get_user(c,
6664               &((unsigned char *) regs->eip)[i])) {
6665 bad:
6666          printk(" Bad EIP value.");
6667          break;
6668        }
6669        printk("%02x ", c);
6670      }
6671    }
6672    printk("\n");
6673 }
6674
6675 spinlock_t die_lock = SPIN_LOCK_UNLOCKED;
6676
6677 void die(const char *str, struct pt_regs *regs, long err)
6678 {
6679    console_verbose();
6680    spin_lock_irq(&die_lock);
6681    printk("%s: %04lx\n", str, err & 0xffff);
```

```
6682    show_registers(regs);
6683
6684    spin_unlock_irq(&die_lock);
6685    do_exit(SIGSEGV);
6686 }
6687
6688 static inline void die_if_kernel(const char *str,
6689    struct pt_regs *regs, long err)
6690 {
6691    if (!(regs->eflags & VM_MASK) && !(3 & regs->xcs))
6692      die(str, regs, err);
6693 }
6694
6695 static inline unsigned long get_cr2(void)
6696 {
6697    unsigned long address;
6698
6699    /* get the address */
6700    __asm__("movl %%cr2,%0":"=r"(address));
6701    return address;
6702 }
6703
6704 static void inline do_trap(int trapnr, int signr,
6705    char *str, int vm86, struct pt_regs *regs,
6706    long error_code, siginfo_t * info)
6707 {
6708    if (vm86 && regs->eflags & VM_MASK)
6709      goto vm86_trap;
6710    if (!(regs->xcs & 3))
6711      goto kernel_trap;
6712
6713    trap_signal:
6714    {
6715      struct task_struct *tsk = current;
6716      tsk->thread.error_code = error_code;
6717      tsk->thread.trap_no = trapnr;
6718      if (info)
6719        force_sig_info(signr, info, tsk);
6720      else
6721        force_sig(signr, tsk);
6722      return;
6723    }
6724
6725    kernel_trap:
6726    {
6727      unsigned long fixup =
6728        search_exception_table(regs->eip);
6729      if (fixup)
6730        regs->eip = fixup;
6731      else
6732        die(str, regs, error_code);
6733      return;
6734    }
6735
6736    vm86_trap:
6737    {
6738      int ret =
6739        handle_vm86_trap((struct kernel_vm86_regs *) regs,
6740                         error_code, trapnr);
6741      if (ret)
6742        goto trap_signal;
6743      return;
6744    }
6745 }
6746
6747 #define DO_ERROR(trapnr, signr, str, name)             \
6748 asmlinkage void do_##name(struct pt_regs * regs,       \
6749                           long error_code)             \
6750 {                                                      \
6751    do_trap(trapnr, signr, str, 0, regs, error_code,   \
6752         NULL);                                        \
6753 }
6754
6755 #define DO_ERROR_INFO(trapnr, signr, str, name, sicode, \
6756                       siaddr)                            \
6757 asmlinkage void do_##name(struct pt_regs * regs,        \
6758                           long error_code)              \
6759 {                                                       \
6760    siginfo_t info;                                     \
6761    info.si_signo = signr;                              \
6762    info.si_errno = 0;                                  \
6763    info.si_code = sicode;                              \
6764    info.si_addr = (void *)siaddr;                      \
6765    do_trap(trapnr, signr, str, 0, regs, error_code,    \
6766         &info);                                        \
6767 }
6768
6769 #define DO_VM86_ERROR(trapnr, signr, str, name)        \
6770 asmlinkage void do_##name(struct pt_regs * regs,       \
6771                           long error_code)             \
6772 {                                                      \
6773    do_trap(trapnr, signr, str, 1, regs, error_code,   \
6774         NULL);                                        \
6775 }
```

```
6776
6777 #define DO_VM86_ERROR_INFO(trapnr, signr, str, name,    \
6778                      sicode, siaddr)    \
6779 asmlinkage void do_##name(struct pt_regs * regs,    \
6780                      long error_code)    \
6781 {    \
6782   siginfo_t info;    \
6783   info.si_signo = signr;    \
6784   info.si_errno = 0;    \
6785   info.si_code = sicode;    \
6786   info.si_addr = (void *)siaddr;    \
6787   do_trap(trapnr, signr, str, 1, regs, error_code,    \
6788        &info);    \
6789 }
6790
6791 DO_VM86_ERROR_INFO(0, SIGFPE, "divide error",
6792                      divide_error, FPE_INTDIV, regs->eip)
6793 DO_VM86_ERROR(3, SIGTRAP, "int3", int3)
6794 DO_VM86_ERROR(4, SIGSEGV, "overflow", overflow)
6795 DO_VM86_ERROR(5, SIGSEGV, "bounds", bounds)
6796 DO_ERROR_INFO(6, SIGILL, "invalid operand",
6797              invalid_op, ILL_ILLOPN, regs->eip)
6798 DO_VM86_ERROR(7, SIGSEGV, "device not available",
6799              device_not_available)
6800 DO_ERROR(8, SIGSEGV, "double fault", double_fault)
6801 DO_ERROR(9, SIGFPE, "coprocessor segment overrun",
6802        coprocessor_segment_overrun)
6803 DO_ERROR(10, SIGSEGV, "invalid TSS", invalid_TSS)
6804 DO_ERROR(11, SIGBUS, "segment not present",
6805        segment_not_present)
6806 DO_ERROR(12, SIGBUS, "stack segment", stack_segment)
6807 DO_ERROR_INFO(17, SIGBUS, "alignment check",
6808              alignment_check, BUS_ADRALN, get_cr2())
6809
6810 asmlinkage void do_general_protection(struct pt_regs
6811      *regs, long error_code)
6812 {
6813   if (regs->eflags & VM_MASK)
6814     goto gp_in_vm86;
6815
6816   if (!(regs->xcs & 3))
6817     goto gp_in_kernel;
6818
6819   current->thread.error_code = error_code;
6820   current->thread.trap_no = 13;
6821   force_sig(SIGSEGV, current);
6822   return;
6823
6824 gp_in_vm86:
6825   handle_vm86_fault((struct kernel_vm86_regs *) regs,
6826      error_code);
6827   return;
6828
6829 gp_in_kernel:
6830   {
6831     unsigned long fixup;
6832     fixup = search_exception_table(regs->eip);
6833     if (fixup) {
6834       regs->eip = fixup;
6835       return;
6836     }
6837     die("general protection fault", regs, error_code);
6838   }
6839 }
6840
6841 static void mem_parity_error(unsigned char reason,
6842     struct pt_regs *regs)
6843 {
6844   printk("Uhhuh. NMI received. Dazed and confused, "
6845        "but trying to continue\n");
6846   printk("You probably have a hardware problem with "
6847        "your RAM chips\n");
6848
6849   /* Clear and disable the memory parity error line. */
6850   reason = (reason & 0xf) | 4;
6851   outb(reason, 0x61);
6852 }
6853
6854 static void io_check_error(unsigned char reason,
6855     struct pt_regs *regs)
6856 {
6857   unsigned long i;
6858
6859   printk("NMI: IOCK error (debug interrupt?)\n");
6860   show_registers(regs);
6861
6862   /* Re-enable the IOCK line, wait for a few seconds */
6863   reason = (reason & 0xf) | 8;
6864   outb(reason, 0x61);
6865   i = 2000;
6866   while (--i)
6867     udelay(1000);
6868   reason &= ~8;
6869   outb(reason, 0x61);
```

```
6870 }
6871
6872 static void unknown_nmi_error(unsigned char reason,
6873     struct pt_regs *regs)
6874 {
6875 #ifdef CONFIG_MCA
6876   /* Might actually be able to figure out what the
6877    * guilty party is. */
6878   if (MCA_bus) {
6879     mca_handle_nmi();
6880     return;
6881   }
6882 #endif
6883   printk("Uhhuh. NMI received for unknown reason "
6884         "%02x.\n", reason);
6885   printk("Dazed and confused, but trying to continue\n");
6886   printk("Do you have a strange power saving mode "
6887         "enabled?\n");
6888 }
6889
6890 #if CONFIG_X86_IO_APIC
6891
6892 int nmi_watchdog = 1;
6893
6894 static int __init setup_nmi_watchdog(char *str)
6895 {
6896   get_option(&str, &nmi_watchdog);
6897   return 1;
6898 }
6899
6900 __setup("nmi_watchdog=", setup_nmi_watchdog);
6901
6902 static spinlock_t nmi_print_lock = SPIN_LOCK_UNLOCKED;
6903
6904 inline void nmi_watchdog_tick(struct pt_regs *regs)
6905 {
6906   /* the best way to detect wether a CPU has a 'hard
6907    * lockup' problem is to check it's local APIC timer
6908    * IRQ counts. If they are not changing then that CPU
6909    * has some problem.
6910    *
6911    * as these watchdog NMI IRQs are broadcasted to every
6912    * CPU, here we only have to check the current
6913    * processor.
6914    *
6915    * since NMIs dont listen to _any_ locks, we have to be
6916    * extremely careful not to rely on unsafe
6917    * variables. The printk might lock up though, so we
6918    * have to break up console_lock first ... [when there
6919    * will be more tty-related locks, break them up here
6920    * too!] */
6921   static unsigned int last_irq_sums[NR_CPUS],
6922       alert_counter[NR_CPUS];
6923
6924   /* Since current-> is always on the stack, and we
6925    * always switch the stack NMI-atomically, it's safe to
6926    * use smp_processor_id(). */
6927   int sum, cpu = smp_processor_id();
6928
6929   sum = apic_timer_irqs[cpu];
6930
6931   if (last_irq_sums[cpu] == sum) {
6932     /* Ayiee, looks like this CPU is stuck ... wait a
6933      * few IRQs (5 seconds) before doing the oops ... */
6934     alert_counter[cpu]++;
6935     if (alert_counter[cpu] == 5 * HZ) {
6936       spin_lock(&nmi_print_lock);
6937       /* We are in trouble anyway, lets at least try to
6938        * get a message out. */
6939       bust_spinlocks();
6940       printk("NMI Watchdog detected LOCKUP on CPU%d, "
6941             "registers:\n", cpu);
6942       show_registers(regs);
6943       printk("console shuts up ...\n");
6944       console_silent();
6945       spin_unlock(&nmi_print_lock);
6946       do_exit(SIGSEGV);
6947     }
6948   } else {
6949     last_irq_sums[cpu] = sum;
6950     alert_counter[cpu] = 0;
6951   }
6952 }
6953 #endif
6954
6955 asmlinkage void do_nmi(struct pt_regs *regs,
6956     long error_code)
6957 {
6958   unsigned char reason = inb(0x61);
6959
6960
6961   ++nmi_count(smp_processor_id());
6962   if (!(reason & 0xc0)) {
6963 #if CONFIG_X86_IO_APIC
```

```
6964        /* Ok, so this is none of the documented NMI sources,
6965         * so it must be the NMI watchdog.  */
6966        if (nmi_watchdog) {
6967          nmi_watchdog_tick(regs);
6968          return;
6969        } else
6970          unknown_nmi_error(reason, regs);
6971 #else
6972        unknown_nmi_error(reason, regs);
6973 #endif
6974        return;
6975      }
6976      if (reason & 0x80)
6977        mem_parity_error(reason, regs);
6978      if (reason & 0x40)
6979        io_check_error(reason, regs);
6980      /* Reassert NMI in case it became active meanwhile as
6981       * it's edge-triggered.  */
6982      outb(0x8f, 0x70);
6983      inb(0x71);                     /* dummy */
6984      outb(0x0f, 0x70);
6985      inb(0x71);                     /* dummy */
6986 }
6987
6988 /* Our handling of the processor debug registers is
6989  * non-trivial.  We do not clear them on entry and exit
6990  * from the kernel. Therefore it is possible to get a
6991  * watchpoint trap here from inside the kernel.  However,
6992  * the code in ./ptrace.c has ensured that the user can
6993  * only set watchpoints on userspace addresses. Therefore
6994  * the in-kernel watchpoint trap can only occur in code
6995  * which is reading/writing from user space. Such code
6996  * must not hold kernel locks (since it can equally take
6997  * a page fault), therefore it is safe to call
6998  * force_sig_info even though that claims and releases
6999  * locks.
7000  *
7001  * Code in ./signal.c ensures that the debug control
7002  * register is restored before we deliver any signal, and
7003  * therefore that user code runs with the correct debug
7004  * control register even though we clear it here.
7005  *
7006  * Being careful here means that we don't have to be as
7007  * careful in a lot of more complicated places (task
7008  * switching can be a bit lazy about restoring all the
7009  * debug state, and ptrace doesn't have to find every
7010  * occurrence of the TF bit that could be saved away even
7011  * by user code) */
7012 asmlinkage void do_debug(struct pt_regs *regs,
7013     long error_code)
7014 {
7015   unsigned int condition;
7016   struct task_struct *tsk = current;
7017   siginfo_t info;
7018
7019   __asm__ __volatile__("movl %%db6,%0":"=r"(condition));
7020
7021   /* Mask out spurious debug traps due to lazy DR7
7022    * setting */
7023   if (condition &
7024       (DR_TRAP0 | DR_TRAP1 | DR_TRAP2 | DR_TRAP3)) {
7025     if (!tsk->thread.debugreg[7])
7026       goto clear_dr7;
7027   }
7028
7029   if (regs->eflags & VM_MASK)
7030     goto debug_vm86;
7031
7032   /* Save debug status register where ptrace can see it
7033    */
7034   tsk->thread.debugreg[6] = condition;
7035
7036   /* Mask out spurious TF errors due to lazy TF clearing
7037    */
7038   if (condition & DR_STEP) {
7039     /* The TF error should be masked out only if the
7040      * current process is not traced and if the TRAP flag
7041      * has been set previously by a tracing process
7042      * (condition detected by the PT_DTRACE flag);
7043      * remember that the i386 TRAP flag can be modified
7044      * by the process itself in user mode, allowing
7045      * programs to debug themselves without the ptrace()
7046      * interface.  */
7047     if ((tsk->ptrace & (PT_DTRACE | PT_PTRACED)) ==
7048         PT_DTRACE)
7049       goto clear_TF;
7050   }
7051
7052   /* Ok, finally something we can handle */
7053   tsk->thread.trap_no = 1;
7054   tsk->thread.error_code = error_code;
7055   info.si_signo = SIGTRAP;
7056   info.si_errno = 0;
7057   info.si_code = TRAP_BRKPT;
```

```
7058
7059    /* If this is a kernel mode trap, save the user PC on
7060     * entry to the kernel, that's what the debugger can
7061     * make sense of. */
7062    info.si_addr = ((regs->xcs & 3) == 0)
7063      ? (void *) tsk->thread.eip
7064      : (void *) regs->eip;
7065    force_sig_info(SIGTRAP, &info, tsk);
7066
7067    /* Disable additional traps. They'll be re-enabled when
7068     * the signal is delivered. */
7069 clear_dr7:
7070    __asm__("movl %0,%%db7": /* no output */ : "r"(0));
7071    return;
7072
7073 debug_vm86:
7074    handle_vm86_trap((struct kernel_vm86_regs *) regs,
7075       error_code, 1);
7076    return;
7077
7078 clear_TF:
7079    regs->eflags &= ~TF_MASK;
7080    return;
7081 }
7082
7083 /* Note that we play around with the 'TS' bit in an
7084  * attempt to get the correct behaviour even in the
7085  * presence of the asynchronous IRQ13 behaviour */
7086 void math_error(void *eip)
7087 {
7088    struct task_struct *task;
7089    siginfo_t info;
7090    unsigned short cwd, swd;
7091
7092    /* Save the info for the exception handler and clear
7093     * the error.  */
7094    task = current;
7095    save_init_fpu(task);
7096    task->thread.trap_no = 16;
7097    task->thread.error_code = 0;
7098    info.si_signo = SIGFPE;
7099    info.si_errno = 0;
7100    info.si_code = __SI_FAULT;
7101    info.si_addr = eip;
7102    /* (~cwd & swd) will mask out exceptions that are not
7103     * set to unmasked status.  0x3f is the exception bits
7104     * in these regs, 0x200 is the C1 reg you need in case
```

```
7105     * of a stack fault, 0x040 is the stack fault bit.  We
7106     * should only be taking one exception at a time, so if
7107     * this combination doesn't produce any single
7108     * exception, then we have a bad program that isn't
7109     * syncronizing its FPU usage and it will suffer the
7110     * consequences since we won't be able to fully
7111     * reproduce the context of the exception */
7112    cwd = get_fpu_cwd(task);
7113    swd = get_fpu_swd(task);
7114    switch (((~cwd) & swd & 0x3f) | (swd & 0x240)) {
7115    case 0x000:
7116    default:
7117      break;
7118    case 0x001:                      /* Invalid Op */
7119    case 0x040:                      /* Stack Fault */
7120    case 0x240:                      /* Stack Fault |
7121                                      * Direction */
7122      info.si_code = FPE_FLTINV;
7123      break;
7124    case 0x002:                      /* Denormalize */
7125    case 0x010:                      /* Underflow */
7126      info.si_code = FPE_FLTUND;
7127      break;
7128    case 0x004:                      /* Zero Divide */
7129      info.si_code = FPE_FLTDIV;
7130      break;
7131    case 0x008:                      /* Overflow */
7132      info.si_code = FPE_FLTOVF;
7133      break;
7134    case 0x020:                      /* Precision */
7135      info.si_code = FPE_FLTRES;
7136      break;
7137    }
7138    force_sig_info(SIGFPE, &info, task);
7139 }
7140
7141 asmlinkage void do_coprocessor_error(struct pt_regs
7142     *regs, long error_code)
7143 {
7144    ignore_irq13 = 1;
7145    math_error((void *) regs->eip);
7146 }
7147
7148 void simd_math_error(void *eip)
7149 {
7150    struct task_struct *task;
7151    siginfo_t info;
```

```
7152    unsigned short mxcsr;
7153
7154    /* Save the info for the exception handler and clear
7155     * the error.  */
7156    task = current;
7157    save_init_fpu(task);
7158    task->thread.trap_no = 19;
7159    task->thread.error_code = 0;
7160    info.si_signo = SIGFPE;
7161    info.si_errno = 0;
7162    info.si_code = __SI_FAULT;
7163    info.si_addr = eip;
7164    /* The SIMD FPU exceptions are handled a little
7165     * differently, as there is only a single
7166     * status/control register.  Thus, to determine which
7167     * unmasked exception was caught we must mask the
7168     * exception mask bits at 0x1f80, and then use these to
7169     * mask the exception bits at 0x3f.  */
7170    mxcsr = get_fpu_mxcsr(task);
7171    switch (~((mxcsr & 0x1f80) >> 7) & (mxcsr & 0x3f)) {
7172    case 0x000:
7173    default:
7174      break;
7175    case 0x001:                    /* Invalid Op */
7176      info.si_code = FPE_FLTINV;
7177      break;
7178    case 0x002:                    /* Denormalize */
7179    case 0x010:                    /* Underflow */
7180      info.si_code = FPE_FLTUND;
7181      break;
7182    case 0x004:                    /* Zero Divide */
7183      info.si_code = FPE_FLTDIV;
7184      break;
7185    case 0x008:                    /* Overflow */
7186      info.si_code = FPE_FLTOVF;
7187      break;
7188    case 0x020:                    /* Precision */
7189      info.si_code = FPE_FLTRES;
7190      break;
7191    }
7192    force_sig_info(SIGFPE, &info, task);
7193 }
7194
7195 asmlinkage void
7196 do_simd_coprocessor_error(struct pt_regs *regs,
7197                                  long error_code)
7198 {
7199    if (cpu_has_xmm) {
7200      /* Handle SIMD FPU exceptions on PIII+ processors. */
7201      ignore_irq13 = 1;
7202      simd_math_error((void *) regs->eip);
7203    } else {
7204      /* Handle strange cache flush from user space
7205       * exception in all other cases.  This is
7206       * undocumented behaviour.  */
7207      if (regs->eflags & VM_MASK) {
7208        handle_vm86_fault((struct kernel_vm86_regs *) regs,
7209            error_code);
7210        return;
7211      }
7212      die_if_kernel("cache flush denied", regs,
7213          error_code);
7214      current->thread.trap_no = 19;
7215      current->thread.error_code = error_code;
7216      force_sig(SIGSEGV, current);
7217    }
7218 }
7219
7220 asmlinkage void
7221 do_spurious_interrupt_bug(struct pt_regs *regs,
7222                                  long error_code)
7223 {
7224 #if 0
7225    /* No need to warn about this any longer. */
7226    printk("Ignoring P6 Local APIC "
7227          "Spurious Interrupt Bug...\n");
7228 #endif
7229 }
7230
7231 /* 'math_state_restore()' saves the current math
7232  * information in the old math state array, and gets the
7233  * new ones from the current task
7234  *
7235  * Careful.. There are problems with IBM-designed IRQ13
7236  * behaviour.  Don't touch unless you *really* know how
7237  * it works.  */
7238 asmlinkage void math_state_restore(struct pt_regs regs)
7239 {
7240    __asm__ __volatile__("clts"); /* Allow maths ops (or
7241                                    * we recurse) */
7242
7243    if (current->used_math) {
7244      restore_fpu(current);
7245    } else {
```

```
7246       init_fpu();
7247   }
7248   current->flags |= PF_USEDFPU; /* So we fnsave on
7249                                  * switch_to() */
7250 }
7251
7252 #ifndef CONFIG_MATH_EMULATION
7253
7254 asmlinkage void math_emulate(long arg)
7255 {
7256   printk("math-emulation not enabled and "
7257          "no coprocessor found.\n");
7258   printk("killing %s.\n", current->comm);
7259   force_sig(SIGFPE, current);
7260   schedule();
7261 }
7262
7263 #endif                           /* CONFIG_MATH_EMULATION */
7264
7265 #ifndef CONFIG_M686
7266 void __init trap_init_f00f_bug(void)
7267 {
7268   unsigned long page;
7269   pgd_t *pgd;
7270   pmd_t *pmd;
7271   pte_t *pte;
7272
7273   /* Allocate a new page in virtual address space, move
7274    * the IDT into it and write protect this page.  */
7275   page = (unsigned long) vmalloc(PAGE_SIZE);
7276   pgd = pgd_offset(&init_mm, page);
7277   pmd = pmd_offset(pgd, page);
7278   pte = pte_offset(pmd, page);
7279   __free_page(pte_page(*pte));
7280   *pte = mk_pte_phys(__pa(&idt_table), PAGE_KERNEL_RO);
7281   /* Not that any PGE-capable kernel should have the f00f
7282    * bug ... */
7283   __flush_tlb_all();
7284
7285   /* "idt" is magic - it overlaps the idt_descr variable
7286    * so that updating idt will automatically update the
7287    * idt descriptor.. */
7288   idt = (struct desc_struct *) page;
7289   __asm__ __volatile__("lidt %0":"=m"(idt_descr));
7290 }
7291
7292 #endif
```

```
7293
7294 #define _set_gate(gate_addr,type,dpl,addr)           \
7295 do {                                                 \
7296   int __d0, __d1;                                     \
7297   __asm__ __volatile__ ("movw %%dx,%%ax\n\t"         \
7298     "movw %4,%%dx\n\t"                               \
7299     "movl %%eax,%0\n\t"                              \
7300     "movl %%edx,%1"                                  \
7301     :"=m" (*((long *) (gate_addr))),                 \
7302     "=m" (*(1+(long *) (gate_addr))),                \
7303     "=&a" (__d0), "=&d" (__d1)                       \
7304     :"i" ((short) (0x8000+(dpl<<13)+(type<<8))),     \
7305     "3" ((char *) (addr)),"2" (__KERNEL_CS << 16));\
7306 } while (0)
7307
7308
7309 /* This needs to use 'idt_table' rather than 'idt', and
7310  * thus use the _nonmapped_ version of the IDT, as the
7311  * Pentium F0 0F bugfix can have resulted in the mapped
7312  * IDT being write-protected.  */
7313 void set_intr_gate(unsigned int n, void *addr)
7314 {
7315   _set_gate(idt_table + n, 14, 0, addr);
7316 }
7317
7318 static void __init set_trap_gate(unsigned int n,
7319     void *addr)
7320 {
7321   _set_gate(idt_table + n, 15, 0, addr);
7322 }
7323
7324 static void __init set_system_gate(unsigned int n,
7325     void *addr)
7326 {
7327   _set_gate(idt_table + n, 15, 3, addr);
7328 }
7329
7330 static void __init set_call_gate(void *a, void *addr)
7331 {
7332   _set_gate(a, 12, 3, addr);
7333 }
7334
7335 #define _set_seg_desc(gate_addr,type,dpl,base,limit) { \
7336         *((gate_addr)+1) = ((base) & 0xff000000) |     \
7337             (((base) & 0x00ff0000)>>16) |              \
7338             ((limit) & 0xf0000) |                      \
7339             ((dpl)<<13) |                              \
```

p 586 ▶ 7313

```
7340                  (0x00408000) |                           \
7341                  ((type)<<8);                             \
7342          *(gate_addr) = (((base) & 0x0000ffff)<<16) |     \
7343                  ((limit) & 0x0ffff); }
7344
7345 #define _set_tssldt_desc(n,addr,limit,type)               \
7346 __asm__ __volatile__ ("movw %w3,0(%2)\n\t"               \
7347         "movw %%ax,2(%2)\n\t"                             \
7348         "rorl $16,%%eax\n\t"                              \
7349         "movb %%al,4(%2)\n\t"                             \
7350         "movb %4,5(%2)\n\t"                               \
7351         "movb $0,6(%2)\n\t"                               \
7352         "movb %%ah,7(%2)\n\t"                             \
7353         "rorl $16,%%eax"                                  \
7354         : "=m"(*(n))                                      \
7355         : "a" (addr), "r"(n), "ir"(limit), "i"(type))
7356
7357 void set_tss_desc(unsigned int n, void *addr)
7358 {
7359   _set_tssldt_desc(gdt_table + __TSS(n), (int) addr, 235,
7360       0x89);
7361 }
7362
7363 void set_ldt_desc(unsigned int n, void *addr,
7364     unsigned int size)
7365 {
7366   _set_tssldt_desc(gdt_table + __LDT(n), (int) addr,
7367       ((size << 3) - 1), 0x82);
7368 }
7369
7370 #ifdef CONFIG_X86_VISWS_APIC
7371
7372 /* On Rev 005 motherboards legacy device interrupt lines
7373  * are wired directly to Lithium from the 307.  But the
7374  * PROM leaves the interrupt type of each 307 logical
7375  * device set appropriate for the 8259.  Later we'll
7376  * actually use the 8259, but for now we have to flip the
7377  * interrupt types to level triggered, active lo as
7378  * required by Lithium.  */
7379 #define REG  0x2e  /* The register to read/write */
7380 #define DEV  0x07  /* Register: Logical device select */
7381 #define VAL  0x2f  /* The value to read/write */
7382
7383 static void superio_outb(int dev, int reg, int val)
7384 {
7385   outb(DEV, REG);
7386   outb(dev, VAL);
7387   outb(reg, REG);
7388   outb(val, VAL);
7389 }
7390
7391 static int __attribute__ ((unused))
7392     superio_inb(int dev, int reg)
7393 {
7394   outb(DEV, REG);
7395   outb(dev, VAL);
7396   outb(reg, REG);
7397   return inb(VAL);
7398 }
7399
7400 #define FLOP    3       /* floppy logical device */
7401 #define PPORT   4       /* parallel logical device */
7402 #define UART5   5       /* uart2 logical device (not wired
7403                          * up) */
7404 #define UART6   6       /* uart1 logical device (THIS is
7405                          * the serial port!) */
7406 #define IDEST   0x70    /* int. destination (which 307 IRQ
7407                          * line) reg. */
7408 #define ITYPE   0x71    /* interrupt type register */
7409
7410 /* interrupt type bits */
7411 #define LEVEL   0x01    /* bit 0, 0 == edge triggered */
7412 #define ACTHI   0x02    /* bit 1, 0 == active lo */
7413
7414 static void superio_init(void)
7415 {
7416   if (visws_board_type == VISWS_320
7417       && visws_board_rev == 5) {
7418     superio_outb(UART6, IDEST, 0);  /* 0 means no intr
7419                                      * propagated */
7420     printk("SGI 320 rev 5: "
7421           "disabling 307 uart1 interrupt\n");
7422   }
7423 }
7424
7425 static void lithium_init(void)
7426 {
7427   set_fixmap(FIX_LI_PCIA, LI_PCI_A_PHYS);
7428   printk("Lithium PCI Bridge A, Bus Number: %d\n",
7429       li_pcia_read16(LI_PCI_BUSNUM) & 0xff);
7430   set_fixmap(FIX_LI_PCIB, LI_PCI_B_PHYS);
7431   printk
7432       ("Lithium PCI Bridge B (PIIX4), Bus Number: %d\n",
7433       li_pcib_read16(LI_PCI_BUSNUM) & 0xff);
```

```
7434
7435     /* XXX blindly enables all interrupts */
7436     li_pcia_write16(LI_PCI_INTEN, 0xffff);
7437     li_pcib_write16(LI_PCI_INTEN, 0xffff);
7438 }
7439
7440 static void cobalt_init(void)
7441 {
7442     /* On normal SMP PC this is used only with SMP, but we
7443      * have to use it and set it up here to start the
7444      * Cobalt clock */
7445     set_fixmap(FIX_APIC_BASE, APIC_DEFAULT_PHYS_BASE);
7446     printk("Local APIC ID %lx\n", apic_read(APIC_ID));
7447     printk("Local APIC Version %lx\n",
7448         apic_read(APIC_LVR));
7449
7450     set_fixmap(FIX_CO_CPU, CO_CPU_PHYS);
7451     printk("Cobalt Revision %lx\n",
7452         co_cpu_read(CO_CPU_REV));
7453
7454     set_fixmap(FIX_CO_APIC, CO_APIC_PHYS);
7455     printk("Cobalt APIC ID %lx\n",
7456         co_apic_read(CO_APIC_ID));
7457
7458     /* Enable Cobalt APIC being careful to NOT change the
7459      * ID! */
7460     co_apic_write(CO_APIC_ID,
7461         co_apic_read(CO_APIC_ID) | CO_APIC_ENABLE);
7462
7463     printk("Cobalt APIC enabled: ID reg %lx\n",
7464         co_apic_read(CO_APIC_ID));
7465 }
7466
7467 #endif
7468 void __init trap_init(void)
7469 {
7470 #ifdef CONFIG_EISA
7471     if (isa_readl(0x0FFFD9) ==
7472         'E' + ('I' << 8) + ('S' << 16) + ('A' << 24))
7473         EISA_bus = 1;
7474 #endif
7475
7476     set_trap_gate(0, &divide_error);
7477     set_trap_gate(1, &debug);
7478     set_intr_gate(2, &nmi);
7479     set_system_gate(3, &int3);      /* int3-5 can be called
7480                                      * from all */
7481     set_system_gate(4, &overflow);
7482     set_system_gate(5, &bounds);
7483     set_trap_gate(6, &invalid_op);
7484     set_trap_gate(7, &device_not_available);
7485     set_trap_gate(8, &double_fault);
7486     set_trap_gate(9, &coprocessor_segment_overrun);
7487     set_trap_gate(10, &invalid_TSS);
7488     set_trap_gate(11, &segment_not_present);
7489     set_trap_gate(12, &stack_segment);
7490     set_trap_gate(13, &general_protection);
7491     set_trap_gate(14, &page_fault);
7492     set_trap_gate(15, &spurious_interrupt_bug);
7493     set_trap_gate(16, &coprocessor_error);
7494     set_trap_gate(17, &alignment_check);
7495     set_trap_gate(18, &machine_check);
7496     set_trap_gate(19, &simd_coprocessor_error);
7497
7498     set_system_gate(SYSCALL_VECTOR, &system_call);
7499
7500     /* default LDT is a single-entry callgate to lcall7 for
7501      * iBCS and a callgate to lcall27 for Solaris/x86
7502      * binaries */
7503     set_call_gate(&default_ldt[0], lcall7);
7504     set_call_gate(&default_ldt[4], lcall27);
7505
7506     /* Should be a barrier for any external CPU state.  */
7507     cpu_init();
7508
7509 #ifdef CONFIG_X86_VISWS_APIC
7510     superio_init();
7511     lithium_init();
7512     cobalt_init();
7513 #endif
7514 }
```

arch/i386/lib/dec_and_lock.c

```
7515 /*
7516  * x86 version of "atomic_dec_and_lock()" using
7517  * the atomic "cmpxchg" instruction.
7518  *
7519  * (For CPU's lacking cmpxchg, we use the slow generic
7520  * version, and this one never even gets compiled).
7521  */
7522
7523 #include <linux/spinlock.h>
7524 #include <asm/atomic.h>
7525
```

```
7526 int atomic_dec_and_lock(atomic_t * atomic,
7527     spinlock_t * lock)
7528 {
7529   int counter;
7530   int newcount;
7531
7532 repeat:
7533   counter = atomic_read(atomic);
7534   newcount = counter - 1;
7535
7536   if (!newcount)
7537     goto slow_path;
7538
7539   asm volatile ("lock; cmpxchgl %1,%2":"=a" (newcount)
7540       :"r"(newcount), "m"(atomic->counter),
7541       "0"(counter));
7542
7543   /* If the above failed, "eax" will have changed */
7544   if (newcount != counter)
7545     goto repeat;
7546   return 0;
7547
7548 slow_path:
7549   spin_lock(lock);
7550   if (atomic_dec_and_test(atomic))
7551     return 1;
7552   spin_unlock(lock);
7553   return 0;
7554 }
```

arch/i386/lib/delay.c

```
7555 /*
7556  *       Precise Delay Loops for i386
7557  *
7558  *       Copyright (C) 1993 Linus Torvalds
7559  *       Copyright (C) 1997 Martin Mares
7560  *                          <mj@atrey.karlin.mff.cuni.cz>
7561  *
7562  * The __delay function must _NOT_ be inlined as its
7563  * execution time depends wildly on alignment on many x86
7564  * processors. The additional jump magic is needed to get
7565  * the timing stable on all the CPU's we have to worry
7566  * about.
7567  */
7568
7569 #include <linux/config.h>
7570 #include <linux/sched.h>
```

```
7571 #include <linux/delay.h>
7572 #include <asm/delay.h>
7573
7574 #ifdef CONFIG_SMP
7575 #include <asm/smp.h>
7576 #endif
7577
7578 int x86_udelay_tsc = 0;          /* Delay via TSC */
7579
7580 /* Do a udelay using the TSC for any CPU that happens to
7581  * have one that we trust.  */
7582 static void __rdtsc_delay(unsigned long loops)
7583 {
7584   unsigned long bclock, now;
7585
7586   rdtscl(bclock);
7587   do {
7588     rdtscl(now);
7589   } while ((now - bclock) < loops);
7590 }
7591
7592 /* Non TSC based delay loop for 386, 486, MediaGX */
7593 static void __loop_delay(unsigned long loops)
7594 {
7595   int d0;
7596   __asm__ __volatile__(
7597       "\tjmp 1f\n"
7598       ".align 16\n"
7599       "1:\tjmp 2f\n"
7600       ".align 16\n"
7601       "2:\tdecl %0\n\tjns 2b":"=&a"(d0)
7602       :"0"(loops));
7603 }
7604
7605 void __delay(unsigned long loops)
7606 {
7607   if (x86_udelay_tsc)
7608     __rdtsc_delay(loops);
7609   else
7610     __loop_delay(loops);
7611 }
7612
7613 inline void __const_udelay(unsigned long xloops)
7614 {
7615   int d0;
7616   __asm__("mull %0":"=d"(xloops), "=&a"(d0)
7617       : "1"(xloops),
```

```
7618              "0"(current_cpu_data.loops_per_jiffy));
7619     __delay(xloops * HZ);
7620 }
7621
7622 void __udelay(unsigned long usecs)
7623 {
7624     /* 2**32 / 1000000 */
7625     __const_udelay(usecs * 0x000010c6);
7626 }
```

arch/i386/lib/getuser.S

```
7627 /*
7628  * __get_user functions.
7629  *
7630  * (C) Copyright 1998 Linus Torvalds
7631  *
7632  * These functions have a non-standard call interface
7633  * to make them more efficient, especially as they
7634  * return an error value in addition to the "real"
7635  * return value.
7636  */
7637
7638 /*
7639  * __get_user_X
7640  *
7641  * Inputs:      %eax contains the address
7642  *
7643  * Outputs:     %eax is error code (0 or -EFAULT)
7644  *              %edx contains zero-extended value
7645  *
7646  * These functions should not modify any other registers,
7647  * as they get called from within inline assembly.
7648  */
7649
7650 addr_limit = 12
7651
7652 .text
7653 .align 4
7654 .globl __get_user_1
7655 __get_user_1:
7656         movl %esp,%edx
7657         andl $0xffffe000,%edx
7658         cmpl addr_limit(%edx),%eax
7659         jae bad_get_user
7660 1:      movzbl (%eax),%edx
7661         xorl %eax,%eax
7662         ret
```

```
7663
7664 .align 4
7665 .globl __get_user_2
7666 __get_user_2:
7667         addl $1,%eax
7668         movl %esp,%edx
7669         jc bad_get_user
7670         andl $0xffffe000,%edx
7671         cmpl addr_limit(%edx),%eax
7672         jae bad_get_user
7673 2:      movzwl -1(%eax),%edx
7674         xorl %eax,%eax
7675         ret
7676
7677 .align 4
7678 .globl __get_user_4
7679 __get_user_4:
7680         addl $3,%eax
7681         movl %esp,%edx
7682         jc bad_get_user
7683         andl $0xffffe000,%edx
7684         cmpl addr_limit(%edx),%eax
7685         jae bad_get_user
7686 3:      movl -3(%eax),%edx
7687         xorl %eax,%eax
7688         ret
7689
7690 bad_get_user:
7691         xorl %edx,%edx
7692         movl $-14,%eax
7693         ret
7694
7695 .section __ex_table,"a"
7696         .long 1b,bad_get_user
7697         .long 2b,bad_get_user
7698         .long 3b,bad_get_user
7699 .previous
```

arch/i386/lib/putuser.S

```
7700 /*
7701  * __put_user functions.
7702  *
7703  * (C) Copyright 1998 Linus Torvalds
7704  *
7705  * These functions have a non-standard call interface
7706  * to make them more efficient.
7707  */
```

```
7708
7709 /*
7710  * __put_user_X
7711  *
7712  * Inputs:       %eax contains the address
7713  *               %edx contains the value
7714  *
7715  * Outputs:      %eax is error code (0 or -EFAULT)
7716  *               %ecx is corrupted (will contain
7717  *                               "current_task").
7718  *
7719  * These functions should not modify any other registers,
7720  * as they get called from within inline assembly.
7721  */
7722
7723 addr_limit = 12
7724
7725 .text
7726 .align 4
7727 .globl __put_user_1
7728 __put_user_1:
7729         movl %esp,%ecx
7730         andl $0xffffe000,%ecx
7731         cmpl addr_limit(%ecx),%eax
7732         jae bad_put_user
7733 1:      movb %dl,(%eax)
7734         xorl %eax,%eax
7735         ret
7736
7737 .align 4
7738 .globl __put_user_2
7739 __put_user_2:
7740         addl $1,%eax
7741         movl %esp,%ecx
7742         jc bad_put_user
7743         andl $0xffffe000,%ecx
7744         cmpl addr_limit(%ecx),%eax
7745         jae bad_put_user
7746 2:      movw %dx,-1(%eax)
7747         xorl %eax,%eax
7748         ret
7749
7750 .align 4
7751 .globl __put_user_4
7752 __put_user_4:
7753         addl $3,%eax
7754         movl %esp,%ecx
```

```
7755         jc bad_put_user
7756         andl $0xffffe000,%ecx
7757         cmpl addr_limit(%ecx),%eax
7758         jae bad_put_user
7759 3:      movl %edx,-3(%eax)
7760         xorl %eax,%eax
7761         ret
7762
7763 bad_put_user:
7764         movl $-14,%eax
7765         ret
7766
7767 .section __ex_table,"a"
7768         .long 1b,bad_put_user
7769         .long 2b,bad_put_user
7770         .long 3b,bad_put_user
7771 .previous
```

arch/i386/lib/usercopy.c

```
7772 /*
7773  * User address space access functions.
7774  * The non inlined parts of asm-i386/uaccess.h are here.
7775  *
7776  * Copyright 1997 Andi Kleen <ak@muc.de>
7777  * Copyright 1997 Linus Torvalds
7778  */
7779 #include <linux/config.h>
7780 #include <asm/uaccess.h>
7781 #include <asm/mmx.h>
7782
7783 #ifdef CONFIG_X86_USE_3DNOW_AND_WORKS
7784
7785 unsigned long
7786 __generic_copy_to_user(void *to, const void *from,
7787     unsigned long n)
7788 {
7789   if (access_ok(VERIFY_WRITE, to, n)) {
7790     if (n < 512)
7791       __copy_user(to, from, n);
7792     else
7793       mmx_copy_user(to, from, n);
7794   }
7795   return n;
7796 }
7797
7798 unsigned long
7799 __generic_copy_from_user(void *to, const void *from,
```

```
7800      unsigned long n)
7801 {
7802    if (access_ok(VERIFY_READ, from, n)) {
7803      if (n < 512)
7804        __copy_user_zeroing(to, from, n);
7805      else
7806        mmx_copy_user_zeroing(to, from, n);
7807    }
7808    return n;
7809 }
7810
7811 #else
7812
7813 unsigned long
7814 __generic_copy_to_user(void *to, const void *from,
7815      unsigned long n)
7816 {
7817    if (access_ok(VERIFY_WRITE, to, n))
7818      __copy_user(to, from, n);
7819    return n;
7820 }
7821
7822 unsigned long
7823 __generic_copy_from_user(void *to, const void *from,
7824      unsigned long n)
7825 {
7826    if (access_ok(VERIFY_READ, from, n))
7827      __copy_user_zeroing(to, from, n);
7828    return n;
7829 }
7830
7831 #endif
7832
7833 /* Copy a null terminated string from userspace.  */
7834 #define __do_strncpy_from_user(dst,src,count,res)       \
7835 do {                                                    \
7836        int __d0, __d1, __d2;                            \
7837        __asm__ __volatile__(                            \
7838                "        testl %1,%1\n"                   \
7839                "        jz 2f\n"                         \
7840                "0:      lodsb\n"                         \
7841                "        stosb\n"                         \
7842                "        testb %%al,%%al\n"               \
7843                "        jz 1f\n"                         \
7844                "        decl %1\n"                       \
7845                "        jnz 0b\n"                        \
7846                "1:      subl %1,%0\n"                    \
```

```
7847                "2:\n"                                   \
7848                ".section .fixup,\"ax\"\n"               \
7849                "3:      movl %5,%0\n"                    \
7850                "        jmp 2b\n"                        \
7851                ".previous\n"                            \
7852                ".section __ex_table,\"a\"\n"            \
7853                "        .align 4\n"                      \
7854                "        .long 0b,3b\n"                   \
7855                ".previous"                              \
7856                : "=d"(res), "=c"(count),                \
7857                  "=&a" (__d0), "=&S" (__d1),            \
7858                  "=&D" (__d2)                           \
7859                : "i"(-EFAULT), "0"(count), "1"(count), \
7860                  "3"(src), "4"(dst)                     \
7861                : "memory");                             \
7862 } while (0)
7863
7864 long
7865 __strncpy_from_user(char *dst, const char *src,
7866                  long count)
7867 {
7868    long res;
7869    __do_strncpy_from_user(dst, src, count, res);
7870    return res;
7871 }
7872
7873 long
7874 strncpy_from_user(char *dst, const char *src, long count)
7875 {
7876    long res = -EFAULT;
7877    if (access_ok(VERIFY_READ, src, 1))
7878      __do_strncpy_from_user(dst, src, count, res);
7879    return res;
7880 }
7881
7882
7883 /* Zero Userspace */
7884 #define __do_clear_user(addr,size)                      \
7885 do {                                                    \
7886        int __d0;                                        \
7887        __asm__ __volatile__(                            \
7888                "0:      rep; stosl\n"                    \
7889                "        movl %2,%0\n"                    \
7890                "1:      rep; stosb\n"                    \
7891                "2:\n"                                   \
7892                ".section .fixup,\"ax\"\n"               \
7893                "3:      lea 0(%2,%0,4),%0\n"             \
```

```
7894                 "       jmp 2b\n"                      \
7895                 ".previous\n"                          \
7896                 ".section __ex_table,\"a\"\n"          \
7897                 "       .align 4\n"                     \
7898                 "       .long 0b,3b\n"                   \
7899                 "       .long 1b,2b\n"                   \
7900                 ".previous"                             \
7901                 : "=&c"(size), "=&D" (__d0)            \
7902                 : "r"(size & 3), "0"(size / 4),        \
7903                 "1"(addr), "a"(0));                    \
7904 } while (0)
7905
7906 unsigned long clear_user(void *to, unsigned long n)
7907 {
7908   if (access_ok(VERIFY_WRITE, to, n))
7909     __do_clear_user(to, n);
7910   return n;
7911 }
7912
7913 unsigned long __clear_user(void *to, unsigned long n)
7914 {
7915   __do_clear_user(to, n);
7916   return n;
7917 }
7918
7919 /* Return the size of a string (including the ending 0)
7920  *
7921  * Return 0 on exception, a value greater than N if too
7922  * long */
7923 long strnlen_user(const char *s, long n)
7924 {
7925   unsigned long mask = -__addr_ok(s);
7926   unsigned long res, tmp;
7927
7928   __asm__ __volatile__(
7929     " andl %0,%%ecx\n"
7930     "0:      repne; scasb\n"
7931     " setne %%al\n"
7932     " subl %%ecx,%0\n"
7933     " addl %0,%%eax\n"
7934     "1:\n"
7935     ".section .fixup,\"ax\"\n"
7936     "2:      xorl %%eax,%%eax\n"
7937     " jmp 1b\n"
7938     ".previous\n"
7939     ".section __ex_table,\"a\"\n"
7940     " .align 4\n"
```

```
7941     " .long 0b,2b\n"
7942     ".previous":"=r"(n), "=D"(s), "=a"(res), "=c"(tmp)
7943     :"0"(n), "1"(s), "2"(0), "3"(mask)
7944     :"cc");
7945   return res & mask;
7946 }
```

arch/i386/mm/extable.c

```
7947 /*
7948  * linux/arch/i386/mm/extable.c
7949  */
7950
7951 #include <linux/config.h>
7952 #include <linux/module.h>
7953 #include <asm/uaccess.h>
7954
7955 extern const struct exception_table_entry
7956     __start___ex_table[];
7957 extern const struct exception_table_entry
7958     __stop___ex_table[];
7959
7960 static inline unsigned long search_one_table(
7961   const struct exception_table_entry *first,
7962   const struct exception_table_entry *last,
7963   unsigned long value)
7964 {
7965   while (first <= last) {
7966     const struct exception_table_entry *mid;
7967     long diff;
7968
7969     mid = (last - first) / 2 + first;
7970     diff = mid->insn - value;
7971     if (diff == 0)
7972       return mid->fixup;
7973     else if (diff < 0)
7974       first = mid + 1;
7975     else
7976       last = mid - 1;
7977   }
7978   return 0;
7979 }
7980
7981 unsigned long search_exception_table(unsigned long addr)
7982 {
7983   unsigned long ret;
7984
7985 #ifndef CONFIG_MODULES
```

```
7986    /* There is only the kernel to search.  */
7987    ret = search_one_table(__start___ex_table,
7988                          __stop___ex_table - 1, addr);
7989    if (ret)
7990      return ret;
7991 #else
7992    /* The kernel is the last "module" - no need to treat
7993     * it special.  */
7994    struct module *mp;
7995    for (mp = module_list; mp != NULL; mp = mp->next) {
7996      if (mp->ex_table_start == NULL)
7997        continue;
7998      ret = search_one_table(mp->ex_table_start,
7999                            mp->ex_table_end - 1, addr);
8000      if (ret)
8001        return ret;
8002    }
8003 #endif
8004
8005    return 0;
8006 }
```

arch/i386/mm/fault.c

```
8007 /*
8008  *  linux/arch/i386/mm/fault.c
8009  *
8010  *  Copyright (C) 1995  Linus Torvalds
8011  */
8012
8013 #include <linux/signal.h>
8014 #include <linux/sched.h>
8015 #include <linux/kernel.h>
8016 #include <linux/errno.h>
8017 #include <linux/string.h>
8018 #include <linux/types.h>
8019 #include <linux/ptrace.h>
8020 #include <linux/mman.h>
8021 #include <linux/mm.h>
8022 #include <linux/smp.h>
8023 #include <linux/smp_lock.h>
8024 #include <linux/interrupt.h>
8025 #include <linux/init.h>
8026
8027 #include <asm/system.h>
8028 #include <asm/uaccess.h>
8029 #include <asm/pgalloc.h>
8030 #include <asm/hardirq.h>
```

```
8031
8032 extern void die(const char *, struct pt_regs *, long);
8033
8034 /* Ugly, ugly, but the goto's result in better assembly..
8035  */
8036 int __verify_write(const void *addr, unsigned long size)
8037 {
8038    struct vm_area_struct *vma;
8039    unsigned long start = (unsigned long) addr;
8040
8041    if (!size)
8042      return 1;
8043
8044    vma = find_vma(current->mm, start);
8045    if (!vma)
8046      goto bad_area;
8047    if (vma->vm_start > start)
8048      goto check_stack;
8049
8050 good_area:
8051    if (!(vma->vm_flags & VM_WRITE))
8052      goto bad_area;
8053    size--;
8054    size += start & ~PAGE_MASK;
8055    size >>= PAGE_SHIFT;
8056    start &= PAGE_MASK;
8057
8058    for (;;) {
8059      if (handle_mm_fault(current->mm, vma, start, 1) <= 0)
8060        goto bad_area;
8061      if (!size)
8062        break;
8063      size--;
8064      start += PAGE_SIZE;
8065      if (start < vma->vm_end)
8066        continue;
8067      vma = vma->vm_next;
8068      if (!vma || vma->vm_start != start)
8069        goto bad_area;
8070      if (!(vma->vm_flags & VM_WRITE))
8071        goto bad_area;;
8072    }
8073    return 1;
8074
8075 check_stack:
8076    if (!(vma->vm_flags & VM_GROWSDOWN))
8077      goto bad_area;
```

```
8078   if (expand_stack(vma, start) == 0)
8079     goto good_area;
8080
8081 bad_area:
8082   return 0;
8083 }
8084
8085 extern spinlock_t console_lock, timerlist_lock;
8086
8087 /* Unlock any spinlocks which will prevent us from
8088  * getting the message out (timerlist_lock is aquired
8089  * through the console unblank code) */
8090 void bust_spinlocks(void)
8091 {
8092   spin_lock_init(&console_lock);
8093   spin_lock_init(&timerlist_lock);
8094 }
8095
8096 asmlinkage void do_invalid_op(struct pt_regs *,
8097     unsigned long);
8098 extern unsigned long idt;
8099
8100 /* This routine handles page faults.  It determines the
8101  * address, and the problem, and then passes it off to
8102  * one of the appropriate routines.
8103  *
8104  * error_code:
8105  *      bit 0 == 0 means no page found,
8106  *              1 means protection fault
8107  *      bit 1 == 0 means read, 1 means write
8108  *      bit 2 == 0 means kernel, 1 means user-mode */
8109 asmlinkage void do_page_fault(struct pt_regs *regs,
8110     unsigned long error_code)
8111 {
8112   struct task_struct *tsk;
8113   struct mm_struct *mm;
8114   struct vm_area_struct *vma;
8115   unsigned long address;
8116   unsigned long page;
8117   unsigned long fixup;
8118   int write;
8119   siginfo_t info;
8120
8121   /* get the address */
8122   __asm__("movl %%cr2,%0":"=r"(address));
8123
8124   tsk = current;
```

p 627

```
8125
8126   /* We fault-in kernel-space virtual memory
8127    * on-demand. The 'reference' page table is
8128    * init_mm.pgd.
8129    *
8130    * NOTE! We MUST NOT take any locks for this case. We
8131    * may be in an interrupt or a critical region, and
8132    * should only copy the information from the master
8133    * page table, nothing more.  */
8134   if (address >= TASK_SIZE)
8135     goto vmalloc_fault;
8136
8137   mm = tsk->mm;
8138   info.si_code = SEGV_MAPERR;
8139
8140   /* If we're in an interrupt or have no user context, we
8141    * must not take the fault..  */
8142   if (in_interrupt() || !mm)
8143     goto no_context;
8144
8145   down(&mm->mmap_sem);
8146
8147   vma = find_vma(mm, address);
8148   if (!vma)
8149     goto bad_area;
8150   if (vma->vm_start <= address)
8151     goto good_area;
8152   if (!(vma->vm_flags & VM_GROWSDOWN))
8153     goto bad_area;
8154   if (error_code & 4) {
8155     /* accessing the stack below %esp is always a bug.
8156      * The "+ 32" is there due to some instructions (like
8157      * pusha) doing post-decrement on the stack and that
8158      * doesn't show up until later..  */
8159     if (address + 32 < regs->esp)
8160       goto bad_area;
8161   }
8162   if (expand_stack(vma, address))
8163     goto bad_area;
8164   /* Ok, we have a good vm_area for this memory access,
8165    * so we can handle it..  */
8166 good_area:
8167   info.si_code = SEGV_ACCERR;
8168   write = 0;
8169   switch (error_code & 3) {
8170     default:                        /* 3: write, present */
8171 #ifdef TEST_VERIFY_AREA
```

```
8172        if (regs->cs == KERNEL_CS)
8173          printk("WP fault at %08lx\n", regs->eip);
8174 #endif
8175        /* fall through */
8176      case 2:                          /* write, not present */
8177        if (!(vma->vm_flags & VM_WRITE))
8178          goto bad_area;
8179        write++;
8180        break;
8181      case 1:                          /* read, present */
8182        goto bad_area;
8183      case 0:                          /* read, not present */
8184        if (!(vma->vm_flags & (VM_READ | VM_EXEC)))
8185          goto bad_area;
8186      }
8187
8188      /* If for any reason at all we couldn't handle the
8189       * fault, make sure we exit gracefully rather than
8190       * endlessly redo the fault.  */
8191      switch (handle_mm_fault(mm, vma, address, write)) {
8192      case 1:
8193        tsk->min_flt++;
8194        break;
8195      case 2:
8196        tsk->maj_flt++;
8197        break;
8198      case 0:
8199        goto do_sigbus;
8200      default:
8201        goto out_of_memory;
8202      }
8203
8204      /* Did it hit the DOS screen memory VA from vm86 mode?
8205       */
8206      if (regs->eflags & VM_MASK) {
8207        unsigned long bit =
8208            (address - 0xA0000) >> PAGE_SHIFT;
8209        if (bit < 32)
8210          tsk->thread.screen_bitmap |= 1 << bit;
8211      }
8212      up(&mm->mmap_sem);
8213      return;
8214
8215      /* Something tried to access memory that isn't in our
8216       * memory map..  Fix it, but check if it's kernel or
8217       * user first..  */
8218 bad_area:
```

```
8219      up(&mm->mmap_sem);
8220
8221 bad_area_nosemaphore:
8222      /* User mode accesses just cause a SIGSEGV */
8223      if (error_code & 4) {
8224        tsk->thread.cr2 = address;
8225        tsk->thread.error_code = error_code;
8226        tsk->thread.trap_no = 14;
8227        info.si_signo = SIGSEGV;
8228        info.si_errno = 0;
8229        /* info.si_code has been set above */
8230        info.si_addr = (void *) address;
8231        force_sig_info(SIGSEGV, &info, tsk);
8232        return;
8233      }
8234
8235      /* Pentium F0 0F C7 C8 bug workaround.  */
8236      if (boot_cpu_data.f00f_bug) {
8237        unsigned long nr;
8238
8239        nr = (address - idt) >> 3;
8240
8241        if (nr == 6) {
8242          do_invalid_op(regs, 0);
8243          return;
8244        }
8245      }
8246
8247 no_context:
8248      /* Are we prepared to handle this kernel fault?  */
8249      if ((fixup = search_exception_table(regs->eip)) != 0) {
8250        regs->eip = fixup;
8251        return;
8252      }
8253
8254      /* Oops. The kernel tried to access some bad
8255       * page. We'll have to terminate things with extreme
8256       * prejudice.  */
8257
8258      bust_spinlocks();
8259
8260      if (address < PAGE_SIZE)
8261        printk(KERN_ALERT "Unable to handle kernel NULL "
8262            "pointer dereference");
8263      else
8264        printk(KERN_ALERT
8265            "Unable to handle kernel paging request");
```

```
8266    printk(" at virtual address %08lx\n", address);
8267    printk(" printing eip:\n");
8268    printk("%08lx\n", regs->eip);
8269    asm("movl %%cr3,%0":"=r"(page));
8270    page = ((unsigned long *) __va(page))[address >> 22];
8271    printk(KERN_ALERT "*pde = %08lx\n", page);
8272    if (page & 1) {
8273      page &= PAGE_MASK;
8274      address &= 0x003ff000;
8275      page = ((unsigned long *) __va(page))[address >>
8276                                      PAGE_SHIFT];
8277      printk(KERN_ALERT "*pte = %08lx\n", page);
8278    }
8279    die("Oops", regs, error_code);
8280    do_exit(SIGKILL);
8281
8282    /* We ran out of memory, or some other thing happened
8283     * to us that made us unable to handle the page fault
8284     * gracefully.  */
8285 out_of_memory:
8286    up(&mm->mmap_sem);
8287    printk("VM: killing process %s\n", tsk->comm);
8288    if (error_code & 4)
8289      do_exit(SIGKILL);
8290    goto no_context;
8291
8292 do_sigbus:
8293    up(&mm->mmap_sem);
8294
8295    /* Send a sigbus, regardless of whether we were in
8296     * kernel or user mode.  */
8297    tsk->thread.cr2 = address;
8298    tsk->thread.error_code = error_code;
8299    tsk->thread.trap_no = 14;
8300    info.si_code = SIGBUS;
8301    info.si_errno = 0;
8302    info.si_code = BUS_ADRERR;
8303    info.si_addr = (void *) address;
8304    force_sig_info(SIGBUS, &info, tsk);
8305
8306    /* Kernel mode? Handle exceptions or die */
8307    if (!(error_code & 4))
8308      goto no_context;
8309    return;
8310
8311 vmalloc_fault:
8312    {
8313      /* Synchronize this task's top level page-table with
8314       * the 'reference' page table.  */
8315      int offset = __pgd_offset(address);
8316      pgd_t *pgd, *pgd_k;
8317      pmd_t *pmd, *pmd_k;
8318
8319      pgd = tsk->active_mm->pgd + offset;
8320      pgd_k = init_mm.pgd + offset;
8321
8322      if (!pgd_present(*pgd)) {
8323        if (!pgd_present(*pgd_k))
8324          goto bad_area_nosemaphore;
8325        set_pgd(pgd, *pgd_k);
8326        return;
8327      }
8328
8329      pmd = pmd_offset(pgd, address);
8330      pmd_k = pmd_offset(pgd_k, address);
8331
8332      if (pmd_present(*pmd) || !pmd_present(*pmd_k))
8333        goto bad_area_nosemaphore;
8334      set_pmd(pmd, *pmd_k);
8335      return;
8336    }
8337 }
```

arch/i386/mm/init.c

```
8338 /*
8339  *  linux/arch/i386/mm/init.c
8340  *
8341  *  Copyright (C) 1995  Linus Torvalds
8342  *
8343  *  Support of BIGMEM added by Gerhard Wichert, Siemens
8344  *  AG, July 1999
8345  */
8346
8347 #include <linux/config.h>
8348 #include <linux/signal.h>
8349 #include <linux/sched.h>
8350 #include <linux/kernel.h>
8351 #include <linux/errno.h>
8352 #include <linux/string.h>
8353 #include <linux/types.h>
8354 #include <linux/ptrace.h>
8355 #include <linux/mman.h>
8356 #include <linux/mm.h>
8357 #include <linux/swap.h>
```

```
8358 #include <linux/smp.h>
8359 #include <linux/init.h>
8360 #ifdef CONFIG_BLK_DEV_INITRD
8361 #include <linux/blk.h>
8362 #endif
8363 #include <linux/highmem.h>
8364 #include <linux/pagemap.h>
8365 #include <linux/bootmem.h>
8366
8367 #include <asm/processor.h>
8368 #include <asm/system.h>
8369 #include <asm/uaccess.h>
8370 #include <asm/pgtable.h>
8371 #include <asm/pgalloc.h>
8372 #include <asm/dma.h>
8373 #include <asm/fixmap.h>
8374 #include <asm/e820.h>
8375 #include <asm/apic.h>
8376
8377 unsigned long highstart_pfn, highend_pfn;
8378 static unsigned long totalram_pages;
8379 static unsigned long totalhigh_pages;
8380
8381 /* BAD_PAGE is the page that is used for page faults when
8382  * linux is out-of-memory. Older versions of linux just
8383  * did a do_exit(), but using this instead means there is
8384  * less risk for a process dying in kernel mode, possibly
8385  * leaving an inode unused etc..
8386  *
8387  * BAD_PAGETABLE is the accompanying page-table: it is
8388  * initialized to point to BAD_PAGE entries.
8389  *
8390  * ZERO_PAGE is a special page that is used for
8391  * zero-initialized data and COW.  */
8392
8393 /* These are allocated in head.S so that we get proper
8394  * page alignment.  If you change the size of these then
8395  * change head.S as well.  */
8396 extern char empty_bad_page[PAGE_SIZE];
8397 #if CONFIG_X86_PAE
8398 extern pmd_t empty_bad_pmd_table[PTRS_PER_PMD];
8399 #endif
8400 extern pte_t empty_bad_pte_table[PTRS_PER_PTE];
8401
8402 /* We init them before every return and make them
8403  * writable-shared.  This guarantees we get out of the
8404  * kernel in some more or less sane way.  */
```

```
8405 #if CONFIG_X86_PAE
8406 static pmd_t *get_bad_pmd_table(void)
8407 {
8408   pmd_t v;
8409   int i;
8410
8411   set_pmd(&v,
8412       __pmd(_PAGE_TABLE + __pa(empty_bad_pte_table)));
8413
8414   for (i = 0; i < PAGE_SIZE / sizeof(pmd_t); i++)
8415     empty_bad_pmd_table[i] = v;
8416
8417   return empty_bad_pmd_table;
8418 }
8419 #endif
8420
8421 static pte_t *get_bad_pte_table(void)
8422 {
8423   pte_t v;
8424   int i;
8425
8426   v = pte_mkdirty(mk_pte_phys(__pa(empty_bad_page),
8427                       PAGE_SHARED));
8428
8429   for (i = 0; i < PAGE_SIZE / sizeof(pte_t); i++)
8430     empty_bad_pte_table[i] = v;
8431
8432   return empty_bad_pte_table;
8433 }
8434
8435
8436
8437 void __handle_bad_pmd(pmd_t * pmd)
8438 {
8439   pmd_ERROR(*pmd);
8440   set_pmd(pmd,
8441       __pmd(_PAGE_TABLE + __pa(get_bad_pte_table())));
8442 }
8443
8444 void __handle_bad_pmd_kernel(pmd_t * pmd)
8445 {
8446   pmd_ERROR(*pmd);
8447   set_pmd(pmd,
8448       __pmd(_KERNPG_TABLE + __pa(get_bad_pte_table())));
8449 }
8450
8451 pte_t *get_pte_kernel_slow(pmd_t * pmd,
```

```
8452    unsigned long offset)
8453 {
8454   pte_t *pte;
8455
8456   pte = (pte_t *) __get_free_page(GFP_KERNEL);
8457   if (pmd_none(*pmd)) {
8458     if (pte) {
8459       clear_page(pte);
8460       set_pmd(pmd, __pmd(_KERNPG_TABLE + __pa(pte)));
8461       return pte + offset;
8462     }
8463     set_pmd(pmd,
8464         __pmd(_KERNPG_TABLE +
8465   __pa(get_bad_pte_table())));
8466     return NULL;
8467   }
8468   free_page((unsigned long) pte);
8469   if (pmd_bad(*pmd)) {
8470     __handle_bad_pmd_kernel(pmd);
8471     return NULL;
8472   }
8473   return (pte_t *) pmd_page(*pmd) + offset;
8474 }
8475
8476 pte_t *get_pte_slow(pmd_t * pmd, unsigned long offset)
8477 {
8478   unsigned long pte;
8479
8480   pte = (unsigned long) __get_free_page(GFP_KERNEL);
8481   if (pmd_none(*pmd)) {
8482     if (pte) {
8483       clear_page((void *) pte);
8484       set_pmd(pmd, __pmd(_PAGE_TABLE + __pa(pte)));
8485       return (pte_t *) pte + offset;
8486     }
8487     set_pmd(pmd,
8488         __pmd(_PAGE_TABLE + __pa(get_bad_pte_table())));
8489     return NULL;
8490   }
8491   free_page(pte);
8492   if (pmd_bad(*pmd)) {
8493     __handle_bad_pmd(pmd);
8494     return NULL;
8495   }
8496   return (pte_t *) pmd_page(*pmd) + offset;
8497 }
8498
8499 int do_check_pgt_cache(int low, int high)
8500 {
8501   int freed = 0;
8502   if (pgtable_cache_size > high) {
8503     do {
8504       if (pgd_quicklist)
8505         free_pgd_slow(get_pgd_fast()), freed++;
8506       if (pmd_quicklist)
8507         free_pmd_slow(get_pmd_fast()), freed++;
8508       if (pte_quicklist)
8509         free_pte_slow(get_pte_fast()), freed++;
8510     } while (pgtable_cache_size > low);
8511   }
8512   return freed;
8513 }
8514
8515 /* NOTE: pagetable_init alloc all the fixmap pagetables
8516  * contiguous on the physical space so we can cache the
8517  * place of the first one and move around without
8518  * checking the pgd every time.  */
8519 #if CONFIG_HIGHMEM
8520 pte_t *kmap_pte;
8521 pgprot_t kmap_prot;
8522
8523 #define kmap_get_fixmap_pte(vaddr)                       \
8524         pte_offset(pmd_offset(pgd_offset_k(vaddr),       \
8525                                 (vaddr)), (vaddr))
8526
8527 void __init kmap_init(void)
8528 {
8529   unsigned long kmap_vstart;
8530
8531   /* cache the first kmap pte */
8532   kmap_vstart = __fix_to_virt(FIX_KMAP_BEGIN);
8533   kmap_pte = kmap_get_fixmap_pte(kmap_vstart);
8534
8535   kmap_prot = PAGE_KERNEL;
8536 }
8537
8538 #endif                                 /* CONFIG_HIGHMEM */
8539
8540 void show_mem(void)
8541 {
8542   int i, total = 0, reserved = 0;
8543   int shared = 0, cached = 0;
8544   int highmem = 0;
8545
```

```
8546   printk("Mem-info:\n");
8547   show_free_areas();
8548   printk("Free swap:       %6dkB\n",
8549       nr_swap_pages << (PAGE_SHIFT - 10));
8550   i = max_mapnr;
8551   while (i- > 0) {
8552     total++;
8553     if (PageHighMem(mem_map + i))
8554       highmem++;
8555     if (PageReserved(mem_map + i))
8556       reserved++;
8557     else if (PageSwapCache(mem_map + i))
8558       cached++;
8559     else if (page_count(mem_map + i))
8560       shared += page_count(mem_map + i) - 1;
8561   }
8562   printk("%d pages of RAM\n", total);
8563   printk("%d pages of HIGHMEM\n", highmem);
8564   printk("%d reserved pages\n", reserved);
8565   printk("%d pages shared\n", shared);
8566   printk("%d pages swap cached\n", cached);
8567   printk("%ld pages in page table cache\n",
8568       pgtable_cache_size);
8569   show_buffers();
8570 }
8571
8572 /* References to section boundaries */
8573 extern char _text, _etext, _edata, __bss_start, _end;
8574 extern char __init_begin, __init_end;
8575
8576 static inline void set_pte_phys(unsigned long vaddr,
8577     unsigned long phys, pgprot_t flags)
8578 {
8579   pgprot_t prot;
8580   pgd_t *pgd;
8581   pmd_t *pmd;
8582   pte_t *pte;
8583
8584   pgd = swapper_pg_dir + __pgd_offset(vaddr);
8585   if (pgd_none(*pgd)) {
8586     printk("PAE BUG #00!\n");
8587     return;
8588   }
8589   pmd = pmd_offset(pgd, vaddr);
8590   if (pmd_none(*pmd)) {
8591     printk("PAE BUG #01!\n");
8592     return;
8593   }
8594   pte = pte_offset(pmd, vaddr);
8595   if (pte_val(*pte))
8596     pte_ERROR(*pte);
8597   pgprot_val(prot) =
8598       pgprot_val(PAGE_KERNEL) | pgprot_val(flags);
8599   set_pte(pte, mk_pte_phys(phys, prot));
8600
8601   /* It's enough to flush this one mapping.  (PGE
8602    * mappings get flushed as well) */
8603   __flush_tlb_one(vaddr);
8604 }
8605
8606 void __set_fixmap(enum fixed_addresses idx,
8607     unsigned long phys, pgprot_t flags)
8608 {
8609   unsigned long address = __fix_to_virt(idx);
8610
8611   if (idx >= __end_of_fixed_addresses) {
8612     printk("Invalid __set_fixmap\n");
8613     return;
8614   }
8615   set_pte_phys(address, phys, flags);
8616 }
8617
8618 static void __init fixrange_init(unsigned long start,
8619     unsigned long end, pgd_t * pgd_base)
8620 {
8621   pgd_t *pgd;
8622   pmd_t *pmd;
8623   pte_t *pte;
8624   int i, j;
8625   unsigned long vaddr;
8626
8627   vaddr = start;
8628   i = __pgd_offset(vaddr);
8629   j = __pmd_offset(vaddr);
8630   pgd = pgd_base + i;
8631
8632   for (; (i < PTRS_PER_PGD) && (vaddr != end);
8633       pgd++, i++) {
8634 #if CONFIG_X86_PAE
8635     if (pgd_none(*pgd)) {
8636       pmd = (pmd_t *) alloc_bootmem_low_pages(PAGE_SIZE);
8637       set_pgd(pgd, __pgd(__pa(pmd) + 0x1));
8638       if (pmd != pmd_offset(pgd, 0))
8639         printk("PAE BUG #02!\n");
```

```
8640        }
8641      pmd = pmd_offset(pgd, vaddr);
8642 #else
8643      pmd = (pmd_t *) pgd;
8644 #endif
8645      for (; (j < PTRS_PER_PMD) && (vaddr != end);
8646          pmd++, j++) {
8647        if (pmd_none(*pmd)) {
8648          pte =
8649              (pte_t *) alloc_bootmem_low_pages(PAGE_SIZE);
8650          set_pmd(pmd, __pmd(_KERNPG_TABLE + __pa(pte)));
8651          if (pte != pte_offset(pmd, 0))
8652            BUG();
8653        }
8654        vaddr += PMD_SIZE;
8655      }
8656      j = 0;
8657    }
8658 }
8659
8660 static void __init pagetable_init(void)
8661 {
8662    unsigned long vaddr, end;
8663    pgd_t *pgd, *pgd_base;
8664    int i, j, k;
8665    pmd_t *pmd;
8666    pte_t *pte, *pte_base;
8667
8668    /* This can be zero as well - no problem, in that case
8669     * we exit the loops anyway due to the PTRS_PER_*
8670     * conditions.  */
8671    end = (unsigned long) __va(max_low_pfn * PAGE_SIZE);
8672
8673    pgd_base = swapper_pg_dir;
8674 #if CONFIG_X86_PAE
8675    for (i = 0; i < PTRS_PER_PGD; i++) {
8676      pgd = pgd_base + i;
8677      __pgd_clear(pgd);
8678    }
8679 #endif
8680    i = __pgd_offset(PAGE_OFFSET);
8681    pgd = pgd_base + i;
8682
8683    for (; i < PTRS_PER_PGD; pgd++, i++) {
8684      vaddr = i * PGDIR_SIZE;
8685      if (end && (vaddr >= end))
8686        break;
```

```
8687 #if CONFIG_X86_PAE
8688      pmd = (pmd_t *) alloc_bootmem_low_pages(PAGE_SIZE);
8689      set_pgd(pgd, __pgd(__pa(pmd) + 0x1));
8690 #else
8691      pmd = (pmd_t *) pgd;
8692 #endif
8693      if (pmd != pmd_offset(pgd, 0))
8694        BUG();
8695      for (j = 0; j < PTRS_PER_PMD; pmd++, j++) {
8696        vaddr = i * PGDIR_SIZE + j * PMD_SIZE;
8697        if (end && (vaddr >= end))
8698          break;
8699        if (cpu_has_pse) {
8700          unsigned long __pe;
8701
8702          set_in_cr4(X86_CR4_PSE);
8703          boot_cpu_data.wp_works_ok = 1;
8704          __pe = _KERNPG_TABLE + _PAGE_PSE + __pa(vaddr);
8705          /* Make it "global" too if supported */
8706          if (cpu_has_pge) {
8707            set_in_cr4(X86_CR4_PGE);
8708            __pe += _PAGE_GLOBAL;
8709          }
8710          set_pmd(pmd, __pmd(__pe));
8711          continue;
8712        }
8713
8714        pte_base = pte =
8715            (pte_t *) alloc_bootmem_low_pages(PAGE_SIZE);
8716
8717        for (k = 0; k < PTRS_PER_PTE; pte++, k++) {
8718          vaddr = i * PGDIR_SIZE + j * PMD_SIZE +
8719              k * PAGE_SIZE;
8720          if (end && (vaddr >= end))
8721            break;
8722          *pte = mk_pte_phys(__pa(vaddr), PAGE_KERNEL);
8723        }
8724        set_pmd(pmd,
8725            __pmd(_KERNPG_TABLE + __pa(pte_base)));
8726        if (pte_base != pte_offset(pmd, 0))
8727          BUG();
8728
8729      }
8730    }
8731
8732    /* Fixed mappings, only the page table structure has to
8733     * be created - mappings will be set by set_fixmap():
```

```
8734      */
8735      vaddr = __fix_to_virt(__end_of_fixed_addresses - 1) &
8736         PMD_MASK;
8737      fixrange_init(vaddr, 0, pgd_base);
8738
8739 #if CONFIG_HIGHMEM
8740      /* Permanent kmaps: */
8741      vaddr = PKMAP_BASE;
8742      fixrange_init(vaddr, vaddr + PAGE_SIZE * LAST_PKMAP,
8743         pgd_base);
8744
8745      pgd = swapper_pg_dir + __pgd_offset(vaddr);
8746      pmd = pmd_offset(pgd, vaddr);
8747      pte = pte_offset(pmd, vaddr);
8748      pkmap_page_table = pte;
8749 #endif
8750
8751 #if CONFIG_X86_PAE
8752      /* Add low memory identity-mappings - SMP needs it when
8753       * starting up on an AP from real-mode. In the non-PAE
8754       * case we already have these mappings through head.S.
8755       * All user-space mappings are explicitly cleared after
8756       * SMP startup. */
8757      pgd_base[0] = pgd_base[USER_PTRS_PER_PGD];
8758 #endif
8759 }
8760
8761 void __init zap_low_mappings(void)
8762 {
8763   int i;
8764   /* Zap initial low-memory mappings.
8765    *
8766    * Note that "pgd_clear()" doesn't do it for us in this
8767    * case, because pgd_clear() is a no-op in the 2-level
8768    * case (pmd_clear() is the thing that clears the
8769    * page-tables in that case).  */
8770   for (i = 0; i < USER_PTRS_PER_PGD; i++)
8771 #if CONFIG_X86_PAE
8772      pgd_clear(swapper_pg_dir + i);
8773 #else
8774      set_pgd(swapper_pg_dir + i, __pgd(0));
8775 #endif
8776   flush_tlb_all();
8777 }
8778
8779 /* paging_init() sets up the page tables - note that the
8780  * first 8MB are already mapped by head.S.
```

```
8781  *
8782  * This routines also unmaps the page at virtual kernel
8783  * address 0, so that we can trap those pesky
8784  * NULL-reference errors in the kernel.  */
8785 void __init paging_init(void)
8786 {
8787   pagetable_init();
8788
8789   __asm__("movl %%ecx,%%cr3\n"
8790           ::"c"(__pa(swapper_pg_dir)));
8791
8792 #if CONFIG_X86_PAE
8793   /* We will bail out later - printk doesnt work right
8794    * now so the user would just see a hanging kernel.  */
8795   if (cpu_has_pae)
8796      set_in_cr4(X86_CR4_PAE);
8797 #endif
8798
8799   __flush_tlb_all();
8800
8801 #ifdef CONFIG_HIGHMEM
8802   kmap_init();
8803 #endif
8804   {
8805      unsigned long zones_size[MAX_NR_ZONES] = { 0, 0, 0 };
8806      unsigned int max_dma, high, low;
8807
8808      max_dma = virt_to_phys((char *) MAX_DMA_ADDRESS) >>
8809                            PAGE_SHIFT;
8810      low = max_low_pfn;
8811      high = highend_pfn;
8812
8813      if (low < max_dma)
8814         zones_size[ZONE_DMA] = low;
8815      else {
8816         zones_size[ZONE_DMA] = max_dma;
8817         zones_size[ZONE_NORMAL] = low - max_dma;
8818 #ifdef CONFIG_HIGHMEM
8819         zones_size[ZONE_HIGHMEM] = high - low;
8820 #endif
8821      }
8822      free_area_init(zones_size);
8823   }
8824   return;
8825 }
8826
8827 /* Test if the WP bit works in supervisor mode. It isn't
```

```
8828   * supported on 386's and also on some strange 486's
8829   * (NexGen etc.). All 586+'s are OK. The jumps before and
8830   * after the test are here to work-around some nasty CPU
8831   * bugs.  */
8832
8833  /* This function cannot be __init, since exceptions don't
8834   * work in that section.  */
8835  static int do_test_wp_bit(unsigned long vaddr);
8836
8837  void __init test_wp_bit(void)
8838  {
8839     /* Ok, all PSE-capable CPUs are definitely handling the
8840      * WP bit right.  */
8841     const unsigned long vaddr = PAGE_OFFSET;
8842     pgd_t *pgd;
8843     pmd_t *pmd;
8844     pte_t *pte, old_pte;
8845
8846     printk("Checking if this processor honours the WP bit "
8847            "even in supervisor mode... ");
8848
8849     pgd = swapper_pg_dir + __pgd_offset(vaddr);
8850     pmd = pmd_offset(pgd, vaddr);
8851     pte = pte_offset(pmd, vaddr);
8852     old_pte = *pte;
8853     *pte = mk_pte_phys(0, PAGE_READONLY);
8854     local_flush_tlb();
8855
8856     boot_cpu_data.wp_works_ok = do_test_wp_bit(vaddr);
8857
8858     *pte = old_pte;
8859     local_flush_tlb();
8860
8861     if (!boot_cpu_data.wp_works_ok) {
8862        printk("No.\n");
8863  #ifdef CONFIG_X86_WP_WORKS_OK
8864        panic("This kernel doesn't support CPU's with "
8865              "broken WP. Recompile it for a 386!");
8866  #endif
8867     } else {
8868        printk("Ok.\n");
8869     }
8870  }
8871
8872  static inline int page_is_ram(unsigned long pagenr)
8873  {
8874     int i;
```

```
8875
8876     for (i = 0; i < e820.nr_map; i++) {
8877        unsigned long addr, end;
8878
8879        if (e820.map[i].type != E820_RAM) /* unusable mem */
8880           continue;
8881        /* !!!FIXME!!! Some BIOSen report areas as RAM that
8882         * are not. Notably the 640->1Mb area. We need a
8883         * sanity check here.  */
8884        addr = (e820.map[i].addr + PAGE_SIZE - 1)
8885           >> PAGE_SHIFT;
8886        end = (e820.map[i].addr + e820.map[i].size)
8887           >> PAGE_SHIFT;
8888        if ((pagenr >= addr) && (pagenr < end))
8889           return 1;
8890     }
8891     return 0;
8892  }
8893
8894  void __init mem_init(void)
8895  {
8896     int codesize, reservedpages, datasize, initsize;
8897     int tmp;
8898
8899     if (!mem_map)
8900        BUG();
8901
8902  #ifdef CONFIG_HIGHMEM
8903     highmem_start_page = mem_map + highstart_pfn;
8904     max_mapnr = num_physpages = highend_pfn;
8905  #else
8906     max_mapnr = num_physpages = max_low_pfn;
8907  #endif
8908     high_memory = (void *) __va(max_low_pfn * PAGE_SIZE);
8909
8910     /* clear the zero-page */
8911     memset(empty_zero_page, 0, PAGE_SIZE);
8912
8913     /* this will put all low memory onto the freelists */
8914     totalram_pages += free_all_bootmem();
8915
8916     reservedpages = 0;
8917     for (tmp = 0; tmp < max_low_pfn; tmp++)
8918        /* Only count reserved RAM pages */
8919        if (page_is_ram(tmp) && PageReserved(mem_map + tmp))
8920           reservedpages++;
8921  #ifdef CONFIG_HIGHMEM
```

```
8922     for (tmp = highstart_pfn; tmp < highend_pfn; tmp++) {
8923       struct page *page = mem_map + tmp;
8924
8925       if (!page_is_ram(tmp)) {
8926         SetPageReserved(page);
8927         continue;
8928       }
8929       ClearPageReserved(page);
8930       set_bit(PG_highmem, &page->flags);
8931       atomic_set(&page->count, 1);
8932       __free_page(page);
8933       totalhigh_pages++;
8934     }
8935     totalram_pages += totalhigh_pages;
8936 #endif
8937     codesize =
8938       (unsigned long) &_etext - (unsigned long) &_text;
8939     datasize =
8940       (unsigned long) &_edata - (unsigned long) &_etext;
8941     initsize =
8942       (unsigned long) &__init_end -
8943       (unsigned long) &__init_begin;
8944
8945     printk("Memory: %luk/%luk available (%dk kernel code, "
8946        "%dk reserved, %dk data, %dk init, "
8947        "%ldk highmem)\n",
8948        (unsigned long) nr_free_pages()
8949        << (PAGE_SHIFT - 10),
8950        max_mapnr << (PAGE_SHIFT - 10),
8951        codesize >> 10,
8952        reservedpages << (PAGE_SHIFT - 10),
8953        datasize >> 10, initsize >> 10,
8954        (unsigned long) (totalhigh_pages
8955                     << (PAGE_SHIFT - 10)));
8956
8957 #if CONFIG_X86_PAE
8958   if (!cpu_has_pae)
8959     panic("cannot execute a PAE-enabled kernel "
8960          "on a PAE-less CPU!");
8961 #endif
8962   if (boot_cpu_data.wp_works_ok < 0)
8963     test_wp_bit();
8964
8965     /* Subtle. SMP is doing it's boot stuff late (because
8966      * it has to fork idle threads) - but it also needs low
8967      * mappings for the protected-mode entry to work. We
8968      * zap these entries only after the WP-bit has been
8969      * tested. */
8970 #ifndef CONFIG_SMP
8971   zap_low_mappings();
8972 #endif
8973
8974 }
8975
8976 /* Put this after the callers, so that it cannot be
8977  * inlined */
8978 static int do_test_wp_bit(unsigned long vaddr)
8979 {
8980   char tmp_reg;
8981   int flag;
8982
8983   __asm__ __volatile__(
8984     " movb %0,%1          \n"
8985     "1:        movb %1,%0         \n"
8986     " xorl %2,%2          \n"
8987     "2:                        \n"
8988     ".section __ex_table,\"a\"\n"
8989     " .align 4        \n"
8990     " .long 1b,2b     \n"
8991     ".previous                \n"
8992     :"=m"(*(char *) vaddr), "=q"(tmp_reg), "=r"(flag)
8993     :"2"(1)
8994     :"memory");
8995
8996   return flag;
8997 }
8998
8999 void free_initmem(void)
9000 {
9001   unsigned long addr;
9002
9003   addr = (unsigned long) (&__init_begin);
9004   for (; addr < (unsigned long) (&__init_end);
9005       addr += PAGE_SIZE) {
9006     ClearPageReserved(virt_to_page(addr));
9007     set_page_count(virt_to_page(addr), 1);
9008     free_page(addr);
9009     totalram_pages++;
9010   }
9011   printk("Freeing unused kernel memory: %dk freed\n",
9012     (&__init_end - &__init_begin) >> 10);
9013 }
9014
9015 #ifdef CONFIG_BLK_DEV_INITRD
```

```
9016 void free_initrd_mem(unsigned long start,
9017     unsigned long end)
9018 {
9019   if (start < end)
9020     printk("Freeing initrd memory: %ldk freed\n",
9021       (end - start) >> 10);
9022   for (; start < end; start += PAGE_SIZE) {
9023     ClearPageReserved(virt_to_page(start));
9024     set_page_count(virt_to_page(start), 1);
9025     free_page(start);
9026     totalram_pages++;
9027   }
9028 }
9029 #endif
9030
9031 void si_meminfo(struct sysinfo *val)
9032 {
9033   val->totalram = totalram_pages;
9034   val->sharedram = 0;
9035   val->freeram = nr_free_pages();
9036   val->bufferram = atomic_read(&buffermem_pages);
9037   val->totalhigh = totalhigh_pages;
9038   val->freehigh = nr_free_highpages();
9039   val->mem_unit = PAGE_SIZE;
9040   return;
9041 }
```

fs/binfmt_elf.c

```
9042 /*
9043  * linux/fs/binfmt_elf.c
9044  *
9045  * These are the functions used to load ELF format
9046  * executables as used on SVr4 machines.  Information on
9047  * the format may be found in the book "UNIX SYSTEM V
9048  * RELEASE 4 Programmers Guide: Ansi C and Programming
9049  * Support Tools".
9050  *
9051  * Copyright 1993, 1994: Eric Youngdale (ericy@cais.com).
9052  */
9053
9054 #include <linux/module.h>
9055
9056 #include <linux/fs.h>
9057 #include <linux/stat.h>
9058 #include <linux/sched.h>
9059 #include <linux/mm.h>
9060 #include <linux/mman.h>
```

```
9061 #include <linux/a.out.h>
9062 #include <linux/errno.h>
9063 #include <linux/signal.h>
9064 #include <linux/binfmts.h>
9065 #include <linux/string.h>
9066 #include <linux/file.h>
9067 #include <linux/fcntl.h>
9068 #include <linux/ptrace.h>
9069 #include <linux/malloc.h>
9070 #include <linux/shm.h>
9071 #include <linux/personality.h>
9072 #include <linux/elfcore.h>
9073 #include <linux/init.h>
9074 #include <linux/highuid.h>
9075 #include <linux/smp_lock.h>
9076
9077 #include <asm/uaccess.h>
9078 #include <asm/param.h>
9079 #include <asm/pgalloc.h>
9080
9081 #define DLINFO_ITEMS 13
9082
9083 #include <linux/elf.h>
9084
9085 static int load_elf_binary(struct linux_binprm *bprm,
9086     struct pt_regs *regs);
9087 static int load_elf_library(struct file *);
9088 static unsigned long elf_map(struct file *,
9089     unsigned long, struct elf_phdr *, int, int);
9090 extern int dump_fpu(struct pt_regs *, elf_fpregset_t *);
9091 extern void dump_thread(struct pt_regs *, struct user *);
9092
9093 #ifndef elf_addr_t
9094 #define elf_addr_t unsigned long
9095 #define elf_caddr_t char *
9096 #endif
9097
9098 /* If we don't support core dumping, then supply a NULL
9099  * so we don't even try.  */
9100 #ifdef USE_ELF_CORE_DUMP
9101 static int elf_core_dump(long signr,
9102     struct pt_regs *regs, struct file *file);
9103 #else
9104 #define elf_core_dump   NULL
9105 #endif
9106
9107 #if ELF_EXEC_PAGESIZE > PAGE_SIZE
```

```
9108 # define ELF_MIN_ALIGN  ELF_EXEC_PAGESIZE
9109 #else
9110 # define ELF_MIN_ALIGN  PAGE_SIZE
9111 #endif
9112
9113 #define ELF_PAGESTART(_v)                               \
9114   ((_v) & ~(unsigned long)(ELF_MIN_ALIGN-1))
9115 #define ELF_PAGEOFFSET(_v) ((_v) & (ELF_MIN_ALIGN-1))
9116 #define ELF_PAGEALIGN(_v)                               \
9117   (((_v) + ELF_MIN_ALIGN - 1) & ~(ELF_MIN_ALIGN - 1))
9118
9119 static struct linux_binfmt elf_format = {
9120   NULL, THIS_MODULE, load_elf_binary, load_elf_library,
9121       elf_core_dump, ELF_EXEC_PAGESIZE
9122 };
9123
9124 static void set_brk(unsigned long start,
9125     unsigned long end)
9126 {
9127   start = ELF_PAGEALIGN(start);
9128   end = ELF_PAGEALIGN(end);
9129   if (end <= start)
9130     return;
9131   do_brk(start, end - start);
9132 }
9133
9134
9135 /* We need to explicitly zero any fractional pages after
9136  * the data section (i.e. bss).  This would contain the
9137  * junk from the file that should not be in memory */
9138 static void padzero(unsigned long elf_bss)
9139 {
9140   unsigned long nbyte;
9141
9142   nbyte = ELF_PAGEOFFSET(elf_bss);
9143   if (nbyte) {
9144     nbyte = ELF_MIN_ALIGN - nbyte;
9145     clear_user((void *) elf_bss, nbyte);
9146   }
9147 }
9148
9149 static elf_addr_t *create_elf_tables(char *p, int argc,
9150     int envc, struct elfhdr *exec,
9151     unsigned long load_addr, unsigned long load_bias,
9152     unsigned long interp_load_addr, int ibcs)
9153 {
9154   elf_caddr_t *argv;
9155   elf_caddr_t *envp;
9156   elf_addr_t *sp, *csp;
9157   char *k_platform, *u_platform;
9158   long hwcap;
9159   size_t platform_len = 0;
9160
9161   /* Get hold of platform and hardware capabilities masks
9162    * for the machine we are running on.  In some cases
9163    * (Sparc), this info is impossible to get, in others
9164    * (i386) it is merely difficult.  */
9165   hwcap = ELF_HWCAP;
9166   k_platform = ELF_PLATFORM;
9167
9168   if (k_platform) {
9169     platform_len = strlen(k_platform) + 1;
9170     u_platform = p - platform_len;
9171     __copy_to_user(u_platform, k_platform, platform_len);
9172   } else
9173     u_platform = p;
9174
9175   /* Force 16 byte _final_ alignment here for generality.
9176    * Leave an extra 16 bytes free so that on the PowerPC
9177    * we can move the aux table up to start on a 16-byte
9178    * boundary.  */
9179   sp = (elf_addr_t *)
9180     ((~15UL & (unsigned long) (u_platform)) - 16UL);
9181   csp = sp;
9182   csp -= ((exec ? DLINFO_ITEMS * 2 : 4) +
9183           (k_platform ? 2 : 0));
9184   csp -= envc + 1;
9185   csp -= argc + 1;
9186   csp -= (!ibcs ? 3 : 1);         /* argc itself */
9187   if ((unsigned long) csp & 15UL)
9188     sp -= ((unsigned long) csp & 15UL) / sizeof(*sp);
9189
9190   /* Put the ELF interpreter info on the stack */
9191 #define NEW_AUX_ENT(nr, id, val)                          \
9192         __put_user ((id), sp+(nr*2));                     \
9193         __put_user ((val), sp+(nr*2+1));                  \
9194
9195   sp -= 2;
9196   NEW_AUX_ENT(0, AT_NULL, 0);
9197   if (k_platform) {
9198     sp -= 2;
9199     NEW_AUX_ENT(0, AT_PLATFORM,
9200         (elf_addr_t) (unsigned long) u_platform);
9201   }
```

```
9202    sp -= 3 * 2;
9203    NEW_AUX_ENT(0, AT_HWCAP, hwcap);
9204    NEW_AUX_ENT(1, AT_PAGESZ, ELF_EXEC_PAGESIZE);
9205    NEW_AUX_ENT(2, AT_CLKTCK, CLOCKS_PER_SEC);
9206
9207    if (exec) {
9208       sp -= 10 * 2;
9209
9210       NEW_AUX_ENT(0, AT_PHDR, load_addr + exec->e_phoff);
9211       NEW_AUX_ENT(1, AT_PHENT, sizeof(struct elf_phdr));
9212       NEW_AUX_ENT(2, AT_PHNUM, exec->e_phnum);
9213       NEW_AUX_ENT(3, AT_BASE, interp_load_addr);
9214       NEW_AUX_ENT(4, AT_FLAGS, 0);
9215       NEW_AUX_ENT(5, AT_ENTRY, load_bias + exec->e_entry);
9216       NEW_AUX_ENT(6, AT_UID, (elf_addr_t) current->uid);
9217       NEW_AUX_ENT(7, AT_EUID, (elf_addr_t) current->euid);
9218       NEW_AUX_ENT(8, AT_GID, (elf_addr_t) current->gid);
9219       NEW_AUX_ENT(9, AT_EGID, (elf_addr_t) current->egid);
9220    }
9221  #undef NEW_AUX_ENT
9222
9223    sp -= envc + 1;
9224    envp = (elf_caddr_t *) sp;
9225    sp -= argc + 1;
9226    argv = (elf_caddr_t *) sp;
9227    if (!ibcs) {
9228       __put_user((elf_addr_t) (unsigned long) envp, -sp);
9229       __put_user((elf_addr_t) (unsigned long) argv, -sp);
9230    }
9231
9232    __put_user((elf_addr_t) argc, -sp);
9233    current->mm->arg_start = (unsigned long) p;
9234    while (argc- > 0) {
9235       __put_user((elf_caddr_t) (unsigned long) p, argv++);
9236       p += strlen_user(p);
9237    }
9238    __put_user(NULL, argv);
9239    current->mm->arg_end = current->mm->env_start =
9240       (unsigned long) p;
9241    while (envc- > 0) {
9242       __put_user((elf_caddr_t) (unsigned long) p, envp++);
9243       p += strlen_user(p);
9244    }
9245    __put_user(NULL, envp);
9246    current->mm->env_end = (unsigned long) p;
9247    return sp;
9248  }
```

```
9249
9250  #ifndef elf_map
9251
9252  static inline unsigned long
9253  elf_map(struct file *filep, unsigned long addr,
9254       struct elf_phdr *eppnt, int prot, int type)
9255  {
9256     unsigned long map_addr;
9257
9258     down(&current->mm->mmap_sem);
9259     map_addr = do_mmap(filep, ELF_PAGESTART(addr),
9260        eppnt->p_filesz + ELF_PAGEOFFSET(eppnt->p_vaddr),
9261        prot, type,
9262        eppnt->p_offset - ELF_PAGEOFFSET(eppnt->p_vaddr));
9263     up(&current->mm->mmap_sem);
9264     return (map_addr);
9265  }
9266
9267  #endif                              /* !elf_map */
9268
9269  /* This is much more generalized than the library
9270   * routine read function, so we keep this separate.
9271   * Technically the library read function is only
9272   * provided so that we can read a.out libraries that
9273   * have an ELF header */
9274  static unsigned long
9275  load_elf_interp(struct elfhdr *interp_elf_ex,
9276                  struct file *interpreter,
9277                  unsigned long *interp_load_addr)
9278  {
9279     struct elf_phdr *elf_phdata;
9280     struct elf_phdr *eppnt;
9281     unsigned long load_addr = 0;
9282     int load_addr_set = 0;
9283     unsigned long last_bss = 0, elf_bss = 0;
9284     unsigned long error = ~0UL;
9285     int retval, i, size;
9286
9287     /* First of all, some simple consistency checks */
9288     if (interp_elf_ex->e_type != ET_EXEC &&
9289        interp_elf_ex->e_type != ET_DYN)
9290       goto out;
9291     if (!elf_check_arch(interp_elf_ex))
9292       goto out;
9293     if (!interpreter->f_op || !interpreter->f_op->mmap)
9294       goto out;
9295
```

```
9296    /* If the size of this structure has changed, then
9297     * punt, since we will be doing the wrong thing.  */
9298    if (interp_elf_ex->e_phentsize !=
9299        sizeof(struct elf_phdr))
9300      goto out;
9301
9302    /* Now read in all of the header information */
9303
9304    size =
9305        sizeof(struct elf_phdr) * interp_elf_ex->e_phnum;
9306    if (size > ELF_MIN_ALIGN)
9307      goto out;
9308    elf_phdata =
9309        (struct elf_phdr *) kmalloc(size, GFP_KERNEL);
9310    if (!elf_phdata)
9311      goto out;
9312
9313    retval =
9314        kernel_read(interpreter, interp_elf_ex->e_phoff,
9315                    (char *) elf_phdata, size);
9316    error = retval;
9317    if (retval < 0)
9318      goto out_close;
9319
9320    eppnt = elf_phdata;
9321    for (i = 0; i < interp_elf_ex->e_phnum; i++, eppnt++) {
9322      if (eppnt->p_type == PT_LOAD) {
9323        int elf_type = MAP_PRIVATE | MAP_DENYWRITE;
9324        int elf_prot = 0;
9325        unsigned long vaddr = 0;
9326        unsigned long k, map_addr;
9327
9328        if (eppnt->p_flags & PF_R)
9329          elf_prot = PROT_READ;
9330        if (eppnt->p_flags & PF_W)
9331          elf_prot |= PROT_WRITE;
9332        if (eppnt->p_flags & PF_X)
9333          elf_prot |= PROT_EXEC;
9334        vaddr = eppnt->p_vaddr;
9335        if (interp_elf_ex->e_type == ET_EXEC
9336            || load_addr_set) elf_type |= MAP_FIXED;
9337
9338        map_addr = elf_map(interpreter, load_addr + vaddr,
9339                           eppnt, elf_prot, elf_type);
9340
9341        if (!load_addr_set
9342            && interp_elf_ex->e_type == ET_DYN) {
9343          load_addr = map_addr - ELF_PAGESTART(vaddr);
9344          load_addr_set = 1;
9345        }
9346
9347        /* Find the end of the file mapping for this phdr,
9348         * and keep track of the largest address we see for
9349         * this.  */
9350        k = load_addr + eppnt->p_vaddr + eppnt->p_filesz;
9351        if (k > elf_bss)
9352          elf_bss = k;
9353
9354        /* Do the same thing for the memory mapping -
9355         * between elf_bss and last_bss is the bss section.
9356         */
9357        k = load_addr + eppnt->p_memsz + eppnt->p_vaddr;
9358        if (k > last_bss)
9359          last_bss = k;
9360      }
9361    }
9362
9363    /* Now use mmap to map the library into memory. */
9364
9365    /* Now fill out the bss section.  First pad the last
9366     * page up to the page boundary, and then perform a
9367     * mmap to make sure that there are zero-mapped pages
9368     * up to and including the last bss page.  */
9369    padzero(elf_bss);
9370    /* What we have mapped so far */
9371    elf_bss = ELF_PAGESTART(elf_bss + ELF_MIN_ALIGN - 1);
9372
9373    /* Map the last of the bss segment */
9374    if (last_bss > elf_bss)
9375      do_brk(elf_bss, last_bss - elf_bss);
9376
9377    *interp_load_addr = load_addr;
9378    error = ((unsigned long) interp_elf_ex->e_entry) +
9379        load_addr;
9380
9381 out_close:
9382    kfree(elf_phdata);
9383 out:
9384    return error;
9385 }
9386
9387 static unsigned long
9388 load_aout_interp(struct exec *interp_ex,
9389                  struct file *interpreter)
```

```
9390 {
9391    unsigned long text_data, elf_entry = ~0UL;
9392    char *addr;
9393    loff_t offset;
9394    int retval;
9395
9396    current->mm->end_code = interp_ex->a_text;
9397    text_data = interp_ex->a_text + interp_ex->a_data;
9398    current->mm->end_data = text_data;
9399    current->mm->brk = interp_ex->a_bss + text_data;
9400
9401    switch (N_MAGIC(*interp_ex)) {
9402    case OMAGIC:
9403      offset = 32;
9404      addr = (char *) 0;
9405      break;
9406    case ZMAGIC:
9407    case QMAGIC:
9408      offset = N_TXTOFF(*interp_ex);
9409      addr = (char *) N_TXTADDR(*interp_ex);
9410      break;
9411    default:
9412      goto out;
9413    }
9414
9415    do_brk(0, text_data);
9416    retval = -ENOEXEC;
9417    if (!interpreter->f_op || !interpreter->f_op->read)
9418      goto out;
9419    retval = interpreter->f_op->read(interpreter, addr,
9420                                     text_data, &offset);
9421    if (retval < 0)
9422      goto out;
9423    flush_icache_range((unsigned long) addr,
9424                       (unsigned long) addr + text_data);
9425
9426    do_brk(ELF_PAGESTART(text_data + ELF_MIN_ALIGN - 1),
9427         interp_ex->a_bss);
9428    elf_entry = interp_ex->a_entry;
9429
9430 out:
9431    return elf_entry;
9432 }
9433
9434 /* These are the functions used to load ELF style
9435  * executables and shared libraries.  There is no binary
9436  * dependent code anywhere else.  */
9437
9438 #define INTERPRETER_NONE 0
9439 #define INTERPRETER_AOUT 1
9440 #define INTERPRETER_ELF 2
9441
9442
9443 static int load_elf_binary(struct linux_binprm *bprm,
9444     struct pt_regs *regs)
9445 {
9446    struct file *interpreter = NULL;    /* to shut gcc up */
9447    unsigned long load_addr = 0, load_bias;
9448    int load_addr_set = 0;
9449    char *elf_interpreter = NULL;
9450    unsigned int interpreter_type = INTERPRETER_NONE;
9451    unsigned char ibcs2_interpreter = 0;
9452    mm_segment_t old_fs;
9453    unsigned long error;
9454    struct elf_phdr *elf_ppnt, *elf_phdata;
9455    unsigned long elf_bss, k, elf_brk;
9456    int elf_exec_fileno;
9457    int retval, size, i;
9458    unsigned long elf_entry, interp_load_addr = 0;
9459    unsigned long start_code, end_code, start_data,
9460        end_data;
9461    struct elfhdr elf_ex;
9462    struct elfhdr interp_elf_ex;
9463    struct exec interp_ex;
9464    char passed_fileno[6];
9465
9466    /* Get the exec-header */
9467    elf_ex = *((struct elfhdr *) bprm->buf);
9468
9469    retval = -ENOEXEC;
9470    /* First of all, some simple consistency checks */
9471    if (memcmp(elf_ex.e_ident, ELFMAG, SELFMAG) != 0)
9472      goto out;
9473
9474    if (elf_ex.e_type != ET_EXEC &&
9475        elf_ex.e_type != ET_DYN)
9476      goto out;
9477    if (!elf_check_arch(&elf_ex))
9478      goto out;
9479    if (!bprm->file->f_op || !bprm->file->f_op->mmap)
9480      goto out;
9481
9482    /* Now read in all of the header information */
9483
```

```
9484    retval = -ENOMEM;
9485    size = elf_ex.e_phentsize * elf_ex.e_phnum;
9486    if (size > 65536)
9487      goto out;
9488    elf_phdata =
9489        (struct elf_phdr *) kmalloc(size, GFP_KERNEL);
9490    if (!elf_phdata)
9491      goto out;
9492
9493    retval = kernel_read(bprm->file, elf_ex.e_phoff,
9494                   (char *) elf_phdata, size);
9495    if (retval < 0)
9496      goto out_free_ph;
9497
9498    retval = get_unused_fd();
9499    if (retval < 0)
9500      goto out_free_ph;
9501    get_file(bprm->file);
9502    fd_install(elf_exec_fileno = retval, bprm->file);
9503
9504    elf_ppnt = elf_phdata;
9505    elf_bss = 0;
9506    elf_brk = 0;
9507
9508    start_code = ~0UL;
9509    end_code = 0;
9510    start_data = 0;
9511    end_data = 0;
9512
9513    for (i = 0; i < elf_ex.e_phnum; i++) {
9514      if (elf_ppnt->p_type == PT_INTERP) {
9515        retval = -EINVAL;
9516        if (elf_interpreter)
9517          goto out_free_dentry;
9518
9519        /* This is the program interpreter used for shared
9520         * libraries - for now assume that this is an a.out
9521         * format binary */
9522
9523        retval = -ENOMEM;
9524        elf_interpreter =
9525            (char *) kmalloc(elf_ppnt->p_filesz,
9526                           GFP_KERNEL);
9527        if (!elf_interpreter)
9528          goto out_free_file;
9529
9530        retval =
9531          kernel_read(bprm->file, elf_ppnt->p_offset,
9532            elf_interpreter, elf_ppnt->p_filesz);
9533        if (retval < 0)
9534          goto out_free_interp;
9535        /* If the program interpreter is one of these two,
9536         * then assume an iBCS2 image. Otherwise assume a
9537         * native linux image. */
9538        if (strcmp(elf_interpreter,
9539                  "/usr/lib/libc.so.1") == 0
9540            || strcmp(elf_interpreter,
9541                  "/usr/lib/ld.so.1") == 0)
9542          ibcs2_interpreter = 1;
9543 #if 0
9544        printk("Using ELF interpreter %s\n",
9545            elf_interpreter);
9546 #endif
9547 #ifdef __sparc__
9548        if (ibcs2_interpreter) {
9549          unsigned long old_pers = current->personality;
9550          struct exec_domain *old_domain =
9551              current->exec_domain;
9552          struct exec_domain *new_domain;
9553          struct fs_struct *old_fs = current->fs, *new_fs;
9554          get_exec_domain(old_domain);
9555          atomic_inc(&old_fs->count);
9556
9557          set_personality(PER_SVR4);
9558          interpreter = open_exec(elf_interpreter);
9559
9560          new_domain = current->exec_domain;
9561          new_fs = current->fs;
9562          current->personality = old_pers;
9563          current->exec_domain = old_domain;
9564          current->fs = old_fs;
9565          put_exec_domain(new_domain);
9566          put_fs_struct(new_fs);
9567        } else
9568 #endif
9569        {
9570          interpreter = open_exec(elf_interpreter);
9571        }
9572        retval = PTR_ERR(interpreter);
9573        if (IS_ERR(interpreter))
9574          goto out_free_interp;
9575        retval = kernel_read(interpreter, 0, bprm->buf,
9576                       BINPRM_BUF_SIZE);
9577        if (retval < 0)
```

```
9578              goto out_free_dentry;
9579
9580          /* Get the exec headers */
9581          interp_ex = *((struct exec *) bprm->buf);
9582          interp_elf_ex = *((struct elfhdr *) bprm->buf);
9583      }
9584      elf_ppnt++;
9585  }
9586
9587  /* Some simple consistency checks for the interpreter*/
9588  if (elf_interpreter) {
9589      interpreter_type =
9590          INTERPRETER_ELF | INTERPRETER_AOUT;
9591
9592      /* Now figure out which format our binary is */
9593      if ((N_MAGIC(interp_ex) != OMAGIC) &&
9594          (N_MAGIC(interp_ex) != ZMAGIC) &&
9595          (N_MAGIC(interp_ex) != QMAGIC))
9596        interpreter_type = INTERPRETER_ELF;
9597
9598      if (memcmp(interp_elf_ex.e_ident, ELFMAG, SELFMAG)
9599          != 0)
9600        interpreter_type &= ~INTERPRETER_ELF;
9601
9602      retval = -ELIBBAD;
9603      if (!interpreter_type)
9604        goto out_free_dentry;
9605
9606      /* Make sure only one type was selected */
9607      if ((interpreter_type & INTERPRETER_ELF) &&
9608          interpreter_type != INTERPRETER_ELF) {
9609        printk(KERN_WARNING
9610           "ELF: Ambiguous type, using ELF\n");
9611        interpreter_type = INTERPRETER_ELF;
9612      }
9613  }
9614
9615  /* OK, we are done with that, now set up the arg
9616   * stuff, and then start this sucker up */
9617
9618  if (!bprm->sh_bang) {
9619    char *passed_p;
9620
9621    if (interpreter_type == INTERPRETER_AOUT) {
9622      sprintf(passed_fileno, "%d", elf_exec_fileno);
9623      passed_p = passed_fileno;
9624
9625      if (elf_interpreter) {
9626        retval = copy_strings_kernel(1, &passed_p, bprm);
9627        if (retval)
9628          goto out_free_dentry;
9629        bprm->argc++;
9630      }
9631    }
9632  }
9633
9634  /* Flush all traces of the currently running
9635   * executable */
9636  retval = flush_old_exec(bprm);
9637  if (retval)
9638    goto out_free_dentry;
9639
9640  /* OK, This is the point of no return */
9641  current->mm->start_data = 0;
9642  current->mm->end_data = 0;
9643  current->mm->end_code = 0;
9644  current->mm->mmap = NULL;
9645  current->flags &= ~PF_FORKNOEXEC;
9646  elf_entry = (unsigned long) elf_ex.e_entry;
9647
9648  /* Do this immediately, since STACK_TOP as used in
9649   * setup_arg_pages may depend on the personality.  */
9650  SET_PERSONALITY(elf_ex, ibcs2_interpreter);
9651
9652  /* Do this so that we can load the interpreter, if
9653   * need be.  We will change some of these later */
9654  current->mm->rss = 0;
9655  setup_arg_pages(bprm);         /* XXX: check error */
9656  current->mm->start_stack = bprm->p;
9657
9658  /* Try and get dynamic programs out of the way of the
9659   * default mmap base, as well as whatever program they
9660   * might try to exec.  This is because the brk will
9661   * follow the loader, and is not movable.  */
9662  load_bias = ELF_PAGESTART(elf_ex.e_type == ET_DYN
9663                    ? ELF_ET_DYN_BASE
9664                    : 0);
9665
9666  /* Now we do a little grungy work by mmaping the ELF
9667   * image into the correct location in memory.  At this
9668   * point, we assume that the image should be loaded at
9669   * fixed address, not at a variable address. */
9670  old_fs = get_fs();
9671  set_fs(get_ds());
```

```
9672    for (i = 0, elf_ppnt = elf_phdata; i < elf_ex.e_phnum;
9673       i++, elf_ppnt++) {
9674      int elf_prot = 0, elf_flags;
9675      unsigned long vaddr;
9676
9677      if (elf_ppnt->p_type != PT_LOAD)
9678        continue;
9679
9680      if (elf_ppnt->p_flags & PF_R)
9681        elf_prot |= PROT_READ;
9682      if (elf_ppnt->p_flags & PF_W)
9683        elf_prot |= PROT_WRITE;
9684      if (elf_ppnt->p_flags & PF_X)
9685        elf_prot |= PROT_EXEC;
9686
9687      elf_flags =
9688          MAP_PRIVATE | MAP_DENYWRITE | MAP_EXECUTABLE;
9689
9690      vaddr = elf_ppnt->p_vaddr;
9691      if (elf_ex.e_type == ET_EXEC || load_addr_set) {
9692        elf_flags |= MAP_FIXED;
9693      }
9694
9695      error = elf_map(bprm->file, load_bias + vaddr,
9696                      elf_ppnt, elf_prot, elf_flags);
9697
9698      if (!load_addr_set) {
9699        load_addr_set = 1;
9700        load_addr =
9701            (elf_ppnt->p_vaddr - elf_ppnt->p_offset);
9702        if (elf_ex.e_type == ET_DYN) {
9703          load_bias += error -
9704              ELF_PAGESTART(load_bias + vaddr);
9705          load_addr += error;
9706        }
9707      }
9708      k = elf_ppnt->p_vaddr;
9709      if (k < start_code)
9710        start_code = k;
9711      if (start_data < k)
9712        start_data = k;
9713
9714      k = elf_ppnt->p_vaddr + elf_ppnt->p_filesz;
9715
9716      if (k > elf_bss)
9717        elf_bss = k;
9718      if ((elf_ppnt->p_flags & PF_X) && end_code < k)
9719        end_code = k;
9720      if (end_data < k)
9721        end_data = k;
9722      k = elf_ppnt->p_vaddr + elf_ppnt->p_memsz;
9723      if (k > elf_brk)
9724        elf_brk = k;
9725    }
9726    set_fs(old_fs);
9727
9728    elf_entry += load_bias;
9729    elf_bss += load_bias;
9730    elf_brk += load_bias;
9731    start_code += load_bias;
9732    end_code += load_bias;
9733    start_data += load_bias;
9734    end_data += load_bias;
9735
9736    if (elf_interpreter) {
9737      if (interpreter_type == INTERPRETER_AOUT)
9738        elf_entry = load_aout_interp(&interp_ex,
9739            interpreter);
9740      else
9741        elf_entry = load_elf_interp(&interp_elf_ex,
9742            interpreter, &interp_load_addr);
9743
9744      allow_write_access(interpreter);
9745      fput(interpreter);
9746      kfree(elf_interpreter);
9747
9748      if (elf_entry == ~0UL) {
9749        printk(KERN_ERR "Unable to load interpreter\n");
9750        kfree(elf_phdata);
9751        send_sig(SIGSEGV, current, 0);
9752        return 0;
9753      }
9754    }
9755
9756    kfree(elf_phdata);
9757
9758    if (interpreter_type != INTERPRETER_AOUT)
9759      sys_close(elf_exec_fileno);
9760
9761    set_binfmt(&elf_format);
9762
9763    compute_creds(bprm);
9764    current->flags &= ~PF_FORKNOEXEC;
9765    bprm->p = (unsigned long)
```

```
9766     create_elf_tables((char *) bprm->p,
9767         bprm->argc, bprm->envc,
9768         (interpreter_type == INTERPRETER_ELF
9769          ? &elf_ex : NULL),
9770         load_addr, load_bias, interp_load_addr,
9771         (interpreter_type == INTERPRETER_AOUT ? 0 : 1));
9772     /* N.B. passed_fileno might not be initialized? */
9773     if (interpreter_type == INTERPRETER_AOUT)
9774       current->mm->arg_start += strlen(passed_fileno) + 1;
9775     current->mm->start_brk = current->mm->brk = elf_brk;
9776     current->mm->end_code = end_code;
9777     current->mm->start_code = start_code;
9778     current->mm->start_data = start_data;
9779     current->mm->end_data = end_data;
9780     current->mm->start_stack = bprm->p;
9781
9782     /* Calling set_brk effectively mmaps the pages that we
9783      * need for the bss and break sections */
9784     set_brk(elf_bss, elf_brk);
9785
9786     padzero(elf_bss);
9787
9788 #if 0
9789     printk("(start_brk) %lx\n",
9790         (long) current->mm->start_brk);
9791     printk("(end_code) %lx\n",
9792         (long) current->mm->end_code);
9793     printk("(start_code) %lx\n",
9794         (long) current->mm->start_code);
9795     printk("(start_data) %lx\n",
9796         (long) current->mm->start_data);
9797     printk("(end_data) %lx\n",
9798         (long) current->mm->end_data);
9799     printk("(start_stack) %lx\n",
9800         (long) current->mm->start_stack);
9801     printk("(brk) %lx\n", (long) current->mm->brk);
9802 #endif
9803
9804     if (current->personality == PER_SVR4) {
9805       /* Why this, you ask??? Well SVr4 maps page 0 as
9806        * read-only, and some applications "depend" upon
9807        * this behavior. Since we do not have the power to
9808        * recompile these, we emulate the SVr4 behavior.
9809        * Sigh. */
9810       /* N.B. Shouldn't the size here be PAGE_SIZE?? */
9811       down(&current->mm->mmap_sem);
9812       error = do_mmap(NULL, 0, 4096, PROT_READ | PROT_EXEC,
9813           MAP_FIXED | MAP_PRIVATE, 0);
9814       up(&current->mm->mmap_sem);
9815     }
9816 #ifdef ELF_PLAT_INIT
9817     /* The ABI may specify that certain registers be set up
9818      * in special ways (on i386 %edx is the address of a
9819      * DT_FINI function, for example.  This macro performs
9820      * whatever initialization to the regs structure is
9821      * required.  */
9822     ELF_PLAT_INIT(regs);
9823 #endif
9824
9825     start_thread(regs, elf_entry, bprm->p);
9826     if (current->ptrace & PT_PTRACED)
9827       send_sig(SIGTRAP, current, 0);
9828     retval = 0;
9829 out:
9830     return retval;
9831
9832     /* error cleanup */
9833 out_free_dentry:
9834     allow_write_access(interpreter);
9835     fput(interpreter);
9836 out_free_interp:
9837     if (elf_interpreter)
9838       kfree(elf_interpreter);
9839 out_free_file:
9840     sys_close(elf_exec_fileno);
9841 out_free_ph:
9842     kfree(elf_phdata);
9843     goto out;
9844 }
9845
9846 /* This is really simpleminded and specialized - we are
9847  * loading an a.out library that is given an ELF header.
9848  */
9849 static int load_elf_library(struct file *file)
9850 {
9851   struct elf_phdr *elf_phdata;
9852   unsigned long elf_bss = 0, bss, len, k;
9853   int retval, error, i, j;
9854   struct elfhdr elf_ex;
9855
9856   error = -ENOEXEC;
9857   retval = kernel_read(file, 0, (char *) &elf_ex,
9858           sizeof(elf_ex));
9859   if (retval != sizeof(elf_ex))
```

```
9860    goto out;
9861
9862    if (memcmp(elf_ex.e_ident, ELFMAG, SELFMAG) != 0)
9863      goto out;
9864
9865    /* First of all, some simple consistency checks */
9866    if (elf_ex.e_type != ET_EXEC || elf_ex.e_phnum > 2 ||
9867        !elf_check_arch(&elf_ex) || !file->f_op ||
9868        !file->f_op->mmap)
9869      goto out;
9870
9871    /* Now read in all of the header information */
9872
9873    j = sizeof(struct elf_phdr) * elf_ex.e_phnum;
9874    if (j > ELF_MIN_ALIGN)
9875      goto out;
9876
9877    error = -ENOMEM;
9878    elf_phdata =
9879        (struct elf_phdr *) kmalloc(j, GFP_KERNEL);
9880    if (!elf_phdata)
9881      goto out;
9882
9883    /* N.B. check for error return?? */
9884    retval =
9885        kernel_read(file, elf_ex.e_phoff, (char *)elf_phdata,
9886                    sizeof(struct elf_phdr) * elf_ex.e_phnum);
9887
9888    error = -ENOEXEC;
9889    for (j = 0, i = 0; i < elf_ex.e_phnum; i++)
9890      if ((elf_phdata + i)->p_type == PT_LOAD)
9891        j++;
9892    if (j != 1)
9893      goto out_free_ph;
9894
9895    while (elf_phdata->p_type != PT_LOAD)
9896      elf_phdata++;
9897
9898    /* Now use mmap to map the library into memory. */
9899    down(&current->mm->mmap_sem);
9900    error =
9901      do_mmap(file,
9902              ELF_PAGESTART(elf_phdata->p_vaddr),
9903              (elf_phdata->p_filesz +
9904               ELF_PAGEOFFSET(elf_phdata->p_vaddr)),
9905              PROT_READ | PROT_WRITE | PROT_EXEC,
9906              MAP_FIXED | MAP_PRIVATE | MAP_DENYWRITE,
9907              (elf_phdata->p_offset -
9908               ELF_PAGEOFFSET(elf_phdata->p_vaddr)));
9909    up(&current->mm->mmap_sem);
9910    if (error != ELF_PAGESTART(elf_phdata->p_vaddr))
9911      goto out_free_ph;
9912
9913    k = elf_phdata->p_vaddr + elf_phdata->p_filesz;
9914    if (k > elf_bss)
9915      elf_bss = k;
9916    padzero(elf_bss);
9917
9918    len = ELF_PAGESTART(elf_phdata->p_filesz +
9919          elf_phdata->p_vaddr + ELF_MIN_ALIGN - 1);
9920    bss = elf_phdata->p_memsz + elf_phdata->p_vaddr;
9921    if (bss > len)
9922      do_brk(len, bss - len);
9923    error = 0;
9924
9925  out_free_ph:
9926    kfree(elf_phdata);
9927  out:
9928    return error;
9929  }
9930
9931  /* Note that some platforms still use traditional core
9932   * dumps and not the ELF core dump.  Each platform can
9933   * select it as appropriate.  */
9934  #ifdef USE_ELF_CORE_DUMP
9935
9936  /* ELF core dumper
9937   *
9938   * Modelled on fs/exec.c:aout_core_dump()
9939   * Jeremy Fitzhardinge <jeremy@sw.oz.au> */
9940  /* These are the only things you should do on a
9941   * core-file: use only these functions to write out all
9942   * the necessary info.  */
9943  static int dump_write(struct file *file,
9944      const void *addr, int nr)
9945  {
9946    return file->f_op->write(file, addr, nr,
9947                             &file->f_pos) == nr;
9948  }
9949
9950  static int dump_seek(struct file *file, off_t off)
9951  {
9952    if (file->f_op->llseek) {
9953      if (file->f_op->llseek(file, off, 0) != off)
```

```
9954       return 0;                                  10001    sz += roundup(strlen(en->name), 4);
9955   } else                                         10002    sz += roundup(en->datasz, 4);
9956     file->f_pos = off;                            10003
9957   return 1;                                       10004    return sz;
9958 }                                                 10005 }
9959                                                   10006
9960 /* Decide whether a segment is worth dumping; default is    10007 /* #define DEBUG */
9961  * yes to be sure (missing info is worse than too much;     10008
9962  * etc).  Personally I'd include everything, and use the    10009 #ifdef DEBUG
9963  * coredump limit...                              10010 static void dump_regs(const char *str, elf_greg_t * r)
9964  *                                                10011 {
9965  * I think we should skip something. But I am not sure       10012   int i;
9966  * how. H.J.  */                                  10013   static const char *regs[] = {
9967 static inline int maydump(struct vm_area_struct *vma)       10014     "ebx", "ecx", "edx", "esi", "edi", "ebp",
9968 {                                                 10015     "eax", "ds", "es", "fs", "gs",
9969   if (!(vma->vm_flags & (VM_READ | VM_WRITE | VM_EXEC)))     10016     "orig_eax", "eip", "cs",
9970     return 0;                                     10017     "efl", "uesp", "ss"
9971                                                   10018   };
9972   /* Do not dump I/O mapped devices! -DaveM */    10019   printk("Registers: %s\n", str);
9973   if (vma->vm_flags & VM_IO)                       10020
9974     return 0;                                     10021   for (i = 0; i < ELF_NGREG; i++) {
9975 #if 1                                              10022     unsigned long val = r[i];
9976   if (vma->vm_flags &                             10023     printk("  %-2d %-5s=%08lx %lu\n", i, regs[i], val,
9977       (VM_WRITE | VM_GROWSUP | VM_GROWSDOWN))      10024       val);
9978     return 1;                                     10025   }
9979   if (vma->vm_flags &                             10026 }
9980       (VM_READ | VM_EXEC | VM_EXECUTABLE | VM_SHARED))     10027
9981     return 0;                                     10028 #endif
9982 #endif                                             10029
9983   return 1;                                       10030 #define DUMP_WRITE(addr, nr)                         \
9984 }                                                 10031   do {                                               \
9985                                                   10032     if (!dump_write(file, (addr), (nr))) return 0;   \
9986 #define roundup(x, y)  ((((x)+((y)-1))/(y))*(y))   10033   } while(0)
9987                                                   10034 #define DUMP_SEEK(off)                               \
9988 /* An ELF note in memory */                       10035   do {                                               \
9989 struct memelfnote {                               10036     if (!dump_seek(file, (off))) return 0;           \
9990   const char *name;                               10037   } while(0)
9991   int type;                                       10038
9992   unsigned int datasz;                            10039 static int writenote(struct memelfnote *men,
9993   void *data;                                     10040     struct file *file)
9994 };                                                10041 {
9995                                                   10042   struct elf_note en;
9996 static int notesize(struct memelfnote *en)        10043
9997 {                                                 10044   en.n_namesz = strlen(men->name);
9998   int sz;                                          10045   en.n_descsz = men->datasz;
9999                                                   10046   en.n_type = men->type;
10000   sz = sizeof(struct elf_note);                   10047
```

```
10048    DUMP_WRITE(&en, sizeof(en));
10049    DUMP_WRITE(men->name, en.n_namesz);
10050    /* XXX - cast from long long to long to avoid need for
10051     * libgcc.a */
10052    /* XXX */
10053    DUMP_SEEK(roundup((unsigned long) file->f_pos, 4));
10054    DUMP_WRITE(men->data, men->datasz);
10055    /* XXX */
10056    DUMP_SEEK(roundup((unsigned long) file->f_pos, 4));
10057
10058    return 1;
10059 }
10060 #undef DUMP_WRITE
10061 #undef DUMP_SEEK
10062
10063 #define DUMP_WRITE(addr, nr)                              \
10064    if ((size += (nr)) > limit ||                         \
10065        !dump_write(file, (addr), (nr)))                  \
10066        goto end_coredump;
10067 #define DUMP_SEEK(off)                                    \
10068    if (!dump_seek(file, (off)))                          \
10069        goto end_coredump;
10070 /* Actual dumper
10071  *
10072  * This is a two-pass process; first we find the offsets
10073  * of the bits, and then they are actually written out.
10074  * If we run out of core limit we just truncate.   */
10075 static int elf_core_dump(long signr,
10076        struct pt_regs *regs, struct file *file)
10077 {
10078    int has_dumped = 0;
10079    mm_segment_t fs;
10080    int segs;
10081    size_t size = 0;
10082    int i;
10083    struct vm_area_struct *vma;
10084    struct elfhdr elf;
10085    off_t offset = 0, dataoff;
10086    unsigned long limit =
10087        current->rlim[RLIMIT_CORE].rlim_cur;
10088    int numnote = 4;
10089    struct memelfnote notes[4];
10090    struct elf_prstatus prstatus; /* NT_PRSTATUS */
10091    elf_fpregset_t fpu;           /* NT_PRFPREG */
10092    struct elf_prpsinfo psinfo;   /* NT_PRPSINFO */
10093
10094    segs = current->mm->map_count;
```

p 652

```
10095
10096 #ifdef DEBUG
10097    printk("elf_core_dump: %d segs %lu limit\n", segs,
10098        limit);
10099 #endif
10100
10101    /* Set up header */
10102    memcpy(elf.e_ident, ELFMAG, SELFMAG);
10103    elf.e_ident[EI_CLASS] = ELF_CLASS;
10104    elf.e_ident[EI_DATA] = ELF_DATA;
10105    elf.e_ident[EI_VERSION] = EV_CURRENT;
10106    memset(elf.e_ident + EI_PAD, 0, EI_NIDENT - EI_PAD);
10107
10108    elf.e_type = ET_CORE;
10109    elf.e_machine = ELF_ARCH;
10110    elf.e_version = EV_CURRENT;
10111    elf.e_entry = 0;
10112    elf.e_phoff = sizeof(elf);
10113    elf.e_shoff = 0;
10114    elf.e_flags = 0;
10115    elf.e_ehsize = sizeof(elf);
10116    elf.e_phentsize = sizeof(struct elf_phdr);
10117    elf.e_phnum = segs + 1;          /* Include notes */
10118    elf.e_shentsize = 0;
10119    elf.e_shnum = 0;
10120    elf.e_shstrndx = 0;
10121
10122    fs = get_fs();
10123    set_fs(KERNEL_DS);
10124
10125    has_dumped = 1;
10126    current->flags |= PF_DUMPCORE;
10127
10128    DUMP_WRITE(&elf, sizeof(elf));
10129    offset += sizeof(elf);           /* Elf header */
10130    /* Program headers */
10131    offset += (segs + 1) * sizeof(struct elf_phdr);
10132
10133    /* Set up the notes in similar form to SVR4 core dumps
10134     * made with info from their /proc.  */
10135    memset(&psinfo, 0, sizeof(psinfo));
10136    memset(&prstatus, 0, sizeof(prstatus));
10137
10138    notes[0].name = "CORE";
10139    notes[0].type = NT_PRSTATUS;
10140    notes[0].datasz = sizeof(prstatus);
10141    notes[0].data = &prstatus;
```

```
10142    prstatus.pr_info.si_signo = prstatus.pr_cursig = signr;
10143    prstatus.pr_sigpend = current->pending.signal.sig[0];
10144    prstatus.pr_sighold = current->blocked.sig[0];
10145    psinfo.pr_pid = prstatus.pr_pid = current->pid;
10146    psinfo.pr_ppid = prstatus.pr_ppid =
10147        current->p_pptr->pid;
10148    psinfo.pr_pgrp = prstatus.pr_pgrp = current->pgrp;
10149    psinfo.pr_sid = prstatus.pr_sid = current->session;
10150    prstatus.pr_utime.tv_sec =
10151        CT_TO_SECS(current->times.tms_utime);
10152    prstatus.pr_utime.tv_usec =
10153        CT_TO_USECS(current->times.tms_utime);
10154    prstatus.pr_stime.tv_sec =
10155        CT_TO_SECS(current->times.tms_stime);
10156    prstatus.pr_stime.tv_usec =
10157        CT_TO_USECS(current->times.tms_stime);
10158    prstatus.pr_cutime.tv_sec =
10159        CT_TO_SECS(current->times.tms_cutime);
10160    prstatus.pr_cutime.tv_usec =
10161        CT_TO_USECS(current->times.tms_cutime);
10162    prstatus.pr_cstime.tv_sec =
10163        CT_TO_SECS(current->times.tms_cstime);
10164    prstatus.pr_cstime.tv_usec =
10165        CT_TO_USECS(current->times.tms_cstime);
10166
10167    /* This transfers the registers from regs into the
10168     * standard coredump arrangement, whatever that is.  */
10169 #ifdef ELF_CORE_COPY_REGS
10170    ELF_CORE_COPY_REGS(prstatus.pr_reg, regs)
10171 #else
10172    if (sizeof(elf_gregset_t) != sizeof(struct pt_regs)) {
10173      printk("sizeof(elf_gregset_t) (%ld) != "
10174          "sizeof(struct pt_regs) (%ld)\n",
10175          (long) sizeof(elf_gregset_t),
10176          (long) sizeof(struct pt_regs));
10177    } else
10178      *(struct pt_regs *) &prstatus.pr_reg = *regs;
10179 #endif
10180
10181 #ifdef DEBUG
10182    dump_regs("Passed in regs", (elf_greg_t *) regs);
10183    dump_regs("prstatus regs",
10184        (elf_greg_t *) & prstatus.pr_reg);
10185 #endif
10186
10187    notes[1].name = "CORE";
10188    notes[1].type = NT_PRPSINFO;
```

```
10189    notes[1].datasz = sizeof(psinfo);
10190    notes[1].data = &psinfo;
10191    i = current->state ? ffz(~current->state) + 1 : 0;
10192    psinfo.pr_state = i;
10193    psinfo.pr_sname = (i < 0 || i > 5) ? '.' : "RSDZTD"[i];
10194    psinfo.pr_zomb = psinfo.pr_sname == 'Z';
10195    psinfo.pr_nice = current->nice;
10196    psinfo.pr_flag = current->flags;
10197    psinfo.pr_uid = NEW_TO_OLD_UID(current->uid);
10198    psinfo.pr_gid = NEW_TO_OLD_GID(current->gid);
10199    {
10200      int i, len;
10201
10202      set_fs(fs);
10203
10204      len = current->mm->arg_end - current->mm->arg_start;
10205      if (len >= ELF_PRARGSZ)
10206        len = ELF_PRARGSZ - 1;
10207      copy_from_user(&psinfo.pr_psargs,
10208          (const char *) current->mm->arg_start, len);
10209      for (i = 0; i < len; i++)
10210        if (psinfo.pr_psargs[i] == 0)
10211          psinfo.pr_psargs[i] = ' ';
10212      psinfo.pr_psargs[len] = 0;
10213
10214      set_fs(KERNEL_DS);
10215    }
10216    strncpy(psinfo.pr_fname, current->comm,
10217        sizeof(psinfo.pr_fname));
10218
10219    notes[2].name = "CORE";
10220    notes[2].type = NT_TASKSTRUCT;
10221    notes[2].datasz = sizeof(*current);
10222    notes[2].data = current;
10223
10224    /* Try to dump the FPU. */
10225    prstatus.pr_fpvalid = dump_fpu(regs, &fpu);
10226    if (!prstatus.pr_fpvalid) {
10227      numnote--;
10228    } else {
10229      notes[3].name = "CORE";
10230      notes[3].type = NT_PRFPREG;
10231      notes[3].datasz = sizeof(fpu);
10232      notes[3].data = &fpu;
10233    }
10234
10235    /* Write notes phdr entry */
```

```
10236   {
10237     struct elf_phdr phdr;
10238     int sz = 0;
10239
10240     for (i = 0; i < numnote; i++)
10241       sz += notesize(&notes[i]);
10242
10243     phdr.p_type = PT_NOTE;
10244     phdr.p_offset = offset;
10245     phdr.p_vaddr = 0;
10246     phdr.p_paddr = 0;
10247     phdr.p_filesz = sz;
10248     phdr.p_memsz = 0;
10249     phdr.p_flags = 0;
10250     phdr.p_align = 0;
10251
10252     offset += phdr.p_filesz;
10253     DUMP_WRITE(&phdr, sizeof(phdr));
10254   }
10255
10256   /* Page-align dumped data */
10257   dataoff = offset = roundup(offset, ELF_EXEC_PAGESIZE);
10258
10259   /* Write program headers for segments dump */
10260   for (vma = current->mm->mmap; vma != NULL;
10261       vma = vma->vm_next) {
10262     struct elf_phdr phdr;
10263     size_t sz;
10264
10265     sz = vma->vm_end - vma->vm_start;
10266
10267     phdr.p_type = PT_LOAD;
10268     phdr.p_offset = offset;
10269     phdr.p_vaddr = vma->vm_start;
10270     phdr.p_paddr = 0;
10271     phdr.p_filesz = maydump(vma) ? sz : 0;
10272     phdr.p_memsz = sz;
10273     offset += phdr.p_filesz;
10274     phdr.p_flags = vma->vm_flags & VM_READ ? PF_R : 0;
10275     if (vma->vm_flags & VM_WRITE)
10276       phdr.p_flags |= PF_W;
10277     if (vma->vm_flags & VM_EXEC)
10278       phdr.p_flags |= PF_X;
10279     phdr.p_align = ELF_EXEC_PAGESIZE;
10280
10281     DUMP_WRITE(&phdr, sizeof(phdr));
10282   }

10283
10284   for (i = 0; i < numnote; i++)
10285     if (!writenote(&notes[i], file))
10286       goto end_coredump;
10287
10288   set_fs(fs);
10289
10290   DUMP_SEEK(dataoff);
10291
10292   for (vma = current->mm->mmap; vma != NULL;
10293       vma = vma->vm_next) {
10294     unsigned long addr;
10295
10296     if (!maydump(vma))
10297       continue;
10298 #ifdef DEBUG
10299     printk("elf_core_dump: writing %08lx %lx\n", addr,
10300         len);
10301 #endif
10302     for (addr = vma->vm_start;
10303         addr < vma->vm_end; addr += PAGE_SIZE) {
10304       pgd_t *pgd;
10305       pmd_t *pmd;
10306       pte_t *pte;
10307
10308       pgd = pgd_offset(vma->vm_mm, addr);
10309       pmd = pmd_alloc(pgd, addr);
10310
10311       if (!pmd)
10312         goto end_coredump;
10313       pte = pte_alloc(pmd, addr);
10314       if (!pte)
10315         goto end_coredump;
10316       if (!pte_present(*pte) && pte_none(*pte)) {
10317         DUMP_SEEK(file->f_pos + PAGE_SIZE);
10318       } else {
10319         DUMP_WRITE((void *) addr, PAGE_SIZE);
10320       }
10321     }
10322   }
10323
10324   if ((off_t) file->f_pos != offset) {
10325     /* Sanity check */
10326     printk("elf_core_dump: file->f_pos (%ld) != "
10327         "offset (%ld)\n", (off_t)file->f_pos, offset);
10328   }
10329
```

```
10330 end_coredump:
10331   set_fs(fs);
10332   return has_dumped;
10333 }
10334 #endif                        /* USE_ELF_CORE_DUMP */
10335
10336 static int __init init_elf_binfmt(void)
10337 {
10338   return register_binfmt(&elf_format);
10339 }
10340
10341 static void __exit exit_elf_binfmt(void)
10342 {
10343   /* Remove the COFF and ELF loaders. */
10344   unregister_binfmt(&elf_format);
10345 }
10346
10347 module_init(init_elf_binfmt)
10348 module_exit(exit_elf_binfmt)
```

fs/binfmt_misc.c

```
10349 /*
10350  *  binfmt_misc.c
10351  *
10352  *  Copyright (C) 1997 Richard Günther
10353  *
10354  *  binfmt_misc detects binaries via a magic or filename
10355  *  extension and invokes a specified wrapper. This
10356  *  should obsolete binfmt_java, binfmt_em86 and
10357  *  binfmt_mz.
10358  *
10359  *  1997-04-25 first version
10360  *  [...]
10361  *  1997-05-19 cleanup
10362  *  1997-06-26 hpa: pass the real filename rather than
10363  *                  argv[0]
10364  *  1997-06-30 minor cleanup
10365  *  1997-08-09 removed extension stripping, locking
10366  *                  cleanup
10367  */
10368
10369 #include <linux/config.h>
10370 #include <linux/module.h>
10371
10372 #include <linux/kernel.h>
10373 #include <linux/errno.h>
10374 #include <linux/fs.h>
10375 #include <linux/malloc.h>
10376 #include <linux/binfmts.h>
10377 #include <linux/init.h>
10378 #include <linux/proc_fs.h>
10379 #include <linux/string.h>
10380 #include <linux/ctype.h>
10381 #include <linux/file.h>
10382 #include <linux/spinlock.h>
10383 #include <asm/uaccess.h>
10384
10385 /* We should make this work with a "stub-only" /proc,
10386  * which would just not be able to be configured.  Right
10387  * now the /proc-fs support is too black and white,
10388  * though, so just remind people that this should be
10389  * fixed..   */
10390 #ifndef CONFIG_PROC_FS
10391 #error You really need /proc support for binfmt_misc.   \
10392   Please reconfigure!
10393 #endif
10394
10395 #define VERBOSE_STATUS    /* undef this to save 400 bytes
10396                            * kernel memory */
10397
10398 struct binfmt_entry {
10399   struct binfmt_entry *next;
10400   long id;
10401   int flags;                /* type, status, etc. */
10402   int offset;               /* offset of magic */
10403   int size;                 /* size of magic/mask */
10404   char *magic;              /* magic or filename extension*/
10405   char *mask;               /* mask, NULL for exact match */
10406   char *interpreter;        /* filename of interpreter */
10407   char *proc_name;
10408   struct proc_dir_entry *proc_dir;
10409 };
10410
10411 #define ENTRY_ENABLED 1   /*the old binfmt_entry.enabled*/
10412 #define ENTRY_MAGIC 8     /* not filename detection */
10413
10414 static int load_misc_binary(struct linux_binprm *bprm,
10415     struct pt_regs *regs);
10416 static void entry_proc_cleanup(struct binfmt_entry *e);
10417 static int entry_proc_setup(struct binfmt_entry *e);
10418
10419 static struct linux_binfmt misc_format = {
10420   NULL, THIS_MODULE, load_misc_binary, NULL, NULL, 0
10421 };
```

p 606

```
10422
10423 static struct proc_dir_entry *bm_dir;
10424
10425 static struct binfmt_entry *entries;
10426 static int free_id = 1;
10427 static int enabled = 1;
10428
10429 static rwlock_t entries_lock __attribute__ ((unused)) =
10430     RW_LOCK_UNLOCKED;
10431
10432
10433 /* Unregister one entry */
10434 static void clear_entry(int id)
10435 {
10436     struct binfmt_entry **ep, *e;
10437
10438     write_lock(&entries_lock);
10439     ep = &entries;
10440     while (*ep && ((*ep)->id != id))
10441         ep = &((*ep)->next);
10442     if ((e = *ep))
10443         *ep = e->next;
10444     write_unlock(&entries_lock);
10445
10446     if (e) {
10447         entry_proc_cleanup(e);
10448         kfree(e);
10449     }
10450 }
10451
10452 /* Clear all registered binary formats */
10453 static void clear_entries(void)
10454 {
10455     struct binfmt_entry *e, *n;
10456
10457     write_lock(&entries_lock);
10458     n = entries;
10459     entries = NULL;
10460     write_unlock(&entries_lock);
10461
10462     while ((e = n)) {
10463         n = e->next;
10464         entry_proc_cleanup(e);
10465         kfree(e);
10466     }
10467 }
10468
10469 /* Find entry through id and lock it */
10470 static struct binfmt_entry *get_entry(int id)
10471 {
10472     struct binfmt_entry *e;
10473
10474     read_lock(&entries_lock);
10475     e = entries;
10476     while (e && (e->id != id))
10477         e = e->next;
10478     if (!e)
10479         read_unlock(&entries_lock);
10480     return e;
10481 }
10482
10483 /* unlock entry */
10484 static inline void put_entry(struct binfmt_entry *e)
10485 {
10486     if (e)
10487         read_unlock(&entries_lock);
10488 }
10489
10490
10491 /* Check if we support the binfmt
10492  * if we do, return the binfmt_entry, else NULL locking
10493  * is done in load_misc_binary */
10494 static struct binfmt_entry *check_file(struct
10495     linux_binprm *bprm)
10496 {
10497     struct binfmt_entry *e;
10498     char *p = strrchr(bprm->filename, '.');
10499     int j;
10500
10501     e = entries;
10502     while (e) {
10503         if (e->flags & ENTRY_ENABLED) {
10504             if (!(e->flags & ENTRY_MAGIC)) {
10505                 if (p && !strcmp(e->magic, p + 1))
10506                     return e;
10507             } else {
10508                 j = 0;
10509                 while ((j < e->size) &&
10510                     !((bprm->buf[e->offset + j] ^ e->magic[j])
10511                         & (e->mask ? e->mask[j] : 0xff)))
10512                     j++;
10513                 if (j == e->size)
10514                     return e;
10515             }
```

p 606

```
10516    }
10517    e = e->next;
10518  };
10519  return NULL;
10520 }
10521
10522 /* the loader itself */
10523 static int load_misc_binary(struct linux_binprm *bprm,
10524    struct pt_regs *regs)
10525 {
10526   struct binfmt_entry *fmt;
10527   struct file *file;
10528   char iname[BINPRM_BUF_SIZE];
10529   char *iname_addr = iname;
10530   int retval;
10531
10532   retval = -ENOEXEC;
10533   if (!enabled)
10534     goto _ret;
10535
10536   /* to keep locking time low, we copy the interpreter
10537    * string */
10538   read_lock(&entries_lock);
10539   fmt = check_file(bprm);
10540   if (fmt) {
10541     strncpy(iname, fmt->interpreter,
10542       BINPRM_BUF_SIZE - 1);
10543     iname[BINPRM_BUF_SIZE - 1] = '\0';
10544   }
10545   read_unlock(&entries_lock);
10546   if (!fmt)
10547     goto _ret;
10548
10549   allow_write_access(bprm->file);
10550   fput(bprm->file);
10551   bprm->file = NULL;
10552
10553   /* Build args for interpreter */
10554   remove_arg_zero(bprm);
10555   retval = copy_strings_kernel(1, &bprm->filename, bprm);
10556   if (retval < 0)
10557     goto _ret;
10558   bprm->argc++;
10559   retval = copy_strings_kernel(1, &iname_addr, bprm);
10560   if (retval < 0)
10561     goto _ret;
10562   bprm->argc++;
10563   bprm->filename = iname;      /* for binfmt_script */
10564
10565   file = open_exec(iname);
10566   retval = PTR_ERR(file);
10567   if (IS_ERR(file))
10568     goto _ret;
10569   bprm->file = file;
10570
10571   retval = prepare_binprm(bprm);
10572   if (retval >= 0)
10573     retval = search_binary_handler(bprm, regs);
10574 _ret:
10575   return retval;
10576 }
10577
10578
10579
10580 /* /proc handling routines */
10581
10582 /* parses and copies one argument enclosed in del from
10583  * *sp to *dp, recognising the \x special.  returns
10584  * pointer to the copied argument or NULL in case of an
10585  * error (and sets err) or null argument length.  */
10586 static char *copyarg(char **dp, const char **sp,
10587    int *count, char del, int special, int *err)
10588 {
10589   char c = 0, *res = *dp;
10590
10591   while (!*err && ((c = *((*sp)++)), (*count)-)
10592     && (c != del)) {
10593     switch (c) {
10594     case '\\':
10595       if (special && (**sp == 'x')) {
10596         if (!isxdigit(c = toupper(*(++*sp))))
10597           *err = -EINVAL;
10598         **dp = (c - (isdigit(c) ? '0' : 'A' - 10)) * 16;
10599         if (!isxdigit(c = toupper(*(++*sp))))
10600           *err = -EINVAL;
10601         *((*dp)++) += c - (isdigit(c) ? '0' : 'A' - 10);
10602         ++*sp;
10603         *count -= 3;
10604         break;
10605       }
10606     default:
10607       *((*dp)++) = c;
10608     }
10609   }
```

```
10610    if (*err || (c != del) || (res == *dp))
10611      res = NULL;
10612    else if (!special)
10613      *((*dp)++) = '\0';
10614    return res;
10615 }
10616
10617 /* This registers a new binary format, it recognises the
10618  * syntax ':name:type:offset:magic:mask:interpreter:'
10619  * where the ':' is the IFS, that can be chosen with the
10620  * first char */
10621 static int proc_write_register(struct file *file,
10622      const char *buffer, unsigned long count, void *data)
10623 {
10624    const char *sp;
10625    char del, *dp;
10626    struct binfmt_entry *e;
10627    int memsize, cnt = count - 1, err;
10628
10629    /* some sanity checks */
10630    err = -EINVAL;
10631    if ((count < 11) || (count > 256))
10632      goto _err;
10633
10634    err = -ENOMEM;
10635    memsize = sizeof(struct binfmt_entry) + count;
10636    if (!(e = (struct binfmt_entry *) kmalloc(memsize,
10637                                    GFP_USER)))
10638      goto _err;
10639
10640    err = 0;
10641    sp = buffer + 1;
10642    del = buffer[0];
10643    dp = (char *) e + sizeof(struct binfmt_entry);
10644
10645    e->proc_name = copyarg(&dp, &sp, &cnt, del, 0, &err);
10646
10647    /* we can use bit 3 of type for ext/magic flag due to
10648     * the nice encoding of E and M */
10649    if ((*sp & ~('E' | 'M')) || (sp[1] != del))
10650      err = -EINVAL;
10651    else
10652      e->flags = (*sp++ & (ENTRY_MAGIC | ENTRY_ENABLED));
10653    cnt -= 2;
10654    sp++;
10655
10656    e->offset = 0;
```

```
10657    while (cnt- && isdigit(*sp))
10658      e->offset = e->offset * 10 + *sp++ - '0';
10659    if (*sp++ != del)
10660      err = -EINVAL;
10661
10662    e->magic = copyarg(&dp, &sp, &cnt, del,
10663                     (e->flags & ENTRY_MAGIC), &err);
10664    e->size = dp - e->magic;
10665    e->mask = copyarg(&dp, &sp, &cnt, del, 1, &err);
10666    if (e->mask && ((dp - e->mask) != e->size))
10667      err = -EINVAL;
10668    e->interpreter = copyarg(&dp, &sp, &cnt, del, 0, &err);
10669    e->id = free_id++;
10670
10671    /* more sanity checks */
10672    if (err || !(!cnt || (!(-cnt) && (*sp == '\n'))) ||
10673        (e->size < 1)
10674        || ((e->size + e->offset) > (BINPRM_BUF_SIZE - 1))
10675        || !(e->proc_name) || !(e->interpreter)
10676        || entry_proc_setup(e))
10677      goto free_err;
10678
10679    write_lock(&entries_lock);
10680    e->next = entries;
10681    entries = e;
10682    write_unlock(&entries_lock);
10683
10684    err = count;
10685 _err:
10686    return err;
10687 free_err:
10688    kfree(e);
10689    err = -EINVAL;
10690    goto _err;
10691 }
10692
10693 /* Get status of entry/binfmt_misc
10694  * FIXME? should an entry be marked disabled if
10695  * binfmt_misc is disabled though entry is enabled? */
10696 static int proc_read_status(char *page, char **start,
10697      off_t off, int count, int *eof, void *data)
10698 {
10699    struct binfmt_entry *e;
10700    char *dp;
10701    int elen, i, err;
10702
10703 #ifndef VERBOSE_STATUS
```

```
10704    if (data) {
10705     if (!(e = get_entry((int) data))) {
10706      err = -ENOENT;
10707      goto _err;
10708     }
10709     i = e->flags & ENTRY_ENABLED;
10710     put_entry(e);
10711    } else {
10712     i = enabled;
10713    }
10714    sprintf(page, "%s\n", (i ? "enabled" : "disabled"));
10715 #else
10716    if (!data)
10717     sprintf(page, "%s\n",
10718            (enabled ? "enabled" : "disabled"));
10719    else {
10720     if (!(e = get_entry((long) data))) {
10721      err = -ENOENT;
10722      goto _err;
10723     }
10724     sprintf(page, "%s\ninterpreter %s\n",
10725            (e->flags & ENTRY_ENABLED
10726            ? "enabled" : "disabled"),
10727            e->interpreter);
10728     dp = page + strlen(page);
10729     if (!(e->flags & ENTRY_MAGIC)) {
10730      sprintf(dp, "extension .%s\n", e->magic);
10731      dp = page + strlen(page);
10732     } else {
10733      sprintf(dp, "offset %i\nmagic ", e->offset);
10734      dp = page + strlen(page);
10735      for (i = 0; i < e->size; i++) {
10736       sprintf(dp, "%02x", 0xff & (int) (e->magic[i]));
10737       dp += 2;
10738      }
10739      if (e->mask) {
10740       sprintf(dp, "\nmask ");
10741       dp += 6;
10742       for (i = 0; i < e->size; i++) {
10743        sprintf(dp, "%02x", 0xff & (int) (e->mask[i]));
10744        dp += 2;
10745       }
10746      }
10747      *dp++ = '\n';
10748      *dp = '\0';
10749     }
10750     put_entry(e);
10751    }
10752 #endif
10753
10754    elen = strlen(page) - off;
10755    if (elen < 0)
10756     elen = 0;
10757    *eof = (elen <= count) ? 1 : 0;
10758    *start = page + off;
10759    err = elen;
10760
10761 _err:
10762    return err;
10763 }
10764
10765 /* Set status of entry/binfmt_misc: '1' enables, '0'
10766  * disables and '-1' clears entry/binfmt_misc */
10767 static int proc_write_status(struct file *file,
10768     const char *buffer, unsigned long count, void *data)
10769 {
10770    struct binfmt_entry *e;
10771    int res = count;
10772
10773    if (buffer[count - 1] == '\n')
10774     count--;
10775    if ((count == 1) && !(buffer[0] & ~('0' | '1'))) {
10776     if (data) {
10777      if ((e = get_entry((long) data)))
10778       e->flags = (e->flags & ~ENTRY_ENABLED)
10779             | (int) (buffer[0] - '0');
10780      put_entry(e);
10781     } else {
10782      enabled = buffer[0] - '0';
10783     }
10784    } else if ((count == 2) && (buffer[0] == '-')
10785             && (buffer[1] == '1')) {
10786     if (data)
10787      clear_entry((long) data);
10788     else
10789      clear_entries();
10790    } else {
10791     res = -EINVAL;
10792    }
10793    return res;
10794 }
10795
10796 /* Remove the /proc-dir entries of one binfmt */
10797 static void entry_proc_cleanup(struct binfmt_entry *e)
```

```
10798 {
10799    remove_proc_entry(e->proc_name, bm_dir);
10800 }
10801
10802 /* Create the /proc-dir entry for binfmt */
10803 static int entry_proc_setup(struct binfmt_entry *e)
10804 {
10805    if (!(e->proc_dir = create_proc_entry(e->proc_name,
10806             S_IFREG | S_IRUGO | S_IWUSR, bm_dir))) {
10807       printk(KERN_WARNING
10808          "Unable to create /proc entry.\n");
10809       return -ENOENT;
10810    }
10811    e->proc_dir->data = (void *) (e->id);
10812    e->proc_dir->read_proc = proc_read_status;
10813    e->proc_dir->write_proc = proc_write_status;
10814    return 0;
10815 }
10816
10817 static int __init init_misc_binfmt(void)
10818 {
10819    int error = -ENOENT;
10820    struct proc_dir_entry *status = NULL, *reg;
10821
10822    /* WTF??? */
10823    bm_dir = proc_mkdir("sys/fs/binfmt_misc", NULL);
10824    if (!bm_dir)
10825       goto out;
10826    bm_dir->owner = THIS_MODULE;
10827
10828    status = create_proc_entry("status",
10829                      S_IFREG | S_IRUGO | S_IWUSR,
10830                      bm_dir);
10831    if (!status)
10832       goto cleanup_bm;
10833    status->read_proc = proc_read_status;
10834    status->write_proc = proc_write_status;
10835
10836    reg = create_proc_entry("register", S_IFREG | S_IWUSR,
10837                      bm_dir);
10838    if (!reg)
10839       goto cleanup_status;
10840    reg->write_proc = proc_write_register;
10841
10842    error = register_binfmt(&misc_format);
10843 out:
10844    return error;
```

```
10845
10846 cleanup_status:
10847    remove_proc_entry("status", bm_dir);
10848 cleanup_bm:
10849    remove_proc_entry("sys/fs/binfmt_misc", NULL);
10850    goto out;
10851 }
10852
10853 static void __exit exit_misc_binfmt(void)
10854 {
10855    unregister_binfmt(&misc_format);
10856    remove_proc_entry("register", bm_dir);
10857    remove_proc_entry("status", bm_dir);
10858    clear_entries();
10859    remove_proc_entry("sys/fs/binfmt_misc", NULL);
10860 }
10861
10862 EXPORT_NO_SYMBOLS;
10863
10864 module_init(init_misc_binfmt);
10865 module_exit(exit_misc_binfmt);
```

fs/binfmt_script.c

```
10866 /*
10867  *  linux/fs/binfmt_script.c
10868  *
10869  *  Copyright (C) 1996  Martin von Löwis
10870  *  original #!-checking implemented by tytso.
10871  */
10872
10873 #include <linux/module.h>
10874 #include <linux/string.h>
10875 #include <linux/stat.h>
10876 #include <linux/malloc.h>
10877 #include <linux/binfmts.h>
10878 #include <linux/init.h>
10879 #include <linux/file.h>
10880 #include <linux/smp_lock.h>
10881
10882 static int load_script(struct linux_binprm *bprm,
10883       struct pt_regs *regs)
10884 {
10885    char *cp, *i_name, *i_arg;
10886    struct file *file;
10887    char interp[BINPRM_BUF_SIZE];
10888    int retval;
10889
```

p 606

```
10890    if ((bprm->buf[0] != '#') || (bprm->buf[1] != '!')
10891        || (bprm->sh_bang))
10892      return -ENOEXEC;
10893    /* This section does the #! interpretation.  Sorta
10894     * complicated, but hopefully it will work.  -TYT */
10895
10896    bprm->sh_bang++;
10897    allow_write_access(bprm->file);
10898    fput(bprm->file);
10899    bprm->file = NULL;
10900
10901    bprm->buf[BINPRM_BUF_SIZE - 1] = '\0';
10902    if ((cp = strchr(bprm->buf, '\n')) == NULL)
10903      cp = bprm->buf + BINPRM_BUF_SIZE - 1;
10904    *cp = '\0';
10905    while (cp > bprm->buf) {
10906      cp--;
10907      if ((*cp == ' ') || (*cp == '\t'))
10908        *cp = '\0';
10909      else
10910        break;
10911    }
10912    for (cp = bprm->buf + 2; (*cp == ' ') || (*cp == '\t');
10913        cp++) ;
10914    if (*cp == '\0')
10915      return -ENOEXEC;        /* No interpreter name found */
10916    i_name = cp;
10917    i_arg = 0;
10918    for (; *cp && (*cp != ' ') && (*cp != '\t'); cp++)
10919      /* nothing */ ;
10920    while ((*cp == ' ') || (*cp == '\t'))
10921      *cp++ = '\0';
10922    if (*cp)
10923      i_arg = cp;
10924    strcpy(interp, i_name);
10925    /* OK, we've parsed out the interpreter name and
10926     * (optional) argument.
10927     * Splice in (1) the interpreter's name for argv[0]
10928     *           (2) (optional) argument to interpreter
10929     *           (3) filename of shell script (replace
10930     *                   argv[0])
10931     *
10932     * This is done in reverse order, because of how the
10933     * user environment and arguments are stored.  */
10934    remove_arg_zero(bprm);
10935    retval = copy_strings_kernel(1, &bprm->filename, bprm);
10936    if (retval < 0)
10937      return retval;
10938    bprm->argc++;
10939    if (i_arg) {
10940      retval = copy_strings_kernel(1, &i_arg, bprm);
10941      if (retval < 0)
10942        return retval;
10943      bprm->argc++;
10944    }
10945    retval = copy_strings_kernel(1, &i_name, bprm);
10946    if (retval)
10947      return retval;
10948    bprm->argc++;
10949    /* OK, now restart the process with the interpreter's
10950     * dentry.  */
10951    file = open_exec(interp);
10952    if (IS_ERR(file))
10953      return PTR_ERR(file);
10954
10955    bprm->file = file;
10956    retval = prepare_binprm(bprm);
10957    if (retval < 0)
10958      return retval;
10959    return search_binary_handler(bprm, regs);
10960 }
10961
10962 struct linux_binfmt script_format = {
10963    NULL, THIS_MODULE, load_script, NULL, NULL, 0
10964 };
10965
10966 static int __init init_script_binfmt(void)
10967 {
10968    return register_binfmt(&script_format);
10969 }
10970
10971 static void __exit exit_script_binfmt(void)
10972 {
10973    unregister_binfmt(&script_format);
10974 }
10975
10976 module_init(init_script_binfmt)
10977 module_exit(exit_script_binfmt)
```

fs/exec.c

```
10978 /*
10979  *  linux/fs/exec.c
10980  *
10981  *  Copyright (C) 1991, 1992  Linus Torvalds
```

```
10982  */
10983
10984  /* #!-checking implemented by tytso. */
10985  /* Demand-loading implemented 01.12.91 - no need to read
10986   * anything but the header into memory. The inode of the
10987   * executable is put into "current->executable", and page
10988   * faults do the actual loading. Clean.
10989   *
10990   * Once more I can proudly say that linux stood up to
10991   * being changed: it was less than 2 hours work to get
10992   * demand-loading completely implemented.
10993   *
10994   * Demand loading changed July 1993 by Eric Youngdale.
10995   * Use mmap instead, current->executable is only used by
10996   * the procfs.  This allows a dispatch table to check for
10997   * several different types of binary formats.  We keep
10998   * trying until we recognize the file or we run out of
10999   * supported binary formats.  */
11000
11001  #include <linux/config.h>
11002  #include <linux/slab.h>
11003  #include <linux/file.h>
11004  #include <linux/mman.h>
11005  #include <linux/a.out.h>
11006  #include <linux/stat.h>
11007  #include <linux/fcntl.h>
11008  #include <linux/smp_lock.h>
11009  #include <linux/init.h>
11010  #include <linux/pagemap.h>
11011  #include <linux/highmem.h>
11012  #include <linux/spinlock.h>
11013  #define __NO_VERSION__
11014  #include <linux/module.h>
11015
11016  #include <asm/uaccess.h>
11017  #include <asm/pgalloc.h>
11018  #include <asm/mmu_context.h>
11019
11020  #ifdef CONFIG_KMOD
11021  #include <linux/kmod.h>
11022  #endif
11023
11024  static struct linux_binfmt *formats;
11025  static rwlock_t binfmt_lock = RW_LOCK_UNLOCKED;
11026
11027  int register_binfmt(struct linux_binfmt *fmt)
11028  {
11029    struct linux_binfmt **tmp = &formats;
11030
11031    if (!fmt)
11032      return -EINVAL;
11033    if (fmt->next)
11034      return -EBUSY;
11035    write_lock(&binfmt_lock);
11036    while (*tmp) {
11037      if (fmt == *tmp) {
11038        write_unlock(&binfmt_lock);
11039        return -EBUSY;
11040      }
11041      tmp = &(*tmp)->next;
11042    }
11043    fmt->next = formats;
11044    formats = fmt;
11045    write_unlock(&binfmt_lock);
11046    return 0;
11047  }
11048
11049  int unregister_binfmt(struct linux_binfmt *fmt)
11050  {
11051    struct linux_binfmt **tmp = &formats;
11052
11053    write_lock(&binfmt_lock);
11054    while (*tmp) {
11055      if (fmt == *tmp) {
11056        *tmp = fmt->next;
11057        write_unlock(&binfmt_lock);
11058        return 0;
11059      }
11060      tmp = &(*tmp)->next;
11061    }
11062    write_unlock(&binfmt_lock);
11063    return -EINVAL;
11064  }
11065
11066  static inline void put_binfmt(struct linux_binfmt *fmt)
11067  {
11068    if (fmt->module)
11069      __MOD_DEC_USE_COUNT(fmt->module);
11070  }
11071
11072  /* Note that a shared library must be both readable and
11073   * executable due to security reasons.
11074   *
11075   * Also note that we take the address to load from from
```

```
11076  * the file itself.  */
11077 asmlinkage long sys_uselib(const char *library)
11078 {
11079   struct file *file;
11080   struct nameidata nd;
11081   int error;
11082
11083   error = user_path_walk(library, &nd);
11084   if (error)
11085     goto out;
11086
11087   error = -EINVAL;
11088   if (!S_ISREG(nd.dentry->d_inode->i_mode))
11089     goto exit;
11090
11091   error = permission(nd.dentry->d_inode,
11092                      MAY_READ | MAY_EXEC);
11093   if (error)
11094     goto exit;
11095
11096   file = dentry_open(nd.dentry, nd.mnt, O_RDONLY);
11097   error = PTR_ERR(file);
11098   if (IS_ERR(file))
11099     goto out;
11100
11101   error = -ENOEXEC;
11102   if (file->f_op && file->f_op->read) {
11103     struct linux_binfmt *fmt;
11104
11105     read_lock(&binfmt_lock);
11106     for (fmt = formats; fmt; fmt = fmt->next) {
11107       if (!fmt->load_shlib)
11108         continue;
11109       if (!try_inc_mod_count(fmt->module))
11110         continue;
11111       read_unlock(&binfmt_lock);
11112       error = fmt->load_shlib(file);
11113       read_lock(&binfmt_lock);
11114       put_binfmt(fmt);
11115       if (error != -ENOEXEC)
11116         break;
11117     }
11118     read_unlock(&binfmt_lock);
11119   }
11120   fput(file);
11121 out:
11122   return error;
```

```
11123 exit:
11124   path_release(&nd);
11125   goto out;
11126 }
11127
11128 /* count() counts the number of arguments/envelopes */
11129 static int count(char **argv, int max)
11130 {
11131   int i = 0;
11132
11133   if (argv != NULL) {
11134     for (;;) {
11135       char *p;
11136       int error;
11137
11138       error = get_user(p, argv);
11139       if (error)
11140         return error;
11141       if (!p)
11142         break;
11143       argv++;
11144       if (++i > max)
11145         return -E2BIG;
11146     }
11147   }
11148   return i;
11149 }
11150
11151 /* 'copy_strings()' copies argument/envelope strings from
11152  * user memory to free pages in kernel mem. These are in
11153  * a format ready to be put directly into the top of new
11154  * user memory.  */
11155 int copy_strings(int argc, char **argv,
11156     struct linux_binprm *bprm)
11157 {
11158   while (argc- > 0) {
11159     char *str;
11160     int len;
11161     unsigned long pos;
11162
11163     if (get_user(str, argv + argc) || !str
11164         || !(len = strnlen_user(str, bprm->p)))
11165       return -EFAULT;
11166     if (bprm->p < len)
11167       return -E2BIG;
11168
11169     bprm->p -= len;
```

```
11170      /* XXX: add architecture specific overflow check
11171       * here. */
11172
11173      pos = bprm->p;
11174      while (len > 0) {
11175        char *kaddr;
11176        int i, new, err;
11177        struct page *page;
11178        int offset, bytes_to_copy;
11179
11180        offset = pos % PAGE_SIZE;
11181        i = pos / PAGE_SIZE;
11182        page = bprm->page[i];
11183        new = 0;
11184        if (!page) {
11185          page = alloc_page(GFP_HIGHUSER);
11186          bprm->page[i] = page;
11187          if (!page)
11188            return -ENOMEM;
11189          new = 1;
11190        }
11191        kaddr = kmap(page);
11192
11193        if (new && offset)
11194          memset(kaddr, 0, offset);
11195        bytes_to_copy = PAGE_SIZE - offset;
11196        if (bytes_to_copy > len) {
11197          bytes_to_copy = len;
11198          if (new)
11199            memset(kaddr + offset + len, 0,
11200                PAGE_SIZE - offset - len);
11201        }
11202        err = copy_from_user(kaddr + offset, str,
11203                            bytes_to_copy);
11204        kunmap(page);
11205
11206        if (err)
11207          return -EFAULT;
11208
11209        pos += bytes_to_copy;
11210        str += bytes_to_copy;
11211        len -= bytes_to_copy;
11212      }
11213    }
11214    return 0;
11215  }
11216
```

```
11217  /* Like copy_strings, but get argv and its values from
11218   * kernel memory.  */
11219  int copy_strings_kernel(int argc, char **argv,
11220      struct linux_binprm *bprm)
11221  {
11222    int r;
11223    mm_segment_t oldfs = get_fs();
11224    set_fs(KERNEL_DS);
11225    r = copy_strings(argc, argv, bprm);
11226    set_fs(oldfs);
11227    return r;
11228  }
11229
11230  /* This routine is used to map in a page into an address
11231   * space: needed by execve() for the initial stack and
11232   * environment pages.  */
11233  void put_dirty_page(struct task_struct *tsk,
11234      struct page *page, unsigned long address)
11235  {
11236    pgd_t *pgd;
11237    pmd_t *pmd;
11238    pte_t *pte;
11239
11240    if (page_count(page) != 1)
11241      printk("mem_map disagrees with %p at %08lx\n", page,
11242          address);
11243    pgd = pgd_offset(tsk->mm, address);
11244    pmd = pmd_alloc(pgd, address);
11245    if (!pmd) {
11246      __free_page(page);
11247      force_sig(SIGKILL, tsk);
11248      return;
11249    }
11250    pte = pte_alloc(pmd, address);
11251    if (!pte) {
11252      __free_page(page);
11253      force_sig(SIGKILL, tsk);
11254      return;
11255    }
11256    if (!pte_none(*pte)) {
11257      pte_ERROR(*pte);
11258      __free_page(page);
11259      return;
11260    }
11261    flush_dcache_page(page);
11262    flush_page_to_ram(page);
11263    set_pte(pte, pte_mkdirty(pte_mkwrite(mk_pte(page,
```

```
11264                     PAGE_COPY)))) ;
11265   /* no need for flush_tlb */
11266 }
11267
11268 int setup_arg_pages(struct linux_binprm *bprm)
11269 {
11270   unsigned long stack_base;
11271   struct vm_area_struct *mpnt;
11272   int i;
11273
11274   stack_base = STACK_TOP - MAX_ARG_PAGES * PAGE_SIZE;
11275
11276   bprm->p += stack_base;
11277   if (bprm->loader)
11278     bprm->loader += stack_base;
11279   bprm->exec += stack_base;
11280
11281   mpnt = kmem_cache_alloc(vm_area_cachep, SLAB_KERNEL);
11282   if (!mpnt)
11283     return -ENOMEM;
11284
11285   down(&current->mm->mmap_sem);
11286   {
11287     mpnt->vm_mm = current->mm;
11288     mpnt->vm_start = PAGE_MASK & (unsigned long) bprm->p;
11289     mpnt->vm_end = STACK_TOP;
11290     mpnt->vm_page_prot = PAGE_COPY;
11291     mpnt->vm_flags = VM_STACK_FLAGS;
11292     mpnt->vm_ops = NULL;
11293     mpnt->vm_pgoff = 0;
11294     mpnt->vm_file = NULL;
11295     mpnt->vm_private_data = (void *) 0;
11296     insert_vm_struct(current->mm, mpnt);
11297     current->mm->total_vm =
11298         (mpnt->vm_end - mpnt->vm_start) >> PAGE_SHIFT;
11299   }
11300
11301   for (i = 0; i < MAX_ARG_PAGES; i++) {
11302     struct page *page = bprm->page[i];
11303     if (page) {
11304       bprm->page[i] = NULL;
11305       current->mm->rss++;
11306       put_dirty_page(current, page, stack_base);
11307     }
11308     stack_base += PAGE_SIZE;
11309   }
11310   up(&current->mm->mmap_sem);
11311
11312   return 0;
11313 }
11314
11315 struct file *open_exec(const char *name)
11316 {
11317   struct nameidata nd;
11318   struct inode *inode;
11319   struct file *file;
11320   int err = 0;
11321
11322   if (path_init(name, LOOKUP_FOLLOW | LOOKUP_POSITIVE,
11323                 &nd))
11324     err = path_walk(name, &nd);
11325   file = ERR_PTR(err);
11326   if (!err) {
11327     inode = nd.dentry->d_inode;
11328     file = ERR_PTR(-EACCES);
11329     if (!IS_NOEXEC(inode) && S_ISREG(inode->i_mode)) {
11330       int err = permission(inode, MAY_EXEC);
11331       file = ERR_PTR(err);
11332       if (!err) {
11333         file = dentry_open(nd.dentry, nd.mnt, O_RDONLY);
11334         if (!IS_ERR(file)) {
11335           err = deny_write_access(file);
11336           if (err) {
11337             fput(file);
11338             file = ERR_PTR(err);
11339           }
11340         }
11341       out:
11342         return file;
11343       }
11344     }
11345     path_release(&nd);
11346   }
11347   goto out;
11348 }
11349
11350 int kernel_read(struct file *file, unsigned long offset,
11351     char *addr, unsigned long count)
11352 {
11353   mm_segment_t old_fs;
11354   loff_t pos = offset;
11355   int result = -ENOSYS;
11356
11357   if (!file->f_op->read)
```

```
11358      goto fail;
11359    old_fs = get_fs();
11360    set_fs(get_ds());
11361    result = file->f_op->read(file, addr, count, &pos);
11362    set_fs(old_fs);
11363 fail:
11364    return result;
11365 }
11366
11367 static int exec_mmap(void)
11368 {
11369    struct mm_struct *mm, *old_mm;
11370
11371    old_mm = current->mm;
11372    if (old_mm && atomic_read(&old_mm->mm_users) == 1) {
11373      mm_release();
11374      exit_mmap(old_mm);
11375      return 0;
11376    }
11377
11378    mm = mm_alloc();
11379    if (mm) {
11380      struct mm_struct *active_mm = current->active_mm;
11381
11382      if (init_new_context(current, mm)) {
11383        mmdrop(mm);
11384        return -ENOMEM;
11385      }
11386
11387      /* Add it to the list of mm's */
11388      spin_lock(&mmlist_lock);
11389      list_add(&mm->mmlist, &init_mm.mmlist);
11390      mmlist_nr++;
11391      spin_unlock(&mmlist_lock);
11392
11393      task_lock(current);
11394      current->mm = mm;
11395      current->active_mm = mm;
11396      task_unlock(current);
11397      activate_mm(active_mm, mm);
11398      mm_release();
11399      if (old_mm) {
11400        if (active_mm != old_mm)
11401          BUG();
11402        mmput(old_mm);
11403        return 0;
11404      }
```

```
11405      mmdrop(active_mm);
11406      return 0;
11407    }
11408    return -ENOMEM;
11409 }
11410
11411 /* This function makes sure the current process has its
11412  * own signal table, so that flush_signal_handlers can
11413  * later reset the handlers without disturbing other
11414  * processes.  (Other processes might share the signal
11415  * table via the CLONE_SIGNAL option to clone().)  */
11416 static inline int make_private_signals(void)
11417 {
11418    struct signal_struct *newsig;
11419
11420    if (atomic_read(&current->sig->count) <= 1)
11421      return 0;
11422    newsig = kmem_cache_alloc(sigact_cachep, GFP_KERNEL);
11423    if (newsig == NULL)
11424      return -ENOMEM;
11425    spin_lock_init(&newsig->siglock);
11426    atomic_set(&newsig->count, 1);
11427    memcpy(newsig->action, current->sig->action,
11428        sizeof(newsig->action));
11429    spin_lock_irq(&current->sigmask_lock);
11430    current->sig = newsig;
11431    spin_unlock_irq(&current->sigmask_lock);
11432    return 0;
11433 }
11434
11435 /* If make_private_signals() made a copy of the signal
11436  * table, decrement the refcount of the original table,
11437  * and free it if necessary.  We don't do that in
11438  * make_private_signals() so that we can back off in
11439  * flush_old_exec() if an error occurs after calling
11440  * make_private_signals().  */
11441 static inline void release_old_signals(struct
11442     signal_struct *oldsig)
11443 {
11444    if (current->sig == oldsig)
11445      return;
11446    if (atomic_dec_and_test(&oldsig->count))
11447      kmem_cache_free(sigact_cachep, oldsig);
11448 }
11449
11450 /* These functions flushes out all traces of the
11451  * currently running executable so that a new one can be
```

```
11452   * started */
11453  static inline void flush_old_files(struct files_struct
11454      *files)
11455  {
11456    long j = -1;
11457
11458    write_lock(&files->file_lock);
11459    for (;;) {
11460      unsigned long set, i;
11461
11462      j++;
11463      i = j * __NFDBITS;
11464      if (i >= files->max_fds || i >= files->max_fdset)
11465        break;
11466      set = files->close_on_exec->fds_bits[j];
11467      if (!set)
11468        continue;
11469      files->close_on_exec->fds_bits[j] = 0;
11470      write_unlock(&files->file_lock);
11471      for (; set; i++, set >>= 1) {
11472        if (set & 1) {
11473          sys_close(i);
11474        }
11475      }
11476      write_lock(&files->file_lock);
11477
11478    }
11479    write_unlock(&files->file_lock);
11480  }
11481
11482  /* An execve() will automatically "de-thread" the
11483   * process.  Note: we don't have to hold the
11484   * tasklist_lock to test whether we migth need to do
11485   * this. If we're not part of a thread group, there is no
11486   * way we can become one dynamically. And if we are, we
11487   * only need to protect the unlink - even if we race with
11488   * the last other thread exit, at worst the
11489   * list_del_init() might end up being a no-op.  */
11490  static inline void de_thread(struct task_struct *tsk)
11491  {
11492    if (!list_empty(&tsk->thread_group)) {
11493      write_lock_irq(&tasklist_lock);
11494      list_del_init(&tsk->thread_group);
11495      write_unlock_irq(&tasklist_lock);
11496    }
11497
11498    /* Minor oddity: this might stay the same. */
11499    tsk->tgid = tsk->pid;
11500  }
11501
11502  int flush_old_exec(struct linux_binprm *bprm)
11503  {
11504    char *name;
11505    int i, ch, retval;
11506    struct signal_struct *oldsig;
11507
11508    /* Make sure we have a private signal table */
11509    oldsig = current->sig;
11510    retval = make_private_signals();
11511    if (retval)
11512      goto flush_failed;
11513
11514    /* Release all of the old mmap stuff */
11515    retval = exec_mmap();
11516    if (retval)
11517      goto mmap_failed;
11518
11519    /* This is the point of no return */
11520    release_old_signals(oldsig);
11521
11522    current->sas_ss_sp = current->sas_ss_size = 0;
11523
11524    if (current->euid == current->uid
11525        && current->egid == current->gid)
11526      current->dumpable = 1;
11527    name = bprm->filename;
11528    for (i = 0; (ch = *(name++)) != '\0';) {
11529      if (ch == '/')
11530        i = 0;
11531      else if (i < 15)
11532        current->comm[i++] = ch;
11533    }
11534    current->comm[i] = '\0';
11535
11536    flush_thread();
11537
11538    de_thread(current);
11539
11540    if (bprm->e_uid != current->euid
11541        || bprm->e_gid != current->egid
11542        || permission(bprm->file->f_dentry->d_inode,
11543                      MAY_READ))
11544      current->dumpable = 0;
11545
```

```
11546    /* An exec changes our domain. We are no longer part
11547     * of the thread group */
11548
11549    current->self_exec_id++;
11550
11551    flush_signal_handlers(current);
11552    flush_old_files(current->files);
11553
11554    return 0;
11555
11556 mmap_failed:
11557 flush_failed:
11558    spin_lock_irq(&current->sigmask_lock);
11559    if (current->sig != oldsig)
11560      kfree(current->sig);
11561    current->sig = oldsig;
11562    spin_unlock_irq(&current->sigmask_lock);
11563    return retval;
11564 }
11565
11566 /* We mustn't allow tracing of suid binaries, unless the
11567  * tracer has the capability to trace anything.. */
11568 static inline int must_not_trace_exec(struct task_struct
11569      *p)
11570 {
11571    return (p->ptrace & PT_PTRACED)
11572        && !cap_raised(p->p_pptr->cap_effective,
11573                 CAP_SYS_PTRACE);
11574 }
11575
11576 /* Fill the binprm structure from the inode.  Check
11577  * permissions, then read the first 128 (BINPRM_BUF_SIZE)
11578  * bytes */
11579 int prepare_binprm(struct linux_binprm *bprm)
11580 {
11581    int mode;
11582    struct inode *inode = bprm->file->f_dentry->d_inode;
11583
11584    mode = inode->i_mode;
11585    /* Huh? We had already checked for MAY_EXEC, WTF do we
11586     * check this? */
11587    if (!(mode & 0111))           /* with at least _one_
11588                                   * execute bit set */
11589      return -EACCES;
11590    if (bprm->file->f_op == NULL)
11591      return -EACCES;
11592
11593    bprm->e_uid = current->euid;
11594    bprm->e_gid = current->egid;
11595
11596    if (!IS_NOSUID(inode)) {
11597      /* Set-uid? */
11598      if (mode & S_ISUID)
11599        bprm->e_uid = inode->i_uid;
11600
11601      /* Set-gid? */
11602      /* If setgid is set but no group execute bit then
11603       * this is a candidate for mandatory locking, not a
11604       * setgid executable.  */
11605      if ((mode & (S_ISGID | S_IXGRP)) ==
11606               (S_ISGID | S_IXGRP))
11607        bprm->e_gid = inode->i_gid;
11608    }
11609
11610    /* We don't have VFS support for capabilities yet */
11611    cap_clear(bprm->cap_inheritable);
11612    cap_clear(bprm->cap_permitted);
11613    cap_clear(bprm->cap_effective);
11614
11615    /* To support inheritance of root-permissions and
11616     * suid-root executables under compatibility mode, we
11617     * raise all three capability sets for the file.  If
11618     * only the real uid is 0, we only raise the
11619     * inheritable and permitted sets of the executable
11620     * file. */
11621
11622    if (!issecure(SECURE_NOROOT)) {
11623      if (bprm->e_uid == 0 || current->uid == 0) {
11624        cap_set_full(bprm->cap_inheritable);
11625        cap_set_full(bprm->cap_permitted);
11626      }
11627      if (bprm->e_uid == 0)
11628        cap_set_full(bprm->cap_effective);
11629    }
11630
11631    memset(bprm->buf, 0, BINPRM_BUF_SIZE);
11632    return kernel_read(bprm->file, 0, bprm->buf,
11633      BINPRM_BUF_SIZE);
11634 }
11635
11636 /* This function is used to produce the new IDs and
11637  * capabilities from the old ones and the file's
11638  * capabilities.
11639  *
```

p 605

```
11640  * The formula used for evolving capabilities is:
11641  *
11642  *        pI' = pI
11643  * (***) pP' = (fP & X) | (fI & pI)
11644  *        pE' = pP' & fE          [NB. fE is 0 or ~0]
11645  *
11646  * I=Inheritable, P=Permitted, E=Effective
11647  * p=process, f=file
11648  * ' indicates post-exec(), and X is the global
11649  * 'cap_bset'. */
11650 void compute_creds(struct linux_binprm *bprm)
11651 {
11652   kernel_cap_t new_permitted, working;
11653   int do_unlock = 0;
11654
11655   new_permitted =
11656       cap_intersect(bprm->cap_permitted, cap_bset);
11657   working = cap_intersect(bprm->cap_inheritable,
11658                       current->cap_inheritable);
11659   new_permitted = cap_combine(new_permitted, working);
11660
11661   if (bprm->e_uid != current->uid
11662       || bprm->e_gid != current->gid
11663       || !cap_issubset(new_permitted,
11664                     current->cap_permitted)) {
11665     current->dumpable = 0;
11666
11667     lock_kernel();
11668     if (must_not_trace_exec(current)
11669         || atomic_read(&current->fs->count) > 1
11670         || atomic_read(&current->files->count) > 1
11671         || atomic_read(&current->sig->count) > 1) {
11672       if (!capable(CAP_SETUID)) {
11673         bprm->e_uid = current->uid;
11674         bprm->e_gid = current->gid;
11675       }
11676       if (!capable(CAP_SETPCAP)) {
11677         new_permitted = cap_intersect(new_permitted,
11678             current->cap_permitted);
11679       }
11680     }
11681     do_unlock = 1;
11682   }
11683
11684
11685   /* For init, we want to retain the capabilities set in
11686    * the init_task struct. Thus we skip the usual
```

```
11687    * capability rules */
11688   if (current->pid != 1) {
11689     current->cap_permitted = new_permitted;
11690     current->cap_effective =
11691       cap_intersect(new_permitted, bprm->cap_effective);
11692   }
11693
11694   /* AUD: Audit candidate if current->cap_effective is
11695    * set */
11696
11697   current->suid = current->euid = current->fsuid =
11698       bprm->e_uid;
11699   current->sgid = current->egid = current->fsgid =
11700       bprm->e_gid;
11701
11702   if (do_unlock)
11703     unlock_kernel();
11704   current->keep_capabilities = 0;
11705 }
11706
11707
11708 void remove_arg_zero(struct linux_binprm *bprm)
11709 {
11710   if (bprm->argc) {
11711     unsigned long offset;
11712     char *kaddr;
11713     struct page *page;
11714
11715     offset = bprm->p % PAGE_SIZE;
11716     goto inside;
11717
11718     while (bprm->p++, *(kaddr + offset++)) {
11719       if (offset != PAGE_SIZE)
11720         continue;
11721       offset = 0;
11722       kunmap(page);
11723     inside:
11724       page = bprm->page[bprm->p / PAGE_SIZE];
11725       kaddr = kmap(page);
11726     }
11727     kunmap(page);
11728     bprm->argc--;
11729   }
11730 }
11731
11732 /* cycle the list of binary formats handler, until one
11733  * recognizes the image */
```

```
11734 int search_binary_handler(struct linux_binprm *bprm,
11735    struct pt_regs *regs)
11736 {
11737    int try, retval = 0;
11738    struct linux_binfmt *fmt;
11739 #ifdef __alpha__
11740    /* handle /sbin/loader.. */
11741    {
11742       struct exec *eh = (struct exec *) bprm->buf;
11743
11744       if (!bprm->loader && eh->fh.f_magic == 0x183 &&
11745          (eh->fh.f_flags & 0x3000) == 0x3000) {
11746          char *dynloader[] = { "/sbin/loader" };
11747          struct file *file;
11748          unsigned long loader;
11749
11750          allow_write_access(bprm->file);
11751          fput(bprm->file);
11752          bprm->file = NULL;
11753
11754          loader =
11755             PAGE_SIZE * MAX_ARG_PAGES - sizeof(void *);
11756
11757          file = open_exec(dynloader[0]);
11758          retval = PTR_ERR(file);
11759          if (IS_ERR(file))
11760             return retval;
11761          bprm->file = file;
11762          bprm->loader = loader;
11763          retval = prepare_binprm(bprm);
11764          if (retval < 0)
11765             return retval;
11766          /* should call search_binary_handler recursively
11767           * here, but it does not matter */
11768       }
11769    }
11770 #endif
11771    for (try = 0; try < 2; try++) {
11772       read_lock(&binfmt_lock);
11773       for (fmt = formats; fmt; fmt = fmt->next) {
11774          int (*fn)(struct linux_binprm *, struct pt_regs *)
11775             = fmt->load_binary;
11776          if (!fn)
11777             continue;
11778          if (!try_inc_mod_count(fmt->module))
11779             continue;
11780          read_unlock(&binfmt_lock);
```

```
11781          retval = fn(bprm, regs);
11782          if (retval >= 0) {
11783             put_binfmt(fmt);
11784             allow_write_access(bprm->file);
11785             if (bprm->file)
11786                fput(bprm->file);
11787             bprm->file = NULL;
11788             current->did_exec = 1;
11789             return retval;
11790          }
11791          read_lock(&binfmt_lock);
11792          put_binfmt(fmt);
11793          if (retval != -ENOEXEC)
11794             break;
11795          if (!bprm->file) {
11796             read_unlock(&binfmt_lock);
11797             return retval;
11798          }
11799       }
11800       read_unlock(&binfmt_lock);
11801       if (retval != -ENOEXEC) {
11802          break;
11803 #ifdef CONFIG_KMOD
11804       } else {
11805 #define printable(c)                                       \
11806    (((c)=='\t') || ((c)=='\n') || (0x20<=(c) && (c)<=0x7e))
11807          char modname[20];
11808          if (printable(bprm->buf[0]) &&
11809             printable(bprm->buf[1]) &&
11810             printable(bprm->buf[2]) &&
11811             printable(bprm->buf[3]))
11812             break; /* -ENOEXEC */
11813          sprintf(modname, "binfmt-%04x",
11814             *(unsigned short *) (&bprm->buf[2]));
11815          request_module(modname);
11816 #endif
11817       }
11818    }
11819    return retval;
11820 }
11821
11822
11823 /* sys_execve() executes a new program.  */
11824 int do_execve(char *filename, char **argv, char **envp,
11825    struct pt_regs *regs)
11826 {
11827    struct linux_binprm bprm;
```

```
11828    struct file *file;
11829    int retval;
11830    int i;
11831
11832    file = open_exec(filename);
11833
11834    retval = PTR_ERR(file);
11835    if (IS_ERR(file))
11836      return retval;
11837
11838    bprm.p = PAGE_SIZE * MAX_ARG_PAGES - sizeof(void *);
11839    memset(bprm.page, 0,
11840        MAX_ARG_PAGES * sizeof(bprm.page[0]));
11841
11842    bprm.file = file;
11843    bprm.filename = filename;
11844    bprm.sh_bang = 0;
11845    bprm.loader = 0;
11846    bprm.exec = 0;
11847    if ((bprm.argc =
11848          count(argv, bprm.p / sizeof(void *))) < 0) {
11849      allow_write_access(file);
11850      fput(file);
11851      return bprm.argc;
11852    }
11853
11854    if ((bprm.envc =
11855          count(envp, bprm.p / sizeof(void *))) < 0) {
11856      allow_write_access(file);
11857      fput(file);
11858      return bprm.envc;
11859    }
11860
11861    retval = prepare_binprm(&bprm);
11862    if (retval < 0)
11863      goto out;
11864
11865    retval = copy_strings_kernel(1, &bprm.filename, &bprm);
11866    if (retval < 0)
11867      goto out;
11868
11869    bprm.exec = bprm.p;
11870    retval = copy_strings(bprm.envc, envp, &bprm);
11871    if (retval < 0)
11872      goto out;
11873
11874    retval = copy_strings(bprm.argc, argv, &bprm);
```

```
11875    if (retval < 0)
11876      goto out;
11877
11878    retval = search_binary_handler(&bprm, regs);
11879    if (retval >= 0)
11880      /* execve success */
11881      return retval;
11882
11883 out:
11884    /* Something went wrong, return the inode and free the
11885     * argument pages */
11886    allow_write_access(bprm.file);
11887    if (bprm.file)
11888      fput(bprm.file);
11889
11890    for (i = 0; i < MAX_ARG_PAGES; i++) {
11891      struct page *page = bprm.page[i];
11892      if (page)
11893        __free_page(page);
11894    }
11895
11896    return retval;
11897 }
11898
11899 void set_binfmt(struct linux_binfmt *new)
11900 {
11901    struct linux_binfmt *old = current->binfmt;
11902    if (new && new->module)
11903      __MOD_INC_USE_COUNT(new->module);
11904    current->binfmt = new;
11905    if (old && old->module)
11906      __MOD_DEC_USE_COUNT(old->module);
11907 }
11908
11909 int do_coredump(long signr, struct pt_regs *regs)
11910 {
11911    struct linux_binfmt *binfmt;
11912    char corename[6 + sizeof(current->comm)];
11913    struct file *file;
11914    struct inode *inode;
11915
11916    lock_kernel();
11917    binfmt = current->binfmt;
11918    if (!binfmt || !binfmt->core_dump)
11919      goto fail;
11920    if (!current->dumpable
11921          || atomic_read(&current->mm->mm_users) != 1)
```

```
11922      goto fail;
11923    current->dumpable = 0;
11924    if (current->rlim[RLIMIT_CORE].rlim_cur <
11925        binfmt->min_coredump)
11926      goto fail;
11927
11928    memcpy(corename, "core.", 5);
11929 #if 0
11930    memcpy(corename + 5, current->comm,
11931        sizeof(current->comm));
11932 #else
11933    corename[4] = '\0';
11934 #endif
11935    file = filp_open(corename, O_CREAT | 2 | O_NOFOLLOW,
11936                     0600);
11937    if (IS_ERR(file))
11938      goto fail;
11939    inode = file->f_dentry->d_inode;
11940    if (inode->i_nlink > 1)
11941      goto close_fail;    /* multiple links - don't dump */
11942    if (d_unhashed(file->f_dentry))
11943      goto close_fail;
11944
11945    if (!S_ISREG(inode->i_mode))
11946      goto close_fail;
11947    if (!file->f_op)
11948      goto close_fail;
11949    if (!file->f_op->write)
11950      goto close_fail;
11951    if (do_truncate(file->f_dentry, 0) != 0)
11952      goto close_fail;
11953    if (!binfmt->core_dump(signr, regs, file))
11954      goto close_fail;
11955    unlock_kernel();
11956    filp_close(file, NULL);
11957    return 1;
11958
11959 close_fail:
11960    filp_close(file, NULL);
11961 fail:
11962    unlock_kernel();
11963    return 0;
11964 }
```

include/asm-generic/pgtable.h

```
11965 #ifndef _ASM_GENERIC_PGTABLE_H
11966 #define _ASM_GENERIC_PGTABLE_H
```

```
11967
11968 static inline int ptep_test_and_clear_young(pte_t * ptep)
11969 {
11970    pte_t pte = *ptep;
11971    if (!pte_young(pte))
11972      return 0;
11973    set_pte(ptep, pte_mkold(pte));
11974    return 1;
11975 }
11976
11977 static inline int ptep_test_and_clear_dirty(pte_t * ptep)
11978 {
11979    pte_t pte = *ptep;
11980    if (!pte_dirty(pte))
11981      return 0;
11982    set_pte(ptep, pte_mkclean(pte));
11983    return 1;
11984 }
11985
11986 static inline pte_t ptep_get_and_clear(pte_t * ptep)
11987 {
11988    pte_t pte = *ptep;
11989    pte_clear(ptep);
11990    return pte;
11991 }
11992
11993 static inline void ptep_set_wrprotect(pte_t * ptep)
11994 {
11995    pte_t old_pte = *ptep;
11996    set_pte(ptep, pte_wrprotect(old_pte));
11997 }
11998
11999 static inline void ptep_mkdirty(pte_t * ptep)
12000 {
12001    pte_t old_pte = *ptep;
12002    set_pte(ptep, pte_mkdirty(old_pte));
12003 }
12004
12005 #define pte_same(A,B)    (pte_val(A) == pte_val(B))
12006
12007 #endif                        /* _ASM_GENERIC_PGTABLE_H */
```

include/asm-generic/smplock.h

```
12008 /*
12009  * <asm/smplock.h>
12010  *
12011  * Default SMP lock implementation
```

```
12012  */
12013 #include <linux/interrupt.h>
12014 #include <linux/spinlock.h>
12015
12016 extern spinlock_t kernel_flag;
12017
12018 #define kernel_locked()  spin_is_locked(&kernel_flag)
12019
12020 /* Release global kernel lock and global interrupt lock
12021  */
12022 #define release_kernel_lock(task, cpu)                 \
12023 do {                                                   \
12024         if (task->lock_depth >= 0)                     \
12025                 spin_unlock(&kernel_flag);             \
12026         release_irqlock(cpu);                          \
12027         __sti();                                       \
12028 } while (0)
12029
12030 /* Re-acquire the kernel lock */
12031 #define reacquire_kernel_lock(task)                    \
12032 do {                                                   \
12033         if (task->lock_depth >= 0)                     \
12034                 spin_lock(&kernel_flag);               \
12035 } while (0)
12036
12037
12038 /* Getting the big kernel lock.
12039  *
12040  * This cannot happen asynchronously, so we only need to
12041  * worry about other CPU's.  */
12042 extern __inline__ void lock_kernel(void)
12043 {
12044   if (!++current->lock_depth)
12045     spin_lock(&kernel_flag);
12046 }
12047
12048 extern __inline__ void unlock_kernel(void)
12049 {
12050   if (--current->lock_depth < 0)
12051     spin_unlock(&kernel_flag);
12052 }
```

include/asm-i386/apic.h

```
12053 #ifndef __ASM_APIC_H
12054 #define __ASM_APIC_H
12055
12056 #include <linux/config.h>
12057 #include <asm/apicdef.h>
12058 #include <asm/system.h>
12059
12060 #define APIC_DEBUG 1
12061
12062 #ifdef CONFIG_X86_LOCAL_APIC
12063
12064 #if APIC_DEBUG
12065 #define Dprintk(x...) printk(x)
12066 #else
12067 #define Dprintk(x...)
12068 #endif
12069
12070 /* Basic functions accessing APICs.  */
12071
12072 extern __inline void apic_write(unsigned long reg,
12073     unsigned long v)
12074 {
12075   *((volatile unsigned long *) (APIC_BASE + reg)) = v;
12076 }
12077
12078 extern __inline void apic_write_atomic(unsigned long reg,
12079     unsigned long v)
12080 {
12081   xchg((volatile unsigned long *) (APIC_BASE + reg), v);
12082 }
12083
12084 extern __inline unsigned long apic_read(unsigned long
12085     reg)
12086 {
12087   return *((volatile unsigned long *) (APIC_BASE + reg));
12088 }
12089
12090 static __inline__ void apic_wait_icr_idle(void)
12091 {
12092   do {} while (apic_read(APIC_ICR) & APIC_ICR_BUSY);
12093 }
12094
12095 extern unsigned int apic_timer_irqs[NR_CPUS];
12096
12097 #ifdef CONFIG_X86_GOOD_APIC
12098 #define FORCE_READ_AROUND_WRITE 0
12099 #define apic_read_around(x)
12100 #define apic_write_around(x,y) apic_write((x),(y))
12101 #else
12102 #define FORCE_READ_AROUND_WRITE 1
12103 #define apic_read_around(x) apic_read(x)
```

```
12104 #define apic_write_around(x,y) apic_write_atomic((x),(y))
12105 #endif
12106
12107 extern inline void ack_APIC_irq(void)
12108 {
12109    /* ack_APIC_irq() actually gets compiled as a single
12110     * instruction:
12111     * - a single rmw on Pentium/82489DX
12112     * - a single write on P6+ cores (CONFIG_X86_GOOD_APIC)
12113     * ... yummie.  */
12114
12115    /* Docs say use 0 for future compatibility */
12116    apic_write_around(APIC_EOI, 0);
12117 }
12118
12119 extern int get_maxlvt(void);
12120 extern void connect_bsp_APIC(void);
12121 extern void disconnect_bsp_APIC(void);
12122 extern void disable_local_APIC(void);
12123 extern int verify_local_APIC(void);
12124 extern void cache_APIC_registers(void);
12125 extern void sync_Arb_IDs(void);
12126 extern void setup_local_APIC(void);
12127 extern void init_apic_mappings(void);
12128 extern void smp_local_timer_interrupt(struct pt_regs
12129     *regs);
12130 extern void setup_APIC_clocks(void);
12131 #endif
12132
12133 #endif
```

include/asm-i386/atomic.h

```
12134 #ifndef __ARCH_I386_ATOMIC__
12135 #define __ARCH_I386_ATOMIC__
12136
12137 #include <linux/config.h>
12138
12139 /* Atomic operations that C can't guarantee us.  Useful
12140  * for resource counting etc..  */
12141
12142 #ifdef CONFIG_SMP
12143 #define LOCK "lock ; "
12144 #else
12145 #define LOCK ""
12146 #endif
12147
12148 /* Make sure gcc doesn't try to be clever and move things
12149  * around on us. We need to use _exactly_ the address the
12150  * user gave us, not some alias that contains the same
12151  * information.  */
12152 typedef struct {
12153    volatile int counter;
12154 } atomic_t;
12155
12156 #define ATOMIC_INIT(i)  { (i) }
12157
12158 #define atomic_read(v)          ((v)->counter)
12159 #define atomic_set(v,i)         (((v)->counter) = (i))
12160
12161 static __inline__ void atomic_add(int i, atomic_t * v)
12162 {
12163    __asm__ __volatile__(LOCK "addl %1,%0"
12164                         :"=m"(v->counter)
12165                         :"ir"(i), "m"(v->counter));
12166 }
12167
12168 static __inline__ void atomic_sub(int i, atomic_t * v)
12169 {
12170    __asm__ __volatile__(LOCK "subl %1,%0"
12171                         :"=m"(v->counter)
12172                         :"ir"(i), "m"(v->counter));
12173 }
12174
12175 static __inline__ int atomic_sub_and_test(int i,
12176     atomic_t * v)
12177 {
12178    unsigned char c;
12179
12180    __asm__ __volatile__(
12181        LOCK "subl %2,%0; sete %1"
12182        :"=m"(v->counter), "=qm"(c)
12183        :"ir"(i), "m"(v->counter)
12184        :"memory");
12185    return c;
12186 }
12187
12188 static __inline__ void atomic_inc(atomic_t * v)
12189 {
12190    __asm__ __volatile__( LOCK "incl %0"
12191                         :"=m"(v->counter)
12192                         :"m"(v->counter));
12193 }
12194
12195 static __inline__ void atomic_dec(atomic_t * v)
```

```
12196 {
12197    __asm__ __volatile__( LOCK "decl %0"
12198                          :"=m"(v->counter)
12199                          :"m"(v->counter));
12200 }
12201
12202 static __inline__ int atomic_dec_and_test(atomic_t * v)
12203 {
12204   unsigned char c;
12205
12206    __asm__ __volatile__(LOCK "decl %0; sete %1"
12207                         :"=m"(v->counter), "=qm"(c)
12208                         :"m"(v->counter):"memory");
12209    return c != 0;
12210 }
12211
12212 static __inline__ int atomic_inc_and_test(atomic_t * v)
12213 {
12214   unsigned char c;
12215
12216    __asm__ __volatile__(LOCK "incl %0; sete %1"
12217                         :"=m"(v->counter), "=qm"(c)
12218                         :"m"(v->counter)
12219                         :"memory");
12220    return c != 0;
12221 }
12222
12223 static __inline__ int atomic_add_negative(int i,
12224     atomic_t * v)
12225 {
12226   unsigned char c;
12227
12228    __asm__ __volatile__(LOCK "addl %2,%0; sets %1"
12229                         :"=m"(v->counter), "=qm"(c)
12230                         :"ir"(i), "m"(v->counter)
12231                         :"memory");
12232    return c;
12233 }
12234
12235 /* These are x86-specific, used by some header files */
12236 #define atomic_clear_mask(mask, addr)                    \
12237 __asm__ __volatile__(                                    \
12238     LOCK "andl %0,%1"                                    \
12239    : : "r" (~(mask)),"m" (*addr) : "memory")
12240
12241 #define atomic_set_mask(mask, addr)                      \
12242 __asm__ __volatile__(                                    \
12243     LOCK "orl %0,%1"                                     \
12244    : : "r" (mask),"m" (*addr) : "memory")
12245
12246 #endif
```

include/asm-i386/bitops.h

```
12247 #ifndef _I386_BITOPS_H
12248 #define _I386_BITOPS_H
12249
12250 /* Copyright 1992, Linus Torvalds.  */
12251
12252 #include <linux/config.h>
12253
12254 /* These have to be done with inline assembly: that way
12255  * the bit-setting is guaranteed to be atomic. All bit
12256  * operations return 0 if the bit was cleared before the
12257  * operation and != 0 if it was not.
12258  *
12259  * bit 0 is the LSB of addr; bit 32 is the LSB of
12260  * (addr+1).  */
12261
12262 #ifdef CONFIG_SMP
12263 #define LOCK_PREFIX "lock ; "
12264 #else
12265 #define LOCK_PREFIX ""
12266 #endif
12267
12268 #define ADDR (*(volatile long *) addr)
12269
12270 static __inline__ void set_bit(int nr,
12271     volatile void *addr)
12272 {
12273    __asm__ __volatile__(LOCK_PREFIX "btsl %1,%0"
12274                         :"=m"(ADDR) :"Ir"(nr));
12275 }
12276
12277 /* WARNING: non atomic and it can be reordered! */
12278 static __inline__ void __set_bit(int nr,
12279     volatile void *addr)
12280 {
12281    __asm__("btsl %1,%0" :"=m"(ADDR) :"Ir"(nr));
12282 }
12283
12284 /* clear_bit() doesn't provide any barrier for the
12285  * compiler.  */
12286 #define smp_mb__before_clear_bit()       barrier()
12287 #define smp_mb__after_clear_bit()        barrier()
```

```
12288 static __inline__ void clear_bit(int nr,
12289     volatile void *addr)
12290 {
12291   __asm__ __volatile__(LOCK_PREFIX "btrl %1,%0"
12292                     :"=m"(ADDR) :"Ir"(nr));
12293 }
12294
12295 static __inline__ void change_bit(int nr,
12296     volatile void *addr)
12297 {
12298   __asm__ __volatile__(LOCK_PREFIX "btcl %1,%0"
12299                     :"=m"(ADDR) :"Ir"(nr));
12300 }
12301
12302 /* It will also imply a memory barrier, thus it must
12303  * clobber memory to make sure to reload anything that
12304  * was cached into registers outside _this_ critical
12305  * section.  */
12306 static __inline__ int test_and_set_bit(int nr,
12307     volatile void *addr)
12308 {
12309   int oldbit;
12310
12311   __asm__ __volatile__(
12312     LOCK_PREFIX "btsl %2,%1\n\tsbbl %0,%0"
12313     :"=r"(oldbit), "=m"(ADDR) :"Ir"(nr) :"memory");
12314   return oldbit;
12315 }
12316
12317 /* WARNING: non atomic and it can be reordered! */
12318 static __inline__ int __test_and_set_bit(int nr,
12319     volatile void *addr)
12320 {
12321   int oldbit;
12322
12323   __asm__("btsl %2,%1\n\tsbbl %0,%0"
12324          : "=r"(oldbit), "=m"(ADDR)
12325          : "Ir"(nr));
12326   return oldbit;
12327 }
12328
12329 static __inline__ int test_and_clear_bit(int nr,
12330     volatile void *addr)
12331 {
12332   int oldbit;
12333
12334   __asm__ __volatile__(
12335     LOCK_PREFIX "btrl %2,%1\n\tsbbl %0,%0"
12336     :"=r"(oldbit), "=m"(ADDR)
12337     :"Ir"(nr)
12338     :"memory");
12339   return oldbit;
12340 }
12341
12342 /* WARNING: non atomic and it can be reordered! */
12343 static __inline__ int __test_and_clear_bit(int nr,
12344     volatile void *addr)
12345 {
12346   int oldbit;
12347
12348   __asm__("btrl %2,%1\n\tsbbl %0,%0"
12349          :"=r"(oldbit), "=m"(ADDR)
12350          :"Ir"(nr));
12351   return oldbit;
12352 }
12353
12354 static __inline__ int test_and_change_bit(int nr,
12355     volatile void *addr)
12356 {
12357   int oldbit;
12358
12359   __asm__ __volatile__(
12360     LOCK_PREFIX "btcl %2,%1\n\tsbbl %0,%0"
12361     :"=r"(oldbit), "=m"(ADDR)
12362     :"Ir"(nr)
12363     :"memory");
12364   return oldbit;
12365 }
12366
12367 /* This routine doesn't need to be atomic.  */
12368 static __inline__ int constant_test_bit(int nr,
12369     const volatile void *addr)
12370 {
12371   return
12372     ((1UL << (nr & 31)) &
12373     (((const volatile unsigned int *) addr)[nr >> 5]))
12374     != 0;
12375 }
12376
12377 static __inline__ int variable_test_bit(int nr,
12378     volatile void *addr)
12379 {
12380   int oldbit;
12381
```

```
12382   __asm__ __volatile__("btl %2,%1\n\tsbbl %0,%0"
12383                   :"=r"(oldbit)
12384                   :"m"(ADDR), "Ir"(nr));
12385     return oldbit;
12386 }
12387
12388 #define test_bit(nr,addr)                              \
12389 (__builtin_constant_p(nr)                             \
12390  ? constant_test_bit((nr),(addr))                     \
12391  : variable_test_bit((nr),(addr)))
12392
12393 /* Find-bit routines.. */
12394 static __inline__ int find_first_zero_bit(void *addr,
12395       unsigned size)
12396 {
12397   int d0, d1, d2;
12398   int res;
12399
12400   if (!size)
12401     return 0;
12402   /* This looks at memory. Mark it volatile to tell gcc
12403    * not to move it around */
12404   __asm__ __volatile__(
12405     "movl $-1,%%eax\n\t"
12406     "xorl %%edx,%%edx\n\t"
12407     "repe; scasl\n\t"
12408     "je 1f\n\t"
12409     "xorl -4(%%edi),%%eax\n\t"
12410     "subl $4,%%edi\n\t"
12411     "bsfl %%eax,%%edx\n"
12412     "1:\tsubl %%ebx,%%edi\n\t"
12413     "shll $3,%%edi\n\t"
12414     "addl %%edi,%%edx"
12415     :"=d"(res), "=&c"(d0), "=&D"(d1), "=&a"(d2)
12416     :"1"((size + 31) >> 5), "2"(addr), "b"(addr));
12417   return res;
12418 }
12419
12420 static __inline__ int find_next_zero_bit(void *addr,
12421       int size, int offset)
12422 {
12423   unsigned long *p =
12424       ((unsigned long *) addr) + (offset >> 5);
12425   int set = 0, bit = offset & 31, res;
12426
12427   if (bit) {
12428     /* Look for zero in first byte */
```

```
12429     __asm__("bsfl %1,%0\n\t"
12430         "jne 1f\n\t"
12431         "movl $32, %0\n"
12432         "1:"
12433         :"=r"(set)
12434         :"r"(~(*p >> bit)));
12435     if (set < (32 - bit))
12436       return set + offset;
12437     set = 32 - bit;
12438     p++;
12439   }
12440   /* No zero yet, search remaining full bytes for a zero
12441    */
12442   res =
12443     find_first_zero_bit(p, size - 32 *
12444                     (p - (unsigned long *) addr));
12445   return (offset + set + res);
12446 }
12447
12448 /* ffz = Find First Zero in word. Undefined if no zero
12449  * exists, so code should check against ~OUL first.. */
12450 static __inline__ unsigned long ffz(unsigned long word)
12451 {
12452   __asm__("bsfl %1,%0" :"=r"(word) : "r"(~word));
12453   return word;
12454 }
12455
12456 #ifdef __KERNEL__
12457
12458 /* ffs: find first bit set. This is defined the same way
12459  * as the libc and compiler builtin ffs routines,
12460  * therefore differs in spirit from the above ffz (man
12461  * ffs). */
12462 static __inline__ int ffs(int x)
12463 {
12464   int r;
12465
12466   __asm__("bsfl %1,%0\n\t"
12467       "jnz 1f\n\t"
12468       "movl $-1,%0\n"
12469       "1:"
12470       :"=r"(r)
12471       :"g"(x));
12472   return r + 1;
12473 }
12474
12475 /* hweightN: returns the hamming weight (i.e. the number
```

```
12476  * of bits set) of a N-bit word */
12477 #define hweight32(x) generic_hweight32(x)
12478 #define hweight16(x) generic_hweight16(x)
12479 #define hweight8(x) generic_hweight8(x)
12480
12481 #endif                              /* __KERNEL__ */
12482
12483 #ifdef __KERNEL__
12484
12485 #define ext2_set_bit            __test_and_set_bit
12486 #define ext2_clear_bit          __test_and_clear_bit
12487 #define ext2_test_bit           test_bit
12488 #define ext2_find_first_zero_bit  find_first_zero_bit
12489 #define ext2_find_next_zero_bit   find_next_zero_bit
12490
12491 /* Bitmap functions for the minix filesystem.  */
12492 #define minix_test_and_set_bit(nr,addr)              \
12493  __test_and_set_bit(nr,addr)
12494 #define minix_set_bit(nr,addr) __set_bit(nr,addr)
12495 #define minix_test_and_clear_bit(nr,addr)            \
12496  __test_and_clear_bit(nr,addr)
12497 #define minix_test_bit(nr,addr) test_bit(nr,addr)
12498 #define minix_find_first_zero_bit(addr,size)         \
12499  find_first_zero_bit(addr,size)
12500
12501 #endif                              /* __KERNEL__ */
12502
12503 #endif                              /* _I386_BITOPS_H */
```

include/asm-i386/cache.h

```
12504 /*
12505  * include/asm-i386/cache.h
12506  */
12507 #ifndef __ARCH_I386_CACHE_H
12508 #define __ARCH_I386_CACHE_H
12509
12510 #include <linux/config.h>
12511
12512 /* L1 cache line size */
12513 #define L1_CACHE_SHIFT  (CONFIG_X86_L1_CACHE_SHIFT)
12514 #define L1_CACHE_BYTES  (1 << L1_CACHE_SHIFT)
12515
12516 #endif
```

include/asm-i386/current.h

```
12517 #ifndef _I386_CURRENT_H
12518 #define _I386_CURRENT_H
12519
12520 struct task_struct;
12521
12522 static inline struct task_struct *get_current(void)
12523 {
12524   struct task_struct *current;
12525   __asm__("andl %%esp,%0; ": "=r"(current):"0"(~8191UL));
12526   return current;
12527 }
12528
12529 #define current get_current()
12530
12531 #endif                              /* !(_I386_CURRENT_H) */
```

include/asm-i386/delay.h

```
12532 #ifndef _I386_DELAY_H
12533 #define _I386_DELAY_H
12534
12535 /*
12536  * Copyright (C) 1993 Linus Torvalds
12537  *
12538  * Delay routines calling functions in
12539  * arch/i386/lib/delay.c
12540  */
12541
12542 extern void __bad_udelay(void);
12543
12544 extern void __udelay(unsigned long usecs);
12545 extern void __const_udelay(unsigned long usecs);
12546 extern void __delay(unsigned long loops);
12547
12548 #define udelay(n)                                      \
12549 (__builtin_constant_p(n)                               \
12550  ? ((n) > 20000 ? __bad_udelay()                       \
12551             : __const_udelay((n) * 0x10c6ul))          \
12552  : __udelay(n))
12553
12554 #endif                              /* defined(_I386_DELAY_H) */
```

include/asm-i386/desc.h

```
12555 #ifndef __ARCH_DESC_H
12556 #define __ARCH_DESC_H
12557
12558 #include <asm/ldt.h>
12559
```

```
12560 /* The layout of the GDT under Linux:
12561  *
12562  *    0 - null
12563  *    1 - not used
12564  *    2 - kernel code segment
12565  *    3 - kernel data segment
12566  *    4 - user code segment          <- new cacheline
12567  *    5 - user data segment
12568  *    6 - not used
12569  *    7 - not used
12570  *    8 - APM BIOS support           <- new cacheline
12571  *    9 - APM BIOS support
12572  *   10 - APM BIOS support
12573  *   11 - APM BIOS support
12574  *
12575  * The TSS+LDT descriptors are spread out a bit so that
12576  * every CPU has an exclusive cacheline for the per-CPU
12577  * TSS and LDT:
12578  *
12579  *   12 - CPU#0 TSS                   <- new cacheline
12580  *   13 - CPU#0 LDT
12581  *   14 - not used
12582  *   15 - not used
12583  *   16 - CPU#1 TSS                   <- new cacheline
12584  *   17 - CPU#1 LDT
12585  *   18 - not used
12586  *   19 - not used
12587  *   ... NR_CPUS per-CPU TSS+LDT's if on SMP
12588  *
12589  * Entry into gdt where to find first TSS. */
12590 #define __FIRST_TSS_ENTRY 12
12591 #define __FIRST_LDT_ENTRY (__FIRST_TSS_ENTRY+1)
12592
12593 #define __TSS(n) (((n)<<2) + __FIRST_TSS_ENTRY)
12594 #define __LDT(n) (((n)<<2) + __FIRST_LDT_ENTRY)
12595
12596 #ifndef __ASSEMBLY__
12597 struct desc_struct {
12598   unsigned long a, b;
12599 };
12600
12601 extern struct desc_struct gdt_table[];
12602 extern struct desc_struct *idt, *gdt;
12603
12604 struct Xgt_desc_struct {
12605   unsigned short size;
12606   unsigned long address __attribute__ ((packed));
12607 };
12608
12609 #define idt_descr                                      \
12610  (*(struct Xgt_desc_struct *)((char *)&idt - 2))
12611 #define gdt_descr                                      \
12612  (*(struct Xgt_desc_struct *)((char *)&gdt - 2))
12613
12614 #define load_TR(n)                                     \
12615   __asm__ __volatile__("ltr %%ax"::"a" (__TSS(n)<<3))
12616
12617 #define __load_LDT(n)                                  \
12618   __asm__ __volatile__("lldt %%ax"::"a" (__LDT(n)<<3))
12619
12620 /* This is the ldt that every process will get unless we
12621  * need something other than this.  */
12622 extern struct desc_struct default_ldt[];
12623 extern void set_intr_gate(unsigned int irq, void *addr);
12624 extern void set_ldt_desc(unsigned int n, void *addr,
12625     unsigned int size);
12626 extern void set_tss_desc(unsigned int n, void *addr);
12627
12628 extern inline void clear_LDT(void)
12629 {
12630   int cpu = smp_processor_id();
12631   set_ldt_desc(cpu, &default_ldt[0], 5);
12632   __load_LDT(cpu);
12633 }
12634
12635 /* load one particular LDT into the current CPU */
12636 extern inline void load_LDT(struct mm_struct *mm)
12637 {
12638   int cpu = smp_processor_id();
12639   void *segments = mm->context.segments;
12640   int count = LDT_ENTRIES;
12641
12642   if (!segments) {
12643     segments = &default_ldt[0];
12644     count = 5;
12645   }
12646
12647   set_ldt_desc(cpu, segments, count);
12648   __load_LDT(cpu);
12649 }
12650
12651 #endif                              /* !__ASSEMBLY__ */
12652
12653 #endif
```

include/asm-i386/hardirq.h

```
12654 #ifndef __ASM_HARDIRQ_H
12655 #define __ASM_HARDIRQ_H
12656
12657 #include <linux/config.h>
12658 #include <linux/threads.h>
12659 #include <linux/irq.h>
12660
12661 /* entry.S is sensitive to the offsets of these fields */
12662 typedef struct {
12663     unsigned int __softirq_active;
12664     unsigned int __softirq_mask;
12665     unsigned int __local_irq_count;
12666     unsigned int __local_bh_count;
12667     unsigned int __syscall_count;
12668     unsigned int __nmi_count;       /* arch dependent */
12669 } ____cacheline_aligned irq_cpustat_t;
12670
12671 #include <linux/irq_cpustat.h>   /* Standard mappings for
12672                                   * irq_cpustat_t above */
12673
12674 /* Are we in an interrupt context? Either doing bottom
12675  * half or hardware interrupt processing?  */
12676 #define in_interrupt()                                    \
12677 ({ int __cpu = smp_processor_id();                        \
12678   (local_irq_count(__cpu) + local_bh_count(__cpu) != 0);\
12679  })
12680
12681 #define in_irq()                                          \
12682   (local_irq_count(smp_processor_id()) != 0)
12683
12684 #ifndef CONFIG_SMP
12685
12686 #define hardirq_trylock(cpu)   (local_irq_count(cpu) == 0)
12687 #define hardirq_endlock(cpu)   do { } while (0)
12688
12689 #define irq_enter(cpu, irq)    (local_irq_count(cpu)++)
12690 #define irq_exit(cpu, irq)     (local_irq_count(cpu)−)
12691
12692 #define synchronize_irq()      barrier()
12693
12694 #else
12695
12696 #include <asm/atomic.h>
12697 #include <asm/smp.h>
12698
12699 extern unsigned char global_irq_holder;
```

```
12700 /* long for set_bit -RR */
12701 extern unsigned volatile long global_irq_lock;
12702
12703 static inline int irqs_running(void)
12704 {
12705     int i;
12706
12707     for (i = 0; i < smp_num_cpus; i++)
12708         if (local_irq_count(i))
12709             return 1;
12710     return 0;
12711 }
12712
12713 static inline void release_irqlock(int cpu)
12714 {
12715     /* if we didn't own the irq lock, just ignore.. */
12716     if (global_irq_holder == (unsigned char) cpu) {
12717         global_irq_holder = NO_PROC_ID;
12718         clear_bit(0, &global_irq_lock);
12719     }
12720 }
12721
12722 static inline void irq_enter(int cpu, int irq)
12723 {
12724     ++local_irq_count(cpu);
12725
12726     while (test_bit(0, &global_irq_lock)) {
12727         /* nothing */ ;
12728     }
12729 }
12730
12731 static inline void irq_exit(int cpu, int irq)
12732 {
12733     −local_irq_count(cpu);
12734 }
12735
12736 static inline int hardirq_trylock(int cpu)
12737 {
12738     return !local_irq_count(cpu)
12739         && !test_bit(0, &global_irq_lock);
12740 }
12741
12742 #define hardirq_endlock(cpu)    do { } while (0)
12743
12744 extern void synchronize_irq(void);
12745
12746 #endif                              /* CONFIG_SMP */
```

```
12747
12748 #endif                              /* __ASM_HARDIRQ_H */
```

include/asm-i386/highmem.h

```
12749 /*
12750  * highmem.h: virtual kernel memory mappings for high
12751  * memory
12752  *
12753  * Used in CONFIG_HIGHMEM systems for memory pages which
12754  * are not addressable by direct kernel virtual adresses.
12755  *
12756  * Copyright (C) 1999 Gerhard Wichert, Siemens AG
12757  *                    Gerhard.Wichert@pdb.siemens.de
12758  *
12759  *
12760  * Redesigned the x86 32-bit VM architecture to deal with
12761  * up to 16 Terrabyte physical memory. With current x86
12762  * CPUs we now support up to 64 Gigabytes physical RAM.
12763  *
12764  * Copyright (C) 1999 Ingo Molnar <mingo@redhat.com>
12765  */
12766
12767 #ifndef _ASM_HIGHMEM_H
12768 #define _ASM_HIGHMEM_H
12769
12770 #ifdef __KERNEL__
12771
12772 #include <linux/config.h>
12773 #include <linux/init.h>
12774 #include <linux/interrupt.h>
12775 #include <asm/kmap_types.h>
12776 #include <asm/pgtable.h>
12777
12778 /* undef for production */
12779 #define HIGHMEM_DEBUG 1
12780
12781 /* declarations for highmem.c */
12782 extern unsigned long highstart_pfn, highend_pfn;
12783
12784 extern pte_t *kmap_pte;
12785 extern pgprot_t kmap_prot;
12786 extern pte_t *pkmap_page_table;
12787
12788 extern void kmap_init(void) __init;
12789
12790 /* Right now we initialize only a single pte table. It
12791  * can be extended easily, subsequent pte tables have to
```

```
12792  * be allocated in one physical chunk of RAM.  */
12793 #define PKMAP_BASE (0xfe000000UL)
12794 #ifdef CONFIG_X86_PAE
12795 #define LAST_PKMAP 512
12796 #else
12797 #define LAST_PKMAP 1024
12798 #endif
12799 #define LAST_PKMAP_MASK (LAST_PKMAP-1)
12800 #define PKMAP_NR(virt)  ((virt-PKMAP_BASE) >> PAGE_SHIFT)
12801 #define PKMAP_ADDR(nr)                                     \
12802   (PKMAP_BASE + ((nr) << PAGE_SHIFT))
12803
12804 extern void *FASTCALL(kmap_high(struct page *page));
12805 extern void FASTCALL(kunmap_high(struct page *page));
12806
12807 static inline void *kmap(struct page *page)
12808 {
12809   if (in_interrupt())
12810     BUG();
12811   if (page < highmem_start_page)
12812     return page_address(page);
12813   return kmap_high(page);
12814 }
12815
12816 static inline void kunmap(struct page *page)
12817 {
12818   if (in_interrupt())
12819     BUG();
12820   if (page < highmem_start_page)
12821     return;
12822   kunmap_high(page);
12823 }
12824
12825 /* The use of kmap_atomic/kunmap_atomic is discouraged -
12826  * kmap/kunmap gives a more generic (and caching)
12827  * interface. But kmap_atomic can be used in IRQ
12828  * contexts, so in some (very limited) cases we need it.
12829  */
12830 static inline void *kmap_atomic(struct page *page,
12831     enum km_type type)
12832 {
12833   enum fixed_addresses idx;
12834   unsigned long vaddr;
12835
12836   if (page < highmem_start_page)
12837     return page_address(page);
12838
```

```
12839    idx = type + KM_TYPE_NR * smp_processor_id();
12840    vaddr = __fix_to_virt(FIX_KMAP_BEGIN + idx);
12841 #if HIGHMEM_DEBUG
12842    if (!pte_none(*(kmap_pte - idx)))
12843      BUG();
12844 #endif
12845    set_pte(kmap_pte - idx, mk_pte(page, kmap_prot));
12846    __flush_tlb_one(vaddr);
12847
12848    return (void *) vaddr;
12849 }
12850
12851 static inline void kunmap_atomic(void *kvaddr,
12852      enum km_type type)
12853 {
12854 #if HIGHMEM_DEBUG
12855    unsigned long vaddr = (unsigned long) kvaddr;
12856    enum fixed_addresses idx =
12857        type + KM_TYPE_NR * smp_processor_id();
12858
12859    if (vaddr < FIXADDR_START)      // FIXME
12860      return;
12861
12862    if (vaddr != __fix_to_virt(FIX_KMAP_BEGIN + idx))
12863      BUG();
12864
12865    /* force other mappings to Oops if they'll try to
12866     * access this pte without first remap it */
12867    pte_clear(kmap_pte - idx);
12868    __flush_tlb_one(vaddr);
12869 #endif
12870 }
12871
12872 #endif                           /* __KERNEL__ */
12873
12874 #endif                           /* _ASM_HIGHMEM_H */
```

include/asm-i386/hw_irq.h

```
12875 #ifndef _ASM_HW_IRQ_H
12876 #define _ASM_HW_IRQ_H
12877
12878 /*
12879  *      linux/include/asm/hw_irq.h
12880  *
12881  *      (C) 1992, 1993 Linus Torvalds, (C) 1997 Ingo
12882  *      Molnar
12883  *
12884  *      moved some of the old arch/i386/kernel/irq.h to
12885  *      here. VY
12886  *
12887  *      IRQ/IPI changes taken from work by Thomas Radke
12888  *      <tomsoft@informatik.tu-chemnitz.de>
12889  */
12890
12891 #include <linux/config.h>
12892 #include <asm/irq.h>
12893
12894 /* IDT vectors usable for external interrupt sources
12895  * start at 0x20: */
12896 #define FIRST_EXTERNAL_VECTOR    0x20
12897
12898 #define SYSCALL_VECTOR           0x80
12899
12900 /* Vectors 0x20-0x2f are used for ISA interrupts.  */
12901
12902 /* Special IRQ vectors used by the SMP architecture,
12903  * 0xf0-0xff
12904  *
12905  * some of the following vectors are 'rare', they are
12906  * merged into a single vector (CALL_FUNCTION_VECTOR) to
12907  * save vector space.  TLB, reschedule and local APIC
12908  * vectors are performance-critical.
12909  *
12910  * Vectors 0xf0-0xfa are free (reserved for future Linux
12911  * use).  */
12912 #define SPURIOUS_APIC_VECTOR     0xff
12913 #define ERROR_APIC_VECTOR        0xfe
12914 #define INVALIDATE_TLB_VECTOR    0xfd
12915 #define RESCHEDULE_VECTOR        0xfc
12916 #define CALL_FUNCTION_VECTOR     0xfb
12917
12918 /* Local APIC timer IRQ vector is on a different priority
12919  * level, to work around the 'lost local interrupt if
12920  * more than 2 IRQ sources per level' errata.  */
12921 #define LOCAL_TIMER_VECTOR       0xef
12922
12923 /* First APIC vector available to drivers: (vectors
12924  * 0x30-0xee) we start at 0x31 to spread out vectors
12925  * evenly between priority levels. (0x80 is the syscall
12926  * vector) */
12927 #define FIRST_DEVICE_VECTOR      0x31
12928 #define FIRST_SYSTEM_VECTOR      0xef
12929
12930 extern int irq_vector[NR_IRQS];
```

```
12931 #define IO_APIC_VECTOR(irq)     irq_vector[irq]
12932
12933 /* Various low-level irq details needed by irq.c,
12934  * process.c, time.c, io_apic.c and smp.c
12935  *
12936  * Interrupt entry/exit code at both C and assembly level
12937  */
12938 extern void mask_irq(unsigned int irq);
12939 extern void unmask_irq(unsigned int irq);
12940 extern void disable_8259A_irq(unsigned int irq);
12941 extern void enable_8259A_irq(unsigned int irq);
12942 extern int i8259A_irq_pending(unsigned int irq);
12943 extern void make_8259A_irq(unsigned int irq);
12944 extern void init_8259A(int aeoi);
12945 extern void FASTCALL(send_IPI_self(int vector));
12946 extern void init_VISWS_APIC_irqs(void);
12947 extern void setup_IO_APIC(void);
12948 extern void disable_IO_APIC(void);
12949 extern void print_IO_APIC(void);
12950 extern int IO_APIC_get_PCI_irq_vector(int bus, int slot,
12951     int fn);
12952 extern void send_IPI(int dest, int vector);
12953
12954 extern unsigned long io_apic_irqs;
12955 extern volatile unsigned long irq_err_count;
12956
12957 extern char _stext, _etext;
12958
12959 #define IO_APIC_IRQ(x)                                    \
12960   (((x) >= 16) || ((1<<(x)) & io_apic_irqs))
12961
12962 #define __STR(x) #x
12963 #define STR(x) __STR(x)
12964
12965 #define SAVE_ALL                                          \
12966         "cld\n\t"                                         \
12967         "pushl %es\n\t"                                   \
12968         "pushl %ds\n\t"                                   \
12969         "pushl %eax\n\t"                                  \
12970         "pushl %ebp\n\t"                                  \
12971         "pushl %edi\n\t"                                  \
12972         "pushl %esi\n\t"                                  \
12973         "pushl %edx\n\t"                                  \
12974         "pushl %ecx\n\t"                                  \
12975         "pushl %ebx\n\t"                                  \
12976         "movl $" STR(__KERNEL_DS) ",%edx\n\t"             \
12977         "movl %edx,%ds\n\t"                               \
12978         "movl %edx,%es\n\t"
12979
12980 #define IRQ_NAME2(nr) nr##_interrupt(void)
12981 #define IRQ_NAME(nr) IRQ_NAME2(IRQ##nr)
12982
12983 #define GET_CURRENT                                       \
12984         "movl %esp, %ebx\n\t"                             \
12985         "andl $-8192, %ebx\n\t"
12986
12987 /* SMP has a few special interrupts for IPI messages */
12988
12989 /* there is a second layer of macro just to get the
12990  * symbolic name for the vector evaluated.  This change
12991  * is for RTLinux */
12992 #define BUILD_SMP_INTERRUPT(x,v)                          \
12993   XBUILD_SMP_INTERRUPT(x,v)
12994 #define XBUILD_SMP_INTERRUPT(x,v)                         \
12995 asmlinkage void x(void);                                  \
12996 asmlinkage void call_##x(void);                           \
12997 __asm__("\n" __ALIGN_STR "\n"                             \
12998         SYMBOL_NAME_STR(x) ":\n\t"                        \
12999         "pushl $"#v"\n\t"                                 \
13000         SAVE_ALL                                          \
13001         SYMBOL_NAME_STR(call_##x)":\n\t"                  \
13002         "call "SYMBOL_NAME_STR(smp_##x)"\n\t"             \
13003         "jmp ret_from_intr\n");
13004
13005 #define BUILD_SMP_TIMER_INTERRUPT(x,v)                    \
13006   XBUILD_SMP_TIMER_INTERRUPT(x,v)
13007 #define XBUILD_SMP_TIMER_INTERRUPT(x,v)                   \
13008 asmlinkage void x(struct pt_regs * regs);                 \
13009 asmlinkage void call_##x(void);                           \
13010 __asm__("\n" __ALIGN_STR "\n"                             \
13011         SYMBOL_NAME_STR(x) ":\n\t"                        \
13012         "pushl $"#v"\n\t"                                 \
13013         SAVE_ALL                                          \
13014         "movl %esp,%eax\n\t"                              \
13015         "pushl %eax\n\t"                                  \
13016         SYMBOL_NAME_STR(call_##x)":\n\t"                  \
13017         "call "SYMBOL_NAME_STR(smp_##x)"\n\t"             \
13018         "addl $4,%esp\n\t"                                \
13019         "jmp ret_from_intr\n");
13020
13021 #define BUILD_COMMON_IRQ()                                \
13022 asmlinkage void call_do_IRQ(void);                        \
13023 __asm__("\n" __ALIGN_STR"\n"                              \
13024         "common_interrupt:\n\t"                          \
```

```
13025          SAVE_ALL                                              \
13026          "pushl $ret_from_intr\n\t"                            \
13027          SYMBOL_NAME_STR(call_do_IRQ)":\n\t"                   \
13028          "jmp "SYMBOL_NAME_STR(do_IRQ));
13029
13030 /* subtle. orig_eax is used by the signal code to
13031  * distinct between system calls and interrupted 'random
13032  * user-space'. Thus we have to put a negative value into
13033  * orig_eax here. (the problem is that both system calls
13034  * and IRQs want to have small integer numbers in
13035  * orig_eax, and the syscall code has won the
13036  * optimization conflict ;)
13037  *
13038  * Subtle as a pigs ear.  VY */
13039
13040 #define BUILD_IRQ(nr)                                           \
13041 asmlinkage void IRQ_NAME(nr);                                  \
13042 __asm__("\n" __ALIGN_STR "\n"                                  \
13043          SYMBOL_NAME_STR(IRQ) #nr "_interrupt:\n\t"            \
13044          "pushl $"#nr"-256\n\t"                                \
13045          "jmp common_interrupt");
13046
13047 extern unsigned long prof_cpu_mask;
13048 extern unsigned int *prof_buffer;
13049 extern unsigned long prof_len;
13050 extern unsigned long prof_shift;
13051
13052 /* x86 profiling function, SMP safe. We might want to do
13053  * this in assembly totally?  */
13054 static inline void x86_do_profile(unsigned long eip)
13055 {
13056   if (!prof_buffer)
13057     return;
13058
13059   /* Only measure the CPUs specified by
13060    * /proc/irq/prof_cpu_mask. (default is all CPUs.)  */
13061   if (!((1 << smp_processor_id()) & prof_cpu_mask))
13062     return;
13063
13064   eip -= (unsigned long) &_stext;
13065   eip >>= prof_shift;
13066   /* Don't ignore out-of-bounds EIP values silently, put
13067    * them into the last histogram slot, so if present,
13068    * they will show up as a sharp peak.  */
13069   if (eip > prof_len - 1)
13070     eip = prof_len - 1;
13071   atomic_inc((atomic_t *) & prof_buffer[eip]);
13072 }
13073
13074 #ifdef CONFIG_SMP                        /* more of this file
13075                                          * should probably be
13076                                          * ifdefed SMP */
13077 static inline void hw_resend_irq(struct hw_interrupt_type
13078    *h, unsigned int i)
13079 {
13080   if (IO_APIC_IRQ(i))
13081     send_IPI_self(IO_APIC_VECTOR(i));
13082 }
13083 #else
13084 static inline void hw_resend_irq(struct hw_interrupt_type
13085    *h, unsigned int i)
13086 {
13087 }
13088
13089 #endif
13090
13091 #endif                                    /* _ASM_HW_IRQ_H */
```

include/asm-i386/ipcbuf.h

```
13092 #ifndef __i386_IPCBUF_H__
13093 #define __i386_IPCBUF_H__
13094
13095 /* The ipc64_perm structure for i386 architecture.  Note
13096  * extra padding because this structure is passed back
13097  * and forth between kernel and user space.
13098  *
13099  * Pad space is left for:
13100  * - 32-bit mode_t and seq
13101  * - 2 miscellaneous 32-bit values */
13102
13103 struct ipc64_perm {
13104   __kernel_key_t key;
13105   __kernel_uid32_t uid;
13106   __kernel_gid32_t gid;
13107   __kernel_uid32_t cuid;
13108   __kernel_gid32_t cgid;
13109   __kernel_mode_t mode;
13110   unsigned short __pad1;
13111   unsigned short seq;
13112   unsigned short __pad2;
13113   unsigned long __unused1;
13114   unsigned long __unused2;
13115 };
13116
13117 #endif                              /* __i386_IPCBUF_H__  */
```

include/asm-i386/ipc.h

```
13118 #ifndef __i386_IPC_H__
13119 #define __i386_IPC_H__
13120
13121 /* These are used to wrap system calls on x86.
13122  *
13123  * See arch/i386/kernel/sys_i386.c for ugly details.. */
13124 struct ipc_kludge {
13125   struct msgbuf *msgp;
13126   long msgtyp;
13127 };
13128
13129 #define SEMOP        1
13130 #define SEMGET       2
13131 #define SEMCTL       3
13132 #define MSGSND      11
13133 #define MSGRCV      12
13134 #define MSGGET      13
13135 #define MSGCTL      14
13136 #define SHMAT       21
13137 #define SHMDT       22
13138 #define SHMGET      23
13139 #define SHMCTL      24
13140
13141 /* Used by the DIPC package, try and avoid reusing it */
13142 #define DIPC        25
13143
13144 #define IPCCALL(version,op)     ((version)<<16 | (op))
13145
13146 #endif
```

include/asm-i386/irq.h

```
13147 #ifndef _ASM_IRQ_H
13148 #define _ASM_IRQ_H
13149
13150 /*
13151  *    linux/include/asm/irq.h
13152  *
13153  *    (C) 1992, 1993 Linus Torvalds, (C) 1997 Ingo Molnar
13154  *
13155  *    IRQ/IPI changes taken from work by Thomas Radke
13156  *    <tomsoft@informatik.tu-chemnitz.de>
13157  */
13158
13159 #define TIMER_IRQ 0
13160
13161 /* 16 8259A IRQ's, 208 potential APIC interrupt sources.
13162  * Right now the APIC is mostly only used for SMP.  256
13163  * vectors is an architectural limit. (we can have more
13164  * than 256 devices theoretically, but they will have to
13165  * use shared interrupts) Since vectors 0x00-0x1f are
13166  * used/reserved for the CPU, the usable vector space is
13167  * 0x20-0xff (224 vectors) */
13168 #define NR_IRQS 224
13169
13170 static __inline__ int irq_cannonicalize(int irq)
13171 {
13172   return ((irq == 2) ? 9 : irq);
13173 }
13174
13175 extern void disable_irq(unsigned int);
13176 extern void disable_irq_nosync(unsigned int);
13177 extern void enable_irq(unsigned int);
13178
13179 #endif                          /* _ASM_IRQ_H */
```

include/asm-i386/ldt.h

```
13180 /*
13181  * ldt.h
13182  *
13183  * Definitions of structures used with the modify_ldt
13184  * system call.
13185  */
13186 #ifndef _LINUX_LDT_H
13187 #define _LINUX_LDT_H
13188
13189 /* Maximum number of LDT entries supported. */
13190 #define LDT_ENTRIES     8192
13191 /* The size of each LDT entry. */
13192 #define LDT_ENTRY_SIZE  8
13193
13194 #ifndef __ASSEMBLY__
13195 struct modify_ldt_ldt_s {
13196   unsigned int entry_number;
13197   unsigned long base_addr;
13198   unsigned int limit;
13199   unsigned int seg_32bit:        1;
13200   unsigned int contents:         2;
13201   unsigned int read_exec_only:   1;
13202   unsigned int limit_in_pages:   1;
13203   unsigned int seg_not_present:  1;
```

```
13204     unsigned int useable:        1;
13205 };
13206
13207 #define MODIFY_LDT_CONTENTS_DATA     0
13208 #define MODIFY_LDT_CONTENTS_STACK    1
13209 #define MODIFY_LDT_CONTENTS_CODE     2
13210
13211 #endif                             /* !__ASSEMBLY__ */
13212 #endif
```

include/asm-i386/mman.h

```
13213 #ifndef __I386_MMAN_H__
13214 #define __I386_MMAN_H__
13215
13216 #define PROT_READ       0x1    /* page can be read */
13217 #define PROT_WRITE      0x2    /* page can be written */
13218 #define PROT_EXEC       0x4    /* page can be
13219                                * executed */
13220 #define PROT_NONE       0x0    /* page can not be
13221                                * accessed */
13222
13223 #define MAP_SHARED      0x01   /* Share changes */
13224 #define MAP_PRIVATE     0x02   /* Changes are private */
13225 #define MAP_TYPE        0x0f   /* Mask for type of
13226                                * mapping */
13227 #define MAP_FIXED       0x10   /* Interpret addr
13228                                * exactly */
13229 #define MAP_ANONYMOUS   0x20   /* don't use a file */
13230
13231 #define MAP_GROWSDOWN   0x0100 /* stack-like segment */
13232 #define MAP_DENYWRITE   0x0800 /* ETXTBSY */
13233 #define MAP_EXECUTABLE  0x1000 /* mark it as an
13234                                * executable */
13235 #define MAP_LOCKED      0x2000 /* pages are locked */
13236 #define MAP_NORESERVE   0x4000 /* don't check for
13237                                * reservations */
13238
13239 #define MS_ASYNC        1      /* sync memory
13240                                * asynchronously */
13241 #define MS_INVALIDATE   2      /* invalidate the caches
13242                                */
13243 #define MS_SYNC         4      /* synchronous memory
13244                                * sync */
13245
13246 #define MCL_CURRENT     1      /* lock all current
13247                                * mappings */
13248 #define MCL_FUTURE      2      /* lock all future
13249                                * mappings */
13250
13251 #define MADV_NORMAL     0x0    /* default page-in
13252                                * behavior */
13253 #define MADV_RANDOM     0x1    /* page-in minimum
13254                                * required */
13255 #define MADV_SEQUENTIAL 0x2    /* read-ahead
13256                                * aggressively */
13257 #define MADV_WILLNEED   0x3    /* pre-fault pages */
13258 #define MADV_DONTNEED   0x4    /* discard these pages */
13259
13260 /* compatibility flags */
13261 #define MAP_ANON        MAP_ANONYMOUS
13262 #define MAP_FILE        0
13263
13264 #endif                             /* __I386_MMAN_H__ */
```

include/asm-i386/mmu_context.h

```
13265 #ifndef __I386_MMU_CONTEXT_H
13266 #define __I386_MMU_CONTEXT_H
13267
13268 #include <linux/config.h>
13269 #include <asm/desc.h>
13270 #include <asm/atomic.h>
13271 #include <asm/pgalloc.h>
13272
13273 /* possibly do the LDT unload here?  */
13274 #define destroy_context(mm)          do { } while(0)
13275 #define init_new_context(tsk,mm)     0
13276
13277 #ifdef CONFIG_SMP
13278
13279 static inline void enter_lazy_tlb(struct mm_struct *mm,
13280     struct task_struct *tsk, unsigned cpu)
13281 {
13282   if (cpu_tlbstate[cpu].state == TLBSTATE_OK)
13283     cpu_tlbstate[cpu].state = TLBSTATE_LAZY;
13284 }
13285 #else
13286 static inline void enter_lazy_tlb(struct mm_struct *mm,
13287     struct task_struct *tsk, unsigned cpu)
13288 {
13289 }
13290
13291 #endif
13292
13293 static inline void switch_mm(struct mm_struct *prev,
```

```
13294     struct mm_struct *next, struct task_struct *tsk,
13295     unsigned cpu)
13296 {
13297   if (prev != next) {
13298     /* stop flush ipis for the previous mm */
13299     clear_bit(cpu, &prev->cpu_vm_mask);
13300     /* Re-load LDT if necessary */
13301     if (prev->context.segments != next->context.segments)
13302       load_LDT(next);
13303 #ifdef CONFIG_SMP
13304     cpu_tlbstate[cpu].state = TLBSTATE_OK;
13305     cpu_tlbstate[cpu].active_mm = next;
13306 #endif
13307     set_bit(cpu, &next->cpu_vm_mask);
13308     /* Re-load page tables */
13309     asm volatile("movl %0,%%cr3"::"r" (__pa(next->pgd)));
13310   }
13311 #ifdef CONFIG_SMP
13312   else {
13313     cpu_tlbstate[cpu].state = TLBSTATE_OK;
13314     if (cpu_tlbstate[cpu].active_mm != next)
13315       BUG();
13316     if (!test_and_set_bit(cpu, &next->cpu_vm_mask)) {
13317       /* We were in lazy tlb mode and leave_mm disabled
13318        * tlb flush IPI delivery. We must flush our tlb.*/
13319       local_flush_tlb();
13320     }
13321   }
13322 #endif
13323 }
13324
13325 #define activate_mm(prev, next)                    \
13326         switch_mm((prev),(next),NULL,smp_processor_id())
13327
13328 #endif
```

include/asm-i386/mmu.h

```
13329 #ifndef __i386_MMU_H
13330 #define __i386_MMU_H
13331
13332 /* The i386 doesn't have a mmu context, but we put the
13333  * segment information here.  */
13334 typedef struct {
13335   void *segments;
13336 } mm_context_t;
13337
13338 #endif
```

include/asm-i386/module.h

```
13339 #ifndef _ASM_I386_MODULE_H
13340 #define _ASM_I386_MODULE_H
13341 /* This file contains the i386 architecture specific
13342  * module code.  */
13343
13344 #define module_map(x)          vmalloc(x)
13345 #define module_unmap(x)        vfree(x)
13346 #define module_arch_init(x)    (0)
13347
13348 #endif                         /* _ASM_I386_MODULE_H */
```

include/asm-i386/msgbuf.h

```
13349 #ifndef _I386_MSGBUF_H
13350 #define _I386_MSGBUF_H
13351
13352 /* The msqid64_ds structure for i386 architecture.  Note
13353  * extra padding because this structure is passed back
13354  * and forth between kernel and user space.
13355  *
13356  * Pad space is left for:
13357  * - 64-bit time_t to solve y2038 problem
13358  * - 2 miscellaneous 32-bit values */
13359
13360 struct msqid64_ds {
13361   struct ipc64_perm msg_perm;
13362   __kernel_time_t msg_stime;    /* last msgsnd time */
13363   unsigned long __unused1;
13364   __kernel_time_t msg_rtime;    /* last msgrcv time */
13365   unsigned long __unused2;
13366   __kernel_time_t msg_ctime;    /* last change time */
13367   unsigned long __unused3;
13368   unsigned long msg_cbytes;     /* current number of
13369                                  * bytes on queue */
13370   unsigned long msg_qnum;       /* number of messages in
13371                                  * queue */
13372   unsigned long msg_qbytes;     /* max number of bytes
13373                                  * on queue */
13374   __kernel_pid_t msg_lspid;     /* pid of last msgsnd */
13375   __kernel_pid_t msg_lrpid;     /* last receive pid */
13376   unsigned long __unused4;
13377   unsigned long __unused5;
13378 };
13379
13380 #endif                         /* _I386_MSGBUF_H */
```

include/asm-i386/page.h

```
13381 #ifndef _I386_PAGE_H
13382 #define _I386_PAGE_H
13383
13384 /* PAGE_SHIFT determines the page size */
13385 #define PAGE_SHIFT        12
13386 #define PAGE_SIZE         (1UL << PAGE_SHIFT)
13387 #define PAGE_MASK         (~(PAGE_SIZE-1))
13388
13389 #ifdef __KERNEL__
13390 #ifndef __ASSEMBLY__
13391
13392 #include <linux/config.h>
13393
13394 #ifdef CONFIG_X86_USE_3DNOW
13395
13396 #include <asm/mmx.h>
13397
13398 #define clear_page(page)         mmx_clear_page(page)
13399 #define copy_page(to,from)       mmx_copy_page(to,from)
13400
13401 #else
13402
13403 /* On older X86 processors its not a win to use MMX here
13404  * it seems.  Maybe the K6-III ?  */
13405
13406 #define clear_page(page)                                \
13407        memset((void *)(page), 0, PAGE_SIZE)
13408 #define copy_page(to,from)                              \
13409        memcpy((void *)(to), (void *)(from), PAGE_SIZE)
13410
13411 #endif
13412
13413 #define clear_user_page(page, vaddr)     clear_page(page)
13414 #define copy_user_page(to, from, vaddr)                 \
13415        copy_page(to, from)
13416
13417 /* These are used to make use of C type-checking..  */
13418 #if CONFIG_X86_PAE
13419 typedef struct {
13420    unsigned long pte_low, pte_high;
13421 } pte_t;
13422 typedef struct {
13423    unsigned long long pmd;
13424 } pmd_t;
13425 typedef struct {
13426    unsigned long long pgd;
```

```
13427 } pgd_t;
13428
13429 #define pte_val(x)                                      \
13430   ((x).pte_low | ((unsigned long long)(x).pte_high << 32))
13431 #else
13432 typedef struct {
13433    unsigned long pte_low;
13434 } pte_t;
13435 typedef struct {
13436    unsigned long pmd;
13437 } pmd_t;
13438 typedef struct {
13439    unsigned long pgd;
13440 } pgd_t;
13441
13442 #define pte_val(x)        ((x).pte_low)
13443 #endif
13444 #define PTE_MASK          PAGE_MASK
13445
13446 typedef struct {
13447    unsigned long pgprot;
13448 } pgprot_t;
13449
13450 #define pmd_val(x)        ((x).pmd)
13451 #define pgd_val(x)        ((x).pgd)
13452 #define pgprot_val(x)     ((x).pgprot)
13453
13454 #define __pte(x) ((pte_t) { (x) } )
13455 #define __pmd(x) ((pmd_t) { (x) } )
13456 #define __pgd(x) ((pgd_t) { (x) } )
13457 #define __pgprot(x)       ((pgprot_t) { (x) } )
13458
13459 #endif                            /* !__ASSEMBLY__ */
13460
13461 /* to align the pointer to the (next) page boundary */
13462 #define PAGE_ALIGN(addr) (((addr)+PAGE_SIZE-1)&PAGE_MASK)
13463
13464 /* This handles the memory map.. We could make this a
13465  * config option, but too many people screw it up, and
13466  * too few need it.
13467  *
13468  * A __PAGE_OFFSET of 0xC0000000 means that the kernel
13469  * has a virtual address space of one gigabyte, which
13470  * limits the amount of physical memory you can use to
13471  * about 950MB.
13472  *
13473  * If you want more physical memory than this then see
13474  * the CONFIG_HIGHMEM4G and CONFIG_HIGHMEM64G options in
```

```
13475  * the kernel configuration.  */
13476
13477 #define __PAGE_OFFSET           (0xC0000000)
13478
13479 #ifndef __ASSEMBLY__
13480
13481 /* Tell the user there is some problem. Beep too, so we
13482  * can see^H^H^Hhear bugs in early bootup as well!  */
13483 #define BUG() do {                                      \
13484   printk("kernel BUG at %s:%d!\n", __FILE__, __LINE__); \
13485   __asm__ __volatile__(".byte 0x0f,0x0b");             \
13486 } while (0)
13487
13488 #define PAGE_BUG(page) do {                             \
13489         BUG();                                          \
13490 } while (0)
13491
13492 /* Pure 2^n version of get_order */
13493 extern __inline__ int get_order(unsigned long size)
13494 {
13495   int order;
13496
13497   size = (size - 1) >> (PAGE_SHIFT - 1);
13498   order = -1;
13499   do {
13500     size >>= 1;
13501     order++;
13502   } while (size);
13503   return order;
13504 }
13505
13506 #endif                          /* __ASSEMBLY__ */
13507
13508 #define PAGE_OFFSET ((unsigned long)__PAGE_OFFSET)
13509 #define __pa(x) ((unsigned long)(x)-PAGE_OFFSET)
13510 #define __va(x) ((void*)((unsigned long)(x)+PAGE_OFFSET))
13511 #define virt_to_page(kaddr)                             \
13512         (mem_map + (__pa(kaddr) >> PAGE_SHIFT))
13513 #define VALID_PAGE(page)   ((page - mem_map) < max_mapnr)
13514
13515
13516 #endif                          /* __KERNEL__ */
13517
13518 #endif                          /* _I386_PAGE_H */
```

include/asm-i386/param.h

```
13519 #ifndef _ASMi386_PARAM_H
13520 #define _ASMi386_PARAM_H
```

```
13521
13522 #ifndef HZ
13523 #define HZ 100
13524 #endif
13525
13526 #define EXEC_PAGESIZE   4096
13527
13528 #ifndef NGROUPS
13529 #define NGROUPS         32
13530 #endif
13531
13532 #ifndef NOGROUP
13533 #define NOGROUP         (-1)
13534 #endif
13535
13536 #define MAXHOSTNAMELEN  64   /* max length of hostname */
13537
13538 #ifdef __KERNEL__
13539 # define CLOCKS_PER_SEC 100   /* frequency at which
13540                                  * times() counts */
13541 #endif
13542
13543 #endif
```

include/asm-i386/pgalloc-2level.h

```
13544 #ifndef _I386_PGALLOC_2LEVEL_H
13545 #define _I386_PGALLOC_2LEVEL_H
13546
13547 /* traditional i386 two-level paging, page table
13548  * allocation routines: */
13549
13550 extern __inline__ pmd_t *get_pmd_fast(void)
13551 {
13552   return (pmd_t *) 0;
13553 }
13554
13555 extern __inline__ void free_pmd_fast(pmd_t * pmd)
13556 {
13557 }
13558 extern __inline__ void free_pmd_slow(pmd_t * pmd)
13559 {
13560 }
13561
13562 extern inline pmd_t *pmd_alloc(pgd_t * pgd,
13563     unsigned long address)
13564 {
```

p 629

```
13565   if (!pgd)
13566     BUG();
13567   return (pmd_t *) pgd;
13568 }
13569
13570 #endif                          /* _I386_PGALLOC_2LEVEL_H */
```

include/asm-i386/pgalloc-3level.h

```
13571 #ifndef _I386_PGALLOC_3LEVEL_H
13572 #define _I386_PGALLOC_3LEVEL_H
13573
13574 /*
13575  * Intel Physical Address Extension (PAE) Mode -
13576  * three-level page tables on PPro+ CPUs. Page-table
13577  * allocation routines.
13578  *
13579  * Copyright (C) 1999 Ingo Molnar <mingo@redhat.com>
13580  */
13581
13582 extern __inline__ pmd_t *get_pmd_slow(void)
13583 {
13584   pmd_t *ret = (pmd_t *) __get_free_page(GFP_KERNEL);
13585
13586   if (ret)
13587     memset(ret, 0, PAGE_SIZE);
13588   return ret;
13589 }
13590
13591 extern __inline__ pmd_t *get_pmd_fast(void)
13592 {
13593   unsigned long *ret;
13594
13595   if ((ret = pmd_quicklist) != NULL) {
13596     pmd_quicklist = (unsigned long *) (*ret);
13597     ret[0] = 0;
13598     pgtable_cache_size--;
13599   } else
13600     ret = (unsigned long *) get_pmd_slow();
13601   return (pmd_t *) ret;
13602 }
13603
13604 extern __inline__ void free_pmd_fast(pmd_t * pmd)
13605 {
13606   *(unsigned long *) pmd = (unsigned long) pmd_quicklist;
13607   pmd_quicklist = (unsigned long *) pmd;
13608   pgtable_cache_size++;
13609 }
```

```
13610
13611 extern __inline__ void free_pmd_slow(pmd_t * pmd)
13612 {
13613   free_page((unsigned long) pmd);
13614 }
13615
13616 extern inline pmd_t *pmd_alloc(pgd_t * pgd,
13617     unsigned long address)
13618 {
13619   if (!pgd)
13620     BUG();
13621   address = (address >> PMD_SHIFT) & (PTRS_PER_PMD - 1);
13622   if (pgd_none(*pgd)) {
13623     pmd_t *page = get_pmd_fast();
13624
13625     if (!page)
13626       page = get_pmd_slow();
13627     if (page) {
13628       if (pgd_none(*pgd)) {
13629         set_pgd(pgd, __pgd(1 + __pa(page)));
13630         __flush_tlb();
13631         return page + address;
13632       } else
13633         free_pmd_fast(page);
13634     } else
13635       return NULL;
13636   }
13637   return (pmd_t *) pgd_page(*pgd) + address;
13638 }
13639
13640 #endif                          /* _I386_PGALLOC_3LEVEL_H */
```

include/asm-i386/pgalloc.h

```
13641 #ifndef _I386_PGALLOC_H
13642 #define _I386_PGALLOC_H
13643
13644 #include <linux/config.h>
13645 #include <asm/processor.h>
13646 #include <asm/fixmap.h>
13647 #include <linux/threads.h>
13648
13649 #define pgd_quicklist (current_cpu_data.pgd_quick)
13650 #define pmd_quicklist (current_cpu_data.pmd_quick)
13651 #define pte_quicklist (current_cpu_data.pte_quick)
13652 #define pgtable_cache_size                              \
13653   (current_cpu_data.pgtable_cache_sz)
```

```
13654
13655 #if CONFIG_X86_PAE
13656 # include <asm/pgalloc-3level.h>
13657 #else
13658 # include <asm/pgalloc-2level.h>
13659 #endif
13660
13661 /* Allocate and free page tables. The xxx_kernel()
13662  * versions are used to allocate a kernel page table -
13663  * this turns on ASN bits if any.  */
13664
13665 extern __inline__ pgd_t *get_pgd_slow(void)
13666 {
13667   pgd_t *ret = (pgd_t *) __get_free_page(GFP_KERNEL);
13668
13669   if (ret) {
13670 #if CONFIG_X86_PAE
13671     int i;
13672     for (i = 0; i < USER_PTRS_PER_PGD; i++)
13673       __pgd_clear(ret + i);
13674 #else
13675     memset(ret, 0, USER_PTRS_PER_PGD * sizeof(pgd_t));
13676 #endif
13677     memcpy(ret + USER_PTRS_PER_PGD,
13678         swapper_pg_dir + USER_PTRS_PER_PGD,
13679         (PTRS_PER_PGD -
13680           USER_PTRS_PER_PGD) * sizeof(pgd_t));
13681   }
13682   return ret;
13683 }
13684
13685 extern __inline__ pgd_t *get_pgd_fast(void)
13686 {
13687   unsigned long *ret;
13688
13689   if ((ret = pgd_quicklist) != NULL) {
13690     pgd_quicklist = (unsigned long *) (*ret);
13691     ret[0] = 0;
13692     pgtable_cache_size-;
13693   } else
13694     ret = (unsigned long *) get_pgd_slow();
13695   return (pgd_t *) ret;
13696 }
13697
13698 extern __inline__ void free_pgd_fast(pgd_t * pgd)
13699 {
13700   *(unsigned long *) pgd = (unsigned long) pgd_quicklist;
13701   pgd_quicklist = (unsigned long *) pgd;
13702   pgtable_cache_size++;
13703 }
13704
13705 extern __inline__ void free_pgd_slow(pgd_t * pgd)
13706 {
13707   free_page((unsigned long) pgd);
13708 }
13709
13710 extern pte_t *get_pte_slow(pmd_t * pmd,
13711     unsigned long address_preadjusted);
13712 extern pte_t *get_pte_kernel_slow(pmd_t * pmd,
13713     unsigned long address_preadjusted);
13714
13715 extern __inline__ pte_t *get_pte_fast(void)
13716 {
13717   unsigned long *ret;
13718
13719   if ((ret = (unsigned long *) pte_quicklist) != NULL) {
13720     pte_quicklist = (unsigned long *) (*ret);
13721     ret[0] = ret[1];
13722     pgtable_cache_size-;
13723   }
13724   return (pte_t *) ret;
13725 }
13726
13727 extern __inline__ void free_pte_fast(pte_t * pte)
13728 {
13729   *(unsigned long *) pte = (unsigned long) pte_quicklist;
13730   pte_quicklist = (unsigned long *) pte;
13731   pgtable_cache_size++;
13732 }
13733
13734 extern __inline__ void free_pte_slow(pte_t * pte)
13735 {
13736   free_page((unsigned long) pte);
13737 }
13738
13739 #define pte_free_kernel(pte)    free_pte_slow(pte)
13740 #define pte_free(pte)        free_pte_slow(pte)
13741 #define pgd_free(pgd)        free_pgd_slow(pgd)
13742 #define pgd_alloc()          get_pgd_fast()
13743
13744 extern inline pte_t *pte_alloc_kernel(pmd_t * pmd,
13745     unsigned long address)
13746 {
13747   if (!pmd)
```

```
13748       BUG();
13749     address = (address >> PAGE_SHIFT) & (PTRS_PER_PTE - 1);
13750     if (pmd_none(*pmd)) {
13751         pte_t *page = (pte_t *) get_pte_fast();
13752
13753         if (!page)
13754             return get_pte_kernel_slow(pmd, address);
13755         set_pmd(pmd, __pmd(_KERNPG_TABLE + __pa(page)));
13756         return page + address;
13757     }
13758     if (pmd_bad(*pmd)) {
13759         __handle_bad_pmd_kernel(pmd);
13760         return NULL;
13761     }
13762     return (pte_t *) pmd_page(*pmd) + address;
13763 }
13764
```

p 629
```
13765 extern inline pte_t *pte_alloc(pmd_t * pmd,
13766     unsigned long address)
13767 {
13768     address = (address >> PAGE_SHIFT) & (PTRS_PER_PTE - 1);
13769
13770     if (pmd_none(*pmd))
13771         goto getnew;
13772     if (pmd_bad(*pmd))
13773         goto fix;
13774     return (pte_t *) pmd_page(*pmd) + address;
13775 getnew:
13776     {
13777         unsigned long page = (unsigned long) get_pte_fast();
13778
13779         if (!page)
13780             return get_pte_slow(pmd, address);
13781         set_pmd(pmd, __pmd(_PAGE_TABLE + __pa(page)));
13782         return (pte_t *) page + address;
13783     }
13784 fix:
13785     __handle_bad_pmd(pmd);
13786     return NULL;
13787 }
13788
13789 /* allocating and freeing a pmd is trivial: the 1-entry
13790  * pmd is inside the pgd, so has no extra memory
13791  * associated with it.  (In the PAE case we free the
13792  * page.)  */
13793 #define pmd_free(pmd)        free_pmd_slow(pmd)
13794
13795 #define pmd_free_kernel        pmd_free
13796 #define pmd_alloc_kernel        pmd_alloc
13797
13798 extern int do_check_pgt_cache(int, int);
13799
13800 /* TLB flushing:
13801  *
13802  *  - flush_tlb() flushes the current mm struct TLBs
13803  *  - flush_tlb_all() flushes all processes TLBs
13804  *  - flush_tlb_mm(mm) flushes the specified mm context
13805  *    TLB's
13806  *  - flush_tlb_page(vma, vmaddr) flushes one page
13807  *  - flush_tlb_range(mm, start, end) flushes a range of
13808  *    pages
13809  *  - flush_tlb_pgtables(mm, start, end) flushes a range
13810  *    of page tables
13811  *
13812  * ..but the i386 has somewhat limited tlb flushing
13813  * capabilities, and page-granular flushes are available
13814  * only on i486 and up.  */
13815
13816 #ifndef CONFIG_SMP
13817
13818 #define flush_tlb() __flush_tlb()
13819 #define flush_tlb_all() __flush_tlb_all()
13820 #define local_flush_tlb() __flush_tlb()
13821
13822 static inline void flush_tlb_mm(struct mm_struct *mm)
13823 {
13824     if (mm == current->active_mm)
13825         __flush_tlb();
13826 }
13827
13828 static inline void flush_tlb_page(struct vm_area_struct
13829     *vma, unsigned long addr)
13830 {
13831     if (vma->vm_mm == current->active_mm)
13832         __flush_tlb_one(addr);
13833 }
13834
13835 static inline void flush_tlb_range(struct mm_struct *mm,
13836     unsigned long start, unsigned long end)
13837 {
13838     if (mm == current->active_mm)
13839         __flush_tlb();
13840 }
13841
```

```
13842 #else
13843
13844 #include <asm/smp.h>
13845
13846 #define local_flush_tlb()                              \
13847         __flush_tlb()
13848
13849 extern void flush_tlb_all(void);
13850 extern void flush_tlb_current_task(void);
13851 extern void flush_tlb_mm(struct mm_struct *);
13852 extern void flush_tlb_page(struct vm_area_struct *,
13853     unsigned long);
13854
13855 #define flush_tlb()     flush_tlb_current_task()
13856
13857 static inline void flush_tlb_range(struct mm_struct *mm,
13858     unsigned long start, unsigned long end)
13859 {
13860   flush_tlb_mm(mm);
13861 }
13862
13863 #define TLBSTATE_OK     1
13864 #define TLBSTATE_LAZY   2
13865
13866 struct tlb_state {
13867   struct mm_struct *active_mm;
13868   int state;
13869 };
13870 extern struct tlb_state cpu_tlbstate[NR_CPUS];
13871
13872
13873 #endif
13874
13875 extern inline void flush_tlb_pgtables(struct mm_struct
13876     *mm, unsigned long start, unsigned long end)
13877 {
13878   /* i386 does not keep any page table caches in TLB */
13879 }
13880
13881 #endif                              /* _I386_PGALLOC_H */
```

include/asm-i386/pgtable-2level.h

```
13882 #ifndef _I386_PGTABLE_2LEVEL_H
13883 #define _I386_PGTABLE_2LEVEL_H
13884
13885 /* traditional i386 two-level paging structure: */
13886
13887 #define PGDIR_SHIFT     22
13888 #define PTRS_PER_PGD    1024
13889
13890 /* the i386 is two-level, so we don't really have any PMD
13891  * directory physically.  */
13892 #define PMD_SHIFT       22
13893 #define PTRS_PER_PMD    1
13894
13895 #define PTRS_PER_PTE    1024
13896
13897 #define pte_ERROR(e)                                   \
13898         printk("%s:%d: bad pte %08lx.\n",              \
13899                 __FILE__, __LINE__, (e).pte_low)
13900 #define pmd_ERROR(e)                                   \
13901         printk("%s:%d: bad pmd %08lx.\n",              \
13902                 __FILE__, __LINE__, pmd_val(e))
13903 #define pgd_ERROR(e)                                   \
13904         printk("%s:%d: bad pgd %08lx.\n",              \
13905                 __FILE__, __LINE__, pgd_val(e))
13906
13907 /* The "pgd_xxx()" functions here are trivial for a
13908  * folded two-level setup: the pgd is never bad, and a
13909  * pmd always exists (as it's folded into the pgd entry)
13910  */
13911 extern inline int pgd_none(pgd_t pgd)
13912 {
13913   return 0;
13914 }
13915 extern inline int pgd_bad(pgd_t pgd)
13916 {
13917   return 0;
13918 }
13919 extern inline int pgd_present(pgd_t pgd)
13920 {
13921   return 1;
13922 }
13923 #define pgd_clear(xp)  do { } while (0)
13924
13925 /* Certain architectures need to do special things when
13926  * PTEs within a page table are directly modified.  Thus,
13927  * the following hook is made available.  */
13928 #define set_pte(pteptr, pteval) (*(pteptr) = pteval)
13929 /* (pmds are folded into pgds so this doesnt get actually
13930  * called, but the define is needed for a generic inline
13931  * function.)  */
13932 #define set_pmd(pmdptr, pmdval) (*(pmdptr) = pmdval)
13933 #define set_pgd(pgdptr, pgdval) (*(pgdptr) = pgdval)
```

```
13934
13935 #define pgd_page(pgd)                                  \
13936 ((unsigned long) __va(pgd_val(pgd) & PAGE_MASK))
13937
13938 extern inline pmd_t *pmd_offset(pgd_t * dir,
13939     unsigned long address)
13940 {
13941   return (pmd_t *) dir;
13942 }
13943 #define ptep_get_and_clear(xp)                          \
13944   __pte(xchg(&(xp)->pte_low, 0))
13945 #define pte_same(a, b)                                  \
13946   ((a).pte_low == (b).pte_low)
13947 #define pte_page(x)                                     \
13948   (mem_map+((unsigned long)(((x).pte_low >> PAGE_SHIFT))))
13949 #define pte_none(x)                    (!(x).pte_low)
13950 #define __mk_pte(page_nr,pgprot)                        \
13951   __pte(((page_nr) << PAGE_SHIFT) | pgprot_val(pgprot))
13952
13953 #endif                               /* _I386_PGTABLE_2LEVEL_H */
```

include/asm-i386/pgtable-3level.h

```
13954 #ifndef _I386_PGTABLE_3LEVEL_H
13955 #define _I386_PGTABLE_3LEVEL_H
13956
13957 /*
13958  * Intel Physical Address Extension (PAE) Mode -
13959  * three-level page tables on PPro+ CPUs.
13960  *
13961  * Copyright (C) 1999 Ingo Molnar <mingo@redhat.com>
13962  */
13963
13964 /* PGDIR_SHIFT determines what a top-level page table
13965  * entry can map */
13966 #define PGDIR_SHIFT     30
13967 #define PTRS_PER_PGD    4
13968
13969 /* PMD_SHIFT determines the size of the area a
13970  * middle-level page table can map */
13971 #define PMD_SHIFT       21
13972 #define PTRS_PER_PMD    512
13973
13974 /* entries per page directory level */
13975 #define PTRS_PER_PTE    512
13976
13977 #define pte_ERROR(e)                                    \
13978         printk("%s:%d: bad pte %p(%08lx%08lx).\n",      \
```

```
13979                 __FILE__, __LINE__,                     \
13980                 &(e), (e).pte_high, (e).pte_low)
13981 #define pmd_ERROR(e)                                    \
13982         printk("%s:%d: bad pmd %p(%016Lx).\n",          \
13983                 __FILE__, __LINE__, &(e), pmd_val(e))
13984 #define pgd_ERROR(e)                                    \
13985         printk("%s:%d: bad pgd %p(%016Lx).\n",          \
13986                 __FILE__, __LINE__, &(e), pgd_val(e))
13987
13988 /* Subtle, in PAE mode we cannot have zeroes in the top
13989  * level page directory, the CPU enforces this. (ie. the
13990  * PGD entry always has to have the present bit set.) The
13991  * CPU caches the 4 pgd entries internally, so there is
13992  * no extra memory load on TLB miss, despite one more
13993  * level of indirection.   */
13994 #define EMPTY_PGD (__pa(empty_zero_page) + 1)
13995 #define pgd_none(x)     (pgd_val(x) == EMPTY_PGD)
13996 extern inline int pgd_bad(pgd_t pgd)
13997 {
13998   return 0;
13999 }
14000 extern inline int pgd_present(pgd_t pgd)
14001 {
14002   return !pgd_none(pgd);
14003 }
14004
14005 /* Rules for using set_pte: the pte being assigned *must*
14006  * be either not present or in a state where the hardware
14007  * will not attempt to update the pte.  In places where
14008  * this is not possible, use pte_get_and_clear to obtain
14009  * the old pte value and then use set_pte to update it.
14010  * -ben */
14011 static inline void set_pte(pte_t * ptep, pte_t pte)
14012 {
14013   ptep->pte_high = pte.pte_high;
14014   smp_wmb();
14015   ptep->pte_low = pte.pte_low;
14016 }
14017
14018 #define set_pmd(pmdptr,pmdval)                          \
14019   set_64bit((unsigned long long *)(pmdptr),             \
14020             pmd_val(pmdval))
14021 #define set_pgd(pgdptr,pgdval)                          \
14022   set_64bit((unsigned long long *)(pgdptr),             \
14023             pgd_val(pgdval))
14024
14025 /* Pentium-II errata A13: in PAE mode we explicitly have
```

```
14026  * to flush the TLB via cr3 if the top-level pgd is
14027  * changed... This was one tough thing to find out -
14028  * guess i should first read all the documentation next
14029  * time around ;) */
14030 extern inline void __pgd_clear(pgd_t * pgd)
14031 {
14032   set_pgd(pgd, __pgd(EMPTY_PGD));
14033 }
14034
14035 extern inline void pgd_clear(pgd_t * pgd)
14036 {
14037   __pgd_clear(pgd);
14038   __flush_tlb();
14039 }
14040
14041 #define pgd_page(pgd)                               \
14042   ((unsigned long) __va(pgd_val(pgd) & PAGE_MASK))
14043
14044 /* Find an entry in the second-level page table.. */
14045 #define pmd_offset(dir, address)                    \
14046   ((pmd_t *) pgd_page(*(dir)) + __pmd_offset(address))
14047
14048 static inline pte_t ptep_get_and_clear(pte_t * ptep)
14049 {
14050   pte_t res;
14051
14052   /* xchg acts as a barrier before the setting of the
14053    * high bits */
14054   res.pte_low = xchg(&ptep->pte_low, 0);
14055   res.pte_high = ptep->pte_high;
14056   ptep->pte_high = 0;
14057
14058   return res;
14059 }
14060
14061 static inline int pte_same(pte_t a, pte_t b)
14062 {
14063   return a.pte_low == b.pte_low
14064       && a.pte_high == b.pte_high;
14065 }
14066
14067 #define pte_page(x)                                 \
14068     (mem_map+(((x).pte_low >> PAGE_SHIFT) |         \
14069              ((x).pte_high << (32 - PAGE_SHIFT)))))
14070 #define pte_none(x)    (!(x).pte_low && !(x).pte_high)
14071
14072 static inline pte_t __mk_pte(unsigned long page_nr,
14073     pgprot_t pgprot)
14074 {
14075   pte_t pte;
14076
14077   pte.pte_high = page_nr >> (32 - PAGE_SHIFT);
14078   pte.pte_low =
14079       (page_nr << PAGE_SHIFT) | pgprot_val(pgprot);
14080   return pte;
14081 }
14082
14083 #endif                        /* _I386_PGTABLE_3LEVEL_H */
```

include/asm-i386/pgtable.h

```
14084 #ifndef _I386_PGTABLE_H
14085 #define _I386_PGTABLE_H
14086
14087 #include <linux/config.h>
14088
14089 /*
14090  * The Linux memory management assumes a three-level page
14091  * table setup. On the i386, we use that, but "fold" the
14092  * mid level into the top-level page table, so that we
14093  * physically have the same two-level page table as the
14094  * i386 mmu expects.
14095  *
14096  * This file contains the functions and defines necessary
14097  * to modify and use the i386 page table tree.   */
14098 #ifndef __ASSEMBLY__
14099 #include <asm/processor.h>
14100 #include <asm/fixmap.h>
14101 #include <linux/threads.h>
14102
14103 #ifndef _I386_BITOPS_H
14104 #include <asm/bitops.h>
14105 #endif
14106
14107 extern pgd_t swapper_pg_dir[1024];
14108 extern void paging_init(void);
14109
14110 /* Caches aren't brain-dead on the intel. */
14111 #define flush_cache_all()                do {} while (0)
14112 #define flush_cache_mm(mm)               do {} while (0)
14113 #define flush_cache_range(mm, start, end) do {} while (0)
14114 #define flush_cache_page(vma, vmaddr)    do {} while (0)
14115 #define flush_page_to_ram(page)          do {} while (0)
14116 #define flush_dcache_page(page)          do {} while (0)
14117 #define flush_icache_range(start, end)   do {} while (0)
```

```
14118 #define flush_icache_page(vma,pg)           do {} while (0)
14119
14120 #define __flush_tlb()                                           \
14121 do {                                                            \
14122   unsigned int tmpreg;                                          \
14123   __asm__ __volatile__(                                         \
14124     "movl %%cr3, %0;  # flush TLB \n"                           \
14125     "movl %0, %%cr3;              \n"                           \
14126     : "=r" (tmpreg)                                              \
14127     :: "memory");                                               \
14128 } while (0)
14129
14130 /* Global pages have to be flushed a bit differently. Not
14131  * a real performance problem because this does not
14132  * happen often.  */
14133 #define __flush_tlb_global()                                     \
14134 do {                                                            \
14135   unsigned int tmpreg;                                          \
14136   __asm__ __volatile__(                                         \
14137     "movl %1, %%cr4;  # turn off PGE     \n"                    \
14138     "movl %%cr3, %0;  # flush TLB        \n"                    \
14139     "movl %0, %%cr3;                     \n"                    \
14140     "movl %2, %%cr4;  # turn PGE back on \n"                    \
14141     : "=&r" (tmpreg)                                            \
14142     : "r" (mmu_cr4_features & ~X86_CR4_PGE),                    \
14143     "r" (mmu_cr4_features)                                      \
14144     : "memory");                                               \
14145 } while (0)
14146
14147 extern unsigned long pgkern_mask;
14148
14149 /* Do not check the PGE bit unnecesserily if this is a
14150  * PPro+ kernel.  */
14151 #ifdef CONFIG_X86_PGE
14152 # define __flush_tlb_all() __flush_tlb_global()
14153 #else
14154 # define __flush_tlb_all()                                       \
14155         do {                                                     \
14156                 if (cpu_has_pge)                                 \
14157                         __flush_tlb_global();                    \
14158                 else                                             \
14159                         __flush_tlb();                           \
14160         } while (0)
14161 #endif
14162
14163 #ifndef CONFIG_X86_INVLPG
14164 #define __flush_tlb_one(addr) __flush_tlb()
14165 #else
14166 #define __flush_tlb_one(addr)                                    \
14167 __asm__ __volatile__("invlpg %0": :"m" (*(char *) addr))
14168 #endif
14169
14170 /* ZERO_PAGE is a global shared page that is always zero:
14171  * used for zero-mapped memory areas etc..  */
14172 extern unsigned long empty_zero_page[1024];
14173 #define ZERO_PAGE(vaddr) (virt_to_page(empty_zero_page))
14174
14175 #endif                                /* !__ASSEMBLY__ */
14176
14177 /* The Linux x86 paging architecture is 'compile-time
14178  * dual-mode', it implements both the traditional 2-level
14179  * x86 page tables and the newer 3-level PAE-mode page
14180  * tables.  */
14181 #ifndef __ASSEMBLY__
14182 #if CONFIG_X86_PAE
14183 # include <asm/pgtable-3level.h>
14184 #else
14185 # include <asm/pgtable-2level.h>
14186 #endif
14187 #endif
14188
14189 #define __beep() asm("movb $0x3,%al; outb %al,$0x61")
14190
14191 #define PMD_SIZE        (1UL << PMD_SHIFT)
14192 #define PMD_MASK        (~(PMD_SIZE-1))
14193 #define PGDIR_SIZE      (1UL << PGDIR_SHIFT)
14194 #define PGDIR_MASK      (~(PGDIR_SIZE-1))
14195
14196 #define USER_PTRS_PER_PGD       (TASK_SIZE/PGDIR_SIZE)
14197 #define FIRST_USER_PGD_NR       0
14198
14199 #define USER_PGD_PTRS (PAGE_OFFSET >> PGDIR_SHIFT)
14200 #define KERNEL_PGD_PTRS (PTRS_PER_PGD-USER_PGD_PTRS)
14201
14202 #define TWOLEVEL_PGDIR_SHIFT    22
14203 #define BOOT_USER_PGD_PTRS                                         \
14204   (__PAGE_OFFSET >> TWOLEVEL_PGDIR_SHIFT)
14205 #define BOOT_KERNEL_PGD_PTRS (1024-BOOT_USER_PGD_PTRS)
14206
14207
14208 #ifndef __ASSEMBLY__
14209 /* Just any arbitrary offset to the start of the vmalloc
14210  * VM area: the current 8MB value just means that there
14211  * will be a 8MB "hole" after the physical memory until
```

p 622

```
14212  * the kernel virtual memory starts.  That means that any
14213  * out-of-bounds memory accesses will hopefully be
14214  * caught. The vmalloc() routines leaves a hole of 4kB
14215  * between each vmalloced area for the same reason. ;) */
14216 #define VMALLOC_OFFSET  (8*1024*1024)
14217 #define VMALLOC_START                                      \
14218   (((unsigned long) high_memory + 2*VMALLOC_OFFSET-1) & \
14219    ~(VMALLOC_OFFSET-1))
14220 #define VMALLOC_VMADDR(x) ((unsigned long)(x))
14221 #if CONFIG_HIGHMEM
14222 # define VMALLOC_END    (PKMAP_BASE-2*PAGE_SIZE)
14223 #else
14224 # define VMALLOC_END    (FIXADDR_START-2*PAGE_SIZE)
14225 #endif
14226
14227 /* The 4MB page is guessing..  Detailed in the infamous
14228  * "Chapter H" of the Pentium details, but assuming intel
14229  * did the straightforward thing, this bit set in the
14230  * page directory entry just means that the page
14231  * directory entry points directly to a 4MB-aligned block
14232  * of memory.  */
14233 #define _PAGE_BIT_PRESENT        0
14234 #define _PAGE_BIT_RW             1
14235 #define _PAGE_BIT_USER           2
14236 #define _PAGE_BIT_PWT            3
14237 #define _PAGE_BIT_PCD            4
14238 #define _PAGE_BIT_ACCESSED       5
14239 #define _PAGE_BIT_DIRTY          6
14240 #define _PAGE_BIT_PSE            7   /* 4 MB (or 2MB) page,
14241                                      * Pentium+, if
14242                                      * present.. */
14243 #define _PAGE_BIT_GLOBAL         8   /* Global TLB entry
14244                                      * PPro+ */
14245
14246 #define _PAGE_PRESENT    0x001
14247 #define _PAGE_RW         0x002
14248 #define _PAGE_USER       0x004
14249 #define _PAGE_PWT        0x008
14250 #define _PAGE_PCD        0x010
14251 #define _PAGE_ACCESSED   0x020
14252 #define _PAGE_DIRTY      0x040
14253 #define _PAGE_PSE        0x080   /* 4 MB (or 2MB) page,
14254                                  * Pentium+, if
14255                                  * present.. */
14256 #define _PAGE_GLOBAL     0x100   /* Global TLB entry
14257                                  * PPro+ */
14258
14259 #define _PAGE_PROTNONE  0x080    /* If not present */
14260
14261 #define _PAGE_TABLE     (_PAGE_PRESENT | _PAGE_RW |    \
14262                          _PAGE_USER | _PAGE_ACCESSED | \
14263                          _PAGE_DIRTY)
14264 #define _KERNPG_TABLE   (_PAGE_PRESENT | _PAGE_RW |    \
14265                          _PAGE_ACCESSED | _PAGE_DIRTY)
14266 #define _PAGE_CHG_MASK  (PTE_MASK | _PAGE_ACCESSED |   \
14267                          _PAGE_DIRTY)
14268
14269 #define PAGE_NONE       __pgprot(_PAGE_PROTNONE |      \
14270                                  _PAGE_ACCESSED)
14271 #define PAGE_SHARED     __pgprot(_PAGE_PRESENT |       \
14272                                  _PAGE_RW | _PAGE_USER |\
14273                                  _PAGE_ACCESSED)
14274 #define PAGE_COPY       __pgprot(_PAGE_PRESENT |       \
14275                                  _PAGE_USER |          \
14276                                  _PAGE_ACCESSED)
14277 #define PAGE_READONLY   __pgprot(_PAGE_PRESENT |       \
14278                                  _PAGE_USER |          \
14279                                  _PAGE_ACCESSED)
14280
14281 #define __PAGE_KERNEL                                  \
14282         (_PAGE_PRESENT | _PAGE_RW |                    \
14283          _PAGE_DIRTY | _PAGE_ACCESSED)
14284 #define __PAGE_KERNEL_NOCACHE                          \
14285         (_PAGE_PRESENT | _PAGE_RW |                    \
14286          _PAGE_DIRTY | _PAGE_PCD | _PAGE_ACCESSED)
14287 #define __PAGE_KERNEL_RO                               \
14288         (_PAGE_PRESENT | _PAGE_DIRTY | _PAGE_ACCESSED)
14289
14290 #ifdef CONFIG_X86_PGE
14291 # define MAKE_GLOBAL(x) __pgprot((x) | _PAGE_GLOBAL)
14292 #else
14293 # define MAKE_GLOBAL(x)                                \
14294 ({                                                     \
14295   pgprot_t __ret;                                      \
14296                                                        \
14297   if (cpu_has_pge)                                     \
14298     __ret = __pgprot((x) | _PAGE_GLOBAL);              \
14299   else                                                 \
14300     __ret = __pgprot(x);                               \
14301   __ret;                                               \
14302 })
14303 #endif
14304
14305 #define PAGE_KERNEL     MAKE_GLOBAL(__PAGE_KERNEL)
```

```
14306 #define PAGE_KERNEL_RO MAKE_GLOBAL(__PAGE_KERNEL_RO)
14307 #define PAGE_KERNEL_NOCACHE                              \
14308                     MAKE_GLOBAL(__PAGE_KERNEL_NOCACHE)
14309
14310 /* The i386 can't do page protection for execute, and
14311  * considers that the same are read. Also, write
14312  * permissions imply read permissions.  This is the
14313  * closest we can get.. */
14314 #define __P000   PAGE_NONE
14315 #define __P001   PAGE_READONLY
14316 #define __P010   PAGE_COPY
14317 #define __P011   PAGE_COPY
14318 #define __P100   PAGE_READONLY
14319 #define __P101   PAGE_READONLY
14320 #define __P110   PAGE_COPY
14321 #define __P111   PAGE_COPY
14322
14323 #define __S000   PAGE_NONE
14324 #define __S001   PAGE_READONLY
14325 #define __S010   PAGE_SHARED
14326 #define __S011   PAGE_SHARED
14327 #define __S100   PAGE_READONLY
14328 #define __S101   PAGE_READONLY
14329 #define __S110   PAGE_SHARED
14330 #define __S111   PAGE_SHARED
14331
14332 /* Define this if things work differently on an i386 and
14333  * an i486: it will (on an i486) warn about kernel memory
14334  * accesses that are done without a
14335  * 'verify_area(VERIFY_WRITE,..)'  */
14336 #undef TEST_VERIFY_AREA
14337
14338 /* page table for 0-4MB for everybody */
14339 extern unsigned long pg0[1024];
14340
14341 /* Handling allocation failures during page table setup.
14342  */
14343 extern void __handle_bad_pmd(pmd_t * pmd);
14344 extern void __handle_bad_pmd_kernel(pmd_t * pmd);
14345
14346 #define pte_present(x)                                   \
14347  ((x).pte_low & (_PAGE_PRESENT | _PAGE_PROTNONE))
14348 #define pte_clear(xp)                                    \
14349   do { set_pte(xp, __pte(0)); } while (0)
14350
14351 #define pmd_none(x)      (!pmd_val(x))
14352 #define pmd_present(x)   (pmd_val(x) & _PAGE_PRESENT)
14353 #define pmd_clear(xp)                                    \
14354   do { set_pmd(xp, __pmd(0)); } while (0)
14355 #define pmd_bad(x)                                       \
14356    ((pmd_val(x) & (~PAGE_MASK & ~_PAGE_USER))            \
14357    != _KERNPG_TABLE)
14358
14359 /* Permanent address of a page. Obviously must never be
14360  * called on a highmem page.  */
14361 #define page_address(page) ((page)->virtual)
14362 #define pages_to_mb(x) ((x) >> (20-PAGE_SHIFT))
14363
14364 /* The following only work if pte_present() is true.
14365  * Undefined behaviour if not.. */
14366 static inline int pte_read(pte_t pte)
14367 {
14368   return (pte).pte_low & _PAGE_USER;
14369 }
14370 static inline int pte_exec(pte_t pte)
14371 {
14372   return (pte).pte_low & _PAGE_USER;
14373 }
14374 static inline int pte_dirty(pte_t pte)
14375 {
14376   return (pte).pte_low & _PAGE_DIRTY;
14377 }
14378 static inline int pte_young(pte_t pte)
14379 {
14380   return (pte).pte_low & _PAGE_ACCESSED;
14381 }
14382 static inline int pte_write(pte_t pte)
14383 {
14384   return (pte).pte_low & _PAGE_RW;
14385 }
14386
14387 static inline pte_t pte_rdprotect(pte_t pte)
14388 {
14389   (pte).pte_low &= ~_PAGE_USER;
14390   return pte;
14391 }
14392 static inline pte_t pte_exprotect(pte_t pte)
14393 {
14394   (pte).pte_low &= ~_PAGE_USER;
14395   return pte;
14396 }
14397 static inline pte_t pte_mkclean(pte_t pte)
14398 {
14399   (pte).pte_low &= ~_PAGE_DIRTY;
```

```
14400   return pte;
14401 }
14402 static inline pte_t pte_mkold(pte_t pte)
14403 {
14404   (pte).pte_low &= ~_PAGE_ACCESSED;
14405   return pte;
14406 }
14407 static inline pte_t pte_wrprotect(pte_t pte)
14408 {
14409   (pte).pte_low &= ~_PAGE_RW;
14410   return pte;
14411 }
14412 static inline pte_t pte_mkread(pte_t pte)
14413 {
14414   (pte).pte_low |= _PAGE_USER;
14415   return pte;
14416 }
14417 static inline pte_t pte_mkexec(pte_t pte)
14418 {
14419   (pte).pte_low |= _PAGE_USER;
14420   return pte;
14421 }
14422 static inline pte_t pte_mkdirty(pte_t pte)
14423 {
14424   (pte).pte_low |= _PAGE_DIRTY;
14425   return pte;
14426 }
14427 static inline pte_t pte_mkyoung(pte_t pte)
14428 {
14429   (pte).pte_low |= _PAGE_ACCESSED;
14430   return pte;
14431 }
14432 static inline pte_t pte_mkwrite(pte_t pte)
14433 {
14434   (pte).pte_low |= _PAGE_RW;
14435   return pte;
14436 }
14437
14438 static inline int ptep_test_and_clear_dirty(pte_t * ptep)
14439 {
14440   return test_and_clear_bit(_PAGE_BIT_DIRTY, ptep);
14441 }
14442 static inline int ptep_test_and_clear_young(pte_t * ptep)
14443 {
14444   return test_and_clear_bit(_PAGE_BIT_ACCESSED, ptep);
14445 }
14446 static inline void ptep_set_wrprotect(pte_t * ptep)
```

```
14447 {
14448   clear_bit(_PAGE_BIT_RW, ptep);
14449 }
14450 static inline void ptep_mkdirty(pte_t * ptep)
14451 {
14452   set_bit(_PAGE_BIT_DIRTY, ptep);
14453 }
14454
14455 /* Conversion functions: convert a page and protection to
14456  * a page entry, and a page entry and page directory to
14457  * the page they refer to.  */
14458 #define mk_pte(page, pgprot)                            \
14459   __mk_pte((page) - mem_map, (pgprot))
14460
14461 /* This takes a physical page address that is used by
14462  * the remapping functions */
14463 #define mk_pte_phys(physpage, pgprot)                   \
14464   __mk_pte((physpage) >> PAGE_SHIFT, pgprot)
14465
14466 static inline pte_t pte_modify(pte_t pte,
14467     pgprot_t newprot)
14468 {
14469   pte.pte_low &= _PAGE_CHG_MASK;
14470   pte.pte_low |= pgprot_val(newprot);
14471   return pte;
14472 }
14473
14474 #define page_pte(page) page_pte_prot(page, __pgprot(0))
14475
14476 #define pmd_page(pmd)                                   \
14477 ((unsigned long) __va(pmd_val(pmd) & PAGE_MASK))
14478
14479 /* to find an entry in a page-table-directory. */
14480 #define pgd_index(address)                              \
14481   ((address >> PGDIR_SHIFT) & (PTRS_PER_PGD-1))
14482
14483 #define __pgd_offset(address) pgd_index(address)
14484
14485 #define pgd_offset(mm, address)                         \
14486   ((mm)->pgd+pgd_index(address))
14487
14488 /* to find an entry in a kernel page-table-directory */
14489 #define pgd_offset_k(address)                           \
14490   pgd_offset(&init_mm, address)
14491
14492 #define __pmd_offset(address)                           \
14493   (((address) >> PMD_SHIFT) & (PTRS_PER_PMD-1))
```

```
14494
14495  /* Find an entry in the third-level page table.. */
14496  #define __pte_offset(address)                               \
14497    ((address >> PAGE_SHIFT) & (PTRS_PER_PTE - 1))
14498  #define pte_offset(dir, address)                            \
14499    ((pte_t *) pmd_page(*(dir)) + __pte_offset(address))
14500
14501  /* The i386 doesn't have any external MMU info: the
14502   * kernel page tables contain all the necessary
14503   * information.  */
14504  #define update_mmu_cache(vma,address,pte) do {} while (0)
14505
14506  /* Encode and de-code a swap entry */
14507  #define SWP_TYPE(x)              (((x).val >> 1) & 0x3f)
14508  #define SWP_OFFSET(x)            ((x).val >> 8)
14509  #define SWP_ENTRY(type, offset)                             \
14510    ((swp_entry_t) { ((type) << 1) | ((offset) << 8) })
14511  #define pte_to_swp_entry(pte)                               \
14512    ((swp_entry_t) { (pte).pte_low })
14513  #define swp_entry_to_pte(x)      ((pte_t) { (x).val })
14514
14515  #endif                           /* !__ASSEMBLY__ */
14516
14517  /* Needs to be defined here and not in linux/mm.h, as it
14518   * is arch dependent */
14519  #define PageSkip(page)           (0)
14520  #define kern_addr_valid(addr)    (1)
14521
14522  #define io_remap_page_range remap_page_range
14523
14524  #endif                           /* _I386_PGTABLE_H */
```

include/asm-i386/processor.h

```
14525  /*
14526   * include/asm-i386/processor.h
14527   *
14528   * Copyright (C) 1994 Linus Torvalds
14529   */
14530
14531  #ifndef __ASM_I386_PROCESSOR_H
14532  #define __ASM_I386_PROCESSOR_H
14533
14534  #include <asm/vm86.h>
14535  #include <asm/math_emu.h>
14536  #include <asm/segment.h>
14537  #include <asm/page.h>
14538  #include <asm/types.h>
14539  #include <asm/sigcontext.h>
14540  #include <asm/cpufeature.h>
14541  #include <linux/config.h>
14542  #include <linux/threads.h>
14543
14544  /* Default implementation of macro that returns current
14545   * instruction pointer ("program counter").  */
14546  #define current_text_addr()                                 \
14547  ({ void *pc; __asm__("movl $1f,%0\n1:":"=g" (pc)); pc; })
14548
14549  /* CPU type and hardware bug flags. Kept separately for
14550   * each CPU.  Members of this structure are referenced in
14551   * head.S, so think twice before touching them. [mj] */
14552  struct cpuinfo_x86 {
14553    __u8 x86;                  /* CPU family */
14554    __u8 x86_vendor;           /* CPU vendor */
14555    __u8 x86_model;
14556    __u8 x86_mask;
14557    char wp_works_ok;          /* It doesn't on 386's */
14558    char hlt_works_ok;         /* Problems on some 486Dx4's
14559                                * and old 386's */
14560    char hard_math;
14561    char rfu;
14562    int cpuid_level;           /* Maximum supported CPUID
14563                                * level, -1=no CPUID */
14564    __u32 x86_capability[NCAPINTS];
14565    char x86_vendor_id[16];
14566    char x86_model_id[64];
14567    int x86_cache_size;        /* in KB - valid for CPUS
14568                                * which support this call */
14569    int fdiv_bug;
14570    int f00f_bug;
14571    int coma_bug;
14572    unsigned long loops_per_jiffy;
14573    unsigned long *pgd_quick;
14574    unsigned long *pmd_quick;
14575    unsigned long *pte_quick;
14576    unsigned long pgtable_cache_sz;
14577  };
14578
14579  #define X86_VENDOR_INTEL 0
14580  #define X86_VENDOR_CYRIX 1
14581  #define X86_VENDOR_AMD 2
14582  #define X86_VENDOR_UMC 3
14583  #define X86_VENDOR_NEXGEN 4
14584  #define X86_VENDOR_CENTAUR 5
14585  #define X86_VENDOR_RISE 6
```

```
14586 #define X86_VENDOR_TRANSMETA 7
14587 #define X86_VENDOR_UNKNOWN 0xff
14588
14589 /* capabilities of CPUs */
14590
14591 extern struct cpuinfo_x86 boot_cpu_data;
14592 extern struct tss_struct init_tss[NR_CPUS];
14593
14594 #ifdef CONFIG_SMP
14595 extern struct cpuinfo_x86 cpu_data[];
14596 #define current_cpu_data cpu_data[smp_processor_id()]
14597 #else
14598 #define cpu_data &boot_cpu_data
14599 #define current_cpu_data boot_cpu_data
14600 #endif
14601
14602 #define cpu_has_pge                                          \
14603 (test_bit(X86_FEATURE_PGE, boot_cpu_data.x86_capability))
14604 #define cpu_has_pse                                          \
14605 (test_bit(X86_FEATURE_PSE, boot_cpu_data.x86_capability))
14606 #define cpu_has_pae                                          \
14607 (test_bit(X86_FEATURE_PAE, boot_cpu_data.x86_capability))
14608 #define cpu_has_tsc                                          \
14609 (test_bit(X86_FEATURE_TSC, boot_cpu_data.x86_capability))
14610 #define cpu_has_de                                           \
14611 (test_bit(X86_FEATURE_DE, boot_cpu_data.x86_capability))
14612 #define cpu_has_vme                                          \
14613 (test_bit(X86_FEATURE_VME, boot_cpu_data.x86_capability))
14614 #define cpu_has_fxsr                                         \
14615 (test_bit(X86_FEATURE_FXSR,boot_cpu_data.x86_capability))
14616 #define cpu_has_xmm                                          \
14617 (test_bit(X86_FEATURE_XMM, boot_cpu_data.x86_capability))
14618 #define cpu_has_fpu                                          \
14619 (test_bit(X86_FEATURE_FPU, boot_cpu_data.x86_capability))
14620
14621 extern char ignore_irq13;
14622
14623 extern void identify_cpu(struct cpuinfo_x86 *);
14624 extern void print_cpu_info(struct cpuinfo_x86 *);
14625 extern void dodgy_tsc(void);
14626
14627 /* EFLAGS bits */
14628 #define X86_EFLAGS_CF    0x00000001   /* Carry Flag */
14629 #define X86_EFLAGS_PF    0x00000004   /* Parity Flag */
14630 #define X86_EFLAGS_AF    0x00000010   /* Auxillary carry
14631                                        * Flag */
14632 #define X86_EFLAGS_ZF    0x00000040   /* Zero Flag */
14633 #define X86_EFLAGS_SF    0x00000080   /* Sign Flag */
14634 #define X86_EFLAGS_TF    0x00000100   /* Trap Flag */
14635 #define X86_EFLAGS_IF    0x00000200   /* Interrupt Flag */
14636 #define X86_EFLAGS_DF    0x00000400   /* Direction Flag */
14637 #define X86_EFLAGS_OF    0x00000800   /* Overflow Flag */
14638 #define X86_EFLAGS_IOPL 0x00003000   /* IOPL mask */
14639 #define X86_EFLAGS_NT    0x00004000   /* Nested Task */
14640 #define X86_EFLAGS_RF    0x00010000   /* Resume Flag */
14641 #define X86_EFLAGS_VM    0x00020000   /* Virtual Mode */
14642 #define X86_EFLAGS_AC    0x00040000   /* Alignment Check */
14643 #define X86_EFLAGS_VIF   0x00080000   /* Virtual Interrupt
14644                                        * Flag */
14645 #define X86_EFLAGS_VIP   0x00100000   /* Virtual Interrupt
14646                                        * Pending */
14647 #define X86_EFLAGS_ID    0x00200000   /* CPUID detection
14648                                        * flag */
14649
14650 /* Generic CPUID function */
14651 extern inline void cpuid(int op, int *eax, int *ebx,
14652     int *ecx, int *edx)
14653 {
14654    __asm__("cpuid"
14655           :"=a"(*eax), "=b"(*ebx), "=c"(*ecx), "=d"(*edx)
14656           :"a"(op));
14657 }
14658
14659 /* CPUID functions returning a single datum */
14660 extern inline unsigned int cpuid_eax(unsigned int op)
14661 {
14662    unsigned int eax, ebx, ecx, edx;
14663
14664    __asm__("cpuid"
14665           :"=a"(eax), "=b"(ebx), "=c"(ecx), "=d"(edx)
14666           :"a"(op));
14667    return eax;
14668 }
14669 extern inline unsigned int cpuid_ebx(unsigned int op)
14670 {
14671    unsigned int eax, ebx, ecx, edx;
14672
14673    __asm__("cpuid"
14674           :"=a"(eax), "=b"(ebx), "=c"(ecx), "=d"(edx)
14675           :"a"(op));
14676    return ebx;
14677 }
14678 extern inline unsigned int cpuid_ecx(unsigned int op)
14679 {
```

```
14680   unsigned int eax, ebx, ecx, edx;
14681
14682   __asm__("cpuid"
14683           :"=a"(eax), "=b"(ebx), "=c"(ecx), "=d"(edx)
14684           :"a"(op));
14685   return ecx;
14686 }
14687 extern inline unsigned int cpuid_edx(unsigned int op)
14688 {
14689   unsigned int eax, ebx, ecx, edx;
14690
14691 __asm__("cpuid"
14692           :"=a"(eax), "=b"(ebx), "=c"(ecx), "=d"(edx)
14693           :"a"(op));
14694   return edx;
14695 }
14696
14697 /* Intel CPU features in CR4 */
14698 #define X86_CR4_VME        0x0001  /* enable vm86
14699                                    * extensions */
14700 #define X86_CR4_PVI        0x0002  /* virtual interrupts
14701                                    * flag enable */
14702 #define X86_CR4_TSD        0x0004  /* disable time stamp
14703                                    * at ipl 3 */
14704 #define X86_CR4_DE         0x0008  /* enable debugging
14705                                    * extensions */
14706 #define X86_CR4_PSE        0x0010  /* enable page size
14707                                    * extensions */
14708 #define X86_CR4_PAE        0x0020  /* enable physical
14709                                    * addr extensions */
14710 #define X86_CR4_MCE        0x0040  /* Machine check
14711                                    * enable */
14712 #define X86_CR4_PGE        0x0080  /* enable global
14713                                    * pages */
14714 #define X86_CR4_PCE        0x0100  /* enable performance
14715                                    * counters @ ipl 3*/
14716 #define X86_CR4_OSFXSR     0x0200  /* enable fast FPU
14717                                    * save and restore*/
14718 #define X86_CR4_OSXMMEXCPT 0x0400  /* enable unmasked
14719                                    * SSE exceptions */
14720
14721 /* Save the cr4 feature set we're using (ie Pentium 4MB
14722  * enable and PPro Global page enable), so that any CPU's
14723  * that boot up after us can get the correct flags.  */
14724 extern unsigned long mmu_cr4_features;
14725
14726 static inline void set_in_cr4(unsigned long mask)
14727 {
14728   mmu_cr4_features |= mask;
14729   __asm__("movl %%cr4,%%eax\n\t"
14730           "orl %0,%%eax\n\t"
14731           "movl %%eax,%%cr4\n"
14732           : :"irg"(mask)
14733           : "ax");
14734 }
14735
14736 static inline void clear_in_cr4(unsigned long mask)
14737 {
14738   mmu_cr4_features &= ~mask;
14739   __asm__("movl %%cr4,%%eax\n\t"
14740           "andl %0,%%eax\n\t"
14741           "movl %%eax,%%cr4\n"
14742           : :"irg"(~mask)
14743           : "ax");
14744 }
14745
14746 /* Cyrix CPU configuration register indexes */
14747 #define CX86_CCR0 0xc0
14748 #define CX86_CCR1 0xc1
14749 #define CX86_CCR2 0xc2
14750 #define CX86_CCR3 0xc3
14751 #define CX86_CCR4 0xe8
14752 #define CX86_CCR5 0xe9
14753 #define CX86_CCR6 0xea
14754 #define CX86_DIR0 0xfe
14755 #define CX86_DIR1 0xff
14756 #define CX86_ARR_BASE 0xc4
14757 #define CX86_RCR_BASE 0xdc
14758
14759 /* Cyrix CPU indexed register access macros */
14760
14761 #define getCx86(reg) ({ outb((reg), 0x22); inb(0x23); })
14762
14763 #define setCx86(reg, data) do {                        \
14764         outb((reg), 0x22);                             \
14765         outb((data), 0x23);                            \
14766 } while (0)
14767
14768 /* Bus types (default is ISA, but people can check others
14769  * with these..)  */
14770 #ifdef CONFIG_EISA
14771 extern int EISA_bus;
14772 #else
14773 #define EISA_bus (0)
```

```
14774 #endif
14775 extern int MCA_bus;
14776
14777 /* from system description table in BIOS.  Mostly for
14778  * MCA use, but others may find it useful. */
14779 extern unsigned int machine_id;
14780 extern unsigned int machine_submodel_id;
14781 extern unsigned int BIOS_revision;
14782 extern unsigned int mca_pentium_flag;
14783
14784 /* User space process size: 3GB (default).  */
14785 #define TASK_SIZE       (PAGE_OFFSET)
14786
14787 /* This decides where the kernel will search for a free
14788  * chunk of vm space during mmap's. */
14789 #define TASK_UNMAPPED_BASE      (TASK_SIZE / 3)
14790
14791 /* Size of io_bitmap in longwords: 32 is ports 0-0x3ff.
14792 */
14793 #define IO_BITMAP_SIZE  32
14794 #define IO_BITMAP_OFFSET                                      \
14795   offsetof(struct tss_struct,io_bitmap)
14796 #define INVALID_IO_BITMAP_OFFSET 0x8000
14797
14798 struct i387_fsave_struct {
14799   long cwd;
14800   long swd;
14801   long twd;
14802   long fip;
14803   long fcs;
14804   long foo;
14805   long fos;
14806   long st_space[20];   /* 8*10 bytes for each FP-reg = 80
14807                         * bytes */
14808   long status;         /* software status information */
14809 };
14810
14811 struct i387_fxsave_struct {
14812   unsigned short cwd;
14813   unsigned short swd;
14814   unsigned short twd;
14815   unsigned short fop;
14816   long fip;
14817   long fcs;
14818   long foo;
14819   long fos;
14820   long mxcsr;
14821   long reserved;
14822   long st_space[32];          /* 8*16 bytes for each
14823                                * FP-reg = 128 bytes */
14824   long xmm_space[32];         /* 8*16 bytes for each
14825                                * XMM-reg = 128 bytes */
14826   long padding[56];
14827 } __attribute__ ((aligned(16)));
14828
14829 struct i387_soft_struct {
14830   long cwd;
14831   long swd;
14832   long twd;
14833   long fip;
14834   long fcs;
14835   long foo;
14836   long fos;
14837   long st_space[20];          /* 8*10 bytes for each
14838                                * FP-reg = 80 bytes */
14839   unsigned char ftop, changed, lookahead, no_update, rm,
14840       alimit;
14841   struct info *info;
14842   unsigned long entry_eip;
14843 };
14844
14845 union i387_union {
14846   struct i387_fsave_struct fsave;
14847   struct i387_fxsave_struct fxsave;
14848   struct i387_soft_struct soft;
14849 };
14850
14851 typedef struct {
14852   unsigned long seg;
14853 } mm_segment_t;
14854
14855 struct tss_struct {
14856   unsigned short back_link, __blh;
14857   unsigned long esp0;
14858   unsigned short ss0, __ss0h;
14859   unsigned long esp1;
14860   unsigned short ss1, __ss1h;
14861   unsigned long esp2;
14862   unsigned short ss2, __ss2h;
14863   unsigned long __cr3;
14864   unsigned long eip;
14865   unsigned long eflags;
14866   unsigned long eax, ecx, edx, ebx;
14867   unsigned long esp;
```

```
14868     unsigned long ebp;
14869     unsigned long esi;
14870     unsigned long edi;
14871     unsigned short es, __esh;
14872     unsigned short cs, __csh;
14873     unsigned short ss, __ssh;
14874     unsigned short ds, __dsh;
14875     unsigned short fs, __fsh;
14876     unsigned short gs, __gsh;
14877     unsigned short ldt, __ldth;
14878     unsigned short trace, bitmap;
14879     unsigned long io_bitmap[IO_BITMAP_SIZE + 1];
14880     /* pads the TSS to be cacheline-aligned (size is 0x100)
14881      */
14882     unsigned long __cacheline_filler[5];
14883 };
14884
14885 struct thread_struct {
14886     unsigned long esp0;
14887     unsigned long eip;
14888     unsigned long esp;
14889     unsigned long fs;
14890     unsigned long gs;
14891     /* Hardware debugging registers */
14892     unsigned long debugreg[8];    /* %%db0-7 debug
14893                                    * registers */
14894     /* fault info */
14895     unsigned long cr2, trap_no, error_code;
14896     /* floating point info */
14897     union i387_union i387;
14898     /* virtual 86 mode info */
14899     struct vm86_struct *vm86_info;
14900     unsigned long screen_bitmap;
14901     unsigned long v86flags, v86mask, v86mode, saved_esp0;
14902     /* IO permissions */
14903     int ioperm;
14904     unsigned long io_bitmap[IO_BITMAP_SIZE + 1];
14905 };
14906
14907 #define INIT_THREAD {                                   \
14908         0,                                              \
14909         0, 0, 0, 0,                                     \
14910         { [0 ... 7] = 0 },    /* debugging registers */ \
14911         0, 0, 0,                                        \
14912         { { 0, }, },          /* 387 state */           \
14913         0,0,0,0,0,0,                                    \
14914         0,{~0,}               /* io permissions */      \
```

```
14915 }
14916
14917 #define INIT_MMAP                                           \
14918 { &init_mm, 0, 0, NULL, PAGE_SHARED,                        \
14919   VM_READ | VM_WRITE | VM_EXEC, 1, NULL, NULL }
14920
14921 #define INIT_TSS  {                                          \
14922         0,0, /* back_link, __blh */                          \
14923         sizeof(init_stack) + (long)&init_stack, /*esp0*/\
14924         __KERNEL_DS, 0, /* ss0 */                            \
14925         0,0,0,0,0,0, /* stack1, stack2 */                    \
14926         0, /* cr3 */                                         \
14927         0,0, /* eip,eflags */                                \
14928         0,0,0,0, /* eax,ecx,edx,ebx */                       \
14929         0,0,0,0, /* esp,ebp,esi,edi */                       \
14930         0,0,0,0,0,0, /* es,cs,ss */                          \
14931         0,0,0,0,0,0, /* ds,fs,gs */                          \
14932         __LDT(0),0, /* ldt */                                \
14933         0, INVALID_IO_BITMAP_OFFSET, /* tace, bitmap */ \
14934         {~0, } /* ioperm */                                  \
14935 }
14936
14937 #define start_thread(regs, new_eip, new_esp)            \
14938 do {                                                    \
14939     __asm__("movl %0,%%fs ; movl %0,%%gs": :"r" (0)); \
14940     set_fs(USER_DS);                                    \
14941     regs->xds = __USER_DS;                              \
14942     regs->xes = __USER_DS;                              \
14943     regs->xss = __USER_DS;                              \
14944     regs->xcs = __USER_CS;                              \
14945     regs->eip = new_eip;                                \
14946     regs->esp = new_esp;                                \
14947 } while (0)
14948
14949 /* Forward declaration, a strange C thing */
14950 struct task_struct;
14951 struct mm_struct;
14952
14953 /* Free all resources held by a thread. */
14954 extern void release_thread(struct task_struct *);
14955 /* create a kernel thread without removing it from
14956  * tasklists */
14957 extern int kernel_thread(int (*fn) (void *), void *arg,
14958     unsigned long flags);
14959
14960 /* Copy and release all segment info associated with a
14961  * VM */
```

```
14962 extern void copy_segments(struct task_struct *p,
14963    struct mm_struct *mm);
14964 extern void release_segments(struct mm_struct *mm);
14965
14966 /* Return saved PC of a blocked thread.  */
14967 extern inline unsigned long thread_saved_pc(struct
14968    thread_struct *t)
14969 {
14970    return ((unsigned long *) t->esp)[3];
14971 }
14972
14973 unsigned long get_wchan(struct task_struct *p);
14974 #define KSTK_EIP(tsk)                                \
14975    (((unsigned long *)(4096+(unsigned long)(tsk)))[1019])
14976 #define KSTK_ESP(tsk)                                \
14977    (((unsigned long *)(4096+(unsigned long)(tsk)))[1022])
14978
14979 #define THREAD_SIZE (2*PAGE_SIZE)
14980 #define alloc_task_struct()                          \
14981    ((struct task_struct *) __get_free_pages(GFP_KERNEL,1))
14982 #define free_task_struct(p)                          \
14983    free_pages((unsigned long) (p), 1)
14984 #define get_task_struct(tsk)                         \
14985    atomic_inc(&virt_to_page(tsk)->count)
14986
14987 #define init_task       (init_task_union.task)
14988 #define init_stack      (init_task_union.stack)
14989
14990 struct microcode {
14991    unsigned int hdrver;
14992    unsigned int rev;
14993    unsigned int date;
14994    unsigned int sig;
14995    unsigned int cksum;
14996    unsigned int ldrver;
14997    unsigned int pf;
14998    unsigned int reserved[5];
14999    unsigned int bits[500];
15000 };
15001
15002 /* '6' because it used to be for P6 only (but now covers
15003  * Pentium 4 as well) */
15004 #define MICROCODE_IOCFREE       _IO('6',0)
15005
15006 /* REP NOP (PAUSE) is a good thing to insert into
15007  * busy-wait loops. */
15008 extern inline void rep_nop(void)
```

```
15009 {
15010    __asm__ __volatile__("rep;nop");
15011 }
15012
15013 #endif                          /* __ASM_I386_PROCESSOR_H */
```

include/asm-i386/ptrace.h

```
15014 #ifndef _I386_PTRACE_H
15015 #define _I386_PTRACE_H
15016
15017 #define EBX        0
15018 #define ECX        1
15019 #define EDX        2
15020 #define ESI        3
15021 #define EDI        4
15022 #define EBP        5
15023 #define EAX        6
15024 #define DS         7
15025 #define ES         8
15026 #define FS         9
15027 #define GS        10
15028 #define ORIG_EAX  11
15029 #define EIP       12
15030 #define CS        13
15031 #define EFL       14
15032 #define UESP      15
15033 #define SS        16
15034
15035
15036 /* this struct defines the way the registers are stored
15037  * on the stack during a system call. */
15038 struct pt_regs {
15039    long ebx;
15040    long ecx;
15041    long edx;
15042    long esi;
15043    long edi;
15044    long ebp;
15045    long eax;
15046    int xds;
15047    int xes;
15048    long orig_eax;
15049    long eip;
15050    int xcs;
15051    long eflags;
15052    long esp;
15053    int xss;
```

```
15054 };
15055
15056 /* Arbitrarily choose the same ptrace numbers as used by
15057  * the Sparc code. */
15058 #define PTRACE_GETREGS          12
15059 #define PTRACE_SETREGS          13
15060 #define PTRACE_GETFPREGS        14
15061 #define PTRACE_SETFPREGS        15
15062 #define PTRACE_GETFPXREGS       18
15063 #define PTRACE_SETFPXREGS       19
15064
15065 #define PTRACE_SETOPTIONS       21
15066
15067 /* options set using PTRACE_SETOPTIONS */
15068 #define PTRACE_O_TRACESYSGOOD    0x00000001
15069
15070 #ifdef __KERNEL__
15071 #define user_mode(regs) ((VM_MASK & (regs)->eflags) || \
15072                         (3 & (regs)->xcs))
15073 #define instruction_pointer(regs) ((regs)->eip)
15074 extern void show_regs(struct pt_regs *);
15075 #endif
15076
15077 #endif
```

include/asm-i386/resource.h

```
15078 #ifndef _I386_RESOURCE_H
15079 #define _I386_RESOURCE_H
15080
15081 /* Resource limits */
15082
15083 #define RLIMIT_CPU      0       /* CPU time in ms */
15084 #define RLIMIT_FSIZE    1       /* Maximum filesize */
15085 #define RLIMIT_DATA     2       /* max data size */
15086 #define RLIMIT_STACK    3       /* max stack size */
15087 #define RLIMIT_CORE     4       /* max core file size */
15088 #define RLIMIT_RSS      5       /* max resident set size
15089                                  */
15090 #define RLIMIT_NPROC    6       /* max number of
15091                                  * processes */
15092 #define RLIMIT_NOFILE   7       /* max number of open
15093                                  * files */
15094 #define RLIMIT_MEMLOCK  8       /* max locked-in-memory
15095                                  * address space */
15096 #define RLIMIT_AS       9       /* address space limit */
15097 #define RLIMIT_LOCKS    10      /* maximum file locks
15098                                  * held */
```

```
15099
15100 #define RLIM_NLIMITS    11
15101
15102 /* SuS says limits have to be unsigned.  Which makes a
15103  * ton more sense anyway.  */
15104 #define RLIM_INFINITY   (~0UL)
15105
15106 #ifdef __KERNEL__
15107
15108 #define INIT_RLIMITS                                    \
15109 {                                                       \
15110         { RLIM_INFINITY, RLIM_INFINITY },               \
15111         { RLIM_INFINITY, RLIM_INFINITY },               \
15112         { RLIM_INFINITY, RLIM_INFINITY },               \
15113         {       _STK_LIM, RLIM_INFINITY },              \
15114         {              0, RLIM_INFINITY },              \
15115         { RLIM_INFINITY, RLIM_INFINITY },               \
15116         {              0,             0 },              \
15117         {       INR_OPEN,      INR_OPEN },              \
15118         { RLIM_INFINITY, RLIM_INFINITY },               \
15119         { RLIM_INFINITY, RLIM_INFINITY },               \
15120         { RLIM_INFINITY, RLIM_INFINITY },               \
15121 }
15122
15123 #endif                          /* __KERNEL__ */
15124
15125 #endif
```

include/asm-i386/rwlock.h

```
15126 /* include/asm-i386/rwlock.h
15127  *
15128  * Helpers used by both rw spinlocks and rw semaphores.
15129  *
15130  * Based in part on code from semaphore.h and spinlock.h
15131  * Copyright 1996 Linus Torvalds.
15132  *
15133  *      Copyright 1999 Red Hat, Inc.
15134  *
15135  *      Written by Benjamin LaHaise.
15136  *
15137  * This program is free software; you can redistribute it
15138  * and/or modify it under the terms of the GNU General
15139  * Public License as published by the Free Software
15140  * Foundation; either version 2 of the License, or (at
15141  * your option) any later version. */
15142 #ifndef _ASM_I386_RWLOCK_H
15143 #define _ASM_I386_RWLOCK_H
```

```
15144
15145 #define RW_LOCK_BIAS              0x01000000
15146 #define RW_LOCK_BIAS_STR          "0x01000000"
15147
15148 #define __build_read_lock_ptr(rw, helper)              \
15149         asm volatile(LOCK "subl $1,(%0)\n\t"           \
15150                      "js 2f\n"                          \
15151                      "1:\n"                             \
15152                      ".section .text.lock,\"ax\"\n"     \
15153                      "2:\tcall " helper "\n\t"          \
15154                      "jmp 1b\n"                         \
15155                      ".previous"                        \
15156                      ::"a" (rw) : "memory")
15157
15158 #define __build_read_lock_const(rw, helper)            \
15159         asm volatile(LOCK "subl $1,%0\n\t"             \
15160                      "js 2f\n"                          \
15161                      "1:\n"                             \
15162                      ".section .text.lock,\"ax\"\n"     \
15163                      "2:\tpushl %%eax\n\t"              \
15164                      "leal %0,%%eax\n\t"                \
15165                      "call " helper "\n\t"              \
15166                      "popl %%eax\n\t"                   \
15167                      "jmp 1b\n"                         \
15168                      ".previous"                        \
15169                      :"=m" (*(volatile int *)rw)        \
15170                      : : "memory")
15171
15172 #define __build_read_lock(rw, helper)                  \
15173 do {                                                   \
15174    if (__builtin_constant_p(rw))                       \
15175      __build_read_lock_const(rw, helper);              \
15176    else                                                \
15177      __build_read_lock_ptr(rw, helper);                \
15178 } while (0)
15179
15180 #define __build_write_lock_ptr(rw, helper)             \
15181         asm volatile(LOCK "subl $"                     \
15182                      RW_LOCK_BIAS_STR ",(%0)\n\t"       \
15183                      "jnz 2f\n"                         \
15184                      "1:\n"                             \
15185                      ".section .text.lock,\"ax\"\n"     \
15186                      "2:\tcall " helper "\n\t"          \
15187                      "jmp 1b\n"                         \
15188                      ".previous"                        \
15189                      ::"a" (rw) : "memory")
15190
15191 #define __build_write_lock_const(rw, helper)           \
15192         asm volatile(LOCK "subl $"                     \
15193                      RW_LOCK_BIAS_STR ",(%0)\n\t"       \
15194                      "jnz 2f\n"                         \
15195                      "1:\n"                             \
15196                      ".section .text.lock,\"ax\"\n"     \
15197                      "2:\tpushl %%eax\n\t"              \
15198                      "leal %0,%%eax\n\t"                \
15199                      "call " helper "\n\t"              \
15200                      "popl %%eax\n\t"                   \
15201                      "jmp 1b\n"                         \
15202                      ".previous"                        \
15203                      :"=m" (*(volatile int *)rw)        \
15204                      : : "memory")
15205
15206 #define __build_write_lock(rw, helper)                 \
15207 do {                                                   \
15208    if (__builtin_constant_p(rw))                       \
15209      __build_write_lock_const(rw, helper);             \
15210    else                                                \
15211      __build_write_lock_ptr(rw, helper);               \
15212 } while (0)
15213
15214 #endif
```

include/asm-i386/segment.h

```
15215 #ifndef _ASM_SEGMENT_H
15216 #define _ASM_SEGMENT_H
15217
15218 #define __KERNEL_CS       0x10
15219 #define __KERNEL_DS       0x18
15220
15221 #define __USER_CS         0x23
15222 #define __USER_DS         0x2B
15223
15224 #endif
```

include/asm-i386/semaphore.h

```
15225 #ifndef _I386_SEMAPHORE_H
15226 #define _I386_SEMAPHORE_H
15227
15228 #include <linux/linkage.h>
15229
15230 #ifdef __KERNEL__
15231
15232 /* SMP- and interrupt-safe semaphores..
```

```
15233  *
15234  * (C) Copyright 1996 Linus Torvalds
15235  *
15236  * Modified 1996-12-23 by Dave Grothe <dave@gcom.com> to
15237  * fix bugs in the original code and to make semaphore
15238  * waits interruptible so that processes waiting on
15239  * semaphores can be killed.
15240  *
15241  * Modified 1999-02-14 by Andrea Arcangeli, split the
15242  * sched.c helper functions in asm/sempahore-helper.h
15243  * while fixing a potential and subtle race discovered by
15244  * Ulrich Schmid in down_interruptible(). Since I started
15245  * to play here I also implemented the 'trylock'
15246  * semaphore operation.
15247  *
15248  *        1999-07-02 Artur Skawina
15249  * <skawina@geocities.com> Optimized "0(ecx)" -> "(ecx)"
15250  * (the assembler does not do this). Changed calling
15251  * sequences from push/jmp to traditional call/ret.
15252  *
15253  * Modified 2001-01-01 Andreas Franck <afranck@gmx.de>
15254  * Some hacks to ensure compatibility with recent GCC
15255  * snapshots, to avoid stack corruption when compiling
15256  * with -fomit-frame-pointer. It's not sure if this will
15257  * be fixed in GCC, as our previous implementation was a
15258  * bit dubious.
15259  *
15260  * If you would like to see an analysis of this
15261  * implementation, please ftp to gcom.com and download
15262  * the file
15263  * /pub/linux/src/semaphore/semaphore-2.0.24.tar.gz.
15264  */
15265
15266 #include <asm/system.h>
15267 #include <asm/atomic.h>
15268 #include <asm/rwlock.h>
15269 #include <linux/wait.h>
15270
15271 struct semaphore {
15272   atomic_t count;
15273   int sleepers;
15274   wait_queue_head_t wait;
15275 #if WAITQUEUE_DEBUG
15276   long __magic;
15277 #endif
15278 };
15279

15280 #if WAITQUEUE_DEBUG
15281 # define __SEM_DEBUG_INIT(name)                      \
15282                   , (int)&(name).__magic
15283 #else
15284 # define __SEM_DEBUG_INIT(name)
15285 #endif
15286
15287 #define __SEMAPHORE_INITIALIZER(name,count)          \
15288 { ATOMIC_INIT(count), 0,                             \
15289   __WAIT_QUEUE_HEAD_INITIALIZER((name).wait)         \
15290   __SEM_DEBUG_INIT(name) }
15291
15292 #define __MUTEX_INITIALIZER(name)                    \
15293         __SEMAPHORE_INITIALIZER(name,1)
15294
15295 #define __DECLARE_SEMAPHORE_GENERIC(name,count)      \
15296         struct semaphore name =                      \
15297             __SEMAPHORE_INITIALIZER(name,count)
15298
15299 #define DECLARE_MUTEX(name)                          \
15300   __DECLARE_SEMAPHORE_GENERIC(name,1)
15301 #define DECLARE_MUTEX_LOCKED(name)                   \
15302   __DECLARE_SEMAPHORE_GENERIC(name,0)
15303
15304 static inline void sema_init(struct semaphore *sem,
15305    int val)
15306 {
15307   /*      *sem = (struct semaphore)
15308    *           __SEMAPHORE_INITIALIZER((*sem),val);
15309    *
15310    * i'd rather use the more flexible initialization
15311    * above, but sadly GCC 2.7.2.3 emits a bogus
15312    * warning. EGCS doesnt. Oh well.  */
15313   atomic_set(&sem->count, val);
15314   sem->sleepers = 0;
15315   init_waitqueue_head(&sem->wait);
15316 #if WAITQUEUE_DEBUG
15317   sem->__magic = (int) &sem->__magic;
15318 #endif
15319 }
15320
15321 static inline void init_MUTEX(struct semaphore *sem)
15322 {
15323   sema_init(sem, 1);
15324 }
15325
15326 static inline void init_MUTEX_LOCKED(struct semaphore
```

```
15327     *sem)
15328 {
15329   sema_init(sem, 0);
15330 }
15331
15332 /* special register calling convention */
15333 asmlinkage void __down_failed(void);
15334 /* params in registers */
15335 asmlinkage int __down_failed_interruptible(void);
15336 /* params in registers */
15337 asmlinkage int __down_failed_trylock(void);
15338 /* special register calling convention */
15339 asmlinkage void __up_wakeup(void);
15340
15341 asmlinkage void __down(struct semaphore *sem);
15342 asmlinkage int __down_interruptible(
15343   struct semaphore *sem);
15344 asmlinkage int __down_trylock(struct semaphore *sem);
15345 asmlinkage void __up(struct semaphore *sem);
15346
15347 /* This is ugly, but we want the default case to fall
15348  * through. "__down_failed" is a special asm handler
15349  * that calls the C routine that actually waits. See
15350  * arch/i386/kernel/semaphore.c */
```
p 683 ▶
```
15351 static inline void down(struct semaphore *sem)
15352 {
15353 #if WAITQUEUE_DEBUG
15354   CHECK_MAGIC(sem->__magic);
15355 #endif
15356
15357   __asm__ __volatile__(
15358     "# atomic down operation\n\t"
15359     LOCK "decl %0\n\t"      /* --sem->count */
15360     "js 2f\n"
15361     "1:\n"
15362     ".section .text.lock,\"ax\"\n"
15363     "2:\tcall __down_failed\n\t"
15364     "jmp 1b\n"
15365     ".previous"
15366     :"=m"(sem->count)
15367     :"c"(sem)
15368     :"memory");
15369 }
15370
```
p 683 ▶
```
15371 static inline int down_interruptible(
15372   struct semaphore *sem)
15373 {
```

```
15374   int result;
15375
15376 #if WAITQUEUE_DEBUG
15377   CHECK_MAGIC(sem->__magic);
15378 #endif
15379
15380   __asm__ __volatile__(
15381     "# atomic interruptible down operation\n\t"
15382     LOCK "decl %1\n\t"      /* --sem->count */
15383     "js 2f\n\t"
15384     "xorl %0,%0\n"
15385     "1:\n"
15386     ".section .text.lock,\"ax\"\n"
15387     "2:\tcall __down_failed_interruptible\n\t"
15388     "jmp 1b\n"
15389     ".previous"
15390     :"=a"(result), "=m"(sem->count)
15391     :"c"(sem)
15392     :"memory");
15393   return result;
15394 }
15395
```
p 684 ▶
```
15396 static inline int down_trylock(struct semaphore *sem)
15397 {
15398   int result;
15399
15400 #if WAITQUEUE_DEBUG
15401   CHECK_MAGIC(sem->__magic);
15402 #endif
15403
15404   __asm__ __volatile__(
15405     "# atomic interruptible down operation\n\t"
15406     LOCK "decl %1\n\t"      /* --sem->count */
15407     "js 2f\n\t"
15408     "xorl %0,%0\n"
15409     "1:\n"
15410     ".section .text.lock,\"ax\"\n"
15411     "2:\tcall __down_failed_trylock\n\t"
15412     "jmp 1b\n"
15413     ".previous"
15414     :"=a"(result), "=m"(sem->count)
15415     :"c"(sem)
15416     :"memory");
15417   return result;
15418 }
15419
15420 /* Note! This is subtle. We jump to wake people up only
```

```
15421  * if the semaphore was negative (== somebody was waiting
15422  * on it).  The default case (no contention) will result
15423  * in NO jumps for both down() and up().  */
15424 static inline void up(struct semaphore *sem)
15425 {
15426 #if WAITQUEUE_DEBUG
15427   CHECK_MAGIC(sem->__magic);
15428 #endif
15429   __asm__ __volatile__(
15430     "# atomic up operation\n\t"
15431     LOCK "incl %0\n\t"    /* ++sem->count */
15432     "jle 2f\n"
15433     "1:\n"
15434     ".section .text.lock,\"ax\"\n"
15435     "2:\tcall __up_wakeup\n\t"
15436     "jmp 1b\n"
15437     ".previous"
15438     :"=m"(sem->count)
15439     :"c"(sem)
15440     :"memory");
15441 }
15442
15443 /* rw mutexes (should that be mutices? =) - throw rw
15444  * spinlocks and semaphores together, and this is what we
15445  * end up with...
15446  *
15447  * The lock is initialized to BIAS.  This way, a writer
15448  * subtracts BIAS ands gets 0 for the case of an
15449  * uncontended lock.  Readers decrement by 1 and see a
15450  * positive value when uncontended, negative if there are
15451  * writers waiting (in which case it goes to sleep).
15452  *
15453  * The value 0x01000000 supports up to 128 processors and
15454  * lots of processes.  BIAS must be chosen such that
15455  * subl'ing BIAS once per CPU will result in the long
15456  * remaining negative.
15457  *
15458  * In terms of fairness, this should result in the lock
15459  * flopping back and forth between readers and writers
15460  * under heavy use.
15461  *
15462  * -ben */
15463 struct rw_semaphore {
15464   atomic_t count;
15465   volatile unsigned char write_bias_granted;
15466   volatile unsigned char read_bias_granted;
15467   volatile unsigned char pad1;
15468   volatile unsigned char pad2;
15469   wait_queue_head_t wait;
15470   wait_queue_head_t write_bias_wait;
15471 #if WAITQUEUE_DEBUG
15472   long __magic;
15473   atomic_t readers;
15474   atomic_t writers;
15475 #endif
15476 };
15477
15478 #if WAITQUEUE_DEBUG
15479 #define __RWSEM_DEBUG_INIT                          \
15480       , ATOMIC_INIT(0), ATOMIC_INIT(0)
15481 #else
15482 #define __RWSEM_DEBUG_INIT        /* */
15483 #endif
15484
15485 #define __RWSEM_INITIALIZER(name,count)             \
15486 { ATOMIC_INIT(count), 0, 0, 0, 0,                   \
15487   __WAIT_QUEUE_HEAD_INITIALIZER((name).wait),       \
15488   __WAIT_QUEUE_HEAD_INITIALIZER((name).write_bias_wait) \
15489   __SEM_DEBUG_INIT(name) __RWSEM_DEBUG_INIT }
15490
15491 #define __DECLARE_RWSEM_GENERIC(name,count)         \
15492         struct rw_semaphore name =                  \
15493             __RWSEM_INITIALIZER(name,count)
15494
15495 #define DECLARE_RWSEM(name)                         \
15496   __DECLARE_RWSEM_GENERIC(name,RW_LOCK_BIAS)
15497 #define DECLARE_RWSEM_READ_LOCKED(name)             \
15498   __DECLARE_RWSEM_GENERIC(name,RW_LOCK_BIAS-1)
15499 #define DECLARE_RWSEM_WRITE_LOCKED(name)            \
15500   __DECLARE_RWSEM_GENERIC(name,0)
15501
15502 static inline void init_rwsem(struct rw_semaphore *sem)
15503 {
15504   atomic_set(&sem->count, RW_LOCK_BIAS);
15505   sem->read_bias_granted = 0;
15506   sem->write_bias_granted = 0;
15507   init_waitqueue_head(&sem->wait);
15508   init_waitqueue_head(&sem->write_bias_wait);
15509 #if WAITQUEUE_DEBUG
15510   sem->__magic = (long) &sem->__magic;
15511   atomic_set(&sem->readers, 0);
15512   atomic_set(&sem->writers, 0);
15513 #endif
15514 }
```

p 686

```
15515
15516 /* we use FASTCALL convention for the helpers */
15517 extern struct rw_semaphore *
15518 FASTCALL(__down_read_failed(struct rw_semaphore *sem));
15519 extern struct rw_semaphore *
15520 FASTCALL(__down_write_failed(struct rw_semaphore *sem));
15521 extern struct rw_semaphore *
15522 FASTCALL(__rwsem_wake(struct rw_semaphore *sem));
15523
15524 static inline void down_read(struct rw_semaphore *sem)
15525 {
15526 #if WAITQUEUE_DEBUG
15527   if (sem->__magic != (long) &sem->__magic)
15528     BUG();
15529 #endif
15530   __build_read_lock(sem, "__down_read_failed");
15531 #if WAITQUEUE_DEBUG
15532   if (sem->write_bias_granted)
15533     BUG();
15534   if (atomic_read(&sem->writers))
15535     BUG();
15536   atomic_inc(&sem->readers);
15537 #endif
15538 }
15539
15540 static inline void down_write(struct rw_semaphore *sem)
15541 {
15542 #if WAITQUEUE_DEBUG
15543   if (sem->__magic != (long) &sem->__magic)
15544     BUG();
15545 #endif
15546   __build_write_lock(sem, "__down_write_failed");
15547 #if WAITQUEUE_DEBUG
15548   if (atomic_read(&sem->writers))
15549     BUG();
15550   if (atomic_read(&sem->readers))
15551     BUG();
15552   if (sem->read_bias_granted)
15553     BUG();
15554   if (sem->write_bias_granted)
15555     BUG();
15556   atomic_inc(&sem->writers);
15557 #endif
15558 }
15559
15560 /* When a reader does a release, the only significant *
15561  * case is when there was a writer waiting, and we've *
15562  * bumped the count to 0: we must wake the writer up. */
15563 static inline void __up_read(struct rw_semaphore *sem)
15564 {
15565   __asm__ __volatile__(
15566     "# up_read\n\t"
15567     LOCK "incl %0\n\t"
15568     /* only do the wake if result == 0 (ie, a writer) */
15569     "jz 2f\n"
15570     "1:\n\t"
15571     ".section .text.lock,\"ax\"\n"
15572     "2:\tcall __rwsem_wake\n\t"
15573     "jmp 1b\n"
15574     ".previous"
15575     :"=m"(sem->count)
15576     :"a"(sem)
15577     :"memory");
15578 }
15579
15580 /* releasing the writer is easy - just release it and *
15581  * wake up any sleepers. */
15582 static inline void __up_write(struct rw_semaphore *sem)
15583 {
15584   __asm__ __volatile__(
15585     "# up_write\n\t"
15586     LOCK "addl $" RW_LOCK_BIAS_STR ",%0\n"
15587     /* only do the wake if the result was -'ve to 0/+'ve
15588      */
15589     "jc 2f\n"
15590     "1:\n\t"
15591     ".section .text.lock,\"ax\"\n"
15592     "2:\tcall __rwsem_wake\n\t"
15593     "jmp 1b\n"
15594     ".previous"
15595     :"=m"(sem->count)
15596     :"a"(sem)
15597     :"memory");
15598 }
15599
15600 static inline void up_read(struct rw_semaphore *sem)
15601 {
15602 #if WAITQUEUE_DEBUG
15603   if (sem->write_bias_granted)
15604     BUG();
15605   if (atomic_read(&sem->writers))
15606     BUG();
15607   atomic_dec(&sem->readers);
15608 #endif
```

```
15609    __up_read(sem);
15610 }
15611
15612 static inline void up_write(struct rw_semaphore *sem)
15613 {
15614 #if WAITQUEUE_DEBUG
15615    if (sem->read_bias_granted)
15616      BUG();
15617    if (sem->write_bias_granted)
15618      BUG();
15619    if (atomic_read(&sem->readers))
15620      BUG();
15621    if (atomic_read(&sem->writers) != 1)
15622      BUG();
15623    atomic_dec(&sem->writers);
15624 #endif
15625    __up_write(sem);
15626 }
15627
15628 #endif
15629 #endif
```

include/asm-i386/sembuf.h

```
15630 #ifndef _I386_SEMBUF_H
15631 #define _I386_SEMBUF_H
15632
15633 /* The semid64_ds structure for i386 architecture.  Note
15634  * extra padding because this structure is passed back
15635  * and forth between kernel and user space.
15636  *
15637  * Pad space is left for:
15638  * - 64-bit time_t to solve y2038 problem
15639  * - 2 miscellaneous 32-bit values */
15640 struct semid64_ds {
15641    struct ipc64_perm sem_perm;   /* permissions .. see
15642                                   * ipc.h */
15643    __kernel_time_t sem_otime;    /* last semop time */
15644    unsigned long __unused1;
15645    __kernel_time_t sem_ctime;    /* last change time */
15646    unsigned long __unused2;
15647    unsigned long sem_nsems;      /* no. of semaphores in
15648                                   * array */
15649    unsigned long __unused3;
15650    unsigned long __unused4;
15651 };
15652
15653 #endif                            /* _I386_SEMBUF_H */
```

include/asm-i386/shmbuf.h

```
15654 #ifndef _I386_SHMBUF_H
15655 #define _I386_SHMBUF_H
15656
15657 /* The shmid64_ds structure for i386 architecture.  Note
15658  * extra padding because this structure is passed back
15659  * and forth between kernel and user space.
15660  *
15661  * Pad space is left for:
15662  * - 64-bit time_t to solve y2038 problem
15663  * - 2 miscellaneous 32-bit values */
15664
15665 struct shmid64_ds {
15666    struct ipc64_perm shm_perm;  /* operation perms */
15667    size_t shm_segsz;            /* segment size (bytes) */
15668    __kernel_time_t shm_atime;   /* last attach time */
15669    unsigned long __unused1;
15670    __kernel_time_t shm_dtime;   /* last detach time */
15671    unsigned long __unused2;
15672    __kernel_time_t shm_ctime;   /* last change time */
15673    unsigned long __unused3;
15674    __kernel_pid_t shm_cpid;     /* pid of creator */
15675    __kernel_pid_t shm_lpid;     /* pid of last operator */
15676    unsigned long shm_nattch;    /* no. of current
15677                                  * attaches */
15678    unsigned long __unused4;
15679    unsigned long __unused5;
15680 };
15681
15682 struct shminfo64 {
15683    unsigned long shmmax;
15684    unsigned long shmmin;
15685    unsigned long shmmni;
15686    unsigned long shmseg;
15687    unsigned long shmall;
15688    unsigned long __unused1;
15689    unsigned long __unused2;
15690    unsigned long __unused3;
15691    unsigned long __unused4;
15692 };
15693
15694 #endif                            /* _I386_SHMBUF_H */
```

include/asm-i386/shmparam.h

```
15695 #ifndef _ASMI386_SHMPARAM_H
15696 #define _ASMI386_SHMPARAM_H
```

```
15697
15698 #define SHMLBA PAGE_SIZE        /* attach addr a
15699                                 * multiple of this */
15700
15701 #endif                          /* _ASMI386_SHMPARAM_H */
```

include/asm-i386/sigcontext.h

```
15702 #ifndef _ASMi386_SIGCONTEXT_H
15703 #define _ASMi386_SIGCONTEXT_H
15704
15705 /*
15706  * As documented in the iBCS2 standard..
15707  *
15708  * The first part of "struct _fpstate" is just the normal
15709  * i387 hardware setup, the extra "status" word is used
15710  * to save the coprocessor status word before entering
15711  * the handler.
15712  *
15713  * Pentium III FXSR, SSE support
15714  *       Gareth Hughes <gareth@valinux.com>, May 2000
15715  *
15716  * The FPU state data structure has had to grow to
15717  * accomodate the extended FPU state required by the
15718  * Streaming SIMD Extensions.  There is no documented
15719  * standard to accomplish this at the moment.
15720  */
15721 struct _fpreg {
15722   unsigned short significand[4];
15723   unsigned short exponent;
15724 };
15725
15726 struct _fpxreg {
15727   unsigned short significand[4];
15728   unsigned short exponent;
15729   unsigned short padding[3];
15730 };
15731
15732 struct _xmmreg {
15733   unsigned long element[4];
15734 };
15735
15736 struct _fpstate {
15737   /* Regular FPU environment */
15738   unsigned long cw;
15739   unsigned long sw;
15740   unsigned long tag;
15741   unsigned long ipoff;
15742   unsigned long cssel;
15743   unsigned long dataoff;
15744   unsigned long datasel;
15745   struct _fpreg _st[8];
15746   unsigned short status;
15747   unsigned short magic;           /* 0xffff = regular FPU
15748                                    * data only */
15749
15750   /* FXSR FPU environment */
15751   unsigned long _fxsr_env[6];     /* FXSR FPU env is
15752                                    * ignored */
15753   unsigned long mxcsr;
15754   unsigned long reserved;
15755   struct _fpxreg _fxsr_st[8];     /* FXSR FPU reg data is
15756                                    * ignored */
15757   struct _xmmreg _xmm[8];
15758   unsigned long padding[56];
15759 };
15760
15761 #define X86_FXSR_MAGIC          0x0000
15762
15763 struct sigcontext {
15764   unsigned short gs, __gsh;
15765   unsigned short fs, __fsh;
15766   unsigned short es, __esh;
15767   unsigned short ds, __dsh;
15768   unsigned long edi;
15769   unsigned long esi;
15770   unsigned long ebp;
15771   unsigned long esp;
15772   unsigned long ebx;
15773   unsigned long edx;
15774   unsigned long ecx;
15775   unsigned long eax;
15776   unsigned long trapno;
15777   unsigned long err;
15778   unsigned long eip;
15779   unsigned short cs, __csh;
15780   unsigned long eflags;
15781   unsigned long esp_at_signal;
15782   unsigned short ss, __ssh;
15783   struct _fpstate *fpstate;
15784   unsigned long oldmask;
15785   unsigned long cr2;
15786 };
15787
15788
15789 #endif
```

include/asm-i386/siginfo.h

```
15790 #ifndef _I386_SIGINFO_H
15791 #define _I386_SIGINFO_H
15792
15793 #include <linux/types.h>
15794
15795 /* XXX: This structure was copied from the Alpha; is
15796  * there an iBCS version?  */
15797 typedef union sigval {
15798   int sival_int;
15799   void *sival_ptr;
15800 } sigval_t;
15801
15802 #define SI_MAX_SIZE     128
15803 #define SI_PAD_SIZE     ((SI_MAX_SIZE/sizeof(int)) - 3)
15804
15805 typedef struct siginfo {
15806   int si_signo;
15807   int si_errno;
15808   int si_code;
15809
15810   union {
15811     int _pad[SI_PAD_SIZE];
15812
15813     /* kill() */
15814     struct {
15815       pid_t _pid;                /* sender's pid */
15816       uid_t _uid;                /* sender's uid */
15817     } _kill;
15818
15819     /* POSIX.1b timers */
15820     struct {
15821       unsigned int _timer1;
15822       unsigned int _timer2;
15823     } _timer;
15824
15825     /* POSIX.1b signals */
15826     struct {
15827       pid_t _pid;                /* sender's pid */
15828       uid_t _uid;                /* sender's uid */
15829       sigval_t _sigval;
15830     } _rt;
15831
15832     /* SIGCHLD */
15833     struct {
15834       pid_t _pid;                /* which child */
15835       uid_t _uid;                /* sender's uid */
15836       int _status;               /* exit code */
15837       clock_t _utime;
15838       clock_t _stime;
15839     } _sigchld;
15840
15841     /* SIGILL, SIGFPE, SIGSEGV, SIGBUS */
15842     struct {
15843       void *_addr;               /* faulting insn/memory
15844                                   * ref. */
15845     } _sigfault;
15846
15847     /* SIGPOLL */
15848     struct {
15849       int _band;                 /* POLL_IN, POLL_OUT,
15850                                   * POLL_MSG */
15851       int _fd;
15852     } _sigpoll;
15853   } _sifields;
15854 } siginfo_t;
15855
15856 /* How these fields are to be accessed.  */
15857 #define si_pid        _sifields._kill._pid
15858 #define si_uid        _sifields._kill._uid
15859 #define si_status     _sifields._sigchld._status
15860 #define si_utime      _sifields._sigchld._utime
15861 #define si_stime      _sifields._sigchld._stime
15862 #define si_value      _sifields._rt._sigval
15863 #define si_int        _sifields._rt._sigval.sival_int
15864 #define si_ptr        _sifields._rt._sigval.sival_ptr
15865 #define si_addr       _sifields._sigfault._addr
15866 #define si_band       _sifields._sigpoll._band
15867 #define si_fd         _sifields._sigpoll._fd
15868
15869 #ifdef __KERNEL__
15870 #define __SI_MASK       0xffff0000
15871 #define __SI_KILL       (0 << 16)
15872 #define __SI_TIMER      (1 << 16)
15873 #define __SI_POLL       (2 << 16)
15874 #define __SI_FAULT      (3 << 16)
15875 #define __SI_CHLD       (4 << 16)
15876 #define __SI_RT         (5 << 16)
15877 #define __SI_CODE(T,N)  ((T) << 16 | ((N) & 0xffff))
15878 #else
15879 #define __SI_KILL       0
15880 #define __SI_TIMER      0
```

p 574

```
15881 #define __SI_POLL        0
15882 #define __SI_FAULT       0
15883 #define __SI_CHLD        0
15884 #define __SI_RT          0
15885 #define __SI_CODE(T,N)   (N)
15886 #endif
15887
15888 /* si_code values
15889  * Digital reserves positive values for kernel-generated
15890  * signals. */
15891 #define SI_USER          0        /* sent by kill,
15892                                    * sigsend, raise */
15893 #define SI_KERNEL        0x80     /* sent by the kernel
15894                                    * from somewhere */
15895 #define SI_QUEUE         -1       /* sent by sigqueue */
15896 #define SI_TIMER __SI_CODE(__SI_TIMER,-2) /* sent by
15897                                    * timer expiration */
15898 #define SI_MESGQ         -3       /* sent by real time
15899                                    * mesq state change */
15900 #define SI_ASYNCIO       -4       /* sent by AIO
15901                                    * completion */
15902 #define SI_SIGIO         -5       /* sent by queued SIGIO*/
15903
15904 #define SI_FROMUSER(siptr)       ((siptr)->si_code <= 0)
15905 #define SI_FROMKERNEL(siptr)     ((siptr)->si_code > 0)
15906
15907 /* SIGILL si_codes */
15908 #define ILL_ILLOPC   (__SI_FAULT|1)  /* illegal opcode */
15909 #define ILL_ILLOPN   (__SI_FAULT|2)  /* illegal operand */
15910 #define ILL_ILLADR   (__SI_FAULT|3)  /* illegal addressing
15911                                       * mode */
15912 #define ILL_ILLTRP   (__SI_FAULT|4)  /* illegal trap */
15913 #define ILL_PRVOPC   (__SI_FAULT|5)  /* privileged opcode
15914                                       */
15915 #define ILL_PRVREG   (__SI_FAULT|6)  /* privileged
15916                                       * register */
15917 #define ILL_COPROC   (__SI_FAULT|7)  /* coprocessor error
15918                                       */
15919 #define ILL_BADSTK   (__SI_FAULT|8)  /* internal stack
15920                                       * error */
15921 #define NSIGILL      8
15922
15923 /* SIGFPE si_codes */
15924 #define FPE_INTDIV   (__SI_FAULT|1)  /* integer divide by
15925                                       * zero */
15926 #define FPE_INTOVF   (__SI_FAULT|2)  /* integer overflow
15927                                       */
15928 #define FPE_FLTDIV   (__SI_FAULT|3)  /* floating point
15929                                       * divide by zero */
15930 #define FPE_FLTOVF   (__SI_FAULT|4)  /* floating point
15931                                       * overflow */
15932 #define FPE_FLTUND   (__SI_FAULT|5)  /* floating point
15933                                       * underflow */
15934 #define FPE_FLTRES   (__SI_FAULT|6)  /* floating point
15935                                       * inexact result */
15936 #define FPE_FLTINV   (__SI_FAULT|7)  /* floating point
15937                                       * invalid operation
15938                                       */
15939 #define FPE_FLTSUB   (__SI_FAULT|8)  /* subscript out of
15940                                       * range */
15941 #define NSIGFPE      8
15942
15943 /* SIGSEGV si_codes */
15944 #define SEGV_MAPERR  (__SI_FAULT|1)  /* address not mapped
15945                                       * to object */
15946 #define SEGV_ACCERR  (__SI_FAULT|2)  /* invalid
15947                                       * permissions for
15948                                       * mapped object */
15949 #define NSIGSEGV     2
15950
15951 /* SIGBUS si_codes */
15952 #define BUS_ADRALN   (__SI_FAULT|1)  /* invalid address
15953                                       * alignment */
15954 #define BUS_ADRERR   (__SI_FAULT|2)  /* non-existant
15955                                       * physical address
15956                                       */
15957 #define BUS_OBJERR   (__SI_FAULT|3)  /* object specific
15958                                       * hardware error */
15959 #define NSIGBUS      3
15960
15961 /* SIGTRAP si_codes */
15962 #define TRAP_BRKPT   (__SI_FAULT|1)  /* process breakpoint
15963                                       */
15964 #define TRAP_TRACE   (__SI_FAULT|2)  /* process trace trap
15965                                       */
15966 #define NSIGTRAP     2
15967
15968 /* SIGCHLD si_codes */
15969 #define CLD_EXITED   (__SI_CHLD|1)   /* child has exited
15970                                       */
15971 #define CLD_KILLED   (__SI_CHLD|2)   /* child was killed
15972                                       */
15973 #define CLD_DUMPED   (__SI_CHLD|3)   /* child terminated
15974                                       * abnormally */
```

```
15975 #define CLD_TRAPPED (__SI_CHLD|4)   /* traced child
15976                                      * has trapped */
15977 #define CLD_STOPPED (__SI_CHLD|5)   /* child has stopped
15978                                      */
15979 #define CLD_CONTINUED (__SI_CHLD|6) /* stopped child has
15980                                      * continued */
15981 #define NSIGCHLD    6
15982
15983 /* SIGPOLL si_codes */
15984 #define POLL_IN     (__SI_POLL|1)   /* data input
15985                                      * available */
15986 #define POLL_OUT    (__SI_POLL|2)   /* output buffers
15987                                      * available */
15988 #define POLL_MSG    (__SI_POLL|3)   /* input message
15989                                      * available */
15990 #define POLL_ERR    (__SI_POLL|4)   /* i/o error */
15991 #define POLL_PRI    (__SI_POLL|5)   /* high priority
15992                                      * input available */
15993 #define POLL_HUP    (__SI_POLL|6)   /* device
15994                                      * disconnected */
15995 #define NSIGPOLL    6
15996
15997 /* sigevent definitions
15998  *
15999  * It seems likely that SIGEV_THREAD will have to be
16000  * handled from userspace, libpthread transmuting it to
16001  * SIGEV_SIGNAL, which the thread manager then catches
16002  * and does the appropriate nonsense.  However,
16003  * everything is written out here so as to not get lost.
16004  */
16005 #define SIGEV_SIGNAL   0        /* notify via signal */
16006 #define SIGEV_NONE     1        /* other notification:
16007                                  * meaningless */
16008 #define SIGEV_THREAD   2        /* deliver via thread
16009                                  * creation */
16010
16011 #define SIGEV_MAX_SIZE 64
16012 #define SIGEV_PAD_SIZE ((SIGEV_MAX_SIZE/sizeof(int)) - 3)
16013
16014 typedef struct sigevent {
16015   sigval_t sigev_value;
16016   int sigev_signo;
16017   int sigev_notify;
16018   union {
16019     int _pad[SIGEV_PAD_SIZE];
16020
16021     struct {
```

```
16022       void (*_function) (sigval_t);
16023       void *_attribute;        /* really pthread_attr_t */
16024     } _sigev_thread;
16025   } _sigev_un;
16026 } sigevent_t;
16027
16028 #define sigev_notify_function                      \
16029   _sigev_un._sigev_thread._function
16030 #define sigev_notify_attributes                    \
16031   _sigev_un._sigev_thread._attribute
16032
16033 #ifdef __KERNEL__
16034 #include <linux/string.h>
16035
16036 extern inline void copy_siginfo(siginfo_t * to,
16037     siginfo_t * from)
16038 {
16039   if (from->si_code < 0)
16040     memcpy(to, from, sizeof(siginfo_t));
16041   else
16042     /* _sigchld is currently the largest know union
16043      * member */
16044     memcpy(to, from,
16045       3 * sizeof(int) +
16046       sizeof(from->_sifields._sigchld));
16047 }
16048
16049 extern int copy_siginfo_to_user(siginfo_t * to,
16050     siginfo_t * from);
16051
16052 #endif                                   /* __KERNEL__ */
16053
16054 #endif
```

include/asm-i386/signal.h

```
16055 #ifndef _ASMi386_SIGNAL_H
16056 #define _ASMi386_SIGNAL_H
16057
16058 #include <linux/types.h>
16059
16060 /* Avoid too many header ordering problems.  */
16061 struct siginfo;
16062
16063 #ifdef __KERNEL__
16064 /* Most things should be clean enough to redefine this
16065  * at will, if care is taken to make libc match.  */
16066
```

```
16067 #define _NSIG            64
16068 #define _NSIG_BPW        32
16069 #define _NSIG_WORDS      (_NSIG / _NSIG_BPW)
16070
16071 typedef unsigned long old_sigset_t; /* at least 32 bits*/
16072
16073 typedef struct {
16074   unsigned long sig[_NSIG_WORDS];
16075 } sigset_t;
16076
16077 #else
16078 /* Here we must cater to libcs that poke about in kernel
16079  * headers.  */
16080
16081 #define NSIG             32
16082 typedef unsigned long sigset_t;
16083
16084 #endif                            /* __KERNEL__ */
16085
16086 #define SIGHUP           1
16087 #define SIGINT           2
16088 #define SIGQUIT          3
16089 #define SIGILL           4
16090 #define SIGTRAP          5
16091 #define SIGABRT          6
16092 #define SIGIOT           6
16093 #define SIGBUS           7
16094 #define SIGFPE           8
16095 #define SIGKILL          9
16096 #define SIGUSR1          10
16097 #define SIGSEGV          11
16098 #define SIGUSR2          12
16099 #define SIGPIPE          13
16100 #define SIGALRM          14
16101 #define SIGTERM          15
16102 #define SIGSTKFLT        16
16103 #define SIGCHLD          17
16104 #define SIGCONT          18
16105 #define SIGSTOP          19
16106 #define SIGTSTP          20
16107 #define SIGTTIN          21
16108 #define SIGTTOU          22
16109 #define SIGURG           23
16110 #define SIGXCPU          24
16111 #define SIGXFSZ          25
16112 #define SIGVTALRM        26
16113 #define SIGPROF          27
```

```
16114 #define SIGWINCH         28
16115 #define SIGIO            29
16116 #define SIGPOLL          SIGIO
16117 /*
16118 #define SIGLOST          29
16119 */
16120 #define SIGPWR           30
16121 #define SIGSYS           31
16122 #define SIGUNUSED        31
16123
16124 /* These should not be considered constants from
16125  * userland.  */
16126 #define SIGRTMIN         32
16127 #define SIGRTMAX         (_NSIG-1)
16128
16129 /* SA_FLAGS values:
16130  *
16131  * SA_ONSTACK indicates that a registered stack_t will be
16132  * used.
16133  * SA_INTERRUPT is a no-op, but left due to historical
16134  * reasons. Use the
16135  * SA_RESTART flag to get restarting signals (which were
16136  * the default long ago)
16137  * SA_NOCLDSTOP flag to turn off SIGCHLD when children
16138  * stop.
16139  * SA_RESETHAND clears the handler when the signal is
16140  * delivered.
16141  * SA_NOCLDWAIT flag on SIGCHLD to inhibit zombies.
16142  * SA_NODEFER prevents the current signal from being
16143  * masked in the handler.
16144  *
16145  * SA_ONESHOT and SA_NOMASK are the historical Linux
16146  * names for the Single Unix names RESETHAND and NODEFER
16147  * respectively.  */
16148 #define SA_NOCLDSTOP     0x00000001
16149 #define SA_NOCLDWAIT     0x00000002   /*not supported yet*/
16150 #define SA_SIGINFO       0x00000004
16151 #define SA_ONSTACK       0x08000000
16152 #define SA_RESTART       0x10000000
16153 #define SA_NODEFER       0x40000000
16154 #define SA_RESETHAND     0x80000000
16155
16156 #define SA_NOMASK        SA_NODEFER
16157 #define SA_ONESHOT       SA_RESETHAND
16158 #define SA_INTERRUPT     0x20000000   /* dummy – ignored*/
16159
16160 #define SA_RESTORER      0x04000000
```

p 573

```
16161
16162 /* sigaltstack controls */
16163 #define SS_ONSTACK      1
16164 #define SS_DISABLE      2
16165
16166 #define MINSIGSTKSZ     2048
16167 #define SIGSTKSZ        8192
16168
16169 #ifdef __KERNEL__
16170
16171 /* These values of sa_flags are used only by the kernel
16172  * as part of the irq handling routines.
16173  *
16174  * SA_INTERRUPT is also used by the irq handling
16175  * routines.
16176  * SA_SHIRQ is for shared interrupt support on PCI and
16177  * EISA.  */
16178 #define SA_PROBE                SA_ONESHOT
16179 #define SA_SAMPLE_RANDOM        SA_RESTART
16180 #define SA_SHIRQ                0x04000000
16181 #endif
16182
16183 #define SIG_BLOCK    0    /* for blocking signals */
16184 #define SIG_UNBLOCK  1    /* for unblocking signals */
16185 #define SIG_SETMASK  2    /* for setting signal mask */
16186
16187 /* Type of a signal handler.  */
16188 typedef void (*__sighandler_t) (int);
16189
16190 #define SIG_DFL ((__sighandler_t)0)    /* default signal
16191                                        * handling */
16192 #define SIG_IGN ((__sighandler_t)1)    /* ignore signal */
16193 #define SIG_ERR ((__sighandler_t)-1)   /* error return
16194                                        * from signal */
16195
16196 #ifdef __KERNEL__
16197 struct old_sigaction {
16198     __sighandler_t sa_handler;
16199     old_sigset_t sa_mask;
16200     unsigned long sa_flags;
16201     void (*sa_restorer) (void);
16202 };
16203
16204 struct sigaction {
16205     __sighandler_t sa_handler;
16206     unsigned long sa_flags;
16207     void (*sa_restorer) (void);
```

```
16208     sigset_t sa_mask;      /* mask last for extensibility */
16209 };
16210
16211 struct k_sigaction {
16212     struct sigaction sa;
16213 };
16214 #else
16215 /* Here we must cater to libcs that poke about in kernel
16216  * headers.  */
16217
16218 struct sigaction {
16219     union {
16220         __sighandler_t _sa_handler;
16221         void (*_sa_sigaction) (int, struct siginfo *,
16222             void *);
16223     } _u;
16224     sigset_t sa_mask;
16225     unsigned long sa_flags;
16226     void (*sa_restorer) (void);
16227 };
16228
16229 #define sa_handler      _u._sa_handler
16230 #define sa_sigaction    _u._sa_sigaction
16231
16232 #endif                              /* __KERNEL__ */
16233
16234 typedef struct sigaltstack {
16235     void *ss_sp;
16236     int ss_flags;
16237     size_t ss_size;
16238 } stack_t;
16239
16240 #ifdef __KERNEL__
16241 #include <asm/sigcontext.h>
16242
16243 #define __HAVE_ARCH_SIG_BITOPS
16244
16245 extern __inline__ void sigaddset(sigset_t * set,
16246     int _sig)
16247 {
16248     __asm__("btsl %1,%0": "=m"(*set): "Ir"(_sig - 1):"cc");
16249 }
16250
16251 extern __inline__ void sigdelset(sigset_t * set,
16252     int _sig)
16253 {
16254     __asm__("btrl %1,%0": "=m"(*set): "Ir"(_sig - 1):"cc");
```

```
16255 }
16256
16257 extern __inline__ int __const_sigismember(sigset_t * set,
16258     int _sig)
16259 {
16260   unsigned long sig = _sig - 1;
16261   return 1 & (set->sig[sig / _NSIG_BPW] >> (sig %
16262         _NSIG_BPW));
16263 }
16264
16265 extern __inline__ int __gen_sigismember(sigset_t * set,
16266     int _sig)
16267 {
16268   int ret;
16269   __asm__("btl %2,%1\n\tsbbl %0,%0"
16270         : "=r"(ret)
16271         : "m"(*set), "Ir"(_sig - 1)
16272         : "cc");
16273   return ret;
16274 }
16275
16276 #define sigismember(set,sig)                       \
16277         (__builtin_constant_p(sig) ?               \
16278         __const_sigismember((set),(sig)) :         \
16279         __gen_sigismember((set),(sig)))
16280
16281 #define sigmask(sig)    (1UL << ((sig) - 1))
16282
16283 extern __inline__ int sigfindinword(unsigned long word)
16284 {
16285   __asm__("bsfl %1,%0": "=r"(word): "rm"(word):"cc");
16286   return word;
16287 }
16288
16289 #endif                                  /* __KERNEL__ */
16290
16291 #endif
```

include/asm-i386/smp.h

```
16292 #ifndef __ASM_SMP_H
16293 #define __ASM_SMP_H
16294
16295 /* We need the APIC definitions automatically as part of
16296  * 'smp.h' */
16297 #ifndef ASSEMBLY
16298 #include <linux/config.h>
16299 #include <linux/threads.h>
16300 #include <linux/ptrace.h>
16301 #endif
16302
16303 #ifdef CONFIG_X86_LOCAL_APIC
16304 #ifndef ASSEMBLY
16305 #include <asm/fixmap.h>
16306 #include <asm/bitops.h>
16307 #include <asm/mpspec.h>
16308 #ifdef CONFIG_X86_IO_APIC
16309 #include <asm/io_apic.h>
16310 #endif
16311 #include <asm/apic.h>
16312 #endif
16313 #endif
16314
16315 #ifdef CONFIG_SMP
16316 #ifndef ASSEMBLY
16317
16318 /* Private routines/data */
16319
16320 extern void smp_alloc_memory(void);
16321 extern unsigned long phys_cpu_present_map;
16322 extern unsigned long cpu_online_map;
16323 extern volatile unsigned long smp_invalidate_needed;
16324 extern int pic_mode;
16325 extern void smp_flush_tlb(void);
16326 extern void smp_message_irq(int cpl, void *dev_id,
16327     struct pt_regs *regs);
16328 extern void smp_send_reschedule(int cpu);
16329 extern void smp_invalidate_rcv(void);    /* Process an
16330                                          * NMI */
16331 extern void (*mtrr_hook) (void);
16332 extern void zap_low_mappings(void);
16333
16334 /* On x86 all CPUs are mapped 1:1 to the APIC space.
16335  * This simplifies scheduling and IPI sending and
16336  * compresses data structures.  */
16337 extern inline int cpu_logical_map(int cpu)
16338 {
16339   return cpu;
16340 }
16341 extern inline int cpu_number_map(int cpu)
16342 {
16343   return cpu;
16344 }
16345
16346 /* Some lowlevel functions might want to know about the
```

```
16347   * real APIC ID <-> CPU # mapping.  */
16348  extern volatile int x86_apicid_to_cpu[NR_CPUS];
16349  extern volatile int x86_cpu_to_apicid[NR_CPUS];
16350
16351  /* General functions that each host system must provide.
16352   */
16353
16354  extern void smp_boot_cpus(void);
16355  /* Store per CPU info (like the initial udelay numbers */
16356  extern void smp_store_cpu_info(int id);
16357
16358  /* This function is needed by all SMP systems. It must
16359   * _always_ be valid from the initial startup. We map
16360   * APIC_BASE very early in page_setup(), so this is
16361   * correct in the x86 case.  */
16362  #define smp_processor_id() (current->processor)
16363
16364  extern __inline int hard_smp_processor_id(void)
16365  {
16366     /* we don't want to mark this access volatile - bad
16367      * code generation */
16368     return GET_APIC_ID(*(unsigned long *) (APIC_BASE +
16369                                    APIC_ID));
16370  }
16371
16372  #endif                          /* !ASSEMBLY */
16373
16374  #define NO_PROC_ID 0xFF  /* No processor magic marker */
16375
16376  /* This magic constant controls our willingness to
16377   * transfer a process across CPUs. Such a transfer incurs
16378   * misses on the L1 cache, and on a P6 or P5 with
16379   * multiple L2 caches L2 hits. My gut feeling is this
16380   * will vary by board in value. For a board with separate
16381   * L2 cache it probably depends also on the RSS, and for
16382   * a board with shared L2 cache it ought to decay fast as
16383   * other processes are run.  */
16384  #define PROC_CHANGE_PENALTY 15  /* Schedule penalty */
16385
16386  #endif
16387  #endif
```

include/asm-i386/smplock.h

```
16388  /*
16389   * <asm/smplock.h>
16390   *
16391   * i386 SMP lock implementation
16392   */
16393  #include <linux/interrupt.h>
16394  #include <linux/spinlock.h>
16395  #include <linux/sched.h>
16396  #include <asm/current.h>
16397
16398  extern spinlock_t kernel_flag;
16399
16400  #define kernel_locked()  spin_is_locked(&kernel_flag)
16401
16402  /* Release global kernel lock and global interrupt lock
16403   */
16404  #define release_kernel_lock(task, cpu)                 \
16405  do {                                                   \
16406          if (task->lock_depth >= 0)                     \
16407                  spin_unlock(&kernel_flag);             \
16408          release_irqlock(cpu);                          \
16409          __sti();                                       \
16410  } while (0)
16411
16412  /* Re-acquire the kernel lock */
16413  #define reacquire_kernel_lock(task)                    \
16414  do {                                                   \
16415          if (task->lock_depth >= 0)                     \
16416                  spin_lock(&kernel_flag);               \
16417  } while (0)
16418
16419
16420  /* Getting the big kernel lock.
16421   *
16422   * This cannot happen asynchronously, so we only need to
16423   * worry about other CPU's.  */
16424  extern __inline__ void lock_kernel(void)
16425  {
16426  #if 1
16427     if (!++current->lock_depth)
16428        spin_lock(&kernel_flag);
16429  #else
16430     __asm__ __volatile__(
16431        "incl %1\n\t"
16432        "jne 9f"
16433        spin_lock_string
16434        "\n9:"
16435        :"=m"(__dummy_lock(&kernel_flag)),
16436         "=m"(current->lock_depth));
16437  #endif
16438  }
```

```
16439
16440 extern __inline__ void unlock_kernel(void)
16441 {
16442   if (current->lock_depth < 0)
16443     BUG();
16444 #if 1
16445   if (--current->lock_depth < 0)
16446     spin_unlock(&kernel_flag);
16447 #else
16448   __asm__ __volatile__(
16449     "decl %1\n\t"
16450     "jns 9f\n\t"
16451     spin_unlock_string
16452     "\n9:"
16453     :"=m"(__dummy_lock(&kernel_flag)),
16454     "=m"(current->lock_depth));
16455 #endif
16456 }
```

include/asm-i386/softirq.h

```
16457 #ifndef __ASM_SOFTIRQ_H
16458 #define __ASM_SOFTIRQ_H
16459
16460 #include <asm/atomic.h>
16461 #include <asm/hardirq.h>
16462
16463 #define cpu_bh_disable(cpu)                        \
16464   do { local_bh_count(cpu)++; barrier(); } while (0)
16465 #define cpu_bh_enable(cpu)                         \
16466   do { barrier(); local_bh_count(cpu)--; } while (0)
16467
16468 #define local_bh_disable()                         \
16469   cpu_bh_disable(smp_processor_id())
16470 #define local_bh_enable()                          \
16471   cpu_bh_enable(smp_processor_id())
16472
16473 #define in_softirq()                               \
16474   (local_bh_count(smp_processor_id()) != 0)
16475
16476 #endif                          /* __ASM_SOFTIRQ_H */
```

include/asm-i386/spinlock.h

```
16477 #ifndef __ASM_SPINLOCK_H
16478 #define __ASM_SPINLOCK_H
16479
16480 #include <asm/atomic.h>
```

```
16481 #include <asm/rwlock.h>
16482 #include <asm/page.h>
16483
16484 extern int printk(const char *fmt, ...)
16485     __attribute__ ((format(printf, 1, 2)));
16486
16487 /* It seems that people are forgetting to initialize
16488  * their spinlocks properly, tsk tsk. Remember to turn
16489  * this off in 2.4. -ben */
16490 #define SPINLOCK_DEBUG   0
16491
16492 /* Your basic SMP spinlocks, allowing only a single CPU
16493  * anywhere */
16494
16495 typedef struct {
16496   volatile unsigned int lock;
16497 #if SPINLOCK_DEBUG
16498   unsigned magic;
16499 #endif
16500 } spinlock_t;
16501
16502 #define SPINLOCK_MAGIC   0xdead4ead
16503
16504 #if SPINLOCK_DEBUG
16505 #define SPINLOCK_MAGIC_INIT      , SPINLOCK_MAGIC
16506 #else
16507 #define SPINLOCK_MAGIC_INIT      /* */
16508 #endif
16509
16510 #define SPIN_LOCK_UNLOCKED                         \
16511   (spinlock_t) { 1 SPINLOCK_MAGIC_INIT }
16512
16513 #define spin_lock_init(x)                          \
16514   do { *(x) = SPIN_LOCK_UNLOCKED; } while(0)
16515
16516 /* Simple spin lock operations.  There are two variants,
16517  * one clears IRQ's on the local processor, one does not.
16518  *
16519  * We make no fairness assumptions. They have a cost.  */
16520
16521 #define spin_is_locked(x)                          \
16522   (*(volatile char *)(&(x)->lock) <= 0)
16523 #define spin_unlock_wait(x)                        \
16524   do { barrier(); } while(spin_is_locked(x))
16525
16526 #define spin_lock_string                           \
16527     "\n1:\t"                                       \
```

p 687

```
16528          "lock ; decb %0\n\t"                            \
16529          "js 2f\n"                                       \
16530          ".section .text.lock,\"ax\"\n"                  \
16531          "2:\t"                                          \
16532          "cmpb $0,%0\n\t"                                \
16533          "rep;nop\n\t"                                   \
16534          "jle 2b\n\t"                                    \
16535          "jmp 1b\n"                                      \
16536          ".previous"
16537
16538 /* This works. Despite all the confusion.  */
16539 #define spin_unlock_string                               \
16540          "movb $1,%0"
16541
16542 static inline int spin_trylock(spinlock_t * lock)
16543 {
16544    char oldval;
16545    __asm__ __volatile__("xchgb %b0,%1"
16546                        :"=q"(oldval), "=m"(lock->lock)
16547                        :"0"(0)
16548                        :"memory");
16549    return oldval > 0;
16550 }
16551
16552 static inline void spin_lock(spinlock_t * lock)
16553 {
16554 #if SPINLOCK_DEBUG
16555    __label__ here;
16556 here:
16557    if (lock->magic != SPINLOCK_MAGIC) {
16558      printk("eip: %p\n", &&here);
16559      BUG();
16560    }
16561 #endif
16562    __asm__ __volatile__(spin_lock_string
16563                        :"=m"(lock->lock)
16564                        ::"memory");
16565 }
16566
16567 static inline void spin_unlock(spinlock_t * lock)
16568 {
16569 #if SPINLOCK_DEBUG
16570    if (lock->magic != SPINLOCK_MAGIC)
16571      BUG();
16572    if (!spin_is_locked(lock))
16573      BUG();
16574 #endif
```

```
16575    __asm__ __volatile__(spin_unlock_string
16576                        :"=m"(lock->lock)
16577                        ::"memory");
16578 }
16579
16580 /* Read-write spinlocks, allowing multiple readers but
16581  * only one writer.
16582  *
16583  * NOTE! it is quite common to have readers in interrupts
16584  * but no interrupt writers. For those circumstances we
16585  * can "mix" irq-safe locks - any writer needs to get a
16586  * irq-safe write-lock, but readers can get non-irqsafe
16587  * read-locks.  */
16588 typedef struct {
16589    volatile unsigned int lock;
16590 #if SPINLOCK_DEBUG
16591    unsigned magic;
16592 #endif
16593 } rwlock_t;
16594
16595 #define RWLOCK_MAGIC     0xdeafleed
16596
16597 #if SPINLOCK_DEBUG
16598 #define RWLOCK_MAGIC_INIT        , RWLOCK_MAGIC
16599 #else
16600 #define RWLOCK_MAGIC_INIT        /* */
16601 #endif
16602
16603 #define RW_LOCK_UNLOCKED                                  \
16604    (rwlock_t) { RW_LOCK_BIAS RWLOCK_MAGIC_INIT }
16605
16606 #define rwlock_init(x)                                    \
16607    do { *(x) = RW_LOCK_UNLOCKED; } while(0)
16608
16609 /* On x86, we implement read-write locks as a 32-bit
16610  * counter with the high bit (sign) being the "contended"
16611  * bit.
16612  *
16613  * The inline assembly is non-obvious. Think about it.
16614  *
16615  * Changed to use the same technique as rw semaphores.
16616  * See semaphore.h for details.  -ben */
16617 /* the spinlock helpers are in
16618  * arch/i386/kernel/semaphore.c */
16619
16620 static inline void read_lock(rwlock_t * rw)
16621 {
```

```
16622 #if SPINLOCK_DEBUG
16623   if (rw->magic != RWLOCK_MAGIC)
16624     BUG();
16625 #endif
16626   __build_read_lock(rw, "__read_lock_failed");
16627 }
16628
16629 static inline void write_lock(rwlock_t * rw)
16630 {
16631 #if SPINLOCK_DEBUG
16632   if (rw->magic != RWLOCK_MAGIC)
16633     BUG();
16634 #endif
16635   __build_write_lock(rw, "__write_lock_failed");
16636 }
16637
16638 #define read_unlock(rw)                                    \
16639   asm volatile("lock ; incl %0"                           \
16640               :"=m" ((rw)->lock) : : "memory")
16641 #define write_unlock(rw)                                   \
16642   asm volatile("lock ; addl $" RW_LOCK_BIAS_STR ",%0"     \
16643               :"=m" ((rw)->lock) : : "memory")
16644
16645 static inline int write_trylock(rwlock_t * lock)
16646 {
16647   atomic_t *count = (atomic_t *) lock;
16648   if (atomic_sub_and_test(RW_LOCK_BIAS, count))
16649     return 1;
16650   atomic_add(RW_LOCK_BIAS, count);
16651   return 0;
16652 }
16653
16654 #endif                            /* __ASM_SPINLOCK_H */
```

include/asm-i386/system.h

```
16655 #ifndef __ASM_SYSTEM_H
16656 #define __ASM_SYSTEM_H
16657
16658 #include <linux/config.h>
16659 #include <linux/kernel.h>
16660 #include <asm/segment.h>
16661 #include <linux/bitops.h>          /* for LOCK_PREFIX */
16662
16663 #ifdef __KERNEL__
16664
16665 /* one of the stranger aspects of C forward
16666  * declarations.. */
16667 struct task_struct;
16668 extern void
16669 FASTCALL(__switch_to(struct task_struct *prev,
16670                     struct task_struct *next));
16671
16672 #define prepare_to_switch()     do { } while(0)
16673 #define switch_to(prev, next, last)                        \
16674 do {                                                       \
16675   asm volatile("pushl %%esi\n\t"                           \
16676               "pushl %%edi\n\t"                            \
16677               "pushl %%ebp\n\t"                            \
16678               "movl %%esp,%0\n\t"   /* save ESP */         \
16679               "movl %3,%%esp\n\t"   /* restore ESP */      \
16680               "movl $1f,%1\n\t"     /* save EIP */         \
16681               "pushl %4\n\t"        /* restore EIP */      \
16682               "jmp __switch_to\n"                          \
16683               "1:\t"                                       \
16684               "popl %%ebp\n\t"                             \
16685              "popl %%edi\n\t"                              \
16686              "popl %%esi\n\t"                              \
16687              :"=m" (prev->thread.esp),                     \
16688              "=m" (prev->thread.eip),                      \
16689              "=b" (last)                                   \
16690             :"m" (next->thread.esp),                       \
16691             "m" (next->thread.eip),                        \
16692             "a" (prev), "d" (next),                        \
16693             "b" (prev));                                   \
16694 } while (0)
16695
16696 #define _set_base(addr, base)                              \
16697 do {                                                       \
16698   unsigned long __pr;                                      \
16699   __asm__ __volatile__ ("movw %%dx,%1\n\t"                 \
16700                        "rorl $16,%%edx\n\t"                 \
16701                        "movb %%dl,%2\n\t"                   \
16702                        "movb %%dh,%3"                       \
16703                       :"=&d" (__pr)                         \
16704                       :"m" (*((addr)+2)),                   \
16705                       "m" (*((addr)+4)),                    \
16706                       "m" (*((addr)+7)),                    \
16707                       "0" (base));                          \
16708 } while(0)
16709
16710 #define _set_limit(addr, limit)                            \
16711 do {                                                       \
16712   unsigned long __lr;                                      \
16713   __asm__ __volatile__ ("movw %%dx,%1\n\t"                 \
```

```
16714                    "rorl $16,%%edx\n\t"              \
16715                    "movb %2,%%dh\n\t"               \
16716                    "andb $0xf0,%%dh\n\t"            \
16717                    "orb %%dh,%%dl\n\t"              \
16718                    "movb %%dl,%2"                   \
16719                    :"=&d" (__lr)                    \
16720                    :"m" (*(addr)),                  \
16721                     "m" (*((addr)+6)),              \
16722                     "0" (limit));                   \
16723 } while(0)
16724
16725 #define set_base(ldt,base)                          \
16726   _set_base( ((char *)&(ldt)) , (base) )
16727 #define set_limit(ldt,limit)                        \
16728   _set_limit( ((char *)&(ldt)) , ((limit)-1)>>12 )
16729
16730 static inline unsigned long _get_base(char *addr)
16731 {
16732   unsigned long __base;
16733   __asm__("movb %3,%%dh\n\t"
16734           "movb %2,%%dl\n\t"
16735           "shll $16,%%edx\n\t"
16736           "movw %1,%%dx"
16737           :"=&d"(__base)
16738           :"m"(*((addr) + 2)),
16739            "m"(*((addr) + 4)), "m"(*((addr) + 7)));
16740   return __base;
16741 }
16742
16743 #define get_base(ldt) _get_base( ((char *)&(ldt)) )
16744
16745 /* Load a segment. Fall back on loading the zero segment
16746  * if something goes wrong..  */
16747 #define loadsegment(seg,value)                        \
16748       asm volatile("\n"                              \
16749                    "1:\t"                            \
16750                    "movl %0,%%" #seg "\n"            \
16751                    "2:\n"                            \
16752                    ".section .fixup,\"ax\"\n"        \
16753                    "3:\t"                            \
16754                    "pushl $0\n\t"                    \
16755                    "popl %%" #seg "\n\t"             \
16756                    "jmp 2b\n"                         \
16757                    ".previous\n"                     \
16758                    ".section __ex_table,\"a\"\n\t"   \
16759                    ".align 4\n\t"                    \
16760                    ".long 1b,3b\n"                   \
```

```
16761                    ".previous"                      \
16762                    : :"m" (*(unsigned int *)&(value)))
16763
16764 /* Clear and set 'TS' bit respectively */
16765 #define clts() __asm__ __volatile__ ("clts")
16766 #define read_cr0() ({                                \
16767       unsigned int __dummy;                          \
16768       __asm__("movl %%cr0,%0\n\t"                     \
16769               :"=r" (__dummy));                       \
16770       __dummy;                                        \
16771 })
16772 #define write_cr0(x)                                 \
16773       __asm__("movl %0,%%cr0": :"r" (x));
16774 #define stts() write_cr0(8 | read_cr0())
16775
16776 #endif                        /* __KERNEL__ */
16777
16778 static inline unsigned long
16779 get_limit(unsigned long segment)
16780 {
16781   unsigned long __limit;
16782   __asm__("lsll %1,%0": "=r"(__limit):"r"(segment));
16783   return __limit + 1;
16784 }
16785
16786 #define nop() __asm__ __volatile__ ("nop")
16787
16788 #define xchg(ptr,v)                                  \
16789   ((__typeof__(*(ptr))) __xchg((unsigned long)(v),(ptr),\
16790                               sizeof(*(ptr))))
16791
16792 #define tas(ptr) (xchg((ptr),1))
16793
16794 struct __xchg_dummy {
16795   unsigned long a[100];
16796 };
16797
16798 #define __xg(x) ((struct __xchg_dummy *)(x))
16799
16800
16801 /* The semantics of XCHGCMP8B are a bit strange, this is
16802  * why there is a loop and the loading of %%eax and %%edx
16803  * has to be inside. This inlines well in most cases, the
16804  * cached cost is around ~38 cycles. (in the future we
16805  * might want to do an SIMD/3DNOW!/MMX/FPU 64-bit store
16806  * here, but that might have an implicit FPU-save as a
16807  * cost, so it's not clear which path to go.)  */
```

```
16808 extern inline void __set_64bit(unsigned long long *ptr,
16809    unsigned int low, unsigned int high)
16810 {
16811    __asm__ __volatile__("1:      movl (%0), %%eax;
16812                                  movl 4(%0), %%edx;
16813                                  cmpxchg8b(%0);
16814                                  jnz 1 b "
16815                    ::"D"(ptr), "b"(low), "c"(high)
16816                    :"ax", "dx", "memory");
16817 }
16818
16819 extern void inline __set_64bit_constant(unsigned long
16820    long *ptr, unsigned long long value)
16821 {
16822    __set_64bit(ptr, (unsigned int) (value),
16823       (unsigned int) ((value) >> 32ULL));
16824 }
16825
16826 #define ll_low(x)     *(((unsigned int*)&(x))+0)
16827 #define ll_high(x)    *(((unsigned int*)&(x))+1)
16828
16829 extern void inline __set_64bit_var(unsigned long long
16830     *ptr, unsigned long long value)
16831 {
16832    __set_64bit(ptr, ll_low(value), ll_high(value));
16833 }
16834
16835 #define set_64bit(ptr,value)                          \
16836 (__builtin_constant_p(value)                         \
16837  ? __set_64bit_constant(ptr, value)                  \
16838  : __set_64bit_var(ptr, value) )
16839
16840 #define _set_64bit(ptr,value)                         \
16841 (__builtin_constant_p(value)                         \
16842  ? __set_64bit(ptr, (unsigned int)(value),           \
16843                (unsigned int)((value)>>32ULL) )       \
16844  : __set_64bit(ptr, ll_low(value), ll_high(value)) )
16845
16846 /* Note: no "lock" prefix even on SMP: xchg always
16847  * implies lock anyway Note 2: xchg has side effect, so
16848  * that attribute volatile is necessary, but generally
16849  * the primitive is invalid, *ptr is output
16850  * argument. —ANK */
16851 static inline unsigned long __xchg(unsigned long x,
16852     volatile void *ptr, int size)
16853 {
16854    switch (size) {
16855    case 1:
16856       __asm__ __volatile__("xchgb %b0,%1":"=q"(x)
16857                            :"m"(*__xg(ptr)), "0"(x)
16858                            :"memory");
16859    break;
16860    case 2:
16861       __asm__ __volatile__("xchgw %w0,%1":"=r"(x)
16862                            :"m"(*__xg(ptr)), "0"(x)
16863                            :"memory");
16864    break;
16865    case 4:
16866       __asm__ __volatile__("xchgl %0,%1":"=r"(x)
16867                            :"m"(*__xg(ptr)), "0"(x)
16868                            :"memory");
16869    break;
16870    }
16871    return x;
16872 }
16873
16874 /* Atomic compare and exchange.  Compare OLD with MEM, if
16875  * identical, store NEW in MEM.  Return the initial value
16876  * in MEM.  Success is indicated by comparing RETURN with
16877  * OLD.  */
16878
16879 #ifdef CONFIG_X86_CMPXCHG
16880 #define __HAVE_ARCH_CMPXCHG 1
16881
16882 static inline unsigned long __cmpxchg(volatile void *ptr,
16883     unsigned long old, unsigned long new, int size)
16884 {
16885    unsigned long prev;
16886    switch (size) {
16887    case 1:
16888       __asm__ __volatile__(LOCK_PREFIX "cmpxchgb %b1,%2":
16889                            "=a"(prev)
16890                            :"q"(new), "m"(*__xg(ptr)),
16891                             "0"(old)
16892                            :"memory");
16893    return prev;
16894    case 2:
16895       __asm__ __volatile__(LOCK_PREFIX "cmpxchgw %w1,%2":
16896                            "=a"(prev)
16897                            :"q"(new), "m"(*__xg(ptr)),
16898                             "0"(old)
16899                            :"memory");
16900    return prev;
16901    case 4:
```

```
16902      __asm__ __volatile__(LOCK_PREFIX "cmpxchgl %1,%2":
16903                            "=a"(prev)
16904                          :"q"(new), "m"(*__xg(ptr)),
16905                            "0"(old)
16906                          :"memory");
16907      return prev;
16908    }
16909    return old;
16910 }
16911
16912 #define cmpxchg(ptr,o,n)                                    \
16913 ((__typeof__(*(ptr)))                                      \
16914   __cmpxchg((ptr),(unsigned long)(o),                      \
16915             (unsigned long)(n),sizeof(*(ptr))))
16916
16917 #else
16918 /* Compiling for a 386 proper.  Is it worth implementing
16919  * via cli/sti?  */
16920 #endif
16921
16922 /* Force strict CPU ordering.  And yes, this is required
16923  * on UP too when we're talking to devices.
16924  *
16925  * For now, "wmb()" doesn't actually do anything, as all
16926  * Intel CPU's follow what Intel calls a *Processor
16927  * Order*, in which all writes are seen in the program
16928  * order even outside the CPU.
16929  *
16930  * I expect future Intel CPU's to have a weaker ordering,
16931  * but I'd also expect them to finally get their act
16932  * together and add some real memory barriers if so.  */
16933 #define mb()    __asm__ __volatile__                        \
16934                 ("lock; addl $0,0(%%esp)": : :"memory")
16935 #define rmb()   mb()
16936 #define wmb()   __asm__ __volatile__ ("": : :"memory")
16937
16938 #ifdef CONFIG_SMP
16939 #define smp_mb()        mb()
16940 #define smp_rmb()       rmb()
16941 #define smp_wmb()       wmb()
16942 #else
16943 #define smp_mb()        barrier()
16944 #define smp_rmb()       barrier()
16945 #define smp_wmb()       barrier()
16946 #endif
16947
16948 #define set_mb(var, value)                                  \
```

```
16949    do { xchg(&var, value); } while (0)
16950 #define set_wmb(var, value)                                \
16951    do { var = value; wmb(); } while (0)
16952
16953 /* interrupt control.. */
16954 #define __save_flags(x)                                    \
16955    __asm__ __volatile__("pushfl ; popl %0"                 \
16956                         :"=g" (x): /* no input */)
16957 #define __restore_flags(x)                                 \
16958    __asm__ __volatile__("pushl %0 ; popfl"                 \
16959                         : /* no output */                  \
16960                         :"g" (x):"memory")
16961 #define __cli() __asm__ __volatile__("cli": : :"memory")
16962 #define __sti() __asm__ __volatile__("sti": : :"memory")
16963 /* used in the idle loop; sti takes one instruction
16964  * cycle to complete */
16965 #define safe_halt()                                        \
16966    __asm__ __volatile__("sti; hlt": : :"memory")
16967
16968 /* For spinlocks etc */
16969 #define local_irq_save(x)       __asm__ __volatile__       \
16970 ("pushfl ; popl %0 ; cli":"=g" (x): /* no input */      \
16971  :"memory")
16972 #define local_irq_restore(x)    __restore_flags(x)
16973 #define local_irq_disable()     __cli()
16974 #define local_irq_enable()      __sti()
16975
16976 #ifdef CONFIG_SMP
16977
16978 extern void __global_cli(void);
16979 extern void __global_sti(void);
16980 extern unsigned long __global_save_flags(void);
16981 extern void __global_restore_flags(unsigned long);
16982 #define cli()           __global_cli()
16983 #define sti()           __global_sti()
16984 #define save_flags(x)   ((x)=__global_save_flags())
16985 #define restore_flags(x) __global_restore_flags(x)
16986
16987 #else
16988
16989 #define cli()           __cli()
16990 #define sti()           __sti()
16991 #define save_flags(x)   __save_flags(x)
16992 #define restore_flags(x) __restore_flags(x)
16993
16994 #endif
16995
```

```
16996 /* disable hlt during certain critical i/o operations */
16997 #define HAVE_DISABLE_HLT
16998 void disable_hlt(void);
16999 void enable_hlt(void);
17000
17001 #endif
```

include/asm-i386/uaccess.h

```
17002 #ifndef __i386_UACCESS_H
17003 #define __i386_UACCESS_H
17004
17005 /* User space memory access functions */
17006 #include <linux/config.h>
17007 #include <linux/sched.h>
17008 #include <asm/page.h>
17009
17010 #define VERIFY_READ 0
17011 #define VERIFY_WRITE 1
17012
17013 /* The fs value determines whether argument validity
17014  * checking should be performed or not.  If get_fs() ==
17015  * USER_DS, checking is performed, with get_fs() ==
17016  * KERNEL_DS, checking is bypassed.
17017  *
17018  * For historical reasons, these macros are grossly
17019  * misnamed.  */
17020
17021 #define MAKE_MM_SEG(s)  ((mm_segment_t) { (s) })
17022
17023
17024 #define KERNEL_DS       MAKE_MM_SEG(0xFFFFFFFF)
17025 #define USER_DS         MAKE_MM_SEG(PAGE_OFFSET)
17026
17027 #define get_ds()        (KERNEL_DS)
17028 #define get_fs()        (current->addr_limit)
17029 #define set_fs(x)       (current->addr_limit = (x))
17030
17031 #define segment_eq(a,b) ((a).seg == (b).seg)
17032
17033 extern int __verify_write(const void *, unsigned long);
17034
17035 #define __addr_ok(addr)                                 \
17036   ((unsigned long)(addr) < (current->addr_limit.seg))
17037
17038 /* Uhhuh, this needs 33-bit arithmetic. We have a carry..
17039  */
17040 #define __range_ok(addr,size) ({                        \
17041      unsigned long flag,sum;                            \
17042      asm("addl %3,%1 ; sbbl %0,%0; "                    \
17043          "cmpl %1,%4; sbbl $0,%0"                       \
17044          :"=&r" (flag), "=r" (sum)                      \
17045          :"1" (addr),"g" ((int)(size)),                 \
17046          "g" (current->addr_limit.seg));                \
17047      flag; })
17048
17049 #ifdef CONFIG_X86_WP_WORKS_OK
17050
17051 #define access_ok(type,addr,size)                       \
17052   (__range_ok(addr,size) == 0)
17053
17054 #else
17055
17056 #define access_ok(type,addr,size)                       \
17057 ((__range_ok(addr,size) == 0) &&                        \
17058 ((type) == VERIFY_READ || boot_cpu_data.wp_works_ok || \
17059  segment_eq(get_fs(),KERNEL_DS) ||                      \
17060  __verify_write((void *)(addr),(size))))
17061
17062 #endif
17063
17064 extern inline int verify_area(int type, const void *addr,
17065     unsigned long size)
17066 {
17067   return access_ok(type, addr, size) ? 0 : -EFAULT;
17068 }
17069
17070
17071 /* The exception table consists of pairs of addresses:
17072  * the first is the address of an instruction that is
17073  * allowed to fault, and the second is the address at
17074  * which the program should continue.  No registers are
17075  * modified, so it is entirely up to the continuation
17076  * code to figure out what to do.
17077  *
17078  * All the routines below use bits of fixup code that are
17079  * out of line with the main instruction path.  This
17080  * means when everything is well, we don't even have to
17081  * jump over them.  Further, they do not intrude on our
17082  * cache or tlb entries.  */
17083
17084 struct exception_table_entry {
17085   unsigned long insn, fixup;
17086 };
17087
```

```
17088 /* Returns 0 if exception not found and fixup otherwise.
17089  */
17090 extern unsigned long
17091 search_exception_table(unsigned long);
17092
17093
17094 /* These are the main single-value transfer routines.
17095  * They automatically use the right size if we just have
17096  * the right pointer type.
17097  *
17098  * This gets kind of ugly. We want to return _two_ values
17099  * in "get_user()" and yet we don't want to do any
17100  * pointers, because that is too much of a performance
17101  * impact. Thus we have a few rather ugly macros here,
17102  * and hide all the uglyness from the user.
17103  *
17104  * The "__xxx" versions of the user access functions are
17105  * versions that do not verify the address space, that
17106  * must have been done previously with a separate
17107  * "access_ok()" call (this is used when we do multiple
17108  * accesses to the same area of user memory).  */
17109
17110 extern void __get_user_1(void);
17111 extern void __get_user_2(void);
17112 extern void __get_user_4(void);
17113
17114 #define __get_user_x(size,ret,x,ptr)                      \
17115         __asm__ __volatile__("call __get_user_" #size  \
17116                 :"=a" (ret),"=d" (x)                     \
17117                 :"0" (ptr))
17118
17119 /* Careful: we have to cast the result to the type of
17120  * the pointer for sign reasons */
17121 #define get_user(x,ptr)                                   \
17122 ({                                                        \
17123 int __ret_gu,__val_gu;                                    \
17124 switch(sizeof (*(ptr))) {                                 \
17125 case 1:  __get_user_x(1,__ret_gu,__val_gu,ptr); break;   \
17126 case 2:  __get_user_x(2,__ret_gu,__val_gu,ptr); break;   \
17127 case 4:  __get_user_x(4,__ret_gu,__val_gu,ptr); break;   \
17128 default: __get_user_x(X,__ret_gu,__val_gu,ptr); break;   \
17129 }                                                         \
17130 (x) = (__typeof__(*(ptr)))__val_gu;                       \
17131 __ret_gu;                                                 \
17132 })
17133
17134 extern void __put_user_1(void);
17135 extern void __put_user_2(void);
17136 extern void __put_user_4(void);
17137
17138 extern void __put_user_bad(void);
17139
17140 #define __put_user_x(size,ret,x,ptr)                      \
17141         __asm__ __volatile__("call __put_user_" #size  \
17142                 :"=a" (ret)                              \
17143                 :"0" (ptr),"d" (x)                       \
17144                 :"cx")
17145
17146 #define put_user(x,ptr)                                   \
17147     __put_user_check((__typeof__(*(ptr)))(x),            \
17148                 (ptr),sizeof(*(ptr)))
17149
17150 #define __get_user(x,ptr)                                 \
17151     __get_user_nocheck((x),(ptr),sizeof(*(ptr)))
17152 #define __put_user(x,ptr)                                 \
17153     __put_user_nocheck((__typeof__(*(ptr)))(x),          \
17154                 (ptr),sizeof(*(ptr)))
17155
17156 #define __put_user_nocheck(x,ptr,size)                    \
17157 ({                                                        \
17158         long __pu_err;                                    \
17159         __put_user_size((x),(ptr),(size),__pu_err);      \
17160         __pu_err;                                         \
17161 })
17162
17163
17164 #define __put_user_check(x,ptr,size)                      \
17165 ({                                                        \
17166         long __pu_err = -EFAULT;                          \
17167         __typeof__(*(ptr)) *__pu_addr = (ptr);           \
17168         if (access_ok(VERIFY_WRITE,__pu_addr,size))      \
17169             __put_user_size((x),__pu_addr,(size),        \
17170                         __pu_err);                        \
17171         __pu_err;                                         \
17172 })
17173
17174 #define __put_user_size(x,ptr,size,retval)                \
17175 do {                                                      \
17176   retval = 0;                                             \
17177   switch (size) {                                         \
17178   case 1: __put_user_asm(x,ptr,retval,"b","b","iq");     \
17179         break;                                            \
17180  case 2: __put_user_asm(x,ptr,retval,"w","w","ir");      \
17181         break;                                            \
```

```
17182   case 4: __put_user_asm(x,ptr,retval,"l","","ir");        \
17183         break;                                             \
17184   default: __put_user_bad();                               \
17185   }                                                        \
17186 } while (0)
17187
17188 struct __large_struct {
17189   unsigned long buf[100];
17190 };
17191
17192 #define __m(x) (*(struct __large_struct *)(x))
17193
17194 /* Tell gcc we read from memory instead of writing: this
17195  * is because we do not write to any memory gcc knows
17196  * about, so there are no aliasing issues.  */
17197 #define __put_user_asm(x,addr,err,itype,rtype,ltype)    \
17198         __asm__ __volatile__(                           \
17199                 "1:     mov"itype" %"rtype"1,%2\n"      \
17200                 "2:\n"                                  \
17201                 ".section .fixup,\"ax\"\n"              \
17202                 "3:     movl %3,%0\n"                   \
17203                 "       jmp 2b\n"                       \
17204                 ".previous\n"                          \
17205                 ".section __ex_table,\"a\"\n"           \
17206                 "       .align 4\n"                     \
17207                 "       .long 1b,3b\n"                  \
17208                 ".previous"                             \
17209                 : "=r"(err)                             \
17210                 : ltype (x), "m"(__m(addr)),            \
17211                   "i"(-EFAULT), "0"(err))
17212
17213
17214 #define __get_user_nocheck(x,ptr,size)                  \
17215 ({                                                      \
17216         long __gu_err, __gu_val;                        \
17217         __get_user_size(__gu_val,(ptr),(size),__gu_err);\
17218         (x) = (__typeof__(*(ptr)))__gu_val;             \
17219         __gu_err;                                       \
17220 })
17221
17222 extern long __get_user_bad(void);
17223
17224 #define __get_user_size(x,ptr,size,retval)              \
17225 do {                                                    \
17226   retval = 0;                                           \
17227   switch (size) {                                       \
17228   case 1: __get_user_asm(x,ptr,retval,"b","b","=q");    \
17229         break;                                          \
17230   case 2: __get_user_asm(x,ptr,retval,"w","w","=r");    \
17231         break;                                          \
17232   case 4: __get_user_asm(x,ptr,retval,"l","","=r");     \
17233         break;                                          \
17234   default: (x) = __get_user_bad();                      \
17235   }                                                     \
17236 } while (0)
17237
17238 #define __get_user_asm(x,addr,err,itype,rtype,ltype)    \
17239         __asm__ __volatile__(                           \
17240                 "1:     mov"itype" %2,%"rtype"1\n"      \
17241                 "2:\n"                                  \
17242                 ".section .fixup,\"ax\"\n"              \
17243                 "3:     movl %3,%0\n"                   \
17244                 "       xor"itype" %"rtype"1,%"rtype"1\n"\
17245                 "       jmp 2b\n"                       \
17246                 ".previous\n"                          \
17247                 ".section __ex_table,\"a\"\n"           \
17248                 "       .align 4\n"                     \
17249                 "       .long 1b,3b\n"                  \
17250                 ".previous"                             \
17251                 : "=r"(err), ltype (x)                  \
17252                 : "m"(__m(addr)), "i"(-EFAULT), "0"(err))
17253
17254
17255 /* Copy To/From Userspace */
17256
17257 /* Generic arbitrary sized copy.  */
17258 #define __copy_user(to,from,size)                       \
17259 do {                                                    \
17260   int __d0, __d1;                                       \
17261   __asm__ __volatile__(                                 \
17262   "0:   rep; movsl\n"                                   \
17263   "     movl %3,%0\n"                                   \
17264   "1:   rep; movsb\n"                                   \
17265   "2:\n"                                                \
17266   ".section .fixup,\"ax\"\n"                            \
17267   "3:   lea 0(%3,%0,4),%0\n"                            \
17268   "     jmp 2b\n"                                       \
17269   ".previous\n"                                         \
17270   ".section __ex_table,\"a\"\n"                         \
17271   "     .align 4\n"                                     \
17272   "     .long 0b,3b\n"                                  \
17273   "     .long 1b,2b\n"                                  \
17274   ".previous"                                           \
17275   : "=&c"(size), "=&D" (__d0), "=&S" (__d1)             \
```

```
17276      : "r"(size & 3), "0"(size / 4), "1"(to), "2"(from)   \
17277      : "memory");                                          \
17278 } while (0)
17279
17280 #define __copy_user_zeroing(to,from,size)                  \
17281 do {                                                        \
17282   int __d0, __d1;                                          \
17283   __asm__ __volatile__(                                    \
17284     "0:      rep; movsl\n"                                 \
17285     "        movl %3,%0\n"                                 \
17286     "1:      rep; movsb\n"                                 \
17287     "2:\n"                                                 \
17288     ".section .fixup,\"ax\"\n"                             \
17289     "3:      lea 0(%3,%0,4),%0\n"                          \
17290     "4:      pushl %0\n"                                   \
17291     "        pushl %%eax\n"                                \
17292     "        xorl %%eax,%%eax\n"                           \
17293     "        rep; stosb\n"                                 \
17294     "        popl %%eax\n"                                 \
17295     "        popl %0\n"                                    \
17296     "        jmp 2b\n"                                     \
17297     ".previous\n"                                          \
17298     ".section __ex_table,\"a\"\n"                          \
17299     "        .align 4\n"                                  \
17300     "        .long 0b,3b\n"                                \
17301     "        .long 1b,4b\n"                                \
17302     ".previous"                                            \
17303     : "=&c"(size), "=&D" (__d0), "=&S" (__d1)              \
17304     : "r"(size & 3), "0"(size / 4), "1"(to), "2"(from)    \
17305     : "memory");                                           \
17306 } while (0)
17307
17308 /* We let the __ versions of copy_from/to_user inline,
17309  * because they're often used in fast paths and have only
17310  * a small space overhead. */
17311 static inline unsigned long
17312 __generic_copy_from_user_nocheck(void *to,
17313     const void *from, unsigned long n)
17314 {
17315   __copy_user_zeroing(to, from, n);
17316   return n;
17317 }
17318
17319 static inline unsigned long
17320 __generic_copy_to_user_nocheck(void *to,
17321     const void *from, unsigned long n)
17322 {
17323   __copy_user(to, from, n);
17324   return n;
17325 }
17326
17327
17328 /* Optimize just a little bit when we know the size of
17329  * the move. */
17330 #define __constant_copy_user(to, from, size)               \
17331 do {                                                        \
17332   int __d0, __d1;                                          \
17333   switch (size & 3) {                                      \
17334   default:                                                 \
17335     __asm__ __volatile__(                                  \
17336       "0:      rep; movsl\n"                               \
17337       "1:\n"                                               \
17338       ".section .fixup,\"ax\"\n"                           \
17339       "2:      shl $2,%0\n"                                \
17340       "        jmp 1b\n"                                   \
17341       ".previous\n"                                        \
17342       ".section __ex_table,\"a\"\n"                        \
17343       "        .align 4\n"                                \
17344       "        .long 0b,2b\n"                              \
17345       ".previous"                                          \
17346       : "=c"(size), "=&S" (__d0), "=&D" (__d1)             \
17347       : "1"(from), "2"(to), "0"(size/4)                   \
17348       : "memory");                                         \
17349     break;                                                 \
17350   case 1:                                                  \
17351     __asm__ __volatile__(                                  \
17352       "0:      rep; movsl\n"                               \
17353       "1:      movsb\n"                                    \
17354       "2:\n"                                               \
17355       ".section .fixup,\"ax\"\n"                           \
17356       "3:      shl $2,%0\n"                                \
17357       "4:      incl %0\n"                                  \
17358       "        jmp 2b\n"                                   \
17359       ".previous\n"                                        \
17360       ".section __ex_table,\"a\"\n"                        \
17361       "        .align 4\n"                                \
17362       "        .long 0b,3b\n"                              \
17363       "        .long 1b,4b\n"                              \
17364       ".previous"                                          \
17365       : "=c"(size), "=&S" (__d0), "=&D" (__d1)             \
17366       : "1"(from), "2"(to), "0"(size/4)                   \
17367       : "memory");                                         \
17368     break;                                                 \
17369   case 2:                                                  \
```

```
17370        __asm__ __volatile__(                              \
17371          "0:      rep; movsl\n"                            \
17372          "1:      movsw\n"                                 \
17373          "2:\n"                                            \
17374          ".section .fixup,\"ax\"\n"                        \
17375          "3:      shl $2,%0\n"                             \
17376          "4:      addl $2,%0\n"                            \
17377          "        jmp 2b\n"                                \
17378          ".previous\n"                                     \
17379          ".section __ex_table,\"a\"\n"                     \
17380          "        .align 4\n"                              \
17381          "        .long 0b,3b\n"                           \
17382          "        .long 1b,4b\n"                           \
17383          ".previous"                                       \
17384          : "=c"(size), "=&S" (__d0), "=&D" (__d1)          \
17385          : "1"(from), "2"(to), "0"(size/4)                 \
17386          : "memory");                                      \
17387        break;                                             \
17388      case 3:                                              \
17389        __asm__ __volatile__(                              \
17390          "0:      rep; movsl\n"                            \
17391          "1:      movsw\n"                                 \
17392          "2:      movsb\n"                                 \
17393          "3:\n"                                            \
17394          ".section .fixup,\"ax\"\n"                        \
17395          "4:      shl $2,%0\n"                             \
17396          "5:      addl $2,%0\n"                            \
17397          "6:      incl %0\n"                               \
17398          "        jmp 3b\n"                                \
17399          ".previous\n"                                     \
17400          ".section __ex_table,\"a\"\n"                     \
17401          "        .align 4\n"                              \
17402          "        .long 0b,4b\n"                           \
17403          "        .long 1b,5b\n"                           \
17404          "        .long 2b,6b\n"                           \
17405          ".previous"                                       \
17406          : "=c"(size), "=&S" (__d0), "=&D" (__d1)          \
17407          : "1"(from), "2"(to), "0"(size/4)                 \
17408          : "memory");                                      \
17409        break;                                             \
17410      }                                                    \
17411    } while (0)
17412
17413    /* Optimize just a little bit when we know the size of
17414     * the move. */
17415    #define __constant_copy_user_zeroing(to, from, size)    \
17416    do {                                                   \
17417      int __d0, __d1;                                       \
17418      switch (size & 3) {                                  \
17419      default:                                             \
17420        __asm__ __volatile__(                              \
17421          "0:      rep; movsl\n"                            \
17422          "1:\n"                                            \
17423          ".section .fixup,\"ax\"\n"                        \
17424          "2:      pushl %0\n"                              \
17425          "        pushl %%eax\n"                           \
17426          "        xorl %%eax,%%eax\n"                      \
17427          "        rep; stosl\n"                            \
17428          "        popl %%eax\n"                            \
17429          "        popl %0\n"                               \
17430          "        shl $2,%0\n"                             \
17431          "        jmp 1b\n"                                \
17432          ".previous\n"                                     \
17433          ".section __ex_table,\"a\"\n"                     \
17434          "        .align 4\n"                              \
17435          "        .long 0b,2b\n"                           \
17436          ".previous"                                       \
17437          : "=c"(size), "=&S" (__d0), "=&D" (__d1)          \
17438          : "1"(from), "2"(to), "0"(size/4)                 \
17439          : "memory");                                      \
17440        break;                                             \
17441      case 1:                                              \
17442        __asm__ __volatile__(                              \
17443          "0:      rep; movsl\n"                            \
17444          "1:      movsb\n"                                 \
17445          "2:\n"                                            \
17446          ".section .fixup,\"ax\"\n"                        \
17447          "3:      pushl %0\n"                              \
17448          "        pushl %%eax\n"                           \
17449          "        xorl %%eax,%%eax\n"                      \
17450          "        rep; stosl\n"                            \
17451          "        stosb\n"                                 \
17452          "        popl %%eax\n"                            \
17453          "        popl %0\n"                               \
17454          "        shl $2,%0\n"                             \
17455          "        incl %0\n"                               \
17456          "        jmp 2b\n"                                \
17457          "4:      pushl %%eax\n"                           \
17458          "        xorl %%eax,%%eax\n"                      \
17459          "        stosb\n"                                 \
17460          "        popl %%eax\n"                            \
17461          "        incl %0\n"                               \
17462          "        jmp 2b\n"                                \
17463          ".previous\n"                                     \
```

```
17464        ".section __ex_table,\"a\"\n"                              \
17465        "       .align 4\n"                                        \
17466        "       .long 0b,3b\n"                                     \
17467        "       .long 1b,4b\n"                                     \
17468        ".previous"                                                \
17469        : "=c"(size), "=&S" (__d0), "=&D" (__d1)                   \
17470        : "1"(from), "2"(to), "0"(size/4)                          \
17471        : "memory");                                               \
17472      break;                                                       \
17473    case 2:                                                        \
17474      __asm__ __volatile__(                                        \
17475        "0:     rep; movsl\n"                                      \
17476        "1:     movsw\n"                                           \
17477        "2:\n"                                                     \
17478        ".section .fixup,\"ax\"\n"                                 \
17479        "3:     pushl %0\n"                                        \
17480        "       pushl %%eax\n"                                     \
17481        "       xorl %%eax,%%eax\n"                                \
17482        "       rep; stosl\n"                                      \
17483        "       stosw\n"                                           \
17484        "       popl %%eax\n"                                      \
17485        "       popl %0\n"                                         \
17486        "       shl $2,%0\n"                                       \
17487        "       addl $2,%0\n"                                      \
17488        "       jmp 2b\n"                                          \
17489        "4:     pushl %%eax\n"                                     \
17490        "       xorl %%eax,%%eax\n"                                \
17491        "       stosw\n"                                           \
17492        "       popl %%eax\n"                                      \
17493        "       addl $2,%0\n"                                      \
17494        "       jmp 2b\n"                                          \
17495        ".previous\n"                                              \
17496        ".section __ex_table,\"a\"\n"                              \
17497        "       .align 4\n"                                        \
17498        "       .long 0b,3b\n"                                     \
17499        "       .long 1b,4b\n"                                     \
17500        ".previous"                                                \
17501        : "=c"(size), "=&S" (__d0), "=&D" (__d1)                   \
17502        : "1"(from), "2"(to), "0"(size/4)                          \
17503        : "memory");                                               \
17504      break;                                                       \
17505    case 3:                                                        \
17506      __asm__ __volatile__(                                        \
17507        "0:     rep; movsl\n"                                      \
17508        "1:     movsw\n"                                           \
17509        "2:     movsb\n"                                           \
17510        "3:\n"                                                     \
17511        ".section .fixup,\"ax\"\n"                                 \
17512        "4:     pushl %0\n"                                        \
17513        "       pushl %%eax\n"                                     \
17514        "       xorl %%eax,%%eax\n"                                \
17515        "       rep; stosl\n"                                      \
17516        "       stosw\n"                                           \
17517        "       stosb\n"                                           \
17518        "       popl %%eax\n"                                      \
17519        "       popl %0\n"                                         \
17520        "       shl $2,%0\n"                                       \
17521        "       addl $3,%0\n"                                      \
17522        "       jmp 2b\n"                                          \
17523        "5:     pushl %%eax\n"                                     \
17524        "       xorl %%eax,%%eax\n"                                \
17525        "       stosw\n"                                           \
17526        "       stosb\n"                                           \
17527        "       popl %%eax\n"                                      \
17528        "       addl $3,%0\n"                                      \
17529        "       jmp 2b\n"                                          \
17530        "6:     pushl %%eax\n"                                     \
17531        "       xorl %%eax,%%eax\n"                                \
17532        "       stosb\n"                                           \
17533        "       popl %%eax\n"                                      \
17534        "       incl %0\n"                                         \
17535        "       jmp 3b\n"                                          \
17536        ".previous\n"                                              \
17537        ".section __ex_table,\"a\"\n"                              \
17538        "       .align 4\n"                                        \
17539        "       .long 0b,4b\n"                                     \
17540        "       .long 1b,5b\n"                                     \
17541        "       .long 2b,6b\n"                                     \
17542        ".previous"                                                \
17543        : "=c"(size), "=&S" (__d0), "=&D" (__d1)                   \
17544        : "1"(from), "2"(to), "0"(size/4)                          \
17545        : "memory");                                               \
17546      break;                                                       \
17547      }                                                            \
17548    } while (0)
17549
17550    unsigned long __generic_copy_to_user(void *,
17551        const void *, unsigned long);
17552    unsigned long __generic_copy_from_user(void *,
17553        const void *, unsigned long);
17554
17555    static inline unsigned long
17556    __constant_copy_to_user(void *to, const void *from,
17557        unsigned long n)
```

```
17558 {
17559   if (access_ok(VERIFY_WRITE, to, n))
17560     __constant_copy_user(to, from, n);
17561   return n;
17562 }
17563
17564 static inline unsigned long
17565 __constant_copy_from_user(void *to, const void *from,
17566     unsigned long n)
17567 {
17568   if (access_ok(VERIFY_READ, from, n))
17569     __constant_copy_user_zeroing(to, from, n);
17570   return n;
17571 }
17572
17573 static inline unsigned long
17574 __constant_copy_to_user_nocheck(void *to,
17575     const void *from, unsigned long n)
17576 {
17577   __constant_copy_user(to, from, n);
17578   return n;
17579 }
17580
17581 static inline unsigned long
17582 __constant_copy_from_user_nocheck(void *to,
17583     const void *from, unsigned long n)
17584 {
17585   __constant_copy_user_zeroing(to, from, n);
17586   return n;
17587 }
17588
17589 #define copy_to_user(to,from,n)                      \
17590 (__builtin_constant_p(n)                             \
17591   ? __constant_copy_to_user((to),(from),(n))         \
17592   : __generic_copy_to_user((to),(from),(n)))
17593
17594 #define copy_from_user(to,from,n)                    \
17595 (__builtin_constant_p(n)                             \
17596   ? __constant_copy_from_user((to),(from),(n))       \
17597   : __generic_copy_from_user((to),(from),(n)))
17598
17599 #define __copy_to_user(to,from,n)                    \
17600 (__builtin_constant_p(n)                             \
17601   ? __constant_copy_to_user_nocheck((to),(from),(n)) \
17602   : __generic_copy_to_user_nocheck((to),(from),(n)))
17603
17604 #define __copy_from_user(to,from,n)                  \
17605 (__builtin_constant_p(n)                             \
17606   ? __constant_copy_from_user_nocheck((to),(from),(n))  \
17607   : __generic_copy_from_user_nocheck((to),(from),(n)))
17608
17609 long strncpy_from_user(char *dst, const char *src,
17610     long count);
17611 long __strncpy_from_user(char *dst, const char *src,
17612     long count);
17613 #define strlen_user(str) strnlen_user(str, ~0UL >> 1)
17614 long strnlen_user(const char *str, long n);
17615 unsigned long clear_user(void *mem, unsigned long len);
17616 unsigned long __clear_user(void *mem, unsigned long len);
17617
17618 #endif                          /* __i386_UACCESS_H */
```

include/asm-i386/ucontext.h

```
17619 #ifndef _ASMi386_UCONTEXT_H
17620 #define _ASMi386_UCONTEXT_H
17621
17622 struct ucontext {
17623   unsigned long     uc_flags;
17624   struct ucontext   *uc_link;
17625   stack_t           uc_stack;
17626   struct sigcontext uc_mcontext;
17627   sigset_t          uc_sigmask;   /* mask last for extensibility */
17628 };
17629
17630 #endif                  /* !_ASMi386_UCONTEXT_H */
```

include/linux/binfmts.h

```
17631 #ifndef _LINUX_BINFMTS_H
17632 #define _LINUX_BINFMTS_H
17633
17634 #include <linux/ptrace.h>
17635 #include <linux/capability.h>
17636
17637 /* MAX_ARG_PAGES defines the number of pages allocated
17638  * for arguments and envelope for the new program. 32
17639  * should suffice, this gives a maximum env+arg of 128kB
17640  * w/4KB pages!  */
17641 #define MAX_ARG_PAGES 32
17642
17643 /* sizeof(linux_binprm->buf) */
17644 #define BINPRM_BUF_SIZE 128
17645
17646 #ifdef __KERNEL__
```

```
17647
17648 /* This structure is used to hold the arguments that are
17649  * used when loading binaries.  */
17650 struct linux_binprm {
17651   char buf[BINPRM_BUF_SIZE];
17652   struct page *page[MAX_ARG_PAGES];
17653   unsigned long p;                 /* current top of mem */
17654   int sh_bang;
17655   struct file *file;
17656   int e_uid, e_gid;
17657   kernel_cap_t cap_inheritable, cap_permitted,
17658      cap_effective;
17659   int argc, envc;
17660   char *filename;                  /* Name of binary */
17661   unsigned long loader, exec;
17662 };
17663
17664 /* This structure defines the functions that are used to
17665  * load the binary formats that linux accepts.  */
17666 struct linux_binfmt {
17667   struct linux_binfmt *next;
17668   struct module *module;
17669   int (*load_binary) (struct linux_binprm *,
17670      struct pt_regs * regs);
17671   int (*load_shlib) (struct file *);
17672   int (*core_dump) (long signr, struct pt_regs * regs,
17673      struct file * file);
17674   unsigned long min_coredump;   /* minimal dump size */
17675 };
17676
17677 extern int register_binfmt(struct linux_binfmt *);
17678 extern int unregister_binfmt(struct linux_binfmt *);
17679
17680 extern int prepare_binprm(struct linux_binprm *);
17681 extern void remove_arg_zero(struct linux_binprm *);
17682 extern int search_binary_handler(struct linux_binprm *,
17683      struct pt_regs *);
17684 extern int flush_old_exec(struct linux_binprm *bprm);
17685 extern int setup_arg_pages(struct linux_binprm *bprm);
17686 extern int copy_strings(int argc, char **argv,
17687      struct linux_binprm *bprm);
17688 extern int copy_strings_kernel(int argc, char **argv,
17689      struct linux_binprm *bprm);
17690 extern void compute_creds(struct linux_binprm *binprm);
17691 extern int do_coredump(long signr, struct pt_regs *regs);
17692 extern void set_binfmt(struct linux_binfmt *new);
17693
```

```
17694
17695 #if 0
17696 /* this went away now */
17697 #define change_ldt(a,b) setup_arg_pages(a,b)
17698 #endif
17699
17700 #endif                           /* __KERNEL__ */
17701 #endif                           /* _LINUX_BINFMTS_H */
```

include/linux/cache.h

```
17702 #ifndef __LINUX_CACHE_H
17703 #define __LINUX_CACHE_H
17704
17705 #include <asm/cache.h>
17706
17707 #ifndef L1_CACHE_ALIGN
17708 #define L1_CACHE_ALIGN(x)                              \
17709   (((x)+(L1_CACHE_BYTES-1))&~(L1_CACHE_BYTES-1))
17710 #endif
17711
17712 #ifndef SMP_CACHE_BYTES
17713 #define SMP_CACHE_BYTES L1_CACHE_BYTES
17714 #endif
17715
17716 #ifndef ____cacheline_aligned
17717 #define ____cacheline_aligned                          \
17718   __attribute__((__aligned__(SMP_CACHE_BYTES)))
17719 #endif
17720
17721 #ifndef __cacheline_aligned
17722 #ifdef MODULE
17723 #define __cacheline_aligned ____cacheline_aligned
17724 #else
17725 #define __cacheline_aligned                            \
17726   __attribute__((__aligned__(SMP_CACHE_BYTES),         \
17727                 __section__(".data.cacheline_aligned")))
17728 #endif
17729 #endif                           /* __cacheline_aligned */
17730
17731 #endif                           /* __LINUX_CACHE_H */
```

include/linux/capability.h

```
17732 /*
17733  * This is <linux/capability.h>
17734  *
17735  * Andrew G. Morgan <morgan@transmeta.com>
```

```
17736  * Alexander Kjeldaas <astor@guardian.no>
17737  * with help from Aleph1, Roland Buresund and
17738  * Andrew Main.
17739  *
17740  * See here for the libcap library ("POSIX draft"
17741  * compliance):
17742  *
17743  * ftp://linux.kernel.org/pub/linux/libs/security/
17744  * linux-privs/kernel-2.2/
17745  */
17746
17747 #ifndef _LINUX_CAPABILITY_H
17748 #define _LINUX_CAPABILITY_H
17749
17750 #include <linux/types.h>
17751 #include <linux/fs.h>
17752
17753 /* User-level do most of the mapping between kernel and
17754  * user capabilities based on the version tag given by
17755  * the kernel. The kernel might be somewhat backwards
17756  * compatible, but don't bet on it. */
17757
17758 /* XXX - Note, cap_t, is defined by POSIX to be an
17759  * "opaque" pointer to a set of three capability sets.
17760  * The transposition of 3*the following structure to
17761  * such a composite is better handled in a user library
17762  * since the draft standard requires the use of
17763  * malloc/free etc.. */
17764
17765 #define _LINUX_CAPABILITY_VERSION  0x19980330
17766
17767 typedef struct __user_cap_header_struct {
17768    __u32 version;
17769    int pid;
17770 } *cap_user_header_t;
17771
17772 typedef struct __user_cap_data_struct {
17773    __u32 effective;
17774    __u32 permitted;
17775    __u32 inheritable;
17776 } *cap_user_data_t;
17777
17778 #ifdef __KERNEL__
17779
17780 /* #define STRICT_CAP_T_TYPECHECKS */
17781
17782 #ifdef STRICT_CAP_T_TYPECHECKS
```

```
17783
17784 typedef struct kernel_cap_struct {
17785    __u32 cap;
17786 } kernel_cap_t;
17787
17788 #else
17789
17790 typedef __u32 kernel_cap_t;
17791
17792 #endif
17793
17794 #define _USER_CAP_HEADER_SIZE  (2*sizeof(__u32))
17795 #define _KERNEL_CAP_T_SIZE     (sizeof(kernel_cap_t))
17796
17797 #endif
17798
17799
17800 /**
17801  ** POSIX-draft defined capabilities.
17802  **/
17803
17804 /* In a system with the [_POSIX_CHOWN_RESTRICTED] option
17805  * defined, this overrides the restriction of changing
17806  * file ownership and group ownership. */
17807 #define CAP_CHOWN          0
17808
17809 /* Override all DAC access, including ACL execute access
17810  * if [_POSIX_ACL] is defined. Excluding DAC access
17811  * covered by CAP_LINUX_IMMUTABLE. */
17812 #define CAP_DAC_OVERRIDE      1
17813
17814 /* Overrides all DAC restrictions regarding read and
17815  * search on files and directories, including ACL
17816  * restrictions if [_POSIX_ACL] is defined. Excluding
17817  * DAC access covered by CAP_LINUX_IMMUTABLE. */
17818 #define CAP_DAC_READ_SEARCH   2
17819
17820 /* Overrides all restrictions about allowed operations
17821  * on files, where file owner ID must be equal to the
17822  * user ID, except where CAP_FSETID is applicable. It
17823  * doesn't override MAC and DAC restrictions. */
17824 #define CAP_FOWNER          3
17825
17826 /* Overrides the following restrictions that the
17827  * effective user ID shall match the file owner ID when
17828  * setting the S_ISUID and S_ISGID bits on that file;
17829  * that the effective group ID (or one of the
```
p 613

```
17830  * supplementary group IDs) shall match the file owner
17831  * ID when setting the S_ISGID bit on that file; that
17832  * the S_ISUID and S_ISGID bits are cleared on
17833  * successful return from chown(2) (not implemented). */
17834 #define CAP_FSETID        4
17835
17836 /* Used to decide between falling back on the old
17837  * suser() or fsuser(). */
17838 #define CAP_FS_MASK       0x1f
17839
17840 /* Overrides the restriction that the real or effective
17841  * user ID of a process sending a signal must match the
17842  * real or effective user ID of the process receiving
17843  * the signal. */
17844 #define CAP_KILL          5
17845
17846 /* Allows setgid(2) manipulation */
17847 /* Allows setgroups(2) */
17848 /* Allows forged gids on socket credentials passing. */
17849 #define CAP_SETGID        6
17850
17851 /* Allows set*uid(2) manipulation (including fsuid). */
17852 /* Allows forged pids on socket credentials passing. */
17853 #define CAP_SETUID        7
17854
17855
17856 /**
17857  ** Linux-specific capabilities
17858  **/
17859
17860 /* Transfer any capability in your permitted set to any
17861  * pid, remove any capability in your permitted set from
17862  * any pid */
17863 #define CAP_SETPCAP       8
17864
17865 /* Allow modification of S_IMMUTABLE and S_APPEND file
17866  * attributes */
17867 #define CAP_LINUX_IMMUTABLE  9
17868
17869 /* Allows binding to TCP/UDP sockets below 1024 */
17870 /* Allows binding to ATM VCIs below 32 */
17871 #define CAP_NET_BIND_SERVICE 10
17872
17873 /* Allow broadcasting, listen to multicast */
17874 #define CAP_NET_BROADCAST    11
17875
17876 /* Allow interface configuration */
17877 /* Allow administration of IP firewall, masquerading and
17878  * accounting */
17879 /* Allow setting debug option on sockets */
17880 /* Allow modification of routing tables */
17881 /* Allow setting arbitrary process / process group
17882  * ownership on sockets */
17883 /* Allow binding to any address for transparent proxying
17884  */
17885 /* Allow setting TOS (type of service) */
17886 /* Allow setting promiscuous mode */
17887 /* Allow clearing driver statistics */
17888 /* Allow multicasting */
17889 /* Allow read/write of device-specific registers */
17890 /* Allow activation of ATM control sockets */
17891 #define CAP_NET_ADMIN     12
17892
17893 /* Allow use of RAW sockets */
17894 /* Allow use of PACKET sockets */
17895 #define CAP_NET_RAW       13
17896
17897 /* Allow locking of shared memory segments */
17898 /* Allow mlock and mlockall (which doesn't really have
17899  * anything to do with IPC) */
17900 #define CAP_IPC_LOCK      14
17901
17902 /* Override IPC ownership checks */
17903 #define CAP_IPC_OWNER     15
17904
17905 /* Insert and remove kernel modules - modify kernel
17906  * without limit */
17907 /* Modify cap_bset */
17908 #define CAP_SYS_MODULE    16
17909
17910 /* Allow ioperm/iopl access */
17911 /* Allow sending USB messages to any device via
17912  * /proc/bus/usb */
17913 #define CAP_SYS_RAWIO     17
17914
17915 /* Allow use of chroot() */
17916 #define CAP_SYS_CHROOT    18
17917
17918 /* Allow ptrace() of any process */
17919 #define CAP_SYS_PTRACE    19
17920
17921 /* Allow configuration of process accounting */
17922 #define CAP_SYS_PACCT     20
17923
```

```
17924 /* Allow configuration of the secure attention key */
17925 /* Allow administration of the random device */
17926 /* Allow examination and configuration of disk quotas */
17927 /* Allow configuring the kernel's syslog (printk
17928  * behaviour) */
17929 /* Allow setting the domainname */
17930 /* Allow setting the hostname */
17931 /* Allow calling bdflush() */
17932 /* Allow mount() and umount(), setting up new smb
17933  * connection */
17934 /* Allow some autofs root ioctls */
17935 /* Allow nfsservctl */
17936 /* Allow VM86_REQUEST_IRQ */
17937 /* Allow to read/write pci config on alpha */
17938 /* Allow irix_prctl on mips (setstacksize) */
17939 /* Allow flushing all cache on m68k (sys_cacheflush) */
17940 /* Allow removing semaphores */
17941 /* Used instead of CAP_CHOWN to "chown" IPC message
17942  * queues, semaphores and shared memory */
17943 /* Allow locking/unlocking of shared memory segment */
17944 /* Allow turning swap on/off */
17945 /* Allow forged pids on socket credentials passing */
17946 /* Allow setting readahead and flushing buffers on block
17947  * devices */
17948 /* Allow setting geometry in floppy driver */
17949 /* Allow turning DMA on/off in xd driver */
17950 /* Allow administration of md devices (mostly the above,
17951  * but some extra ioctls) */
17952 /* Allow tuning the ide driver */
17953 /* Allow access to the nvram device */
17954 /* Allow administration of apm_bios, serial and bttv
17955  * (TV) device */
17956 /* Allow manufacturer commands in isdn CAPI support
17957  * driver */
17958 /* Allow reading non-standardized portions of pci
17959  * configuration space */
17960 /* Allow DDI debug ioctl on sbpcd driver */
17961 /* Allow setting up serial ports */
17962 /* Allow sending raw qic-117 commands */
17963 /* Allow enabling/disabling tagged queuing on SCSI
17964  * controllers and sending arbitrary SCSI commands */
17965 /* Allow setting encryption key on loopback filesystem */
17966 #define CAP_SYS_ADMIN        21
17967
17968 /* Allow use of reboot() */
17969 #define CAP_SYS_BOOT          22
17970
17971 /* Allow raising priority and setting priority on other
17972  * (different UID) processes */
17973 /* Allow use of FIFO and round-robin (realtime)
17974  * scheduling on own processes and setting the
17975  * scheduling algorithm used by another process. */
17976 #define CAP_SYS_NICE          23
17977
17978 /* Override resource limits. Set resource limits. */
17979 /* Override quota limits. */
17980 /* Override reserved space on ext2 filesystem */
17981 /* NOTE: ext2 honors fsuid when checking for resource
17982  * overrides, so you can override using fsuid too */
17983 /* Override size restrictions on IPC message queues */
17984 /* Allow more than 64hz interrupts from the real-time
17985  * clock */
17986 /* Override max number of consoles on console allocation
17987  */
17988 /* Override max number of keymaps */
17989 #define CAP_SYS_RESOURCE      24
17990
17991 /* Allow manipulation of system clock */
17992 /* Allow irix_stime on mips */
17993 /* Allow setting the real-time clock */
17994 #define CAP_SYS_TIME          25
17995
17996 /* Allow configuration of tty devices */
17997 /* Allow vhangup() of tty */
17998 #define CAP_SYS_TTY_CONFIG    26
17999
18000 /* Allow the privileged aspects of mknod() */
18001 #define CAP_MKNOD             27
18002
18003 /* Allow taking of leases on files */
18004 #define CAP_LEASE             28
18005
18006 #ifdef __KERNEL__
18007 /* Bounding set */
18008 extern kernel_cap_t cap_bset;
18009
18010 /* Internal kernel functions only */
18011
18012 #ifdef STRICT_CAP_T_TYPECHECKS
18013
18014 #define to_cap_t(x) { x }
18015 #define cap_t(x) (x).cap
18016
18017 #else
```

```
18018
18019 #define to_cap_t(x) (x)
18020 #define cap_t(x) (x)
18021
18022 #endif
18023
18024 #define CAP_EMPTY_SET      to_cap_t(0)
18025 #define CAP_FULL_SET       to_cap_t(~0)
18026 #define CAP_INIT_EFF_SET                                        \
18027    to_cap_t(~0 & ~CAP_TO_MASK(CAP_SETPCAP))
18028 #define CAP_INIT_INH_SET    to_cap_t(0)
18029
18030 #define CAP_TO_MASK(x) (1 << (x))
18031 #define cap_raise(c, flag)                                     \
18032    (cap_t(c) |= CAP_TO_MASK(flag))
18033 #define cap_lower(c, flag)                                     \
18034    (cap_t(c) &= ~CAP_TO_MASK(flag))
18035 #define cap_raised(c, flag)                                    \
18036    (cap_t(c) & CAP_TO_MASK(flag))
18037
18038 static inline kernel_cap_t cap_combine(kernel_cap_t a,
18039     kernel_cap_t b)
18040 {
18041    kernel_cap_t dest;
18042    cap_t(dest) = cap_t(a) | cap_t(b);
18043    return dest;
18044 }
18045
18046 static inline kernel_cap_t cap_intersect(kernel_cap_t a,
18047     kernel_cap_t b)
18048 {
18049    kernel_cap_t dest;
18050    cap_t(dest) = cap_t(a) & cap_t(b);
18051    return dest;
18052 }
18053
18054 static inline kernel_cap_t cap_drop(kernel_cap_t a,
18055     kernel_cap_t drop)
18056 {
18057    kernel_cap_t dest;
18058    cap_t(dest) = cap_t(a) & ~cap_t(drop);
18059    return dest;
18060 }
18061
18062 static inline kernel_cap_t cap_invert(kernel_cap_t c)
18063 {
18064    kernel_cap_t dest;
18065    cap_t(dest) = ~cap_t(c);
18066    return dest;
18067 }
18068
18069 #define cap_isclear(c)      (!cap_t(c))
18070 #define cap_issubset(a,set) (!(cap_t(a) & ~cap_t(set)))
18071
18072 #define cap_clear(c)        do { cap_t(c) =  0; } while(0)
18073 #define cap_set_full(c)     do { cap_t(c) = ~0; } while(0)
18074 #define cap_mask(c,mask)                                        \
18075    do { cap_t(c) &= cap_t(mask); } while(0)
18076
18077 #define cap_is_fs_cap(c)    (CAP_TO_MASK(c) & CAP_FS_MASK)
18078
18079 #endif                      /* __KERNEL__ */
18080
18081 #endif                      /* !_LINUX_CAPABILITY_H */
```

include/linux/delay.h

```
18082 #ifndef _LINUX_DELAY_H
18083 #define _LINUX_DELAY_H
18084
18085 /*
18086  * Copyright (C) 1993 Linus Torvalds
18087  *
18088  * Delay routines, using a pre-computed "loops_per_jiffy"
18089  * value.
18090  */
18091
18092 extern unsigned long loops_per_jiffy;
18093
18094 #include <asm/delay.h>
18095
18096 /* Using udelay() for intervals greater than a few
18097  * milliseconds can risk overflow for high
18098  * loops_per_jiffy (high bogomips) machines. The mdelay()
18099  * provides a wrapper to prevent this.  For delays
18100  * greater than MAX_UDELAY_MS milliseconds, the wrapper
18101  * is used.  Architecture specific values can be defined
18102  * in asm-???/delay.h as an override.  The 2nd mdelay()
18103  * definition ensures GCC will optimize away the while
18104  * loop for the common cases where n <= MAX_UDELAY_MS —
18105  * Paul G.  */
18106
18107 #ifndef MAX_UDELAY_MS
18108 #define MAX_UDELAY_MS    5
18109 #endif
```

```
18110
18111 #ifdef notdef
18112 #define mdelay(n)                                          \
18113   ({unsigned long msec=(n); while (msec−) udelay(1000);})
18114 #else
18115 #define mdelay(n)                                          \
18116 ((__builtin_constant_p(n) && (n)<=MAX_UDELAY_MS)          \
18117   ? udelay((n)*1000)                                       \
18118   : ({ unsigned long msec=(n);                             \
18119        while (msec−) udelay(1000);}))
18120 #endif
18121
18122 #endif                          /* defined(_LINUX_DELAY_H) */
```

include/linux/elfcore.h

```
18123 #ifndef _LINUX_ELFCORE_H
18124 #define _LINUX_ELFCORE_H
18125
18126 #include <linux/types.h>
18127 #include <linux/signal.h>
18128 #include <linux/time.h>
18129 #include <linux/ptrace.h>
18130 #include <linux/user.h>
18131
18132 struct elf_siginfo {
18133   int si_signo;                 /* signal number */
18134   int si_code;                  /* extra code */
18135   int si_errno;                 /* errno */
18136 };
18137
18138 #include <asm/elf.h>
18139
18140 #ifndef __KERNEL__
18141 typedef elf_greg_t greg_t;
18142 typedef elf_gregset_t gregset_t;
18143 typedef elf_fpregset_t fpregset_t;
18144 typedef elf_fpxregset_t fpxregset_t;
18145 #define NGREG ELF_NGREG
18146 #endif
18147
18148 /* Definitions to generate Intel SVR4-like core files. */
18149  * These mostly have the same names as the SVR4 types
18150  * with "elf_" tacked on the front to prevent clashes
18151  * with linux definitions, and the typedef forms have
18152  * been avoided.  This is mostly like the SVR4 structure,
18153  * but more Linuxy, with things that Linux does not
18154  * support and which gdb doesn't really use excluded.
18155  * Fields present but not used are marked with "XXX".  */
18156 struct elf_prstatus {
18157 #if 0
18158   long pr_flags;                /* XXX Process flags */
18159   short pr_why;                 /* XXX Reason for
18160                                  * process halt */
18161   short pr_what;                /* XXX More detailed
18162                                  * reason */
18163 #endif
18164   struct elf_siginfo pr_info;   /* Info associated with
18165                                  * signal */
18166   short pr_cursig;              /* Current signal */
18167   unsigned long pr_sigpend;     /* Set of pending
18168                                  * signals */
18169   unsigned long pr_sighold;     /* Set of held signals */
18170 #if 0
18171   struct sigaltstack pr_altstack;      /* Alternate
18172                                         * stack info */
18173   struct sigaction pr_action;   /* Signal action for
18174                                  * current sig */
18175 #endif
18176   pid_t pr_pid;
18177   pid_t pr_ppid;
18178   pid_t pr_pgrp;
18179   pid_t pr_sid;
18180   struct timeval pr_utime;      /* User time */
18181   struct timeval pr_stime;      /* System time */
18182   struct timeval pr_cutime;     /* Cumulative user time*/
18183   struct timeval pr_cstime;     /* Cumulative system
18184                                  * time */
18185 #if 0
18186   long pr_instr;                /* Current instruction */
18187 #endif
18188   elf_gregset_t pr_reg;         /* GP registers */
18189   int pr_fpvalid;               /* True if math
18190                                  * co-processor being
18191                                  * used.  */
18192 };
18193
18194 #define ELF_PRARGSZ     (80)    /* Number of chars for
18195                                  * args */
18196
18197 struct elf_prpsinfo {
18198   char pr_state;                /* numeric process state
18199                                  */
18200   char pr_sname;                /* char for pr_state */
18201   char pr_zomb;                 /* zombie */
```

```
18202    char pr_nice;                /* nice val */
18203    unsigned long pr_flag;       /* flags */
18204    __kernel_uid_t pr_uid;
18205    __kernel_gid_t pr_gid;
18206    pid_t pr_pid, pr_ppid, pr_pgrp, pr_sid;
18207    /* Lots missing */
18208    char pr_fname[16];           /* filename of
18209                                  * executable */
18210    char pr_psargs[ELF_PRARGSZ]; /* initial part of arg
18211                                  * list */
18212 };
18213
18214 #ifndef __KERNEL__
18215 typedef struct elf_prstatus prstatus_t;
18216 typedef struct elf_prpsinfo prpsinfo_t;
18217 #define PRARGSZ ELF_PRARGSZ
18218 #endif
18219
18220 #endif                          /* _LINUX_ELFCORE_H */
```

include/linux/elf.h

```
18221 #ifndef _LINUX_ELF_H
18222 #define _LINUX_ELF_H
18223
18224 #include <linux/types.h>
18225 #include <asm/elf.h>
18226
18227 /* 32-bit ELF base types. */
18228 typedef __u32 Elf32_Addr;
18229 typedef __u16 Elf32_Half;
18230 typedef __u32 Elf32_Off;
18231 typedef __s32 Elf32_Sword;
18232 typedef __u32 Elf32_Word;
18233
18234 /* 64-bit ELF base types. */
18235 typedef __u64 Elf64_Addr;
18236 typedef __u16 Elf64_Half;
18237 typedef __s16 Elf64_SHalf;
18238 typedef __u64 Elf64_Off;
18239 typedef __s64 Elf64_Sword;
18240 typedef __u64 Elf64_Word;
18241
18242 /* These constants are for the segment types stored in
18243  * the image headers */
18244 #define PT_NULL          0
18245 #define PT_LOAD          1
18246 #define PT_DYNAMIC       2
```

```
18247 #define PT_INTERP         3
18248 #define PT_NOTE           4
18249 #define PT_SHLIB          5
18250 #define PT_PHDR           6
18251 #define PT_LOPROC         0x70000000
18252 #define PT_HIPROC         0x7fffffff
18253 #define PT_MIPS_REGINFO   0x70000000
18254
18255 /* Flags in the e_flags field of the header */
18256 #define EF_MIPS_NOREORDER 0x00000001
18257 #define EF_MIPS_PIC       0x00000002
18258 #define EF_MIPS_CPIC      0x00000004
18259 #define EF_MIPS_ARCH      0xf0000000
18260
18261 /* These constants define the different elf file types */
18262 #define ET_NONE   0
18263 #define ET_REL    1
18264 #define ET_EXEC   2
18265 #define ET_DYN    3
18266 #define ET_CORE   4
18267 #define ET_LOPROC 0xff00
18268 #define ET_HIPROC 0xffff
18269
18270 /* These constants define the various ELF target
18271  * machines */
18272 #define EM_NONE        0
18273 #define EM_M32         1
18274 #define EM_SPARC       2
18275 #define EM_386         3
18276 #define EM_68K         4
18277 #define EM_88K         5
18278 #define EM_486         6   /* Perhaps disused */
18279 #define EM_860         7
18280
18281 #define EM_MIPS        8   /* MIPS R3000 (officially,
18282                            * big-endian only) */
18283 #define EM_MIPS_RS4_BE 10  /* MIPS R4000 big-endian */
18284 #define EM_PARISC      15  /* HPPA */
18285 #define EM_SPARC32PLUS 18  /* Sun's "v8plus" */
18286 #define EM_PPC         20  /* PowerPC */
18287 #define EM_SH          42  /* SuperH */
18288 #define EM_SPARCV9     43  /* SPARC v9 64-bit */
18289 #define EM_IA_64       50  /* HP/Intel IA-64 */
18290 #define EM_X8664       62  /* AMD x86-64 */
18291
18292 /* This is an interim value that we will use until the
18293  * committee comes up with a final number.  */
```

```
18294 #define EM_ALPHA          0x9026
18295
18296 /* This is an interim value for S390 architecture */
18297 #define EM_S390          0xA390
18298
18299 /* This is the info that is needed to parse the dynamic
18300  * section of the file */
18301 #define DT_NULL           0
18302 #define DT_NEEDED         1
18303 #define DT_PLTRELSZ       2
18304 #define DT_PLTGOT         3
18305 #define DT_HASH           4
18306 #define DT_STRTAB         5
18307 #define DT_SYMTAB         6
18308 #define DT_RELA           7
18309 #define DT_RELASZ         8
18310 #define DT_RELAENT        9
18311 #define DT_STRSZ          10
18312 #define DT_SYMENT         11
18313 #define DT_INIT           12
18314 #define DT_FINI           13
18315 #define DT_SONAME         14
18316 #define DT_RPATH          15
18317 #define DT_SYMBOLIC       16
18318 #define DT_REL            17
18319 #define DT_RELSZ          18
18320 #define DT_RELENT         19
18321 #define DT_PLTREL         20
18322 #define DT_DEBUG          21
18323 #define DT_TEXTREL        22
18324 #define DT_JMPREL         23
18325 #define DT_LOPROC         0x70000000
18326 #define DT_HIPROC         0x7fffffff
18327 #define DT_MIPS_RLD_VERSION   0x70000001
18328 #define DT_MIPS_TIME_STAMP    0x70000002
18329 #define DT_MIPS_ICHECKSUM     0x70000003
18330 #define DT_MIPS_IVERSION      0x70000004
18331 #define DT_MIPS_FLAGS         0x70000005
18332 #define RHF_NONE          0
18333 #define RHF_HARDWAY       1
18334 #define RHF_NOTPOT        2
18335 #define DT_MIPS_BASE_ADDRESS  0x70000006
18336 #define DT_MIPS_CONFLICT      0x70000008
18337 #define DT_MIPS_LIBLIST       0x70000009
18338 #define DT_MIPS_LOCAL_GOTNO   0x7000000a
18339 #define DT_MIPS_CONFLICTNO    0x7000000b
18340 #define DT_MIPS_LIBLISTNO     0x70000010
18341 #define DT_MIPS_SYMTABNO      0x70000011
18342 #define DT_MIPS_UNREFEXTNO    0x70000012
18343 #define DT_MIPS_GOTSYM        0x70000013
18344 #define DT_MIPS_HIPAGENO      0x70000014
18345 #define DT_MIPS_RLD_MAP       0x70000016
18346
18347 /* This info is needed when parsing the symbol table */
18348 #define STB_LOCAL  0
18349 #define STB_GLOBAL 1
18350 #define STB_WEAK   2
18351
18352 #define STT_NOTYPE  0
18353 #define STT_OBJECT  1
18354 #define STT_FUNC    2
18355 #define STT_SECTION 3
18356 #define STT_FILE    4
18357
18358 #define ELF32_ST_BIND(x) ((x) >> 4)
18359 #define ELF32_ST_TYPE(x) (((unsigned int) x) & 0xf)
18360
18361 /* Symbolic values for the entries in the auxiliary
18362  * table put on the initial stack */
18363 #define AT_NULL     0          /* end of vector */
18364 #define AT_IGNORE   1          /* entry should be
18365                                 * ignored */
18366 #define AT_EXECFD   2          /* file descriptor of
18367                                 * program */
18368 #define AT_PHDR     3          /* program headers for
18369                                 * program */
18370 #define AT_PHENT    4          /* size of program
18371                                 * header entry */
18372 #define AT_PHNUM    5          /* number of program
18373                                 * headers */
18374 #define AT_PAGESZ   6          /* system page size */
18375 #define AT_BASE     7          /* base address of
18376                                 * interpreter */
18377 #define AT_FLAGS    8          /* flags */
18378 #define AT_ENTRY    9          /* entry point of
18379                                 * program */
18380 #define AT_NOTELF   10         /* program is not ELF */
18381 #define AT_UID      11         /* real uid */
18382 #define AT_EUID     12         /* effective uid */
18383 #define AT_GID      13         /* real gid */
18384 #define AT_EGID     14         /* effective gid */
18385 #define AT_PLATFORM 15         /* string identifying
18386                                 * CPU for optimizations
18387                                 */
```

```
18388 #define AT_HWCAP    16          /* arch dependent hints
18389                                  * at CPU capabilities */
18390 #define AT_CLKTCK   17          /* frequency at which
18391                                  * times() increments */
18392
18393 typedef struct dynamic {
18394   Elf32_Sword d_tag;
18395   union {
18396     Elf32_Sword d_val;
18397     Elf32_Addr d_ptr;
18398   } d_un;
18399 } Elf32_Dyn;
18400
18401 typedef struct {
18402   Elf64_Word d_tag;                /* entry tag value */
18403   union {
18404     Elf64_Word d_val;
18405     Elf64_Word d_ptr;
18406   } d_un;
18407 } Elf64_Dyn;
18408
18409 /* The following are used with relocations */
18410 #define ELF32_R_SYM(x) ((x) >> 8)
18411 #define ELF32_R_TYPE(x) ((x) & 0xff)
18412
18413 #define R_386_NONE      0
18414 #define R_386_32        1
18415 #define R_386_PC32      2
18416 #define R_386_GOT32     3
18417 #define R_386_PLT32     4
18418 #define R_386_COPY      5
18419 #define R_386_GLOB_DAT  6
18420 #define R_386_JMP_SLOT  7
18421 #define R_386_RELATIVE  8
18422 #define R_386_GOTOFF    9
18423 #define R_386_GOTPC     10
18424 #define R_386_NUM       11
18425
18426 #define R_MIPS_NONE         0
18427 #define R_MIPS_16           1
18428 #define R_MIPS_32           2
18429 #define R_MIPS_REL32        3
18430 #define R_MIPS_26           4
18431 #define R_MIPS_HI16         5
18432 #define R_MIPS_LO16         6
18433 #define R_MIPS_GPREL16      7
18434 #define R_MIPS_LITERAL      8
```

```
18435 #define R_MIPS_GOT16        9
18436 #define R_MIPS_PC16         10
18437 #define R_MIPS_CALL16       11
18438 #define R_MIPS_GPREL32      12
18439 /* The remaining relocs are defined on Irix, although
18440  * they are not in the MIPS ELF ABI.  */
18441 #define R_MIPS_UNUSED1      13
18442 #define R_MIPS_UNUSED2      14
18443 #define R_MIPS_UNUSED3      15
18444 #define R_MIPS_SHIFT5       16
18445 #define R_MIPS_SHIFT6       17
18446 #define R_MIPS_64           18
18447 #define R_MIPS_GOT_DISP     19
18448 #define R_MIPS_GOT_PAGE     20
18449 #define R_MIPS_GOT_OFST     21
18450 /* The following two relocation types are specified in
18451  * the the MIPS ABI conformance guide version 1.2 but not
18452  * yet in the psABI.  */
18453 #define R_MIPS_GOTHI16      22
18454 #define R_MIPS_GOTLO16      23
18455 #define R_MIPS_SUB          24
18456 #define R_MIPS_INSERT_A     25
18457 #define R_MIPS_INSERT_B     26
18458 #define R_MIPS_DELETE       27
18459 #define R_MIPS_HIGHER       28
18460 #define R_MIPS_HIGHEST      29
18461 /* The following two relocation types are specified in
18462  * the the MIPS ABI conformance guide version 1.2 but not
18463  * yet in the psABI.  */
18464 #define R_MIPS_CALLHI16     30
18465 #define R_MIPS_CALLLO16     31
18466 /* This range is reserved for vendor specific
18467  * relocations.  */
18468 #define R_MIPS_LOVENDOR     100
18469 #define R_MIPS_HIVENDOR     127
18470
18471
18472 /* Sparc ELF relocation types */
18473 #define R_SPARC_NONE        0
18474 #define R_SPARC_8           1
18475 #define R_SPARC_16          2
18476 #define R_SPARC_32          3
18477 #define R_SPARC_DISP8       4
18478 #define R_SPARC_DISP16      5
18479 #define R_SPARC_DISP32      6
18480 #define R_SPARC_WDISP30     7
18481 #define R_SPARC_WDISP22     8
```

```
18482 #define R_SPARC_HI22            9
18483 #define R_SPARC_22              10
18484 #define R_SPARC_13              11
18485 #define R_SPARC_LO10            12
18486 #define R_SPARC_GOT10           13
18487 #define R_SPARC_GOT13           14
18488 #define R_SPARC_GOT22           15
18489 #define R_SPARC_PC10            16
18490 #define R_SPARC_PC22            17
18491 #define R_SPARC_WPLT30          18
18492 #define R_SPARC_COPY            19
18493 #define R_SPARC_GLOB_DAT        20
18494 #define R_SPARC_JMP_SLOT        21
18495 #define R_SPARC_RELATIVE        22
18496 #define R_SPARC_UA32            23
18497 #define R_SPARC_PLT32           24
18498 #define R_SPARC_HIPLT22         25
18499 #define R_SPARC_LOPLT10         26
18500 #define R_SPARC_PCPLT32         27
18501 #define R_SPARC_PCPLT22         28
18502 #define R_SPARC_PCPLT10         29
18503 #define R_SPARC_10              30
18504 #define R_SPARC_11              31
18505 #define R_SPARC_WDISP16         40
18506 #define R_SPARC_WDISP19         41
18507 #define R_SPARC_7               43
18508 #define R_SPARC_5               44
18509 #define R_SPARC_6               45
18510
18511 /* Bits present in AT_HWCAP, primarily for Sparc32.  */
18512
18513 #define HWCAP_SPARC_FLUSH       1   /* CPU supports flush
18514                                     * instruction. */
18515 #define HWCAP_SPARC_STBAR       2
18516 #define HWCAP_SPARC_SWAP        4
18517 #define HWCAP_SPARC_MULDIV      8
18518 #define HWCAP_SPARC_V9          16
18519
18520
18521 /* 68k ELF relocation types */
18522 #define R_68K_NONE      0
18523 #define R_68K_32        1
18524 #define R_68K_16        2
18525 #define R_68K_8         3
18526 #define R_68K_PC32      4
18527 #define R_68K_PC16      5
18528 #define R_68K_PC8       6
18529 #define R_68K_GOT32     7
18530 #define R_68K_GOT16     8
18531 #define R_68K_GOT8      9
18532 #define R_68K_GOT320    10
18533 #define R_68K_GOT160    11
18534 #define R_68K_GOT80     12
18535 #define R_68K_PLT32     13
18536 #define R_68K_PLT16     14
18537 #define R_68K_PLT8      15
18538 #define R_68K_PLT320    16
18539 #define R_68K_PLT160    17
18540 #define R_68K_PLT80     18
18541 #define R_68K_COPY      19
18542 #define R_68K_GLOB_DAT  20
18543 #define R_68K_JMP_SLOT  21
18544 #define R_68K_RELATIVE  22
18545
18546 /* Alpha ELF relocation types */
18547 #define R_ALPHA_NONE            0   /* No reloc */
18548 #define R_ALPHA_REFLONG         1   /* Direct 32 bit */
18549 #define R_ALPHA_REFQUAD         2   /* Direct 64 bit */
18550 #define R_ALPHA_GPREL32         3   /* GP relative 32 bit
18551                                     */
18552 #define R_ALPHA_LITERAL         4   /* GP relative 16 bit
18553                                     * w/optimization */
18554 #define R_ALPHA_LITUSE          5   /* Optimization hint
18555                                     * for LITERAL */
18556 #define R_ALPHA_GPDISP          6   /* Add displacement
18557                                     * to GP */
18558 #define R_ALPHA_BRADDR          7   /* PC+4 relative 23
18559                                     * bit shifted */
18560 #define R_ALPHA_HINT            8   /* PC+4 relative 16
18561                                     * bit shifted */
18562 #define R_ALPHA_SREL16          9   /* PC relative 16 bit
18563                                     */
18564 #define R_ALPHA_SREL32          10  /* PC relative 32 bit
18565                                     */
18566 #define R_ALPHA_SREL64          11  /* PC relative 64 bit
18567                                     */
18568 #define R_ALPHA_OP_PUSH         12  /* OP stack push */
18569 #define R_ALPHA_OP_STORE        13  /* OP stack pop and
18570                                     * store */
18571 #define R_ALPHA_OP_PSUB         14  /* OP stack subtract
18572                                     */
18573 #define R_ALPHA_OP_PRSHIFT      15  /* OP stack right
18574                                     * shift */
18575 #define R_ALPHA_GPVALUE         16
```

```
18576 #define R_ALPHA_GPRELHIGH        17
18577 #define R_ALPHA_GPRELLOW         18
18578 #define R_ALPHA_IMMED_GP_16      19
18579 #define R_ALPHA_IMMED_GP_HI32    20
18580 #define R_ALPHA_IMMED_SCN_HI32   21
18581 #define R_ALPHA_IMMED_BR_HI32    22
18582 #define R_ALPHA_IMMED_LO32       23
18583 #define R_ALPHA_COPY             24   /* Copy symbol at
18584                                       * runtime */
18585 #define R_ALPHA_GLOB_DAT         25   /* Create GOT entry
18586                                       */
18587 #define R_ALPHA_JMP_SLOT         26   /* Create PLT entry
18588                                       */
18589 #define R_ALPHA_RELATIVE         27   /* Adjust by program
18590                                       * base */
18591
18592 /* Legal values for e_flags field of Elf64_Ehdr.  */
18593
18594 #define EF_ALPHA_32BIT           1    /* All addresses are
18595                                       * below 2GB */
18596
18597
18598 typedef struct elf32_rel {
18599   Elf32_Addr r_offset;
18600   Elf32_Word r_info;
18601 } Elf32_Rel;
18602
18603 typedef struct elf64_rel {
18604   Elf64_Addr r_offset;  /* Location at which to apply the
18605                          * action */
18606   Elf64_Word r_info;    /* index and type of relocation*/
18607 } Elf64_Rel;
18608
18609 typedef struct elf32_rela {
18610   Elf32_Addr r_offset;
18611   Elf32_Word r_info;
18612   Elf32_Sword r_addend;
18613 } Elf32_Rela;
18614
18615 typedef struct elf64_rela {
18616   Elf64_Addr r_offset;  /* Location at which to apply the
18617                          * action */
18618   Elf64_Word r_info;    /* index and type of relocation*/
18619   Elf64_Word r_addend;  /* Constant addend used to
18620                          * compute value */
18621 } Elf64_Rela;
18622
```

```
18623 typedef struct elf32_sym {
18624   Elf32_Word st_name;
18625   Elf32_Addr st_value;
18626   Elf32_Word st_size;
18627   unsigned char st_info;
18628   unsigned char st_other;
18629   Elf32_Half st_shndx;
18630 } Elf32_Sym;
18631
18632 typedef struct elf64_sym {
18633   Elf32_Word st_name;       /* Symbol name, index in
18634                              * string tbl (yes, Elf32) */
18635   unsigned char st_info;    /* Type and binding attributes
18636                              */
18637   unsigned char st_other;   /* No defined meaning, 0 */
18638   Elf64_Half st_shndx;      /* Associated section index */
18639   Elf64_Addr st_value;      /* Value of the symbol */
18640   Elf64_Word st_size;       /* Associated symbol size */
18641 } Elf64_Sym;
18642
18643
18644 #define EI_NIDENT      16
18645
18646 typedef struct elf32_hdr {
18647   unsigned char e_ident[EI_NIDENT];
18648   Elf32_Half e_type;
18649   Elf32_Half e_machine;
18650   Elf32_Word e_version;
18651   Elf32_Addr e_entry;         /* Entry point */
18652   Elf32_Off e_phoff;
18653   Elf32_Off e_shoff;
18654   Elf32_Word e_flags;
18655   Elf32_Half e_ehsize;
18656   Elf32_Half e_phentsize;
18657   Elf32_Half e_phnum;
18658   Elf32_Half e_shentsize;
18659   Elf32_Half e_shnum;
18660   Elf32_Half e_shstrndx;
18661 } Elf32_Ehdr;
18662
18663 typedef struct elf64_hdr {
18664   unsigned char e_ident[16];    /* ELF "magic number" */
18665   Elf64_SHalf e_type;
18666   Elf64_Half e_machine;
18667   __s32 e_version;
18668   Elf64_Addr e_entry;  /* Entry point virtual address */
18669   Elf64_Off e_phoff;   /* Program header table file
```

```
18670                   * offset */
18671    Elf64_Off e_shoff;    /* Section header table file
18672                   * offset */
18673    __s32 e_flags;
18674    Elf64_SHalf e_ehsize;
18675    Elf64_SHalf e_phentsize;
18676    Elf64_SHalf e_phnum;
18677    Elf64_SHalf e_shentsize;
18678    Elf64_SHalf e_shnum;
18679    Elf64_SHalf e_shstrndx;
18680 } Elf64_Ehdr;
18681
18682 /* These constants define the permissions on sections in
18683  * the program header, p_flags. */
18684 #define PF_R            0x4
18685 #define PF_W            0x2
18686 #define PF_X            0x1
18687
18688 typedef struct elf32_phdr {
18689    Elf32_Word p_type;
18690    Elf32_Off p_offset;
18691    Elf32_Addr p_vaddr;
18692    Elf32_Addr p_paddr;
18693    Elf32_Word p_filesz;
18694    Elf32_Word p_memsz;
18695    Elf32_Word p_flags;
18696    Elf32_Word p_align;
18697 } Elf32_Phdr;
18698
18699 typedef struct elf64_phdr {
18700    __s32 p_type;
18701    __s32 p_flags;
18702    Elf64_Off p_offset;    /* Segment file offset */
18703    Elf64_Addr p_vaddr;    /* Segment virtual address */
18704    Elf64_Addr p_paddr;    /* Segment physical address */
18705    Elf64_Word p_filesz;   /* Segment size in file */
18706    Elf64_Word p_memsz;    /* Segment size in memory */
18707    Elf64_Word p_align;    /* Segment alignment, file &
18708                    * memory */
18709 } Elf64_Phdr;
18710
18711 /* sh_type */
18712 #define SHT_NULL          0
18713 #define SHT_PROGBITS      1
18714 #define SHT_SYMTAB        2
18715 #define SHT_STRTAB        3
18716 #define SHT_RELA          4
```

```
18717 #define SHT_HASH          5
18718 #define SHT_DYNAMIC       6
18719 #define SHT_NOTE          7
18720 #define SHT_NOBITS        8
18721 #define SHT_REL           9
18722 #define SHT_SHLIB         10
18723 #define SHT_DYNSYM        11
18724 #define SHT_NUM           12
18725 #define SHT_LOPROC        0x70000000
18726 #define SHT_HIPROC        0x7fffffff
18727 #define SHT_LOUSER        0x80000000
18728 #define SHT_HIUSER        0xffffffff
18729 #define SHT_MIPS_LIST     0x70000000
18730 #define SHT_MIPS_CONFLICT 0x70000002
18731 #define SHT_MIPS_GPTAB    0x70000003
18732 #define SHT_MIPS_UCODE    0x70000004
18733
18734 /* sh_flags */
18735 #define SHF_WRITE         0x1
18736 #define SHF_ALLOC         0x2
18737 #define SHF_EXECINSTR     0x4
18738 #define SHF_MASKPROC      0xf0000000
18739 #define SHF_MIPS_GPREL    0x10000000
18740
18741 /* special section indexes */
18742 #define SHN_UNDEF         0
18743 #define SHN_LORESERVE     0xff00
18744 #define SHN_LOPROC        0xff00
18745 #define SHN_HIPROC        0xff1f
18746 #define SHN_ABS           0xfff1
18747 #define SHN_COMMON        0xfff2
18748 #define SHN_HIRESERVE     0xffff
18749 #define SHN_MIPS_ACCOMON  0xff00
18750
18751 typedef struct {
18752    Elf32_Word sh_name;
18753    Elf32_Word sh_type;
18754    Elf32_Word sh_flags;
18755    Elf32_Addr sh_addr;
18756    Elf32_Off sh_offset;
18757    Elf32_Word sh_size;
18758    Elf32_Word sh_link;
18759    Elf32_Word sh_info;
18760    Elf32_Word sh_addralign;
18761    Elf32_Word sh_entsize;
18762 } Elf32_Shdr;
18763
```

```
18764 typedef struct elf64_shdr {
18765    Elf32_Word sh_name;        /* Section name, index in
18766                               * string tbl (yes Elf32) */
18767    Elf32_Word sh_type;        /* Type of section (yes
18768                               * Elf32) */
18769    Elf64_Word sh_flags;       /* Miscellaneous section
18770                               * attributes */
18771    Elf64_Addr sh_addr;        /* Section virtual addr at
18772                               * execution */
18773    Elf64_Off sh_offset;       /* Section file offset */
18774    Elf64_Word sh_size;        /* Size of section in bytes*/
18775    Elf32_Word sh_link;        /* Index of another section
18776                               * (yes Elf32) */
18777    Elf32_Word sh_info;        /* Additional section
18778                               * information (yes Elf32) */
18779    Elf64_Word sh_addralign;   /* Section alignment */
18780    Elf64_Word sh_entsize;     /* Entry size if section
18781                               * holds table */
18782 } Elf64_Shdr;
18783
18784 #define EI_MAG0        0      /* e_ident[] indexes */
18785 #define EI_MAG1        1
18786 #define EI_MAG2        2
18787 #define EI_MAG3        3
18788 #define EI_CLASS       4
18789 #define EI_DATA        5
18790 #define EI_VERSION     6
18791 #define EI_PAD         7
18792
18793 #define ELFMAG0        0x7f   /* EI_MAG */
18794 #define ELFMAG1        'E'
18795 #define ELFMAG2        'L'
18796 #define ELFMAG3        'F'
18797 #define ELFMAG         "\177ELF"
18798 #define SELFMAG        4
18799
18800 #define ELFCLASSNONE   0      /* EI_CLASS */
18801 #define ELFCLASS32     1
18802 #define ELFCLASS64     2
18803 #define ELFCLASSNUM    3
18804
18805 #define ELFDATANONE    0      /* e_ident[EI_DATA] */
18806 #define ELFDATA2LSB    1
18807 #define ELFDATA2MSB    2
18808
18809 #define EV_NONE        0      /* e_version, EI_VERSION */
18810 #define EV_CURRENT     1
18811 #define EV_NUM         2
18812
18813 /* Notes used in ET_CORE */
18814 #define NT_PRSTATUS    1
18815 #define NT_PRFPREG     2
18816 #define NT_PRPSINFO    3
18817 #define NT_TASKSTRUCT  4
18818 #define NT_PRFPXREG    20
18819
18820 /* Note header in a PT_NOTE section */
18821 typedef struct elf32_note {
18822    Elf32_Word n_namesz;       /* Name size */
18823    Elf32_Word n_descsz;       /* Content size */
18824    Elf32_Word n_type;         /* Content type */
18825 } Elf32_Nhdr;
18826
18827 /* Note header in a PT_NOTE section */
18828 /* For now we use the 32 bit version of the structure
18829  * until we figure out whether we need anything
18830  * better. Note - on the Alpha, "unsigned int" is only 32
18831  * bits.  */
18832 typedef struct elf64_note {
18833    Elf32_Word n_namesz;       /* Name size */
18834    Elf32_Word n_descsz;       /* Content size */
18835    Elf32_Word n_type;         /* Content type */
18836 } Elf64_Nhdr;
18837
18838 #if ELF_CLASS == ELFCLASS32
18839
18840 extern Elf32_Dyn _DYNAMIC[];
18841 #define elfhdr          elf32_hdr
18842 #define elf_phdr        elf32_phdr
18843 #define elf_note        elf32_note
18844
18845 #else
18846
18847 extern Elf64_Dyn _DYNAMIC[];
18848 #define elfhdr          elf64_hdr
18849 #define elf_phdr        elf64_phdr
18850 #define elf_note        elf64_note
18851
18852 #endif
18853
18854
18855 #endif                                    /* _LINUX_ELF_H */
```

include/linux/highmem.h

```
18856 #ifndef _LINUX_HIGHMEM_H
18857 #define _LINUX_HIGHMEM_H
18858
18859 #include <linux/config.h>
18860 #include <asm/pgalloc.h>
18861
18862 #ifdef CONFIG_HIGHMEM
18863
18864 extern struct page *highmem_start_page;
18865
18866 #include <asm/highmem.h>
18867
18868 /* declarations for linux/mm/highmem.c */
18869 FASTCALL(unsigned int nr_free_highpages(void));
18870
18871 extern struct buffer_head *create_bounce(int rw,
18872     struct buffer_head *bh_orig);
18873
18874
18875 static inline char *bh_kmap(struct buffer_head *bh)
18876 {
18877   return kmap(bh->b_page) + bh_offset(bh);
18878 }
18879
18880 static inline void bh_kunmap(struct buffer_head *bh)
18881 {
18882   kunmap(bh->b_page);
18883 }
18884
18885 #else                           /* CONFIG_HIGHMEM */
18886
18887 static inline unsigned int nr_free_highpages(void)
18888 {
18889   return 0;
18890 }
18891
18892 static inline void *kmap(struct page *page)
18893 {
18894   return page_address(page);
18895 }
18896
18897 #define kunmap(page) do { } while (0)
18898
18899 #define kmap_atomic(page,idx)          kmap(page)
18900 #define kunmap_atomic(page,idx)        kunmap(page)
18901
18902 #define bh_kmap(bh)      ((bh)->b_data)
```

```
18903 #define bh_kunmap(bh)   do { } while (0);
18904
18905 #endif                          /* CONFIG_HIGHMEM */
18906
18907 /* when CONFIG_HIGHMEM is not set these will be plain
18908  * clear/copy_page */
18909 static inline void clear_user_highpage(struct page *page,
18910     unsigned long vaddr)
18911 {
18912   clear_user_page(kmap(page), vaddr);
18913   kunmap(page);
18914 }
18915
18916 static inline void clear_highpage(struct page *page)
18917 {
18918   clear_page(kmap(page));
18919   kunmap(page);
18920 }
18921
18922 static inline void memclear_highpage(struct page *page,
18923     unsigned int offset, unsigned int size)
18924 {
18925   char *kaddr;
18926
18927   if (offset + size > PAGE_SIZE)
18928     BUG();
18929   kaddr = kmap(page);
18930   memset(kaddr + offset, 0, size);
18931   kunmap(page);
18932 }
18933
18934 /* Same but also flushes aliased cache contents to RAM.
18935  */
18936 static inline void memclear_highpage_flush(struct page
18937     *page, unsigned int offset, unsigned int size)
18938 {
18939   char *kaddr;
18940
18941   if (offset + size > PAGE_SIZE)
18942     BUG();
18943   kaddr = kmap(page);
18944   memset(kaddr + offset, 0, size);
18945   flush_page_to_ram(page);
18946   kunmap(page);
18947 }
18948
18949 static inline void copy_user_highpage(struct page *to,
```

```
18950      struct page *from, unsigned long vaddr)
18951 {
18952    char *vfrom, *vto;
18953
18954    vfrom = kmap(from);
18955    vto = kmap(to);
18956    copy_user_page(vto, vfrom, vaddr);
18957    kunmap(from);
18958    kunmap(to);
18959 }
18960
18961 static inline void copy_highpage(struct page *to,
18962      struct page *from)
18963 {
18964    char *vfrom, *vto;
18965
18966    vfrom = kmap(from);
18967    vto = kmap(to);
18968    copy_page(vto, vfrom);
18969    kunmap(from);
18970    kunmap(to);
18971 }
18972
18973 #endif                        /* _LINUX_HIGHMEM_H */
```

include/linux/init.h

```
18974 #ifndef _LINUX_INIT_H
18975 #define _LINUX_INIT_H
18976
18977 #include <linux/config.h>
18978
18979 /* These macros are used to mark some functions or
18980  * initialized data (doesn't apply to uninitialized data)
18981  * as 'initialization' functions. The kernel can take
18982  * this as hint that the function is used only during the
18983  * initialization phase and free up used memory resources
18984  * after
18985  *
18986  * Usage:
18987  * For functions:
18988  *
18989  * You should add __init immediately before the function
18990  * name, like:
18991  *
18992  * static void __init initme(int x, int y)
18993  * {
18994  *   extern int z;  z = x * y;
18995  * }
18996  *
18997  * If the function has a prototype somewhere, you can
18998  * also add __init between closing brace of the prototype
18999  * and semicolon:
19000  *
19001  * extern int initialize_foobar_device(int, int, int)
19002  * __init;
19003  *
19004  * For initialized data:
19005  * You should insert __initdata between the variable name
19006  * and equal sign followed by value, e.g.:
19007  *
19008  * static int init_variable __initdata = 0;
19009  * static char linux_logo[] __initdata = {
19010  *   0x32, 0x36, ...
19011  * };
19012  *
19013  * Don't forget to initialize data not at file scope,
19014  * i.e. within a function, as gcc otherwise puts the data
19015  * into the bss section and not into the init section.
19016  */
19017
19018 #ifndef MODULE
19019
19020 #ifndef __ASSEMBLY__
19021
19022 /* Used for initialization calls..  */
19023 typedef int (*initcall_t) (void);
19024 typedef void (*exitcall_t) (void);
19025
19026 extern initcall_t __initcall_start, __initcall_end;
19027
19028 #define __initcall(fn)                              \
19029      static initcall_t __initcall_##fn __init_call = fn
19030 #define __exitcall(fn)                              \
19031      static exitcall_t __exitcall_##fn __exit_call = fn
19032
19033 /* Used for kernel command line parameter setup */
19034 struct kernel_param {
19035    const char *str;
19036    int (*setup_func) (char *);
19037 };
19038
19039 extern struct kernel_param __setup_start, __setup_end;
19040
19041 #define __setup(str, fn)                            \
```

```
19042      static char __setup_str_##fn[] __initdata = str;    \
19043      static struct kernel_param __setup_##fn              \
19044          __attribute__((unused)) __initsetup =           \
19045      { __setup_str_##fn, fn }
19046
19047 #endif                              /* __ASSEMBLY__ */
19048
19049 /* Mark functions and data as being used at
19050  * initialization or exit time.  */
19051 #define __init                                             \
19052   __attribute__ ((__section__ (".text.init")))
19053 #define __exit                                             \
19054   __attribute__ ((unused, __section__(".text.exit")))
19055 #define __initdata                                         \
19056   __attribute__ ((__section__ (".data.init")))
19057 #define __exitdata                                         \
19058   __attribute__ ((unused, __section__ (".data.exit")))
19059 #define __initsetup                                        \
19060   __attribute__ ((unused,__section__ (".setup.init")))
19061 #define __init_call                                        \
19062   __attribute__ ((unused,__section__ (".initcall.init")))
19063 #define __exit_call                                        \
19064   __attribute__ ((unused,__section__ (".exitcall.exit")))
19065
19066 /* For assembly routines */
19067 #define __INIT           .section      ".text.init","ax"
19068 #define __FINIT          .previous
19069 #define __INITDATA       .section      ".data.init","aw"
19070
19071 #define module_init(x)   __initcall(x);
19072 #define module_exit(x)   __exitcall(x);
19073
19074 #else
19075
19076 #define __init
19077 #define __exit
19078 #define __initdata
19079 #define __exitdata
19080 #define __initcall(fn)
19081 /* For assembly routines */
19082 #define __INIT
19083 #define __FINIT
19084 #define __INITDATA
19085
19086 /* These macros create a dummy inline: gcc 2.9x does not
19087  * count alias as usage, hence the 'unused function'
19088  * warning when __init functions are declared static. We
```

```
19089  * use the dummy __*_module_inline functions both to
19090  * kill the warning and check the type of the
19091  * init/cleanup function. */
19092 typedef int (*__init_module_func_t) (void);
19093 typedef void (*__cleanup_module_func_t) (void);
19094 #define module_init(x)                                      \
19095   int init_module(void) __attribute__((alias(#x)));    \
19096   extern inline __init_module_func_t                   \
19097   __init_module_inline(void)  { return x; }
19098 #define module_exit(x)                                      \
19099   void cleanup_module(void) __attribute__((alias(#x))); \
19100   extern inline __cleanup_module_func_t                \
19101   __cleanup_module_inline(void)  { return x; }
19102
19103 #define __setup(str,func)       /* nothing */
19104
19105 #endif
19106
19107 #ifdef CONFIG_HOTPLUG
19108 #define __devinit
19109 #define __devinitdata
19110 #define __devexit
19111 #define __devexitdata
19112 #else
19113 #define __devinit __init
19114 #define __devinitdata __initdata
19115 #define __devexit __exit
19116 #define __devexitdata __exitdata
19117 #endif
19118
19119 #endif                              /* _LINUX_INIT_H */
```

include/linux/interrupt.h

```
19120 /* interrupt.h */
19121 #ifndef _LINUX_INTERRUPT_H
19122 #define _LINUX_INTERRUPT_H
19123
19124 #include <linux/config.h>
19125 #include <linux/kernel.h>
19126 #include <linux/smp.h>
19127 #include <linux/cache.h>
19128
19129 #include <asm/bitops.h>
19130 #include <asm/atomic.h>
19131 #include <asm/ptrace.h>
19132
19133 struct irqaction {
```

```
19134    void (*handler) (int, void *, struct pt_regs *);
19135    unsigned long flags;
19136    unsigned long mask;
19137    const char *name;
19138    void *dev_id;
19139    struct irqaction *next;
19140 };
19141
19142
19143 /* Who gets which entry in bh_base.  Things which will
19144  * occur most often should come first */
19145 enum {
19146    TIMER_BH = 0,
19147    TQUEUE_BH,
19148    DIGI_BH,
19149    SERIAL_BH,
19150    RISCOM8_BH,
19151    SPECIALIX_BH,
19152    AURORA_BH,
19153    ESP_BH,
19154    SCSI_BH,
19155    IMMEDIATE_BH,
19156    CYCLADES_BH,
19157    CM206_BH,
19158    JS_BH,
19159    MACSERIAL_BH,
19160    ISICOM_BH
19161 };
19162
19163 #include <asm/hardirq.h>
19164 #include <asm/softirq.h>
19165
19166
19167
19168 /* PLEASE, avoid to allocate new softirqs, if you need
19169  * not _really_ high frequency threaded job scheduling.
19170  * For almost all the purposes tasklets are more than
19171  * enough. F.e. all serial device BHs et al. should be
19172  * converted to tasklets, not to softirqs. */
19173 enum {
19174    HI_SOFTIRQ = 0,
19175    NET_TX_SOFTIRQ,
19176    NET_RX_SOFTIRQ,
19177    TASKLET_SOFTIRQ
19178 };
19179
19180 /* softirq mask and active fields moved to irq_cpustat_t
```

```
19181  * in asm/hardirq.h to get better cache usage.  KAO */
19182 struct softirq_action {
19183    void (*action) (struct softirq_action *);
19184    void *data;
19185 };
19186
19187 asmlinkage void do_softirq(void);
19188 extern void open_softirq(int nr,
19189    void (*action) (struct softirq_action *),
19190    void *data);
19191
19192 static inline void __cpu_raise_softirq(int cpu, int nr)
19193 {
19194    softirq_active(cpu) |= (1 << nr);
19195 }
19196
19197
19198 /* I do not want to use atomic variables now, so that
19199  * cli/sti */
19200 static inline void raise_softirq(int nr)
19201 {
19202    unsigned long flags;
19203
19204    local_irq_save(flags);
19205    __cpu_raise_softirq(smp_processor_id(), nr);
19206    local_irq_restore(flags);
19207 }
19208
19209 extern void softirq_init(void);
19210
19211
19212
19213 /* Tasklets — multithreaded analogue of BHs.
19214  *
19215  * Main feature differing them of generic softirqs:
19216  * tasklet is running only on one CPU simultaneously.
19217  *
19218  * Main feature differing them of BHs: different
19219  * tasklets may be run simultaneously on different CPUs.
19220  *
19221  * Properties:
19222  * If tasklet_schedule() is called, then tasklet is
19223  * guaranteed to be executed on some cpu at least once
19224  * after this.
19225  * If the tasklet is already scheduled, but its
19226  * excecution is still not started, it will be executed
19227  * only once.
```

```
19228   * If this tasklet is already running on another CPU (or
19229   * schedule is called from tasklet itself), it is
19230   * rescheduled for later.
19231   *
19232   * Tasklet is strictly serialized wrt itself, but not wrt
19233   * another tasklets. If client needs some intertask
19234   * synchronization, he makes it with spinlocks. */
19235
19236 struct tasklet_struct {
19237   struct tasklet_struct *next;
19238   unsigned long state;
19239   atomic_t count;
19240   void (*func) (unsigned long);
19241   unsigned long data;
19242 };
19243
19244 #define DECLARE_TASKLET(name, func, data)          \
19245   struct tasklet_struct name =                     \
19246     { NULL, 0, ATOMIC_INIT(0), func, data }
19247
19248 #define DECLARE_TASKLET_DISABLED(name, func, data)  \
19249   struct tasklet_struct name =                     \
19250     { NULL, 0, ATOMIC_INIT(1), func, data }
19251
19252
19253 enum {
19254   TASKLET_STATE_SCHED,   /* Tasklet is scheduled for
19255                           * execution */
19256   TASKLET_STATE_RUN      /* Tasklet is running (SMP only)
19257                           */
19258 };
19259
19260 struct tasklet_head {
19261   struct tasklet_struct *list;
19262 } __attribute__ ((__aligned__(SMP_CACHE_BYTES)));
19263
19264 extern struct tasklet_head tasklet_vec[NR_CPUS];
19265 extern struct tasklet_head tasklet_hi_vec[NR_CPUS];
19266
19267 #ifdef CONFIG_SMP
19268 #define tasklet_trylock(t)                          \
19269   (!test_and_set_bit(TASKLET_STATE_RUN, &(t)->state))
19270 #define tasklet_unlock_wait(t)                      \
19271   while (test_bit(TASKLET_STATE_RUN, &(t)->state))  \
19272   { /* NOTHING */ }
19273 #define tasklet_unlock(t)                           \
19274   clear_bit(TASKLET_STATE_RUN, &(t)->state)
19275 #else
19276 #define tasklet_trylock(t)      1
19277 #define tasklet_unlock_wait(t) do {} while (0)
19278 #define tasklet_unlock(t)       do {} while (0)
19279 #endif
19280
19281 static inline void tasklet_schedule(
19282   struct tasklet_struct *t)
19283 {
19284   if (!test_and_set_bit(TASKLET_STATE_SCHED,
19285                         &t->state)) {
19286     int cpu = smp_processor_id();
19287     unsigned long flags;
19288
19289     local_irq_save(flags);
19290     t->next = tasklet_vec[cpu].list;
19291     tasklet_vec[cpu].list = t;
19292     __cpu_raise_softirq(cpu, TASKLET_SOFTIRQ);
19293     local_irq_restore(flags);
19294   }
19295 }
19296
19297 static inline void tasklet_hi_schedule(
19298   struct tasklet_struct *t)
19299 {
19300   if (!test_and_set_bit(TASKLET_STATE_SCHED,
19301                         &t->state)) {
19302     int cpu = smp_processor_id();
19303     unsigned long flags;
19304
19305     local_irq_save(flags);
19306     t->next = tasklet_hi_vec[cpu].list;
19307     tasklet_hi_vec[cpu].list = t;
19308     __cpu_raise_softirq(cpu, HI_SOFTIRQ);
19309     local_irq_restore(flags);
19310   }
19311 }
19312
19313
19314 static inline void tasklet_disable_nosync(
19315   struct tasklet_struct *t)
19316 {
19317   atomic_inc(&t->count);
19318 }
19319
19320 static inline void tasklet_disable(
19321   struct tasklet_struct *t)
```

```
19322 {
19323   tasklet_disable_nosync(t);
19324   tasklet_unlock_wait(t);
19325 }
19326
19327 static inline void tasklet_enable(
19328   struct tasklet_struct *t)
19329 {
19330   atomic_dec(&t->count);
19331 }
19332
19333 extern void tasklet_kill(struct tasklet_struct *t);
19334 extern void tasklet_init(struct tasklet_struct *t,
19335     void (*func) (unsigned long), unsigned long data);
19336
19337 #ifdef CONFIG_SMP
19338
19339 #define SMP_TIMER_NAME(name) name##__thr
19340
19341 #define SMP_TIMER_DEFINE(name, task)                    \
19342 DECLARE_TASKLET(task, name##__thr, 0);                 \
19343 static void name (unsigned long dummy)                 \
19344 {                                                      \
19345         tasklet_schedule(&(task));                     \
19346 }
19347
19348 #else                            /* CONFIG_SMP */
19349
19350 #define SMP_TIMER_NAME(name) name
19351 #define SMP_TIMER_DEFINE(name, task)
19352
19353 #endif                           /* CONFIG_SMP */
19354
19355
19356 /* Old BH definitions */
19357
19358 extern struct tasklet_struct bh_task_vec[];
19359
19360 /* It is exported _ONLY_ for wait_on_irq(). */
19361 extern spinlock_t global_bh_lock;
19362
19363 static inline void mark_bh(int nr)
19364 {
19365   tasklet_hi_schedule(bh_task_vec + nr);
19366 }
19367
19368 extern void init_bh(int nr, void (*routine) (void));
```

```
19369 extern void remove_bh(int nr);
19370
19371
19372 /* Autoprobing for irqs:
19373  *
19374  * probe_irq_on() and probe_irq_off() provide robust
19375  * primitives for accurate IRQ probing during kernel
19376  * initialization.  They are reasonably simple to use,
19377  * are not "fooled" by spurious interrupts, and, unlike
19378  * other attempts at IRQ probing, they do not get hung on
19379  * stuck interrupts (such as unused PS2 mouse interfaces
19380  * on ASUS boards).
19381  *
19382  * For reasonably foolproof probing, use them as follows:
19383  *
19384  * 1. clear and/or mask the device's internal interrupt.
19385  * 2. sti();
19386  * 3. irqs = probe_irq_on(); // "take over" all
19387  *                          // unassigned idle IRQs
19388  * 4. enable the device and cause it to trigger an
19389  * interrupt.
19390  * 5. wait for the device to interrupt, using
19391  * non-intrusive polling or a delay.
19392  * 6. irq = probe_irq_off(irqs);  // get IRQ number,
19393  *                          // 0=none, negative=multiple
19394  * 7. service the device to clear its pending interrupt.
19395  * 8. loop again if paranoia is required.
19396  *
19397  * probe_irq_on() returns a mask of allocated irq's.
19398  *
19399  * probe_irq_off() takes the mask as a parameter,
19400  * and returns the irq number which occurred,
19401  * or zero if none occurred, or a negative irq number
19402  * if more than one irq occurred.  */
19403 /* returns 0 on failure */
19404 extern unsigned long probe_irq_on(void);
19405 /* returns 0 or negative on failure */
19406 extern int probe_irq_off(unsigned long);
19407 /* returns mask of ISA interrupts */
19408 extern unsigned int probe_irq_mask(unsigned long);
19409
19410 #endif
```

include/linux/ipc.h

```
19411 #ifndef _LINUX_IPC_H
19412 #define _LINUX_IPC_H
19413
```

```
19414 #include <linux/types.h>
19415
19416 #define IPC_PRIVATE ((__kernel_key_t) 0)
19417
19418 /* Obsolete, used only for backwards compatibility and
19419  * libc5 compiles */
19420 struct ipc_perm {
19421   __kernel_key_t key;
19422   __kernel_uid_t uid;
19423   __kernel_gid_t gid;
19424   __kernel_uid_t cuid;
19425   __kernel_gid_t cgid;
19426   __kernel_mode_t mode;
19427   unsigned short seq;
19428 };
19429
19430 /* Include the definition of ipc64_perm */
19431 #include <asm/ipcbuf.h>
19432
19433 /* resource get request flags */
19434 #define IPC_CREAT  00001000      /* create if key is
19435                                  * nonexistent */
19436 #define IPC_EXCL   00002000      /* fail if key exists */
19437 #define IPC_NOWAIT 00004000      /* return error on wait*/
19438
19439 /* these fields are used by the DIPC package so the
19440  * kernel as standard should avoid using them if
19441  * possible */
19442
19443 #define IPC_DIPC 00010000        /* make it distributed */
19444 #define IPC_OWN  00020000        /* this machine is the
19445                                  * DIPC owner */
19446
19447 /* Control commands used with semctl, msgctl and shmctl
19448  * see also specific commands in sem.h, msg.h and shm.h
19449  */
19450 #define IPC_RMID 0               /* remove resource */
19451 #define IPC_SET  1               /* set ipc_perm options*/
19452 #define IPC_STAT 2               /* get ipc_perm options*/
19453 #define IPC_INFO 3               /* see ipcs */
19454
19455 /* Version flags for semctl, msgctl, and shmctl commands
19456  * These are passed as bitflags or-ed with the actual
19457  * command */
19458 #define IPC_OLD 0                /* Old version (no
19459                                  * 32-bit UID support on
19460                                  * many architectures) */
19461 #define IPC_64   0x0100          /* New version (support
19462                                  * 32-bit UIDs, bigger
19463                                  * message sizes, etc. */
19464
19465 #ifdef __KERNEL__
19466
19467 #define IPCMNI 32768             /* <= MAX_INT limit for
19468                                  * ipc arrays (including
19469                                  * sysctl changes) */
19470
19471 /* used by in-kernel data structures */
19472 struct kern_ipc_perm {
19473   key_t key;
19474   uid_t uid;
19475   gid_t gid;
19476   uid_t cuid;
19477   gid_t cgid;
19478   mode_t mode;
19479   unsigned long seq;
19480 };
19481
19482 #endif                           /* __KERNEL__ */
19483
19484 #endif                           /* _LINUX_IPC_H */
```

include/linux/irq_cpustat.h

```
19485 #ifndef __irq_cpustat_h
19486 #define __irq_cpustat_h
19487
19488 /*
19489  * Contains default mappings for irq_cpustat_t, used by
19490  * almost every architecture.  Some arch (like s390) have
19491  * per cpu hardware pages and they define their own
19492  * mappings for irq_stat.
19493  *
19494  * Keith Owens <kaos@ocs.com.au> July 2000.
19495  */
19496
19497 #include <linux/config.h>
19498
19499 /* Simple wrappers reducing source bloat.  Define all
19500  * irq_stat fields here, even ones that are arch
19501  * dependent.  That way we get common definitions instead
19502  * of differing sets for each arch.  */
19503
19504 /* defined in asm/hardirq.h */
19505 extern irq_cpustat_t irq_stat[];
```

```
19506
19507 #ifdef CONFIG_SMP
19508 #define __IRQ_STAT(cpu, member) (irq_stat[cpu].member)
19509 #else
19510 #define __IRQ_STAT(cpu, member)                        \
19511   ((void)(cpu), irq_stat[0].member)
19512 #endif
19513
19514   /* arch independent irq_stat fields */
19515 #define softirq_active(cpu)                            \
19516   __IRQ_STAT((cpu), __softirq_active)
19517 #define softirq_mask(cpu)                              \
19518   __IRQ_STAT((cpu), __softirq_mask)
19519 #define local_irq_count(cpu)                           \
19520   __IRQ_STAT((cpu), __local_irq_count)
19521 #define local_bh_count(cpu)                            \
19522   __IRQ_STAT((cpu), __local_bh_count)
19523 #define syscall_count(cpu)                             \
19524   __IRQ_STAT((cpu), __syscall_count)
19525   /* arch dependent irq_stat fields */
19526 #define nmi_count(cpu)                                 \
19527   __IRQ_STAT((cpu), __nmi_count)  /* i386, ia64 */
19528
19529 #endif                            /* __irq_cpustat_h */
```

include/linux/irq.h

```
19530 #ifndef __irq_h
19531 #define __irq_h
19532
19533 #include <linux/cache.h>
19534 #include <linux/spinlock.h>
19535
19536 #include <asm/irq.h>
19537 #include <asm/ptrace.h>
19538
19539 /* IRQ line status. */
19540 #define IRQ_INPROGRESS  1       /* IRQ handler active -
19541                                  * do not enter! */
19542 #define IRQ_DISABLED    2       /* IRQ disabled - do not
19543                                  * enter! */
19544 #define IRQ_PENDING     4       /* IRQ pending - replay
19545                                  * on enable */
19546 #define IRQ_REPLAY      8       /* IRQ has been replayed
19547                                  * but not acked yet */
19548 #define IRQ_AUTODETECT  16      /* IRQ is being
19549                                  * autodetected */
19550 #define IRQ_WAITING     32      /* IRQ not yet seen -
19551                                  * for autodetection */
19552 #define IRQ_LEVEL       64      /* IRQ level triggered */
19553 #define IRQ_MASKED      128     /* IRQ masked -
19554                                  * shouldn't be seen
19555                                  * again */
19556 #define IRQ_PER_CPU     256     /* IRQ is per CPU */
19557
19558 /* Interrupt controller descriptor. This is all we need
19559  * to describe about the low-level hardware.  */
19560 struct hw_interrupt_type {
19561   const char *typename;
19562   unsigned int (*startup) (unsigned int irq);
19563   void (*shutdown) (unsigned int irq);
19564   void (*enable) (unsigned int irq);
19565   void (*disable) (unsigned int irq);
19566   void (*ack) (unsigned int irq);
19567   void (*end) (unsigned int irq);
19568   void (*set_affinity) (unsigned int irq,
19569                         unsigned long mask);
19570 };
19571
19572 typedef struct hw_interrupt_type hw_irq_controller;
19573
19574 /* This is the "IRQ descriptor", which contains various
19575  * information about the irq, including what kind of
19576  * hardware handling it has, whether it is disabled etc
19577  * etc.
19578  *
19579  * Pad this out to 32 bytes for cache and indexing
19580  * reasons.  */
19581 typedef struct {
19582   unsigned int status;          /* IRQ status */
19583   hw_irq_controller *handler;
19584   struct irqaction *action;     /* IRQ action list */
19585   unsigned int depth;           /* nested irq disables */
19586   spinlock_t lock;
19587 } ____cacheline_aligned irq_desc_t;
19588
19589 extern irq_desc_t irq_desc[NR_IRQS];
19590
19591 #include <asm/hw_irq.h>     /* the arch dependent stuff */
19592
19593 extern int handle_IRQ_event(unsigned int,
19594     struct pt_regs *, struct irqaction *);
19595 extern int setup_irq(unsigned int, struct irqaction *);
19596
19597 extern hw_irq_controller no_irq_type;   /* needed in
```

```
19598                                    * every arch? */
19599 extern void no_action(int cpl, void *dev_id,
19600     struct pt_regs *regs);
19601
19602 extern volatile unsigned long irq_err_count;
19603
19604 #endif                          /* __asm_h */
```

include/linux/kernel.h

```
19605 #ifndef _LINUX_KERNEL_H
19606 #define _LINUX_KERNEL_H
19607
19608 /* 'kernel.h' contains some often-used function
19609  * prototypes etc */
19610
19611 #ifdef __KERNEL__
19612
19613 #include <stdarg.h>
19614 #include <linux/linkage.h>
19615 #include <linux/stddef.h>
19616
19617 /* Optimization barrier */
19618 /* The "volatile" is due to gcc bugs */
19619 #define barrier() __asm__ __volatile__("": : :"memory")
19620
19621 #define INT_MAX        ((int)(~0U>>1))
19622 #define INT_MIN        (-INT_MAX - 1)
19623 #define UINT_MAX       (~0U)
19624 #define LONG_MAX       ((long)(~0UL>>1))
19625 #define LONG_MIN       (-LONG_MAX - 1)
19626 #define ULONG_MAX      (~0UL)
19627
19628 #define STACK_MAGIC    0xdeadbeef
19629
19630 #define ARRAY_SIZE(x)  (sizeof(x) / sizeof((x)[0]))
19631
19632 #define KERN_EMERG     "<0>"   /* system is unusable */
19633 #define KERN_ALERT     "<1>"   /* action must be taken
19634                                 * immediately  */
19635 #define KERN_CRIT      "<2>"   /* critical conditions */
19636 #define KERN_ERR       "<3>"   /* error conditions */
19637 #define KERN_WARNING   "<4>"   /* warning conditions */
19638 #define KERN_NOTICE    "<5>"   /* normal but significant
19639                                 * condition */
19640 #define KERN_INFO      "<6>"   /* informational */
19641 #define KERN_DEBUG     "<7>"   /* debug-level messages*/
19642
```

```
19643 # define NORET_TYPE     /**/
19644 # define ATTRIB_NORET   __attribute__((noreturn))
19645 # define NORET_AND      noreturn,
19646 #ifdef __i386__
19647 #define FASTCALL(x)     x __attribute__((regparm(3)))
19648 #else
19649 #define FASTCALL(x)     x
19650 #endif
19651 struct semaphore;
19652
19653 extern struct notifier_block *panic_notifier_list;
19654 NORET_TYPE void panic(const char *fmt, ...)
19655     __attribute__ ((NORET_AND format(printf, 1, 2)));
19656 NORET_TYPE void do_exit(long error_code) ATTRIB_NORET;
19657 NORET_TYPE void up_and_exit(struct semaphore *, long)
19658     ATTRIB_NORET;
19659 extern unsigned long simple_strtoul(const char *,
19660     char **, unsigned int);
19661 extern long simple_strtol(const char *, char **,
19662     unsigned int);
19663 extern unsigned long long simple_strtoull(const char *,
19664     char **, unsigned int);
19665 extern long long simple_strtoll(const char *, char **,
19666     unsigned int);
19667 extern int sprintf(char *buf, const char *fmt, ...);
19668 extern int vsprintf(char *buf, const char *, va_list);
19669 extern int get_option(char **str, int *pint);
19670 extern char *get_options(char *str, int nints,
19671     int *ints);
19672 extern unsigned long memparse(char *ptr, char **retptr);
19673 extern void dev_probe_lock(void);
19674 extern void dev_probe_unlock(void);
19675
19676 extern int session_of_pgrp(int pgrp);
19677
19678 asmlinkage int printk(const char *fmt, ...)
19679     __attribute__ ((format(printf, 1, 2)));
19680
19681 extern int console_loglevel;
19682
19683 static inline void console_silent(void)
19684 {
19685    console_loglevel = 0;
19686 }
19687
19688 static inline void console_verbose(void)
19689 {
```

```
19690   if (console_loglevel)
19691     console_loglevel = 15;
19692 }
19693
19694 #if DEBUG
19695 #define pr_debug(fmt,arg...)                          \
19696         printk(KERN_DEBUG fmt,##arg)
19697 #else
19698 #define pr_debug(fmt,arg...)                          \
19699         do { } while (0)
19700 #endif
19701
19702 #define pr_info(fmt,arg...)                            \
19703         printk(KERN_INFO fmt,##arg)
19704
19705 /* Display an IP address in readable format.  */
19706
19707 #define NIPQUAD(addr)                                  \
19708         ((unsigned char *)&addr)[0],                   \
19709         ((unsigned char *)&addr)[1],                   \
19710         ((unsigned char *)&addr)[2],                   \
19711         ((unsigned char *)&addr)[3]
19712
19713 #define HIPQUAD(addr)                                  \
19714         ((unsigned char *)&addr)[3],                   \
19715         ((unsigned char *)&addr)[2],                   \
19716         ((unsigned char *)&addr)[1],                   \
19717         ((unsigned char *)&addr)[0]
19718
19719 #endif                             /* __KERNEL__ */
19720
19721 #define SI_LOAD_SHIFT   16
19722 struct sysinfo {
19723   long uptime;                /* Seconds since boot */
19724   unsigned long loads[3];     /* 1, 5, and 15 minute load
19725                                * averages */
19726   unsigned long totalram;     /* Total usable main memory
19727                                * size */
19728   unsigned long freeram;      /* Available memory size */
19729   unsigned long sharedram;    /* Amount of shared memory */
19730   unsigned long bufferram;    /* Memory used by buffers */
19731   unsigned long totalswap;    /* Total swap space size */
19732   unsigned long freeswap;     /* swap space still available
19733                                */
19734   unsigned short procs;       /* Number of current
19735                                * processes */
19736   unsigned long totalhigh;    /* Total high memory size */
19737   unsigned long freehigh;     /* Available high memory size
19738                                */
19739   unsigned int mem_unit;      /* Memory unit size in bytes
19740                                */
19741   /* Padding: libc5 uses this..  */
19742   char _f[20 - 2 * sizeof(long) - sizeof(int)];
19743 };
19744
19745 #endif
```

include/linux/kernel_stat.h

```
19746 #ifndef _LINUX_KERNEL_STAT_H
19747 #define _LINUX_KERNEL_STAT_H
19748
19749 #include <linux/config.h>
19750 #include <asm/irq.h>
19751 #include <linux/smp.h>
19752 #include <linux/threads.h>
19753
19754 /* 'kernel_stat.h' contains the definitions needed for
19755  * doing some kernel statistics (CPU usage, context
19756  * switches ...), used by rstatd/perfmeter */
19757
19758 #define DK_MAX_MAJOR 16
19759 #define DK_MAX_DISK 16
19760
19761 struct kernel_stat {
19762   unsigned int per_cpu_user[NR_CPUS],
19763       per_cpu_nice[NR_CPUS], per_cpu_system[NR_CPUS];
19764   unsigned int dk_drive[DK_MAX_MAJOR][DK_MAX_DISK];
19765   unsigned int dk_drive_rio[DK_MAX_MAJOR][DK_MAX_DISK];
19766   unsigned int dk_drive_wio[DK_MAX_MAJOR][DK_MAX_DISK];
19767   unsigned int dk_drive_rblk[DK_MAX_MAJOR][DK_MAX_DISK];
19768   unsigned int dk_drive_wblk[DK_MAX_MAJOR][DK_MAX_DISK];
19769   unsigned int pgpgin, pgpgout;
19770   unsigned int pswpin, pswpout;
19771 #if !defined(CONFIG_ARCH_S390)
19772   unsigned int irqs[NR_CPUS][NR_IRQS];
19773 #endif
19774   unsigned int ipackets, opackets;
19775   unsigned int ierrors, oerrors;
19776   unsigned int collisions;
19777   unsigned int context_swtch;
19778 };
19779
19780 extern struct kernel_stat kstat;
19781
```

```
19782 #if !defined(CONFIG_ARCH_S390)
19783 /* Number of interrupts per specific IRQ source, since
19784  * bootup */
19785 extern inline int kstat_irqs(int irq)
19786 {
19787   int i, sum = 0;
19788
19789   for (i = 0; i < smp_num_cpus; i++)
19790     sum += kstat.irqs[cpu_logical_map(i)][irq];
19791
19792   return sum;
19793 }
19794 #endif
19795
19796 #endif                          /* _LINUX_KERNEL_STAT_H */
```

include/linux/linkage.h

```
19797 #ifndef _LINUX_LINKAGE_H
19798 #define _LINUX_LINKAGE_H
19799
19800 #include <linux/config.h>
19801
19802 #ifdef __cplusplus
19803 #define CPP_ASMLINKAGE extern "C"
19804 #else
19805 #define CPP_ASMLINKAGE
19806 #endif
19807
19808 #if defined __i386__
19809 #define asmlinkage                                          \
19810   CPP_ASMLINKAGE __attribute__((regparm(0)))
19811 #elif defined __ia64__
19812 #define asmlinkage                                          \
19813   CPP_ASMLINKAGE __attribute__((syscall_linkage))
19814 #else
19815 #define asmlinkage CPP_ASMLINKAGE
19816 #endif
19817
19818 #define SYMBOL_NAME_STR(X) #X
19819 #define SYMBOL_NAME(X) X
19820 #ifdef __STDC__
19821 #define SYMBOL_NAME_LABEL(X) X##:
19822 #else
19823 #define SYMBOL_NAME_LABEL(X) X/**/:
19824 #endif
19825
19826 #ifdef __arm__
```

```
19827 #define __ALIGN .align 0
19828 #define __ALIGN_STR ".align 0"
19829 #else
19830 #ifdef __mc68000__
19831 #define __ALIGN .align 4
19832 #define __ALIGN_STR ".align 4"
19833 #else
19834 #ifdef __sh__
19835 #define __ALIGN .balign 4
19836 #define __ALIGN_STR ".balign 4"
19837 #else
19838 #if defined(__i386__) && defined(CONFIG_X86_ALIGNMENT_16)
19839 #define __ALIGN .align 16,0x90
19840 #define __ALIGN_STR ".align 16,0x90"
19841 #else
19842 #define __ALIGN .align 4,0x90
19843 #define __ALIGN_STR ".align 4,0x90"
19844 #endif
19845 #endif                          /* __sh__ */
19846 #endif                          /* __mc68000__ */
19847 #endif                          /* __arm__ */
19848
19849 #ifdef __ASSEMBLY__
19850
19851 #define ALIGN __ALIGN
19852 #define ALIGN_STR __ALIGN_STR
19853
19854 #define ENTRY(name)                                          \
19855   .globl SYMBOL_NAME(name);                                  \
19856   ALIGN;                                                     \
19857   SYMBOL_NAME_LABEL(name)
19858
19859 #endif
19860
19861 #endif
```

include/linux/list.h

```
19862 #ifndef _LINUX_LIST_H
19863 #define _LINUX_LIST_H
19864
19865 #ifdef __KERNEL__
19866
19867 /*
19868  * Simple doubly linked list implementation.
19869  *
19870  * Some of the internal functions ("__xxx") are useful
19871  * when manipulating whole lists rather than single
```

```
19872  * entries, as sometimes we already know the next/prev
19873  * entries and we can generate better code by using them
19874  * directly rather than using the generic single-entry
19875  * routines.
19876  */
19877
19878 struct list_head {
19879   struct list_head *next, *prev;
19880 };
19881
19882 #define LIST_HEAD_INIT(name) { &(name), &(name) }
19883
19884 #define LIST_HEAD(name)                                 \
19885         struct list_head name = LIST_HEAD_INIT(name)
19886
19887 #define INIT_LIST_HEAD(ptr) do {                        \
19888         (ptr)->next = (ptr); (ptr)->prev = (ptr);       \
19889 } while (0)
19890
19891 /* Insert a new entry between two known consecutive
19892  * entries.
19893  *
19894  * This is only for internal list manipulation where we
19895  * know the prev/next entries already!  */
19896 static __inline__ void __list_add(struct list_head *new,
19897       struct list_head *prev, struct list_head *next)
19898 {
19899   next->prev = new;
19900   new->next = next;
19901   new->prev = prev;
19902   prev->next = new;
19903 }
19904
19905 /**
19906  * list_add - add a new entry
19907  * @new: new entry to be added
19908  * @head: list head to add it after
19909  *
19910  * Insert a new entry after the specified head.  This is
19911  * good for implementing stacks.  */
19912 static __inline__ void list_add(struct list_head *new,
19913       struct list_head *head)
19914 {
19915   __list_add(new, head, head->next);
19916 }
19917
19918 /**
```

```
19919  * list_add_tail - add a new entry
19920  * @new: new entry to be added
19921  * @head: list head to add it before
19922  *
19923  * Insert a new entry before the specified head.  This is
19924  * useful for implementing queues.  */
19925 static __inline__ void
19926 list_add_tail(struct list_head *new,
19927             struct list_head *head)
19928 {
19929   __list_add(new, head->prev, head);
19930 }
19931
19932 /* Delete a list entry by making the prev/next entries
19933  * point to each other.
19934  *
19935  * This is only for internal list manipulation where we
19936  * know the prev/next entries already!  */
19937 static __inline__ void __list_del(struct list_head *prev,
19938     struct list_head *next)
19939 {
19940   next->prev = prev;
19941   prev->next = next;
19942 }
19943
19944 /**
19945  * list_del - deletes entry from list.
19946  * @entry: the element to delete from the list.
19947  * Note: list_empty on entry does not return true after
19948  * this, the entry is in an undefined state.  */
19949 static __inline__ void list_del(struct list_head *entry)
19950 {
19951   __list_del(entry->prev, entry->next);
19952 }
19953
19954 /**
19955  * list_del_init - deletes entry from list and
19956  * reinitialize it.
19957  * @entry: the element to delete from the list.  */
19958 static __inline__ void list_del_init(struct list_head
19959     *entry)
19960 {
19961   __list_del(entry->prev, entry->next);
19962   INIT_LIST_HEAD(entry);
19963 }
19964
19965 /**
```

```
19966  * list_empty - tests whether a list is empty
19967  * @head: the list to test. */
19968 static __inline__ int list_empty(struct list_head *head)
19969 {
19970    return head->next == head;
19971 }
19972
19973 /**
19974  * list_splice - join two lists
19975  * @list: the new list to add.
19976  * @head: the place to add it in the first list. */
19977 static __inline__ void
19978 list_splice(struct list_head *list,
19979              struct list_head *head)
19980 {
19981    struct list_head *first = list->next;
19982
19983    if (first != list) {
19984       struct list_head *last = list->prev;
19985       struct list_head *at = head->next;
19986
19987       first->prev = head;
19988       head->next = first;
19989
19990       last->next = at;
19991       at->prev = last;
19992    }
19993 }
19994
19995 /**
19996  * list_entry - get the struct for this entry
19997  * @ptr:    the &struct list_head pointer.
19998  * @type:   the type of the struct this is embedded in.
19999  * @member: the name of the list_struct within the
20000  *          struct. */
20001 #define list_entry(ptr, type, member)                  \
20002         ((type *)((char *)(ptr)-                        \
20003                 (unsigned long)(&((type *)0)->member)))
20004
20005 /**
20006  * list_for_each     -        iterate over a list
20007  * @pos: the &struct list_head to use as a loop counter.
20008  * @head: the head for your list. */
20009 #define list_for_each(pos, head)                       \
20010    for (pos = (head)->next; pos != (head); pos = pos->next)
20011
20012 #endif                              /* __KERNEL__ */
```

(p 541 ► at line 20001)
(p 541 ► at line 20009)

```
20013
20014 #endif
```

include/linux/mm.h

```
20015 #ifndef _LINUX_MM_H
20016 #define _LINUX_MM_H
20017
20018 #include <linux/sched.h>
20019 #include <linux/errno.h>
20020
20021 #ifdef __KERNEL__
20022
20023 #include <linux/config.h>
20024 #include <linux/string.h>
20025 #include <linux/list.h>
20026 #include <linux/mmzone.h>
20027
20028 extern unsigned long max_mapnr;
20029 extern unsigned long num_physpages;
20030 extern void *high_memory;
20031 extern int page_cluster;
20032 /* The inactive_clean lists are per zone. */
20033 extern struct list_head active_list;
20034 extern struct list_head inactive_dirty_list;
20035
20036 #include <asm/page.h>
20037 #include <asm/pgtable.h>
20038 #include <asm/atomic.h>
20039
20040 /* Linux kernel virtual memory manager primitives.  The
20041  * idea being to have a "virtual" mm in the same way we
20042  * have a virtual fs - giving a cleaner interface to the
20043  * mm details, and allowing different kinds of memory
20044  * mappings (from shared memory to executable loading to
20045  * arbitrary mmap() functions).  */
20046
20047 /* This struct defines a memory VMM memory area. There is
20048  * one of these per VM-area/task.  A VM area is any part
20049  * of the process virtual memory space that has a special
20050  * rule for the page-fault handlers (ie a shared library,
20051  * the executable area etc).  */
20052 struct vm_area_struct {
20053    struct mm_struct *vm_mm;      /* VM area parameters */
20054    unsigned long vm_start;
20055    unsigned long vm_end;
20056
20057    /* linked list of VM areas per task, sorted by address
```

```
20058    */
20059    struct vm_area_struct *vm_next;
20060
20061    pgprot_t vm_page_prot;
20062    unsigned long vm_flags;
20063
20064    /* AVL tree of VM areas per task, sorted by address */
20065    short vm_avl_height;
20066    struct vm_area_struct *vm_avl_left;
20067    struct vm_area_struct *vm_avl_right;
20068
20069    /* For areas with an address space and backing store,
20070     * one of the address_space->i_mmap{,shared} lists, for
20071     * shm areas, the list of attaches, otherwise
20072     * unused. */
20073    struct vm_area_struct *vm_next_share;
20074    struct vm_area_struct **vm_pprev_share;
20075
20076    struct vm_operations_struct *vm_ops;
20077    unsigned long vm_pgoff;  /* offset in PAGE_SIZE units,
20078                             * *not* PAGE_CACHE_SIZE */
20079    struct file *vm_file;
20080    unsigned long vm_raend;
20081    void *vm_private_data;   /* was vm_pte (shared mem) */
20082 };
20083
20084 /* vm_flags.. */
20085 #define VM_READ        0x00000001  /* currently active
20086                                    * flags */
20087 #define VM_WRITE       0x00000002
20088 #define VM_EXEC        0x00000004
20089 #define VM_SHARED      0x00000008
20090
20091 #define VM_MAYREAD     0x00000010  /* limits for
20092                                    * mprotect() etc */
20093 #define VM_MAYWRITE    0x00000020
20094 #define VM_MAYEXEC     0x00000040
20095 #define VM_MAYSHARE    0x00000080
20096
20097 #define VM_GROWSDOWN   0x00000100  /* general info on
20098                                    * the segment */
20099 #define VM_GROWSUP     0x00000200
20100 #define VM_SHM         0x00000400  /* shared memory
20101                                    * area, don't swap
20102                                    * out */
20103 #define VM_DENYWRITE   0x00000800  /* ETXTBSY on write
20104                                    * attempts.. */
```

```
20105
20106 #define VM_EXECUTABLE  0x00001000
20107 #define VM_LOCKED      0x00002000
20108 #define VM_IO          0x00004000  /* Memory mapped I/O
20109                                    * or similar */
20110
20111 #define VM_SEQ_READ    0x00008000  /* App will access
20112                                    * data sequentially
20113                                    */
20114 #define VM_RAND_READ   0x00010000  /* App will not
20115                                    * benefit from
20116                                    * clustered reads */
20117
20118 #define VM_DONTCOPY    0x00020000  /* Do not copy this
20119                                    * vma on fork */
20120 #define VM_DONTEXPAND  0x00040000  /* Cannot expand with
20121                                    * mremap() */
20122 #define VM_RESERVED    0x00080000  /* Don't unmap it
20123                                    * from swap_out */
20124
20125 #define VM_STACK_FLAGS 0x00000177
20126
20127 #define VM_READHINTMASK                           \
20128   (VM_SEQ_READ | VM_RAND_READ)
20129 #define VM_ClearReadHint(v)                       \
20130   (v)->vm_flags &= ~VM_READHINTMASK
20131 #define VM_NormalReadHint(v)                      \
20132   (!((v)->vm_flags & VM_READHINTMASK))
20133 #define VM_SequentialReadHint(v)                  \
20134   ((v)->vm_flags & VM_SEQ_READ)
20135 #define VM_RandomReadHint(v)                      \
20136   ((v)->vm_flags & VM_RAND_READ)
20137
20138 /* mapping from the currently active vm_flags protection
20139  * bits (the low four bits) to a page protection mask..
20140  */
20141 extern pgprot_t protection_map[16];
20142
20143
20144 /* These are the virtual MM functions - opening of an
20145  * area, closing and unmapping it (needed to keep files
20146  * on disk up-to-date etc), pointer to the functions
20147  * called when a no-page or a wp-page exception occurs.
20148  */
20149 struct vm_operations_struct {
20150   void (*open) (struct vm_area_struct * area);
20151   void (*close) (struct vm_area_struct * area);
```

```
20152   struct page *(*nopage) (struct vm_area_struct * area,
20153       unsigned long address, int write_access);
20154 };
20155
20156 /* Try to keep the most commonly accessed fields in
20157  * single cache lines here (16 bytes or greater).  This
20158  * ordering should be particularly beneficial on 32-bit
20159  * processors.
20160  *
20161  * The first line is data used in page cache lookup, the
20162  * second line is used for linear searches (eg. clock
20163  * algorithm scans).  */
20164 typedef struct page {
20165   struct list_head list;
20166   struct address_space *mapping;
20167   unsigned long index;
20168   struct page *next_hash;
20169   atomic_t count;
20170   unsigned long flags;   /* atomic flags, some possibly
20171                           * updated asynchronously */
20172   struct list_head lru;
20173   unsigned long age;
20174   wait_queue_head_t wait;
20175   struct page **pprev_hash;
20176   struct buffer_head *buffers;
20177   void *virtual;              /* non-NULL if kmapped */
20178   struct zone_struct *zone;
20179 } mem_map_t;
20180
20181 #define get_page(p)          atomic_inc(&(p)->count)
20182 #define put_page(p)          __free_page(p)
20183 #define put_page_testzero(p)                           \
20184   atomic_dec_and_test(&(p)->count)
20185 #define page_count(p)        atomic_read(&(p)->count)
20186 #define set_page_count(p,v)  atomic_set(&(p)->count, v)
20187
20188 /* Page flag bit values */
20189 #define PG_locked           0
20190 #define PG_error            1
20191 #define PG_referenced       2
20192 #define PG_uptodate         3
20193 #define PG_dirty            4
20194 #define PG_decr_after       5
20195 #define PG_active           6
20196 #define PG_inactive_dirty   7
20197 #define PG_slab             8
20198 #define PG_swap_cache       9
```

```
20199 #define PG_skip             10
20200 #define PG_inactive_clean   11
20201 #define PG_highmem          12
20202                             /* bits 21-29 unused */
20203 #define PG_arch_1           30
20204 #define PG_reserved         31
20205
20206 /* Make it prettier to test the above... */
20207 #define Page_Uptodate(page)                            \
20208   test_bit(PG_uptodate, &(page)->flags)
20209 #define SetPageUptodate(page)                          \
20210   set_bit(PG_uptodate, &(page)->flags)
20211 #define ClearPageUptodate(page)                        \
20212   clear_bit(PG_uptodate, &(page)->flags)
20213 #define PageDirty(page)                                \
20214   test_bit(PG_dirty, &(page)->flags)
20215 #define SetPageDirty(page)                             \
20216   set_bit(PG_dirty, &(page)->flags)
20217 #define ClearPageDirty(page)                           \
20218   clear_bit(PG_dirty, &(page)->flags)
20219 #define PageLocked(page)                               \
20220   test_bit(PG_locked, &(page)->flags)
20221 #define LockPage(page)                                 \
20222   set_bit(PG_locked, &(page)->flags)
20223 #define TryLockPage(page)                              \
20224   test_and_set_bit(PG_locked, &(page)->flags)
20225
20226 extern void __set_page_dirty(struct page *);
20227
20228 static inline void set_page_dirty(struct page *page)
20229 {
20230   if (!test_and_set_bit(PG_dirty, &page->flags))
20231     __set_page_dirty(page);
20232 }
20233
20234 /* The first mb is necessary to safely close the critical
20235  * section opened by the TryLockPage(), the second mb is
20236  * necessary to enforce ordering between the clear_bit
20237  * and the read of the waitqueue (to avoid SMP races with
20238  * a parallel wait_on_page).  */
20239 #define UnlockPage(page)                               \
20240 do {                                                   \
20241   smp_mb__before_clear_bit();                          \
20242   if (!test_and_clear_bit(PG_locked, &(page)->flags))  \
20243     BUG();                                             \
20244   smp_mb__after_clear_bit();                           \
20245   if (waitqueue_active(&page->wait))                   \
```

```
20246     wake_up(&page->wait);                             \
20247 } while (0)
20248 #define PageError(page)                               \
20249   test_bit(PG_error, &(page)->flags)
20250 #define SetPageError(page)                            \
20251   set_bit(PG_error, &(page)->flags)
20252 #define ClearPageError(page)                          \
20253   clear_bit(PG_error, &(page)->flags)
20254 #define PageReferenced(page)                          \
20255   test_bit(PG_referenced, &(page)->flags)
20256 #define SetPageReferenced(page)                       \
20257   set_bit(PG_referenced, &(page)->flags)
20258 #define ClearPageReferenced(page)                     \
20259   clear_bit(PG_referenced, &(page)->flags)
20260 #define PageTestandClearReferenced(page)              \
20261   test_and_clear_bit(PG_referenced, &(page)->flags)
20262 #define PageDecrAfter(page)                           \
20263   test_bit(PG_decr_after, &(page)->flags)
20264 #define SetPageDecrAfter(page)                        \
20265   set_bit(PG_decr_after, &(page)->flags)
20266 #define PageTestandClearDecrAfter(page)               \
20267   test_and_clear_bit(PG_decr_after, &(page)->flags)
20268 #define PageSlab(page)                                \
20269   test_bit(PG_slab, &(page)->flags)
20270 #define PageSwapCache(page)                           \
20271   test_bit(PG_swap_cache, &(page)->flags)
20272 #define PageReserved(page)                            \
20273   test_bit(PG_reserved, &(page)->flags)
20274
20275 #define PageSetSlab(page)                             \
20276   set_bit(PG_slab, &(page)->flags)
20277 #define PageSetSwapCache(page)                        \
20278   set_bit(PG_swap_cache, &(page)->flags)
20279
20280 #define PageTestandSetSwapCache(page)                 \
20281   test_and_set_bit(PG_swap_cache, &(page)->flags)
20282
20283 #define PageClearSlab(page)                           \
20284   clear_bit(PG_slab, &(page)->flags)
20285 #define PageClearSwapCache(page)                      \
20286   clear_bit(PG_swap_cache, &(page)->flags)
20287
20288 #define PageTestandClearSwapCache(page)               \
20289   test_and_clear_bit(PG_swap_cache, &(page)->flags)
20290
20291 #define PageActive(page)                              \
20292   test_bit(PG_active, &(page)->flags)
20293 #define SetPageActive(page)                           \
20294   set_bit(PG_active, &(page)->flags)
20295 #define ClearPageActive(page)                         \
20296   clear_bit(PG_active, &(page)->flags)
20297
20298 #define PageInactiveDirty(page)                       \
20299   test_bit(PG_inactive_dirty, &(page)->flags)
20300 #define SetPageInactiveDirty(page)                    \
20301   set_bit(PG_inactive_dirty, &(page)->flags)
20302 #define ClearPageInactiveDirty(page)                  \
20303   clear_bit(PG_inactive_dirty, &(page)->flags)
20304
20305 #define PageInactiveClean(page)                       \
20306   test_bit(PG_inactive_clean, &(page)->flags)
20307 #define SetPageInactiveClean(page)                    \
20308   set_bit(PG_inactive_clean, &(page)->flags)
20309 #define ClearPageInactiveClean(page)                  \
20310   clear_bit(PG_inactive_clean, &(page)->flags)
20311
20312 #ifdef CONFIG_HIGHMEM
20313 #define PageHighMem(page)                             \
20314   test_bit(PG_highmem, &(page)->flags)
20315 #else
20316 /* needed to optimize away at compile time */
20317 #define PageHighMem(page)                 0
20318 #endif
20319
20320 #define SetPageReserved(page)                         \
20321   set_bit(PG_reserved, &(page)->flags)
20322 #define ClearPageReserved(page)                       \
20323   clear_bit(PG_reserved, &(page)->flags)
20324
20325 /* Error return values for the *_nopage functions */
20326 #define NOPAGE_SIGBUS    (NULL)
20327 #define NOPAGE_OOM       ((struct page *) (-1))
20328
20329
20330 /* Various page->flags bits:
20331  *
20332  * PG_reserved is set for a page which must never be
20333  * accessed (which may not even be present).
20334  *
20335  * PG_DMA has been removed, page->zone now tells exactly
20336  * wether the page is suited to do DMAing into.
20337  *
20338  * Multiple processes may "see" the same page. E.g. for
20339  * untouched mappings of /dev/null, all processes see the
```

```
20340  * same page full of zeroes, and text pages of
20341  * executables and shared libraries have only one copy in
20342  * memory, at most, normally.
20343  *
20344  * For the non-reserved pages, page->count denotes a
20345  * reference count.
20346  *   page->count == 0 means the page is free.
20347  *   page->count == 1 means the page is used for exactly
20348  *                 one purpose (e.g. a private data
20349  *                 page of one process).
20350  *
20351  * A page may be used for kmalloc() or anyone else who
20352  * does a __get_free_page(). In this case the page->count
20353  * is at least 1, and all other fields are unused but
20354  * should be 0 or NULL. The management of this page is
20355  * the responsibility of the one who uses it.
20356  *
20357  * The other pages (we may call them "process pages") are
20358  * completely managed by the Linux memory manager: I/O,
20359  * buffers, swapping etc.  The following discussion
20360  * applies only to them.
20361  *
20362  * A page may belong to an inode's memory mapping. In
20363  * this case, page->inode is the pointer to the inode,
20364  * and page->offset is the file offset of the page (not
20365  * necessarily a multiple of PAGE_SIZE).
20366  *
20367  * A page may have buffers allocated to it. In this case,
20368  * page->buffers is a circular list of these buffer
20369  * heads. Else, page->buffers == NULL.
20370  *
20371  * For pages belonging to inodes, the page->count is the
20372  * number of attaches, plus 1 if buffers are allocated to
20373  * the page.
20374  *
20375  * All pages belonging to an inode make up a doubly
20376  * linked list inode->i_pages, using the fields
20377  * page->next and page->prev. (These fields are also used
20378  * for freelist management when page->count==0.)  There
20379  * is also a hash table mapping (inode,offset) to the
20380  * page in memory if present. The lists for this hash
20381  * table use the fields page->next_hash and
20382  * page->pprev_hash.
20383  *
20384  * All process pages can do I/O:
20385  * - inode pages may need to be read from disk,
20386  * - inode pages which have been modified and are
20387  *   MAP_SHARED may need to be written to disk,
20388  * - private pages which have been modified may need to
20389  *   be swapped out to swap space and (later) to be read
20390  *   back into memory.
20391  *
20392  * During disk I/O, PG_locked is used. This bit is set
20393  * before I/O and reset when I/O completes. page->wait is
20394  * a wait queue of all tasks waiting for the I/O on this
20395  * page to complete.  PG_uptodate tells whether the
20396  * page's contents is valid.  When a read completes, the
20397  * page becomes uptodate, unless a disk I/O error
20398  * happened.
20399  *
20400  * For choosing which pages to swap out, inode pages
20401  * carry a PG_referenced bit, which is set any time the
20402  * system accesses that page through the (inode,offset)
20403  * hash table.
20404  *
20405  * PG_skip is used on sparc/sparc64 architectures to
20406  * "skip" certain parts of the address space.
20407  *
20408  * PG_error is set to indicate that an I/O error occurred
20409  * on this page.
20410  *
20411  * PG_arch_1 is an architecture specific page state bit.
20412  * The generic code guarentees that this bit is cleared
20413  * for a page when it first is entered into the page
20414  * cache.  */
20415
20416  extern mem_map_t *mem_map;
20417
20418  /* There is only one page-allocator function, and two
20419   * main namespaces to it. The alloc_page*() variants
20420   * return 'struct page *' and as such can allocate
20421   * highmem pages, the *get*page*() variants return
20422   * virtual kernel addresses to the allocated page(s).  */
20423  extern struct page *FASTCALL(__alloc_pages(zonelist_t *
20424          zonelist, unsigned long order));
20425  extern struct page *alloc_pages_node(int nid,
20426      int gfp_mask, unsigned long order);
20427
20428  #ifndef CONFIG_DISCONTIGMEM
20429  static inline struct page *alloc_pages(int gfp_mask,
20430      unsigned long order)
20431  {
20432    /* Gets optimized away by the compiler.  */
20433    if (order >= MAX_ORDER)
```

```
20434     return NULL;
20435   return __alloc_pages(contig_page_data.node_zonelists +
20436                     (gfp_mask), order);
20437 }
20438 #else                           /* !CONFIG_DISCONTIGMEM */
20439 extern struct page *alloc_pages(int gfp_mask,
20440     unsigned long order);
20441 #endif                          /* !CONFIG_DISCONTIGMEM */
20442
20443 #define alloc_page(gfp_mask) alloc_pages(gfp_mask, 0)
20444
20445 extern unsigned long
20446 FASTCALL(__get_free_pages(int gfp_mask,
20447                     unsigned long order));
20448 extern unsigned long
20449 FASTCALL(get_zeroed_page(int gfp_mask));
20450
20451 #define __get_free_page(gfp_mask)                   \
20452   __get_free_pages((gfp_mask),0)
20453
20454 #define __get_dma_pages(gfp_mask, order)            \
20455   __get_free_pages((gfp_mask) | GFP_DMA,(order))
20456
20457 /* The old interface name will be removed in 2.5: */
20458 #define get_free_page get_zeroed_page
20459
20460 /* There is only one 'core' page-freeing function.  */
20461 extern void FASTCALL(__free_pages(struct page *page,
20462         unsigned long order));
20463 extern void FASTCALL(free_pages(unsigned long addr,
20464         unsigned long order));
20465
20466 #define __free_page(page) __free_pages((page), 0)
20467 #define free_page(addr) free_pages((addr),0)
20468
20469 extern void show_free_areas(void);
20470 extern void show_free_areas_node(pg_data_t * pgdat);
20471
20472 extern void clear_page_tables(struct mm_struct *,
20473     unsigned long, int);
20474
20475 struct page *shmem_nopage(struct vm_area_struct *vma,
20476     unsigned long address, int no_share);
20477 struct file *shmem_file_setup(char *name, loff_t size);
20478 extern void shmem_lock(struct file *file, int lock);
20479 extern int shmem_zero_setup(struct vm_area_struct *);
20480
20481 extern void zap_page_range(struct mm_struct *mm,
20482     unsigned long address, unsigned long size);
20483 extern int copy_page_range(struct mm_struct *dst,
20484     struct mm_struct *src, struct vm_area_struct *vma);
20485 extern int remap_page_range(unsigned long from,
20486     unsigned long to, unsigned long size, pgprot_t prot);
20487 extern int zeromap_page_range(unsigned long from,
20488     unsigned long size, pgprot_t prot);
20489
20490 extern void vmtruncate(struct inode *inode,
20491     loff_t offset);
20492 extern int handle_mm_fault(struct mm_struct *mm,
20493     struct vm_area_struct *vma, unsigned long address,
20494     int write_access);
20495 extern int make_pages_present(unsigned long addr,
20496     unsigned long end);
20497 extern int access_process_vm(struct task_struct *tsk,
20498     unsigned long addr, void *buf, int len, int write);
20499 extern int ptrace_readdata(struct task_struct *tsk,
20500     unsigned long src, char *dst, int len);
20501 extern int ptrace_writedata(struct task_struct *tsk,
20502     char *src, unsigned long dst, int len);
20503
20504 extern int pgt_cache_water[2];
20505 extern int check_pgt_cache(void);
20506
20507 extern void free_area_init(unsigned long *zones_size);
20508 extern void free_area_init_node(int nid,
20509     pg_data_t * pgdat, struct page *pmap,
20510     unsigned long *zones_size,
20511     unsigned long zone_start_paddr,
20512     unsigned long *zholes_size);
20513 extern void mem_init(void);
20514 extern void show_mem(void);
20515 extern void si_meminfo(struct sysinfo *val);
20516 extern void swapin_readahead(swp_entry_t);
20517
20518 /* mmap.c */
20519 extern void lock_vma_mappings(struct vm_area_struct *);
20520 extern void unlock_vma_mappings(struct vm_area_struct *);
20521 extern void insert_vm_struct(struct mm_struct *,
20522     struct vm_area_struct *);
20523 extern void __insert_vm_struct(struct mm_struct *,
20524     struct vm_area_struct *);
20525 extern void build_mmap_avl(struct mm_struct *);
20526 extern void exit_mmap(struct mm_struct *);
20527 extern unsigned long get_unmapped_area(unsigned long,
```

```
20528     unsigned long);
20529
20530 extern unsigned long do_mmap_pgoff(struct file *file,
20531     unsigned long addr, unsigned long len,
20532     unsigned long prot, unsigned long flag,
20533     unsigned long pgoff);
20534
20535 static inline unsigned long do_mmap(struct file *file,
20536     unsigned long addr, unsigned long len,
20537     unsigned long prot, unsigned long flag,
20538     unsigned long offset)
20539 {
20540     unsigned long ret = -EINVAL;
20541     if ((offset + PAGE_ALIGN(len)) < offset)
20542         goto out;
20543     if (!(offset & ~PAGE_MASK))
20544         ret = do_mmap_pgoff(file, addr, len, prot, flag,
20545                             offset >> PAGE_SHIFT);
20546 out:
20547     return ret;
20548 }
20549
20550 extern int do_munmap(struct mm_struct *, unsigned long,
20551     size_t);
20552
20553 extern unsigned long do_brk(unsigned long,
20554     unsigned long);
20555
20556 struct zone_t;
20557 /* filemap.c */
20558 extern void remove_inode_page(struct page *);
20559 extern unsigned long page_unuse(struct page *);
20560 extern void truncate_inode_pages(struct address_space *,
20561     loff_t);
20562
20563 /* generic vm_area_ops exported for stackable file
20564  * systems */
20565 extern int filemap_sync(struct vm_area_struct *,
20566     unsigned long, size_t, unsigned int);
20567 extern struct page *filemap_nopage(
20568     struct vm_area_struct *, unsigned long, int);
20569
20570 /* GFP bitmasks.. */
20571 #define __GFP_WAIT      0x01
20572 #define __GFP_HIGH      0x02
20573 #define __GFP_IO        0x04
20574 #define __GFP_DMA       0x08
20575 #ifdef CONFIG_HIGHMEM
20576 #define __GFP_HIGHMEM   0x10
20577 #else
20578 #define __GFP_HIGHMEM   0x0      /* noop */
20579 #endif
20580 #define __GFP_VM        0x20
20581
20582
20583 #define GFP_BUFFER    (__GFP_HIGH | __GFP_WAIT)
20584 #define GFP_ATOMIC    (__GFP_HIGH)
20585 #define GFP_USER      (             __GFP_WAIT | __GFP_IO)
20586 #define GFP_HIGHUSER  (             __GFP_WAIT | __GFP_IO\
20587                                   | __GFP_HIGHMEM)
20588 #define GFP_KERNEL    (__GFP_HIGH | __GFP_WAIT | __GFP_IO)
20589 #define GFP_NFS       (__GFP_HIGH | __GFP_WAIT | __GFP_IO)
20590 #define GFP_KSWAPD    (                          __GFP_IO)
20591
20592 /* Flag - indicates that the buffer will be suitable for
20593  * DMA.  Ignored on some platforms, used as appropriate
20594  * on others */
20595
20596 #define GFP_DMA         __GFP_DMA
20597
20598 /* Flag - indicates that the buffer can be taken from
20599  * high memory which is not permanently mapped by the
20600  * kernel */
20601
20602 #define GFP_HIGHMEM     __GFP_HIGHMEM
20603
20604 /* vma is the first one with address < vma->vm_end, and
20605  * even address < vma->vm_start. Have to extend vma. */
20606 static inline int expand_stack(struct vm_area_struct
20607     *vma, unsigned long address)
20608 {
20609     unsigned long grow;
20610
20611     address &= PAGE_MASK;
20612     grow = (vma->vm_start - address) >> PAGE_SHIFT;
20613     if (vma->vm_end - address >
20614         current->rlim[RLIMIT_STACK].rlim_cur
20615         || ((vma->vm_mm->total_vm + grow) << PAGE_SHIFT) >
20616         current->rlim[RLIMIT_AS].rlim_cur)
20617         return -ENOMEM;
20618     vma->vm_start = address;
20619     vma->vm_pgoff -= grow;
20620     vma->vm_mm->total_vm += grow;
20621     if (vma->vm_flags & VM_LOCKED)
```

```
20622       vma->vm_mm->locked_vm += grow;
20623     return 0;
20624 }
20625
20626 /* Look up the first VMA which satisfies  addr < vm_end,
20627  * NULL if none. */
20628 extern struct vm_area_struct *find_vma(
20629    struct mm_struct *mm, unsigned long addr);
20630 extern struct vm_area_struct *find_vma_prev(
20631    struct mm_struct *mm, unsigned long addr,
20632    struct vm_area_struct **pprev);
20633
20634 /* Look up the first VMA which intersects the interval
20635  * start_addr..end_addr-1, NULL if none.  Assume
20636  * start_addr < end_addr. */
20637 static inline struct vm_area_struct *
20638 find_vma_intersection(struct mm_struct *mm,
20639      unsigned long start_addr, unsigned long end_addr)
20640 {
20641    struct vm_area_struct *vma = find_vma(mm, start_addr);
20642
20643    if (vma && end_addr <= vma->vm_start)
20644      vma = NULL;
20645    return vma;
20646 }
20647
20648 extern struct vm_area_struct *find_extend_vma(struct
20649      mm_struct *mm, unsigned long addr);
20650
20651 #define buffer_under_min()                              \
20652    (atomic_read(&buffermem_pages) * 100 <               \
20653      buffer_mem.min_percent * num_physpages)
20654 #define pgcache_under_min()                             \
20655    (atomic_read(&page_cache_size) * 100 <               \
20656      page_cache.min_percent * num_physpages)
20657
20658 #endif                              /* __KERNEL__ */
20659
20660 #endif
```

include/linux/mmzone.h

```
20661 #ifndef _LINUX_MMZONE_H
20662 #define _LINUX_MMZONE_H
20663
20664 #ifdef __KERNEL__
20665 #ifndef __ASSEMBLY__
20666
20667 #include <linux/config.h>
20668 #include <linux/spinlock.h>
20669 #include <linux/list.h>
20670
20671 /* Free memory management - zoned buddy allocator.  */
20672
20673 #define MAX_ORDER 10
20674
20675 typedef struct free_area_struct {
20676    struct list_head free_list;
20677    unsigned int *map;
20678 } free_area_t;
20679
20680 struct pglist_data;
20681
20682 typedef struct zone_struct {
20683    /* Commonly accessed fields: */
20684    spinlock_t lock;
20685    unsigned long offset;
20686    unsigned long free_pages;
20687    unsigned long inactive_clean_pages;
20688    unsigned long inactive_dirty_pages;
20689    unsigned long pages_min, pages_low, pages_high;
20690
20691    /* free areas of different sizes */
20692    struct list_head inactive_clean_list;
20693    free_area_t free_area[MAX_ORDER];
20694
20695    /* rarely used fields: */
20696    char *name;
20697    unsigned long size;
20698    /* Discontig memory support fields.  */
20699    struct pglist_data *zone_pgdat;
20700    unsigned long zone_start_paddr;
20701    unsigned long zone_start_mapnr;
20702    struct page *zone_mem_map;
20703 } zone_t;
20704
20705 #define ZONE_DMA           0
20706 #define ZONE_NORMAL        1
20707 #define ZONE_HIGHMEM       2
20708 #define MAX_NR_ZONES       3
20709
20710 /* One allocation request operates on a zonelist. A
20711  * zonelist is a list of zones, the first one is the
20712  * 'goal' of the allocation, the other zones are fallback
20713  * zones, in decreasing priority.
```

```
20714  *
20715  * Right now a zonelist takes up less than a
20716  * cacheline. We never modify it apart from boot-up, and
20717  * only a few indices are used, so despite the zonelist
20718  * table being relatively big, the cache footprint of
20719  * this construct is very small.  */
20720 typedef struct zonelist_struct {
20721   zone_t *zones[MAX_NR_ZONES + 1];      // NULL delimited
20722   int gfp_mask;
20723 } zonelist_t;
20724
20725 #define NR_GFPINDEX            0x100
20726
20727 struct bootmem_data;
20728 typedef struct pglist_data {
20729   zone_t node_zones[MAX_NR_ZONES];
20730   zonelist_t node_zonelists[NR_GFPINDEX];
20731   struct page *node_mem_map;
20732   unsigned long *valid_addr_bitmap;
20733   struct bootmem_data *bdata;
20734   unsigned long node_start_paddr;
20735   unsigned long node_start_mapnr;
20736   unsigned long node_size;
20737   int node_id;
20738   struct pglist_data *node_next;
20739 } pg_data_t;
20740
20741 extern int numnodes;
20742 extern pg_data_t *pgdat_list;
20743
20744 #define memclass(pgzone, tzone)                       \
20745   (((pgzone)->zone_pgdat == (tzone)->zone_pgdat)      \
20746    && (((pgzone) - (pgzone)->zone_pgdat->node_zones) <= \
20747       ((tzone) - (pgzone)->zone_pgdat->node_zones)))
20748
20749 /* The following two are not meant for general
20750  * usage. They are here as prototypes for the discontig
20751  * memory code.  */
20752 struct page;
20753 extern void show_free_areas_core(pg_data_t * pgdat);
20754 extern void free_area_init_core(int nid,
20755     pg_data_t * pgdat, struct page **gmap,
20756     unsigned long *zones_size, unsigned long paddr,
20757     unsigned long *zholes_size, struct page *pmap);
20758
20759 extern pg_data_t contig_page_data;
20760
20761 #ifndef CONFIG_DISCONTIGMEM
20762
20763 #define NODE_DATA(nid)            (&contig_page_data)
20764 #define NODE_MEM_MAP(nid)         mem_map
20765
20766 #else                             /* !CONFIG_DISCONTIGMEM */
20767
20768 #include <asm/mmzone.h>
20769
20770 #endif                            /* !CONFIG_DISCONTIGMEM */
20771
20772 #define MAP_ALIGN(x)                                   \
20773 (((((x) % sizeof(mem_map_t)) == 0)                     \
20774   ? (x)                                                \
20775   : ((x) + sizeof(mem_map_t) - ((x) % sizeof(mem_map_t))))
20776
20777 #endif                            /* !__ASSEMBLY__ */
20778 #endif                            /* __KERNEL__ */
20779 #endif                            /* _LINUX_MMZONE_H */
```

include/linux/modsetver.h

```
20780 /* Symbol versioning nastiness.  */
20781
20782 #define __SYMBOL_VERSION(x)       __ver_ ## x
20783 #define __VERSIONED_SYMBOL2(x,v)  x ## _R ## v
20784 #define __VERSIONED_SYMBOL1(x,v)  __VERSIONED_SYMBOL2(x,v)
20785 #define __VERSIONED_SYMBOL(x)                          \
20786   __VERSIONED_SYMBOL1(x,__SYMBOL_VERSION(x))
20787
20788 #ifndef _set_ver
20789 #define _set_ver(x)               __VERSIONED_SYMBOL(x)
20790 #endif
```

include/linux/module.h

```
20791 /*
20792  * Dynamic loading of modules into the kernel.
20793  *
20794  * Rewritten by Richard Henderson <rth@tamu.edu> Dec 1996
20795  */
20796
20797 #ifndef _LINUX_MODULE_H
20798 #define _LINUX_MODULE_H
20799
20800 #include <linux/config.h>
20801 #include <linux/spinlock.h>
20802 #include <linux/list.h>
```

```
20803
20804 #ifdef __GENKSYMS__
20805 #  define _set_ver(sym) sym
20806 #  undef  MODVERSIONS
20807 #  define MODVERSIONS
20808 #else                              /* ! __GENKSYMS__ */
20809 # if !defined(MODVERSIONS) && defined(EXPORT_SYMTAB)
20810 #   define _set_ver(sym) sym
20811 #   include <linux/modversions.h>
20812 # endif
20813 #endif                             /* __GENKSYMS__ */
20814
20815 #include <asm/atomic.h>
20816
20817 /* Don't need to bring in all of uaccess.h just for this
20818  * decl.  */
20819 struct exception_table_entry;
20820
20821 /* Used by get_kernel_syms, which is obsolete.  */
20822 struct kernel_sym {
20823   unsigned long value;
20824   char name[60];  /* should have been 64-sizeof(long); oh
20825                    * well */
20826 };
20827
20828 struct module_symbol {
20829   unsigned long value;
20830   const char *name;
20831 };
20832
20833 struct module_ref {
20834   struct module *dep;         /* "parent" pointer */
20835   struct module *ref;         /* "child" pointer */
20836   struct module_ref *next_ref;
20837 };
20838
20839 /* TBD */
20840 struct module_persist;
20841
20842 struct module {
20843   unsigned long size_of_struct; /* == sizeof(module) */
20844   struct module *next;
20845   const char *name;
20846   unsigned long size;
20847
20848   union {
20849     atomic_t usecount;
20850     long pad;
20851   } uc;           /* Needs to keep its size - so says rth */
20852
20853   unsigned long flags;            /* AUTOCLEAN et al */
20854
20855   unsigned nsyms;
20856   unsigned ndeps;
20857
20858   struct module_symbol *syms;
20859   struct module_ref *deps;
20860   struct module_ref *refs;
20861   int (*init) (void);
20862   void (*cleanup) (void);
20863   const struct exception_table_entry *ex_table_start;
20864   const struct exception_table_entry *ex_table_end;
20865 #ifdef __alpha__
20866   unsigned long gp;
20867 #endif
20868   /* Members past this point are extensions to the basic
20869    * module support and are optional.  Use
20870    * mod_member_present() to examine them.  */
20871   const struct module_persist *persist_start;
20872   const struct module_persist *persist_end;
20873   int (*can_unload) (void);
20874   int runsize;                    /* In modutils, not
20875                                    * currently used */
20876   const char *kallsyms_start;     /* All symbols for
20877                                    * kernel debugging */
20878   const char *kallsyms_end;
20879   const char *archdata_start;     /* arch specific data
20880                                    * for module */
20881   const char *archdata_end;
20882   const char *kernel_data;        /* Reserved for kernel
20883                                    * internal use */
20884 };
20885
20886 struct module_info {
20887   unsigned long addr;
20888   unsigned long size;
20889   unsigned long flags;
20890   long usecount;
20891 };
20892
20893 /* Bits of module.flags.  */
20894 #define MOD_UNINITIALIZED       0
20895 #define MOD_RUNNING             1
20896 #define MOD_DELETED             2
```

```
20897 #define MOD_AUTOCLEAN          4
20898 #define MOD_VISITED           8
20899 #define MOD_USED_ONCE         16
20900 #define MOD_JUST_FREED        32
20901 #define MOD_INITIALIZING      64
20902
20903 /* Values for query_module's which. */
20904 #define QM_MODULES     1
20905 #define QM_DEPS        2
20906 #define QM_REFS        3
20907 #define QM_SYMBOLS     4
20908 #define QM_INFO        5
20909
20910 /* Can the module be queried? */
20911 #define MOD_CAN_QUERY(mod)                              \
20912   (((mod)->flags & (MOD_RUNNING | MOD_INITIALIZING)) && \
20913   !((mod)->flags & MOD_DELETED))
20914
20915 /* When struct module is extended, we must test whether
20916  * the new member is present in the header received from
20917  * insmod before we can use it. This function returns
20918  * true if the member is present.  */
20919 #define mod_member_present(mod,member)                  \
20920   ((unsigned long)(&((struct module *)0L)->member + 1)  \
20921         <= (mod)->size_of_struct)
20922
20923 /* Check if an address p with number of entries n is
20924  * within the body of module m */
20925 #define mod_bound(p, n, m)                              \
20926   ((unsigned long)(p) >=                                \
20927   ((unsigned long)(m) + ((m)->size_of_struct)) &&       \
20928   (unsigned long)((p)+(n)) <=                            \
20929   (unsigned long)(m) + (m)->size)
20930
20931 /* Backwards compatibility definition.  */
20932 #define GET_USE_COUNT(module)                           \
20933   (atomic_read(&(module)->uc.usecount))
20934
20935 /* Poke the use count of a module.  */
20936
20937 #define __MOD_INC_USE_COUNT(mod)                        \
20938   (atomic_inc(&(mod)->uc.usecount),                     \
20939   (mod)->flags |= MOD_VISITED|MOD_USED_ONCE)
20940 #define __MOD_DEC_USE_COUNT(mod)                        \
20941   (atomic_dec(&(mod)->uc.usecount),                     \
20942   (mod)->flags |= MOD_VISITED)
20943 #define __MOD_IN_USE(mod)                               \
20944   (mod_member_present((mod), can_unload) &&             \
20945   (mod)->can_unload                                     \
20946   ? (mod)->can_unload()                                 \
20947   : atomic_read(&(mod)->uc.usecount))
20948
20949 /* Indirect stringification.  */
20950
20951 #define __MODULE_STRING_1(x)     #x
20952 #define __MODULE_STRING(x)       __MODULE_STRING_1(x)
20953
20954 /* Generic inter module communication.
20955  *
20956  * NOTE: This interface is intended for small amounts of
20957  * data that are passed between two objects and either or
20958  * both of the objects might be compiled as modules.  Do
20959  * not over use this interface.
20960  *
20961  * If more than two objects need to communicate then you
20962  * probably need a specific interface instead of abusing
20963  * this generic interface.  If both objects are *always*
20964  * built into the kernel then a global extern variable is
20965  * good enough, you do not need this interface.
20966  *
20967  * Keith Owens
20968  * <kaos@ocs.com.au> 28 Oct 2000. */
20969
20970 #ifdef __KERNEL__
20971 #define HAVE_INTER_MODULE
20972 extern void inter_module_register(const char *,
20973     struct module *, const void *);
20974 extern void inter_module_unregister(const char *);
20975 extern const void *inter_module_get(const char *);
20976 extern const void *inter_module_get_request(const char *,
20977     const char *);
20978 extern void inter_module_put(const char *);
20979
20980 struct inter_module_entry {
20981   struct list_head list;
20982   const char *im_name;
20983   struct module *owner;
20984   const void *userdata;
20985 };
20986
20987 extern int try_inc_mod_count(struct module *mod);
20988 #endif                          /* __KERNEL__ */
20989
20990 #if defined(MODULE) && !defined(__GENKSYMS__)
```

```
20991
20992 /* Embedded module documentation macros.  */
20993
20994 /* For documentation purposes only.  */
20995
20996 #define MODULE_AUTHOR(name)                          \
20997 const char __module_author[]                         \
20998 __attribute__((section(".modinfo"))) = "author=" name
20999
21000 #define MODULE_DESCRIPTION(desc)                     \
21001 const char __module_description[]                    \
21002 __attribute__((section(".modinfo"))) =               \
21003  "description=" desc
21004
21005 /* Could potentially be used by kmod...  */
21006 #define MODULE_SUPPORTED_DEVICE(dev)                 \
21007 const char __module_device[]                         \
21008 __attribute__((section(".modinfo"))) = "device=" dev
21009
21010 /* Used to verify parameters given to the module.  The
21011  * TYPE arg should be a string in the following format:
21012  * [min[-max]]{b,h,i,l,s} The MIN and MAX specifiers
21013  * delimit the length of the array.  If MAX is omitted,
21014  * it defaults to MIN; if both are omitted, the default
21015  * is 1. The final character is a type specifier: b
21016  * byte h       short i int l   long s  string */
21017
21018 #define MODULE_PARM(var,type)                        \
21019 const char __module_parm_##var[]                     \
21020 __attribute__((section(".modinfo"))) =               \
21021 "parm_" __MODULE_STRING(var) "=" type
21022
21023 #define MODULE_PARM_DESC(var,desc)                   \
21024 const char __module_parm_desc_##var[]                \
21025 __attribute__((section(".modinfo"))) =               \
21026 "parm_desc_" __MODULE_STRING(var) "=" desc
21027
21028 /* MODULE_DEVICE_TABLE exports information about devices
21029  * currently supported by this module.  A device type,
21030  * such as PCI, is a C-like identifier passed as the
21031  * first arg to this macro.  The second macro arg is the
21032  * variable containing the device information being made
21033  * public.
21034  *
21035  * The following is a list of known device types (arg 1),
21036  * and the C types which are to be passed as arg 2.
21037  * pci - struct pci_device_id - List of PCI ids supported
21038  * by this module
21039  * isapnp - struct isapnp_device_id - List of ISA PnP ids
21040  * supported by this module
21041  * usb - struct usb_device_id - List of USB ids supported
21042  * by this module */
21043 #define MODULE_GENERIC_TABLE(gtype,name)             \
21044 static const unsigned long __module_##gtype##_size   \
21045   __attribute__ ((unused)) = sizeof(struct gtype##_id); \
21046 static const struct gtype##_id *                     \
21047 __module_##gtype##_table __attribute__ ((unused)) = name
21048 #define MODULE_DEVICE_TABLE(type,name)               \
21049   MODULE_GENERIC_TABLE(type##_device,name)
21050 /* not put to .modinfo section to avoid section type
21051  * conflicts */
21052
21053 /* The attributes of a section are set the first time
21054  * the section is seen; we want .modinfo to not be
21055  * allocated.  */
21056 __asm__(".section .modinfo\n\t.previous");
21057
21058 /* Define the module variable, and usage macros.  */
21059 extern struct module __this_module;
21060
21061 #define THIS_MODULE                 (&__this_module)
21062 #define MOD_INC_USE_COUNT                            \
21063   __MOD_INC_USE_COUNT(THIS_MODULE)
21064 #define MOD_DEC_USE_COUNT                            \
21065   __MOD_DEC_USE_COUNT(THIS_MODULE)
21066 #define MOD_IN_USE              __MOD_IN_USE(THIS_MODULE)
21067
21068 #include <linux/version.h>
21069 static const char __module_kernel_version[]
21070     __attribute__ ((section(".modinfo"))) =
21071     "kernel_version=" UTS_RELEASE;
21072 #ifdef MODVERSIONS
21073 static const char __module_using_checksums[]
21074     __attribute__ ((section(".modinfo"))) =
21075     "using_checksums=1";
21076 #endif
21077
21078 #else                               /* MODULE */
21079
21080 #define MODULE_AUTHOR(name)
21081 #define MODULE_DESCRIPTION(desc)
21082 #define MODULE_SUPPORTED_DEVICE(name)
21083 #define MODULE_PARM(var,type)
21084 #define MODULE_PARM_DESC(var,desc)
```

```
21085 #define MODULE_GENERIC_TABLE(gtype,name)
21086 #define MODULE_DEVICE_TABLE(type,name)
21087
21088 #ifndef __GENKSYMS__
21089
21090 #define THIS_MODULE            NULL
21091 #define MOD_INC_USE_COUNT      do { } while (0)
21092 #define MOD_DEC_USE_COUNT      do { } while (0)
21093 #define MOD_IN_USE             1
21094
21095 extern struct module *module_list;
21096
21097 #endif                         /* !__GENKSYMS__ */
21098
21099 #endif                         /* MODULE */
21100
21101 /* Export a symbol either from the kernel or a module.
21102  *
21103  * In the kernel, the symbol is added to the kernel's
21104  * global symbol table.
21105  *
21106  * In a module, it controls which variables are
21107  * exported.  If no variables are explicitly exported,
21108  * the action is controled by the insmod -[xX] flags.
21109  * Otherwise, only the variables listed are exported.
21110  * This obviates the need for the old register_symtab()
21111  * function.  */
21112
21113 #if defined(__GENKSYMS__)
21114
21115 /* We want the EXPORT_SYMBOL tag left intact for
21116  * recognition.  */
21117
21118 #elif !defined(AUTOCONF_INCLUDED)
21119
21120 #define __EXPORT_SYMBOL(sym,str)                           \
21121   error config_must_be_included_before_module
21122 #define EXPORT_SYMBOL(var)                                 \
21123   error config_must_be_included_before_module
21124 #define EXPORT_SYMBOL_NOVERS(var)                          \
21125   error config_must_be_included_before_module
21126
21127 #elif !defined(CONFIG_MODULES)
21128
21129 #define __EXPORT_SYMBOL(sym,str)
21130 #define EXPORT_SYMBOL(var)
21131 #define EXPORT_SYMBOL_NOVERS(var)
21132
21133 #else
21134
21135 #define __EXPORT_SYMBOL(sym, str)                          \
21136 const char __kstrtab_##sym[]                               \
21137 __attribute__((section(".kstrtab"))) = str;               \
21138 const struct module_symbol __ksymtab_##sym                \
21139 __attribute__((section("__ksymtab"))) =                   \
21140 { (unsigned long)&sym, __kstrtab_##sym }
21141
21142 #if defined(MODVERSIONS) || !defined(CONFIG_MODVERSIONS)
21143 #define EXPORT_SYMBOL(var)                                 \
21144   __EXPORT_SYMBOL(var, __MODULE_STRING(var))
21145 #else
21146 #define EXPORT_SYMBOL(var)                                 \
21147   __EXPORT_SYMBOL(var,                                     \
21148     __MODULE_STRING(__VERSIONED_SYMBOL(var)))
21149 #endif
21150
21151 #define EXPORT_SYMBOL_NOVERS(var)                          \
21152   __EXPORT_SYMBOL(var, __MODULE_STRING(var))
21153
21154 #endif                         /* __GENKSYMS__ */
21155
21156 #ifdef MODULE
21157 /* Force a module to export no symbols.  */
21158 #define EXPORT_NO_SYMBOLS                                  \
21159   __asm__(".section __ksymtab\n.previous")
21160 #else
21161 #define EXPORT_NO_SYMBOLS
21162 #endif                         /* MODULE */
21163
21164 #ifdef CONFIG_MODULES
21165 #define SET_MODULE_OWNER(some_struct)                      \
21166   do { (some_struct)->owner = THIS_MODULE; } while (0)
21167 #else
21168 #define SET_MODULE_OWNER(some_struct) do { } while (0)
21169 #endif
21170
21171 #endif                         /* _LINUX_MODULE_H */
```

include/linux/msg.h

```
21172 #ifndef _LINUX_MSG_H
21173 #define _LINUX_MSG_H
21174
21175 #include <linux/ipc.h>
21176
```

```
21177 /* ipcs ctl commands */
21178 #define MSG_STAT 11
21179 #define MSG_INFO 12
21180
21181 /* msgrcv options */
21182 #define MSG_NOERROR    010000  /* no error if message
21183                                * is too big */
21184 #define MSG_EXCEPT     020000  /* recv any msg except
21185                                * of specified type. */
21186
21187 /* Obsolete, used only for backwards compatibility and
21188  * libc5 compiles */
21189 struct msqid_ds {
21190   struct ipc_perm msg_perm;
21191   struct msg *msg_first;       /* first message on
21192                                * queue,unused  */
21193   struct msg *msg_last;        /* last message in
21194                                * queue,unused */
21195   __kernel_time_t msg_stime;   /* last msgsnd time */
21196   __kernel_time_t msg_rtime;   /* last msgrcv time */
21197   __kernel_time_t msg_ctime;   /* last change time */
21198   unsigned long msg_lcbytes;   /* Reuse junk fields for
21199                                * 32 bit */
21200   unsigned long msg_lqbytes;   /* ditto */
21201   unsigned short msg_cbytes;   /* current number of
21202                                * bytes on queue */
21203   unsigned short msg_qnum;     /* number of messages in
21204                                * queue */
21205   unsigned short msg_qbytes;   /* max number of bytes
21206                                * on queue */
21207   __kernel_ipc_pid_t msg_lspid; /* pid of last msgsnd */
21208   __kernel_ipc_pid_t msg_lrpid; /* last receive pid */
21209 };
21210
21211 /* Include the definition of msqid64_ds */
21212 #include <asm/msgbuf.h>
21213
21214 /* message buffer for msgsnd and msgrcv calls */
21215 struct msgbuf {
21216   long mtype;                  /* type of message */
21217   char mtext[1];               /* message text */
21218 };
21219
21220 /* buffer for msgctl calls IPC_INFO, MSG_INFO */
21221 struct msginfo {
21222   int msgpool;
21223   int msgmap;
```

```
21224   int msgmax;
21225   int msgmnb;
21226   int msgmni;
21227   int msgssz;
21228   int msgtql;
21229   unsigned short msgseg;
21230 };
21231
21232 #define MSGMNI    16 /* <= IPCMNI */  /* max # of msg
21233                                      * queue
21234                                      * identifiers */
21235 #define MSGMAX  8192 /* <= INT_MAX */ /* max size of
21236                                      * message
21237                                      * (bytes) */
21238 #define MSGMNB 16384 /* <= INT_MAX */ /* default max size
21239                                      * of a message
21240                                      * queue */
21241
21242 /* unused */
21243 #define MSGPOOL (MSGMNI*MSGMNB/1024)    /* size in
21244                                        * kilobytes of
21245                                        * message pool*/
21246 #define MSGTQL   MSGMNB          /* number of system
21247                                 * message headers */
21248 #define MSGMAP   MSGMNB          /* number of entries in
21249                                 * message map */
21250 #define MSGSSZ  16               /* message segment size*/
21251 /* max no.  of segments */
21252 #define __MSGSEG ((MSGPOOL*1024)/ MSGSSZ)
21253 #define MSGSEG (__MSGSEG <= 0xffff ? __MSGSEG : 0xffff)
21254
21255 #ifdef __KERNEL__
21256
21257 asmlinkage long sys_msgget(key_t key, int msgflg);
21258 asmlinkage long sys_msgsnd(int msqid,
21259     struct msgbuf *msgp, size_t msgsz, int msgflg);
21260 asmlinkage long sys_msgrcv(int msqid,
21261     struct msgbuf *msgp, size_t msgsz, long msgtyp,
21262     int msgflg);
21263 asmlinkage long sys_msgctl(int msqid, int cmd,
21264     struct msqid_ds *buf);
21265
21266 #endif                           /* __KERNEL__ */
21267
21268 #endif                           /* _LINUX_MSG_H */
```

include/linux/notifier.h

```
21269 /*
21270  * Routines to manage notifier chains for passing status
21271  * changes to any interested routines. We need this
21272  * instead of hard coded call lists so that modules can
21273  * poke their nose into the innards. The network devices
21274  * needed them so here they are for the rest of you.
21275  *
21276  *                    Alan Cox <Alan.Cox@linux.org>
21277  */
21278
21279 #ifndef _LINUX_NOTIFIER_H
21280 #define _LINUX_NOTIFIER_H
21281 #include <linux/errno.h>
21282
21283 struct notifier_block {
21284   int (*notifier_call) (struct notifier_block * self,
21285                          unsigned long, void *);
21286   struct notifier_block *next;
21287   int priority;
21288 };
21289
21290
21291 #ifdef __KERNEL__
21292
21293 extern int
21294 notifier_chain_register(struct notifier_block **list,
21295                          struct notifier_block *n);
21296 extern int
21297 notifier_chain_unregister(struct notifier_block **nl,
21298                            struct notifier_block *n);
21299 extern int notifier_call_chain(struct notifier_block **n,
21300    unsigned long val, void *v);
21301
21302 #define NOTIFY_DONE       0x0000  /* Don't care */
21303 #define NOTIFY_OK         0x0001  /* Suits me */
21304 #define NOTIFY_STOP_MASK  0x8000  /* Don't call further
21305                                    */
21306 /* Bad/Veto action */
21307 #define NOTIFY_BAD        (NOTIFY_STOP_MASK|0x0002)
21308
21309 /* Declared notifiers so far. I can imagine quite a few
21310  * more chains over time (eg laptop power reset chains,
21311  * reboot chain (to clean device units up), device
21312  * [un]mount chain, module load/unload chain, low memory
21313  * chain, screenblank chain (for plug in modular
21314  * screenblankers) VC switch chains (for loadable kernel
21315  * svgalib VC switch helpers) etc...  */
21316
21317 /* netdevice notifier chain */
21318 #define NETDEV_UP         0x0001  /* For now you can't
21319                                    * veto a device up/down
21320                                    */
21321 #define NETDEV_DOWN       0x0002
21322 #define NETDEV_REBOOT     0x0003  /* Tell a protocol stack
21323                                    * a network interface
21324                                    * detected a hardware
21325                                    * crash and restarted -
21326                                    * we can use this eg to
21327                                    * kick tcp sessions
21328                                    * once done */
21329 #define NETDEV_CHANGE     0x0004  /* Notify device state
21330                                    * change */
21331 #define NETDEV_REGISTER 0x0005
21332 #define NETDEV_UNREGISTER      0x0006
21333 #define NETDEV_CHANGEMTU       0x0007
21334 #define NETDEV_CHANGEADDR      0x0008
21335 #define NETDEV_GOING_DOWN      0x0009
21336 #define NETDEV_CHANGENAME      0x000A
21337
21338 #define SYS_DOWN          0x0001  /* Notify of system down
21339                                    */
21340 #define SYS_RESTART       SYS_DOWN
21341 #define SYS_HALT          0x0002  /* Notify of system halt
21342                                    */
21343 #define SYS_POWER_OFF     0x0003  /* Notify of system
21344                                    * power off */
21345
21346 #endif                          /* __KERNEL__ */
21347 #endif                          /* _LINUX_NOTIFIER_H */
```

include/linux/pagemap.h

```
21348 #ifndef _LINUX_PAGEMAP_H
21349 #define _LINUX_PAGEMAP_H
21350
21351 /*
21352  * Page-mapping primitive inline functions
21353  *
21354  * Copyright 1995 Linus Torvalds
21355  */
21356
21357 #include <linux/mm.h>
21358 #include <linux/fs.h>
21359 #include <linux/list.h>
21360
```

```
21361 #include <asm/system.h>
21362 #include <asm/pgtable.h>
21363 #include <linux/highmem.h>
21364
21365 /* The page cache can done in larger chunks than one
21366  * page, because it allows for more efficient throughput
21367  * (it can then be mapped into user space in smaller
21368  * chunks for same flexibility).
21369  *
21370  * Or rather, it _will_ be done in larger chunks.  */
21371 #define PAGE_CACHE_SHIFT     PAGE_SHIFT
21372 #define PAGE_CACHE_SIZE      PAGE_SIZE
21373 #define PAGE_CACHE_MASK      PAGE_MASK
21374 #define PAGE_CACHE_ALIGN(addr)                       \
21375   (((addr)+PAGE_CACHE_SIZE-1)&PAGE_CACHE_MASK)
21376
21377 #define page_cache_get(x)     get_page(x)
21378 #define page_cache_alloc()    alloc_pages(GFP_HIGHUSER, 0)
21379 #define page_cache_free(x)      __free_page(x)
21380 #define page_cache_release(x)   __free_page(x)
21381
21382 /* From a kernel address, get the "struct page *" */
21383 #define page_cache_entry(x)     virt_to_page(x)
21384
21385 extern unsigned int page_hash_bits;
21386 #define PAGE_HASH_BITS (page_hash_bits)
21387 #define PAGE_HASH_SIZE (1 << PAGE_HASH_BITS)
21388
21389 /* # of pages currently in the hash table */
21390 extern atomic_t page_cache_size;
21391 extern struct page **page_hash_table;
21392
21393 extern void page_cache_init(unsigned long);
21394
21395 /* We use a power-of-two hash table to avoid a modulus,
21396  * and get a reasonable hash by knowing roughly how the
21397  * inode pointer and indexes are distributed (ie, we
21398  * roughly know which bits are "significant")
21399  *
21400  * For the time being it will work for struct
21401  * address_space too (most of them sitting inside the
21402  * inodes). We might want to change it later.  */
21403 extern inline unsigned long _page_hashfn(struct
21404     address_space *mapping, unsigned long index)
21405 {
21406 #define i (((unsigned long) mapping) /                \
```

```
21407    (sizeof(struct inode) & ~ (sizeof(struct inode) - 1)))
21408 #define s(x) ((x)+((x)>>PAGE_HASH_BITS))
21409    return s(i + index) & (PAGE_HASH_SIZE - 1);
21410 #undef i
21411 #undef s
21412 }
21413
21414 #define page_hash(mapping,index)                     \
21415   (page_hash_table+_page_hashfn(mapping,index))
21416
21417 extern struct page *
21418 __find_get_page(struct address_space *mapping,
21419   unsigned long offset, struct page **hash);
21420 extern struct page *
21421 __find_lock_page(struct address_space *mapping,
21422   unsigned long index, struct page **hash);
21423 extern void lock_page(struct page *page);
21424 #define find_lock_page(mapping, index)               \
21425   __find_lock_page(mapping, index,                   \
21426                 page_hash(mapping, index))
21427
21428 extern void __add_page_to_hash_queue(struct page *page,
21429     struct page **p);
21430
21431 extern void add_to_page_cache(struct page *page,
21432     struct address_space *mapping, unsigned long index);
21433 extern void add_to_page_cache_locked(struct page *page,
21434     struct address_space *mapping, unsigned long index);
21435
21436 extern void ___wait_on_page(struct page *);
21437
21438 extern inline void wait_on_page(struct page *page)
21439 {
21440    if (PageLocked(page))
21441      ___wait_on_page(page);
21442 }
21443
21444 extern struct page *
21445 grab_cache_page(struct address_space *, unsigned long);
21446
21447 typedef int filler_t(void *, struct page *);
21448
21449 extern struct page *
21450 read_cache_page(struct address_space *,
21451                 unsigned long, filler_t *, void *);
21452 #endif
```

include/linux/personality.h

```
21453 #ifndef _PERSONALITY_H
21454 #define _PERSONALITY_H
21455
21456 #include <linux/linkage.h>
21457 #include <linux/ptrace.h>
21458 #include <asm/current.h>
21459
21460 /* Flags for bug emulation. These occupy the top three
21461  * bytes. */
21462 #define STICKY_TIMEOUTS     0x4000000
21463 #define WHOLE_SECONDS       0x2000000
21464 #define ADDR_LIMIT_32BIT    0x0800000
21465
21466 /* Personality types. These go in the low byte. Avoid
21467  * using the top bit, it will conflict with error
21468  * returns. */
21469 #define PER_MASK         (0x00ff)
21470 #define PER_LINUX        (0x0000)
21471 #define PER_LINUX_32BIT  (0x0000 | ADDR_LIMIT_32BIT)
21472 #define PER_SVR4         (0x0001 | STICKY_TIMEOUTS)
21473 #define PER_SVR3         (0x0002 | STICKY_TIMEOUTS)
21474 #define PER_SCOSVR3      (0x0003 | STICKY_TIMEOUTS |  \
21475                                   WHOLE_SECONDS)
21476 #define PER_WYSEV386     (0x0004 | STICKY_TIMEOUTS)
21477 #define PER_ISCR4        (0x0005 | STICKY_TIMEOUTS)
21478 #define PER_BSD          (0x0006)
21479 #define PER_SUNOS        (PER_BSD | STICKY_TIMEOUTS)
21480 #define PER_XENIX        (0x0007 | STICKY_TIMEOUTS)
21481 #define PER_LINUX32      (0x0008)
21482 /* IRIX5 32-bit */
21483 #define PER_IRIX32       (0x0009 | STICKY_TIMEOUTS)
21484 /* IRIX6 new 32-bit */
21485 #define PER_IRIXN32      (0x000a | STICKY_TIMEOUTS)
21486 /* IRIX6 64-bit */
21487 #define PER_IRIX64       (0x000b | STICKY_TIMEOUTS)
21488 #define PER_RISCOS       (0x000c)
21489 #define PER_SOLARIS      (0x000d | STICKY_TIMEOUTS)
21490
21491 /* Prototype for an lcall7 syscall handler. */
21492 typedef void (*lcall7_func) (int, struct pt_regs *);
21493
21494
21495 /* Description of an execution domain - personality range
21496  * supported, lcall7 syscall handler, start up / shut
21497  * down functions etc.  N.B. The name and lcall7 handler
21498  * must be where they are since the offset of the handler
21499  * is hard coded in kernel/sys_call.S. */
```

```
21500 struct exec_domain {
21501   const char *name;
21502   lcall7_func handler;
21503   unsigned char pers_low, pers_high;
21504   unsigned long *signal_map;
21505   unsigned long *signal_invmap;
21506   struct module *module;
21507   struct exec_domain *next;
21508 };
21509
21510 extern struct exec_domain default_exec_domain;
21511
21512 extern int register_exec_domain(struct exec_domain *it);
21513 extern int unregister_exec_domain(struct exec_domain
21514     *it);
21515 #define put_exec_domain(it)                           \
21516   if (it && it->module) __MOD_DEC_USE_COUNT(it->module);
21517 #define get_exec_domain(it)                           \
21518   if (it && it->module) __MOD_INC_USE_COUNT(it->module);
21519 extern void __set_personality(unsigned long personality);
21520 #define set_personality(pers) do {                    \
21521         if (current->personality != pers)             \
21522               __set_personality(pers);                \
21523 } while (0)
21524 asmlinkage long sys_personality(unsigned long
21525     personality);
21526
21527 #endif                          /* _PERSONALITY_H */
```

include/linux/reboot.h

```
21528 #ifndef _LINUX_REBOOT_H
21529 #define _LINUX_REBOOT_H
21530
21531 /* Magic values required to use _reboot() system call. */
21532
21533 #define LINUX_REBOOT_MAGIC1     0xfee1dead
21534 #define LINUX_REBOOT_MAGIC2     672274793
21535 #define LINUX_REBOOT_MAGIC2A    85072278
21536 #define LINUX_REBOOT_MAGIC2B    369367448
21537
21538
21539 /* Commands accepted by the _reboot() system call.
21540  *
21541  * RESTART     Restart system using default command and
21542  *             mode.
21543  * HALT        Stop OS and give system control to ROM
21544  *             monitor, if any.
```

```
21545  * CAD_ON      Ctrl-Alt-Del sequence causes RESTART
21546  *             command.
21547  * CAD_OFF     Ctrl-Alt-Del sequence sends SIGINT to init
21548  *             task.
21549  * POWER_OFF   Stop OS and remove all power from system,
21550  *             if possible.
21551  * RESTART2 Restart system using given command string. */
21552
21553  #define LINUX_REBOOT_CMD_RESTART    0x01234567
21554  #define LINUX_REBOOT_CMD_HALT       0xCDEF0123
21555  #define LINUX_REBOOT_CMD_CAD_ON     0x89ABCDEF
21556  #define LINUX_REBOOT_CMD_CAD_OFF    0x00000000
21557  #define LINUX_REBOOT_CMD_POWER_OFF  0x4321FEDC
21558  #define LINUX_REBOOT_CMD_RESTART2   0xA1B2C3D4
21559
21560
21561  #ifdef __KERNEL__
21562
21563  #include <linux/notifier.h>
21564
21565  extern int register_reboot_notifier(
21566    struct notifier_block *);
21567  extern int unregister_reboot_notifier(
21568    struct notifier_block *);
21569
21570
21571  /* Architecture-specific implementations of sys_reboot
21572   * commands.  */
21573
21574  extern void machine_restart(char *cmd);
21575  extern void machine_halt(void);
21576  extern void machine_power_off(void);
21577
21578  #endif
21579
21580  #endif                              /* _LINUX_REBOOT_H */
```

include/linux/resource.h

```
21581  #ifndef _LINUX_RESOURCE_H
21582  #define _LINUX_RESOURCE_H
21583
21584  #include <linux/time.h>
21585
21586  /* Resource control/accounting header file for linux */
21587
21588  /* Definition of struct rusage taken from BSD 4.3 Reno
21589   *
21590   * We don't support all of these yet, but we might as
21591   * well have them....  Otherwise, each time we add new
21592   * items, programs which depend on this structure will
21593   * lose.  This reduces the chances of that happening.  */
21594  #define RUSAGE_SELF      0
21595  #define RUSAGE_CHILDREN (-1)
21596  #define RUSAGE_BOTH     (-2)  /* sys_wait4() uses this */
21597
21598  struct rusage {
21599    struct timeval ru_utime;  /* user time used */
21600    struct timeval ru_stime;  /* system time used */
21601    long ru_maxrss;           /* maximum resident set size
21602                               */
21603    long ru_ixrss;            /* integral shared memory
21604                               * size */
21605    long ru_idrss;            /* integral unshared data
21606                               * size */
21607    long ru_isrss;            /* integral unshared stack
21608                               * size */
21609    long ru_minflt;           /* page reclaims */
21610    long ru_majflt;           /* page faults */
21611    long ru_nswap;            /* swaps */
21612    long ru_inblock;          /* block input operations */
21613    long ru_oublock;          /* block output operations */
21614    long ru_msgsnd;           /* messages sent */
21615    long ru_msgrcv;           /* messages received */
21616    long ru_nsignals;         /* signals received */
21617    long ru_nvcsw;            /* voluntary context switches
21618                               */
21619    long ru_nivcsw;           /* involuntary " */
21620  };
21621
21622  struct rlimit {
21623    unsigned long rlim_cur;
21624    unsigned long rlim_max;
21625  };
21626
21627  #define PRIO_MIN        (-20)
21628  #define PRIO_MAX        20
21629
21630  #define PRIO_PROCESS    0
21631  #define PRIO_PGRP       1
21632  #define PRIO_USER       2
21633
21634  /* Due to binary compatibility, the actual resource
21635   * numbers may be different for different linux
21636   * versions..  */
```

```
21637 #include <asm/resource.h>
21638
21639 #endif
```

include/linux/sched.h

```
21640 #ifndef _LINUX_SCHED_H
21641 #define _LINUX_SCHED_H
21642
21643 #include <asm/param.h>            /* for HZ */
21644
21645 extern unsigned long event;
21646
21647 #include <linux/config.h>
21648 #include <linux/binfmts.h>
21649 #include <linux/personality.h>
21650 #include <linux/threads.h>
21651 #include <linux/kernel.h>
21652 #include <linux/types.h>
21653 #include <linux/times.h>
21654 #include <linux/timex.h>
21655
21656 #include <asm/system.h>
21657 #include <asm/semaphore.h>
21658 #include <asm/page.h>
21659 #include <asm/ptrace.h>
21660 #include <asm/mmu.h>
21661
21662 #include <linux/smp.h>
21663 #include <linux/tty.h>
21664 #include <linux/sem.h>
21665 #include <linux/signal.h>
21666 #include <linux/securebits.h>
21667 #include <linux/fs_struct.h>
21668
21669 /* cloning flags: */
21670 #define CSIGNAL         0x000000ff  /* signal mask to be
21671                                      * sent at exit */
21672 #define CLONE_VM        0x00000100  /* set if VM shared
21673                                      * between processes */
21674 #define CLONE_FS        0x00000200  /* set if fs info
21675                                      * shared between
21676                                      * processes */
21677 #define CLONE_FILES     0x00000400  /* set if open files
21678                                      * shared between
21679                                      * processes */
21680 #define CLONE_SIGHAND 0x00000800    /* set if signal
21681                                      * handlers and blocked
21682                                      * signals shared */
21683 #define CLONE_PID       0x00001000  /* set if pid shared */
21684 #define CLONE_PTRACE    0x00002000  /* set if we want to
21685                                      * let tracing continue
21686                                      * on the child too */
21687 #define CLONE_VFORK     0x00004000  /* set if the parent
21688                                      * wants the child to
21689                                      * wake it up on
21690                                      * mm_release */
21691 #define CLONE_PARENT    0x00008000  /* set if we want to
21692                                      * have the same parent
21693                                      * as the cloner */
21694 #define CLONE_THREAD    0x00010000  /* Same thread group?*/
21695
21696 #define CLONE_SIGNAL  (CLONE_SIGHAND | CLONE_THREAD)
21697
21698 /* These are the constant used to fake the fixed-point
21699  * load-average counting. Some notes:
21700  *  - 11 bit fractions expand to 22 bits by the
21701  *     multiplies: this gives a load-average precision of
21702  *     10 bits integer + 11 bits fractional
21703  *  - if you want to count load-averages more often, you
21704  *     need more precision, or rounding will get you. With
21705  *     2-second counting freq, the EXP_n values would be
21706  *     1981, 2034 and 2043 if still using only 11 bit
21707  *     fractions.  */
21708 extern unsigned long avenrun[]; /* Load averages */
21709
21710 #define FSHIFT        11       /* nr of bits of precision
21711                                  */
21712 #define FIXED_1       (1<<FSHIFT) /* 1.0 as fixed-point*/
21713 #define LOAD_FREQ     (5*HZ)   /* 5 sec intervals */
21714 #define EXP_1         1884     /* 1/exp(5sec/1min) as
21715                                  * fixed-point */
21716 #define EXP_5         2014     /* 1/exp(5sec/5min) */
21717 #define EXP_15        2037     /* 1/exp(5sec/15min) */
21718
21719 #define CALC_LOAD(load,exp,n)                          \
21720         load *= exp;                                   \
21721         load += n*(FIXED_1-exp);                       \
21722         load >>= FSHIFT;
21723
21724 #define CT_TO_SECS(x)   ((x) / HZ)
21725 #define CT_TO_USECS(x)  (((x) % HZ) * 1000000/HZ)
21726
21727 extern int nr_running, nr_threads;
21728 extern int last_pid;
```

```
21729
21730 #include <linux/fs.h>
21731 #include <linux/time.h>
21732 #include <linux/param.h>
21733 #include <linux/resource.h>
21734 #include <linux/timer.h>
21735
21736 #include <asm/processor.h>
21737
21738 #define TASK_RUNNING            0
21739 #define TASK_INTERRUPTIBLE      1
21740 #define TASK_UNINTERRUPTIBLE    2
21741 #define TASK_ZOMBIE             4
21742 #define TASK_STOPPED            8
21743
21744 #define __set_task_state(tsk, state_value)           \
21745         do { (tsk)->state = (state_value); } while (0)
21746 #ifdef CONFIG_SMP
21747 #define set_task_state(tsk, state_value)             \
21748         set_mb((tsk)->state, (state_value))
21749 #else
21750 #define set_task_state(tsk, state_value)             \
21751         __set_task_state((tsk), (state_value))
21752 #endif
21753
21754 #define __set_current_state(state_value)             \
21755         do { current->state = (state_value); } while (0)
21756 #ifdef CONFIG_SMP
21757 #define set_current_state(state_value)               \
21758         set_mb(current->state, (state_value))
21759 #else
21760 #define set_current_state(state_value)               \
21761         __set_current_state(state_value)
21762 #endif
21763
21764 /* Scheduling policies */
21765 #define SCHED_OTHER             0
21766 #define SCHED_FIFO              1
21767 #define SCHED_RR                2
21768
21769 /* This is an additional bit set when we want to yield
21770  * the CPU for one re-schedule.. */
21771 #define SCHED_YIELD             0x10
21772
21773 struct sched_param {
21774   int sched_priority;
21775 };
```

```
21776
21777 #ifdef __KERNEL__
21778
21779 #include <linux/spinlock.h>
21780
21781 /* This serializes "schedule()" and also protects the
21782  * run-queue from deletions/modifications (but _adding_
21783  * to the beginning of the run-queue has a separate
21784  * lock).  */
21785 extern rwlock_t tasklist_lock;
21786 extern spinlock_t runqueue_lock;
21787 extern spinlock_t mmlist_lock;
21788
21789 extern void sched_init(void);
21790 extern void init_idle(void);
21791 extern void show_state(void);
21792 extern void cpu_init(void);
21793 extern void trap_init(void);
21794 extern void update_process_times(int user);
21795 extern void update_one_process(struct task_struct *p,
21796     unsigned long user, unsigned long system, int cpu);
21797
21798 #define MAX_SCHEDULE_TIMEOUT    LONG_MAX
21799 extern signed long FASTCALL(schedule_timeout(signed long
21800         timeout));
21801 asmlinkage void schedule(void);
21802
21803 extern int schedule_task(struct tq_struct *task);
21804 extern void flush_scheduled_tasks(void);
21805 extern int start_context_thread(void);
21806 extern int current_is_keventd(void);
21807
21808 /* The default fd array needs to be at least
21809  * BITS_PER_LONG, as this is the granularity returned by
21810  * copy_fdset().  */
21811 #define NR_OPEN_DEFAULT BITS_PER_LONG
21812
21813 /* Open file table structure */
21814 struct files_struct {
21815   atomic_t count;
21816   rwlock_t file_lock;
21817   int max_fds;
21818   int max_fdset;
21819   int next_fd;
21820   struct file **fd;                  /* current fd array */
21821   fd_set *close_on_exec;
21822   fd_set *open_fds;
```

```
21823    fd_set close_on_exec_init;
21824    fd_set open_fds_init;
21825    struct file *fd_array[NR_OPEN_DEFAULT];
21826 };
21827
21828 #define INIT_FILES                                          \
21829 {                                                           \
21830         count:          ATOMIC_INIT(1),                     \
21831         file_lock:      RW_LOCK_UNLOCKED,                   \
21832         max_fds:        NR_OPEN_DEFAULT,                    \
21833         max_fdset:      __FD_SETSIZE,                       \
21834         next_fd:        0,                                  \
21835         fd:             &init_files.fd_array[0],            \
21836         close_on_exec:  &init_files.close_on_exec_init,    \
21837         open_fds:       &init_files.open_fds_init,          \
21838         close_on_exec_init: { { 0, } },                     \
21839         open_fds_init:  { { 0, } },                         \
21840         fd_array:       { NULL, }                           \
21841 }
21842
21843 /* Maximum number of active map areas.. This is a random
21844  * (large) number */
21845 #define MAX_MAP_COUNT   (65536)
21846
21847 /* Number of map areas at which the AVL tree is
21848  * activated. This is arbitrary. */
21849 #define AVL_MIN_MAP_COUNT       32
21850
21851 struct mm_struct {
21852   struct vm_area_struct *mmap;  /* list of VMAs */
21853   struct vm_area_struct *mmap_avl;  /* tree of VMAs */
21854   struct vm_area_struct *mmap_cache;   /* last find_vma
21855                                          * result */
21856   pgd_t *pgd;
21857   atomic_t mm_users;  /* How many users with user space?
21858                        */
21859   atomic_t mm_count;  /* How many references to "struct
21860                        * mm_struct" (users count as 1) */
21861   int map_count;      /* number of VMAs */
21862   struct semaphore mmap_sem;
21863   spinlock_t page_table_lock;
21864
21865   struct list_head mmlist;  /* List of all active mm's */
21866
21867   unsigned long start_code, end_code, start_data,
21868       end_data;
21869   unsigned long start_brk, brk, start_stack;
```

```
21870    unsigned long arg_start, arg_end, env_start, env_end;
21871    unsigned long rss, total_vm, locked_vm;
21872    unsigned long def_flags;
21873    unsigned long cpu_vm_mask;
21874    unsigned long swap_address;
21875
21876    /* Architecture-specific MM context */
21877    mm_context_t context;
21878 };
21879
21880 extern int mmlist_nr;
21881
21882 #define INIT_MM(name)                                        \
21883 {                                                            \
21884         mmap:       &init_mmap,                              \
21885         mmap_avl:   NULL,                                    \
21886         mmap_cache: NULL,                                    \
21887         pgd:        swapper_pg_dir,                          \
21888         mm_users:   ATOMIC_INIT(2),                          \
21889         mm_count:   ATOMIC_INIT(1),                          \
21890         map_count:  1,                                       \
21891         mmap_sem:   __MUTEX_INITIALIZER(name.mmap_sem),     \
21892         page_table_lock: SPIN_LOCK_UNLOCKED,               \
21893         mmlist:     LIST_HEAD_INIT(name.mmlist),            \
21894 }
21895
21896 struct signal_struct {
21897   atomic_t count;
21898   struct k_sigaction action[_NSIG];
21899   spinlock_t siglock;
21900 };
21901
21902
21903 #define INIT_SIGNALS {                                       \
21904         count:          ATOMIC_INIT(1),                     \
21905         action:         { {{0,}}, },                        \
21906         siglock:        SPIN_LOCK_UNLOCKED                  \
21907 }
21908
21909 /* Some day this will be a full-fledged user tracking
21910  * system.. */
21911 struct user_struct {
21912   atomic_t __count;            /* reference count */
21913   atomic_t processes;          /* How many processes
21914                                 * does this user have?*/
21915   atomic_t files;              /* How many open files
21916                                 * does this user have?*/
```

```
21917
21918    /* Hash table maintenance information */
21919    struct user_struct *next, **pprev;
21920    uid_t uid;
21921 };
21922
21923 #define get_current_user() ({                              \
21924         struct user_struct *__user = current->user;        \
21925         atomic_inc(&__user->__count);                      \
21926         __user; })
21927
21928 extern struct user_struct root_user;
21929 #define INIT_USER (&root_user)
21930
21931 struct task_struct {
21932    /* offsets of these are hardcoded elsewhere - touch
21933     * with care */
21934    volatile long state;        /* -1 unrunnable, 0
21935                                 * runnable, >0 stopped */
21936    unsigned long flags;        /* per process flags,
21937                                 * defined below */
21938    int sigpending;
21939    mm_segment_t addr_limit;    /* thread address space:
21940                                 * 0-0xBFFFFFFF for
21941                                 * user-thead 0-0xFFFFFFFF
21942                                 * for kernel-thread */
21943    struct exec_domain *exec_domain;
21944    volatile long need_resched;
21945    unsigned long ptrace;
21946
21947    int lock_depth;             /* Lock depth */
21948
21949    /* offset 32 begins here on 32-bit platforms. We keep
21950     * all fields in a single cacheline that are needed for
21951     * the goodness() loop in schedule().  */
21952    long counter;
21953    long nice;
21954    unsigned long policy;
21955    struct mm_struct *mm;
21956    int has_cpu, processor;
21957    unsigned long cpus_allowed;
21958    /* (only the 'next' pointer fits into the cacheline,
21959     * but that's just fine.)  */
21960    struct list_head run_list;
21961    unsigned long sleep_time;
21962
21963    struct task_struct *next_task, *prev_task;
21964    struct mm_struct *active_mm;
21965
21966    /* task state */
21967    struct linux_binfmt *binfmt;
21968    int exit_code, exit_signal;
21969    int pdeath_signal;              /* The signal sent when
21970                                     * the parent dies  */
21971    /* ??? */
21972    unsigned long personality;
21973    int dumpable: 1;
21974    int did_exec: 1;
21975    pid_t pid;
21976    pid_t pgrp;
21977    pid_t tty_old_pgrp;
21978    pid_t session;
21979    pid_t tgid;
21980    /* boolean value for session group leader */
21981    int leader;
21982    /* pointers to (original) parent process, youngest
21983     * child, younger sibling, older sibling, respectively.
21984     * (p->father can be replaced with p->p_pptr->pid) */
21985    struct task_struct *p_opptr, *p_pptr, *p_cptr,
21986        *p_ysptr, *p_osptr;
21987    struct list_head thread_group;
21988
21989    /* PID hash table linkage. */
21990    struct task_struct *pidhash_next;
21991    struct task_struct **pidhash_pprev;
21992
21993    wait_queue_head_t wait_chldexit;    /* for wait4() */
21994    struct semaphore *vfork_sem;  /* for vfork() */
21995    unsigned long rt_priority;
21996    unsigned long it_real_value, it_prof_value,
21997        it_virt_value;
21998    unsigned long it_real_incr, it_prof_incr, it_virt_incr;
21999    struct timer_list real_timer;
22000    struct tms times;
22001    unsigned long start_time;
22002    long per_cpu_utime[NR_CPUS], per_cpu_stime[NR_CPUS];
22003    /* mm fault and swap info: this can arguably be seen
22004     * as either mm-specific or thread-specific */
22005    unsigned long min_flt, maj_flt, nswap, cmin_flt,
22006        cmaj_flt, cnswap;
22007    int swappable: 1;
22008    /* process credentials */
22009    uid_t uid, euid, suid, fsuid;
22010    gid_t gid, egid, sgid, fsgid;
```

```
22011    int ngroups;
22012    gid_t groups[NGROUPS];
22013    kernel_cap_t cap_effective, cap_inheritable,
22014       cap_permitted;
22015    int keep_capabilities: 1;
22016    struct user_struct *user;
22017    /* limits */
22018    struct rlimit rlim[RLIM_NLIMITS];
22019    unsigned short used_math;
22020    char comm[16];
22021    /* file system info */
22022    int link_count;
22023    struct tty_struct *tty;      /* NULL if no tty */
22024    unsigned int locks;         /* How many file locks
22025                                 * are being held */
22026    /* ipc stuff */
22027    struct sem_undo *semundo;
22028    struct sem_queue *semsleeping;
22029    /* CPU-specific state of this task */
22030    struct thread_struct thread;
22031    /* filesystem information */
22032    struct fs_struct *fs;
22033    /* open file information */
22034    struct files_struct *files;
22035    /* signal handlers */
22036    spinlock_t sigmask_lock;     /* Protects signal and
22037                                 * blocked */
22038    struct signal_struct *sig;
22039
22040    sigset_t blocked;
22041    struct sigpending pending;
22042
22043    unsigned long sas_ss_sp;
22044    size_t sas_ss_size;
22045    int (*notifier) (void *priv);
22046    void *notifier_data;
22047    sigset_t *notifier_mask;
22048
22049    /* Thread group tracking */
22050    u32 parent_exec_id;
22051    u32 self_exec_id;
22052    /* Protection of (de-)allocation: mm, files, fs, tty */
22053    spinlock_t alloc_lock;
22054 };
22055
22056 /* Per process flags */
22057 #define PF_ALIGNWARN    0x00000001  /* Print alignment
```

```
22058                                  * warning msgs */
22059                                  /* Not implemented
22060                                  * yet, only for 486
22061                                  */
22062 #define PF_STARTING    0x00000002 /* being created */
22063 #define PF_EXITING     0x00000004 /* getting shut down
22064                                  */
22065 #define PF_FORKNOEXEC  0x00000040 /* forked but didn't
22066                                  * exec */
22067 #define PF_SUPERPRIV   0x00000100 /* used super-user
22068                                  * privileges */
22069 #define PF_DUMPCORE    0x00000200 /* dumped core */
22070 #define PF_SIGNALED    0x00000400 /* killed by a signal
22071                                  */
22072 #define PF_MEMALLOC    0x00000800 /* Allocating
22073                                  * memory */
22074 #define PF_VFORK       0x00001000 /* Wake up parent in
22075                                  * mm_release */
22076
22077 #define PF_USEDFPU     0x00100000 /* task used FPU this
22078                                  * quantum (SMP) */
22079
22080 /* Ptrace flags */
22081
22082 #define PT_PTRACED     0x00000001
22083 #define PT_TRACESYS    0x00000002
22084 #define PT_DTRACE      0x00000004 /* delayed trace
22085                                  * (used on m68k,
22086                                  * i386) */
22087 #define PT_TRACESYSGOOD 0x00000008
22088
22089 /* Limit the stack by to some sane default: root can
22090  * always increase this limit if needed..  8MB seems
22091  * reasonable.  */
22092 #define _STK_LIM      (8*1024*1024)
22093
22094 #define DEF_COUNTER (10*HZ/100)   /* 100 ms time slice */
22095 #define MAX_COUNTER (20*HZ/100)
22096 #define DEF_NICE    (0)
22097
22098 /* INIT_TASK is used to set up the first task table,
22099  * touch at your own risk!. Base=0, limit=0x1fffff (=2MB)
22100  */
22101 #define INIT_TASK(tsk)                                \
22102 {                                                     \
22103     state:              0,                            \
22104     flags:              0,                            \
```

```
22105     sigpending:         0,                              \
22106     addr_limit:         KERNEL_DS,                      \
22107     exec_domain:        &default_exec_domain,           \
22108     lock_depth:         -1,                             \
22109     counter:            DEF_COUNTER,                    \
22110     nice:               DEF_NICE,                       \
22111     policy:             SCHED_OTHER,                    \
22112     mm:                 NULL,                           \
22113     active_mm:          &init_mm,                       \
22114     cpus_allowed:       -1,                             \
22115     run_list:           LIST_HEAD_INIT(tsk.run_list),   \
22116     next_task:          &tsk,                           \
22117     prev_task:          &tsk,                           \
22118     p_opptr:            &tsk,                           \
22119     p_pptr:             &tsk,                           \
22120     thread_group:       LIST_HEAD_INIT(tsk.thread_group),\
22121     wait_chldexit:                                      \
22122         __WAIT_QUEUE_HEAD_INITIALIZER(tsk.wait_chldexit),\
22123     real_timer:         {                               \
22124         function:               it_real_fn              \
22125     },                                                  \
22126     cap_effective:      CAP_INIT_EFF_SET,               \
22127     cap_inheritable:    CAP_INIT_INH_SET,               \
22128     cap_permitted:      CAP_FULL_SET,                   \
22129     keep_capabilities: 0,                               \
22130     rlim:               INIT_RLIMITS,                   \
22131     user:               INIT_USER,                      \
22132     comm:               "swapper",                      \
22133     thread:             INIT_THREAD,                    \
22134     fs:                 &init_fs,                       \
22135     files:              &init_files,                    \
22136     sigmask_lock:       SPIN_LOCK_UNLOCKED,             \
22137     sig:                &init_signals,                  \
22138     pending:            {NULL, &tsk.pending.head, {{0}}},\
22139     blocked:            {{0}},                          \
22140     alloc_lock:         SPIN_LOCK_UNLOCKED              \
22141 }
22142
22143
22144 #ifndef INIT_TASK_SIZE
22145 # define INIT_TASK_SIZE 2048*sizeof(long)
22146 #endif
22147
22148 union task_union {
22149   struct task_struct task;
22150   unsigned long stack[INIT_TASK_SIZE / sizeof(long)];
22151 };
```

```
22152
22153 extern union task_union init_task_union;
22154
22155 extern struct mm_struct init_mm;
22156 extern struct task_struct *init_tasks[NR_CPUS];
22157
22158 /* PID hashing. (shouldnt this be dynamic?) */
22159 #define PIDHASH_SZ (4096 >> 2)
22160 extern struct task_struct *pidhash[PIDHASH_SZ];
22161
22162 #define pid_hashfn(x)                                   \
22163   ((((x) >> 8) ^ (x)) & (PIDHASH_SZ - 1))
22164
22165 static inline void hash_pid(struct task_struct *p)
22166 {
22167   struct task_struct **htable =
22168       &pidhash[pid_hashfn(p->pid)];
22169
22170   if ((p->pidhash_next = *htable) != NULL)
22171     (*htable)->pidhash_pprev = &p->pidhash_next;
22172   *htable = p;
22173   p->pidhash_pprev = htable;
22174 }
22175
22176 static inline void unhash_pid(struct task_struct *p)
22177 {
22178   if (p->pidhash_next)
22179     p->pidhash_next->pidhash_pprev = p->pidhash_pprev;
22180   *p->pidhash_pprev = p->pidhash_next;
22181 }
22182
22183 static inline struct task_struct *
22184 find_task_by_pid(int pid)
22185 {
22186   struct task_struct *p, **htable =
22187       &pidhash[pid_hashfn(pid)];
22188
22189   for (p = *htable; p && p->pid != pid;
22190       p = p->pidhash_next) ;
22191
22192   return p;
22193 }
22194
22195 /* per-UID process charging. */
22196 extern struct user_struct *alloc_uid(uid_t);
22197 extern void free_uid(struct user_struct *);
22198
```

```
22199 #include <asm/current.h>
22200
22201 extern unsigned long volatile jiffies;
22202 extern unsigned long itimer_ticks;
22203 extern unsigned long itimer_next;
22204 extern struct timeval xtime;
22205 extern void do_timer(struct pt_regs *);
22206
22207 extern unsigned int *prof_buffer;
22208 extern unsigned long prof_len;
22209 extern unsigned long prof_shift;
22210
22211 #define CURRENT_TIME (xtime.tv_sec)
22212
22213 extern void FASTCALL(__wake_up(wait_queue_head_t * q,
22214   unsigned int mode, int nr));
22215 extern void FASTCALL(__wake_up_sync(
22216   wait_queue_head_t * q, unsigned int mode, int nr));
22217 extern void FASTCALL(sleep_on(wait_queue_head_t * q));
22218 extern long FASTCALL(sleep_on_timeout(
22219   wait_queue_head_t * q, signed long timeout));
22220 extern void
22221 FASTCALL(interruptible_sleep_on(wait_queue_head_t * q));
22222 extern long
22223 FASTCALL(interruptible_sleep_on_timeout(
22224   wait_queue_head_t * q, signed long timeout));
22225 extern void
22226 FASTCALL(wake_up_process(struct task_struct *tsk));
22227
22228 #define wake_up(x)                                  \
22229   __wake_up((x),TASK_UNINTERRUPTIBLE|TASK_INTERRUPTIBLE,\
22230           1)
22231 #define wake_up_nr(x, nr)                           \
22232   __wake_up((x),TASK_UNINTERRUPTIBLE|TASK_INTERRUPTIBLE,\
22233           nr)
22234 #define wake_up_all(x)                              \
22235   __wake_up((x),TASK_UNINTERRUPTIBLE|TASK_INTERRUPTIBLE,\
22236           0)
22237 #define wake_up_sync(x)                             \
22238   __wake_up_sync((x),                               \
22239           TASK_UNINTERRUPTIBLE | TASK_INTERRUPTIBLE, 1)
22240 #define wake_up_sync_nr(x, nr)                      \
22241   __wake_up_sync((x),                               \
22242           TASK_UNINTERRUPTIBLE | TASK_INTERRUPTIBLE, nr)
22243 #define wake_up_interruptible(x)                    \
22244   __wake_up((x),TASK_INTERRUPTIBLE, 1)
22245 #define wake_up_interruptible_nr(x, nr)             \
22246   __wake_up((x),TASK_INTERRUPTIBLE, nr)
22247 #define wake_up_interruptible_all(x)                \
22248   __wake_up((x),TASK_INTERRUPTIBLE, 0)
22249 #define wake_up_interruptible_sync(x)               \
22250   __wake_up_sync((x),TASK_INTERRUPTIBLE, 1)
22251 #define wake_up_interruptible_sync_nr(x)            \
22252   __wake_up_sync((x),TASK_INTERRUPTIBLE,  nr)
22253 asmlinkage long sys_wait4(pid_t pid,
22254     unsigned int *stat_addr, int options,
22255     struct rusage *ru);
22256
22257 extern int in_group_p(gid_t);
22258 extern int in_egroup_p(gid_t);
22259
22260 extern void proc_caches_init(void);
22261 extern void flush_signals(struct task_struct *);
22262 extern void flush_signal_handlers(struct task_struct *);
22263 extern int dequeue_signal(sigset_t *, siginfo_t *);
22264 extern void
22265 block_all_signals(int (*notifier) (void *priv),
22266                   void *priv, sigset_t * mask);
22267 extern void unblock_all_signals(void);
22268 extern int send_sig_info(int, struct siginfo *,
22269     struct task_struct *);
22270 extern int force_sig_info(int, struct siginfo *,
22271     struct task_struct *);
22272 extern int kill_pg_info(int, struct siginfo *, pid_t);
22273 extern int kill_sl_info(int, struct siginfo *, pid_t);
22274 extern int kill_proc_info(int, struct siginfo *, pid_t);
22275 extern void notify_parent(struct task_struct *, int);
22276 extern void do_notify_parent(struct task_struct *, int);
22277 extern void force_sig(int, struct task_struct *);
22278 extern int send_sig(int, struct task_struct *, int);
22279 extern int kill_pg(pid_t, int, int);
22280 extern int kill_sl(pid_t, int, int);
22281 extern int kill_proc(pid_t, int, int);
22282 extern int do_sigaction(int, const struct k_sigaction *,
22283     struct k_sigaction *);
22284 extern int do_sigaltstack(const stack_t *, stack_t *,
22285     unsigned long);
22286
22287 static inline int signal_pending(struct task_struct *p)
22288 {
22289   return (p->sigpending != 0);
22290 }
22291
22292 /* Re-calculate pending state from the set of locally
```

```
22293  * pending signals, globally pending signals, and blocked
22294  * signals. */
22295  static inline int has_pending_signals(sigset_t * signal,
22296       sigset_t * blocked)
22297  {
22298    unsigned long ready;
22299    long i;
22300
22301    switch (_NSIG_WORDS) {
22302    default:
22303      for (i = _NSIG_WORDS, ready = 0; --i >= 0;)
22304        ready |= signal->sig[i] & ~blocked->sig[i];
22305      break;
22306
22307    case 4:
22308      ready  = signal->sig[3] & ~blocked->sig[3];
22309      ready |= signal->sig[2] & ~blocked->sig[2];
22310      ready |= signal->sig[1] & ~blocked->sig[1];
22311      ready |= signal->sig[0] & ~blocked->sig[0];
22312      break;
22313
22314    case 2:
22315      ready  = signal->sig[1] & ~blocked->sig[1];
22316      ready |= signal->sig[0] & ~blocked->sig[0];
22317      break;
22318
22319    case 1:
22320      ready = signal->sig[0] & ~blocked->sig[0];
22321    }
22322    return ready != 0;
22323  }
22324
22325  /* Reevaluate whether the task has signals pending
22326   * delivery. This is required every time the blocked
22327   * sigset_t changes. All callers should have
22328   * t->sigmask_lock. */
22329  static inline void recalc_sigpending(
22330    struct task_struct *t)
22331  {
22332    t->sigpending = has_pending_signals(&t->pending.signal,
22333                                        &t->blocked);
22334  }
22335
22336  /* True if we are on the alternate signal stack. */
22337  static inline int on_sig_stack(unsigned long sp)
22338  {
22339    return (sp - current->sas_ss_sp <
```

```
22340       current->sas_ss_size);
22341  }
22342
22343  static inline int sas_ss_flags(unsigned long sp)
22344  {
22345    return (current->sas_ss_size == 0
22346            ? SS_DISABLE
22347            : on_sig_stack(sp) ? SS_ONSTACK : 0);
22348  }
22349
22350  extern int request_irq(unsigned int,
22351      void (*handler) (int, void *, struct pt_regs *),
22352      unsigned long, const char *, void *);
22353  extern void free_irq(unsigned int, void *);
22354
22355  /* This has now become a routine instead of a macro, it
22356   * sets a flag if it returns true (to do BSD-style
22357   * accounting where the process is flagged if it uses
22358   * root privs). The implication of this is that you
22359   * should do normal permissions checks first, and check
22360   * suser() last.
22361   *
22362   * [Dec 1997 - Chris Evans]
22363   * For correctness, the above considerations need to be
22364   * extended to fsuser(). This is done, along with moving
22365   * fsuser() checks to be last.
22366   *
22367   * These will be removed, but in the mean time, when the
22368   * SECURE_NOROOT flag is set, uids don't grant privilege.
22369   */
22370  static inline int suser(void)
22371  {
22372    if (!issecure(SECURE_NOROOT) && current->euid == 0) {
22373      current->flags |= PF_SUPERPRIV;
22374      return 1;
22375    }
22376    return 0;
22377  }
22378
22379  static inline int fsuser(void)
22380  {
22381    if (!issecure(SECURE_NOROOT) && current->fsuid == 0) {
22382      current->flags |= PF_SUPERPRIV;
22383      return 1;
22384    }
22385    return 0;
22386  }
```

```
22387
22388 /* capable() checks for a particular capability.  New
22389  * privilege checks should use this interface, rather
22390  * than suser() or fsuser(). See
22391  * include/linux/capability.h for defined capabilities.
22392  */
22393 static inline int capable(int cap)
22394 {
22395 #if 1                                  /* ok now */
22396    if (cap_raised(current->cap_effective, cap))
22397 #else
22398    if (cap_is_fs_cap(cap)
22399        ? current->fsuid == 0
22400        : current->euid  == 0)
22401 #endif
22402    {
22403      current->flags |= PF_SUPERPRIV;
22404      return 1;
22405    }
22406    return 0;
22407 }
22408
22409 /* Routines for handling mm_structs */
22410 extern struct mm_struct *mm_alloc(void);
22411
22412 extern struct mm_struct *start_lazy_tlb(void);
22413 extern void end_lazy_tlb(struct mm_struct *mm);
22414
22415 /* mmdrop drops the mm and the page tables */
22416 extern inline void
22417 FASTCALL(__mmdrop(struct mm_struct *));
22418 static inline void mmdrop(struct mm_struct *mm)
22419 {
22420    if (atomic_dec_and_test(&mm->mm_count))
22421      __mmdrop(mm);
22422 }
22423
22424 /* mmput gets rid of the mappings and all user-space */
22425 extern void mmput(struct mm_struct *);
22426 /* Remove the current tasks stale references to the old
22427  * mm_struct */
22428 extern void mm_release(void);
22429
22430 /* Routines for handling the fd arrays */
22431 extern struct file **alloc_fd_array(int);
22432 extern int expand_fd_array(struct files_struct *,
22433     int nr);
```

```
22434 extern void free_fd_array(struct file **, int);
22435
22436 extern fd_set *alloc_fdset(int);
22437 extern int expand_fdset(struct files_struct *, int nr);
22438 extern void free_fdset(fd_set *, int);
22439
22440 extern int copy_thread(int, unsigned long, unsigned long,
22441     unsigned long, struct task_struct *,
22442     struct pt_regs *);
22443 extern void flush_thread(void);
22444 extern void exit_thread(void);
22445
22446 extern void exit_mm(struct task_struct *);
22447 extern void exit_files(struct task_struct *);
22448 extern void exit_sighand(struct task_struct *);
22449
22450 extern void daemonize(void);
22451
22452 extern int do_execve(char *, char **, char **,
22453     struct pt_regs *);
22454 extern int do_fork(unsigned long, unsigned long,
22455     struct pt_regs *, unsigned long);
22456
22457 extern void
22458 FASTCALL(add_wait_queue(wait_queue_head_t * q,
22459                         wait_queue_t * wait));
22460 extern void
22461 FASTCALL(add_wait_queue_exclusive(wait_queue_head_t * q,
22462                         wait_queue_t * wait));
22463 extern void
22464 FASTCALL(remove_wait_queue(wait_queue_head_t * q,
22465                         wait_queue_t * wait));
22466
22467 #define __wait_event(wq, condition)                    \
22468 do {                                                   \
22469        wait_queue_t __wait;                            \
22470        init_waitqueue_entry(&__wait, current);         \
22471                                                        \
22472        add_wait_queue(&wq, &__wait);                   \
22473        for (;;) {                                      \
22474                set_current_state(TASK_UNINTERRUPTIBLE);\
22475                if (condition)                          \
22476                        break;                          \
22477                schedule();                             \
22478        }                                               \
22479        current->state = TASK_RUNNING;                  \
22480        remove_wait_queue(&wq, &__wait);                \
```

p 539

```
22481 } while (0)
22482
22483 #define wait_event(wq, condition)                       \
22484 do {                                                    \
22485         if (condition)                                  \
22486                 break;                                  \
22487         __wait_event(wq, condition);                    \
22488 } while (0)
22489
22490 #define __wait_event_interruptible(wq, condition, ret)  \
22491 do {                                                    \
22492         wait_queue_t __wait;                            \
22493         init_waitqueue_entry(&__wait, current);         \
22494                                                         \
22495         add_wait_queue(&wq, &__wait);                   \
22496         for (;;) {                                      \
22497                 set_current_state(TASK_INTERRUPTIBLE);  \
22498                 if (condition)                          \
22499                         break;                          \
22500                 if (!signal_pending(current)) {         \
22501                         schedule();                     \
22502                         continue;                       \
22503                 }                                       \
22504                 ret = -ERESTARTSYS;                     \
22505                 break;                                  \
22506         }                                               \
22507         current->state = TASK_RUNNING;                  \
22508         remove_wait_queue(&wq, &__wait);                \
22509 } while (0)
22510
22511 #define wait_event_interruptible(wq, condition)         \
22512 ({                                                      \
22513         int __ret = 0;                                  \
22514         if (!(condition))                               \
22515                 __wait_event_interruptible(wq,          \
22516                                 condition, __ret);      \
22517         __ret;                                          \
22518 })
22519
22520 #define REMOVE_LINKS(p) do {                            \
22521         (p)->next_task->prev_task = (p)->prev_task;     \
22522         (p)->prev_task->next_task = (p)->next_task;     \
22523         if ((p)->p_osptr)                               \
22524                 (p)->p_osptr->p_ysptr = (p)->p_ysptr;   \
22525         if ((p)->p_ysptr)                               \
22526                 (p)->p_ysptr->p_osptr = (p)->p_osptr;   \
22527         else                                            \
```

```
22528                 (p)->p_pptr->p_cptr = (p)->p_osptr;     \
22529         } while (0)
22530
22531 #define SET_LINKS(p) do {                               \
22532         (p)->next_task = &init_task;                    \
22533         (p)->prev_task = init_task.prev_task;           \
22534         init_task.prev_task->next_task = (p);           \
22535         init_task.prev_task = (p);                      \
22536         (p)->p_ysptr = NULL;                            \
22537         if(((p)->p_osptr = (p)->p_pptr->p_cptr) != NULL)\
22538                 (p)->p_osptr->p_ysptr = p;              \
22539         (p)->p_pptr->p_cptr = p;                        \
22540         } while (0)
22541
22542 #define for_each_task(p)                                \
22543   for (p = &init_task; (p = p->next_task) != &init_task;)
22544
22545 #define next_thread(p)                                  \
22546         list_entry((p)->thread_group.next,              \
22547                 struct task_struct, thread_group)
22548
22549 static inline void del_from_runqueue(
22550   struct task_struct *p)
22551 {
22552   nr_running--;
22553   p->sleep_time = jiffies;
22554   list_del(&p->run_list);
22555   p->run_list.next = NULL;
22556 }
22557
22558 static inline int task_on_runqueue(struct task_struct *p)
22559 {
22560   return (p->run_list.next != NULL);
22561 }
22562
22563 static inline void unhash_process(struct task_struct *p)
22564 {
22565   if (task_on_runqueue(p))
22566     BUG();
22567   write_lock_irq(&tasklist_lock);
22568   nr_threads--;
22569   unhash_pid(p);
22570   REMOVE_LINKS(p);
22571   list_del(&p->thread_group);
22572   write_unlock_irq(&tasklist_lock);
22573 }
22574
```

```
22575 static inline void task_lock(struct task_struct *p)
22576 {
22577   spin_lock(&p->alloc_lock);
22578 }
22579
22580 static inline void task_unlock(struct task_struct *p)
22581 {
22582   spin_unlock(&p->alloc_lock);
22583 }
22584
22585 /* write full pathname into buffer and return start of
22586  * pathname */
22587 static inline char *d_path(struct dentry *dentry,
22588      struct vfsmount *vfsmnt, char *buf, int buflen)
22589 {
22590   char *res;
22591   struct vfsmount *rootmnt;
22592   struct dentry *root;
22593   read_lock(&current->fs->lock);
22594   rootmnt = mntget(current->fs->rootmnt);
22595   root = dget(current->fs->root);
22596   read_unlock(&current->fs->lock);
22597   spin_lock(&dcache_lock);
22598   res = __d_path(dentry, vfsmnt, root, rootmnt, buf,
22599                  buflen);
22600   spin_unlock(&dcache_lock);
22601   dput(root);
22602   mntput(rootmnt);
22603   return res;
22604 }
22605
22606 #endif                        /* __KERNEL__ */
22607
22608 #endif
```

include/linux/securebits.h

```
22609 #ifndef _LINUX_SECUREBITS_H
22610 #define _LINUX_SECUREBITS_H 1
22611
22612 #define SECUREBITS_DEFAULT 0x00000000
22613
22614 extern unsigned securebits;
22615
22616 /* When set UID 0 has no special privileges. When unset,
22617  * we support inheritance of root-permissions and
22618  * suid-root executablew under compatibility mode. We
22619  * raise the effective and inheritable bitmasks *of the
22620  * executable file* if the effective uid of the new
22621  * process is 0. If the real uid is 0, we raise the
22622  * inheritable bitmask of the executable file. */
22623 #define SECURE_NOROOT            0
22624
22625 /* When set, setuid to/from uid 0 does not trigger
22626  * capability-"fixes" to be compatible with old programs
22627  * relying on set*uid to loose privileges. When unset,
22628  * setuid doesn't change privileges. */
22629 #define SECURE_NO_SETUID_FIXUP    2
22630
22631 /* Each securesetting is implemented using two bits. One
22632  * bit specify whether the setting is on or off. The
22633  * other bit specify whether the setting is fixed or
22634  * not. A setting which is fixed cannot be changed from
22635  * user-level. */
22636 #define issecure(X) ( (1 << (X+1)) & SECUREBITS_DEFAULT \
22637                     ? (1 << (X)) & SECUREBITS_DEFAULT \
22638                     : (1 << (X)) & securebits )
22639
22640 #endif                        /* !_LINUX_SECUREBITS_H */
```

include/linux/sem.h

```
22641 #ifndef _LINUX_SEM_H
22642 #define _LINUX_SEM_H
22643
22644 #include <linux/ipc.h>
22645
22646 /* semop flags */
22647 #define SEM_UNDO  0x1000 /* undo the operation on exit */
22648
22649 /* semctl Command Definitions. */
22650 #define GETPID   11           /* get sempid */
22651 #define GETVAL   12           /* get semval */
22652 #define GETALL   13           /* get all semval's */
22653 #define GETNCNT  14           /* get semncnt */
22654 #define GETZCNT  15           /* get semzcnt */
22655 #define SETVAL   16           /* set semval */
22656 #define SETALL   17           /* set all semval's */
22657
22658 /* ipcs ctl cmds */
22659 #define SEM_STAT 18
22660 #define SEM_INFO 19
22661
22662 /* Obsolete, used only for backwards compatibility and
22663  * libc5 compiles */
22664 struct semid_ds {
```

```
22665   struct ipc_perm sem_perm;    /* permissions .. see
22666                                 * ipc.h */
22667   __kernel_time_t sem_otime;   /* last semop time */
22668   __kernel_time_t sem_ctime;   /* last change time */
22669   struct sem *sem_base;        /* ptr to first
22670                                 * semaphore in array */
22671   struct sem_queue *sem_pending;/* pending operations to
22672                                 * be processed */
22673   struct sem_queue **sem_pending_last;  /* last pending
22674                                         * operation */
22675   struct sem_undo *undo;       /* undo requests on this
22676                                 * array */
22677   unsigned short sem_nsems;    /* no. of semaphores in
22678                                 * array */
22679 };
22680
22681 /* Include the definition of semid64_ds */
22682 #include <asm/sembuf.h>
22683
22684 /* semop system calls takes an array of these. */
22685 struct sembuf {
22686   unsigned short sem_num;      /* semaphore index in
22687                                 * array */
22688   short sem_op;                /* semaphore operation */
22689   short sem_flg;               /* operation flags */
22690 };
22691
22692 /* arg for semctl system calls. */
22693 union semun {
22694   int val;                     /* value for SETVAL */
22695   struct semid_ds *buf;        /* buffer for IPC_STAT &
22696                                 * IPC_SET */
22697   unsigned short *array;       /* array for GETALL &
22698                                 * SETALL */
22699   struct seminfo *__buf;       /* buffer for IPC_INFO */
22700   void *__pad;
22701 };
22702
22703 struct seminfo {
22704   int semmap;
22705   int semmni;
22706   int semmns;
22707   int semmnu;
22708   int semmsl;
22709   int semopm;
22710   int semume;
22711   int semusz;
```

```
22712   int semvmx;
22713   int semaem;
22714 };
22715
22716 #define SEMMNI  128           /* <= IPCMNI   max # of
22717                               * semaphore identifiers
22718                               */
22719 #define SEMMSL  250           /* <= 8 000 max num of
22720                               * semaphores per id */
22721 #define SEMMNS  (SEMMNI*SEMMSL) /* <= INT_MAX max # of
22722                               * semaphores in system*/
22723 #define SEMOPM  32            /* <= 1 000 max num of
22724                               * ops per semop call */
22725 #define SEMVMX  32767         /* <= 32767 semaphore
22726                               * maximum value */
22727
22728 /* unused */
22729 #define SEMUME  SEMOPM        /* max num of undo
22730                               * entries per process */
22731 #define SEMMNU  SEMMNS        /* num of undo
22732                               * structures system
22733                               * wide */
22734 #define SEMAEM  (SEMVMX >> 1) /* adjust on exit max
22735                               * value */
22736 #define SEMMAP  SEMMNS        /* # of entries in
22737                               * semaphore map */
22738 #define SEMUSZ  20            /* sizeof struct
22739                               * sem_undo */
22740
22741 #ifdef __KERNEL__
22742
22743 /* One semaphore structure for each semaphore in the
22744  * system. */
22745 struct sem {
22746   int semval;                  /* current value */
22747   int sempid;                  /* pid of last operation
22748                                 */
22749 };
22750
22751 /* One sem_array data structure for each set of
22752  * semaphores in the system. */
22753 struct sem_array {
22754   struct kern_ipc_perm sem_perm;/* permissions
22755                                 * .. see ipc.h */
22756   time_t sem_otime;            /* last semop time */
22757   time_t sem_ctime;            /* last change time */
22758   struct sem *sem_base;        /* ptr to first
```

```
22759                         * semaphore in array */
22760    struct sem_queue *sem_pending;/* pending operations to
22761                         * be processed */
22762    struct sem_queue **sem_pending_last;  /* last pending
22763                             * operation */
22764    struct sem_undo *undo;        /* undo requests on this
22765                         * array */
22766    unsigned long sem_nsems;      /* no. of semaphores in
22767                         * array */
22768 };
22769
22770 /* One queue for each sleeping process in the system. */
```
p 668 ▶
```
22771 struct sem_queue {
22772    struct sem_queue *next;       /* next entry in the
22773                         * queue */
22774    struct sem_queue **prev;      /* previous entry in the
22775                         * queue, *(q->prev) ==
22776                         * q */
22777    struct task_struct *sleeper;  /* this process */
22778    struct sem_undo *undo;        /* undo structure */
22779    int pid;                      /* process id of
22780                         * requesting process */
22781    int status;                   /* completion status of
22782                         * operation */
22783    struct sem_array *sma;        /* semaphore array for
22784                         * operations */
22785    int id;                       /* internal sem id */
22786    struct sembuf *sops;          /* array of pending
22787                         * operations */
22788    int nsops;                    /* number of operations*/
22789    int alter;                    /* operation will alter
22790                         * semaphore */
22791 };
22792
22793 /* Each task has a list of undo requests. They are
22794  * executed automatically when the process exits. */
```
p 669 ▶
```
22795 struct sem_undo {
22796    struct sem_undo *proc_next;   /* next entry on this
22797                         * process */
22798    struct sem_undo *id_next;     /* next entry on this
22799                         * semaphore set */
22800    int semid;                    /* semaphore set
22801                         * identifier */
22802    short *semadj;                /* array of adjustments,
22803                         * one per semaphore */
22804 };
22805
```

```
22806 asmlinkage long sys_semget(key_t key, int nsems,
22807    int semflg);
22808 asmlinkage long sys_semop(int semid, struct sembuf *sops,
22809    unsigned nsops);
22810 asmlinkage long sys_semctl(int semid, int semnum,
22811    int cmd, union semun arg);
22812
22813 #endif                              /* __KERNEL__ */
22814
22815 #endif                              /* _LINUX_SEM_H */
```

include/linux/shm.h

```
22816 #ifndef _LINUX_SHM_H_
22817 #define _LINUX_SHM_H_
22818
22819 #include <linux/ipc.h>
22820 #include <asm/page.h>
22821
22822 /* SHMMAX, SHMMNI and SHMALL are upper limits are
22823  * defaults which can be increased by sysctl */
22824
22825 #define SHMMAX 0x2000000 /* max shared seg size (bytes)*/
22826 #define SHMMIN 1          /* min shared seg size (bytes)*/
22827 #define SHMMNI 4096       /* max num of segs system wide*/
22828 /* max shm system wide (pages) */
22829 #define SHMALL (SHMMAX/PAGE_SIZE*(SHMMNI/16))
22830 #define SHMSEG SHMMNI     /* max shared segs per process*/
22831
22832 #include <asm/shmparam.h>
22833
22834 /* Obsolete, used only for backwards compatibility and
22835  * libc5 compiles */
22836 struct shmid_ds {
22837    struct ipc_perm shm_perm;     /* operation perms */
22838    int shm_segsz;                /* size of segment
22839                         * (bytes) */
22840    __kernel_time_t shm_atime;    /* last attach time */
22841    __kernel_time_t shm_dtime;    /* last detach time */
22842    __kernel_time_t shm_ctime;    /* last change time */
22843    __kernel_ipc_pid_t shm_cpid;  /* pid of creator */
22844    __kernel_ipc_pid_t shm_lpid;  /* pid of last operator*/
22845    unsigned short shm_nattch;    /* no. of current
22846                         * attaches */
22847    unsigned short shm_unused;    /* compatibility */
22848    void *shm_unused2;            /* ditto - used by DIPC*/
22849    void *shm_unused3;            /* unused */
22850 };
```

```
22851
22852 /* Include the definition of shmid64_ds and shminfo64 */
22853 #include <asm/shmbuf.h>
22854
22855 /* permission flag for shmget */
22856 #define SHM_R          0400    /* or S_IRUGO from
22857                                 * <linux/stat.h> */
22858 #define SHM_W          0200    /* or S_IWUGO from
22859                                 * <linux/stat.h> */
22860
22861 /* mode for attach */
22862 #define SHM_RDONLY     010000  /* read-only access */
22863 #define SHM_RND        020000  /* round attach address
22864                                 * to SHMLBA boundary */
22865 #define SHM_REMAP      040000  /* take-over region on
22866                                 * attach */
22867
22868 /* super user shmctl commands */
22869 #define SHM_LOCK       11
22870 #define SHM_UNLOCK     12
22871
22872 /* ipcs ctl commands */
22873 #define SHM_STAT       13
22874 #define SHM_INFO       14
22875
22876 /* Obsolete, used only for backwards compatibility */
22877 struct shminfo {
22878   int shmmax;
22879   int shmmin;
22880   int shmmni;
22881   int shmseg;
22882   int shmall;
22883 };
22884
22885 struct shm_info {
22886   int used_ids;
22887   unsigned long shm_tot;      /* total allocated shm */
22888   unsigned long shm_rss;      /* total resident shm */
22889   unsigned long shm_swp;      /* total swapped shm */
22890   unsigned long swap_attempts;
22891   unsigned long swap_successes;
22892 };
22893
22894 #ifdef __KERNEL__
22895
22896 /* shm_mode upper byte flags */
22897 #define SHM_DEST    01000   /* segment will be destroyed
22898                              * on last detach */
22899 #define SHM_LOCKED  02000   /* segment will not be
22900                              * swapped */
22901
22902 asmlinkage long sys_shmget(key_t key, size_t size,
22903     int flag);
22904 asmlinkage long sys_shmat(int shmid, char *shmaddr,
22905     int shmflg, unsigned long *addr);
22906 asmlinkage long sys_shmdt(char *shmaddr);
22907 asmlinkage long sys_shmctl(int shmid, int cmd,
22908     struct shmid_ds *buf);
22909 extern void shm_unuse(swp_entry_t entry,
22910     struct page *page);
22911
22912 #endif                           /* __KERNEL__ */
22913
22914 #endif                           /* _LINUX_SHM_H_ */
```

include/linux/signal.h

```
22915 #ifndef _LINUX_SIGNAL_H
22916 #define _LINUX_SIGNAL_H
22917
22918 #include <asm/signal.h>
22919 #include <asm/siginfo.h>
22920
22921 #ifdef __KERNEL__
22922 /* Real Time signals may be queued.  */
22923
22924 struct sigqueue {
22925     struct sigqueue *next;
22926     siginfo_t info;
22927 };
22928
22929 struct sigpending {
22930     struct sigqueue *head, **tail;
22931     sigset_t signal;
22932 };
22933
22934 /* Define some primitives to manipulate sigset_t. */
22935
22936 #ifndef __HAVE_ARCH_SIG_BITOPS
22937 #include <asm/bitops.h>
22938
22939 /* We don't use <asm/bitops.h> for these because there
22940  * is no need to be atomic.  */
22941 static inline void sigaddset(sigset_t * set, int _sig)
22942 {
```

```
22943    unsigned long sig = _sig - 1;
22944    if (_NSIG_WORDS == 1)
22945      set->sig[0] |= 1UL << sig;
22946    else
22947      set->sig[sig / _NSIG_BPW] |=
22948                    1UL << (sig % _NSIG_BPW);
22949 }
22950
22951 static inline void sigdelset(sigset_t * set, int _sig)
22952 {
22953    unsigned long sig = _sig - 1;
22954    if (_NSIG_WORDS == 1)
22955      set->sig[0] &= ~(1UL << sig);
22956    else
22957      set->sig[sig / _NSIG_BPW] &=
22958                    ~(1UL << (sig % _NSIG_BPW));
22959 }
22960
22961 static inline int sigismember(sigset_t * set, int _sig)
22962 {
22963    unsigned long sig = _sig - 1;
22964    if (_NSIG_WORDS == 1)
22965      return 1 & (set->sig[0] >> sig);
22966    else
22967      return 1 & (set->sig[sig / _NSIG_BPW] >>
22968                        (sig % _NSIG_BPW));
22969 }
22970
22971 static inline int sigfindinword(unsigned long word)
22972 {
22973    return ffz(~word);
22974 }
22975
22976 #define sigmask(sig)    (1UL << ((sig) - 1))
22977
22978 #endif                    /* __HAVE_ARCH_SIG_BITOPS */
22979
22980 #ifndef __HAVE_ARCH_SIG_SETOPS
22981 #include <linux/string.h>
22982
22983 #define _SIG_SET_BINOP(name, op)                    \
22984 static inline void name(sigset_t *r,                \
22985   const sigset_t *a, const sigset_t *b)            \
22986 {                                                   \
22987         unsigned long a0, a1, a2, a3, b0, b1, b2, b3; \
22988         unsigned long i;                            \
22989                                                     \
22990         for (i = 0; i < _NSIG_WORDS/4; ++i) {       \
22991             a0 = a->sig[4*i+0]; a1 = a->sig[4*i+1]; \
22992             a2 = a->sig[4*i+2]; a3 = a->sig[4*i+3]; \
22993             b0 = b->sig[4*i+0]; b1 = b->sig[4*i+1]; \
22994             b2 = b->sig[4*i+2]; b3 = b->sig[4*i+3]; \
22995             r->sig[4*i+0] = op(a0, b0);             \
22996             r->sig[4*i+1] = op(a1, b1);             \
22997             r->sig[4*i+2] = op(a2, b2);             \
22998             r->sig[4*i+3] = op(a3, b3);             \
22999         }                                           \
23000         switch (_NSIG_WORDS % 4) {                  \
23001             case 3:                                 \
23002                 a0 = a->sig[4*i+0];                 \
23003                 a1 = a->sig[4*i+1]; a2 = a->sig[4*i+2]; \
23004                 b0 = b->sig[4*i+0];                 \
23005                 b1 = b->sig[4*i+1]; b2 = b->sig[4*i+2]; \
23006                 r->sig[4*i+0] = op(a0, b0);         \
23007                 r->sig[4*i+1] = op(a1, b1);         \
23008                 r->sig[4*i+2] = op(a2, b2);         \
23009                 break;                              \
23010             case 2:                                 \
23011                 a0 = a->sig[4*i+0]; a1 = a->sig[4*i+1]; \
23012                 b0 = b->sig[4*i+0]; b1 = b->sig[4*i+1]; \
23013                 r->sig[4*i+0] = op(a0, b0);         \
23014                 r->sig[4*i+1] = op(a1, b1);         \
23015                 break;                              \
23016             case 1:                                 \
23017                 a0 = a->sig[4*i+0]; b0 = b->sig[4*i+0]; \
23018                 r->sig[4*i+0] = op(a0, b0);         \
23019                 break;                              \
23020         }                                           \
23021 }
23022
23023 #define _sig_or(x,y)     ((x) | (y))
23024     _SIG_SET_BINOP(sigorsets, _sig_or)
23025 #define _sig_and(x,y)    ((x) & (y))
23026     _SIG_SET_BINOP(sigandsets, _sig_and)
23027 #define _sig_nand(x,y)  ((x) & ~(y))
23028     _SIG_SET_BINOP(signandsets, _sig_nand)
23029 #undef _SIG_SET_BINOP
23030 #undef _sig_or
23031 #undef _sig_and
23032 #undef _sig_nand
23033 #define _SIG_SET_OP(name, op)                       \
23034 static inline void name(sigset_t *set)              \
23035 {                                                   \
23036         unsigned long i;                            \
```

```
23037                                                                      \
23038          for (i = 0; i < _NSIG_WORDS/4; ++i) {                       \
23039                  set->sig[4*i+0] = op(set->sig[4*i+0]);  \
23040                  set->sig[4*i+1] = op(set->sig[4*i+1]);  \
23041                  set->sig[4*i+2] = op(set->sig[4*i+2]);  \
23042                  set->sig[4*i+3] = op(set->sig[4*i+3]);  \
23043          }                                                           \
23044          switch (_NSIG_WORDS % 4) {                                  \
23045          case 3: set->sig[4*i+2] = op(set->sig[4*i+2]);  \
23046          case 2: set->sig[4*i+1] = op(set->sig[4*i+1]);  \
23047          case 1: set->sig[4*i+0] = op(set->sig[4*i+0]);  \
23048          }                                                           \
23049 }
23050 #define _sig_not(x)     (~(x))
23051     _SIG_SET_OP(signotset, _sig_not)
23052 #undef _SIG_SET_OP
23053 #undef _sig_not
23054 static inline void sigemptyset(sigset_t * set)
23055 {
23056   switch (_NSIG_WORDS) {
23057   default:
23058     memset(set, 0, sizeof(sigset_t));
23059     break;
23060   case 2:
23061     set->sig[1] = 0;
23062   case 1:
23063     set->sig[0] = 0;
23064     break;
23065   }
23066 }
23067
23068 static inline void sigfillset(sigset_t * set)
23069 {
23070   switch (_NSIG_WORDS) {
23071   default:
23072     memset(set, -1, sizeof(sigset_t));
23073     break;
23074   case 2:
23075     set->sig[1] = -1;
23076   case 1:
23077     set->sig[0] = -1;
23078     break;
23079   }
23080 }
23081
23082 extern char *render_sigset_t(sigset_t * set,
23083     char *buffer);
```

```
23084
23085 /* Some extensions for manipulating the low 32 signals
23086  * in particular.  */
23087
23088 static inline void sigaddsetmask(sigset_t * set,
23089     unsigned long mask)
23090 {
23091   set->sig[0] |= mask;
23092 }
23093
23094 static inline void sigdelsetmask(sigset_t * set,
23095     unsigned long mask)
23096 {
23097   set->sig[0] &= ~mask;
23098 }
23099
23100 static inline int sigtestsetmask(sigset_t * set,
23101     unsigned long mask)
23102 {
23103   return (set->sig[0] & mask) != 0;
23104 }
23105
23106 static inline void siginitset(sigset_t * set,
23107     unsigned long mask)
23108 {
23109   set->sig[0] = mask;
23110   switch (_NSIG_WORDS) {
23111   default:
23112     memset(&set->sig[1], 0,
23113         sizeof(long) * (_NSIG_WORDS - 1));
23114     break;
23115   case 2:
23116     set->sig[1] = 0;
23117   case 1::
23118   }
23119 }
23120
23121 static inline void siginitsetinv(sigset_t * set,
23122     unsigned long mask)
23123 {
23124   set->sig[0] = ~mask;
23125   switch (_NSIG_WORDS) {
23126   default:
23127     memset(&set->sig[1], -1,
23128         sizeof(long) * (_NSIG_WORDS - 1));
23129     break;
23130   case 2:
```

```
23131      set->sig[1] = -1;
23132   case 1::
23133   }
23134 }
23135
23136 #endif                           /* __HAVE_ARCH_SIG_SETOPS */
23137
23138 static inline void init_sigpending(
23139   struct sigpending *sig)
23140 {
23141   sigemptyset(&sig->signal);
23142   sig->head = NULL;
23143   sig->tail = &sig->head;
23144 }
23145
23146 extern long do_sigpending(void *, unsigned long);
23147
23148 #endif                           /* __KERNEL__ */
23149
23150 #endif                           /* _LINUX_SIGNAL_H */
```

include/linux/slab.h

```
23151 /*
23152  * linux/mm/slab.h
23153  * Written by Mark Hemment, 1996.
23154  * (markhe@nextd.demon.co.uk)
23155  */
23156
23157 #if    !defined(_LINUX_SLAB_H)
23158 #define _LINUX_SLAB_H
23159
23160 #if    defined(__KERNEL__)
23161
23162 typedef struct kmem_cache_s kmem_cache_t;
23163
23164 #include        <linux/mm.h>
23165 #include        <linux/cache.h>
23166
23167 /* flags for kmem_cache_alloc() */
23168 #define SLAB_BUFFER       GFP_BUFFER
23169 #define SLAB_ATOMIC       GFP_ATOMIC
23170 #define SLAB_USER         GFP_USER
23171 #define SLAB_KERNEL       GFP_KERNEL
23172 #define SLAB_NFS          GFP_NFS
23173 #define SLAB_DMA          GFP_DMA
23174
23175 #define SLAB_LEVEL_MASK   (__GFP_WAIT|__GFP_HIGH|__GFP_IO)
```

```
23176 #define SLAB_NO_GROW      0x00001000UL    /* don't grow a
23177                                          * cache */
23178
23179 /* flags to pass to kmem_cache_create().  The first 3 are
23180  * only valid when the allocator as been build
23181  * SLAB_DEBUG_SUPPORT. */
23182 /* Peform (expensive) checks on free */
23183 #define SLAB_DEBUG_FREE        0x00000100UL
23184 /* Call constructor (as verifier) */
23185 #define SLAB_DEBUG_INITIAL     0x00000200UL
23186 /* Red zone objs in a cache */
23187 #define SLAB_RED_ZONE          0x00000400UL
23188 /* Poison objects */
23189 #define SLAB_POISON            0x00000800UL
23190 /* never reap from the cache */
23191 #define SLAB_NO_REAP           0x00001000UL
23192 /* align objs on a h/w cache lines */
23193 #define SLAB_HWCACHE_ALIGN     0x00002000UL
23194 /* use GFP_DMA memory */
23195 #define SLAB_CACHE_DMA         0x00004000UL
23196
23197 /* flags passed to a constructor func */
23198 /* if not set, then deconstructor */
23199 #define SLAB_CTOR_CONSTRUCTOR   0x001UL
23200 /* tell constructor it can't sleep */
23201 #define SLAB_CTOR_ATOMIC        0x002UL
23202 /* tell constructor it's a verify call */
23203 #define SLAB_CTOR_VERIFY        0x004UL
23204
23205 /* prototypes */
23206 extern void kmem_cache_init(void);
23207 extern void kmem_cache_sizes_init(void);
23208
23209 extern kmem_cache_t *kmem_find_general_cachep(size_t,
23210     int gfpflags);
23211 extern kmem_cache_t * kmem_cache_create(const char *,
23212   size_t, size_t, unsigned long,
23213   void (*)(void *, kmem_cache_t *, unsigned long),
23214   void (*)(void *, kmem_cache_t *, unsigned long));
23215 extern int kmem_cache_destroy(kmem_cache_t *);
23216 extern int kmem_cache_shrink(kmem_cache_t *);
23217 extern void *kmem_cache_alloc(kmem_cache_t *, int);
23218 extern void kmem_cache_free(kmem_cache_t *, void *);
23219
23220 extern void *kmalloc(size_t, int);
23221 extern void kfree(const void *);
23222
```

```
23223 extern void kmem_cache_reap(int);
23224 extern int slabinfo_read_proc(char *page, char **start,
23225     off_t off, int count, int *eof, void *data);
23226 extern int slabinfo_write_proc(struct file *file,
23227     const char *buffer, unsigned long count, void *data);
23228
23229 /* System wide caches */
23230 extern kmem_cache_t *vm_area_cachep;
23231 extern kmem_cache_t *mm_cachep;
23232 extern kmem_cache_t *names_cachep;
23233 extern kmem_cache_t *files_cachep;
23234 extern kmem_cache_t *filp_cachep;
23235 extern kmem_cache_t *dquot_cachep;
23236 extern kmem_cache_t *bh_cachep;
23237 extern kmem_cache_t *fs_cachep;
23238 extern kmem_cache_t *sigact_cachep;
23239
23240 #endif                          /* __KERNEL__ */
23241
23242 #endif                          /* _LINUX_SLAB_H */
```

include/linux/smp.h

```
23243 #ifndef __LINUX_SMP_H
23244 #define __LINUX_SMP_H
23245
23246 /*
23247  *      Generic SMP support
23248  *              Alan Cox. <alan@redhat.com>
23249  */
23250
23251 #include <linux/config.h>
23252
23253 #ifdef CONFIG_SMP
23254
23255 #include <linux/kernel.h>
23256 #include <asm/smp.h>
23257
23258 /* main cross-CPU interfaces, handles INIT, TLB flush,
23259  * STOP, etc.  (defined in asm header): */
23260
23261 /* stops all CPUs but the current one: */
23262 extern void smp_send_stop(void);
23263
23264 /* sends a 'reschedule' event to another CPU: */
23265 extern void FASTCALL(smp_send_reschedule(int cpu));
23266
23267
23268 /* Boot processor call to load the other CPU's */
23269 extern void smp_boot_cpus(void);
23270
23271 /* Processor call in. Must hold processors until .. */
23272 extern void smp_callin(void);
23273
23274 /* Multiprocessors may now schedule */
23275 extern void smp_commence(void);
23276
23277 /* Call a function on all other processors */
23278 extern int smp_call_function(void (*func) (void *info),
23279     void *info, int retry, int wait);
23280
23281 /* True once the per process idle is forked */
23282 extern int smp_threads_ready;
23283
23284 extern int smp_num_cpus;
23285
23286 extern volatile unsigned long smp_msg_data;
23287 extern volatile int smp_src_cpu;
23288 extern volatile int smp_msg_id;
23289
23290 #define MSG_ALL_BUT_SELF    0x8000  /* Assume <32768
23291                                     * CPU's */
23292 #define MSG_ALL             0x8001
23293
23294 #define MSG_INVALIDATE_TLB  0x0001  /* Remote processor
23295                                     * TLB invalidate */
23296 #define MSG_STOP_CPU        0x0002  /* Sent to shut down
23297                                     * slave CPU's when
23298                                     * rebooting */
23299 #define MSG_RESCHEDULE      0x0003  /* Reschedule request
23300                                     * from master CPU */
23301 #define MSG_CALL_FUNCTION   0x0004  /* Call function on
23302                                     * all other CPUs */
23303
23304 #else
23305
23306 /* These macros fold the SMP functionality into a single
23307  * CPU system */
23308
23309 #define smp_num_cpus                    1
23310 #define smp_processor_id()              0
23311 #define hard_smp_processor_id()         0
23312 #define smp_threads_ready               1
23313 #define kernel_lock()
23314 #define cpu_logical_map(cpu)            0
```

```
23315 #define cpu_number_map(cpu)                      0
23316 #define smp_call_function(func,info,retry,wait) ({ 0; })
23317 #define cpu_online_map                           1
23318
23319 #endif
23320 #endif
```

include/linux/smp_lock.h

```
23321 #ifndef __LINUX_SMPLOCK_H
23322 #define __LINUX_SMPLOCK_H
23323
23324 #include <linux/config.h>
23325
23326 #ifndef CONFIG_SMP
23327
23328 #define lock_kernel()                 do { } while(0)
23329 #define unlock_kernel()               do { } while(0)
23330 #define release_kernel_lock(task, cpu) do { } while(0)
23331 #define reacquire_kernel_lock(task)   do { } while(0)
23332 #define kernel_locked() 1
23333
23334 #else
23335
23336 #include <asm/smplock.h>
23337
23338 #endif                                /* CONFIG_SMP */
23339
23340 #endif
```

include/linux/spinlock.h

```
23341 #ifndef __LINUX_SPINLOCK_H
23342 #define __LINUX_SPINLOCK_H
23343
23344 #include <linux/config.h>
23345
23346 /* These are the generic versions of the spinlocks and
23347  * read-write locks.. */
23348 #define spin_lock_irqsave(lock, flags)                \
23349 do { local_irq_save(flags);  spin_lock(lock); } while (0)
23350 #define spin_lock_irq(lock)                           \
23351 do { local_irq_disable();  spin_lock(lock); } while (0)
23352 #define spin_lock_bh(lock)                            \
23353 do { local_bh_disable();  spin_lock(lock); } while (0)
23354
23355 #define read_lock_irqsave(lock, flags)                \
23356 do { local_irq_save(flags);  read_lock(lock); } while (0)
23357 #define read_lock_irq(lock)                           \
23358 do { local_irq_disable();  read_lock(lock); } while (0)
23359 #define read_lock_bh(lock)                            \
23360 do { local_bh_disable();  read_lock(lock); } while (0)
23361
23362 #define write_lock_irqsave(lock, flags)               \
23363 do { local_irq_save(flags); write_lock(lock); } while (0)
23364 #define write_lock_irq(lock)                          \
23365 do { local_irq_disable();  write_lock(lock); } while (0)
23366 #define write_lock_bh(lock)                           \
23367 do { local_bh_disable();  write_lock(lock); } while (0)
23368
23369 #define spin_unlock_irqrestore(lock, flags)           \
23370 do { spin_unlock(lock);                               \
23371      local_irq_restore(flags); } while (0)
23372 #define spin_unlock_irq(lock)                         \
23373 do { spin_unlock(lock);   local_irq_enable(); } while (0)
23374 #define spin_unlock_bh(lock)                          \
23375 do { spin_unlock(lock);  local_bh_enable(); } while (0)
23376
23377 #define read_unlock_irqrestore(lock, flags)           \
23378 do { read_unlock(lock);                               \
23379      local_irq_restore(flags); } while (0)
23380 #define read_unlock_irq(lock)                         \
23381 do { read_unlock(lock);  local_irq_enable(); } while (0)
23382 #define read_unlock_bh(lock)                          \
23383 do { read_unlock(lock);  local_bh_enable(); } while (0)
23384
23385 #define write_unlock_irqrestore(lock, flags)          \
23386 do { write_unlock(lock);                              \
23387      local_irq_restore(flags); } while (0)
23388 #define write_unlock_irq(lock)                        \
23389 do { write_unlock(lock); local_irq_enable(); } while (0)
23390 #define write_unlock_bh(lock)                         \
23391 do { write_unlock(lock); local_bh_enable(); } while (0)
23392
23393 #ifdef CONFIG_SMP
23394 #include <asm/spinlock.h>
23395
23396 #else                                 /* !SMP */
23397
23398 #define DEBUG_SPINLOCKS 0  /* 0 == no debugging,
23399                             * 1 == maintain lock state,
23400                             * 2 == full debug */
23401
23402 #if (DEBUG_SPINLOCKS < 1)
23403
```

```
23404 #define atomic_dec_and_lock(atomic,lock)            \
23405   atomic_dec_and_test(atomic)
23406
23407 /* Your basic spinlocks, allowing only a single CPU
23408  * anywhere
23409  *
23410  * Most gcc versions have a nasty bug with empty
23411  * initializers.  */
23412 #if (__GNUC__ > 2)
23413 typedef struct {
23414 } spinlock_t;
23415
23416 #define SPIN_LOCK_UNLOCKED (spinlock_t) { }
23417 #else
23418 typedef struct {
23419   int gcc_is_buggy;
23420 } spinlock_t;
23421
23422 #define SPIN_LOCK_UNLOCKED (spinlock_t) { 0 }
23423 #endif
23424
23425 #define spin_lock_init(lock)    do { } while(0)
23426 /* Not "unused variable". */
23427 #define spin_lock(lock)         (void)(lock)
23428 #define spin_is_locked(lock)    (0)
23429 #define spin_trylock(lock)      ({1; })
23430 #define spin_unlock_wait(lock)  do { } while(0)
23431 #define spin_unlock(lock)       do { } while(0)
23432
23433 #elif (DEBUG_SPINLOCKS < 2)
23434
23435 typedef struct {
23436   volatile unsigned long lock;
23437 } spinlock_t;
23438
23439 #define SPIN_LOCK_UNLOCKED (spinlock_t) { 0 }
23440
23441 #define spin_lock_init(x)                             \
23442   do { (x)->lock = 0; } while (0)
23443 #define spin_is_locked(lock)    (test_bit(0,(lock)))
23444 #define spin_trylock(lock)                            \
23445   (!test_and_set_bit(0,(lock)))
23446
23447 #define spin_lock(x)      do { (x)->lock = 1; } while (0)
23448 #define spin_unlock_wait(x)     do { } while (0)
23449 #define spin_unlock(x)    do { (x)->lock = 0; } while (0)
23450
23451 #else                              /* (DEBUG_SPINLOCKS >= 2) */
23452
23453 typedef struct {
23454   volatile unsigned long lock;
23455   volatile unsigned int babble;
23456   const char *module;
23457 } spinlock_t;
23458
23459 #define SPIN_LOCK_UNLOCKED                            \
23460   (spinlock_t) { 0, 25, __BASE_FILE__ }
23461
23462 #include <linux/kernel.h>
23463
23464 #define spin_lock_init(x) do { (x)->lock = 0; } while (0)
23465 #define spin_is_locked(lock)    (test_bit(0,(lock)))
23466 #define spin_trylock(lock)  (!test_and_set_bit(0,(lock)))
23467
23468 #define spin_lock(x)                                  \
23469 do {                                                  \
23470   unsigned long __spinflags;                          \
23471   save_flags(__spinflags);                            \
23472   cli();                                              \
23473   if ((x)->lock&&(x)->babble) {                       \
23474     printk("%s:%d: spin_lock(%s:%p) already locked\n", \
23475            __BASE_FILE__,__LINE__, (x)->module, (x)); \
23476     (x)->babble--;                                    \
23477   }                                                   \
23478   (x)->lock = 1;                                      \
23479   restore_flags(__spinflags);                         \
23480 } while (0)
23481 #define spin_unlock_wait(x)                           \
23482 do {                                                  \
23483   unsigned long __spinflags;                          \
23484   save_flags(__spinflags);                            \
23485   cli();                                              \
23486   if ((x)->lock&&(x)->babble) {                       \
23487     printk("%s:%d: spin_unlock_wait(%s:%p) deadlock\n", \
23488            __BASE_FILE__,__LINE__, (x)->module, (x)); \
23489     (x)->babble--;                                    \
23490   }                                                   \
23491   restore_flags(__spinflags);                         \
23492 } while (0)
23493 #define spin_unlock(x)                                \
23494 do {                                                  \
23495   unsigned long __spinflags;                          \
23496   save_flags(__spinflags);                            \
23497   cli();                                              \
```

```
23498   if (!(x)->lock&&(x)->babble) {                      \
23499     printk("%s:%d: spin_unlock(%s:%p) not locked\n",  \
23500             __BASE_FILE__,__LINE__, (x)->module, (x)); \
23501     (x)->babble—;                                      \
23502   }                                                    \
23503   (x)->lock = 0;                                       \
23504   restore_flags(__spinflags);                          \
23505 } while (0)
23506
23507 #endif                              /* DEBUG_SPINLOCKS */
23508
23509 /* Read-write spinlocks, allowing multiple readers but
23510  * only one writer.
23511  *
23512  * NOTE! it is quite common to have readers in interrupts
23513  * but no interrupt writers. For those circumstances we
23514  * can "mix" irq-safe locks - any writer needs to get a
23515  * irq-safe write-lock, but readers can get non-irqsafe
23516  * read-locks.
23517  *
23518  * Most gcc versions have a nasty bug with empty
23519  * initializers.  */
23520 #if (__GNUC__ > 2)
23521 typedef struct {
23522 } rwlock_t;
23523
23524 #define RW_LOCK_UNLOCKED (rwlock_t) { }
23525 #else
23526 typedef struct {
23527   int gcc_is_buggy;
23528 } rwlock_t;
23529
23530 #define RW_LOCK_UNLOCKED (rwlock_t) { 0 }
23531 #endif
23532
23533 #define rwlock_init(lock)       do { } while(0)
23534 /* Not "unused variable".  */
23535 #define read_lock(lock)         (void)(lock)
23536 #define read_unlock(lock)       do { } while(0)
23537 /* Not "unused variable".  */
23538 #define write_lock(lock)        (void)(lock)
23539 #define write_unlock(lock)      do { } while(0)
23540
23541 #endif                              /* !SMP */
23542
23543 /* "lock on reference count zero" */
23544 #ifndef atomic_dec_and_lock
```

```
23545 #include <asm/atomic.h>
23546 extern int atomic_dec_and_lock(atomic_t * atomic,
23547     spinlock_t * lock);
23548 #endif
23549
23550 #endif                         /* __LINUX_SPINLOCK_H */
```

include/linux/swapctl.h

```
23551 #ifndef _LINUX_SWAPCTL_H
23552 #define _LINUX_SWAPCTL_H
23553
23554 #include <asm/page.h>
23555 #include <linux/fs.h>
23556
23557 typedef struct buffer_mem_v1 {
23558   unsigned int min_percent;
23559   unsigned int borrow_percent;
23560   unsigned int max_percent;
23561 } buffer_mem_v1;
23562 typedef buffer_mem_v1 buffer_mem_t;
23563 extern buffer_mem_t buffer_mem;
23564 extern buffer_mem_t page_cache;
23565
23566 typedef struct freepages_v1 {
23567   unsigned int min;
23568   unsigned int low;
23569   unsigned int high;
23570 } freepages_v1;
23571 typedef freepages_v1 freepages_t;
23572 extern freepages_t freepages;
23573
23574 typedef struct pager_daemon_v1 {
23575   unsigned int tries_base;
23576   unsigned int tries_min;
23577   unsigned int swap_cluster;
23578 } pager_daemon_v1;
23579 typedef pager_daemon_v1 pager_daemon_t;
23580 extern pager_daemon_t pager_daemon;
23581
23582 #endif                          /* _LINUX_SWAPCTL_H */
```

include/linux/swap.h

```
23583 #ifndef _LINUX_SWAP_H
23584 #define _LINUX_SWAP_H
23585
23586 #include <linux/spinlock.h>
```

```
23587 #include <asm/page.h>
23588
23589 #define SWAP_FLAG_PREFER      0x8000  /* set if swap
23590                                       * priority
23591                                       * specified */
23592 #define SWAP_FLAG_PRIO_MASK   0x7fff
23593 #define SWAP_FLAG_PRIO_SHIFT  0
23594
23595 #define MAX_SWAPFILES 8
23596
23597 union swap_header {
23598   struct {
23599     char reserved[PAGE_SIZE - 10];
23600     char magic[10];
23601   } magic;
23602   struct {
23603     char bootbits[1024];  /* Space for disklabel etc. */
23604     unsigned int version;
23605     unsigned int last_page;
23606     unsigned int nr_badpages;
23607     unsigned int padding[125];
23608     unsigned int badpages[1];
23609   } info;
23610 };
23611
23612 #ifdef __KERNEL__
23613
23614 /* Max bad pages in the new format..  */
23615 #define __swapoffset(x)                                    \
23616   ((unsigned long)&((union swap_header *)0)->x)
23617 #define MAX_SWAP_BADPAGES                                  \
23618   ((__swapoffset(magic.magic) -                           \
23619     __swapoffset(info.badpages)) / sizeof(int))
23620
23621 #include <asm/atomic.h>
23622
23623 #define SWP_USED      1
23624 #define SWP_WRITEOK   3
23625
23626 #define SWAP_CLUSTER_MAX 32
23627
23628 #define SWAP_MAP_MAX    0x7fff
23629 #define SWAP_MAP_BAD    0x8000
23630
23631 struct swap_info_struct {
23632   unsigned int flags;
23633   kdev_t swap_device;
```

```
23634   spinlock_t sdev_lock;
23635   struct dentry *swap_file;
23636   struct vfsmount *swap_vfsmnt;
23637   unsigned short *swap_map;
23638   unsigned int lowest_bit;
23639   unsigned int highest_bit;
23640   unsigned int cluster_next;
23641   unsigned int cluster_nr;
23642   int prio;                  /* swap priority */
23643   int pages;
23644   unsigned long max;
23645   int next;                  /* next entry on swap list */
23646 };
23647
23648 extern int nr_swap_pages;
23649 FASTCALL(unsigned int nr_free_pages(void));
23650 FASTCALL(unsigned int nr_inactive_clean_pages(void));
23651 FASTCALL(unsigned int nr_free_buffer_pages(void));
23652 extern int nr_active_pages;
23653 extern int nr_inactive_dirty_pages;
23654 extern atomic_t nr_async_pages;
23655 extern struct address_space swapper_space;
23656 extern atomic_t page_cache_size;
23657 extern atomic_t buffermem_pages;
23658 extern spinlock_t pagecache_lock;
23659 extern void __remove_inode_page(struct page *);
23660
23661 /* Incomplete types for prototype declarations: */
23662 struct task_struct;
23663 struct vm_area_struct;
23664 struct sysinfo;
23665
23666 struct zone_t;
23667
23668 /* linux/mm/swap.c */
23669 extern int memory_pressure;
23670 extern void age_page_up(struct page *);
23671 extern void age_page_up_nolock(struct page *);
23672 extern void age_page_down(struct page *);
23673 extern void age_page_down_nolock(struct page *);
23674 extern void age_page_down_ageonly(struct page *);
23675 extern void deactivate_page(struct page *);
23676 extern void deactivate_page_nolock(struct page *);
23677 extern void activate_page(struct page *);
23678 extern void activate_page_nolock(struct page *);
23679 extern void lru_cache_add(struct page *);
23680 extern void __lru_cache_del(struct page *);
```

```
23681 extern void lru_cache_del(struct page *);
23682 extern void recalculate_vm_stats(void);
23683 extern void swap_setup(void);
23684
23685 /* linux/mm/vmscan.c */
23686 extern struct page *reclaim_page(zone_t *);
23687 extern wait_queue_head_t kswapd_wait;
23688 extern wait_queue_head_t kreclaimd_wait;
23689 extern int page_launder(int, int);
23690 extern int free_shortage(void);
23691 extern int inactive_shortage(void);
23692 extern void wakeup_kswapd(void);
23693 extern int try_to_free_pages(unsigned int gfp_mask);
23694
23695 /* linux/mm/page_io.c */
23696 extern void rw_swap_page(int, struct page *, int);
23697 extern void rw_swap_page_nolock(int, swp_entry_t, char *,
23698     int);
23699
23700 /* linux/mm/page_alloc.c */
23701
23702 /* linux/mm/swap_state.c */
23703 extern void show_swap_cache_info(void);
23704 extern void add_to_swap_cache(struct page *,
23705     swp_entry_t);
23706 extern int swap_check_entry(unsigned long);
23707 extern struct page *lookup_swap_cache(swp_entry_t);
23708 extern struct page *read_swap_cache_async(swp_entry_t,
23709     int);
23710 #define read_swap_cache(entry)                          \
23711   read_swap_cache_async(entry, 1);
23712
23713 /* linux/mm/oom_kill.c */
23714 extern int out_of_memory(void);
23715 extern void oom_kill(void);
23716
23717 /* Make these inline later once they are working
23718  * properly. */
23719 extern void __delete_from_swap_cache(struct page *page);
23720 extern void delete_from_swap_cache(struct page *page);
23721 extern void delete_from_swap_cache_nolock(
23722   struct page *page);
23723 extern void free_page_and_swap_cache(struct page *page);
23724
23725 /* linux/mm/swapfile.c */
23726 extern unsigned int nr_swapfiles;
23727 extern struct swap_info_struct swap_info[];
23728 extern int is_swap_partition(kdev_t);
23729 extern void si_swapinfo(struct sysinfo *);
23730 extern swp_entry_t __get_swap_page(unsigned short);
23731 extern void get_swaphandle_info(swp_entry_t,
23732     unsigned long *, kdev_t *, struct inode **);
23733 extern int swap_duplicate(swp_entry_t);
23734 extern int swap_count(struct page *);
23735 extern int valid_swaphandles(swp_entry_t,
23736     unsigned long *);
23737 #define get_swap_page() __get_swap_page(1)
23738 extern void __swap_free(swp_entry_t, unsigned short);
23739 #define swap_free(entry) __swap_free((entry), 1)
23740 struct swap_list_t {
23741   int head;  /* head of priority-ordered swapfile list */
23742   int next;  /* swapfile to be used next */
23743 };
23744 extern struct swap_list_t swap_list;
23745 asmlinkage long sys_swapoff(const char *);
23746 asmlinkage long sys_swapon(const char *, int);
23747
23748 #define SWAP_CACHE_INFO
23749
23750 #ifdef SWAP_CACHE_INFO
23751 extern unsigned long swap_cache_add_total;
23752 extern unsigned long swap_cache_del_total;
23753 extern unsigned long swap_cache_find_total;
23754 extern unsigned long swap_cache_find_success;
23755 #endif
23756
23757 /* Work out if there are any other processes sharing this
23758  * page, ignoring any page reference coming from the swap
23759  * cache, or from outstanding swap IO on this page.  (The
23760  * page cache _does_ count as another valid reference to
23761  * the page, however.)  */
23762 static inline int is_page_shared(struct page *page)
23763 {
23764   unsigned int count;
23765   if (PageReserved(page))
23766     return 1;
23767   count = page_count(page);
23768   if (PageSwapCache(page))
23769     count += swap_count(page) - 2 - !!page->buffers;
23770   return count > 1;
23771 }
23772
23773 extern spinlock_t pagemap_lru_lock;
23774
```

```
23775 /* Page aging defines.  Since we do exponential decay of
23776  * the page age, we can chose a fairly large maximum.  */
23777 #define PAGE_AGE_START 2
23778 #define PAGE_AGE_ADV 3
23779 #define PAGE_AGE_MAX 64
23780
23781 /* List add/del helper macros. These must be called with
23782  * the pagemap_lru_lock held!  */
23783 #define DEBUG_ADD_PAGE                                       \
23784   if (PageActive(page) || PageInactiveDirty(page) ||        \
23785       PageInactiveClean(page)) BUG();
23786
23787 #define ZERO_PAGE_BUG                                        \
23788         if (page_count(page) == 0) BUG();
23789
23790 #define add_page_to_active_list(page) {                      \
23791         DEBUG_ADD_PAGE                                       \
23792         ZERO_PAGE_BUG                                        \
23793         SetPageActive(page);                                 \
23794         list_add(&(page)->lru, &active_list);                \
23795         nr_active_pages++;                                   \
23796 }
23797
23798 #define add_page_to_inactive_dirty_list(page) {              \
23799         DEBUG_ADD_PAGE                                       \
23800         ZERO_PAGE_BUG                                        \
23801         SetPageInactiveDirty(page);                          \
23802         list_add(&(page)->lru, &inactive_dirty_list);        \
23803         nr_inactive_dirty_pages++;                           \
23804         page->zone->inactive_dirty_pages++;                  \
23805 }
23806
23807 #define add_page_to_inactive_clean_list(page) {              \
23808         DEBUG_ADD_PAGE                                       \
23809         ZERO_PAGE_BUG                                        \
23810         SetPageInactiveClean(page);                          \
23811         list_add(&(page)->lru,                               \
23812                 &page->zone->inactive_clean_list);           \
23813         page->zone->inactive_clean_pages++;                  \
23814 }
23815
23816 #define del_page_from_active_list(page) {                    \
23817         list_del(&(page)->lru);                              \
23818         ClearPageActive(page);                               \
23819         nr_active_pages-;                                    \
23820         DEBUG_ADD_PAGE                                       \
23821         ZERO_PAGE_BUG                                        \
23822 }
23823
23824 #define del_page_from_inactive_dirty_list(page) {            \
23825         list_del(&(page)->lru);                              \
23826         ClearPageInactiveDirty(page);                        \
23827         nr_inactive_dirty_pages-;                            \
23828         page->zone->inactive_dirty_pages-;                   \
23829         DEBUG_ADD_PAGE                                       \
23830         ZERO_PAGE_BUG                                        \
23831 }
23832
23833 #define del_page_from_inactive_clean_list(page) {            \
23834         list_del(&(page)->lru);                              \
23835         ClearPageInactiveClean(page);                        \
23836         page->zone->inactive_clean_pages-;                   \
23837         DEBUG_ADD_PAGE                                       \
23838         ZERO_PAGE_BUG                                        \
23839 }
23840
23841 /* In mm/swap.c::recalculate_vm_stats(), we substract
23842  * inactive_target from memory_pressure every second.
23843  * This means that memory_pressure is smoothed over 64 (1
23844  * << INACTIVE_SHIFT) seconds.  */
23845 #define INACTIVE_SHIFT 6
23846 #define inactive_min(a,b) ((a) < (b) ? (a) : (b))
23847 #define inactive_target                                      \
23848   inactive_min((memory_pressure >> INACTIVE_SHIFT),          \
23849                 (num_physpages / 4))
23850
23851 /* Ugly ugly ugly HACK to make sure the inactive lists
23852  * don't fill up with unfreeable ramdisk pages. We really
23853  * want to fix the ramdisk driver to mark its pages as
23854  * unfreeable instead of using dirty buffer magic, but
23855  * the next code-change time is when 2.5 is forked...  */
23856 #ifndef _LINUX_KDEV_T_H
23857 #include <linux/kdev_t.h>
23858 #endif
23859 #ifndef _LINUX_MAJOR_H
23860 #include <linux/major.h>
23861 #endif
23862
23863 #define page_ramdisk(page)                                   \
23864         (page->buffers &&                                    \
23865         (MAJOR(page->buffers->b_dev) == RAMDISK_MAJOR))
23866
23867 extern spinlock_t swaplock;
23868
```

```
23869 #define swap_list_lock()        spin_lock(&swaplock)
23870 #define swap_list_unlock()      spin_unlock(&swaplock)
23871 #define swap_device_lock(p)     spin_lock(&p->sdev_lock)
23872 #define swap_device_unlock(p)   spin_unlock(&p->sdev_lock)
23873
23874 extern void shmem_unuse(swp_entry_t entry,
23875     struct page *page);
23876
23877 #endif                          /* __KERNEL__ */
23878
23879 #endif                          /* _LINUX_SWAP_H */
```

include/linux/sysctl.h

```
23880 /*
23881  * sysctl.h: General linux system control interface
23882  *
23883  * Begun 24 March 1995, Stephen Tweedie
23884  *
23885  ***************************************************************
23886  ***************************************************************
23887  **
23888  **   WARNING: The values in this file are exported to
23889  **   user space via the sysctl() binary interface.  Do
23890  **   *NOT* change the numbering of any existing values
23891  **   here, and do not change any numbers within any one
23892  **   set of values.  If you have to redefine an existing
23893  **   interface, use a new number for it.  The kernel will
23894  **   then return ENOTDIR to any application using the old
23895  **   binary interface.
23896  **
23897  **   —sct
23898  **
23899  ***************************************************************
23900  ***************************************************************
23901  */
23902
23903 #ifndef _LINUX_SYSCTL_H
23904 #define _LINUX_SYSCTL_H
23905
23906 #include <linux/kernel.h>
23907 #include <linux/types.h>
23908 #include <linux/list.h>
23909
23910 struct file;
23911
23912 #define CTL_MAXNAME 10
23913
23914 struct __sysctl_args {
23915   int *name;
23916   int nlen;
23917   void *oldval;
23918   size_t *oldlenp;
23919   void *newval;
23920   size_t newlen;
23921   unsigned long __unused[4];
23922 };
23923
23924 /* Define sysctl names first */
23925
23926 /* Top-level names: */
23927
23928 /* For internal pattern-matching use only: */
23929 #ifdef __KERNEL__
23930 #define CTL_ANY         -1       /* Matches any name */
23931 #define CTL_NONE        0
23932 #endif
23933
23934 enum {
23935   CTL_KERN = 1,    /* General kernel info and control */
23936   CTL_VM = 2,      /* VM management */
23937   CTL_NET = 3,     /* Networking */
23938   CTL_PROC = 4,    /* Process info */
23939   CTL_FS = 5,      /* Filesystems */
23940   CTL_DEBUG = 6,   /* Debugging */
23941   CTL_DEV = 7,     /* Devices */
23942   CTL_BUS = 8      /* Buses */
23943 };
23944
23945 /* CTL_BUS names: */
23946 enum {
23947   BUS_ISA = 1      /* ISA */
23948 };
23949
23950 /* CTL_KERN names: */
23951 enum {
23952   KERN_OSTYPE = 1,         /* string: system version */
23953   KERN_OSRELEASE = 2,      /* string: system release */
23954   KERN_OSREV = 3,          /* int: system revision*/
23955   KERN_VERSION = 4,        /* string: compile time info*/
23956   KERN_SECUREMASK = 5,     /* struct: maximum rights mask
23957                               */
23958   KERN_PROF = 6,           /* table: profiling info */
23959   KERN_NODENAME = 7,
23960   KERN_DOMAINNAME = 8,
```

```
23961
23962    KERN_CAP_BSET = 14,        /* int: capability bounding
23963                               * set */
23964    KERN_PANIC = 15,           /* int: panic timeout */
23965    KERN_REALROOTDEV = 16,     /* real root device to mount
23966                               * after initrd */
23967
23968    KERN_SPARC_REBOOT = 21,    /* reboot command on Sparc */
23969    KERN_CTLALTDEL = 22,       /* int: allow ctl-alt-del to
23970                               * reboot */
23971    KERN_PRINTK = 23,          /* struct: control printk
23972                               * logging parameters */
23973    KERN_NAMETRANS = 24,       /* Name translation */
23974    KERN_PPC_HTABRECLAIM = 25, /* turn htab reclaimation
23975                               * on/off on PPC */
23976    KERN_PPC_ZEROPAGED = 26,   /* turn idle page zeroing
23977                               * on/off on PPC */
23978    KERN_PPC_POWERSAVE_NAP = 27,/* use nap mode for power
23979                               * saving */
23980    KERN_MODPROBE = 28,
23981    KERN_SG_BIG_BUFF = 29,
23982    KERN_ACCT = 30,            /* BSD process accounting
23983                               * parameters */
23984    KERN_PPC_L2CR = 31,        /* l2cr register on PPC*/
23985
23986    KERN_RTSIGNR = 32,         /* Number of rt sigs queued */
23987    KERN_RTSIGMAX = 33,        /* Max queueable */
23988
23989    KERN_SHMMAX = 34,          /* long: Maximum shared memory
23990                               * segment */
23991    KERN_MSGMAX = 35,          /* int: Maximum size of a
23992                               * messege */
23993    KERN_MSGMNB = 36,          /* int: Maximum message queue
23994                               * size */
23995    KERN_MSGPOOL = 37,         /* int: Maximum system message
23996                               * pool size */
23997    KERN_SYSRQ = 38,           /* int: Sysreq enable */
23998    KERN_MAX_THREADS = 39,     /* int: Maximum nr of threads
23999                               * in the system */
24000    KERN_RANDOM = 40,          /* Random driver */
24001    KERN_SHMALL = 41,          /* int: Maximum size of shared
24002                               * memory */
24003    KERN_MSGMNI = 42,          /* int: msg queue identifiers
24004                               */
24005    KERN_SEM = 43,             /* struct: sysv semaphore
24006                               * limits */
24007    KERN_SPARC_STOP_A = 44,    /* int: Sparc Stop-A enable */
24008    KERN_SHMMNI = 45,          /* int: shm array IDs */
24009    KERN_OVERFLOWUID = 46,     /* int: overflow UID */
24010    KERN_OVERFLOWGID = 47,     /* int: overflow GID */
24011    KERN_SHMPATH = 48,         /* string: path to shm fs */
24012    KERN_HOTPLUG = 49,         /* string: path to hotplug
24013                               * policy agent*/
24014 };
24015
24016
24017 /* CTL_VM names: */
24018 enum {
24019    VM_SWAPCTL = 1,            /* struct: Set vm swapping
24020                               * control */
24021    VM_SWAPOUT = 2,            /* int: Linear or sqrt()
24022                               * swapout for hogs */
24023    VM_FREEPG = 3,             /* struct: Set free page
24024                               * thresholds */
24025    VM_BDFLUSH = 4,            /* struct: Control buffer
24026                               * cache flushing */
24027    VM_OVERCOMMIT_MEMORY = 5,  /* Turn off the virtual memory
24028                               * safety limit */
24029    VM_BUFFERMEM = 6,          /* struct: Set buffer memory
24030                               * thresholds */
24031    VM_PAGECACHE = 7,          /* struct: Set cache memory
24032                               * thresholds */
24033    VM_PAGERDAEMON = 8,        /* struct: Control kswapd
24034                               * behaviour */
24035    VM_PGT_CACHE = 9,          /* struct: Set page table
24036                               * cache parameters */
24037    VM_PAGE_CLUSTER = 10       /* int: set number of pages to
24038                               * swap together */
24039 };
24040
24041
24042 /* CTL_NET names: */
24043 enum {
24044    NET_CORE = 1,
24045    NET_ETHER = 2,
24046    NET_802 = 3,
24047    NET_UNIX = 4,
24048    NET_IPV4 = 5,
24049    NET_IPX = 6,
24050    NET_ATALK = 7,
24051    NET_NETROM = 8,
24052    NET_AX25 = 9,
24053    NET_BRIDGE = 10,
24054    NET_ROSE = 11,
```

```
24055    NET_IPV6 = 12,
24056    NET_X25 = 13,
24057    NET_TR = 14,
24058    NET_DECNET = 15,
24059    NET_ECONET = 16,
24060    NET_KHTTPD = 17
24061 };
24062
24063 /* /proc/sys/kernel/random */
24064 enum {
24065    RANDOM_POOLSIZE = 1,
24066    RANDOM_ENTROPY_COUNT = 2,
24067    RANDOM_READ_THRESH = 3,
24068    RANDOM_WRITE_THRESH = 4,
24069    RANDOM_BOOT_ID = 5,
24070    RANDOM_UUID = 6
24071 };
24072
24073 /* /proc/sys/bus/isa */
24074 enum {
24075    BUS_ISA_MEM_BASE = 1,
24076    BUS_ISA_PORT_BASE = 2,
24077    BUS_ISA_PORT_SHIFT = 3
24078 };
24079
24080 /* /proc/sys/net/core */
24081 enum {
24082    NET_CORE_WMEM_MAX = 1,
24083    NET_CORE_RMEM_MAX = 2,
24084    NET_CORE_WMEM_DEFAULT = 3,
24085    NET_CORE_RMEM_DEFAULT = 4,
24086    /* was  NET_CORE_DESTROY_DELAY */
24087    NET_CORE_MAX_BACKLOG = 6,
24088    NET_CORE_FASTROUTE = 7,
24089    NET_CORE_MSG_COST = 8,
24090    NET_CORE_MSG_BURST = 9,
24091    NET_CORE_OPTMEM_MAX = 10,
24092    NET_CORE_HOT_LIST_LENGTH = 11,
24093    NET_CORE_DIVERT_VERSION = 12,
24094    NET_CORE_NO_CONG_THRESH = 13,
24095    NET_CORE_NO_CONG = 14,
24096    NET_CORE_LO_CONG = 15,
24097    NET_CORE_MOD_CONG = 16
24098 };
24099
24100 /* /proc/sys/net/ethernet */
24101
24102 /* /proc/sys/net/802 */
24103
24104 /* /proc/sys/net/unix */
24105
24106 enum {
24107    NET_UNIX_DESTROY_DELAY = 1,
24108    NET_UNIX_DELETE_DELAY = 2,
24109    NET_UNIX_MAX_DGRAM_QLEN = 3,
24110 };
24111
24112 /* /proc/sys/net/ipv4 */
24113 enum {
24114    /* v2.0 compatibile variables */
24115    NET_IPV4_FORWARD = 8,
24116    NET_IPV4_DYNADDR = 9,
24117
24118    NET_IPV4_CONF = 16,
24119    NET_IPV4_NEIGH = 17,
24120    NET_IPV4_ROUTE = 18,
24121    NET_IPV4_FIB_HASH = 19,
24122
24123    NET_IPV4_TCP_TIMESTAMPS = 33,
24124    NET_IPV4_TCP_WINDOW_SCALING = 34,
24125    NET_IPV4_TCP_SACK = 35,
24126    NET_IPV4_TCP_RETRANS_COLLAPSE = 36,
24127    NET_IPV4_DEFAULT_TTL = 37,
24128    NET_IPV4_AUTOCONFIG = 38,
24129    NET_IPV4_NO_PMTU_DISC = 39,
24130    NET_IPV4_TCP_SYN_RETRIES = 40,
24131    NET_IPV4_IPFRAG_HIGH_THRESH = 41,
24132    NET_IPV4_IPFRAG_LOW_THRESH = 42,
24133    NET_IPV4_IPFRAG_TIME = 43,
24134    NET_IPV4_TCP_MAX_KA_PROBES = 44,
24135    NET_IPV4_TCP_KEEPALIVE_TIME = 45,
24136    NET_IPV4_TCP_KEEPALIVE_PROBES = 46,
24137    NET_IPV4_TCP_RETRIES1 = 47,
24138    NET_IPV4_TCP_RETRIES2 = 48,
24139    NET_IPV4_TCP_FIN_TIMEOUT = 49,
24140    NET_IPV4_IP_MASQ_DEBUG = 50,
24141    NET_TCP_SYNCOOKIES = 51,
24142    NET_TCP_STDURG = 52,
24143    NET_TCP_RFC1337 = 53,
24144    NET_TCP_SYN_TAILDROP = 54,
24145    NET_TCP_MAX_SYN_BACKLOG = 55,
24146    NET_IPV4_LOCAL_PORT_RANGE = 56,
24147    NET_IPV4_ICMP_ECHO_IGNORE_ALL = 57,
24148    NET_IPV4_ICMP_ECHO_IGNORE_BROADCASTS = 58,
```

```
24149    NET_IPV4_ICMP_SOURCEQUENCH_RATE = 59,
24150    NET_IPV4_ICMP_DESTUNREACH_RATE = 60,
24151    NET_IPV4_ICMP_TIMEEXCEED_RATE = 61,
24152    NET_IPV4_ICMP_PARAMPROB_RATE = 62,
24153    NET_IPV4_ICMP_ECHOREPLY_RATE = 63,
24154    NET_IPV4_ICMP_IGNORE_BOGUS_ERROR_RESPONSES = 64,
24155    NET_IPV4_IGMP_MAX_MEMBERSHIPS = 65,
24156    NET_TCP_TW_RECYCLE = 66,
24157    NET_IPV4_ALWAYS_DEFRAG = 67,
24158    NET_IPV4_TCP_KEEPALIVE_INTVL = 68,
24159    NET_IPV4_INET_PEER_THRESHOLD = 69,
24160    NET_IPV4_INET_PEER_MINTTL = 70,
24161    NET_IPV4_INET_PEER_MAXTTL = 71,
24162    NET_IPV4_INET_PEER_GC_MINTIME = 72,
24163    NET_IPV4_INET_PEER_GC_MAXTIME = 73,
24164    NET_TCP_ORPHAN_RETRIES = 74,
24165    NET_TCP_ABORT_ON_OVERFLOW = 75,
24166    NET_TCP_SYNACK_RETRIES = 76,
24167    NET_TCP_MAX_ORPHANS = 77,
24168    NET_TCP_MAX_TW_BUCKETS = 78,
24169    NET_TCP_FACK = 79,
24170    NET_TCP_REORDERING = 80,
24171    NET_TCP_ECN = 81,
24172    NET_TCP_DSACK = 82,
24173    NET_TCP_MEM = 83,
24174    NET_TCP_WMEM = 84,
24175    NET_TCP_RMEM = 85,
24176    NET_TCP_APP_WIN = 86,
24177    NET_TCP_ADV_WIN_SCALE = 87,
24178    NET_IPV4_NONLOCAL_BIND = 88,
24179 };
24180
24181 enum {
24182    NET_IPV4_ROUTE_FLUSH = 1,
24183    NET_IPV4_ROUTE_MIN_DELAY = 2,
24184    NET_IPV4_ROUTE_MAX_DELAY = 3,
24185    NET_IPV4_ROUTE_GC_THRESH = 4,
24186    NET_IPV4_ROUTE_MAX_SIZE = 5,
24187    NET_IPV4_ROUTE_GC_MIN_INTERVAL = 6,
24188    NET_IPV4_ROUTE_GC_TIMEOUT = 7,
24189    NET_IPV4_ROUTE_GC_INTERVAL = 8,
24190    NET_IPV4_ROUTE_REDIRECT_LOAD = 9,
24191    NET_IPV4_ROUTE_REDIRECT_NUMBER = 10,
24192    NET_IPV4_ROUTE_REDIRECT_SILENCE = 11,
24193    NET_IPV4_ROUTE_ERROR_COST = 12,
24194    NET_IPV4_ROUTE_ERROR_BURST = 13,
24195    NET_IPV4_ROUTE_GC_ELASTICITY = 14,
24196    NET_IPV4_ROUTE_MTU_EXPIRES = 15,
24197    NET_IPV4_ROUTE_MIN_PMTU = 16,
24198    NET_IPV4_ROUTE_MIN_ADVMSS = 17
24199 };
24200
24201 enum {
24202    NET_PROTO_CONF_ALL = -2,
24203    NET_PROTO_CONF_DEFAULT = -3
24204        /* And device ifindices ... */
24205 };
24206
24207 enum {
24208    NET_IPV4_CONF_FORWARDING = 1,
24209    NET_IPV4_CONF_MC_FORWARDING = 2,
24210    NET_IPV4_CONF_PROXY_ARP = 3,
24211    NET_IPV4_CONF_ACCEPT_REDIRECTS = 4,
24212    NET_IPV4_CONF_SECURE_REDIRECTS = 5,
24213    NET_IPV4_CONF_SEND_REDIRECTS = 6,
24214    NET_IPV4_CONF_SHARED_MEDIA = 7,
24215    NET_IPV4_CONF_RP_FILTER = 8,
24216    NET_IPV4_CONF_ACCEPT_SOURCE_ROUTE = 9,
24217    NET_IPV4_CONF_BOOTP_RELAY = 10,
24218    NET_IPV4_CONF_LOG_MARTIANS = 11,
24219    NET_IPV4_CONF_TAG = 12
24220 };
24221
24222 /* /proc/sys/net/ipv6 */
24223 enum {
24224    NET_IPV6_CONF = 16,
24225    NET_IPV6_NEIGH = 17,
24226    NET_IPV6_ROUTE = 18
24227 };
24228
24229 enum {
24230    NET_IPV6_ROUTE_FLUSH = 1,
24231    NET_IPV6_ROUTE_GC_THRESH = 2,
24232    NET_IPV6_ROUTE_MAX_SIZE = 3,
24233    NET_IPV6_ROUTE_GC_MIN_INTERVAL = 4,
24234    NET_IPV6_ROUTE_GC_TIMEOUT = 5,
24235    NET_IPV6_ROUTE_GC_INTERVAL = 6,
24236    NET_IPV6_ROUTE_GC_ELASTICITY = 7,
24237    NET_IPV6_ROUTE_MTU_EXPIRES = 8,
24238    NET_IPV6_ROUTE_MIN_ADVMSS = 9
24239 };
24240
24241 enum {
24242    NET_IPV6_FORWARDING = 1,
```

```
24243    NET_IPV6_HOP_LIMIT = 2,
24244    NET_IPV6_MTU = 3,
24245    NET_IPV6_ACCEPT_RA = 4,
24246    NET_IPV6_ACCEPT_REDIRECTS = 5,
24247    NET_IPV6_AUTOCONF = 6,
24248    NET_IPV6_DAD_TRANSMITS = 7,
24249    NET_IPV6_RTR_SOLICITS = 8,
24250    NET_IPV6_RTR_SOLICIT_INTERVAL = 9,
24251    NET_IPV6_RTR_SOLICIT_DELAY = 10
24252 };
24253
24254 /* /proc/sys/net/<protocol>/neigh/<dev> */
24255 enum {
24256    NET_NEIGH_MCAST_SOLICIT = 1,
24257    NET_NEIGH_UCAST_SOLICIT = 2,
24258    NET_NEIGH_APP_SOLICIT = 3,
24259    NET_NEIGH_RETRANS_TIME = 4,
24260    NET_NEIGH_REACHABLE_TIME = 5,
24261    NET_NEIGH_DELAY_PROBE_TIME = 6,
24262    NET_NEIGH_GC_STALE_TIME = 7,
24263    NET_NEIGH_UNRES_QLEN = 8,
24264    NET_NEIGH_PROXY_QLEN = 9,
24265    NET_NEIGH_ANYCAST_DELAY = 10,
24266    NET_NEIGH_PROXY_DELAY = 11,
24267    NET_NEIGH_LOCKTIME = 12,
24268    NET_NEIGH_GC_INTERVAL = 13,
24269    NET_NEIGH_GC_THRESH1 = 14,
24270    NET_NEIGH_GC_THRESH2 = 15,
24271    NET_NEIGH_GC_THRESH3 = 16
24272 };
24273
24274 /* /proc/sys/net/ipx */
24275
24276
24277 /* /proc/sys/net/appletalk */
24278 enum {
24279    NET_ATALK_AARP_EXPIRY_TIME = 1,
24280    NET_ATALK_AARP_TICK_TIME = 2,
24281    NET_ATALK_AARP_RETRANSMIT_LIMIT = 3,
24282    NET_ATALK_AARP_RESOLVE_TIME = 4
24283 };
24284
24285
24286 /* /proc/sys/net/netrom */
24287 enum {
24288    NET_NETROM_DEFAULT_PATH_QUALITY = 1,
24289    NET_NETROM_OBSOLESCENCE_COUNT_INITIALISER = 2,
```

```
24290    NET_NETROM_NETWORK_TTL_INITIALISER = 3,
24291    NET_NETROM_TRANSPORT_TIMEOUT = 4,
24292    NET_NETROM_TRANSPORT_MAXIMUM_TRIES = 5,
24293    NET_NETROM_TRANSPORT_ACKNOWLEDGE_DELAY = 6,
24294    NET_NETROM_TRANSPORT_BUSY_DELAY = 7,
24295    NET_NETROM_TRANSPORT_REQUESTED_WINDOW_SIZE = 8,
24296    NET_NETROM_TRANSPORT_NO_ACTIVITY_TIMEOUT = 9,
24297    NET_NETROM_ROUTING_CONTROL = 10,
24298    NET_NETROM_LINK_FAILS_COUNT = 11
24299 };
24300
24301 /* /proc/sys/net/ax25 */
24302 enum {
24303    NET_AX25_IP_DEFAULT_MODE = 1,
24304    NET_AX25_DEFAULT_MODE = 2,
24305    NET_AX25_BACKOFF_TYPE = 3,
24306    NET_AX25_CONNECT_MODE = 4,
24307    NET_AX25_STANDARD_WINDOW = 5,
24308    NET_AX25_EXTENDED_WINDOW = 6,
24309    NET_AX25_T1_TIMEOUT = 7,
24310    NET_AX25_T2_TIMEOUT = 8,
24311    NET_AX25_T3_TIMEOUT = 9,
24312    NET_AX25_IDLE_TIMEOUT = 10,
24313    NET_AX25_N2 = 11,
24314    NET_AX25_PACLEN = 12,
24315    NET_AX25_PROTOCOL = 13,
24316    NET_AX25_DAMA_SLAVE_TIMEOUT = 14
24317 };
24318
24319 /* /proc/sys/net/rose */
24320 enum {
24321    NET_ROSE_RESTART_REQUEST_TIMEOUT = 1,
24322    NET_ROSE_CALL_REQUEST_TIMEOUT = 2,
24323    NET_ROSE_RESET_REQUEST_TIMEOUT = 3,
24324    NET_ROSE_CLEAR_REQUEST_TIMEOUT = 4,
24325    NET_ROSE_ACK_HOLD_BACK_TIMEOUT = 5,
24326    NET_ROSE_ROUTING_CONTROL = 6,
24327    NET_ROSE_LINK_FAIL_TIMEOUT = 7,
24328    NET_ROSE_MAX_VCS = 8,
24329    NET_ROSE_WINDOW_SIZE = 9,
24330    NET_ROSE_NO_ACTIVITY_TIMEOUT = 10
24331 };
24332
24333 /* /proc/sys/net/x25 */
24334 enum {
24335    NET_X25_RESTART_REQUEST_TIMEOUT = 1,
24336    NET_X25_CALL_REQUEST_TIMEOUT = 2,
```

```
24337    NET_X25_RESET_REQUEST_TIMEOUT = 3,
24338    NET_X25_CLEAR_REQUEST_TIMEOUT = 4,
24339    NET_X25_ACK_HOLD_BACK_TIMEOUT = 5
24340 };
24341
24342 /* /proc/sys/net/token-ring */
24343 enum {
24344    NET_TR_RIF_TIMEOUT = 1
24345 };
24346
24347 /* /proc/sys/net/decnet/ */
24348 enum {
24349    NET_DECNET_NODE_TYPE = 1,
24350    NET_DECNET_NODE_ADDRESS = 2,
24351    NET_DECNET_NODE_NAME = 3,
24352    NET_DECNET_DEFAULT_DEVICE = 4,
24353    NET_DECNET_TIME_WAIT = 5,
24354    NET_DECNET_DN_COUNT = 6,
24355    NET_DECNET_DI_COUNT = 7,
24356    NET_DECNET_DR_COUNT = 8,
24357    NET_DECNET_DST_GC_INTERVAL = 9,
24358    NET_DECNET_CONF = 10,
24359    NET_DECNET_DEBUG_LEVEL = 255
24360 };
24361
24362 /* /proc/sys/net/khttpd/ */
24363 enum {
24364    NET_KHTTPD_DOCROOT = 1,
24365    NET_KHTTPD_START = 2,
24366    NET_KHTTPD_STOP = 3,
24367    NET_KHTTPD_UNLOAD = 4,
24368    NET_KHTTPD_CLIENTPORT = 5,
24369    NET_KHTTPD_PERMREQ = 6,
24370    NET_KHTTPD_PERMFORBID = 7,
24371    NET_KHTTPD_LOGGING = 8,
24372    NET_KHTTPD_SERVERPORT = 9,
24373    NET_KHTTPD_DYNAMICSTRING = 10,
24374    NET_KHTTPD_SLOPPYMIME = 11,
24375    NET_KHTTPD_THREADS = 12,
24376    NET_KHTTPD_MAXCONNECT = 13
24377 };
24378
24379 /* /proc/sys/net/decnet/conf/<dev> */
24380 enum {
24381    NET_DECNET_CONF_LOOPBACK = -2,
24382    NET_DECNET_CONF_DDCMP = -3,
24383    NET_DECNET_CONF_PPP = -4,
```

```
24384    NET_DECNET_CONF_X25 = -5,
24385    NET_DECNET_CONF_GRE = -6,
24386    NET_DECNET_CONF_ETHER = -7
24387        /* ... and ifindex of devices */
24388 };
24389
24390 /* /proc/sys/net/decnet/conf/<dev>/ */
24391 enum {
24392    NET_DECNET_CONF_DEV_PRIORITY = 1,
24393    NET_DECNET_CONF_DEV_T1 = 2,
24394    NET_DECNET_CONF_DEV_T2 = 3,
24395    NET_DECNET_CONF_DEV_T3 = 4,
24396    NET_DECNET_CONF_DEV_FORWARDING = 5,
24397    NET_DECNET_CONF_DEV_BLKSIZE = 6,
24398    NET_DECNET_CONF_DEV_STATE = 7
24399 };
24400
24401 /* CTL_PROC names: */
24402
24403 /* CTL_FS names: */
24404 enum {
24405    FS_NRINODE = 1,        /* int:current number of
24406                           * allocated inodes */
24407    FS_STATINODE = 2,
24408    FS_MAXINODE = 3,       /* int:maximum number of inodes
24409                           * that can be allocated */
24410    FS_NRDQUOT = 4,        /* int:current number of
24411                           * allocated dquots */
24412    FS_MAXDQUOT = 5,       /* int:maximum number of dquots
24413                           * that can be allocated */
24414    FS_NRFILE = 6,         /* int:current number of
24415                           * allocated filedescriptors */
24416    FS_MAXFILE = 7,        /* int:maximum number of
24417                           * filedescriptors that can be
24418                           * allocated */
24419    FS_DENTRY = 8,
24420    FS_NRSUPER = 9,        /* int:current number of
24421                           * allocated super_blocks */
24422    FS_MAXSUPER = 10,      /* int:maximum number of
24423                           * super_blocks that can be
24424                           * allocated */
24425    FS_OVERFLOWUID = 11,   /* int: overflow UID */
24426    FS_OVERFLOWGID = 12,   /* int: overflow GID */
24427    FS_LEASES = 13,        /* int: leases enabled */
24428    FS_DIR_NOTIFY = 14,    /* int: directory notification
24429                           * enabled*/
24430    FS_LEASE_TIME = 15,    /* int: maximum time to wait for
```

```
24431                        * a lease break */
24432 };
24433
24434 /* CTL_DEBUG names: */
24435
24436 /* CTL_DEV names: */
24437 enum {
24438   DEV_CDROM = 1,
24439   DEV_HWMON = 2,
24440   DEV_PARPORT = 3,
24441   DEV_RAID = 4,
24442   DEV_MAC_HID = 5
24443 };
24444
24445 /* /proc/sys/dev/cdrom */
24446 enum {
24447   DEV_CDROM_INFO = 1,
24448   DEV_CDROM_AUTOCLOSE = 2,
24449   DEV_CDROM_AUTOEJECT = 3,
24450   DEV_CDROM_DEBUG = 4,
24451   DEV_CDROM_LOCK = 5,
24452   DEV_CDROM_CHECK_MEDIA = 6
24453 };
24454
24455 /* /proc/sys/dev/parport */
24456 enum {
24457   DEV_PARPORT_DEFAULT = -3
24458 };
24459
24460 /* /proc/sys/dev/raid */
24461 enum {
24462   DEV_RAID_SPEED_LIMIT_MIN = 1,
24463   DEV_RAID_SPEED_LIMIT_MAX = 2
24464 };
24465
24466 /* /proc/sys/dev/parport/default */
24467 enum {
24468   DEV_PARPORT_DEFAULT_TIMESLICE = 1,
24469   DEV_PARPORT_DEFAULT_SPINTIME = 2
24470 };
24471
24472 /* /proc/sys/dev/parport/parport n */
24473 enum {
24474   DEV_PARPORT_SPINTIME = 1,
24475   DEV_PARPORT_BASE_ADDR = 2,
24476   DEV_PARPORT_IRQ = 3,
24477   DEV_PARPORT_DMA = 4,
```

```
24478   DEV_PARPORT_MODES = 5,
24479   DEV_PARPORT_DEVICES = 6,
24480   DEV_PARPORT_AUTOPROBE = 16
24481 };
24482
24483 /* /proc/sys/dev/parport/parport n/devices/ */
24484 enum {
24485   DEV_PARPORT_DEVICES_ACTIVE = -3,
24486 };
24487
24488 /* /proc/sys/dev/parport/parport n/devices/device n */
24489 enum {
24490   DEV_PARPORT_DEVICE_TIMESLICE = 1,
24491 };
24492
24493 /* /proc/sys/dev/mac_hid */
24494 enum {
24495   DEV_MAC_HID_KEYBOARD_SENDS_LINUX_KEYCODES = 1,
24496   DEV_MAC_HID_KEYBOARD_LOCK_KEYCODES = 2,
24497   DEV_MAC_HID_MOUSE_BUTTON_EMULATION = 3,
24498   DEV_MAC_HID_MOUSE_BUTTON2_KEYCODE = 4,
24499   DEV_MAC_HID_MOUSE_BUTTON3_KEYCODE = 5,
24500   DEV_MAC_HID_ADB_MOUSE_SENDS_KEYCODES = 6
24501 };
24502
24503 #ifdef __KERNEL__
24504
24505 extern asmlinkage long sys_sysctl(struct __sysctl_args*);
24506 extern void sysctl_init(void);
24507
24508 typedef struct ctl_table ctl_table;
24509
24510 typedef int ctl_handler(ctl_table * table, int *name,
24511     int nlen, void *oldval, size_t * oldlenp,
24512     void *newval, size_t newlen, void **context);
24513
24514 typedef int proc_handler(ctl_table * ctl, int write,
24515     struct file *filp, void *buffer, size_t * lenp);
24516
24517 extern int proc_dostring(ctl_table *, int, struct file *,
24518     void *, size_t *);
24519 extern int proc_dointvec(ctl_table *, int, struct file *,
24520     void *, size_t *);
24521 extern int proc_dointvec_bset(ctl_table *, int,
24522     struct file *, void *, size_t *);
24523 extern int proc_dointvec_minmax(ctl_table *, int,
24524     struct file *, void *, size_t *);
```

```
24525  extern int proc_dointvec_jiffies(ctl_table *, int,
24526      struct file *, void *, size_t *);
24527  extern int proc_doulongvec_minmax(ctl_table *, int,
24528      struct file *, void *, size_t *);
24529  extern int proc_doulongvec_ms_jiffies_minmax(ctl_table *
24530      table, int, struct file *, void *, size_t *);
24531
24532  extern int do_sysctl(int *name, int nlen,
24533      void *oldval, size_t * oldlenp,
24534      void *newval, size_t newlen);
24535
24536  extern int do_sysctl_strategy(ctl_table * table,
24537      int *name, int nlen,
24538      void *oldval, size_t * oldlenp,
24539      void *newval, size_t newlen, void **context);
24540
24541  extern ctl_handler sysctl_string;
24542  extern ctl_handler sysctl_intvec;
24543  extern ctl_handler sysctl_jiffies;
24544
24545
24546  /* Register a set of sysctl names by calling
24547   * register_sysctl_table with an initialised array of
24548   * ctl_table's.  An entry with zero ctl_name terminates
24549   * the table.  table->de will be set up by the
24550   * registration and need not be initialised in advance.
24551   *
24552   * sysctl names can be mirrored automatically under
24553   * /proc/sys.  The procname supplied controls /proc
24554   * naming.
24555   *
24556   * The table's mode will be honoured both for
24557   * sys_sysctl(2) and proc-fs access.
24558   *
24559   * Leaf nodes in the sysctl tree will be represented by a
24560   * single file under /proc; non-leaf nodes will be
24561   * represented by directories.  A null procname disables
24562   * /proc mirroring at this node.
24563   *
24564   * sysctl(2) can automatically manage read and write
24565   * requests through the sysctl table.  The data and
24566   * maxlen fields of the ctl_table struct enable minimal
24567   * validation of the values being written to be
24568   * performed, and the mode field allows minimal
24569   * authentication.
24570   *
24571   * More sophisticated management can be enabled by the
```

```
24572   * provision of a strategy routine with the table entry.
24573   * This will be called before any automatic read or write
24574   * of the data is performed.
24575   *
24576   * The strategy routine may return:
24577   * <0: Error occurred (error is passed to user process)
24578   * 0:  OK - proceed with automatic read or write.
24579   * >0: OK - read or write has been done by the strategy
24580   *     routine, so return immediately.
24581   *
24582   * There must be a proc_handler routine for any terminal
24583   * nodes mirrored under /proc/sys (non-terminals are
24584   * handled by a built-in directory handler).  Several
24585   * default handlers are available to cover common cases.
24586   */
24587
24588  /* A sysctl table is an array of struct ctl_table: */
24589  struct ctl_table {
24590      int ctl_name;                   /* Binary ID */
24591      const char *procname;           /* Text ID for
24592                                       * /proc/sys, or zero */
24593      void *data;
24594      int maxlen;
24595      mode_t mode;
24596      ctl_table *child;
24597      proc_handler *proc_handler;     /* Callback for text
24598                                       * formatting */
24599      ctl_handler *strategy;          /* Callback function for
24600                                       * all r/w */
24601      struct proc_dir_entry *de;      /* /proc control block */
24602      void *extra1;
24603      void *extra2;
24604  };
24605
24606  /* struct ctl_table_header is used to maintain dynamic
24607   * lists of ctl_table trees. */
24608  struct ctl_table_header {
24609      ctl_table *ctl_table;
24610      struct list_head ctl_entry;
24611  };
24612
24613  struct ctl_table_header *
24614  register_sysctl_table(ctl_table * table,
24615                        int insert_at_head);
24616  void
24617  unregister_sysctl_table(struct ctl_table_header *table);
24618
```

p 693

```
24619 #else                            /* __KERNEL__ */
24620
24621 #endif                           /* __KERNEL__ */
24622
24623 #endif                           /* _LINUX_SYSCTL_H */
```

include/linux/threads.h

```
24624 #ifndef _LINUX_THREADS_H
24625 #define _LINUX_THREADS_H
24626
24627 #include <linux/config.h>
24628
24629 /* The default limit for the nr of threads is now in
24630  * /proc/sys/kernel/max-threads.  */
24631
24632 #ifdef CONFIG_SMP
24633 #define NR_CPUS 32               /* Max processors that can
24634                                  * be running in SMP */
24635 #else
24636 #define NR_CPUS 1
24637 #endif
24638
24639 #define MIN_THREADS_LEFT_FOR_ROOT 4
24640
24641 /* This controls the maximum pid allocated to a process
24642  */
24643 #define PID_MAX 0x8000
24644
24645 #endif
```

include/linux/time.h

```
24646 #ifndef _LINUX_TIME_H
24647 #define _LINUX_TIME_H
24648
24649 #include <asm/param.h>
24650 #include <linux/types.h>
24651
24652 #ifndef _STRUCT_TIMESPEC
24653 #define _STRUCT_TIMESPEC
24654 struct timespec {
24655   time_t tv_sec;                 /* seconds */
24656   long tv_nsec;                  /* nanoseconds */
24657 };
24658 #endif                           /* _STRUCT_TIMESPEC */
24659
24660 #ifdef __KERNEL__
```

```
24661
24662 /* Change timeval to jiffies, trying to avoid the most
24663  * obvious overflows..
24664  *
24665  * And some not so obvious.
24666  *
24667  * Note that we don't want to return MAX_LONG, because
24668  * for various timeout reasons we often end up having
24669  * to wait "jiffies+1" in order to guarantee that we wait
24670  * at _least_ "jiffies" - so "jiffies+1" had better still
24671  * be positive.  */
24672 #define MAX_JIFFY_OFFSET ((~0UL >> 1)-1)
24673
24674 static __inline__ unsigned long
24675 timespec_to_jiffies(struct timespec *value)
24676 {
24677   unsigned long sec = value->tv_sec;
24678   long nsec = value->tv_nsec;
24679
24680   if (sec >= (MAX_JIFFY_OFFSET / HZ))
24681     return MAX_JIFFY_OFFSET;
24682   nsec += 1000000000L / HZ - 1;
24683   nsec /= 1000000000L / HZ;
24684   return HZ * sec + nsec;
24685 }
24686
24687 static __inline__ void
24688 jiffies_to_timespec(unsigned long jiffies,
24689       struct timespec *value)
24690 {
24691   value->tv_nsec = (jiffies % HZ) * (1000000000L / HZ);
24692   value->tv_sec = jiffies / HZ;
24693 }
24694
24695
24696 /* Converts Gregorian date to seconds since 1970-01-01
24697  * 00:00:00.  Assumes input in normal date format, i.e.
24698  * 1980-12-31 23:59:59 => year=1980, mon=12, day=31,
24699  * hour=23, min=59, sec=59.
24700  *
24701  * [For the Julian calendar (which was used in Russia
24702  * before 1917,Britain & colonies before 1752, anywhere
24703  * else before 1582, and is still in use by some
24704  * communities) leave out the -year/100+year/400 terms,
24705  * and add 10.]
24706  *
24707  * This algorithm was first published by Gauss (I
```

```
24708   * think).
24709   *
24710   * WARNING: this function will overflow on 2106-02-07
24711   * 06:28:16 onmachines were long is 32-bit!  (However, as
24712   * time_t is signed, wewill already get problems at other
24713   * places on 2038-01-19 03:14:08) */
24714  static inline unsigned long
24715  mktime(unsigned int year, unsigned int mon,
24716         unsigned int day, unsigned int hour,
24717         unsigned int min, unsigned int sec)
24718  {
24719    if (0 >= (int) (mon -= 2)) { /* 1..12 -> 11,12,1..10 */
24720      mon += 12;                 /* Puts Feb last since
24721                                  * it has leap day */
24722      year -= 1;
24723    }
24724
24725    return (((((unsigned long) (year / 4 - year / 100 +
24726                                year / 400 +
24727                                367 * mon / 12 + day) +
24728              year * 365 - 719499) * 24 + hour
24729            /* now have hours */
24730          ) * 60 + min            /* now have minutes */
24731        ) * 60 + sec;             /* finally seconds */
24732  }
24733
24734  #endif                          /* __KERNEL__ */
24735
24736
24737  struct timeval {
24738    time_t tv_sec;                 /* seconds */
24739    suseconds_t tv_usec;           /* microseconds */
24740  };
24741
24742  struct timezone {
24743    int tz_minuteswest;  /* minutes west of Greenwich */
24744    int tz_dsttime;      /* type of dst correction */
24745  };
24746
24747  #define NFDBITS                 __NFDBITS
24748
24749  #ifdef __KERNEL__
24750  extern void do_gettimeofday(struct timeval *tv);
24751  extern void do_settimeofday(struct timeval *tv);
24752  extern void get_fast_time(struct timeval *tv);
24753  extern void (*do_get_fast_time) (struct timeval *);
24754  #endif
```

```
24755
24756  #define FD_SETSIZE              __FD_SETSIZE
24757  #define FD_SET(fd,fdsetp)       __FD_SET(fd,fdsetp)
24758  #define FD_CLR(fd,fdsetp)       __FD_CLR(fd,fdsetp)
24759  #define FD_ISSET(fd,fdsetp)     __FD_ISSET(fd,fdsetp)
24760  #define FD_ZERO(fdsetp)         __FD_ZERO(fdsetp)
24761
24762  /* Names of the interval timers, and structure defining a
24763   * timer setting.  */
24764  #define ITIMER_REAL     0
24765  #define ITIMER_VIRTUAL  1
24766  #define ITIMER_PROF     2
24767
24768  struct itimerspec {
24769    struct timespec it_interval;  /* timer period */
24770    struct timespec it_value;     /* timer expiration */
24771  };
24772
24773  struct itimerval {
24774    struct timeval it_interval;   /* timer interval */
24775    struct timeval it_value;      /* current value */
24776  };
24777
24778  #endif
```

include/linux/timer.h

```
24779  #ifndef _LINUX_TIMER_H
24780  #define _LINUX_TIMER_H
24781
24782  #include <linux/config.h>
24783  #include <linux/list.h>
24784
24785  /* This is completely separate from the above, and is the
24786   * "new and improved" way of handling timers more
24787   * dynamically.  Hopefully efficient and general enough
24788   * for most things.
24789   *
24790   * The "hardcoded" timers above are still useful for
24791   * well-defined problems, but the timer-list is probably
24792   * better when you need multiple outstanding timers or
24793   * similar.
24794   *
24795   * The "data" field is in case you want to use the same
24796   * timeout function for several timeouts. You can use
24797   * this to distinguish between the different invocations.
24798   */
24799  struct timer_list {
```

```
24800    struct list_head list;
24801    unsigned long expires;
24802    unsigned long data;
24803    void (*function) (unsigned long);
24804 };
24805
24806 extern void add_timer(struct timer_list *timer);
24807 extern int del_timer(struct timer_list *timer);
24808
24809 #ifdef CONFIG_SMP
24810 extern int del_timer_sync(struct timer_list *timer);
24811 extern void sync_timers(void);
24812 #else
24813 #define del_timer_sync(t)      del_timer(t)
24814 #define sync_timers()          do { } while (0)
24815 #endif
24816
24817 /* mod_timer is a more efficient way to update the expire
24818  * field of an active timer (if the timer is inactive it
24819  * will be activated) mod_timer(a,b) is equivalent to
24820  * del_timer(a); a->expires = b; add_timer(a).  If the
24821  * timer is known to be not pending (ie, in the handler),
24822  * mod_timer is less efficient than a->expires = b;
24823  * add_timer(a).  */
24824 int mod_timer(struct timer_list *timer,
24825     unsigned long expires);
24826
24827 extern void it_real_fn(unsigned long);
24828
24829 static inline void init_timer(struct timer_list *timer)
24830 {
24831    timer->list.next = timer->list.prev = NULL;
24832 }
24833
24834 static inline int timer_pending(const struct timer_list
24835     *timer)
24836 {
24837    return timer->list.next != NULL;
24838 }
24839
24840 /* These inlines deal with timer wrapping correctly. You
24841  * are strongly encouraged to use them
24842  *     1. Because people otherwise forget
24843  *     2. Because if the timer wrap changes in future
24844  *        you wont have to alter your driver code.
24845  *
24846  * Do this with "<0" and ">=0" to only test the sign of
24847  * the result. A good compiler would generate better code
24848  * (and a really good compiler wouldn't care). Gcc is
24849  * currently neither.  */
24850 #define time_after(a,b)      ((long)(b) - (long)(a) < 0)
24851 #define time_before(a,b)     time_after(b,a)
24852
24853 #define time_after_eq(a,b)   ((long)(a) - (long)(b) >= 0)
24854 #define time_before_eq(a,b)  time_after_eq(b,a)
24855
24856 #endif
```

include/linux/times.h

```
24857 #ifndef _LINUX_TIMES_H
24858 #define _LINUX_TIMES_H
24859
24860 struct tms {
24861    clock_t tms_utime;
24862    clock_t tms_stime;
24863    clock_t tms_cutime;
24864    clock_t tms_cstime;
24865 };
24866
24867 #endif
```

include/linux/tqueue.h

```
24868 /*
24869  * tqueue.h — task queue handling for Linux.
24870  *
24871  * Mostly based on a proposed bottom-half replacement
24872  * code written by Kai Petzke,
24873  * wpp@marie.physik.tu-berlin.de.
24874  *
24875  * Modified for use in the Linux kernel by Theodore Ts'o,
24876  * tytso@mit.edu.  Any bugs are my fault, not Kai's.
24877  *
24878  * The original comment follows below.  */
24879
24880 #ifndef _LINUX_TQUEUE_H
24881 #define _LINUX_TQUEUE_H
24882
24883 #include <linux/spinlock.h>
24884 #include <linux/list.h>
24885 #include <asm/bitops.h>
24886 #include <asm/system.h>
24887
24888 /* New proposed "bottom half" handlers:
```

```
24889  * (C) 1994 Kai Petzke, wpp@marie.physik.tu-berlin.de
24890  *
24891  * Advantages:
24892  * - Bottom halves are implemented as a linked list.  You
24893  *   can have as many of them, as you want.
24894  * - No more scanning of a bit field is required upon
24895  *   call of a bottom half.
24896  * - Support for chained bottom half lists.  The
24897  *   run_task_queue() function can be used as a bottom
24898  *   half handler.  This is for example useful for bottom
24899  *   halves, which want to be delayed until the next clock
24900  *   tick.
24901  *
24902  * Notes:
24903  * - Bottom halves are called in the reverse order that
24904  *   they were linked into the list.  */
24905
24906 struct tq_struct {
24907   struct list_head list;      /* linked list of active
24908                                * bh's */
24909   unsigned long sync;         /* must be initialized to
24910                                * zero */
24911   void (*routine) (void *);   /* function to call */
24912   void *data;                 /* argument to function */
24913 };
24914
24915 typedef struct list_head task_queue;
24916
24917 #define DECLARE_TASK_QUEUE(q)   LIST_HEAD(q)
24918 #define TQ_ACTIVE(q)            (!list_empty(&q))
24919
24920 extern task_queue tq_timer, tq_immediate, tq_disk;
24921
24922 /* To implement your own list of active bottom halfs, use
24923  * the following two definitions:
24924  *
24925  * DECLARE_TASK_QUEUE(my_tqueue);
24926  * struct tq_struct my_task = {
24927  *      routine: (void (*)(void *)) my_routine,
24928  *      data: &my_data
24929  * };
24930  *
24931  * To activate a bottom half on a list, use:
24932  *
24933  *      queue_task(&my_task, &my_tqueue);
24934  *
24935  * To later run the queued tasks use
```

```
24936  *
24937  *      run_task_queue(&my_tqueue);
24938  *
24939  * This allows you to do deferred processing.  For
24940  * example, you could have a task queue called tq_timer,
24941  * which is executed within the timer interrupt.  */
24942
24943 extern spinlock_t tqueue_lock;
24944
24945 /* Queue a task on a tq.  Return non-zero if it was
24946  * successfully added.  */
24947 static inline int
24948 queue_task(struct tq_struct *bh_pointer,
24949            task_queue * bh_list)
24950 {
24951   int ret = 0;
24952   if (!test_and_set_bit(0, &bh_pointer->sync)) {
24953     unsigned long flags;
24954     spin_lock_irqsave(&tqueue_lock, flags);
24955     list_add_tail(&bh_pointer->list, bh_list);
24956     spin_unlock_irqrestore(&tqueue_lock, flags);
24957     ret = 1;
24958   }
24959   return ret;
24960 }
24961
24962 /* Call all "bottom halfs" on a given list.  */
24963
24964 extern void __run_task_queue(task_queue * list);
24965
24966 static inline void run_task_queue(task_queue * list)
24967 {
24968   if (TQ_ACTIVE(*list))
24969     __run_task_queue(list);
24970 }
24971
24972 #endif                          /* _LINUX_TQUEUE_H */
```

include/linux/utsname.h

```
24973 #ifndef _LINUX_UTSNAME_H
24974 #define _LINUX_UTSNAME_H
24975
24976 #define __OLD_UTS_LEN 8
24977
24978 struct oldold_utsname {
24979   char sysname[9];
24980   char nodename[9];
```

```
24981   char release[9];
24982   char version[9];
24983   char machine[9];
24984 };
24985
24986 #define __NEW_UTS_LEN 64
24987
24988 struct old_utsname {
24989   char sysname[65];
24990   char nodename[65];
24991   char release[65];
24992   char version[65];
24993   char machine[65];
24994 };
24995
24996 struct new_utsname {
24997   char sysname[65];
24998   char nodename[65];
24999   char release[65];
25000   char version[65];
25001   char machine[65];
25002   char domainname[65];
25003 };
25004
25005 extern struct new_utsname system_utsname;
25006
25007 extern struct rw_semaphore uts_sem;
25008 #endif
```

include/linux/vmalloc.h

```
25009 #ifndef __LINUX_VMALLOC_H
25010 #define __LINUX_VMALLOC_H
25011
25012 #include <linux/sched.h>
25013 #include <linux/mm.h>
25014 #include <linux/spinlock.h>
25015
25016 #include <asm/pgtable.h>
25017
25018 /* bits in vm_struct->flags */
25019 #define VM_IOREMAP  0x00000001 /* ioremap() and friends*/
25020 #define VM_ALLOC    0x00000002 /* vmalloc() */
25021
25022 struct vm_struct {
25023   unsigned long flags;
25024   void *addr;
25025   unsigned long size;
```

```
25026   struct vm_struct *next;
25027 };
25028
25029 extern struct vm_struct *get_vm_area(unsigned long size,
25030     unsigned long flags);
25031 extern void vfree(void *addr);
25032 extern void *__vmalloc(unsigned long size, int gfp_mask,
25033     pgprot_t prot);
25034 extern long vread(char *buf, char *addr,
25035     unsigned long count);
25036 extern void vmfree_area_pages(unsigned long address,
25037     unsigned long size);
25038 extern int vmalloc_area_pages(unsigned long address,
25039     unsigned long size, int gfp_mask, pgprot_t prot);
25040
25041 /* Allocate any pages */
25042 static inline void *vmalloc(unsigned long size)
25043 {
25044    return __vmalloc(size, GFP_KERNEL | __GFP_HIGHMEM,
25045                PAGE_KERNEL);
25046 }
25047
25048 /* Allocate ISA addressable pages for broke crap */
25049 static inline void *vmalloc_dma(unsigned long size)
25050 {
25051    return __vmalloc(size, GFP_KERNEL | GFP_DMA,
25052                PAGE_KERNEL);
25053 }
25054
25055 /* vmalloc 32bit PA addressable pages - eg for PCI 32bit
25056  * devices */
25057 static inline void *vmalloc_32(unsigned long size)
25058 {
25059    return __vmalloc(size, GFP_KERNEL, PAGE_KERNEL);
25060 }
25061
25062 /* vmlist_lock is a read-write spinlock that protects
25063  * vmlist Used in mm/vmalloc.c (get_vm_area() and
25064  * vfree()) and fs/proc/kcore.c.  */
25065 extern rwlock_t vmlist_lock;
25066
25067 extern struct vm_struct *vmlist;
25068 #endif
```

include/linux/wait.h

```
25069 #ifndef _LINUX_WAIT_H
25070 #define _LINUX_WAIT_H
```

p 641

```
25071
25072 #define WNOHANG          0x00000001
25073 #define WUNTRACED        0x00000002
25074
25075 #define __WNOTHREAD  0x20000000  /* Don't wait on
25076                                   * children of other
25077                                   * threads in this group
25078                                   */
25079 #define __WALL       0x40000000  /* Wait on all children,
25080                                   * regardless of type */
25081 #define __WCLONE     0x80000000  /* Wait only on
25082                                   * non-SIGCHLD children
25083                                   */
25084
25085 #ifdef __KERNEL__
25086
25087 #include <linux/kernel.h>
25088 #include <linux/list.h>
25089 #include <linux/stddef.h>
25090 #include <linux/spinlock.h>
25091
25092 #include <asm/page.h>
25093 #include <asm/processor.h>
25094
25095 /* Temporary debugging help until all code is converted
25096  * to the new waitqueue usage.  */
25097 #define WAITQUEUE_DEBUG 0
25098
25099 #if WAITQUEUE_DEBUG
25100 extern int printk(const char *fmt, ...);
25101 #define WQ_BUG() do {                                      \
25102         printk("wq bug, forcing oops.\n");                 \
25103         BUG();                                             \
25104 } while (0)
25105
25106 #define CHECK_MAGIC(x) if (x != (long)&(x))                \
25107   { printk("bad magic %lx (should be %lx), ",              \
25108          (long)x, (long)&(x)); WQ_BUG(); }
25109
25110 #define CHECK_MAGIC_WQHEAD(x) do {                         \
25111 if (x->__magic != (long)&(x->__magic)) {                   \
25112   printk("bad magic %lx (should be %lx, creator %lx), ",\
25113         x->__magic, (long)&(x->__magic), x->__creator); \
25114   WQ_BUG();                                                \
25115 }                                                          \
25116 } while (0)
25117 #endif
```

```
25118
25119 struct __wait_queue {
25120   unsigned int flags;
25121 #define WQ_FLAG_EXCLUSIVE        0x01
25122   struct task_struct *task;
25123   struct list_head task_list;
25124 #if WAITQUEUE_DEBUG
25125   long __magic;
25126   long __waker;
25127 #endif
25128 };
25129 typedef struct __wait_queue wait_queue_t;
25130
25131 /* 'dual' spinlock architecture. Can be switched between
25132  * spinlock_t and rwlock_t locks via changing this
25133  * define. Since waitqueues are quite decoupled in the
25134  * new architecture, lightweight 'simple' spinlocks give
25135  * us slightly better latencies and smaller waitqueue
25136  * structure size.  */
25137 #define USE_RW_WAIT_QUEUE_SPINLOCK 0
25138
25139 #if USE_RW_WAIT_QUEUE_SPINLOCK
25140 # define wq_lock_t rwlock_t
25141 # define WAITQUEUE_RW_LOCK_UNLOCKED RW_LOCK_UNLOCKED
25142
25143 # define wq_read_lock read_lock
25144 # define wq_read_lock_irqsave read_lock_irqsave
25145 # define wq_read_unlock_irqrestore read_unlock_irqrestore
25146 # define wq_read_unlock read_unlock
25147 # define wq_write_lock_irq write_lock_irq
25148 # define wq_write_lock_irqsave write_lock_irqsave
25149 # define wq_write_unlock_irqrestore                        \
25150     write_unlock_irqrestore
25151 # define wq_write_unlock write_unlock
25152 #else
25153 # define wq_lock_t spinlock_t
25154 # define WAITQUEUE_RW_LOCK_UNLOCKED SPIN_LOCK_UNLOCKED
25155
25156 # define wq_read_lock spin_lock
25157 # define wq_read_lock_irqsave spin_lock_irqsave
25158 # define wq_read_unlock spin_unlock
25159 # define wq_read_unlock_irqrestore spin_unlock_irqrestore
25160 # define wq_write_lock_irq spin_lock_irq
25161 # define wq_write_lock_irqsave spin_lock_irqsave
25162 # define wq_write_unlock_irqrestore                        \
25163     spin_unlock_irqrestore
25164 # define wq_write_unlock spin_unlock
```

p 538 ▶ (line 25119)

```
25165 #endif
25166
25167 struct __wait_queue_head {
25168   wq_lock_t lock;
25169   struct list_head task_list;
25170 #if WAITQUEUE_DEBUG
25171   long __magic;
25172   long __creator;
25173 #endif
25174 };
25175 typedef struct __wait_queue_head wait_queue_head_t;
25176
25177 #if WAITQUEUE_DEBUG
25178 # define __WAITQUEUE_DEBUG_INIT(name)                \
25179   , (long)&(name).__magic, 0
25180 # define __WAITQUEUE_HEAD_DEBUG_INIT(name)           \
25181   , (long)&(name).__magic, (long)&(name).__magic
25182 #else
25183 # define __WAITQUEUE_DEBUG_INIT(name)
25184 # define __WAITQUEUE_HEAD_DEBUG_INIT(name)
25185 #endif
25186
25187 #define __WAITQUEUE_INITIALIZER(name,task)           \
25188 { 0x0, task, { NULL, NULL } __WAITQUEUE_DEBUG_INIT(name)}
25189 #define DECLARE_WAITQUEUE(name,task)                 \
25190   wait_queue_t name = __WAITQUEUE_INITIALIZER(name,task)
25191
25192 #define __WAIT_QUEUE_HEAD_INITIALIZER(name)          \
25193   { WAITQUEUE_RW_LOCK_UNLOCKED,                      \
25194     { &(name).task_list, &(name).task_list }        \
25195     __WAITQUEUE_HEAD_DEBUG_INIT(name)}
25196
25197 #define DECLARE_WAIT_QUEUE_HEAD(name)                \
25198   wait_queue_head_t name =                          \
25199     __WAIT_QUEUE_HEAD_INITIALIZER(name)
25200
25201 static inline void
25202 init_waitqueue_head(wait_queue_head_t * q)
25203 {
25204 #if WAITQUEUE_DEBUG
25205   if (!q)
25206     WQ_BUG();
25207 #endif
25208   q->lock = WAITQUEUE_RW_LOCK_UNLOCKED;
25209   INIT_LIST_HEAD(&q->task_list);
25210 #if WAITQUEUE_DEBUG
25211   q->__magic = (long) &q->__magic;
25212   q->__creator = (long) current_text_addr();
25213 #endif
25214 }
25215
25216 static inline void init_waitqueue_entry(wait_queue_t * q,
25217     struct task_struct *p)
25218 {
25219 #if WAITQUEUE_DEBUG
25220   if (!q || !p)
25221     WQ_BUG();
25222 #endif
25223   q->flags = 0;
25224   q->task = p;
25225 #if WAITQUEUE_DEBUG
25226   q->__magic = (long) &q->__magic;
25227 #endif
25228 }
25229
25230 static inline int waitqueue_active(wait_queue_head_t * q)
25231 {
25232 #if WAITQUEUE_DEBUG
25233   if (!q)
25234     WQ_BUG();
25235   CHECK_MAGIC_WQHEAD(q);
25236 #endif
25237
25238   return !list_empty(&q->task_list);
25239 }
25240
25241 static inline void __add_wait_queue(wait_queue_head_t *
25242     head, wait_queue_t * new)
25243 {
25244 #if WAITQUEUE_DEBUG
25245   if (!head || !new)
25246     WQ_BUG();
25247   CHECK_MAGIC_WQHEAD(head);
25248   CHECK_MAGIC(new->__magic);
25249   if (!head->task_list.next || !head->task_list.prev)
25250     WQ_BUG();
25251 #endif
25252   list_add(&new->task_list, &head->task_list);
25253 }
25254
25255 /* Used for wake-one threads: */
25256 static inline void
25257 __add_wait_queue_tail(wait_queue_head_t * head,
25258     wait_queue_t * new)
```

```
25259 {
25260 #if WAITQUEUE_DEBUG
25261   if (!head || !new)
25262     WQ_BUG();
25263   CHECK_MAGIC_WQHEAD(head);
25264   CHECK_MAGIC(new->__magic);
25265   if (!head->task_list.next || !head->task_list.prev)
25266     WQ_BUG();
25267 #endif
25268   list_add_tail(&new->task_list, &head->task_list);
25269 }
25270
25271 static inline void
25272 __remove_wait_queue(wait_queue_head_t * head,
25273                     wait_queue_t * old)
25274 {
25275 #if WAITQUEUE_DEBUG
25276   if (!old)
25277     WQ_BUG();
25278   CHECK_MAGIC(old->__magic);
25279 #endif
25280   list_del(&old->task_list);
25281 }
25282
25283 #endif                          /* __KERNEL__ */
25284
25285 #endif
```

init/main.c

```
25286 /*
25287  *  linux/init/main.c
25288  *
25289  *  Copyright (C) 1991, 1992  Linus Torvalds
25290  *
25291  *  GK 2/5/95 - Changed to support mounting root fs via
25292  *  NFS
25293  *  Added initrd & change_root: Werner Almesberger & Hans
25294  *  Lermen, Feb '96
25295  *  Moan early if gcc is old, avoiding bogus kernels -
25296  *  Paul Gortmaker, May '96
25297  *  Simplified starting of init: Michael A. Griffith
25298  *  <grif@acm.org>
25299  */
25300
25301 #define __KERNEL_SYSCALLS__
25302
25303 #include <linux/config.h>
```

```
25304 #include <linux/proc_fs.h>
25305 #include <linux/devfs_fs_kernel.h>
25306 #include <linux/unistd.h>
25307 #include <linux/string.h>
25308 #include <linux/ctype.h>
25309 #include <linux/delay.h>
25310 #include <linux/utsname.h>
25311 #include <linux/ioport.h>
25312 #include <linux/init.h>
25313 #include <linux/raid/md.h>
25314 #include <linux/smp_lock.h>
25315 #include <linux/blk.h>
25316 #include <linux/hdreg.h>
25317 #include <linux/iobuf.h>
25318 #include <linux/bootmem.h>
25319
25320 #include <asm/io.h>
25321 #include <asm/bugs.h>
25322
25323 #ifdef CONFIG_PCI
25324 #include <linux/pci.h>
25325 #endif
25326
25327 #ifdef CONFIG_DIO
25328 #include <linux/dio.h>
25329 #endif
25330
25331 #ifdef CONFIG_ZORRO
25332 #include <linux/zorro.h>
25333 #endif
25334
25335 #ifdef CONFIG_MTRR
25336 #  include <asm/mtrr.h>
25337 #endif
25338
25339 #ifdef CONFIG_3215_CONSOLE
25340 extern int con3215_activate(void);
25341 #endif
25342
25343 #ifdef CONFIG_NUBUS
25344 #include <linux/nubus.h>
25345 #endif
25346
25347 #ifdef CONFIG_ISAPNP
25348 #include <linux/isapnp.h>
25349 #endif
25350
```

```
25351 #ifdef CONFIG_IRDA
25352 #include <net/irda/irda_device.h>
25353 #endif
25354
25355 #ifdef CONFIG_X86_IO_APIC
25356 #include <asm/smp.h>
25357 #endif
25358
25359 /* Versions of gcc older than that listed below may
25360  * actually compile and link okay, but the end product
25361  * can have subtle run time bugs.  To avoid associated
25362  * bogus bug reports, we flatly refuse to compile with a
25363  * gcc that is known to be too old from the very
25364  * beginning. */
25365 #if __GNUC__ < 2 || (__GNUC__ ==2 && __GNUC_MINOR__ < 91)
25366 #error Sorry, your GCC is too old.                    \
25367  It builds incorrect kernels.
25368 #endif
25369
25370 extern char _stext, _etext;
25371 extern char *linux_banner;
25372
25373 static int init(void *);
25374
25375 extern void init_IRQ(void);
25376 extern void init_modules(void);
25377 extern void sock_init(void);
25378 extern void fork_init(unsigned long);
25379 extern void mca_init(void);
25380 extern void sbus_init(void);
25381 extern void ppc_init(void);
25382 extern void sysctl_init(void);
25383 extern void signals_init(void);
25384 extern void bdev_init(void);
25385 extern int init_pcmcia_ds(void);
25386 extern void net_notifier_init(void);
25387
25388 extern void free_initmem(void);
25389 extern void filesystem_setup(void);
25390
25391 #ifdef CONFIG_TC
25392 extern void tc_init(void);
25393 #endif
25394
25395 extern void ecard_init(void);
25396
25397 #if defined(CONFIG_SYSVIPC)
```

```
25398 extern void ipc_init(void);
25399 #endif
25400 #if defined(CONFIG_QUOTA)
25401 extern void dquot_init_hash(void);
25402 #endif
25403
25404 /* Boot command-line arguments */
25405 #define MAX_INIT_ARGS 8
25406 #define MAX_INIT_ENVS 8
25407
25408 extern void time_init(void);
25409 extern void softirq_init(void);
25410
25411 int rows, cols;
25412
25413 #ifdef CONFIG_BLK_DEV_INITRD
25414 kdev_t real_root_dev;
25415 #endif
25416
25417 int root_mountflags = MS_RDONLY;
25418 char *execute_command;
25419 char root_device_name[64];
25420
25421
25422 static char *argv_init[MAX_INIT_ARGS + 2] =
25423    { "init", NULL, };
25424 static char *envp_init[MAX_INIT_ENVS + 2] =
25425    { "HOME=/", "TERM=linux", NULL, };
25426
25427 static int __init profile_setup(char *str)
25428 {
25429    int par;
25430    if (get_option(&str, &par))
25431      prof_shift = par;
25432    return 1;
25433 }
25434
25435 __setup("profile=", profile_setup);
25436
25437
25438 static struct dev_name_struct {
25439    const char *name;
25440    const int num;
25441 } root_dev_names[] __initdata = {
25442    { "nfs", 0x00ff },
25443    { "hda", 0x0300 },
25444    { "hdb", 0x0340 },
```

p 561

```
25445    { "hdc", 0x1600 },
25446    { "hdd", 0x1640 },
25447    { "hde", 0x2100 },
25448    { "hdf", 0x2140 },
25449    { "hdg", 0x2200 },
25450    { "hdh", 0x2240 },
25451    { "hdi", 0x3800 },
25452    { "hdj", 0x3840 },
25453    { "hdk", 0x3900 },
25454    { "hdl", 0x3940 },
25455    { "hdm", 0x5800 },
25456    { "hdn", 0x5840 },
25457    { "hdo", 0x5900 },
25458    { "hdp", 0x5940 },
25459    { "hdq", 0x5A00 },
25460    { "hdr", 0x5A40 },
25461    { "hds", 0x5B00 },
25462    { "hdt", 0x5B40 },
25463    { "sda", 0x0800 },
25464    { "sdb", 0x0810 },
25465    { "sdc", 0x0820 },
25466    { "sdd", 0x0830 },
25467    { "sde", 0x0840 },
25468    { "sdf", 0x0850 },
25469    { "sdg", 0x0860 },
25470    { "sdh", 0x0870 },
25471    { "sdi", 0x0880 },
25472    { "sdj", 0x0890 },
25473    { "sdk", 0x08a0 },
25474    { "sdl", 0x08b0 },
25475    { "sdm", 0x08c0 },
25476    { "sdn", 0x08d0 },
25477    { "sdo", 0x08e0 },
25478    { "sdp", 0x08f0 },
25479    { "ada", 0x1c00 },
25480    { "adb", 0x1c10 },
25481    { "adc", 0x1c20 },
25482    { "add", 0x1c30 },
25483    { "ade", 0x1c40 },
25484    { "fd", 0x0200 },
25485    { "md", 0x0900 },
25486    { "xda", 0x0d00 },
25487    { "xdb", 0x0d40 },
25488    { "ram", 0x0100 },
25489    { "scd", 0x0b00 },
25490    { "mcd", 0x1700 },
25491    { "cdu535", 0x1800 },
25492    { "sonycd", 0x1800 },
25493    { "aztcd", 0x1d00 },
25494    { "cm206cd", 0x2000 },
25495    { "gscd", 0x1000 },
25496    { "sbpcd", 0x1900 },
25497    { "eda", 0x2400 },
25498    { "edb", 0x2440 },
25499    { "pda", 0x2d00 },
25500    { "pdb", 0x2d10 },
25501    { "pdc", 0x2d20 },
25502    { "pdd", 0x2d30 },
25503    { "pcd", 0x2e00 },
25504    { "pf", 0x2f00 },
25505    { "apblock", APBLOCK_MAJOR << 8 },
25506    { "ddv", DDV_MAJOR << 8 },
25507    { "jsfd", JSFD_MAJOR << 8  },
25508 #ifdef CONFIG_MDISK
25509    { "mnda", (MDISK_MAJOR << MINORBITS) },
25510    { "mndb", (MDISK_MAJOR << MINORBITS) + 1 },
25511    { "mndc", (MDISK_MAJOR << MINORBITS) + 2 },
25512    { "mndd", (MDISK_MAJOR << MINORBITS) + 3 },
25513    { "mnde", (MDISK_MAJOR << MINORBITS) + 4 },
25514    { "mndf", (MDISK_MAJOR << MINORBITS) + 5 },
25515    { "mndg", (MDISK_MAJOR << MINORBITS) + 6 },
25516    { "mndh", (MDISK_MAJOR << MINORBITS) + 7 },
25517 #endif
25518 #ifdef CONFIG_DASD
25519    { "dasda", (DASD_MAJOR << MINORBITS) },
25520    { "dasdb", (DASD_MAJOR << MINORBITS) + (1 << 2) },
25521    { "dasdc", (DASD_MAJOR << MINORBITS) + (2 << 2) },
25522    { "dasdd", (DASD_MAJOR << MINORBITS) + (3 << 2) },
25523    { "dasde", (DASD_MAJOR << MINORBITS) + (4 << 2) },
25524    { "dasdf", (DASD_MAJOR << MINORBITS) + (5 << 2) },
25525    { "dasdg", (DASD_MAJOR << MINORBITS) + (6 << 2) },
25526    { "dasdh", (DASD_MAJOR << MINORBITS) + (7 << 2) },
25527 #endif
25528 #if defined(CONFIG_BLK_CPQ_DA) ||                                  \
25529     defined(CONFIG_BLK_CPQ_DA_MODULE)
25530    { "ida/c0d0p", 0x4800 },
25531    { "ida/c0d1p", 0x4810 },
25532    { "ida/c0d2p", 0x4820 },
25533    { "ida/c0d3p", 0x4830 },
25534    { "ida/c0d4p", 0x4840 },
25535    { "ida/c0d5p", 0x4850 },
25536    { "ida/c0d6p", 0x4860 },
25537    { "ida/c0d7p", 0x4870 },
25538    { "ida/c0d8p", 0x4880 },
```

```
25539    { "ida/c0d9p", 0x4890 },
25540    { "ida/c0d10p", 0x48A0 },
25541    { "ida/c0d11p", 0x48B0 },
25542    { "ida/c0d12p", 0x48C0 },
25543    { "ida/c0d13p", 0x48D0 },
25544    { "ida/c0d14p", 0x48E0 },
25545    { "ida/c0d15p", 0x48F0 },
25546 #endif
25547 #if defined(CONFIG_BLK_CPQ_CISS_DA) ||          \
25548     defined(CONFIG_BLK_CPQ_CISS_DA_MODULE)
25549    { "cciss/c0d0p", 0x6800 },
25550    { "cciss/c0d1p", 0x6810 },
25551    { "cciss/c0d2p", 0x6820 },
25552    { "cciss/c0d3p", 0x6830 },
25553    { "cciss/c0d4p", 0x6840 },
25554    { "cciss/c0d5p", 0x6850 },
25555    { "cciss/c0d6p", 0x6860 },
25556    { "cciss/c0d7p", 0x6870 },
25557    { "cciss/c0d8p", 0x6880 },
25558    { "cciss/c0d9p", 0x6890 },
25559    { "cciss/c0d10p", 0x68A0 },
25560    { "cciss/c0d11p", 0x68B0 },
25561    { "cciss/c0d12p", 0x68C0 },
25562    { "cciss/c0d13p", 0x68D0 },
25563    { "cciss/c0d14p", 0x68E0 },
25564    { "cciss/c0d15p", 0x68F0 },
25565 #endif
25566 #ifdef CONFIG_NFTL
25567    { "nftla", 0x5d00 },
25568 #endif
25569    { NULL, 0 }
25570 };
25571
25572 kdev_t __init name_to_kdev_t(char *line)
25573 {
25574    int base = 0;
25575
25576    if (strncmp(line, "/dev/", 5) == 0) {
25577      struct dev_name_struct *dev = root_dev_names;
25578      line += 5;
25579      do {
25580        int len = strlen(dev->name);
25581        if (strncmp(line, dev->name, len) == 0) {
25582          line += len;
25583          base = dev->num;
25584          break;
25585        }
```

```
25586      dev++;
25587    } while (dev->name);
25588  }
25589  return to_kdev_t(base + simple_strtoul(line, NULL,
25590                                         base ? 10 : 16));
25591 }
25592
25593 static int __init root_dev_setup(char *line)
25594 {
25595   int i;
25596   char ch;
25597
25598   ROOT_DEV = name_to_kdev_t(line);
25599   memset(root_device_name, 0, sizeof root_device_name);
25600   if (strncmp(line, "/dev/", 5) == 0)
25601     line += 5;
25602   for (i = 0; i < sizeof root_device_name - 1; ++i) {
25603     ch = line[i];
25604     if (isspace(ch) || (ch == ',') || (ch == '\0'))
25605       break;
25606     root_device_name[i] = ch;
25607   }
25608   return 1;
25609 }
25610
25611 __setup("root=", root_dev_setup);
25612
25613 static int __init checksetup(char *line)
25614 {
25615   struct kernel_param *p;
25616
25617   p = &__setup_start;
25618   do {
25619     int n = strlen(p->str);
25620     if (!strncmp(line, p->str, n)) {
25621       if (p->setup_func(line + n))
25622         return 1;
25623     }
25624     p++;
25625   } while (p < &__setup_end);
25626   return 0;
25627 }
25628
25629 /* this should be approx 2 Bo*oMips to start (note
25630  * initial shift), and will still work even if initially
25631  * too large, it will just take slightly longer */
25632 unsigned long loops_per_jiffy = (1 << 12);
```

p 559

```
25633
25634 /* This is the number of bits of precision for the
25635  * loops_per_jiffy.  Each bit takes on average 1.5/HZ
25636  * seconds.  This (like the original) is a little better
25637  * than 1% */
25638 #define LPS_PREC 8
25639
25640 void __init calibrate_delay(void)
25641 {
25642   unsigned long ticks, loopbit;
25643   int lps_precision = LPS_PREC;
25644
25645   loops_per_jiffy = (1 << 12);
25646
25647   printk("Calibrating delay loop... ");
25648   while (loops_per_jiffy <<= 1) {
25649     /* wait for "start of" clock tick */
25650     ticks = jiffies;
25651     while (ticks == jiffies)
25652       /* nothing */ ;
25653     /* Go .. */
25654     ticks = jiffies;
25655     __delay(loops_per_jiffy);
25656     ticks = jiffies - ticks;
25657     if (ticks)
25658       break;
25659   }
25660
25661   /* Do a binary approximation to get loops_per_jiffy
25662    * set to equal one clock (up to lps_precision bits) */
25663   loops_per_jiffy >>= 1;
25664   loopbit = loops_per_jiffy;
25665   while (lps_precision-- && (loopbit >>= 1)) {
25666     loops_per_jiffy |= loopbit;
25667     ticks = jiffies;
25668     while (ticks == jiffies) ;
25669     ticks = jiffies;
25670     __delay(loops_per_jiffy);
25671     if (jiffies != ticks)        /* longer than 1 tick */
25672       loops_per_jiffy &= ~loopbit;
25673   }
25674
25675   /* Round the value and print it */
25676   printk("%lu.%02lu BogoMIPS\n",
25677       loops_per_jiffy / (500000 / HZ),
25678       (loops_per_jiffy / (5000 / HZ)) % 100);
25679 }
```

```
25680
25681 static int __init readonly(char *str)
25682 {
25683   if (*str)
25684     return 0;
25685   root_mountflags |= MS_RDONLY;
25686   return 1;
25687 }
25688
25689 static int __init readwrite(char *str)
25690 {
25691   if (*str)
25692     return 0;
25693   root_mountflags &= ~MS_RDONLY;
25694   return 1;
25695 }
25696
25697 static int __init debug_kernel(char *str)
25698 {
25699   if (*str)
25700     return 0;
25701   console_loglevel = 10;
25702   return 1;
25703 }
25704
25705 static int __init quiet_kernel(char *str)
25706 {
25707   if (*str)
25708     return 0;
25709   console_loglevel = 4;
25710   return 1;
25711 }
25712
25713 __setup("ro", readonly);
25714 __setup("rw", readwrite);
25715 __setup("debug", debug_kernel);
25716 __setup("quiet", quiet_kernel);
25717
25718 /* This is a simple kernel command line parsing function:
25719  * it parses the command line, and fills in the
25720  * arguments/environment to init as appropriate. Any
25721  * cmd-line option is taken to be an environment variable
25722  * if it contains the character '='.
25723  *
25724  * This routine also checks for options meant for the
25725  * kernel.  These options are not given to init - they
25726  * are for internal kernel use only.  */
```

```
p 558  25727 static void __init parse_options(char *line)
       25728 {
       25729   char *next, *quote;
       25730   int args, envs;
       25731
       25732   if (!*line)
       25733     return;
       25734   args = 0;
       25735   envs = 1;          /* TERM is set to 'linux' by default */
       25736   next = line;
       25737   while ((line = next) != NULL) {
       25738     quote = strchr(line, '"');
       25739     next = strchr(line, ' ');
       25740     while (next != NULL && quote != NULL &&
       25741            quote < next) {
       25742       /* we found a left quote before the next blank now
       25743        * we have to find the matching right quote */
       25744       next = strchr(quote + 1, '"');
       25745       if (next != NULL) {
       25746         quote = strchr(next + 1, '"');
       25747         next = strchr(next + 1, ' ');
       25748       }
       25749     }
       25750     if (next != NULL)
       25751       *next++ = 0;
       25752     if (!strncmp(line, "init=", 5)) {
       25753       line += 5;
       25754       execute_command = line;
       25755       /* In case LILO is going to boot us with default
       25756        * command line, it prepends "auto" before the
       25757        * whole cmdline which makes the shell think it
       25758        * should execute a script with such name. So we
       25759        * ignore all arguments entered _before_ init=...
       25760        * [MJ] */
       25761       args = 0;
       25762       continue;
       25763     }
       25764     if (checksetup(line))
       25765       continue;
       25766
       25767     /* Then check if it's an environment variable or an
       25768      * option.  */
       25769     if (strchr(line, '=')) {
       25770       if (envs >= MAX_INIT_ENVS)
       25771         break;
       25772       envp_init[++envs] = line;
       25773     } else {
```

```
       25774       if (args >= MAX_INIT_ARGS)
       25775         break;
       25776       if (*line)
       25777         argv_init[++args] = line;
       25778     }
       25779   }
       25780   argv_init[args + 1] = NULL;
       25781   envp_init[envs + 1] = NULL;
       25782 }
       25783
       25784
       25785 extern void setup_arch(char **);
       25786 extern void cpu_idle(void);
       25787
       25788 #ifndef CONFIG_SMP
       25789
       25790 #ifdef CONFIG_X86_IO_APIC
       25791 static void __init smp_init(void)
       25792 {
       25793   IO_APIC_init_uniprocessor();
       25794 }
       25795
       25796 #else
       25797 #define smp_init()      do { } while (0)
       25798 #endif
       25799
       25800 #else
       25801
       25802 /* Called by boot processor to activate the rest. */
       25803 static void __init smp_init(void)
       25804 {
       25805   /* Get other processors into their bootup holding
       25806    * patterns. */
       25807   smp_boot_cpus();
       25808   smp_threads_ready = 1;
       25809   smp_commence();
       25810 }
       25811
       25812 #endif
       25813
       25814 /* Activate the first processor.  */
p 556  25815 asmlinkage void __init start_kernel(void)
       25816 {
       25817   char *command_line;
       25818   unsigned long mempages;
       25819   extern char saved_command_line[];
       25820   /* Interrupts are still disabled. Do necessary setups,
```

```
25821      * then enable them */
25822     lock_kernel();
25823     printk(linux_banner);
25824     setup_arch(&command_line);
25825     printk("Kernel command line: %s\n",
25826         saved_command_line);
25827     parse_options(command_line);
25828     trap_init();
25829     init_IRQ();
25830     sched_init();
25831     time_init();
25832     softirq_init();
25833
25834     /* HACK ALERT! This is early. We're enabling the
25835      * console before we've done PCI setups etc, and
25836      * console_init() must be aware of this. But we do want
25837      * output early, in case something goes wrong.  */
25838     console_init();
25839 #ifdef CONFIG_MODULES
25840     init_modules();
25841 #endif
25842     if (prof_shift) {
25843       unsigned int size;
25844       /* only text is profiled */
25845       prof_len = (unsigned long) &_etext -
25846                  (unsigned long) &_stext;
25847       prof_len >>= prof_shift;
25848
25849       size =
25850           prof_len * sizeof(unsigned int) + PAGE_SIZE - 1;
25851       prof_buffer = (unsigned int *) alloc_bootmem(size);
25852     }
25853
25854     kmem_cache_init();
25855     sti();
25856     calibrate_delay();
25857 #ifdef CONFIG_BLK_DEV_INITRD
25858     if (initrd_start && !initrd_below_start_ok &&
25859         initrd_start < min_low_pfn << PAGE_SHIFT) {
25860       printk(KERN_CRIT
25861           "initrd overwritten (0x%08lx < 0x%08lx) - "
25862           "disabling it.\n", initrd_start,
25863           min_low_pfn << PAGE_SHIFT);
25864       initrd_start = 0;
25865     }
25866 #endif
25867     mem_init();
25868     kmem_cache_sizes_init();
25869 #ifdef CONFIG_3215_CONSOLE
25870     con3215_activate();
25871 #endif
25872 #ifdef CONFIG_PROC_FS
25873     proc_root_init();
25874 #endif
25875     mempages = num_physpages;
25876
25877     fork_init(mempages);
25878     proc_caches_init();
25879     vfs_caches_init(mempages);
25880     buffer_init(mempages);
25881     page_cache_init(mempages);
25882     kiobuf_setup();
25883     signals_init();
25884     bdev_init();
25885     inode_init(mempages);
25886 #if defined(CONFIG_SYSVIPC)
25887     ipc_init();
25888 #endif
25889 #if defined(CONFIG_QUOTA)
25890     dquot_init_hash();
25891 #endif
25892     check_bugs();
25893     printk("POSIX conformance testing by UNIFIX\n");
25894
25895     /* We count on the initial thread going ok Like idlers
25896      * init is an unlocked kernel thread, which will make
25897      * syscalls (and thus be locked).  */
25898     smp_init();
25899     kernel_thread(init, NULL,
25900         CLONE_FS | CLONE_FILES | CLONE_SIGNAL);
25901     unlock_kernel();
25902     current->need_resched = 1;
25903     cpu_idle();
25904 }
25905
25906 #ifdef CONFIG_BLK_DEV_INITRD
25907 static int do_linuxrc(void *shell)
25908 {
25909     static char *argv[] = { "linuxrc", NULL, };
25910
25911     close(0);
25912     close(1);
25913     close(2);
25914     setsid();
```

```
25915    (void) open("/dev/console", O_RDWR, 0);
25916    (void) dup(0);
25917    (void) dup(0);
25918    return execve(shell, argv, envp_init);
25919  }
25920
25921  #endif
25922
25923  struct task_struct *child_reaper = &init_task;
25924
25925  static void __init do_initcalls(void)
25926  {
25927    initcall_t *call;
25928
25929    call = &__initcall_start;
25930    do {
25931      (*call) ();
25932      call++;
25933    } while (call < &__initcall_end);
25934
25935    /* Make sure there is no pending stuff from the
25936     * initcall sequence */
25937    flush_scheduled_tasks();
25938  }
25939
25940  /* Ok, the machine is now initialized. None of the
25941   * devices have been touched yet, but the CPU subsystem
25942   * is up and running, and memory and process management
25943   * works.
25944   *
25945   * Now we can finally start doing some real work.. */
25946  static void __init do_basic_setup(void)
25947  {
25948  #ifdef CONFIG_BLK_DEV_INITRD
25949    int real_root_mountflags;
25950  #endif
25951
25952    /* Tell the world that we're going to be the grim
25953     * reaper of innocent orphaned children.
25954     *
25955     * We don't want people to have to make incorrect
25956     * assumptions about where in the task array this
25957     * can be found. */
25958    child_reaper = current;
25959
25960  #if defined(CONFIG_MTRR)     /* Do this after SMP
25961                               * initialization */
```

```
25962    /* We should probably create some
25963     * architecture-dependent "fixup after everything is
25964     * up" style function where this would belong better
25965     * than in init/main.c..  */
25966    mtrr_init();
25967  #endif
25968
25969  #ifdef CONFIG_SYSCTL
25970    sysctl_init();
25971  #endif
25972
25973    /* Ok, at this point all CPU's should be initialized,
25974     * so we can start looking into devices..  */
25975  #ifdef CONFIG_PCI
25976    pci_init();
25977  #endif
25978  #ifdef CONFIG_SBUS
25979    sbus_init();
25980  #endif
25981  #if defined(CONFIG_PPC)
25982    ppc_init();
25983  #endif
25984  #ifdef CONFIG_MCA
25985    mca_init();
25986  #endif
25987  #ifdef CONFIG_ARCH_ACORN
25988    ecard_init();
25989  #endif
25990  #ifdef CONFIG_ZORRO
25991    zorro_init();
25992  #endif
25993  #ifdef CONFIG_DIO
25994    dio_init();
25995  #endif
25996  #ifdef CONFIG_NUBUS
25997    nubus_init();
25998  #endif
25999  #ifdef CONFIG_ISAPNP
26000    isapnp_init();
26001  #endif
26002  #ifdef CONFIG_TC
26003    tc_init();
26004  #endif
26005
26006    /* Networking initialization needs a process context */
26007    sock_init();
26008
```

```
26009 #ifdef CONFIG_BLK_DEV_INITRD
26010   real_root_dev = ROOT_DEV;
26011   real_root_mountflags = root_mountflags;
26012   if (initrd_start && mount_initrd)
26013     root_mountflags &= ~MS_RDONLY;
26014   else
26015     mount_initrd = 0;
26016 #endif
26017
26018   start_context_thread();
26019   do_initcalls();
26020
26021   /* .. filesystems .. */
26022   filesystem_setup();
26023
26024 #ifdef CONFIG_IRDA
26025   irda_device_init();    /* Must be done after protocol
26026                           * initialization */
26027 #endif
26028 #ifdef CONFIG_PCMCIA
26029   init_pcmcia_ds();              /* Do this last */
26030 #endif
26031
26032   /* Mount the root filesystem.. */
26033   mount_root();
26034
26035   mount_devfs_fs();
26036
26037 #ifdef CONFIG_BLK_DEV_INITRD
26038   root_mountflags = real_root_mountflags;
26039   if (mount_initrd && ROOT_DEV != real_root_dev
26040       && MAJOR(ROOT_DEV) == RAMDISK_MAJOR
26041       && MINOR(ROOT_DEV) == 0) {
26042   int error;
26043   int i, pid;
26044
26045   pid = kernel_thread(do_linuxrc, "/linuxrc", SIGCHLD);
26046   if (pid > 0)
26047     while (pid != wait(&i)) ;
26048   if (MAJOR(real_root_dev) != RAMDISK_MAJOR
26049       || MINOR(real_root_dev) != 0) {
26050     error = change_root(real_root_dev, "/initrd");
26051     if (error)
26052       printk(KERN_ERR "Change root to /initrd: "
26053             "error %d\n", error);
26054   }
26055   }
```

```
26056 #endif
26057 }
26058
26059 static int init(void *unused)
26060 {
26061   lock_kernel();
26062   do_basic_setup();
26063
26064   /* Ok, we have completed the initial bootup, and we're
26065    * essentially up and running. Get rid of the initmem
26066    * segments and start the user-mode stuff.. */
26067   free_initmem();
26068   unlock_kernel();
26069
26070   if (open("/dev/console", O_RDWR, 0) < 0)
26071     printk("Warning: unable to open "
26072           "an initial console.\n");
26073
26074   (void) dup(0);
26075   (void) dup(0);
26076
26077   /* We try each of these until one succeeds.
26078    *
26079    * The Bourne shell can be used instead of init if we
26080    * are trying to recover a really broken machine.  */
26081
26082   if (execute_command)
26083     execve(execute_command, argv_init, envp_init);
26084   execve("/sbin/init", argv_init, envp_init);
26085   execve("/etc/init", argv_init, envp_init);
26086   execve("/bin/init", argv_init, envp_init);
26087   execve("/bin/sh", argv_init, envp_init);
26088   panic("No init found.  "
26089         "Try passing init= option to kernel.");
26090 }
```

init/version.c

```
26091 /*
26092  *  linux/version.c
26093  *
26094  *  Copyright (C) 1992  Theodore Ts'o
26095  *
26096  *  May be freely distributed as part of Linux.
26097  */
26098
26099 #include <linux/uts.h>
26100 #include <linux/utsname.h>
```

```
26101 #include <linux/version.h>
26102 #include <linux/compile.h>
26103
26104 #define version(a) Version_ ## a
26105 #define version_string(a) version(a)
26106
26107 int version_string(LINUX_VERSION_CODE);
26108
26109 struct new_utsname system_utsname = {
26110   UTS_SYSNAME, UTS_NODENAME, UTS_RELEASE, UTS_VERSION,
26111   UTS_MACHINE, UTS_DOMAINNAME
26112 };
26113
26114 const char *linux_banner =
26115     "Linux version " UTS_RELEASE " (" LINUX_COMPILE_BY
26116     "@" LINUX_COMPILE_HOST ") (" LINUX_COMPILER ") "
26117     UTS_VERSION "\n";
```

ipc/msg.c

```
26118 /*
26119  * linux/ipc/msg.c
26120  * Copyright (C) 1992 Krishna Balasubramanian
26121  *
26122  * Removed all the remaining kerneld mess
26123  * Catch the -EFAULT stuff properly
26124  * Use GFP_KERNEL for messages as in 1.2
26125  * Fixed up the unchecked user space derefs
26126  * Copyright (C) 1998 Alan Cox & Andi Kleen
26127  *
26128  * /proc/sysvipc/msg support (c) 1999 Dragos
26129  * Acostachioaie <dragos@iname.com>
26130  *
26131  * mostly rewritten, threaded and wake-one semantics
26132  * added MSGMAX limit removed, sysctl's added
26133  * (c) 1999 Manfred Spraul <manfreds@colorfullife.com>
26134  */
26135
26136 #include <linux/config.h>
26137 #include <linux/malloc.h>
26138 #include <linux/msg.h>
26139 #include <linux/spinlock.h>
26140 #include <linux/init.h>
26141 #include <linux/proc_fs.h>
26142 #include <linux/list.h>
26143 #include <asm/uaccess.h>
26144 #include "util.h"
26145
```

```
26146 /* sysctl: */
26147 int msg_ctlmax = MSGMAX;
26148 int msg_ctlmnb = MSGMNB;
26149 int msg_ctlmni = MSGMNI;
26150
26151 /* one msg_receiver structure for each sleeping receiver
26152  */
26153 struct msg_receiver {
26154   struct list_head r_list;
26155   struct task_struct *r_tsk;
26156
26157   int r_mode;
26158   long r_msgtype;
26159   long r_maxsize;
26160
26161   struct msg_msg *volatile r_msg;
26162 };
26163
26164 /* one msg_sender for each sleeping sender */
26165 struct msg_sender {
26166   struct list_head list;
26167   struct task_struct *tsk;
26168 };
26169
26170 struct msg_msgseg {
26171   struct msg_msgseg *next;
26172   /* the next part of the message follows immediately */
26173 };
26174
26175 /* one msg_msg structure for each message */
26176 struct msg_msg {
26177   struct list_head m_list;
26178   long m_type;
26179   int m_ts;                    /* message text size */
26180   struct msg_msgseg *next;
26181   /* the actual message follows immediately */
26182 };
26183
26184 #define DATALEN_MSG (PAGE_SIZE-sizeof(struct msg_msg))
26185 #define DATALEN_SEG (PAGE_SIZE-sizeof(struct msg_msgseg))
26186
26187 /* one msq_queue structure for each present queue on the
26188  * system */
26189 struct msg_queue {
26190   struct kern_ipc_perm q_perm;
26191   time_t q_stime;              /* last msgsnd time */
26192   time_t q_rtime;              /* last msgrcv time */
```

```
26193    time_t q_ctime;              /* last change time */
26194    unsigned long q_cbytes;      /* current number of
26195                                  * bytes on queue */
26196    unsigned long q_qnum;        /* number of messages in
26197                                  * queue */
26198    unsigned long q_qbytes;      /* max number of bytes
26199                                  * on queue */
26200    pid_t q_lspid;               /* pid of last msgsnd */
26201    pid_t q_lrpid;               /* last receive pid */
26202
26203    struct list_head q_messages;
26204    struct list_head q_receivers;
26205    struct list_head q_senders;
26206 };
26207
26208 #define SEARCH_ANY          1
26209 #define SEARCH_EQUAL        2
26210 #define SEARCH_NOTEQUAL     3
26211 #define SEARCH_LESSEQUAL    4
26212
26213 static atomic_t msg_bytes = ATOMIC_INIT(0);
26214 static atomic_t msg_hdrs = ATOMIC_INIT(0);
26215
26216 static struct ipc_ids msg_ids;
26217
26218 #define msg_lock(id)                                \
26219    ((struct msg_queue*)ipc_lock(&msg_ids,id))
26220 #define msg_unlock(id)  ipc_unlock(&msg_ids,id)
26221 #define msg_rmid(id)                                \
26222    ((struct msg_queue*)ipc_rmid(&msg_ids,id))
26223 #define msg_checkid(msq, msgid)                     \
26224        ipc_checkid(&msg_ids,&msq->q_perm,msgid)
26225 #define msg_buildid(id, seq)                        \
26226        ipc_buildid(&msg_ids, id, seq)
26227
26228 static void freeque(int id);
26229 static int newque(key_t key, int msgflg);
26230 #ifdef CONFIG_PROC_FS
26231 static int sysvipc_msg_read_proc(char *buffer,
26232    char **start, off_t offset, int length, int *eof,
26233    void *data);
26234 #endif
26235
26236 void __init msg_init(void)
26237 {
26238    ipc_init_ids(&msg_ids, msg_ctlmni);
26239
```

```
26240 #ifdef CONFIG_PROC_FS
26241    create_proc_read_entry("sysvipc/msg", 0, 0,
26242        sysvipc_msg_read_proc, NULL);
26243 #endif
26244 }
26245
26246 static int newque(key_t key, int msgflg)
26247 {
26248    int id;
26249    struct msg_queue *msq;
26250
26251    msq = (struct msg_queue *) kmalloc(sizeof(*msq),
26252                                    GFP_KERNEL);
26253    if (!msq)
26254      return -ENOMEM;
26255    id = ipc_addid(&msg_ids, &msq->q_perm, msg_ctlmni);
26256    if (id == -1) {
26257      kfree(msq);
26258      return -ENOSPC;
26259    }
26260    msq->q_perm.mode = (msgflg & S_IRWXUGO);
26261    msq->q_perm.key = key;
26262
26263    msq->q_stime = msq->q_rtime = 0;
26264    msq->q_ctime = CURRENT_TIME;
26265    msq->q_cbytes = msq->q_qnum = 0;
26266    msq->q_qbytes = msg_ctlmnb;
26267    msq->q_lspid = msq->q_lrpid = 0;
26268    INIT_LIST_HEAD(&msq->q_messages);
26269    INIT_LIST_HEAD(&msq->q_receivers);
26270    INIT_LIST_HEAD(&msq->q_senders);
26271    msg_unlock(id);
26272
26273    return msg_buildid(id, msq->q_perm.seq);
26274 }
26275
26276 static void free_msg(struct msg_msg *msg)
26277 {
26278    struct msg_msgseg *seg;
26279    seg = msg->next;
26280    kfree(msg);
26281    while (seg != NULL) {
26282      struct msg_msgseg *tmp = seg->next;
26283      kfree(seg);
26284      seg = tmp;
26285    }
26286 }
```

```
26287
26288 static struct msg_msg *load_msg(void *src, int len)
26289 {
26290   struct msg_msg *msg;
26291   struct msg_msgseg **pseg;
26292   int err;
26293   int alen;
26294
26295   alen = len;
26296   if (alen > DATALEN_MSG)
26297     alen = DATALEN_MSG;
26298
26299   msg = (struct msg_msg *) kmalloc(sizeof(*msg) + alen,
26300                                     GFP_KERNEL);
26301   if (msg == NULL)
26302     return ERR_PTR(-ENOMEM);
26303
26304   msg->next = NULL;
26305
26306   if (copy_from_user(msg + 1, src, alen)) {
26307     err = -EFAULT;
26308     goto out_err;
26309   }
26310
26311   len -= alen;
26312   src = ((char *) src) + alen;
26313   pseg = &msg->next;
26314   while (len > 0) {
26315     struct msg_msgseg *seg;
26316     alen = len;
26317     if (alen > DATALEN_SEG)
26318       alen = DATALEN_SEG;
26319     seg = (struct msg_msgseg *)kmalloc(sizeof(*seg) +
26320                                 alen, GFP_KERNEL);
26321     if (seg == NULL) {
26322       err = -ENOMEM;
26323       goto out_err;
26324     }
26325     *pseg = seg;
26326     seg->next = NULL;
26327     if (copy_from_user(seg + 1, src, alen)) {
26328       err = -EFAULT;
26329       goto out_err;
26330     }
26331     pseg = &seg->next;
26332     len -= alen;
26333     src = ((char *) src) + alen;
```

```
26334   }
26335   return msg;
26336
26337 out_err:
26338   free_msg(msg);
26339   return ERR_PTR(err);
26340 }
26341
26342 static int store_msg(void *dest, struct msg_msg *msg,
26343     int len)
26344 {
26345   int alen;
26346   struct msg_msgseg *seg;
26347
26348   alen = len;
26349   if (alen > DATALEN_MSG)
26350     alen = DATALEN_MSG;
26351   if (copy_to_user(dest, msg + 1, alen))
26352     return -1;
26353
26354   len -= alen;
26355   dest = ((char *) dest) + alen;
26356   seg = msg->next;
26357   while (len > 0) {
26358     alen = len;
26359     if (alen > DATALEN_SEG)
26360       alen = DATALEN_SEG;
26361     if (copy_to_user(dest, seg + 1, alen))
26362       return -1;
26363     len -= alen;
26364     dest = ((char *) dest) + alen;
26365     seg = seg->next;
26366   }
26367   return 0;
26368 }
26369
26370 static inline void ss_add(struct msg_queue *msq,
26371     struct msg_sender *mss)
26372 {
26373   mss->tsk = current;
26374   current->state = TASK_INTERRUPTIBLE;
26375   list_add_tail(&mss->list, &msq->q_senders);
26376 }
26377
26378 static inline void ss_del(struct msg_sender *mss)
26379 {
26380   if (mss->list.next != NULL)
```

```
26381        list_del(&mss->list);
26382 }
26383
26384 static void ss_wakeup(struct list_head *h, int kill)
26385 {
26386    struct list_head *tmp;
26387
26388    tmp = h->next;
26389    while (tmp != h) {
26390       struct msg_sender *mss;
26391
26392       mss = list_entry(tmp, struct msg_sender, list);
26393       tmp = tmp->next;
26394       if (kill)
26395          mss->list.next = NULL;
26396       wake_up_process(mss->tsk);
26397    }
26398 }
26399
26400 static void expunge_all(struct msg_queue *msq, int res)
26401 {
26402    struct list_head *tmp;
26403
26404    tmp = msq->q_receivers.next;
26405    while (tmp != &msq->q_receivers) {
26406       struct msg_receiver *msr;
26407
26408       msr = list_entry(tmp, struct msg_receiver, r_list);
26409       tmp = tmp->next;
26410       msr->r_msg = ERR_PTR(res);
26411       wake_up_process(msr->r_tsk);
26412    }
26413 }
26414
26415 static void freeque(int id)
26416 {
26417    struct msg_queue *msq;
26418    struct list_head *tmp;
26419
26420    msq = msg_rmid(id);
26421
26422    expunge_all(msq, -EIDRM);
26423    ss_wakeup(&msq->q_senders, 1);
26424    msg_unlock(id);
26425
26426    tmp = msq->q_messages.next;
26427    while (tmp != &msq->q_messages) {
```

p 667 (line 26415)

```
26428       struct msg_msg *msg =
26429          list_entry(tmp, struct msg_msg, m_list);
26430       tmp = tmp->next;
26431       atomic_dec(&msg_hdrs);
26432       free_msg(msg);
26433    }
26434    atomic_sub(msq->q_cbytes, &msg_bytes);
26435    kfree(msq);
26436 }
26437
26438 asmlinkage long sys_msgget(key_t key, int msgflg)
26439 {
26440    int id, ret = -EPERM;
26441    struct msg_queue *msq;
26442
26443    down(&msg_ids.sem);
26444    if (key == IPC_PRIVATE)
26445       ret = newque(key, msgflg);
26446    else if ((id = ipc_findkey(&msg_ids, key)) == -1) {
26447       /* key not used */
26448       if (!(msgflg & IPC_CREAT))
26449          ret = -ENOENT;
26450       else
26451          ret = newque(key, msgflg);
26452    } else if (msgflg & IPC_CREAT && msgflg & IPC_EXCL) {
26453       ret = -EEXIST;
26454    } else {
26455       msq = msg_lock(id);
26456       if (msq == NULL)
26457          BUG();
26458       if (ipcperms(&msq->q_perm, msgflg))
26459          ret = -EACCES;
26460       else
26461          ret = msg_buildid(id, msq->q_perm.seq);
26462       msg_unlock(id);
26463    }
26464    up(&msg_ids.sem);
26465    return ret;
26466 }
26467
26468 static inline unsigned long copy_msqid_to_user(void *buf,
26469    struct msqid64_ds *in, int version)
26470 {
26471    switch (version) {
26472    case IPC_64:
26473       return copy_to_user(buf, in, sizeof(*in));
26474    case IPC_OLD:
```

p 658 (line 26438)

```
26475    {
26476      struct msqid_ds out;
26477
26478      memset(&out, 0, sizeof(out));
26479
26480      ipc64_perm_to_ipc_perm(&in->msg_perm,
26481                             &out.msg_perm);
26482
26483      out.msg_stime = in->msg_stime;
26484      out.msg_rtime = in->msg_rtime;
26485      out.msg_ctime = in->msg_ctime;
26486
26487      if (in->msg_cbytes > USHRT_MAX)
26488        out.msg_cbytes = USHRT_MAX;
26489      else
26490        out.msg_cbytes = in->msg_cbytes;
26491      out.msg_lcbytes = in->msg_cbytes;
26492
26493      if (in->msg_qnum > USHRT_MAX)
26494        out.msg_qnum = USHRT_MAX;
26495      else
26496        out.msg_qnum = in->msg_qnum;
26497
26498      if (in->msg_qbytes > USHRT_MAX)
26499        out.msg_qbytes = USHRT_MAX;
26500      else
26501        out.msg_qbytes = in->msg_qbytes;
26502      out.msg_lqbytes = in->msg_qbytes;
26503
26504      out.msg_lspid = in->msg_lspid;
26505      out.msg_lrpid = in->msg_lrpid;
26506
26507      return copy_to_user(buf, &out, sizeof(out));
26508    }
26509    default:
26510      return -EINVAL;
26511    }
26512 }
26513
26514 struct msq_setbuf {
26515   unsigned long qbytes;
26516   uid_t uid;
26517   gid_t gid;
26518   mode_t mode;
26519 };
26520
26521 static inline unsigned long copy_msqid_from_user(struct
```

```
26522      msq_setbuf *out, void *buf, int version)
26523 {
26524   switch (version) {
26525   case IPC_64:
26526   {
26527     struct msqid64_ds tbuf;
26528
26529     if (copy_from_user(&tbuf, buf, sizeof(tbuf)))
26530       return -EFAULT;
26531
26532     out->qbytes = tbuf.msg_qbytes;
26533     out->uid = tbuf.msg_perm.uid;
26534     out->gid = tbuf.msg_perm.gid;
26535     out->mode = tbuf.msg_perm.mode;
26536
26537     return 0;
26538   }
26539   case IPC_OLD:
26540   {
26541     struct msqid_ds tbuf_old;
26542
26543     if (copy_from_user(&tbuf_old, buf,
26544                        sizeof(tbuf_old)))
26545       return -EFAULT;
26546
26547     out->uid = tbuf_old.msg_perm.uid;
26548     out->gid = tbuf_old.msg_perm.gid;
26549     out->mode = tbuf_old.msg_perm.mode;
26550
26551     if (tbuf_old.msg_qbytes == 0)
26552       out->qbytes = tbuf_old.msg_lqbytes;
26553     else
26554       out->qbytes = tbuf_old.msg_qbytes;
26555
26556     return 0;
26557   }
26558   default:
26559     return -EINVAL;
26560   }
26561 }
26562
26563 asmlinkage long sys_msgctl(int msqid, int cmd,
26564     struct msqid_ds *buf)
26565 {
26566   int err, version;
26567   struct msg_queue *msq;
26568   struct msq_setbuf setbuf;
```

p 665

```
26569    struct kern_ipc_perm *ipcp;
26570
26571    if (msqid < 0 || cmd < 0)
26572      return -EINVAL;
26573
26574    version = ipc_parse_version(&cmd);
26575
26576    switch (cmd) {
26577    case IPC_INFO:
26578    case MSG_INFO:
26579    {
26580      struct msginfo msginfo;
26581      int max_id;
26582      if (!buf)
26583        return -EFAULT;
26584      /* We must not return kernel stack data.  due to
26585       * padding, it's not enough to set all member
26586       * fields. */
26587      memset(&msginfo, 0, sizeof(msginfo));
26588      msginfo.msgmni = msg_ctlmni;
26589      msginfo.msgmax = msg_ctlmax;
26590      msginfo.msgmnb = msg_ctlmnb;
26591      msginfo.msgssz = MSGSSZ;
26592      msginfo.msgseg = MSGSEG;
26593      down(&msg_ids.sem);
26594      if (cmd == MSG_INFO) {
26595        msginfo.msgpool = msg_ids.in_use;
26596        msginfo.msgmap = atomic_read(&msg_hdrs);
26597        msginfo.msgtql = atomic_read(&msg_bytes);
26598      } else {
26599        msginfo.msgmap = MSGMAP;
26600        msginfo.msgpool = MSGPOOL;
26601        msginfo.msgtql = MSGTQL;
26602      }
26603      max_id = msg_ids.max_id;
26604      up(&msg_ids.sem);
26605      if (copy_to_user(buf, &msginfo,
26606                       sizeof(struct msginfo)))
26607        return -EFAULT;
26608      return (max_id < 0) ? 0 : max_id;
26609    }
26610    case MSG_STAT:
26611    case IPC_STAT:
26612    {
26613      struct msqid64_ds tbuf;
26614      int success_return;
26615      if (!buf)
26616        return -EFAULT;
26617      if (cmd == MSG_STAT && msqid > msg_ids.size)
26618        return -EINVAL;
26619
26620      memset(&tbuf, 0, sizeof(tbuf));
26621
26622      msq = msg_lock(msqid);
26623      if (msq == NULL)
26624        return -EINVAL;
26625
26626      if (cmd == MSG_STAT) {
26627        success_return =
26628          msg_buildid(msqid, msq->q_perm.seq);
26629      } else {
26630        err = -EIDRM;
26631        if (msg_checkid(msq, msqid))
26632          goto out_unlock;
26633        success_return = 0;
26634      }
26635      err = -EACCES;
26636      if (ipcperms(&msq->q_perm, S_IRUGO))
26637        goto out_unlock;
26638
26639      kernel_to_ipc64_perm(&msq->q_perm, &tbuf.msg_perm);
26640      tbuf.msg_stime = msq->q_stime;
26641      tbuf.msg_rtime = msq->q_rtime;
26642      tbuf.msg_ctime = msq->q_ctime;
26643      tbuf.msg_cbytes = msq->q_cbytes;
26644      tbuf.msg_qnum = msq->q_qnum;
26645      tbuf.msg_qbytes = msq->q_qbytes;
26646      tbuf.msg_lspid = msq->q_lspid;
26647      tbuf.msg_lrpid = msq->q_lrpid;
26648      msg_unlock(msqid);
26649      if (copy_msqid_to_user(buf, &tbuf, version))
26650        return -EFAULT;
26651      return success_return;
26652    }
26653    case IPC_SET:
26654      if (!buf)
26655        return -EFAULT;
26656      if (copy_msqid_from_user(&setbuf, buf, version))
26657        return -EFAULT;
26658      break;
26659    case IPC_RMID:
26660      break;
26661    default:
26662      return -EINVAL;
```

```
26663    }
26664
26665    down(&msg_ids.sem);
26666    msq = msg_lock(msqid);
26667    err = -EINVAL;
26668    if (msq == NULL)
26669      goto out_up;
26670
26671    err = -EIDRM;
26672    if (msg_checkid(msq, msqid))
26673      goto out_unlock_up;
26674    ipcp = &msq->q_perm;
26675    err = -EPERM;
26676    if (current->euid != ipcp->cuid &&
26677        current->euid != ipcp->uid
26678        && !capable(CAP_SYS_ADMIN))
26679      /* We _could_ check for CAP_CHOWN above, but we don't
26680       */
26681      goto out_unlock_up;
26682
26683    switch (cmd) {
26684    case IPC_SET:
26685    {
26686      if (setbuf.qbytes > msg_ctlmnb
26687          && !capable(CAP_SYS_RESOURCE))
26688        goto out_unlock_up;
26689      msq->q_qbytes = setbuf.qbytes;
26690
26691      ipcp->uid = setbuf.uid;
26692      ipcp->gid = setbuf.gid;
26693      ipcp->mode = (ipcp->mode & ~S_IRWXUGO) |
26694        (S_IRWXUGO & setbuf.mode);
26695      msq->q_ctime = CURRENT_TIME;
26696      /* sleeping receivers might be excluded by stricter
26697       * permissions. */
26698      expunge_all(msq, -EAGAIN);
26699      /* sleeping senders might be able to send due to a
26700       * larger queue size. */
26701      ss_wakeup(&msq->q_senders, 0);
26702      msg_unlock(msqid);
26703      break;
26704    }
26705    case IPC_RMID:
26706      freeque(msqid);
26707      break;
26708    }
26709    err = 0;
```

```
26710  out_up:
26711    up(&msg_ids.sem);
26712    return err;
26713  out_unlock_up:
26714    msg_unlock(msqid);
26715    goto out_up;
26716  out_unlock:
26717    msg_unlock(msqid);
26718    return err;
26719  }
26720
26721  static int testmsg(struct msg_msg *msg, long type,
26722      int mode)
26723  {
26724    switch (mode) {
26725    case SEARCH_ANY:
26726      return 1;
26727    case SEARCH_LESSEQUAL:
26728      if (msg->m_type <= type)
26729        return 1;
26730      break;
26731    case SEARCH_EQUAL:
26732      if (msg->m_type == type)
26733        return 1;
26734      break;
26735    case SEARCH_NOTEQUAL:
26736      if (msg->m_type != type)
26737        return 1;
26738      break;
26739    }
26740    return 0;
26741  }
26742
26743  int inline pipelined_send(struct msg_queue *msq,
26744      struct msg_msg *msg)
26745  {
26746    struct list_head *tmp;
26747
26748    tmp = msq->q_receivers.next;
26749    while (tmp != &msq->q_receivers) {
26750      struct msg_receiver *msr;
26751      msr = list_entry(tmp, struct msg_receiver, r_list);
26752      tmp = tmp->next;
26753      if (testmsg(msg, msr->r_msgtype, msr->r_mode)) {
26754        list_del(&msr->r_list);
26755        if (msr->r_maxsize < msg->m_ts) {
26756          msr->r_msg = ERR_PTR(-E2BIG);
```

p 663 (at line 26721)

p 663 (at line 26743)

```
26757              wake_up_process(msr->r_tsk);
26758          } else {
26759              msr->r_msg = msg;
26760              msq->q_lspid = msr->r_tsk->pid;
26761              msq->q_rtime = CURRENT_TIME;
26762              wake_up_process(msr->r_tsk);
26763              return 1;
26764          }
26765      }
26766  }
26767  return 0;
26768 }
26769
26770 asmlinkage long sys_msgsnd(int msqid,
26771     struct msgbuf *msgp, size_t msgsz, int msgflg)
26772 {
26773   struct msg_queue *msq;
26774   struct msg_msg *msg;
26775   long mtype;
26776   int err;
26777
26778   if(msgsz > msg_ctlmax || (long) msgsz < 0 || msqid < 0)
26779     return -EINVAL;
26780   if (get_user(mtype, &msgp->mtype))
26781     return -EFAULT;
26782   if (mtype < 1)
26783     return -EINVAL;
26784
26785   msg = load_msg(msgp->mtext, msgsz);
26786   if (IS_ERR(msg))
26787     return PTR_ERR(msg);
26788
26789   msg->m_type = mtype;
26790   msg->m_ts = msgsz;
26791
26792   msq = msg_lock(msqid);
26793   err = -EINVAL;
26794   if (msq == NULL)
26795     goto out_free;
26796 retry:
26797   err = -EIDRM;
26798   if (msg_checkid(msq, msqid))
26799     goto out_unlock_free;
26800
26801   err = -EACCES;
26802   if (ipcperms(&msq->q_perm, S_IWUGO))
26803     goto out_unlock_free;
```

```
26804
26805   if (msgsz + msq->q_cbytes > msq->q_qbytes ||
26806       1 + msq->q_qnum > msq->q_qbytes) {
26807     struct msg_sender s;
26808
26809     if (msgflg & IPC_NOWAIT) {
26810       err = -EAGAIN;
26811       goto out_unlock_free;
26812     }
26813     ss_add(msq, &s);
26814     msg_unlock(msqid);
26815     schedule();
26816     current->state = TASK_RUNNING;
26817
26818     msq = msg_lock(msqid);
26819     err = -EIDRM;
26820     if (msq == NULL)
26821       goto out_free;
26822     ss_del(&s);
26823
26824     if (signal_pending(current)) {
26825       err = -EINTR;
26826       goto out_unlock_free;
26827     }
26828     goto retry;
26829   }
26830
26831   if (!pipelined_send(msq, msg)) {
26832     /* noone is waiting for this message, enqueue it */
26833     list_add_tail(&msg->m_list, &msq->q_messages);
26834     msq->q_cbytes += msgsz;
26835     msq->q_qnum++;
26836     atomic_add(msgsz, &msg_bytes);
26837     atomic_inc(&msg_hdrs);
26838   }
26839
26840   err = 0;
26841   msg = NULL;
26842   msq->q_lspid = current->pid;
26843   msq->q_stime = CURRENT_TIME;
26844
26845 out_unlock_free:
26846   msg_unlock(msqid);
26847 out_free:
26848   if (msg != NULL)
26849     free_msg(msg);
26850   return err;
```

```
26851 }
26852
26853 int inline convert_mode(long *msgtyp, int msgflg)
26854 {
26855   /*
26856    *  find message of correct type.
26857    *  msgtyp = 0 => get first.
26858    *  msgtyp > 0 => get first message of matching type.
26859    *  msgtyp < 0 => get message with least type must
26860    *                be < abs(msgtype). */
26861   if (*msgtyp == 0)
26862     return SEARCH_ANY;
26863   if (*msgtyp < 0) {
26864     *msgtyp = -(*msgtyp);
26865     return SEARCH_LESSEQUAL;
26866   }
26867   if (msgflg & MSG_EXCEPT)
26868     return SEARCH_NOTEQUAL;
26869   return SEARCH_EQUAL;
26870 }
26871
26872 asmlinkage long sys_msgrcv(int msqid,
26873       struct msgbuf *msgp, size_t msgsz, long msgtyp,
26874       int msgflg)
26875 {
26876   struct msg_queue *msq;
26877   struct msg_receiver msr_d;
26878   struct list_head *tmp;
26879   struct msg_msg *msg, *found_msg;
26880   int err;
26881   int mode;
26882
26883   if (msqid < 0 || (long) msgsz < 0)
26884     return -EINVAL;
26885   mode = convert_mode(&msgtyp, msgflg);
26886
26887   msq = msg_lock(msqid);
26888   if (msq == NULL)
26889     return -EINVAL;
26890 retry:
26891   err = -EACCES;
26892   if (ipcperms(&msq->q_perm, S_IRUGO))
26893     goto out_unlock;
26894
26895   tmp = msq->q_messages.next;
26896   found_msg = NULL;
26897   while (tmp != &msq->q_messages) {
```

```
26898     msg = list_entry(tmp, struct msg_msg, m_list);
26899     if (testmsg(msg, msgtyp, mode)) {
26900       found_msg = msg;
26901       if (mode == SEARCH_LESSEQUAL && msg->m_type != 1) {
26902         found_msg = msg;
26903         msgtyp = msg->m_type - 1;
26904       } else {
26905         found_msg = msg;
26906         break;
26907       }
26908     }
26909     tmp = tmp->next;
26910   }
26911   if (found_msg) {
26912     msg = found_msg;
26913     if ((msgsz < msg->m_ts) && !(msgflg & MSG_NOERROR)) {
26914       err = -E2BIG;
26915       goto out_unlock;
26916     }
26917     list_del(&msg->m_list);
26918     msq->q_qnum--;
26919     msq->q_rtime = CURRENT_TIME;
26920     msq->q_lrpid = current->pid;
26921     msq->q_cbytes -= msg->m_ts;
26922     atomic_sub(msg->m_ts, &msg_bytes);
26923     atomic_dec(&msg_hdrs);
26924     ss_wakeup(&msq->q_senders, 0);
26925     msg_unlock(msqid);
26926 out_success:
26927     msgsz = (msgsz > msg->m_ts) ? msg->m_ts : msgsz;
26928     if (put_user(msg->m_type, &msgp->mtype) ||
26929         store_msg(msgp->mtext, msg, msgsz)) {
26930       msgsz = -EFAULT;
26931     }
26932     free_msg(msg);
26933     return msgsz;
26934   } else {
26935     struct msg_queue *t;
26936     /* no message waiting. Prepare for pipelined
26937      * receive. */
26938     if (msgflg & IPC_NOWAIT) {
26939       err = -ENOMSG;
26940       goto out_unlock;
26941     }
26942     list_add_tail(&msr_d.r_list, &msq->q_receivers);
26943     msr_d.r_tsk = current;
26944     msr_d.r_msgtype = msgtyp;
```

```
26945      msr_d.r_mode = mode;
26946      if (msgflg & MSG_NOERROR)
26947        msr_d.r_maxsize = INT_MAX;
26948      else
26949        msr_d.r_maxsize = msgsz;
26950      msr_d.r_msg = ERR_PTR(-EAGAIN);
26951      current->state = TASK_INTERRUPTIBLE;
26952      msg_unlock(msqid);
26953
26954      schedule();
26955      current->state = TASK_RUNNING;
26956
26957      msg = (struct msg_msg *) msr_d.r_msg;
26958      if (!IS_ERR(msg))
26959        goto out_success;
26960
26961      t = msg_lock(msqid);
26962      if (t == NULL)
26963        msqid = -1;
26964      msg = (struct msg_msg *) msr_d.r_msg;
26965      if (!IS_ERR(msg)) {
26966        /* our message arived while we waited for the
26967         * spinlock. Process it. */
26968        if (msqid != -1)
26969          msg_unlock(msqid);
26970        goto out_success;
26971      }
26972      err = PTR_ERR(msg);
26973      if (err == -EAGAIN) {
26974        if (msqid == -1)
26975          BUG();
26976        list_del(&msr_d.r_list);
26977        if (signal_pending(current))
26978          err = -EINTR;
26979        else
26980          goto retry;
26981      }
26982    }
26983 out_unlock:
26984    if (msqid != -1)
26985      msg_unlock(msqid);
26986    return err;
26987 }
26988
26989 #ifdef CONFIG_PROC_FS
26990 static int sysvipc_msg_read_proc(char *buffer,
26991      char **start, off_t offset, int length, int *eof,
```

```
26992      void *data)
26993 {
26994    off_t pos = 0;
26995    off_t begin = 0;
26996    int i, len = 0;
26997
26998    down(&msg_ids.sem);
26999    len +=
27000      sprintf(buffer, "       key       msqid perms       "
27001              "cbytes       qnum lspid lrpid   uid    gid"
27002              "cuid cgid       stime      rtime       "
27003              "ctime\n");
27004
27005    for (i = 0; i <= msg_ids.max_id; i++) {
27006      struct msg_queue *msq;
27007      msq = msg_lock(i);
27008      if (msq != NULL) {
27009        len += sprintf(buffer + len,
27010                "%10d %10d  %4o  %10lu %10lu %5u "
27011                "%5u %5u %5u %5u %5u %10lu %10lu "
27012                "%10lu\n",
27013                msq->q_perm.key,
27014                msg_buildid(i, msq->q_perm.seq),
27015                msq->q_perm.mode, msq->q_cbytes,
27016                msq->q_qnum, msq->q_lspid,
27017                msq->q_lrpid, msq->q_perm.uid,
27018                msq->q_perm.gid, msq->q_perm.cuid,
27019                msq->q_perm.cgid, msq->q_stime,
27020                msq->q_rtime, msq->q_ctime);
27021        msg_unlock(i);
27022
27023        pos += len;
27024        if (pos < offset) {
27025          len = 0;
27026          begin = pos;
27027        }
27028        if (pos > offset + length)
27029          goto done;
27030      }
27031
27032    }
27033    *eof = 1;
27034 done:
27035    up(&msg_ids.sem);
27036    *start = buffer + (offset - begin);
27037    len -= (offset - begin);
27038    if (len > length)
```

```
27039    len = length;
27040   if (len < 0)
27041     len = 0;
27042   return len;
27043 }
27044 #endif
```

ipc/sem.c

```
27045 /*
27046  * linux/ipc/sem.c
27047  * Copyright (C) 1992 Krishna Balasubramanian
27048  * Copyright (C) 1995 Eric Schenk, Bruno Haible
27049  *
27050  * IMPLEMENTATION NOTES ON CODE REWRITE (Eric Schenk,
27051  * January 1995): This code underwent a massive rewrite
27052  * in order to solve some problems with the original
27053  * code. In particular the original code failed to wake
27054  * up processes that were waiting for semval to go to 0
27055  * if the value went to 0 and was then incremented
27056  * rapidly enough. In solving this problem I have also
27057  * modified the implementation so that it processes
27058  * pending operations in a FIFO manner, thus give a
27059  * guarantee that processes waiting for a lock on the
27060  * semaphore won't starve unless another locking process
27061  * fails to unlock.  In addition the following two
27062  * changes in behavior have been introduced:
27063  * - The original implementation of semop returned the
27064  *   value last semaphore element examined on
27065  *   success. This does not match the manual page
27066  *   specifications, and effectively allows the user to
27067  *   read the semaphore even if they do not have read
27068  *   permissions. The implementation now returns 0 on
27069  *   success as stated in the manual page.
27070  * - There is some confusion over whether the set of undo
27071  *   adjustments to be performed at exit should be done
27072  *   in an atomic manner.  That is, if we are attempting
27073  *   to decrement the semval should we queue up and wait
27074  *   until we can do so legally?  The original
27075  *   implementation attempted to do this.  The current
27076  *   implementation does not do so. This is because I
27077  *   don't think it is the right thing (TM) to do, and
27078  *   because I couldn't see a clean way to get the old
27079  *   behavior with the new design.  The POSIX standard
27080  *   and SVID should be consulted to determine what
27081  *   behavior is mandated.
27082  *
27083  * Further notes on refinement (Christoph Rohland,
27084  *                                December 1998):
27085  * - The POSIX standard says, that the undo adjustments
27086  *   simply should redo. So the current implementation is
27087  *   o.K.
27088  * - The previous code had two flaws:
27089  * 1) It actively gave the semaphore to the next waiting
27090  *     process sleeping on the semaphore. Since this
27091  *     process did not have the cpu this led to many
27092  *     unnecessary context switches and bad
27093  *     performance. Now we only check which process
27094  *     should be able to get the semaphore and if this
27095  *     process wants to reduce some semaphore value we
27096  *     simply wake it up without doing the operation. So
27097  *     it has to try to get it later. Thus e.g. the
27098  *     running process may reacquire the semaphore
27099  *     during the current time slice. If it only waits
27100  *     for zero or increases the semaphore, we do the
27101  *     operation in advance and wake it up.
27102  * 2) It did not wake up all zero waiting processes. We
27103  *     try to do better but only get the semops right
27104  *     which only wait for zero or increase. If there
27105  *     are decrement operations in the operations array
27106  *     we do the same as before.
27107  *
27108  * /proc/sysvipc/sem support
27109  * (c) 1999 Dragos Acostachioaie <dragos@iname.com>
27110  *
27111  * SMP-threaded, sysctl's added
27112  * (c) 1999 Manfred Spraul <manfreds@colorfullife.com>
27113  */
27114
27115 #include <linux/config.h>
27116 #include <linux/malloc.h>
27117 #include <linux/spinlock.h>
27118 #include <linux/init.h>
27119 #include <linux/proc_fs.h>
27120 #include <asm/uaccess.h>
27121 #include "util.h"
27122
27123
27124 #define sem_lock(id)                                      \
27125   ((struct sem_array*)ipc_lock(&sem_ids,id))
27126 #define sem_unlock(id)  ipc_unlock(&sem_ids,id)
27127 #define sem_rmid(id)                                      \
27128   ((struct sem_array*)ipc_rmid(&sem_ids,id))
27129 #define sem_checkid(sma, semid)                           \
27130       ipc_checkid(&sem_ids,&sma->sem_perm,semid)
```

```
27131 #define sem_buildid(id, seq)                              \
27132        ipc_buildid(&sem_ids, id, seq)
27133 static struct ipc_ids sem_ids;
27134
27135 static int newary(key_t, int, int);
27136 static void freeary(int id);
27137 #ifdef CONFIG_PROC_FS
27138 static int sysvipc_sem_read_proc(char *buffer,
27139    char **start, off_t offset, int length, int *eof,
27140    void *data);
27141 #endif
27142
27143 #define SEMMSL_FAST    256      /* 512 bytes on stack */
27144 #define SEMOPM_FAST    64       /* ~ 372 bytes on stack */
27145
27146 /* linked list protection:
27147  *       sem_undo.id_next,
27148  *       sem_array.sem_pending{,last},
27149  *       sem_array.sem_undo: sem_lock() for read/write
27150  *       sem_undo.proc_next: only "current" is allowed to
27151  *                           read/write that field. */
27152
27153 int sem_ctls[4] = { SEMMSL, SEMMNS, SEMOPM, SEMMNI };
27154
27155 #define sc_semmsl    (sem_ctls[0])
27156 #define sc_semmns    (sem_ctls[1])
27157 #define sc_semopm    (sem_ctls[2])
27158 #define sc_semmni    (sem_ctls[3])
27159
27160 static int used_sems;
27161
27162 void __init sem_init(void)
27163 {
27164    used_sems = 0;
27165    ipc_init_ids(&sem_ids, sc_semmni);
27166
27167 #ifdef CONFIG_PROC_FS
27168    create_proc_read_entry("sysvipc/sem", 0, 0,
27169                           sysvipc_sem_read_proc, NULL);
27170 #endif
27171 }
27172
27173 static int newary(key_t key, int nsems, int semflg)
27174 {
27175    int id;
27176    struct sem_array *sma;
27177    int size;

27178
27179    if (!nsems)
27180       return -EINVAL;
27181    if (used_sems + nsems > sc_semmns)
27182       return -ENOSPC;
27183
27184    size = sizeof(*sma) + nsems * sizeof(struct sem);
27185    sma = (struct sem_array *) ipc_alloc(size);
27186    if (!sma) {
27187       return -ENOMEM;
27188    }
27189    memset(sma, 0, size);
27190    id = ipc_addid(&sem_ids, &sma->sem_perm, sc_semmni);
27191    if (id == -1) {
27192       ipc_free(sma, size);
27193       return -ENOSPC;
27194    }
27195    used_sems += nsems;
27196
27197    sma->sem_perm.mode = (semflg & S_IRWXUGO);
27198    sma->sem_perm.key = key;
27199
27200    sma->sem_base = (struct sem *) &sma[1];
27201    /* sma->sem_pending = NULL; */
27202    sma->sem_pending_last = &sma->sem_pending;
27203    /* sma->undo = NULL; */
27204    sma->sem_nsems = nsems;
27205    sma->sem_ctime = CURRENT_TIME;
27206    sem_unlock(id);
27207
27208    return sem_buildid(id, sma->sem_perm.seq);
27209 }
27210
27211 asmlinkage long sys_semget(key_t key, int nsems,
27212    int semflg)
27213 {
27214    int id, err = -EINVAL;
27215    struct sem_array *sma;
27216
27217    if (nsems < 0 || nsems > sc_semmsl)
27218       return -EINVAL;
27219    down(&sem_ids.sem);
27220
27221    if (key == IPC_PRIVATE) {
27222       err = newary(key, nsems, semflg);
27223    } else if ((id = ipc_findkey(&sem_ids, key)) == -1) {
27224       /* key not used */
```

```
27225    if (!(semflg & IPC_CREAT))
27226      err = -ENOENT;
27227    else
27228      err = newary(key, nsems, semflg);
27229  } else if (semflg & IPC_CREAT && semflg & IPC_EXCL) {
27230    err = -EEXIST;
27231  } else {
27232    sma = sem_lock(id);
27233    if (sma == NULL)
27234      BUG();
27235    if (nsems > sma->sem_nsems)
27236      err = -EINVAL;
27237    else if (ipcperms(&sma->sem_perm, semflg))
27238      err = -EACCES;
27239    else
27240      err = sem_buildid(id, sma->sem_perm.seq);
27241    sem_unlock(id);
27242  }
27243
27244  up(&sem_ids.sem);
27245  return err;
27246 }
27247
27248 /* doesn't acquire the sem_lock on error! */
27249 static int sem_revalidate(int semid,
27250     struct sem_array *sma, int nsems, short flg)
27251 {
27252   struct sem_array *smanew;
27253
27254   smanew = sem_lock(semid);
27255   if (smanew == NULL)
27256     return -EIDRM;
27257   if (smanew != sma || sem_checkid(sma, semid)
27258       || sma->sem_nsems != nsems) {
27259     sem_unlock(semid);
27260     return -EIDRM;
27261   }
27262
27263   if (ipcperms(&sma->sem_perm, flg)) {
27264     sem_unlock(semid);
27265     return -EACCES;
27266   }
27267   return 0;
27268 }
27269
27270 /* Manage the doubly linked list sma->sem_pending as a
27271  * FIFO: insert new queue elements at the tail
```

```
27272  * sma->sem_pending_last. */
27273 static inline void append_to_queue(struct sem_array *sma,
27274     struct sem_queue *q)
27275 {
27276   *(q->prev = sma->sem_pending_last) = q;
27277   *(sma->sem_pending_last = &q->next) = NULL;
27278 }
27279
27280 static inline void
27281 prepend_to_queue(struct sem_array *sma,
27282                  struct sem_queue *q)
27283 {
27284   q->next = sma->sem_pending;
27285   *(q->prev = &sma->sem_pending) = q;
27286   if (q->next)
27287     q->next->prev = &q->next;
27288   else    /* sma->sem_pending_last == &sma->sem_pending */
27289     sma->sem_pending_last = &q->next;
27290 }
27291
27292 static inline void
27293 remove_from_queue(struct sem_array *sma,
27294                   struct sem_queue *q)
27295 {
27296   *(q->prev) = q->next;
27297   if (q->next)
27298     q->next->prev = q->prev;
27299   else              /* sma->sem_pending_last == &q->next */
27300     sma->sem_pending_last = q->prev;
27301   q->prev = NULL;                    /* mark as removed */
27302 }
27303
27304 /* Determine whether a sequence of semaphore operations
27305  * would succeed all at once. Return 0 if yes, 1 if need
27306  * to sleep, else return error code.  */
27307 static int try_atomic_semop(struct sem_array *sma,
27308     struct sembuf *sops, int nsops, struct sem_undo *un,
27309     int pid, int do_undo)
27310 {
27311   int result, sem_op;
27312   struct sembuf *sop;
27313   struct sem *curr;
27314
27315   for (sop = sops; sop < sops + nsops; sop++) {
27316     curr = sma->sem_base + sop->sem_num;
27317     sem_op = sop->sem_op;
27318
```

```
27319      if (!sem_op && curr->semval)
27320        goto would_block;
27321
27322      curr->sempid = (curr->sempid << 16) | pid;
27323      curr->semval += sem_op;
27324      if (sop->sem_flg & SEM_UNDO)
27325        un->semadj[sop->sem_num] -= sem_op;
27326
27327      if (curr->semval < 0)
27328        goto would_block;
27329      if (curr->semval > SEMVMX)
27330        goto out_of_range;
27331    }
27332
27333    if (do_undo) {
27334      sop--;
27335      result = 0;
27336      goto undo;
27337    }
27338
27339    sma->sem_otime = CURRENT_TIME;
27340    return 0;
27341
27342 out_of_range:
27343    result = -ERANGE;
27344    goto undo;
27345
27346 would_block:
27347    if (sop->sem_flg & IPC_NOWAIT)
27348      result = -EAGAIN;
27349    else
27350      result = 1;
27351
27352 undo:
27353    while (sop >= sops) {
27354      curr = sma->sem_base + sop->sem_num;
27355      curr->semval -= sop->sem_op;
27356      curr->sempid >>= 16;
27357
27358      if (sop->sem_flg & SEM_UNDO)
27359        un->semadj[sop->sem_num] += sop->sem_op;
27360      sop--;
27361    }
27362
27363    return result;
27364 }
27365
```

```
27366 /* Go through the pending queue for the indicated
27367  * semaphore looking for tasks that can be completed. */
```
p 672 ►
```
27368 static void update_queue(struct sem_array *sma)
27369 {
27370   int error;
27371   struct sem_queue *q;
27372
27373   for (q = sma->sem_pending; q; q = q->next) {
27374
27375     if (q->status == 1)
27376       continue;  /* this one was woken up before */
27377
27378     error = try_atomic_semop(sma, q->sops, q->nsops,
27379        q->undo, q->pid, q->alter);
27380
27381     /* Does q->sleeper still need to sleep? */
27382     if (error <= 0) {
27383       /* Found one, wake it up */
27384       wake_up_process(q->sleeper);
27385       if (error == 0 && q->alter) {
27386         /* if q-> alter let it self try */
27387         q->status = 1;
27388         return;
27389       }
27390       q->status = error;
27391       remove_from_queue(sma, q);
27392     }
27393   }
27394 }
27395
27396 /* The following counts are associated to each
27397  * semaphore:
27398  *   semncnt        number of tasks waiting on semval
27399  *                  being nonzero
27400  *   semzcnt        number of tasks waiting on semval
27401  *                  being zero
27402  * This model assumes that a task waits on exactly one
27403  * semaphore.
27404  *
27405  * Since semaphore operations are to be performed
27406  * atomically, tasks actually wait on a whole sequence of
27407  * semaphores simultaneously.  The counts we return here
27408  * are a rough approximation, but still warrant that
27409  * semncnt+semzcnt>0 if the task is on the pending
27410  * queue. */
```
p 674 ►
```
27411 static int count_semncnt(struct sem_array *sma,
27412     ushort semnum)
```

```
27413 {
27414   int semncnt;
27415   struct sem_queue *q;
27416
27417   semncnt = 0;
27418   for (q = sma->sem_pending; q; q = q->next) {
27419     struct sembuf *sops = q->sops;
27420     int nsops = q->nsops;
27421     int i;
27422     for (i = 0; i < nsops; i++)
27423       if (sops[i].sem_num == semnum &&
27424         (sops[i].sem_op < 0) &&
27425         !(sops[i].sem_flg & IPC_NOWAIT))
27426       semncnt++;
27427   }
27428   return semncnt;
27429 }
27430
27431 static int count_semzcnt(struct sem_array *sma,
27432     ushort semnum)
27433 {
27434   int semzcnt;
27435   struct sem_queue *q;
27436
27437   semzcnt = 0;
27438   for (q = sma->sem_pending; q; q = q->next) {
27439     struct sembuf *sops = q->sops;
27440     int nsops = q->nsops;
27441     int i;
27442     for (i = 0; i < nsops; i++)
27443       if (sops[i].sem_num == semnum &&
27444         (sops[i].sem_op == 0) &&
27445         !(sops[i].sem_flg & IPC_NOWAIT))
27446       semzcnt++;
27447   }
27448   return semzcnt;
27449 }
27450
27451 /* Free a semaphore set. */
27452 static void freeary(int id)
27453 {
27454   struct sem_array *sma;
27455   struct sem_undo *un;
27456   struct sem_queue *q;
27457   int size;
27458
27459   sma = sem_rmid(id);
```

```
27460
27461   /* Invalidate the existing undo structures for this
27462    * semaphore set.  (They will be freed without any
27463    * further action in sem_exit() or during the next
27464    * semop.) */
27465   for (un = sma->undo; un; un = un->id_next)
27466     un->semid = -1;
27467
27468   /* Wake up all pending processes and let them fail
27469    * with EIDRM. */
27470   for (q = sma->sem_pending; q; q = q->next) {
27471     q->status = -EIDRM;
27472     q->prev = NULL;
27473     wake_up_process(q->sleeper);      /* doesn't sleep */
27474   }
27475   sem_unlock(id);
27476
27477   used_sems -= sma->sem_nsems;
27478   size =
27479       sizeof(*sma) + sma->sem_nsems * sizeof(struct sem);
27480   ipc_free(sma, size);
27481 }
27482
27483 static unsigned long copy_semid_to_user(void *buf,
27484     struct semid64_ds *in, int version)
27485 {
27486   switch (version) {
27487   case IPC_64:
27488     return copy_to_user(buf, in, sizeof(*in));
27489   case IPC_OLD:
27490   {
27491     struct semid_ds out;
27492
27493     ipc64_perm_to_ipc_perm(&in->sem_perm,
27494                            &out.sem_perm);
27495
27496     out.sem_otime = in->sem_otime;
27497     out.sem_ctime = in->sem_ctime;
27498     out.sem_nsems = in->sem_nsems;
27499
27500     return copy_to_user(buf, &out, sizeof(out));
27501   }
27502   default:
27503     return -EINVAL;
27504   }
27505 }
27506
```

```
p 673  27507 int semctl_nolock(int semid, int semnum, int cmd,
       27508    int version, union semun arg)
       27509 {
       27510   int err = -EINVAL;
       27511
       27512   switch (cmd) {
       27513   case IPC_INFO:
       27514   case SEM_INFO:
       27515   {
       27516     struct seminfo seminfo;
       27517     int max_id;
       27518
       27519     memset(&seminfo, 0, sizeof(seminfo));
       27520     seminfo.semmni = sc_semmni;
       27521     seminfo.semmns = sc_semmns;
       27522     seminfo.semmsl = sc_semmsl;
       27523     seminfo.semopm = sc_semopm;
       27524     seminfo.semvmx = SEMVMX;
       27525     seminfo.semmnu = SEMMNU;
       27526     seminfo.semmap = SEMMAP;
       27527     seminfo.semume = SEMUME;
       27528     down(&sem_ids.sem);
       27529     if (cmd == SEM_INFO) {
       27530       seminfo.semusz = sem_ids.in_use;
       27531       seminfo.semaem = used_sems;
       27532     } else {
       27533       seminfo.semusz = SEMUSZ;
       27534       seminfo.semaem = SEMAEM;
       27535     }
       27536     max_id = sem_ids.max_id;
       27537     up(&sem_ids.sem);
       27538     if (copy_to_user(arg.__buf, &seminfo,
       27539                      sizeof(struct seminfo)))
       27540       return -EFAULT;
       27541     return (max_id < 0) ? 0 : max_id;
       27542   }
       27543   case SEM_STAT:
       27544   {
       27545     struct sem_array *sma;
       27546     struct semid64_ds tbuf;
       27547     int id;
       27548
       27549     if (semid > sem_ids.size)
       27550       return -EINVAL;
       27551
       27552     memset(&tbuf, 0, sizeof(tbuf));
       27553
       27554     sma = sem_lock(semid);
       27555     if (sma == NULL)
       27556       return -EINVAL;
       27557
       27558     err = -EACCES;
       27559     if (ipcperms(&sma->sem_perm, S_IRUGO))
       27560       goto out_unlock;
       27561     id = sem_buildid(semid, sma->sem_perm.seq);
       27562
       27563     kernel_to_ipc64_perm(&sma->sem_perm,
       27564                          &tbuf.sem_perm);
       27565     tbuf.sem_otime = sma->sem_otime;
       27566     tbuf.sem_ctime = sma->sem_ctime;
       27567     tbuf.sem_nsems = sma->sem_nsems;
       27568     sem_unlock(semid);
       27569     if (copy_semid_to_user(arg.buf, &tbuf, version))
       27570       return -EFAULT;
       27571     return id;
       27572   }
       27573   default:
       27574     return -EINVAL;
       27575   }
       27576   return err;
       27577 out_unlock:
       27578   sem_unlock(semid);
       27579   return err;
       27580 }
       27581
p 673  27582 int semctl_main(int semid, int semnum, int cmd,
       27583    int version, union semun arg)
       27584 {
       27585   struct sem_array *sma;
       27586   struct sem *curr;
       27587   int err;
       27588   ushort fast_sem_io[SEMMSL_FAST];
       27589   ushort *sem_io = fast_sem_io;
       27590   int nsems;
       27591
       27592   sma = sem_lock(semid);
       27593   if (sma == NULL)
       27594     return -EINVAL;
       27595
       27596   nsems = sma->sem_nsems;
       27597
       27598   err = -EIDRM;
       27599   if (sem_checkid(sma, semid))
       27600     goto out_unlock;
```

```
27601
27602    err = -EACCES;
27603    if (ipcperms(&sma->sem_perm,
27604                 (cmd == SETVAL || cmd == SETALL)
27605                 ? S_IWUGO : S_IRUGO))
27606      goto out_unlock;
27607
27608    switch (cmd) {
27609    case GETALL:
27610    {
27611      ushort *array = arg.array;
27612      int i;
27613
27614      if (nsems > SEMMSL_FAST) {
27615        sem_unlock(semid);
27616        sem_io = ipc_alloc(sizeof(ushort) * nsems);
27617        if (sem_io == NULL)
27618          return -ENOMEM;
27619        err = sem_revalidate(semid, sma, nsems, S_IRUGO);
27620        if (err)
27621          goto out_free;
27622      }
27623
27624      for (i = 0; i < sma->sem_nsems; i++)
27625        sem_io[i] = sma->sem_base[i].semval;
27626      sem_unlock(semid);
27627      err = 0;
27628      if (copy_to_user(array, sem_io,
27629                       nsems * sizeof(ushort)))
27630        err = -EFAULT;
27631      goto out_free;
27632    }
27633    case SETALL:
27634    {
27635      int i;
27636      struct sem_undo *un;
27637
27638      sem_unlock(semid);
27639
27640      if (nsems > SEMMSL_FAST) {
27641        sem_io = ipc_alloc(sizeof(ushort) * nsems);
27642        if (sem_io == NULL)
27643          return -ENOMEM;
27644      }
27645
27646      if (copy_from_user(sem_io, arg.array,
27647                         nsems * sizeof(ushort))) {
27648        err = -EFAULT;
27649        goto out_free;
27650      }
27651
27652      for (i = 0; i < nsems; i++) {
27653        if (sem_io[i] > SEMVMX) {
27654          err = -ERANGE;
27655          goto out_free;
27656        }
27657      }
27658      err = sem_revalidate(semid, sma, nsems, S_IWUGO);
27659      if (err)
27660        goto out_free;
27661
27662      for (i = 0; i < nsems; i++)
27663        sma->sem_base[i].semval = sem_io[i];
27664      for (un = sma->undo; un; un = un->id_next)
27665        for (i = 0; i < nsems; i++)
27666          un->semadj[i] = 0;
27667      sma->sem_ctime = CURRENT_TIME;
27668      /* maybe some queued-up processes were waiting for
27669       * this */
27670      update_queue(sma);
27671      err = 0;
27672      goto out_unlock;
27673    }
27674    case IPC_STAT:
27675    {
27676      struct semid64_ds tbuf;
27677      memset(&tbuf, 0, sizeof(tbuf));
27678      kernel_to_ipc64_perm(&sma->sem_perm, &tbuf.sem_perm);
27679      tbuf.sem_otime = sma->sem_otime;
27680      tbuf.sem_ctime = sma->sem_ctime;
27681      tbuf.sem_nsems = sma->sem_nsems;
27682      sem_unlock(semid);
27683      if (copy_semid_to_user(arg.buf, &tbuf, version))
27684        return -EFAULT;
27685      return 0;
27686    }
27687    /* GETVAL, GETPID, GETNCTN, GETZCNT, SETVAL:
27688     * fall-through */
27689    }
27690    err = -EINVAL;
27691    if (semnum < 0 || semnum >= nsems)
27692      goto out_unlock;
27693
27694    curr = &sma->sem_base[semnum];
```

```
27695
27696    switch (cmd) {
27697    case GETVAL:
27698      err = curr->semval;
27699      goto out_unlock;
27700    case GETPID:
27701      err = curr->sempid & 0xffff;
27702      goto out_unlock;
27703    case GETNCNT:
27704      err = count_semncnt(sma, semnum);
27705      goto out_unlock;
27706    case GETZCNT:
27707      err = count_semzcnt(sma, semnum);
27708      goto out_unlock;
27709    case SETVAL:
27710    {
27711      int val = arg.val;
27712      struct sem_undo *un;
27713      err = -ERANGE;
27714      if (val > SEMVMX || val < 0)
27715        goto out_unlock;
27716
27717      for (un = sma->undo; un; un = un->id_next)
27718        un->semadj[semnum] = 0;
27719      curr->semval = val;
27720      sma->sem_ctime = CURRENT_TIME;
27721      /* maybe some queued-up processes were waiting for
27722       * this */
27723      update_queue(sma);
27724      err = 0;
27725      goto out_unlock;
27726    }
27727    }
27728  out_unlock:
27729    sem_unlock(semid);
27730  out_free:
27731    if (sem_io != fast_sem_io)
27732      ipc_free(sem_io, sizeof(ushort) * nsems);
27733    return err;
27734  }
27735
27736  struct sem_setbuf {
27737    uid_t uid;
27738    gid_t gid;
27739    mode_t mode;
27740  };
27741
```

```
27742  static inline unsigned long copy_semid_from_user(struct
27743      sem_setbuf *out, void *buf, int version)
27744  {
27745    switch (version) {
27746    case IPC_64:
27747    {
27748      struct semid64_ds tbuf;
27749
27750      if (copy_from_user(&tbuf, buf, sizeof(tbuf)))
27751        return -EFAULT;
27752
27753      out->uid = tbuf.sem_perm.uid;
27754      out->gid = tbuf.sem_perm.gid;
27755      out->mode = tbuf.sem_perm.mode;
27756
27757      return 0;
27758    }
27759    case IPC_OLD:
27760    {
27761      struct semid_ds tbuf_old;
27762
27763      if (copy_from_user(&tbuf_old, buf, sizeof(tbuf_old)))
27764        return -EFAULT;
27765
27766      out->uid = tbuf_old.sem_perm.uid;
27767      out->gid = tbuf_old.sem_perm.gid;
27768      out->mode = tbuf_old.sem_perm.mode;
27769
27770      return 0;
27771    }
27772    default:
27773      return -EINVAL;
27774    }
27775  }
27776
27777  int semctl_down(int semid, int semnum, int cmd,
27778      int version, union semun arg)
27779  {
27780    struct sem_array *sma;
27781    int err;
27782    struct sem_setbuf setbuf;
27783    struct kern_ipc_perm *ipcp;
27784
27785    if (cmd == IPC_SET) {
27786      if (copy_semid_from_user(&setbuf, arg.buf, version))
27787        return -EFAULT;
27788    }
```

p 674

```
27789    sma = sem_lock(semid);
27790    if (sma == NULL)
27791      return -EINVAL;
27792
27793    if (sem_checkid(sma, semid)) {
27794      err = -EIDRM;
27795      goto out_unlock;
27796    }
27797    ipcp = &sma->sem_perm;
27798
27799    if (current->euid != ipcp->cuid &&
27800        current->euid != ipcp->uid &&
27801        !capable(CAP_SYS_ADMIN)) {
27802      err = -EPERM;
27803      goto out_unlock;
27804    }
27805
27806    switch (cmd) {
27807    case IPC_RMID:
27808      freeary(semid);
27809      err = 0;
27810      break;
27811    case IPC_SET:
27812      ipcp->uid = setbuf.uid;
27813      ipcp->gid = setbuf.gid;
27814      ipcp->mode = (ipcp->mode & ~S_IRWXUGO)
27815          | (setbuf.mode & S_IRWXUGO);
27816      sma->sem_ctime = CURRENT_TIME;
27817      sem_unlock(semid);
27818      err = 0;
27819      break;
27820    default:
27821      sem_unlock(semid);
27822      err = -EINVAL;
27823      break;
27824    }
27825    return err;
27826
27827 out_unlock:
27828    sem_unlock(semid);
27829    return err;
27830 }
27831
27832 asmlinkage long sys_semctl(int semid, int semnum,
27833      int cmd, union semun arg)
27834 {
27835    int err = -EINVAL;
```

```
27836    int version;
27837
27838    if (semid < 0)
27839      return -EINVAL;
27840
27841    version = ipc_parse_version(&cmd);
27842
27843    switch (cmd) {
27844    case IPC_INFO:
27845    case SEM_INFO:
27846    case SEM_STAT:
27847      err =
27848        semctl_nolock(semid, semnum, cmd, version, arg);
27849      return err;
27850    case GETALL:
27851    case GETVAL:
27852    case GETPID:
27853    case GETNCNT:
27854    case GETZCNT:
27855    case IPC_STAT:
27856    case SETVAL:
27857    case SETALL:
27858      err = semctl_main(semid, semnum, cmd, version, arg);
27859      return err;
27860    case IPC_RMID:
27861    case IPC_SET:
27862      down(&sem_ids.sem);
27863      err = semctl_down(semid, semnum, cmd, version, arg);
27864      up(&sem_ids.sem);
27865      return err;
27866    default:
27867      return -EINVAL;
27868    }
27869 }
27870
27871 static struct sem_undo *freeundos(struct sem_array *sma,
27872      struct sem_undo *un)
27873 {
27874    struct sem_undo *u;
27875    struct sem_undo **up;
27876
27877    for (up = &current->semundo;
27878        (u = *up);
27879        up = &u->proc_next) {
27880      if (un == u) {
27881        un = u->proc_next;
27882        *up = un;
```

```
27883        kfree(u);
27884        return un;
27885      }
27886    }
27887    printk("freeundos undo list error id=%d\n", un->semid);
27888    return un->proc_next;
27889 }
27890
27891 /* returns without sem_lock on error! */
27892 static int alloc_undo(struct sem_array *sma,
27893      struct sem_undo **unp, int semid, int alter)
27894 {
27895    int size, nsems, error;
27896    struct sem_undo *un;
27897
27898    nsems = sma->sem_nsems;
27899    size = sizeof(struct sem_undo) + sizeof(short) * nsems;
27900    sem_unlock(semid);
27901
27902    un = (struct sem_undo *) kmalloc(size, GFP_KERNEL);
27903    if (!un)
27904      return -ENOMEM;
27905
27906    memset(un, 0, size);
27907    error = sem_revalidate(semid, sma, nsems,
27908                          alter ? S_IWUGO : S_IRUGO);
27909    if (error) {
27910      kfree(un);
27911      return error;
27912    }
27913
27914    un->semadj = (short *) &un[1];
27915    un->semid = semid;
27916    un->proc_next = current->semundo;
27917    current->semundo = un;
27918    un->id_next = sma->undo;
27919    sma->undo = un;
27920    *unp = un;
27921    return 0;
27922 }
27923
27924 asmlinkage long sys_semop(int semid,
27925      struct sembuf *tsops, unsigned nsops)
27926 {
27927    int error = -EINVAL;
27928    struct sem_array *sma;
27929    struct sembuf fast_sops[SEMOPM_FAST];
```

```
27930    struct sembuf *sops = fast_sops, *sop;
27931    struct sem_undo *un;
27932    int undos = 0, decrease = 0, alter = 0;
27933    struct sem_queue queue;
27934
27935    if (nsops < 1 || semid < 0)
27936      return -EINVAL;
27937    if (nsops > sc_semopm)
27938      return -E2BIG;
27939    if (nsops > SEMOPM_FAST) {
27940      sops = kmalloc(sizeof(*sops) * nsops, GFP_KERNEL);
27941      if (sops == NULL)
27942        return -ENOMEM;
27943    }
27944    if (copy_from_user(sops, tsops,
27945            nsops * sizeof(*tsops))) {
27946      error = -EFAULT;
27947      goto out_free;
27948    }
27949    sma = sem_lock(semid);
27950    error = -EINVAL;
27951    if (sma == NULL)
27952      goto out_free;
27953    error = -EIDRM;
27954    if (sem_checkid(sma, semid))
27955      goto out_unlock_free;
27956    error = -EFBIG;
27957    for (sop = sops; sop < sops + nsops; sop++) {
27958      if (sop->sem_num >= sma->sem_nsems)
27959        goto out_unlock_free;
27960      if (sop->sem_flg & SEM_UNDO)
27961        undos++;
27962      if (sop->sem_op < 0)
27963        decrease = 1;
27964      if (sop->sem_op > 0)
27965        alter = 1;
27966    }
27967    alter |= decrease;
27968
27969    error = -EACCES;
27970    if (ipcperms(&sma->sem_perm,
27971            alter ? S_IWUGO : S_IRUGO))
27972      goto out_unlock_free;
27973    if (undos) {
27974      /* Make sure we have an undo structure for this
27975       * process and this semaphore set. */
27976      un = current->semundo;
```

```
27977      while (un != NULL) {
27978        if (un->semid == semid)
27979          break;
27980        if (un->semid == -1)
27981          un = freeundos(sma, un);
27982        else
27983          un = un->proc_next;
27984      }
27985      if (!un) {
27986        error = alloc_undo(sma, &un, semid, alter);
27987        if (error)
27988          goto out_free;
27989      }
27990    } else
27991      un = NULL;
27992
27993    error = try_atomic_semop(sma, sops, nsops, un,
27994                            current->pid, 0);
27995    if (error <= 0)
27996      goto update;
27997
27998    /* We need to sleep on this operation, so we put the
27999     * current task into the pending queue and go to
28000     * sleep. */
28001    queue.sma = sma;
28002    queue.sops = sops;
28003    queue.nsops = nsops;
28004    queue.undo = un;
28005    queue.pid = current->pid;
28006    queue.alter = decrease;
28007    queue.id = semid;
28008    if (alter)
28009      append_to_queue(sma, &queue);
28010    else
28011      prepend_to_queue(sma, &queue);
28012    current->semsleeping = &queue;
28013
28014    for (;;) {
28015      struct sem_array *tmp;
28016      queue.status = -EINTR;
28017      queue.sleeper = current;
28018      current->state = TASK_INTERRUPTIBLE;
28019      sem_unlock(semid);
28020
28021      schedule();
28022
28023      tmp = sem_lock(semid);
28024      if (tmp == NULL) {
28025        if (queue.status != -EIDRM)
28026          BUG();
28027        current->semsleeping = NULL;
28028        error = -EIDRM;
28029        goto out_free;
28030      }
28031      /* If queue.status == 1 we where woken up and have to
28032       * retry else we simply return.  If an interrupt
28033       * occurred we have to clean up the queue */
28034      if (queue.status == 1) {
28035        error = try_atomic_semop(sma, sops, nsops, un,
28036            current->pid, 0);
28037        if (error <= 0)
28038          break;
28039      } else {
28040        error = queue.status;
28041        if (queue.prev)            /* got Interrupt */
28042          break;
28043        /* Everything done by update_queue */
28044        current->semsleeping = NULL;
28045        goto out_unlock_free;
28046      }
28047    }
28048    current->semsleeping = NULL;
28049    remove_from_queue(sma, &queue);
28050  update:
28051    if (alter)
28052      update_queue(sma);
28053  out_unlock_free:
28054    sem_unlock(semid);
28055  out_free:
28056    if (sops != fast_sops)
28057      kfree(sops);
28058    return error;
28059  }
28060
28061  /* add semadj values to semaphores, free undo structures.
28062   * undo structures are not freed when semaphore arrays
28063   * are destroyed so some of them may be out of date.
28064   * IMPLEMENTATION NOTE: There is some confusion over
28065   * whether the set of adjustments that needs to be done
28066   * should be done in an atomic manner or not. That is, if
28067   * we are attempting to decrement the semval should we
28068   * queue up and wait until we can do so legally?  The
28069   * original implementation attempted to do this (queue
28070   * and wait).  The current implementation does not do
```

```
28071    * so. The POSIX standard and SVID should be consulted to
28072    * determine what behavior is mandated.  */
28073 void sem_exit(void)
28074 {
28075    struct sem_queue *q;
28076    struct sem_undo *u, *un = NULL, **up, **unp;
28077    struct sem_array *sma;
28078    int nsems, i;
28079
28080    /* If the current process was sleeping for a semaphore,
28081     * remove it from the queue. */
28082    if ((q = current->semsleeping)) {
28083      int semid = q->id;
28084      sma = sem_lock(semid);
28085      current->semsleeping = NULL;
28086
28087      if (q->prev) {
28088        if (sma == NULL)
28089          BUG();
28090        remove_from_queue(q->sma, q);
28091      }
28092      if (sma != NULL)
28093        sem_unlock(semid);
28094    }
28095
28096    for (up = &current->semundo;
28097         (u = *up);
28098         *up = u->proc_next, kfree(u)) {
28099      int semid = u->semid;
28100      if (semid == -1)
28101        continue;
28102      sma = sem_lock(semid);
28103      if (sma == NULL)
28104        continue;
28105
28106      if (u->semid == -1)
28107        goto next_entry;
28108
28109      if (sem_checkid(sma, u->semid))
28110        goto next_entry;
28111
28112      /* remove u from the sma->undo list */
28113      for (unp = &sma->undo;
28114           (un = *unp);
28115           unp = &un->id_next) {
28116        if (u == un)
28117          goto found;
28118      }
28119      printk("sem_exit undo list error id=%d\n", u->semid);
28120      goto next_entry;
28121    found:
28122      *unp = un->id_next;
28123      /* perform adjustments registered in u */
28124      nsems = sma->sem_nsems;
28125      for (i = 0; i < nsems; i++) {
28126        struct sem *sem = &sma->sem_base[i];
28127        sem->semval += u->semadj[i];
28128        if (sem->semval < 0)
28129          sem->semval = 0;          /* shouldn't happen */
28130        sem->sempid = current->pid;
28131      }
28132      sma->sem_otime = CURRENT_TIME;
28133      /* maybe some queued-up processes were waiting for
28134       * this */
28135      update_queue(sma);
28136    next_entry:
28137      sem_unlock(semid);
28138    }
28139    current->semundo = NULL;
28140 }
28141
28142 #ifdef CONFIG_PROC_FS
28143 static int sysvipc_sem_read_proc(char *buffer,
28144     char **start, off_t offset, int length, int *eof,
28145     void *data)
28146 {
28147    off_t pos = 0;
28148    off_t begin = 0;
28149    int i, len = 0;
28150
28151    len += sprintf(buffer,
28152                "       key      semid perms      nsems"
28153                "  uid   gid  cuid  cgid      otime"
28154                "          ctime\n");
28155    down(&sem_ids.sem);
28156
28157    for (i = 0; i <= sem_ids.max_id; i++) {
28158      struct sem_array *sma;
28159      sma = sem_lock(i);
28160      if (sma) {
28161        len +=
28162            sprintf(buffer + len,
28163                "%10d %10d  %4o %10lu %5u %5u %5u %5u "
28164                "%10lu %10lu\n",
```

```
28165                    sma->sem_perm.key,
28166                    sem_buildid(i, sma->sem_perm.seq),
28167                    sma->sem_perm.mode,
28168                    sma->sem_nsems, sma->sem_perm.uid,
28169                    sma->sem_perm.gid, sma->sem_perm.cuid,
28170                    sma->sem_perm.cgid, sma->sem_otime,
28171                    sma->sem_ctime);
28172        sem_unlock(i);
28173
28174        pos += len;
28175        if (pos < offset) {
28176          len = 0;
28177          begin = pos;
28178        }
28179        if (pos > offset + length)
28180          goto done;
28181      }
28182    }
28183    *eof = 1;
28184 done:
28185    up(&sem_ids.sem);
28186    *start = buffer + (offset - begin);
28187    len -= (offset - begin);
28188    if (len > length)
28189      len = length;
28190    if (len < 0)
28191      len = 0;
28192    return len;
28193 }
28194 #endif
```

ipc/shm.c

```
28195 /*
28196  * linux/ipc/shm.c
28197  * Copyright (C) 1992, 1993 Krishna Balasubramanian
28198  *       Many improvements/fixes by Bruno Haible.
28199  * Replaced 'struct shm_desc' by 'struct vm_area_struct',
28200  * July 1994.
28201  * Fixed the shm swap deallocation (shm_unuse()), August
28202  * 1998 Andrea Arcangeli.
28203  *
28204  * /proc/sysvipc/shm support (c) 1999 Dragos
28205  * Acostachioaie <dragos@iname.com>
28206  * BIGMEM support, Andrea Arcangeli <andrea@suse.de>
28207  * SMP thread shm, Jean-Luc Boyard
28208  * <jean-luc.boyard@siemens.fr>
28209  * HIGHMEM support, Ingo Molnar <mingo@redhat.com>
```

```
28210  * Make shmmax, shmall, shmmni sysctl'able, Christoph
28211  * Rohland <cr@sap.com>
28212  * Shared /dev/zero support, Kanoj Sarcar <kanoj@sgi.com>
28213  * Move the mm functionality over to mm/shmem.c,
28214  * Christoph Rohland <cr@sap.com>
28215  */
28216
28217 #include <linux/config.h>
28218 #include <linux/malloc.h>
28219 #include <linux/shm.h>
28220 #include <linux/init.h>
28221 #include <linux/file.h>
28222 #include <linux/mman.h>
28223 #include <linux/proc_fs.h>
28224 #include <asm/uaccess.h>
28225
28226 #include "util.h"
28227
28228 struct shmid_kernel {            /* private to the kernel */
28229    struct kern_ipc_perm shm_perm;
28230    struct file *shm_file;
28231    int id;
28232    unsigned long shm_nattch;
28233    unsigned long shm_segsz;
28234    time_t shm_atim;
28235    time_t shm_dtim;
28236    time_t shm_ctim;
28237    pid_t shm_cprid;
28238    pid_t shm_lprid;
28239 };
28240
28241 #define shm_flags        shm_perm.mode
28242
28243 static struct file_operations shm_file_operations;
28244 static struct vm_operations_struct shm_vm_ops;
28245
28246 static struct ipc_ids shm_ids;
28247
28248 #define shm_lock(id)                                     \
28249    ((struct shmid_kernel*)ipc_lock(&shm_ids,id))
28250 #define shm_unlock(id)  ipc_unlock(&shm_ids,id)
28251 #define shm_lockall()    ipc_lockall(&shm_ids)
28252 #define shm_unlockall() ipc_unlockall(&shm_ids)
28253 #define shm_get(id)                                      \
28254    ((struct shmid_kernel*)ipc_get(&shm_ids,id))
28255 #define shm_buildid(id, seq)                             \
28256         ipc_buildid(&shm_ids, id, seq)
```

```
28257
28258 static int newseg(key_t key, int shmflg, size_t size);
28259 static void shm_open(struct vm_area_struct *shmd);
28260 static void shm_close(struct vm_area_struct *shmd);
28261 #ifdef CONFIG_PROC_FS
28262 static int sysvipc_shm_read_proc(char *buffer,
28263     char **start, off_t offset, int length, int *eof,
28264     void *data);
28265 #endif
28266
28267 size_t shm_ctlmax = SHMMAX;
28268 size_t shm_ctlall = SHMALL;
28269 int shm_ctlmni = SHMMNI;
28270
28271 /* total number of shared memory pages */
28272 static int shm_tot;
28273
28274 void __init shm_init(void)
28275 {
28276   ipc_init_ids(&shm_ids, 1);
28277   create_proc_read_entry("sysvipc/shm", 0, 0,
28278       sysvipc_shm_read_proc, NULL);
28279 }
28280
28281 static inline int shm_checkid(struct shmid_kernel *s,
28282     int id)
28283 {
28284   if (ipc_checkid(&shm_ids, &s->shm_perm, id))
28285     return -EIDRM;
28286   return 0;
28287 }
28288
28289 static inline struct shmid_kernel *shm_rmid(int id)
28290 {
28291   return (struct shmid_kernel *) ipc_rmid(&shm_ids, id);
28292 }
28293
28294 static inline int shm_addid(struct shmid_kernel *shp)
28295 {
28296   return ipc_addid(&shm_ids, &shp->shm_perm,
28297       shm_ctlmni + 1);
28298 }
28299
28300
28301
28302 static inline void shm_inc(int id)
28303 {
28304   struct shmid_kernel *shp;
28305
28306   if (!(shp = shm_lock(id)))
28307     BUG();
28308   shp->shm_atim = CURRENT_TIME;
28309   shp->shm_lprid = current->pid;
28310   shp->shm_nattch++;
28311   shm_unlock(id);
28312 }
28313
28314 /* This is called by fork, once for every shm attach. */
28315 static void shm_open(struct vm_area_struct *shmd)
28316 {
28317   shm_inc(shmd->vm_file->f_dentry->d_inode->i_ino);
28318 }
28319
28320 /* shm_destroy - free the struct shmid_kernel
28321  *
28322  * @shp: struct to free
28323  *
28324  * It has to be called with shp and shm_ids.sem locked */
28325 static void shm_destroy(struct shmid_kernel *shp)
28326 {
28327   shm_tot -=
28328       (shp->shm_segsz + PAGE_SIZE - 1) >> PAGE_SHIFT;
28329   shm_rmid(shp->id);
28330   shmem_lock(shp->shm_file, 0);
28331   fput(shp->shm_file);
28332   kfree(shp);
28333 }
28334
28335 /* remove the attach descriptor shmd.
28336  * free memory for segment if it is marked destroyed.
28337  * The descriptor has already been removed from the
28338  * current->mm->mmap list and will later be kfree()d.  */
28339 static void shm_close(struct vm_area_struct *shmd)
28340 {
28341   struct file *file = shmd->vm_file;
28342   int id = file->f_dentry->d_inode->i_ino;
28343   struct shmid_kernel *shp;
28344
28345   down(&shm_ids.sem);
28346   /* remove from the list of attaches of the shm segment
28347    */
28348   if (!(shp = shm_lock(id)))
28349     BUG();
28350   shp->shm_lprid = current->pid;
```

p 678

```
28351    shp->shm_dtim = CURRENT_TIME;
28352    shp->shm_nattch--;
28353    if (shp->shm_nattch == 0 && shp->shm_flags & SHM_DEST)
28354      shm_destroy(shp);
28355
28356    shm_unlock(id);
28357    up(&shm_ids.sem);
28358 }
28359
28360 static int shm_mmap(struct file *file,
28361      struct vm_area_struct *vma)
28362 {
28363    UPDATE_ATIME(file->f_dentry->d_inode);
28364    vma->vm_ops = &shm_vm_ops;
28365    shm_inc(file->f_dentry->d_inode->i_ino);
28366    return 0;
28367 }
28368
28369 static struct file_operations shm_file_operations = {
28370    mmap: shm_mmap
28371 };
28372
28373 static struct vm_operations_struct shm_vm_ops = {
28374    open:     shm_open,        /* callback for a new
28375                               * vm-area open */
28376    close:    shm_close,       /* callback for when the
28377                               * vm-area is released */
28378    nopage:   shmem_nopage,
28379 };
28380
28381 static int newseg(key_t key, int shmflg, size_t size)
28382 {
28383    int error;
28384    struct shmid_kernel *shp;
28385    int numpages = (size + PAGE_SIZE - 1) >> PAGE_SHIFT;
28386    struct file *file;
28387    char name[13];
28388    int id;
28389
28390    if (size < SHMMIN || size > shm_ctlmax)
28391      return -EINVAL;
28392
28393    if (shm_tot + numpages >= shm_ctlall)
28394      return -ENOSPC;
28395
28396    shp = (struct shmid_kernel *) kmalloc(sizeof(*shp),
28397                                    GFP_USER);
```

```
28398    if (!shp)
28399      return -ENOMEM;
28400    sprintf(name, "SYSV%08x", key);
28401    file = shmem_file_setup(name, size);
28402    error = PTR_ERR(file);
28403    if (IS_ERR(file))
28404      goto no_file;
28405
28406    error = -ENOSPC;
28407    id = shm_addid(shp);
28408    if (id == -1)
28409      goto no_id;
28410    shp->shm_perm.key = key;
28411    shp->shm_flags = (shmflg & S_IRWXUGO);
28412    shp->shm_cprid = current->pid;
28413    shp->shm_lprid = 0;
28414    shp->shm_atim = shp->shm_dtim = 0;
28415    shp->shm_ctim = CURRENT_TIME;
28416    shp->shm_segsz = size;
28417    shp->shm_nattch = 0;
28418    shp->id = shm_buildid(id, shp->shm_perm.seq);
28419    shp->shm_file = file;
28420    file->f_dentry->d_inode->i_ino = shp->id;
28421    file->f_op = &shm_file_operations;
28422    shm_tot += numpages;
28423    shm_unlock(id);
28424    return shp->id;
28425
28426 no_id:
28427    fput(file);
28428 no_file:
28429    kfree(shp);
28430    return error;
28431 }
28432
28433 asmlinkage long sys_shmget(key_t key, size_t size,
28434      int shmflg)
28435 {
28436    struct shmid_kernel *shp;
28437    int err, id = 0;
28438
28439    down(&shm_ids.sem);
28440    if (key == IPC_PRIVATE) {
28441      err = newseg(key, shmflg, size);
28442    } else if ((id = ipc_findkey(&shm_ids, key)) == -1) {
28443      if (!(shmflg & IPC_CREAT))
28444        err = -ENOENT;
```

```
28445       else
28446         err = newseg(key, shmflg, size);
28447     } else if ((shmflg & IPC_CREAT) &&
28448             (shmflg & IPC_EXCL)) {
28449       err = -EEXIST;
28450     } else {
28451       shp = shm_lock(id);
28452       if (shp == NULL)
28453         BUG();
28454       if (shp->shm_segsz < size)
28455         err = -EINVAL;
28456       else if (ipcperms(&shp->shm_perm, shmflg))
28457         err = -EACCES;
28458       else
28459         err = shm_buildid(id, shp->shm_perm.seq);
28460       shm_unlock(id);
28461     }
28462     up(&shm_ids.sem);
28463     return err;
28464 }
28465
28466 static inline unsigned long copy_shmid_to_user(void *buf,
28467     struct shmid64_ds *in, int version)
28468 {
28469   switch (version) {
28470   case IPC_64:
28471     return copy_to_user(buf, in, sizeof(*in));
28472   case IPC_OLD:
28473     {
28474       struct shmid_ds out;
28475
28476       ipc64_perm_to_ipc_perm(&in->shm_perm,
28477                         &out.shm_perm);
28478       out.shm_segsz = in->shm_segsz;
28479       out.shm_atime = in->shm_atime;
28480       out.shm_dtime = in->shm_dtime;
28481       out.shm_ctime = in->shm_ctime;
28482       out.shm_cpid = in->shm_cpid;
28483       out.shm_lpid = in->shm_lpid;
28484       out.shm_nattch = in->shm_nattch;
28485
28486       return copy_to_user(buf, &out, sizeof(out));
28487     }
28488   default:
28489     return -EINVAL;
28490   }
28491 }
28492
28493 struct shm_setbuf {
28494   uid_t uid;
28495   gid_t gid;
28496   mode_t mode;
28497 };
28498
28499 static inline unsigned long copy_shmid_from_user(struct
28500     shm_setbuf *out, void *buf, int version)
28501 {
28502   switch (version) {
28503   case IPC_64:
28504   {
28505     struct shmid64_ds tbuf;
28506
28507     if (copy_from_user(&tbuf, buf, sizeof(tbuf)))
28508       return -EFAULT;
28509
28510     out->uid = tbuf.shm_perm.uid;
28511     out->gid = tbuf.shm_perm.gid;
28512     out->mode = tbuf.shm_flags;
28513
28514     return 0;
28515   }
28516   case IPC_OLD:
28517   {
28518     struct shmid_ds tbuf_old;
28519
28520     if (copy_from_user(&tbuf_old, buf,
28521                   sizeof(tbuf_old)))
28522       return -EFAULT;
28523
28524     out->uid = tbuf_old.shm_perm.uid;
28525     out->gid = tbuf_old.shm_perm.gid;
28526     out->mode = tbuf_old.shm_flags;
28527
28528     return 0;
28529   }
28530   default:
28531     return -EINVAL;
28532   }
28533 }
28534
28535 static inline unsigned long
28536 copy_shminfo_to_user(void *buf, struct shminfo64 *in,
28537                   int version)
28538 {
```

```
28539    switch (version) {
28540    case IPC_64:
28541      return copy_to_user(buf, in, sizeof(*in));
28542    case IPC_OLD:
28543    {
28544      struct shminfo out;
28545
28546      if (in->shmmax > INT_MAX)
28547        out.shmmax = INT_MAX;
28548      else
28549        out.shmmax = (int) in->shmmax;
28550
28551      out.shmmin = in->shmmin;
28552      out.shmmni = in->shmmni;
28553      out.shmseg = in->shmseg;
28554      out.shmall = in->shmall;
28555
28556      return copy_to_user(buf, &out, sizeof(out));
28557    }
28558    default:
28559      return -EINVAL;
28560    }
28561 }
28562
28563 static void shm_get_stat(unsigned long *rss,
28564      unsigned long *swp)
28565 {
28566   int i;
28567
28568   *rss = 0;
28569   *swp = 0;
28570
28571   for (i = 0; i <= shm_ids.max_id; i++) {
28572     struct shmid_kernel *shp;
28573     struct inode *inode;
28574
28575     shp = shm_get(i);
28576     if (shp == NULL)
28577       continue;
28578     inode = shp->shm_file->f_dentry->d_inode;
28579     spin_lock(&inode->u.shmem_i.lock);
28580     *rss += inode->i_mapping->nrpages;
28581     *swp += inode->u.shmem_i.swapped;
28582     spin_unlock(&inode->u.shmem_i.lock);
28583   }
28584 }
28585
```

```
                 28586 asmlinkage long sys_shmctl(int shmid, int cmd,
p 678            28587      struct shmid_ds *buf)
                 28588 {
28589   struct shm_setbuf setbuf;
28590   struct shmid_kernel *shp;
28591   int err, version;
28592
28593   if (cmd < 0 || shmid < 0)
28594     return -EINVAL;
28595
28596   version = ipc_parse_version(&cmd);
28597
28598   switch (cmd) {          /* replace with proc interface ? */
28599   case IPC_INFO:
28600   {
28601     struct shminfo64 shminfo;
28602
28603     memset(&shminfo, 0, sizeof(shminfo));
28604     shminfo.shmmni = shminfo.shmseg = shm_ctlmni;
28605     shminfo.shmmax = shm_ctlmax;
28606     shminfo.shmall = shm_ctlall;
28607
28608     shminfo.shmmin = SHMMIN;
28609     if (copy_shminfo_to_user(buf, &shminfo, version))
28610       return -EFAULT;
28611     /* reading a integer is always atomic */
28612     err = shm_ids.max_id;
28613     if (err < 0)
28614       err = 0;
28615     return err;
28616   }
28617   case SHM_INFO:
28618   {
28619     struct shm_info shm_info;
28620
28621     memset(&shm_info, 0, sizeof(shm_info));
28622     down(&shm_ids.sem);
28623     shm_lockall();
28624     shm_info.used_ids = shm_ids.in_use;
28625     shm_get_stat(&shm_info.shm_rss, &shm_info.shm_swp);
28626     shm_info.shm_tot = shm_tot;
28627     shm_info.swap_attempts = 0;
28628     shm_info.swap_successes = 0;
28629     err = shm_ids.max_id;
28630     shm_unlockall();
28631     up(&shm_ids.sem);
28632     if (copy_to_user(buf, &shm_info, sizeof(shm_info)))
```

```
28633        return -EFAULT;
28634
28635      return err < 0 ? 0 : err;
28636    }
28637    case SHM_STAT:
28638    case IPC_STAT:
28639    {
28640      struct shmid64_ds tbuf;
28641      int result;
28642      memset(&tbuf, 0, sizeof(tbuf));
28643      shp = shm_lock(shmid);
28644      if (shp == NULL)
28645        return -EINVAL;
28646      if (cmd == SHM_STAT) {
28647        err = -EINVAL;
28648        if (shmid > shm_ids.max_id)
28649          goto out_unlock;
28650        result = shm_buildid(shmid, shp->shm_perm.seq);
28651      } else {
28652        err = shm_checkid(shp, shmid);
28653        if (err)
28654          goto out_unlock;
28655        result = 0;
28656      }
28657      err = -EACCES;
28658      if (ipcperms(&shp->shm_perm, S_IRUGO))
28659        goto out_unlock;
28660      kernel_to_ipc64_perm(&shp->shm_perm,
28661                           &tbuf.shm_perm);
28662      tbuf.shm_segsz = shp->shm_segsz;
28663      tbuf.shm_atime = shp->shm_atim;
28664      tbuf.shm_dtime = shp->shm_dtim;
28665      tbuf.shm_ctime = shp->shm_ctim;
28666      tbuf.shm_cpid = shp->shm_cprid;
28667      tbuf.shm_lpid = shp->shm_lprid;
28668      tbuf.shm_nattch = shp->shm_nattch;
28669      shm_unlock(shmid);
28670      if (copy_shmid_to_user(buf, &tbuf, version))
28671        return -EFAULT;
28672      return result;
28673    }
28674    case SHM_LOCK:
28675    case SHM_UNLOCK:
28676    {
28677      /* Allow superuser to lock segment in memory */
28678      /* Should the pages be faulted in here or leave it
28679       * to user? */
28680      /* need to determine interaction with
28681       * current->swappable */
28682      if (!capable(CAP_IPC_LOCK))
28683        return -EPERM;
28684
28685      shp = shm_lock(shmid);
28686      if (shp == NULL)
28687        return -EINVAL;
28688      err = shm_checkid(shp, shmid);
28689      if (err)
28690        goto out_unlock;
28691      if (cmd == SHM_LOCK) {
28692        shmem_lock(shp->shm_file, 1);
28693        shp->shm_flags |= SHM_LOCKED;
28694      } else {
28695        shmem_lock(shp->shm_file, 0);
28696        shp->shm_flags &= ~SHM_LOCKED;
28697      }
28698      shm_unlock(shmid);
28699      return err;
28700    }
28701    case IPC_RMID:
28702    {
28703      /* We cannot simply remove the file. The SVID
28704       * states that the block remains until the last
28705       * person detaches from it, then is deleted. A
28706       * shmat() on an RMID segment is legal in older
28707       * Linux and if we change it apps break...
28708       *
28709       * Instead we set a destroyed flag, and then blow
28710       * the name away when the usage hits zero.  */
28711      down(&shm_ids.sem);
28712      shp = shm_lock(shmid);
28713      err = -EINVAL;
28714      if (shp == NULL)
28715        goto out_up;
28716      err = shm_checkid(shp, shmid);
28717      if (err == 0) {
28718        if (shp->shm_nattch) {
28719          shp->shm_flags |= SHM_DEST;
28720          /* Do not find it any more */
28721          shp->shm_perm.key = IPC_PRIVATE;
28722        } else
28723          shm_destroy(shp);
28724      }
28725      /* Unlock */
28726      shm_unlock(shmid);
```

```
28727      up(&shm_ids.sem);
28728      return err;
28729   }
28730
28731   case IPC_SET:
28732   {
28733      if (copy_shmid_from_user(&setbuf, buf, version))
28734        return -EFAULT;
28735      down(&shm_ids.sem);
28736      shp = shm_lock(shmid);
28737      err = -EINVAL;
28738      if (shp == NULL)
28739        goto out_up;
28740      err = shm_checkid(shp, shmid);
28741      if (err)
28742        goto out_unlock_up;
28743      err = -EPERM;
28744      if (current->euid != shp->shm_perm.uid &&
28745          current->euid != shp->shm_perm.cuid &&
28746          !capable(CAP_SYS_ADMIN)) {
28747        goto out_unlock_up;
28748      }
28749
28750      shp->shm_perm.uid = setbuf.uid;
28751      shp->shm_perm.gid = setbuf.gid;
28752      shp->shm_flags = (shp->shm_flags & ~S_IRWXUGO)
28753         | (setbuf.mode & S_IRWXUGO);
28754      shp->shm_ctim = CURRENT_TIME;
28755      break;
28756   }
28757
28758   default:
28759      return -EINVAL;
28760   }
28761
28762   err = 0;
28763 out_unlock_up:
28764   shm_unlock(shmid);
28765 out_up:
28766   up(&shm_ids.sem);
28767   return err;
28768 out_unlock:
28769   shm_unlock(shmid);
28770   return err;
28771 }
28772
28773 /* Fix shmaddr, allocate descriptor, map shm, add attach
28774  * descriptor to lists.  */
28775 asmlinkage long sys_shmat(int shmid, char *shmaddr,
28776     int shmflg, ulong * raddr)
28777 {
28778   struct shmid_kernel *shp;
28779   unsigned long addr;
28780   struct file *file;
28781   int err;
28782   unsigned long flags;
28783   unsigned long prot;
28784   unsigned long o_flags;
28785   int acc_mode;
28786   void *user_addr;
28787
28788   if (shmid < 0)
28789     return -EINVAL;
28790
28791   if ((addr = (ulong) shmaddr)) {
28792     if (addr & (SHMLBA - 1)) {
28793       if (shmflg & SHM_RND)
28794         addr &= ~(SHMLBA - 1);   /* round down */
28795       else
28796         return -EINVAL;
28797     }
28798     flags = MAP_SHARED | MAP_FIXED;
28799   } else
28800     flags = MAP_SHARED;
28801
28802   if (shmflg & SHM_RDONLY) {
28803     prot = PROT_READ;
28804     o_flags = O_RDONLY;
28805     acc_mode = S_IRUGO;
28806   } else {
28807     prot = PROT_READ | PROT_WRITE;
28808     o_flags = O_RDWR;
28809     acc_mode = S_IRUGO | S_IWUGO;
28810   }
28811
28812   /* We cannot rely on the fs check since SYSV IPC does
28813    * have an aditional creator id... */
28814   shp = shm_lock(shmid);
28815   if (shp == NULL)
28816     return -EINVAL;
28817   if (ipcperms(&shp->shm_perm, acc_mode)) {
28818     shm_unlock(shmid);
28819     return -EACCES;
28820   }
```

p 677

```
28821    file = shp->shm_file;
28822    shp->shm_nattch++;
28823    shm_unlock(shmid);
28824
28825    down(&current->mm->mmap_sem);
28826    user_addr =
28827      (void *) do_mmap(file, addr,
28828                       file->f_dentry->d_inode->i_size,
28829                       prot, flags, 0);
28830    up(&current->mm->mmap_sem);
28831
28832    down(&shm_ids.sem);
28833    if (!(shp = shm_lock(shmid)))
28834      BUG();
28835    shp->shm_nattch-;
28836    if (shp->shm_nattch == 0 && shp->shm_flags & SHM_DEST)
28837      shm_destroy(shp);
28838    shm_unlock(shmid);
28839    up(&shm_ids.sem);
28840
28841    *raddr = (unsigned long) user_addr;
28842    err = 0;
28843    if (IS_ERR(user_addr))
28844      err = PTR_ERR(user_addr);
28845    return err;
28846
28847 }
28848
28849 /* detach and kill segment if marked destroyed.  The work
28850  * is done in shm_close.  */
28851 asmlinkage long sys_shmdt(char *shmaddr)
28852 {
28853    struct mm_struct *mm = current->mm;
28854    struct vm_area_struct *shmd, *shmdnext;
28855
28856    down(&mm->mmap_sem);
28857    for (shmd = mm->mmap; shmd; shmd = shmdnext) {
28858      shmdnext = shmd->vm_next;
28859      if (shmd->vm_ops == &shm_vm_ops &&
28860          shmd->vm_start - (shmd->vm_pgoff <<PAGE_SHIFT) ==
28861          (ulong) shmaddr)
28862        do_munmap(mm, shmd->vm_start,
28863                  shmd->vm_end - shmd->vm_start);
28864    }
28865    up(&mm->mmap_sem);
28866    return 0;
28867 }
```

p 678

```
28868
28869 #ifdef CONFIG_PROC_FS
28870 static int sysvipc_shm_read_proc(char *buffer,
28871     char **start, off_t offset, int length, int *eof,
28872     void *data)
28873 {
28874    off_t pos = 0;
28875    off_t begin = 0;
28876    int i, len = 0;
28877
28878    down(&shm_ids.sem);
28879    len +=
28880        sprintf(buffer,
28881                "       key       shmid perms       size  "
28882                "cpid  lpid nattch   uid   gid  cuid  cgid"
28883                "       atime       dtime       ctime\n");
28884
28885    for (i = 0; i <= shm_ids.max_id; i++) {
28886      struct shmid_kernel *shp;
28887
28888      shp = shm_lock(i);
28889      if (shp != NULL) {
28890 #define SMALL_STRING "%10d %10d  %4o %10u %5u %5u  %5d" \
28891    " %5u %5u %5u %5u %10lu %10lu %10lu\n"
28892 #define BIG_STRING   "%10d %10d  %4o %21u %5u %5u  %5d" \
28893    " %5u %5u %5u %5u %10lu %10lu %10lu\n"
28894      char *format;
28895
28896      if (sizeof(size_t) <= sizeof(int))
28897        format = SMALL_STRING;
28898      else
28899        format = BIG_STRING;
28900      len += sprintf(buffer + len, format,
28901        shp->shm_perm.key,
28902        shm_buildid(i, shp->shm_perm.seq),
28903        shp->shm_flags,
28904        shp->shm_segsz,
28905        shp->shm_cprid,
28906        shp->shm_lprid,
28907        shp->shm_nattch,
28908        shp->shm_perm.uid,
28909        shp->shm_perm.gid,
28910        shp->shm_perm.cuid,
28911        shp->shm_perm.cgid,
28912        shp->shm_atim, shp->shm_dtim, shp->shm_ctim);
28913      shm_unlock(i);
28914
```

```
28915       pos += len;
28916       if (pos < offset) {
28917         len = 0;
28918         begin = pos;
28919       }
28920       if (pos > offset + length)
28921         goto done;
28922     }
28923   }
28924   *eof = 1;
28925 done:
28926   up(&shm_ids.sem);
28927   *start = buffer + (offset - begin);
28928   len -= (offset - begin);
28929   if (len > length)
28930     len = length;
28931   if (len < 0)
28932     len = 0;
28933   return len;
28934 }
28935 #endif
```

ipc/util.c

```
28936 /*
28937  * linux/ipc/util.c
28938  * Copyright (C) 1992 Krishna Balasubramanian
28939  *
28940  * Sep 1997 - Call suser() last after "normal" permission
28941  *            checks so we get BSD style process
28942  *            accounting right.  Occurs in several places
28943  *            in the IPC code.  Chris Evans,
28944  *            <chris@ferret.lmh.ox.ac.uk>
28945  * Nov 1999 - ipc helper functions, unified SMP locking
28946  *            Manfred Spraul <manfreds@colorfullife.com>
28947  */
28948
28949 #include <linux/config.h>
28950 #include <linux/mm.h>
28951 #include <linux/shm.h>
28952 #include <linux/init.h>
28953 #include <linux/msg.h>
28954 #include <linux/smp_lock.h>
28955 #include <linux/vmalloc.h>
28956 #include <linux/malloc.h>
28957 #include <linux/highuid.h>
28958
28959 #if defined(CONFIG_SYSVIPC)
28960
28961 #include "util.h"
28962
28963 /**
28964  *      ipc_init       -       initialise IPC subsystem
28965  *
28966  * The various system5 IPC resources (semaphores,
28967  * messages and shared memory are initialised */
28968 void __init ipc_init(void)
28969 {
28970   sem_init();
28971   msg_init();
28972   shm_init();
28973   return;
28974 }
28975
28976 /**
28977  *      ipc_init_ids   -       initialise IPC identifiers
28978  *      @ids: Identifier set
28979  *      @size: Number of identifiers
28980  *
28981  * Given a size for the ipc identifier range (limited
28982  * below IPCMNI) set up the sequence range to use then
28983  * allocate and initialise the array itself.  */
28984 void __init ipc_init_ids(struct ipc_ids *ids, int size)
28985 {
28986   int i;
28987   sema_init(&ids->sem, 1);
28988
28989   if (size > IPCMNI)
28990     size = IPCMNI;
28991   ids->size = size;
28992   ids->in_use = 0;
28993   ids->max_id = -1;
28994   ids->seq = 0;
28995   {
28996     int seq_limit = INT_MAX / SEQ_MULTIPLIER;
28997     if (seq_limit > USHRT_MAX)
28998       ids->seq_max = USHRT_MAX;
28999     else
29000       ids->seq_max = seq_limit;
29001   }
29002
29003   ids->entries = ipc_alloc(sizeof(struct ipc_id) * size);
29004
29005   if (ids->entries == NULL) {
29006     printk(KERN_ERR "ipc_init_ids() failed, "
```

p 658

```
29007                "ipc service disabled.\n");
29008     ids->size = 0;
29009   }
29010   ids->ary = SPIN_LOCK_UNLOCKED;
29011   for (i = 0; i < size; i++)
29012     ids->entries[i].p = NULL;
29013 }
29014
29015 /**
29016  *      ipc_findkey - find a key in an ipc identifier set
29017  *      @ids: Identifier set
29018  *      @key: The key to find
29019  *
29020  * Returns the identifier if found or -1 if not.  */
29021 int ipc_findkey(struct ipc_ids *ids, key_t key)
29022 {
29023   int id;
29024   struct kern_ipc_perm *p;
29025
29026   for (id = 0; id <= ids->max_id; id++) {
29027     p = ids->entries[id].p;
29028     if (p == NULL)
29029       continue;
29030     if (key == p->key)
29031       return id;
29032   }
29033   return -1;
29034 }
29035
29036 static int grow_ary(struct ipc_ids *ids, int newsize)
29037 {
29038   struct ipc_id *new;
29039   struct ipc_id *old;
29040   int i;
29041
29042   if (newsize > IPCMNI)
29043     newsize = IPCMNI;
29044   if (newsize <= ids->size)
29045     return newsize;
29046
29047   new = ipc_alloc(sizeof(struct ipc_id) * newsize);
29048   if (new == NULL)
29049     return ids->size;
29050   memcpy(new, ids->entries,
29051       sizeof(struct ipc_id) * ids->size);
29052   for (i = ids->size; i < newsize; i++) {
29053     new[i].p = NULL;
```

```
29054   }
29055   spin_lock(&ids->ary);
29056
29057   old = ids->entries;
29058   ids->entries = new;
29059   i = ids->size;
29060   ids->size = newsize;
29061   spin_unlock(&ids->ary);
29062   ipc_free(old, sizeof(struct ipc_id) * i);
29063   return ids->size;
29064 }
29065
29066 /**
29067  *      ipc_addid          -          add an IPC identifier
29068  *      @ids: IPC identifier set
29069  *      @new: new IPC permission set
29070  *      @size: new size limit for the id array
29071  *
29072  * Add an entry 'new' to the IPC arrays. The permissions
29073  * object is initialised and the first free entry is set
29074  * up and the id assigned is returned. The list is
29075  * returned in a locked state on success.  On failure the
29076  * list is not locked and -1 is returned.  */
29077 int ipc_addid(struct ipc_ids *ids,
29078       struct kern_ipc_perm *new, int size)
29079 {
29080   int id;
29081
29082   size = grow_ary(ids, size);
29083   for (id = 0; id < size; id++) {
29084     if (ids->entries[id].p == NULL)
29085       goto found;
29086   }
29087   return -1;
29088 found:
29089   ids->in_use++;
29090   if (id > ids->max_id)
29091     ids->max_id = id;
29092
29093   new->cuid = new->uid = current->euid;
29094   new->gid = new->cgid = current->egid;
29095
29096   new->seq = ids->seq++;
29097   if (ids->seq > ids->seq_max)
29098     ids->seq = 0;
29099
29100   spin_lock(&ids->ary);
```

```
29101    ids->entries[id].p = new;
29102    return id;
29103 }
29104
29105 /**
29106  *      ipc_rmid         -        remove an IPC identifier
29107  *      @ids: identifier set
29108  *      @id: Identifier to remove
29109  *
29110  * The identifier must be valid, and in use. The kernel
29111  * will panic if fed an invalid identifier. The entry is
29112  * removed and internal variables recomputed. The object
29113  * associated with the identifier is returned.  */
29114 struct kern_ipc_perm *ipc_rmid(struct ipc_ids *ids,
29115      int id)
29116 {
29117    struct kern_ipc_perm *p;
29118    int lid = id % SEQ_MULTIPLIER;
29119    if (lid > ids->size)
29120      BUG();
29121    p = ids->entries[lid].p;
29122    ids->entries[lid].p = NULL;
29123    if (p == NULL)
29124      BUG();
29125    ids->in_use--;
29126
29127    if (lid == ids->max_id) {
29128      do {
29129        lid--;
29130        if (lid == -1)
29131          break;
29132      } while (ids->entries[lid].p == NULL);
29133      ids->max_id = lid;
29134    }
29135    return p;
29136 }
29137
29138 /**
29139  *      ipc_alloc        -        allocate ipc space
29140  *      @size: size desired
29141  *
29142  * Allocate memory from the appropriate pools and return
29143  * a pointer to it.  NULL is returned if the allocation
29144  * fails */
29145 void *ipc_alloc(int size)
29146 {
29147    void *out;
```

```
29148    if (size > PAGE_SIZE)
29149      out = vmalloc(size);
29150    else
29151      out = kmalloc(size, GFP_KERNEL);
29152    return out;
29153 }
29154
29155 /**
29156  *      ipc_free         -         free ipc space
29157  *      @ptr: pointer returned by ipc_alloc
29158  *      @size: size of block
29159  *
29160  * Free a block created with ipc_alloc. The caller must
29161  * know the size used in the allocation call.  */
29162 void ipc_free(void *ptr, int size)
29163 {
29164    if (size > PAGE_SIZE)
29165      vfree(ptr);
29166    else
29167      kfree(ptr);
29168 }
29169
29170 /**
29171  *      ipcperms         -         check IPC permissions
29172  *      @ipcp: IPC permission set
29173  *      @flag: desired permission set.
29174  *
29175  * Check user, group, other permissions for access to ipc
29176  * resources. return 0 if allowed */
29177 int ipcperms(struct kern_ipc_perm *ipcp, short flag)
29178 {                            /* flag will most
29179                              * probably be 0 or
29180                              * S_...UGO from
29181                              * <linux/stat.h> */
29182    int requested_mode, granted_mode;
29183
29184    requested_mode = (flag >> 6) | (flag >> 3) | flag;
29185    granted_mode = ipcp->mode;
29186    if (current->euid == ipcp->cuid ||
29187        current->euid == ipcp->uid)
29188      granted_mode >>= 6;
29189    else if (in_group_p(ipcp->cgid) ||
29190           in_group_p(ipcp->gid))
29191      granted_mode >>= 3;
29192    /* is there some bit set in requested_mode but not in
29193     * granted_mode? */
29194    if ((requested_mode & ~granted_mode & 0007) &&
```

p 667

```
29195        !capable(CAP_IPC_OWNER))
29196      return -1;
29197
29198    return 0;
29199 }
29200
29201 /* Functions to convert between the kern_ipc_perm
29202  * structure and the old/new ipc_perm structures */
29203
29204 /**
29205  *      kernel_to_ipc64_perm - convert kernel ipc
29206  *                             permissions to user
29207  *      @in: kernel permissions
29208  *      @out: new style IPC permissions
29209  *
29210  * Turn the kernel object 'in' into a set of permissions
29211  * descriptions for returning to userspace (out).  */
29212 void kernel_to_ipc64_perm(struct kern_ipc_perm *in,
29213     struct ipc64_perm *out)
29214 {
29215   out->key = in->key;
29216   out->uid = in->uid;
29217   out->gid = in->gid;
29218   out->cuid = in->cuid;
29219   out->cgid = in->cgid;
29220   out->mode = in->mode;
29221   out->seq = in->seq;
29222 }
29223
29224 /**
29225  *      ipc64_perm_to_ipc_perm  - convert old ipc
29226  *                                permissions to new
29227  *      @in: new style IPC permissions
29228  *      @out: old style IPC permissions
29229  *
29230  * Turn the new style permissions object in into a
29231  * compatibility object and store it into the 'out'
29232  * pointer.  */
29233 void ipc64_perm_to_ipc_perm(struct ipc64_perm *in,
29234     struct ipc_perm *out)
29235 {
29236   out->key  = in->key;
29237   out->uid  = NEW_TO_OLD_UID(in->uid);
29238   out->gid  = NEW_TO_OLD_GID(in->gid);
29239   out->cuid = NEW_TO_OLD_UID(in->cuid);
29240   out->cgid = NEW_TO_OLD_GID(in->cgid);
29241   out->mode = in->mode;
```

```
29242   out->seq  = in->seq;
29243 }
29244
29245 #ifndef __ia64__
29246
29247 /**
29248  *      ipc_parse_version    -        IPC call version
29249  *      @cmd: pointer to command
29250  *
29251  * Return IPC_64 for new style IPC and IPC_OLD for old
29252  * style IPC.  The cmd value is turned from an encoding
29253  * command and version into just the command code.  */
29254 int ipc_parse_version(int *cmd)
29255 {
29256   if (*cmd & IPC_64) {
29257     *cmd ^= IPC_64;
29258     return IPC_64;
29259   } else {
29260     return IPC_OLD;
29261   }
29262 }
29263
29264 #endif                        /* __ia64__ */
29265
29266 #else
29267 /* Dummy functions when SYSV IPC isn't configured */
29268
29269 void sem_exit(void)
29270 {
29271   return;
29272 }
29273
29274 asmlinkage long sys_semget(key_t key, int nsems,
29275     int semflg)
29276 {
29277   return -ENOSYS;
29278 }
29279
29280 asmlinkage long sys_semop(int semid, struct sembuf *sops,
29281     unsigned nsops)
29282 {
29283   return -ENOSYS;
29284 }
29285
29286 asmlinkage long sys_semctl(int semid, int semnum,
29287     int cmd, union semun arg)
29288 {
```

```
29289    return -ENOSYS;
29290 }
29291
29292 asmlinkage long sys_msgget(key_t key, int msgflg)
29293 {
29294    return -ENOSYS;
29295 }
29296
29297 asmlinkage long sys_msgsnd(int msqid,
29298      struct msgbuf *msgp, size_t msgsz, int msgflg)
29299 {
29300    return -ENOSYS;
29301 }
29302
29303 asmlinkage long sys_msgrcv(int msqid,
29304      struct msgbuf *msgp, size_t msgsz, long msgtyp,
29305      int msgflg)
29306 {
29307    return -ENOSYS;
29308 }
29309
29310 asmlinkage long sys_msgctl(int msqid, int cmd,
29311      struct msqid_ds *buf)
29312 {
29313    return -ENOSYS;
29314 }
29315
29316 asmlinkage long sys_shmget(key_t key, size_t size,
29317      int shmflag)
29318 {
29319    return -ENOSYS;
29320 }
29321
29322 asmlinkage long sys_shmat(int shmid, char *shmaddr,
29323      int shmflg, ulong * addr)
29324 {
29325    return -ENOSYS;
29326 }
29327
29328 asmlinkage long sys_shmdt(char *shmaddr)
29329 {
29330    return -ENOSYS;
29331 }
29332
29333 asmlinkage long sys_shmctl(int shmid, int cmd,
29334      struct shmid_ds *buf)
29335 {
```

```
29336    return -ENOSYS;
29337 }
29338
29339 #endif                          /* CONFIG_SYSVIPC */
```

ipc/util.h

```
29340 /*
29341  * linux/ipc/util.h
29342  * Copyright (C) 1999 Christoph Rohland
29343  *
29344  * ipc helper functions (c) 1999 Manfred Spraul
29345  * <manfreds@colorfullife.com>
29346  */
29347
29348 #define USHRT_MAX 0xffff
29349 #define SEQ_MULTIPLIER  (IPCMNI)
29350
29351 void sem_init(void);
29352 void msg_init(void);
29353 void shm_init(void);
29354
29355 struct ipc_ids {
29356    int size;
29357    int in_use;
29358    int max_id;
29359    unsigned short seq;
29360    unsigned short seq_max;
29361    struct semaphore sem;
29362    spinlock_t ary;
29363    struct ipc_id *entries;
29364 };
29365
29366 struct ipc_id {
29367    struct kern_ipc_perm *p;
29368 };
29369
29370
29371 void __init ipc_init_ids(struct ipc_ids *ids, int size);
29372
29373 /* must be called with ids->sem acquired. */
29374 int ipc_findkey(struct ipc_ids *ids, key_t key);
29375 int ipc_addid(struct ipc_ids *ids,
29376      struct kern_ipc_perm *new, int size);
29377
29378 /* must be called with both locks acquired. */
29379 struct kern_ipc_perm *ipc_rmid(struct ipc_ids *ids,
29380      int id);
```

p 657

```
29381
29382 int ipcperms(struct kern_ipc_perm *ipcp, short flg);
29383
29384 /* for rare, potentially huge allocations. both function
29385  * can sleep */
29386 void *ipc_alloc(int size);
29387 void ipc_free(void *ptr, int size);
29388
29389 extern inline void ipc_lockall(struct ipc_ids *ids)
29390 {
29391   spin_lock(&ids->ary);
29392 }
29393
29394 extern inline struct kern_ipc_perm *ipc_get(struct
29395     ipc_ids *ids, int id)
29396 {
29397   struct kern_ipc_perm *out;
29398   int lid = id % SEQ_MULTIPLIER;
29399   if (lid > ids->size)
29400     return NULL;
29401
29402   out = ids->entries[lid].p;
29403   return out;
29404 }
29405
29406 extern inline void ipc_unlockall(struct ipc_ids *ids)
29407 {
29408   spin_unlock(&ids->ary);
29409 }
29410 extern inline struct kern_ipc_perm *ipc_lock(struct
29411     ipc_ids *ids, int id)
29412 {
29413   struct kern_ipc_perm *out;
29414   int lid = id % SEQ_MULTIPLIER;
29415   if (lid > ids->size)
29416     return NULL;
29417
29418   spin_lock(&ids->ary);
29419   out = ids->entries[lid].p;
29420   if (out == NULL)
29421     spin_unlock(&ids->ary);
29422   return out;
29423 }
29424
29425 extern inline void ipc_unlock(struct ipc_ids *ids,
29426     int id)
29427 {
```

```
29428   spin_unlock(&ids->ary);
29429 }
29430
29431 extern inline int ipc_buildid(struct ipc_ids *ids,
29432     int id, int seq)
29433 {
29434   return SEQ_MULTIPLIER * seq + id;
29435 }
29436
29437 extern inline int ipc_checkid(struct ipc_ids *ids,
29438     struct kern_ipc_perm *ipcp, int uid)
29439 {
29440   if (uid / SEQ_MULTIPLIER != ipcp->seq)
29441     return 1;
29442   return 0;
29443 }
29444
29445 void kernel_to_ipc64_perm(struct kern_ipc_perm *in,
29446     struct ipc64_perm *out);
29447 void ipc64_perm_to_ipc_perm(struct ipc64_perm *in,
29448     struct ipc_perm *out);
29449
29450 #ifdef __ia64__
29451   /* On IA-64, we always use the "64-bit version" of the
29452    * IPC structures.  */
29453 # define ipc_parse_version(cmd) IPC_64
29454 #else
29455 int ipc_parse_version(int *cmd);
29456 #endif
```

kernel/capability.c

```
29457 /*
29458  * linux/kernel/capability.c
29459  *
29460  * Copyright (C) 1997  Andrew Main <zefram@fysh.org>
29461  * Integrated into 2.1.97+, Andrew G. Morgan
29462  * <morgan@transmeta.com>
29463  */
29464
29465 #include <linux/mm.h>
29466 #include <asm/uaccess.h>
29467
29468 kernel_cap_t cap_bset = CAP_INIT_EFF_SET;
29469
29470 /* Note: never hold tasklist_lock while spinning for
29471  * this one */
29472 spinlock_t task_capability_lock = SPIN_LOCK_UNLOCKED;
```

```
29473
29474 /* For sys_getproccap() and sys_setproccap(), any of the
29475  * three capability set pointers may be NULL —
29476  * indicating that that set is uninteresting and/or not
29477  * to be changed.  */
29478
29479 asmlinkage long sys_capget(cap_user_header_t header,
29480     cap_user_data_t dataptr)
29481 {
29482   int error, pid;
29483   __u32 version;
29484   struct task_struct *target;
29485   struct __user_cap_data_struct data;
29486
29487   if (get_user(version, &header->version))
29488     return -EFAULT;
29489
29490   error = -EINVAL;
29491   if (version != _LINUX_CAPABILITY_VERSION) {
29492     version = _LINUX_CAPABILITY_VERSION;
29493     if (put_user(version, &header->version))
29494       error = -EFAULT;
29495     return error;
29496   }
29497
29498   if (get_user(pid, &header->pid))
29499     return -EFAULT;
29500
29501   if (pid < 0)
29502     return -EINVAL;
29503
29504   error = 0;
29505
29506   spin_lock(&task_capability_lock);
29507
29508   if (pid && pid != current->pid) {
29509     read_lock(&tasklist_lock);
29510     target = find_task_by_pid(pid);  /* identify target
29511                                       * of query */
29512     if (!target)
29513       error = -ESRCH;
29514   } else {
29515     target = current;
29516   }
29517
29518   if (!error) {
29519     data.permitted   = cap_t(target->cap_permitted);
```

```
29520     data.inheritable = cap_t(target->cap_inheritable);
29521     data.effective   = cap_t(target->cap_effective);
29522   }
29523
29524   if (target != current)
29525     read_unlock(&tasklist_lock);
29526   spin_unlock(&task_capability_lock);
29527
29528   if (!error) {
29529     if (copy_to_user(dataptr, &data, sizeof data))
29530       return -EFAULT;
29531   }
29532
29533   return error;
29534 }
29535
29536 /* set capabilities for all processes in a given process
29537  * group */
29538 static void cap_set_pg(int pgrp,
29539     kernel_cap_t * effective,
29540     kernel_cap_t * inheritable, kernel_cap_t * permitted)
29541 {
29542   struct task_struct *target;
29543
29544   /* FIXME: do we need to have a write lock here..? */
29545   read_lock(&tasklist_lock);
29546   for_each_task(target) {
29547     if (target->pgrp != pgrp)
29548       continue;
29549     target->cap_effective = *effective;
29550     target->cap_inheritable = *inheritable;
29551     target->cap_permitted = *permitted;
29552   }
29553   read_unlock(&tasklist_lock);
29554 }
29555
29556 /* set capabilities for all processes other than 1 and
29557  * self */
29558 static void cap_set_all(kernel_cap_t * effective,
29559     kernel_cap_t * inheritable, kernel_cap_t * permitted)
29560 {
29561   struct task_struct *target;
29562
29563   /* FIXME: do we need to have a write lock here..? */
29564   read_lock(&tasklist_lock);
29565   /* ALL means everyone other than self or 'init' */
29566   for_each_task(target) {
```

```
29567        if (target == current || target->pid == 1)
29568          continue;
29569        target->cap_effective = *effective;
29570        target->cap_inheritable = *inheritable;
29571        target->cap_permitted = *permitted;
29572      }
29573      read_unlock(&tasklist_lock);
29574 }
29575
29576 /* The restrictions on setting capabilities are specified
29577  * as:
29578  *
29579  * [pid is for the 'target' task.  'current' is the
29580  * calling task.]
29581  *
29582  * I: any raised capabilities must be a subset of the
29583  * (old current) Permitted
29584  * P: any raised capabilities must be a subset of the
29585  * (old current) permitted
29586  * E: must be set to a subset of (new target) Permitted
29587  */
29588 asmlinkage long sys_capset(cap_user_header_t header,
29589      const cap_user_data_t data)
29590 {
29591   kernel_cap_t inheritable, permitted, effective;
29592   __u32 version;
29593   struct task_struct *target;
29594   int error, pid;
29595
29596   if (get_user(version, &header->version))
29597     return -EFAULT;
29598
29599   if (version != _LINUX_CAPABILITY_VERSION) {
29600     version = _LINUX_CAPABILITY_VERSION;
29601     if (put_user(version, &header->version))
29602       return -EFAULT;
29603     return -EINVAL;
29604   }
29605
29606   if (get_user(pid, &header->pid))
29607     return -EFAULT;
29608
29609   if (pid && !capable(CAP_SETPCAP))
29610     return -EPERM;
29611
29612   if (copy_from_user(&effective, &data->effective,
29613            sizeof(effective))
29614     || copy_from_user(&inheritable, &data->inheritable,
29615            sizeof(inheritable))
29616     || copy_from_user(&permitted, &data->permitted,
29617            sizeof(permitted)))
29618     return -EFAULT;
29619
29620   error = -EPERM;
29621   spin_lock(&task_capability_lock);
29622
29623   if (pid > 0 && pid != current->pid) {
29624     read_lock(&tasklist_lock);
29625     target = find_task_by_pid(pid);  /* identify target
29626                                       * of query */
29627     if (!target) {
29628       error = -ESRCH;
29629       goto out;
29630     }
29631   } else {
29632     target = current;
29633   }
29634
29635
29636   /* verify restrictions on target's new Inheritable set
29637    */
29638   if (!cap_issubset(inheritable,
29639         cap_combine(target->cap_inheritable,
29640                 current->cap_permitted))) {
29641     goto out;
29642   }
29643
29644   /* verify restrictions on target's new Permitted set */
29645   if (!cap_issubset(permitted,
29646         cap_combine(target->cap_permitted,
29647                 current->cap_permitted))) {
29648     goto out;
29649   }
29650
29651   /* verify the _new_Effective_ is a subset of the
29652    * _new_Permitted_ */
29653   if (!cap_issubset(effective, permitted)) {
29654     goto out;
29655   }
29656
29657   /* having verified that the proposed changes are
29658    * legal, we now put them into effect. */
29659   error = 0;
29660
```

```
29661    if (pid < 0) {
29662      if (pid == -1)                /* all procs other than
29663                                      * current and init */
29664        cap_set_all(&effective, &inheritable, &permitted);
29665      else                          /* all procs in process group */
29666        cap_set_pg(-pid, &effective, &inheritable,
29667             &permitted);
29668      goto spin_out;
29669    } else {
29670      /* FIXME: do we need to have a write lock here..? */
29671      target->cap_effective = effective;
29672      target->cap_inheritable = inheritable;
29673      target->cap_permitted = permitted;
29674    }
29675
29676 out:
29677    if (target != current) {
29678      read_unlock(&tasklist_lock);
29679    }
29680 spin_out:
29681    spin_unlock(&task_capability_lock);
29682    return error;
29683 }
```

kernel/exec_domain.c

```
29684 #include <linux/mm.h>
29685 #include <linux/smp_lock.h>
29686 #include <linux/module.h>
29687
29688 static asmlinkage void no_lcall7(int segment,
29689     struct pt_regs *regs);
29690
29691
29692 static unsigned long ident_map[32] = {
29693    0, 1, 2, 3, 4, 5, 6, 7,
29694    8, 9, 10, 11, 12, 13, 14, 15,
29695    16, 17, 18, 19, 20, 21, 22, 23,
29696    24, 25, 26, 27, 28, 29, 30, 31
29697 };
29698
29699 struct exec_domain default_exec_domain = {
29700    "Linux",            /* name */
29701    no_lcall7,          /* lcall7 causes a seg fault. */
29702    0, 0xff,            /* All personalities. */
29703    ident_map,          /* Identity map signals.  */
29704    ident_map,          /* - both ways. */
29705    NULL,               /* No usage counter. */
29706    NULL                /* Nothing after this in the list. */
29707 };
29708
29709 static struct exec_domain *exec_domains =
29710    &default_exec_domain;
29711 static rwlock_t exec_domains_lock = RW_LOCK_UNLOCKED;
29712
29713 static asmlinkage void no_lcall7(int segment,
29714     struct pt_regs *regs)
29715 {
29716    /* This may have been a static linked SVr4 binary, so
29717     * we would have the personality set incorrectly.
29718     * Check to see whether SVr4 is available, and use it,
29719     * otherwise give the user a SEGV.  */
29720    set_personality(PER_SVR4);
29721
29722    if (current->exec_domain
29723       && current->exec_domain->handler
29724       && current->exec_domain->handler != no_lcall7) {
29725      current->exec_domain->handler(segment, regs);
29726      return;
29727    }
29728
29729    send_sig(SIGSEGV, current, 1);
29730 }
29731
29732 static struct exec_domain *lookup_exec_domain(unsigned
29733     long personality)
29734 {
29735    unsigned long pers = personality & PER_MASK;
29736    struct exec_domain *it;
29737
29738    read_lock(&exec_domains_lock);
29739    for (it = exec_domains; it; it = it->next)
29740      if (pers >= it->pers_low && pers <= it->pers_high) {
29741        if (!try_inc_mod_count(it->module))
29742          continue;
29743        read_unlock(&exec_domains_lock);
29744        return it;
29745      }
29746    read_unlock(&exec_domains_lock);
29747
29748    /* Should never get this far. */
29749    printk(KERN_ERR
29750       "No execution domain for personality 0x%02lx\n",
29751       pers);
29752    return NULL;
```

```
29753 }
29754
29755 int register_exec_domain(struct exec_domain *it)
29756 {
29757   struct exec_domain *tmp;
29758
29759   if (!it)
29760     return -EINVAL;
29761   if (it->next)
29762     return -EBUSY;
29763   write_lock(&exec_domains_lock);
29764   for (tmp = exec_domains; tmp; tmp = tmp->next)
29765     if (tmp == it) {
29766       write_unlock(&exec_domains_lock);
29767       return -EBUSY;
29768     }
29769   it->next = exec_domains;
29770   exec_domains = it;
29771   write_unlock(&exec_domains_lock);
29772   return 0;
29773 }
29774
29775 int unregister_exec_domain(struct exec_domain *it)
29776 {
29777   struct exec_domain **tmp;
29778
29779   tmp = &exec_domains;
29780   write_lock(&exec_domains_lock);
29781   while (*tmp) {
29782     if (it == *tmp) {
29783       *tmp = it->next;
29784       it->next = NULL;
29785       write_unlock(&exec_domains_lock);
29786       return 0;
29787     }
29788     tmp = &(*tmp)->next;
29789   }
29790   write_unlock(&exec_domains_lock);
29791   return -EINVAL;
29792 }
29793
29794 void __set_personality(unsigned long personality)
29795 {
29796   struct exec_domain *it, *prev;
29797
29798   it = lookup_exec_domain(personality);
29799   if (it == current->exec_domain) {
29800     current->personality = personality;
29801     return;
29802   }
29803   if (!it)
29804     return;
29805   if (atomic_read(&current->fs->count) != 1) {
29806     struct fs_struct *new = copy_fs_struct(current->fs);
29807     struct fs_struct *old;
29808     if (!new) {
29809       put_exec_domain(it);
29810       return;
29811     }
29812     task_lock(current);
29813     old = current->fs;
29814     current->fs = new;
29815     task_unlock(current);
29816     put_fs_struct(old);
29817   }
29818   /* At that point we are guaranteed to be the sole owner
29819    * of current->fs.  */
29820   current->personality = personality;
29821   prev = current->exec_domain;
29822   current->exec_domain = it;
29823   set_fs_altroot();
29824   put_exec_domain(prev);
29825 }
29826
29827 asmlinkage long sys_personality(unsigned long
29828     personality)
29829 {
29830   int ret = current->personality;
29831   if (personality != 0xffffffff) {
29832     set_personality(personality);
29833     if (current->personality != personality)
29834       ret = -EINVAL;
29835   }
29836   return ret;
29837 }
29838
29839 int get_exec_domain_list(char *page)
29840 {
29841   int len = 0;
29842   struct exec_domain *e;
29843
29844   read_lock(&exec_domains_lock);
29845   for (e = exec_domains; e && len < PAGE_SIZE - 80;
29846     e = e->next)
```

```
29847      len += sprintf(page + len, "%d-%d\t%-16s\t[%s]\n",
29848                    e->pers_low, e->pers_high, e->name,
29849                    e->module
29850                    ? e->module->name
29851                    : "kernel");
29852    read_unlock(&exec_domains_lock);
29853    return len;
29854 }
```

kernel/exit.c

```
29855 /*
29856  *  linux/kernel/exit.c
29857  *
29858  *  Copyright (C) 1991, 1992  Linus Torvalds
29859  */
29860
29861 #include <linux/config.h>
29862 #include <linux/malloc.h>
29863 #include <linux/interrupt.h>
29864 #include <linux/smp_lock.h>
29865 #include <linux/module.h>
29866 #ifdef CONFIG_BSD_PROCESS_ACCT
29867 #include <linux/acct.h>
29868 #endif
29869
29870 #include <asm/uaccess.h>
29871 #include <asm/pgtable.h>
29872 #include <asm/mmu_context.h>
29873
29874 extern void sem_exit(void);
29875 extern struct task_struct *child_reaper;
29876
29877 int getrusage(struct task_struct *, int,
29878     struct rusage *);
29879
29880 static void release_task(struct task_struct *p)
29881 {
29882    if (p != current) {
29883 #ifdef CONFIG_SMP
29884    /* Wait to make sure the process isn't on the
29885     * runqueue (active on some other CPU still) */
29886    for (;;) {
29887      task_lock(p);
29888      if (!p->has_cpu)
29889        break;
29890      task_unlock(p);
29891      do {
```

> p 617 (line 29880)
> p 691 (line 29881)

```
29892      barrier();
29893    } while (p->has_cpu);
29894    }
29895    task_unlock(p);
29896 #endif
29897    atomic_dec(&p->user->processes);
29898    free_uid(p->user);
29899    unhash_process(p);
29900
29901    release_thread(p);
29902    current->cmin_flt += p->min_flt + p->cmin_flt;
29903    current->cmaj_flt += p->maj_flt + p->cmaj_flt;
29904    current->cnswap += p->nswap + p->cnswap;
29905    /* Potentially available timeslices are retrieved
29906     * here - this way the parent does not get penalized
29907     * for creating too many processes.
29908     *
29909     * (this cannot be used to artificially 'generate'
29910     * timeslices, because any timeslice recovered here
29911     * was given away by the parent in the first place.)
29912     */
29913    current->counter += p->counter;
29914    if (current->counter >= MAX_COUNTER)
29915      current->counter = MAX_COUNTER;
29916    free_task_struct(p);
29917 } else {
29918    printk("task releasing itself\n");
29919 }
29920 }
29921
29922 /* This checks not only the pgrp, but falls back on the
29923  * pid if no satisfactory pgrp is found. I dunno - gdb
29924  * doesn't work correctly without this...  */
29925 int session_of_pgrp(int pgrp)
29926 {
29927   struct task_struct *p;
29928   int fallback;
29929
29930   fallback = -1;
29931   read_lock(&tasklist_lock);
29932   for_each_task(p) {
29933     if (p->session <= 0)
29934       continue;
29935     if (p->pgrp == pgrp) {
29936       fallback = p->session;
29937       break;
29938     }
```

```
29939      if (p->pid == pgrp)
29940        fallback = p->session;
29941    }
29942    read_unlock(&tasklist_lock);
29943    return fallback;
29944 }
29945
29946 /* Determine if a process group is "orphaned", according
29947  * to the POSIX definition in 2.2.2.52.  Orphaned process
29948  * groups are not to be affected by terminal-generated
29949  * stop signals.  Newly orphaned process groups are to
29950  * receive a SIGHUP and a SIGCONT.
29951  *
29952  * "I ask you, have you ever known what it is to be an
29953  * orphan?" */
29954 static int will_become_orphaned_pgrp(int pgrp,
29955      struct task_struct *ignored_task)
29956 {
29957    struct task_struct *p;
29958
29959    read_lock(&tasklist_lock);
29960    for_each_task(p) {
29961      if ((p == ignored_task) || (p->pgrp != pgrp) ||
29962         (p->state == TASK_ZOMBIE) ||
29963         (p->p_pptr->pid == 1))
29964       continue;
29965      if ((p->p_pptr->pgrp != pgrp) &&
29966         (p->p_pptr->session == p->session)) {
29967       read_unlock(&tasklist_lock);
29968       return 0;
29969      }
29970    }
29971    read_unlock(&tasklist_lock);
29972    return 1;                    /* (sighing) "Often!" */
29973 }
29974
29975 int is_orphaned_pgrp(int pgrp)
29976 {
29977    return will_become_orphaned_pgrp(pgrp, 0);
29978 }
29979
29980 static inline int has_stopped_jobs(int pgrp)
29981 {
29982    int retval = 0;
29983    struct task_struct *p;
29984
29985    read_lock(&tasklist_lock);
```

```
29986    for_each_task(p) {
29987      if (p->pgrp != pgrp)
29988        continue;
29989      if (p->state != TASK_STOPPED)
29990        continue;
29991      retval = 1;
29992      break;
29993    }
29994    read_unlock(&tasklist_lock);
29995    return retval;
29996 }
29997
29998 /* When we die, we re-parent all our children.  Try to
29999  * give them to another thread in our process group, and
30000  * if no such member exists, give it to the global child
30001  * reaper process (ie "init") */
30002 static inline void forget_original_parent(
30003    struct task_struct *father)
30004 {
30005    struct task_struct *p, *reaper;
30006
30007    read_lock(&tasklist_lock);
30008
30009    /* Next in our thread group */
30010    reaper = next_thread(father);
30011    if (reaper == father)
30012      reaper = child_reaper;
30013
30014    for_each_task(p) {
30015      if (p->p_opptr == father) {
30016        /* We dont want people slaying init */
30017        p->exit_signal = SIGCHLD;
30018        p->self_exec_id++;
30019        p->p_opptr = reaper;
30020        if (p->pdeath_signal)
30021          send_sig(p->pdeath_signal, p, 0);
30022      }
30023    }
30024    read_unlock(&tasklist_lock);
30025 }
30026
30027 static inline void close_files(
30028    struct files_struct *files)
30029 {
30030    int i, j;
30031
30032    j = 0;
```

```
30033   for (;;) {
30034     unsigned long set;
30035     i = j * __NFDBITS;
30036     if (i >= files->max_fdset || i >= files->max_fds)
30037       break;
30038     set = files->open_fds->fds_bits[j++];
30039     while (set) {
30040       if (set & 1) {
30041         struct file *file = xchg(&files->fd[i], NULL);
30042         if (file)
30043           filp_close(file, files);
30044       }
30045       i++;
30046       set >>= 1;
30047     }
30048   }
30049 }
30050
30051 void put_files_struct(struct files_struct *files)
30052 {
30053   if (atomic_dec_and_test(&files->count)) {
30054     close_files(files);
30055     /* Free the fd and fdset arrays if we expanded them.
30056      */
30057     if (files->fd != &files->fd_array[0])
30058       free_fd_array(files->fd, files->max_fds);
30059     if (files->max_fdset > __FD_SETSIZE) {
30060       free_fdset(files->open_fds, files->max_fdset);
30061       free_fdset(files->close_on_exec, files->max_fdset);
30062     }
30063     kmem_cache_free(files_cachep, files);
30064   }
30065 }
30066
30067 static inline void __exit_files(struct task_struct *tsk)
30068 {
30069   struct files_struct *files = tsk->files;
30070
30071   if (files) {
30072     task_lock(tsk);
30073     tsk->files = NULL;
30074     task_unlock(tsk);
30075     put_files_struct(files);
30076   }
30077 }
30078
30079 void exit_files(struct task_struct *tsk)
```

```
30080 {
30081   __exit_files(tsk);
30082 }
30083
30084 static inline void __put_fs_struct(struct fs_struct *fs)
30085 {
30086   /* No need to hold fs->lock if we are killing it */
30087   if (atomic_dec_and_test(&fs->count)) {
30088     dput(fs->root);
30089     mntput(fs->rootmnt);
30090     dput(fs->pwd);
30091     mntput(fs->pwdmnt);
30092     if (fs->altroot) {
30093       dput(fs->altroot);
30094       mntput(fs->altrootmnt);
30095     }
30096     kmem_cache_free(fs_cachep, fs);
30097   }
30098 }
30099
30100 void put_fs_struct(struct fs_struct *fs)
30101 {
30102   __put_fs_struct(fs);
30103 }
30104
30105 static inline void __exit_fs(struct task_struct *tsk)
30106 {
30107   struct fs_struct *fs = tsk->fs;
30108
30109   if (fs) {
30110     task_lock(tsk);
30111     tsk->fs = NULL;
30112     task_unlock(tsk);
30113     __put_fs_struct(fs);
30114   }
30115 }
30116
30117 void exit_fs(struct task_struct *tsk)
30118 {
30119   __exit_fs(tsk);
30120 }
30121
30122 /* We can use these to temporarily drop into "lazy TLB"
30123  * mode and back.  */
30124 struct mm_struct *start_lazy_tlb(void)
30125 {
30126   struct mm_struct *mm = current->mm;
```

p 615

```
30127    current->mm = NULL;
30128    /* active_mm is still 'mm' */
30129    atomic_inc(&mm->mm_count);
30130    enter_lazy_tlb(mm, current, smp_processor_id());
30131    return mm;
30132 }
30133
30134 void end_lazy_tlb(struct mm_struct *mm)
30135 {
30136    struct mm_struct *active_mm = current->active_mm;
30137
30138    current->mm = mm;
30139    if (mm != active_mm) {
30140      current->active_mm = mm;
30141      activate_mm(active_mm, mm);
30142    }
30143    mmdrop(active_mm);
30144 }
30145
30146 /* Turn us into a lazy TLB process if we aren't already.. 
30147  */
30148 static inline void __exit_mm(struct task_struct *tsk)
30149 {
30150    struct mm_struct *mm = tsk->mm;
30151
30152    mm_release();
30153    if (mm) {
30154      atomic_inc(&mm->mm_count);
30155      if (mm != tsk->active_mm)
30156        BUG();
30157      /* more a memory barrier than a real lock */
30158      task_lock(tsk);
30159      tsk->mm = NULL;
30160      task_unlock(tsk);
30161      enter_lazy_tlb(mm, current, smp_processor_id());
30162      mmput(mm);
30163    }
30164 }
30165
30166 void exit_mm(struct task_struct *tsk)
30167 {
30168    __exit_mm(tsk);
30169 }
30170
30171 /* Send signals to all our closest relatives so that they
30172  * know to properly mourn us..   */
30173 static void exit_notify(void)
30174 {
30175    struct task_struct *p, *t;
30176
30177    forget_original_parent(current);
30178    /* Check to see if any process groups have become
30179     * orphaned as a result of our exiting, and if they
30180     * have any stopped jobs, send them a SIGHUP and then a
30181     * SIGCONT.  (POSIX 3.2.2.2)
30182     *
30183     * Case i: Our father is in a different pgrp than we
30184     * are and we were the only connection outside, so our
30185     * pgrp is about to become orphaned.  */
30186
30187    t = current->p_pptr;
30188
30189    if ((t->pgrp != current->pgrp) &&
30190        (t->session == current->session) &&
30191        will_become_orphaned_pgrp(current->pgrp, current)
30192        && has_stopped_jobs(current->pgrp)) {
30193      kill_pg(current->pgrp, SIGHUP, 1);
30194      kill_pg(current->pgrp, SIGCONT, 1);
30195    }
30196
30197    /* Let father know we died
30198     *
30199     * Thread signals are configurable, but you aren't
30200     * going to use that to send signals to arbitary
30201     * processes.  That stops right now.
30202     *
30203     * If the parent exec id doesn't match the exec id we
30204     * saved when we started then we know the parent has
30205     * changed security domain.
30206     *
30207     * If our self_exec id doesn't match our parent_exec_id
30208     * then we have changed execution domain as these two
30209     * values started the same after a fork. */
30210
30211    if (current->exit_signal != SIGCHLD &&
30212        (current->parent_exec_id != t->self_exec_id ||
30213         current->self_exec_id != current->parent_exec_id)
30214        && !capable(CAP_KILL))
30215      current->exit_signal = SIGCHLD;
30216
30217
30218    /* This loop does two things:
30219     *
30220     * A.  Make init inherit all the child processes
```

```
30221    * B.   Check to see if any process groups have become
30222    *      orphaned as a result of our exiting, and if
30223    *      they have any stopped jobs, send them a SIGHUP
30224    *      and then a SIGCONT.  (POSIX 3.2.2.2) */
30225
30226   write_lock_irq(&tasklist_lock);
30227   current->state = TASK_ZOMBIE;
30228   do_notify_parent(current, current->exit_signal);
30229   while (current->p_cptr != NULL) {
30230     p = current->p_cptr;
30231     current->p_cptr = p->p_osptr;
30232     p->p_ysptr = NULL;
30233     p->ptrace = 0;
30234
30235     p->p_pptr = p->p_opptr;
30236     p->p_osptr = p->p_pptr->p_cptr;
30237     if (p->p_osptr)
30238       p->p_osptr->p_ysptr = p;
30239     p->p_pptr->p_cptr = p;
30240     if (p->state == TASK_ZOMBIE)
30241       do_notify_parent(p, p->exit_signal);
30242     /* process group orphan check
30243      * Case ii: Our child is in a different pgrp than we
30244      * are, and it was the only connection outside, so
30245      * the child pgrp is now orphaned.  */
30246     if ((p->pgrp != current->pgrp) &&
30247         (p->session == current->session)) {
30248       int pgrp = p->pgrp;
30249
30250       write_unlock_irq(&tasklist_lock);
30251       if (is_orphaned_pgrp(pgrp)
30252           && has_stopped_jobs(pgrp)) {
30253         kill_pg(pgrp, SIGHUP, 1);
30254         kill_pg(pgrp, SIGCONT, 1);
30255       }
30256       write_lock_irq(&tasklist_lock);
30257     }
30258   }
30259   write_unlock_irq(&tasklist_lock);
30260 }
30261
30262 NORET_TYPE void do_exit(long code)
30263 {
30264   struct task_struct *tsk = current;
30265
30266   if (in_interrupt())
30267     panic("Aiee, killing interrupt handler!");
```

```
30268   if (!tsk->pid)
30269     panic("Attempted to kill the idle task!");
30270   if (tsk->pid == 1)
30271     panic("Attempted to kill init!");
30272   tsk->flags |= PF_EXITING;
30273   del_timer_sync(&tsk->real_timer);
30274
30275 fake_volatile:
30276 #ifdef CONFIG_BSD_PROCESS_ACCT
30277   acct_process(code);
30278 #endif
30279   __exit_mm(tsk);
30280
30281   lock_kernel();
30282   sem_exit();
30283   __exit_files(tsk);
30284   __exit_fs(tsk);
30285   exit_sighand(tsk);
30286   exit_thread();
30287
30288   if (current->leader)
30289     disassociate_ctty(1);
30290
30291   put_exec_domain(tsk->exec_domain);
30292   if (tsk->binfmt && tsk->binfmt->module)
30293     __MOD_DEC_USE_COUNT(tsk->binfmt->module);
30294
30295   tsk->exit_code = code;
30296   exit_notify();
30297   schedule();
30298   BUG();
30299   /* In order to get rid of the "volatile function does
30300    * return" message I did this little loop that confuses
30301    * gcc to think do_exit really is volatile. In fact
30302    * it's schedule() that is volatile in some
30303    * circumstances: when current->state = ZOMBIE,
30304    * schedule() never returns.
30305    *
30306    * In fact the natural way to do all this is to have
30307    * the label and the goto right after each other, but I
30308    * put the fake_volatile label at the start of the
30309    * function just in case something /really/ bad
30310    * happens, and the schedule returns. This way we can
30311    * try again. I'm not paranoid: it's just that
30312    * everybody is out to get me.  */
30313   goto fake_volatile;
30314 }
```

p 615

```
30315
30316 NORET_TYPE void up_and_exit(struct semaphore *sem,
30317       long code)
30318 {
30319   if (sem)
30320     up(sem);
30321
30322   do_exit(code);
30323 }
30324
30325 asmlinkage long sys_exit(int error_code)
30326 {
30327   do_exit((error_code & 0xff) << 8);
30328 }
30329
30330 asmlinkage long sys_wait4(pid_t pid,
30331       unsigned int *stat_addr, int options,
30332       struct rusage *ru)
30333 {
30334   int flag, retval;
30335   DECLARE_WAITQUEUE(wait, current);
30336   struct task_struct *tsk;
30337
30338   if (options & ~(WNOHANG | WUNTRACED | __WNOTHREAD |
30339                   __WCLONE | __WALL))
30340     return -EINVAL;
30341
30342   add_wait_queue(&current->wait_chldexit, &wait);
30343 repeat:
30344   flag = 0;
30345   current->state = TASK_INTERRUPTIBLE;
30346   read_lock(&tasklist_lock);
30347   tsk = current;
30348   do {
30349     struct task_struct *p;
30350     for (p = tsk->p_cptr; p; p = p->p_osptr) {
30351       if (pid > 0) {
30352         if (p->pid != pid)
30353           continue;
30354       } else if (!pid) {
30355         if (p->pgrp != current->pgrp)
30356           continue;
30357       } else if (pid != -1) {
30358         if (p->pgrp != -pid)
30359           continue;
30360       }
30361       /* Wait for all children (clone and not) if __WALL
```

```
30362      * is set; otherwise, wait for clone children
30363      * *only* if __WCLONE is set; otherwise, wait for
30364      * non-clone children *only*.  (Note: A "clone"
30365      * child here is one that reports to its parent
30366      * using a signal other than SIGCHLD.) */
30367     if (((p->exit_signal != SIGCHLD) ^
30368         ((options & __WCLONE) != 0))
30369         && !(options & __WALL))
30370       continue;
30371     flag = 1;
30372     switch (p->state) {
30373     case TASK_STOPPED:
30374       if (!p->exit_code)
30375         continue;
30376       if (!(options & WUNTRACED)
30377           && !(p->ptrace & PT_PTRACED))
30378         continue;
30379       read_unlock(&tasklist_lock);
30380       retval = ru ? getrusage(p, RUSAGE_BOTH, ru) : 0;
30381       if (!retval && stat_addr)
30382         retval = put_user((p->exit_code << 8) | 0x7f,
30383                       stat_addr);
30384       if (!retval) {
30385         p->exit_code = 0;
30386         retval = p->pid;
30387       }
30388       goto end_wait4;
30389     case TASK_ZOMBIE:
30390       current->times.tms_cutime +=
30391           p->times.tms_utime + p->times.tms_cutime;
30392       current->times.tms_cstime +=
30393           p->times.tms_stime + p->times.tms_cstime;
30394       read_unlock(&tasklist_lock);
30395       retval = ru ? getrusage(p, RUSAGE_BOTH, ru) : 0;
30396       if (!retval && stat_addr)
30397         retval = put_user(p->exit_code, stat_addr);
30398       if (retval)
30399         goto end_wait4;
30400       retval = p->pid;
30401       if (p->p_opptr != p->p_pptr) {
30402         write_lock_irq(&tasklist_lock);
30403         REMOVE_LINKS(p);
30404         p->p_pptr = p->p_opptr;
30405         SET_LINKS(p);
30406         do_notify_parent(p, SIGCHLD);
30407         write_unlock_irq(&tasklist_lock);
30408       } else
```

```
30409          release_task(p);
30410        goto end_wait4;
30411      default:
30412        continue;
30413      }
30414    }
30415    if (options & __WNOTHREAD)
30416      break;
30417    tsk = next_thread(tsk);
30418  } while (tsk != current);
30419  read_unlock(&tasklist_lock);
30420  if (flag) {
30421    retval = 0;
30422    if (options & WNOHANG)
30423      goto end_wait4;
30424    retval = -ERESTARTSYS;
30425    if (signal_pending(current))
30426      goto end_wait4;
30427    schedule();
30428    goto repeat;
30429  }
30430  retval = -ECHILD;
30431 end_wait4:
30432  current->state = TASK_RUNNING;
30433  remove_wait_queue(&current->wait_chldexit, &wait);
30434  return retval;
30435 }
30436
30437 #if !defined(__alpha__) && !defined(__ia64__)
30438
30439 /* sys_waitpid() remains for compatibility. waitpid()
30440  * should be implemented by calling sys_wait4() from
30441  * libc.a.  */
30442 asmlinkage long sys_waitpid(pid_t pid,
30443      unsigned int *stat_addr, int options)
30444 {
30445    return sys_wait4(pid, stat_addr, options, NULL);
30446 }
30447
30448 #endif
```

kernel/fork.c

```
30449 /*
30450  *  linux/kernel/fork.c
30451  *
30452  *  Copyright (C) 1991, 1992  Linus Torvalds
30453  */
30454
30455 /* 'fork.c' contains the help-routines for the 'fork'
30456  * system call (see also entry.S and others).  Fork is
30457  * rather simple, once you get the hang of it, but the
30458  * memory management can be a bitch. See 'mm/memory.c':
30459  * 'copy_page_tables()' */
30460
30461 #include <linux/config.h>
30462 #include <linux/malloc.h>
30463 #include <linux/init.h>
30464 #include <linux/unistd.h>
30465 #include <linux/smp_lock.h>
30466 #include <linux/module.h>
30467 #include <linux/vmalloc.h>
30468
30469 #include <asm/pgtable.h>
30470 #include <asm/pgalloc.h>
30471 #include <asm/uaccess.h>
30472 #include <asm/mmu_context.h>
30473
30474 /* The idle threads do not count.. */
30475 int nr_threads;
30476 int nr_running;
30477
30478 int max_threads;
30479 unsigned long total_forks;      /* Handle normal Linux
30480                                  * uptimes. */
30481 int last_pid;
30482
30483 struct task_struct *pidhash[PIDHASH_SZ];
30484
30485 void add_wait_queue(wait_queue_head_t * q,
30486      wait_queue_t * wait)
30487 {
30488    unsigned long flags;
30489
30490    wq_write_lock_irqsave(&q->lock, flags);
30491    wait->flags = 0;
30492    __add_wait_queue(q, wait);
30493    wq_write_unlock_irqrestore(&q->lock, flags);
30494 }
30495
30496 void add_wait_queue_exclusive(wait_queue_head_t * q,
30497      wait_queue_t * wait)
30498 {
30499    unsigned long flags;
30500
```

```
30501    wq_write_lock_irqsave(&q->lock, flags);
30502    wait->flags = WQ_FLAG_EXCLUSIVE;
30503    __add_wait_queue_tail(q, wait);
30504    wq_write_unlock_irqrestore(&q->lock, flags);
30505 }
30506
30507 void remove_wait_queue(wait_queue_head_t * q,
30508      wait_queue_t * wait)
30509 {
30510    unsigned long flags;
30511
30512    wq_write_lock_irqsave(&q->lock, flags);
30513    __remove_wait_queue(q, wait);
30514    wq_write_unlock_irqrestore(&q->lock, flags);
30515 }
30516
30517 void __init fork_init(unsigned long mempages)
30518 {
30519    /* The default maximum number of threads is set to a
30520     * safe value: the thread structures can take up at
30521     * most half of memory.  */
30522    max_threads = mempages / (THREAD_SIZE / PAGE_SIZE) / 2;
30523
30524    init_task.rlim[RLIMIT_NPROC].rlim_cur =
30525        max_threads / 2;
30526    init_task.rlim[RLIMIT_NPROC].rlim_max =
30527        max_threads / 2;
30528 }
30529
30530 /* Protects next_safe and last_pid. */
30531 spinlock_t lastpid_lock = SPIN_LOCK_UNLOCKED;
30532
30533 static int get_pid(unsigned long flags)
30534 {
30535    static int next_safe = PID_MAX;
30536    struct task_struct *p;
30537
30538    if (flags & CLONE_PID)
30539      return current->pid;
30540
30541    spin_lock(&lastpid_lock);
30542    if ((++last_pid) & 0xffff8000) {
30543      last_pid = 300;                /* Skip daemons etc. */
30544      goto inside;
30545    }
30546    if (last_pid >= next_safe) {
30547    inside:
```

```
30548      next_safe = PID_MAX;
30549      read_lock(&tasklist_lock);
30550    repeat:
30551      for_each_task(p) {
30552        if (p->pid == last_pid ||
30553            p->pgrp == last_pid ||
30554            p->session == last_pid) {
30555          if (++last_pid >= next_safe) {
30556            if (last_pid & 0xffff8000)
30557              last_pid = 300;
30558            next_safe = PID_MAX;
30559          }
30560          goto repeat;
30561        }
30562        if (p->pid > last_pid && next_safe > p->pid)
30563          next_safe = p->pid;
30564        if (p->pgrp > last_pid && next_safe > p->pgrp)
30565          next_safe = p->pgrp;
30566        if (p->session > last_pid
30567            && next_safe > p->session)
30568          next_safe = p->session;
30569      }
30570      read_unlock(&tasklist_lock);
30571    }
30572    spin_unlock(&lastpid_lock);
30573
30574    return last_pid;
30575 }
30576
30577 static inline int dup_mmap(struct mm_struct *mm)
30578 {
30579    struct vm_area_struct *mpnt, *tmp, **pprev;
30580    int retval;
30581
30582    flush_cache_mm(current->mm);
30583    mm->locked_vm = 0;
30584    mm->mmap = NULL;
30585    mm->mmap_avl = NULL;
30586    mm->mmap_cache = NULL;
30587    mm->map_count = 0;
30588    mm->cpu_vm_mask = 0;
30589    mm->swap_address = 0;
30590    pprev = &mm->mmap;
30591    for (mpnt = current->mm->mmap; mpnt;
30592        mpnt = mpnt->vm_next) {
30593      struct file *file;
30594
```

```
30595    retval = -ENOMEM;
30596    if (mpnt->vm_flags & VM_DONTCOPY)
30597      continue;
30598    tmp = kmem_cache_alloc(vm_area_cachep, SLAB_KERNEL);
30599    if (!tmp)
30600      goto fail_nomem;
30601    *tmp = *mpnt;
30602    tmp->vm_flags &= ~VM_LOCKED;
30603    tmp->vm_mm = mm;
30604    mm->map_count++;
30605    tmp->vm_next = NULL;
30606    file = tmp->vm_file;
30607    if (file) {
30608      struct inode *inode = file->f_dentry->d_inode;
30609      get_file(file);
30610      if (tmp->vm_flags & VM_DENYWRITE)
30611        atomic_dec(&inode->i_writecount);
30612
30613      /* insert tmp into the share list, just after mpnt
30614       */
30615      spin_lock(&inode->i_mapping->i_shared_lock);
30616      if ((tmp->vm_next_share = mpnt->vm_next_share)
30617          != NULL)
30618        mpnt->vm_next_share->vm_pprev_share =
30619          &tmp->vm_next_share;
30620      mpnt->vm_next_share = tmp;
30621      tmp->vm_pprev_share = &mpnt->vm_next_share;
30622      spin_unlock(&inode->i_mapping->i_shared_lock);
30623    }
30624
30625    /* Copy the pages, but defer checking for errors */
30626    retval = copy_page_range(mm, current->mm, tmp);
30627    if (!retval && tmp->vm_ops && tmp->vm_ops->open)
30628      tmp->vm_ops->open(tmp);
30629
30630    /* Link in the new vma even if an error occurred, so
30631     * that exit_mmap() can clean up the mess.  */
30632    *pprev = tmp;
30633    pprev = &tmp->vm_next;
30634
30635    if (retval)
30636      goto fail_nomem;
30637  }
30638  retval = 0;
30639  if (mm->map_count >= AVL_MIN_MAP_COUNT)
30640    build_mmap_avl(mm);
30641
30642 fail_nomem:
30643   flush_tlb_mm(current->mm);
30644   return retval;
30645 }
30646
30647 spinlock_t mmlist_lock __cacheline_aligned =
30648     SPIN_LOCK_UNLOCKED;
30649 int mmlist_nr;
30650
30651 #define allocate_mm()                                      \
30652   (kmem_cache_alloc(mm_cachep, SLAB_KERNEL))
30653 #define free_mm(mm)                                        \
30654   (kmem_cache_free(mm_cachep, (mm)))
30655
30656 static struct mm_struct *mm_init(struct mm_struct *mm)
30657 {
30658   atomic_set(&mm->mm_users, 1);
30659   atomic_set(&mm->mm_count, 1);
30660   init_MUTEX(&mm->mmap_sem);
30661   mm->page_table_lock = SPIN_LOCK_UNLOCKED;
30662   mm->pgd = pgd_alloc();
30663   if (mm->pgd)
30664     return mm;
30665   free_mm(mm);
30666   return NULL;
30667 }
30668
30669
30670 /* Allocate and initialize an mm_struct.  */
30671 struct mm_struct *mm_alloc(void)
30672 {
30673   struct mm_struct *mm;
30674
30675   mm = allocate_mm();
30676   if (mm) {
30677     memset(mm, 0, sizeof(*mm));
30678     return mm_init(mm);
30679   }
30680   return NULL;
30681 }
30682
30683 /* Called when the last reference to the mm is dropped:
30684  * either by a lazy thread or by mmput. Free the page
30685  * directory and the mm.  */
30686 inline void __mmdrop(struct mm_struct *mm)
30687 {
30688   if (mm == &init_mm)
```

```
30689      BUG();
30690    pgd_free(mm->pgd);
30691    destroy_context(mm);
30692    free_mm(mm);
30693 }
30694
30695 /* Decrement the use count and release all resources for
30696  * an mm.  */
30697 void mmput(struct mm_struct *mm)
30698 {
30699    if (atomic_dec_and_lock(&mm->mm_users, &mmlist_lock)) {
30700      list_del(&mm->mmlist);
30701      mmlist_nr--;
30702      spin_unlock(&mmlist_lock);
30703      exit_mmap(mm);
30704      mmdrop(mm);
30705    }
30706 }
30707
30708 /* Please note the differences between mmput and
30709  * mm_release.  mmput is called whenever we stop holding
30710  * onto a mm_struct, error success whatever.
30711  *
30712  * mm_release is called after a mm_struct has been
30713  * removed from the current process.
30714  *
30715  * This difference is important for error handling, when
30716  * we only half set up a mm_struct for a new process and
30717  * need to restore the old one.  Because we mmput the new
30718  * mm_struct before restoring the old one. . .
30719  *
30720  * Eric Biederman 10 January 1998 */
30721 void mm_release(void)
30722 {
30723    struct task_struct *tsk = current;
30724
30725    /* notify parent sleeping on vfork() */
30726    if (tsk->flags & PF_VFORK) {
30727      tsk->flags &= ~PF_VFORK;
30728      up(tsk->p_opptr->vfork_sem);
30729    }
30730 }
30731
30732 static int copy_mm(unsigned long clone_flags,
30733      struct task_struct *tsk)
30734 {
30735    struct mm_struct *mm, *oldmm;
30736    int retval;
30737
30738    tsk->min_flt = tsk->maj_flt = 0;
30739    tsk->cmin_flt = tsk->cmaj_flt = 0;
30740    tsk->nswap = tsk->cnswap = 0;
30741
30742    tsk->mm = NULL;
30743    tsk->active_mm = NULL;
30744
30745    /* Are we cloning a kernel thread?
30746     *
30747     * We need to steal a active VM for that..  */
30748    oldmm = current->mm;
30749    if (!oldmm)
30750      return 0;
30751
30752    if (clone_flags & CLONE_VM) {
30753      atomic_inc(&oldmm->mm_users);
30754      mm = oldmm;
30755      goto good_mm;
30756    }
30757
30758    retval = -ENOMEM;
30759    mm = allocate_mm();
30760    if (!mm)
30761      goto fail_nomem;
30762
30763    /* Copy the current MM stuff.. */
30764    memcpy(mm, oldmm, sizeof(*mm));
30765    if (!mm_init(mm))
30766      goto fail_nomem;
30767
30768    down(&oldmm->mmap_sem);
30769    retval = dup_mmap(mm);
30770    up(&oldmm->mmap_sem);
30771
30772    /* Add it to the mmlist after the parent.
30773     *
30774     * Doing it this way means that we can order the list,
30775     * and fork() won't mess up the ordering significantly.
30776     */
30777    spin_lock(&mmlist_lock);
30778    list_add(&mm->mmlist, &oldmm->mmlist);
30779    mmlist_nr++;
30780    spin_unlock(&mmlist_lock);
30781
30782    if (retval)
```

```
30783      goto free_pt;
30784
30785    /* child gets a private LDT (if there was an LDT in the
30786     * parent) */
30787    copy_segments(tsk, mm);
30788
30789    if (init_new_context(tsk, mm))
30790      goto free_pt;
30791
30792 good_mm:
30793   tsk->mm = mm;
30794   tsk->active_mm = mm;
30795   return 0;
30796
30797 free_pt:
30798   mmput(mm);
30799 fail_nomem:
30800   return retval;
30801 }
30802
30803 static inline struct fs_struct *__copy_fs_struct(struct
30804     fs_struct *old)
30805 {
30806   struct fs_struct *fs =
30807       kmem_cache_alloc(fs_cachep, GFP_KERNEL);
30808   /* We don't need to lock fs - think why ;-) */
30809   if (fs) {
30810     atomic_set(&fs->count, 1);
30811     fs->lock = RW_LOCK_UNLOCKED;
30812     fs->umask = old->umask;
30813     read_lock(&old->lock);
30814     fs->rootmnt = mntget(old->rootmnt);
30815     fs->root = dget(old->root);
30816     fs->pwdmnt = mntget(old->pwdmnt);
30817     fs->pwd = dget(old->pwd);
30818     if (old->altroot) {
30819       fs->altrootmnt = mntget(old->altrootmnt);
30820       fs->altroot = dget(old->altroot);
30821     } else {
30822       fs->altrootmnt = NULL;
30823       fs->altroot = NULL;
30824     }
30825     read_unlock(&old->lock);
30826   }
30827   return fs;
30828 }
30829
```

```
30830 struct fs_struct *copy_fs_struct(struct fs_struct *old)
30831 {
30832   return __copy_fs_struct(old);
30833 }
30834
30835 static inline int copy_fs(unsigned long clone_flags,
30836     struct task_struct *tsk)
30837 {
30838   if (clone_flags & CLONE_FS) {
30839     atomic_inc(&current->fs->count);
30840     return 0;
30841   }
30842   tsk->fs = __copy_fs_struct(current->fs);
30843   if (!tsk->fs)
30844     return -1;
30845   return 0;
30846 }
30847
30848 static int count_open_files(struct files_struct *files,
30849     int size)
30850 {
30851   int i;
30852
30853   /* Find the last open fd */
30854   for (i = size / (8 * sizeof(long)); i > 0;) {
30855     if (files->open_fds->fds_bits[-i])
30856       break;
30857   }
30858   i = (i + 1) * 8 * sizeof(long);
30859   return i;
30860 }
30861
30862 static int copy_files(unsigned long clone_flags,
30863     struct task_struct *tsk)
30864 {
30865   struct files_struct *oldf, *newf;
30866   struct file **old_fds, **new_fds;
30867   int open_files, nfds, size, i, error = 0;
30868
30869   /* A background process may not have any files ...  */
30870   oldf = current->files;
30871   if (!oldf)
30872     goto out;
30873
30874   if (clone_flags & CLONE_FILES) {
30875     atomic_inc(&oldf->count);
30876     goto out;
```

```
30877    }
30878
30879    tsk->files = NULL;
30880    error = -ENOMEM;
30881    newf = kmem_cache_alloc(files_cachep, SLAB_KERNEL);
30882    if (!newf)
30883      goto out;
30884
30885    atomic_set(&newf->count, 1);
30886
30887    newf->file_lock = RW_LOCK_UNLOCKED;
30888    newf->next_fd = 0;
30889    newf->max_fds = NR_OPEN_DEFAULT;
30890    newf->max_fdset = __FD_SETSIZE;
30891    newf->close_on_exec = &newf->close_on_exec_init;
30892    newf->open_fds = &newf->open_fds_init;
30893    newf->fd = &newf->fd_array[0];
30894
30895    /* We don't yet have the oldf readlock, but even if
30896     * the old fdset gets grown now, we'll only copy up to
30897     * "size" fds */
30898    size = oldf->max_fdset;
30899    if (size > __FD_SETSIZE) {
30900      newf->max_fdset = 0;
30901      write_lock(&newf->file_lock);
30902      error = expand_fdset(newf, size - 1);
30903      write_unlock(&newf->file_lock);
30904      if (error)
30905        goto out_release;
30906    }
30907    read_lock(&oldf->file_lock);
30908
30909    open_files = count_open_files(oldf, size);
30910
30911    /* Check whether we need to allocate a larger fd array.
30912     * Note: we're not a clone task, so the open count
30913     * won't change.  */
30914    nfds = NR_OPEN_DEFAULT;
30915    if (open_files > nfds) {
30916      read_unlock(&oldf->file_lock);
30917      newf->max_fds = 0;
30918      write_lock(&newf->file_lock);
30919      error = expand_fd_array(newf, open_files - 1);
30920      write_unlock(&newf->file_lock);
30921      if (error)
30922        goto out_release;
30923      nfds = newf->max_fds;
30924      read_lock(&oldf->file_lock);
30925    }
30926
30927    old_fds = oldf->fd;
30928    new_fds = newf->fd;
30929
30930    memcpy(newf->open_fds->fds_bits,
30931           oldf->open_fds->fds_bits, open_files / 8);
30932    memcpy(newf->close_on_exec->fds_bits,
30933           oldf->close_on_exec->fds_bits, open_files / 8);
30934
30935    for (i = open_files; i != 0; i--) {
30936      struct file *f = *old_fds++;
30937      if (f)
30938        get_file(f);
30939      *new_fds++ = f;
30940    }
30941    read_unlock(&oldf->file_lock);
30942
30943    /* compute the remainder to be cleared */
30944    size = (newf->max_fds - open_files) *
30945      sizeof(struct file *);
30946
30947    /* This is long word aligned thus could use a
30948     * optimized version */
30949    memset(new_fds, 0, size);
30950
30951    if (newf->max_fdset > open_files) {
30952      int left = (newf->max_fdset - open_files) / 8;
30953      int start = open_files / (8 * sizeof(unsigned long));
30954
30955      memset(&newf->open_fds->fds_bits[start], 0, left);
30956      memset(&newf->close_on_exec->fds_bits[start], 0,
30957        left);
30958    }
30959
30960    tsk->files = newf;
30961    error = 0;
30962 out:
30963    return error;
30964
30965 out_release:
30966    free_fdset(newf->close_on_exec, newf->max_fdset);
30967    free_fdset(newf->open_fds, newf->max_fdset);
30968    kmem_cache_free(files_cachep, newf);
30969    goto out;
30970 }
```

```
30971
30972 static inline int copy_sighand(unsigned long clone_flags,
30973     struct task_struct *tsk)
30974 {
30975   struct signal_struct *sig;
30976
30977   if (clone_flags & CLONE_SIGHAND) {
30978     atomic_inc(&current->sig->count);
30979     return 0;
30980   }
30981   sig = kmem_cache_alloc(sigact_cachep, GFP_KERNEL);
30982   tsk->sig = sig;
30983   if (!sig)
30984     return -1;
30985   spin_lock_init(&sig->siglock);
30986   atomic_set(&sig->count, 1);
30987   memcpy(tsk->sig->action, current->sig->action,
30988        sizeof(tsk->sig->action));
30989   return 0;
30990 }
30991
30992 static inline void copy_flags(unsigned long clone_flags,
30993     struct task_struct *p)
30994 {
30995   unsigned long new_flags = p->flags;
30996
30997   new_flags &= ~(PF_SUPERPRIV | PF_USEDFPU | PF_VFORK);
30998   new_flags |= PF_FORKNOEXEC;
30999   if (!(clone_flags & CLONE_PTRACE))
31000     p->ptrace = 0;
31001   if (clone_flags & CLONE_VFORK)
31002     new_flags |= PF_VFORK;
31003   p->flags = new_flags;
31004 }
31005
31006 /* Ok, this is the main fork-routine. It copies the
31007  * system process information (task[nr]) and sets up the
31008  * necessary registers. It also copies the data segment
31009  * in its entirety.  The "stack_start" and "stack_top"
31010  * arguments are simply passed along to the platform
31011  * specific copy_thread() routine.  Most platforms ignore
31012  * stack_top.  For an example that's using stack_top, see
31013  * arch/ia64/kernel/process.c.  */
31014 int do_fork(unsigned long clone_flags,
31015     unsigned long stack_start, struct pt_regs *regs,
31016     unsigned long stack_size)
31017 {
31018   int retval = -ENOMEM;
31019   struct task_struct *p;
31020   DECLARE_MUTEX_LOCKED(sem);
31021
31022   if (clone_flags & CLONE_PID) {
31023     /* This is only allowed from the boot up thread */
31024     if (current->pid)
31025       return -EPERM;
31026   }
31027
31028   current->vfork_sem = &sem;
31029
31030   p = alloc_task_struct();
31031   if (!p)
31032     goto fork_out;
31033
31034   *p = *current;
31035
31036   retval = -EAGAIN;
31037   if (atomic_read(&p->user->processes) >=
31038       p->rlim[RLIMIT_NPROC].rlim_cur)
31039     goto bad_fork_free;
31040   atomic_inc(&p->user->__count);
31041   atomic_inc(&p->user->processes);
31042
31043   /* Counter increases are protected by the kernel lock
31044    * so nr_threads can't increase under us (but it may
31045    * decrease).  */
31046   if (nr_threads >= max_threads)
31047     goto bad_fork_cleanup_count;
31048
31049   get_exec_domain(p->exec_domain);
31050
31051   if (p->binfmt && p->binfmt->module)
31052     __MOD_INC_USE_COUNT(p->binfmt->module);
31053
31054   p->did_exec = 0;
31055   p->swappable = 0;
31056   p->state = TASK_UNINTERRUPTIBLE;
31057
31058   copy_flags(clone_flags, p);
31059   p->pid = get_pid(clone_flags);
31060
31061   p->run_list.next = NULL;
31062   p->run_list.prev = NULL;
31063
31064   if ((clone_flags & CLONE_VFORK)
```

p 602

```
31065        || !(clone_flags & CLONE_PARENT)) {
31066      p->p_opptr = current;
31067      if (!(p->ptrace & PT_PTRACED))
31068        p->p_pptr = current;
31069    }
31070    p->p_cptr = NULL;
31071    init_waitqueue_head(&p->wait_chldexit);
31072    p->vfork_sem = NULL;
31073    spin_lock_init(&p->alloc_lock);
31074
31075    p->sigpending = 0;
31076    init_sigpending(&p->pending);
31077
31078    p->it_real_value = p->it_virt_value =
31079        p->it_prof_value = 0;
31080    p->it_real_incr = p->it_virt_incr =
31081        p->it_prof_incr = 0;
31082    init_timer(&p->real_timer);
31083    p->real_timer.data = (unsigned long) p;
31084
31085    p->leader = 0; /* session leadership doesn't inherit */
31086    p->tty_old_pgrp = 0;
31087    p->times.tms_utime = p->times.tms_stime = 0;
31088    p->times.tms_cutime = p->times.tms_cstime = 0;
31089 #ifdef CONFIG_SMP
31090    {
31091      int i;
31092      p->has_cpu = 0;
31093      p->processor = current->processor;
31094      /* ?? should we just memset this ?? */
31095      for (i = 0; i < smp_num_cpus; i++)
31096        p->per_cpu_utime[i] = p->per_cpu_stime[i] = 0;
31097      spin_lock_init(&p->sigmask_lock);
31098    }
31099 #endif
31100    p->lock_depth = -1;           /* -1 = no lock */
31101    p->start_time = jiffies;
31102
31103    retval = -ENOMEM;
31104    /* copy all the process information */
31105    if (copy_files(clone_flags, p))
31106      goto bad_fork_cleanup;
31107    if (copy_fs(clone_flags, p))
31108      goto bad_fork_cleanup_files;
31109    if (copy_sighand(clone_flags, p))
31110      goto bad_fork_cleanup_fs;
31111    if (copy_mm(clone_flags, p))
31112      goto bad_fork_cleanup_sighand;
31113    retval = copy_thread(0, clone_flags, stack_start,
31114                    stack_size, p, regs);
31115    if (retval)
31116      goto bad_fork_cleanup_sighand;
31117    p->semundo = NULL;
31118
31119    /* Our parent execution domain becomes current domain
31120     * These must match for thread signalling to apply */
31121
31122    p->parent_exec_id = p->self_exec_id;
31123
31124    /* ok, now we should be set up.. */
31125    p->swappable = 1;
31126    p->exit_signal = clone_flags & CSIGNAL;
31127    p->pdeath_signal = 0;
31128
31129    /* "share" dynamic priority between parent and child,
31130     * thus the total amount of dynamic priorities in the
31131     * system doesnt change, more scheduling fairness. This
31132     * is only important in the first timeslice, on the
31133     * long run the scheduling behaviour is unchanged.  */
31134    p->counter = (current->counter + 1) >> 1;
31135    current->counter >>= 1;
31136    if (!current->counter)
31137      current->need_resched = 1;
31138
31139    /* Ok, add it to the run-queues and make it visible to
31140     * the rest of the system.
31141     *
31142     * Let it rip!  */
31143    retval = p->pid;
31144    p->tgid = retval;
31145    INIT_LIST_HEAD(&p->thread_group);
31146    write_lock_irq(&tasklist_lock);
31147    if (clone_flags & CLONE_THREAD) {
31148      p->tgid = current->tgid;
31149      list_add(&p->thread_group, &current->thread_group);
31150    }
31151    SET_LINKS(p);
31152    hash_pid(p);
31153    nr_threads++;
31154    write_unlock_irq(&tasklist_lock);
31155
31156    if (p->ptrace & PT_PTRACED)
31157      send_sig(SIGSTOP, p, 1);
31158
```

```
31159    wake_up_process(p);          /* do this last */
31160    ++total_forks;
31161
31162 fork_out:
31163    if ((clone_flags & CLONE_VFORK) && (retval > 0))
31164      down(&sem);
31165    return retval;
31166
31167 bad_fork_cleanup_sighand:
31168    exit_sighand(p);
31169 bad_fork_cleanup_fs:
31170    exit_fs(p);                  /* blocking */
31171 bad_fork_cleanup_files:
31172    exit_files(p);               /* blocking */
31173 bad_fork_cleanup:
31174    put_exec_domain(p->exec_domain);
31175    if (p->binfmt && p->binfmt->module)
31176      __MOD_DEC_USE_COUNT(p->binfmt->module);
31177 bad_fork_cleanup_count:
31178    atomic_dec(&p->user->processes);
31179    free_uid(p->user);
31180 bad_fork_free:
31181    free_task_struct(p);
31182    goto fork_out;
31183 }
31184
31185 /* SLAB cache for signal_struct structures (tsk->sig) */
31186 kmem_cache_t *sigact_cachep;
31187
31188 /* SLAB cache for files_struct structures (tsk->files) */
31189 kmem_cache_t *files_cachep;
31190
31191 /* SLAB cache for fs_struct structures (tsk->fs) */
31192 kmem_cache_t *fs_cachep;
31193
31194 /* SLAB cache for vm_area_struct structures */
31195 kmem_cache_t *vm_area_cachep;
31196
31197 /* SLAB cache for mm_struct structures (tsk->mm) */
31198 kmem_cache_t *mm_cachep;
31199
31200 void __init proc_caches_init(void)
31201 {
31202    sigact_cachep = kmem_cache_create("signal_act",
31203        sizeof(struct signal_struct), 0,
31204        SLAB_HWCACHE_ALIGN, NULL, NULL);
31205    if (!sigact_cachep)
```

```
31206      panic("Cannot create signal action SLAB cache");
31207
31208    files_cachep = kmem_cache_create("files_cache",
31209        sizeof(struct files_struct), 0,
31210        SLAB_HWCACHE_ALIGN, NULL, NULL);
31211    if (!files_cachep)
31212      panic("Cannot create files SLAB cache");
31213
31214    fs_cachep = kmem_cache_create("fs_cache",
31215        sizeof(struct fs_struct), 0,
31216        SLAB_HWCACHE_ALIGN, NULL, NULL);
31217    if (!fs_cachep)
31218      panic("Cannot create fs_struct SLAB cache");
31219
31220    vm_area_cachep = kmem_cache_create("vm_area_struct",
31221        sizeof(struct vm_area_struct), 0,
31222        SLAB_HWCACHE_ALIGN, NULL, NULL);
31223    if (!vm_area_cachep)
31224      panic("vma_init: Cannot alloc vm_area_struct SLAB "
31225          "cache");
31226
31227    mm_cachep = kmem_cache_create("mm_struct",
31228        sizeof(struct mm_struct), 0,
31229        SLAB_HWCACHE_ALIGN, NULL, NULL);
31230    if (!mm_cachep)
31231      panic("vma_init: Cannot alloc mm_struct SLAB cache");
31232 }
```

kernel/info.c

```
31233 /*
31234  * linux/kernel/info.c
31235  *
31236  * Copyright (C) 1992 Darren Senn
31237  */
31238
31239 /* This implements the sysinfo() system call */
31240
31241 #include <linux/mm.h>
31242 #include <linux/unistd.h>
31243 #include <linux/swap.h>
31244 #include <linux/smp_lock.h>
31245
31246 #include <asm/uaccess.h>
31247
31248 asmlinkage long sys_sysinfo(struct sysinfo *info)
31249 {
31250    struct sysinfo val;
```
p 570

```
31251
31252    memset((char *) &val, 0, sizeof(struct sysinfo));
31253
31254    cli();
31255    val.uptime = jiffies / HZ;
31256
31257    val.loads[0] = avenrun[0] << (SI_LOAD_SHIFT - FSHIFT);
31258    val.loads[1] = avenrun[1] << (SI_LOAD_SHIFT - FSHIFT);
31259    val.loads[2] = avenrun[2] << (SI_LOAD_SHIFT - FSHIFT);
31260
31261    val.procs = nr_threads - 1;
31262    sti();
31263
31264    si_meminfo(&val);
31265    si_swapinfo(&val);
31266
31267    {
31268        /* If the sum of all the available memory (i.e. ram +
31269         * swap + highmem) is less then can be stored in a 32
31270         * bit unsigned long then we can be binary compatible
31271         * with 2.2.x kernels.  If not, well, who cares since
31272         * in that case 2.2.x was broken anyways...
31273         *   -Erik Andersen <andersee@debian.org> */
31274
31275        unsigned long mem_total =
31276            val.totalram + val.totalswap;
31277        if (!(mem_total < val.totalram
31278                || mem_total < val.totalswap)) {
31279            unsigned long mem_total2 =
31280                mem_total + val.totalhigh;
31281            if (!(mem_total2 < mem_total
31282                    || mem_total2 < val.totalhigh)) {
31283                /* If mem_total did not overflow.  Divide all
31284                 * memory values by mem_unit and set mem_unit=1.
31285                 * This leaves things compatible with 2.2.x, and
31286                 * also retains compatibility with earlier 2.4.x
31287                 * kernels...  */
31288
31289                int bitcount = 0;
31290                while (val.mem_unit > 1) {
31291                    bitcount++;
31292                    val.mem_unit >>= 1;
31293                }
31294                val.totalram <<= bitcount;
31295                val.freeram <<= bitcount;
31296                val.sharedram <<= bitcount;
31297                val.bufferram <<= bitcount;
31298                val.totalswap <<= bitcount;
31299                val.freeswap <<= bitcount;
31300                val.totalhigh <<= bitcount;
31301                val.freehigh <<= bitcount;
31302            }
31303        }
31304    }
31305
31306    if (copy_to_user(info, &val, sizeof(struct sysinfo)))
31307        return -EFAULT;
31308    return 0;
31309 }
```

kernel/itimer.c

```
31310 /*
31311  * linux/kernel/itimer.c
31312  *
31313  * Copyright (C) 1992 Darren Senn
31314  */
31315
31316 /* These are all the functions necessary to implement
31317  * itimers */
31318
31319 #include <linux/mm.h>
31320 #include <linux/smp_lock.h>
31321 #include <linux/interrupt.h>
31322
31323 #include <asm/uaccess.h>
31324
31325 /* change timeval to jiffies, trying to avoid the most
31326  * obvious overflows..
31327  *
31328  * The tv_*sec values are signed, but nothing seems to
31329  * indicate whether we really should use them as signed
31330  * values when doing itimers. POSIX doesn't mention this
31331  * (but if alarm() uses itimers without checking, we have
31332  * to use unsigned arithmetic).  */
31333 static unsigned long tvtojiffies(struct timeval *value)
31334 {
31335    unsigned long sec = (unsigned) value->tv_sec;
31336    unsigned long usec = (unsigned) value->tv_usec;
31337
31338    if (sec > (ULONG_MAX / HZ))
31339        return ULONG_MAX;
31340    usec += 1000000 / HZ - 1;
31341    usec /= 1000000 / HZ;
31342    return HZ * sec + usec;
```

```
31343 }
31344
31345 static void jiffiestotv(unsigned long jiffies,
31346     struct timeval *value)
31347 {
31348   value->tv_usec = (jiffies % HZ) * (1000000 / HZ);
31349   value->tv_sec = jiffies / HZ;
31350 }
31351
31352 int do_getitimer(int which, struct itimerval *value)
31353 {
31354   register unsigned long val, interval;
31355
31356   switch (which) {
31357   case ITIMER_REAL:
31358     interval = current->it_real_incr;
31359     val = 0;
31360     /* FIXME! This needs to be atomic, in case the kernel
31361      * timer happens!  */
31362     if (timer_pending(&current->real_timer)) {
31363       val = current->real_timer.expires - jiffies;
31364
31365       /* look out for negative/zero itimer.. */
31366       if ((long) val <= 0)
31367         val = 1;
31368     }
31369     break;
31370   case ITIMER_VIRTUAL:
31371     val = current->it_virt_value;
31372     interval = current->it_virt_incr;
31373     break;
31374   case ITIMER_PROF:
31375     val = current->it_prof_value;
31376     interval = current->it_prof_incr;
31377     break;
31378   default:
31379     return (-EINVAL);
31380   }
31381   jiffiestotv(val, &value->it_value);
31382   jiffiestotv(interval, &value->it_interval);
31383   return 0;
31384 }
31385
31386 /* SMP: Only we modify our itimer values. */
31387 asmlinkage long sys_getitimer(int which,
31388     struct itimerval *value)
31389 {
31390   int error = -EFAULT;
31391   struct itimerval get_buffer;
31392
31393   if (value) {
31394     error = do_getitimer(which, &get_buffer);
31395     if (!error && copy_to_user(value, &get_buffer,
31396                                 sizeof(get_buffer)))
31397       error = -EFAULT;
31398   }
31399   return error;
31400 }
31401
31402 void it_real_fn(unsigned long __data)
31403 {
31404   struct task_struct *p = (struct task_struct *) __data;
31405   unsigned long interval;
31406
31407   send_sig(SIGALRM, p, 1);
31408   interval = p->it_real_incr;
31409   if (interval) {
31410     if (interval > (unsigned long) LONG_MAX)
31411       interval = LONG_MAX;
31412     p->real_timer.expires = jiffies + interval;
31413     add_timer(&p->real_timer);
31414   }
31415 }
31416
31417 int do_setitimer(int which, struct itimerval *value,
31418     struct itimerval *ovalue)
31419 {
31420   register unsigned long i, j;
31421   int k;
31422
31423   i = tvtojiffies(&value->it_interval);
31424   j = tvtojiffies(&value->it_value);
31425   if (ovalue && (k = do_getitimer(which, ovalue)) < 0)
31426     return k;
31427   switch (which) {
31428   case ITIMER_REAL:
31429     del_timer_sync(&current->real_timer);
31430     current->it_real_value = j;
31431     current->it_real_incr = i;
31432     if (!j)
31433       break;
31434     if (j > (unsigned long) LONG_MAX)
31435       j = LONG_MAX;
31436     i = j + jiffies;
```

```
31437      current->real_timer.expires = i;
31438      add_timer(&current->real_timer);
31439      break;
31440    case ITIMER_VIRTUAL:
31441      if (j)
31442        j++;
31443      current->it_virt_value = j;
31444      current->it_virt_incr = i;
31445      break;
31446    case ITIMER_PROF:
31447      if (j)
31448        j++;
31449      current->it_prof_value = j;
31450      current->it_prof_incr = i;
31451      break;
31452    default:
31453      return -EINVAL;
31454    }
31455    return 0;
31456 }
31457
31458 /* SMP: Again, only we play with our itimers, and signals
31459  * are SMP safe now so that is not an issue at all
31460  * anymore. */
31461 asmlinkage long sys_setitimer(int which,
31462      struct itimerval *value, struct itimerval *ovalue)
31463 {
31464    struct itimerval set_buffer, get_buffer;
31465    int error;
31466
31467    if (value) {
31468      if (copy_from_user(&set_buffer, value,
31469                    sizeof(set_buffer)))
31470        return -EFAULT;
31471    } else
31472      memset((char *) &set_buffer, 0, sizeof(set_buffer));
31473
31474    error = do_setitimer(which, &set_buffer,
31475                    ovalue ? &get_buffer : 0);
31476    if (error || !ovalue)
31477      return error;
31478
31479    if (copy_to_user(ovalue, &get_buffer,
31480                    sizeof(get_buffer)))
31481      return -EFAULT;
31482    return 0;
31483 }
```

kernel/kmod.c

```
31484 /*
31485  * kmod, the new module loader (replaces kerneld) Kirk
31486  * Petersen
31487  *
31488  * Reorganized not to be a daemon by Adam Richter, with
31489  * guidance from Greg Zornetzer.
31490  *
31491  * Modified to avoid chroot and file sharing problems.
31492  * Mikael Pettersson
31493  *
31494  * Limit the concurrent number of kmod modprobes to
31495  * catch loops from "modprobe needs a service that is in
31496  * a module". Keith Owens <kaos@ocs.com.au> December
31497  * 1999
31498  *
31499  * Unblock all signals when we exec a usermode process.
31500  * Shuu Yamaguchi <shuu@wondernetworkresources.com>
31501  * December 2000
31502  */
31503
31504 #define __KERNEL_SYSCALLS__
31505
31506 #include <linux/config.h>
31507 #include <linux/module.h>
31508 #include <linux/sched.h>
31509 #include <linux/unistd.h>
31510 #include <linux/kmod.h>
31511 #include <linux/smp_lock.h>
31512
31513 #include <asm/uaccess.h>
31514
31515 extern int max_threads;
31516
31517 static inline void use_init_fs_context(void)
31518 {
31519    struct fs_struct *our_fs, *init_fs;
31520    struct dentry *root, *pwd;
31521    struct vfsmount *rootmnt, *pwdmnt;
31522
31523    /* Make modprobe's fs context be a copy of init's.
31524     *
31525     * We cannot use the user's fs context, because it may
31526     * have a different root than init.  Since init was
31527     * created with CLONE_FS, we can grab its fs context
31528     * from "init_task".
31529     *
```

```
31530     * The fs context has to be a copy. If it is shared
31531     * with init, then any chdir() call in modprobe will
31532     * also affect init and the other threads sharing
31533     * init_task's fs context.
31534     *
31535     * We created the exec_modprobe thread without
31536     * CLONE_FS, so we can update the fields in our fs
31537     * context freely.  */
31538
31539     init_fs = init_task.fs;
31540     read_lock(&init_fs->lock);
31541     rootmnt = mntget(init_fs->rootmnt);
31542     root = dget(init_fs->root);
31543     pwdmnt = mntget(init_fs->pwdmnt);
31544     pwd = dget(init_fs->pwd);
31545     read_unlock(&init_fs->lock);
31546
31547     /* FIXME - unsafe ->fs access */
31548     our_fs = current->fs;
31549     our_fs->umask = init_fs->umask;
31550     set_fs_root(our_fs, rootmnt, root);
31551     set_fs_pwd(our_fs, pwdmnt, pwd);
31552     write_lock(&our_fs->lock);
31553     if (our_fs->altroot) {
31554       struct vfsmount *mnt = our_fs->altrootmnt;
31555       struct dentry *dentry = our_fs->altroot;
31556       our_fs->altrootmnt = NULL;
31557       our_fs->altroot = NULL;
31558       write_unlock(&our_fs->lock);
31559       dput(dentry);
31560       mntput(mnt);
31561     } else
31562       write_unlock(&our_fs->lock);
31563     dput(root);
31564     mntput(rootmnt);
31565     dput(pwd);
31566     mntput(pwdmnt);
31567 }
31568
31569 int exec_usermodehelper(char *program_path, char *argv[],
31570     char *envp[])
31571 {
31572   int i;
31573   struct task_struct *curtask = current;
31574
31575   curtask->session = 1;
31576   curtask->pgrp = 1;
```

```
31577
31578   use_init_fs_context();
31579
31580   /* Prevent parent user process from sending signals to
31581    * child. Otherwise, if the modprobe program does not
31582    * exist, it might be possible to get a user defined
31583    * signal handler to execute as the super user right
31584    * after the execve fails if you time the signal just
31585    * right. */
31586   spin_lock_irq(&curtask->sigmask_lock);
31587   sigemptyset(&curtask->blocked);
31588   flush_signals(curtask);
31589   flush_signal_handlers(curtask);
31590   recalc_sigpending(curtask);
31591   spin_unlock_irq(&curtask->sigmask_lock);
31592
31593   for (i = 0; i < curtask->files->max_fds; i++) {
31594     if (curtask->files->fd[i])
31595       close(i);
31596   }
31597
31598   /* Drop the "current user" thing */
31599   {
31600     struct user_struct *user = curtask->user;
31601     curtask->user = INIT_USER;
31602     atomic_inc(&INIT_USER->__count);
31603     atomic_inc(&INIT_USER->processes);
31604     atomic_dec(&user->processes);
31605     free_uid(user);
31606   }
31607
31608   /* Give kmod all effective privileges.. */
31609   curtask->euid = curtask->fsuid = 0;
31610   curtask->egid = curtask->fsgid = 0;
31611   cap_set_full(curtask->cap_effective);
31612
31613   /* Allow execve args to be in kernel space. */
31614   set_fs(KERNEL_DS);
31615
31616   /* Go, go, go... */
31617   if (execve(program_path, argv, envp) < 0)
31618     return -errno;
31619   return 0;
31620 }
31621
31622 #ifdef CONFIG_KMOD
31623
```

```
31624 /* modprobe_path is set via /proc/sys. */
31625 char modprobe_path[256] = "/sbin/modprobe";
31626
31627 static int exec_modprobe(void *module_name)
31628 {
31629   static char *envp[] =
31630   { "HOME=/", "TERM=linux",
31631     "PATH=/sbin:/usr/sbin:/bin:/usr/bin", NULL };
31632   char *argv[] =
31633   { modprobe_path, "-s", "-k", "-",
31634     (char *) module_name, NULL };
31635   int ret;
31636
31637   ret = exec_usermodehelper(modprobe_path, argv, envp);
31638   if (ret) {
31639     printk(KERN_ERR
31640       "kmod: failed to exec %s -s -k %s, errno = %d\n",
31641       modprobe_path, (char *) module_name, errno);
31642   }
31643   return ret;
31644 }
31645
31646 /**
31647  *      request_module - try to load a kernel module
31648  *      @module_name: Name of module
31649  *
31650  * Load a module using the user mode module loader. The
31651  * function returns zero on success or a negative errno
31652  * code on failure. Note that a successful module load
31653  * does not mean the module did not then unload and exit
31654  * on an error of its own. Callers must check that the
31655  * service they requested is now available not blindly
31656  * invoke it.
31657  *
31658  * If module auto-loading support is disabled then this
31659  * function becomes a no-operation.  */
31660 int request_module(const char *module_name)
31661 {
31662   pid_t pid;
31663   int waitpid_result;
31664   sigset_t tmpsig;
31665   int i;
31666   static atomic_t kmod_concurrent = ATOMIC_INIT(0);
31667 #define MAX_KMOD_CONCURRENT 50   /* Completely arbitrary
31668                                   * value - KAO */
31669   static int kmod_loop_msg;
31670
31671   /* Don't allow request_module() before the root fs is
31672    * mounted!  */
31673   if (!current->fs->root) {
31674     printk(KERN_ERR
31675       "request_module[%s]: Root fs not mounted\n",
31676       module_name);
31677     return -EPERM;
31678   }
31679
31680   /* If modprobe needs a service that is in a module, we
31681    * get a recursive loop.  Limit the number of running
31682    * kmod threads to max_threads/2 or
31683    * MAX_KMOD_CONCURRENT, whichever is the smaller.  A
31684    * cleaner method would be to run the parents of this
31685    * process, counting how many times kmod was invoked.
31686    * That would mean accessing the internals of the
31687    * process tables to get the command line,
31688    * proc_pid_cmdline is static and it is not worth
31689    * changing the proc code just to handle this case.
31690    *
31691    * KAO. */
31692   i = max_threads / 2;
31693   if (i > MAX_KMOD_CONCURRENT)
31694     i = MAX_KMOD_CONCURRENT;
31695   atomic_inc(&kmod_concurrent);
31696   if (atomic_read(&kmod_concurrent) > i) {
31697     if (kmod_loop_msg++ < 5)
31698       printk(KERN_ERR "kmod: runaway modprobe loop "
31699             "assumed and stopped\n");
31700     atomic_dec(&kmod_concurrent);
31701     return -ENOMEM;
31702   }
31703
31704   pid = kernel_thread(exec_modprobe,
31705                 (void *) module_name, 0);
31706   if (pid < 0) {
31707     printk(KERN_ERR
31708       "request_module[%s]: fork failed, errno %d\n",
31709       module_name, -pid);
31710     atomic_dec(&kmod_concurrent);
31711     return pid;
31712   }
31713
31714   /* Block everything but SIGKILL/SIGSTOP */
31715   spin_lock_irq(&current->sigmask_lock);
31716   tmpsig = current->blocked;
31717   siginitsetinv(&current->blocked,
```

```
31718       sigmask(SIGKILL) | sigmask(SIGSTOP));
31719   recalc_sigpending(current);
31720   spin_unlock_irq(&current->sigmask_lock);
31721
31722   waitpid_result = waitpid(pid, NULL, __WCLONE);
31723   atomic_dec(&kmod_concurrent);
31724
31725   /* Allow signals again.. */
31726   spin_lock_irq(&current->sigmask_lock);
31727   current->blocked = tmpsig;
31728   recalc_sigpending(current);
31729   spin_unlock_irq(&current->sigmask_lock);
31730
31731   if (waitpid_result != pid) {
31732     printk(KERN_ERR "request_module[%s]: waitpid(%d,...)"
31733           " failed, errno %d\n",
31734           module_name, pid, -waitpid_result);
31735   }
31736   return 0;
31737 }
31738 #endif                              /* CONFIG_KMOD */
31739
31740
31741 #ifdef CONFIG_HOTPLUG
31742 /* hotplug path is set via /proc/sys invoked by
31743  * hotplug-aware bus drivers, with exec_usermodehelper
31744  * and some thread-spawner
31745  *
31746  * argv [0] = hotplug_path; argv [1] = "usb", "scsi",
31747  * "pci", "network", etc; ... plus optional
31748  * type-specific parameters argv [n] = 0;
31749  *
31750  * envp [*] = HOME, PATH; optional type-specific
31751  * parameters
31752  *
31753  * a hotplug bus should invoke this for device
31754  * add/remove events.  the command is expected to load
31755  * drivers when necessary, and may perform additional
31756  * system setup. */
31757 char hotplug_path[256] = "/sbin/hotplug";
31758
31759 EXPORT_SYMBOL(hotplug_path);
31760
31761 #endif                              /* CONFIG_HOTPLUG */
31762
31763 struct subprocess_info {
31764   struct semaphore *sem;
31765   char *path;
31766   char **argv;
31767   char **envp;
31768   pid_t retval;
31769 };
31770
31771 /* This is the task which runs the usermode application
31772  */
31773 static int ____call_usermodehelper(void *data)
31774 {
31775   struct subprocess_info *sub_info = data;
31776   int retval;
31777
31778   retval = -EPERM;
31779   if (current->fs->root)
31780     retval = exec_usermodehelper(sub_info->path,
31781                           sub_info->argv,
31782                           sub_info->envp);
31783
31784   /* Exec failed? */
31785   sub_info->retval = (pid_t) retval;
31786   do_exit(0);
31787 }
31788
31789 /* This is run by keventd.  */
31790 static void __call_usermodehelper(void *data)
31791 {
31792   struct subprocess_info *sub_info = data;
31793   pid_t pid;
31794
31795   /* CLONE_VFORK: wait until the usermode helper has
31796    * execve'd successfully We need the data structures to
31797    * stay around until that is done.  */
31798   pid = kernel_thread(____call_usermodehelper, sub_info,
31799                 CLONE_VFORK | SIGCHLD);
31800   if (pid < 0)
31801     sub_info->retval = pid;
31802   up(sub_info->sem);
31803 }
31804
31805 /**
31806  * call_usermodehelper - start a usermode application
31807  * @path: pathname for the application
31808  * @argv: null-terminated argument list
31809  * @envp: null-terminated environment list
31810  *
31811  * Runs a user-space application.  The application is
```

```
31812    * started asynchronously.  It runs as a child of
31813    * keventd.  It runs with full root capabilities.
31814    * keventd silently reaps the child when it exits.
31815    *
31816    * Must be called from process context.  Returns zero on
31817    * success, else a negative error code.  */
31818   int call_usermodehelper(char *path, char **argv,
31819        char **envp)
31820   {
31821     DECLARE_MUTEX_LOCKED(sem);
31822     struct subprocess_info sub_info = {
31823       sem:     &sem,
31824       path:    path,
31825       argv:    argv,
31826       envp:    envp,
31827       retval:  0,
31828     };
31829     struct tq_struct tqs = {
31830       routine: __call_usermodehelper,
31831       data:    &sub_info,
31832     };
31833
31834     if (path[0] == '\0')
31835       goto out;
31836
31837     if (current_is_keventd()) {
31838       /* We can't wait on keventd! */
31839       __call_usermodehelper(&sub_info);
31840     } else {
31841       schedule_task(&tqs);
31842       down(&sem); /* Wait until keventd has started the
31843                    * subprocess */
31844     }
31845   out:
31846     return sub_info.retval;
31847   }
31848
31849   /* This is for the serialisation of device probe()
31850    * functions against device open() functions */
31851   static DECLARE_MUTEX(dev_probe_sem);
31852
31853   void dev_probe_lock(void)
31854   {
31855     down(&dev_probe_sem);
31856   }
31857
31858   void dev_probe_unlock(void)
31859   {
31860     up(&dev_probe_sem);
31861   }
31862
31863   EXPORT_SYMBOL(exec_usermodehelper);
31864   EXPORT_SYMBOL(call_usermodehelper);
31865
31866   #ifdef CONFIG_KMOD
31867   EXPORT_SYMBOL(request_module);
31868   #endif
```

kernel/module.c

```
31869   #include <linux/config.h>
31870   #include <linux/mm.h>
31871   #include <linux/module.h>
31872   #include <asm/module.h>
31873   #include <asm/uaccess.h>
31874   #include <linux/vmalloc.h>
31875   #include <linux/smp_lock.h>
31876   #include <asm/pgalloc.h>
31877   #include <linux/init.h>
31878   #include <linux/slab.h>
31879   #include <linux/kmod.h>
31880
31881   /*
31882    * Originally by Anonymous (as far as I know...)
31883    * Linux version by Bas Laarhoven <bas@vimec.nl>
31884    * 0.99.14 version by Jon Tombs <jon@gtex02.us.es>,
31885    * Heavily modified by Bjorn Ekwall <bj0rn@blox.se> May
31886    * 1994 (C)
31887    * Rewritten by Richard Henderson <rth@tamu.edu> Dec 1996
31888    * Add MOD_INITIALIZING Keith Owens <kaos@ocs.com.au> Nov
31889    * 1999
31890    * Add kallsyms support, Keith Owens <kaos@ocs.com.au>
31891    * Apr 2000
31892    * Add asm/module support, IA64 has special requirements.
31893    * Keith Owens <kaos@ocs.com.au> Sep 2000
31894    * Fix assorted bugs in module verification.  Keith Owens
31895    * <kaos@ocs.com.au> Sep 2000
31896    * Fix sys_init_module race, Andrew Morton
31897    * <andrewm@uow.edu.au> Oct 2000
31898    * http://www.uwsg.iu.edu/hypermail/linux/kernel/0008.3/
31899    * 0379.html
31900    * Replace xxx_module_symbol with inter_module_xxx.
31901    * Keith Owens <kaos@ocs.com.au> Oct 2000
31902    *
31903    * This source is covered by the GNU GPL, the same as all
```

```
31904  * kernel sources.
31905  */
31906
31907 #if defined(CONFIG_MODULES) || defined(CONFIG_KALLSYMS)
31908
31909 extern struct module_symbol __start___ksymtab[];
31910 extern struct module_symbol __stop___ksymtab[];
31911
31912 extern const struct exception_table_entry
31913     __start___ex_table[];
31914 extern const struct exception_table_entry
31915     __stop___ex_table[];
31916
31917 extern const char __start___kallsyms[]
31918     __attribute__ ((weak));
31919 extern const char __stop___kallsyms[]
31920     __attribute__ ((weak));
31921
31922 static struct module kernel_module = {
31923   size_of_struct:   sizeof(struct module),
31924   name:             "",
31925   uc:               { ATOMIC_INIT(1) },
31926   flags:            MOD_RUNNING,
31927   syms:             __start___ksymtab,
31928   ex_table_start:   __start___ex_table,
31929   ex_table_end:     __stop___ex_table,
31930   kallsyms_start:   __start___kallsyms,
31931   kallsyms_end:     __stop___kallsyms,
31932 };
31933
31934 struct module *module_list = &kernel_module;
31935
31936 #endif /* defined(CONFIG_MODULES) ||
31937         * defined(CONFIG_KALLSYMS) */
31938
31939 /* inter_module functions are always available, even when
31940  * the kernel is compiled without modules.  Consumers of
31941  * inter_module_xxx routines will always work, even when
31942  * both are built into the kernel, this approach removes
31943  * lots of #ifdefs in mainline code. */
31944
31945 static struct list_head ime_list =
31946   LIST_HEAD_INIT(ime_list);
31947 static spinlock_t ime_lock = SPIN_LOCK_UNLOCKED;
31948 static int kmalloc_failed;
31949
31950 /**
```

```
31951  * inter_module_register - register a new set of inter
31952  * module data.
31953  * @im_name: an arbitrary string to identify the data,
31954  * must be unique
31955  * @owner: module that is registering the data, always
31956  * use THIS_MODULE
31957  * @userdata: pointer to arbitrary userdata to be
31958  * registered
31959  *
31960  * Description: Check that the im_name has not already
31961  * been registered, complain if it has.  For new data,
31962  * add it to the inter_module_entry list.  */
31963 void inter_module_register(const char *im_name,
31964     struct module *owner, const void *userdata)
31965 {
31966   struct list_head *tmp;
31967   struct inter_module_entry *ime, *ime_new;
31968
31969   if (!(ime_new = kmalloc(sizeof(*ime), GFP_KERNEL))) {
31970     /* Overloaded kernel, not fatal */
31971     printk(KERN_ERR
31972         "Aiee, inter_module_register: "
31973         "cannot kmalloc entry for '%s'\n", im_name);
31974     kmalloc_failed = 1;
31975     return;
31976   }
31977   memset(ime_new, 0, sizeof(*ime_new));
31978   ime_new->im_name = im_name;
31979   ime_new->owner = owner;
31980   ime_new->userdata = userdata;
31981
31982   spin_lock(&ime_lock);
31983   list_for_each(tmp, &ime_list) {
31984     ime =
31985       list_entry(tmp, struct inter_module_entry, list);
31986     if (strcmp(ime->im_name, im_name) == 0) {
31987       spin_unlock(&ime_lock);
31988       kfree(ime_new);
31989       /* Program logic error, fatal */
31990       printk(KERN_ERR "inter_module_register: "
31991             "duplicate im_name '%s'", im_name);
31992       BUG();
31993     }
31994   }
31995   list_add(&(ime_new->list), &ime_list);
31996   spin_unlock(&ime_lock);
31997 }
```

```
31998
31999 /**
32000  * inter_module_unregister - unregister a set of inter
32001  * module data.
32002  * @im_name: an arbitrary string to identify the data,
32003  * must be unique
32004  *
32005  * Description: Check that the im_name has been
32006  * registered, complain if it has not.  For existing
32007  * data, remove it from the inter_module_entry list.  */
32008 void inter_module_unregister(const char *im_name)
32009 {
32010    struct list_head *tmp;
32011    struct inter_module_entry *ime;
32012
32013    spin_lock(&ime_lock);
32014    list_for_each(tmp, &ime_list) {
32015      ime =
32016          list_entry(tmp, struct inter_module_entry, list);
32017      if (strcmp(ime->im_name, im_name) == 0) {
32018        list_del(&(ime->list));
32019        spin_unlock(&ime_lock);
32020        kfree(ime);
32021        return;
32022      }
32023    }
32024    spin_unlock(&ime_lock);
32025    if (kmalloc_failed) {
32026      printk(KERN_ERR
32027          "inter_module_unregister: no entry for '%s', "
32028          "probably caused by previous kmalloc failure\n",
32029          im_name);
32030      return;
32031    } else {
32032      /* Program logic error, fatal */
32033      printk(KERN_ERR
32034          "inter_module_unregister: no entry for '%s'",
32035          im_name);
32036      BUG();
32037    }
32038 }
32039
32040 /**
32041  * inter_module_get - return arbitrary userdata from
32042  * another module.
32043  * @im_name: an arbitrary string to identify the data,
32044  * must be unique
32045  *
32046  * Description: If the im_name has not been registered,
32047  * return NULL.  Try to increment the use count on the
32048  * owning module, if that fails then return NULL.
32049  * Otherwise return the userdata.  */
32050 const void *inter_module_get(const char *im_name)
32051 {
32052    struct list_head *tmp;
32053    struct inter_module_entry *ime;
32054    const void *result = NULL;
32055
32056    spin_lock(&ime_lock);
32057    list_for_each(tmp, &ime_list) {
32058      ime =
32059          list_entry(tmp, struct inter_module_entry, list);
32060      if (strcmp(ime->im_name, im_name) == 0) {
32061        if (try_inc_mod_count(ime->owner))
32062          result = ime->userdata;
32063        break;
32064      }
32065    }
32066    spin_unlock(&ime_lock);
32067    return (result);
32068 }
32069
32070 /**
32071  * inter_module_get_request - im get with automatic
32072  * request_module.
32073  * @im_name: an arbitrary string to identify the data,
32074  * must be unique
32075  * @modname: module that is expected to register im_name
32076  *
32077  * Description: If inter_module_get fails, do
32078  * request_module then retry.  */
32079 const void *inter_module_get_request(const char *im_name,
32080      const char *modname)
32081 {
32082    const void *result = inter_module_get(im_name);
32083    if (!result) {
32084      request_module(modname);
32085      result = inter_module_get(im_name);
32086    }
32087    return (result);
32088 }
32089
32090 /**
32091  * inter_module_put - release use of data from another
```

```
32092  * module.
32093  * @im_name: an arbitrary string to identify the data,
32094  * must be unique
32095  *
32096  * Description: If the im_name has not been registered,
32097  * complain, otherwise decrement the use count on the
32098  * owning module.  */
32099  void inter_module_put(const char *im_name)
32100  {
32101    struct list_head *tmp;
32102    struct inter_module_entry *ime;
32103
32104    spin_lock(&ime_lock);
32105    list_for_each(tmp, &ime_list) {
32106      ime =
32107          list_entry(tmp, struct inter_module_entry, list);
32108      if (strcmp(ime->im_name, im_name) == 0) {
32109        if (ime->owner)
32110          __MOD_DEC_USE_COUNT(ime->owner);
32111        spin_unlock(&ime_lock);
32112        return;
32113      }
32114    }
32115    spin_unlock(&ime_lock);
32116    printk(KERN_ERR "inter_module_put: no entry for '%s'",
32117        im_name);
32118    BUG();
32119  }
32120
32121
32122  #if defined(CONFIG_MODULES)   /* The rest of the source */
32123
32124  static long get_mod_name(const char *user_name,
32125      char **buf);
32126  static void put_mod_name(char *buf);
32127  struct module *find_module(const char *name);
32128  void free_module(struct module *, int tag_freed);
32129
32130
32131  /* Called at boot time */
32132  void __init init_modules(void)
32133  {
32134    kernel_module.nsyms =
32135        __stop___ksymtab - __start___ksymtab;
32136
32137  #ifdef __alpha__
32138    __asm__("stq $29,%0":"=m"(kernel_module.gp));
```

```
32139  #endif
32140  }
32141
32142  /* Copy the name of a module from user space.  */
32143  static inline long
32144  get_mod_name(const char *user_name, char **buf)
32145  {
32146    unsigned long page;
32147    long retval;
32148
32149    page = __get_free_page(GFP_KERNEL);
32150    if (!page)
32151      return -ENOMEM;
32152
32153    retval = strncpy_from_user((char *) page, user_name,
32154                        PAGE_SIZE);
32155    if (retval > 0) {
32156      if (retval < PAGE_SIZE) {
32157        *buf = (char *) page;
32158        return retval;
32159      }
32160      retval = -ENAMETOOLONG;
32161    } else if (!retval)
32162      retval = -EINVAL;
32163
32164    free_page(page);
32165    return retval;
32166  }
32167
32168  static inline void put_mod_name(char *buf)
32169  {
32170    free_page((unsigned long) buf);
32171  }
32172
32173  /* Allocate space for a module.  */
32174  asmlinkage unsigned long
32175  sys_create_module(const char *name_user, size_t size)
32176  {
32177    char *name;
32178    long namelen, error;
32179    struct module *mod;
32180
32181    if (!capable(CAP_SYS_MODULE))
32182      return -EPERM;
32183    lock_kernel();
32184    if ((namelen = get_mod_name(name_user, &name)) < 0) {
32185      error = namelen;
```

```
32186        goto err0;
32187    }
32188    if (size < sizeof(struct module) + namelen) {
32189        error = -EINVAL;
32190        goto err1;
32191    }
32192    if (find_module(name) != NULL) {
32193        error = -EEXIST;
32194        goto err1;
32195    }
32196    if((mod = (struct module *)module_map(size)) == NULL) {
32197        error = -ENOMEM;
32198        goto err1;
32199    }
32200
32201    memset(mod, 0, sizeof(*mod));
32202    mod->size_of_struct = sizeof(*mod);
32203    mod->next = module_list;
32204    mod->name = (char *) (mod + 1);
32205    mod->size = size;
32206    memcpy((char *) (mod + 1), name, namelen + 1);
32207
32208    put_mod_name(name);
32209
32210    module_list = mod;                /* link it in */
32211
32212    error = (long) mod;
32213    goto err0;
32214 err1:
32215    put_mod_name(name);
32216 err0:
32217    unlock_kernel();
32218    return error;
32219 }
32220
32221 /* Initialize a module.  */
32222 asmlinkage long
32223 sys_init_module(const char *name_user,
32224 struct module *mod_user)
32225 {
32226    struct module mod_tmp, *mod;
32227    char *name, *n_name, *name_tmp = NULL;
32228    long namelen, n_namelen, i, error;
32229    unsigned long mod_user_size;
32230    struct module_ref *dep;
32231
32232    if (!capable(CAP_SYS_MODULE))
```

```
32233        return -EPERM;
32234    lock_kernel();
32235    if ((namelen = get_mod_name(name_user, &name)) < 0) {
32236        error = namelen;
32237        goto err0;
32238    }
32239    if ((mod = find_module(name)) == NULL) {
32240        error = -ENOENT;
32241        goto err1;
32242    }
32243
32244    /* Check module header size.  We allow a bit of slop
32245     * over the size we are familiar with to cope with a
32246     * version of insmod for a newer kernel.  But don't
32247     * over do it. */
32248    if ((error = get_user(mod_user_size,
32249                      &mod_user->size_of_struct)) != 0)
32250        goto err1;
32251    if (mod_user_size < (unsigned long)
32252            &((struct module *) 0L)->persist_start
32253        || mod_user_size >
32254            sizeof(struct module) + 16 * sizeof(void *)) {
32255        printk(KERN_ERR
32256            "init_module: Invalid module header size.\n"
32257            KERN_ERR
32258            "A new version of the modutils is likely "
32259            "needed.\n");
32260        error = -EINVAL;
32261        goto err1;
32262    }
32263
32264    /* Hold the current contents while we play with the
32265     * user's idea of righteousness.  */
32266    mod_tmp = *mod;
32267    /* Where's kstrdup()?  */
32268    name_tmp = kmalloc(strlen(mod->name) + 1, GFP_KERNEL);
32269    if (name_tmp == NULL) {
32270        error = -ENOMEM;
32271        goto err1;
32272    }
32273    strcpy(name_tmp, mod->name);
32274
32275    error = copy_from_user(mod, mod_user, mod_user_size);
32276    if (error) {
32277        error = -EFAULT;
32278        goto err2;
32279    }
```

```
32280
32281    /* Sanity check the size of the module.  */
32282    error = -EINVAL;
32283
32284    if (mod->size > mod_tmp.size) {
32285      printk(KERN_ERR
32286          "init_module: Size of initialized module "
32287          "exceeds size of created module.\n");
32288      goto err2;
32289    }
32290
32291    /* Make sure all interesting pointers are sane.  */
32292
32293    if (!mod_bound(mod->name, namelen, mod)) {
32294      printk(KERN_ERR
32295          "init_module: mod->name out of bounds.\n");
32296      goto err2;
32297    }
32298    if (mod->nsyms
32299        && !mod_bound(mod->syms, mod->nsyms, mod)) {
32300      printk(KERN_ERR
32301          "init_module: mod->syms out of bounds.\n");
32302      goto err2;
32303    }
32304    if (mod->ndeps
32305        && !mod_bound(mod->deps, mod->ndeps, mod)) {
32306      printk(KERN_ERR
32307          "init_module: mod->deps out of bounds.\n");
32308      goto err2;
32309    }
32310    if (mod->init && !mod_bound(mod->init, 0, mod)) {
32311      printk(KERN_ERR
32312          "init_module: mod->init out of bounds.\n");
32313      goto err2;
32314    }
32315    if (mod->cleanup && !mod_bound(mod->cleanup, 0, mod)) {
32316      printk(KERN_ERR
32317          "init_module: mod->cleanup out of bounds.\n");
32318      goto err2;
32319    }
32320    if (mod->ex_table_start > mod->ex_table_end
32321        || (mod->ex_table_start &&
32322          !((unsigned long) mod->ex_table_start >=
32323              ((unsigned long) mod + mod->size_of_struct)
32324            && ((unsigned long) mod->ex_table_end <
32325                (unsigned long) mod + mod->size)))
32326        || (((unsigned long) mod->ex_table_start -
32327              (unsigned long) mod->ex_table_end)
32328            % sizeof(struct exception_table_entry))) {
32329      printk(KERN_ERR
32330          "init_module: mod->ex_table_* invalid.\n");
32331      goto err2;
32332    }
32333    if (mod->flags & ~MOD_AUTOCLEAN) {
32334      printk(KERN_ERR
32335          "init_module: mod->flags invalid.\n");
32336      goto err2;
32337    }
32338 #ifdef __alpha__
32339    if (!mod_bound(mod->gp - 0x8000, 0, mod)) {
32340      printk(KERN_ERR
32341          "init_module: mod->gp out of bounds.\n");
32342      goto err2;
32343    }
32344 #endif
32345    if (mod_member_present(mod, can_unload)
32346        && mod->can_unload
32347        && !mod_bound(mod->can_unload, 0, mod)) {
32348      printk(KERN_ERR
32349          "init_module: mod->can_unload out of bounds.\n");
32350      goto err2;
32351    }
32352    if (mod_member_present(mod, kallsyms_end)) {
32353      if (mod->kallsyms_end &&
32354          (!mod_bound(mod->kallsyms_start, 0, mod) ||
32355            !mod_bound(mod->kallsyms_end, 0, mod))) {
32356        printk(KERN_ERR
32357            "init_module: mod->kallsyms out of bounds.\n");
32358        goto err2;
32359      }
32360      if (mod->kallsyms_start > mod->kallsyms_end) {
32361        printk(KERN_ERR
32362            "init_module: mod->kallsyms invalid.\n");
32363        goto err2;
32364      }
32365    }
32366    if (mod_member_present(mod, archdata_end)) {
32367      if (mod->archdata_end &&
32368          (!mod_bound(mod->archdata_start, 0, mod) ||
32369            !mod_bound(mod->archdata_end, 0, mod))) {
32370        printk(KERN_ERR
32371            "init_module: mod->archdata out of bounds.\n");
32372        goto err2;
32373      }
```

```
32374        if (mod->archdata_start > mod->archdata_end) {
32375            printk(KERN_ERR
32376                "init_module: mod->archdata invalid.\n");
32377            goto err2;
32378        }
32379    }
32380    if (mod_member_present(mod, kernel_data)
32381        && mod->kernel_data) {
32382        printk(KERN_ERR
32383            "init_module: mod->kernel_data must be zero.\n");
32384        goto err2;
32385    }
32386
32387    /* Check that the user isn't doing something silly
32388     * with the name.  */
32389
32390    if ((n_namelen =
32391            get_mod_name(mod->name - (unsigned long) mod +
32392                (unsigned long) mod_user, &n_name)) < 0) {
32393        printk(KERN_ERR
32394            "init_module: get_mod_name failure.\n");
32395        error = n_namelen;
32396        goto err2;
32397    }
32398    if (namelen != n_namelen
32399        || strcmp(n_name, mod_tmp.name) != 0) {
32400        printk(KERN_ERR
32401            "init_module: changed module name to "
32402            "`%s' from `%s'\n", n_name, mod_tmp.name);
32403        goto err3;
32404    }
32405
32406    /* Ok, that's about all the sanity we can stomach;
32407     * copy the rest.  */
32408
32409    if (copy_from_user((char *) mod + mod_user_size,
32410            (char *) mod_user + mod_user_size,
32411            mod->size - mod_user_size)) {
32412        error = -EFAULT;
32413        goto err3;
32414    }
32415
32416    if (module_arch_init(mod))
32417        goto err3;
32418
32419    /* On some machines it is necessary to do something
32420     * here to make the I and D caches consistent.  */
```

```
32421    flush_icache_range((unsigned long) mod,
32422                        (unsigned long) mod + mod->size);
32423
32424    mod->next = mod_tmp.next;
32425    mod->refs = NULL;
32426
32427    /* Sanity check the module's dependents */
32428    for (i = 0, dep = mod->deps; i < mod->ndeps;
32429        ++i, ++dep) {
32430        struct module *o, *d = dep->dep;
32431
32432        /* Make sure the indicated dependencies are really
32433         * modules.  */
32434        if (d == mod) {
32435            printk(KERN_ERR "init_module: self-referential "
32436                "dependency in mod->deps.\n");
32437            goto err3;
32438        }
32439
32440        /* Scan the current modules for this dependency */
32441        for (o = module_list; o != &kernel_module && o != d;
32442            o = o->next) ;
32443
32444        if (o != d) {
32445            printk(KERN_ERR
32446                "init_module: found dependency that is "
32447                "(no longer?) a module.\n");
32448            goto err3;
32449        }
32450    }
32451
32452    /* Update module references.  */
32453    for (i = 0, dep = mod->deps; i < mod->ndeps;
32454        ++i, ++dep) {
32455        struct module *d = dep->dep;
32456
32457        dep->ref = mod;
32458        dep->next_ref = d->refs;
32459        d->refs = dep;
32460        /* Being referenced by a dependent module counts as
32461         * a use as far as kmod is concerned.  */
32462        d->flags |= MOD_USED_ONCE;
32463    }
32464
32465    /* Free our temporary memory.  */
32466    put_mod_name(n_name);
32467    put_mod_name(name);
```

```
32468
32469    /* Initialize the module.  */
32470    mod->flags |= MOD_INITIALIZING;
32471    atomic_set(&mod->uc.usecount, 1);
32472    if (mod->init && (error = mod->init()) != 0) {
32473      atomic_set(&mod->uc.usecount, 0);
32474      mod->flags &= ~MOD_INITIALIZING;
32475      if (error > 0)                    /* Buggy module */
32476        error = -EBUSY;
32477      goto err0;
32478    }
32479    atomic_dec(&mod->uc.usecount);
32480
32481    /* And set it running.  */
32482    mod->flags =
32483        (mod->flags | MOD_RUNNING) & ~MOD_INITIALIZING;
32484    error = 0;
32485    goto err0;
32486
32487 err3:
32488    put_mod_name(n_name);
32489 err2:
32490    *mod = mod_tmp;
32491    /* We know there is room for this */
32492    strcpy((char *) mod->name, name_tmp);
32493 err1:
32494    put_mod_name(name);
32495 err0:
32496    unlock_kernel();
32497    kfree(name_tmp);
32498    return error;
32499 }
32500
32501 static spinlock_t unload_lock = SPIN_LOCK_UNLOCKED;
32502 int try_inc_mod_count(struct module *mod)
32503 {
32504    int res = 1;
32505    if (mod) {
32506      spin_lock(&unload_lock);
32507      if (mod->flags & MOD_DELETED)
32508        res = 0;
32509      else
32510        __MOD_INC_USE_COUNT(mod);
32511      spin_unlock(&unload_lock);
32512    }
32513    return res;
32514 }
```

```
32515
32516 asmlinkage long sys_delete_module(const char *name_user)
32517 {
32518    struct module *mod, *next;
32519    char *name;
32520    long error;
32521    int something_changed;
32522
32523    if (!capable(CAP_SYS_MODULE))
32524      return -EPERM;
32525
32526    lock_kernel();
32527    if (name_user) {
32528      if ((error = get_mod_name(name_user, &name)) < 0)
32529        goto out;
32530      if (error == 0) {
32531        error = -EINVAL;
32532        put_mod_name(name);
32533        goto out;
32534      }
32535      error = -ENOENT;
32536      if ((mod = find_module(name)) == NULL) {
32537        put_mod_name(name);
32538        goto out;
32539      }
32540      put_mod_name(name);
32541      error = -EBUSY;
32542      if (mod->refs != NULL)
32543        goto out;
32544
32545      spin_lock(&unload_lock);
32546      if (!__MOD_IN_USE(mod)) {
32547        mod->flags |= MOD_DELETED;
32548        spin_unlock(&unload_lock);
32549        free_module(mod, 0);
32550        error = 0;
32551      } else {
32552        spin_unlock(&unload_lock);
32553      }
32554      goto out;
32555    }
32556
32557    /* Do automatic reaping */
32558 restart:
32559    something_changed = 0;
32560    for (mod = module_list; mod != &kernel_module;
32561         mod = next) {
```

```
32562      next = mod->next;
32563      spin_lock(&unload_lock);
32564      if (mod->refs == NULL && (mod->flags & MOD_AUTOCLEAN)
32565          && (mod->flags & MOD_RUNNING)
32566          && !(mod->flags & MOD_DELETED)
32567          && (mod->flags & MOD_USED_ONCE)
32568          && !__MOD_IN_USE(mod)) {
32569        if ((mod->flags & MOD_VISITED)
32570            && !(mod->flags & MOD_JUST_FREED)) {
32571          spin_unlock(&unload_lock);
32572          mod->flags &= ~MOD_VISITED;
32573        } else {
32574          mod->flags |= MOD_DELETED;
32575          spin_unlock(&unload_lock);
32576          free_module(mod, 1);
32577          something_changed = 1;
32578        }
32579      } else {
32580        spin_unlock(&unload_lock);
32581      }
32582    }
32583    if (something_changed)
32584      goto restart;
32585    for (mod = module_list; mod != &kernel_module;
32586         mod = mod->next) mod->flags &= ~MOD_JUST_FREED;
32587    error = 0;
32588  out:
32589    unlock_kernel();
32590    return error;
32591  }
32592
32593  /* Query various bits about modules.  */
32594  static int
32595  qm_modules(char *buf, size_t bufsize, size_t * ret)
32596  {
32597    struct module *mod;
32598    size_t nmod, space, len;
32599
32600    nmod = space = 0;
32601
32602    for (mod = module_list; mod != &kernel_module;
32603         mod = mod->next, ++nmod) {
32604      len = strlen(mod->name) + 1;
32605      if (len > bufsize)
32606        goto calc_space_needed;
32607      if (copy_to_user(buf, mod->name, len))
32608        return -EFAULT;
32609      buf += len;
32610      bufsize -= len;
32611      space += len;
32612    }
32613
32614    if (put_user(nmod, ret))
32615      return -EFAULT;
32616    else
32617      return 0;
32618
32619  calc_space_needed:
32620    space += len;
32621    while ((mod = mod->next) != &kernel_module)
32622      space += strlen(mod->name) + 1;
32623
32624    if (put_user(space, ret))
32625      return -EFAULT;
32626    else
32627      return -ENOSPC;
32628  }
32629
32630  static int
32631  qm_deps(struct module *mod, char *buf, size_t bufsize,
32632      size_t * ret)
32633  {
32634    size_t i, space, len;
32635
32636    if (mod == &kernel_module)
32637      return -EINVAL;
32638    if (!MOD_CAN_QUERY(mod))
32639      if (put_user(0, ret))
32640        return -EFAULT;
32641      else
32642        return 0;
32643
32644    space = 0;
32645    for (i = 0; i < mod->ndeps; ++i) {
32646      const char *dep_name = mod->deps[i].dep->name;
32647
32648      len = strlen(dep_name) + 1;
32649      if (len > bufsize)
32650        goto calc_space_needed;
32651      if (copy_to_user(buf, dep_name, len))
32652        return -EFAULT;
32653      buf += len;
32654      bufsize -= len;
32655      space += len;
```

```
32656    }
32657
32658    if (put_user(i, ret))
32659      return -EFAULT;
32660    else
32661      return 0;
32662
32663 calc_space_needed:
32664    space += len;
32665    while (++i < mod->ndeps)
32666      space += strlen(mod->deps[i].dep->name) + 1;
32667
32668    if (put_user(space, ret))
32669      return -EFAULT;
32670    else
32671      return -ENOSPC;
32672 }
32673
32674 static int
32675 qm_refs(struct module *mod, char *buf, size_t bufsize,
32676      size_t * ret)
32677 {
32678    size_t nrefs, space, len;
32679    struct module_ref *ref;
32680
32681    if (mod == &kernel_module)
32682      return -EINVAL;
32683    if (!MOD_CAN_QUERY(mod))
32684      if (put_user(0, ret))
32685        return -EFAULT;
32686      else
32687        return 0;
32688
32689    space = 0;
32690    for (nrefs = 0, ref = mod->refs; ref;
32691        ++nrefs, ref = ref->next_ref) {
32692      const char *ref_name = ref->ref->name;
32693
32694      len = strlen(ref_name) + 1;
32695      if (len > bufsize)
32696        goto calc_space_needed;
32697      if (copy_to_user(buf, ref_name, len))
32698        return -EFAULT;
32699      buf += len;
32700      bufsize -= len;
32701      space += len;
32702    }
```

```
32703
32704    if (put_user(nrefs, ret))
32705      return -EFAULT;
32706    else
32707      return 0;
32708
32709 calc_space_needed:
32710    space += len;
32711    while ((ref = ref->next_ref) != NULL)
32712      space += strlen(ref->ref->name) + 1;
32713
32714    if (put_user(space, ret))
32715      return -EFAULT;
32716    else
32717      return -ENOSPC;
32718 }
32719
32720 static int
32721 qm_symbols(struct module *mod, char *buf, size_t bufsize,
32722      size_t * ret)
32723 {
32724    size_t i, space, len;
32725    struct module_symbol *s;
32726    char *strings;
32727    unsigned long *vals;
32728
32729    if (!MOD_CAN_QUERY(mod))
32730      if (put_user(0, ret))
32731        return -EFAULT;
32732      else
32733        return 0;
32734
32735    space = mod->nsyms * 2 * sizeof(void *);
32736
32737    i = len = 0;
32738    s = mod->syms;
32739
32740    if (space > bufsize)
32741      goto calc_space_needed;
32742
32743    if (!access_ok(VERIFY_WRITE, buf, space))
32744      return -EFAULT;
32745
32746    bufsize -= space;
32747    vals = (unsigned long *) buf;
32748    strings = buf + space;
32749
```

```
32750    for (; i < mod->nsyms; ++i, ++s, vals += 2) {
32751      len = strlen(s->name) + 1;
32752      if (len > bufsize)
32753        goto calc_space_needed;
32754
32755      if (copy_to_user(strings, s->name, len)
32756          || __put_user(s->value, vals + 0)
32757          || __put_user(space, vals + 1))
32758        return -EFAULT;
32759
32760      strings += len;
32761      bufsize -= len;
32762      space += len;
32763    }
32764
32765    if (put_user(i, ret))
32766      return -EFAULT;
32767    else
32768      return 0;
32769
32770 calc_space_needed:
32771    for (; i < mod->nsyms; ++i, ++s)
32772      space += strlen(s->name) + 1;
32773
32774    if (put_user(space, ret))
32775      return -EFAULT;
32776    else
32777      return -ENOSPC;
32778 }
32779
32780 static int
32781 qm_info(struct module *mod, char *buf, size_t bufsize,
32782      size_t * ret)
32783 {
32784    int error = 0;
32785
32786    if (mod == &kernel_module)
32787      return -EINVAL;
32788
32789    if (sizeof(struct module_info) <= bufsize) {
32790      struct module_info info;
32791      info.addr = (unsigned long) mod;
32792      info.size = mod->size;
32793      info.flags = mod->flags;
32794      info.usecount = (mod_member_present(mod, can_unload)
32795          && mod->can_unload
32796                    ? -1
```

```
32797                    : atomic_read(&mod->uc.usecount));
32798
32799      if (copy_to_user(buf, &info,
32800                  sizeof(struct module_info)))
32801        return -EFAULT;
32802    } else
32803      error = -ENOSPC;
32804
32805    if (put_user(sizeof(struct module_info), ret))
32806      return -EFAULT;
32807
32808    return error;
32809 }
32810
32811 asmlinkage long
32812 sys_query_module(const char *name_user, int which,
32813      char *buf, size_t bufsize, size_t * ret)
32814 {
32815    struct module *mod;
32816    int err;
32817
32818    lock_kernel();
32819    if (name_user == NULL)
32820      mod = &kernel_module;
32821    else {
32822      long namelen;
32823      char *name;
32824
32825      if ((namelen = get_mod_name(name_user, &name)) < 0) {
32826        err = namelen;
32827        goto out;
32828      }
32829      err = -ENOENT;
32830      if (namelen == 0)
32831        mod = &kernel_module;
32832      else if ((mod = find_module(name)) == NULL) {
32833        put_mod_name(name);
32834        goto out;
32835      }
32836      put_mod_name(name);
32837    }
32838
32839    switch (which) {
32840    case 0:
32841      err = 0;
32842      break;
32843    case QM_MODULES:
```

```
32844      err = qm_modules(buf, bufsize, ret);
32845      break;
32846    case QM_DEPS:
32847      err = qm_deps(mod, buf, bufsize, ret);
32848      break;
32849    case QM_REFS:
32850      err = qm_refs(mod, buf, bufsize, ret);
32851      break;
32852    case QM_SYMBOLS:
32853      err = qm_symbols(mod, buf, bufsize, ret);
32854      break;
32855    case QM_INFO:
32856      err = qm_info(mod, buf, bufsize, ret);
32857      break;
32858    default:
32859      err = -EINVAL;
32860      break;
32861    }
32862 out:
32863    unlock_kernel();
32864    return err;
32865 }
32866
32867 /* Copy the kernel symbol table to user space.  If the
32868  * argument is NULL, just return the size of the table.
32869  *
32870  * This call is obsolete.  New programs should use
32871  * query_module+QM_SYMBOLS which does not arbitrarily
32872  * limit the length of symbols.  */
32873 asmlinkage long
32874 sys_get_kernel_syms(struct kernel_sym *table)
32875 {
32876    struct module *mod;
32877    int i;
32878    struct kernel_sym ksym;
32879
32880    lock_kernel();
32881    for (mod = module_list, i = 0; mod; mod = mod->next) {
32882      /* include the count for the module name! */
32883      i += mod->nsyms + 1;
32884    }
32885
32886    if (table == NULL)
32887      goto out;
32888
32889    /* So that we don't give the user our stack content */
32890    memset(&ksym, 0, sizeof(ksym));
32891
32892    for (mod = module_list, i = 0; mod; mod = mod->next) {
32893      struct module_symbol *msym;
32894      unsigned int j;
32895
32896      if (!MOD_CAN_QUERY(mod))
32897        continue;
32898
32899      /* magic: write module info as a pseudo symbol */
32900      ksym.value = (unsigned long) mod;
32901      ksym.name[0] = '#';
32902      strncpy(ksym.name + 1, mod->name,
32903          sizeof(ksym.name) - 1);
32904      ksym.name[sizeof(ksym.name) - 1] = '\0';
32905
32906      if (copy_to_user(table, &ksym, sizeof(ksym)) != 0)
32907        goto out;
32908      ++i, ++table;
32909
32910      if (mod->nsyms == 0)
32911        continue;
32912
32913      for (j = 0, msym = mod->syms; j < mod->nsyms;
32914          ++j, ++msym) {
32915        ksym.value = msym->value;
32916        strncpy(ksym.name, msym->name, sizeof(ksym.name));
32917        ksym.name[sizeof(ksym.name) - 1] = '\0';
32918
32919        if (copy_to_user(table, &ksym, sizeof(ksym)) != 0)
32920          goto out;
32921        ++i, ++table;
32922      }
32923    }
32924 out:
32925    unlock_kernel();
32926    return i;
32927 }
32928
32929 /* Look for a module by name, ignoring modules marked for
32930  * deletion.  */
32931 struct module *find_module(const char *name)
32932 {
32933    struct module *mod;
32934
32935    for (mod = module_list; mod; mod = mod->next) {
32936      if (mod->flags & MOD_DELETED)
32937        continue;
```

```
32938      if (!strcmp(mod->name, name))
32939        break;
32940    }
32941
32942    return mod;
32943  }
32944
32945  /* Free the given module. */
32946  void free_module(struct module *mod, int tag_freed)
32947  {
32948    struct module_ref *dep;
32949    unsigned i;
32950
32951    /* Let the module clean up. */
32952
32953    if (mod->flags & MOD_RUNNING) {
32954      if (mod->cleanup)
32955        mod->cleanup();
32956      mod->flags &= ~MOD_RUNNING;
32957    }
32958
32959    /* Remove the module from the dependency lists. */
32960
32961    for (i = 0, dep = mod->deps; i < mod->ndeps;
32962         ++i, ++dep) {
32963      struct module_ref **pp;
32964      for (pp = &dep->dep->refs; *pp != dep;
32965           pp = &(*pp)->next_ref)
32966        continue;
32967      *pp = dep->next_ref;
32968      if (tag_freed && dep->dep->refs == NULL)
32969        dep->dep->flags |= MOD_JUST_FREED;
32970    }
32971
32972    /* And from the main module list. */
32973
32974    if (mod == module_list) {
32975      module_list = mod->next;
32976    } else {
32977      struct module *p;
32978      for (p = module_list; p->next != mod; p = p->next)
32979        continue;
32980      p->next = mod->next;
32981    }
32982
32983    /* And free the memory. */
32984
32985    module_unmap(mod);
32986  }
32987
32988  /* Called by the /proc file system to return a current
32989   * list of modules. */
32990  int get_module_list(char *p)
32991  {
32992    size_t left = PAGE_SIZE;
32993    struct module *mod;
32994    char tmpstr[64];
32995    struct module_ref *ref;
32996
32997    for (mod = module_list; mod != &kernel_module;
32998         mod = mod->next) {
32999      long len;
33000      const char *q;
33001
33002  #define safe_copy_str(str, len)                          \
33003    do {                                                   \
33004      if (left < len)                                      \
33005        goto fini;                                          \
33006      memcpy(p, str, len); p += len, left -= len;          \
33007    } while (0)
33008  #define safe_copy_cstr(str)                              \
33009    safe_copy_str(str, sizeof(str)-1)
33010
33011      len = strlen(mod->name);
33012      safe_copy_str(mod->name, len);
33013
33014      if ((len = 20 - len) > 0) {
33015        if (left < len)
33016          goto fini;
33017        memset(p, ' ', len);
33018        p += len;
33019        left -= len;
33020      }
33021
33022      len = sprintf(tmpstr, "%8lu", mod->size);
33023      safe_copy_str(tmpstr, len);
33024
33025      if (mod->flags & MOD_RUNNING) {
33026        len = sprintf(tmpstr, "%4ld",
33027             (mod_member_present(mod, can_unload)
33028              && mod->can_unload
33029              ? -1L
33030              : (long) atomic_read(&mod->uc. usecount)));
33031        safe_copy_str(tmpstr, len);
```

```
33032      }
33033
33034      if (mod->flags & MOD_DELETED)
33035        safe_copy_cstr(" (deleted)");
33036      else if (mod->flags & MOD_RUNNING) {
33037        if (mod->flags & MOD_AUTOCLEAN)
33038          safe_copy_cstr(" (autoclean)");
33039        if (!(mod->flags & MOD_USED_ONCE))
33040          safe_copy_cstr(" (unused)");
33041      } else if (mod->flags & MOD_INITIALIZING)
33042        safe_copy_cstr(" (initializing)");
33043      else
33044        safe_copy_cstr(" (uninitialized)");
33045
33046      if ((ref = mod->refs) != NULL) {
33047        safe_copy_cstr(" [");
33048        while (1) {
33049          q = ref->ref->name;
33050          len = strlen(q);
33051          safe_copy_str(q, len);
33052
33053          if ((ref = ref->next_ref) != NULL)
33054            safe_copy_cstr(" ");
33055          else
33056            break;
33057        }
33058        safe_copy_cstr("]");
33059      }
33060      safe_copy_cstr("\n");
33061
33062 #undef safe_copy_str
33063 #undef safe_copy_cstr
33064    }
33065
33066 fini:
33067    return PAGE_SIZE - left;
33068 }
33069
33070 /* Called by the /proc file system to return a current
33071  * list of ksyms.  */
33072 int
33073 get_ksyms_list(char *buf, char **start, off_t offset,
33074 int length)
33075 {
33076    struct module *mod;
33077    char *p = buf;
33078    int len = 0;              /* code from net/ipv4/proc.c */
33079    off_t pos = 0;
33080    off_t begin = 0;
33081
33082    for (mod = module_list; mod; mod = mod->next) {
33083      unsigned i;
33084      struct module_symbol *sym;
33085
33086      if (!MOD_CAN_QUERY(mod))
33087        continue;
33088
33089      for (i = mod->nsyms, sym = mod->syms; i > 0;
33090          -i, ++sym) {
33091        p = buf + len;
33092        if (*mod->name) {
33093          len += sprintf(p, "%0*lx %s\t[%s]\n",
33094              (int) (2 * sizeof(void *)),
33095              sym->value, sym->name, mod->name);
33096        } else {
33097          len += sprintf(p, "%0*lx %s\n",
33098              (int) (2 * sizeof(void *)),
33099              sym->value, sym->name);
33100        }
33101        pos = begin + len;
33102        if (pos < offset) {
33103          len = 0;
33104          begin = pos;
33105        }
33106        pos = begin + len;
33107        if (pos > offset + length)
33108          goto leave_the_loop;
33109      }
33110    }
33111 leave_the_loop:
33112    *start = buf + (offset - begin);
33113    len -= (offset - begin);
33114    if (len > length)
33115      len = length;
33116    return len;
33117 }
33118
33119 #else                          /* CONFIG_MODULES */
33120
33121 /* Dummy syscalls for people who don't want modules */
33122
33123 asmlinkage unsigned long
33124 sys_create_module(const char *name_user, size_t size)
33125 {
```

```
33126    return -ENOSYS;
33127 }
33128
33129 asmlinkage long
33130 sys_init_module(const char *name_user,
33131 struct module *mod_user)
33132 {
33133    return -ENOSYS;
33134 }
33135
33136 asmlinkage long sys_delete_module(const char *name_user)
33137 {
33138    return -ENOSYS;
33139 }
33140
33141 asmlinkage long
33142 sys_query_module(const char *name_user, int which,
33143     char *buf, size_t bufsize, size_t * ret)
33144 {
33145    /* Let the program know about the new interface.  Not
33146     * that it'll do them much good.  */
33147    if (which == 0)
33148      return 0;
33149
33150    return -ENOSYS;
33151 }
33152
33153 asmlinkage long
33154 sys_get_kernel_syms(struct kernel_sym *table)
33155 {
33156    return -ENOSYS;
33157 }
33158
33159 int try_inc_mod_count(struct module *mod)
33160 {
33161    return 1;
33162 }
33163
33164 #endif                         /* CONFIG_MODULES */
```

kernel/panic.c

```
33165 /*
33166  *  linux/kernel/panic.c
33167  *
33168  *  Copyright (C) 1991, 1992  Linus Torvalds
33169  */
33170
33171 /* This function is used through-out the kernel
33172  * (including mm and fs) to indicate a major problem.  */
33173 #include <linux/config.h>
33174 #include <linux/sched.h>
33175 #include <linux/delay.h>
33176 #include <linux/reboot.h>
33177 #include <linux/notifier.h>
33178 #include <linux/init.h>
33179 #include <linux/sysrq.h>
33180 #include <linux/interrupt.h>
33181
33182 asmlinkage void sys_sync(void); /* it's really int */
33183 extern void unblank_console(void);
33184
33185 int panic_timeout;
33186
33187 struct notifier_block *panic_notifier_list;
33188
33189 static int __init panic_setup(char *str)
33190 {
33191    panic_timeout = simple_strtoul(str, NULL, 0);
33192    return 1;
33193 }
33194
33195 __setup("panic=", panic_setup);
33196
33197 /**
33198  *     panic - halt the system
33199  *     @fmt: The text string to print
33200  *
33201  * Display a message, then unblank the console and
33202  * perform cleanups. Functions in the panic notifier list
33203  * are called after the filesystem cache is flushed (when
33204  * possible).
33205  *
33206  * This function never returns.  */
33207 NORET_TYPE void panic(const char *fmt, ...)
33208 {
33209    static char buf[1024];
33210    va_list args;
33211 #if defined(CONFIG_ARCH_S390)
33212    unsigned long caller =
33213       (unsigned long) __builtin_return_address(0);
33214 #endif
33215
33216    va_start(args, fmt);
33217    vsprintf(buf, fmt, args);
```

```
33218    va_end(args);
33219    printk(KERN_EMERG "Kernel panic: %s\n", buf);
33220    if (in_interrupt())
33221      printk(KERN_EMERG
33222          "In interrupt handler - not syncing\n");
33223    else if (!current->pid)
33224      printk(KERN_EMERG "In idle task - not syncing\n");
33225    else
33226      sys_sync();
33227
33228    unblank_console();
33229
33230 #ifdef CONFIG_SMP
33231    smp_send_stop();
33232 #endif
33233
33234    notifier_call_chain(&panic_notifier_list, 0, NULL);
33235
33236    if (panic_timeout > 0) {
33237      /* Delay timeout seconds before rebooting the
33238       * machine.  We can't use the "normal" timers since
33239       * we just panicked..   */
33240      printk(KERN_EMERG "Rebooting in %d seconds..",
33241          panic_timeout);
33242      mdelay(panic_timeout * 1000);
33243      /* Should we run the reboot notifier. For the moment
33244       * Im choosing not too. It might crash, be corrupt or
33245       * do more harm than good for other reasons.  */
33246      machine_restart(NULL);
33247    }
33248 #ifdef __sparc__
33249    {
33250      extern int stop_a_enabled;
33251      /* Make sure the user can actually press L1-A */
33252      stop_a_enabled = 1;
33253      printk("Press L1-A to return to the boot prom\n");
33254    }
33255 #endif
33256 #if defined(CONFIG_ARCH_S390)
33257    disabled_wait(caller);
33258 #endif
33259    sti();
33260    for (;;) {
33261    CHECK_EMERGENCY_SYNC}
33262 }
```

kernel/printk.c

```
33263 /*
33264  *  linux/kernel/printk.c
33265  *
33266  *  Copyright (C) 1991, 1992  Linus Torvalds
33267  *
33268  * Modified to make sys_syslog() more flexible: added
33269  * commands to return the last 4k of kernel messages,
33270  * regardless of whether they've been read or not.  Added
33271  * option to suppress kernel printk's to the console.
33272  * Added hook for sending the console messages elsewhere,
33273  * in preparation for a serial line console (someday).
33274  * Ted Ts'o, 2/11/93.
33275  * Modified for sysctl support, 1/8/97, Chris Horn.
33276  * Fixed SMP synchronization, 08/08/99, Manfred Spraul
33277  *       manfreds@colorfullife.com
33278  */
33279
33280 #include <linux/mm.h>
33281 #include <linux/tty_driver.h>
33282 #include <linux/smp_lock.h>
33283 #include <linux/console.h>
33284 #include <linux/init.h>
33285
33286 #include <asm/uaccess.h>
33287
33288 #define LOG_BUF_LEN     (16384)
33289 #define LOG_BUF_MASK    (LOG_BUF_LEN-1)
33290
33291 static char buf[1024];
33292
33293 /* printk's without a loglevel use this.. */
33294 #define DEFAULT_MESSAGE_LOGLEVEL 4  /* KERN_WARNING */
33295
33296 /* We show everything that is MORE important than this..
33297  */
33298 #define MINIMUM_CONSOLE_LOGLEVEL 1 /* Minimum loglevel we
33299                                     * let people use */
33300 #define DEFAULT_CONSOLE_LOGLEVEL 7 /* anything MORE
33301                                     * serious than
33302                                     * KERN_DEBUG */
33303
33304 unsigned long log_size;
33305 DECLARE_WAIT_QUEUE_HEAD(log_wait);
33306
33307 /* Keep together for sysctl support */
```

```
33308 int console_loglevel = DEFAULT_CONSOLE_LOGLEVEL;
33309 int default_message_loglevel = DEFAULT_MESSAGE_LOGLEVEL;
33310 int minimum_console_loglevel = MINIMUM_CONSOLE_LOGLEVEL;
33311 int default_console_loglevel = DEFAULT_CONSOLE_LOGLEVEL;
33312
33313 spinlock_t console_lock = SPIN_LOCK_UNLOCKED;
33314
33315 struct console *console_drivers;
33316 static char log_buf[LOG_BUF_LEN];
33317 static unsigned long log_start;
33318 static unsigned long logged_chars;
33319 struct console_cmdline
33320     console_cmdline[MAX_CMDLINECONSOLES];
33321 static int preferred_console = -1;
33322
33323 /* Setup a list of consoles. Called from init/main.c */
33324 static int __init console_setup(char *str)
33325 {
33326   struct console_cmdline *c;
33327   char name[sizeof(c->name)];
33328   char *s, *options;
33329   int i, idx;
33330
33331   /* Decode str into name, index, options.  */
33332   if (str[0] >= '0' && str[0] <= '9') {
33333     strcpy(name, "ttyS");
33334     strncpy(name + 4, str, sizeof(name) - 5);
33335   } else
33336     strncpy(name, str, sizeof(name) - 1);
33337   name[sizeof(name) - 1] = 0;
33338   if ((options = strchr(str, ',')) != NULL)
33339     *(options++) = 0;
33340 #ifdef __sparc__
33341   if (!strcmp(str, "ttya"))
33342     strcpy(name, "ttyS0");
33343   if (!strcmp(str, "ttyb"))
33344     strcpy(name, "ttyS1");
33345 #endif
33346   for (s = name; *s; s++)
33347     if (*s >= '0' && *s <= '9')
33348       break;
33349   idx = simple_strtoul(s, NULL, 10);
33350   *s = 0;
33351
33352   /* See if this tty is not yet registered, and if we
33353    * have a slot free.  */
33354   for (i = 0;
33355       i < MAX_CMDLINECONSOLES
33356       && console_cmdline[i].name[0]; i++)
33357     if (strcmp(console_cmdline[i].name, name) == 0
33358         && console_cmdline[i].index == idx) {
33359       preferred_console = i;
33360       return 1;
33361     }
33362   if (i == MAX_CMDLINECONSOLES)
33363     return 1;
33364   preferred_console = i;
33365   c = &console_cmdline[i];
33366   memcpy(c->name, name, sizeof(c->name));
33367   c->options = options;
33368   c->index = idx;
33369   return 1;
33370 }
33371
33372 __setup("console=", console_setup);
33373
33374 /* Commands to do_syslog:
33375  *
33376  *      0 - Close the log.  Currently a NOP.
33377  *      1 - Open the log. Currently a NOP.
33378  *      2 - Read from the log.
33379  *      3 - Read all messages remaining in the ring
33380  *          buffer.
33381  *      4 - Read and clear all messages remaining in the
33382  *          ring buffer
33383  *      5 - Clear ring buffer.
33384  *      6 - Disable printk's to console
33385  *      7 - Enable printk's to console
33386  *      8 - Set level of messages printed to console */
33387 int do_syslog(int type, char *buf, int len)
33388 {
33389   unsigned long i, j, limit, count;
33390   int do_clear = 0;
33391   char c;
33392   int error = -EPERM;
33393
33394   error = 0;
33395   switch (type) {
33396   case 0:                           /* Close log */
33397     break;
33398   case 1:                           /* Open log */
33399     break;
33400   case 2:                           /* Read from log */
33401     error = -EINVAL;
33402     if (!buf || len < 0)
33403       goto out;
```

```
33404      error = 0;
33405      if (!len)
33406        goto out;
33407      error = verify_area(VERIFY_WRITE, buf, len);
33408      if (error)
33409        goto out;
33410      error = wait_event_interruptible(log_wait, log_size);
33411      if (error)
33412        goto out;
33413      i = 0;
33414      spin_lock_irq(&console_lock);
33415      while (log_size && i < len) {
33416        c = log_buf[log_start & LOG_BUF_MASK];
33417        log_start++;
33418        log_size--;
33419        spin_unlock_irq(&console_lock);
33420        __put_user(c, buf);
33421        buf++;
33422        i++;
33423        spin_lock_irq(&console_lock);
33424      }
33425      spin_unlock_irq(&console_lock);
33426      error = i;
33427      break;
33428    case 4:            /* Read/clear last kernel messages */
33429      do_clear = 1;
33430      /* FALL THRU */
33431    case 3:            /* Read last kernel messages */
33432      error = -EINVAL;
33433      if (!buf || len < 0)
33434        goto out;
33435      error = 0;
33436      if (!len)
33437        goto out;
33438      error = verify_area(VERIFY_WRITE, buf, len);
33439      if (error)
33440        goto out;
33441      count = len;
33442      if (count > LOG_BUF_LEN)
33443        count = LOG_BUF_LEN;
33444      spin_lock_irq(&console_lock);
33445      if (count > logged_chars)
33446        count = logged_chars;
33447      if (do_clear)
33448        logged_chars = 0;
33449      limit = log_start + log_size;
33450      /* __put_user() could sleep, and while we sleep
33451       * printk() could overwrite the messages we try to
33452       * copy to user space. Therefore the messages are
33453       * copied in reverse. <manfreds> */
33454      for (i = 0; i < count; i++) {
33455        j = limit - 1 - i;
33456        if (j + LOG_BUF_LEN < log_start + log_size)
33457          break;
33458        c = log_buf[j & LOG_BUF_MASK];
33459        spin_unlock_irq(&console_lock);
33460        __put_user(c, &buf[count - 1 - i]);
33461        spin_lock_irq(&console_lock);
33462      }
33463      spin_unlock_irq(&console_lock);
33464      error = i;
33465      if (i != count) {
33466        int offset = count - error;
33467        /* buffer overflow during copy, correct user
33468         * buffer. */
33469        for (i = 0; i < error; i++) {
33470          __get_user(c, &buf[i + offset]);
33471          __put_user(c, &buf[i]);
33472        }
33473      }
33474
33475      break;
33476    case 5:            /* Clear ring buffer */
33477      spin_lock_irq(&console_lock);
33478      logged_chars = 0;
33479      spin_unlock_irq(&console_lock);
33480      break;
33481    case 6:            /* Disable logging to console */
33482      spin_lock_irq(&console_lock);
33483      console_loglevel = minimum_console_loglevel;
33484      spin_unlock_irq(&console_lock);
33485      break;
33486    case 7:            /* Enable logging to console */
33487      spin_lock_irq(&console_lock);
33488      console_loglevel = default_console_loglevel;
33489      spin_unlock_irq(&console_lock);
33490      break;
33491    case 8:
33492      error = -EINVAL;
33493      if (len < 1 || len > 8)
33494        goto out;
33495      if (len < minimum_console_loglevel)
33496        len = minimum_console_loglevel;
33497      spin_lock_irq(&console_lock);
```

```
33498      console_loglevel = len;
33499      spin_unlock_irq(&console_lock);
33500      error = 0;
33501      break;
33502    default:
33503      error = -EINVAL;
33504      break;
33505    }
33506 out:
33507    return error;
33508 }
33509
33510 asmlinkage long sys_syslog(int type, char *buf, int len)
33511 {
33512    if ((type != 3) && !capable(CAP_SYS_ADMIN))
33513      return -EPERM;
33514    return do_syslog(type, buf, len);
33515 }
33516
33517 asmlinkage int printk(const char *fmt, ...)
33518 {
33519    va_list args;
33520    int i;
33521    char *msg, *p, *buf_end;
33522    int line_feed;
33523    static signed char msg_level = -1;
33524    long flags;
33525
33526    spin_lock_irqsave(&console_lock, flags);
33527    va_start(args, fmt);
33528    /* hopefully i < sizeof(buf)-4 */
33529    i = vsprintf(buf + 3, fmt, args);
33530    buf_end = buf + 3 + i;
33531    va_end(args);
33532    for (p = buf + 3; p < buf_end; p++) {
33533      msg = p;
33534      if (msg_level < 0) {
33535        if (p[0] != '<' ||
33536            p[1] < '0' || p[1] > '7' || p[2] != '>') {
33537          p -= 3;
33538          p[0] = '<';
33539          p[1] = default_message_loglevel + '0';
33540          p[2] = '>';
33541        } else
33542          msg += 3;
33543        msg_level = p[1] - '0';
33544      }
```

The arrow marker on the left margin reads: **p 536** → 33517

```
33545      line_feed = 0;
33546      for (; p < buf_end; p++) {
33547        log_buf[(log_start + log_size) & LOG_BUF_MASK] =
33548          *p;
33549        if (log_size < LOG_BUF_LEN)
33550          log_size++;
33551        else
33552          log_start++;
33553
33554        logged_chars++;
33555        if (*p == '\n') {
33556          line_feed = 1;
33557          break;
33558        }
33559      }
33560      if(msg_level < console_loglevel && console_drivers) {
33561        struct console *c = console_drivers;
33562        while (c) {
33563          if ((c->flags & CON_ENABLED) && c->write)
33564            c->write(c, msg, p - msg + line_feed);
33565          c = c->next;
33566        }
33567      }
33568      if (line_feed)
33569        msg_level = -1;
33570    }
33571    spin_unlock_irqrestore(&console_lock, flags);
33572    wake_up_interruptible(&log_wait);
33573    return i;
33574 }
33575
33576 void console_print(const char *s)
33577 {
33578    struct console *c;
33579    unsigned long flags;
33580    int len = strlen(s);
33581
33582    spin_lock_irqsave(&console_lock, flags);
33583    c = console_drivers;
33584    while (c) {
33585      if ((c->flags & CON_ENABLED) && c->write)
33586        c->write(c, s, len);
33587      c = c->next;
33588    }
33589    spin_unlock_irqrestore(&console_lock, flags);
33590 }
33591
```

```
33592 void unblank_console(void)
33593 {
33594   struct console *c;
33595   unsigned long flags;
33596
33597   spin_lock_irqsave(&console_lock, flags);
33598   c = console_drivers;
33599   while (c) {
33600     if ((c->flags & CON_ENABLED) && c->unblank)
33601       c->unblank();
33602     c = c->next;
33603   }
33604   spin_unlock_irqrestore(&console_lock, flags);
33605 }
33606
33607 /* The console driver calls this routine during kernel
33608  * initialization to register the console printing
33609  * procedure with printk() and to print any messages that
33610  * were printed by the kernel before the console driver
33611  * was initialized.  */
33612 void register_console(struct console *console)
33613 {
33614   int i, j, len;
33615   int p;
33616   char buf[16];
33617   signed char msg_level = -1;
33618   char *q;
33619   unsigned long flags;
33620
33621   /* See if we want to use this console driver. If we
33622    * didn't select a console we take the first one that
33623    * registers here.  */
33624   if (preferred_console < 0) {
33625     if (console->index < 0)
33626       console->index = 0;
33627     if (console->setup == NULL ||
33628       console->setup(console, NULL) == 0) {
33629       console->flags |= CON_ENABLED | CON_CONSDEV;
33630       preferred_console = 0;
33631     }
33632   }
33633
33634   /* See if this console matches one we selected on the
33635    * command line.  */
33636   for (i = 0;
33637        i < MAX_CMDLINECONSOLES
33638        && console_cmdline[i].name[0]; i++) {
```

```
33639     if (strcmp(console_cmdline[i].name,
33640             console->name) != 0)
33641       continue;
33642     if (console->index >= 0
33643       && console->index != console_cmdline[i].index)
33644       continue;
33645     if (console->index < 0)
33646       console->index = console_cmdline[i].index;
33647     if (console->setup &&
33648       console->setup(console,
33649                   console_cmdline[i].options) != 0)
33650       break;
33651     console->flags |= CON_ENABLED;
33652     console->index = console_cmdline[i].index;
33653     if (i == preferred_console)
33654       console->flags |= CON_CONSDEV;
33655     break;
33656   }
33657
33658   if (!(console->flags & CON_ENABLED))
33659     return;
33660
33661   /* Put this console in the list - keep the preferred
33662    * driver at the head of the list.  */
33663   spin_lock_irqsave(&console_lock, flags);
33664   if ((console->flags & CON_CONSDEV)
33665       || console_drivers == NULL) {
33666     console->next = console_drivers;
33667     console_drivers = console;
33668   } else {
33669     console->next = console_drivers->next;
33670     console_drivers->next = console;
33671   }
33672   if ((console->flags & CON_PRINTBUFFER) == 0)
33673     goto done;
33674   /* Print out buffered log messages.  */
33675   p = log_start & LOG_BUF_MASK;
33676
33677   for (i = 0, j = 0; i < log_size; i++) {
33678     buf[j++] = log_buf[p];
33679     p = (p + 1) & LOG_BUF_MASK;
33680     if (buf[j - 1] != '\n' && i < log_size - 1
33681         && j < sizeof(buf) - 1)
33682       continue;
33683     buf[j] = 0;
33684     q = buf;
33685     len = j;
```

```
33686     if (msg_level < 0) {
33687       if (buf[0] == '<' &&
33688           buf[1] >= '0' &&
33689           buf[1] <= '7' && buf[2] == '>') {
33690         msg_level = buf[1] - '0';
33691         q = buf + 3;
33692         len -= 3;
33693       } else {
33694         msg_level = default_message_loglevel;
33695       }
33696     }
33697     if (msg_level < console_loglevel)
33698       console->write(console, q, len);
33699     if (buf[j - 1] == '\n')
33700       msg_level = -1;
33701     j = 0;
33702   }
33703 done:
33704   spin_unlock_irqrestore(&console_lock, flags);
33705 }
33706
33707
33708 int unregister_console(struct console *console)
33709 {
33710   struct console *a, *b;
33711   unsigned long flags;
33712   int res = 1;
33713
33714   spin_lock_irqsave(&console_lock, flags);
33715   if (console_drivers == console) {
33716     console_drivers = console->next;
33717     res = 0;
33718   } else {
33719     for (a = console_drivers->next, b = console_drivers;
33720          a; b = a, a = b->next) {
33721       if (a == console) {
33722         b->next = a->next;
33723         res = 0;
33724         break;
33725       }
33726     }
33727   }
33728
33729   /* If last console is removed, we re-enable picking the
33730    * first one that gets registered. Without that, pmac
33731    * early boot console would prevent fbcon from taking
33732    * over. */
```

```
33733   if (console_drivers == NULL)
33734     preferred_console = -1;
33735
33736   spin_unlock_irqrestore(&console_lock, flags);
33737   return res;
33738 }
33739
33740 /* Write a message to a certain tty, not just the
33741  * console. This is used for messages that need to be
33742  * redirected to a specific tty.  We don't put it into
33743  * the syslog queue right now maybe in the future if
33744  * really needed.  */
33745 void tty_write_message(struct tty_struct *tty, char *msg)
33746 {
33747   if (tty && tty->driver.write)
33748     tty->driver.write(tty, 0, msg, strlen(msg));
33749   return;
33750 }
```

kernel/sched.c

```
33751 /*
33752  *  linux/kernel/sched.c
33753  *
33754  *  Kernel scheduler and related syscalls
33755  *
33756  *  Copyright (C) 1991, 1992  Linus Torvalds
33757  *
33758  * 1996-12-23 Modified by Dave Grothe to fix bugs in
33759  *            semaphores and make semaphores SMP safe
33760  * 1998-11-19 Implemented schedule_timeout() and related
33761  *            stuff by Andrea Arcangeli
33762  * 1998-12-28 Implemented better SMP scheduling by Ingo
33763  *            Molnar
33764  */
33765
33766 /* 'sched.c' is the main kernel file. It contains
33767  * scheduling primitives (sleep_on, wakeup, schedule etc)
33768  * as well as a number of simple system call functions
33769  * (type getpid()), which just extract a field from
33770  * current-task */
33771
33772 #include <linux/config.h>
33773 #include <linux/mm.h>
33774 #include <linux/init.h>
33775 #include <linux/smp_lock.h>
33776 #include <linux/interrupt.h>
33777 #include <linux/kernel_stat.h>
```

```
33778
33779 #include <asm/uaccess.h>
33780 #include <asm/mmu_context.h>
33781
33782 extern void timer_bh(void);
33783 extern void tqueue_bh(void);
33784 extern void immediate_bh(void);
33785
33786 /* scheduler variables */
33787
33788 /* systemwide security settings */
33789 unsigned securebits = SECUREBITS_DEFAULT;
33790
33791 extern void mem_use(void);
33792
33793 /* Scheduling quanta.
33794  *
33795  * NOTE! The unix "nice" value influences how long a
33796  * process gets. The nice value ranges from -20 to +19,
33797  * where a -20 is a "high-priority" task, and a "+10" is
33798  * a low-priority task.
33799  *
33800  * We want the time-slice to be around 50ms or so, so
33801  * this calculation depends on the value of HZ. */
33802 #if HZ < 200
33803 #define TICK_SCALE(x)   ((x) >> 2)
33804 #elif HZ < 400
33805 #define TICK_SCALE(x)   ((x) >> 1)
33806 #elif HZ < 800
33807 #define TICK_SCALE(x)   (x)
33808 #elif HZ < 1600
33809 #define TICK_SCALE(x)   ((x) << 1)
33810 #else
33811 #define TICK_SCALE(x)   ((x) << 2)
33812 #endif
33813
33814 #define NICE_TO_TICKS(nice)   (TICK_SCALE(20-(nice))+1)
33815
33816
33817 /* Init task must be ok at boot for the ix86 as we will
33818  * check its signals via the SMP irq return path. */
33819
33820 struct task_struct *init_tasks[NR_CPUS] =
33821     { &init_task, };
33822
33823 /* The tasklist_lock protects the linked list of
33824  * processes.
33825  *
33826  * The runqueue_lock locks the parts that actually access
33827  * and change the run-queues, and have to be
33828  * interrupt-safe.
33829  *
33830  * If both locks are to be concurrently held, the
33831  * runqueue_lock nests inside the tasklist_lock. */
33832 spinlock_t runqueue_lock
33833 __cacheline_aligned = SPIN_LOCK_UNLOCKED; /* inner */
33834 rwlock_t tasklist_lock
33835 __cacheline_aligned = RW_LOCK_UNLOCKED;  /* outer */
33836
33837 static LIST_HEAD(runqueue_head);
33838
33839 /* We align per-CPU scheduling data on cacheline
33840  * boundaries, to prevent cacheline ping-pong.  */
33841 static union {
33842   struct schedule_data {
33843     struct task_struct *curr;
33844     cycles_t last_schedule;
33845   } schedule_data;
33846   char __pad[SMP_CACHE_BYTES];
33847 } aligned_data[NR_CPUS] __cacheline_aligned =
33848 { { { &init_task, 0 } } };
33849
33850 #define cpu_curr(cpu)                                    \
33851   aligned_data[(cpu)].schedule_data.curr
33852 #define last_schedule(cpu)                               \
33853   aligned_data[(cpu)].schedule_data.last_schedule
33854
33855 struct kernel_stat kstat;
33856
33857 #ifdef CONFIG_SMP
33858
33859 #define idle_task(cpu) (init_tasks[cpu_number_map(cpu)])
33860 #define can_schedule(p,cpu)                              \
33861   (((!(p)->has_cpu) && ((p)->cpus_allowed & (1 << cpu)))
33862
33863 #else
33864
33865 #define idle_task(cpu) (&init_task)
33866 #define can_schedule(p,cpu) (1)
33867
33868 #endif
33869
33870 void scheduling_functions_start_here(void)
33871 {
```

```
33872 }
33873
33874 /* This is the function that decides how desirable a
33875  * process is..  You can weigh different processes
33876  * against each other depending on what CPU they've run
33877  * on lately etc to try to handle cache and TLB miss
33878  * penalties.
33879  *
33880  * Return values:
33881  *          -1000: never select this
33882  *              0: out of time, recalculate counters (but it
33883  *                 might still be selected)
33884  *            +ve: "goodness" value (the larger, the better)
33885  *          +1000: realtime process, select this.  */
33886 static inline int goodness(struct task_struct *p,
33887     int this_cpu, struct mm_struct *this_mm)
33888 {
33889   int weight;
33890
33891   /* select the current process after every other
33892    * runnable process, but before the idle thread.  Also,
33893    * dont trigger a counter recalculation.  */
33894   weight = -1;
33895   if (p->policy & SCHED_YIELD)
33896     goto out;
33897
33898   /* Non-RT process - normal case first.  */
33899   if (p->policy == SCHED_OTHER) {
33900     /* Give the process a first-approximation goodness
33901      * value according to the number of clock-ticks it
33902      * has left.
33903      *
33904      * Don't do any other calculations if the time slice
33905      * is over..  */
33906     weight = p->counter;
33907     if (!weight)
33908       goto out;
33909
33910 #ifdef CONFIG_SMP
33911     /* Give a largish advantage to the same processor...
33912      */
33913     /* (this is equivalent to penalizing other
33914      * processors) */
33915     if (p->processor == this_cpu)
33916       weight += PROC_CHANGE_PENALTY;
33917 #endif
33918
33919     /* .. and a slight advantage to the current MM */
33920     if (p->mm == this_mm || !p->mm)
33921       weight += 1;
33922     weight += 20 - p->nice;
33923     goto out;
33924   }
33925
33926   /* Realtime process, select the first one on the
33927    * runqueue (taking priorities within processes into
33928    * account).  */
33929   weight = 1000 + p->rt_priority;
33930 out:
33931   return weight;
33932 }
33933
33934 /* the 'goodness value' of replacing a process on a given
33935  * CPU.  positive value means 'replace', zero or negative
33936  * means 'dont'.  */
33937 static inline int
33938 preemption_goodness(struct task_struct *prev,
33939                 struct task_struct *p, int cpu)
33940 {
33941   return goodness(p,    cpu, prev->active_mm) -
33942         goodness(prev, cpu, prev->active_mm);
33943 }
33944
33945 /* This is ugly, but reschedule_idle() is very
33946  * timing-critical.  We are called with the runqueue
33947  * spinlock held and we must not claim the tasklist_lock.
33948  */
33949 static FASTCALL(void reschedule_idle(
33950   struct task_struct *p));
33951
33952 static void reschedule_idle(struct task_struct *p)
33953 {
33954 #ifdef CONFIG_SMP
33955   int this_cpu = smp_processor_id();
33956   struct task_struct *tsk, *target_tsk;
33957   int cpu, best_cpu, i, max_prio;
33958   cycles_t oldest_idle;
33959
33960   /* shortcut if the woken up task's last CPU is idle
33961    * now.  */
33962   best_cpu = p->processor;
33963   if (can_schedule(p, best_cpu)) {
33964     tsk = idle_task(best_cpu);
33965     if (cpu_curr(best_cpu) == tsk) {
```

p 609
p 690

```
33966        int need_resched;
33967     send_now_idle:
33968        /* If need_resched == -1 then we can skip sending
33969         * the IPI altogether, tsk->need_resched is
33970         * actively watched by the idle thread.  */
33971        need_resched = tsk->need_resched;
33972        tsk->need_resched = 1;
33973        if ((best_cpu != this_cpu) && !need_resched)
33974          smp_send_reschedule(best_cpu);
33975        return;
33976      }
33977    }
33978
33979  /* We know that the preferred CPU has a cache-affine
33980   * current process, lets try to find a new idle CPU for
33981   * the woken-up process. Select the least recently
33982   * active idle CPU. (that one will have the least
33983   * active cache context.) Also find the executing
33984   * process which has the least priority.  */
33985  oldest_idle = (cycles_t) - 1;
33986  target_tsk = NULL;
33987  max_prio = 1;
33988
33989  for (i = 0; i < smp_num_cpus; i++) {
33990    cpu = cpu_logical_map(i);
33991    if (!can_schedule(p, cpu))
33992      continue;
33993    tsk = cpu_curr(cpu);
33994    /* We use the first available idle CPU. This creates
33995     * a priority list between idle CPUs, but this is not
33996     * a problem.  */
33997    if (tsk == idle_task(cpu)) {
33998      if (last_schedule(cpu) < oldest_idle) {
33999        oldest_idle = last_schedule(cpu);
34000        target_tsk = tsk;
34001      }
34002    } else {
34003      if (oldest_idle == -1ULL) {
34004        int prio = preemption_goodness(tsk, p, cpu);
34005
34006        if (prio > max_prio) {
34007          max_prio = prio;
34008          target_tsk = tsk;
34009        }
34010      }
34011    }
34012  }
34013  tsk = target_tsk;
34014  if (tsk) {
34015    if (oldest_idle != -1ULL) {
34016      best_cpu = tsk->processor;
34017      goto send_now_idle;
34018    }
34019    tsk->need_resched = 1;
34020    if (tsk->processor != this_cpu)
34021      smp_send_reschedule(tsk->processor);
34022  }
34023  return;
34024
34025
34026 #else                            /* UP */
34027   int this_cpu = smp_processor_id();
34028   struct task_struct *tsk;
34029
34030   tsk = cpu_curr(this_cpu);
34031   if (preemption_goodness(tsk, p, this_cpu) > 1)
34032     tsk->need_resched = 1;
34033 #endif
34034 }
34035
34036 /* Careful!
34037  *
34038  * This has to add the process to the _beginning_ of the
34039  * run-queue, not the end. See the comment about "This is
34040  * subtle" in the scheduler proper..  */
34041 static inline void add_to_runqueue(struct task_struct *p)
34042 {
34043   list_add(&p->run_list, &runqueue_head);
34044   nr_running++;
34045 }
34046
34047 static inline void
34048 move_last_runqueue(struct task_struct *p)
34049 {
34050   list_del(&p->run_list);
34051   list_add_tail(&p->run_list, &runqueue_head);
34052 }
34053
34054 static inline void
34055 move_first_runqueue(struct task_struct *p)
34056 {
34057   list_del(&p->run_list);
34058   list_add(&p->run_list, &runqueue_head);
34059 }
```

```
34060
34061 /* Wake up a process. Put it on the run-queue if it's not
34062  * already there.  The "current" process is always on the
34063  * run-queue (except when the actual re-schedule is in
34064  * progress), and as such you're allowed to do the
34065  * simpler "current->state = TASK_RUNNING" to mark
34066  * yourself runnable without the overhead of this.  */
34067 inline void wake_up_process(struct task_struct *p)
34068 {
34069   unsigned long flags;
34070
34071   /* We want the common case fall through straight, thus
34072    * the goto.  */
34073   spin_lock_irqsave(&runqueue_lock, flags);
34074   p->state = TASK_RUNNING;
34075   if (task_on_runqueue(p))
34076     goto out;
34077   add_to_runqueue(p);
34078   reschedule_idle(p);
34079 out:
34080   spin_unlock_irqrestore(&runqueue_lock, flags);
34081 }
34082
34083 static inline void
34084 wake_up_process_synchronous(struct task_struct *p)
34085 {
34086   unsigned long flags;
34087
34088   /* We want the common case fall through straight, thus
34089    * the goto.  */
34090   spin_lock_irqsave(&runqueue_lock, flags);
34091   p->state = TASK_RUNNING;
34092   if (task_on_runqueue(p))
34093     goto out;
34094   add_to_runqueue(p);
34095 out:
34096   spin_unlock_irqrestore(&runqueue_lock, flags);
34097 }
34098
34099 static void process_timeout(unsigned long __data)
34100 {
34101   struct task_struct *p = (struct task_struct *) __data;
34102
34103   wake_up_process(p);
34104 }
34105
34106 signed long schedule_timeout(signed long timeout)
34107 {
34108   struct timer_list timer;
34109   unsigned long expire;
34110
34111   switch (timeout) {
34112   case MAX_SCHEDULE_TIMEOUT:
34113     /* These two special cases are useful to be
34114      * comfortable in the caller. Nothing more. We could
34115      * take MAX_SCHEDULE_TIMEOUT from one of the negative
34116      * value but I' d like to return a valid offset (>=0)
34117      * to allow the caller to do everything it want with
34118      * the retval.  */
34119     schedule();
34120     goto out;
34121   default:
34122     /* Another bit of PARANOID. Note that the retval will
34123      * be 0 since no piece of kernel is supposed to do a
34124      * check for a negative retval of schedule_timeout()
34125      * (since it should never happens anyway). You just
34126      * have the printk() that will tell you if something
34127      * is gone wrong and where.  */
34128     if (timeout < 0) {
34129       printk(KERN_ERR "schedule_timeout: wrong timeout "
34130         "value %lx from %p\n", timeout,
34131         __builtin_return_address(0));
34132       current->state = TASK_RUNNING;
34133       goto out;
34134     }
34135   }
34136
34137   expire = timeout + jiffies;
34138
34139   init_timer(&timer);
34140   timer.expires = expire;
34141   timer.data = (unsigned long) current;
34142   timer.function = process_timeout;
34143
34144   add_timer(&timer);
34145   schedule();
34146   del_timer_sync(&timer);
34147
34148   timeout = expire - jiffies;
34149
34150 out:
34151   return timeout < 0 ? 0 : timeout;
34152 }
34153
```

```
34154 /* schedule_tail() is getting called from the fork return
34155  * path. This cleans up all remaining scheduler things,
34156  * without impacting the common case.  */
34157 static inline void
34158 __schedule_tail(struct task_struct *prev)
34159 {
34160 #ifdef CONFIG_SMP
34161   int policy;
34162
34163   /* prev->policy can be written from here only before
34164    * 'prev' can be scheduled (before setting
34165    * prev->has_cpu to zero).  Of course it must also be
34166    * read before allowing prev to be rescheduled, but
34167    * since the write depends on the read to complete,
34168    * wmb() is enough. (the spin_lock() acquired before
34169    * setting has_cpu is not enough because the
34170    * spin_lock() common code semantics allows code
34171    * outside the critical section to enter inside the
34172    * critical section) */
34173   policy = prev->policy;
34174   prev->policy = policy & ~SCHED_YIELD;
34175   wmb();
34176
34177   /* fast path falls through. We have to clear has_cpu
34178    * before checking prev->state to avoid a wakeup race -
34179    * thus we also have to protect against the task
34180    * exiting early.  */
34181   task_lock(prev);
34182   prev->has_cpu = 0;
34183   mb();
34184   if (prev->state == TASK_RUNNING)
34185     goto needs_resched;
34186
34187 out_unlock:
34188   /* Synchronise here with release_task() if prev is
34189    * TASK_ZOMBIE */
34190   task_unlock(prev);
34191   return;
34192
34193   /* Slow path - we 'push' the previous process and
34194    * reschedule_idle() will attempt to find a new
34195    * processor for it. (but it might preempt the current
34196    * process as well.) We must take the runqueue lock and
34197    * re-check prev->state to be correct. It might still
34198    * happen that this process has a preemption 'in
34199    * progress' already - but this is not a problem and
34200    * might happen in other circumstances as well.  */
34201 needs_resched:
34202   {
34203     unsigned long flags;
34204
34205     /* Avoid taking the runqueue lock in cases where no
34206      * preemption-check is necessery: */
34207     if ((prev == idle_task(smp_processor_id())) ||
34208         (policy & SCHED_YIELD))
34209       goto out_unlock;
34210
34211     spin_lock_irqsave(&runqueue_lock, flags);
34212     if (prev->state == TASK_RUNNING)
34213       reschedule_idle(prev);
34214     spin_unlock_irqrestore(&runqueue_lock, flags);
34215     goto out_unlock;
34216   }
34217 #else
34218   prev->policy &= ~SCHED_YIELD;
34219 #endif                            /* CONFIG_SMP */
34220 }
34221
34222 void schedule_tail(struct task_struct *prev)
34223 {
34224   __schedule_tail(prev);
34225 }
34226
34227 /* 'schedule()' is the scheduler function. It's a very
34228  * simple and nice scheduler: it's not perfect, but
34229  * certainly works for most things.
34230  *
34231  * The goto is "interesting".
34232  *
34233  * NOTE!!  Task 0 is the 'idle' task, which gets called
34234  * when no other tasks can run. It can not be killed, and
34235  * it cannot sleep. The 'state' information in task[0] is
34236  * never used.  */
34237 asmlinkage void schedule(void)
34238 {
34239   struct schedule_data *sched_data;
34240   struct task_struct *prev, *next, *p;
34241   struct list_head *tmp;
34242   int this_cpu, c;
34243
34244   if (!current->active_mm)
34245     BUG();
34246 need_resched_back:
34247   prev = current;
```

```
34248    this_cpu = prev->processor;
34249
34250    if (in_interrupt())
34251      goto scheduling_in_interrupt;
34252
34253    release_kernel_lock(prev, this_cpu);
34254
34255    /* Do "administrative" work here while we don't hold
34256     * any locks */
34257    if (softirq_active(this_cpu) & softirq_mask(this_cpu))
34258      goto handle_softirq;
34259  handle_softirq_back:
34260
34261    /* 'sched_data' is protected by the fact that we can
34262     * run only one process per CPU. */
34263    sched_data = &aligned_data[this_cpu].schedule_data;
34264
34265    spin_lock_irq(&runqueue_lock);
34266
34267    /* move an exhausted RR process to be last.. */
34268    if (prev->policy == SCHED_RR)
34269      goto move_rr_last;
34270  move_rr_back:
34271
34272    switch (prev->state) {
34273    case TASK_INTERRUPTIBLE:
34274      if (signal_pending(prev)) {
34275        prev->state = TASK_RUNNING;
34276        break;
34277      }
34278    default:
34279      del_from_runqueue(prev);
34280    case TASK_RUNNING:
34281    }
34282    prev->need_resched = 0;
34283
34284    /* this is the scheduler proper: */
34285
34286  repeat_schedule:
34287    /* Default process to select.. */
34288    next = idle_task(this_cpu);
34289    c = -1000;
34290    if (prev->state == TASK_RUNNING)
34291      goto still_running;
34292
34293  still_running_back:
34294    list_for_each(tmp, &runqueue_head) {
34295      p = list_entry(tmp, struct task_struct, run_list);
34296      if (can_schedule(p, this_cpu)) {
34297        int weight =
34298          goodness(p, this_cpu, prev->active_mm);
34299        if (weight > c)
34300          c = weight, next = p;
34301      }
34302    }
34303
34304    /* Do we need to re-calculate counters? */
34305    if (!c)
34306      goto recalculate;
34307    /* from this point on nothing can prevent us from
34308     * switching to the next task, save this fact in
34309     * sched_data.  */
34310    sched_data->curr = next;
34311  #ifdef CONFIG_SMP
34312    next->has_cpu = 1;
34313    next->processor = this_cpu;
34314  #endif
34315    spin_unlock_irq(&runqueue_lock);
34316
34317    if (prev == next)
34318      goto same_process;
34319
34320  #ifdef CONFIG_SMP
34321    /* maintain the per-process 'last schedule' value.
34322     * (this has to be recalculated even if we reschedule
34323     * to the same process) Currently this is only used on
34324     * SMP, and it's approximate, so we do not have to
34325     * maintain it while holding the runqueue spinlock.  */
34326    sched_data->last_schedule = get_cycles();
34327
34328    /* We drop the scheduler lock early (it's a global
34329     * spinlock), thus we have to lock the previous process
34330     * from getting rescheduled during switch_to().  */
34331
34332  #endif                                    /* CONFIG_SMP */
34333
34334    kstat.context_swtch++;
34335    /* there are 3 processes which are affected by a
34336     * context switch:
34337     *
34338     * prev == .... ==> (last => next)
34339     *
34340     * It's the 'much more previous' 'prev' that is on
34341     * next's stack, but prev is set to (the just run)
```

```
34342    * 'last' process by switch_to().  This might sound
34343    * slightly confusing but makes tons of sense.  */
34344   prepare_to_switch();
34345   {
34346     struct mm_struct *mm = next->mm;
34347     struct mm_struct *oldmm = prev->active_mm;
34348     if (!mm) {
34349       if (next->active_mm)
34350         BUG();
34351       next->active_mm = oldmm;
34352       atomic_inc(&oldmm->mm_count);
34353       enter_lazy_tlb(oldmm, next, this_cpu);
34354     } else {
34355       if (next->active_mm != mm)
34356         BUG();
34357       switch_mm(oldmm, mm, next, this_cpu);
34358     }
34359
34360     if (!prev->mm) {
34361       prev->active_mm = NULL;
34362       mmdrop(oldmm);
34363     }
34364   }
34365
34366   /* This just switches the register state and the stack.
34367    */
34368   switch_to(prev, next, prev);
34369   __schedule_tail(prev);
34370
34371 same_process:
34372   reacquire_kernel_lock(current);
34373   if (current->need_resched)
34374     goto need_resched_back;
34375
34376   return;
34377
34378 recalculate:
34379   {
34380     struct task_struct *p;
34381     spin_unlock_irq(&runqueue_lock);
34382     read_lock(&tasklist_lock);
34383     for_each_task(p)
34384       p->counter = (p->counter >> 1) +
34385                    NICE_TO_TICKS(p->nice);
34386     read_unlock(&tasklist_lock);
34387     spin_lock_irq(&runqueue_lock);
34388   }
```

```
34389   goto repeat_schedule;
34390
34391 still_running:
34392   c = goodness(prev, this_cpu, prev->active_mm);
34393   next = prev;
34394   goto still_running_back;
34395
34396 handle_softirq:
34397   do_softirq();
34398   goto handle_softirq_back;
34399
34400 move_rr_last:
34401   if (!prev->counter) {
34402     prev->counter = NICE_TO_TICKS(prev->nice);
34403     move_last_runqueue(prev);
34404   }
34405   goto move_rr_back;
34406
34407 scheduling_in_interrupt:
34408   printk("Scheduling in interrupt\n");
34409   BUG();
34410   return;
34411 }
34412
34413 static inline void
34414 __wake_up_common(wait_queue_head_t * q,
34415   unsigned int mode, int nr_exclusive, const int sync)
34416 {
34417   struct list_head *tmp, *head;
34418   struct task_struct *p;
34419   unsigned long flags;
34420
34421   if (!q)
34422     goto out;
34423
34424   wq_write_lock_irqsave(&q->lock, flags);
34425
34426 #if WAITQUEUE_DEBUG
34427   CHECK_MAGIC_WQHEAD(q);
34428 #endif
34429
34430   head = &q->task_list;
34431 #if WAITQUEUE_DEBUG
34432   if (!head->next || !head->prev)
34433     WQ_BUG();
34434 #endif
34435   tmp = head->next;
```

p 624
p 540

```
34436    while (tmp != head) {
34437        unsigned int state;
34438        wait_queue_t *curr =
34439            list_entry(tmp, wait_queue_t, task_list);
34440
34441        tmp = tmp->next;
34442
34443 #if WAITQUEUE_DEBUG
34444        CHECK_MAGIC(curr->__magic);
34445 #endif
34446        p = curr->task;
34447        state = p->state;
34448        if (state & mode) {
34449 #if WAITQUEUE_DEBUG
34450            curr->__waker = (long) __builtin_return_address(0);
34451 #endif
34452            if (sync)
34453                wake_up_process_synchronous(p);
34454            else
34455                wake_up_process(p);
34456            if ((curr->flags & WQ_FLAG_EXCLUSIVE) &&
34457                !--nr_exclusive)
34458                break;
34459        }
34460    } wq_write_unlock_irqrestore(&q->lock, flags);
34461 out:
34462    return;
34463 }
34464
34465 void __wake_up(wait_queue_head_t * q,
34466                unsigned int mode, int nr)
34467 {
34468    __wake_up_common(q, mode, nr, 0);
34469 }
34470
34471 void __wake_up_sync(wait_queue_head_t * q,
34472                unsigned int mode, int nr)
34473 {
34474    __wake_up_common(q, mode, nr, 1);
34475 }
34476
34477 #define SLEEP_ON_VAR                                          \
34478        unsigned long flags;                                  \
34479        wait_queue_t wait;                                    \
34480        init_waitqueue_entry(&wait, current);
34481
34482 #define SLEEP_ON_HEAD                                         \
34483        wq_write_lock_irqsave(&q->lock,flags);               \
34484        __add_wait_queue(q, &wait);                          \
34485        wq_write_unlock(&q->lock);
34486
34487 #define SLEEP_ON_TAIL                                         \
34488        wq_write_lock_irq(&q->lock);                         \
34489        __remove_wait_queue(q, &wait);                       \
34490        wq_write_unlock_irqrestore(&q->lock,flags);
34491
34492 void interruptible_sleep_on(wait_queue_head_t * q)
34493 {
34494    SLEEP_ON_VAR
34495    current->state = TASK_INTERRUPTIBLE;
34496
34497    SLEEP_ON_HEAD
34498    schedule();
34499    SLEEP_ON_TAIL
34500 }
34501
34502 long interruptible_sleep_on_timeout(wait_queue_head_t *q,
34503                                long timeout)
34504 {
34505    SLEEP_ON_VAR
34506    current->state = TASK_INTERRUPTIBLE;
34507
34508    SLEEP_ON_HEAD
34509    timeout = schedule_timeout(timeout);
34510    SLEEP_ON_TAIL
34511    return timeout;
34512 }
34513
34514 void sleep_on(wait_queue_head_t * q)
34515 {
34516    SLEEP_ON_VAR
34517    current->state = TASK_UNINTERRUPTIBLE;
34518
34519    SLEEP_ON_HEAD
34520    schedule();
34521    SLEEP_ON_TAIL
34522 }
34523
34524 long sleep_on_timeout(wait_queue_head_t * q,
34525                       long timeout)
34526 {
34527    SLEEP_ON_VAR
34528    current->state = TASK_UNINTERRUPTIBLE;
34529
```

```
34530   SLEEP_ON_HEAD
34531   timeout = schedule_timeout(timeout);
34532   SLEEP_ON_TAIL
34533   return timeout;
34534 }
34535
34536 void scheduling_functions_end_here(void) {}
34537
34538 #ifndef __alpha__
34539 /* This has been replaced by sys_setpriority.  Maybe it
34540  * should be moved into the arch dependent tree for those
34541  * ports that require it for backward compatibility?  */
34542 asmlinkage long sys_nice(int increment)
34543 {
34544   long newprio;
34545
34546   /* Setpriority might change our priority at the same
34547    * moment.  We don't have to worry.  Conceptually one
34548    * call occurs first and we have a single winner.  */
34549   if (increment < 0) {
34550     if (!capable(CAP_SYS_NICE))
34551       return -EPERM;
34552     if (increment < -40)
34553       increment = -40;
34554   }
34555   if (increment > 40)
34556     increment = 40;
34557
34558   newprio = current->nice + increment;
34559   if (newprio < -20)
34560     newprio = -20;
34561   if (newprio > 19)
34562     newprio = 19;
34563   current->nice = newprio;
34564   return 0;
34565 }
34566
34567 #endif
34568
34569 static inline
34570 struct task_struct * find_process_by_pid(pid_t pid)
34571 {
34572   struct task_struct *tsk = current;
34573
34574   if (pid)
34575     tsk = find_task_by_pid(pid);
34576   return tsk;
```

```
34577 }
34578
34579 static int setscheduler(pid_t pid, int policy,
34580                         struct sched_param *param)
34581 {
34582   struct sched_param lp;
34583   struct task_struct *p;
34584   int retval;
34585
34586   retval = -EINVAL;
34587   if (!param || pid < 0)
34588     goto out_nounlock;
34589
34590   retval = -EFAULT;
34591   if (copy_from_user(&lp, param,
34592                      sizeof(struct sched_param)))
34593     goto out_nounlock;
34594
34595   /* We play safe to avoid deadlocks.  */
34596   read_lock_irq(&tasklist_lock);
34597   spin_lock(&runqueue_lock);
34598
34599   p = find_process_by_pid(pid);
34600
34601   retval = -ESRCH;
34602   if (!p)
34603     goto out_unlock;
34604
34605   if (policy < 0)
34606     policy = p->policy;
34607   else {
34608     retval = -EINVAL;
34609     if (policy != SCHED_FIFO &&
34610         policy != SCHED_RR &&
34611         policy != SCHED_OTHER)
34612       goto out_unlock;
34613   }
34614   /* Valid priorities for SCHED_FIFO and SCHED_RR are
34615    * 1..99, valid priority for SCHED_OTHER is 0.  */
34616   retval = -EINVAL;
34617   if (lp.sched_priority < 0 || lp.sched_priority > 99)
34618     goto out_unlock;
34619   if ((policy == SCHED_OTHER) !=
34620       (lp.sched_priority == 0))
34621     goto out_unlock;
34622
34623   retval = -EPERM;
```

p 611

```
34624    if ((policy == SCHED_FIFO || policy == SCHED_RR) &&
34625        !capable(CAP_SYS_NICE))
34626      goto out_unlock;
34627    if ((current->euid != p->euid) &&
34628        (current->euid != p->uid) &&
34629        !capable(CAP_SYS_NICE))
34630      goto out_unlock;
34631
34632    retval = 0;
34633    p->policy = policy;
34634    p->rt_priority = lp.sched_priority;
34635    if (task_on_runqueue(p))
34636      move_first_runqueue(p);
34637
34638    current->need_resched = 1;
34639
34640  out_unlock:
34641    spin_unlock(&runqueue_lock);
34642    read_unlock_irq(&tasklist_lock);
34643
34644  out_nounlock:
34645    return retval;
34646  }
34647
34648  asmlinkage long sys_sched_setscheduler(pid_t pid,
34649    int policy, struct sched_param *param)
34650  {
34651    return setscheduler(pid, policy, param);
34652  }
34653
34654  asmlinkage long sys_sched_setparam(pid_t pid,
34655    struct sched_param *param)
34656  {
34657    return setscheduler(pid, -1, param);
34658  }
34659
34660  asmlinkage long sys_sched_getscheduler(pid_t pid)
34661  {
34662    struct task_struct *p;
34663    int retval;
34664
34665    retval = -EINVAL;
34666    if (pid < 0)
34667      goto out_nounlock;
34668
34669    retval = -ESRCH;
34670    read_lock(&tasklist_lock);
34671    p = find_process_by_pid(pid);
34672    if (p)
34673      retval = p->policy & ~SCHED_YIELD;
34674    read_unlock(&tasklist_lock);
34675
34676  out_nounlock:
34677    return retval;
34678  }
34679
34680  asmlinkage long sys_sched_getparam(pid_t pid,
34681    struct sched_param *param)
34682  {
34683    struct task_struct *p;
34684    struct sched_param lp;
34685    int retval;
34686
34687    retval = -EINVAL;
34688    if (!param || pid < 0)
34689      goto out_nounlock;
34690
34691    read_lock(&tasklist_lock);
34692    p = find_process_by_pid(pid);
34693    retval = -ESRCH;
34694    if (!p)
34695      goto out_unlock;
34696    lp.sched_priority = p->rt_priority;
34697    read_unlock(&tasklist_lock);
34698
34699    /* This one might sleep, we cannot do it with a
34700     * spinlock held ...  */
34701
34702    retval = copy_to_user(param, &lp,
34703                          sizeof(*param)) ? -EFAULT : 0;
34704
34705  out_nounlock:
34706    return retval;
34707
34708  out_unlock:
34709    read_unlock(&tasklist_lock);
34710    return retval;
34711  }
34712
34713  asmlinkage long sys_sched_yield(void)
34714  {
34715    /* Trick. sched_yield() first counts the number of
34716     * truly 'pending' runnable processes, then returns if
34717     * it's only the current processes. (This test does not
```

```
34718     * have to be atomic.) In threaded applications this
34719     * optimization gets triggered quite often.  */
34720
34721    int nr_pending = nr_running;
34722
34723 #if CONFIG_SMP
34724    int i;
34725
34726    // Substract non-idle processes running on other
34727    // CPUs.
34728    for (i = 0; i < smp_num_cpus; i++)
34729      if (aligned_data[i].schedule_data.curr !=
34730          idle_task(i))
34731        nr_pending--;
34732 #else
34733    // on UP this process is on the runqueue as well
34734    nr_pending--;
34735 #endif
34736    if (nr_pending) {
34737      /* This process can only be rescheduled by us, so
34738       * this is safe without any locking.  */
34739      if (current->policy == SCHED_OTHER)
34740        current->policy |= SCHED_YIELD;
34741      current->need_resched = 1;
34742    }
34743    return 0;
34744 }
34745
34746 asmlinkage long sys_sched_get_priority_max(int policy)
34747 {
34748    int ret = -EINVAL;
34749
34750    switch (policy) {
34751    case SCHED_FIFO:
34752    case SCHED_RR:
34753      ret = 99;
34754      break;
34755    case SCHED_OTHER:
34756      ret = 0;
34757      break;
34758    }
34759    return ret;
34760 }
34761
34762 asmlinkage long sys_sched_get_priority_min(int policy)
34763 {
34764    int ret = -EINVAL;
34765
34766    switch (policy) {
34767    case SCHED_FIFO:
34768    case SCHED_RR:
34769      ret = 1;
34770      break;
34771    case SCHED_OTHER:
34772      ret = 0;
34773    }
34774    return ret;
34775 }
34776
34777 asmlinkage long sys_sched_rr_get_interval(pid_t pid,
34778    struct timespec *interval)
34779 {
34780    struct timespec t;
34781    struct task_struct *p;
34782    int retval = -EINVAL;
34783
34784    if (pid < 0)
34785      goto out_nounlock;
34786
34787    retval = -ESRCH;
34788    read_lock(&tasklist_lock);
34789    p = find_process_by_pid(pid);
34790    if (p)
34791      jiffies_to_timespec(p->policy & SCHED_FIFO
34792                     ? 0 : NICE_TO_TICKS(p->nice),
34793                     &t);
34794    read_unlock(&tasklist_lock);
34795    if (p)
34796      retval = copy_to_user(interval, &t, sizeof(t))
34797         ? -EFAULT
34798         : 0;
34799 out_nounlock:
34800    return retval;
34801 }
34802
34803 static void show_task(struct task_struct *p)
34804 {
34805    unsigned long free = 0;
34806    int state;
34807    static const char *stat_nam[] =
34808      { "R", "S", "D", "Z", "T", "W" };
34809
34810    printk("%-8s  ", p->comm);
34811    state = p->state ?  ffz(~p->state) + 1  :  0;
```

```
34812    if (((unsigned) state) <
34813        sizeof(stat_nam) / sizeof(char *))
34814      printk(stat_nam[state]);
34815    else
34816      printk(" ");
34817  #if (BITS_PER_LONG == 32)
34818    if (p == current)
34819      printk(" current ");
34820    else
34821      printk(" %08lX ", thread_saved_pc(&p->thread));
34822  #else
34823    if (p == current)
34824      printk("   current task   ");
34825    else
34826      printk(" %016lx ", thread_saved_pc(&p->thread));
34827  #endif
34828    {
34829      unsigned long *n = (unsigned long *) (p + 1);
34830      while (!*n)
34831        n++;
34832      free = (unsigned long) n - (unsigned long) (p + 1);
34833    }
34834    printk("%5lu %5d %6d ", free, p->pid, p->p_pptr->pid);
34835
34836    if (p->p_cptr)
34837      printk("%5d ", p->p_cptr->pid);
34838    else
34839      printk("      ");
34840
34841    if (!p->mm)
34842      printk(" (L-TLB) ");
34843    else
34844      printk(" (NOTLB) ");
34845
34846    if (p->p_ysptr)
34847      printk("%7d", p->p_ysptr->pid);
34848    else
34849      printk("       ");
34850
34851    if (p->p_osptr)
34852      printk(" %5d\n", p->p_osptr->pid);
34853    else
34854      printk("\n");
34855
34856  #ifdef CONFIG_X86
34857    /* This is very useful, but only works on x86 right
34858     * now */
34859    {
34860      extern void show_trace(unsigned long);
34861      show_trace(p->thread.esp);
34862    }
34863  #endif
34864  }
34865
34866  char *render_sigset_t(sigset_t * set, char *buffer)
34867  {
34868    int i = _NSIG, x;
34869    do {
34870      i -= 4, x = 0;
34871      if (sigismember(set, i + 1))   x |= 1;
34872      if (sigismember(set, i + 2))   x |= 2;
34873      if (sigismember(set, i + 3))   x |= 4;
34874      if (sigismember(set, i + 4))   x |= 8;
34875      *buffer++ = (x < 10 ? '0' : 'a' - 10) + x;
34876    } while (i >= 4);
34877    *buffer = 0;
34878    return buffer;
34879  }
34880
34881  void show_state(void)
34882  {
34883    struct task_struct *p;
34884
34885  #if (BITS_PER_LONG == 32)
34886    printk("\n"
34887           "                                         free                 "
34888           "         sibling\n");
34889
34890    printk("  task             PC    stack   pid father "
34891           "child younger older\n");
34892  #else
34893    printk("\n"
34894           "                                           free             "
34895           "         sibling\n");
34896
34897    printk("  task                 PC        stack    pid "
34898           "father child younger older\n");
34899  #endif
34900    read_lock(&tasklist_lock);
34901    for_each_task(p) show_task(p);
34902    read_unlock(&tasklist_lock);
34903  }
34904
34905  /* Put all the gunge required to become a kernel thread
```

```
34906    * without attached user resources in one place where it
34907    * belongs.  */
34908   void daemonize(void)
34909   {
34910      struct fs_struct *fs;
34911
34912      /* If we were started as result of loading a module,
34913       * close all of the user space pages.  We don't need
34914       * them, and if we didn't close them they would be
34915       * locked into memory.  */
34916      exit_mm(current);
34917
34918      current->session = 1;
34919      current->pgrp = 1;
34920
34921      /* Become as one with the init task */
34922
34923      exit_fs(current);            /* current->fs->count--; */
34924      fs = init_task.fs;
34925      current->fs = fs;
34926      atomic_inc(&fs->count);
34927      exit_files(current);
34928      current->files = init_task.files;
34929      atomic_inc(&current->files->count);
34930   }
34931
34932   void __init init_idle(void)
34933   {
34934      struct schedule_data *sched_data;
34935      sched_data =
34936        &aligned_data[smp_processor_id()].schedule_data;
34937
34938      if (current != &init_task
34939          && task_on_runqueue(current)) {
34940        printk
34941          ("UGH! (%d:%d) was on the runqueue, removing.\n",
34942           smp_processor_id(), current->pid);
34943        del_from_runqueue(current);
34944      }
34945      sched_data->curr = current;
34946      sched_data->last_schedule = get_cycles();
34947   }
34948
34949   extern void init_timervecs(void);
34950
34951   void __init sched_init(void)
34952   {
```

```
34953      /* We have to do a little magic to get the first
34954       * process right in SMP mode.  */
34955      int cpu = smp_processor_id();
34956      int nr;
34957
34958      init_task.processor = cpu;
34959
34960      for (nr = 0; nr < PIDHASH_SZ; nr++)
34961        pidhash[nr] = NULL;
34962
34963      init_timervecs();
34964
34965      init_bh(TIMER_BH, timer_bh);
34966      init_bh(TQUEUE_BH, tqueue_bh);
34967      init_bh(IMMEDIATE_BH, immediate_bh);
34968
34969      /* The boot idle thread does lazy MMU switching as
34970       * well: */
34971      atomic_inc(&init_mm.mm_count);
34972      enter_lazy_tlb(&init_mm, current, cpu);
34973   }
```

kernel/signal.c

```
34974   /*
34975    *  linux/kernel/signal.c
34976    *
34977    *  Copyright (C) 1991, 1992  Linus Torvalds
34978    *
34979    *  1997-11-02 Modified for POSIX.1b signals by Richard
34980    *  Henderson
34981    */
34982
34983   #include <linux/config.h>
34984   #include <linux/slab.h>
34985   #include <linux/module.h>
34986   #include <linux/unistd.h>
34987   #include <linux/smp_lock.h>
34988   #include <linux/init.h>
34989   #include <linux/sched.h>
34990
34991   #include <asm/uaccess.h>
34992
34993   /* SLAB caches for signal bits.  */
34994
34995   #define DEBUG_SIG 0
34996
34997   #if DEBUG_SIG
```

```
34998 #define SIG_SLAB_DEBUG
34999   (SLAB_DEBUG_FREE | SLAB_RED_ZONE /* | SLAB_POISON */)    \
35000 #else
35001 #define SIG_SLAB_DEBUG  0
35002 #endif
35003
35004 static kmem_cache_t *sigqueue_cachep;
35005
35006 atomic_t nr_queued_signals;
35007 int max_queued_signals = 1024;
35008
35009 void __init signals_init(void)
35010 {
35011   sigqueue_cachep =
35012     kmem_cache_create("sigqueue",
35013                       sizeof(struct sigqueue),
35014                       __alignof__(struct sigqueue),
35015                       SIG_SLAB_DEBUG, NULL, NULL);
35016   if (!sigqueue_cachep)
35017     panic("signals_init(): "
35018           "cannot create sigqueue SLAB cache");
35019 }
35020
35021
35022 /* Given the mask, find the first available signal that
35023  * should be serviced. */
35024 static int
35025 next_signal(struct task_struct *tsk, sigset_t * mask)
35026 {
35027   unsigned long i, *s, *m, x;
35028   int sig = 0;
35029
35030   s = tsk->pending.signal.sig;
35031   m = mask->sig;
35032   switch (_NSIG_WORDS) {
35033   default:
35034     for (i = 0; i < _NSIG_WORDS; ++i, ++s, ++m)
35035       if ((x = *s & ~*m) != 0) {
35036         sig = ffz(~x) + i * _NSIG_BPW + 1;
35037         break;
35038       }
35039     break;
35040
35041   case 2:
35042     if ((x = s[0] & ~m[0]) != 0)
35043       sig = 1;
35044     else if ((x = s[1] & ~m[1]) != 0)
```

```
35045       sig = _NSIG_BPW + 1;
35046     else
35047       break;
35048     sig += ffz(~x);
35049     break;
35050
35051   case 1:
35052     if ((x = *s & ~*m) != 0)
35053       sig = ffz(~x) + 1;
35054     break;
35055   }
35056
35057   return sig;
35058 }
35059
35060 static void flush_sigqueue(struct sigpending *queue)
35061 {
35062   struct sigqueue *q, *n;
35063
35064   sigemptyset(&queue->signal);
35065   q = queue->head;
35066   queue->head = NULL;
35067   queue->tail = &queue->head;
35068
35069   while (q) {
35070     n = q->next;
35071     kmem_cache_free(sigqueue_cachep, q);
35072     atomic_dec(&nr_queued_signals);
35073     q = n;
35074   }
35075 }
35076
35077 /* Flush all pending signals for a task.  */
35078 void flush_signals(struct task_struct *t)
35079 {
35080   t->sigpending = 0;
35081   flush_sigqueue(&t->pending);
35082 }
35083
35084 void exit_sighand(struct task_struct *tsk)
35085 {
35086   struct signal_struct *sig = tsk->sig;
35087
35088   spin_lock_irq(&tsk->sigmask_lock);
35089   if (sig) {
35090     tsk->sig = NULL;
35091     if (atomic_dec_and_test(&sig->count))
```

p 581

```
35092        kmem_cache_free(sigact_cachep, sig);
35093    }
35094    tsk->sigpending = 0;
35095    flush_sigqueue(&tsk->pending);
35096    spin_unlock_irq(&tsk->sigmask_lock);
35097 }
35098
35099 /* Flush all handlers for a task.  */
35100 void flush_signal_handlers(struct task_struct *t)
35101 {
35102    int i;
35103    struct k_sigaction *ka = &t->sig->action[0];
35104    for (i = _NSIG; i != 0; i-) {
35105      if (ka->sa.sa_handler != SIG_IGN)
35106        ka->sa.sa_handler = SIG_DFL;
35107      ka->sa.sa_flags = 0;
35108      sigemptyset(&ka->sa.sa_mask);
35109      ka++;
35110    }
35111 }
35112
35113 /* Notify the system that a driver wants to block all
35114  * signals for this process, and wants to be notified if
35115  * any signals at all were to be sent/acted upon.  If the
35116  * notifier routine returns non-zero, then the signal
35117  * will be acted upon after all.  If the notifier routine
35118  * returns 0, then then signal will be blocked.  Only one
35119  * block per process is allowed.  priv is a pointer to
35120  * private data that the notifier routine can use to
35121  * determine if the signal should be blocked or not.  */
35122 void
35123 block_all_signals(int (*notifier) (void *priv),
35124 void *priv, sigset_t * mask)
35125 {
35126    unsigned long flags;
35127
35128    spin_lock_irqsave(&current->sigmask_lock, flags);
35129    current->notifier_mask = mask;
35130    current->notifier_data = priv;
35131    current->notifier = notifier;
35132    spin_unlock_irqrestore(&current->sigmask_lock, flags);
35133 }
35134
35135 /* Notify the system that blocking has ended. */
35136 void unblock_all_signals(void)
35137 {
35138    unsigned long flags;
```

```
35139
35140    spin_lock_irqsave(&current->sigmask_lock, flags);
35141    current->notifier = NULL;
35142    current->notifier_data = NULL;
35143    recalc_sigpending(current);
35144    spin_unlock_irqrestore(&current->sigmask_lock, flags);
35145 }
35146
35147 static int collect_signal(int sig,
35148     struct sigpending *list, siginfo_t * info)
35149 {
35150    if (sigismember(&list->signal, sig)) {
35151      /* Collect the siginfo appropriate to this signal. */
35152      struct sigqueue *q, **pp;
35153      pp = &list->head;
35154      while ((q = *pp) != NULL) {
35155        if (q->info.si_signo == sig)
35156          goto found_it;
35157        pp = &q->next;
35158      }
35159
35160      /* Ok, it wasn't in the queue.  We must have been
35161       * out of queue space.  So zero out the info.  */
35162      sigdelset(&list->signal, sig);
35163      info->si_signo = sig;
35164      info->si_errno = 0;
35165      info->si_code = 0;
35166      info->si_pid = 0;
35167      info->si_uid = 0;
35168      return 1;
35169
35170    found_it:
35171      if ((*pp = q->next) == NULL)
35172        list->tail = pp;
35173
35174      /* Copy the sigqueue information and free the queue
35175       * entry */
35176      copy_siginfo(info, &q->info);
35177      kmem_cache_free(sigqueue_cachep, q);
35178      atomic_dec(&nr_queued_signals);
35179
35180      /* Non-RT signals can exist multiple times.. */
35181      if (sig >= SIGRTMIN) {
35182        while ((q = *pp) != NULL) {
35183          if (q->info.si_signo == sig)
35184            goto found_another;
35185          pp = &q->next;
```

p 582

```
35186        }
35187      }
35188
35189      sigdelset(&list->signal, sig);
35190    found_another:
35191      return 1;
35192    }
35193    return 0;
35194  }
35195
35196  /* Dequeue a signal and return the element to the caller,
35197   * which is expected to free it.
35198   *
35199   * All callers must be holding current->sigmask_lock.  */
35200  int dequeue_signal(sigset_t * mask, siginfo_t * info)
35201  {
35202    int sig = 0;
35203
35204  #if DEBUG_SIG
35205    printk("SIG dequeue (%s:%d): %d ", current->comm,
35206        current->pid, signal_pending(current));
35207  #endif
35208
35209    sig = next_signal(current, mask);
35210    if (current->notifier) {
35211      if (sigismember(current->notifier_mask, sig)) {
35212        if(!(current->notifier) (current->notifier_data)) {
35213          current->sigpending = 0;
35214          return 0;
35215        }
35216      }
35217    }
35218
35219    if (sig) {
35220      if (!collect_signal(sig, &current->pending, info))
35221        sig = 0;
35222
35223      /* XXX: Once POSIX.1b timers are in, if si_code ==
35224       * SI_TIMER, we need to xchg out the timer overrun
35225       * values.  */
35226    }
35227    recalc_sigpending(current);
35228
35229  #if DEBUG_SIG
35230    printk(" %d -> %d\n", signal_pending(current), sig);
35231  #endif
35232
35233    return sig;
35234  }
35235
35236  static int rm_from_queue(int sig, struct sigpending *s)
35237  {
35238    struct sigqueue *q, **pp;
35239
35240    if (!sigismember(&s->signal, sig))
35241      return 0;
35242
35243    sigdelset(&s->signal, sig);
35244
35245    pp = &s->head;
35246
35247    while ((q = *pp) != NULL) {
35248      if (q->info.si_signo == sig) {
35249        if ((*pp = q->next) == NULL)
35250          s->tail = pp;
35251        kmem_cache_free(sigqueue_cachep, q);
35252        atomic_dec(&nr_queued_signals);
35253        continue;
35254      }
35255      pp = &q->next;
35256    }
35257    return 1;
35258  }
35259
35260  /* Remove signal sig from t->pending.  Returns 1 if sig
35261   * was found.
35262   *
35263   * All callers must be holding t->sigmask_lock.  */
35264  static int rm_sig_from_queue(int sig,
35265      struct task_struct *t)
35266  {
35267    return rm_from_queue(sig, &t->pending);
35268  }
35269
35270  /* Bad permissions for sending the signal */
35271  int bad_signal(int sig, struct siginfo *info,
35272      struct task_struct *t)
35273  {
35274    return
35275      (!info ||
35276       ((unsigned long) info != 1 && SI_FROMUSER(info)))
35277      && ((sig != SIGCONT)
35278          || (current->session != t->session))
35279      && (current->euid ^ t->suid)
```

p 581 (35200)
p 578 (35271)

```
35280        && (current->euid ^ t->uid)
35281        && (current->uid ^ t->suid)
35282        && (current->uid ^ t->uid)
35283        && !capable(CAP_KILL);
35284 }
35285
35286 /* Signal type:
35287  *    < 0 : global action (kill - spread to all
35288  *                         non-blocked threads)
35289  *    = 0 : ignored
35290  *    > 0 : wake up. */
35291 static int signal_type(int sig,
35292     struct signal_struct *signals)
35293 {
35294   unsigned long handler;
35295
35296   if (!signals)
35297     return 0;
35298
35299   handler = (unsigned long)
35300     signals->action[sig - 1].sa.sa_handler;
35301   if (handler > 1)
35302     return 1;
35303
35304   /* "Ignore" handler.. Illogical, but that has an
35305    * implicit handler for SIGCHLD */
35306   if (handler == 1)
35307     return sig == SIGCHLD;
35308
35309   /* Default handler. Normally lethal, but.. */
35310   switch (sig) {
35311
35312     /* Ignored */
35313   case SIGCONT:
35314   case SIGWINCH:
35315   case SIGCHLD:
35316   case SIGURG:
35317     return 0;
35318
35319     /* Implicit behaviour */
35320   case SIGTSTP:
35321   case SIGTTIN:
35322   case SIGTTOU:
35323     return 1;
35324
35325     /* Implicit actions (kill or do special stuff) */
35326   default:
35327     return -1;
35328   }
35329 }
35330
35331
35332 /* Determine whether a signal should be posted or not.
35333  *
35334  * Signals with SIG_IGN can be ignored, except for the
35335  * special case of a SIGCHLD.
35336  *
35337  * Some signals with SIG_DFL default to a non-action. */
35338 static int ignored_signal(int sig, struct task_struct *t)
35339 {
35340   /* Don't ignore traced or blocked signals */
35341   if ((t->ptrace & PT_PTRACED)
35342       || sigismember(&t->blocked, sig))
35343     return 0;
35344
35345   return signal_type(sig, t->sig) == 0;
35346 }
35347
35348 /* Handle TASK_STOPPED cases etc implicit behaviour of
35349  * certain magical signals.
35350  *
35351  * SIGKILL gets spread out to every thread. */
35352 static void handle_stop_signal(int sig,
35353     struct task_struct *t)
35354 {
35355   switch (sig) {
35356   case SIGKILL:
35357   case SIGCONT:
35358     /* Wake up the process if stopped. */
35359     if (t->state == TASK_STOPPED)
35360       wake_up_process(t);
35361     t->exit_code = 0;
35362     rm_sig_from_queue(SIGSTOP, t);
35363     rm_sig_from_queue(SIGTSTP, t);
35364     rm_sig_from_queue(SIGTTOU, t);
35365     rm_sig_from_queue(SIGTTIN, t);
35366     break;
35367
35368   case SIGSTOP:
35369   case SIGTSTP:
35370   case SIGTTIN:
35371   case SIGTTOU:
35372     /* If we're stopping again, cancel SIGCONT */
35373     rm_sig_from_queue(SIGCONT, t);
```

```
35374        break;
35375    }
35376 }
35377
35378 static int send_signal(int sig, struct siginfo *info,
35379        struct sigpending *signals)
35380 {
35381    struct sigqueue *q = NULL;
35382
35383    /* Real-time signals must be queued if sent by
35384     * sigqueue, or some other real-time mechanism.  It is
35385     * implementation defined whether kill() does so.  We
35386     * attempt to do so, on the principle of least
35387     * surprise, but since kill is not allowed to fail
35388     * with EAGAIN when low on memory we just make sure at
35389     * least one signal gets delivered and don't pass on
35390     * the info struct.  */
35391
35392    if (atomic_read(&nr_queued_signals) <
35393        max_queued_signals) {
35394      q = kmem_cache_alloc(sigqueue_cachep, GFP_ATOMIC);
35395    }
35396
35397    if (q) {
35398      atomic_inc(&nr_queued_signals);
35399      q->next = NULL;
35400      *signals->tail = q;
35401      signals->tail = &q->next;
35402      switch ((unsigned long) info) {
35403      case 0:
35404        q->info.si_signo = sig;
35405        q->info.si_errno = 0;
35406        q->info.si_code = SI_USER;
35407        q->info.si_pid = current->pid;
35408        q->info.si_uid = current->uid;
35409        break;
35410      case 1:
35411        q->info.si_signo = sig;
35412        q->info.si_errno = 0;
35413        q->info.si_code = SI_KERNEL;
35414        q->info.si_pid = 0;
35415        q->info.si_uid = 0;
35416        break;
35417      default:
35418        copy_siginfo(&q->info, info);
35419        break;
35420      }
```

```
35421    } else if (sig >= SIGRTMIN && info
35422            && (unsigned long) info != 1
35423            && info->si_code != SI_USER) {
35424      /* Queue overflow, abort.  We may abort if the signal
35425       * was rt and sent by user using something other than
35426       * kill().  */
35427      return -EAGAIN;
35428    }
35429
35430    sigaddset(&signals->signal, sig);
35431    return 0;
35432 }
35433
35434 /* Tell a process that it has a new active signal..
35435  *
35436  * NOTE! we rely on the previous spin_lock to lock
35437  * interrupts for us! We can only be called with
35438  * "sigmask_lock" held, and the local interrupt must have
35439  * been disabled when that got acquired!
35440  *
35441  * No need to set need_resched since signal event passing
35442  * goes through ->blocked */
35443 static inline void signal_wake_up(struct task_struct *t)
35444 {
35445    t->sigpending = 1;
35446
35447    if (t->state & TASK_INTERRUPTIBLE) {
35448      wake_up_process(t);
35449      return;
35450    }
35451 #ifdef CONFIG_SMP
35452    /* If the task is running on a different CPU force a
35453     * reschedule on the other CPU to make it notice the
35454     * new signal quickly.
35455     *
35456     * The code below is a tad loose and might occasionally
35457     * kick the wrong CPU if we catch the process in the
35458     * process of changing - but no harm is done by that
35459     * other than doing an extra (lightweight) IPI
35460     * interrupt.  */
35461    spin_lock(&runqueue_lock);
35462    if (t->has_cpu && t->processor != smp_processor_id())
35463      smp_send_reschedule(t->processor);
35464    spin_unlock(&runqueue_lock);
35465 #endif                           /* CONFIG_SMP */
35466 }
35467
```

```
p 579  35468 static int deliver_signal(int sig, struct siginfo *info,
       35469     struct task_struct *t)
       35470 {
       35471   int retval = send_signal(sig, info, &t->pending);
       35472
       35473   if (!retval && !sigismember(&t->blocked, sig))
       35474     signal_wake_up(t);
       35475
       35476   return retval;
       35477 }
       35478
       35479 int
p 577  35480 send_sig_info(int sig, struct siginfo *info,
       35481 struct task_struct *t)
       35482 {
       35483   unsigned long flags;
       35484   int ret;
       35485
       35486
       35487 #if DEBUG_SIG
       35488   printk("SIG queue (%s:%d): %d ", t->comm, t->pid, sig);
       35489 #endif
       35490
       35491   ret = -EINVAL;
       35492   if (sig < 0 || sig > _NSIG)
       35493     goto out_nolock;
       35494   /* The somewhat baroque permissions check... */
       35495   ret = -EPERM;
       35496   if (bad_signal(sig, info, t))
       35497     goto out_nolock;
       35498
       35499   /* The null signal is a permissions and process
       35500    * existance probe. No signal is actually delivered.
       35501    * Same goes for zombies. */
       35502   ret = 0;
       35503   if (!sig || !t->sig)
       35504     goto out_nolock;
       35505
       35506   spin_lock_irqsave(&t->sigmask_lock, flags);
       35507   handle_stop_signal(sig, t);
       35508
       35509   /* Optimize away the signal, if it's a signal that can
       35510    * be handled immediately (ie non-blocked and
       35511    * untraced) and that is ignored (either explicitly or
       35512    * by default). */
       35513   if (ignored_signal(sig, t))
       35514     goto out;
```

```
       35515
       35516   /* Support queueing exactly one non-rt signal, so that
       35517    * we can get more detailed information about the
       35518    * cause of the signal. */
       35519   if (sig < SIGRTMIN &&
       35520       sigismember(&t->pending.signal, sig))
       35521     goto out;
       35522
       35523   ret = deliver_signal(sig, info, t);
       35524 out:
       35525   spin_unlock_irqrestore(&t->sigmask_lock, flags);
       35526   if ((t->state & TASK_INTERRUPTIBLE)
       35527       && signal_pending(t))
       35528     wake_up_process(t);
       35529 out_nolock:
       35530 #if DEBUG_SIG
       35531   printk(" %d -> %d\n", signal_pending(t), ret);
       35532 #endif
       35533
       35534   return ret;
       35535 }
       35536
       35537 /* Force a signal that the process can't ignore: if
       35538  * necessary we unblock the signal and change any SIG_IGN
       35539  * to SIG_DFL.  */
       35540 int
p 579  35541 force_sig_info(int sig, struct siginfo *info,
       35542 struct task_struct *t)
       35543 {
       35544   unsigned long int flags;
       35545
       35546   spin_lock_irqsave(&t->sigmask_lock, flags);
       35547   if (t->sig == NULL) {
       35548     spin_unlock_irqrestore(&t->sigmask_lock, flags);
       35549     return -ESRCH;
       35550   }
       35551
       35552   if (t->sig->action[sig - 1].sa.sa_handler == SIG_IGN)
       35553     t->sig->action[sig - 1].sa.sa_handler = SIG_DFL;
       35554   sigdelset(&t->blocked, sig);
       35555   recalc_sigpending(t);
       35556   spin_unlock_irqrestore(&t->sigmask_lock, flags);
       35557
       35558   return send_sig_info(sig, info, t);
       35559 }
       35560
       35561 /* kill_pg_info() sends a signal to a process group: this
```

```
35562    * is what the tty control characters do (^C, ^Z etc) */
35563 int
35564 kill_pg_info(int sig, struct siginfo *info, pid_t pgrp)
35565 {
35566    int retval = -EINVAL;
35567    if (pgrp > 0) {
35568      struct task_struct *p;
35569
35570      retval = -ESRCH;
35571      read_lock(&tasklist_lock);
35572      for_each_task(p) {
35573        if (p->pgrp == pgrp) {
35574          int err = send_sig_info(sig, info, p);
35575          if (retval)
35576            retval = err;
35577        }
35578      }
35579      read_unlock(&tasklist_lock);
35580    }
35581    return retval;
35582 }
35583
35584 /* kill_sl_info() sends a signal to the session leader:
35585  * this is used to send SIGHUP to the controlling process
35586  * of a terminal when the connection is lost.  */
35587 int
35588 kill_sl_info(int sig, struct siginfo *info, pid_t sess)
35589 {
35590    int retval = -EINVAL;
35591    if (sess > 0) {
35592      struct task_struct *p;
35593
35594      retval = -ESRCH;
35595      read_lock(&tasklist_lock);
35596      for_each_task(p) {
35597        if (p->leader && p->session == sess) {
35598          int err = send_sig_info(sig, info, p);
35599          if (retval)
35600            retval = err;
35601        }
35602      }
35603      read_unlock(&tasklist_lock);
35604    }
35605    return retval;
35606 }
35607
35608 inline int
```

```
35609 kill_proc_info(int sig, struct siginfo *info, pid_t pid)
35610 {
35611    int error;
35612    struct task_struct *p;
35613
35614    read_lock(&tasklist_lock);
35615    p = find_task_by_pid(pid);
35616    error = -ESRCH;
35617    if (p)
35618      error = send_sig_info(sig, info, p);
35619    read_unlock(&tasklist_lock);
35620    return error;
35621 }
35622
35623
35624 /* kill_something_info() interprets pid in interesting
35625  * ways just like kill(2).
35626  *
35627  * POSIX specifies that kill(-1,sig) is unspecified, but
35628  * what we have is probably wrong.  Should make it like
35629  * BSD or SYSV.  */
35630 static int kill_something_info(int sig,
35631      struct siginfo *info, int pid)
35632 {
35633    if (!pid) {
35634      return kill_pg_info(sig, info, current->pgrp);
35635    } else if (pid == -1) {
35636      int retval = 0, count = 0;
35637      struct task_struct *p;
35638
35639      read_lock(&tasklist_lock);
35640      for_each_task(p) {
35641        if (p->pid > 1 && p != current) {
35642          int err = send_sig_info(sig, info, p);
35643          ++count;
35644          if (err != -EPERM)
35645            retval = err;
35646        }
35647      }
35648      read_unlock(&tasklist_lock);
35649      return count ? retval : -ESRCH;
35650    } else if (pid < 0) {
35651      return kill_pg_info(sig, info, -pid);
35652    } else {
35653      return kill_proc_info(sig, info, pid);
35654    }
35655 }
```

```
35656
35657  /* These are for backward compatibility with the rest of
35658   * the kernel source.  */
35659
35660  int send_sig(int sig, struct task_struct *p, int priv)
35661  {
35662    return send_sig_info(sig, (void *) (long) (priv != 0),
35663                              p);
35664  }
35665
35666  void force_sig(int sig, struct task_struct *p)
35667  {
35668    force_sig_info(sig, (void *) 1L, p);
35669  }
35670
35671  int kill_pg(pid_t pgrp, int sig, int priv)
35672  {
35673    return kill_pg_info(sig, (void *) (long) (priv != 0),
35674                            pgrp);
35675  }
35676
35677  int kill_sl(pid_t sess, int sig, int priv)
35678  {
35679    return kill_sl_info(sig, (void *) (long) (priv != 0),
35680                            sess);
35681  }
35682
35683  int kill_proc(pid_t pid, int sig, int priv)
35684  {
35685    return kill_proc_info(sig, (void *) (long) (priv != 0),
35686                              pid);
35687  }
35688
35689  /* Joy. Or not. Pthread wants us to wake up every thread
35690   * in our parent group.  */
35691  static void wake_up_parent(struct task_struct *parent)
35692  {
35693    struct task_struct *tsk = parent;
35694
35695    do {
35696      wake_up_interruptible(&tsk->wait_chldexit);
35697      tsk = next_thread(tsk);
35698    } while (tsk != parent);
35699  }
35700
35701  /* Let a parent know about a status change of a child. */
35702  void do_notify_parent(struct task_struct *tsk, int sig)
35703  {
35704    struct siginfo info;
35705    int why, status;
35706
35707    info.si_signo = sig;
35708    info.si_errno = 0;
35709    info.si_pid = tsk->pid;
35710    info.si_uid = tsk->uid;
35711
35712    /* FIXME: find out whether or not this is supposed to
35713     * be c*time. */
35714    info.si_utime = tsk->times.tms_utime;
35715    info.si_stime = tsk->times.tms_stime;
35716
35717    status = tsk->exit_code & 0x7f;
35718    why = SI_KERNEL;                   /* shouldn't happen */
35719    switch (tsk->state) {
35720    case TASK_STOPPED:
35721      /* FIXME - can we deduce CLD_TRAPPED or
35722       * CLD_CONTINUED? */
35723      if (tsk->ptrace & PT_PTRACED)
35724        why = CLD_TRAPPED;
35725      else
35726        why = CLD_STOPPED;
35727      break;
35728
35729    default:
35730      if (tsk->exit_code & 0x80)
35731        why = CLD_DUMPED;
35732      else if (tsk->exit_code & 0x7f)
35733        why = CLD_KILLED;
35734      else {
35735        why = CLD_EXITED;
35736        status = tsk->exit_code >> 8;
35737      }
35738      break;
35739    }
35740    info.si_code = why;
35741    info.si_status = status;
35742
35743    send_sig_info(sig, &info, tsk->p_pptr);
35744    wake_up_parent(tsk->p_pptr);
35745  }
35746
35747
35748  /* We need the tasklist lock because it's the only thing
35749   * that protects out "parent" pointer.
```

```
35750  *
35751  * exit.c calls "do_notify_parent()" directly, because
35752  * it already has the tasklist lock.  */
35753 void notify_parent(struct task_struct *tsk, int sig)
35754 {
35755    read_lock(&tasklist_lock);
35756    do_notify_parent(tsk, sig);
35757    read_unlock(&tasklist_lock);
35758 }
35759
35760 EXPORT_SYMBOL(dequeue_signal);
35761 EXPORT_SYMBOL(flush_signals);
35762 EXPORT_SYMBOL(force_sig);
35763 EXPORT_SYMBOL(force_sig_info);
35764 EXPORT_SYMBOL(kill_pg);
35765 EXPORT_SYMBOL(kill_pg_info);
35766 EXPORT_SYMBOL(kill_proc);
35767 EXPORT_SYMBOL(kill_proc_info);
35768 EXPORT_SYMBOL(kill_sl);
35769 EXPORT_SYMBOL(kill_sl_info);
35770 EXPORT_SYMBOL(notify_parent);
35771 EXPORT_SYMBOL(recalc_sigpending);
35772 EXPORT_SYMBOL(send_sig);
35773 EXPORT_SYMBOL(send_sig_info);
35774 EXPORT_SYMBOL(block_all_signals);
35775 EXPORT_SYMBOL(unblock_all_signals);
35776
35777
35778 /* System call entry points.  */
35779
35780 /* We don't need to get the kernel lock - this is all
35781  * local to this particular thread.. (and that's good,
35782  * because this is _heavily_ used by various programs) */
35783 asmlinkage long
35784 sys_rt_sigprocmask(int how, sigset_t * set,
35785      sigset_t * oset, size_t sigsetsize)
35786 {
35787   int error = -EINVAL;
35788   sigset_t old_set, new_set;
35789
35790   /* XXX: Don't preclude handling different sized
35791    * sigset_t's.  */
35792   if (sigsetsize != sizeof(sigset_t))
35793     goto out;
35794
35795   if (set) {
35796     error = -EFAULT;
```

```
35797     if (copy_from_user(&new_set, set, sizeof(*set)))
35798       goto out;
35799     sigdelsetmask(&new_set,
35800         sigmask(SIGKILL) | sigmask(SIGSTOP));
35801
35802     spin_lock_irq(&current->sigmask_lock);
35803     old_set = current->blocked;
35804
35805     error = 0;
35806     switch (how) {
35807     default:
35808       error = -EINVAL;
35809       break;
35810     case SIG_BLOCK:
35811       sigorsets(&new_set, &old_set, &new_set);
35812       break;
35813     case SIG_UNBLOCK:
35814       signandsets(&new_set, &old_set, &new_set);
35815       break;
35816     case SIG_SETMASK:
35817       break;
35818     }
35819
35820     current->blocked = new_set;
35821     recalc_sigpending(current);
35822     spin_unlock_irq(&current->sigmask_lock);
35823     if (error)
35824       goto out;
35825     if (oset)
35826       goto set_old;
35827   } else if (oset) {
35828     spin_lock_irq(&current->sigmask_lock);
35829     old_set = current->blocked;
35830     spin_unlock_irq(&current->sigmask_lock);
35831
35832 set_old:
35833     error = -EFAULT;
35834     if (copy_to_user(oset, &old_set, sizeof(*oset)))
35835       goto out;
35836   }
35837   error = 0;
35838 out:
35839   return error;
35840 }
35841
35842 long do_sigpending(void *set, unsigned long sigsetsize)
35843 {
```

```
35844    long error = -EINVAL;
35845    sigset_t pending;
35846
35847    if (sigsetsize > sizeof(sigset_t))
35848      goto out;
35849
35850    spin_lock_irq(&current->sigmask_lock);
35851    sigandsets(&pending, &current->blocked,
35852        &current->pending.signal);
35853    spin_unlock_irq(&current->sigmask_lock);
35854
35855    error = -EFAULT;
35856    if (!copy_to_user(set, &pending, sigsetsize))
35857      error = 0;
35858 out:
35859    return error;
35860 }
35861
35862 asmlinkage long
35863 sys_rt_sigpending(sigset_t * set, size_t sigsetsize)
35864 {
35865    return do_sigpending(set, sigsetsize);
35866 }
35867
35868 asmlinkage long
35869 sys_rt_sigtimedwait(const sigset_t * uthese,
35870      siginfo_t * uinfo, const struct timespec *uts,
35871      size_t sigsetsize)
35872 {
35873    int ret, sig;
35874    sigset_t these;
35875    struct timespec ts;
35876    siginfo_t info;
35877    long timeout = 0;
35878
35879    /* XXX: Don't preclude handling different sized
35880     * sigset_t's. */
35881    if (sigsetsize != sizeof(sigset_t))
35882      return -EINVAL;
35883
35884    if (copy_from_user(&these, uthese, sizeof(these)))
35885      return -EFAULT;
35886
35887    /* Invert the set of allowed signals to get those we
35888     * want to block. */
35889    sigdelsetmask(&these,
35890        sigmask(SIGKILL) | sigmask(SIGSTOP));
```

```
35891    signotset(&these);
35892
35893    if (uts) {
35894      if (copy_from_user(&ts, uts, sizeof(ts)))
35895        return -EFAULT;
35896      if (ts.tv_nsec >= 1000000000L || ts.tv_nsec < 0
35897          || ts.tv_sec < 0)
35898        return -EINVAL;
35899    }
35900
35901    spin_lock_irq(&current->sigmask_lock);
35902    sig = dequeue_signal(&these, &info);
35903    if (!sig) {
35904      timeout = MAX_SCHEDULE_TIMEOUT;
35905      if (uts)
35906        timeout = (timespec_to_jiffies(&ts)
35907            + (ts.tv_sec || ts.tv_nsec));
35908
35909      if (timeout) {
35910        /* None ready — temporarily unblock those we're
35911         * interested while we are sleeping in so that
35912         * we'll be awakened when they arrive.  */
35913        sigset_t oldblocked = current->blocked;
35914        sigandsets(&current->blocked, &current->blocked,
35915            &these);
35916        recalc_sigpending(current);
35917        spin_unlock_irq(&current->sigmask_lock);
35918
35919        current->state = TASK_INTERRUPTIBLE;
35920        timeout = schedule_timeout(timeout);
35921
35922        spin_lock_irq(&current->sigmask_lock);
35923        sig = dequeue_signal(&these, &info);
35924        current->blocked = oldblocked;
35925        recalc_sigpending(current);
35926      }
35927    }
35928    spin_unlock_irq(&current->sigmask_lock);
35929
35930    if (sig) {
35931      ret = sig;
35932      if (uinfo) {
35933        if (copy_siginfo_to_user(uinfo, &info))
35934          ret = -EFAULT;
35935      }
35936    } else {
35937      ret = -EAGAIN;
```

p 583

```
35938        if (timeout)
35939            ret = -EINTR;
35940    }
35941
35942    return ret;
35943 }
35944
```
p 577 ►
```
35945 asmlinkage long sys_kill(int pid, int sig)
35946 {
35947    struct siginfo info;
35948
35949    info.si_signo = sig;
35950    info.si_errno = 0;
35951    info.si_code = SI_USER;
35952    info.si_pid = current->pid;
35953    info.si_uid = current->uid;
35954
35955    return kill_something_info(sig, &info, pid);
35956 }
35957
35958 asmlinkage long
35959 sys_rt_sigqueueinfo(int pid, int sig, siginfo_t * uinfo)
35960 {
35961    siginfo_t info;
35962
35963    if (copy_from_user(&info, uinfo, sizeof(siginfo_t)))
35964        return -EFAULT;
35965
35966    /* Not even root can pretend to send signals from the
35967     * kernel. Nor can they impersonate a kill(), which
35968     * adds source info.  */
35969    if (info.si_code >= 0)
35970        return -EPERM;
35971    info.si_signo = sig;
35972
35973    /* POSIX.1b doesn't mention process groups.  */
35974    return kill_proc_info(sig, &info, pid);
35975 }
35976
35977 int
```
p 583 ►
```
35978 do_sigaction(int sig, const struct k_sigaction *act,
35979 struct k_sigaction *oact)
35980 {
35981    struct k_sigaction *k;
35982
35983    if (sig < 1 || sig > _NSIG ||
35984        (act && (sig == SIGKILL || sig == SIGSTOP)))
```

```
35985        return -EINVAL;
35986
35987    k = &current->sig->action[sig - 1];
35988
35989    spin_lock(&current->sig->siglock);
35990
35991    if (oact)
35992        *oact = *k;
35993
35994    if (act) {
35995        *k = *act;
35996        sigdelsetmask(&k->sa.sa_mask,
35997            sigmask(SIGKILL) | sigmask(SIGSTOP));
35998
35999        /* POSIX 3.3.1.3:
36000         * "Setting a signal action to SIG_IGN for a signal
36001         * that is pending shall cause the pending signal to
36002         * be discarded, whether or not it is blocked."
36003         *
36004         * "Setting a signal action to SIG_DFL for a signal
36005         * that is pending and whose default action is to
36006         * ignore the signal (for example, SIGCHLD), shall
36007         * cause the pending signal to be discarded, whether
36008         * or not it is blocked"
36009         *
36010         * Note the silly behaviour of SIGCHLD: SIG_IGN means
36011         * that the signal isn't actually ignored, but does
36012         * automatic child reaping, while SIG_DFL is
36013         * explicitly said by POSIX to force the signal to be
36014         * ignored.  */
36015
36016        if (k->sa.sa_handler == SIG_IGN
36017            || (k->sa.sa_handler == SIG_DFL
36018                && (sig == SIGCONT ||
36019                    sig == SIGCHLD || sig == SIGWINCH))) {
36020            spin_lock_irq(&current->sigmask_lock);
36021            if (rm_sig_from_queue(sig, current))
36022                recalc_sigpending(current);
36023            spin_unlock_irq(&current->sigmask_lock);
36024        }
36025    }
36026
36027    spin_unlock(&current->sig->siglock);
36028    return 0;
36029 }
36030
36031 int
```

```
36032 do_sigaltstack(const stack_t * uss, stack_t * uoss,      36079     current->sas_ss_sp = (unsigned long) ss_sp;
36033 unsigned long sp)                                        36080     current->sas_ss_size = ss_size;
36034 {                                                        36081   }
36035   stack_t oss;                                          36082
36036   int error;                                            36083   if (uoss) {
36037                                                          36084     error = -EFAULT;
36038   if (uoss) {                                           36085     if (copy_to_user(uoss, &oss, sizeof(oss)))
36039     oss.ss_sp = (void *) current->sas_ss_sp;            36086       goto out;
36040     oss.ss_size = current->sas_ss_size;                 36087   }
36041     oss.ss_flags = sas_ss_flags(sp);                    36088
36042   }                                                     36089   error = 0;
36043                                                          36090 out:
36044   if (uss) {                                            36091   return error;
36045     void *ss_sp;                                        36092 }
36046     size_t ss_size;                                     36093
36047     int ss_flags;                                       36094 asmlinkage long sys_sigpending(old_sigset_t * set)
36048                                                          36095 {
36049     error = -EFAULT;                                    36096   return do_sigpending(set, sizeof(*set));
36050     if (verify_area(VERIFY_READ, uss, sizeof(*uss))     36097 }
36051         || __get_user(ss_sp, &uss->ss_sp)               36098
36052         || __get_user(ss_flags, &uss->ss_flags)         36099 #if !defined(__alpha__)
36053         || __get_user(ss_size, &uss->ss_size))          36100 /* Alpha has its own versions with special arguments.  */
36054       goto out;                                         36101
36055                                                          36102 asmlinkage long
36056     error = -EPERM;                                     36103 sys_sigprocmask(int how, old_sigset_t * set,
36057     if (on_sig_stack(sp))                               36104     old_sigset_t * oset)
36058       goto out;                                         36105 {
36059                                                          36106   int error;
36060     error = -EINVAL;                                    36107   old_sigset_t old_set, new_set;
36061     /* Note - this code used to test ss_flags incorrectly 36108
36062      *        old code may have been written using      36109   if (set) {
36063      *        ss_flags==0 to mean ss_flags==SS_ONSTACK  36110     error = -EFAULT;
36064      *        (as this was the only way that worked) -  36111     if (copy_from_user(&new_set, set, sizeof(*set)))
36065      *        this fix preserves that older mechanism */ 36112       goto out;
36066     if (ss_flags != SS_DISABLE && ss_flags != SS_ONSTACK 36113     new_set &= ~(sigmask(SIGKILL) | sigmask(SIGSTOP));
36067         && ss_flags != 0)                               36114
36068       goto out;                                         36115     spin_lock_irq(&current->sigmask_lock);
36069                                                          36116     old_set = current->blocked.sig[0];
36070     if (ss_flags == SS_DISABLE) {                       36117
36071       ss_size = 0;                                      36118     error = 0;
36072       ss_sp = NULL;                                     36119     switch (how) {
36073     } else {                                            36120     default:
36074       error = -ENOMEM;                                  36121       error = -EINVAL;
36075       if (ss_size < MINSIGSTKSZ)                        36122       break;
36076         goto out;                                       36123     case SIG_BLOCK:
36077     }                                                   36124       sigaddsetmask(&current->blocked, new_set);
36078                                                          36125       break;
```

```
36126      case SIG_UNBLOCK:
36127        sigdelsetmask(&current->blocked, new_set);
36128        break;
36129      case SIG_SETMASK:
36130        current->blocked.sig[0] = new_set;
36131        break;
36132      }
36133
36134      recalc_sigpending(current);
36135      spin_unlock_irq(&current->sigmask_lock);
36136      if (error)
36137        goto out;
36138      if (oset)
36139        goto set_old;
36140    } else if (oset) {
36141      old_set = current->blocked.sig[0];
36142    set_old:
36143      error = -EFAULT;
36144      if (copy_to_user(oset, &old_set, sizeof(*oset)))
36145        goto out;
36146    }
36147    error = 0;
36148 out:
36149    return error;
36150 }
36151
36152 #ifndef __sparc__
36153 asmlinkage long
36154 sys_rt_sigaction(int sig, const struct sigaction *act,
36155      struct sigaction *oact, size_t sigsetsize)
36156 {
36157    struct k_sigaction new_sa, old_sa;
36158    int ret = -EINVAL;
36159
36160    /* XXX: Don't preclude handling different sized
36161     * sigset_t's. */
36162    if (sigsetsize != sizeof(sigset_t))
36163      goto out;
36164
36165    if (act) {
36166      if (copy_from_user(&new_sa.sa, act,
36167                         sizeof(new_sa.sa)))
36168        return -EFAULT;
36169    }
36170
36171    ret = do_sigaction(sig,
36172                       act ? &new_sa : NULL,
36173                       oact ? &old_sa : NULL);
36174
36175    if (!ret && oact) {
36176      if(copy_to_user(oact, &old_sa.sa, sizeof(old_sa.sa)))
36177        return -EFAULT;
36178    }
36179 out:
36180    return ret;
36181 }
36182 #endif
36183 #endif                              /* __sparc__ */
36184
36185 #if !defined(__alpha__) && !defined(__ia64__)
36186 /* For backwards compatibility.  Functionality superseded
36187  * by sigprocmask.  */
36188 asmlinkage long sys_sgetmask(void)
36189 {
36190    /* SMP safe */
36191    return current->blocked.sig[0];
36192 }
36193
36194 asmlinkage long sys_ssetmask(int newmask)
36195 {
36196    int old;
36197
36198    spin_lock_irq(&current->sigmask_lock);
36199    old = current->blocked.sig[0];
36200
36201    siginitset(&current->blocked,
36202        newmask & ~(sigmask(SIGKILL) | sigmask(SIGSTOP)));
36203    recalc_sigpending(current);
36204    spin_unlock_irq(&current->sigmask_lock);
36205
36206    return old;
36207 }
36208 #endif                              /* !defined(__alpha__) */
36209
36210 #if !defined(__alpha__) && !defined(__ia64__) &&         \
36211      !defined(__mips__)
36212 /* For backwards compatibility.  Functionality superseded
36213  * by sigaction.  */
36214 asmlinkage unsigned long
36215 sys_signal(int sig, __sighandler_t handler)
36216 {
36217    struct k_sigaction new_sa, old_sa;
36218    int ret;
36219
```

```
36220    new_sa.sa.sa_handler = handler;
36221    new_sa.sa.sa_flags = SA_ONESHOT | SA_NOMASK;
36222
36223    ret = do_sigaction(sig, &new_sa, &old_sa);
36224
36225    return ret
36226      ? ret
36227      : (unsigned long) old_sa.sa.sa_handler;
36228 }
36229
36230 #endif    /* !alpha && !__ia64__ && !defined(__mips__) */
```

kernel/softirq.c

```
36231 /*
36232  *       linux/kernel/softirq.c
36233  *
36234  *       Copyright (C) 1992 Linus Torvalds
36235  *
36236  * Fixed a disable_bh()/enable_bh() race (was causing a
36237  * console lockup) due bh_mask_count not atomic
36238  * handling. Copyright (C) 1998 Andrea Arcangeli
36239  *
36240  * Rewritten. Old one was good in 2.2, but in 2.3 it was
36241  * immoral. —ANK (990903)
36242  */
36243
36244 #include <linux/config.h>
36245 #include <linux/mm.h>
36246 #include <linux/kernel_stat.h>
36247 #include <linux/interrupt.h>
36248 #include <linux/smp_lock.h>
36249 #include <linux/init.h>
36250 #include <linux/tqueue.h>
36251
36252 /* - No shared variables, all the data are CPU local.
36253  * - If a softirq needs serialization, let it serialize
36254  * itself by its own spinlocks.
36255  * - Even if softirq is serialized, only local cpu is
36256  * marked for execution.  Hence, we get something sort of
36257  * weak cpu binding.  Though it is still not clear, will
36258  * it result in better locality or will not.
36259  * - These softirqs are not masked by global cli() and
36260  * start_bh_atomic() (by clear reasons). Hence, old parts
36261  * of code still using global locks MUST NOT use
36262  * softirqs, but insert interfacing routines acquiring
36263  * global locks. F.e.  look at BHs implementation.
36264  *
36265  * Examples:
36266  * - NET RX softirq. It is multithreaded and does not
36267  * require any global serialization.
36268  * - NET TX softirq. It kicks software netdevice queues,
36269  * hence it is logically serialized per device, but this
36270  * serialization is invisible to common code.
36271  * - Tasklets: serialized wrt itself.
36272  * - Bottom halves: globally serialized, grr... */
36273
36274 /* No separate irq_stat for s390, it is part of PSA */
36275 #if !defined(CONFIG_ARCH_S390)
36276 irq_cpustat_t irq_stat[NR_CPUS];
36277 #endif                           /* CONFIG_ARCH_S390 */
36278
36279 static struct softirq_action softirq_vec[32]
36280     __cacheline_aligned;
36281
36282 asmlinkage void do_softirq()
36283 {
36284    int cpu = smp_processor_id();
36285    __u32 active, mask;
36286
36287    if (in_interrupt())
36288      return;
36289
36290    local_bh_disable();
36291
36292    local_irq_disable();
36293    mask = softirq_mask(cpu);
36294    active = softirq_active(cpu) & mask;
36295
36296    if (active) {
36297      struct softirq_action *h;
36298
36299 restart:
36300      /* Reset active bitmask before enabling irqs */
36301      softirq_active(cpu) &= ~active;
36302
36303      local_irq_enable();
36304
36305      h = softirq_vec;
36306      mask &= ~active;
36307
36308      do {
36309        if (active & 1)
36310          h->action(h);
36311        h++;
```

p 590

```
36312        active >>= 1;
36313      } while (active);
36314
36315      local_irq_disable();
36316
36317      active = softirq_active(cpu);
36318      if ((active &= mask) != 0)
36319        goto retry;
36320    }
36321
36322    local_bh_enable();
36323
36324    /* Leave with locally disabled hard irqs. It is
36325     * critical to close window for infinite recursion,
36326     * while we help local bh count, it protected us. Now
36327     * we are defenceless. */
36328    return;
36329
36330 retry:
36331    goto restart;
36332 }
36333
36334
36335 static spinlock_t softirq_mask_lock = SPIN_LOCK_UNLOCKED;
36336
36337 void open_softirq(int nr,
36338      void (*action) (struct softirq_action *), void *data)
36339 {
36340    unsigned long flags;
36341    int i;
36342
36343    spin_lock_irqsave(&softirq_mask_lock, flags);
36344    softirq_vec[nr].data = data;
36345    softirq_vec[nr].action = action;
36346
36347    for (i = 0; i < NR_CPUS; i++)
36348      softirq_mask(i) |= (1 << nr);
36349    spin_unlock_irqrestore(&softirq_mask_lock, flags);
36350 }
36351
36352
36353 /* Tasklets */
36354
36355 struct tasklet_head tasklet_vec[NR_CPUS]
36356      __cacheline_aligned;
36357
36358 static void tasklet_action(struct softirq_action *a)
36359 {
36360    int cpu = smp_processor_id();
36361    struct tasklet_struct *list;
36362
36363    local_irq_disable();
36364    list = tasklet_vec[cpu].list;
36365    tasklet_vec[cpu].list = NULL;
36366    local_irq_enable();
36367
36368    while (list != NULL) {
36369      struct tasklet_struct *t = list;
36370
36371      list = list->next;
36372
36373      if (tasklet_trylock(t)) {
36374        if (atomic_read(&t->count) == 0) {
36375          clear_bit(TASKLET_STATE_SCHED, &t->state);
36376
36377          t->func(t->data);
36378          /* talklet_trylock() uses test_and_set_bit that
36379           * imply an mb when it returns zero, thus we need
36380           * the explicit mb only here: while closing the
36381           * critical section.  */
36382 #ifdef CONFIG_SMP
36383          smp_mb__before_clear_bit();
36384 #endif
36385          tasklet_unlock(t);
36386          continue;
36387        }
36388        tasklet_unlock(t);
36389      }
36390      local_irq_disable();
36391      t->next = tasklet_vec[cpu].list;
36392      tasklet_vec[cpu].list = t;
36393      __cpu_raise_softirq(cpu, TASKLET_SOFTIRQ);
36394      local_irq_enable();
36395    }
36396 }
36397
36398
36399
36400 struct tasklet_head tasklet_hi_vec[NR_CPUS]
36401      __cacheline_aligned;
36402
36403 static void tasklet_hi_action(struct softirq_action *a)
36404 {
36405    int cpu = smp_processor_id();
```

```
36406    struct tasklet_struct *list;                       36453        current->state = TASK_RUNNING;
36407                                                        36454        do {
36408    local_irq_disable();                                36455          current->policy |= SCHED_YIELD;
36409    list = tasklet_hi_vec[cpu].list;                    36456          schedule();
36410    tasklet_hi_vec[cpu].list = NULL;                    36457        } while (test_bit(TASKLET_STATE_SCHED, &t->state));
36411    local_irq_enable();                                 36458      }
36412                                                        36459      tasklet_unlock_wait(t);
36413    while (list != NULL) {                              36460      clear_bit(TASKLET_STATE_SCHED, &t->state);
36414      struct tasklet_struct *t = list;                 36461  }
36415                                                        36462
36416      list = list->next;                               36463
36417                                                        36464
36418      if (tasklet_trylock(t)) {                        36465  /* Old style BHs */
36419        if (atomic_read(&t->count) == 0) {             36466
36420          clear_bit(TASKLET_STATE_SCHED, &t->state);   36467  static void (*bh_base[32]) (void);
36421                                                        36468  struct tasklet_struct bh_task_vec[32];
36422          t->func(t->data);                            36469
36423          tasklet_unlock(t);                           36470  /* BHs are serialized by spinlock global_bh_lock.
36424          continue;                                    36471   *
36425        }                                              36472   * It is still possible to make synchronize_bh() as
36426        tasklet_unlock(t);                             36473   * spin_unlock_wait(&global_bh_lock). This operation is
36427      }                                                36474   * not used by kernel now, so that this lock is not made
36428      local_irq_disable();                             36475   * private only due to wait_on_irq().
36429      t->next = tasklet_hi_vec[cpu].list;              36476   *
36430      tasklet_hi_vec[cpu].list = t;                    36477   * It can be removed only after auditing all the BHs. */
36431      __cpu_raise_softirq(cpu, HI_SOFTIRQ);            36478  spinlock_t global_bh_lock = SPIN_LOCK_UNLOCKED;
36432      local_irq_enable();                              36479
36433    }                                                  36480  static void bh_action(unsigned long nr)
36434  }                                                    36481  {
36435                                                       36482    int cpu = smp_processor_id();
36436                                                       36483
36437  void tasklet_init(struct tasklet_struct *t,          36484    if (!spin_trylock(&global_bh_lock))
36438        void (*func) (unsigned long), unsigned long data) 36485      goto resched;
36439  {                                                    36486
36440    t->func = func;                                    36487    if (!hardirq_trylock(cpu))
36441    t->data = data;                                    36488      goto resched_unlock;
36442    t->state = 0;                                      36489
36443    atomic_set(&t->count, 0);                          36490    if (bh_base[nr])
36444  }                                                    36491      bh_base[nr] ();
36445                                                       36492
36446  void tasklet_kill(struct tasklet_struct *t)          36493    hardirq_endlock(cpu);
36447  {                                                    36494    spin_unlock(&global_bh_lock);
36448    if (in_interrupt())                                36495    return;
36449      printk("Attempt to kill tasklet from interrupt\n"); 36496
36450                                                       36497  resched_unlock:
36451    while (test_and_set_bit(TASKLET_STATE_SCHED,       36498    spin_unlock(&global_bh_lock);
36452                           &t->state)) {               36499  resched:
```

```
36500   mark_bh(nr);
36501 }
36502
36503 void init_bh(int nr, void (*routine) (void))
36504 {
36505   bh_base[nr] = routine;
36506   mb();
36507 }
36508
36509 void remove_bh(int nr)
36510 {
36511   tasklet_kill(bh_task_vec + nr);
36512   bh_base[nr] = NULL;
36513 }
36514
36515 void __init softirq_init()
36516 {
36517   int i;
36518
36519   for (i = 0; i < 32; i++)
36520     tasklet_init(bh_task_vec + i, bh_action, i);
36521
36522   open_softirq(TASKLET_SOFTIRQ, tasklet_action, NULL);
36523   open_softirq(HI_SOFTIRQ, tasklet_hi_action, NULL);
36524 }
36525
36526 void __run_task_queue(task_queue * list)
36527 {
36528   struct list_head head, *next;
36529   unsigned long flags;
36530
36531   spin_lock_irqsave(&tqueue_lock, flags);
36532   list_add(&head, list);
36533   list_del_init(list);
36534   spin_unlock_irqrestore(&tqueue_lock, flags);
36535
36536   next = head.next;
36537   while (next != &head) {
36538     void (*f) (void *);
36539     struct tq_struct *p;
36540     void *data;
36541
36542     p = list_entry(next, struct tq_struct, list);
36543     next = next->next;
36544     f = p->routine;
36545     data = p->data;
36546     wmb();
```

p 590

```
36547     p->sync = 0;
36548     if (f)
36549       f(data);
36550   }
36551 }
```

kernel/sys.c

```
36552 /*
36553  *  linux/kernel/sys.c
36554  *
36555  *  Copyright (C) 1991, 1992  Linus Torvalds
36556  */
36557
36558 #include <linux/module.h>
36559 #include <linux/mm.h>
36560 #include <linux/utsname.h>
36561 #include <linux/mman.h>
36562 #include <linux/smp_lock.h>
36563 #include <linux/notifier.h>
36564 #include <linux/reboot.h>
36565 #include <linux/prctl.h>
36566 #include <linux/init.h>
36567 #include <linux/highuid.h>
36568
36569 #include <asm/uaccess.h>
36570 #include <asm/io.h>
36571
36572 /* this is where the system-wide overflow UID and GID are
36573  * defined, for architectures that now have 32-bit
36574  * UID/GID but didn't in the past */
36575 int overflowuid = DEFAULT_OVERFLOWUID;
36576 int overflowgid = DEFAULT_OVERFLOWGID;
36577
36578 /* the same as above, but for filesystems which can only
36579  * store a 16-bit UID and GID. as such, this is needed on
36580  * all architectures */
36581 int fs_overflowuid = DEFAULT_FS_OVERFLOWUID;
36582 int fs_overflowgid = DEFAULT_FS_OVERFLOWUID;
36583
36584 /* this indicates whether you can reboot with
36585  * ctrl-alt-del: the default is yes */
36586 int C_A_D = 1;
36587
36588
36589 /* Notifier list for kernel code which wants to be called
36590  * at shutdown. This is used to stop any idling DMA
36591  * operations and the like.  */
```

```
36592 static struct notifier_block *reboot_notifier_list;
36593 rwlock_t notifier_lock = RW_LOCK_UNLOCKED;
36594
36595 /**
36596  *      notifier_chain_register - Add notifier to a
36597  *                              notifier chain
36598  *      @list: Pointer to root list pointer
36599  *      @n: New entry in notifier chain
36600  *
36601  *      Adds a notifier to a notifier chain.
36602  *
36603  *      Currently always returns zero. */
36604 int notifier_chain_register(struct notifier_block **list,
36605     struct notifier_block *n)
36606 {
36607   write_lock(&notifier_lock);
36608   while (*list) {
36609     if (n->priority > (*list)->priority)
36610       break;
36611     list = &((*list)->next);
36612   }
36613   n->next = *list;
36614   *list = n;
36615   write_unlock(&notifier_lock);
36616   return 0;
36617 }
36618
36619 /**
36620  *      notifier_chain_unregister - Remove notifier from
36621  *                              a notifier chain
36622  *      @nl: Pointer to root list pointer
36623  *      @n: New entry in notifier chain
36624  *
36625  *      Removes a notifier from a notifier chain.
36626  *
36627  *      Returns zero on success, or %-ENOENT on failure.
36628  */
36629 int notifier_chain_unregister(struct notifier_block **nl,
36630     struct notifier_block *n)
36631 {
36632   write_lock(&notifier_lock);
36633   while ((*nl) != NULL) {
36634     if ((*nl) == n) {
36635       *nl = n->next;
36636       write_unlock(&notifier_lock);
36637       return 0;
36638     }
36639     nl = &((*nl)->next);
36640   }
36641   write_unlock(&notifier_lock);
36642   return -ENOENT;
36643 }
36644
36645 /**
36646  *      notifier_call_chain - Call functions in a
36647  *                              notifier chain
36648  *      @n: Pointer to root pointer of notifier chain
36649  *      @val: Value passed unmodified to notifier
36650  *          function
36651  *      @v: Pointer passed unmodified to notifier
36652  *          function
36653  *
36654  *      Calls each function in a notifier chain in turn.
36655  *
36656  * If the return value of the notifier can be and'd with
36657  * %NOTIFY_STOP_MASK, then notifier_call_chain will
36658  * return immediately, with the return value of the
36659  * notifier function which halted execution.  Otherwise,
36660  * the return value is the return value of the last
36661  * notifier function called.  */
36662 int notifier_call_chain(struct notifier_block **n,
36663     unsigned long val, void *v)
36664 {
36665   int ret = NOTIFY_DONE;
36666   struct notifier_block *nb = *n;
36667
36668   while (nb) {
36669     ret = nb->notifier_call(nb, val, v);
36670     if (ret & NOTIFY_STOP_MASK) {
36671       return ret;
36672     }
36673     nb = nb->next;
36674   }
36675   return ret;
36676 }
36677
36678 /**
36679  *      register_reboot_notifier - Register function to
36680  *                              be called at reboot time
36681  *      @nb: Info about notifier function to be called
36682  *
36683  *      Registers a function with the list of functions
36684  *      to be called at reboot time.
36685  *
```

```
36686  *       Currently always returns zero, as
36687  *       notifier_chain_register always returns zero.  */
36688 int register_reboot_notifier(struct notifier_block *nb)
36689 {
36690   return notifier_chain_register(&reboot_notifier_list,
36691       nb);
36692 }
36693
36694 /**
36695  *       unregister_reboot_notifier - Unregister
36696  *                previously registered reboot notifier
36697  *       @nb: Hook to be unregistered
36698  *
36699  *       Unregisters a previously registered reboot
36700  *       notifier function.
36701  *
36702  *       Returns zero on success, or %-ENOENT on failure.
36703  */
36704 int unregister_reboot_notifier(struct notifier_block *nb)
36705 {
36706   return notifier_chain_unregister(&reboot_notifier_list,
36707       nb);
36708 }
36709
36710 asmlinkage long sys_ni_syscall(void)
36711 {
36712   return -ENOSYS;
36713 }
36714
36715 static int proc_sel(struct task_struct *p, int which,
36716     int who)
36717 {
36718   if (p->pid) {
36719     switch (which) {
36720     case PRIO_PROCESS:
36721       if (!who && p == current)
36722         return 1;
36723       return (p->pid == who);
36724     case PRIO_PGRP:
36725       if (!who)
36726         who = current->pgrp;
36727       return (p->pgrp == who);
36728     case PRIO_USER:
36729       if (!who)
36730         who = current->uid;
36731       return (p->uid == who);
36732     }
```

```
36733   }
36734   return 0;
36735 }
36736
36737 asmlinkage long sys_setpriority(int which, int who,
36738     int niceval)
36739 {
36740   struct task_struct *p;
36741   int error;
36742
36743   if (which > 2 || which < 0)
36744     return -EINVAL;
36745
36746   /* normalize: avoid signed division (rounding
36747    * problems) */
36748   error = -ESRCH;
36749   if (niceval < -20)
36750     niceval = -20;
36751   if (niceval > 19)
36752     niceval = 19;
36753
36754   read_lock(&tasklist_lock);
36755   for_each_task(p) {
36756     if (!proc_sel(p, which, who))
36757       continue;
36758     if (p->uid != current->euid &&
36759         p->uid != current->uid &&
36760         !capable(CAP_SYS_NICE)) {
36761       error = -EPERM;
36762       continue;
36763     }
36764     if (error == -ESRCH)
36765       error = 0;
36766     if (niceval < p->nice && !capable(CAP_SYS_NICE))
36767       error = -EACCES;
36768     else
36769       p->nice = niceval;
36770   }
36771   read_unlock(&tasklist_lock);
36772
36773   return error;
36774 }
36775
36776 /* Ugh. To avoid negative return values, "getpriority()"
36777  * will not return the normal nice-value, but a negated
36778  * value that has been offset by 20 (ie it returns 40..1
36779  * instead of -20..19) to stay compatible.  */
```

```
36780 asmlinkage long sys_getpriority(int which, int who)
36781 {
36782   struct task_struct *p;
36783   long retval = -ESRCH;
36784
36785   if (which > 2 || which < 0)
36786     return -EINVAL;
36787
36788   read_lock(&tasklist_lock);
36789   for_each_task(p) {
36790     long niceval;
36791     if (!proc_sel(p, which, who))
36792       continue;
36793     niceval = 20 - p->nice;
36794     if (niceval > retval)
36795       retval = niceval;
36796   }
36797   read_unlock(&tasklist_lock);
36798
36799   return retval;
36800 }
36801
36802
36803 /* Reboot system call: for obvious reasons only root may
36804  * call it, and even root needs to set up some magic
36805  * numbers in the registers so that some mistake won't
36806  * make this reboot the whole machine.  You can also set
36807  * the meaning of the ctrl-alt-del-key here.
36808  *
36809  * reboot doesn't sync: do that yourself before calling
36810  * this. */
36811 asmlinkage long sys_reboot(int magic1, int magic2,
36812     unsigned int cmd, void *arg)
36813 {
36814   char buffer[256];
36815
36816   /* We only trust the superuser with rebooting the
36817    * system. */
36818   if (!capable(CAP_SYS_BOOT))
36819     return -EPERM;
36820
36821   /* For safety, we require "magic" arguments. */
36822   if (magic1 != LINUX_REBOOT_MAGIC1 ||
36823       (magic2 != LINUX_REBOOT_MAGIC2 &&
36824        magic2 != LINUX_REBOOT_MAGIC2A &&
36825        magic2 != LINUX_REBOOT_MAGIC2B))
36826     return -EINVAL;
```

p 569

```
36827
36828   lock_kernel();
36829   switch (cmd) {
36830   case LINUX_REBOOT_CMD_RESTART:
36831     notifier_call_chain(&reboot_notifier_list,
36832         SYS_RESTART, NULL);
36833     printk(KERN_EMERG "Restarting system.\n");
36834     machine_restart(NULL);
36835     break;
36836
36837   case LINUX_REBOOT_CMD_CAD_ON:
36838     C_A_D = 1;
36839     break;
36840
36841   case LINUX_REBOOT_CMD_CAD_OFF:
36842     C_A_D = 0;
36843     break;
36844
36845   case LINUX_REBOOT_CMD_HALT:
36846     notifier_call_chain(&reboot_notifier_list, SYS_HALT,
36847         NULL);
36848     printk(KERN_EMERG "System halted.\n");
36849     machine_halt();
36850     do_exit(0);
36851     break;
36852
36853   case LINUX_REBOOT_CMD_POWER_OFF:
36854     notifier_call_chain(&reboot_notifier_list,
36855         SYS_POWER_OFF, NULL);
36856     printk(KERN_EMERG "Power down.\n");
36857     machine_power_off();
36858     do_exit(0);
36859     break;
36860
36861   case LINUX_REBOOT_CMD_RESTART2:
36862     if (strncpy_from_user(&buffer[0], (char *) arg,
36863         sizeof(buffer) - 1) < 0) {
36864       unlock_kernel();
36865       return -EFAULT;
36866     }
36867     buffer[sizeof(buffer) - 1] = '\0';
36868
36869     notifier_call_chain(&reboot_notifier_list,
36870         SYS_RESTART, buffer);
36871     printk(KERN_EMERG
36872         "Restarting system with command '%s'.\n",
36873         buffer);
```

```
36874      machine_restart(buffer);
36875      break;
36876
36877    default:
36878      unlock_kernel();
36879      return -EINVAL;
36880    }
36881    unlock_kernel();
36882    return 0;
36883 }
36884
36885 /* This function gets called by ctrl-alt-del - ie the
36886  * keyboard interrupt.  As it's called within an
36887  * interrupt, it may NOT sync: the only choice is whether
36888  * to reboot at once, or just ignore the ctrl-alt-del. */
36889 void ctrl_alt_del(void)
36890 {
36891    if (C_A_D) {
36892      notifier_call_chain(&reboot_notifier_list,
36893          SYS_RESTART, NULL);
36894      machine_restart(NULL);
36895    } else
36896      kill_proc(1, SIGINT, 1);
36897 }
36898
36899
36900 /* Unprivileged users may change the real gid to the
36901  * effective gid or vice versa.  (BSD-style)
36902  *
36903  * If you set the real gid at all, or set the effective
36904  * gid to a value not equal to the real gid, then the
36905  * saved gid is set to the new effective gid.
36906  *
36907  * This makes it possible for a setgid program to
36908  * completely drop its privileges, which is often a
36909  * useful assertion to make when you are doing a security
36910  * audit over a program.
36911  *
36912  * The general idea is that a program which uses just
36913  * setregid() will be 100% compatible with BSD.  A
36914  * program which uses just setgid() will be 100%
36915  * compatible with POSIX with saved IDs.
36916  *
36917  * SMP: There are not races, the GIDs are checked only by
36918  * filesystem operations (as far as semantic preservation
36919  * is concerned).  */
36920 asmlinkage long sys_setregid(gid_t rgid, gid_t egid)
36921 {
36922    int old_rgid = current->gid;
36923    int old_egid = current->egid;
36924
36925    if (rgid != (gid_t) - 1) {
36926      if ((old_rgid == rgid) ||
36927          (current->egid == rgid) || capable(CAP_SETGID))
36928        current->gid = rgid;
36929      else
36930        return -EPERM;
36931    }
36932    if (egid != (gid_t) - 1) {
36933      if ((old_rgid == egid) ||
36934          (current->egid == egid) ||
36935          (current->sgid == egid) || capable(CAP_SETGID))
36936        current->fsgid = current->egid = egid;
36937      else {
36938        current->gid = old_rgid;
36939        return -EPERM;
36940      }
36941    }
36942    if (rgid != (gid_t) - 1 ||
36943        (egid != (gid_t) - 1 && egid != old_rgid))
36944      current->sgid = current->egid;
36945    current->fsgid = current->egid;
36946    if (current->egid != old_egid)
36947      current->dumpable = 0;
36948    return 0;
36949 }
36950
36951 /* setgid() is implemented like SysV w/ SAVED_IDS
36952  *
36953  * SMP: Same implicit races as above.  */
36954 asmlinkage long sys_setgid(gid_t gid)
36955 {
36956    int old_egid = current->egid;
36957
36958    if (capable(CAP_SETGID))
36959      current->gid = current->egid = current->sgid =
36960        current->fsgid = gid;
36961    else if ((gid == current->gid) ||
36962        (gid == current->sgid))
36963      current->egid = current->fsgid = gid;
36964    else
36965      return -EPERM;
36966
36967    if (current->egid != old_egid)
```

```
36968      current->dumpable = 0;
36969   return 0;
36970 }
36971
36972 /* cap_emulate_setxuid() fixes the effective / permitted
36973  * capabilities of a process after a call to setuid,
36974  * setreuid, or setresuid.
36975  *
36976  *  1) When set*uiding _from_ one of {r,e,s}uid == 0 _to_
36977  *  all of {r,e,s}uid != 0, the permitted and effective
36978  *  capabilities are cleared.
36979  *
36980  *  2) When set*uiding _from_ euid == 0 _to_ euid != 0,
36981  *  the effective capabilities of the process are
36982  *  cleared.
36983  *
36984  *  3) When set*uiding _from_ euid != 0 _to_ euid == 0,
36985  *  the effective capabilities are set to the permitted
36986  *  capabilities.
36987  *
36988  *  fsuid is handled elsewhere. fsuid == 0 and
36989  *  {r,e,s}uid!= 0 should never happen.
36990  *
36991  *  -astor
36992  *
36993  * cevans - New behaviour, Oct '99
36994  * A process may, via prctl(), elect to keep its
36995  * capabilities when it calls setuid() and switches away
36996  * from uid==0. Both permitted and effective sets will be
36997  * retained.  Without this change, it was impossible for
36998  * a daemon to drop only some of its privilege. The call
36999  * to setuid(!=0) would drop all privileges!  Keeping uid
37000  * 0 is not an option because uid 0 owns too many vital
37001  * files..  Thanks to Olaf Kirch and Peter Benie for
37002  * spotting this. */
37003 extern inline void cap_emulate_setxuid(int old_ruid,
37004     int old_euid, int old_suid)
37005 {
37006   if ((old_ruid == 0 || old_euid == 0 || old_suid == 0)
37007       && (current->uid != 0 && current->euid != 0
37008           && current->suid != 0)
37009       && !current->keep_capabilities) {
37010     cap_clear(current->cap_permitted);
37011     cap_clear(current->cap_effective);
37012   }
37013   if (old_euid == 0 && current->euid != 0) {
37014     cap_clear(current->cap_effective);
37015   }
37016   if (old_euid != 0 && current->euid == 0) {
37017     current->cap_effective = current->cap_permitted;
37018   }
37019 }
37020
37021 static int set_user(uid_t new_ruid)
37022 {
37023   struct user_struct *new_user, *old_user;
37024
37025   /* What if a process setreuid()'s and this brings the
37026    * new uid over his NPROC rlimit?  We can check this
37027    * now cheaply with the new uid cache, so if it matters
37028    * we should be checking for it.   -DaveM */
37029   new_user = alloc_uid(new_ruid);
37030   if (!new_user)
37031     return -EAGAIN;
37032   old_user = current->user;
37033   atomic_dec(&old_user->processes);
37034   atomic_inc(&new_user->processes);
37035
37036   current->uid = new_ruid;
37037   current->user = new_user;
37038   free_uid(old_user);
37039   return 0;
37040 }
37041
37042 /* Unprivileged users may change the real uid to the
37043  * effective uid or vice versa.  (BSD-style)
37044  *
37045  * If you set the real uid at all, or set the effective
37046  * uid to a value not equal to the real uid, then the
37047  * saved uid is set to the new effective uid.
37048  *
37049  * This makes it possible for a setuid program to
37050  * completely drop its privileges, which is often a
37051  * useful assertion to make when you are doing a security
37052  * audit over a program.
37053  *
37054  * The general idea is that a program which uses just
37055  * setreuid() will be 100% compatible with BSD.  A
37056  * program which uses just setuid() will be 100%
37057  * compatible with POSIX with saved IDs.   */
37058 asmlinkage long sys_setreuid(uid_t ruid, uid_t euid)
37059 {
37060   int old_ruid, old_euid, old_suid, new_ruid, new_euid;
37061
```

```
37062   new_ruid = old_ruid = current->uid;
37063   new_euid = old_euid = current->euid;
37064   old_suid = current->suid;
37065
37066   if (ruid != (uid_t) -1) {
37067     new_ruid = ruid;
37068     if ((old_ruid != ruid) &&
37069         (current->euid != ruid) && !capable(CAP_SETUID))
37070       return -EPERM;
37071   }
37072
37073   if (euid != (uid_t) -1) {
37074     new_euid = euid;
37075     if ((old_ruid != euid) &&
37076         (current->euid != euid) &&
37077         (current->suid != euid) && !capable(CAP_SETUID))
37078       return -EPERM;
37079   }
37080
37081   if (new_ruid != old_ruid && set_user(new_ruid) < 0)
37082     return -EAGAIN;
37083
37084   current->fsuid = current->euid = new_euid;
37085   if (ruid != (uid_t) -1 ||
37086       (euid != (uid_t) -1 && euid != old_ruid))
37087     current->suid = current->euid;
37088   current->fsuid = current->euid;
37089   if (current->euid != old_euid)
37090     current->dumpable = 0;
37091
37092   if (!issecure(SECURE_NO_SETUID_FIXUP)) {
37093     cap_emulate_setxuid(old_ruid, old_euid, old_suid);
37094   }
37095
37096   return 0;
37097 }
37098
37099
37100
37101 /* setuid() is implemented like SysV with SAVED_IDS
37102  *
37103  * Note that SAVED_ID's is deficient in that a setuid
37104  * root program like sendmail, for example, cannot set
37105  * its uid to be a normal user and then switch back,
37106  * because if you're root, setuid() sets the saved uid
37107  * too.  If you don't like this, blame the bright people
37108  * in the POSIX committee and/or USG.  Note that the
37109  * BSD-style setreuid() will allow a root program to
37110  * temporarily drop privileges and be able to regain them
37111  * by swapping the real and effective uid.  */
37112 asmlinkage long sys_setuid(uid_t uid)
37113 {
37114   int old_euid = current->euid;
37115   int old_ruid, old_suid, new_ruid;
37116
37117   old_ruid = new_ruid = current->uid;
37118   old_suid = current->suid;
37119   if (capable(CAP_SETUID)) {
37120     if (uid != old_ruid && set_user(uid) < 0)
37121       return -EAGAIN;
37122     current->suid = uid;
37123   } else if ((uid != current->uid) &&
37124             (uid != current->suid))
37125     return -EPERM;
37126
37127   current->fsuid = current->euid = uid;
37128
37129   if (old_euid != uid)
37130     current->dumpable = 0;
37131
37132   if (!issecure(SECURE_NO_SETUID_FIXUP)) {
37133     cap_emulate_setxuid(old_ruid, old_euid, old_suid);
37134   }
37135
37136   return 0;
37137 }
37138
37139
37140 /* This function implements a generic ability to update
37141  * ruid, euid, and suid.  This allows you to implement
37142  * the 4.4 compatible seteuid().  */
37143 asmlinkage long sys_setresuid(uid_t ruid, uid_t euid,
37144     uid_t suid)
37145 {
37146   int old_ruid = current->uid;
37147   int old_euid = current->euid;
37148   int old_suid = current->suid;
37149
37150   if (!capable(CAP_SETUID)) {
37151     if ((ruid != (uid_t) -1) && (ruid != current->uid)
37152         && (ruid != current->euid)
37153         && (ruid != current->suid))
37154       return -EPERM;
37155     if ((euid != (uid_t) -1) && (euid != current->uid)
```

```
37156          && (euid != current->euid)
37157          && (euid != current->suid))
37158        return -EPERM;
37159     if ((suid != (uid_t) -1) && (suid != current->uid)
37160          && (suid != current->euid)
37161          && (suid != current->suid))
37162        return -EPERM;
37163    }
37164    if (ruid != (uid_t) -1) {
37165      if (ruid != current->uid && set_user(ruid) < 0)
37166        return -EAGAIN;
37167    }
37168    if (euid != (uid_t) -1) {
37169      if (euid != current->euid)
37170        current->dumpable = 0;
37171      current->euid = euid;
37172      current->fsuid = euid;
37173    }
37174    if (suid != (uid_t) -1)
37175      current->suid = suid;
37176
37177    if (!issecure(SECURE_NO_SETUID_FIXUP)) {
37178      cap_emulate_setxuid(old_ruid, old_euid, old_suid);
37179    }
37180
37181    return 0;
37182 }
37183
37184 asmlinkage long sys_getresuid(uid_t * ruid, uid_t * euid,
37185      uid_t * suid)
37186 {
37187    int retval;
37188
37189    if (!(retval = put_user(current->uid, ruid)) &&
37190        !(retval = put_user(current->euid, euid)))
37191      retval = put_user(current->suid, suid);
37192
37193    return retval;
37194 }
37195
37196 /* Same as above, but for rgid, egid, sgid.  */
37197 asmlinkage long sys_setresgid(gid_t rgid, gid_t egid,
37198      gid_t sgid)
37199 {
37200    if (!capable(CAP_SETGID)) {
37201      if ((rgid != (gid_t) -1) && (rgid != current->gid)
37202          && (rgid != current->egid)
37203          && (rgid != current->sgid))
37204        return -EPERM;
37205      if ((egid != (gid_t) -1) && (egid != current->gid)
37206          && (egid != current->egid)
37207          && (egid != current->sgid))
37208        return -EPERM;
37209      if ((sgid != (gid_t) -1) && (sgid != current->gid)
37210          && (sgid != current->egid)
37211          && (sgid != current->sgid))
37212        return -EPERM;
37213    }
37214    if (rgid != (gid_t) -1)
37215      current->gid = rgid;
37216    if (egid != (gid_t) -1) {
37217      if (egid != current->egid)
37218        current->dumpable = 0;
37219      current->egid = egid;
37220      current->fsgid = egid;
37221    }
37222    if (sgid != (gid_t) -1)
37223      current->sgid = sgid;
37224    return 0;
37225 }
37226
37227 asmlinkage long sys_getresgid(gid_t * rgid, gid_t * egid,
37228      gid_t * sgid)
37229 {
37230    int retval;
37231
37232    if (!(retval = put_user(current->gid, rgid)) &&
37233        !(retval = put_user(current->egid, egid)))
37234      retval = put_user(current->sgid, sgid);
37235
37236    return retval;
37237 }
37238
37239
37240 /* "setfsuid()" sets the fsuid - the uid used for
37241  * filesystem checks. This is used for "access()" and for
37242  * the NFS daemon (letting nfsd stay at whatever uid it
37243  * wants to). It normally shadows "euid", except when
37244  * explicitly set by setfsuid() or for access..  */
37245 asmlinkage long sys_setfsuid(uid_t uid)
37246 {
37247    int old_fsuid;
37248
37249    old_fsuid = current->fsuid;
```

```
37250    if (uid == current->uid || uid == current->euid ||
37251        uid == current->suid || uid == current->fsuid ||
37252        capable(CAP_SETUID))
37253      current->fsuid = uid;
37254    if (current->fsuid != old_fsuid)
37255      current->dumpable = 0;
37256
37257    /* We emulate fsuid by essentially doing a scaled-down
37258     * version of what we did in setresuid and friends.
37259     * However, we only operate on the fs-specific bits of
37260     * the process' effective capabilities
37261     * FIXME
37262     * - is fsuser used for all CAP_FS_MASK capabilities?
37263     *  if not, we might be a bit too harsh here. */
37264
37265    if (!issecure(SECURE_NO_SETUID_FIXUP)) {
37266      if (old_fsuid == 0 && current->fsuid != 0) {
37267        cap_t(current->cap_effective) &= ~CAP_FS_MASK;
37268      }
37269      if (old_fsuid != 0 && current->fsuid == 0) {
37270        cap_t(current->cap_effective) |=
37271            (cap_t(current->cap_permitted) & CAP_FS_MASK);
37272      }
37273    }
37274
37275    return old_fsuid;
37276  }
37277
37278  /* Samma på svenska.. */
37279  asmlinkage long sys_setfsgid(gid_t gid)
37280  {
37281    int old_fsgid;
37282
37283    old_fsgid = current->fsgid;
37284    if (gid == current->gid || gid == current->egid ||
37285        gid == current->sgid || gid == current->fsgid ||
37286        capable(CAP_SETGID))
37287      current->fsgid = gid;
37288    if (current->fsgid != old_fsgid)
37289      current->dumpable = 0;
37290
37291    return old_fsgid;
37292  }
37293
37294  asmlinkage long sys_times(struct tms *tbuf)
37295  {
37296    /* In the SMP world we might just be unlucky and have
37297     * one of the times increment as we use it. Since the
37298     * value is an atomically safe type this is just
37299     * fine. Conceptually its as if the syscall took an
37300     * instant longer to occur. */
37301    if (tbuf)
37302      if (copy_to_user(tbuf, &current->times,
37303            sizeof(struct tms)))
37304        return -EFAULT;
37305    return jiffies;
37306  }
37307
37308  /* This needs some heavy checking ... I just haven't the
37309   * stomach for it. I also don't fully understand
37310   * sessions/pgrp etc. Let somebody who does explain it.
37311   *
37312   * OK, I think I have the protection semantics
37313   * right.... this is really only important on a
37314   * multi-user system anyway, to make sure one user can't
37315   * send a signal to a process owned by another. -TYT,
37316   * 12/12/91
37317   *
37318   * Auch. Had to add the 'did_exec' flag to conform
37319   * completely to POSIX. LBT 04.03.94 */
37320  asmlinkage long sys_setpgid(pid_t pid, pid_t pgid)
37321  {
37322    struct task_struct *p;
37323    int err = -EINVAL;
37324
37325    if (!pid)
37326      pid = current->pid;
37327    if (!pgid)
37328      pgid = pid;
37329    if (pgid < 0)
37330      return -EINVAL;
37331
37332    /* From this point forward we keep holding onto the
37333     * tasklist lock so that our parent does not change
37334     * from under us. -DaveM */
37335    read_lock(&tasklist_lock);
37336
37337    err = -ESRCH;
37338    p = find_task_by_pid(pid);
37339    if (!p)
37340      goto out;
37341
37342    if (p->p_pptr == current || p->p_opptr == current) {
37343      err = -EPERM;
```

```
37344     if (p->session != current->session)
37345       goto out;
37346     err = -EACCES;
37347     if (p->did_exec)
37348       goto out;
37349   } else if (p != current)
37350     goto out;
37351   err = -EPERM;
37352   if (p->leader)
37353     goto out;
37354   if (pgid != pid) {
37355     struct task_struct *tmp;
37356     for_each_task(tmp) {
37357       if (tmp->pgrp == pgid &&
37358           tmp->session == current->session)
37359         goto ok_pgid;
37360     }
37361     goto out;
37362   }
37363
37364 ok_pgid:
37365   p->pgrp = pgid;
37366   err = 0;
37367 out:
37368   /* All paths lead to here, thus we are safe. -DaveM */
37369   read_unlock(&tasklist_lock);
37370   return err;
37371 }
37372
37373 asmlinkage long sys_getpgid(pid_t pid)
37374 {
37375   if (!pid) {
37376     return current->pgrp;
37377   } else {
37378     int retval;
37379     struct task_struct *p;
37380
37381     read_lock(&tasklist_lock);
37382     p = find_task_by_pid(pid);
37383
37384     retval = -ESRCH;
37385     if (p)
37386       retval = p->pgrp;
37387     read_unlock(&tasklist_lock);
37388     return retval;
37389   }
37390 }
```

```
37391
37392 asmlinkage long sys_getpgrp(void)
37393 {
37394   /* SMP - assuming writes are word atomic this is fine*/
37395   return current->pgrp;
37396 }
37397
37398 asmlinkage long sys_getsid(pid_t pid)
37399 {
37400   if (!pid) {
37401     return current->session;
37402   } else {
37403     int retval;
37404     struct task_struct *p;
37405
37406     read_lock(&tasklist_lock);
37407     p = find_task_by_pid(pid);
37408
37409     retval = -ESRCH;
37410     if (p)
37411       retval = p->session;
37412     read_unlock(&tasklist_lock);
37413     return retval;
37414   }
37415 }
37416
37417 asmlinkage long sys_setsid(void)
37418 {
37419   struct task_struct *p;
37420   int err = -EPERM;
37421
37422   read_lock(&tasklist_lock);
37423   for_each_task(p) {
37424     if (p->pgrp == current->pid)
37425       goto out;
37426   }
37427
37428   current->leader = 1;
37429   current->session = current->pgrp = current->pid;
37430   current->tty = NULL;
37431   current->tty_old_pgrp = 0;
37432   err = current->pgrp;
37433 out:
37434   read_unlock(&tasklist_lock);
37435   return err;
37436 }
37437
```

```
37438 /* Supplementary group IDs */
37439 asmlinkage long sys_getgroups(int gidsetsize,
37440     gid_t * grouplist)
37441 {
37442   int i;
37443
37444   /* SMP: Nobody else can change our grouplist. Thus we
37445    * are safe.  */
37446
37447   if (gidsetsize < 0)
37448     return -EINVAL;
37449   i = current->ngroups;
37450   if (gidsetsize) {
37451     if (i > gidsetsize)
37452       return -EINVAL;
37453     if (copy_to_user(grouplist, current->groups,
37454           sizeof(gid_t) * i))
37455       return -EFAULT;
37456   }
37457   return i;
37458 }
37459
37460 /* SMP: Our groups are not shared. We can copy to/from
37461  * them safely without another task interfering.  */
37462
37463 asmlinkage long sys_setgroups(int gidsetsize,
37464     gid_t * grouplist)
37465 {
37466   if (!capable(CAP_SETGID))
37467     return -EPERM;
37468   if ((unsigned) gidsetsize > NGROUPS)
37469     return -EINVAL;
37470   if (copy_from_user(current->groups, grouplist,
37471         gidsetsize * sizeof(gid_t)))
37472     return -EFAULT;
37473   current->ngroups = gidsetsize;
37474   return 0;
37475 }
37476
37477 static int supplemental_group_member(gid_t grp)
37478 {
37479   int i = current->ngroups;
37480
37481   if (i) {
37482     gid_t *groups = current->groups;
37483     do {
37484       if (*groups == grp)
```

```
37485         return 1;
37486       groups++;
37487       i--;
37488     } while (i);
37489   }
37490   return 0;
37491 }
37492
37493 /* Check whether we're fsgid/egid or in the supplemental
37494  * group..  */
37495 int in_group_p(gid_t grp)
37496 {
37497   int retval = 1;
37498   if (grp != current->fsgid)
37499     retval = supplemental_group_member(grp);
37500   return retval;
37501 }
37502
37503 int in_egroup_p(gid_t grp)
37504 {
37505   int retval = 1;
37506   if (grp != current->egid)
37507     retval = supplemental_group_member(grp);
37508   return retval;
37509 }
37510
37511 DECLARE_RWSEM(uts_sem);
37512
37513 asmlinkage long sys_newuname(struct new_utsname *name)
37514 {
37515   int errno = 0;
37516
37517   down_read(&uts_sem);
37518   if (copy_to_user(name, &system_utsname, sizeof *name))
37519     errno = -EFAULT;
37520   up_read(&uts_sem);
37521   return errno;
37522 }
37523
37524 asmlinkage long sys_sethostname(char *name, int len)
37525 {
37526   int errno;
37527
37528   if (!capable(CAP_SYS_ADMIN))
37529     return -EPERM;
37530   if (len < 0 || len > __NEW_UTS_LEN)
37531     return -EINVAL;
```

```
37532   down_write(&uts_sem);
37533   errno = -EFAULT;
37534   if (!copy_from_user(system_utsname.nodename, name,
37535           len)) {
37536     system_utsname.nodename[len] = 0;
37537     errno = 0;
37538   }
37539   up_write(&uts_sem);
37540   return errno;
37541 }
37542
37543 asmlinkage long sys_gethostname(char *name, int len)
37544 {
37545   int i, errno;
37546
37547   if (len < 0)
37548     return -EINVAL;
37549   down_read(&uts_sem);
37550   i = 1 + strlen(system_utsname.nodename);
37551   if (i > len)
37552     i = len;
37553   errno = 0;
37554   if (copy_to_user(name, system_utsname.nodename, i))
37555     errno = -EFAULT;
37556   up_read(&uts_sem);
37557   return errno;
37558 }
37559
37560 /* Only setdomainname; getdomainname can be implemented
37561  * by calling uname() */
37562 asmlinkage long sys_setdomainname(char *name, int len)
37563 {
37564   int errno;
37565
37566   if (!capable(CAP_SYS_ADMIN))
37567     return -EPERM;
37568   if (len < 0 || len > __NEW_UTS_LEN)
37569     return -EINVAL;
37570
37571   down_write(&uts_sem);
37572   errno = -EFAULT;
37573   if (!copy_from_user(system_utsname.domainname, name,
37574           len)) {
37575     errno = 0;
37576     system_utsname.domainname[len] = 0;
37577   }
37578   up_write(&uts_sem);
```

```
37579   return errno;
37580 }
37581
37582 asmlinkage long sys_getrlimit(unsigned int resource,
37583     struct rlimit *rlim)
37584 {
37585   if (resource >= RLIM_NLIMITS)
37586     return -EINVAL;
37587   else
37588     return copy_to_user(rlim, current->rlim + resource,
37589                   sizeof(*rlim))
37590       ? -EFAULT
37591       : 0;
37592 }
37593
37594 #if !defined(__ia64__) && !defined(__s390__)
37595
37596 /* Back compatibility for getrlimit. Needed for some
37597  * apps.  */
37598 asmlinkage long sys_old_getrlimit(unsigned int resource,
37599     struct rlimit *rlim)
37600 {
37601   struct rlimit x;
37602   if (resource >= RLIM_NLIMITS)
37603     return -EINVAL;
37604
37605   memcpy(&x, current->rlim + resource, sizeof(*rlim));
37606   if (x.rlim_cur > 0x7FFFFFFF)
37607     x.rlim_cur = 0x7FFFFFFF;
37608   if (x.rlim_max > 0x7FFFFFFF)
37609     x.rlim_max = 0x7FFFFFFF;
37610   return copy_to_user(rlim, &x, sizeof(x)) ? -EFAULT : 0;
37611 }
37612
37613 #endif
37614
37615 asmlinkage long sys_setrlimit(unsigned int resource,
37616     struct rlimit *rlim)
37617 {
37618   struct rlimit new_rlim, *old_rlim;
37619
37620   if (resource >= RLIM_NLIMITS)
37621     return -EINVAL;
37622   if (copy_from_user(&new_rlim, rlim, sizeof(*rlim)))
37623     return -EFAULT;
37624   if (new_rlim.rlim_cur < 0 || new_rlim.rlim_max < 0)
37625     return -EINVAL;
```

```
37626    old_rlim = current->rlim + resource;
37627    if (((new_rlim.rlim_cur > old_rlim->rlim_max) ||
37628            (new_rlim.rlim_max > old_rlim->rlim_max)) &&
37629        !capable(CAP_SYS_RESOURCE))
37630      return -EPERM;
37631    if (resource == RLIMIT_NOFILE) {
37632      if (new_rlim.rlim_cur > NR_OPEN
37633          || new_rlim.rlim_max > NR_OPEN)
37634        return -EPERM;
37635    }
37636    *old_rlim = new_rlim;
37637    return 0;
37638 }
37639
37640 /* It would make sense to put struct rusage in the
37641  * task_struct, except that would make the task_struct be
37642  * *really big*.  After task_struct gets moved into
37643  * malloc'ed memory, it would make sense to do this.  It
37644  * will make moving the rest of the information a lot
37645  * simpler!  (Which we're not doing right now because
37646  * we're not measuring them yet).
37647  *
37648  * This is SMP safe.  Either we are called from
37649  * sys_getrusage on ourselves below (we know we aren't
37650  * going to exit/disappear and only we change our rusage
37651  * counters), or we are called from wait4() on a process
37652  * which is either stopped or zombied.  In the zombied
37653  * case the task won't get reaped till shortly after the
37654  * call to getrusage(), in both cases the task being
37655  * examined is in a frozen state so the counters won't
37656  * change.
37657  *
37658  * FIXME! Get the fault counts properly!  */
37659 int getrusage(struct task_struct *p, int who,
37660        struct rusage *ru)
37661 {
37662    struct rusage r;
37663
37664    memset((char *) &r, 0, sizeof(r));
37665    switch (who) {
37666    case RUSAGE_SELF:
37667      r.ru_utime.tv_sec = CT_TO_SECS(p->times.tms_utime);
37668      r.ru_utime.tv_usec = CT_TO_USECS(p->times.tms_utime);
37669      r.ru_stime.tv_sec = CT_TO_SECS(p->times.tms_stime);
37670      r.ru_stime.tv_usec = CT_TO_USECS(p->times.tms_stime);
37671      r.ru_minflt = p->min_flt;
37672      r.ru_majflt = p->maj_flt;
37673      r.ru_nswap = p->nswap;
37674      break;
37675    case RUSAGE_CHILDREN:
37676      r.ru_utime.tv_sec = CT_TO_SECS(p->times.tms_cutime);
37677      r.ru_utime.tv_usec =
37678         CT_TO_USECS(p->times.tms_cutime);
37679      r.ru_stime.tv_sec = CT_TO_SECS(p->times.tms_cstime);
37680      r.ru_stime.tv_usec =
37681         CT_TO_USECS(p->times.tms_cstime);
37682      r.ru_minflt = p->cmin_flt;
37683      r.ru_majflt = p->cmaj_flt;
37684      r.ru_nswap = p->cnswap;
37685      break;
37686    default:
37687      r.ru_utime.tv_sec =
37688         CT_TO_SECS(p->times.tms_utime +
37689                    p->times.tms_cutime);
37690      r.ru_utime.tv_usec =
37691         CT_TO_USECS(p->times.tms_utime +
37692                     p->times.tms_cutime);
37693      r.ru_stime.tv_sec =
37694         CT_TO_SECS(p->times.tms_stime +
37695                    p->times.tms_cstime);
37696      r.ru_stime.tv_usec =
37697         CT_TO_USECS(p->times.tms_stime +
37698                     p->times.tms_cstime);
37699      r.ru_minflt = p->min_flt + p->cmin_flt;
37700      r.ru_majflt = p->maj_flt + p->cmaj_flt;
37701      r.ru_nswap = p->nswap + p->cnswap;
37702      break;
37703    }
37704    return copy_to_user(ru, &r, sizeof(r)) ? -EFAULT : 0;
37705 }
37706
37707 asmlinkage long sys_getrusage(int who, struct rusage *ru)
37708 {
37709    if (who != RUSAGE_SELF && who != RUSAGE_CHILDREN)
37710      return -EINVAL;
37711    return getrusage(current, who, ru);
37712 }
37713
37714 asmlinkage long sys_umask(int mask)
37715 {
37716    mask = xchg(&current->fs->umask, mask & S_IRWXUGO);
37717    return mask;
37718 }
37719
```

```
37720 asmlinkage long sys_prctl(int option, unsigned long arg2,
37721     unsigned long arg3, unsigned long arg4,
37722     unsigned long arg5)
37723 {
37724   int error = 0;
37725   int sig;
37726
37727   switch (option) {
37728   case PR_SET_PDEATHSIG:
37729     sig = arg2;
37730     if (sig > _NSIG) {
37731       error = -EINVAL;
37732       break;
37733     }
37734     current->pdeath_signal = sig;
37735     break;
37736   case PR_GET_PDEATHSIG:
37737     error =
37738        put_user(current->pdeath_signal, (int *) arg2);
37739     break;
37740   case PR_GET_DUMPABLE:
37741     if (current->dumpable)
37742       error = 1;
37743     break;
37744   case PR_SET_DUMPABLE:
37745     if (arg2 != 0 && arg2 != 1) {
37746       error = -EINVAL;
37747       break;
37748     }
37749     current->dumpable = arg2;
37750     break;
37751   case PR_SET_UNALIGN:
37752 #ifdef SET_UNALIGN_CTL
37753     error = SET_UNALIGN_CTL(current, arg2);
37754 #else
37755     error = -EINVAL;
37756 #endif
37757     break;
37758
37759   case PR_GET_UNALIGN:
37760 #ifdef GET_UNALIGN_CTL
37761     error = GET_UNALIGN_CTL(current, arg2);
37762 #else
37763     error = -EINVAL;
37764 #endif
37765     break;
37766
37767   case PR_GET_KEEPCAPS:
37768     if (current->keep_capabilities)
37769       error = 1;
37770     break;
37771   case PR_SET_KEEPCAPS:
37772     if (arg2 != 0 && arg2 != 1) {
37773       error = -EINVAL;
37774       break;
37775     }
37776     current->keep_capabilities = arg2;
37777     break;
37778   default:
37779     error = -EINVAL;
37780     break;
37781   }
37782   return error;
37783 }
37784
37785 EXPORT_SYMBOL(notifier_chain_register);
37786 EXPORT_SYMBOL(notifier_chain_unregister);
37787 EXPORT_SYMBOL(notifier_call_chain);
37788 EXPORT_SYMBOL(register_reboot_notifier);
37789 EXPORT_SYMBOL(unregister_reboot_notifier);
37790 EXPORT_SYMBOL(in_group_p);
37791 EXPORT_SYMBOL(in_egroup_p);
```

kernel/sysctl.c

```
37792 /*
37793  * sysctl.c: General linux system control interface
37794  *
37795  * Begun 24 March 1995, Stephen Tweedie
37796  * Added /proc support, Dec 1995
37797  * Added bdflush entry and intvec min/max checking,
37798  * 2/23/96, Tom Dyas.
37799  * Added hooks for /proc/sys/net (minor, minor patch),
37800  * 96/4/1, Mike Shaver.
37801  * Added kernel/java-{interpreter,appletviewer}, 96/5/10,
37802  * Mike Shaver.
37803  * Dynamic registration fixes, Stephen Tweedie.
37804  * Added kswapd-interval, ctrl-alt-del, printk stuff,
37805  * 1/8/97, Chris Horn.
37806  * Made sysctl support optional via CONFIG_SYSCTL,
37807  *  1/10/97, Chris Horn.
37808  * Added proc_doulongvec_ms_jiffies_minmax, 09/08/99,
37809  * Carlos H. Bauer.
37810  * Added proc_doulongvec_minmax, 09/08/99, Carlos
37811  * H. Bauer.
```

```
37812   * Changed linked lists to use list.h instead of lists.h,
37813   * 02/24/00, Bill Wendling.
37814   * The list_for_each() macro wasn't appropriate for the
37815   * sysctl loop.  Removed it and replaced it with older
37816   * style, 03/23/00, Bill Wendling
37817   */
37818
37819  #include <linux/config.h>
37820  #include <linux/malloc.h>
37821  #include <linux/sysctl.h>
37822  #include <linux/swapctl.h>
37823  #include <linux/proc_fs.h>
37824  #include <linux/ctype.h>
37825  #include <linux/utsname.h>
37826  #include <linux/capability.h>
37827  #include <linux/smp_lock.h>
37828  #include <linux/init.h>
37829  #include <linux/sysrq.h>
37830  #include <linux/highuid.h>
37831
37832  #include <asm/uaccess.h>
37833
37834  #ifdef CONFIG_ROOT_NFS
37835  #include <linux/nfs_fs.h>
37836  #endif
37837
37838  #if defined(CONFIG_SYSCTL)
37839
37840  /* External variables not in a header file. */
37841  extern int panic_timeout;
37842  extern int C_A_D;
37843  extern int bdf_prm[], bdflush_min[], bdflush_max[];
37844  extern int sysctl_overcommit_memory;
37845  extern int max_threads;
37846  extern int nr_queued_signals, max_queued_signals;
37847  extern int sysrq_enabled;
37848
37849  /* this is needed for the proc_dointvec_minmax for
37850   * [fs_]overflow UID and GID */
37851  static int maxolduid = 65535;
37852  static int minolduid;
37853
37854  #ifdef CONFIG_KMOD
37855  extern char modprobe_path[];
37856  #endif
37857  #ifdef CONFIG_HOTPLUG
37858  extern char hotplug_path[];
37859  #endif
37860  #ifdef CONFIG_CHR_DEV_SG
37861  extern int sg_big_buff;
37862  #endif
37863  #ifdef CONFIG_SYSVIPC
37864  extern size_t shm_ctlmax;
37865  extern size_t shm_ctlall;
37866  extern int shm_ctlmni;
37867  extern int msg_ctlmax;
37868  extern int msg_ctlmnb;
37869  extern int msg_ctlmni;
37870  extern int sem_ctls[];
37871  #endif
37872
37873  #ifdef __sparc__
37874  extern char reboot_command[];
37875  extern int stop_a_enabled;
37876  #endif
37877  #ifdef __powerpc__
37878  extern unsigned long htab_reclaim_on, zero_paged_on,
37879      powersave_nap;
37880  int proc_dol2crvec(ctl_table * table, int write,
37881      struct file *filp, void *buffer, size_t * lenp);
37882  #endif
37883
37884  #ifdef CONFIG_BSD_PROCESS_ACCT
37885  extern int acct_parm[];
37886  #endif
37887
37888  extern int pgt_cache_water[];
37889
37890  static int parse_table(int *, int, void *, size_t *,
37891      void *, size_t, ctl_table *, void **);
37892  static int proc_doutsstring(ctl_table * table, int write,
37893      struct file *filp, void *buffer, size_t * lenp);
37894
37895  static ctl_table root_table[];
37896  static struct ctl_table_header root_table_header =
37897      { root_table,
37898        LIST_HEAD_INIT(root_table_header.ctl_entry) };
37899
37900  static ctl_table kern_table[];
37901  static ctl_table vm_table[];
37902  #ifdef CONFIG_NET
37903  extern ctl_table net_table[];
37904  #endif
37905  static ctl_table proc_table[];
```

```
37906 static ctl_table fs_table[];
37907 static ctl_table debug_table[];
37908 static ctl_table dev_table[];
37909 extern ctl_table random_table[];
37910
37911 /* /proc declarations: */
37912
37913 #ifdef CONFIG_PROC_FS
37914
37915 static ssize_t proc_readsys(struct file *, char *,
37916     size_t, loff_t *);
37917 static ssize_t proc_writesys(struct file *, const char *,
37918     size_t, loff_t *);
37919 static int proc_sys_permission(struct inode *, int);
37920
37921 struct file_operations proc_sys_file_operations = {
37922   read:   proc_readsys,
37923   write:  proc_writesys,
37924 };
37925
37926 static struct inode_operations
37927 proc_sys_inode_operations = {
37928   permission:  proc_sys_permission,
37929 };
37930
37931 extern struct proc_dir_entry *proc_sys_root;
37932
37933 static void register_proc_table(ctl_table *,
37934     struct proc_dir_entry *);
37935 static void unregister_proc_table(ctl_table *,
37936     struct proc_dir_entry *);
37937 #endif
37938
37939 extern int inodes_stat[];
37940 extern int dentry_stat[];
37941
37942 /* The default sysctl tables: */
37943
37944 static ctl_table root_table[] = {
37945   {CTL_KERN, "kernel", NULL, 0, 0555, kern_table},
37946   {CTL_VM, "vm", NULL, 0, 0555, vm_table},
37947 #ifdef CONFIG_NET
37948   {CTL_NET, "net", NULL, 0, 0555, net_table},
37949 #endif
37950   {CTL_PROC, "proc", NULL, 0, 0555, proc_table},
37951   {CTL_FS, "fs", NULL, 0, 0555, fs_table},
37952   {CTL_DEBUG, "debug", NULL, 0, 0555, debug_table},
37953   {CTL_DEV, "dev", NULL, 0, 0555, dev_table},
37954   {0}
37955 };
37956
37957 static ctl_table kern_table[] = {
37958   {KERN_OSTYPE, "ostype", system_utsname.sysname, 64,
37959    0444, NULL, &proc_doutsstring, &sysctl_string},
37960   {KERN_OSRELEASE, "osrelease", system_utsname.release,
37961    64, 0444, NULL, &proc_doutsstring, &sysctl_string},
37962   {KERN_VERSION, "version", system_utsname.version, 64,
37963    0444, NULL, &proc_doutsstring, &sysctl_string},
37964   {KERN_NODENAME, "hostname", system_utsname.nodename,
37965    64, 0644, NULL, &proc_doutsstring, &sysctl_string},
37966   {KERN_DOMAINNAME, "domainname",
37967    system_utsname.domainname, 64,
37968    0644, NULL, &proc_doutsstring, &sysctl_string},
37969   {KERN_PANIC, "panic", &panic_timeout, sizeof(int),
37970    0644, NULL, &proc_dointvec},
37971   {KERN_CAP_BSET, "cap-bound", &cap_bset,
37972    sizeof(kernel_cap_t), 0600, NULL,&proc_dointvec_bset},
37973 #ifdef CONFIG_BLK_DEV_INITRD
37974
37975   {KERN_REALROOTDEV, "real-root-dev", &real_root_dev,
37976    sizeof(int), 0644, NULL, &proc_dointvec},
37977 #endif
37978 #ifdef __sparc__
37979   {KERN_SPARC_REBOOT, "reboot-cmd", reboot_command,
37980    256, 0644, NULL, &proc_dostring, &sysctl_string},
37981   {KERN_SPARC_STOP_A, "stop-a", &stop_a_enabled,
37982    sizeof(int), 0644, NULL, &proc_dointvec},
37983 #endif
37984 #ifdef __powerpc__
37985
37986   {KERN_PPC_HTABRECLAIM, "htab-reclaim",
37987    &htab_reclaim_on, sizeof(int), 0644, NULL,
37988    &proc_dointvec},
37989   {KERN_PPC_ZEROPAGED, "zero-paged", &zero_paged_on,
37990    sizeof(int), 0644, NULL, &proc_dointvec},
37991   {KERN_PPC_POWERSAVE_NAP, "powersave-nap",
37992    &powersave_nap, sizeof(int), 0644, NULL,
37993    &proc_dointvec},
37994   {KERN_PPC_L2CR, "l2cr", NULL, 0, 0644, NULL,
37995    &proc_dol2crvec},
37996 #endif
37997   {KERN_CTLALTDEL, "ctrl-alt-del", &C_A_D, sizeof(int),
37998    0644, NULL, &proc_dointvec},
37999   {KERN_PRINTK, "printk", &console_loglevel,
```

```
38000    4 * sizeof(int), 0644, NULL, &proc_dointvec},
38001 #ifdef CONFIG_KMOD
38002    {KERN_MODPROBE, "modprobe", &modprobe_path, 256,
38003     0644, NULL, &proc_dostring, &sysctl_string},
38004 #endif
38005 #ifdef CONFIG_HOTPLUG
38006    {KERN_HOTPLUG, "hotplug", &hotplug_path, 256,
38007     0644, NULL, &proc_dostring, &sysctl_string},
38008 #endif
38009 #ifdef CONFIG_CHR_DEV_SG
38010    {KERN_SG_BIG_BUFF, "sg-big-buff", &sg_big_buff,
38011     sizeof(int), 0444, NULL, &proc_dointvec},
38012 #endif
38013 #ifdef CONFIG_BSD_PROCESS_ACCT
38014    {KERN_ACCT, "acct", &acct_parm, 3 * sizeof(int),
38015     0644, NULL, &proc_dointvec},
38016 #endif
38017    {KERN_RTSIGNR, "rtsig-nr", &nr_queued_signals,
38018     sizeof(int), 0444, NULL, &proc_dointvec},
38019    {KERN_RTSIGMAX, "rtsig-max", &max_queued_signals,
38020     sizeof(int), 0644, NULL, &proc_dointvec},
38021 #ifdef CONFIG_SYSVIPC
38022    {KERN_SHMMAX, "shmmax", &shm_ctlmax, sizeof(size_t),
38023     0644, NULL, &proc_doulongvec_minmax},
38024    {KERN_SHMALL, "shmall", &shm_ctlall, sizeof(size_t),
38025     0644, NULL, &proc_doulongvec_minmax},
38026    {KERN_SHMMNI, "shmmni", &shm_ctlmni, sizeof(int),
38027     0644, NULL, &proc_dointvec},
38028    {KERN_MSGMAX, "msgmax", &msg_ctlmax, sizeof(int),
38029     0644, NULL, &proc_dointvec},
38030    {KERN_MSGMNI, "msgmni", &msg_ctlmni, sizeof(int),
38031     0644, NULL, &proc_dointvec},
38032    {KERN_MSGMNB, "msgmnb", &msg_ctlmnb, sizeof(int),
38033     0644, NULL, &proc_dointvec},
38034    {KERN_SEM, "sem", &sem_ctls, 4 * sizeof(int),
38035     0644, NULL, &proc_dointvec},
38036 #endif
38037 #ifdef CONFIG_MAGIC_SYSRQ
38038    {KERN_SYSRQ, "sysrq", &sysrq_enabled, sizeof(int),
38039     0644, NULL, &proc_dointvec},
38040 #endif
38041    {KERN_MAX_THREADS, "threads-max", &max_threads,
38042     sizeof(int), 0644, NULL, &proc_dointvec},
38043    {KERN_RANDOM, "random", NULL, 0, 0555, random_table},
38044
38045    {KERN_OVERFLOWUID, "overflowuid", &overflowuid,
38046     sizeof(int), 0644, NULL, &proc_dointvec_minmax,
38047     &sysctl_intvec, NULL, &minolduid, &maxolduid},
38048
38049    {KERN_OVERFLOWGID, "overflowgid", &overflowgid,
38050     sizeof(int), 0644, NULL, &proc_dointvec_minmax,
38051     &sysctl_intvec, NULL, &minolduid, &maxolduid},
38052    {0}
38053 };
38054
38055 static ctl_table vm_table[] = {
38056    {VM_FREEPG, "freepages", &freepages,
38057     sizeof(freepages_t), 0444, NULL, &proc_dointvec},
38058    {VM_BDFLUSH, "bdflush", &bdf_prm, 9 * sizeof(int),
38059     0644, NULL, &proc_dointvec_minmax, &sysctl_intvec,
38060     NULL, &bdflush_min, &bdflush_max},
38061    {VM_OVERCOMMIT_MEMORY, "overcommit_memory",
38062     &sysctl_overcommit_memory,
38063     sizeof(sysctl_overcommit_memory), 0644, NULL,
38064     &proc_dointvec},
38065    {VM_BUFFERMEM, "buffermem", &buffer_mem,
38066     sizeof(buffer_mem_t), 0644, NULL, &proc_dointvec},
38067    {VM_PAGECACHE, "pagecache", &page_cache,
38068     sizeof(buffer_mem_t), 0644, NULL, &proc_dointvec},
38069    {VM_PAGERDAEMON, "kswapd", &pager_daemon,
38070     sizeof(pager_daemon_t), 0644, NULL, &proc_dointvec},
38071    {VM_PGT_CACHE, "pagetable_cache", &pgt_cache_water,
38072     2 * sizeof(int), 0644, NULL, &proc_dointvec},
38073    {VM_PAGE_CLUSTER, "page-cluster", &page_cluster,
38074     sizeof(int), 0644, NULL, &proc_dointvec},
38075    {0}
38076 };
38077
38078 static ctl_table proc_table[] = {
38079    {0}
38080 };
38081
38082 static ctl_table fs_table[] = {
38083    {FS_NRINODE, "inode-nr", &inodes_stat, 2 * sizeof(int),
38084     0444, NULL, &proc_dointvec},
38085    {FS_STATINODE, "inode-state", &inodes_stat,
38086     7 * sizeof(int), 0444, NULL, &proc_dointvec},
38087    {FS_NRFILE, "file-nr", &files_stat, 3 * sizeof(int),
38088     0444, NULL, &proc_dointvec},
38089    {FS_MAXFILE, "file-max", &files_stat.max_files,
38090     sizeof(int), 0644, NULL, &proc_dointvec},
38091    {FS_NRSUPER, "super-nr", &nr_super_blocks, sizeof(int),
38092     0444, NULL, &proc_dointvec},
38093    {FS_MAXSUPER, "super-max", &max_super_blocks,
```

```
38094      sizeof(int), 0644, NULL, &proc_dointvec},
38095     {FS_NRDQUOT, "dquot-nr", &nr_dquots, 2 * sizeof(int),
38096      0444, NULL, &proc_dointvec},
38097     {FS_MAXDQUOT, "dquot-max", &max_dquots, sizeof(int),
38098      0644, NULL, &proc_dointvec},
38099     {FS_DENTRY, "dentry-state", &dentry_stat,
38100      6 * sizeof(int), 0444, NULL, &proc_dointvec},
38101     {FS_OVERFLOWUID, "overflowuid", &fs_overflowuid,
38102      sizeof(int), 0644, NULL, &proc_dointvec_minmax,
38103      &sysctl_intvec, NULL, &minolduid, &maxolduid},
38104     {FS_OVERFLOWGID, "overflowgid", &fs_overflowgid,
38105      sizeof(int), 0644, NULL, &proc_dointvec_minmax,
38106      &sysctl_intvec, NULL, &minolduid, &maxolduid},
38107     {FS_LEASES, "leases-enable", &leases_enable,
38108      sizeof(int), 0644, NULL, &proc_dointvec},
38109     {FS_DIR_NOTIFY, "dir-notify-enable",
38110      &dir_notify_enable, sizeof(int), 0644, NULL,
38111      &proc_dointvec},
38112     {FS_LEASE_TIME, "lease-break-time", &lease_break_time,
38113      sizeof(int), 0644, NULL, &proc_dointvec},
38114     {0}
38115 };
38116
38117 static ctl_table debug_table[] = {
38118    {0}
38119 };
38120
38121 static ctl_table dev_table[] = {
38122    {0}
38123 };
38124
38125 extern void init_irq_proc(void);
38126
38127 void __init sysctl_init(void)
38128 {
38129 #ifdef CONFIG_PROC_FS
38130    register_proc_table(root_table, proc_sys_root);
38131    init_irq_proc();
38132 #endif
38133 }
38134
38135 int do_sysctl(int *name, int nlen, void *oldval,
38136     size_t * oldlenp, void *newval, size_t newlen)
38137 {
38138    struct list_head *tmp;
38139
38140    if (nlen == 0 || nlen >= CTL_MAXNAME)
```

```
38141      return -ENOTDIR;
38142    if (oldval) {
38143      int old_len;
38144      if (!oldlenp || get_user(old_len, oldlenp))
38145        return -EFAULT;
38146    }
38147    tmp = &root_table_header.ctl_entry;
38148    do {
38149      struct ctl_table_header *head =
38150          list_entry(tmp, struct ctl_table_header,
38151                     ctl_entry);
38152      void *context = NULL;
38153      int error = parse_table(name, nlen, oldval, oldlenp,
38154                        newval, newlen,
38155                        head->ctl_table, &context);
38156      if (context)
38157        kfree(context);
38158      if (error != -ENOTDIR)
38159        return error;
38160      tmp = tmp->next;
38161    } while (tmp != &root_table_header.ctl_entry);
38162    return -ENOTDIR;
38163 }
38164
38165 extern asmlinkage long sys_sysctl(struct __sysctl_args
38166     *args)
38167 {
38168    struct __sysctl_args tmp;
38169    int error;
38170
38171    if (copy_from_user(&tmp, args, sizeof(tmp)))
38172      return -EFAULT;
38173
38174    lock_kernel();
38175    error = do_sysctl(tmp.name, tmp.nlen, tmp.oldval,
38176                  tmp.oldlenp, tmp.newval, tmp.newlen);
38177    unlock_kernel();
38178    return error;
38179 }
38180
38181 /* ctl_perm does NOT grant the superuser all rights
38182  * automatically, because some sysctl variables are
38183  * readonly even to root.  */
38184
38185 static int test_perm(int mode, int op)
38186 {
38187    if (!current->euid)
```

p 698

```
38188        mode >>= 6;
38189      else if (in_egroup_p(0))
38190        mode >>= 3;
38191      if ((mode & op & 0007) == op)
38192        return 0;
38193      return -EACCES;
38194  }
38195
38196  static inline int ctl_perm(ctl_table * table, int op)
38197  {
38198      return test_perm(table->mode, op);
38199  }
38200
38201  static int parse_table(int *name, int nlen,
38202          void *oldval, size_t * oldlenp,
38203          void *newval, size_t newlen,
38204          ctl_table * table, void **context)
38205  {
38206    int n;
38207  repeat:
38208    if (!nlen)
38209      return -ENOTDIR;
38210    if (get_user(n, name))
38211      return -EFAULT;
38212    for (; table->ctl_name; table++) {
38213      if (n == table->ctl_name
38214          || table->ctl_name == CTL_ANY) {
38215        int error;
38216        if (table->child) {
38217          if (ctl_perm(table, 001))
38218            return -EPERM;
38219          if (table->strategy) {
38220            error = table->strategy(table, name, nlen,
38221                oldval, oldlenp, newval, newlen, context);
38222            if (error)
38223              return error;
38224          }
38225          name++;
38226          nlen--;
38227          table = table->child;
38228          goto repeat;
38229        }
38230        error = do_sysctl_strategy(table, name, nlen,
38231            oldval, oldlenp, newval, newlen, context);
38232        return error;
38233      }
38234    }
```

p 699 at line 38201

```
38235    return -ENOTDIR;
38236  }
38237
38238  /* Perform the actual read/write of a sysctl table
38239   * entry. */
38240  int do_sysctl_strategy(ctl_table * table,
38241      int *name, int nlen,
38242      void *oldval, size_t * oldlenp,
38243      void *newval, size_t newlen, void **context)
38244  {
38245    int op = 0, rc, len;
38246
38247    if (oldval)
38248      op |= 004;
38249    if (newval)
38250      op |= 002;
38251    if (ctl_perm(table, op))
38252      return -EPERM;
38253
38254    if (table->strategy) {
38255      rc = table->strategy(table, name, nlen, oldval,
38256          oldlenp, newval, newlen, context);
38257      if (rc < 0)
38258        return rc;
38259      if (rc > 0)
38260        return 0;
38261    }
38262
38263    /* If there is no strategy routine, or if the strategy
38264     * returns zero, proceed with automatic r/w */
38265    if (table->data && table->maxlen) {
38266      if (oldval && oldlenp) {
38267        get_user(len, oldlenp);
38268        if (len) {
38269          if (len > table->maxlen)
38270            len = table->maxlen;
38271          if (copy_to_user(oldval, table->data, len))
38272            return -EFAULT;
38273          if (put_user(len, oldlenp))
38274            return -EFAULT;
38275        }
38276      }
38277      if (newval && newlen) {
38278        len = newlen;
38279        if (len > table->maxlen)
38280          len = table->maxlen;
38281        if (copy_from_user(table->data, newval, len))
```

p 699 at line 38240

```
38282          return -EFAULT;
38283      }
38284   }
38285   return 0;
38286 }
38287
38288 struct ctl_table_header *
38289 register_sysctl_table(ctl_table * table,
38290                       int insert_at_head)
38291 {
38292   struct ctl_table_header *tmp;
38293   tmp = kmalloc(sizeof(struct ctl_table_header),
38294           GFP_KERNEL);
38295   if (!tmp)
38296     return 0;
38297   tmp->ctl_table = table;
38298   INIT_LIST_HEAD(&tmp->ctl_entry);
38299   if (insert_at_head)
38300     list_add(&tmp->ctl_entry,
38301         &root_table_header.ctl_entry);
38302   else
38303     list_add_tail(&tmp->ctl_entry,
38304         &root_table_header.ctl_entry);
38305 #ifdef CONFIG_PROC_FS
38306   register_proc_table(table, proc_sys_root);
38307 #endif
38308   return tmp;
38309 }
38310
38311 /* Unlink and free a ctl_table.  */
38312 void unregister_sysctl_table(
38313   struct ctl_table_header *header)
38314 {
38315   list_del(&header->ctl_entry);
38316 #ifdef CONFIG_PROC_FS
38317   unregister_proc_table(header->ctl_table,
38318       proc_sys_root);
38319 #endif
38320   kfree(header);
38321 }
38322
38323 /* /proc/sys support */
38324
38325 #ifdef CONFIG_PROC_FS
38326
38327 /* Scan the sysctl entries in table and add them all
38328  * into /proc */
```

```
38329 static void register_proc_table(ctl_table * table,
38330     struct proc_dir_entry *root)
38331 {
38332   struct proc_dir_entry *de;
38333   int len;
38334   mode_t mode;
38335
38336   for (; table->ctl_name; table++) {
38337     /* Can't do anything without a proc name. */
38338     if (!table->procname)
38339       continue;
38340     /* Maybe we can't do anything with it... */
38341     if (!table->proc_handler && !table->child) {
38342       printk(KERN_WARNING "SYSCTL: Can't register %s\n",
38343           table->procname);
38344       continue;
38345     }
38346
38347     len = strlen(table->procname);
38348     mode = table->mode;
38349
38350     de = NULL;
38351     if (table->proc_handler)
38352       mode |= S_IFREG;
38353     else {
38354       mode |= S_IFDIR;
38355       for (de = root->subdir; de; de = de->next) {
38356         if (proc_match(len, table->procname, de))
38357           break;
38358       }
38359       /* If the subdir exists already, de is non-NULL */
38360     }
38361
38362     if (!de) {
38363       de =
38364           create_proc_entry(table->procname, mode, root);
38365       if (!de)
38366         continue;
38367       de->data = (void *) table;
38368       if (table->proc_handler) {
38369         de->proc_fops = &proc_sys_file_operations;
38370         de->proc_iops = &proc_sys_inode_operations;
38371       }
38372     }
38373     table->de = de;
38374     if (de->mode & S_IFDIR)
38375       register_proc_table(table->child, de);
```

```
38376    }
38377 }
38378
38379 /* Unregister a /proc sysctl table and any
38380  * subdirectories.  */
```
p 695
```
38381 static void unregister_proc_table(ctl_table * table,
38382     struct proc_dir_entry *root)
38383 {
38384   struct proc_dir_entry *de;
38385   for (; table->ctl_name; table++) {
38386     if (!(de = table->de))
38387       continue;
38388     if (de->mode & S_IFDIR) {
38389       if (!table->child) {
38390         printk(KERN_ALERT
38391           "Help - malformed sysctl tree on free\n");
38392         continue;
38393       }
38394       unregister_proc_table(table->child, de);
38395
38396       /* Don't unregister directories which still have
38397        * entries.. */
38398       if (de->subdir)
38399         continue;
38400     }
38401
38402     /* Don't unregister proc entries that are still
38403      * being used.. */
38404     if (atomic_read(&de->count))
38405       continue;
38406
38407     table->de = NULL;
38408     remove_proc_entry(table->procname, root);
38409   }
38410 }
38411
```
p 696
```
38412 static ssize_t do_rw_proc(int write, struct file *file,
38413     char *buf, size_t count, loff_t * ppos)
38414 {
38415   int op;
38416   struct proc_dir_entry *de;
38417   struct ctl_table *table;
38418   size_t res;
38419   ssize_t error;
38420
38421   de = (struct proc_dir_entry *)
38422     file->f_dentry->d_inode->u.generic_ip;
```

```
38423   if (!de || !de->data)
38424     return -ENOTDIR;
38425   table = (struct ctl_table *) de->data;
38426   if (!table || !table->proc_handler)
38427     return -ENOTDIR;
38428   op = (write ? 002 : 004);
38429   if (ctl_perm(table, op))
38430     return -EPERM;
38431
38432   res = count;
38433
38434   /* FIXME: we need to pass on ppos to the handler.  */
38435
38436   error = (*table->proc_handler)(table, write, file, buf,
38437                                  &res);
38438   if (error)
38439     return error;
38440   return res;
38441 }
38442
38443 static ssize_t proc_readsys(struct file *file, char *buf,
38444     size_t count, loff_t * ppos)
38445 {
38446   return do_rw_proc(0, file, buf, count, ppos);
38447 }
38448
38449 static ssize_t proc_writesys(struct file *file,
38450     const char *buf, size_t count, loff_t * ppos)
38451 {
38452   return do_rw_proc(1, file, (char *) buf, count, ppos);
38453 }
38454
38455 static int proc_sys_permission(struct inode *inode,
38456     int op)
38457 {
38458   return test_perm(inode->i_mode, op);
38459 }
38460
```
p 696
```
38461 int proc_dostring(ctl_table * table, int write,
38462     struct file *filp, void *buffer, size_t * lenp)
38463 {
38464   int len;
38465   char *p, c;
38466
38467   if (!table->data || !table->maxlen || !*lenp ||
38468       (filp->f_pos && !write)) {
38469     *lenp = 0;
```

```
38470        return 0;
38471    }
38472
38473    if (write) {
38474      len = 0;
38475      p = buffer;
38476      while (len < *lenp) {
38477        if (get_user(c, p++))
38478          return -EFAULT;
38479        if (c == 0 || c == '\n')
38480          break;
38481        len++;
38482      }
38483      if (len >= table->maxlen)
38484        len = table->maxlen - 1;
38485      if (copy_from_user(table->data, buffer, len))
38486        return -EFAULT;
38487      ((char *) table->data)[len] = 0;
38488      filp->f_pos += *lenp;
38489    } else {
38490      len = strlen(table->data);
38491      if (len > table->maxlen)
38492        len = table->maxlen;
38493      if (len > *lenp)
38494        len = *lenp;
38495      if (len)
38496        if (copy_to_user(buffer, table->data, len))
38497          return -EFAULT;
38498      if (len < *lenp) {
38499        if (put_user('\n', ((char *) buffer) + len))
38500          return -EFAULT;
38501        len++;
38502      }
38503      *lenp = len;
38504      filp->f_pos += len;
38505    }
38506    return 0;
38507  }
38508
38509  /* Special case of dostring for the UTS structure. This
38510   * has locks to observe. Should this be in kernel/sys.c
38511   * ????  */
38512  static int proc_doutsstring(ctl_table * table, int write,
38513      struct file *filp, void *buffer, size_t * lenp)
38514  {
38515    int r;
38516
38517    if (!write) {
38518      down_read(&uts_sem);
38519      r = proc_dostring(table, 0, filp, buffer, lenp);
38520      up_read(&uts_sem);
38521    } else {
38522      down_write(&uts_sem);
38523      r = proc_dostring(table, 1, filp, buffer, lenp);
38524      up_write(&uts_sem);
38525    }
38526    return r;
38527  }
38528
38529  #define OP_SET  0
38530  #define OP_AND  1
38531  #define OP_OR   2
38532  #define OP_MAX  3
38533  #define OP_MIN  4
38534
38535  static int do_proc_dointvec(ctl_table * table, int write,
38536      struct file *filp, void *buffer, size_t * lenp,
38537      int conv, int op)
38538  {
38539    int *i, vleft, first = 1, len, left, neg, val;
38540  #define TMPBUFLEN 20
38541    char buf[TMPBUFLEN], *p;
38542
38543    if (!table->data || !table->maxlen || !*lenp ||
38544        (filp->f_pos && !write)) {
38545      *lenp = 0;
38546      return 0;
38547    }
38548
38549    i = (int *) table->data;
38550    vleft = table->maxlen / sizeof(int);
38551    left = *lenp;
38552
38553    for (; left && vleft--; i++, first = 0) {
38554      if (write) {
38555        while (left) {
38556          char c;
38557          if (get_user(c, (char *) buffer))
38558            return -EFAULT;
38559          if (!isspace(c))
38560            break;
38561          left--;
38562          ((char *) buffer)++;
38563        }
```

```
38564        if (!left)
38565          break;
38566        neg = 0;
38567        len = left;
38568        if (len > TMPBUFLEN - 1)
38569          len = TMPBUFLEN - 1;
38570        if (copy_from_user(buf, buffer, len))
38571          return -EFAULT;
38572        buf[len] = 0;
38573        p = buf;
38574        if (*p == '-' && left > 1) {
38575          neg = 1;
38576          left-, p++;
38577        }
38578        if (*p < '0' || *p > '9')
38579          break;
38580        val = simple_strtoul(p, &p, 0) * conv;
38581        len = p - buf;
38582        if ((len < left) && *p && !isspace(*p))
38583          break;
38584        if (neg)
38585          val = -val;
38586        buffer += len;
38587        left -= len;
38588        switch (op) {
38589        case OP_SET:
38590          *i = val;
38591          break;
38592        case OP_AND:
38593          *i &= val;
38594          break;
38595        case OP_OR:
38596          *i |= val;
38597          break;
38598        case OP_MAX:
38599          if (*i < val)
38600            *i = val;
38601          break;
38602        case OP_MIN:
38603          if (*i > val)
38604            *i = val;
38605          break;
38606        }
38607      } else {
38608        p = buf;
38609        if (!first)
38610          *p++ = '\t';
38611          sprintf(p, "%d", (*i) / conv);
38612          len = strlen(buf);
38613          if (len > left)
38614            len = left;
38615          if (copy_to_user(buffer, buf, len))
38616            return -EFAULT;
38617          left -= len;
38618          buffer += len;
38619        }
38620      }
38621
38622      if (!write && !first && left) {
38623        if (put_user('\n', (char *) buffer))
38624          return -EFAULT;
38625        left-, buffer++;
38626      }
38627      if (write) {
38628        p = (char *) buffer;
38629        while (left) {
38630          char c;
38631          if (get_user(c, p++))
38632            return -EFAULT;
38633          if (!isspace(c))
38634            break;
38635          left-;
38636        }
38637      }
38638      if (write && first)
38639        return -EINVAL;
38640      *lenp -= left;
38641      filp->f_pos += *lenp;
38642      return 0;
38643 }
38644
38645 int proc_dointvec(ctl_table * table, int write,
38646      struct file *filp, void *buffer, size_t * lenp)
38647 {
38648    return do_proc_dointvec(table, write, filp, buffer,
38649        lenp, 1, OP_SET);
38650 }
38651
38652 /* init may raise the set.  */
38653
38654 int proc_dointvec_bset(ctl_table * table, int write,
38655      struct file *filp, void *buffer, size_t * lenp)
38656 {
38657    if (!capable(CAP_SYS_MODULE)) {
```

```
38658    return -EPERM;
38659  }
38660  return do_proc_dointvec(table, write, filp, buffer,
38661      lenp, 1, (current->pid == 1) ? OP_SET : OP_AND);
38662 }
38663
38664 int proc_dointvec_minmax(ctl_table * table, int write,
38665      struct file *filp, void *buffer, size_t * lenp)
38666 {
38667   int *i, *min, *max, vleft, first = 1,
38668     len, left, neg, val;
38669 #define TMPBUFLEN 20
38670   char buf[TMPBUFLEN], *p;
38671
38672   if (!table->data || !table->maxlen || !*lenp ||
38673       (filp->f_pos && !write)) {
38674    *lenp = 0;
38675    return 0;
38676   }
38677
38678   i = (int *) table->data;
38679   min = (int *) table->extra1;
38680   max = (int *) table->extra2;
38681   vleft = table->maxlen / sizeof(int);
38682   left = *lenp;
38683
38684   for (; left && vleft--; i++, first = 0) {
38685    if (write) {
38686     while (left) {
38687      char c;
38688      if (get_user(c, (char *) buffer))
38689        return -EFAULT;
38690      if (!isspace(c))
38691        break;
38692      left--;
38693      ((char *) buffer)++;
38694     }
38695     if (!left)
38696      break;
38697     neg = 0;
38698     len = left;
38699     if (len > TMPBUFLEN - 1)
38700      len = TMPBUFLEN - 1;
38701     if (copy_from_user(buf, buffer, len))
38702      return -EFAULT;
38703     buf[len] = 0;
38704     p = buf;
```

```
38705      if (*p == '-' && left > 1) {
38706       neg = 1;
38707       left--, p++;
38708      }
38709      if (*p < '0' || *p > '9')
38710       break;
38711      val = simple_strtoul(p, &p, 0);
38712      len = p - buf;
38713      if ((len < left) && *p && !isspace(*p))
38714       break;
38715      if (neg)
38716       val = -val;
38717      buffer += len;
38718      left -= len;
38719
38720      if (min && val < *min++)
38721       continue;
38722      if (max && val > *max++)
38723       continue;
38724      *i = val;
38725    } else {
38726      p = buf;
38727      if (!first)
38728       *p++ = '\t';
38729      sprintf(p, "%d", *i);
38730      len = strlen(buf);
38731      if (len > left)
38732       len = left;
38733      if (copy_to_user(buffer, buf, len))
38734       return -EFAULT;
38735      left -= len;
38736      buffer += len;
38737    }
38738   }
38739
38740   if (!write && !first && left) {
38741    if (put_user('\n', (char *) buffer))
38742     return -EFAULT;
38743    left--, buffer++;
38744   }
38745   if (write) {
38746    p = (char *) buffer;
38747    while (left) {
38748     char c;
38749     if (get_user(c, p++))
38750       return -EFAULT;
38751     if (!isspace(c))
```

```
38752          break;
38753        left--;
38754      }
38755    }
38756    if (write && first)
38757      return -EINVAL;
38758    *lenp -= left;
38759    filp->f_pos += *lenp;
38760    return 0;
38761 }
38762
38763 /* an unsigned long function version */
38764 static int do_proc_doulongvec_minmax(ctl_table * table,
38765      int write, struct file *filp, void *buffer,
38766      size_t * lenp, unsigned long convmul,
38767      unsigned long convdiv)
38768 {
38769 #define TMPBUFLEN 20
38770    unsigned long *i, *min, *max, val;
38771    int vleft, first = 1, len, left, neg;
38772    char buf[TMPBUFLEN], *p;
38773
38774    if (!table->data || !table->maxlen || !*lenp ||
38775        (filp->f_pos && !write)) {
38776      *lenp = 0;
38777      return 0;
38778    }
38779
38780    i = (unsigned long *) table->data;
38781    min = (unsigned long *) table->extra1;
38782    max = (unsigned long *) table->extra2;
38783    vleft = table->maxlen / sizeof(unsigned long);
38784    left = *lenp;
38785
38786    for (; left && vleft--; i++, first = 0) {
38787      if (write) {
38788        while (left) {
38789          char c;
38790          if (get_user(c, (char *) buffer))
38791            return -EFAULT;
38792          if (!isspace(c))
38793            break;
38794          left--;
38795          ((char *) buffer)++;
38796        }
38797        if (!left)
38798          break;
```

```
38799        neg = 0;
38800        len = left;
38801        if (len > TMPBUFLEN - 1)
38802          len = TMPBUFLEN - 1;
38803        if (copy_from_user(buf, buffer, len))
38804          return -EFAULT;
38805        buf[len] = 0;
38806        p = buf;
38807        if (*p == '-' && left > 1) {
38808          neg = 1;
38809          left--, p++;
38810        }
38811        if (*p < '0' || *p > '9')
38812          break;
38813        val = simple_strtoul(p, &p, 0) * convmul / convdiv;
38814        len = p - buf;
38815        if ((len < left) && *p && !isspace(*p))
38816          break;
38817        if (neg)
38818          val = -val;
38819        buffer += len;
38820        left -= len;
38821
38822        if (neg)
38823          continue;
38824        if (min && val < *min++)
38825          continue;
38826        if (max && val > *max++)
38827          continue;
38828        *i = val;
38829      } else {
38830        p = buf;
38831        if (!first)
38832          *p++ = '\t';
38833        sprintf(p, "%lu", convdiv * (*i) / convmul);
38834        len = strlen(buf);
38835        if (len > left)
38836          len = left;
38837        if (copy_to_user(buffer, buf, len))
38838          return -EFAULT;
38839        left -= len;
38840        buffer += len;
38841      }
38842    }
38843
38844    if (!write && !first && left) {
38845      if (put_user('\n', (char *) buffer))
```

```
38846        return -EFAULT;
38847      left--, buffer++;
38848    }
38849    if (write) {
38850      p = (char *) buffer;
38851      while (left) {
38852        char c;
38853        if (get_user(c, p++))
38854          return -EFAULT;
38855        if (!isspace(c))
38856          break;
38857        left--;
38858      }
38859    }
38860    if (write && first)
38861      return -EINVAL;
38862    *lenp -= left;
38863    filp->f_pos += *lenp;
38864    return 0;
38865 #undef TMPBUFLEN
38866 }
38867
38868 int proc_doulongvec_minmax(ctl_table * table, int write,
38869      struct file *filp, void *buffer, size_t * lenp)
38870 {
38871    return do_proc_doulongvec_minmax(table, write, filp,
38872        buffer, lenp, 1l, 1l);
38873 }
38874
38875 int proc_doulongvec_ms_jiffies_minmax(ctl_table * table,
38876      int write, struct file *filp, void *buffer,
38877      size_t * lenp)
38878 {
38879    return do_proc_doulongvec_minmax(table, write, filp,
38880        buffer, lenp, HZ, 1000l);
38881 }
38882
38883
38884 /* Like proc_dointvec, but converts seconds to jiffies */
38885 int proc_dointvec_jiffies(ctl_table * table, int write,
38886      struct file *filp, void *buffer, size_t * lenp)
38887 {
38888    return do_proc_dointvec(table, write, filp, buffer,
38889        lenp, HZ, OP_SET);
38890 }
38891
38892 #else                              /* CONFIG_PROC_FS */
38893
38894 int proc_dostring(ctl_table * table, int write,
38895      struct file *filp, void *buffer, size_t * lenp)
38896 {
38897    return -ENOSYS;
38898 }
38899
38900 static int proc_doutsstring(ctl_table * table, int write,
38901      struct file *filp, void *buffer, size_t * lenp)
38902 {
38903    return -ENOSYS;
38904 }
38905
38906 int proc_dointvec(ctl_table * table, int write,
38907      struct file *filp, void *buffer, size_t * lenp)
38908 {
38909    return -ENOSYS;
38910 }
38911
38912 int proc_dointvec_bset(ctl_table * table, int write,
38913      struct file *filp, void *buffer, size_t * lenp)
38914 {
38915    return -ENOSYS;
38916 }
38917
38918 int proc_dointvec_minmax(ctl_table * table, int write,
38919      struct file *filp, void *buffer, size_t * lenp)
38920 {
38921    return -ENOSYS;
38922 }
38923
38924 int proc_dointvec_jiffies(ctl_table * table, int write,
38925      struct file *filp, void *buffer, size_t * lenp)
38926 {
38927    return -ENOSYS;
38928 }
38929
38930 int proc_doulongvec_minmax(ctl_table * table, int write,
38931      struct file *filp, void *buffer, size_t * lenp)
38932 {
38933    return -ENOSYS;
38934 }
38935
38936 int proc_doulongvec_ms_jiffies_minmax(ctl_table * table,
38937      int write, struct file *filp, void *buffer,
38938      size_t * lenp)
38939 {
```

```
38940    return -ENOSYS;
38941 }
38942
38943
38944 #endif                              /* CONFIG_PROC_FS */
38945
38946
38947 /* General sysctl support routines */
38948
38949 /* The generic string strategy routine: */
38950 int sysctl_string(ctl_table * table, int *name, int nlen,
38951     void *oldval, size_t * oldlenp,
38952     void *newval, size_t newlen, void **context)
38953 {
38954   int l, len;
38955
38956   if (!table->data || !table->maxlen)
38957     return -ENOTDIR;
38958
38959   if (oldval && oldlenp) {
38960     if (get_user(len, oldlenp))
38961       return -EFAULT;
38962     if (len) {
38963       l = strlen(table->data);
38964       if (len > l)
38965         len = l;
38966       if (len >= table->maxlen)
38967         len = table->maxlen;
38968       if (copy_to_user(oldval, table->data, len))
38969         return -EFAULT;
38970       if (put_user(0, ((char *) oldval) + len))
38971         return -EFAULT;
38972       if (put_user(len, oldlenp))
38973         return -EFAULT;
38974     }
38975   }
38976   if (newval && newlen) {
38977     len = newlen;
38978     if (len > table->maxlen)
38979       len = table->maxlen;
38980     if (copy_from_user(table->data, newval, len))
38981       return -EFAULT;
38982     if (len == table->maxlen)
38983       len--;
38984     ((char *) table->data)[len] = 0;
38985   }
38986   return 0;
38987 }
38988
38989 /* This function makes sure that all of the integers in
38990  * the vector are between the minimum and maximum values
38991  * given in the arrays table->extra1 and table->extra2,
38992  * respectively.  */
38993 int sysctl_intvec(ctl_table * table, int *name, int nlen,
38994     void *oldval, size_t * oldlenp,
38995     void *newval, size_t newlen, void **context)
38996 {
38997   int i, length, *vec, *min, *max;
38998
38999   if (newval && newlen) {
39000     if (newlen % sizeof(int) != 0)
39001       return -EINVAL;
39002
39003     if (!table->extra1 && !table->extra2)
39004       return 0;
39005
39006     if (newlen > table->maxlen)
39007       newlen = table->maxlen;
39008     length = newlen / sizeof(int);
39009
39010     vec = (int *) newval;
39011     min = (int *) table->extra1;
39012     max = (int *) table->extra2;
39013
39014     for (i = 0; i < length; i++) {
39015       int value;
39016       get_user(value, vec + i);
39017       if (min && value < min[i])
39018         return -EINVAL;
39019       if (max && value > max[i])
39020         return -EINVAL;
39021     }
39022   }
39023   return 0;
39024 }
39025
39026 /* Strategy function to convert jiffies to seconds */
39027 int sysctl_jiffies(ctl_table * table, int *name,
39028     int nlen, void *oldval, size_t * oldlenp,
39029     void *newval, size_t newlen, void **context)
39030 {
39031   if (oldval) {
39032     size_t olen;
39033     if (oldlenp) {
```

```
39034      if (get_user(olen, oldlenp))
39035        return -EFAULT;
39036      if (olen != sizeof(int))
39037        return -EINVAL;
39038    }
39039    if (put_user(*(int *) (table->data) / HZ,
39040              (int *) oldval) ||
39041        (oldlenp && put_user(sizeof(int), oldlenp)))
39042      return -EFAULT;
39043   }
39044   if (newval && newlen) {
39045     int new;
39046     if (newlen != sizeof(int))
39047       return -EINVAL;
39048     if (get_user(new, (int *) newval))
39049       return -EFAULT;
39050     *(int *) (table->data) = new * HZ;
39051   }
39052   return 1;
39053 }
39054
39055
39056 #else                          /* CONFIG_SYSCTL */
39057
39058
39059 extern asmlinkage
39060 long sys_sysctl(struct __sysctl_args *args)
39061 {
39062   return -ENOSYS;
39063 }
39064
39065 int sysctl_string(ctl_table * table, int *name, int nlen,
39066     void *oldval, size_t * oldlenp,
39067     void *newval, size_t newlen, void **context)
39068 {
39069   return -ENOSYS;
39070 }
39071
39072 int sysctl_intvec(ctl_table * table, int *name, int nlen,
39073     void *oldval, size_t * oldlenp,
39074     void *newval, size_t newlen, void **context)
39075 {
39076   return -ENOSYS;
39077 }
39078
39079 int sysctl_jiffies(ctl_table * table, int *name,
39080     int nlen, void *oldval, size_t * oldlenp,
39081     void *newval, size_t newlen, void **context)
39082 {
39083   return -ENOSYS;
39084 }
39085
39086 int proc_dostring(ctl_table * table, int write,
39087     struct file *filp, void *buffer, size_t * lenp)
39088 {
39089   return -ENOSYS;
39090 }
39091
39092 int proc_dointvec(ctl_table * table, int write,
39093     struct file *filp, void *buffer, size_t * lenp)
39094 {
39095   return -ENOSYS;
39096 }
39097
39098 int proc_dointvec_bset(ctl_table * table, int write,
39099     struct file *filp, void *buffer, size_t * lenp)
39100 {
39101   return -ENOSYS;
39102 }
39103
39104 int proc_dointvec_minmax(ctl_table * table, int write,
39105     struct file *filp, void *buffer, size_t * lenp)
39106 {
39107   return -ENOSYS;
39108 }
39109
39110 int proc_dointvec_jiffies(ctl_table * table, int write,
39111     struct file *filp, void *buffer, size_t * lenp)
39112 {
39113   return -ENOSYS;
39114 }
39115
39116 int proc_doulongvec_minmax(ctl_table * table, int write,
39117     struct file *filp, void *buffer, size_t * lenp)
39118 {
39119   return -ENOSYS;
39120 }
39121
39122 int proc_doulongvec_ms_jiffies_minmax(ctl_table * table,
39123     int write, struct file *filp, void *buffer,
39124     size_t * lenp)
39125 {
39126   return -ENOSYS;
39127 }
```

```
39128
39129 struct ctl_table_header *register_sysctl_table(
39130   ctl_table * table, int insert_at_head)
39131 {
39132   return 0;
39133 }
39134
39135 void unregister_sysctl_table(struct ctl_table_header
39136     *table)
39137 {
39138 }
39139
39140 #endif                          /* CONFIG_SYSCTL */
```

kernel/time.c

```
39141 /*
39142  *   linux/kernel/time.c
39143  *
39144  *   Copyright (C) 1991, 1992   Linus Torvalds
39145  *
39146  *   This file contains the interface functions for the
39147  *   various time related system calls: time, stime,
39148  *   gettimeofday, settimeofday, adjtime
39149  */
39150
39151 /*
39152  * Modification history kernel/time.c
39153  *
39154  * 1993-09-02 Philip Gladstone
39155  * Created file with time related functions from sched.c
39156  * and adjtimex()
39157  * 1993-10-08    Torsten Duwe
39158  *       adjtime interface update and CMOS clock write
39159  *       code
39160  * 1995-08-13    Torsten Duwe
39161  *       kernel PLL updated to 1994-12-13 specs (rfc-1589)
39162  * 1999-01-16    Ulrich Windl
39163  *       Introduced error checking for many cases in
39164  *       adjtimex().  Updated NTP code according to
39165  *       technical memorandum Jan '96 "A Kernel Model for
39166  *       Precision Timekeeping" by Dave Mills Allow
39167  *       time_constant larger than MAXTC(6) for NTP v4
39168  *       (MAXTC == 10) (Even though the technical
39169  *       memorandum forbids it)
39170  */
39171
39172 #include <linux/mm.h>
```

```
39173 #include <linux/timex.h>
39174 #include <linux/smp_lock.h>
39175
39176 #include <asm/uaccess.h>
39177
39178 /* The timezone where the local system is located.  Used
39179  * as a default by some programs who obtain this value by
39180  * using gettimeofday.  */
39181 struct timezone sys_tz;
39182
39183 static void do_normal_gettime(struct timeval *tm)
39184 {
39185   *tm = xtime;
39186 }
39187
39188 void (*do_get_fast_time) (struct timeval *) =
39189     do_normal_gettime;
39190
39191 /* Generic way to access 'xtime' (the current time of
39192  * day).  This can be changed if the platform provides a
39193  * more accurate (and fast!)  version.  */
39194 void get_fast_time(struct timeval *t)
39195 {
39196   do_get_fast_time(t);
39197 }
39198
39199 /* The xtime_lock is not only serializing the xtime
39200  * read/writes but it's also serializing all accesses to
39201  * the global NTP variables now. */
39202 extern rwlock_t xtime_lock;
39203
39204 #if !defined(__alpha__) && !defined(__ia64__)
39205
39206 /* sys_time() can be implemented in user-level using
39207  * sys_gettimeofday().  Is this for backwards
39208  * compatibility?  If so, why not move it into the
39209  * appropriate arch directory (for those architectures
39210  * that need it).
39211  *
39212  * XXX This function is NOT 64-bit clean!  */
39213 asmlinkage long sys_time(int *tloc)
39214 {
39215   int i;
39216
39217   /* SMP: This is fairly trivial. We grab CURRENT_TIME
39218    * and stuff it to user space. No side effects */
39219   i = CURRENT_TIME;
```

p 569

```
39220    if (tloc) {
39221      if (put_user(i, tloc))
39222        i = -EFAULT;
39223    }
39224    return i;
39225 }
39226
39227 /* sys_stime() can be implemented in user-level using
39228  * sys_settimeofday().  Is this for backwards
39229  * compatibility?  If so, why not move it into the
39230  * appropriate arch directory (for those architectures
39231  * that need it).  */
39232 asmlinkage long sys_stime(int *tptr)
39233 {
39234   int value;
39235
39236   if (!capable(CAP_SYS_TIME))
39237     return -EPERM;
39238   if (get_user(value, tptr))
39239     return -EFAULT;
39240   write_lock_irq(&xtime_lock);
39241   xtime.tv_sec = value;
39242   xtime.tv_usec = 0;
39243   time_adjust = 0;               /* stop active adjtime() */
39244   time_status |= STA_UNSYNC;
39245   time_maxerror = NTP_PHASE_LIMIT;
39246   time_esterror = NTP_PHASE_LIMIT;
39247   write_unlock_irq(&xtime_lock);
39248   return 0;
39249 }
39250
39251 #endif
39252
39253 asmlinkage long sys_gettimeofday(struct timeval *tv,
39254     struct timezone *tz)
39255 {
39256   if (tv) {
39257     struct timeval ktv;
39258     do_gettimeofday(&ktv);
39259     if (copy_to_user(tv, &ktv, sizeof(ktv)))
39260       return -EFAULT;
39261   }
39262   if (tz) {
39263     if (copy_to_user(tz, &sys_tz, sizeof(sys_tz)))
39264       return -EFAULT;
39265   }
39266   return 0;
39267 }
39268
39269 /* Adjust the time obtained from the CMOS to be UTC time
39270  * instead of local time.
39271  *
39272  * This is ugly, but preferable to the alternatives.
39273  * Otherwise we would either need to write a program to
39274  * do it in /etc/rc (and risk confusion if the program
39275  * gets run more than once; it would also be hard to make
39276  * the program warp the clock precisely n hours) or
39277  * compile in the timezone information into the kernel.
39278  * Bad, bad....
39279  *
39280  *                                   - TYT, 1992-01-01
39281  *
39282  * The best thing to do is to keep the CMOS clock in
39283  * universal time (UTC) as real UNIX machines always do
39284  * it. This avoids all headaches about daylight saving
39285  * times and warping kernel clocks.   */
39286 inline static void warp_clock(void)
39287 {
39288   write_lock_irq(&xtime_lock);
39289   xtime.tv_sec += sys_tz.tz_minuteswest * 60;
39290   write_unlock_irq(&xtime_lock);
39291 }
39292
39293 /* In case for some reason the CMOS clock has not already
39294  * been running in UTC, but in some local time: The first
39295  * time we set the timezone, we will warp the clock so
39296  * that it is ticking UTC time instead of local
39297  * time. Presumably, if someone is setting the timezone
39298  * then we are running in an environment where the
39299  * programs understand about timezones. This should be
39300  * done at boot time in the /etc/rc script, as soon as
39301  * possible, so that the clock can be set
39302  * right. Otherwise, various programs will get confused
39303  * when the clock gets warped.   */
39304
39305 int do_sys_settimeofday(struct timeval *tv,
39306     struct timezone *tz)
39307 {
39308   static int firsttime = 1;
39309
39310   if (!capable(CAP_SYS_TIME))
39311     return -EPERM;
39312
39313   if (tz) {
```

```
39314        /* SMP safe, global irq locking makes it work. */       39361  int pps_shift = PPS_SHIFT;    /* interval duration (s)
39315        sys_tz = *tz;                                           39362                                * (shift) */
39316        if (firsttime) {                                        39363
39317          firsttime = 0;                                        39364  long pps_jitcnt;             /* jitter limit exceeded */
39318          if (!tv)                                               39365  long pps_calcnt;             /* calibration intervals */
39319            warp_clock();                                        39366  long pps_errcnt;             /* calibration errors */
39320        }                                                        39367  long pps_stbcnt;             /* stability limit exceeded*/
39321      }                                                          39368
39322      if (tv) {                                                  39369  /* hook for a loadable hardpps kernel module */
39323        /* SMP safe, again the code in arch/foo/time.c should   39370  void (*hardpps_ptr) (struct timeval *);
39324         * globally block out interrupts when it runs. */       39371
39325        do_settimeofday(tv);                                    39372  /* adjtimex mainly allows reading (and writing, if
39326      }                                                          39373   * superuser) of kernel time-keeping variables. used by
39327      return 0;                                                  39374   * xntpd. */
39328  }                                                              39375  int do_adjtimex(struct timex *txc)
39329                                                                 39376  {
39330  asmlinkage long sys_settimeofday(struct timeval *tv,           39377    long ltemp, mtemp, save_adjust;
39331      struct timezone *tz)                                       39378    int result;
39332  {                                                              39379
39333    struct timeval new_tv;                                       39380    /* In order to modify anything, you gotta be
39334    struct timezone new_tz;                                      39381     * super-user! */
39335                                                                 39382    if (txc->modes && !capable(CAP_SYS_TIME))
39336    if (tv) {                                                    39383      return -EPERM;
39337      if (copy_from_user(&new_tv, tv, sizeof(*tv)))              39384
39338        return -EFAULT;                                          39385    /* Now we validate the data before disabling
39339    }                                                            39386     * interrupts */
39340    if (tz) {                                                    39387
39341      if (copy_from_user(&new_tz, tz, sizeof(*tz)))              39388    if (txc->modes != ADJ_OFFSET_SINGLESHOT
39342        return -EFAULT;                                          39389        && (txc->modes & ADJ_OFFSET))
39343    }                                                            39390      /* adjustment Offset limited to +- .512 seconds */
39344                                                                 39391      if (txc->offset <= -MAXPHASE ||
39345    return do_sys_settimeofday(tv ? &new_tv : NULL,              39392          txc->offset >= MAXPHASE)
39346        tz ? &new_tz : NULL);                                    39393        return -EINVAL;
39347  }                                                              39394
39348                                                                 39395    /* if the quartz is off by more than 10% something is
39349  long pps_offset;            /* pps time offset (us) */          39396     * VERY wrong ! */
39350  long pps_jitter = MAXTIME;  /* time dispersion                 39397    if (txc->modes & ADJ_TICK)
39351                              * (jitter) (us) */                 39398      if (txc->tick < 900000 / HZ ||
39352                                                                 39399          txc->tick > 1100000 / HZ)
39353  long pps_freq;             /* frequency offset                 39400        return -EINVAL;
39354                              * (scaled ppm) */                  39401
39355  long pps_stabil = MAXFREQ;  /* frequency dispersion            39402    write_lock_irq(&xtime_lock);
39356                              * (scaled ppm) */                  39403    result = time_state;          /* mostly 'TIME_OK' */
39357                                                                 39404
39358  long pps_valid = PPS_VALID; /* pps signal watchdog             39405    /* Save for later - semantics of adjtime is to return
39359                              * counter */                       39406     * old value */
39360                                                                 39407    save_adjust = time_adjust;
```

```
39408
39409 #if 0                              /* STA_CLOCKERR is never
39410                                   * set yet */
39411     time_status &= ~STA_CLOCKERR; /* reset STA_CLOCKERR */
39412 #endif
39413     /* If there are input parameters, then process them */
39414     if (txc->modes) {
39415       if (txc->modes & ADJ_STATUS) /* only set
39416                                   * allowed bits */
39417         time_status = (txc->status & ~STA_RONLY) |
39418             (time_status & STA_RONLY);
39419
39420       if (txc->modes & ADJ_FREQUENCY) {   /* p. 22 */
39421         if (txc->freq > MAXFREQ || txc->freq < -MAXFREQ) {
39422           result = -EINVAL;
39423           goto leave;
39424         }
39425         time_freq = txc->freq - pps_freq;
39426       }
39427
39428       if (txc->modes & ADJ_MAXERROR) {
39429         if (txc->maxerror < 0
39430             || txc->maxerror >= NTP_PHASE_LIMIT) {
39431           result = -EINVAL;
39432           goto leave;
39433         }
39434         time_maxerror = txc->maxerror;
39435       }
39436
39437       if (txc->modes & ADJ_ESTERROR) {
39438         if (txc->esterror < 0
39439             || txc->esterror >= NTP_PHASE_LIMIT) {
39440           result = -EINVAL;
39441           goto leave;
39442         }
39443         time_esterror = txc->esterror;
39444       }
39445
39446       if (txc->modes & ADJ_TIMECONST) {   /* p. 24 */
39447         if (txc->constant < 0) {  /* NTP v4 uses values >
39448                                   * 6 */
39449           result = -EINVAL;
39450           goto leave;
39451         }
39452         time_constant = txc->constant;
39453       }
39454
39455       if (txc->modes & ADJ_OFFSET) {       /* values
39456                                   * checked
39457                                   * earlier */
39458         if (txc->modes == ADJ_OFFSET_SINGLESHOT) {
39459           /* adjtime() is independent from ntp_adjtime() */
39460           time_adjust = txc->offset;
39461         } else if (time_status & (STA_PLL | STA_PPSTIME)) {
39462           ltemp =
39463             (time_status & (STA_PPSTIME | STA_PPSSIGNAL))
39464             == (STA_PPSTIME | STA_PPSSIGNAL)
39465             ? pps_offset : txc->offset;
39466
39467           /* Scale the phase adjustment and clamp to the
39468            * operating range.  */
39469           if (ltemp > MAXPHASE)
39470             time_offset = MAXPHASE << SHIFT_UPDATE;
39471           else if (ltemp < -MAXPHASE)
39472             time_offset = -(MAXPHASE << SHIFT_UPDATE);
39473           else
39474             time_offset = ltemp << SHIFT_UPDATE;
39475
39476           /* Select whether the frequency is to be
39477            * controlled and in which mode (PLL or
39478            * FLL). Clamp to the operating range. Ugly
39479            * multiply/divide should be replaced someday. */
39480
39481           if (time_status & STA_FREQHOLD
39482               || time_reftime == 0)
39483             time_reftime = xtime.tv_sec;
39484           mtemp = xtime.tv_sec - time_reftime;
39485           time_reftime = xtime.tv_sec;
39486           if (time_status & STA_FLL) {
39487             if (mtemp >= MINSEC) {
39488               ltemp =
39489                 (time_offset / mtemp) << (SHIFT_USEC -
39490                                     SHIFT_UPDATE);
39491               if (ltemp < 0)
39492                 time_freq -= -ltemp >> SHIFT_KH;
39493               else
39494                 time_freq += ltemp >> SHIFT_KH;
39495             } else              /* calibration interval
39496                                 * too short (p. 12) */
39497               result = TIME_ERROR;
39498           } else {              /* PLL mode */
39499             if (mtemp < MAXSEC) {
39500               ltemp *= mtemp;
39501               if (ltemp < 0)
```

```
39502              time_freq -= -ltemp >> (time_constant +
39503                    time_constant + SHIFT_KF - SHIFT_USEC);
39504            else
39505              time_freq += ltemp >> (time_constant +
39506                    time_constant + SHIFT_KF - SHIFT_USEC);
39507          } else                    /* calibration interval
39508                                     * too long (p. 12) */
39509            result = TIME_ERROR;
39510        }
39511        if (time_freq > time_tolerance)
39512          time_freq = time_tolerance;
39513        else if (time_freq < -time_tolerance)
39514          time_freq = -time_tolerance;
39515      }                    /* STA_PLL || STA_PPSTIME */
39516    }                      /* txc->modes & ADJ_OFFSET */
39517    if (txc->modes & ADJ_TICK) {
39518      /* if the quartz is off by more than 10% something
39519       * is VERY wrong ! */
39520      if (txc->tick < 900000 / HZ
39521          || txc->tick > 1100000 / HZ) {
39522        result = -EINVAL;
39523        goto leave;
39524      }
39525      tick = txc->tick;
39526    }
39527  }                                 /* txc->modes */
39528 leave:
39529  if ((time_status & (STA_UNSYNC | STA_CLOCKERR)) != 0
39530      || ((time_status & (STA_PPSFREQ | STA_PPSTIME)) !=0
39531          && (time_status & STA_PPSSIGNAL) == 0)
39532      /* p. 24, (b) */
39533      || ((time_status & (STA_PPSTIME | STA_PPSJITTER))
39534          == (STA_PPSTIME | STA_PPSJITTER))
39535      /* p. 24, (c) */
39536      || ((time_status & STA_PPSFREQ) != 0
39537          && (time_status & (STA_PPSWANDER |
39538                         STA_PPSERROR)) != 0))
39539      /* p. 24, (d) */
39540      result = TIME_ERROR;
39541
39542  if ((txc->modes & ADJ_OFFSET_SINGLESHOT) ==
39543      ADJ_OFFSET_SINGLESHOT)
39544    txc->offset = save_adjust;
39545  else {
39546    if (time_offset < 0)
39547      txc->offset = -(-time_offset >> SHIFT_UPDATE);
39548    else
39549      txc->offset = time_offset >> SHIFT_UPDATE;
39550  }
39551  txc->freq = time_freq + pps_freq;
39552  txc->maxerror = time_maxerror;
39553  txc->esterror = time_esterror;
39554  txc->status = time_status;
39555  txc->constant = time_constant;
39556  txc->precision = time_precision;
39557  txc->tolerance = time_tolerance;
39558  txc->tick = tick;
39559  txc->ppsfreq = pps_freq;
39560  txc->jitter = pps_jitter >> PPS_AVG;
39561  txc->shift = pps_shift;
39562  txc->stabil = pps_stabil;
39563  txc->jitcnt = pps_jitcnt;
39564  txc->calcnt = pps_calcnt;
39565  txc->errcnt = pps_errcnt;
39566  txc->stbcnt = pps_stbcnt;
39567  write_unlock_irq(&xtime_lock);
39568  do_gettimeofday(&txc->time);
39569  return (result);
39570 }
39571
39572 asmlinkage long sys_adjtimex(struct timex *txc_p)
39573 {
39574   struct timex txc;          /* Local copy of parameter */
39575   int ret;
39576
39577   /* Copy the user data space into the kernel copy
39578    * structure. But bear in mind that the structures may
39579    * change */
39580   if (copy_from_user(&txc, txc_p, sizeof(struct timex)))
39581     return -EFAULT;
39582   ret = do_adjtimex(&txc);
39583   return copy_to_user(txc_p, &txc, sizeof(struct timex))
39584     ? -EFAULT
39585     : ret;
39586 }
```

kernel/timer.c

```
39587 /*
39588  *  linux/kernel/timer.c
39589  *
39590  *  Kernel internal timers, kernel timekeeping, basic
39591  *  process system calls
39592  *
39593  *  Copyright (C) 1991, 1992  Linus Torvalds
```

```
39594  *
39595  *  1997-01-28 Modified by Finn Arne Gangstad to make
39596  *  timers scale better.
39597  *
39598  *  1997-09-10 Updated NTP code according to technical
39599  *  memorandum Jan '96 "A Kernel Model for Precision
39600  *  Timekeeping" by Dave Mills
39601  *  1998-12-24 Fixed a xtime SMP race (we need the
39602  *  xtime_lock rw spinlock to serialize accesses to
39603  *  xtime/lost_ticks).  Copyright (C) 1998 Andrea
39604  *  Arcangeli
39605  *  1999-03-10 Improved NTP compatibility by Ulrich Windl
39606  */
39607
39608 #include <linux/config.h>
39609 #include <linux/mm.h>
39610 #include <linux/timex.h>
39611 #include <linux/delay.h>
39612 #include <linux/smp_lock.h>
39613 #include <linux/interrupt.h>
39614 #include <linux/kernel_stat.h>
39615
39616 #include <asm/uaccess.h>
39617
39618 /* Timekeeping variables */
39619
39620 /* timer interrupt period */
39621 long tick = (1000000 + HZ / 2) / HZ;
39622
39623 /* The current time */
39624 volatile struct timeval xtime
39625     __attribute__ ((aligned(16)));
39626
39627 /* Don't completely fail for HZ > 500.  */
39628 int tickadj = 500 / HZ ? : 1;   /* microsecs */
39629
39630 DECLARE_TASK_QUEUE(tq_timer);
39631 DECLARE_TASK_QUEUE(tq_immediate);
39632
39633 /* phase-lock loop variables */
39634 /* TIME_ERROR prevents overwriting the CMOS clock */
39635 int time_state = TIME_OK;  /* clock synchronization
39636                             * status */
39637 int time_status = STA_UNSYNC;  /* clock status bits */
39638 long time_offset;          /* time adjustment (us) */
39639 long time_constant = 2;    /* pll time constant */
39640 long time_tolerance = MAXFREQ;  /* frequency tolerance
39641                             * (ppm) */
39642 long time_precision = 1;   /* clock precision (us) */
39643 long time_maxerror = NTP_PHASE_LIMIT;  /* maximum error
39644                             * (us) */
39645 long time_esterror = NTP_PHASE_LIMIT;  /* estimated
39646                             * error (us) */
39647 long time_phase;           /* phase offset (scaled us) */
39648 long time_freq =           /* frequency offset (scaled ppm) */
39649     ((1000000 + HZ / 2) % HZ - HZ / 2) << SHIFT_USEC;
39650 long time_adj;             /* tick adjust (scaled 1/HZ)*/
39651 long time_reftime;         /* time @ last adjustment(s)*/
39652
39653 long time_adjust;
39654 long time_adjust_step;
39655
39656 unsigned long event;
39657
39658 extern int do_setitimer(int, struct itimerval *,
39659     struct itimerval *);
39660
39661 unsigned long volatile jiffies;
39662
39663 unsigned int *prof_buffer;
39664 unsigned long prof_len;
39665 unsigned long prof_shift;
39666
39667 /* Event timer code */
39668 #define TVN_BITS 6
39669 #define TVR_BITS 8
39670 #define TVN_SIZE (1 << TVN_BITS)
39671 #define TVR_SIZE (1 << TVR_BITS)
39672 #define TVN_MASK (TVN_SIZE - 1)
39673 #define TVR_MASK (TVR_SIZE - 1)
39674
39675 struct timer_vec {
39676   int index;
39677   struct list_head vec[TVN_SIZE];
39678 };
39679
39680 struct timer_vec_root {
39681   int index;
39682   struct list_head vec[TVR_SIZE];
39683 };
39684
39685 static struct timer_vec tv5;
39686 static struct timer_vec tv4;
39687 static struct timer_vec tv3;
```

```
39688 static struct timer_vec tv2;
39689 static struct timer_vec_root tv1;
39690
39691 static struct timer_vec *const tvecs[] = {
39692   (struct timer_vec *) &tv1, &tv2, &tv3, &tv4, &tv5
39693 };
39694
39695 #define NOOF_TVECS (sizeof(tvecs) / sizeof(tvecs[0]))
39696
39697 void init_timervecs(void)
39698 {
39699   int i;
39700
39701   for (i = 0; i < TVN_SIZE; i++) {
39702     INIT_LIST_HEAD(tv5.vec + i);
39703     INIT_LIST_HEAD(tv4.vec + i);
39704     INIT_LIST_HEAD(tv3.vec + i);
39705     INIT_LIST_HEAD(tv2.vec + i);
39706   }
39707   for (i = 0; i < TVR_SIZE; i++)
39708     INIT_LIST_HEAD(tv1.vec + i);
39709 }
39710
39711 static unsigned long timer_jiffies;
39712
39713 static inline void
39714 internal_add_timer(struct timer_list *timer)
39715 {
39716   /* must be cli-ed when calling this */
39717   unsigned long expires = timer->expires;
39718   unsigned long idx = expires - timer_jiffies;
39719   struct list_head *vec;
39720
39721   if (idx < TVR_SIZE) {
39722     int i = expires & TVR_MASK;
39723     vec = tv1.vec + i;
39724   } else if (idx < 1 << (TVR_BITS + TVN_BITS)) {
39725     int i = (expires >> TVR_BITS) & TVN_MASK;
39726     vec = tv2.vec + i;
39727   } else if (idx < 1 << (TVR_BITS + 2 * TVN_BITS)) {
39728     int i =
39729         (expires >> (TVR_BITS + TVN_BITS)) & TVN_MASK;
39730     vec = tv3.vec + i;
39731   } else if (idx < 1 << (TVR_BITS + 3 * TVN_BITS)) {
39732     int i = (expires >> (TVR_BITS + 2 * TVN_BITS)) &
39733                                               TVN_MASK;
39734     vec = tv4.vec + i;
39735   } else if ((signed long) idx < 0) {
39736     /* can happen if you add a timer with expires ==
39737      * jiffies, or you set a timer to go off in the past
39738      */
39739     vec = tv1.vec + tv1.index;
39740   } else if (idx <= 0xffffffffUL) {
39741     int i =
39742         (expires >> (TVR_BITS + 3 * TVN_BITS)) &
39743                                               TVN_MASK;
39744     vec = tv5.vec + i;
39745   } else {
39746     /* Can only get here on architectures with 64-bit
39747      * jiffies */
39748     INIT_LIST_HEAD(&timer->list);
39749     return;
39750   }
39751   /* Timers are FIFO!  */
39752   list_add(&timer->list, vec->prev);
39753 }
39754
39755 /* Initialize both explicitly - let's try to have them
39756  * in the same cache line */
39757 spinlock_t timerlist_lock = SPIN_LOCK_UNLOCKED;
39758
39759 #ifdef CONFIG_SMP
39760 volatile struct timer_list *volatile running_timer;
39761 #define timer_enter(t)                                  \
39762   do { running_timer = t; mb(); } while (0)
39763 #define timer_exit()                                    \
39764   do { running_timer = NULL; } while (0)
39765 #define timer_is_running(t) (running_timer == t)
39766 #define timer_synchronize(t)                            \
39767   while (timer_is_running(t)) barrier()
39768 #else
39769 #define timer_enter(t)          do { } while (0)
39770 #define timer_exit()            do { } while (0)
39771 #endif
39772
39773 void add_timer(struct timer_list *timer)
39774 {
39775   unsigned long flags;
39776
39777   spin_lock_irqsave(&timerlist_lock, flags);
39778   if (timer_pending(timer))
39779     goto bug;
39780   internal_add_timer(timer);
39781   spin_unlock_irqrestore(&timerlist_lock, flags);
```

```
39782    return;
39783 bug:
39784    spin_unlock_irqrestore(&timerlist_lock, flags);
39785    printk("bug: kernel timer added twice at %p.\n",
39786        __builtin_return_address(0));
39787 }
39788
39789 static inline int detach_timer(struct timer_list *timer)
39790 {
39791    if (!timer_pending(timer))
39792      return 0;
39793    list_del(&timer->list);
39794    return 1;
39795 }
39796
39797 int mod_timer(struct timer_list *timer,
39798      unsigned long expires)
39799 {
39800    int ret;
39801    unsigned long flags;
39802
39803    spin_lock_irqsave(&timerlist_lock, flags);
39804    timer->expires = expires;
39805    ret = detach_timer(timer);
39806    internal_add_timer(timer);
39807    spin_unlock_irqrestore(&timerlist_lock, flags);
39808    return ret;
39809 }
39810
39811 int del_timer(struct timer_list *timer)
39812 {
39813    int ret;
39814    unsigned long flags;
39815
39816    spin_lock_irqsave(&timerlist_lock, flags);
39817    ret = detach_timer(timer);
39818    timer->list.next = timer->list.prev = NULL;
39819    spin_unlock_irqrestore(&timerlist_lock, flags);
39820    return ret;
39821 }
39822
39823 #ifdef CONFIG_SMP
39824 void sync_timers(void)
39825 {
39826    spin_unlock_wait(&global_bh_lock);
39827 }
39828
39829 /* SMP specific function to delete periodic timer.
39830  * Caller must disable by some means restarting the timer
39831  * for new. Upon exit the timer is not queued and handler
39832  * is not running on any CPU. It returns number of times,
39833  * which timer was deleted (for reference counting).  */
39834
39835 int del_timer_sync(struct timer_list *timer)
39836 {
39837    int ret = 0;
39838
39839    for (;;) {
39840      unsigned long flags;
39841      int running;
39842
39843      spin_lock_irqsave(&timerlist_lock, flags);
39844      ret += detach_timer(timer);
39845      timer->list.next = timer->list.prev = 0;
39846      running = timer_is_running(timer);
39847      spin_unlock_irqrestore(&timerlist_lock, flags);
39848
39849      if (!running)
39850        break;
39851
39852      timer_synchronize(timer);
39853    }
39854
39855    return ret;
39856 }
39857 #endif
39858
39859
39860 static inline void cascade_timers(struct timer_vec *tv)
39861 {
39862    /* cascade all the timers from tv up one level */
39863    struct list_head *head, *curr, *next;
39864
39865    head = tv->vec + tv->index;
39866    curr = head->next;
39867    /* We are removing _all_ timers from the list, so we
39868     * don't have to detach them individually, just clear
39869     * the list afterwards.  */
39870    while (curr != head) {
39871      struct timer_list *tmp;
39872
39873      tmp = list_entry(curr, struct timer_list, list);
39874      next = curr->next;
39875      list_del(curr);               // not needed
```

```
39876        internal_add_timer(tmp);
39877        curr = next;
39878      }
39879      INIT_LIST_HEAD(head);
39880      tv->index = (tv->index + 1) & TVN_MASK;
39881 }
39882
39883 static inline void run_timer_list(void)
39884 {
39885    spin_lock_irq(&timerlist_lock);
39886    while ((long) (jiffies - timer_jiffies) >= 0) {
39887      struct list_head *head, *curr;
39888      if (!tv1.index) {
39889        int n = 1;
39890        do {
39891          cascade_timers(tvecs[n]);
39892        } while (tvecs[n]->index == 1 && ++n < NOOF_TVECS);
39893      }
39894    repeat:
39895      head = tv1.vec + tv1.index;
39896      curr = head->next;
39897      if (curr != head) {
39898        struct timer_list *timer;
39899        void (*fn) (unsigned long);
39900        unsigned long data;
39901
39902        timer = list_entry(curr, struct timer_list, list);
39903        fn = timer->function;
39904        data = timer->data;
39905
39906        detach_timer(timer);
39907        timer->list.next = timer->list.prev = NULL;
39908        timer_enter(timer);
39909        spin_unlock_irq(&timerlist_lock);
39910        fn(data);
39911        spin_lock_irq(&timerlist_lock);
39912        timer_exit();
39913        goto repeat;
39914      }
39915      ++timer_jiffies;
39916      tv1.index = (tv1.index + 1) & TVR_MASK;
39917    }
39918    spin_unlock_irq(&timerlist_lock);
39919 }
39920
39921 spinlock_t tqueue_lock = SPIN_LOCK_UNLOCKED;
39922
39923 void tqueue_bh(void)
39924 {
39925    run_task_queue(&tq_timer);
39926 }
39927
39928 void immediate_bh(void)
39929 {
39930    run_task_queue(&tq_immediate);
39931 }
39932
39933 /* this routine handles the overflow of the microsecond
39934  * field
39935  *
39936  * The tricky bits of code to handle the accurate clock
39937  * support were provided by Dave Mills (Mills@UDEL.EDU)
39938  * of NTP fame.  They were originally developed for SUN
39939  * and DEC kernels.  All the kudos should go to Dave for
39940  * this stuff. */
39941 static void second_overflow(void)
39942 {
39943    long ltemp;
39944
39945    /* Bump the maxerror field */
39946    time_maxerror += time_tolerance >> SHIFT_USEC;
39947    if (time_maxerror > NTP_PHASE_LIMIT) {
39948      time_maxerror = NTP_PHASE_LIMIT;
39949      time_status |= STA_UNSYNC;
39950    }
39951
39952    /* Leap second processing. If in leap-insert state at
39953     * the end of the day, the system clock is set back one
39954     * second; if in leap-delete state, the system clock is
39955     * set ahead one second. The microtime() routine or
39956     * external clock driver will insure that reported time
39957     * is always monotonic. The ugly divides should be
39958     * replaced.  */
39959    switch (time_state) {
39960
39961    case TIME_OK:
39962      if (time_status & STA_INS)
39963        time_state = TIME_INS;
39964      else if (time_status & STA_DEL)
39965        time_state = TIME_DEL;
39966      break;
39967
39968    case TIME_INS:
39969      if (xtime.tv_sec % 86400 == 0) {
```

```
39970      xtime.tv_sec-;
39971      time_state = TIME_OOP;
39972      printk(KERN_NOTICE
39973          "Clock: inserting leap second 23:59:60 UTC\n");
39974    }
39975    break;
39976
39977  case TIME_DEL:
39978    if ((xtime.tv_sec + 1) % 86400 == 0) {
39979      xtime.tv_sec++;
39980      time_state = TIME_WAIT;
39981      printk(KERN_NOTICE
39982          "Clock: deleting leap second 23:59:59 UTC\n");
39983    }
39984    break;
39985
39986  case TIME_OOP:
39987    time_state = TIME_WAIT;
39988    break;
39989
39990  case TIME_WAIT:
39991    if (!(time_status & (STA_INS | STA_DEL)))
39992      time_state = TIME_OK;
39993  }
39994
39995  /* Compute the phase adjustment for the next second. In
39996   * PLL mode, the offset is reduced by a fixed factor
39997   * times the time constant. In FLL mode the offset is
39998   * used directly. In either mode, the maximum phase
39999   * adjustment for each second is clamped so as to
40000   * spread the adjustment over not more than the number
40001   * of seconds between updates.  */
40002  if (time_offset < 0) {
40003    ltemp = -time_offset;
40004    if (!(time_status & STA_FLL))
40005      ltemp >>= SHIFT_KG + time_constant;
40006    if (ltemp > (MAXPHASE / MINSEC) << SHIFT_UPDATE)
40007      ltemp = (MAXPHASE / MINSEC) << SHIFT_UPDATE;
40008    time_offset += ltemp;
40009    time_adj = -ltemp << (SHIFT_SCALE - SHIFT_HZ -
40010                          SHIFT_UPDATE);
40011  } else {
40012    ltemp = time_offset;
40013    if (!(time_status & STA_FLL))
40014      ltemp >>= SHIFT_KG + time_constant;
40015    if (ltemp > (MAXPHASE / MINSEC) << SHIFT_UPDATE)
40016      ltemp = (MAXPHASE / MINSEC) << SHIFT_UPDATE;
40017    time_offset -= ltemp;
40018    time_adj =
40019        ltemp << (SHIFT_SCALE - SHIFT_HZ - SHIFT_UPDATE);
40020  }
40021
40022  /* Compute the frequency estimate and additional phase
40023   * adjustment due to frequency error for the next
40024   * second. When the PPS signal is engaged, gnaw on the
40025   * watchdog counter and update the frequency computed
40026   * by the pll and the PPS signal.  */
40027  pps_valid++;
40028  if (pps_valid == PPS_VALID) { /* PPS signal lost */
40029    pps_jitter = MAXTIME;
40030    pps_stabil = MAXFREQ;
40031    time_status &= ~(STA_PPSSIGNAL | STA_PPSJITTER |
40032                     STA_PPSWANDER | STA_PPSERROR);
40033  }
40034  ltemp = time_freq + pps_freq;
40035  if (ltemp < 0)
40036    time_adj -= -ltemp >>
40037        (SHIFT_USEC + SHIFT_HZ - SHIFT_SCALE);
40038  else
40039    time_adj += ltemp >>
40040        (SHIFT_USEC + SHIFT_HZ - SHIFT_SCALE);
40041
40042 #if HZ == 100
40043  /* Compensate for (HZ==100) != (1 << SHIFT_HZ). Add 25%
40044   * and 3.125% to get 128.125; => only 0.125% error
40045   * (p. 14) */
40046  if (time_adj < 0)
40047    time_adj -= (-time_adj >> 2) + (-time_adj >> 5);
40048  else
40049    time_adj += (time_adj >> 2) + (time_adj >> 5);
40050 #endif
40051 }
40052
40053 /* in the NTP reference this is called "hardclock()" */
40054 static void update_wall_time_one_tick(void)
40055 {
40056   if ((time_adjust_step = time_adjust) != 0) {
40057     /* We are doing an adjtime thing.
40058      *
40059      * Prepare time_adjust_step to be within bounds.
40060      * Note that a positive time_adjust means we want the
40061      * clock to run faster.
40062      *
40063      * Limit the amount of the step to be in the range
```

```
40064        *  -tickadj .. +tickadj */
40065       if (time_adjust > tickadj)
40066         time_adjust_step = tickadj;
40067       else if (time_adjust < -tickadj)
40068         time_adjust_step = -tickadj;
40069
40070       /* Reduce by this step the amount of time left  */
40071       time_adjust -= time_adjust_step;
40072     }
40073     xtime.tv_usec += tick + time_adjust_step;
40074     /* Advance the phase, once it gets to one microsecond,
40075      * then advance the tick more.  */
40076     time_phase += time_adj;
40077     if (time_phase <= -FINEUSEC) {
40078       long ltemp = -time_phase >> SHIFT_SCALE;
40079       time_phase += ltemp << SHIFT_SCALE;
40080       xtime.tv_usec -= ltemp;
40081     } else if (time_phase >= FINEUSEC) {
40082       long ltemp = time_phase >> SHIFT_SCALE;
40083       time_phase -= ltemp << SHIFT_SCALE;
40084       xtime.tv_usec += ltemp;
40085     }
40086 }
40087
40088 /* Using a loop looks inefficient, but "ticks" is usually
40089  * just one (we shouldn't be losing ticks, we're doing
40090  * this this way mainly for interrupt latency reasons,
40091  * not because we think we'll have lots of lost timer
40092  * ticks */
40093 static void update_wall_time(unsigned long ticks)
40094 {
40095   do {
40096     ticks--;
40097     update_wall_time_one_tick();
40098   } while (ticks);
40099
40100   if (xtime.tv_usec >= 1000000) {
40101     xtime.tv_usec -= 1000000;
40102     xtime.tv_sec++;
40103     second_overflow();
40104   }
40105 }
40106
40107 static inline void
40108 do_process_times(struct task_struct *p,
40109   unsigned long user, unsigned long system)
40110 {
40111   unsigned long psecs;
40112
40113   psecs  = (p->times.tms_utime += user);
40114   psecs += (p->times.tms_stime += system);
40115   if (psecs / HZ > p->rlim[RLIMIT_CPU].rlim_cur) {
40116     /* Send SIGXCPU every second.. */
40117     if (!(psecs % HZ))
40118       send_sig(SIGXCPU, p, 1);
40119     /* and SIGKILL when we go over max.. */
40120     if (psecs / HZ > p->rlim[RLIMIT_CPU].rlim_max)
40121       send_sig(SIGKILL, p, 1);
40122   }
40123 }
40124
40125 static inline void do_it_virt(struct task_struct *p,
40126     unsigned long ticks)
40127 {
40128   unsigned long it_virt = p->it_virt_value;
40129
40130   if (it_virt) {
40131     it_virt -= ticks;
40132     if (!it_virt) {
40133       it_virt = p->it_virt_incr;
40134       send_sig(SIGVTALRM, p, 1);
40135     }
40136     p->it_virt_value = it_virt;
40137   }
40138 }
40139
40140 static inline void do_it_prof(struct task_struct *p)
40141 {
40142   unsigned long it_prof = p->it_prof_value;
40143
40144   if (it_prof) {
40145     if (--it_prof == 0) {
40146       it_prof = p->it_prof_incr;
40147       send_sig(SIGPROF, p, 1);
40148     }
40149     p->it_prof_value = it_prof;
40150   }
40151 }
40152
40153 void update_one_process(struct task_struct *p,
40154     unsigned long user, unsigned long system, int cpu)
40155 {
40156   p->per_cpu_utime[cpu] += user;
40157   p->per_cpu_stime[cpu] += system;
```

p 594

```
40158   do_process_times(p, user, system);
40159   do_it_virt(p, user);
40160   do_it_prof(p);
40161 }
40162
40163 /* Called from the timer interrupt handler to charge one
40164  * tick to the current process.  user_tick is 1 if the
40165  * tick is user time, 0 for system.  */
40166 void update_process_times(int user_tick)
40167 {
40168   struct task_struct *p = current;
40169   int cpu = smp_processor_id(), system = user_tick ^ 1;
40170
40171   update_one_process(p, user_tick, system, cpu);
40172   if (p->pid) {
40173     if (--p->counter <= 0) {
40174       p->counter = 0;
40175       p->need_resched = 1;
40176     }
40177     if (p->nice > 0)
40178       kstat.per_cpu_nice[cpu] += user_tick;
40179     else
40180       kstat.per_cpu_user[cpu] += user_tick;
40181     kstat.per_cpu_system[cpu] += system;
40182   } else if (local_bh_count(cpu)
40183       || local_irq_count(cpu) > 1)
40184     kstat.per_cpu_system[cpu] += system;
40185 }
40186
40187 /* Nr of active tasks - counted in fixed-point numbers */
40188 static unsigned long count_active_tasks(void)
40189 {
40190   struct task_struct *p;
40191   unsigned long nr = 0;
40192
40193   read_lock(&tasklist_lock);
40194   for_each_task(p) {
40195     if ((p->state == TASK_RUNNING ||
40196         (p->state & TASK_UNINTERRUPTIBLE)))
40197       nr += FIXED_1;
40198   }
40199   read_unlock(&tasklist_lock);
40200   return nr;
40201 }
40202
40203 /* Hmm.. Changed this, as the GNU make sources (load.c)
40204  * seems to imply that avenrun[] is the standard name for
```

```
40205  * this kind of thing.  Nothing else seems to be
40206  * standardized: the fractional size etc all seem to
40207  * differ on different machines.  */
40208 unsigned long avenrun[3];
40209
40210 static inline void calc_load(unsigned long ticks)
40211 {
40212   unsigned long active_tasks;   /* fixed-point */
40213   static int count = LOAD_FREQ;
40214
40215   count -= ticks;
40216   if (count < 0) {
40217     count += LOAD_FREQ;
40218     active_tasks = count_active_tasks();
40219     CALC_LOAD(avenrun[0], EXP_1, active_tasks);
40220     CALC_LOAD(avenrun[1], EXP_5, active_tasks);
40221     CALC_LOAD(avenrun[2], EXP_15, active_tasks);
40222   }
40223 }
40224
40225 /* jiffies at the most recent update of wall time */
40226 unsigned long wall_jiffies;
40227
40228 /* This spinlock protect us from races in SMP while
40229  * playing with xtime. -arca */
40230 rwlock_t xtime_lock = RW_LOCK_UNLOCKED;
40231
40232 static inline void update_times(void)
40233 {
40234   unsigned long ticks;
40235
40236   /* update_times() is run from the raw timer_bh handler
40237    * so we just know that the irqs are locally enabled
40238    * and so we don't need to save/restore the flags of
40239    * the local CPU here. -arca */
40240   write_lock_irq(&xtime_lock);
40241
40242   ticks = jiffies - wall_jiffies;
40243   if (ticks) {
40244     wall_jiffies += ticks;
40245     update_wall_time(ticks);
40246   }
40247   write_unlock_irq(&xtime_lock);
40248   calc_load(ticks);
40249 }
40250
40251 void timer_bh(void)
```

```
40252 {
40253   update_times();
40254   run_timer_list();
40255 }
40256
40257 void do_timer(struct pt_regs *regs)
40258 {
40259   (*(unsigned long *) &jiffies)++;
40260 #ifndef CONFIG_SMP
40261   /* SMP process accounting uses the local APIC timer */
40262
40263   update_process_times(user_mode(regs));
40264 #endif
40265   mark_bh(TIMER_BH);
40266   if (TQ_ACTIVE(tq_timer))
40267     mark_bh(TQUEUE_BH);
40268 }
40269
40270 #if !defined(__alpha__) && !defined(__ia64__)
40271
40272 /* For backwards compatibility?  This can be done in libc
40273  * so Alpha and all newer ports shouldn't need it.  */
40274 asmlinkage unsigned long sys_alarm(unsigned int seconds)
40275 {
40276   struct itimerval it_new, it_old;
40277   unsigned int oldalarm;
40278
40279   it_new.it_interval.tv_sec =
40280       it_new.it_interval.tv_usec = 0;
40281   it_new.it_value.tv_sec = seconds;
40282   it_new.it_value.tv_usec = 0;
40283   do_setitimer(ITIMER_REAL, &it_new, &it_old);
40284   oldalarm = it_old.it_value.tv_sec;
40285   /* ehhh.. We can't return 0 if we have an alarm
40286    * pending.. */
40287   /* And we'd better return too much than too little
40288    * anyway */
40289   if (it_old.it_value.tv_usec)
40290     oldalarm++;
40291   return oldalarm;
40292 }
40293
40294 #endif
40295
40296 #ifndef __alpha__
40297
40298 /* The Alpha uses getxpid, getxuid, and getxgid instead.
```

```
40299  * Maybe this should be moved into arch/i386 instead?  */
40300
40301 asmlinkage long sys_getpid(void)
40302 {
40303   /* This is SMP safe - current->pid doesn't change */
40304   return current->tgid;
40305 }
40306
40307 /* This is not strictly SMP safe: p_opptr could change
40308  * from under us. However, rather than getting any lock
40309  * we can use an optimistic algorithm: get the parent
40310  * pid, and go back and check that the parent is still
40311  * the same. If it has changed (which is extremely
40312  * unlikely indeed), we just try again..
40313  *
40314  * NOTE! This depends on the fact that even if we _do_
40315  * get an old value of "parent", we can happily
40316  * dereference the pointer: we just can't necessarily
40317  * trust the result until we know that the parent pointer
40318  * is valid.
40319  *
40320  * The "mb()" macro is a memory barrier - a synchronizing
40321  * event. It also makes sure that gcc doesn't optimize
40322  * away the necessary memory references.. The barrier
40323  * doesn't have to have all that strong semantics: on x86
40324  * we don't really require a synchronizing instruction,
40325  * for example.  The barrier is more important for code
40326  * generation than for any real memory ordering semantics
40327  * (even if there is a small window for a race, using the
40328  * old pointer is harmless for a while).  */
40329 asmlinkage long sys_getppid(void)
40330 {
40331   int pid;
40332   struct task_struct *me = current;
40333   struct task_struct *parent;
40334
40335   parent = me->p_opptr;
40336   for (;;) {
40337     pid = parent->pid;
40338 #if CONFIG_SMP
40339   {
40340     struct task_struct *old = parent;
40341     mb();
40342     parent = me->p_opptr;
40343     if (old != parent)
40344       continue;
40345   }
```

```
40346 #endif
40347    break;
40348  }
40349  return pid;
40350 }
40351
40352 asmlinkage long sys_getuid(void)
40353 {
40354   /* Only we change this so SMP safe */
40355   return current->uid;
40356 }
40357
40358 asmlinkage long sys_geteuid(void)
40359 {
40360   /* Only we change this so SMP safe */
40361   return current->euid;
40362 }
40363
40364 asmlinkage long sys_getgid(void)
40365 {
40366   /* Only we change this so SMP safe */
40367   return current->gid;
40368 }
40369
40370 asmlinkage long sys_getegid(void)
40371 {
40372   /* Only we change this so SMP safe */
40373   return current->egid;
40374 }
40375
40376 #endif
40377
40378 asmlinkage long sys_nanosleep(struct timespec *rqtp,
40379      struct timespec *rmtp)
40380 {
40381   struct timespec t;
40382   unsigned long expire;
40383
40384   if (copy_from_user(&t, rqtp, sizeof(struct timespec)))
40385     return -EFAULT;
40386
40387   if (t.tv_nsec >= 1000000000L || t.tv_nsec < 0
40388       || t.tv_sec < 0)
40389     return -EINVAL;
40390
40391
40392   if (t.tv_sec == 0 && t.tv_nsec <= 2000000L &&
```

```
40393      current->policy != SCHED_OTHER) {
40394     /* Short delay requests up to 2 ms will be handled
40395      * with high precision by a busy wait for all
40396      * real-time processes.
40397      *
40398      * Its important on SMP not to do this holding locks.
40399      */
40400     udelay((t.tv_nsec + 999) / 1000);
40401     return 0;
40402   }
40403
40404   expire = timespec_to_jiffies(&t) +
40405     (t.tv_sec || t.tv_nsec);
40406
40407   current->state = TASK_INTERRUPTIBLE;
40408   expire = schedule_timeout(expire);
40409
40410   if (expire) {
40411     if (rmtp) {
40412       jiffies_to_timespec(expire, &t);
40413       if (copy_to_user(rmtp, &t,
40414                  sizeof(struct timespec)))
40415         return -EFAULT;
40416     }
40417     return -EINTR;
40418   }
40419   return 0;
40420 }
```

kernel/user.c

```
40421 /*
40422  * The "user cache".
40423  *
40424  * (C) Copyright 1991-2000 Linus Torvalds
40425  *
40426  * We have a per-user structure to keep track of how many
40427  * processes, files etc the user has claimed, in order to
40428  * be able to have per-user limits for system resources.
40429  */
40430
40431 #include <linux/init.h>
40432 #include <linux/sched.h>
40433 #include <linux/slab.h>
40434
40435 /* UID task count cache, to get fast user lookup in
40436  * "alloc_uid" when changing user ID's (ie setuid() and
40437  * friends).  */
```

```
40438 #define UIDHASH_BITS            8
40439 #define UIDHASH_SZ              (1 << UIDHASH_BITS)
40440 #define UIDHASH_MASK            (UIDHASH_SZ - 1)
40441 #define __uidhashfn(uid)                              \
40442   (((uid >> UIDHASH_BITS) ^ uid) & UIDHASH_MASK)
40443 #define uidhashentry(uid)                             \
40444   (uidhash_table + __uidhashfn(uid))
40445
40446 static kmem_cache_t *uid_cachep;
40447 static struct user_struct *uidhash_table[UIDHASH_SZ];
40448 static spinlock_t uidhash_lock = SPIN_LOCK_UNLOCKED;
40449
40450 struct user_struct root_user = {
40451   __count:    ATOMIC_INIT(1),
40452   processes:  ATOMIC_INIT(1),
40453   files:      ATOMIC_INIT(0)
40454 };
40455
40456 /* These routines must be called with the uidhash
40457  * spinlock held!  */
40458 static inline void
40459 uid_hash_insert(struct user_struct *up,
40460                 struct user_struct **hashent)
40461 {
40462   struct user_struct *next = *hashent;
40463
40464   up->next = next;
40465   if (next)
40466     next->pprev = &up->next;
40467   up->pprev = hashent;
40468   *hashent = up;
40469 }
40470
40471 static inline void
40472 uid_hash_remove(struct user_struct *up)
40473 {
40474   struct user_struct *next = up->next;
40475   struct user_struct **pprev = up->pprev;
40476
40477   if (next)
40478     next->pprev = pprev;
40479   *pprev = next;
40480 }
40481
40482 static inline struct user_struct *
40483 uid_hash_find(uid_t uid, struct user_struct **hashent)
40484 {
40485   struct user_struct *next;
40486
40487   next = *hashent;
40488   for (;;) {
40489     struct user_struct *up = next;
40490     if (next) {
40491       next = up->next;
40492       if (up->uid != uid)
40493         continue;
40494       atomic_inc(&up->__count);
40495     }
40496     return up;
40497   }
40498 }
40499
40500 void free_uid(struct user_struct *up)
40501 {
40502   if (up &&
40503       atomic_dec_and_lock(&up->__count, &uidhash_lock)) {
40504     uid_hash_remove(up);
40505     kmem_cache_free(uid_cachep, up);
40506     spin_unlock(&uidhash_lock);
40507   }
40508 }
40509
40510 struct user_struct *alloc_uid(uid_t uid)
40511 {
40512   struct user_struct **hashent = uidhashentry(uid);
40513   struct user_struct *up;
40514
40515   spin_lock(&uidhash_lock);
40516   up = uid_hash_find(uid, hashent);
40517   spin_unlock(&uidhash_lock);
40518
40519   if (!up) {
40520     struct user_struct *new;
40521
40522     new = kmem_cache_alloc(uid_cachep, SLAB_KERNEL);
40523     if (!new)
40524       return NULL;
40525     new->uid = uid;
40526     atomic_set(&new->__count, 1);
40527     atomic_set(&new->processes, 0);
40528     atomic_set(&new->files, 0);
40529
40530     /* Before adding this, check whether we raced on
40531      * adding the same user already..  */
```

```
40532      spin_lock(&uidhash_lock);
40533      up = uid_hash_find(uid, hashent);
40534      if (up) {
40535        kmem_cache_free(uid_cachep, new);
40536      } else {
40537        uid_hash_insert(new, hashent);
40538        up = new;
40539      }
40540      spin_unlock(&uidhash_lock);
40541
40542    }
40543    return up;
40544  }
40545
40546
40547  static int __init uid_cache_init(void)
40548  {
40549    uid_cachep =
40550        kmem_cache_create("uid_cache",
40551                          sizeof(struct user_struct), 0,
40552                          SLAB_HWCACHE_ALIGN,
40553                          NULL, NULL);
40554    if (!uid_cachep)
40555      panic("Cannot create uid taskcount SLAB cache\n");
40556
40557    /* Insert the root user immediately - init already
40558     * runs with this */
40559    uid_hash_insert(&root_user, uidhashentry(0));
40560    return 0;
40561  }
40562
40563  module_init(uid_cache_init);
```

lib/cmdline.c

```
40564  /*
40565   * linux/lib/cmdline.c
40566   * Helper functions generally used for parsing kernel
40567   * command line and module options.
40568   *
40569   * Code and copyrights come from init/main.c and
40570   * arch/i386/kernel/setup.c.
40571   *
40572   * This source code is licensed under the GNU General
40573   * Public License, Version 2.  See the file COPYING for
40574   * more details.
40575   *
40576   * GNU Indent formatting options for this file: -kr -i8
40577   * -npsl -pcs
40578   */
40579
40580  #include <linux/module.h>
40581  #include <linux/kernel.h>
40582  #include <linux/string.h>
40583
40584
40585  /**
40586   *      get_option - Parse integer from an option string
40587   *      @str: option string
40588   *      @pint: (output) integer value parsed from @str
40589   *
40590   * Read an int from an option string; if available accept
40591   * a subsequent comma as well.
40592   *
40593   * Return values:
40594   *    0: no int in string
40595   *    1: int found, no subsequent comma
40596   *    2: int found including a subsequent comma */
40597  int get_option(char **str, int *pint)
40598  {
40599    char *cur = *str;
40600
40601    if (!cur || !(*cur))
40602      return 0;
40603    *pint = simple_strtol(cur, str, 0);
40604    if (cur == *str)
40605      return 0;
40606    if (**str == ',') {
40607      (*str)++;
40608      return 2;
40609    }
40610
40611    return 1;
40612  }
40613
40614  /**
40615   *      get_options - Parse a string into a list of
40616   *                         integers
40617   *      @str: String to be parsed
40618   *      @nints: size of integer array
40619   *      @ints: integer array
40620   *
40621   * This function parses a string containing a
40622   * comma-separated list of integers.   The parse halts
40623   * when the array is full, or when no more numbers can be
```

```
40624  * retrieved from the string.
40625  *
40626  * Return value is the character in the string which
40627  * caused the parse to end (typically a null terminator,
40628  * if @str is completely parseable).  */
40629 char *get_options(char *str, int nints, int *ints)
40630 {
40631   int res, i = 1;
40632
40633   while (i < nints) {
40634     res = get_option(&str, ints + i);
40635     if (res == 0)
40636       break;
40637     i++;
40638     if (res == 1)
40639       break;
40640   }
40641   ints[0] = i - 1;
40642   return (str);
40643 }
40644
40645 /**
40646  *      memparse - parse a string with mem suffixes into
40647  *                 a number
40648  *      @ptr: Where parse begins
40649  *      @retptr: (output) Pointer to next char after
40650  *                parse completes
40651  *
40652  * Parses a string into a number.  The number stored at
40653  * @ptr is potentially suffixed with %K (for kilobytes,
40654  * or 1024 bytes), %M (for megabytes, or 1048576 bytes),
40655  * or %G (for gigabytes, or 1073741824).  If the number
40656  * is suffixed with K, M, or G, then the return value is
40657  * the number multiplied by one kilobyte, one megabyte,
40658  * or one gigabyte, respectively.  */
40659 unsigned long memparse(char *ptr, char **retptr)
40660 {
40661   unsigned long ret = simple_strtoul(ptr, retptr, 0);
40662
40663   switch (**retptr) {
40664   case 'G':
40665   case 'g':
40666     ret <<= 10;
40667   case 'M':
40668   case 'm':
40669     ret <<= 10;
40670   case 'K':
```

```
40671   case 'k':
40672     ret <<= 10;
40673     (*retptr)++;
40674   default:
40675     break;
40676   }
40677   return ret;
40678 }
40679
40680
40681 EXPORT_SYMBOL(memparse);
40682 EXPORT_SYMBOL(get_option);
40683 EXPORT_SYMBOL(get_options);
```

mm/memory.c

```
40684 /*
40685  * linux/mm/memory.c
40686  *
40687  * Copyright (C) 1991, 1992, 1993, 1994  Linus Torvalds
40688  */
40689
40690 /* demand-loading started 01.12.91 - seems it is high on
40691  * the list of things wanted, and it should be easy to
40692  * implement. - Linus */
40693
40694 /* Ok, demand-loading was easy, shared pages a little bit
40695  * tricker. Shared pages started 02.12.91, seems to
40696  * work. - Linus.
40697  *
40698  * Tested sharing by executing about 30 /bin/sh: under
40699  * the old kernel it would have taken more than the 6M I
40700  * have free, but it worked well as far as I could see.
40701  *
40702  * Also corrected some "invalidate()"s - I wasn't doing
40703  * enough of them.   */
40704
40705 /* Real VM (paging to/from disk) started 18.12.91. Much
40706  * more work and thought has to go into this. Oh, well..
40707  * 19.12.91 - works, somewhat. Sometimes I get faults,
40708  * don't know why.  Found it. Everything seems to work
40709  * now.
40710  * 20.12.91 - Ok, making the swap-device changeable like
40711  * the root.   */
40712
40713 /* 05.04.94 - Multi-page memory management added for
40714  *            v1.1.  Idea by Alex Bligh
40715  *            (alex@cconcepts.co.uk)
```

```
40716  *
40717  * 16.07.99 - Support of BIGMEM added by Gerhard Wichert,
40718  *              Siemens AG
40719  *              (Gerhard.Wichert@pdb.siemens.de) */
40720
40721 #include <linux/mm.h>
40722 #include <linux/mman.h>
40723 #include <linux/swap.h>
40724 #include <linux/smp_lock.h>
40725 #include <linux/swapctl.h>
40726 #include <linux/iobuf.h>
40727 #include <asm/uaccess.h>
40728 #include <asm/pgalloc.h>
40729 #include <linux/highmem.h>
40730 #include <linux/pagemap.h>
40731
40732
40733 unsigned long max_mapnr;
40734 unsigned long num_physpages;
40735 void *high_memory;
40736 struct page *highmem_start_page;
40737
40738 /* We special-case the C-O-W ZERO_PAGE, because it's such
40739  * a common occurrence (no need to read the page to know
40740  * that it's zero - better for the cache and memory
40741  * subsystem).  */
40742 static inline void copy_cow_page(struct page *from,
40743     struct page *to, unsigned long address)
40744 {
40745   if (from == ZERO_PAGE(address)) {
40746     clear_user_highpage(to, address);
40747     return;
40748   }
40749   copy_user_highpage(to, from, address);
40750 }
40751
40752 mem_map_t *mem_map;
40753
40754 /* Note: this doesn't free the actual pages
40755  * themselves. That has been handled earlier when
40756  * unmapping all the memory regions.  */
40757 static inline void free_one_pmd(pmd_t * dir)
40758 {
40759   pte_t *pte;
40760
40761   if (pmd_none(*dir))
40762     return;
```

```
40763   if (pmd_bad(*dir)) {
40764     pmd_ERROR(*dir);
40765     pmd_clear(dir);
40766     return;
40767   }
40768   pte = pte_offset(dir, 0);
40769   pmd_clear(dir);
40770   pte_free(pte);
40771 }
40772
40773 static inline void free_one_pgd(pgd_t * dir)
40774 {
40775   int j;
40776   pmd_t *pmd;
40777
40778   if (pgd_none(*dir))
40779     return;
40780   if (pgd_bad(*dir)) {
40781     pgd_ERROR(*dir);
40782     pgd_clear(dir);
40783     return;
40784   }
40785   pmd = pmd_offset(dir, 0);
40786   pgd_clear(dir);
40787   for (j = 0; j < PTRS_PER_PMD; j++)
40788     free_one_pmd(pmd + j);
40789   pmd_free(pmd);
40790 }
40791
40792 /* Low and high watermarks for page table cache. The
40793  * system should try to have pgt_water[0] <= cache
40794  * elements <= pgt_water[1] */
40795 int pgt_cache_water[2] = { 25, 50 };
40796
40797 /* Returns the number of pages freed */
40798 int check_pgt_cache(void)
40799 {
40800   return do_check_pgt_cache(pgt_cache_water[0],
40801       pgt_cache_water[1]);
40802 }
40803
40804
40805 /* This function clears all user-level page tables of a
40806  * process - this is needed by execve(), so that old
40807  * pages aren't in the way.  */
40808 void clear_page_tables(struct mm_struct *mm,
40809     unsigned long first, int nr)
```

```
40810 {
40811   pgd_t *page_dir = mm->pgd;
40812
40813   page_dir += first;
40814   do {
40815     free_one_pgd(page_dir);
40816     page_dir++;
40817   } while (-nr);
40818
40819   /* keep the page table cache within bounds */
40820   check_pgt_cache();
40821 }
40822
40823 #define PTE_TABLE_MASK ((PTRS_PER_PTE-1) * sizeof(pte_t))
40824 #define PMD_TABLE_MASK ((PTRS_PER_PMD-1) * sizeof(pmd_t))
40825
40826 /* copy one vm_area from one task to the other. Assumes
40827  * the page tables already present in the new task to be
40828  * cleared in the whole range covered by this vma.
40829  *
40830  * 08Jan98 Merged into one routine from several inline
40831  * routines to reduce variable count and make things
40832  * faster. -jj */
40833 int copy_page_range(struct mm_struct *dst,
40834     struct mm_struct *src, struct vm_area_struct *vma)
40835 {
40836   pgd_t *src_pgd, *dst_pgd;
40837   unsigned long address = vma->vm_start;
40838   unsigned long end = vma->vm_end;
40839   unsigned long cow =
40840       (vma->vm_flags & (VM_SHARED | VM_MAYWRITE)) ==
40841       VM_MAYWRITE;
40842
40843   src_pgd = pgd_offset(src, address) - 1;
40844   dst_pgd = pgd_offset(dst, address) - 1;
40845
40846   for (;;) {
40847     pmd_t *src_pmd, *dst_pmd;
40848
40849     src_pgd++;
40850     dst_pgd++;
40851
40852     /* copy_pmd_range */
40853
40854     if (pgd_none(*src_pgd))
40855       goto skip_copy_pmd_range;
40856     if (pgd_bad(*src_pgd)) {
40857       pgd_ERROR(*src_pgd);
40858       pgd_clear(src_pgd);
40859     skip_copy_pmd_range:
40860       address = (address + PGDIR_SIZE) & PGDIR_MASK;
40861       if (!address || (address >= end))
40862         goto out;
40863       continue;
40864     }
40865     if (pgd_none(*dst_pgd)) {
40866       if (!pmd_alloc(dst_pgd, 0))
40867         goto nomem;
40868     }
40869
40870     src_pmd = pmd_offset(src_pgd, address);
40871     dst_pmd = pmd_offset(dst_pgd, address);
40872
40873     do {
40874       pte_t *src_pte, *dst_pte;
40875
40876       /* copy_pte_range */
40877
40878       if (pmd_none(*src_pmd))
40879         goto skip_copy_pte_range;
40880       if (pmd_bad(*src_pmd)) {
40881         pmd_ERROR(*src_pmd);
40882         pmd_clear(src_pmd);
40883       skip_copy_pte_range:
40884         address = (address + PMD_SIZE) & PMD_MASK;
40885         if (address >= end)
40886           goto out;
40887         goto cont_copy_pmd_range;
40888       }
40889       if (pmd_none(*dst_pmd)) {
40890         if (!pte_alloc(dst_pmd, 0))
40891           goto nomem;
40892       }
40893
40894       src_pte = pte_offset(src_pmd, address);
40895       dst_pte = pte_offset(dst_pmd, address);
40896
40897       spin_lock(&src->page_table_lock);
40898       do {
40899         pte_t pte = *src_pte;
40900         struct page *ptepage;
40901
40902         /* copy_one_pte */
40903
```

```
40904          if (pte_none(pte))
40905            goto cont_copy_pte_range_noset;
40906          if (!pte_present(pte)) {
40907            swap_duplicate(pte_to_swp_entry(pte));
40908            goto cont_copy_pte_range;
40909          }
40910          ptepage = pte_page(pte);
40911          if ((!VALID_PAGE(ptepage)) ||
40912              PageReserved(ptepage))
40913                goto cont_copy_pte_range;
40914
40915          /* If it's a COW mapping, write protect it both
40916           * in the parent and the child */
40917          if (cow) {
40918            ptep_set_wrprotect(src_pte);
40919            pte = *src_pte;
40920          }
40921
40922          /* If it's a shared mapping, mark it clean in
40923           * the child */
40924          if (vma->vm_flags & VM_SHARED)
40925            pte = pte_mkclean(pte);
40926          pte = pte_mkold(pte);
40927          get_page(ptepage);
40928
40929        cont_copy_pte_range:
40930          set_pte(dst_pte, pte);
40931        cont_copy_pte_range_noset:
40932          address += PAGE_SIZE;
40933          if (address >= end)
40934            goto out_unlock;
40935          src_pte++;
40936          dst_pte++;
40937        } while ((unsigned long) src_pte & PTE_TABLE_MASK);
40938        spin_unlock(&src->page_table_lock);
40939
40940      cont_copy_pmd_range:
40941        src_pmd++;
40942        dst_pmd++;
40943      } while ((unsigned long) src_pmd & PMD_TABLE_MASK);
40944    }
40945 out:
40946    return 0;
40947
40948 out_unlock:
40949    spin_unlock(&src->page_table_lock);
40950    return 0;
40951
40952 nomem:
40953    return -ENOMEM;
40954 }
40955
40956 /* Return indicates whether a page was freed so caller
40957  * can adjust rss */
40958 static inline int free_pte(pte_t pte)
40959 {
40960    if (pte_present(pte)) {
40961      struct page *page = pte_page(pte);
40962      if ((!VALID_PAGE(page)) || PageReserved(page))
40963        return 0;
40964      /* free_page() used to be able to clear swap cache
40965       * entries.  We may now have to do it manually.  */
40966      if (pte_dirty(pte) && page->mapping)
40967        set_page_dirty(page);
40968      free_page_and_swap_cache(page);
40969      return 1;
40970    }
40971    swap_free(pte_to_swp_entry(pte));
40972    return 0;
40973 }
40974
40975 static inline void forget_pte(pte_t page)
40976 {
40977    if (!pte_none(page)) {
40978      printk("forget_pte: old mapping existed!\n");
40979      free_pte(page);
40980    }
40981 }
40982
40983 static inline int zap_pte_range(struct mm_struct *mm,
40984      pmd_t * pmd, unsigned long address,
40985      unsigned long size)
40986 {
40987    pte_t *pte;
40988    int freed;
40989
40990    if (pmd_none(*pmd))
40991      return 0;
40992    if (pmd_bad(*pmd)) {
40993      pmd_ERROR(*pmd);
40994      pmd_clear(pmd);
40995      return 0;
40996    }
40997    pte = pte_offset(pmd, address);
```

```
40998    address &= ~PMD_MASK;
40999    if (address + size > PMD_SIZE)
41000      size = PMD_SIZE - address;
41001    size >>= PAGE_SHIFT;
41002    freed = 0;
41003    for (;;) {
41004      pte_t page;
41005      if (!size)
41006        break;
41007      page = ptep_get_and_clear(pte);
41008      pte++;
41009      size--;
41010      if (pte_none(page))
41011        continue;
41012      freed += free_pte(page);
41013    }
41014    return freed;
41015 }
41016
41017 static inline int zap_pmd_range(struct mm_struct *mm,
41018      pgd_t * dir, unsigned long address,
41019      unsigned long size)
41020 {
41021    pmd_t *pmd;
41022    unsigned long end;
41023    int freed;
41024
41025    if (pgd_none(*dir))
41026      return 0;
41027    if (pgd_bad(*dir)) {
41028      pgd_ERROR(*dir);
41029      pgd_clear(dir);
41030      return 0;
41031    }
41032    pmd = pmd_offset(dir, address);
41033    address &= ~PGDIR_MASK;
41034    end = address + size;
41035    if (end > PGDIR_SIZE)
41036      end = PGDIR_SIZE;
41037    freed = 0;
41038    do {
41039      freed +=
41040          zap_pte_range(mm, pmd, address, end - address);
41041      address = (address + PMD_SIZE) & PMD_MASK;
41042      pmd++;
41043    } while (address < end);
41044    return freed;
```

```
41045 }
41046
41047 /* remove user pages in a given range.  */
41048 void zap_page_range(struct mm_struct *mm,
41049      unsigned long address, unsigned long size)
41050 {
41051    pgd_t *dir;
41052    unsigned long end = address + size;
41053    int freed = 0;
41054
41055    dir = pgd_offset(mm, address);
41056
41057    /* This is a long-lived spinlock. That's fine.  There's
41058     * no contention, because the page table lock only
41059     * protects against kswapd anyway, and even if kswapd
41060     * happened to be looking at this process we _want_ it
41061     * to get stuck.  */
41062    if (address >= end)
41063      BUG();
41064    spin_lock(&mm->page_table_lock);
41065    do {
41066      freed +=
41067          zap_pmd_range(mm, dir, address, end - address);
41068      address = (address + PGDIR_SIZE) & PGDIR_MASK;
41069      dir++;
41070    } while (address && (address < end));
41071    spin_unlock(&mm->page_table_lock);
41072    /* Update rss for the mm_struct (not necessarily
41073     * current->mm) Notice that rss is an unsigned long. */
41074    if (mm->rss > freed)
41075      mm->rss -= freed;
41076    else
41077      mm->rss = 0;
41078 }
41079
41080
41081 /* Do a quick page-table lookup for a single page.  */
41082 static struct page *follow_page(unsigned long address)
41083 {
41084    pgd_t *pgd;
41085    pmd_t *pmd;
41086
41087    pgd = pgd_offset(current->mm, address);
41088    pmd = pmd_offset(pgd, address);
41089    if (pmd) {
41090      pte_t *pte = pte_offset(pmd, address);
41091      if (pte && pte_present(*pte))
```

```
41092        return pte_page(*pte);
41093   }
41094
41095   return NULL;
41096 }
41097
41098 /* Given a physical address, is there a useful struct
41099  * page pointing to it?  This may become more complex in
41100  * the future if we start dealing with IO-aperture pages
41101  * in kiobufs. */
41102 static inline struct page *get_page_map(
41103   struct page *page)
41104 {
41105   if (!VALID_PAGE(page))
41106     return 0;
41107   return page;
41108 }
41109
41110 /* Force in an entire range of pages from the current
41111  * process's user VA, and pin them in physical memory.
41112  */
41113 #define dprintk(x...)
41114 int map_user_kiobuf(int rw, struct kiobuf *iobuf,
41115     unsigned long va, size_t len)
41116 {
41117   unsigned long ptr, end;
41118   int err;
41119   struct mm_struct *mm;
41120   struct vm_area_struct *vma = 0;
41121   struct page *map;
41122   int i;
41123   int datain = (rw == READ);
41124
41125   /* Make sure the iobuf is not already mapped
41126    * somewhere. */
41127   if (iobuf->nr_pages)
41128     return -EINVAL;
41129
41130   mm = current->mm;
41131   dprintk("map_user_kiobuf: begin\n");
41132
41133   ptr = va & PAGE_MASK;
41134   end = (va + len + PAGE_SIZE - 1) & PAGE_MASK;
41135   err = expand_kiobuf(iobuf, (end - ptr) >> PAGE_SHIFT);
41136   if (err)
41137     return err;
41138
41139   down(&mm->mmap_sem);
41140
41141   err = -EFAULT;
41142   iobuf->locked = 0;
41143   iobuf->offset = va & ~PAGE_MASK;
41144   iobuf->length = len;
41145
41146   i = 0;
41147
41148   /* First of all, try to fault in all of the necessary
41149    * pages */
41150   while (ptr < end) {
41151     if (!vma || ptr >= vma->vm_end) {
41152       vma = find_vma(current->mm, ptr);
41153       if (!vma)
41154         goto out_unlock;
41155       if (vma->vm_start > ptr) {
41156         if (!(vma->vm_flags & VM_GROWSDOWN))
41157           goto out_unlock;
41158         if (expand_stack(vma, ptr))
41159           goto out_unlock;
41160       }
41161       if (((datain) && (!(vma->vm_flags & VM_WRITE))) ||
41162           (!(vma->vm_flags & VM_READ))) {
41163         err = -EACCES;
41164         goto out_unlock;
41165       }
41166     }
41167     if (handle_mm_fault(current->mm, vma, ptr,
41168                         datain) <= 0)
41169       goto out_unlock;
41170     spin_lock(&mm->page_table_lock);
41171     map = follow_page(ptr);
41172     if (!map) {
41173       spin_unlock(&mm->page_table_lock);
41174       dprintk(KERN_ERR
41175           "Missing page in map_user_kiobuf\n");
41176       goto out_unlock;
41177     }
41178     map = get_page_map(map);
41179     if (map) {
41180       flush_dcache_page(map);
41181       atomic_inc(&map->count);
41182     } else
41183       printk(KERN_INFO "Mapped page missing [%d]\n", i);
41184     spin_unlock(&mm->page_table_lock);
41185     iobuf->maplist[i] = map;
```

```
41186      iobuf->nr_pages = ++i;
41187
41188      ptr += PAGE_SIZE;
41189    }
41190
41191    up(&mm->mmap_sem);
41192    dprintk("map_user_kiobuf: end OK\n");
41193    return 0;
41194
41195 out_unlock:
41196    up(&mm->mmap_sem);
41197    unmap_kiobuf(iobuf);
41198    dprintk("map_user_kiobuf: end %d\n", err);
41199    return err;
41200 }
41201
41202
41203 /* Unmap all of the pages referenced by a kiobuf.  We
41204  * release the pages, and unlock them if they were
41205  * locked.  */
41206 void unmap_kiobuf(struct kiobuf *iobuf)
41207 {
41208    int i;
41209    struct page *map;
41210
41211    for (i = 0; i < iobuf->nr_pages; i++) {
41212      map = iobuf->maplist[i];
41213      if (map) {
41214        if (iobuf->locked)
41215          UnlockPage(map);
41216        __free_page(map);
41217      }
41218    }
41219
41220    iobuf->nr_pages = 0;
41221    iobuf->locked = 0;
41222 }
41223
41224
41225 /* Lock down all of the pages of a kiovec for IO.
41226  *
41227  * If any page is mapped twice in the kiovec, we return
41228  * the error -EINVAL.
41229  *
41230  * The optional wait parameter causes the lock call to
41231  * block until all pages can be locked if set.  If
41232  * wait==0, the lock operation is aborted if any locked
```

```
41233  * pages are found and -EAGAIN is returned.  */
41234 int lock_kiovec(int nr, struct kiobuf *iovec[], int wait)
41235 {
41236    struct kiobuf *iobuf;
41237    int i, j;
41238    struct page *page, **ppage;
41239    int doublepage = 0;
41240    int repeat = 0;
41241
41242 repeat:
41243
41244    for (i = 0; i < nr; i++) {
41245      iobuf = iovec[i];
41246
41247      if (iobuf->locked)
41248        continue;
41249      iobuf->locked = 1;
41250
41251      ppage = iobuf->maplist;
41252      for (j = 0; j < iobuf->nr_pages; ppage++, j++) {
41253        page = *ppage;
41254        if (!page)
41255          continue;
41256
41257        if (TryLockPage(page))
41258          goto retry;
41259      }
41260    }
41261
41262    return 0;
41263
41264 retry:
41265
41266    /* We couldn't lock one of the pages.  Undo the locking
41267     * so far, wait on the page we got to, and try again.*/
41268
41269    unlock_kiovec(nr, iovec);
41270    if (!wait)
41271      return -EAGAIN;
41272
41273    /* Did the release also unlock the page we got stuck
41274     * on? */
41275    if (!PageLocked(page)) {
41276      /* If so, we may well have the page mapped twice in
41277       * the IO address range.  Bad news.  Of course, it
41278       * _might_ just be a coincidence, but if it happens
41279       * more than once, chances are we have a
```

```
41280      * double-mapped page.  */
41281     if (++doublepage >= 3)
41282       return -EINVAL;
41283
41284     /* Try again...  */
41285     wait_on_page(page);
41286   }
41287
41288   if (++repeat < 16)
41289     goto repeat;
41290   return -EAGAIN;
41291 }
41292
41293 /* Unlock all of the pages of a kiovec after IO.  */
41294 int unlock_kiovec(int nr, struct kiobuf *iovec[])
41295 {
41296   struct kiobuf *iobuf;
41297   int i, j;
41298   struct page *page, **ppage;
41299
41300   for (i = 0; i < nr; i++) {
41301     iobuf = iovec[i];
41302
41303     if (!iobuf->locked)
41304       continue;
41305     iobuf->locked = 0;
41306
41307     ppage = iobuf->maplist;
41308     for (j = 0; j < iobuf->nr_pages; ppage++, j++) {
41309       page = *ppage;
41310       if (!page)
41311         continue;
41312       UnlockPage(page);
41313     }
41314   }
41315   return 0;
41316 }
41317
41318 static inline void zeromap_pte_range(pte_t * pte,
41319     unsigned long address, unsigned long size,
41320     pgprot_t prot)
41321 {
41322   unsigned long end;
41323
41324   address &= ~PMD_MASK;
41325   end = address + size;
41326   if (end > PMD_SIZE)
41327     end = PMD_SIZE;
41328   do {
41329     pte_t zero_pte =
41330         pte_wrprotect(mk_pte(ZERO_PAGE(address), prot));
41331     pte_t oldpage = ptep_get_and_clear(pte);
41332     set_pte(pte, zero_pte);
41333     forget_pte(oldpage);
41334     address += PAGE_SIZE;
41335     pte++;
41336   } while (address && (address < end));
41337 }
41338
41339 static inline int zeromap_pmd_range(pmd_t * pmd,
41340     unsigned long address, unsigned long size,
41341     pgprot_t prot)
41342 {
41343   unsigned long end;
41344
41345   address &= ~PGDIR_MASK;
41346   end = address + size;
41347   if (end > PGDIR_SIZE)
41348     end = PGDIR_SIZE;
41349   do {
41350     pte_t *pte = pte_alloc(pmd, address);
41351     if (!pte)
41352       return -ENOMEM;
41353     zeromap_pte_range(pte, address, end - address, prot);
41354     address = (address + PMD_SIZE) & PMD_MASK;
41355     pmd++;
41356   } while (address && (address < end));
41357   return 0;
41358 }
41359
41360 int zeromap_page_range(unsigned long address,
41361     unsigned long size, pgprot_t prot)
41362 {
41363   int error = 0;
41364   pgd_t *dir;
41365   unsigned long beg = address;
41366   unsigned long end = address + size;
41367
41368   dir = pgd_offset(current->mm, address);
41369   flush_cache_range(current->mm, beg, end);
41370   if (address >= end)
41371     BUG();
41372   do {
41373     pmd_t *pmd = pmd_alloc(dir, address);
```

```
41374      error = -ENOMEM;
41375      if (!pmd)
41376        break;
41377      error = zeromap_pmd_range(pmd, address,
41378                              end - address, prot);
41379      if (error)
41380        break;
41381      address = (address + PGDIR_SIZE) & PGDIR_MASK;
41382      dir++;
41383    } while (address && (address < end));
41384    flush_tlb_range(current->mm, beg, end);
41385    return error;
41386 }
41387
41388 /* maps a range of physical memory into the requested
41389  * pages. the old mappings are removed. any references to
41390  * nonexistent pages results in null mappings (currently
41391  * treated as "copy-on-access") */
41392 static inline void remap_pte_range(pte_t * pte,
41393      unsigned long address, unsigned long size,
41394      unsigned long phys_addr, pgprot_t prot)
41395 {
41396    unsigned long end;
41397
41398    address &= ~PMD_MASK;
41399    end = address + size;
41400    if (end > PMD_SIZE)
41401      end = PMD_SIZE;
41402    do {
41403      struct page *page;
41404      pte_t oldpage;
41405      oldpage = ptep_get_and_clear(pte);
41406
41407      page = virt_to_page(__va(phys_addr));
41408      if ((!VALID_PAGE(page)) || PageReserved(page))
41409        set_pte(pte, mk_pte_phys(phys_addr, prot));
41410      forget_pte(oldpage);
41411      address += PAGE_SIZE;
41412      phys_addr += PAGE_SIZE;
41413      pte++;
41414    } while (address && (address < end));
41415 }
41416
41417 static inline int remap_pmd_range(pmd_t * pmd,
41418      unsigned long address, unsigned long size,
41419      unsigned long phys_addr, pgprot_t prot)
41420 {
41421      unsigned long end;
41422
41423      address &= ~PGDIR_MASK;
41424      end = address + size;
41425      if (end > PGDIR_SIZE)
41426        end = PGDIR_SIZE;
41427      phys_addr -= address;
41428      do {
41429        pte_t *pte = pte_alloc(pmd, address);
41430        if (!pte)
41431          return -ENOMEM;
41432        remap_pte_range(pte, address, end - address,
41433            address + phys_addr, prot);
41434        address = (address + PMD_SIZE) & PMD_MASK;
41435        pmd++;
41436      } while (address && (address < end));
41437      return 0;
41438 }
41439
41440 /* Note: this is only safe if the mm semaphore is held
41441  * when called. */
41442 int remap_page_range(unsigned long from,
41443      unsigned long phys_addr, unsigned long size,
41444      pgprot_t prot)
41445 {
41446    int error = 0;
41447    pgd_t *dir;
41448    unsigned long beg = from;
41449    unsigned long end = from + size;
41450
41451    phys_addr -= from;
41452    dir = pgd_offset(current->mm, from);
41453    flush_cache_range(current->mm, beg, end);
41454    if (from >= end)
41455      BUG();
41456    do {
41457      pmd_t *pmd = pmd_alloc(dir, from);
41458      error = -ENOMEM;
41459      if (!pmd)
41460        break;
41461      error = remap_pmd_range(pmd, from, end - from,
41462                              phys_addr + from, prot);
41463      if (error)
41464        break;
41465      from = (from + PGDIR_SIZE) & PGDIR_MASK;
41466      dir++;
41467    } while (from && (from < end));
```

```
41468     flush_tlb_range(current->mm, beg, end);
41469     return error;
41470 }
41471
41472 /* Establish a new mapping:
41473  *  - flush the old one
41474  *  - update the page tables
41475  *  - inform the TLB about the new one */
41476 static inline void
41477 establish_pte(struct vm_area_struct *vma,
41478                 unsigned long address, pte_t * page_table,
41479                 pte_t entry)
41480 {
41481     set_pte(page_table, entry);
41482     flush_tlb_page(vma, address);
41483     update_mmu_cache(vma, address, entry);
41484 }
41485
41486 static inline void break_cow(struct vm_area_struct *vma,
41487     struct page *old_page, struct page *new_page,
41488     unsigned long address, pte_t * page_table)
41489 {
41490     copy_cow_page(old_page, new_page, address);
41491     flush_page_to_ram(new_page);
41492     flush_cache_page(vma, address);
41493     establish_pte(vma, address, page_table,
41494         pte_mkwrite(pte_mkdirty(mk_pte(new_page,
41495                     vma->vm_page_prot))));
41496 }
41497
41498 /* This routine handles present pages, when users try to
41499  * write to a shared page. It is done by copying the page
41500  * to a new address and decrementing the shared-page
41501  * counter for the old page.
41502  *
41503  * Goto-purists beware: the only reason for goto's here
41504  * is that it results in better assembly code.. The
41505  * "default" path will see no jumps at all.
41506  *
41507  * Note that this routine assumes that the protection
41508  * checks have been done by the caller (the low-level
41509  * page fault routine in most cases).  Thus we can safely
41510  * just mark it writable once we've done any necessary
41511  * COW.
41512  *
41513  * We also mark the page dirty at this point even though
41514  * the page will change only once the write actually
```

```
41515  * happens. This avoids a few races, and potentially
41516  * makes it more efficient.
41517  *
41518  * We enter with the page table read-lock held, and need
41519  * to exit without it.  */
```
p 629 ►
```
41520 static int do_wp_page(struct mm_struct *mm,
41521     struct vm_area_struct *vma, unsigned long address,
41522     pte_t * page_table, pte_t pte)
41523 {
41524     struct page *old_page, *new_page;
41525
41526     old_page = pte_page(pte);
41527     if (!VALID_PAGE(old_page))
41528         goto bad_wp_page;
41529
41530     /* We can avoid the copy if:
41531      * - we're the only user (count == 1)
41532      * - the only other user is the swap cache,
41533      *   and the only swap cache user is itself,
41534      *   in which case we can just continue to
41535      *   use the same swap cache (it will be
41536      *   marked dirty). */
41537     switch (page_count(old_page)) {
41538     case 2:
41539         /* Lock the page so that no one can look it up from
41540          * the swap cache, grab a reference and start using
41541          * it.  Can not do lock_page, holding
41542          * page_table_lock.  */
41543         if (!PageSwapCache(old_page)
41544             || TryLockPage(old_page))
41545             break;
41546         if (is_page_shared(old_page)) {
41547             UnlockPage(old_page);
41548             break;
41549         }
41550         UnlockPage(old_page);
41551         /* FallThrough */
41552     case 1:
41553         flush_cache_page(vma, address);
41554         establish_pte(vma, address, page_table,
41555             pte_mkyoung(pte_mkdirty(pte_mkwrite(pte))));
41556         spin_unlock(&mm->page_table_lock);
41557         return 1;                    /* Minor fault */
41558     }
41559
41560     /* Ok, we need to copy. Oh, well..  */
41561     spin_unlock(&mm->page_table_lock);
```

```
41562    new_page = page_cache_alloc();
41563    if (!new_page)
41564      return -1;
41565    spin_lock(&mm->page_table_lock);
41566
41567    /* Re-check the pte - we dropped the lock */
41568    if (pte_same(*page_table, pte)) {
41569      if (PageReserved(old_page))
41570        ++mm->rss;
41571      break_cow(vma, old_page, new_page, address,
41572        page_table);
41573
41574      /* Free the old page.. */
41575      new_page = old_page;
41576    }
41577    spin_unlock(&mm->page_table_lock);
41578    page_cache_release(new_page);
41579    return 1;                      /* Minor fault */
41580
41581 bad_wp_page:
41582    spin_unlock(&mm->page_table_lock);
41583    printk("do_wp_page: bogus page at address %08lx "
41584          "(page 0x%lx)\n",
41585          address, (unsigned long) old_page);
41586    return -1;
41587 }
41588
41589 static void vmtruncate_list(struct vm_area_struct *mpnt,
41590      unsigned long pgoff, unsigned long partial)
41591 {
41592    do {
41593      struct mm_struct *mm = mpnt->vm_mm;
41594      unsigned long start = mpnt->vm_start;
41595      unsigned long end = mpnt->vm_end;
41596      unsigned long len = end - start;
41597      unsigned long diff;
41598
41599      /* mapping wholly truncated? */
41600      if (mpnt->vm_pgoff >= pgoff) {
41601        flush_cache_range(mm, start, end);
41602        zap_page_range(mm, start, len);
41603        flush_tlb_range(mm, start, end);
41604        continue;
41605      }
41606
41607      /* mapping wholly unaffected? */
41608      len = len >> PAGE_SHIFT;
41609      diff = pgoff - mpnt->vm_pgoff;
41610      if (diff >= len)
41611        continue;
41612
41613      /* Ok, partially affected.. */
41614      start += diff << PAGE_SHIFT;
41615      len = (len - diff) << PAGE_SHIFT;
41616      flush_cache_range(mm, start, end);
41617      zap_page_range(mm, start, len);
41618      flush_tlb_range(mm, start, end);
41619    } while ((mpnt = mpnt->vm_next_share) != NULL);
41620 }
41621
41622
41623 /* Handle all mappings that got truncated by a
41624  * "truncate()" system call.
41625  *
41626  * NOTE! We have to be ready to update the memory sharing
41627  * between the file and the memory map for a potential
41628  * last incomplete page.  Ugly, but necessary.  */
41629 void vmtruncate(struct inode *inode, loff_t offset)
41630 {
41631    unsigned long partial, pgoff;
41632    struct address_space *mapping = inode->i_mapping;
41633    unsigned long limit;
41634
41635    if (inode->i_size < offset)
41636      goto do_expand;
41637    inode->i_size = offset;
41638    spin_lock(&mapping->i_shared_lock);
41639    if (!mapping->i_mmap && !mapping->i_mmap_shared)
41640      goto out_unlock;
41641
41642    pgoff =
41643        (offset + PAGE_CACHE_SIZE - 1) >> PAGE_CACHE_SHIFT;
41644    partial =
41645        (unsigned long) offset & (PAGE_CACHE_SIZE - 1);
41646
41647    if (mapping->i_mmap != NULL)
41648      vmtruncate_list(mapping->i_mmap, pgoff, partial);
41649    if (mapping->i_mmap_shared != NULL)
41650      vmtruncate_list(mapping->i_mmap_shared, pgoff,
41651        partial);
41652
41653 out_unlock:
41654    spin_unlock(&mapping->i_shared_lock);
41655    truncate_inode_pages(mapping, offset);
```

```
41656    if (inode->i_op && inode->i_op->truncate)
41657      inode->i_op->truncate(inode);
41658    return;
41659
41660 do_expand:
41661    limit = current->rlim[RLIMIT_FSIZE].rlim_cur;
41662    if (limit != RLIM_INFINITY) {
41663      if (inode->i_size >= limit) {
41664        send_sig(SIGXFSZ, current, 0);
41665        goto out;
41666      }
41667      if (offset > limit) {
41668        send_sig(SIGXFSZ, current, 0);
41669        offset = limit;
41670      }
41671    }
41672    inode->i_size = offset;
41673    if (inode->i_op && inode->i_op->truncate)
41674      inode->i_op->truncate(inode);
41675 out:
41676    return;
41677 }
41678
41679
41680
41681 /* Primitive swap readahead code. We simply read an
41682  * aligned block of (1 << page_cluster) entries in the
41683  * swap area. This method is chosen because it doesn't
41684  * cost us any seek time.  We also make sure to queue the
41685  * 'original' request together with the readahead
41686  * ones... */
41687 void swapin_readahead(swp_entry_t entry)
41688 {
41689    int i, num;
41690    struct page *new_page;
41691    unsigned long offset;
41692
41693    /* Get the number of handles we should do readahead io
41694     * to. Also, grab temporary references on them,
41695     * releasing them as io completes.  */
41696    num = valid_swaphandles(entry, &offset);
41697    for (i = 0; i < num; offset++, i++) {
41698      /* Don't block on I/O for read-ahead */
41699      if (atomic_read(&nr_async_pages) >=
41700          pager_daemon.swap_cluster * (1 << page_cluster)){
41701        while (i++ < num)
41702          swap_free(SWP_ENTRY(SWP_TYPE(entry), offset++));
41703        break;
41704      }
41705      /* Ok, do the async read-ahead now */
41706      new_page =
41707          read_swap_cache_async(SWP_ENTRY(SWP_TYPE(entry),
41708                                          offset), 0);
41709      if (new_page != NULL)
41710        page_cache_release(new_page);
41711      swap_free(SWP_ENTRY(SWP_TYPE(entry), offset));
41712    }
41713    return;
41714 }
41715
41716 static int do_swap_page(struct mm_struct *mm,
41717      struct vm_area_struct *vma, unsigned long address,
41718      pte_t * page_table, swp_entry_t entry,
41719      int write_access)
41720 {
41721    struct page *page = lookup_swap_cache(entry);
41722    pte_t pte;
41723
41724    if (!page) {
41725      lock_kernel();
41726      swapin_readahead(entry);
41727      page = read_swap_cache(entry);
41728      unlock_kernel();
41729      if (!page)
41730        return -1;
41731
41732      flush_page_to_ram(page);
41733      flush_icache_page(vma, page);
41734    }
41735
41736    mm->rss++;
41737
41738    pte = mk_pte(page, vma->vm_page_prot);
41739
41740    /* Freeze the "shared"ness of the page, ie page_count +
41741     * swap_count.  Must lock page before transferring our
41742     * swap count to already obtained page count.  */
41743    lock_page(page);
41744    swap_free(entry);
41745    if (write_access && !is_page_shared(page))
41746      pte = pte_mkwrite(pte_mkdirty(pte));
41747    UnlockPage(page);
41748
41749    set_pte(page_table, pte);
```

```
41750     /* No need to invalidate - it was non-present before */
41751     update_mmu_cache(vma, address, pte);
41752     return 1;                        /* Minor fault */
41753 }
41754
41755 /* This only needs the MM semaphore */
41756 static int do_anonymous_page(struct mm_struct *mm,
41757     struct vm_area_struct *vma, pte_t * page_table,
41758     int write_access, unsigned long addr)
41759 {
41760     struct page *page = NULL;
41761     pte_t entry =
41762         pte_wrprotect(mk_pte(ZERO_PAGE(addr),
41763                         vma->vm_page_prot));
41764     if (write_access) {
41765       page = alloc_page(GFP_HIGHUSER);
41766       if (!page)
41767         return -1;
41768       clear_user_highpage(page, addr);
41769       entry = pte_mkwrite(pte_mkdirty(mk_pte(page,
41770                         vma->vm_page_prot)));
41771       mm->rss++;
41772       flush_page_to_ram(page);
41773     }
41774     set_pte(page_table, entry);
41775     /* No need to invalidate - it was non-present before */
41776     update_mmu_cache(vma, addr, entry);
41777     return 1;                        /* Minor fault */
41778 }
41779
41780 /* do_no_page() tries to create a new page mapping. It
41781  * aggressively tries to share with existing pages, but
41782  * makes a separate copy if the "write_access" parameter
41783  * is true in order to avoid the next page fault.
41784  *
41785  * As this is called only for pages that do not currently
41786  * exist, we do not need to flush old virtual caches or
41787  * the TLB.
41788  *
41789  * This is called with the MM semaphore held.  */
41790 static int do_no_page(struct mm_struct *mm,
41791     struct vm_area_struct *vma, unsigned long address,
41792     int write_access, pte_t * page_table)
41793 {
41794   struct page *new_page;
41795   pte_t entry;
41796
41797   if (!vma->vm_ops || !vma->vm_ops->nopage)
41798     return do_anonymous_page(mm, vma, page_table,
41799         write_access, address);
41800
41801   /* The third argument is "no_share", which tells the
41802    * low-level code to copy, not share the page even if
41803    * sharing is possible.  It's essentially an early COW
41804    * detection.  */
41805   new_page =
41806       vma->vm_ops->nopage(vma, address & PAGE_MASK,
41807                       (vma->vm_flags & VM_SHARED)
41808                       ? 0
41809                       : write_access);
41810   if (new_page == NULL)            /* no page was available
41811                                     * - SIGBUS */
41812     return 0;
41813   if (new_page == NOPAGE_OOM)
41814     return -1;
41815   ++mm->rss;
41816   /* This silly early PAGE_DIRTY setting removes a race
41817    * due to the bad i386 page protection. But it's valid
41818    * for other architectures too.
41819    *
41820    * Note that if write_access is true, we either now
41821    * have an exclusive copy of the page, or this is a
41822    * shared mapping, so we can make it writable and dirty
41823    * to avoid having to handle that later.  */
41824   flush_page_to_ram(new_page);
41825   flush_icache_page(vma, new_page);
41826   entry = mk_pte(new_page, vma->vm_page_prot);
41827   if (write_access) {
41828     entry = pte_mkwrite(pte_mkdirty(entry));
41829   } else if (page_count(new_page) > 1 &&
41830             !(vma->vm_flags & VM_SHARED))
41831     entry = pte_wrprotect(entry);
41832   set_pte(page_table, entry);
41833   /* no need to invalidate: a not-present page shouldn't
41834    * be cached */
41835   update_mmu_cache(vma, address, entry);
41836   return 2;                        /* Major fault */
41837 }
41838
41839 /* These routines also need to handle stuff like marking
41840  * pages dirty and/or accessed for architectures that
41841  * don't do it in hardware (most RISC architectures).
41842  * The early dirtying is also good on the i386.
41843  *
```

```
41844  * There is also a hook called "update_mmu_cache()" that
41845  * architectures with external mmu caches can use to
41846  * update those (ie the Sparc or PowerPC hashed page
41847  * tables that act as extended TLBs).
41848  *
41849  * Note the "page_table_lock". It is to protect against
41850  * kswapd removing pages from under us. Note that kswapd
41851  * only ever _removes_ pages, never adds them. As such,
41852  * once we have noticed that the page is not present, we
41853  * can drop the lock early.
41854  *
41855  * The adding of pages is protected by the MM semaphore
41856  * (which we hold), so we don't need to worry about a
41857  * page being suddenly been added into our VM.  */
41858 static inline int handle_pte_fault(struct mm_struct *mm,
41859      struct vm_area_struct *vma, unsigned long address,
41860      int write_access, pte_t * pte)
41861 {
41862   pte_t entry;
41863
41864   /* We need the page table lock to synchronize with
41865    * kswapd and the SMP-safe atomic PTE updates.  */
41866   spin_lock(&mm->page_table_lock);
41867   entry = *pte;
41868   if (!pte_present(entry)) {
41869     /* If it truly wasn't present, we know that kswapd
41870      * and the PTE updates will not touch it later. So
41871      * drop the lock.  */
41872     spin_unlock(&mm->page_table_lock);
41873     if (pte_none(entry))
41874       return do_no_page(mm, vma, address, write_access,
41875                               pte);
41876     return do_swap_page(mm, vma, address, pte,
41877                           pte_to_swp_entry(entry),
41878                           write_access);
41879   }
41880
41881   if (write_access) {
41882     if (!pte_write(entry))
41883       return do_wp_page(mm, vma, address, pte, entry);
41884
41885     entry = pte_mkdirty(entry);
41886   }
41887   entry = pte_mkyoung(entry);
41888   establish_pte(vma, address, pte, entry);
41889   spin_unlock(&mm->page_table_lock);
41890   return 1;
41891 }
41892
41893 /* By the time we get here, we already hold the mm
41894  semaphore */
41895 int handle_mm_fault(struct mm_struct *mm,
41896      struct vm_area_struct *vma, unsigned long address,
41897      int write_access)
41898 {
41899   int ret = -1;
41900   pgd_t *pgd;
41901   pmd_t *pmd;
41902
41903   pgd = pgd_offset(mm, address);
41904   pmd = pmd_alloc(pgd, address);
41905
41906   if (pmd) {
41907     pte_t *pte = pte_alloc(pmd, address);
41908     if (pte)
41909       ret = handle_pte_fault(mm, vma, address,
41910                                 write_access, pte);
41911   }
41912   return ret;
41913 }
41914
41915 /* Simplistic page force-in..  */
41916 int make_pages_present(unsigned long addr,
41917      unsigned long end)
41918 {
41919   int write;
41920   struct mm_struct *mm = current->mm;
41921   struct vm_area_struct *vma;
41922
41923   vma = find_vma(mm, addr);
41924   write = (vma->vm_flags & VM_WRITE) != 0;
41925   if (addr >= end)
41926     BUG();
41927   do {
41928     if (handle_mm_fault(mm, vma, addr, write) < 0)
41929       return -1;
41930     addr += PAGE_SIZE;
41931   } while (addr < end);
41932   return 0;
41933 }
```

mm/mmap.c

```
41934 /*
41935  *      linux/mm/mmap.c
```

```
41936  *
41937  * Written by obz.
41938  */
41939  #include <linux/slab.h>
41940  #include <linux/shm.h>
41941  #include <linux/mman.h>
41942  #include <linux/pagemap.h>
41943  #include <linux/swap.h>
41944  #include <linux/swapctl.h>
41945  #include <linux/smp_lock.h>
41946  #include <linux/init.h>
41947  #include <linux/file.h>
41948
41949  #include <asm/uaccess.h>
41950  #include <asm/pgalloc.h>
41951
41952  /* description of effects of mapping type and prot in
41953   * current implementation.  this is due to the limited
41954   * x86 page protection hardware.  The expected behavior
41955   * is in parens (Y = yes, N = no, C = copy):
41956   *
41957   * map_type      prot
41958   *              PROT_NONE  PROT_READ  PROT_WRITE  PROT_EXEC
41959   * MAP_SHARED   r: (N) N   r: (Y) Y   r: (N) Y    r: (N) Y
41960   *              w: (N) N   w: (N) N   w: (Y) Y    w: (N) N
41961   *              x: (N) N   x: (N) Y   x: (N) Y    x: (Y) Y
41962   *
41963   * MAP_PRIVATE  r: (N) N   r: (Y) Y   r: (N) Y    r: (N) Y
41964   *              w: (N) N   w: (N) N   w: (C) C    w: (N) N
41965   *              x: (N) N   x: (N) Y   x: (N) Y    x: (Y) Y
41966   */
41967  pgprot_t protection_map[16] = {
41968      __P000, __P001, __P010, __P011,
41969      __P100, __P101, __P110, __P111,
41970      __S000, __S001, __S010, __S011,
41971      __S100, __S101, __S110, __S111
41972  };
41973
41974  int sysctl_overcommit_memory;
41975
41976  /* Check that a process has enough memory to allocate a
41977   * new virtual mapping. */
41978  int vm_enough_memory(long pages)
41979  {
41980      /* Stupid algorithm to decide if we have enough memory:
41981       * while simple, it hopefully works in most obvious
41982       * cases.. Easy to fool it, but this should catch most
41983       * mistakes. */
41984      /* 23/11/98 NJC: Somewhat less stupid version of
41985       * algorithm, which tries to do "TheRightThing".
41986       * Instead of using half of (buffers+cache), use the
41987       * minimum values.  Allow an extra 2% of num_physpages
41988       * for safety margin. */
41989
41990      long free;
41991
41992      /* Sometimes we want to use more memory than we
41993       * have. */
41994      if (sysctl_overcommit_memory)
41995          return 1;
41996
41997      free = atomic_read(&buffermem_pages);
41998      free += atomic_read(&page_cache_size);
41999      free += nr_free_pages();
42000      free += nr_swap_pages;
42001      return free > pages;
42002  }
42003
42004  /* Remove one vm structure from the inode's i_mapping
42005   * address space. */
42006  static inline void __remove_shared_vm_struct(
42007      struct vm_area_struct *vma)
42008  {
42009      struct file *file = vma->vm_file;
42010
42011      if (file) {
42012          struct inode *inode = file->f_dentry->d_inode;
42013          if (vma->vm_flags & VM_DENYWRITE)
42014              atomic_inc(&inode->i_writecount);
42015          if (vma->vm_next_share)
42016              vma->vm_next_share->vm_pprev_share =
42017                  vma->vm_pprev_share;
42018          *vma->vm_pprev_share = vma->vm_next_share;
42019      }
42020  }
42021
42022  static inline void remove_shared_vm_struct(
42023      struct vm_area_struct *vma)
42024  {
42025      lock_vma_mappings(vma);
42026      __remove_shared_vm_struct(vma);
42027      unlock_vma_mappings(vma);
42028  }
42029
```

```
42030 void lock_vma_mappings(struct vm_area_struct *vma)
42031 {
42032   struct address_space *mapping;
42033
42034   mapping = NULL;
42035   if (vma->vm_file)
42036     mapping = vma->vm_file->f_dentry->d_inode->i_mapping;
42037   if (mapping)
42038     spin_lock(&mapping->i_shared_lock);
42039 }
42040
42041 void unlock_vma_mappings(struct vm_area_struct *vma)
42042 {
42043   struct address_space *mapping;
42044
42045   mapping = NULL;
42046   if (vma->vm_file)
42047     mapping = vma->vm_file->f_dentry->d_inode->i_mapping;
42048   if (mapping)
42049     spin_unlock(&mapping->i_shared_lock);
42050 }
42051
42052 /* sys_brk() for the most part doesn't need the global
42053  * kernel lock, except when an application is doing
42054  * something nasty like trying to un-brk an area that has
42055  * already been mapped to a regular file.  in this case,
42056  * the unmapping will need to invoke file system routines
42057  * that need the global lock.  */
42058 asmlinkage unsigned long sys_brk(unsigned long brk)
42059 {
42060   unsigned long rlim, retval;
42061   unsigned long newbrk, oldbrk;
42062   struct mm_struct *mm = current->mm;
42063
42064   down(&mm->mmap_sem);
42065
42066   if (brk < mm->end_code)
42067     goto out;
42068   newbrk = PAGE_ALIGN(brk);
42069   oldbrk = PAGE_ALIGN(mm->brk);
42070   if (oldbrk == newbrk)
42071     goto set_brk;
42072
42073   /* Always allow shrinking brk. */
42074   if (brk <= mm->brk) {
42075     if (!do_munmap(mm, newbrk, oldbrk - newbrk))
42076       goto set_brk;
```
(p 636) at line 42058

```
42077     goto out;
42078   }
42079
42080   /* Check against rlimit.. */
42081   rlim = current->rlim[RLIMIT_DATA].rlim_cur;
42082   if (rlim < RLIM_INFINITY &&
42083       brk - mm->start_data > rlim)
42084     goto out;
42085
42086   /* Check against existing mmap mappings. */
42087   if (find_vma_intersection(mm, oldbrk,
42088                             newbrk + PAGE_SIZE))
42089     goto out;
42090
42091   /* Check if we have enough memory.. */
42092   if (!vm_enough_memory((newbrk - oldbrk) >> PAGE_SHIFT))
42093     goto out;
42094
42095   /* Ok, looks good - let it rip. */
42096   if (do_brk(oldbrk, newbrk - oldbrk) != oldbrk)
42097     goto out;
42098 set_brk:
42099   mm->brk = brk;
42100 out:
42101   retval = mm->brk;
42102   up(&mm->mmap_sem);
42103   return retval;
42104 }
42105
42106 /* Combine the mmap "prot" and "flags" argument into one
42107  * "vm_flags" used internally. Essentially, translate the
42108  * "PROT_xxx" and "MAP_xxx" bits into "VM_xxx". */
42109 static inline unsigned long vm_flags(unsigned long prot,
42110     unsigned long flags)
42111 {
42112 #define _trans(x,bit1,bit2)                                \
42113   ((bit1==bit2)?(x&bit1):(x&bit1)?bit2:0)
42114
42115   unsigned long prot_bits, flag_bits;
42116   prot_bits = _trans(prot, PROT_READ, VM_READ)   |
42117               _trans(prot, PROT_WRITE, VM_WRITE) |
42118               _trans(prot, PROT_EXEC, VM_EXEC);
42119   flag_bits =
42120       _trans(flags, MAP_GROWSDOWN, VM_GROWSDOWN) |
42121       _trans(flags, MAP_DENYWRITE, VM_DENYWRITE) |
42122       _trans(flags, MAP_EXECUTABLE, VM_EXECUTABLE);
42123   return prot_bits | flag_bits;
```

```
42124 #undef _trans
42125 }
42126
42127 unsigned long do_mmap_pgoff(struct file *file,
42128     unsigned long addr, unsigned long len,
42129     unsigned long prot, unsigned long flags,
42130     unsigned long pgoff)
42131 {
42132   struct mm_struct *mm = current->mm;
42133   struct vm_area_struct *vma;
42134   int correct_wcount = 0;
42135   int error;
42136
42137   if (file && (!file->f_op || !file->f_op->mmap))
42138     return -ENODEV;
42139
42140   if ((len = PAGE_ALIGN(len)) == 0)
42141     return addr;
42142
42143   if (len > TASK_SIZE || addr > TASK_SIZE - len)
42144     return -EINVAL;
42145
42146   /* offset overflow? */
42147   if ((pgoff + (len >> PAGE_SHIFT)) < pgoff)
42148     return -EINVAL;
42149
42150   /* Too many mappings? */
42151   if (mm->map_count > MAX_MAP_COUNT)
42152     return -ENOMEM;
42153
42154   /* mlock MCL_FUTURE? */
42155   if (mm->def_flags & VM_LOCKED) {
42156     unsigned long locked = mm->locked_vm << PAGE_SHIFT;
42157     locked += len;
42158     if (locked > current->rlim[RLIMIT_MEMLOCK].rlim_cur)
42159       return -EAGAIN;
42160   }
42161
42162   /* Do simple checking here so the lower-level routines
42163    * won't have to. we assume access permissions have
42164    * been handled by the open of the memory object, so we
42165    * don't do any here. */
42166   if (file != NULL) {
42167     switch (flags & MAP_TYPE) {
42168     case MAP_SHARED:
42169       if ((prot & PROT_WRITE) &&
42170           !(file->f_mode & FMODE_WRITE))
42171         return -EACCES;
42172
42173       /* Make sure we don't allow writing to an
42174        * append-only file.. */
42175       if (IS_APPEND(file->f_dentry->d_inode) &&
42176           (file->f_mode & FMODE_WRITE))
42177         return -EACCES;
42178
42179       /* make sure there are no mandatory locks on the
42180        * file. */
42181       if (locks_verify_locked(file->f_dentry->d_inode))
42182         return -EAGAIN;
42183
42184       /* fall through */
42185     case MAP_PRIVATE:
42186       if (!(file->f_mode & FMODE_READ))
42187         return -EACCES;
42188       break;
42189
42190     default:
42191       return -EINVAL;
42192     }
42193   }
42194
42195   /* Obtain the address to map to. we verify (or select)
42196    * it and ensure that it represents a valid section of
42197    * the address space. */
42198   if (flags & MAP_FIXED) {
42199     if (addr & ~PAGE_MASK)
42200       return -EINVAL;
42201   } else {
42202     addr = get_unmapped_area(addr, len);
42203     if (!addr)
42204       return -ENOMEM;
42205   }
42206
42207   /* Determine the object being mapped and call the
42208    * appropriate specific mapper. the address has already
42209    * been validated, but not unmapped, but the maps are
42210    * removed from the list. */
42211   vma = kmem_cache_alloc(vm_area_cachep, SLAB_KERNEL);
42212   if (!vma)
42213     return -ENOMEM;
42214
42215   vma->vm_mm = mm;
42216   vma->vm_start = addr;
42217   vma->vm_end = addr + len;
```

```
42218    vma->vm_flags = vm_flags(prot, flags) | mm->def_flags;
42219
42220    if (file) {
42221      VM_ClearReadHint(vma);
42222      vma->vm_raend = 0;
42223
42224      if (file->f_mode & FMODE_READ)
42225        vma->vm_flags |=
42226            VM_MAYREAD | VM_MAYWRITE | VM_MAYEXEC;
42227      if (flags & MAP_SHARED) {
42228        vma->vm_flags |= VM_SHARED | VM_MAYSHARE;
42229
42230        /* This looks strange, but when we don't have the
42231         * file open for writing, we can demote the shared
42232         * mapping to a simpler private mapping.  That also
42233         * takes care of a security hole with ptrace()
42234         * writing to a shared mapping without write
42235         * permissions.
42236         *
42237         * We leave the VM_MAYSHARE bit on, just to get
42238         * correct output * from /proc/xxx/maps.. */
42239        if (!(file->f_mode & FMODE_WRITE))
42240          vma->vm_flags &= ~(VM_MAYWRITE | VM_SHARED);
42241      }
42242    } else {
42243      vma->vm_flags |=
42244          VM_MAYREAD | VM_MAYWRITE | VM_MAYEXEC;
42245      if (flags & MAP_SHARED)
42246        vma->vm_flags |= VM_SHARED | VM_MAYSHARE;
42247    }
42248    vma->vm_page_prot =
42249        protection_map[vma->vm_flags & 0x0f];
42250    vma->vm_ops = NULL;
42251    vma->vm_pgoff = pgoff;
42252    vma->vm_file = NULL;
42253    vma->vm_private_data = NULL;
42254
42255    /* Clear old maps */
42256    error = -ENOMEM;
42257    if (do_munmap(mm, addr, len))
42258      goto free_vma;
42259
42260    /* Check against address space limit. */
42261    if ((mm->total_vm << PAGE_SHIFT) + len
42262        > current->rlim[RLIMIT_AS].rlim_cur)
42263      goto free_vma;
42264
42265    /* Private writable mapping? Check memory
42266     * availability.. */
42267    if ((vma->vm_flags & (VM_SHARED | VM_WRITE)) ==
42268        VM_WRITE && !(flags & MAP_NORESERVE)
42269        && !vm_enough_memory(len >> PAGE_SHIFT))
42270      goto free_vma;
42271
42272    if (file) {
42273      if (vma->vm_flags & VM_DENYWRITE) {
42274        error = deny_write_access(file);
42275        if (error)
42276          goto free_vma;
42277        correct_wcount = 1;
42278      }
42279      vma->vm_file = file;
42280      get_file(file);
42281      error = file->f_op->mmap(file, vma);
42282      if (error)
42283        goto unmap_and_free_vma;
42284    } else if (flags & MAP_SHARED) {
42285      error = shmem_zero_setup(vma);
42286      if (error)
42287        goto free_vma;
42288    }
42289
42290    /* Can addr have changed??
42291     *
42292     * Answer: Yes, several device drivers can do it in
42293     * their f_op->mmap method. -DaveM */
42294    flags = vma->vm_flags;
42295    addr = vma->vm_start;
42296
42297    insert_vm_struct(mm, vma);
42298    if (correct_wcount)
42299      atomic_inc(&file->f_dentry->d_inode->i_writecount);
42300
42301    mm->total_vm += len >> PAGE_SHIFT;
42302    if (flags & VM_LOCKED) {
42303      mm->locked_vm += len >> PAGE_SHIFT;
42304      make_pages_present(addr, addr + len);
42305    }
42306    return addr;
42307
42308 unmap_and_free_vma:
42309    if (correct_wcount)
42310      atomic_inc(&file->f_dentry->d_inode->i_writecount);
42311    vma->vm_file = NULL;
```

```
42312      fput(file);
42313      /* Undo any partial mapping done by a device driver. */
42314      flush_cache_range(mm, vma->vm_start, vma->vm_end);
42315      zap_page_range(mm, vma->vm_start,
42316          vma->vm_end - vma->vm_start);
42317      flush_tlb_range(mm, vma->vm_start, vma->vm_end);
42318 free_vma:
42319      kmem_cache_free(vm_area_cachep, vma);
42320      return error;
42321 }
42322
42323 /* Get an address range which is currently unmapped.  For
42324  * mmap() without MAP_FIXED and shmat() with addr=0.
42325  * Return value 0 means ENOMEM. */
42326 #ifndef HAVE_ARCH_UNMAPPED_AREA
42327 unsigned long get_unmapped_area(unsigned long addr,
42328      unsigned long len)
42329 {
42330      struct vm_area_struct *vmm;
42331
42332      if (len > TASK_SIZE)
42333          return 0;
42334      if (!addr)
42335          addr = TASK_UNMAPPED_BASE;
42336      addr = PAGE_ALIGN(addr);
42337
42338      for (vmm = find_vma(current->mm, addr);;
42339          vmm = vmm->vm_next) {
42340          /* At this point: (!vmm || addr < vmm->vm_end). */
42341          if (TASK_SIZE - len < addr)
42342              return 0;
42343          if (!vmm || addr + len <= vmm->vm_start)
42344              return addr;
42345          addr = vmm->vm_end;
42346      }
42347 }
42348 #endif
42349
42350 #define vm_avl_empty    (struct vm_area_struct *) NULL
42351
42352 #include "mmap_avl.c"
42353
42354 /* Look up the first VMA which satisfies  addr < vm_end,
42355  * NULL if none. */
42356 struct vm_area_struct *find_vma(struct mm_struct *mm,
42357      unsigned long addr)
42358 {
```
p 625

```
42359      struct vm_area_struct *vma = NULL;
42360
42361      if (mm) {
42362          /* Check the cache first. */
42363          /* (Cache hit rate is typically around 35%.) */
42364          vma = mm->mmap_cache;
42365          if (!(vma && vma->vm_end > addr
42366                  && vma->vm_start <= addr)) {
42367              if (!mm->mmap_avl) {
42368                  /* Go through the linear list. */
42369                  vma = mm->mmap;
42370                  while (vma && vma->vm_end <= addr)
42371                      vma = vma->vm_next;
42372              } else {
42373                  /* Then go through the AVL tree quickly. */
42374                  struct vm_area_struct *tree = mm->mmap_avl;
42375                  vma = NULL;
42376                  for (;;) {
42377                      if (tree == vm_avl_empty)
42378                          break;
42379                      if (tree->vm_end > addr) {
42380                          vma = tree;
42381                          if (tree->vm_start <= addr)
42382                              break;
42383                          tree = tree->vm_avl_left;
42384                      } else
42385                          tree = tree->vm_avl_right;
42386                  }
42387              }
42388              if (vma)
42389                  mm->mmap_cache = vma;
42390          }
42391      }
42392      return vma;
42393 }
42394
42395 /* Same as find_vma, but also return a pointer to the
42396  * previous VMA in *pprev. */
42397 struct vm_area_struct *find_vma_prev(
42398      struct mm_struct *mm, unsigned long addr,
42399      struct vm_area_struct **pprev)
42400 {
42401      if (mm) {
42402          if (!mm->mmap_avl) {
42403              /* Go through the linear list. */
42404              struct vm_area_struct *prev = NULL;
42405              struct vm_area_struct *vma = mm->mmap;
```
p 625

```
42406        while (vma && vma->vm_end <= addr) {          42453      struct vm_area_struct *vma;
42407          prev = vma;                                 42454      unsigned long start;
42408          vma = vma->vm_next;                         42455
42409        }                                             42456      addr &= PAGE_MASK;
42410        *pprev = prev;                                42457      vma = find_vma(mm, addr);
42411        return vma;                                   42458      if (!vma)
42412      } else {                                        42459        return NULL;
42413        /* Go through the AVL tree quickly. */        42460      if (vma->vm_start <= addr)
42414        struct vm_area_struct *vma = NULL;            42461        return vma;
42415        struct vm_area_struct *last_turn_right = NULL; 42462     if (!(vma->vm_flags & VM_GROWSDOWN))
42416        struct vm_area_struct *prev = NULL;           42463        return NULL;
42417        struct vm_area_struct *tree = mm->mmap_avl;   42464      start = vma->vm_start;
42418        for (;;) {                                    42465      if (expand_stack(vma, addr))
42419          if (tree == vm_avl_empty)                   42466        return NULL;
42420            break;                                    42467      if (vma->vm_flags & VM_LOCKED) {
42421          if (tree->vm_end > addr) {                  42468        make_pages_present(addr, start);
42422            vma = tree;                               42469      }
42423            prev = last_turn_right;                   42470      return vma;
42424            if (tree->vm_start <= addr)               42471 }
42425              break;                                  42472
42426            tree = tree->vm_avl_left;                 42473 /* Normal function to fix up a mapping This function is
42427          } else {                                    42474  * the default for when an area has no specific function.
42428            last_turn_right = tree;                   42475  * This may be used as part of a more specific routine.
42429            tree = tree->vm_avl_right;                42476  * This function works out what part of an area is
42430          }                                           42477  * affected and adjusts the mapping information.  Since
42431        }                                             42478  * the actual page manipulation is done in do_mmap(),
42432        if (vma) {                                    42479  * none need be done here, though it would probably be
42433          if (vma->vm_avl_left != vm_avl_empty) {     42480  * more appropriate.
42434            prev = vma->vm_avl_left;                  42481  *
42435            while (prev->vm_avl_right != vm_avl_empty) 42482  * By the time this function is called, the area struct
42436              prev = prev->vm_avl_right;              42483  * has been removed from the process mapping list, so it
42437          }                                           42484  * needs to be reinserted if necessary.
42438          if ((prev ? prev->vm_next : mm->mmap) != vma) 42485 *
42439            printk("find_vma_prev: "                  42486  * The 4 main cases are:
42440                    "tree inconsistent with list\n");  42487  *    Unmapping the whole area
42441          *pprev = prev;                              42488  *    Unmapping from the start of the segment to a point
42442          return vma;                                 42489  *       in it
42443        }                                             42490  *    Unmapping from an intermediate point to the end
42444      }                                               42491  *    Unmapping between to intermediate points, making a
42445    }                                                 42492  *       hole.
42446    *pprev = NULL;                                    42493  *
42447    return NULL;                                      42494  * Case 4 involves the creation of 2 new areas, for each
42448 }                                                    42495  * side of the hole.  If possible, we reuse the existing
42449                                                       42496  * area rather than allocate a new one, and the return
42450 struct vm_area_struct *find_extend_vma(               42497  * indicates whether the old area was reused.  */
42451   struct mm_struct *mm, unsigned long addr)          42498 static struct vm_area_struct *unmap_fixup(
42452 {                                                     42499      struct mm_struct *mm, struct vm_area_struct *area,
```

p 635

```
42500    unsigned long addr, size_t len,
42501    struct vm_area_struct *extra)
42502 {
42503    struct vm_area_struct *mpnt;
42504    unsigned long end = addr + len;
42505
42506    area->vm_mm->total_vm -= len >> PAGE_SHIFT;
42507    if (area->vm_flags & VM_LOCKED)
42508      area->vm_mm->locked_vm -= len >> PAGE_SHIFT;
42509
42510    /* Unmapping the whole area. */
42511    if (addr == area->vm_start && end == area->vm_end) {
42512      if (area->vm_ops && area->vm_ops->close)
42513        area->vm_ops->close(area);
42514      if (area->vm_file)
42515        fput(area->vm_file);
42516      kmem_cache_free(vm_area_cachep, area);
42517      return extra;
42518    }
42519
42520    /* Work out to one of the ends. */
42521    if (end == area->vm_end) {
42522      area->vm_end = addr;
42523      lock_vma_mappings(area);
42524      spin_lock(&mm->page_table_lock);
42525    } else if (addr == area->vm_start) {
42526      area->vm_pgoff +=
42527          (end - area->vm_start) >> PAGE_SHIFT;
42528      area->vm_start = end;
42529      lock_vma_mappings(area);
42530      spin_lock(&mm->page_table_lock);
42531    } else {
42532    /* Unmapping a hole: area->vm_start < addr <= end <
42533     * area->vm_end */
42534    /* Add end mapping — leave beginning for below */
42535      mpnt = extra;
42536      extra = NULL;
42537
42538      mpnt->vm_mm = area->vm_mm;
42539      mpnt->vm_start = end;
42540      mpnt->vm_end = area->vm_end;
42541      mpnt->vm_page_prot = area->vm_page_prot;
42542      mpnt->vm_flags = area->vm_flags;
42543      mpnt->vm_raend = 0;
42544      mpnt->vm_ops = area->vm_ops;
42545      mpnt->vm_pgoff = area->vm_pgoff +
42546        ((end - area->vm_start) >> PAGE_SHIFT);
42547      mpnt->vm_file = area->vm_file;
42548      mpnt->vm_private_data = area->vm_private_data;
42549      if (mpnt->vm_file)
42550        get_file(mpnt->vm_file);
42551      if (mpnt->vm_ops && mpnt->vm_ops->open)
42552        mpnt->vm_ops->open(mpnt);
42553      area->vm_end = addr;          /* Truncate area */
42554
42555      /* Because mpnt->vm_file == area->vm_file this locks
42556       * things correctly. */
42557      lock_vma_mappings(area);
42558      spin_lock(&mm->page_table_lock);
42559      __insert_vm_struct(mm, mpnt);
42560    }
42561
42562    __insert_vm_struct(mm, area);
42563    spin_unlock(&mm->page_table_lock);
42564    unlock_vma_mappings(area);
42565    return extra;
42566 }
42567
42568 /*
42569  * Try to free as many page directory entries as we can,
42570  * without having to work very hard at actually scanning
42571  * the page tables themselves.
42572  *
42573  * Right now we try to free page tables if we have a nice
42574  * PGDIR-aligned area that got free'd up. We could be
42575  * more granular if we want to, but this is fast and
42576  * simple, and covers the bad cases.
42577  *
42578  * "prev", if it exists, points to a vma before the one
42579  * we just free'd - but there's no telling how much
42580  * before.  */
42581 static void free_pgtables(struct mm_struct *mm,
42582      struct vm_area_struct *prev, unsigned long start,
42583      unsigned long end)
42584 {
42585    unsigned long first = start & PGDIR_MASK;
42586    unsigned long last = end + PGDIR_SIZE - 1;
42587    unsigned long start_index, end_index;
42588
42589    if (!prev) {
42590      prev = mm->mmap;
42591      if (!prev)
42592        goto no_mmaps;
42593      if (prev->vm_end > start) {
```

```
42594        if (last > prev->vm_start)
42595          last = prev->vm_start;
42596        goto no_mmaps;
42597      }
42598    }
42599    for (;;) {
42600      struct vm_area_struct *next = prev->vm_next;
42601
42602      if (next) {
42603        if (next->vm_start < start) {
42604          prev = next;
42605          continue;
42606        }
42607        if (last > next->vm_start)
42608          last = next->vm_start;
42609      }
42610      if (prev->vm_end > first)
42611        first = prev->vm_end + PGDIR_SIZE - 1;
42612      break;
42613    }
42614 no_mmaps:
42615    /* If the PGD bits are not consecutive in the virtual
42616     * address, the old method of shifting the VA >> by
42617     * PGDIR_SHIFT doesn't work. */
42618    start_index = pgd_index(first);
42619    end_index = pgd_index(last);
42620    if (end_index > start_index) {
42621      clear_page_tables(mm, start_index,
42622          end_index - start_index);
42623      flush_tlb_pgtables(mm, first & PGDIR_MASK,
42624                         last & PGDIR_MASK);
42625    }
42626 }
42627
42628 /* Munmap is split into 2 main parts — this part which
42629  * finds what needs doing, and the areas themselves,
42630  * which do the work.  This now handles partial
42631  * unmappings.
42632  * Jeremy Fitzhardine <jeremy@sw.oz.au> */
42633 int do_munmap(struct mm_struct *mm, unsigned long addr,
42634     size_t len)
42635 {
42636    struct vm_area_struct *mpnt, *prev, **npp, *free,
42637        *extra;
42638
42639    if ((addr & ~PAGE_MASK) || addr > TASK_SIZE
42640        || len > TASK_SIZE - addr)
42641      return -EINVAL;
42642
42643    if ((len = PAGE_ALIGN(len)) == 0)
42644      return -EINVAL;
42645
42646    /* Check if this memory area is ok - put it on the
42647     * temporary list if so..  The checks here are pretty
42648     * simple — every area affected in some way (by any
42649     * overlap) is put on the list.  If nothing is put on,
42650     * nothing is affected. */
42651    mpnt = find_vma_prev(mm, addr, &prev);
42652    if (!mpnt)
42653      return 0;
42654    /* we have  addr < mpnt->vm_end  */
42655
42656    if (mpnt->vm_start >= addr + len)
42657      return 0;
42658
42659    /* If we'll make "hole", check the vm areas limit */
42660    if ((mpnt->vm_start < addr
42661            && mpnt->vm_end > addr + len)
42662        && mm->map_count >= MAX_MAP_COUNT)
42663      return -ENOMEM;
42664
42665    /* We may need one additional vma to fix up the
42666     * mappings ...  and this is the last chance for an
42667     * easy error exit.  */
42668    extra = kmem_cache_alloc(vm_area_cachep, SLAB_KERNEL);
42669    if (!extra)
42670      return -ENOMEM;
42671
42672    npp = (prev ? &prev->vm_next : &mm->mmap);
42673    free = NULL;
42674    spin_lock(&mm->page_table_lock);
42675    for (; mpnt && mpnt->vm_start < addr + len;
42676        mpnt = *npp) {
42677      *npp = mpnt->vm_next;
42678      mpnt->vm_next = free;
42679      free = mpnt;
42680      if (mm->mmap_avl)
42681        avl_remove(mpnt, &mm->mmap_avl);
42682    }
42683    mm->mmap_cache = NULL;         /* Kill the cache. */
42684    spin_unlock(&mm->page_table_lock);
42685
42686    /* Ok - we have the memory areas we should free on the
42687     * 'free' list, so release them, and unmap the page
```

p 634

```
42688    * range..  If the one of the segments is only being
42689    * partially unmapped, it will put new
42690    * vm_area_struct(s) into the address space.  In that
42691    * case we have to be careful with VM_DENYWRITE. */
42692   while ((mpnt = free) != NULL) {
42693     unsigned long st, end, size;
42694     struct file *file = NULL;
42695
42696     free = free->vm_next;
42697
42698     st = addr < mpnt->vm_start ? mpnt->vm_start : addr;
42699     end = addr + len;
42700     end = end > mpnt->vm_end ? mpnt->vm_end : end;
42701     size = end - st;
42702
42703     if (mpnt->vm_flags & VM_DENYWRITE &&
42704         (st != mpnt->vm_start || end != mpnt->vm_end) &&
42705         (file = mpnt->vm_file) != NULL) {
42706       atomic_dec(&file->f_dentry->d_inode->i_writecount);
42707     }
42708     remove_shared_vm_struct(mpnt);
42709     mm->map_count--;
42710
42711     flush_cache_range(mm, st, end);
42712     zap_page_range(mm, st, size);
42713     flush_tlb_range(mm, st, end);
42714
42715     /* Fix the mapping, and free the old area if it
42716      * wasn't reused.  */
42717     extra = unmap_fixup(mm, mpnt, st, size, extra);
42718     if (file)
42719       atomic_inc(&file->f_dentry->d_inode->i_writecount);
42720   }
42721
42722   /* Release the extra vma struct if it wasn't used */
42723   if (extra)
42724     kmem_cache_free(vm_area_cachep, extra);
42725
42726   free_pgtables(mm, prev, addr, addr + len);
42727
42728   return 0;
42729 }
42730
42731 asmlinkage long sys_munmap(unsigned long addr,
42732     size_t len)
42733 {
42734   int ret;
42735   struct mm_struct *mm = current->mm;
42736
42737   down(&mm->mmap_sem);
42738   ret = do_munmap(mm, addr, len);
42739   up(&mm->mmap_sem);
42740   return ret;
42741 }
42742
42743 /* this is really a simplified "do_mmap".  it only
42744  * handles anonymous maps.  eventually we may be able to
42745  * do some brk-specific accounting here.  */
42746 unsigned long do_brk(unsigned long addr,
42747     unsigned long len)
42748 {
42749   struct mm_struct *mm = current->mm;
42750   struct vm_area_struct *vma;
42751   unsigned long flags, retval;
42752
42753   len = PAGE_ALIGN(len);
42754   if (!len)
42755     return addr;
42756
42757   /* mlock MCL_FUTURE?  */
42758   if (mm->def_flags & VM_LOCKED) {
42759     unsigned long locked = mm->locked_vm << PAGE_SHIFT;
42760     locked += len;
42761     if (locked > current->rlim[RLIMIT_MEMLOCK].rlim_cur)
42762       return -EAGAIN;
42763   }
42764
42765   /* Clear old maps.  this also does some error checking
42766    * for us */
42767   retval = do_munmap(mm, addr, len);
42768   if (retval != 0)
42769     return retval;
42770
42771   /* Check against address space limits *after* clearing
42772    * old maps... */
42773   if ((mm->total_vm << PAGE_SHIFT) + len
42774       > current->rlim[RLIMIT_AS].rlim_cur)
42775     return -ENOMEM;
42776
42777   if (mm->map_count > MAX_MAP_COUNT)
42778     return -ENOMEM;
42779
42780   if (!vm_enough_memory(len >> PAGE_SHIFT))
42781     return -ENOMEM;
```

```
42782
42783    flags = vm_flags(PROT_READ | PROT_WRITE | PROT_EXEC,
42784                     MAP_FIXED | MAP_PRIVATE)
42785      | mm->def_flags;
42786
42787    flags |= VM_MAYREAD | VM_MAYWRITE | VM_MAYEXEC;
42788
42789
42790    /* Can we just expand an old anonymous mapping? */
42791    if (addr) {
42792      struct vm_area_struct *vma = find_vma(mm, addr - 1);
42793      if (vma && vma->vm_end == addr && !vma->vm_file &&
42794          vma->vm_flags == flags) {
42795        vma->vm_end = addr + len;
42796        goto out;
42797      }
42798    }
42799
42800
42801    /* create a vma struct for an anonymous mapping */
42802    vma = kmem_cache_alloc(vm_area_cachep, SLAB_KERNEL);
42803    if (!vma)
42804      return -ENOMEM;
42805
42806    vma->vm_mm = mm;
42807    vma->vm_start = addr;
42808    vma->vm_end = addr + len;
42809    vma->vm_flags = flags;
42810    vma->vm_page_prot = protection_map[flags & 0x0f];
42811    vma->vm_ops = NULL;
42812    vma->vm_pgoff = 0;
42813    vma->vm_file = NULL;
42814    vma->vm_private_data = NULL;
42815
42816    insert_vm_struct(mm, vma);
42817
42818 out:
42819    mm->total_vm += len >> PAGE_SHIFT;
42820    if (flags & VM_LOCKED) {
42821      mm->locked_vm += len >> PAGE_SHIFT;
42822      make_pages_present(addr, addr + len);
42823    }
42824    return addr;
42825 }
42826
42827 /* Build the AVL tree corresponding to the VMA list. */
42828 void build_mmap_avl(struct mm_struct *mm)
42829 {
42830    struct vm_area_struct *vma;
42831
42832    mm->mmap_avl = NULL;
42833    for (vma = mm->mmap; vma; vma = vma->vm_next)
42834      avl_insert(vma, &mm->mmap_avl);
42835 }
42836
42837 /* Release all mmaps. */
42838 void exit_mmap(struct mm_struct *mm)
42839 {
42840    struct vm_area_struct *mpnt;
42841
42842    release_segments(mm);
42843    spin_lock(&mm->page_table_lock);
42844    mpnt = mm->mmap;
42845    mm->mmap = mm->mmap_avl = mm->mmap_cache = NULL;
42846    spin_unlock(&mm->page_table_lock);
42847    mm->rss = 0;
42848    mm->total_vm = 0;
42849    mm->locked_vm = 0;
42850
42851    flush_cache_mm(mm);
42852    while (mpnt) {
42853      struct vm_area_struct *next = mpnt->vm_next;
42854      unsigned long start = mpnt->vm_start;
42855      unsigned long end = mpnt->vm_end;
42856      unsigned long size = end - start;
42857
42858      if (mpnt->vm_ops) {
42859        if (mpnt->vm_ops->close)
42860          mpnt->vm_ops->close(mpnt);
42861      }
42862      mm->map_count-;
42863      remove_shared_vm_struct(mpnt);
42864      zap_page_range(mm, start, size);
42865      if (mpnt->vm_file)
42866        fput(mpnt->vm_file);
42867      kmem_cache_free(vm_area_cachep, mpnt);
42868      mpnt = next;
42869    }
42870    flush_tlb_mm(mm);
42871
42872    /* This is just debugging */
42873    if (mm->map_count)
42874      printk("exit_mmap: map count is %d\n",
42875          mm->map_count);
```

```
42876
42877   clear_page_tables(mm, FIRST_USER_PGD_NR,
42878        USER_PTRS_PER_PGD);
42879 }
42880
42881 /* Insert vm structure into process list sorted by
42882  * address and into the inode's i_mmap ring.  If vm_file
42883  * is non-NULL then the i_shared_lock must be held
42884  * here. */
42885 void __insert_vm_struct(struct mm_struct *mm,
42886      struct vm_area_struct *vmp)
42887 {
42888   struct vm_area_struct **pprev;
42889   struct file *file;
42890
42891   if (!mm->mmap_avl) {
42892     pprev = &mm->mmap;
42893     while (*pprev && (*pprev)->vm_start <= vmp->vm_start)
42894       pprev = &(*pprev)->vm_next;
42895   } else {
42896     struct vm_area_struct *prev, *next;
42897     avl_insert_neighbours(vmp, &mm->mmap_avl, &prev,
42898         &next);
42899     pprev = (prev ? &prev->vm_next : &mm->mmap);
42900     if (*pprev != next)
42901       printk("insert_vm_struct: "
42902             "tree inconsistent with list\n");
42903   }
42904   vmp->vm_next = *pprev;
42905   *pprev = vmp;
42906
42907   mm->map_count++;
42908   if (mm->map_count >= AVL_MIN_MAP_COUNT
42909       && !mm->mmap_avl)
42910     build_mmap_avl(mm);
42911
42912   file = vmp->vm_file;
42913   if (file) {
42914     struct inode *inode = file->f_dentry->d_inode;
42915     struct address_space *mapping = inode->i_mapping;
42916     struct vm_area_struct **head;
42917
42918     if (vmp->vm_flags & VM_DENYWRITE)
42919       atomic_dec(&inode->i_writecount);
42920
42921     head = &mapping->i_mmap;
42922     if (vmp->vm_flags & VM_SHARED)
42923       head = &mapping->i_mmap_shared;
42924
42925     /* insert vmp into inode's share list */
42926     if ((vmp->vm_next_share = *head) != NULL)
42927       (*head)->vm_pprev_share = &vmp->vm_next_share;
42928     *head = vmp;
42929     vmp->vm_pprev_share = head;
42930   }
42931 }
42932
42933 void insert_vm_struct(struct mm_struct *mm,
42934      struct vm_area_struct *vmp)
42935 {
42936   lock_vma_mappings(vmp);
42937   spin_lock(&current->mm->page_table_lock);
42938   __insert_vm_struct(mm, vmp);
42939   spin_unlock(&current->mm->page_table_lock);
42940   unlock_vma_mappings(vmp);
42941 }
```

mm/page_alloc.c

```
42942 /*
42943  *  linux/mm/page_alloc.c
42944  *
42945  *  Copyright (C) 1991, 1992, 1993, 1994  Linus Torvalds
42946  *  Swap reorganised 29.12.95, Stephen Tweedie
42947  *  Support of BIGMEM added by Gerhard Wichert, Siemens
42948  *  AG, July 1999
42949  *  Reshaped it to be a zoned allocator, Ingo Molnar, Red
42950  *  Hat, 1999
42951  *  Discontiguous memory support, Kanoj Sarcar, SGI, Nov
42952  *  1999
42953  *  Zone balancing, Kanoj Sarcar, SGI, Jan 2000
42954  */
42955
42956 #include <linux/config.h>
42957 #include <linux/mm.h>
42958 #include <linux/swap.h>
42959 #include <linux/swapctl.h>
42960 #include <linux/interrupt.h>
42961 #include <linux/pagemap.h>
42962 #include <linux/bootmem.h>
42963 #include <linux/slab.h>
42964
42965 int nr_swap_pages;
42966 int nr_active_pages;
42967 int nr_inactive_dirty_pages;
```

```
42968 pg_data_t *pgdat_list;
42969
42970 static char *zone_names[MAX_NR_ZONES] =
42971     { "DMA", "Normal", "HighMem" };
42972 static int zone_balance_ratio[MAX_NR_ZONES] =
42973     { 32, 128, 128, };
42974 static int zone_balance_min[MAX_NR_ZONES] =
42975     { 10, 10, 10, };
42976 static int zone_balance_max[MAX_NR_ZONES] =
42977     { 255, 255, 255, };
42978
42979 struct list_head active_list;
42980 struct list_head inactive_dirty_list;
42981 /* Free_page() adds the page to the free lists. This is
42982  * optimized for fast normal cases (no error jumps taken
42983  * normally).
42984  *
42985  * The way to optimize jumps for gcc-2.2.2 is to:
42986  *  - select the "normal" case and put it inside the
42987  *    if () { XXX }
42988  *  - no else-statements if you can avoid them
42989  *
42990  * With the above two rules, you get a straight-line
42991  * execution path for the normal case, giving better
42992  * asm-code.   */
42993
42994 #define memlist_init(x) INIT_LIST_HEAD(x)
42995 #define memlist_add_head list_add
42996 #define memlist_add_tail list_add_tail
42997 #define memlist_del list_del
42998 #define memlist_entry list_entry
42999 #define memlist_next(x) ((x)->next)
43000 #define memlist_prev(x) ((x)->prev)
43001
43002 /* Temporary debugging check.  */
43003 #define BAD_RANGE(zone,x)                           \
43004    (((zone) != (x)->zone) ||                        \
43005    (((x)-mem_map) < (zone)->offset) ||              \
43006    (((x)-mem_map) >= (zone)->offset+(zone)->size))
43007
43008 /* Buddy system. Hairy. You really aren't expected to
43009  * understand this
43010  *
43011  * Hint: -mask = 1+~mask */
43012
43013 static void FASTCALL(__free_pages_ok(struct page *page,
43014           unsigned long order));
```

```
p 639  43015 static void __free_pages_ok(struct page *page,
43016     unsigned long order)
43017 {
43018   unsigned long index, page_idx, mask, flags;
43019   free_area_t *area;
43020   struct page *base;
43021   zone_t *zone;
43022
43023   if (page->buffers)
43024     BUG();
43025   if (page->mapping)
43026     BUG();
43027   if (!VALID_PAGE(page))
43028     BUG();
43029   if (PageSwapCache(page))
43030     BUG();
43031   if (PageLocked(page))
43032     BUG();
43033   if (PageDecrAfter(page))
43034     BUG();
43035   if (PageActive(page))
43036     BUG();
43037   if (PageInactiveDirty(page))
43038     BUG();
43039   if (PageInactiveClean(page))
43040     BUG();
43041
43042   page->flags &=
43043      ~((1 << PG_referenced) | (1 << PG_dirty));
43044   page->age = PAGE_AGE_START;
43045
43046   zone = page->zone;
43047
43048   mask = (~0UL) << order;
43049   base = mem_map + zone->offset;
43050   page_idx = page - base;
43051   if (page_idx & ~mask)
43052     BUG();
43053   index = page_idx >> (1 + order);
43054
43055   area = zone->free_area + order;
43056
43057   spin_lock_irqsave(&zone->lock, flags);
43058
43059   zone->free_pages -= mask;
43060
43061   while (mask + (1 << (MAX_ORDER - 1))) {
```

```
43062      struct page *buddy1, *buddy2;
43063
43064      if (area >= zone->free_area + MAX_ORDER)
43065        BUG();
43066      if (!test_and_change_bit(index, area->map))
43067        /* the buddy page is still allocated.  */
43068        break;
43069      /* Move the buddy up one level.  */
43070      buddy1 = base + (page_idx ^ -mask);
43071      buddy2 = base + page_idx;
43072      if (BAD_RANGE(zone, buddy1))
43073        BUG();
43074      if (BAD_RANGE(zone, buddy2))
43075        BUG();
43076
43077      memlist_del(&buddy1->list);
43078      mask <<= 1;
43079      area++;
43080      index >>= 1;
43081      page_idx &= mask;
43082    }
43083    memlist_add_head(&(base + page_idx)->list,
43084        &area->free_list);
43085
43086    spin_unlock_irqrestore(&zone->lock, flags);
43087
43088    /* We don't want to protect this variable from race
43089     * conditions since it's nothing important, but we do
43090     * want to make sure it never gets negative.  */
43091    if (memory_pressure > NR_CPUS)
43092      memory_pressure--;
43093 }
43094
43095 #define MARK_USED(index, order, area)                    \
43096        change_bit((index) >> (1+(order)), (area)->map)
43097
43098 static inline struct page *expand(zone_t * zone,
43099      struct page *page, unsigned long index, int low,
43100      int high, free_area_t * area)
43101 {
43102    unsigned long size = 1 << high;
43103
43104    while (high > low) {
43105      if (BAD_RANGE(zone, page))
43106        BUG();
43107      area--;
43108      high--;
```

```
43109      size >>= 1;
43110      memlist_add_head(&(page)->list, &(area)->free_list);
43111      MARK_USED(index, high, area);
43112      index += size;
43113      page += size;
43114    }
43115    if (BAD_RANGE(zone, page))
43116      BUG();
43117    return page;
43118 }
43119
43120 static FASTCALL(struct page *rmqueue(zone_t * zone,
43121        unsigned long order));
43122 static struct page *rmqueue(zone_t * zone,
43123      unsigned long order)
43124 {
43125    free_area_t *area = zone->free_area + order;
43126    unsigned long curr_order = order;
43127    struct list_head *head, *curr;
43128    unsigned long flags;
43129    struct page *page;
43130
43131    spin_lock_irqsave(&zone->lock, flags);
43132    do {
43133      head = &area->free_list;
43134      curr = memlist_next(head);
43135
43136      if (curr != head) {
43137        unsigned int index;
43138
43139        page = memlist_entry(curr, struct page, list);
43140        if (BAD_RANGE(zone, page))
43141          BUG();
43142        memlist_del(curr);
43143        index = (page - mem_map) - zone->offset;
43144        MARK_USED(index, curr_order, area);
43145        zone->free_pages -= 1 << order;
43146
43147        page = expand(zone, page, index, order,
43148                    curr_order, area);
43149        spin_unlock_irqrestore(&zone->lock, flags);
43150
43151        set_page_count(page, 1);
43152        if (BAD_RANGE(zone, page))
43153          BUG();
43154        DEBUG_ADD_PAGE
43155        return page;
```

```
43156        }
43157      curr_order++;
43158      area++;
43159    } while (curr_order < MAX_ORDER);
43160    spin_unlock_irqrestore(&zone->lock, flags);
43161
43162    return NULL;
43163 }
43164
43165 #define PAGES_MIN     0
43166 #define PAGES_LOW     1
43167 #define PAGES_HIGH    2
43168
43169 /* This function does the dirty work for __alloc_pages
43170  * and is separated out to keep the code size smaller.
43171  * (suggested by Davem at 1:30 AM, typed by Rik at 6 AM)
43172  */
43173 static struct page *__alloc_pages_limit(zonelist_t *
43174     zonelist, unsigned long order, int limit,
43175     int direct_reclaim)
43176 {
43177    zone_t **zone = zonelist->zones;
43178
43179    for (;;) {
43180      zone_t *z = *(zone++);
43181      unsigned long water_mark;
43182
43183      if (!z)
43184        break;
43185      if (!z->size)
43186        BUG();
43187
43188      /* We allocate if the number of free + inactive_clean
43189       * pages is above the watermark.  */
43190      switch (limit) {
43191      default:
43192      case PAGES_MIN:
43193        water_mark = z->pages_min;
43194        break;
43195      case PAGES_LOW:
43196        water_mark = z->pages_low;
43197        break;
43198      case PAGES_HIGH:
43199        water_mark = z->pages_high;
43200      }
43201
43202      if (z->free_pages + z->inactive_clean_pages >
```

```
43203          water_mark) {
43204        struct page *page = NULL;
43205        /* If possible, reclaim a page directly. */
43206        if (direct_reclaim
43207            && z->free_pages < z->pages_min + 8)
43208          page = reclaim_page(z);
43209        /* If that fails, fall back to rmqueue. */
43210        if (!page)
43211          page = rmqueue(z, order);
43212        if (page)
43213          return page;
43214      }
43215    }
43216
43217    /* Found nothing. */
43218    return NULL;
43219 }
43220
43221
43222 /* This is the 'heart' of the zoned buddy allocator: */
43223 struct page *__alloc_pages(zonelist_t * zonelist,
43224     unsigned long order)
43225 {
43226    zone_t **zone;
43227    int direct_reclaim = 0;
43228    unsigned int gfp_mask = zonelist->gfp_mask;
43229    struct page *page;
43230
43231    /* Allocations put pressure on the VM subsystem.  */
43232    memory_pressure++;
43233
43234    /* (If anyone calls gfp from interrupts nonatomically
43235     * then it will sooner or later tripped up by a
43236     * schedule().)
43237     *
43238     * We are falling back to lower-level zones if
43239     * allocation in a higher zone fails.  */
43240
43241    /* Can we take pages directly from the inactive_clean
43242     * list?  */
43243    if (order == 0 && (gfp_mask & __GFP_WAIT) &&
43244        !(current->flags & PF_MEMALLOC))
43245      direct_reclaim = 1;
43246
43247    /* If we are about to get low on free pages and we also
43248     * have an inactive page shortage, wake up kswapd.  */
43249    if (inactive_shortage() > inactive_target / 2
```

p 637

```
43250        && free_shortage())
43251      wakeup_kswapd();
43252    /* If we are about to get low on free pages and
43253     * cleaning the inactive_dirty pages would fix the
43254     * situation, wake up bdflush. */
43255    else if (free_shortage()
43256        && nr_inactive_dirty_pages > free_shortage()
43257        && nr_inactive_dirty_pages >= freepages.high)
43258      wakeup_bdflush(0);
43259
43260 try_again:
43261    /* First, see if we have any zones with lots of free
43262     *memory.
43263     *
43264     * We allocate free memory first because it doesn't
43265     * contain any data ... DUH! */
43266    zone = zonelist->zones;
43267    for (;;) {
43268      zone_t *z = *(zone++);
43269      if (!z)
43270        break;
43271      if (!z->size)
43272        BUG();
43273
43274      if (z->free_pages >= z->pages_low) {
43275        page = rmqueue(z, order);
43276        if (page)
43277          return page;
43278      } else if (z->free_pages < z->pages_min &&
43279          waitqueue_active(&kreclaimd_wait)) {
43280        wake_up_interruptible(&kreclaimd_wait);
43281      }
43282    }
43283
43284    /* Try to allocate a page from a zone with a HIGH
43285     * amount of free + inactive_clean pages.
43286     *
43287     * If there is a lot of activity, inactive_target will
43288     * be high and we'll have a good chance of finding a
43289     * page using the HIGH limit. */
43290    page = __alloc_pages_limit(zonelist, order, PAGES_HIGH,
43291                          direct_reclaim);
43292    if (page)
43293      return page;
43294
43295    /* Then try to allocate a page from a zone with more
43296     * than zone->pages_low free + inactive_clean pages.
43297     *
43298     * When the working set is very large and VM activity
43299     * is low, we're most likely to have our allocation
43300     * succeed here. */
43301    page = __alloc_pages_limit(zonelist, order, PAGES_LOW,
43302                          direct_reclaim);
43303    if (page)
43304      return page;
43305
43306    /* OK, none of the zones on our zonelist has lots of
43307     * pages free.
43308     *
43309     * We wake up kswapd, in the hope that kswapd will
43310     * resolve this situation before memory gets tight.
43311     *
43312     * We also yield the CPU, because that:
43313     * - gives kswapd a chance to do something
43314     * - slows down allocations, in particular the
43315     *   allocations from the fast allocator that's
43316     *   causing the problems ...
43317     * - ... which minimises the impact the "bad guys"
43318     *   have on the rest of the system
43319     * - if we don't have __GFP_IO set, kswapd may be
43320     *   able to free some memory we can't free ourselves
43321     */
43322    wakeup_kswapd();
43323    if (gfp_mask & __GFP_WAIT) {
43324      __set_current_state(TASK_RUNNING);
43325      current->policy |= SCHED_YIELD;
43326      schedule();
43327    }
43328
43329    /* After waking up kswapd, we try to allocate a page
43330     * from any zone which isn't critical yet.
43331     *
43332     * Kswapd should, in most situations, bring the
43333     * situation back to normal in no time. */
43334    page = __alloc_pages_limit(zonelist, order, PAGES_MIN,
43335                          direct_reclaim);
43336    if (page)
43337      return page;
43338
43339    /* Damn, we didn't succeed.
43340     *
43341     * This can be due to 2 reasons:
43342     * - we're doing a higher-order allocation
43343     *     -> move pages to the free list until we succeed
```

```
43344    * - we're /really/ tight on memory
43345    *    -> try to free pages ourselves with page_launder
43346    */
43347   if (!(current->flags & PF_MEMALLOC)) {
43348     /* Are we dealing with a higher order allocation?
43349      *
43350      * Move pages from the inactive_clean to the free
43351      * list in the hope of creating a large, physically
43352      * contiguous piece of free memory.  */
43353     if (order > 0 && (gfp_mask & __GFP_WAIT)) {
43354       zone = zonelist->zones;
43355       /* First, clean some dirty pages. */
43356       current->flags |= PF_MEMALLOC;
43357       page_launder(gfp_mask, 1);
43358       current->flags &= ~PF_MEMALLOC;
43359       for (;;) {
43360         zone_t *z = *(zone++);
43361         if (!z)
43362           break;
43363         if (!z->size)
43364           continue;
43365         while (z->inactive_clean_pages) {
43366           struct page *page;
43367           /* Move one page to the free list. */
43368           page = reclaim_page(z);
43369           if (!page)
43370             break;
43371           __free_page(page);
43372           /* Try if the allocation succeeds. */
43373           page = rmqueue(z, order);
43374           if (page)
43375             return page;
43376         }
43377       }
43378     }
43379     /* When we arrive here, we are really tight on
43380      * memory.
43381      *
43382      * We try to free pages ourselves by:
43383      *      - shrinking the i/d caches.
43384      *      - reclaiming unused memory from the slab
43385      *        caches.
43386      *      - swapping/syncing pages to disk (done by
43387      *        page_launder)
43388      *      - moving clean pages from the inactive dirty
43389      *        list to the inactive clean list. (done by
43390      *        page_launder) */
43391     if (gfp_mask & __GFP_WAIT) {
43392       memory_pressure++;
43393       try_to_free_pages(gfp_mask);
43394       wakeup_bdflush(0);
43395       if (!order)
43396         goto try_again;
43397     }
43398   }
43399
43400   /* Final phase: allocate anything we can!
43401    *
43402    * Higher order allocations, GFP_ATOMIC allocations and
43403    * recursive allocations (PF_MEMALLOC) end up here.
43404    *
43405    * Only recursive allocations can use the very last
43406    * pages in the system, otherwise it would be just too
43407    * easy to deadlock the system...  */
43408   zone = zonelist->zones;
43409   for (;;) {
43410     zone_t *z = *(zone++);
43411     struct page *page = NULL;
43412     if (!z)
43413       break;
43414     if (!z->size)
43415       BUG();
43416
43417     /* SUBTLE: direct_reclaim is only possible if the
43418      * task becomes PF_MEMALLOC while looping above. This
43419      * will happen when the OOM killer selects this task
43420      * for instant execution...  */
43421     if (direct_reclaim) {
43422       page = reclaim_page(z);
43423       if (page)
43424         return page;
43425     }
43426
43427     /* XXX: is pages_min/4 a good amount to reserve for
43428      * this? */
43429     if (z->free_pages < z->pages_min / 4 &&
43430         !(current->flags & PF_MEMALLOC))
43431       continue;
43432     page = rmqueue(z, order);
43433     if (page)
43434       return page;
43435   }
43436
43437   /* No luck.. */
```

```
43438    printk(KERN_ERR
43439        "__alloc_pages: %lu-order allocation failed.\n",
43440        order);
43441    return NULL;
43442 }
43443
43444 /* Common helper functions.  */
43445 unsigned long __get_free_pages(int gfp_mask,
43446        unsigned long order)
43447 {
43448    struct page *page;
43449
43450    page = alloc_pages(gfp_mask, order);
43451    if (!page)
43452      return 0;
43453    return (unsigned long) page_address(page);
43454 }
43455
43456 unsigned long get_zeroed_page(int gfp_mask)
43457 {
43458    struct page *page;
43459
43460    page = alloc_pages(gfp_mask, 0);
43461    if (page) {
43462      void *address = page_address(page);
43463      clear_page(address);
43464      return (unsigned long) address;
43465    }
43466    return 0;
43467 }
43468
43469 void __free_pages(struct page *page, unsigned long order)
43470 {
43471    if (!PageReserved(page) && put_page_testzero(page))
43472      __free_pages_ok(page, order);
43473 }
43474
43475 void free_pages(unsigned long addr, unsigned long order)
43476 {
43477    if (addr != 0)
43478      __free_pages(virt_to_page(addr), order);
43479 }
43480
43481 /* Total amount of free (allocatable) RAM: */
43482 unsigned int nr_free_pages(void)
43483 {
43484    unsigned int sum;
43485    zone_t *zone;
43486    pg_data_t *pgdat = pgdat_list;
43487
43488    sum = 0;
43489    while (pgdat) {
43490      for (zone = pgdat->node_zones;
43491          zone < pgdat->node_zones + MAX_NR_ZONES; zone++)
43492        sum += zone->free_pages;
43493      pgdat = pgdat->node_next;
43494    }
43495    return sum;
43496 }
43497
43498 /* Total amount of inactive_clean (allocatable) RAM: */
43499 unsigned int nr_inactive_clean_pages(void)
43500 {
43501    unsigned int sum;
43502    zone_t *zone;
43503    pg_data_t *pgdat = pgdat_list;
43504
43505    sum = 0;
43506    while (pgdat) {
43507      for (zone = pgdat->node_zones;
43508          zone < pgdat->node_zones + MAX_NR_ZONES; zone++)
43509        sum += zone->inactive_clean_pages;
43510      pgdat = pgdat->node_next;
43511    }
43512    return sum;
43513 }
43514
43515 /* Amount of free RAM allocatable as buffer memory: */
43516 unsigned int nr_free_buffer_pages(void)
43517 {
43518    unsigned int sum;
43519
43520    sum = nr_free_pages();
43521    sum += nr_inactive_clean_pages();
43522    sum += nr_inactive_dirty_pages;
43523
43524    /* Keep our write behind queue filled, even if kswapd
43525     * lags a bit right now.  */
43526    if (sum < freepages.high + inactive_target)
43527      sum = freepages.high + inactive_target;
43528    /* We don't want dirty page writebehind to put too much
43529     * pressure on the working set, but we want it to be
43530     * possible to have some dirty pages in the working set
43531     * without upsetting the writebehind logic.  */
```

```
43532    sum += nr_active_pages >> 4;
43533
43534    return sum;
43535 }
43536
43537 #if CONFIG_HIGHMEM
43538 unsigned int nr_free_highpages(void)
43539 {
43540    pg_data_t *pgdat = pgdat_list;
43541    unsigned int pages = 0;
43542
43543    while (pgdat) {
43544       pages += pgdat->node_zones[ZONE_HIGHMEM].free_pages;
43545       pgdat = pgdat->node_next;
43546    }
43547    return pages;
43548 }
43549 #endif
43550
43551 /* Show free area list (used inside shift_scroll-lock
43552  * stuff)
43553  * We also calculate the percentage fragmentation. We do
43554  * this by counting the memory on each free list with the
43555  * exception of the first item on the list.  */
43556 void show_free_areas_core(pg_data_t * pgdat)
43557 {
43558    unsigned long order;
43559    unsigned type;
43560
43561    printk("Free pages:      %6dkB (%6dkB HighMem)\n",
43562         nr_free_pages() << (PAGE_SHIFT - 10),
43563         nr_free_highpages() << (PAGE_SHIFT - 10));
43564
43565    printk("( Active: %d, inactive_dirty: %d, "
43566          "inactive_clean: %d, free: %d (%d %d %d) )\n",
43567          nr_active_pages, nr_inactive_dirty_pages,
43568          nr_inactive_clean_pages(), nr_free_pages(),
43569          freepages.min, freepages.low, freepages.high);
43570
43571    for (type = 0; type < MAX_NR_ZONES; type++) {
43572       struct list_head *head, *curr;
43573       zone_t *zone = pgdat->node_zones + type;
43574       unsigned long nr, total, flags;
43575
43576       total = 0;
43577       if (zone->size) {
43578          spin_lock_irqsave(&zone->lock, flags);
43579          for (order = 0; order < MAX_ORDER; order++) {
43580             head = &(zone->free_area + order)->free_list;
43581             curr = head;
43582             nr = 0;
43583             for (;;) {
43584                curr = memlist_next(curr);
43585                if (curr == head)
43586                   break;
43587                nr++;
43588             }
43589             total += nr * (1 << order);
43590             printk("%lu*%lukB ", nr,
43591                  (PAGE_SIZE >> 10) << order);
43592          }
43593          spin_unlock_irqrestore(&zone->lock, flags);
43594       }
43595       printk("= %lukB)\n", total * (PAGE_SIZE >> 10));
43596    }
43597
43598 #ifdef SWAP_CACHE_INFO
43599    show_swap_cache_info();
43600 #endif
43601 }
43602
43603 void show_free_areas(void)
43604 {
43605    show_free_areas_core(pgdat_list);
43606 }
43607
43608 /* Builds allocation fallback zone lists.  */
43609 static inline void build_zonelists(pg_data_t * pgdat)
43610 {
43611    int i, j, k;
43612
43613    for (i = 0; i < NR_GFPINDEX; i++) {
43614       zonelist_t *zonelist;
43615       zone_t *zone;
43616
43617       zonelist = pgdat->node_zonelists + i;
43618       memset(zonelist, 0, sizeof(*zonelist));
43619
43620       zonelist->gfp_mask = i;
43621       j = 0;
43622       k = ZONE_NORMAL;
43623       if (i & __GFP_HIGHMEM)
43624          k = ZONE_HIGHMEM;
43625       if (i & __GFP_DMA)
```

```
43626        k = ZONE_DMA;
43627
43628      switch (k) {
43629      default:
43630        BUG();
43631        /* fallthrough: */
43632      case ZONE_HIGHMEM:
43633        zone = pgdat->node_zones + ZONE_HIGHMEM;
43634        if (zone->size) {
43635 #ifndef CONFIG_HIGHMEM
43636          BUG();
43637 #endif
43638          zonelist->zones[j++] = zone;
43639        }
43640      case ZONE_NORMAL:
43641        zone = pgdat->node_zones + ZONE_NORMAL;
43642        if (zone->size)
43643          zonelist->zones[j++] = zone;
43644      case ZONE_DMA:
43645        zone = pgdat->node_zones + ZONE_DMA;
43646        if (zone->size)
43647          zonelist->zones[j++] = zone;
43648      }
43649      zonelist->zones[j++] = NULL;
43650    }
43651 }
43652
43653 #define LONG_ALIGN(x)                                                   \
43654    (((x)+(sizeof(long))-1)&~((sizeof(long))-1))
43655
43656 /* Set up the zone data structures:
43657  *   - mark all pages reserved
43658  *   - mark all memory queues empty
43659  *   - clear the memory bitmaps */
43660 void __init free_area_init_core(int nid,
43661    pg_data_t * pgdat, struct page **gmap,
43662    unsigned long *zones_size,
43663    unsigned long zone_start_paddr,
43664    unsigned long *zholes_size, struct page *lmem_map)
43665 {
43666    struct page *p;
43667    unsigned long i, j;
43668    unsigned long map_size;
43669    unsigned long totalpages, offset, realtotalpages;
43670    unsigned int cumulative = 0;
43671
43672    totalpages = 0;
43673    for (i = 0; i < MAX_NR_ZONES; i++) {
43674      unsigned long size = zones_size[i];
43675      totalpages += size;
43676    }
43677    realtotalpages = totalpages;
43678    if (zholes_size)
43679      for (i = 0; i < MAX_NR_ZONES; i++)
43680        realtotalpages -= zholes_size[i];
43681
43682    printk("On node %d totalpages: %lu\n", nid,
43683      realtotalpages);
43684
43685    memlist_init(&active_list);
43686    memlist_init(&inactive_dirty_list);
43687
43688    /* Some architectures (with lots of mem and
43689     * discontinous memory maps) have to search for a good
43690     * mem_map area: For discontigmem, the conceptual mem
43691     * map array starts from PAGE_OFFSET, we need to align
43692     * the actual array onto a mem map boundary, so that
43693     * MAP_NR works.  */
43694    map_size = (totalpages + 1) * sizeof(struct page);
43695    if (lmem_map == (struct page *) 0) {
43696      lmem_map = (struct page *)
43697        alloc_bootmem_node(pgdat, map_size);
43698      lmem_map = (struct page *)
43699        (PAGE_OFFSET + MAP_ALIGN((unsigned long) lmem_map -
43700                               PAGE_OFFSET));
43701    }
43702    *gmap = pgdat->node_mem_map = lmem_map;
43703    pgdat->node_size = totalpages;
43704    pgdat->node_start_paddr = zone_start_paddr;
43705    pgdat->node_start_mapnr = (lmem_map - mem_map);
43706
43707    /* Initially all pages are reserved - free ones are
43708     * freed up by free_all_bootmem() once the early boot
43709     * process is done.  */
43710    for (p = lmem_map; p < lmem_map + totalpages; p++) {
43711      set_page_count(p, 0);
43712      SetPageReserved(p);
43713      init_waitqueue_head(&p->wait);
43714      memlist_init(&p->list);
43715    }
43716
43717    offset = lmem_map - mem_map;
43718    for (j = 0; j < MAX_NR_ZONES; j++) {
43719      zone_t *zone = pgdat->node_zones + j;
```

```
43720    unsigned long mask;
43721    unsigned long size, realsize;
43722
43723    realsize = size = zones_size[j];
43724    if (zholes_size)
43725      realsize -= zholes_size[j];
43726
43727    printk("zone(%lu): %lu pages.\n", j, size);
43728    zone->size = size;
43729    zone->name = zone_names[j];
43730    zone->lock = SPIN_LOCK_UNLOCKED;
43731    zone->zone_pgdat = pgdat;
43732    zone->free_pages = 0;
43733    zone->inactive_clean_pages = 0;
43734    zone->inactive_dirty_pages = 0;
43735    memlist_init(&zone->inactive_clean_list);
43736    if (!size)
43737      continue;
43738
43739    zone->offset = offset;
43740    cumulative += size;
43741    mask = (realsize / zone_balance_ratio[j]);
43742    if (mask < zone_balance_min[j])
43743      mask = zone_balance_min[j];
43744    else if (mask > zone_balance_max[j])
43745      mask = zone_balance_max[j];
43746    zone->pages_min = mask;
43747    zone->pages_low = mask * 2;
43748    zone->pages_high = mask * 3;
43749    /* Add these free targets to the global free target;
43750     * we have to be SURE that freepages.high is higher
43751     * than SUM [zone->pages_min] for all zones,
43752     * otherwise we may have bad bad problems.
43753     *
43754     * This means we cannot make the freepages array
43755     * writable in /proc, but have to add a separate
43756     * extra_free_target for people who require it to
43757     * catch load spikes in eg. gigabit ethernet
43758     * routing... */
43759    freepages.min += mask;
43760    freepages.low += mask * 2;
43761    freepages.high += mask * 3;
43762    zone->zone_mem_map = mem_map + offset;
43763    zone->zone_start_mapnr = offset;
43764    zone->zone_start_paddr = zone_start_paddr;
43765
43766    for (i = 0; i < size; i++) {
43767      struct page *page = mem_map + offset + i;
43768      page->zone = zone;
43769      if (j != ZONE_HIGHMEM) {
43770        page->virtual = __va(zone_start_paddr);
43771        zone_start_paddr += PAGE_SIZE;
43772      }
43773    }
43774
43775    offset += size;
43776    mask = -1;
43777    for (i = 0; i < MAX_ORDER; i++) {
43778      unsigned long bitmap_size;
43779
43780      memlist_init(&zone->free_area[i].free_list);
43781      mask += mask;
43782      size = (size + ~mask) & mask;
43783      bitmap_size = size >> i;
43784      bitmap_size = (bitmap_size + 7) >> 3;
43785      bitmap_size = LONG_ALIGN(bitmap_size);
43786      zone->free_area[i].map = (unsigned int *)
43787        alloc_bootmem_node(pgdat, bitmap_size);
43788    }
43789  }
43790  build_zonelists(pgdat);
43791 }
43792
43793 void __init free_area_init(unsigned long *zones_size)
43794 {
43795   free_area_init_core(0, &contig_page_data, &mem_map,
43796       zones_size, 0, 0, 0);
43797 }
43798
43799 static int __init setup_mem_frac(char *str)
43800 {
43801   int j = 0;
43802
43803   while (get_option(&str,
43804           &zone_balance_ratio[j++]) == 2) ;
43805   printk("setup_mem_frac: ");
43806   for (j = 0; j < MAX_NR_ZONES; j++)
43807     printk("%d  ", zone_balance_ratio[j]);
43808   printk("\n");
43809   return 1;
43810 }
43811
43812 __setup("memfrac=", setup_mem_frac);
```

mm/page_io.c

```
43813  /*
43814   *  linux/mm/page_io.c
43815   *
43816   *  Copyright (C) 1991, 1992, 1993, 1994  Linus Torvalds
43817   *
43818   *  Swap reorganised 29.12.95,
43819   *  Asynchronous swapping added 30.12.95. Stephen Tweedie
43820   *  Removed race in async swapping. 14.4.1996. Bruno
43821   *  Haible
43822   *  Add swap of shared pages through the page
43823   *  cache. 20.2.1998. Stephen Tweedie
43824   *  Always use brw_page, life becomes simpler. 12 May
43825   *  1998 Eric Biederman
43826   */
43827
43828  #include <linux/mm.h>
43829  #include <linux/kernel_stat.h>
43830  #include <linux/swap.h>
43831  #include <linux/locks.h>
43832  #include <linux/swapctl.h>
43833
43834  #include <asm/pgtable.h>
43835
43836  /* Reads or writes a swap page.
43837   * wait=1: start I/O and wait for completion. wait=0:
43838   * start asynchronous I/O.
43839   * Important prevention of race condition: the caller
43840   * *must* atomically create a unique swap cache entry for
43841   * this swap page before calling rw_swap_page, and must
43842   * lock that page.  By ensuring that there is a single
43843   * page of memory reserved for the swap entry, the normal
43844   * VM page lock on that page also doubles as a lock on
43845   * swap entries.  Having only one lock to deal with per
43846   * swap entry (rather than locking swap and memory
43847   * independently) also makes it easier to make certain
43848   * swapping operations atomic, which is particularly
43849   * important when we are trying to ensure that shared
43850   * pages stay shared while being swapped.  */
43851  static int rw_swap_page_base(int rw, swp_entry_t entry,
43852      struct page *page, int wait)
43853  {
43854    unsigned long offset;
43855    int zones[PAGE_SIZE / 512];
43856    int zones_used;
43857    kdev_t dev = 0;
43858    int block_size;
```

```
43859    struct inode *swapf = 0;
43860
43861    /* Don't allow too many pending pages in flight.. */
43862    if ((rw == WRITE) && atomic_read(&nr_async_pages) >
43863        pager_daemon.swap_cluster * (1 << page_cluster))
43864      wait = 1;
43865
43866    if (rw == READ) {
43867      ClearPageUptodate(page);
43868      kstat.pswpin++;
43869    } else
43870      kstat.pswpout++;
43871
43872    get_swaphandle_info(entry, &offset, &dev, &swapf);
43873    if (dev) {
43874      zones[0] = offset;
43875      zones_used = 1;
43876      block_size = PAGE_SIZE;
43877    } else if (swapf) {
43878      int i, j;
43879      unsigned int block = offset
43880          << (PAGE_SHIFT - swapf->i_sb->s_blocksize_bits);
43881
43882      block_size = swapf->i_sb->s_blocksize;
43883      for (i = 0, j = 0; j < PAGE_SIZE;
43884          i++, j += block_size)
43885        if (!(zones[i] = bmap(swapf, block++))) {
43886          printk("rw_swap_page: bad swap file\n");
43887          return 0;
43888        }
43889      zones_used = i;
43890      dev = swapf->i_dev;
43891    } else {
43892      return 0;
43893    }
43894    if (!wait) {
43895      SetPageDecrAfter(page);
43896      atomic_inc(&nr_async_pages);
43897    }
43898
43899    /* block_size == PAGE_SIZE/zones_used */
43900    brw_page(rw, page, dev, zones, block_size);
43901
43902    /* Note! For consistency we do all of the logic,
43903     * decrementing the page count, and unlocking the page
43904     * in the swap lock map - in the IO completion
43905     * handler. */
```

```
43906    if (!wait)
43907      return 1;
43908
43909    wait_on_page(page);
43910    /* This shouldn't happen, but check to be sure. */
43911    if (page_count(page) == 0)
43912      printk(KERN_ERR
43913            "rw_swap_page: page unused while waiting!\n");
43914
43915    return 1;
43916  }
43917
43918  /* A simple wrapper so the base function doesn't need to
43919   * enforce that all swap pages go through the swap cache!
43920   * We verify that:
43921   *  - the page is locked
43922   *  - it's marked as being swap-cache
43923   *  - it's associated with the swap inode */
43924  void rw_swap_page(int rw, struct page *page, int wait)
43925  {
43926    swp_entry_t entry;
43927
43928    entry.val = page->index;
43929
43930    if (!PageLocked(page))
43931      PAGE_BUG(page);
43932    if (!PageSwapCache(page))
43933      PAGE_BUG(page);
43934    if (page->mapping != &swapper_space)
43935      PAGE_BUG(page);
43936    if (!rw_swap_page_base(rw, entry, page, wait))
43937      UnlockPage(page);
43938  }
43939
43940  /* The swap lock map insists that pages be in the page
43941   * cache!  Therefore we can't use it.  Later when we can
43942   * remove the need for the lock map and we can reduce the
43943   * number of functions exported.  */
43944  void rw_swap_page_nolock(int rw, swp_entry_t entry,
43945       char *buf, int wait)
43946  {
43947    struct page *page = virt_to_page(buf);
43948
43949    if (!PageLocked(page))
43950      PAGE_BUG(page);
43951    if (PageSwapCache(page))
43952      PAGE_BUG(page);
```

```
43953    if (page->mapping)
43954      PAGE_BUG(page);
43955    /* needs sync_page to wait I/O completation */
43956    page->mapping = &swapper_space;
43957    if (!rw_swap_page_base(rw, entry, page, wait))
43958      UnlockPage(page);
43959    page->mapping = NULL;
43960  }
```

mm/slab.c

```
43961  /*
43962   * linux/mm/slab.c
43963   * Written by Mark Hemment, 1996/97.
43964   * (markhe@nextd.demon.co.uk)
43965   *
43966   * kmem_cache_destroy() + some cleanup - 1999 Andrea
43967   * Arcangeli
43968   *
43969   * Major cleanup, different bufctl logic, per-cpu arrays
43970   *      (c) 2000 Manfred Spraul
43971   *
43972   * An implementation of the Slab Allocator as described
43973   * in outline in;
43974   *    UNIX Internals: The New Frontiers by Uresh Vahalia
43975   *    Pub: Prentice Hall      ISBN 0-13-101908-2
43976   * or with a little more detail in;
43977   *    The Slab Allocator: An Object-Caching
43978   *                        Kernel Memory Allocator
43979   *    Jeff Bonwick (Sun Microsystems).
43980   *    Presented at: USENIX Summer 1994 Technical
43981   *                  Conference
43982   *
43983   *
43984   * The memory is organized in caches, one cache for each
43985   * object type. (e.g. inode_cache, dentry_cache,
43986   * buffer_head, vm_area_struct) Each cache consists out
43987   * of many slabs (they are small (usually one page long)
43988   * and always contiguous), and each slab contains
43989   * multiple initialized objects.
43990   *
43991   * Each cache can only support one memory type (GFP_DMA,
43992   * GFP_HIGHMEM, normal). If you need a special memory
43993   * type, then must create a new cache for that memory
43994   * type.
43995   *
43996   * In order to reduce fragmentation, the slabs are sorted
43997   * in 3 groups:
```

```
43998  *      full slabs with 0 free objects
43999  *      partial slabs
44000  *      empty slabs with no allocated objects
44001  *
44002  * If partial slabs exist, then new allocations come from
44003  * these slabs, otherwise from empty slabs or new slabs
44004  * are allocated.
44005  *
44006  * kmem_cache_destroy() CAN CRASH if you try to allocate
44007  * from the cache during kmem_cache_destroy(). The caller
44008  * must prevent concurrent allocs.
44009  *
44010  * On SMP systems, each cache has a short per-cpu head
44011  * array, most allocs and frees go into that array, and
44012  * if that array overflows, then 1/2 of the entries in
44013  * the array are given back into the global cache.  This
44014  * reduces the number of spinlock operations.
44015  *
44016  * The c_cpuarray may not be read with enabled local
44017  * interrupts.
44018  *
44019  * SMP synchronization:
44020  *   constructors and destructors are called without any
44021  *     locking.
44022  *   Several members in kmem_cache_t and slab_t never
44023  *   change, they are accessed without any locking.  The
44024  *   per-cpu arrays are never accessed from the wrong cpu,
44025  *   no locking.  The non-constant members are protected
44026  *   with a per-cache irq spinlock.
44027  *
44028  * Further notes from the original documentation:
44029  *
44030  * 11 April '97.  Started multi-threading - markhe
44031  *     The global cache-chain is protected by the
44032  *     semaphore 'cache_chain_sem'.  The sem is only
44033  *     needed when accessing/extending the cache-chain,
44034  *     which can never happen inside an interrupt
44035  *     (kmem_cache_create(), kmem_cache_shrink() and
44036  *     kmem_cache_reap()).
44037  *
44038  *     To prevent kmem_cache_shrink() trying to shrink a
44039  *     'growing' cache (which maybe be sleeping and
44040  *     therefore not holding the semaphore/lock), the
44041  *     growing field is used.  This also prevents
44042  *     reaping from a cache.
44043  *
44044  *     At present, each engine can be growing a cache.
```

```
44045  *      This should be blocked.
44046  */
44047
44048  #include         <linux/config.h>
44049  #include         <linux/slab.h>
44050  #include         <linux/interrupt.h>
44051  #include         <linux/init.h>
44052  #include         <asm/uaccess.h>
44053
44054  /* DEBUG        - 1 for kmem_cache_create() to honour;
44055   *                SLAB_DEBUG_INITIAL, SLAB_RED_ZONE &
44056   *                SLAB_POISON.
44057   *                0 for faster, smaller code (especially
44058   *                in the critical paths).
44059   *
44060   * STATS        - 1 to collect stats for /proc/slabinfo.
44061   *                0 for faster, smaller code (especially
44062   *                in the critical paths).
44063   *
44064   * FORCED_DEBUG - 1 enables SLAB_RED_ZONE and SLAB_POISON
44065   *                (if possible) */
44066
44067  #define DEBUG          0
44068  #define STATS          0
44069  #define FORCED_DEBUG   0
44070
44071  /* Parameters for kmem_cache_reap */
44072  #define REAP_SCANLEN   10
44073  #define REAP_PERFECT   10
44074
44075  /* Shouldn't this be in a header file somewhere? */
44076  #define BYTES_PER_WORD      sizeof(void *)
44077
44078  /* Legal flag mask for kmem_cache_create(). */
44079  #if DEBUG
44080  # define CREATE_MASK                                    \
44081      (SLAB_DEBUG_INITIAL | SLAB_RED_ZONE |               \
44082       SLAB_POISON | SLAB_HWCACHE_ALIGN |                 \
44083       SLAB_NO_REAP | SLAB_CACHE_DMA)
44084  #else
44085  # define CREATE_MASK                                    \
44086      (SLAB_HWCACHE_ALIGN | SLAB_NO_REAP | SLAB_CACHE_DMA)
44087  #endif
44088
44089  /* kmem_bufctl_t:
44090   *
44091   * Bufctl's are used for linking objs within a slab
```

```
44092   * linked offsets.
44093   *
44094   * This implementaion relies on "struct page" for
44095   * locating the cache & slab an object belongs to.  This
44096   * allows the bufctl structure to be small (one int), but
44097   * limits the number of objects a slab (not a cache) can
44098   * contain when off-slab bufctls are used. The limit is
44099   * the size of the largest general cache that does not
44100   * use off-slab slabs.  For 32bit archs with 4 kB pages,
44101   * is this 56.  This is not serious, as it is only for
44102   * large objects, when it is unwise to have too many per
44103   * slab.  Note: This limit can be raised by introducing a
44104   * general cache whose size is less than 512
44105   * (PAGE_SIZE<<3), but greater than 256.  */
44106
44107  #define BUFCTL_END 0xffffFFFF
44108  #define SLAB_LIMIT 0xffffFFFE
44109  typedef unsigned int kmem_bufctl_t;
44110
44111  /* Max number of objs-per-slab for caches which use
44112   * off-slab slabs.  Needed to avoid a possible looping
44113   * condition in kmem_cache_grow(). */
44114  static unsigned long offslab_limit;
44115
44116  /* slab_t
44117   *
44118   * Manages the objs in a slab. Placed either at the
44119   * beginning of mem allocated for a slab, or allocated
44120   * from an general cache.  Slabs are chained into one
44121   * ordered list: fully used, partial, then fully free
44122   * slabs.  */
44123  typedef struct slab_s {
44124    struct list_head list;
44125    unsigned long colouroff;
44126    void *s_mem;                    /* including colour
44127                                     * offset */
44128    unsigned int inuse;             /* num of objs active in
44129                                     * slab */
44130    kmem_bufctl_t free;
44131  } slab_t;
44132
44133  #define slab_bufctl(slabp)                               \
44134          ((kmem_bufctl_t *)(((slab_t*)slabp)+1))
44135
44136  /* cpucache_t
44137   *
44138   * Per cpu structures
44139   * The limit is stored in the per-cpu structure to reduce
44140   * the data cache footprint.  */
44141  typedef struct cpucache_s {
44142    unsigned int avail;
44143    unsigned int limit;
44144  } cpucache_t;
44145
44146  #define cc_entry(cpucache)                               \
44147          ((void **)(((cpucache_t*)cpucache)+1))
44148  #define cc_data(cachep)                                  \
44149          ((cachep)->cpudata[smp_processor_id()])
44150
44151  /* kmem_cache_t
44152   *
44153   * manages a cache.  */
44154
44155  #define CACHE_NAMELEN   20        /* max name length for a
44156                                     * slab cache */
44157
44158  struct kmem_cache_s {
44159    /* 1) each alloc & free */
44160    /* full, partial first, then free */
44161    struct list_head slabs;
44162    struct list_head *firstnotfull;
44163    unsigned int objsize;
44164    unsigned int flags;             /* constant flags */
44165    unsigned int num;               /* # of objs per slab */
44166    spinlock_t spinlock;
44167  #ifdef CONFIG_SMP
44168    unsigned int batchcount;
44169  #endif
44170
44171    /* 2) slab additions /removals */
44172    /* order of pgs per slab (2^n) */
44173    unsigned int gfporder;
44174
44175    /* force GFP flags, e.g. GFP_DMA */
44176    unsigned int gfpflags;
44177
44178    size_t colour;                  /* cache colouring range */
44179    unsigned int colour_off;        /* colour offset */
44180    unsigned int colour_next;       /* cache colouring */
44181    kmem_cache_t *slabp_cache;
44182    unsigned int growing;
44183    unsigned int dflags;            /* dynamic flags */
44184
44185    /* constructor func */
```

```
44186    void (*ctor) (void *, kmem_cache_t *, unsigned long);
44187
44188    /* de-constructor func */
44189    void (*dtor) (void *, kmem_cache_t *, unsigned long);
44190
44191    unsigned long failures;
44192
44193    /* 3) cache creation/removal */
44194    char name[CACHE_NAMELEN];
44195    struct list_head next;
44196 #ifdef CONFIG_SMP
44197    /* 4) per-cpu data */
44198    cpucache_t *cpudata[NR_CPUS];
44199 #endif
44200 #if STATS
44201    unsigned long num_active;
44202    unsigned long num_allocations;
44203    unsigned long high_mark;
44204    unsigned long grown;
44205    unsigned long reaped;
44206    unsigned long errors;
44207 #ifdef CONFIG_SMP
44208    atomic_t allochit;
44209    atomic_t allocmiss;
44210    atomic_t freehit;
44211    atomic_t freemiss;
44212 #endif
44213 #endif
44214 };
44215
44216 /* internal c_flags */
44217 #define CFLGS_OFF_SLAB  0x010000UL  /* slab management in
44218                                     * own cache */
44219 #define CFLGS_OPTIMIZE  0x020000UL /* optimized slab
44220                                     * lookup */
44221
44222 /* c_dflags (dynamic flags). Need to hold the spinlock
44223  * to access this member */
44224 #define DFLGS_GROWN     0x000001UL /* don't reap a
44225                                     * recently grown */
44226
44227 #define OFF_SLAB(x)     ((x)->flags & CFLGS_OFF_SLAB)
44228 #define OPTIMIZE(x)     ((x)->flags & CFLGS_OPTIMIZE)
44229 #define GROWN(x)        ((x)->dlags & DFLGS_GROWN)
44230
44231 #if STATS
44232 #define STATS_INC_ACTIVE(x)     ((x)->num_active++)
```

```
44233 #define STATS_DEC_ACTIVE(x)     ((x)->num_active-)
44234 #define STATS_INC_ALLOCED(x)    ((x)->num_allocations++)
44235 #define STATS_INC_GROWN(x)      ((x)->grown++)
44236 #define STATS_INC_REAPED(x)     ((x)->reaped++)
44237 #define STATS_SET_HIGH(x)                               \
44238 do { if ((x)->num_active > (x)->high_mark)              \
44239    (x)->high_mark = (x)->num_active;                    \
44240 } while (0)
44241 #define STATS_INC_ERR(x)        ((x)->errors++)
44242 #else
44243 #define STATS_INC_ACTIVE(x)     do { } while (0)
44244 #define STATS_DEC_ACTIVE(x)     do { } while (0)
44245 #define STATS_INC_ALLOCED(x)    do { } while (0)
44246 #define STATS_INC_GROWN(x)      do { } while (0)
44247 #define STATS_INC_REAPED(x)     do { } while (0)
44248 #define STATS_SET_HIGH(x)       do { } while (0)
44249 #define STATS_INC_ERR(x)        do { } while (0)
44250 #endif
44251
44252 #if STATS && defined(CONFIG_SMP)
44253 #define STATS_INC_ALLOCHIT(x)   atomic_inc(&(x)->allochit)
44254 #define STATS_INC_ALLOCMISS(x)                          \
44255                         atomic_inc(&(x)->allocmiss)
44256 #define STATS_INC_FREEHIT(x)    atomic_inc(&(x)->freehit)
44257 #define STATS_INC_FREEMISS(x)   atomic_inc(&(x)->freemiss)
44258 #else
44259 #define STATS_INC_ALLOCHIT(x)   do { } while (0)
44260 #define STATS_INC_ALLOCMISS(x)  do { } while (0)
44261 #define STATS_INC_FREEHIT(x)    do { } while (0)
44262 #define STATS_INC_FREEMISS(x)   do { } while (0)
44263 #endif
44264
44265 #if DEBUG
44266 /* Magic nums for obj red zoning. Placed in the first
44267  * word before and the first word after an obj. */
44268 #define RED_MAGIC1      0x5A2CF071UL     /* when obj is
44269                                          * active */
44270 #define RED_MAGIC2      0x170FC2A5UL     /* when obj is
44271                                          * inactive */
44272
44273 /* ...and for poisoning */
44274 #define POISON_BYTE 0x5a  /* byte value for poisoning */
44275 #define POISON_END  0xa5  /* end-byte of poisoning */
44276
44277 #endif
44278
44279 /* maximum size of an obj (in 2^order pages) */
```

```
44280 #define MAX_OBJ_ORDER    5          /* 32 pages */
44281
44282 /* Do not go above this order unless 0 objects fit into
44283  * the slab.  */
44284 #define BREAK_GFP_ORDER_HI    2
44285 #define BREAK_GFP_ORDER_LO    1
44286 static int slab_break_gfp_order = BREAK_GFP_ORDER_LO;
44287
44288 /* Absolute limit for the gfp order */
44289 #define MAX_GFP_ORDER    5          /* 32 pages */
44290
44291
44292 /* Macros for storing/retrieving the cachep and or slab
44293  * from the global 'mem_map'. These are used to find the
44294  * slab an obj belongs to.  With kfree(), these are used
44295  * to find the cache which an obj belongs to. */
44296 #define SET_PAGE_CACHE(pg,x)                              \
44297   ((pg)->list.next = (struct list_head *)(x))
44298 #define GET_PAGE_CACHE(pg)                               \
44299   ((kmem_cache_t *)(pg)->list.next)
44300 #define SET_PAGE_SLAB(pg,x)                              \
44301   ((pg)->list.prev = (struct list_head *)(x))
44302 #define GET_PAGE_SLAB(pg)      ((slab_t *)(pg)->list.prev)
44303
44304 /* Size description struct for general caches. */
44305 typedef struct cache_sizes {
44306   size_t cs_size;
44307   kmem_cache_t *cs_cachep;
44308   kmem_cache_t *cs_dmacachep;
44309 } cache_sizes_t;
44310
44311 static cache_sizes_t cache_sizes[] = {
44312 #if PAGE_SIZE == 4096
44313   { 32,      NULL, NULL },
44314 #endif
44315   { 64,      NULL, NULL },
44316   { 128,     NULL, NULL },
44317   { 256,     NULL, NULL },
44318   { 512,     NULL, NULL },
44319   { 1024,    NULL, NULL },
44320   { 2048,    NULL, NULL },
44321   { 4096,    NULL, NULL },
44322   { 8192,    NULL, NULL },
44323   { 16384,   NULL, NULL },
44324   { 32768,   NULL, NULL },
44325   { 65536,   NULL, NULL },
44326   { 131072,  NULL, NULL },
44327   { 0,       NULL, NULL }
44328 };
44329
44330 /* internal cache of cache description objs */
44331 static kmem_cache_t cache_cache = {
44332   slabs:          LIST_HEAD_INIT(cache_cache.slabs),
44333   firstnotfull:   &cache_cache.slabs,
44334   objsize:        sizeof(kmem_cache_t),
44335   flags:          SLAB_NO_REAP,
44336   spinlock:       SPIN_LOCK_UNLOCKED,
44337   colour_off:     L1_CACHE_BYTES,
44338   name:           "kmem_cache",
44339 };
44340
44341 /* Guard access to the cache-chain. */
44342 static struct semaphore cache_chain_sem;
44343
44344 /* Place maintainer for reaping. */
44345 static kmem_cache_t *clock_searchp = &cache_cache;
44346
44347 #define cache_chain (cache_cache.next)
44348
44349 #ifdef CONFIG_SMP
44350 /* chicken and egg problem: delay the per-cpu array
44351  * allocation until the general caches are up.  */
44352 static int g_cpucache_up;
44353
44354 static void enable_cpucache(kmem_cache_t * cachep);
44355 static void enable_all_cpucaches(void);
44356 #endif
44357
44358 /* Cal the num objs, wastage, and bytes left over for a
44359  * given slab size. */
44360 static void kmem_cache_estimate(unsigned long gfporder,
44361     size_t size, int flags, size_t * left_over,
44362     unsigned int *num)
44363 {
44364   int i;
44365   size_t wastage = PAGE_SIZE << gfporder;
44366   size_t extra = 0;
44367   size_t base = 0;
44368
44369   if (!(flags & CFLGS_OFF_SLAB)) {
44370     base = sizeof(slab_t);
44371     extra = sizeof(kmem_bufctl_t);
44372   }
44373   i = 0;
```

p 644

```
44374     while (i * size + L1_CACHE_ALIGN(base + i * extra) <=
44375           wastage)
44376       i++;
44377     if (i > 0)
44378       i--;
44379
44380     if (i > SLAB_LIMIT)
44381       i = SLAB_LIMIT;
44382
44383     *num = i;
44384     wastage -= i * size;
44385     wastage -= L1_CACHE_ALIGN(base + i * extra);
44386     *left_over = wastage;
44387 }
44388
44389 /* Initialisation - setup the 'cache' cache. */
44390 void __init kmem_cache_init(void)
44391 {
44392   size_t left_over;
44393
44394   init_MUTEX(&cache_chain_sem);
44395   INIT_LIST_HEAD(&cache_chain);
44396
44397   kmem_cache_estimate(0, cache_cache.objsize, 0,
44398     &left_over, &cache_cache.num);
44399   if (!cache_cache.num)
44400     BUG();
44401
44402   cache_cache.colour =
44403     left_over / cache_cache.colour_off;
44404   cache_cache.colour_next = 0;
44405 }
44406
44407
44408 /* Initialisation - setup remaining internal and general
44409  * caches.  Called after the gfp() functions have been
44410  * enabled, and before smp_init(). */
44411 void __init kmem_cache_sizes_init(void)
44412 {
44413   cache_sizes_t *sizes = cache_sizes;
44414   char name[20];
44415   /* Fragmentation resistance on low memory - only use
44416    * bigger page orders on machines with more than 32MB
44417    * of memory.  */
44418   if (num_physpages > (32 << 20) >> PAGE_SHIFT)
44419     slab_break_gfp_order = BREAK_GFP_ORDER_HI;
44420   do {
```

```
44421     /* For performance, all the general caches are L1
44422      * aligned.  This should be particularly beneficial
44423      * on SMP boxes, as it eliminates "false sharing".
44424      *
44425      * Note for systems short on memory removing the
44426      * alignment will allow tighter packing of the
44427      * smaller caches. */
44428     sprintf(name, "size-%Zd", sizes->cs_size);
44429     if (!(sizes->cs_cachep =
44430         kmem_cache_create(name, sizes->cs_size,
44431                 0, SLAB_HWCACHE_ALIGN,
44432                 NULL, NULL))) {
44433       BUG();
44434     }
44435
44436     /* Inc off-slab bufctl limit until the ceiling is
44437      * hit. */
44438     if (!(OFF_SLAB(sizes->cs_cachep))) {
44439       offslab_limit = sizes->cs_size - sizeof(slab_t);
44440       offslab_limit /= 2;
44441     }
44442     sprintf(name, "size-%Zd(DMA)", sizes->cs_size);
44443     sizes->cs_dmacachep =
44444         kmem_cache_create(name, sizes->cs_size, 0,
44445                 SLAB_CACHE_DMA |
44446                 SLAB_HWCACHE_ALIGN,
44447                 NULL, NULL);
44448     if (!sizes->cs_dmacachep)
44449       BUG();
44450     sizes++;
44451   } while (sizes->cs_size);
44452 }
44453
44454 int __init kmem_cpucache_init(void)
44455 {
44456 #ifdef CONFIG_SMP
44457   g_cpucache_up = 1;
44458   enable_all_cpucaches();
44459 #endif
44460   return 0;
44461 }
44462
44463 __initcall(kmem_cpucache_init);
44464
44465 /* Interface to system's page allocator. No need to hold
44466  * the cache-lock. */
44467 static inline void *kmem_getpages(kmem_cache_t * cachep,
```

```
44468    unsigned long flags)
44469 {
44470   void *addr;
44471
44472   /* If we requested dmaable memory, we will get it. Even
44473    * if we did not request dmaable memory, we might get
44474    * it, but that would be relatively rare and
44475    * ignorable. */
44476   flags |= cachep->gfpflags;
44477   addr =
44478       (void *) __get_free_pages(flags, cachep->gfporder);
44479   /* Assume that now we have the pages no one else can
44480    * legally messes with the 'struct page's.  However
44481    * vm_scan() might try to test the structure to see if
44482    * it is a named-page or buffer-page.  The members it
44483    * tests are of no interest here..... */
44484   return addr;
44485 }
44486
44487 /* Interface to system's page release. */
44488 static inline void kmem_freepages(kmem_cache_t * cachep,
44489     void *addr)
44490 {
44491   unsigned long i = (1 << cachep->gfporder);
44492   struct page *page = virt_to_page(addr);
44493
44494   /* free_pages() does not clear the type bit - we do
44495    * that.  The pages have been unlinked from their
44496    * cache-slab, but their 'struct page's might be
44497    * accessed in vm_scan(). Shouldn't be a worry. */
44498   while (i--) {
44499     PageClearSlab(page);
44500     page++;
44501   }
44502   free_pages((unsigned long) addr, cachep->gfporder);
44503 }
44504
44505 #if DEBUG
44506 static inline void kmem_poison_obj(kmem_cache_t * cachep,
44507     void *addr)
44508 {
44509   int size = cachep->objsize;
44510   if (cachep->flags & SLAB_RED_ZONE) {
44511     addr += BYTES_PER_WORD;
44512     size -= 2 * BYTES_PER_WORD;
44513   }
44514   memset(addr, POISON_BYTE, size);
```

```
44515    *(unsigned char *) (addr + size - 1) = POISON_END;
44516 }
44517
44518 static inline int kmem_check_poison_obj(
44519    kmem_cache_t * cachep, void *addr)
44520 {
44521   int size = cachep->objsize;
44522   void *end;
44523   if (cachep->flags & SLAB_RED_ZONE) {
44524     addr += BYTES_PER_WORD;
44525     size -= 2 * BYTES_PER_WORD;
44526   }
44527   end = memchr(addr, POISON_END, size);
44528   if (end != (addr + size - 1))
44529     return 1;
44530   return 0;
44531 }
44532 #endif
44533
44534 /* Destroy all the objs in a slab, and release the mem
44535  * back to the system.  Before calling the slab must have
44536  * been unlinked from the cache.  The cache-lock is not
44537  * held/needed. */
44538 static void kmem_slab_destroy(kmem_cache_t * cachep,
44539     slab_t * slabp)
44540 {
44541   if (cachep->dtor
44542 #if DEBUG
44543       || cachep->flags & (SLAB_POISON | SLAB_RED_ZONE)
44544 #endif
44545       ) {
44546     int i;
44547     for (i = 0; i < cachep->num; i++) {
44548       void *objp = slabp->s_mem + cachep->objsize * i;
44549 #if DEBUG
44550       if (cachep->flags & SLAB_RED_ZONE) {
44551         if (*((unsigned long *) (objp)) != RED_MAGIC1)
44552           BUG();
44553         if (*((unsigned long *) (objp + cachep->objsize
44554                 - BYTES_PER_WORD)) != RED_MAGIC1)
44555           BUG();
44556         objp += BYTES_PER_WORD;
44557       }
44558 #endif
44559       if (cachep->dtor)
44560         (cachep->dtor) (objp, cachep, 0);
44561 #if DEBUG
```

p 651

```
44562          if (cachep->flags & SLAB_RED_ZONE) {
44563              objp -= BYTES_PER_WORD;
44564          }
44565          if ((cachep->flags & SLAB_POISON) &&
44566              kmem_check_poison_obj(cachep, objp))
44567              BUG();
44568 #endif
44569      }
44570    }
44571
44572    kmem_freepages(cachep,
44573                  slabp->s_mem - slabp->colouroff);
44574    if (OFF_SLAB(cachep))
44575      kmem_cache_free(cachep->slabp_cache, slabp);
44576 }
44577
44578 /**
44579  * kmem_cache_create - Create a cache.
44580  * @name: A string which is used in /proc/slabinfo to
44581  * identify this cache.
44582  * @size: The size of objects to be created in this
44583  * cache.
44584  * @offset: The offset to use within the page.
44585  * @flags: SLAB flags
44586  * @ctor: A constructor for the objects.
44587  * @dtor: A destructor for the objects.
44588  *
44589  * Returns a ptr to the cache on success, NULL on
44590  * failure.  Cannot be called within a int, but can be
44591  * interrupted.  The @ctor is run when new pages are
44592  * allocated by the cache and the @dtor is run before the
44593  * pages are handed back.  The flags are
44594  *
44595  * %SLAB_POISON - Poison the slab with a known test
44596  * pattern (a5a5a5a5) to catch references to
44597  * uninitialised memory.
44598  *
44599  * %SLAB_RED_ZONE - Insert 'Red' zones around the
44600  * allocated memory to check for buffer overruns.
44601  *
44602  * %SLAB_NO_REAP - Don't automatically reap this cache
44603  * when we're under memory pressure.
44604  *
44605  * %SLAB_HWCACHE_ALIGN - Align the objects in this cache
44606  * to a hardware cacheline.  This can be beneficial if
44607  * you're counting cycles as closely as davem.  */
44608 kmem_cache_t *kmem_cache_create(const char *name,
```

p 644

```
44609          size_t size, size_t offset, unsigned long flags,
44610          void (*ctor) (void *, kmem_cache_t *, unsigned long),
44611          void (*dtor) (void *, kmem_cache_t *, unsigned long))
44612 {
44613    const char *func_nm = KERN_ERR "kmem_create: ";
44614    size_t left_over, align, slab_size;
44615    kmem_cache_t *cachep = NULL;
44616
44617    /* Sanity checks... these are all serious usage bugs.
44618     */
44619    if ((!name) ||
44620        ((strlen(name) >= CACHE_NAMELEN - 1)) ||
44621        in_interrupt() ||
44622        (size < BYTES_PER_WORD) ||
44623        (size > (1 << MAX_OBJ_ORDER) * PAGE_SIZE) ||
44624        (dtor && !ctor) || (offset < 0 || offset > size))
44625      BUG();
44626
44627 #if DEBUG
44628    if ((flags & SLAB_DEBUG_INITIAL) && !ctor) {
44629      /* No constructor, but inital state check requested*/
44630      printk("%sNo con, but init state check requested - "
44631             "%s\n", func_nm, name);
44632      flags &= ~SLAB_DEBUG_INITIAL;
44633    }
44634
44635    if ((flags & SLAB_POISON) && ctor) {
44636      /* request for poisoning, but we can't do that with
44637       * a constructor */
44638      printk("%sPoisoning requested, but con given - %s\n",
44639             func_nm, name);
44640      flags &= ~SLAB_POISON;
44641    }
44642 #if FORCED_DEBUG
44643    if (size < (PAGE_SIZE >> 3))
44644      /* do not red zone large object, causes severe
44645       * fragmentation.  */
44646      flags |= SLAB_RED_ZONE;
44647    if (!ctor)
44648      flags |= SLAB_POISON;
44649 #endif
44650 #endif
44651
44652    /* Always checks flags, a caller might be expecting
44653     * debug support which isn't available.  */
44654    if (flags & ~CREATE_MASK)
44655      BUG();
```

```
44656
44657    /* Get cache's description obj. */
44658    cachep = (kmem_cache_t *)
44659      kmem_cache_alloc(&cache_cache, SLAB_KERNEL);
44660    if (!cachep)
44661      goto opps;
44662    memset(cachep, 0, sizeof(kmem_cache_t));
44663
44664    /* Check that size is in terms of words.  This is
44665     * needed to avoid unaligned accesses for some archs
44666     * when redzoning is used, and makes sure any on-slab
44667     * bufctl's are also correctly aligned. */
44668    if (size & (BYTES_PER_WORD - 1)) {
44669      size += (BYTES_PER_WORD - 1);
44670      size &= ~(BYTES_PER_WORD - 1);
44671      printk("%sForcing size word alignment - %s\n",
44672          func_nm, name);
44673    }
44674 #if DEBUG
44675    if (flags & SLAB_RED_ZONE) {
44676      /* There is no point trying to honour cache alignment
44677       * when redzoning.  */
44678      flags &= ~SLAB_HWCACHE_ALIGN;
44679      size += 2 * BYTES_PER_WORD; /* words for redzone */
44680    }
44681 #endif
44682    align = BYTES_PER_WORD;
44683    if (flags & SLAB_HWCACHE_ALIGN)
44684      align = L1_CACHE_BYTES;
44685
44686    /* Determine if the slab management is 'on' or 'off'
44687     * slab. */
44688    if (size >= (PAGE_SIZE >> 3))
44689      /* Size is large, assume best to place the slab
44690       * management obj off-slab (should allow better
44691       * packing of objs).  */
44692      flags |= CFLGS_OFF_SLAB;
44693
44694    if (flags & SLAB_HWCACHE_ALIGN) {
44695      /* Need to adjust size so that objs are cache
44696       * aligned. */
44697      /* Small obj size, can get at least two per cache
44698       * line. */
44699      /* FIXME: only power of 2 supported, was better */
44700      while (size < align / 2)
44701        align /= 2;
44702      size = (size + align - 1) & (~(align - 1));
44703    }
44704
44705    /* Cal size (in pages) of slabs, and the num of objs
44706     * per slab.  This could be made much more intelligent.
44707     * For now, try to avoid using high page-orders for
44708     * slabs.  When the gfp() funcs are more friendly
44709     * towards high-order requests, this should be
44710     * changed. */
44711    do {
44712      unsigned int break_flag = 0;
44713    cal_wastage:
44714      kmem_cache_estimate(cachep->gfporder, size, flags,
44715                    &left_over, &cachep->num);
44716      if (break_flag)
44717        break;
44718      if (cachep->gfporder >= MAX_GFP_ORDER)
44719        break;
44720      if (!cachep->num)
44721        goto next;
44722      if (flags & CFLGS_OFF_SLAB
44723        && cachep->num > offslab_limit) {
44724        /* Oops, this num of objs will cause problems. */
44725        cachep->gfporder--;
44726        break_flag++;
44727        goto cal_wastage;
44728      }
44729
44730      /* Large num of objs is good, but v. large slabs are
44731       * currently bad for the gfp()s.  */
44732      if (cachep->gfporder >= slab_break_gfp_order)
44733        break;
44734
44735      if ((left_over * 8) <=
44736          (PAGE_SIZE << cachep->gfporder))
44737        break;     /* Acceptable internal fragmentation. */
44738
44739    next:
44740      cachep->gfporder++;
44741    } while (1);
44742
44743    if (!cachep->num) {
44744      printk("kmem_cache_create: couldn't create cache "
44745          "%s.\n", name);
44746      kmem_cache_free(&cache_cache, cachep);
44747      cachep = NULL;
44748      goto opps;
44749    }
```

```
44750    slab_size = L1_CACHE_ALIGN(cachep->num *
44751                               sizeof(kmem_bufctl_t) +
44752                               sizeof(slab_t));
44753
44754    /* If the slab has been placed off-slab, and we have
44755     * enough space then move it on-slab. This is at the
44756     * expense of any extra colouring.  */
44757    if (flags & CFLGS_OFF_SLAB && left_over >= slab_size) {
44758      flags &= ~CFLGS_OFF_SLAB;
44759      left_over -= slab_size;
44760    }
44761
44762    /* Offset must be a multiple of the alignment. */
44763    offset += (align - 1);
44764    offset &= ~(align - 1);
44765    if (!offset)
44766      offset = L1_CACHE_BYTES;
44767    cachep->colour_off = offset;
44768    cachep->colour = left_over / offset;
44769
44770    /* init remaining fields */
44771    if (!cachep->gfporder && !(flags & CFLGS_OFF_SLAB))
44772      flags |= CFLGS_OPTIMIZE;
44773
44774    cachep->flags = flags;
44775    cachep->gfpflags = 0;
44776    if (flags & SLAB_CACHE_DMA)
44777      cachep->gfpflags |= GFP_DMA;
44778    spin_lock_init(&cachep->spinlock);
44779    cachep->objsize = size;
44780    INIT_LIST_HEAD(&cachep->slabs);
44781    cachep->firstnotfull = &cachep->slabs;
44782
44783    if (flags & CFLGS_OFF_SLAB)
44784      cachep->slabp_cache =
44785          kmem_find_general_cachep(slab_size, 0);
44786    cachep->ctor = ctor;
44787    cachep->dtor = dtor;
44788    /* Copy name over so we don't have problems with
44789     * unloaded modules */
44790    strcpy(cachep->name, name);
44791
44792 #ifdef CONFIG_SMP
44793    if (g_cpucache_up)
44794      enable_cpucache(cachep);
44795 #endif
44796    /* Need the semaphore to access the chain. */
44797    down(&cache_chain_sem);
44798    {
44799      struct list_head *p;
44800
44801      list_for_each(p, &cache_chain) {
44802        kmem_cache_t *pc =
44803            list_entry(p, kmem_cache_t, next);
44804
44805        /* The name field is constant - no lock needed. */
44806        if (!strcmp(pc->name, name))
44807          BUG();
44808      }
44809    }
44810
44811    /* There is no reason to lock our new cache before we
44812     * link it in - no one knows about it yet... */
44813    list_add(&cachep->next, &cache_chain);
44814    up(&cache_chain_sem);
44815 opps:
44816    return cachep;
44817 }
44818
44819 /* This check if the kmem_cache_t pointer is chained in
44820  * the cache_cache list. -arca */
44821 static int is_chained_kmem_cache(kmem_cache_t * cachep)
44822 {
44823    struct list_head *p;
44824    int ret = 0;
44825
44826    /* Find the cache in the chain of caches. */
44827    down(&cache_chain_sem);
44828    list_for_each(p, &cache_chain) {
44829      if (p == &cachep->next) {
44830        ret = 1;
44831        break;
44832      }
44833    }
44834    up(&cache_chain_sem);
44835
44836    return ret;
44837 }
44838
44839 #ifdef CONFIG_SMP
44840 /* Waits for all CPUs to execute func().  */
44841 static void
44842 smp_call_function_all_cpus(void (*func) (void *arg),
44843                                         void *arg)
```

```
44844 {
44845   local_irq_disable();
44846   func(arg);
44847   local_irq_enable();
44848
44849   if (smp_call_function(func, arg, 1, 1))
44850     BUG();
44851 }
44852 typedef struct ccupdate_struct_s {
44853   kmem_cache_t *cachep;
44854   cpucache_t *new[NR_CPUS];
44855 } ccupdate_struct_t;
44856
44857 static void do_ccupdate_local(void *info)
44858 {
44859   ccupdate_struct_t *new = (ccupdate_struct_t *) info;
44860   cpucache_t *old = cc_data(new->cachep);
44861
44862   cc_data(new->cachep) = new->new[smp_processor_id()];
44863   new->new[smp_processor_id()] = old;
44864 }
44865
44866 static void free_block(kmem_cache_t * cachep,
44867     void **objpp, int len);
44868
44869 static void drain_cpu_caches(kmem_cache_t * cachep)
44870 {
44871   ccupdate_struct_t new;
44872   int i;
44873
44874   memset(&new.new, 0, sizeof(new.new));
44875
44876   new.cachep = cachep;
44877
44878   down(&cache_chain_sem);
44879   smp_call_function_all_cpus(do_ccupdate_local,
44880       (void *) &new);
44881
44882   for (i = 0; i < smp_num_cpus; i++) {
44883     cpucache_t *ccold = new.new[cpu_logical_map(i)];
44884     if (!ccold || (ccold->avail == 0))
44885       continue;
44886     local_irq_disable();
44887     free_block(cachep, cc_entry(ccold), ccold->avail);
44888     local_irq_enable();
44889     ccold->avail = 0;
44890   }
```

```
44891   smp_call_function_all_cpus(do_ccupdate_local,
44892       (void *) &new);
44893   up(&cache_chain_sem);
44894 }
44895
44896 #else
44897 #define drain_cpu_caches(cachep)        do { } while (0)
44898 #endif
44899
44900 static int __kmem_cache_shrink(kmem_cache_t * cachep)
44901 {
44902   slab_t *slabp;
44903   int ret;
44904
44905   drain_cpu_caches(cachep);
44906
44907   spin_lock_irq(&cachep->spinlock);
44908
44909   /* If the cache is growing, stop shrinking. */
44910   while (!cachep->growing) {
44911     struct list_head *p;
44912
44913     p = cachep->slabs.prev;
44914     if (p == &cachep->slabs)
44915       break;
44916
44917     slabp = list_entry(cachep->slabs.prev, slab_t, list);
44918     if (slabp->inuse)
44919       break;
44920
44921     list_del(&slabp->list);
44922     if (cachep->firstnotfull == &slabp->list)
44923       cachep->firstnotfull = &cachep->slabs;
44924
44925     spin_unlock_irq(&cachep->spinlock);
44926     kmem_slab_destroy(cachep, slabp);
44927     spin_lock_irq(&cachep->spinlock);
44928   }
44929   ret = !list_empty(&cachep->slabs);
44930   spin_unlock_irq(&cachep->spinlock);
44931   return ret;
44932 }
44933
44934 /**
44935  * kmem_cache_shrink - Shrink a cache.
44936  * @cachep: The cache to shrink.
44937  *
```

p 650

```
44938   * Releases as many slabs as possible for a cache.  To
44939   * help debugging, a zero exit status indicates all slabs
44940   * were released.  */
44941 int kmem_cache_shrink(kmem_cache_t * cachep)
44942 {
44943   if (!cachep || in_interrupt()
44944       || !is_chained_kmem_cache(cachep)) BUG();
44945
44946   return __kmem_cache_shrink(cachep);
44947 }
44948
44949 /**
44950  * kmem_cache_destroy - delete a cache
44951  * @cachep: the cache to destroy
44952  *
44953  * Remove a kmem_cache_t object from the slab cache.
44954  * Returns 0 on success.
44955  *
44956  * It is expected this function will be called by a
44957  * module when it is unloaded.  This will remove the
44958  * cache completely, and avoid a duplicate cache being
44959  * allocated each time a module is loaded and unloaded,
44960  * if the module doesn't have persistent in-kernel
44961  * storage across loads and unloads.
44962  *
44963  * The caller must guarantee that noone will allocate
44964  * memory from the cache during the kmem_cache_destroy().
44965  */
44966 int kmem_cache_destroy(kmem_cache_t * cachep)
44967 {
44968   if (!cachep || in_interrupt() || cachep->growing)
44969     BUG();
44970
44971   /* Find the cache in the chain of caches. */
44972   down(&cache_chain_sem);
44973   /* the chain is never empty, cache_cache is never
44974    * destroyed */
44975   if (clock_searchp == cachep)
44976     clock_searchp = list_entry(cachep->next.next,
44977                        kmem_cache_t, next);
44978   list_del(&cachep->next);
44979   up(&cache_chain_sem);
44980
44981   if (__kmem_cache_shrink(cachep)) {
44982     printk(KERN_ERR
44983         "kmem_cache_destroy: "
44984         "Can't free all objects %p\n", cachep);
```

p 650 → line 44966

```
44985     down(&cache_chain_sem);
44986     list_add(&cachep->next, &cache_chain);
44987     up(&cache_chain_sem);
44988     return 1;
44989   }
44990 #ifdef CONFIG_SMP
44991   {
44992     int i;
44993     for (i = 0; i < NR_CPUS; i++)
44994       kfree(cachep->cpudata[i]);
44995   }
44996 #endif
44997   kmem_cache_free(&cache_cache, cachep);
44998
44999   return 0;
45000 }
45001
45002 /* Get the memory for a slab management obj. */
45003 static inline slab_t *kmem_cache_slabmgmt(kmem_cache_t *
45004     cachep, void *objp, int colour_off, int local_flags)
45005 {
45006   slab_t *slabp;
45007
45008   if (OFF_SLAB(cachep)) {
45009     /* Slab management obj is off-slab. */
45010     slabp = kmem_cache_alloc(cachep->slabp_cache,
45011                     local_flags);
45012     if (!slabp)
45013       return NULL;
45014   } else {
45015     /* FIXME: change to slabp = objp if you enable
45016      * OPTIMIZE */
45017     slabp = objp + colour_off;
45018     colour_off += L1_CACHE_ALIGN(cachep->num *
45019                     sizeof(kmem_bufctl_t) +
45020                     sizeof(slab_t));
45021   }
45022   slabp->inuse = 0;
45023   slabp->colouroff = colour_off;
45024   slabp->s_mem = objp + colour_off;
45025
45026   return slabp;
45027 }
45028
45029 static inline void kmem_cache_init_objs(
45030   kmem_cache_t * cachep, slab_t * slabp,
45031   unsigned long ctor_flags)
```

p 649 → line 45029

```
45032 {
45033   int i;
45034
45035   for (i = 0; i < cachep->num; i++) {
45036     void *objp = slabp->s_mem + cachep->objsize * i;
45037 #if DEBUG
45038     if (cachep->flags & SLAB_RED_ZONE) {
45039       *((unsigned long *) (objp)) = RED_MAGIC1;
45040       *((unsigned long *) (objp + cachep->objsize -
45041                     BYTES_PER_WORD)) = RED_MAGIC1;
45042       objp += BYTES_PER_WORD;
45043     }
45044 #endif
45045
45046     /* Constructors are not allowed to allocate memory
45047      * from the same cache which they are a constructor
45048      * for.  Otherwise, deadlock. They must also be
45049      * threaded.  */
45050     if (cachep->ctor)
45051       cachep->ctor(objp, cachep, ctor_flags);
45052 #if DEBUG
45053     if (cachep->flags & SLAB_RED_ZONE)
45054       objp -= BYTES_PER_WORD;
45055     if (cachep->flags & SLAB_POISON)
45056       /* need to poison the objs */
45057       kmem_poison_obj(cachep, objp);
45058     if (cachep->flags & SLAB_RED_ZONE) {
45059       if (*((unsigned long *) (objp)) != RED_MAGIC1)
45060         BUG();
45061       if (*((unsigned long *) (objp + cachep->objsize -
45062                     BYTES_PER_WORD))
45063           != RED_MAGIC1)
45064         BUG();
45065     }
45066 #endif
45067     slab_bufctl(slabp)[i] = i + 1;
45068   }
45069   slab_bufctl(slabp)[i - 1] = BUFCTL_END;
45070   slabp->free = 0;
45071 }
45072
45073 /* Grow (by 1) the number of slabs within a cache.  This
45074  * is called by kmem_cache_alloc() when there are no
45075  * active objs left in a cache.  */
45076 static int kmem_cache_grow(kmem_cache_t * cachep,
45077      int flags)
45078 {
45079   slab_t *slabp;
45080   struct page *page;
45081   void *objp;
45082   size_t offset;
45083   unsigned int i, local_flags;
45084   unsigned long ctor_flags;
45085   unsigned long save_flags;
45086
45087   /* Be lazy and only check for valid flags here, keeping
45088    * it out of the critical path in
45089    * kmem_cache_alloc(). */
45090   if (flags &
45091     ~(SLAB_DMA | SLAB_LEVEL_MASK | SLAB_NO_GROW))
45092     BUG();
45093   if (flags & SLAB_NO_GROW)
45094     return 0;
45095
45096   /* The test for missing atomic flag is performed here,
45097    * rather than the more obvious place, simply to reduce
45098    * the critical path length in kmem_cache_alloc(). If a
45099    * caller is seriously mis-behaving they will
45100    * eventually be caught here (where it matters).  */
45101   if (in_interrupt()
45102       && (flags & SLAB_LEVEL_MASK) != SLAB_ATOMIC)
45103     BUG();
45104
45105   ctor_flags = SLAB_CTOR_CONSTRUCTOR;
45106   local_flags = (flags & SLAB_LEVEL_MASK);
45107   if (local_flags == SLAB_ATOMIC)
45108     /* Not allowed to sleep.  Need to tell a constructor
45109      * about this - it might need to know...  */
45110     ctor_flags |= SLAB_CTOR_ATOMIC;
45111
45112   /* About to mess with non-constant members - lock. */
45113   spin_lock_irqsave(&cachep->spinlock, save_flags);
45114
45115   /* Get colour for the slab, and cal the next value. */
45116   offset = cachep->colour_next;
45117   cachep->colour_next++;
45118   if (cachep->colour_next >= cachep->colour)
45119     cachep->colour_next = 0;
45120   offset *= cachep->colour_off;
45121   cachep->dflags |= DFLGS_GROWN;
45122
45123   cachep->growing++;
45124   spin_unlock_irqrestore(&cachep->spinlock, save_flags);
45125
```

p 648

```
45126    /* A series of memory allocations for a new slab.
45127     * Neither the cache-chain semaphore, or cache-lock,
45128     * are held, but the incrementing c_growing prevents
45129     * this cache from being reaped or shrunk.  Note: The
45130     * cache could be selected in for reaping in
45131     * kmem_cache_reap(), but when the final test is made
45132     * the growing value will be seen. */
45133
45134    /* Get mem for the objs. */
45135    if (!(objp = kmem_getpages(cachep, flags)))
45136      goto failed;
45137
45138    /* Get slab management. */
45139    if (!(slabp = kmem_cache_slabmgmt(cachep, objp, offset,
45140                                       local_flags)))
45141      goto opps1;
45142
45143    /* Nasty!!!!!! I hope this is OK. */
45144    i = 1 << cachep->gfporder;
45145    page = virt_to_page(objp);
45146    do {
45147      SET_PAGE_CACHE(page, cachep);
45148      SET_PAGE_SLAB(page, slabp);
45149      PageSetSlab(page);
45150      page++;
45151    } while (-i);
45152
45153    kmem_cache_init_objs(cachep, slabp, ctor_flags);
45154
45155    spin_lock_irqsave(&cachep->spinlock, save_flags);
45156    cachep->growing-;
45157
45158    /* Make slab active. */
45159    list_add_tail(&slabp->list, &cachep->slabs);
45160    if (cachep->firstnotfull == &cachep->slabs)
45161      cachep->firstnotfull = &slabp->list;
45162    STATS_INC_GROWN(cachep);
45163    cachep->failures = 0;
45164
45165    spin_unlock_irqrestore(&cachep->spinlock, save_flags);
45166    return 1;
45167 opps1:
45168    kmem_freepages(cachep, objp);
45169 failed:
45170    spin_lock_irqsave(&cachep->spinlock, save_flags);
45171    cachep->growing-;
45172    spin_unlock_irqrestore(&cachep->spinlock, save_flags);
45173    return 0;
45174 }
45175
45176 /* Perform extra freeing checks:
45177  * - detect double free
45178  * - detect bad pointers.
45179  * Called with the cache-lock held. */
45180
45181 #if DEBUG
45182 static int kmem_extra_free_checks(kmem_cache_t * cachep,
45183     slab_t * slabp, void *objp)
45184 {
45185    int i;
45186    unsigned int objnr =
45187       (objp - slabp->s_mem) / cachep->objsize;
45188
45189    if (objnr >= cachep->num)
45190      BUG();
45191    if (objp != slabp->s_mem + objnr * cachep->objsize)
45192      BUG();
45193
45194    /* Check slab's freelist to see if this obj is there.*/
45195    for (i = slabp->free; i != BUFCTL_END;
45196        i = slab_bufctl(slabp)[i]) {
45197      if (i == objnr)
45198        BUG();
45199    }
45200    return 0;
45201 }
45202 #endif
45203
45204 static inline
45205 void kmem_cache_alloc_head(kmem_cache_t * cachep,
45206                            int flags)
45207 {
45208 #if DEBUG
45209    if (flags & SLAB_DMA) {
45210      if (!(cachep->gfpflags & GFP_DMA))
45211        BUG();
45212    } else {
45213      if (cachep->gfpflags & GFP_DMA)
45214        BUG();
45215    }
45216 #endif
45217 }
45218
45219 static inline void *
```

```
p 647  45220 kmem_cache_alloc_one_tail(kmem_cache_t * cachep,
        45221                             slab_t * slabp)
        45222 {
        45223   void *objp;
        45224
        45225   STATS_INC_ALLOCED(cachep);
        45226   STATS_INC_ACTIVE(cachep);
        45227   STATS_SET_HIGH(cachep);
        45228
        45229   /* get obj pointer */
        45230   slabp->inuse++;
        45231   objp = slabp->s_mem + slabp->free * cachep->objsize;
        45232   slabp->free = slab_bufctl(slabp)[slabp->free];
        45233
        45234   if (slabp->free == BUFCTL_END)
        45235     /* slab now full: move to next slab for next alloc */
        45236     cachep->firstnotfull = slabp->list.next;
        45237 #if DEBUG
        45238   if (cachep->flags & SLAB_POISON)
        45239     if (kmem_check_poison_obj(cachep, objp))
        45240       BUG();
        45241   if (cachep->flags & SLAB_RED_ZONE) {
        45242     /* Set alloc red-zone, and check old one. */
        45243     if (xchg((unsigned long *) objp, RED_MAGIC2) !=
        45244         RED_MAGIC1)
        45245       BUG();
        45246     if (xchg((unsigned long *) (objp + cachep->objsize -
        45247                             BYTES_PER_WORD),
        45248           RED_MAGIC2)
        45249       != RED_MAGIC1)
        45250       BUG();
        45251     objp += BYTES_PER_WORD;
        45252   }
        45253 #endif
        45254   return objp;
        45255 }
        45256
        45257 /* Returns a ptr to an obj in the given cache.  caller
        45258  * must guarantee synchronization #define for the goto
        45259  * optimization 8-) */
        45260 #define kmem_cache_alloc_one(cachep)                  \
        45261 ({                                                   \
        45262   slab_t  *slabp;                                    \
        45263                                                      \
        45264   /* Get slab alloc is to come from. */              \
        45265   {                                                  \
        45266     struct list_head* p = cachep->firstnotfull;      \
```

```
        45267     if (p == &cachep->slabs)                         \
        45268       goto alloc_new_slab;                           \
        45269     slabp = list_entry(p,slab_t, list);              \
        45270   }                                                  \
        45271   kmem_cache_alloc_one_tail(cachep, slabp);          \
        45272 })
        45273
        45274 #ifdef CONFIG_SMP
        45275 void *kmem_cache_alloc_batch(kmem_cache_t * cachep,
        45276     int flags)
        45277 {
        45278   int batchcount = cachep->batchcount;
        45279   cpucache_t *cc = cc_data(cachep);
        45280
        45281   spin_lock(&cachep->spinlock);
        45282   while (batchcount—) {
        45283     /* Get slab alloc is to come from. */
        45284     struct list_head *p = cachep->firstnotfull;
        45285     slab_t *slabp;
        45286
        45287     if (p == &cachep->slabs)
        45288       break;
        45289     slabp = list_entry(p, slab_t, list);
        45290     cc_entry(cc)[cc->avail++] =
        45291         kmem_cache_alloc_one_tail(cachep, slabp);
        45292   }
        45293   spin_unlock(&cachep->spinlock);
        45294
        45295   if (cc->avail)
        45296     return cc_entry(cc)[—cc->avail];
        45297   return NULL;
        45298 }
        45299 #endif
        45300
p 646  45301 static inline void *__kmem_cache_alloc(kmem_cache_t *
        45302     cachep, int flags)
        45303 {
        45304   unsigned long save_flags;
        45305   void *objp;
        45306
        45307   kmem_cache_alloc_head(cachep, flags);
        45308 try_again:
        45309   local_irq_save(save_flags);
        45310 #ifdef CONFIG_SMP
        45311   {
        45312     cpucache_t *cc = cc_data(cachep);
        45313
```

```
45314      if (cc) {
45315        if (cc->avail) {
45316          STATS_INC_ALLOCHIT(cachep);
45317          objp = cc_entry(cc)[--cc->avail];
45318        } else {
45319          STATS_INC_ALLOCMISS(cachep);
45320          objp = kmem_cache_alloc_batch(cachep, flags);
45321          if (!objp)
45322            goto alloc_new_slab_nolock;
45323        }
45324      } else {
45325        spin_lock(&cachep->spinlock);
45326        objp = kmem_cache_alloc_one(cachep);
45327        spin_unlock(&cachep->spinlock);
45328      }
45329    }
45330 #else
45331    objp = kmem_cache_alloc_one(cachep);
45332 #endif
45333    local_irq_restore(save_flags);
45334    return objp;
45335 alloc_new_slab:
45336 #ifdef CONFIG_SMP
45337    spin_unlock(&cachep->spinlock);
45338 alloc_new_slab_nolock:
45339 #endif
45340    local_irq_restore(save_flags);
45341    if (kmem_cache_grow(cachep, flags))
45342      /* Someone may have stolen our objs.  Doesn't matter,
45343       * we'll just come back here again. */
45344      goto try_again;
45345    return NULL;
45346 }
45347
45348 /* Release an obj back to its cache. If the obj has a
45349  * constructed state, it should be in this state _before_
45350  * it is released.  - caller is responsible for the
45351  * synchronization */
45352
45353 #if DEBUG
45354 # define CHECK_NR(pg)                                        \
45355 do {                                                         \
45356    if (!VALID_PAGE(pg)) {                                     \
45357      printk(KERN_ERR "kfree: out of range ptr %lxh.\n",     \
45358        (unsigned long)objp);                                 \
45359      BUG();                                                  \
45360    }                                                         \
45361 } while (0)
45362 # define CHECK_PAGE(page)                                    \
45363 do {                                                         \
45364    CHECK_NR(page);                                           \
45365    if (!PageSlab(page)) {                                     \
45366      printk(KERN_ERR "kfree: bad ptr %lxh.\n",              \
45367        (unsigned long)objp);                                 \
45368      BUG();                                                  \
45369    }                                                         \
45370 } while (0)
45371
45372 #else
45373 # define CHECK_PAGE(pg) do { } while (0)
45374 #endif
45375
45376 static inline void kmem_cache_free_one(kmem_cache_t *
45377      cachep, void *objp)
45378 {
45379    slab_t *slabp;
45380
45381    CHECK_PAGE(virt_to_page(objp));
45382    /* reduces memory footprint
45383     * if (OPTIMIZE(cachep))
45384     *   slabp = (void*)((unsigned long)objp &
45385     *                   (~(PAGE_SIZE-1)));
45386     * else */
45387    slabp = GET_PAGE_SLAB(virt_to_page(objp));
45388
45389 #if DEBUG
45390    if (cachep->flags & SLAB_DEBUG_INITIAL)
45391      /* Need to call the slab's constructor so the caller
45392       * can perform a verify of its state (debugging).
45393       * Called without the cache-lock held. */
45394      cachep->ctor(objp, cachep,
45395          SLAB_CTOR_CONSTRUCTOR | SLAB_CTOR_VERIFY);
45396
45397    if (cachep->flags & SLAB_RED_ZONE) {
45398      objp -= BYTES_PER_WORD;
45399      if (xchg((unsigned long *) objp,
45400            RED_MAGIC1) != RED_MAGIC2)
45401        /* Either write before start, or a double free. */
45402        BUG();
45403      if (xchg((unsigned long *) (objp + cachep->objsize -
45404                                  BYTES_PER_WORD),
45405            RED_MAGIC1) != RED_MAGIC2)
45406        /* Either write past end, or a double free. */
45407        BUG();
```

p 649

```
45408   }
45409   if (cachep->flags & SLAB_POISON)
45410     kmem_poison_obj(cachep, objp);
45411   if (kmem_extra_free_checks(cachep, slabp, objp))
45412     return;
45413 #endif
45414   {
45415     unsigned int objnr =
45416       (objp - slabp->s_mem) / cachep->objsize;
45417
45418     slab_bufctl(slabp)[objnr] = slabp->free;
45419     slabp->free = objnr;
45420   }
45421   STATS_DEC_ACTIVE(cachep);
45422
45423   /* fixup slab chain */
45424   if (slabp->inuse-- == cachep->num)
45425     goto moveslab_partial;
45426   if (!slabp->inuse)
45427     goto moveslab_free;
45428   return;
45429
45430 moveslab_partial:
45431   /* was full. Even if the page is now empty, we can set
45432    * c_firstnotfull to slabp: there are no partial slabs
45433    * in this case */
45434   {
45435     struct list_head *t = cachep->firstnotfull;
45436
45437     cachep->firstnotfull = &slabp->list;
45438     if (slabp->list.next == t)
45439       return;
45440     list_del(&slabp->list);
45441     list_add_tail(&slabp->list, t);
45442     return;
45443   }
45444 moveslab_free:
45445   /* was partial, now empty.  c_firstnotfull might point
45446    * to slabp
45447    * FIXME: optimize */
45448   {
45449     struct list_head *t = cachep->firstnotfull->prev;
45450
45451     list_del(&slabp->list);
45452     list_add_tail(&slabp->list, &cachep->slabs);
45453     if (cachep->firstnotfull == &slabp->list)
45454       cachep->firstnotfull = t->next;
```

```
45455     return;
45456   }
45457 }
45458
45459 #ifdef CONFIG_SMP
45460 static inline void __free_block(kmem_cache_t * cachep,
45461     void **objpp, int len)
45462 {
45463   for (; len > 0; len--, objpp++)
45464     kmem_cache_free_one(cachep, *objpp);
45465 }
45466
45467 static void free_block(kmem_cache_t * cachep,
45468     void **objpp, int len)
45469 {
45470   spin_lock(&cachep->spinlock);
45471   __free_block(cachep, objpp, len);
45472   spin_unlock(&cachep->spinlock);
45473 }
45474
45475 #endif
45476
45477 /* __kmem_cache_free
45478  * called with disabled ints */
45479 static inline void __kmem_cache_free(
45480   kmem_cache_t * cachep, void *objp)
45481 {
45482 #ifdef CONFIG_SMP
45483   cpucache_t *cc = cc_data(cachep);
45484
45485   CHECK_PAGE(virt_to_page(objp));
45486   if (cc) {
45487     int batchcount;
45488     if (cc->avail < cc->limit) {
45489       STATS_INC_FREEHIT(cachep);
45490       cc_entry(cc)[cc->avail++] = objp;
45491       return;
45492     }
45493     STATS_INC_FREEMISS(cachep);
45494     batchcount = cachep->batchcount;
45495     cc->avail -= batchcount;
45496     free_block(cachep,
45497         &cc_entry(cc)[cc->avail], batchcount);
45498     cc_entry(cc)[cc->avail++] = objp;
45499     return;
45500   } else {
45501     free_block(cachep, &objp, 1);
```

p 649

```
45502   }
45503 #else
45504   kmem_cache_free_one(cachep, objp);
45505 #endif
45506 }
45507
45508 /**
45509  * kmem_cache_alloc - Allocate an object
45510  * @cachep: The cache to allocate from.
45511  * @flags: See kmalloc().
45512  *
45513  * Allocate an object from this cache.  The flags are
45514  * only relevant if the cache has no available objects.
45515  */
45516 void *kmem_cache_alloc(kmem_cache_t * cachep, int flags)
45517 {
45518   return __kmem_cache_alloc(cachep, flags);
45519 }
45520
45521 /**
45522  * kmalloc - allocate memory
45523  * @size: how many bytes of memory are required.
45524  * @flags: the type of memory to allocate.
45525  *
45526  * kmalloc is the normal method of allocating memory
45527  * in the kernel.  The @flags argument may be one of:
45528  *
45529  * %GFP_BUFFER - XXX
45530  *
45531  * %GFP_ATOMIC - allocation will not sleep.  Use inside
45532  * interrupt handlers.
45533  *
45534  * %GFP_USER - allocate memory on behalf of user.  May
45535  * sleep.
45536  *
45537  * %GFP_KERNEL - allocate normal kernel ram.  May sleep.
45538  *
45539  * %GFP_NFS - has a slightly lower probability of
45540  * sleeping than %GFP_KERNEL.  Don't use unless you're in
45541  * the NFS code.
45542  *
45543  * %GFP_KSWAPD - Don't use unless you're modifying
45544  * kswapd.  */
45545 void *kmalloc(size_t size, int flags)
45546 {
45547   cache_sizes_t *csizep = cache_sizes;
45548
45549   for (; csizep->cs_size; csizep++) {
45550     if (size > csizep->cs_size)
45551       continue;
45552     return __kmem_cache_alloc(flags & GFP_DMA
45553                               ? csizep->cs_dmacachep
45554                               : csizep->cs_cachep,
45555                               flags);
45556   }
45557   BUG();                           // too big size
45558   return NULL;
45559 }
45560
45561 /**
45562  * kmem_cache_free - Deallocate an object
45563  * @cachep: The cache the allocation was from.
45564  * @objp: The previously allocated object.
45565  *
45566  * Free an object which was previously allocated from
45567  * this cache.  */
45568 void kmem_cache_free(kmem_cache_t * cachep, void *objp)
45569 {
45570   unsigned long flags;
45571 #if DEBUG
45572   CHECK_PAGE(virt_to_page(objp));
45573   if (cachep != GET_PAGE_CACHE(virt_to_page(objp)))
45574     BUG();
45575 #endif
45576
45577   local_irq_save(flags);
45578   __kmem_cache_free(cachep, objp);
45579   local_irq_restore(flags);
45580 }
45581
45582 /**
45583  * kfree - free previously allocated memory
45584  * @objp: pointer returned by kmalloc.
45585  *
45586  * Don't free memory not originally allocated by
45587  * kmalloc() or you will run into trouble.  */
45588 void kfree(const void *objp)
45589 {
45590   kmem_cache_t *c;
45591   unsigned long flags;
45592
45593   if (!objp)
45594     return;
45595   local_irq_save(flags);
```

```
45596   CHECK_PAGE(virt_to_page(objp));
45597   c = GET_PAGE_CACHE(virt_to_page(objp));
45598   __kmem_cache_free(c, (void *) objp);
45599   local_irq_restore(flags);
45600 }
45601
45602 kmem_cache_t *kmem_find_general_cachep(size_t size,
45603     int gfpflags)
45604 {
45605   cache_sizes_t *csizep = cache_sizes;
45606
45607   /* This function could be moved to the header file, and
45608    * made inline so consumers can quickly determine what
45609    * cache pointer they require. */
45610   for (; csizep->cs_size; csizep++) {
45611     if (size > csizep->cs_size)
45612       continue;
45613     break;
45614   }
45615   return (gfpflags & GFP_DMA)
45616     ? csizep->cs_dmacachep
45617     : csizep->cs_cachep;
45618 }
45619
45620 #ifdef CONFIG_SMP
45621
45622 /* called with cache_chain_sem acquired.  */
45623 static int kmem_tune_cpucache(kmem_cache_t * cachep,
45624     int limit, int batchcount)
45625 {
45626   ccupdate_struct_t new;
45627   int i;
45628
45629   /* These are admin-provided, so we are more graceful.
45630    */
45631   if (limit < 0)
45632     return -EINVAL;
45633   if (batchcount < 0)
45634     return -EINVAL;
45635   if (batchcount > limit)
45636     return -EINVAL;
45637   if (limit != 0 && !batchcount)
45638     return -EINVAL;
45639
45640   memset(&new.new, 0, sizeof(new.new));
45641   if (limit) {
45642     for (i = 0; i < smp_num_cpus; i++) {
```

```
45643       cpucache_t *ccnew;
45644
45645       ccnew = kmalloc(sizeof(void *) * limit +
45646                   sizeof(cpucache_t), GFP_KERNEL);
45647       if (!ccnew)
45648         goto oom;
45649       ccnew->limit = limit;
45650       ccnew->avail = 0;
45651       new.new[cpu_logical_map(i)] = ccnew;
45652     }
45653   }
45654   new.cachep = cachep;
45655   spin_lock_irq(&cachep->spinlock);
45656   cachep->batchcount = batchcount;
45657   spin_unlock_irq(&cachep->spinlock);
45658
45659   smp_call_function_all_cpus(do_ccupdate_local,
45660     (void *) &new);
45661
45662   for (i = 0; i < smp_num_cpus; i++) {
45663     cpucache_t *ccold = new.new[cpu_logical_map(i)];
45664     if (!ccold)
45665       continue;
45666     local_irq_disable();
45667     free_block(cachep, cc_entry(ccold), ccold->avail);
45668     local_irq_enable();
45669     kfree(ccold);
45670   }
45671   return 0;
45672 oom:
45673   for (i--; i >= 0; i--)
45674     kfree(new.new[cpu_logical_map(i)]);
45675   return -ENOMEM;
45676 }
45677
45678 static void enable_cpucache(kmem_cache_t * cachep)
45679 {
45680   int err;
45681   int limit;
45682
45683   /* FIXME: optimize */
45684   if (cachep->objsize > PAGE_SIZE)
45685     return;
45686   if (cachep->objsize > 1024)
45687     limit = 60;
45688   else if (cachep->objsize > 256)
45689     limit = 124;
```

```
45690    else
45691      limit = 252;
45692
45693    err = kmem_tune_cpucache(cachep, limit, limit / 2);
45694    if (err)
45695      printk(KERN_ERR
45696        "enable_cpucache failed for %s, error %d.\n",
45697        cachep->name, -err);
45698  }
45699
45700  static void enable_all_cpucaches(void)
45701  {
45702    struct list_head *p;
45703
45704    down(&cache_chain_sem);
45705
45706    p = &cache_cache.next;
45707    do {
45708      kmem_cache_t *cachep =
45709        list_entry(p, kmem_cache_t, next);
45710
45711      enable_cpucache(cachep);
45712      p = cachep->next.next;
45713    } while (p != &cache_cache.next);
45714
45715    up(&cache_chain_sem);
45716  }
45717  #endif
45718
45719  /**
45720   * kmem_cache_reap - Reclaim memory from caches.
45721   * @gfp_mask: the type of memory required.
45722   *
45723   * Called from do_try_to_free_pages() and __alloc_pages()
45724   */
45725  void kmem_cache_reap(int gfp_mask)
45726  {
45727    slab_t *slabp;
45728    kmem_cache_t *searchp;
45729    kmem_cache_t *best_cachep;
45730    unsigned int best_pages;
45731    unsigned int best_len;
45732    unsigned int scan;
45733
45734    if (gfp_mask & __GFP_WAIT)
45735      down(&cache_chain_sem);
45736    else if (down_trylock(&cache_chain_sem))
```

```
45737      return;
45738
45739    scan = REAP_SCANLEN;
45740    best_len = 0;
45741    best_pages = 0;
45742    best_cachep = NULL;
45743    searchp = clock_searchp;
45744    do {
45745      unsigned int pages;
45746      struct list_head *p;
45747      unsigned int full_free;
45748
45749      /* It's safe to test this without holding the
45750       * cache-lock. */
45751      if (searchp->flags & SLAB_NO_REAP)
45752        goto next;
45753      spin_lock_irq(&searchp->spinlock);
45754      if (searchp->growing)
45755        goto next_unlock;
45756      if (searchp->dflags & DFLGS_GROWN) {
45757        searchp->dflags &= ~DFLGS_GROWN;
45758        goto next_unlock;
45759      }
45760  #ifdef CONFIG_SMP
45761      {
45762        cpucache_t *cc = cc_data(searchp);
45763        if (cc && cc->avail) {
45764          __free_block(searchp, cc_entry(cc), cc->avail);
45765          cc->avail = 0;
45766        }
45767      }
45768  #endif
45769
45770      full_free = 0;
45771      p = searchp->slabs.prev;
45772      while (p != &searchp->slabs) {
45773        slabp = list_entry(p, slab_t, list);
45774        if (slabp->inuse)
45775          break;
45776        full_free++;
45777        p = p->prev;
45778      }
45779
45780      /* Try to avoid slabs with constructors and/or more
45781       * than one page per slab (as it can be difficult to
45782       * get high orders from gfp()).  */
45783      pages = full_free * (1 << searchp->gfporder);
```

```
45784      if (searchp->ctor)
45785        pages = (pages * 4 + 1) / 5;
45786      if (searchp->gfporder)
45787        pages = (pages * 4 + 1) / 5;
45788      if (pages > best_pages) {
45789        best_cachep = searchp;
45790        best_len = full_free;
45791        best_pages = pages;
45792        if (full_free >= REAP_PERFECT) {
45793          clock_searchp = list_entry(searchp->next.next,
45794                                     kmem_cache_t, next);
45795          goto perfect;
45796        }
45797      }
45798  next_unlock:
45799      spin_unlock_irq(&searchp->spinlock);
45800  next:
45801      searchp = list_entry(searchp->next.next,
45802                           kmem_cache_t, next);
45803  } while (—scan && searchp != clock_searchp);
45804
45805  clock_searchp = searchp;
45806
45807  if (!best_cachep)
45808    /* couldn't find anything to reap */
45809    goto out;
45810
45811  spin_lock_irq(&best_cachep->spinlock);
45812 perfect:
45813  /* free only 80% of the free slabs */
45814  best_len = (best_len * 4 + 1) / 5;
45815  for (scan = 0; scan < best_len; scan++) {
45816    struct list_head *p;
45817
45818    if (best_cachep->growing)
45819      break;
45820    p = best_cachep->slabs.prev;
45821    if (p == &best_cachep->slabs)
45822      break;
45823    slabp = list_entry(p, slab_t, list);
45824    if (slabp->inuse)
45825      break;
45826    list_del(&slabp->list);
45827    if (best_cachep->firstnotfull == &slabp->list)
45828      best_cachep->firstnotfull = &best_cachep->slabs;
45829    STATS_INC_REAPED(best_cachep);
45830
45831    /* Safe to drop the lock. The slab is no longer
45832     * linked to the cache. */
45833    spin_unlock_irq(&best_cachep->spinlock);
45834    kmem_slab_destroy(best_cachep, slabp);
45835    spin_lock_irq(&best_cachep->spinlock);
45836  }
45837  spin_unlock_irq(&best_cachep->spinlock);
45838 out:
45839  up(&cache_chain_sem);
45840  return;
45841 }
45842
45843 #ifdef CONFIG_PROC_FS
45844 /* /proc/slabinfo
45845  *      cache-name num-active-objs total-objs
45846  *      obj-size num-active-slabs total-slabs
45847  *      num-pages-per-slab */
45848 #define FIXUP(t)                                         \
45849         do {                                             \
45850                 if (len <= off) {                        \
45851                         off -= len;                      \
45852                         len = 0;                         \
45853                 } else {                                 \
45854                         if (len-off > count)             \
45855                                 goto t;                  \
45856                 }                                        \
45857         } while (0)
45858
45859 static int proc_getdata(char *page, char **start,
45860     off_t off, int count)
45861 {
45862   struct list_head *p;
45863   int len = 0;
45864
45865   /* Output format version, so at least we can change it
45866    * without _too_ many complaints. */
45867   len += sprintf(page + len, "slabinfo - version: 1.1"
45868 #if STATS
45869        " (statistics)"
45870 #endif
45871 #ifdef CONFIG_SMP
45872        " (SMP)"
45873 #endif
45874        "\n");
45875   FIXUP(got_data);
45876
45877   down(&cache_chain_sem);
```

```
45878      p = &cache_cache.next;
45879      do {
45880          kmem_cache_t *cachep;
45881          struct list_head *q;
45882          slab_t *slabp;
45883          unsigned long active_objs;
45884          unsigned long num_objs;
45885          unsigned long active_slabs = 0;
45886          unsigned long num_slabs;
45887          cachep = list_entry(p, kmem_cache_t, next);
45888
45889          spin_lock_irq(&cachep->spinlock);
45890          active_objs = 0;
45891          num_slabs = 0;
45892          list_for_each(q, &cachep->slabs) {
45893            slabp = list_entry(q, slab_t, list);
45894            active_objs += slabp->inuse;
45895            num_objs += cachep->num;
45896            if (slabp->inuse)
45897              active_slabs++;
45898            else
45899              num_slabs++;
45900          }
45901          num_slabs += active_slabs;
45902          num_objs = num_slabs * cachep->num;
45903
45904          len +=
45905              sprintf(page + len,
45906                  "%-17s %6lu %6lu %6u %4lu %4lu %4u",
45907                  cachep->name, active_objs, num_objs,
45908                  cachep->objsize, active_slabs, num_slabs,
45909                  (1 << cachep->gfporder));
45910
45911 #if STATS
45912      {
45913          unsigned long errors = cachep->errors;
45914          unsigned long high = cachep->high_mark;
45915          unsigned long grown = cachep->grown;
45916          unsigned long reaped = cachep->reaped;
45917          unsigned long allocs = cachep->num_allocations;
45918
45919          len +=
45920              sprintf(page + len,
45921                  " : %6lu %7lu %5lu %4lu %4lu",
45922                  high, allocs, grown, reaped, errors);
45923      }
45924 #endif
45925 #ifdef CONFIG_SMP
45926      {
45927          unsigned int batchcount = cachep->batchcount;
45928          unsigned int limit;
45929
45930          if (cc_data(cachep))
45931            limit = cc_data(cachep)->limit;
45932          else
45933            limit = 0;
45934          len += sprintf(page + len, " : %4u %4u",
45935                  limit, batchcount);
45936      }
45937 #endif
45938 #if STATS && defined(CONFIG_SMP)
45939      {
45940          unsigned long allochit =
45941              atomic_read(&cachep->allochit);
45942          unsigned long allocmiss =
45943              atomic_read(&cachep->allocmiss);
45944          unsigned long freehit =
45945              atomic_read(&cachep->freehit);
45946          unsigned long freemiss =
45947              atomic_read(&cachep->freemiss);
45948          len +=
45949              sprintf(page + len, " : %6lu %6lu %6lu %6lu",
45950                  allochit, allocmiss,
45951                  freehit, freemiss);
45952      }
45953 #endif
45954      len += sprintf(page + len, "\n");
45955      spin_unlock_irq(&cachep->spinlock);
45956      FIXUP(got_data_up);
45957      p = cachep->next.next;
45958      } while (p != &cache_cache.next);
45959 got_data_up:
45960      up(&cache_chain_sem);
45961
45962 got_data:
45963      *start = page + off;
45964      return len;
45965 }
45966
45967 /**
45968  * slabinfo_read_proc - generates /proc/slabinfo
45969  * @page: scratch area, one page long
45970  * @start: pointer to the pointer to the output buffer
45971  * @off: offset within /proc/slabinfo the caller is
```

```
45972  *          interested in
45973  * @count: requested len in bytes
45974  * @eof: eof marker
45975  * @data: unused
45976  *
45977  * The contents of the buffer are
45978  * cache-name
45979  * num-active-objs
45980  * total-objs
45981  * object size
45982  * num-active-slabs
45983  * total-slabs
45984  * num-pages-per-slab
45985  * + further values on SMP and with statistics enabled */
45986 int slabinfo_read_proc(char *page, char **start,
45987      off_t off, int count, int *eof, void *data)
45988 {
45989    int len = proc_getdata(page, start, off, count);
45990    len -= (*start - page);
45991    if (len <= count)
45992      *eof = 1;
45993    if (len > count)
45994      len = count;
45995    if (len < 0)
45996      len = 0;
45997    return len;
45998 }
45999
46000 #define MAX_SLABINFO_WRITE 128
46001 /**
46002  * slabinfo_write_proc - SMP tuning for the slab
46003  *                       allocator
46004  * @file: unused
46005  * @buffer: user buffer
46006  * @count: data len
46007  * @data: unused */
46008 int slabinfo_write_proc(struct file *file,
46009      const char *buffer, unsigned long count, void *data)
46010 {
46011 #ifdef CONFIG_SMP
46012    char kbuf[MAX_SLABINFO_WRITE], *tmp;
46013    int limit, batchcount, res;
46014    struct list_head *p;
46015
46016    if (count > MAX_SLABINFO_WRITE)
46017      return -EINVAL;
46018    if (copy_from_user(&kbuf, buffer, count))
```

```
46019      return -EFAULT;
46020
46021    tmp = strchr(kbuf, ' ');
46022    if (!tmp)
46023      return -EINVAL;
46024    *tmp = '\0';
46025    tmp++;
46026    limit = simple_strtol(tmp, &tmp, 10);
46027    while (*tmp == ' ')
46028      tmp++;
46029    batchcount = simple_strtol(tmp, &tmp, 10);
46030
46031    /* Find the cache in the chain of caches. */
46032    down(&cache_chain_sem);
46033    res = -EINVAL;
46034    list_for_each(p, &cache_chain) {
46035      kmem_cache_t *cachep =
46036          list_entry(p, kmem_cache_t, next);
46037
46038      if (!strcmp(cachep->name, kbuf)) {
46039        res =
46040            kmem_tune_cpucache(cachep, limit, batchcount);
46041        break;
46042      }
46043    }
46044    up(&cache_chain_sem);
46045    if (res >= 0)
46046      res = count;
46047    return res;
46048 #else
46049    return -EINVAL;
46050 #endif
46051 }
46052 #endif
```

mm/swap.c

```
46053 /*
46054  *  linux/mm/swap.c
46055  *
46056  *  Copyright (C) 1991, 1992, 1993, 1994  Linus Torvalds
46057  */
46058
46059 /* This file contains the default values for the
46060  * opereation of the Linux VM subsystem. Fine-tuning
46061  * documentation can be found in
46062  * linux/Documentation/sysctl/vm.txt.
46063  * Started 18.12.91
```

```
46064  * Swap aging added 23.2.95, Stephen Tweedie.
46065  * Buffermem limits added 12.3.98, Rik van Riel.
46066  */
46067
46068 #include <linux/mm.h>
46069 #include <linux/kernel_stat.h>
46070 #include <linux/swap.h>
46071 #include <linux/swapctl.h>
46072 #include <linux/pagemap.h>
46073 #include <linux/init.h>
46074
46075 #include <asm/dma.h>
46076 #include <asm/uaccess.h>       /* for copy_to/from_user */
46077 #include <asm/pgtable.h>
46078
46079 /* We identify three levels of free memory.  We never let
46080  * free mem fall below the freepages.min except for
46081  * atomic allocations.  We start background swapping if
46082  * we fall below freepages.high free pages, and we begin
46083  * intensive swapping below freepages.low.
46084  *
46085  * Actual initialization is done in mm/page_alloc.c */
46086 freepages_t freepages = {
46087   0,                         /* freepages.min */
46088   0,                         /* freepages.low */
46089   0                          /* freepages.high */
46090 };
46091
46092 /* How many pages do we try to swap or page in/out
46093  * together? */
46094 int page_cluster;
46095
46096 /* This variable contains the amount of page steals the
46097  * system is doing, averaged over a minute. We use this
46098  * to determine how many inactive pages we should have.
46099  *
46100  * In reclaim_page and __alloc_pages: memory_pressure++
46101  * In __free_pages_ok: memory_pressure-
46102  * In recalculate_vm_stats the value is decayed (once a
46103  * second) */
46104 int memory_pressure;
46105
46106 /* We track the number of pages currently being
46107  * asynchronously swapped out, so that we don't try to
46108  * swap TOO many pages out at once */
46109 atomic_t nr_async_pages = ATOMIC_INIT(0);
46110
46111 buffer_mem_t buffer_mem = {
46112   2,                 /* minimum percent buffer */
46113   10,                /* borrow percent buffer */
46114   60                 /* maximum percent buffer */
46115 };
46116
46117 buffer_mem_t page_cache = {
46118   2,                 /* minimum percent page cache */
46119   15,                /* borrow percent page cache */
46120   75                 /* maximum */
46121 };
46122
46123 pager_daemon_t pager_daemon = {
46124   512,               /* base number for calculating the
46125                       * number of tries */
46126   SWAP_CLUSTER_MAX,  /* minimum number of tries */
46127   8,                 /* do swap I/O in clusters of this
46128                       * size */
46129 };
46130
46131 /**
46132  * age_page_{up,down} - page aging helper functions
46133  * @page - the page we want to age
46134  * @nolock - are we already holding the
46135  *           pagelist_lru_lock?
46136  *
46137  * If the page is on one of the lists (active,
46138  * inactive_dirty or inactive_clean), we will grab the
46139  * pagelist_lru_lock as needed.  If you're already
46140  * holding the lock, call this function with the nolock
46141  * argument non-zero.  */
46142 void age_page_up_nolock(struct page *page)
46143 {
46144   /* We're dealing with an inactive page, move the page
46145    * to the active list.  */
46146   if (!page->age)
46147     activate_page_nolock(page);
46148
46149   /* The actual page aging bit */
46150   page->age += PAGE_AGE_ADV;
46151   if (page->age > PAGE_AGE_MAX)
46152     page->age = PAGE_AGE_MAX;
46153 }
46154
46155 /* We use this (minimal) function in the case where we
46156  * know we can't deactivate the page (yet).  */
46157 void age_page_down_ageonly(struct page *page)
```

```
46158 {
46159   page->age /= 2;
46160 }
46161
46162 void age_page_down_nolock(struct page *page)
46163 {
46164   /* The actual page aging bit */
46165   page->age /= 2;
46166
46167   /* The page is now an old page. Move to the inactive
46168    * list (if possible ... see below).  */
46169   if (!page->age)
46170     deactivate_page_nolock(page);
46171 }
46172
46173 void age_page_up(struct page *page)
46174 {
46175   /* We're dealing with an inactive page, move the page
46176    * to the active list.  */
46177   if (!page->age)
46178     activate_page(page);
46179
46180   /* The actual page aging bit */
46181   page->age += PAGE_AGE_ADV;
46182   if (page->age > PAGE_AGE_MAX)
46183     page->age = PAGE_AGE_MAX;
46184 }
46185
46186 void age_page_down(struct page *page)
46187 {
46188   /* The actual page aging bit */
46189   page->age /= 2;
46190
46191   /* The page is now an old page. Move to the inactive
46192    * list (if possible ... see below).  */
46193   if (!page->age)
46194     deactivate_page(page);
46195 }
46196
46197
46198 /**
46199  * (de)activate_page - move pages from/to active and
46200  *                     inactive lists
46201  * @page: the page we want to move
46202  * @nolock - are we already holding the pagemap_lru_lock?
46203  *
46204  * Deactivate_page will move an active page to the right
```

```
46205  * inactive list, while activate_page will move a page
46206  * back from one of the inactive lists to the active
46207  * list. If called on a page which is not on any of the
46208  * lists, the page is left alone.  */
46209 void deactivate_page_nolock(struct page *page)
46210 {
46211   /* One for the cache, one for the extra reference the
46212    * caller has and (maybe) one for the buffers.
46213    *
46214    * This isn't perfect, but works for just about
46215    * everything.  Besides, as long as we don't move
46216    * unfreeable pages to the inactive_clean list it
46217    * doesn't need to be perfect...  */
46218   int maxcount = (page->buffers ? 3 : 2);
46219   page->age = 0;
46220   ClearPageReferenced(page);
46221
46222   /* Don't touch it if it's not on the active list.
46223    * (some pages aren't on any list at all) */
46224   if (PageActive(page) && page_count(page) <= maxcount
46225       && !page_ramdisk(page)) {
46226     del_page_from_active_list(page);
46227     add_page_to_inactive_dirty_list(page);
46228   }
46229 }
46230
46231 void deactivate_page(struct page *page)
46232 {
46233   spin_lock(&pagemap_lru_lock);
46234   deactivate_page_nolock(page);
46235   spin_unlock(&pagemap_lru_lock);
46236 }
46237
46238 /* Move an inactive page to the active list.  */
46239 void activate_page_nolock(struct page *page)
46240 {
46241   if (PageInactiveDirty(page)) {
46242     del_page_from_inactive_dirty_list(page);
46243     add_page_to_active_list(page);
46244   } else if (PageInactiveClean(page)) {
46245     del_page_from_inactive_clean_list(page);
46246     add_page_to_active_list(page);
46247   } else {
46248     /* The page was not on any list, so we take care not
46249      * to do anything.  */
46250   }
46251
```

```
46252    /* Make sure the page gets a fair chance at staying
46253     * active. */
46254    if (page->age < PAGE_AGE_START)
46255      page->age = PAGE_AGE_START;
46256  }
46257
46258  void activate_page(struct page *page)
46259  {
46260    spin_lock(&pagemap_lru_lock);
46261    activate_page_nolock(page);
46262    spin_unlock(&pagemap_lru_lock);
46263  }
46264
46265  /**
46266   * lru_cache_add: add a page to the page lists
46267   * @page: the page to add */
46268  void lru_cache_add(struct page *page)
46269  {
46270    spin_lock(&pagemap_lru_lock);
46271    if (!PageLocked(page))
46272      BUG();
46273    DEBUG_ADD_PAGE
46274    add_page_to_active_list(page);
46275    /* This should be relatively rare */
46276    if (!page->age)
46277      deactivate_page_nolock(page);
46278    spin_unlock(&pagemap_lru_lock);
46279  }
46280
46281  /**
46282   * __lru_cache_del: remove a page from the page lists
46283   * @page: the page to add
46284   *
46285   * This function is for when the caller already holds
46286   * the pagemap_lru_lock. */
46287  void __lru_cache_del(struct page *page)
46288  {
46289    if (PageActive(page)) {
46290      del_page_from_active_list(page);
46291    } else if (PageInactiveDirty(page)) {
46292      del_page_from_inactive_dirty_list(page);
46293    } else if (PageInactiveClean(page)) {
46294      del_page_from_inactive_clean_list(page);
46295    } else {
46296      printk
46297        ("VM: __lru_cache_del, found unknown page ?!\n");
46298    }
46299    DEBUG_ADD_PAGE
46300  }
46301
46302  /**
46303   * lru_cache_del: remove a page from the page lists
46304   * @page: the page to remove */
46305  void lru_cache_del(struct page *page)
46306  {
46307    if (!PageLocked(page))
46308      BUG();
46309    spin_lock(&pagemap_lru_lock);
46310    __lru_cache_del(page);
46311    spin_unlock(&pagemap_lru_lock);
46312  }
46313
46314  /**
46315   * recalculate_vm_stats - recalculate VM statistics
46316   *
46317   * This function should be called once a second to
46318   * recalculate some useful statistics the VM subsystem
46319   * uses to determine its behaviour.  */
46320  void recalculate_vm_stats(void)
46321  {
46322    /* Substract one second worth of memory_pressure from
46323     * memory_pressure.  */
46324    memory_pressure -= (memory_pressure >> INACTIVE_SHIFT);
46325  }
46326
46327  /* Perform any setup for the swap system */
46328  void __init swap_setup(void)
46329  {
46330    /* Use a smaller cluster for memory <16MB or <32MB */
46331    if (num_physpages < ((16 * 1024 * 1024) >> PAGE_SHIFT))
46332      page_cluster = 2;
46333    else if (num_physpages < ((32 * 1024 * 1024)
46334                               >> PAGE_SHIFT))
46335      page_cluster = 3;
46336    else
46337      page_cluster = 4;
46338  }
```

mm/swapfile.c

```
46339  /*
46340   *  linux/mm/swapfile.c
46341   *
46342   *  Copyright (C) 1991, 1992, 1993, 1994  Linus Torvalds
46343   *  Swap reorganised 29.12.95, Stephen Tweedie
```

```
46344  */
46345
46346 #include <linux/malloc.h>
46347 #include <linux/smp_lock.h>
46348 #include <linux/kernel_stat.h>
46349 #include <linux/swap.h>
46350 #include <linux/swapctl.h>
46351 #include <linux/blkdev.h>        /* for blk_size */
46352 #include <linux/vmalloc.h>
46353 #include <linux/pagemap.h>
46354 #include <linux/shm.h>
46355
46356 #include <asm/pgtable.h>
46357
46358 spinlock_t swaplock = SPIN_LOCK_UNLOCKED;
46359 unsigned int nr_swapfiles;
46360
46361 struct swap_list_t swap_list = { -1, -1 };
46362
46363 struct swap_info_struct swap_info[MAX_SWAPFILES];
46364
46365 #define SWAPFILE_CLUSTER 256
46366
46367 static inline int scan_swap_map(
46368    struct swap_info_struct *si, unsigned short count)
46369 {
46370    unsigned long offset;
46371    /* We try to cluster swap pages by allocating them
46372     * sequentially in swap.  Once we've allocated
46373     * SWAPFILE_CLUSTER pages this way, however, we resort
46374     * to first-free allocation, starting a new cluster.
46375     * This prevents us from scattering swap pages all over
46376     * the entire swap partition, so that we reduce overall
46377     * disk seek times between swap pages.  - sct */
46378    if (si->cluster_nr) {
46379      while (si->cluster_next <= si->highest_bit) {
46380        offset = si->cluster_next++;
46381        if (si->swap_map[offset])
46382          continue;
46383        si->cluster_nr--;
46384        goto got_page;
46385      }
46386    }
46387    si->cluster_nr = SWAPFILE_CLUSTER;
46388
46389    /* try to find an empty (even not aligned) cluster. */
46390    offset = si->lowest_bit;
```

```
46391 check_next_cluster:
46392    if (offset + SWAPFILE_CLUSTER - 1 <= si->highest_bit) {
46393      int nr;
46394      for (nr = offset; nr < offset + SWAPFILE_CLUSTER;
46395          nr++)
46396        if (si->swap_map[nr]) {
46397          offset = nr + 1;
46398          goto check_next_cluster;
46399        }
46400      /* We found a completly empty cluster, so start using
46401       * it. */
46402      goto got_page;
46403    }
46404    /* No luck, so now go finegrined as usual. -Andrea */
46405    for (offset = si->lowest_bit;
46406        offset <= si->highest_bit; offset++) {
46407      if (si->swap_map[offset])
46408        continue;
46409  got_page:
46410      if (offset == si->lowest_bit)
46411        si->lowest_bit++;
46412      if (offset == si->highest_bit)
46413        si->highest_bit--;
46414      si->swap_map[offset] = count;
46415      nr_swap_pages--;
46416      si->cluster_next = offset + 1;
46417      return offset;
46418    }
46419    return 0;
46420 }
46421
46422 swp_entry_t __get_swap_page(unsigned short count)
46423 {
46424    struct swap_info_struct *p;
46425    unsigned long offset;
46426    swp_entry_t entry;
46427    int type, wrapped = 0;
46428
46429    entry.val = 0;                    /* Out of memory */
46430    if (count >= SWAP_MAP_MAX)
46431      goto bad_count;
46432    swap_list_lock();
46433    type = swap_list.next;
46434    if (type < 0)
46435      goto out;
46436    if (nr_swap_pages == 0)
46437      goto out;
```

p 631

```
46438
46439   while (1) {
46440     p = &swap_info[type];
46441     if ((p->flags & SWP_WRITEOK) == SWP_WRITEOK) {
46442       swap_device_lock(p);
46443       offset = scan_swap_map(p, count);
46444       swap_device_unlock(p);
46445       if (offset) {
46446         entry = SWP_ENTRY(type, offset);
46447         type = swap_info[type].next;
46448         if(type < 0 || p->prio != swap_info[type].prio) {
46449           swap_list.next = swap_list.head;
46450         } else {
46451           swap_list.next = type;
46452         }
46453         goto out;
46454       }
46455     }
46456     type = p->next;
46457     if (!wrapped) {
46458       if (type < 0 || p->prio != swap_info[type].prio) {
46459         type = swap_list.head;
46460         wrapped = 1;
46461       }
46462     } else if (type < 0)
46463       goto out;                        /* out of swap space */
46464   }
46465 out:
46466   swap_list_unlock();
46467   return entry;
46468
46469 bad_count:
46470   printk(KERN_ERR
46471     "get_swap_page: bad count %hd from %p\n", count,
46472     __builtin_return_address(0));
46473   goto out;
46474 }
46475
46476
46477 /* Caller has made sure that the swapdevice corresponding
46478  * to entry is still around or has not been recycled.  */
46479 void __swap_free(swp_entry_t entry, unsigned short count)
46480 {
46481   struct swap_info_struct *p;
46482   unsigned long offset, type;
46483
46484   if (!entry.val)
46485     goto out;
46486
46487   type = SWP_TYPE(entry);
46488   if (type >= nr_swapfiles)
46489     goto bad_nofile;
46490   p = &swap_info[type];
46491   if (!(p->flags & SWP_USED))
46492     goto bad_device;
46493   offset = SWP_OFFSET(entry);
46494   if (offset >= p->max)
46495     goto bad_offset;
46496   if (!p->swap_map[offset])
46497     goto bad_free;
46498   swap_list_lock();
46499   if (p->prio > swap_info[swap_list.next].prio)
46500     swap_list.next = type;
46501   swap_device_lock(p);
46502   if (p->swap_map[offset] < SWAP_MAP_MAX) {
46503     if (p->swap_map[offset] < count)
46504       goto bad_count;
46505     if (!(p->swap_map[offset] -= count)) {
46506       if (offset < p->lowest_bit)
46507         p->lowest_bit = offset;
46508       if (offset > p->highest_bit)
46509         p->highest_bit = offset;
46510       nr_swap_pages++;
46511     }
46512   }
46513   swap_device_unlock(p);
46514   swap_list_unlock();
46515 out:
46516   return;
46517
46518 bad_nofile:
46519   printk("swap_free: Trying to free nonexistent "
46520         "swap-page\n");
46521   goto out;
46522 bad_device:
46523   printk("swap_free: Trying to free swap from unused "
46524         "swap-device\n");
46525   goto out;
46526 bad_offset:
46527   printk("swap_free: offset exceeds max\n");
46528   goto out;
46529 bad_free:
46530   printk("VM: Bad swap entry %08lx\n", entry.val);
46531   goto out;
```

p 631

```
46532 bad_count:
46533   swap_device_unlock(p);
46534   swap_list_unlock();
46535   printk(KERN_ERR
46536       "VM: Bad count %hd current count %hd\n", count,
46537       p->swap_map[offset]);
46538   goto out;
46539 }
46540
46541 /* The swap entry has been read in advance, and we return
46542  * 1 to indicate that the page has been used or is no
46543  * longer needed.
46544  *
46545  * Always set the resulting pte to be nowrite (the same
46546  * as COW pages after one process has exited).  We don't
46547  * know just how many PTEs will share this swap entry, so
46548  * be cautious and let do_wp_page work out what to do if
46549  * a write is requested later.  */
46550 static inline void unuse_pte(struct vm_area_struct *vma,
46551     unsigned long address, pte_t * dir,
46552     swp_entry_t entry, struct page *page)
46553 {
46554   pte_t pte = *dir;
46555
46556   if (pte_none(pte))
46557     return;
46558   if (pte_present(pte)) {
46559     /* If this entry is swap-cached, then page must
46560      * already hold the right address for any copies in
46561      * physical memory */
46562     if (pte_page(pte) != page)
46563       return;
46564     /* We will be removing the swap cache in a moment,
46565      * so... */
46566     ptep_mkdirty(dir);
46567     return;
46568   }
46569   if (pte_to_swp_entry(pte).val != entry.val)
46570     return;
46571   set_pte(dir,
46572         pte_mkdirty(mk_pte(page, vma->vm_page_prot)));
46573   swap_free(entry);
46574   get_page(page);
46575   ++vma->vm_mm->rss;
46576 }
46577
46578 static inline void unuse_pmd(struct vm_area_struct *vma,
46579     pmd_t * dir, unsigned long address,
46580     unsigned long size, unsigned long offset,
46581     swp_entry_t entry, struct page *page)
46582 {
46583   pte_t *pte;
46584   unsigned long end;
46585
46586   if (pmd_none(*dir))
46587     return;
46588   if (pmd_bad(*dir)) {
46589     pmd_ERROR(*dir);
46590     pmd_clear(dir);
46591     return;
46592   }
46593   pte = pte_offset(dir, address);
46594   offset += address & PMD_MASK;
46595   address &= ~PMD_MASK;
46596   end = address + size;
46597   if (end > PMD_SIZE)
46598     end = PMD_SIZE;
46599   do {
46600     unuse_pte(vma, offset + address - vma->vm_start, pte,
46601         entry, page);
46602     address += PAGE_SIZE;
46603     pte++;
46604   } while (address && (address < end));
46605 }
46606
46607 static inline void unuse_pgd(struct vm_area_struct *vma,
46608     pgd_t * dir, unsigned long address,
46609     unsigned long size, swp_entry_t entry,
46610     struct page *page)
46611 {
46612   pmd_t *pmd;
46613   unsigned long offset, end;
46614
46615   if (pgd_none(*dir))
46616     return;
46617   if (pgd_bad(*dir)) {
46618     pgd_ERROR(*dir);
46619     pgd_clear(dir);
46620     return;
46621   }
46622   pmd = pmd_offset(dir, address);
46623   offset = address & PGDIR_MASK;
46624   address &= ~PGDIR_MASK;
46625   end = address + size;
```

```
46626     if (end > PGDIR_SIZE)
46627         end = PGDIR_SIZE;
46628     if (address >= end)
46629         BUG();
46630     do {
46631         unuse_pmd(vma, pmd, address, end - address, offset,
46632             entry, page);
46633         address = (address + PMD_SIZE) & PMD_MASK;
46634         pmd++;
46635     } while (address && (address < end));
46636 }
46637
46638 static void unuse_vma(struct vm_area_struct *vma,
46639     pgd_t * pgdir, swp_entry_t entry, struct page *page)
46640 {
46641     unsigned long start = vma->vm_start, end = vma->vm_end;
46642
46643     if (start >= end)
46644         BUG();
46645     do {
46646         unuse_pgd(vma, pgdir, start, end - start, entry,
46647             page);
46648         start = (start + PGDIR_SIZE) & PGDIR_MASK;
46649         pgdir++;
46650     } while (start && (start < end));
46651 }
46652
46653 static void unuse_process(struct mm_struct *mm,
46654     swp_entry_t entry, struct page *page)
46655 {
46656     struct vm_area_struct *vma;
46657
46658     /* Go through process' page directory.  */
46659     if (!mm)
46660         return;
46661     spin_lock(&mm->page_table_lock);
46662     for (vma = mm->mmap; vma; vma = vma->vm_next) {
46663         pgd_t *pgd = pgd_offset(mm, vma->vm_start);
46664         unuse_vma(vma, pgd, entry, page);
46665     }
46666     spin_unlock(&mm->page_table_lock);
46667     return;
46668 }
46669
46670 /* We completely avoid races by reading each swap page in
46671  * advance, and then search for the process using it.
46672  * All the necessary page table adjustments can then be
46673  * made atomically.  */
46674 static int try_to_unuse(unsigned int type)
46675 {
46676     struct swap_info_struct *si = &swap_info[type];
46677     struct task_struct *p;
46678     struct page *page;
46679     swp_entry_t entry;
46680     int i;
46681
46682     while (1) {
46683         /* Find a swap page in use and read it in. */
46684         swap_device_lock(si);
46685         for (i = 1; i < si->max; i++) {
46686             if (si->swap_map[i] > 0
46687                 && si->swap_map[i] != SWAP_MAP_BAD) {
46688                 /* Prevent swaphandle from being completely
46689                  * unused by swap_free while we are trying to
46690                  * read in the page - this prevents warning
46691                  * messages from rw_swap_page_base.  */
46692                 if (si->swap_map[i] != SWAP_MAP_MAX)
46693                     si->swap_map[i]++;
46694                 swap_device_unlock(si);
46695                 goto found_entry;
46696             }
46697         }
46698         swap_device_unlock(si);
46699         break;
46700
46701 found_entry:
46702         entry = SWP_ENTRY(type, i);
46703
46704         /* Get a page for the entry, using the existing swap
46705          * cache page if there is one.  Otherwise, get a
46706          * clean page and read the swap into it. */
46707         page = read_swap_cache(entry);
46708         if (!page) {
46709             swap_free(entry);
46710             return -ENOMEM;
46711         }
46712         if (PageSwapCache(page))
46713             delete_from_swap_cache(page);
46714         read_lock(&tasklist_lock);
46715         for_each_task(p)
46716             unuse_process(p->mm, entry, page);
46717         read_unlock(&tasklist_lock);
46718         shmem_unuse(entry, page);
46719         /* Now get rid of the extra reference to the
```

```
46720      * temporary page we've been using. */
46721     page_cache_release(page);
46722     /* Check for and clear any overflowed swap map
46723      * counts.  */
46724     swap_free(entry);
46725     swap_list_lock();
46726     swap_device_lock(si);
46727     if (si->swap_map[i] > 0) {
46728       if (si->swap_map[i] != SWAP_MAP_MAX)
46729         printk("VM: Undead swap entry %08lx\n",
46730             entry.val);
46731       nr_swap_pages++;
46732       si->swap_map[i] = 0;
46733     }
46734     swap_device_unlock(si);
46735     swap_list_unlock();
46736   }
46737   return 0;
46738 }
46739
46740 asmlinkage long sys_swapoff(const char *specialfile)
46741 {
46742   struct swap_info_struct *p = NULL;
46743   struct nameidata nd;
46744   int i, type, prev;
46745   int err;
46746
46747   if (!capable(CAP_SYS_ADMIN))
46748     return -EPERM;
46749
46750   err = user_path_walk(specialfile, &nd);
46751   if (err)
46752     goto out;
46753
46754   lock_kernel();
46755   prev = -1;
46756   swap_list_lock();
46757   for (type = swap_list.head; type >= 0;
46758       type = swap_info[type].next) {
46759     p = swap_info + type;
46760     if ((p->flags & SWP_WRITEOK) == SWP_WRITEOK) {
46761       if (p->swap_file) {
46762         if (p->swap_file == nd.dentry)
46763           break;
46764       } else {
46765         if (S_ISBLK(nd.dentry->d_inode->i_mode)
46766             && (p->swap_device ==
46767             nd.dentry->d_inode->i_rdev))
46768           break;
46769       }
46770     }
46771     prev = type;
46772   }
46773   err = -EINVAL;
46774   if (type < 0) {
46775     swap_list_unlock();
46776     goto out_dput;
46777   }
46778
46779   if (prev < 0) {
46780     swap_list.head = p->next;
46781   } else {
46782     swap_info[prev].next = p->next;
46783   }
46784   if (type == swap_list.next) {
46785     /* just pick something that's safe... */
46786     swap_list.next = swap_list.head;
46787   }
46788   nr_swap_pages -= p->pages;
46789   swap_list_unlock();
46790   p->flags = SWP_USED;
46791   err = try_to_unuse(type);
46792   if (err) {
46793     /* re-insert swap space back into swap_list */
46794     swap_list_lock();
46795     for (prev = -1, i = swap_list.head; i >= 0;
46796         prev = i, i = swap_info[i].next)
46797       if (p->prio >= swap_info[i].prio)
46798         break;
46799     p->next = i;
46800     if (prev < 0)
46801       swap_list.head = swap_list.next = p - swap_info;
46802     else
46803       swap_info[prev].next = p - swap_info;
46804     nr_swap_pages += p->pages;
46805     swap_list_unlock();
46806     p->flags = SWP_WRITEOK;
46807     goto out_dput;
46808   }
46809   if (p->swap_device)
46810     blkdev_put(nd.dentry->d_inode->i_bdev, BDEV_SWAP);
46811   path_release(&nd);
46812
46813   nd.dentry = p->swap_file;
```

```
46814    p->swap_file = NULL;
46815    nd.mnt = p->swap_vfsmnt;
46816    p->swap_vfsmnt = NULL;
46817    p->swap_device = 0;
46818    vfree(p->swap_map);
46819    p->swap_map = NULL;
46820    p->flags = 0;
46821    err = 0;
46822
46823 out_dput:
46824    unlock_kernel();
46825    path_release(&nd);
46826 out:
46827    return err;
46828 }
46829
46830 int get_swaparea_info(char *buf)
46831 {
46832    char *page = (char *) __get_free_page(GFP_KERNEL);
46833    struct swap_info_struct *ptr = swap_info;
46834    int i, j, len = 0, usedswap;
46835
46836    if (!page)
46837       return -ENOMEM;
46838
46839    len +=
46840       sprintf(buf,
46841          "Filename\t\t\tType\t\tSize\tUsed\tPriority\n");
46842    for (i = 0; i < nr_swapfiles; i++, ptr++) {
46843       if (ptr->flags & SWP_USED) {
46844          char *path = d_path(ptr->swap_file,
46845                             ptr->swap_vfsmnt,
46846                             page, PAGE_SIZE);
46847
46848          len += sprintf(buf + len, "%-31s ", path);
46849
46850          if (!ptr->swap_device)
46851             len += sprintf(buf + len, "file\t\t");
46852          else
46853             len += sprintf(buf + len, "partition\t");
46854
46855          usedswap = 0;
46856          for (j = 0; j < ptr->max; ++j)
46857             switch (ptr->swap_map[j]) {
46858             case SWAP_MAP_BAD:
46859             case 0:
46860                continue;
46861             default:
46862                usedswap++;
46863             }
46864          len +=
46865             sprintf(buf + len, "%d\t%d\t%d\n",
46866                     ptr->pages << (PAGE_SHIFT - 10),
46867                     usedswap << (PAGE_SHIFT - 10),
46868                     ptr->prio);
46869       }
46870    }
46871    free_page((unsigned long) page);
46872    return len;
46873 }
46874
46875 int is_swap_partition(kdev_t dev)
46876 {
46877    struct swap_info_struct *ptr = swap_info;
46878    int i;
46879
46880    for (i = 0; i < nr_swapfiles; i++, ptr++) {
46881       if (ptr->flags & SWP_USED)
46882          if (ptr->swap_device == dev)
46883             return 1;
46884    }
46885    return 0;
46886 }
46887
46888 /* Written 01/25/92 by Simmule Turner, heavily changed by
46889  * Linus.
46890  *
46891  * The swapon system call */
46892 asmlinkage long sys_swapon(const char *specialfile,
46893    int swap_flags)
46894 {
46895    struct swap_info_struct *p;
46896    struct nameidata nd;
46897    struct inode *swap_inode;
46898    unsigned int type;
46899    int i, j, prev;
46900    int error;
46901    static int least_priority = 0;
46902    union swap_header *swap_header = 0;
46903    int swap_header_version;
46904    int nr_good_pages = 0;
46905    unsigned long maxpages;
46906    int swapfilesize;
46907    struct block_device *bdev = NULL;
```

p 632

```
46908
46909    if (!capable(CAP_SYS_ADMIN))
46910      return -EPERM;
46911    lock_kernel();
46912    p = swap_info;
46913    for (type = 0; type < nr_swapfiles; type++, p++)
46914      if (!(p->flags & SWP_USED))
46915        break;
46916    error = -EPERM;
46917    if (type >= MAX_SWAPFILES)
46918      goto out;
46919    if (type >= nr_swapfiles)
46920      nr_swapfiles = type + 1;
46921    p->flags = SWP_USED;
46922    p->swap_file = NULL;
46923    p->swap_vfsmnt = NULL;
46924    p->swap_device = 0;
46925    p->swap_map = NULL;
46926    p->lowest_bit = 0;
46927    p->highest_bit = 0;
46928    p->cluster_nr = 0;
46929    p->sdev_lock = SPIN_LOCK_UNLOCKED;
46930    p->max = 1;
46931    p->next = -1;
46932    if (swap_flags & SWAP_FLAG_PREFER) {
46933      p->prio = (swap_flags & SWAP_FLAG_PRIO_MASK) >>
46934        SWAP_FLAG_PRIO_SHIFT;
46935    } else {
46936      p->prio = -least_priority;
46937    }
46938    error = user_path_walk(specialfile, &nd);
46939    if (error)
46940      goto bad_swap_2;
46941
46942    p->swap_file = nd.dentry;
46943    p->swap_vfsmnt = nd.mnt;
46944    swap_inode = nd.dentry->d_inode;
46945    error = -EINVAL;
46946
46947    if (S_ISBLK(swap_inode->i_mode)) {
46948      kdev_t dev = swap_inode->i_rdev;
46949      struct block_device_operations *bdops;
46950
46951      p->swap_device = dev;
46952      set_blocksize(dev, PAGE_SIZE);
46953
46954      bdev = swap_inode->i_bdev;
```

```
46955      bdops = devfs_get_ops(devfs_get_handle_from_inode
46956                                          (swap_inode));
46957      if (bdops)
46958        bdev->bd_op = bdops;
46959
46960      error = blkdev_get(bdev, FMODE_READ | FMODE_WRITE, 0,
46961                      BDEV_SWAP);
46962      if (error)
46963        goto bad_swap_2;
46964      set_blocksize(dev, PAGE_SIZE);
46965      error = -ENODEV;
46966      if (!dev || (blk_size[MAJOR(dev)] &&
46967          !blk_size[MAJOR(dev)][MINOR(dev)]))
46968        goto bad_swap;
46969      error = -EBUSY;
46970      for (i = 0; i < nr_swapfiles; i++) {
46971        if (i == type)
46972          continue;
46973        if (dev == swap_info[i].swap_device)
46974          goto bad_swap;
46975      }
46976      swapfilesize = 0;
46977      if (blk_size[MAJOR(dev)])
46978        swapfilesize = blk_size[MAJOR(dev)][MINOR(dev)]
46979            >> (PAGE_SHIFT - 10);
46980    } else if (S_ISREG(swap_inode->i_mode)) {
46981      error = -EBUSY;
46982      for (i = 0; i < nr_swapfiles; i++) {
46983        if (i == type || !swap_info[i].swap_file)
46984          continue;
46985        if (swap_inode == swap_info[i].swap_file->d_inode)
46986          goto bad_swap;
46987      }
46988      swapfilesize = swap_inode->i_size >> PAGE_SHIFT;
46989    } else
46990      goto bad_swap;
46991
46992    swap_header = (void *) __get_free_page(GFP_USER);
46993    if (!swap_header) {
46994      printk("Unable to start swapping: "
46995            "out of memory :-)\n");
46996      error = -ENOMEM;
46997      goto bad_swap;
46998    }
46999
47000    lock_page(virt_to_page(swap_header));
47001    rw_swap_page_nolock(READ, SWP_ENTRY(type, 0),
```

```
47002         (char *) swap_header, 1);
47003
47004     if (!memcmp("SWAP-SPACE", swap_header->magic.magic,
47005              10))
47006       swap_header_version = 1;
47007     else if (!memcmp("SWAPSPACE2",
47008            swap_header->magic.magic, 10))
47009       swap_header_version = 2;
47010     else {
47011       printk("Unable to find swap-space signature\n");
47012       error = -EINVAL;
47013       goto bad_swap;
47014     }
47015
47016     switch (swap_header_version) {
47017     case 1:
47018       memset(((char *) swap_header) + PAGE_SIZE - 10, 0,
47019              10);
47020       j = 0;
47021       p->lowest_bit = 0;
47022       p->highest_bit = 0;
47023       for (i = 1; i < 8 * PAGE_SIZE; i++) {
47024         if (test_bit(i, (char *) swap_header)) {
47025           if (!p->lowest_bit)
47026             p->lowest_bit = i;
47027           p->highest_bit = i;
47028           p->max = i + 1;
47029           j++;
47030         }
47031       }
47032       nr_good_pages = j;
47033       p->swap_map = vmalloc(p->max * sizeof(short));
47034       if (!p->swap_map) {
47035         error = -ENOMEM;
47036         goto bad_swap;
47037       }
47038       for (i = 1; i < p->max; i++) {
47039         if (test_bit(i, (char *) swap_header))
47040           p->swap_map[i] = 0;
47041         else
47042           p->swap_map[i] = SWAP_MAP_BAD;
47043       }
47044       break;
47045
47046     case 2:
47047       /* Check the swap header's sub-version and the size
47048        * of the swap file and bad block lists */
```

```
47049       if (swap_header->info.version != 1) {
47050         printk(KERN_WARNING
47051           "Unable to handle swap header version %d\n",
47052           swap_header->info.version);
47053         error = -EINVAL;
47054         goto bad_swap;
47055       }
47056
47057       p->lowest_bit = 1;
47058       p->highest_bit = swap_header->info.last_page - 1;
47059       p->max = swap_header->info.last_page;
47060
47061       maxpages = SWP_OFFSET(SWP_ENTRY(0, ~0UL));
47062       if (p->max >= maxpages)
47063         p->max = maxpages - 1;
47064
47065       error = -EINVAL;
47066       if(swap_header->info.nr_badpages > MAX_SWAP_BADPAGES)
47067         goto bad_swap;
47068
47069       /* OK, set up the swap map and apply the bad block
47070        * list */
47071       if (!(p->swap_map =
47072             vmalloc(p->max * sizeof(short)))) {
47073         error = -ENOMEM;
47074         goto bad_swap;
47075       }
47076
47077       error = 0;
47078       memset(p->swap_map, 0, p->max * sizeof(short));
47079       for (i = 0; i < swap_header->info.nr_badpages; i++) {
47080         int page = swap_header->info.badpages[i];
47081         if (page <= 0
47082            || page >= swap_header->info.last_page)
47083           error = -EINVAL;
47084         else
47085           p->swap_map[page] = SWAP_MAP_BAD;
47086       }
47087       nr_good_pages = swap_header->info.last_page -
47088         swap_header->info.nr_badpages - 1 /*header page*/;
47089       if (error)
47090         goto bad_swap;
47091     }
47092
47093     if (swapfilesize && p->max > swapfilesize) {
47094       printk(KERN_WARNING
47095         "Swap area shorter than signature indicates\n");
```

```
47096      error = -EINVAL;
47097      goto bad_swap;
47098   }
47099   if (!nr_good_pages) {
47100      printk(KERN_WARNING "Empty swap-file\n");
47101      error = -EINVAL;
47102      goto bad_swap;
47103   }
47104   p->swap_map[0] = SWAP_MAP_BAD;
47105   p->flags = SWP_WRITEOK;
47106   p->pages = nr_good_pages;
47107   swap_list_lock();
47108   nr_swap_pages += nr_good_pages;
47109   printk(KERN_INFO
47110      "Adding Swap: %dk swap-space (priority %d)\n",
47111      nr_good_pages << (PAGE_SHIFT - 10), p->prio);
47112
47113   /* insert swap space into swap_list: */
47114   prev = -1;
47115   for (i = swap_list.head;
47116        i >= 0;
47117        i = swap_info[i].next) {
47118     if (p->prio >= swap_info[i].prio) {
47119       break;
47120     }
47121     prev = i;
47122   }
47123   p->next = i;
47124   if (prev < 0) {
47125     swap_list.head = swap_list.next = p - swap_info;
47126   } else {
47127     swap_info[prev].next = p - swap_info;
47128   }
47129   swap_list_unlock();
47130   error = 0;
47131   goto out;
47132 bad_swap:
47133   if (bdev)
47134     blkdev_put(bdev, BDEV_SWAP);
47135 bad_swap_2:
47136   if (p->swap_map)
47137     vfree(p->swap_map);
47138   nd.mnt = p->swap_vfsmnt;
47139   nd.dentry = p->swap_file;
47140   p->swap_device = 0;
47141   p->swap_file = NULL;
47142   p->swap_vfsmnt = NULL;
47143   p->swap_map = NULL;
47144   p->flags = 0;
47145   if (!(swap_flags & SWAP_FLAG_PREFER))
47146     ++least_priority;
47147   path_release(&nd);
47148 out:
47149   if (swap_header)
47150     free_page((long) swap_header);
47151   unlock_kernel();
47152   return error;
47153 }
47154
47155 void si_swapinfo(struct sysinfo *val)
47156 {
47157   unsigned int i;
47158   unsigned long freeswap = 0;
47159   unsigned long totalswap = 0;
47160
47161   for (i = 0; i < nr_swapfiles; i++) {
47162     unsigned int j;
47163     if ((swap_info[i].flags & SWP_WRITEOK) !=
47164         SWP_WRITEOK)
47165       continue;
47166     for (j = 0; j < swap_info[i].max; ++j) {
47167       switch (swap_info[i].swap_map[j]) {
47168       case SWAP_MAP_BAD:
47169         continue;
47170       case 0:
47171         freeswap++;
47172       default:
47173         totalswap++;
47174       }
47175     }
47176   }
47177   val->freeswap = freeswap;
47178   val->totalswap = totalswap;
47179   return;
47180 }
47181
47182 /* Verify that a swap entry is valid and increment its
47183  * swap map count.  Kernel_lock is held, which guarantees
47184  * existance of swap device.
47185  *
47186  * Note: if swap_map[] reaches SWAP_MAP_MAX the entries
47187  * are treated as "permanent", but will be reclaimed by
47188  * the next swapoff.  */
47189 int swap_duplicate(swp_entry_t entry)
```

```
47190 {
47191     struct swap_info_struct *p;
47192     unsigned long offset, type;
47193     int result = 0;
47194
47195     /* Swap entry 0 is illegal */
47196     if (!entry.val)
47197       goto out;
47198     type = SWP_TYPE(entry);
47199     if (type >= nr_swapfiles)
47200       goto bad_file;
47201     p = type + swap_info;
47202     offset = SWP_OFFSET(entry);
47203     if (offset >= p->max)
47204       goto bad_offset;
47205     if (!p->swap_map[offset])
47206       goto bad_unused;
47207     /* Entry is valid, so increment the map count.  */
47208     swap_device_lock(p);
47209     if (p->swap_map[offset] < SWAP_MAP_MAX)
47210       p->swap_map[offset]++;
47211     else {
47212       static int overflow = 0;
47213       if (overflow++ < 5)
47214         printk("VM: swap entry overflow\n");
47215       p->swap_map[offset] = SWAP_MAP_MAX;
47216     }
47217     swap_device_unlock(p);
47218     result = 1;
47219 out:
47220     return result;
47221
47222 bad_file:
47223     printk("Bad swap file entry %08lx\n", entry.val);
47224     goto out;
47225 bad_offset:
47226     printk("Bad swap offset entry %08lx\n", entry.val);
47227     goto out;
47228 bad_unused:
47229     printk("Unused swap offset entry in swap_dup %08lx\n",
47230         entry.val);
47231     goto out;
47232 }
47233
47234 /* Page lock needs to be held in all cases to prevent
47235  * races with swap file deletion.  */
47236 int swap_count(struct page *page)
47237 {
47238     struct swap_info_struct *p;
47239     unsigned long offset, type;
47240     swp_entry_t entry;
47241     int retval = 0;
47242
47243     entry.val = page->index;
47244     if (!entry.val)
47245       goto bad_entry;
47246     type = SWP_TYPE(entry);
47247     if (type >= nr_swapfiles)
47248       goto bad_file;
47249     p = type + swap_info;
47250     offset = SWP_OFFSET(entry);
47251     if (offset >= p->max)
47252       goto bad_offset;
47253     if (!p->swap_map[offset])
47254       goto bad_unused;
47255     retval = p->swap_map[offset];
47256 out:
47257     return retval;
47258
47259 bad_entry:
47260     printk(KERN_ERR "swap_count: null entry!\n");
47261     goto out;
47262 bad_file:
47263     printk("Bad swap file entry %08lx\n", entry.val);
47264     goto out;
47265 bad_offset:
47266     printk("Bad swap offset entry %08lx\n", entry.val);
47267     goto out;
47268 bad_unused:
47269     printk
47270         ("Unused swap offset entry in swap_count %08lx\n",
47271         entry.val);
47272     goto out;
47273 }
47274
47275 /* Kernel_lock protects against swap device deletion.  */
47276 void get_swaphandle_info(swp_entry_t entry,
47277     unsigned long *offset, kdev_t * dev,
47278     struct inode **swapf)
47279 {
47280     unsigned long type;
47281     struct swap_info_struct *p;
47282
47283     type = SWP_TYPE(entry);
```

```
47284   if (type >= nr_swapfiles) {
47285     printk("Internal error: bad swap-device\n");
47286     return;
47287   }
47288
47289   p = &swap_info[type];
47290   *offset = SWP_OFFSET(entry);
47291   if (*offset >= p->max) {
47292     printk("rw_swap_page: weirdness\n");
47293     return;
47294   }
47295   if (p->swap_map && !p->swap_map[*offset]) {
47296     printk("VM: Bad swap entry %08lx\n", entry.val);
47297     return;
47298   }
47299   if (!(p->flags & SWP_USED)) {
47300     printk(KERN_ERR "rw_swap_page: "
47301         "Trying to swap to unused swap-device\n");
47302     return;
47303   }
47304
47305   if (p->swap_device) {
47306     *dev = p->swap_device;
47307   } else if (p->swap_file) {
47308     *swapf = p->swap_file->d_inode;
47309   } else {
47310     printk(KERN_ERR
47311         "rw_swap_page: no swap file or device\n");
47312   }
47313   return;
47314 }
47315
47316 /* Kernel_lock protects against swap device
47317  * deletion. Grab an extra reference on the swaphandle so
47318  * that it dos not become unused.  */
47319 int valid_swaphandles(swp_entry_t entry,
47320     unsigned long *offset)
47321 {
47322   int ret = 0, i = 1 << page_cluster;
47323   unsigned long toff;
47324   struct swap_info_struct *swapdev =
47325       SWP_TYPE(entry) + swap_info;
47326
47327   *offset = SWP_OFFSET(entry);
47328   toff = *offset =
47329       (*offset >> page_cluster) << page_cluster;
47330
47331   swap_device_lock(swapdev);
47332   do {
47333     /* Don't read-ahead past the end of the swap area */
47334     if (toff >= swapdev->max)
47335       break;
47336     /* Don't read in bad or busy pages */
47337     if (!swapdev->swap_map[toff])
47338       break;
47339     if (swapdev->swap_map[toff] == SWAP_MAP_BAD)
47340       break;
47341     swapdev->swap_map[toff]++;
47342     toff++;
47343     ret++;
47344   } while (--i);
47345   swap_device_unlock(swapdev);
47346   return ret;
47347 }
```

mm/swap_state.c

```
47348 /*
47349  *  linux/mm/swap_state.c
47350  *
47351  *  Copyright (C) 1991, 1992, 1993, 1994  Linus Torvalds
47352  *  Swap reorganised 29.12.95, Stephen Tweedie
47353  *
47354  *  Rewritten to use page cache, (C) 1998 Stephen Tweedie
47355  */
47356
47357 #include <linux/mm.h>
47358 #include <linux/kernel_stat.h>
47359 #include <linux/swap.h>
47360 #include <linux/swapctl.h>
47361 #include <linux/init.h>
47362 #include <linux/pagemap.h>
47363 #include <linux/smp_lock.h>
47364
47365 #include <asm/pgtable.h>
47366
47367 static int swap_writepage(struct page *page)
47368 {
47369   rw_swap_page(WRITE, page, 0);
47370   return 0;
47371 }
47372
47373 static struct address_space_operations swap_aops = {
47374   writepage: swap_writepage,
47375   sync_page: block_sync_page,
```

```
47376 };
47377
47378 struct address_space swapper_space = {
47379   LIST_HEAD_INIT(swapper_space.clean_pages),
47380   LIST_HEAD_INIT(swapper_space.dirty_pages),
47381   LIST_HEAD_INIT(swapper_space.locked_pages),
47382   0,                              /* nrpages    */
47383   &swap_aops,
47384 };
47385
47386 #ifdef SWAP_CACHE_INFO
47387 unsigned long swap_cache_add_total;
47388 unsigned long swap_cache_del_total;
47389 unsigned long swap_cache_find_total;
47390 unsigned long swap_cache_find_success;
47391
47392 void show_swap_cache_info(void)
47393 {
47394   printk
47395       ("Swap cache: add %ld, delete %ld, find %ld/%ld\n",
47396       swap_cache_add_total, swap_cache_del_total,
47397       swap_cache_find_success, swap_cache_find_total);
47398 }
47399
47400 #endif
47401
47402 void add_to_swap_cache(struct page *page,
47403     swp_entry_t entry)
47404 {
47405   unsigned long flags;
47406
47407 #ifdef SWAP_CACHE_INFO
47408   swap_cache_add_total++;
47409 #endif
47410   if (!PageLocked(page))
47411     BUG();
47412   if (PageTestandSetSwapCache(page))
47413     BUG();
47414   if (page->mapping)
47415     BUG();
47416   flags = page->flags &
47417     ~((1 << PG_error) | (1 << PG_arch_1));
47418   page->flags = flags | (1 << PG_uptodate);
47419   add_to_page_cache_locked(page, &swapper_space,
47420       entry.val);
47421 }
47422
47423 static inline void
47424 remove_from_swap_cache(struct page *page)
47425 {
47426   struct address_space *mapping = page->mapping;
47427
47428   if (mapping != &swapper_space)
47429     BUG();
47430   if (!PageSwapCache(page) || !PageLocked(page))
47431     PAGE_BUG(page);
47432
47433   PageClearSwapCache(page);
47434   ClearPageDirty(page);
47435   __remove_inode_page(page);
47436 }
47437
47438 /* This must be called only on pages that have been
47439  * verified to be in the swap cache.   */
47440 void __delete_from_swap_cache(struct page *page)
47441 {
47442   swp_entry_t entry;
47443
47444   entry.val = page->index;
47445
47446 #ifdef SWAP_CACHE_INFO
47447   swap_cache_del_total++;
47448 #endif
47449   remove_from_swap_cache(page);
47450   swap_free(entry);
47451 }
47452
47453 /* This will never put the page into the free list, the
47454  * caller has a reference on the page.   */
47455 void delete_from_swap_cache_nolock(struct page *page)
47456 {
47457   if (!PageLocked(page))
47458     BUG();
47459
47460   if (block_flushpage(page, 0))
47461     lru_cache_del(page);
47462
47463   spin_lock(&pagecache_lock);
47464   ClearPageDirty(page);
47465   __delete_from_swap_cache(page);
47466   spin_unlock(&pagecache_lock);
47467   page_cache_release(page);
47468 }
47469
```

```
47470 /* This must be called only on pages that have been
47471  * verified to be in the swap cache and locked.  */
47472 void delete_from_swap_cache(struct page *page)
47473 {
47474   lock_page(page);
47475   delete_from_swap_cache_nolock(page);
47476   UnlockPage(page);
47477 }
47478
47479 /* Perform a free_page(), also freeing any swap cache
47480  * associated with this page if it is the last user of
47481  * the page. Can not do a lock_page, as we are holding
47482  * the page_table_lock spinlock.  */
47483 void free_page_and_swap_cache(struct page *page)
47484 {
47485   /* If we are the only user, then try to free up the
47486    swap cache.  */
47487   if (PageSwapCache(page) && !TryLockPage(page)) {
47488     if (!is_page_shared(page)) {
47489       delete_from_swap_cache_nolock(page);
47490     }
47491     UnlockPage(page);
47492   }
47493   page_cache_release(page);
47494 }
47495
47496
47497 /* Lookup a swap entry in the swap cache. A found page
47498  * will be returned unlocked and with its refcount
47499  * incremented - we rely on the kernel lock getting page
47500  * table operations atomic even if we drop the page lock
47501  * before returning.  */
47502 struct page *lookup_swap_cache(swp_entry_t entry)
47503 {
47504   struct page *found;
47505
47506 #ifdef SWAP_CACHE_INFO
47507   swap_cache_find_total++;
47508 #endif
47509   while (1) {
47510     /* Right now the pagecache is 32-bit only.  But it's
47511      a 32 bit index. =) */
47512   repeat:
47513     found = find_lock_page(&swapper_space, entry.val);
47514     if (!found)
47515       return 0;
47516     /* Though the "found" page was in the swap cache an
47517      * instant earlier, it might have been removed by
47518      * refill_inactive etc.  Re search ... Since
47519      * find_lock_page grabs a reference on the page, it
47520      * can not be reused for anything else, namely it can
47521      * not be associated with another swaphandle, so it
47522      * is enough to check whether the page is still in
47523      * the scache.  */
47524     if (!PageSwapCache(found)) {
47525       UnlockPage(found);
47526       page_cache_release(found);
47527       goto repeat;
47528     }
47529     if (found->mapping != &swapper_space)
47530       goto out_bad;
47531 #ifdef SWAP_CACHE_INFO
47532     swap_cache_find_success++;
47533 #endif
47534     UnlockPage(found);
47535     return found;
47536   }
47537
47538 out_bad:
47539   printk(KERN_ERR
47540       "VM: Found a non-swapper swap page!\n");
47541   UnlockPage(found);
47542   page_cache_release(found);
47543   return 0;
47544 }
47545
47546 /* Locate a page of swap in physical memory, reserving
47547  * swap cache space and reading the disk if it is not
47548  * already cached.  If wait==0, we are only doing
47549  * readahead, so don't worry if the page is already
47550  * locked.
47551  *
47552  * A failure return means that either the page allocation
47553  * failed or that the swap entry is no longer in use.  */
47554 struct page *read_swap_cache_async(swp_entry_t entry,
47555     int wait)
47556 {
47557   struct page *found_page = 0, *new_page;
47558   unsigned long new_page_addr;
47559
47560   /* Make sure the swap entry is still in use.  */
47561   if (!swap_duplicate(entry))   /* Account for the swap
47562                                    * cache */
47563     goto out;
```

```
47564    /* Look for the page in the swap cache. */
47565    found_page = lookup_swap_cache(entry);
47566    if (found_page)
47567      goto out_free_swap;
47568
47569    new_page_addr = __get_free_page(GFP_USER);
47570    if (!new_page_addr)
47571      goto out_free_swap;           /* Out of memory */
47572    new_page = virt_to_page(new_page_addr);
47573
47574    /* Check the swap cache again, in case we stalled
47575     above.  */
47576    found_page = lookup_swap_cache(entry);
47577    if (found_page)
47578      goto out_free_page;
47579    /* Add it to the swap cache and read its contents.  */
47580    lock_page(new_page);
47581    add_to_swap_cache(new_page, entry);
47582    rw_swap_page(READ, new_page, wait);
47583    return new_page;
47584
47585 out_free_page:
47586    page_cache_release(new_page);
47587 out_free_swap:
47588    swap_free(entry);
47589 out:
47590    return found_page;
47591 }
```

mm/vmalloc.c

```
47592 /*
47593  *  linux/mm/vmalloc.c
47594  *
47595  *  Copyright (C) 1993  Linus Torvalds
47596  *  Support of BIGMEM added by Gerhard Wichert, Siemens
47597  *  AG, July 1999
47598  *  SMP-safe vmalloc/vfree/ioremap, Tigran Aivazian
47599  *  <tigran@veritas.com>, May 2000
47600  */
47601
47602 #include <linux/malloc.h>
47603 #include <linux/vmalloc.h>
47604 #include <linux/spinlock.h>
47605 #include <linux/highmem.h>
47606 #include <linux/smp_lock.h>
47607
47608 #include <asm/uaccess.h>
```

```
47609 #include <asm/pgalloc.h>
47610
47611 rwlock_t vmlist_lock = RW_LOCK_UNLOCKED;
47612 struct vm_struct *vmlist;
47613
47614 static inline void free_area_pte(pmd_t * pmd,
47615    unsigned long address, unsigned long size)
47616 {
47617    pte_t *pte;
47618    unsigned long end;
47619
47620    if (pmd_none(*pmd))
47621      return;
47622    if (pmd_bad(*pmd)) {
47623      pmd_ERROR(*pmd);
47624      pmd_clear(pmd);
47625      return;
47626    }
47627    pte = pte_offset(pmd, address);
47628    address &= ~PMD_MASK;
47629    end = address + size;
47630    if (end > PMD_SIZE)
47631      end = PMD_SIZE;
47632    do {
47633      pte_t page;
47634      page = ptep_get_and_clear(pte);
47635      address += PAGE_SIZE;
47636      pte++;
47637      if (pte_none(page))
47638        continue;
47639      if (pte_present(page)) {
47640        struct page *ptpage = pte_page(page);
47641        if (VALID_PAGE(ptpage) && (!PageReserved(ptpage)))
47642          __free_page(ptpage);
47643        continue;
47644      }
47645      printk(KERN_CRIT "Whee.. Swapped out page in "
47646          "kernel page table\n");
47647    } while (address < end);
47648 }
47649
47650 static inline void free_area_pmd(pgd_t * dir,
47651    unsigned long address, unsigned long size)
47652 {
47653    pmd_t *pmd;
47654    unsigned long end;
47655
```

```
47656    if (pgd_none(*dir))
47657      return;
47658    if (pgd_bad(*dir)) {
47659      pgd_ERROR(*dir);
47660      pgd_clear(dir);
47661      return;
47662    }
47663    pmd = pmd_offset(dir, address);
47664    address &= ~PGDIR_MASK;
47665    end = address + size;
47666    if (end > PGDIR_SIZE)
47667      end = PGDIR_SIZE;
47668    do {
47669      free_area_pte(pmd, address, end - address);
47670      address = (address + PMD_SIZE) & PMD_MASK;
47671      pmd++;
47672    } while (address < end);
47673  }
47674
47675  void vmfree_area_pages(unsigned long address,
47676      unsigned long size)
47677  {
47678    pgd_t *dir;
47679    unsigned long end = address + size;
47680
47681    dir = pgd_offset_k(address);
47682    flush_cache_all();
47683    do {
47684      free_area_pmd(dir, address, end - address);
47685      address = (address + PGDIR_SIZE) & PGDIR_MASK;
47686      dir++;
47687    } while (address && (address < end));
47688    flush_tlb_all();
47689  }
47690
47691  static inline int alloc_area_pte(pte_t * pte,
47692      unsigned long address, unsigned long size,
47693      int gfp_mask, pgprot_t prot)
47694  {
47695    unsigned long end;
47696
47697    address &= ~PMD_MASK;
47698    end = address + size;
47699    if (end > PMD_SIZE)
47700      end = PMD_SIZE;
47701    do {
47702      struct page *page;
```

```
47703      if (!pte_none(*pte))
47704        printk(KERN_ERR
47705            "alloc_area_pte: page already exists\n");
47706      page = alloc_page(gfp_mask);
47707      if (!page)
47708        return -ENOMEM;
47709      set_pte(pte, mk_pte(page, prot));
47710      address += PAGE_SIZE;
47711      pte++;
47712    } while (address < end);
47713    return 0;
47714  }
47715
47716  static inline int alloc_area_pmd(pmd_t * pmd,
47717      unsigned long address, unsigned long size,
47718      int gfp_mask, pgprot_t prot)
47719  {
47720    unsigned long end;
47721
47722    address &= ~PGDIR_MASK;
47723    end = address + size;
47724    if (end > PGDIR_SIZE)
47725      end = PGDIR_SIZE;
47726    do {
47727      pte_t *pte = pte_alloc_kernel(pmd, address);
47728      if (!pte)
47729        return -ENOMEM;
47730      if (alloc_area_pte(pte, address, end - address,
47731            gfp_mask, prot))
47732        return -ENOMEM;
47733      address = (address + PMD_SIZE) & PMD_MASK;
47734      pmd++;
47735    } while (address < end);
47736    return 0;
47737  }
47738
47739  inline int vmalloc_area_pages(unsigned long address,
47740      unsigned long size, int gfp_mask, pgprot_t prot)
47741  {
47742    pgd_t *dir;
47743    unsigned long end = address + size;
47744    int ret;
47745
47746    dir = pgd_offset_k(address);
47747    flush_cache_all();
47748    lock_kernel();
47749    do {
```

```
47750      pmd_t *pmd;
47751
47752      pmd = pmd_alloc_kernel(dir, address);
47753      ret = -ENOMEM;
47754      if (!pmd)
47755        break;
47756
47757      ret = -ENOMEM;
47758      if (alloc_area_pmd(pmd, address, end - address,
47759              gfp_mask, prot))
47760        break;
47761
47762      address = (address + PGDIR_SIZE) & PGDIR_MASK;
47763      dir++;
47764
47765      ret = 0;
47766    } while (address && (address < end));
47767    unlock_kernel();
47768    flush_tlb_all();
47769    return ret;
47770 }
47771
```

◀ p 641
```
47772 struct vm_struct *get_vm_area(unsigned long size,
47773        unsigned long flags)
47774 {
47775    unsigned long addr;
47776    struct vm_struct **p, *tmp, *area;
47777
47778    area = (struct vm_struct *) kmalloc(sizeof(*area),
47779                                GFP_KERNEL);
47780    if (!area)
47781      return NULL;
47782    size += PAGE_SIZE;
47783    addr = VMALLOC_START;
47784    write_lock(&vmlist_lock);
47785    for (p = &vmlist; (tmp = *p); p = &tmp->next) {
47786      if ((size + addr) < addr) {
47787        write_unlock(&vmlist_lock);
47788        kfree(area);
47789        return NULL;
47790      }
47791      if (size + addr < (unsigned long) tmp->addr)
47792        break;
47793      addr = tmp->size + (unsigned long) tmp->addr;
47794      if (addr > VMALLOC_END - size) {
47795        write_unlock(&vmlist_lock);
47796        kfree(area);
```

```
47797        return NULL;
47798      }
47799    }
47800    area->flags = flags;
47801    area->addr = (void *) addr;
47802    area->size = size;
47803    area->next = *p;
47804    *p = area;
47805    write_unlock(&vmlist_lock);
47806    return area;
47807 }
47808
```

◀ p 642
```
47809 void vfree(void *addr)
47810 {
47811    struct vm_struct **p, *tmp;
47812
47813    if (!addr)
47814      return;
47815    if ((PAGE_SIZE - 1) & (unsigned long) addr) {
47816      printk(KERN_ERR
47817          "Trying to vfree() bad address (%p)\n", addr);
47818      return;
47819    }
47820    write_lock(&vmlist_lock);
47821    for (p = &vmlist; (tmp = *p); p = &tmp->next) {
47822      if (tmp->addr == addr) {
47823        *p = tmp->next;
47824        vmfree_area_pages(VMALLOC_VMADDR(tmp->addr),
47825            tmp->size);
47826        write_unlock(&vmlist_lock);
47827        kfree(tmp);
47828        return;
47829      }
47830    }
47831    write_unlock(&vmlist_lock);
47832    printk(KERN_ERR
47833        "Trying to vfree() nonexistent vm area (%p)\n",
47834        addr);
47835 }
47836
```

◀ p 641
```
47837 void *__vmalloc(unsigned long size, int gfp_mask,
47838     pgprot_t prot)
47839 {
47840    void *addr;
47841    struct vm_struct *area;
47842
47843    size = PAGE_ALIGN(size);
```

```
47844    if (!size || (size >> PAGE_SHIFT) > num_physpages) {
47845      BUG();
47846      return NULL;
47847    }
47848    area = get_vm_area(size, VM_ALLOC);
47849    if (!area)
47850      return NULL;
47851    addr = area->addr;
47852    if (vmalloc_area_pages(VMALLOC_VMADDR(addr), size,
47853          gfp_mask, prot)) {
47854      vfree(addr);
47855      return NULL;
47856    }
47857    return addr;
47858 }
47859
47860 long vread(char *buf, char *addr, unsigned long count)
47861 {
47862    struct vm_struct *tmp;
47863    char *vaddr, *buf_start = buf;
47864    unsigned long n;
47865
47866    /* Don't allow overflow */
47867    if ((unsigned long) addr + count < count)
47868      count = -(unsigned long) addr;
47869
47870    read_lock(&vmlist_lock);
47871    for (tmp = vmlist; tmp; tmp = tmp->next) {
47872      vaddr = (char *) tmp->addr;
47873      if (addr >= vaddr + tmp->size - PAGE_SIZE)
47874        continue;
47875      while (addr < vaddr) {
47876        if (count == 0)
47877          goto finished;
47878        *buf = '\0';
47879        buf++;
47880        addr++;
47881        count--;
47882      }
47883      n = vaddr + tmp->size - PAGE_SIZE - addr;
47884      do {
47885        if (count == 0)
47886          goto finished;
47887        *buf = *addr;
47888        buf++;
47889        addr++;
47890        count--;
```

```
47891      } while (--n > 0);
47892    }
47893 finished:
47894    read_unlock(&vmlist_lock);
47895    return buf - buf_start;
47896 }
```

mm/vmscan.c

```
47897 /*
47898  *  linux/mm/vmscan.c
47899  *
47900  *  Copyright (C) 1991, 1992, 1993, 1994  Linus Torvalds
47901  *
47902  *  Swap reorganised 29.12.95, Stephen Tweedie.
47903  *  kswapd added: 7.1.96  sct
47904  *  Removed kswapd_ctl limits, and swap out as many pages
47905  *  as needed to bring the system back to freepages.high:
47906  *  2.4.97, Rik van Riel.
47907  *  Version: $Id: vmscan.c,v 1.5 1998/02/23 22:14:28 sct
47908  *  Exp $
47909  *  Zone aware kswapd started 02/00, Kanoj Sarcar
47910  *  (kanoj@sgi.com).
47911  *  Multiqueue VM started 5.8.00, Rik van Riel.
47912  */
47913
47914 #include <linux/slab.h>
47915 #include <linux/kernel_stat.h>
47916 #include <linux/swap.h>
47917 #include <linux/swapctl.h>
47918 #include <linux/smp_lock.h>
47919 #include <linux/pagemap.h>
47920 #include <linux/init.h>
47921 #include <linux/highmem.h>
47922 #include <linux/file.h>
47923
47924 #include <asm/pgalloc.h>
47925
47926 /* The swap-out functions return 1 if they successfully
47927  * threw something out, and we got a free page. It
47928  * returns zero if it couldn't do anything, and any other
47929  * value indicates it decreased rss, but the page was
47930  * shared.
47931  *
47932  * NOTE! If it sleeps, it *must* return 1 to make sure we
47933  * don't continue with the swap-out. Otherwise we may be
47934  * using a process that no longer actually exists (it
47935  * might have died while we slept).  */
```

```
p 630  47936 static void try_to_swap_out(struct mm_struct *mm,
       47937     struct vm_area_struct *vma, unsigned long address,
       47938     pte_t * page_table, struct page *page)
       47939 {
       47940   pte_t pte;
       47941   swp_entry_t entry;
       47942
       47943   /* Don't look at this pte if it's been accessed
       47944    * recently. */
       47945   if (ptep_test_and_clear_young(page_table)) {
       47946     page->age += PAGE_AGE_ADV;
       47947     if (page->age > PAGE_AGE_MAX)
       47948       page->age = PAGE_AGE_MAX;
       47949     return;
       47950   }
       47951
       47952   if (TryLockPage(page))
       47953     return;
       47954
       47955   /* From this point on, the odds are that we're going to
       47956    * nuke this pte, so read and clear the pte.  This hook
       47957    * is needed on CPUs which update the accessed and
       47958    * dirty bits in hardware. */
       47959   pte = ptep_get_and_clear(page_table);
       47960   flush_tlb_page(vma, address);
       47961
       47962   /* Is the page already in the swap cache? If so, then
       47963    * we can just drop our reference to it without doing
       47964    * any IO - it's already up-to-date on disk.  */
       47965   if (PageSwapCache(page)) {
       47966     entry.val = page->index;
       47967     if (pte_dirty(pte))
       47968       set_page_dirty(page);
       47969 set_swap_pte:
       47970     swap_duplicate(entry);
       47971     set_pte(page_table, swp_entry_to_pte(entry));
       47972 drop_pte:
       47973     mm->rss--;
       47974     if (!page->age)
       47975       deactivate_page(page);
       47976     UnlockPage(page);
       47977     page_cache_release(page);
       47978     return;
       47979   }
       47980
       47981   /* Is it a clean page? Then it must be recoverable by
       47982    * just paging it in again, and we can just drop it..
```

```
47983    *
47984    * However, this won't actually free any real memory,
47985    * as the page will just be in the page cache
47986    * somewhere, and as such we should just continue our
47987    * scan.
47988    *
47989    * Basically, this just makes it possible for us to do
47990    * some real work in the future in "refill_inactive()".
47991    */
47992   flush_cache_page(vma, address);
47993   if (!pte_dirty(pte))
47994     goto drop_pte;
47995
47996   /* Ok, it's really dirty. That means that we should
47997    * either create a new swap cache entry for it, or we
47998    * should write it back to its own backing store.  */
47999   if (page->mapping) {
48000     set_page_dirty(page);
48001     goto drop_pte;
48002   }
48003
48004   /* This is a dirty, swappable page.  First of all, get
48005    * a suitable swap entry for it, and make sure we have
48006    * the swap cache set up to associate the page with
48007    * that swap entry.  */
48008   entry = get_swap_page();
48009   if (!entry.val)
48010     goto out_unlock_restore;   /* No swap space left */
48011
48012   /* Add it to the swap cache and mark it dirty */
48013   add_to_swap_cache(page, entry);
48014   set_page_dirty(page);
48015   goto set_swap_pte;
48016
48017 out_unlock_restore:
48018   set_pte(page_table, pte);
48019   UnlockPage(page);
48020   return;
48021 }
48022
48023 static int swap_out_pmd(struct mm_struct *mm,
48024     struct vm_area_struct *vma, pmd_t * dir,
48025     unsigned long address, unsigned long end, int count)
48026 {
48027   pte_t *pte;
48028   unsigned long pmd_end;
48029
```

```
48030   if (pmd_none(*dir))
48031     return count;
48032   if (pmd_bad(*dir)) {
48033     pmd_ERROR(*dir);
48034     pmd_clear(dir);
48035     return count;
48036   }
48037
48038   pte = pte_offset(dir, address);
48039
48040   pmd_end = (address + PMD_SIZE) & PMD_MASK;
48041   if (end > pmd_end)
48042     end = pmd_end;
48043
48044   do {
48045     if (pte_present(*pte)) {
48046       struct page *page = pte_page(*pte);
48047
48048       if (VALID_PAGE(page) && !PageReserved(page)) {
48049         try_to_swap_out(mm, vma, address, pte, page);
48050         if (!--count)
48051           break;
48052       }
48053     }
48054     address += PAGE_SIZE;
48055     pte++;
48056   } while (address && (address < end));
48057   mm->swap_address = address + PAGE_SIZE;
48058   return count;
48059 }
48060
48061 static inline int swap_out_pgd(struct mm_struct *mm,
48062     struct vm_area_struct *vma, pgd_t * dir,
48063     unsigned long address, unsigned long end, int count)
48064 {
48065   pmd_t *pmd;
48066   unsigned long pgd_end;
48067
48068   if (pgd_none(*dir))
48069     return count;
48070   if (pgd_bad(*dir)) {
48071     pgd_ERROR(*dir);
48072     pgd_clear(dir);
48073     return count;
48074   }
48075
48076   pmd = pmd_offset(dir, address);
```

```
48077
48078   pgd_end = (address + PGDIR_SIZE) & PGDIR_MASK;
48079   if (pgd_end && (end > pgd_end))
48080     end = pgd_end;
48081
48082   do {
48083     count =
48084         swap_out_pmd(mm, vma, pmd, address, end, count);
48085     if (!count)
48086       break;
48087     address = (address + PMD_SIZE) & PMD_MASK;
48088     pmd++;
48089   } while (address && (address < end));
48090   return count;
48091 }
48092
48093 static int swap_out_vma(struct mm_struct *mm,
48094     struct vm_area_struct *vma, unsigned long address,
48095     int count)
48096 {
48097   pgd_t *pgdir;
48098   unsigned long end;
48099
48100   /* Don't swap out areas which are locked down */
48101   if (vma->vm_flags & (VM_LOCKED | VM_RESERVED))
48102     return count;
48103
48104   pgdir = pgd_offset(mm, address);
48105
48106   end = vma->vm_end;
48107   if (address >= end)
48108     BUG();
48109   do {
48110     count = swap_out_pgd(mm, vma, pgdir, address, end,
48111                          count);
48112     if (!count)
48113       break;
48114     address = (address + PGDIR_SIZE) & PGDIR_MASK;
48115     pgdir++;
48116   } while (address && (address < end));
48117   return count;
48118 }
48119
48120 static int swap_out_mm(struct mm_struct *mm, int count)
48121 {
48122   unsigned long address;
48123   struct vm_area_struct *vma;
```

```
48124
48125    /* Go through process' page directory.  */
48126
48127    /* Find the proper vm-area after freezing the vma chain
48128     * and ptes.  */
48129    spin_lock(&mm->page_table_lock);
48130    address = mm->swap_address;
48131    vma = find_vma(mm, address);
48132    if (vma) {
48133      if (address < vma->vm_start)
48134        address = vma->vm_start;
48135
48136      for (;;) {
48137        count = swap_out_vma(mm, vma, address, count);
48138        if (!count)
48139          goto out_unlock;
48140        vma = vma->vm_next;
48141        if (!vma)
48142          break;
48143        address = vma->vm_start;
48144      }
48145    }
48146    /* Reset to 0 when we reach the end of address space */
48147    mm->swap_address = 0;
48148
48149 out_unlock:
48150    spin_unlock(&mm->page_table_lock);
48151    return !count;
48152 }
48153
48154 /* N.B. This function returns only 0 or 1.  Return values
48155  * != 1 from the lower level routines result in continued
48156  * processing.  */
48157 #define SWAP_SHIFT 5
48158 #define SWAP_MIN 8
48159
48160 static inline int swap_amount(struct mm_struct *mm)
48161 {
48162    int nr = mm->rss >> SWAP_SHIFT;
48163    return nr < SWAP_MIN ? SWAP_MIN : nr;
48164 }
48165
48166 static int swap_out(unsigned int priority, int gfp_mask)
48167 {
48168    int counter;
48169    int retval = 0;
48170    struct mm_struct *mm = current->mm;
48171
48172    /* Always start by trying to penalize the process that
48173     * is allocating memory */
48174    if (mm)
48175      retval = swap_out_mm(mm, swap_amount(mm));
48176
48177    /* Then, look at the other mm's */
48178    counter = mmlist_nr >> priority;
48179    do {
48180      struct list_head *p;
48181
48182      spin_lock(&mmlist_lock);
48183      p = init_mm.mmlist.next;
48184      if (p == &init_mm.mmlist)
48185        goto empty;
48186
48187      /* Move it to the back of the queue.. */
48188      list_del(p);
48189      list_add_tail(p, &init_mm.mmlist);
48190      mm = list_entry(p, struct mm_struct, mmlist);
48191
48192      /* Make sure the mm doesn't disappear when we drop
48193       * the lock.. */
48194      atomic_inc(&mm->mm_users);
48195      spin_unlock(&mmlist_lock);
48196
48197      /* Walk about 6% of the address space each time */
48198      retval |= swap_out_mm(mm, swap_amount(mm));
48199      mmput(mm);
48200    } while (--counter >= 0);
48201    return retval;
48202
48203 empty:
48204    spin_unlock(&mmlist_lock);
48205    return 0;
48206 }
48207
48208
48209 /**
48210  * reclaim_page - reclaims one page from the
48211  *                  inactive_clean list
48212  * @zone: reclaim a page from this zone
48213  *
48214  * The pages on the inactive_clean can be instantly
48215  * reclaimed.  The tests look impressive, but most of the
48216  * time we'll grab the first page of the list and exit
48217  * successfully.  */
```

```
48218 struct page *reclaim_page(zone_t * zone)
48219 {
48220   struct page *page = NULL;
48221   struct list_head *page_lru;
48222   int maxscan;
48223
48224   /* We only need the pagemap_lru_lock if we don't
48225    * reclaim the page, but we have to grab the
48226    * pagecache_lock before the pagemap_lru_lock to avoid
48227    * deadlocks and most of the time we'll succeed anyway.
48228    */
48229   spin_lock(&pagecache_lock);
48230   spin_lock(&pagemap_lru_lock);
48231   maxscan = zone->inactive_clean_pages;
48232   while ((page_lru = zone->inactive_clean_list.prev) !=
48233      &zone->inactive_clean_list && maxscan--) {
48234    page = list_entry(page_lru, struct page, lru);
48235
48236     /* Wrong page on list?! (list corruption, should not
48237      * happen) */
48238     if (!PageInactiveClean(page)) {
48239       printk("VM: reclaim_page, wrong page on list.\n");
48240       list_del(page_lru);
48241       `page->zone->inactive_clean_pages--;
48242       continue;
48243     }
48244
48245     /* Page is or was in use?  Move it to the active
48246      * list. */
48247     if (PageTestandClearReferenced(page) || page->age > 0
48248        || (!page->buffers && page_count(page) > 1)) {
48249       del_page_from_inactive_clean_list(page);
48250       add_page_to_active_list(page);
48251       continue;
48252     }
48253
48254     /* The page is dirty, or locked, move to
48255      * inactive_dirty list. */
48256     if (page->buffers || PageDirty(page)
48257        || TryLockPage(page)) {
48258       del_page_from_inactive_clean_list(page);
48259       add_page_to_inactive_dirty_list(page);
48260       continue;
48261     }
48262
48263     /* OK, remove the page from the caches. */
48264       if (PageSwapCache(page)) {
48265         __delete_from_swap_cache(page);
48266         goto found_page;
48267       }
48268
48269       if (page->mapping) {
48270         __remove_inode_page(page);
48271         goto found_page;
48272       }
48273
48274       /* We should never ever get here. */
48275       printk(KERN_ERR
48276         "VM: reclaim_page, found unknown page\n");
48277       list_del(page_lru);
48278       zone->inactive_clean_pages--;
48279       UnlockPage(page);
48280     }
48281     /* Reset page pointer, maybe we encountered an
48282      * unfreeable page. */
48283     page = NULL;
48284     goto out;
48285
48286 found_page:
48287     del_page_from_inactive_clean_list(page);
48288     UnlockPage(page);
48289     page->age = PAGE_AGE_START;
48290     if (page_count(page) != 1)
48291       printk
48292         ("VM: reclaim_page, found page with count %d!\n",
48293         page_count(page));
48294 out:
48295     spin_unlock(&pagemap_lru_lock);
48296     spin_unlock(&pagecache_lock);
48297     memory_pressure++;
48298     return page;
48299 }
48300
48301 /**
48302  * page_launder - clean dirty inactive pages, move to
48303  *                inactive_clean list
48304  * @gfp_mask: what operations we are allowed to do
48305  * @sync: should we wait synchronously for the cleaning
48306  *        of pages
48307  *
48308  * When this function is called, we are most likely low
48309  * on free + inactive_clean pages. Since we want to
48310  * refill those pages as soon as possible, we'll make two
48311  * loops over the inactive list, one to move the already
```

```
48312   * cleaned pages to the inactive_clean lists and one to
48313   * (often asynchronously) clean the dirty inactive pages.
48314   *
48315   * In situations where kswapd cannot keep up, user
48316   * processes will end up calling this function. Since the
48317   * user process needs to have a page before it can
48318   * continue with its allocation, we'll do synchronous
48319   * page flushing in that case.
48320   *
48321   * This code is heavily inspired by the FreeBSD source
48322   * code. Thanks go out to Matthew Dillon.  */
48323 #define MAX_LAUNDER            (4 * (1 << page_cluster))
48324 int page_launder(int gfp_mask, int sync)
48325 {
48326   int launder_loop, maxscan, cleaned_pages, maxlaunder;
48327   int can_get_io_locks;
48328   struct list_head *page_lru;
48329   struct page *page;
48330
48331   /* We can only grab the IO locks (eg. for flushing
48332    * dirty buffers to disk) if __GFP_IO is set.  */
48333   can_get_io_locks = gfp_mask & __GFP_IO;
48334
48335   launder_loop = 0;
48336   maxlaunder = 0;
48337   cleaned_pages = 0;
48338
48339 dirty_page_rescan:
48340   spin_lock(&pagemap_lru_lock);
48341   maxscan = nr_inactive_dirty_pages;
48342   while ((page_lru = inactive_dirty_list.prev) !=
48343           &inactive_dirty_list
48344           && maxscan- > 0) {
48345     page = list_entry(page_lru, struct page, lru);
48346
48347     /* Wrong page on list?! (list corruption, should not
48348      * happen) */
48349     if (!PageInactiveDirty(page)) {
48350       printk("VM: page_launder, wrong page on list.\n");
48351       list_del(page_lru);
48352       nr_inactive_dirty_pages--;
48353       page->zone->inactive_dirty_pages--;
48354       continue;
48355     }
48356
48357     /* Page is or was in use?  Move it to the active
48358      * list. */
48359     if (PageTestandClearReferenced(page) || page->age > 0
48360         || (!page->buffers && page_count(page) > 1)
48361         || page_ramdisk(page)) {
48362       del_page_from_inactive_dirty_list(page);
48363       add_page_to_active_list(page);
48364       continue;
48365     }
48366
48367     /* The page is locked. IO in progress?  Move it to
48368      * the back of the list.  */
48369     if (TryLockPage(page)) {
48370       list_del(page_lru);
48371       list_add(page_lru, &inactive_dirty_list);
48372       continue;
48373     }
48374
48375     /* Dirty swap-cache page? Write it out if last copy..
48376      */
48377     if (PageDirty(page)) {
48378       int (*writepage) (struct page *) =
48379           page->mapping->a_ops->writepage;
48380
48381       if (!writepage)
48382         goto page_active;
48383
48384       /* First time through? Move it to the back of the
48385        * list */
48386       if (!launder_loop) {
48387         list_del(page_lru);
48388         list_add(page_lru, &inactive_dirty_list);
48389         UnlockPage(page);
48390         continue;
48391       }
48392
48393       /* OK, do a physical asynchronous write to swap. */
48394       ClearPageDirty(page);
48395       page_cache_get(page);
48396       spin_unlock(&pagemap_lru_lock);
48397
48398       writepage(page);
48399       page_cache_release(page);
48400
48401       /* And re-start the thing.. */
48402       spin_lock(&pagemap_lru_lock);
48403       continue;
48404     }
48405
```

```
48406    /* If the page has buffers, try to free the buffer
48407     * mappings associated with this page. If we succeed
48408     * we either free the page (in case it was a
48409     * buffercache only page) or we move the page to the
48410     * inactive_clean list.
48411     *
48412     * On the first round, we should free all previously
48413     * cleaned buffer pages */
48414    if (page->buffers) {
48415     int wait, clearedbuf;
48416     int freed_page = 0;
48417     /* Since we might be doing disk IO, we have to drop
48418      * the spinlock and take an extra reference on the
48419      * page so it doesn't go away from under us.  */
48420     del_page_from_inactive_dirty_list(page);
48421     page_cache_get(page);
48422     spin_unlock(&pagemap_lru_lock);
48423
48424     /* Will we do (asynchronous) IO? */
48425     if (launder_loop && maxlaunder == 0 && sync)
48426       wait = 2;                /* Synchrounous IO */
48427     else if (launder_loop && maxlaunder- > 0)
48428       wait = 1;                /* Async IO */
48429     else
48430       wait = 0;                /* No IO */
48431
48432     /* Try to free the page buffers. */
48433     clearedbuf = try_to_free_buffers(page, wait);
48434
48435     /* Re-take the spinlock. Note that we cannot unlock
48436      * the page yet since we're still accessing the
48437      * page_struct here...  */
48438     spin_lock(&pagemap_lru_lock);
48439
48440     /* The buffers were not freed. */
48441     if (!clearedbuf) {
48442       add_page_to_inactive_dirty_list(page);
48443
48444       /* The page was only in the buffer cache. */
48445     } else if (!page->mapping) {
48446       atomic_dec(&buffermem_pages);
48447       freed_page = 1;
48448       cleaned_pages++;
48449
48450       /* The page has more users besides the cache and
48451        * us. */
48452     } else if (page_count(page) > 2) {
```

```
48453       add_page_to_active_list(page);
48454
48455       /* OK, we "created" a freeable page. */
48456     } else { /*page->mapping && page_count(page) == 2*/
48457       add_page_to_inactive_clean_list(page);
48458       cleaned_pages++;
48459     }
48460
48461     /* Unlock the page and drop the extra reference.
48462      * We can only do it here because we ar accessing
48463      * the page struct above.  */
48464     UnlockPage(page);
48465     page_cache_release(page);
48466
48467     /* If we're freeing buffer cache pages, stop when
48468      * we've got enough free memory.  */
48469     if (freed_page && !free_shortage())
48470       break;
48471     continue;
48472   } else if (page->mapping && !PageDirty(page)) {
48473     /* If a page had an extra reference in
48474      * deactivate_page(), we will find it here.  Now
48475      * the page is really freeable, so we move it to
48476      * the inactive_clean list.  */
48477     del_page_from_inactive_dirty_list(page);
48478     add_page_to_inactive_clean_list(page);
48479     UnlockPage(page);
48480     cleaned_pages++;
48481   } else {
48482   page_active:
48483     /* OK, we don't know what to do with the page.
48484      * It's no use keeping it here, so we move it to
48485      * the active list.  */
48486     del_page_from_inactive_dirty_list(page);
48487     add_page_to_active_list(page);
48488     UnlockPage(page);
48489   }
48490 }
48491 spin_unlock(&pagemap_lru_lock);
48492
48493 /* If we don't have enough free pages, we loop back
48494  * once to queue the dirty pages for writeout. When we
48495  * were called by a user process (that /needs/ a free
48496  * page) and we didn't free anything yet, we wait
48497  * synchronously on the writeout of MAX_SYNC_LAUNDER
48498  * pages.
48499  *
```

```
48500        * We also wake up bdflush, since bdflush should, under
48501        * most loads, flush out the dirty pages before we have
48502        * to wait on IO. */
48503      if (can_get_io_locks && !launder_loop
48504            && free_shortage()) {
48505        launder_loop = 1;
48506        /* If we cleaned pages, never do synchronous IO. */
48507        if (cleaned_pages)
48508          sync = 0;
48509        /* We only do a few "out of order" flushes. */
48510        maxlaunder = MAX_LAUNDER;
48511        /* Kflushd takes care of the rest. */
48512        wakeup_bdflush(0);
48513        goto dirty_page_rescan;
48514      }
48515
48516      /* Return the number of pages moved to the
48517       * inactive_clean list. */
48518      return cleaned_pages;
48519 }
48520
48521 /**
48522  * refill_inactive_scan - scan the active list and find
48523  *                             pages to deactivate
48524  * @priority: the priority at which to scan
48525  * @oneshot: exit after deactivating one page
48526  *
48527  * This function will scan a portion of the active list
48528  * to find unused pages, those pages will then be moved
48529  * to the inactive list.  */
48530 int refill_inactive_scan(unsigned int priority,
48531     int oneshot)
48532 {
48533   struct list_head *page_lru;
48534   struct page *page;
48535   int maxscan, page_active = 0;
48536   int ret = 0;
48537
48538   /* Take the lock while messing with the list... */
48539   spin_lock(&pagemap_lru_lock);
48540   maxscan = nr_active_pages >> priority;
48541   while (maxscan- > 0
48542        && (page_lru = active_list.prev) != &active_list) {
48543     page = list_entry(page_lru, struct page, lru);
48544
48545     /* Wrong page on list?! (list corruption, should not
48546      * happen) */
```

```
48547     if (!PageActive(page)) {
48548       printk
48549         ("VM: refill_inactive, wrong page on list.\n");
48550       list_del(page_lru);
48551       nr_active_pages-;
48552       continue;
48553     }
48554
48555     /* Do aging on the pages. */
48556     if (PageTestandClearReferenced(page)) {
48557       age_page_up_nolock(page);
48558       page_active = 1;
48559     } else {
48560       age_page_down_ageonly(page);
48561       /* Since we don't hold a reference on the page
48562        * ourselves, we have to do our test a bit more
48563        * strict then deactivate_page(). This is needed
48564        * since otherwise the system could hang shuffling
48565        * unfreeable pages from the active list to the
48566        * inactive_dirty list and back again...
48567        *
48568        * SUBTLE: we can have buffer pages with count 1.*/
48569       if (page->age == 0 &&
48570           page_count(page) <= (page->buffers ? 2 : 1)) {
48571         deactivate_page_nolock(page);
48572         page_active = 0;
48573       } else {
48574         page_active = 1;
48575       }
48576     }
48577     /* If the page is still on the active list, move it
48578      * to the other end of the list. Otherwise it was
48579      * deactivated by age_page_down and we exit
48580      * successfully.  */
48581     if (page_active || PageActive(page)) {
48582       list_del(page_lru);
48583       list_add(page_lru, &active_list);
48584     } else {
48585       ret = 1;
48586       if (oneshot)
48587         break;
48588     }
48589   }
48590   spin_unlock(&pagemap_lru_lock);
48591
48592   return ret;
48593 }
```

```
48594
48595 /* Check if there are zones with a severe shortage of
48596  * free pages, or if all zones have a minor shortage.  */
48597 int free_shortage(void)
48598 {
48599   pg_data_t *pgdat = pgdat_list;
48600   int sum = 0;
48601   int freeable =
48602       nr_free_pages() + nr_inactive_clean_pages();
48603   int freetarget = freepages.high + inactive_target / 3;
48604
48605   /* Are we low on free pages globally? */
48606   if (freeable < freetarget)
48607     return freetarget - freeable;
48608
48609   /* If not, are we very low on any particular zone? */
48610   do {
48611     int i;
48612     for (i = 0; i < MAX_NR_ZONES; i++) {
48613       zone_t *zone = pgdat->node_zones + i;
48614       if (zone->size &&
48615           (zone->inactive_clean_pages +
48616           zone->free_pages < zone->pages_min + 1)) {
48617         /* + 1 to have overlap with alloc_pages() !! */
48618         sum += zone->pages_min + 1;
48619         sum -= zone->free_pages;
48620         sum -= zone->inactive_clean_pages;
48621       }
48622     }
48623     pgdat = pgdat->node_next;
48624   } while (pgdat);
48625
48626   return sum;
48627 }
48628
48629 /* How many inactive pages are we short?  */
48630 int inactive_shortage(void)
48631 {
48632   int shortage = 0;
48633   pg_data_t *pgdat = pgdat_list;
48634
48635   /* Is the inactive dirty list too small? */
48636
48637   shortage += freepages.high;
48638   shortage += inactive_target;
48639   shortage -= nr_free_pages();
48640   shortage -= nr_inactive_clean_pages();
48641   shortage -= nr_inactive_dirty_pages;
48642
48643   if (shortage > 0)
48644     return shortage;
48645
48646   /* If not, do we have enough per-zone pages on the
48647    * inactive list? */
48648
48649   shortage = 0;
48650
48651   do {
48652     int i;
48653     for (i = 0; i < MAX_NR_ZONES; i++) {
48654       int zone_shortage;
48655       zone_t *zone = pgdat->node_zones + i;
48656
48657       zone_shortage  = zone->pages_high;
48658       zone_shortage -= zone->inactive_dirty_pages;
48659       zone_shortage -= zone->inactive_clean_pages;
48660       zone_shortage -= zone->free_pages;
48661       if (zone_shortage > 0)
48662         shortage += zone_shortage;
48663     }
48664     pgdat = pgdat->node_next;
48665   } while (pgdat);
48666
48667   return shortage;
48668 }
48669
48670 /* We need to make the locks finer granularity, but right
48671  * now we need this so that we can do page allocations
48672  * without holding the kernel lock etc.
48673  *
48674  * We want to try to free "count" pages, and we want to
48675  * cluster them so that we get good swap-out behaviour.
48676  *
48677  * OTOH, if we're a user process (and not kswapd), we
48678  * really care about latency. In that case we don't try
48679  * to free too many pages.  */
48680 #define DEF_PRIORITY (6)
48681 static int refill_inactive(unsigned int gfp_mask,
48682     int user)
48683 {
48684   int count, start_count, maxtry;
48685
48686   count = inactive_shortage() + free_shortage();
48687   if (user)
```

```
48688       count = (1 << page_cluster);
48689     start_count = count;
48690
48691     maxtry = 6;
48692     do {
48693       if (current->need_resched) {
48694         __set_current_state(TASK_RUNNING);
48695         schedule();
48696       }
48697
48698       while (refill_inactive_scan(DEF_PRIORITY, 1)) {
48699         if (--count <= 0)
48700           goto done;
48701       }
48702
48703       /* If refill_inactive_scan failed, try to page stuff
48704        * out.. */
48705       swap_out(DEF_PRIORITY, gfp_mask);
48706
48707       if (--maxtry <= 0)
48708         return 0;
48709
48710     } while (inactive_shortage());
48711
48712 done:
48713     return (count < start_count);
48714 }
48715
48716 static int do_try_to_free_pages(unsigned int gfp_mask,
48717       int user)
48718 {
48719   int ret = 0;
48720
48721   /* If we're low on free pages, move pages from the
48722    * inactive_dirty list to the inactive_clean list.
48723    *
48724    * Usually bdflush will have pre-cleaned the pages
48725    * before we get around to moving them to the other
48726    * list, so this is a relatively cheap operation.  */
48727   if (free_shortage()
48728       || nr_inactive_dirty_pages >
48729         nr_free_pages() + nr_inactive_clean_pages())
48730     ret += page_launder(gfp_mask, user);
48731
48732   /* If needed, we move pages from the active list to the
48733    * inactive list.  */
48734   if (inactive_shortage())
48735     ret += refill_inactive(gfp_mask, user);
48736
48737   /* Delete pages from the inode and dentry caches and
48738    * reclaim unused slab cache if memory is low.  */
48739   if (free_shortage()) {
48740     shrink_dcache_memory(DEF_PRIORITY, gfp_mask);
48741     shrink_icache_memory(DEF_PRIORITY, gfp_mask);
48742   } else {
48743     /* Illogical, but true. At least for now.
48744      *
48745      * If we're _not_ under shortage any more, we reap
48746      * the caches. Why? Because a noticeable part of the
48747      * caches are the buffer-heads, which we'll want to
48748      * keep if under shortage.  */
48749     kmem_cache_reap(gfp_mask);
48750   }
48751
48752   return ret;
48753 }
48754
48755 DECLARE_WAIT_QUEUE_HEAD(kswapd_wait);
48756 DECLARE_WAIT_QUEUE_HEAD(kswapd_done);
48757 struct task_struct *kswapd_task;
48758
48759 /* The background pageout daemon, started as a kernel
48760  * thread from the init process.
48761  *
48762  * This basically trickles out pages so that we have
48763  * _some_ free memory available even if there is no other
48764  * activity that frees anything up. This is needed for
48765  * things like routing etc, where we otherwise might have
48766  * all activity going on in asynchronous contexts that
48767  * cannot page things out.
48768  *
48769  * If there are applications that are active
48770  * memory-allocators (most normal use), this basically
48771  * shouldn't matter.  */
48772 int kswapd(void *unused)
48773 {
48774   struct task_struct *tsk = current;
48775
48776   tsk->session = 1;
48777   tsk->pgrp = 1;
48778   strcpy(tsk->comm, "kswapd");
48779   sigfillset(&tsk->blocked);
48780   kswapd_task = tsk;
48781
```

```
48782    /* Tell the memory management that we're a "memory
48783     * allocator", and that if we need more memory we
48784     * should get access to it regardless (see
48785     * "__alloc_pages()"). "kswapd" should never get caught
48786     * in the normal page freeing logic.
48787     *
48788     * (Kswapd normally doesn't need memory anyway, but
48789     * sometimes you need a small amount of memory in order
48790     * to be able to page out something else, and this flag
48791     * essentially protects us from recursively trying to
48792     * free more memory as we're trying to free the first
48793     * piece of memory in the first place). */
48794    tsk->flags |= PF_MEMALLOC;
48795
48796    /* Kswapd main loop. */
48797    for (;;) {
48798      static int recalc = 0;
48799
48800      /* If needed, try to free some memory. */
48801      if (inactive_shortage() || free_shortage())
48802        do_try_to_free_pages(GFP_KSWAPD, 0);
48803
48804      /* Do some (very minimal) background scanning. This
48805       * will scan all pages on the active list once every
48806       * minute. This clears old referenced bits and moves
48807       * unused pages to the inactive list. */
48808      refill_inactive_scan(DEF_PRIORITY, 0);
48809
48810      /* Once a second, recalculate some VM stats. */
48811      if (time_after(jiffies, recalc + HZ)) {
48812        recalc = jiffies;
48813        recalculate_vm_stats();
48814      }
48815
48816      run_task_queue(&tq_disk);
48817
48818      /* We go to sleep if either the free page shortage
48819       * or the inactive page shortage is gone. We do this
48820       * because:
48821       * 1) we need no more free pages   or
48822       * 2) the inactive pages need to be flushed to disk,
48823       *    it wouldn't help to eat CPU time now ...
48824       *
48825       * We go to sleep for one second, but if it's needed
48826       * we'll be woken up earlier... */
48827      if (!free_shortage() || !inactive_shortage()) {
48828        interruptible_sleep_on_timeout(&kswapd_wait, HZ);
```

```
48829        /* If we couldn't free enough memory, we see if it
48830         * was due to the system just not having enough
48831         * memory.  If that is the case, the only solution
48832         * is to kill a process (the alternative is
48833         * enternal deadlock).
48834         *
48835         * If there still is enough memory around, we just
48836         * loop and try free some more memory... */
48837      } else if (out_of_memory()) {
48838        oom_kill();
48839      }
48840    }
48841  }
48842
48843  void wakeup_kswapd(void)
48844  {
48845    if (current != kswapd_task)
48846      wake_up_process(kswapd_task);
48847  }
48848
48849  /* Called by non-kswapd processes when they want more
48850   * memory but are unable to sleep on kswapd because they
48851   * might be holding some IO locks ... */
48852  int try_to_free_pages(unsigned int gfp_mask)
48853  {
48854    int ret = 1;
48855
48856    if (gfp_mask & __GFP_WAIT) {
48857      current->flags |= PF_MEMALLOC;
48858      ret = do_try_to_free_pages(gfp_mask, 1);
48859      current->flags &= ~PF_MEMALLOC;
48860    }
48861
48862    return ret;
48863  }
48864
48865  DECLARE_WAIT_QUEUE_HEAD(kreclaimd_wait);
48866  /* Kreclaimd will move pages from the inactive_clean list
48867   * to the free list, in order to keep atomic allocations
48868   * possible under all circumstances. */
48869  int kreclaimd(void *unused)
48870  {
48871    struct task_struct *tsk = current;
48872    pg_data_t *pgdat;
48873
48874    tsk->session = 1;
48875    tsk->pgrp = 1;
```

```
48876    strcpy(tsk->comm, "kreclaimd");
48877    sigfillset(&tsk->blocked);
48878    current->flags |= PF_MEMALLOC;
48879
48880    while (1) {
48881
48882      /* We sleep until someone wakes us up from
48883       * page_alloc.c::__alloc_pages().  */
48884      interruptible_sleep_on(&kreclaimd_wait);
48885
48886      /* Move some pages from the inactive_clean lists to
48887       * the free lists, if it is needed.  */
48888      pgdat = pgdat_list;
48889      do {
48890        int i;
48891        for (i = 0; i < MAX_NR_ZONES; i++) {
48892          zone_t *zone = pgdat->node_zones + i;
48893          if (!zone->size)
48894            continue;
48895
48896          while (zone->free_pages < zone->pages_low) {
48897            struct page *page;
48898            page = reclaim_page(zone);
48899            if (!page)
48900              break;
48901            __free_page(page);
48902          }
48903        }
48904        pgdat = pgdat->node_next;
48905      } while (pgdat);
48906    }
48907 }
48908
48909
48910 static int __init kswapd_init(void)
48911 {
48912   printk("Starting kswapd v1.8\n");
48913   swap_setup();
48914   kernel_thread(kswapd, NULL,
48915                 CLONE_FS | CLONE_FILES | CLONE_SIGNAL);
48916   kernel_thread(kreclaimd, NULL,
48917                 CLONE_FS | CLONE_FILES | CLONE_SIGNAL);
48918   return 0;
48919 }
48920
48921 module_init(kswapd_init)
```

Part II

**Linux Core Kernel
Commentary**

Chapter 1

Introduction to Linux

You probably will never know in any detail how most real operating systems work, because the source code for most operating systems is a closely guarded secret. Many of the exceptions are research systems; many others are designed explicitly for teaching about operating systems. (Some are both.) Although research and teaching are fine goals, such systems can hope to demonstrate little in the way of the tradeoffs that are the stuff of real-world software development, much less the peculiar resolutions to these tradeoffs that apply to real operating systems.

Only a few operating systems intended for the real world make their source code freely available to all comers—to anyone who wants to learn, admire, and improve. This book is about one of those few operating systems: Linux.

Linux is a free, open-source, standards-compliant, 32-bit (and 64-bit, on 64-bit CPUs), Unix-workalike operating system. Linux has everything you would expect in a modern operating system, including the following:

- True preemptive multitasking, including full support for multiple users

- Memory protection

- Virtual memory

- Support for symmetric multiprocessing (SMP) machines—that is, machines with multiple CPUs—as well as the more common uniprocessor (UP) machines

- POSIX compliance

- Networking

- Graphical user interface (GUI) and desktop environment (more than one desktop environment, in fact)

- Speed and stability

Strictly speaking, Linux is not the whole operating system. When you install what is often called Linux, you're installing a huge number of tools that work together to make a truly functional system. Linux itself is the *kernel* of this operating system, its heart, its mind, its nerve center. (The whole shebang is often called *GNU/Linux*, for reasons that will become clear later in the chapter.) The kernel is exclusively responsible for carrying out the lowest-level tasks that make everything else possible—juggling many processes simultaneously, managing their memory so that they don't interfere with one another, satisfying their requests to use the disk, and much more.

In this book, I'll explain how the Linux kernel does some of these critical jobs.

A Brief History of Linux (and Unix)

To give you a little better understanding of what you're looking at in this book, let's take a short tour of Linux's history. Linux is based on Unix, so the story begins there.

Ken Thompson and Dennis Ritchie originally developed Unix in 1969 at AT&T's Bell Laboratories, employing a generally disused PDP-7. It was initially a single-user operating system written in assembler. In short order, it was rewritten in C (which was invented partly for the purpose) on a more powerful PDP-11—after Thompson and Ritchie persuaded their management to buy the newer machine so the team could implement a text-processing system. And it *did* become a text-processing system—a little later. There was just the small matter of writing an OS first. . . .

Eventually, the text-processing tools were implemented, and Unix (and the tools that ran on it) became widely used within AT&T. Thompson and Ritchie presented a paper on the system at an OS conference in 1973, sparking interest in the system in the academic community.

AT&T was not able to enter the computer business because of a 1956 antitrust suit, but it was allowed to distribute the system for a nominal fee. And it did, to academic users at first, and later to government and industry.

One of the academic users was the University of California at Berkeley, where the Computer Systems Research Group adopted Unix in a big way. The modifications developed there led to a strain of Unix known as *Berkeley Software Distribution (BSD) Unix*, which became the most influential strain of the operating system, excepting only the main line of development from AT&T itself. BSD added such notable features as TCP/IP networking, a better file system (the Berkeley Fast File System, or FFS), job control, and improvements to AT&T's memory-management code.

For years, BSD maintained a lead in academic environments, while AT&T's versions, which culminated in a version known as System V, dominated commercial environments. In part, this was for sociological reasons: Universities were comfortable with obtaining the unofficial, but often better, BSD flavor of Unix, whereas businesses preferred to get their Unix from AT&T.

Being user-driven and user-developed, BSD's flavor of Unix was generally the more innovative and rapidly developed of the two. Nevertheless, by the time of the last official AT&T Unix, System V Release 4 (SVR4), System V Unix had absorbed the majority of BSD's most important advances and had added some of its own. Partly because AT&T became able to market Unix commercially in 1984, Berkeley's Unix development efforts withered and died by 1993, following the release of BSD 4.4, although the effort was continued by outside developers and is still active to this day. At least four separate branches of ongoing Unix development are derived directly from BSD 4.4, not to mention that several commercial vendors' Unix versions, such as Hewlett-Packard's HP-UX, are wholly or partly BSD-based.

BSD and System V were not the only Unix variants. Because Unix was written mostly in C, it was relatively easy to port it to new machines, and its simplicity made it relatively easy to rewrite from scratch. These qualities made Unix a popular choice for vendors who were mainly in business to sell hardware—Sun, SGI, Hewlett-Packard, IBM (which has implemented Unix more than once), Digital Equipment Corporation, Amdahl, and dozens of others. A vendor would design and build new hardware and then port Unix to it simply so the hardware would do something useful on delivery. Over time, each of these vendors ended up with its own variation of Unix, and these variations were deliberately pushed in different directions to help lock in customers.

The resulting confusion gave rise to several standardization efforts, the most important of which has been the Portable Operating System Interface (POSIX) family of standards, which defines a standard OS interface and tools. POSIX-compliant code theoretically is portable to any POSIX-compliant OS, and the rigid POSIX test suites have largely made this theoretical portability a practical reality. Today, almost any serious OS aims at POSIX compliance.

Now rewind. In 1984, hacker extraordinaire Richard Stallman kicked off a completely independent effort to implement a Unix-like OS, complete with kernel, development tools, and end-user applications. Dubbed Project GNU (for "GNU's Not Unix"—perhaps the first-ever recursive acronym), Stallman's goal was as much ideological as technical: He wanted an operating system that was not only of high quality but also free. Stallman uses the word "free" not only in its sense of "available at no cost," but also, and more importantly, to mean something closer to "liberated"—unencumbered by licenses that restrict the user's freedom to use, copy, inspect, reuse, modify, or redistribute the software. ("Think 'free speech,'" as Stallman puts it, "not 'free beer.'") This is the sense of the word as used in the name of the Free Software Foundation (FSF), a charitable organization Stallman founded principally to fund GNU software development. (The FSF also has a side interest in other intellectual property matters.)

In its 17-year history, the GNU project has generated and adopted an enormous number of programs, not the least of which are Emacs, gcc (the GNU Compiler Collection, formerly known as the GNU C Compiler), and bash (a command shell), all familiar utilities to any Linux user. The project is currently developing a kernel, the

GNU Hurd, the last major component of the GNU OS. (The Hurd is already working, but its current release number, 0.3, is a fair statement of how far it has to go before it is finished.)

The Hurd continues to be developed, despite Linux's popularity, for several reasons. For one thing, the Hurd's architecture more clearly embodies Stallman's idea of how an operating system should work. For example, any user can change or replace some pieces of the Hurd while it is running. (The changes aren't visible to everyone, only to that user, and only in ways consistent with security.) Another reason is that the Hurd purportedly scales to multiprocessor machines better than the Linux kernel does. Also, you could say that the Hurd is being developed simply because there is interest in developing it—programmers working for free work on what they please, and as long as some of them want to work on the Hurd, the Hurd will be worked on. If it lives up to its promise, the Hurd will someday rival Linux. Today, however, Linux is the undisputed king of the free kernels.

In 1991, in the middle of all this GNU development, a Finnish undergraduate student named Linus Torvalds wanted to learn about Intel's new CPU, the 80386, and he decided that writing his own OS kernel would be a good way to go about it. This desire, plus his dissatisfaction with the weak Unix variants then available for 80386-class machines, led to a resolve to implement a complete, full-featured, POSIX-compliant, Unix-like kernel, one that would draw from the best of BSD and System V while avoiding their worst flaws. Linus (I know I should refer to him as "Torvalds," but everybody calls him "Linus") developed this kernel up to version 0.02 by himself, at which point it was able to run gcc, bash, and a few other utilities, but that was about all. He then began recruiting help over the Internet.

Within three years, Linus's Unix—Linux—had reached version 1.0. Its source code base had grown by more than an order of magnitude, and a preliminary TCP/IP implementation was in place. (This networking code was later re-implemented, and it might yet be re-implemented again.) It also had an estimated 100,000 users.

Today, the Linux kernel is composed of more than 3 million lines of code, and it has an estimated 17 million users. (Because Linux can be obtained and copied for free, it's impossible to count its users precisely.) GNU/Linux—the Linux kernel, surrounded by GNU tools—is believed to make up more than 50 percent of the Unix market. Several companies, Red Hat and SuSE prominent among them, produce GNU/Linux *distributions*— a packaging of the kernel with a variety of utilities and applications, together with installation software. Such industry powerhouses as Sun, IBM, and SGI have taken notice of and support GNU/Linux. IBM promised to invest $1 billion in GNU/Linux in 2001, and SGI plans to ship GNU/Linux instead of its own Unix variant, IRIX, on its new Intel IA-64-based machines.

The GNU General Public License

An operating system so popular and so widely respected surely merits study. The fact that Linux's source code is made freely available under the GNU General Public License (GPL) is a tremendous help in such study. The GPL is an unusual software license that expresses Stallman's aforementioned philosophy: It grants you the right to use, copy, inspect, reuse, modify, and redistribute the software, as long as your modifications are equally free. In this way, the GPL guarantees that Linux (and the huge amount of other software covered by the same license) not only is free today, but also will continue to be free to use and modify forever.

Note that "free," in this context, doesn't imply that nobody may charge money for the software—thriving businesses such as Red Hat, which produces the most popular GNU/Linux distribution, are proof of that. (Red Hat is a billion-dollar company with $100 million in annual revenue—not bad for a company whose main product is free.) You simply aren't allowed to keep others from giving away the software or from making changes that aren't equally free.

The complete text of the GNU General Public License is included in this book, in the Appendix.

The Linux Development Process

Linux is available to study because it is free, and Linux is worth studying because it is great. If it were a lousy OS kernel, it wouldn't be worth using, nor would there be much reason to read a book about it. (Except horrified amusement, possibly.) It is a great operating system for several inextricably intertwined reasons.

One of the reasons Linux is great is that it was developed by great minds. Linus Torvalds, who as a student started the whole ball rolling, is a genius. (And not only with respect to programming. His organizational skills are rarely given the credit they deserve.) The kernel has since been extended and improved by some of the best programmers on the planet, cooperating over the Internet to build the OS they wanted, for the fun of it and for the well-justified pride they take in their work.

Another reason Linux is great is that it is based on great concepts. Unix is a simple and elegant OS model. Unix had 20 years to mature before Linux was created, and Linux draws from the strengths of all strains of Unix, emulating the best features and eschewing the worst. The result is a best-of-breed Unix—fast, robust, complete, and largely free from irrelevant historical baggage.

But Linux's greatest strength is its open development process. Because the kernel's source code is freely available to all, anyone can make improvements, which then are made freely available to everyone else. If you find a bug, you can fix it yourself, rather than beg a faceless company to fix it for you. If you think of an optimization or a great new feature, you can just add it, rather than try to explain your idea to your OS vendor and hope that it adds it someday. When a security hole appears, you can close it yourself, rather than shut down your systems until your vendor decides it's ready to release a fix. Because you have access to the source code, you can read through it to find bugs, slow parts, or security holes, and take care of them before they bite you.

This might sound like small comfort, unless you're a programmer. But even if you aren't a programmer, this development model is still good for you, in two ways:

- You benefit indirectly from the activities of the thousands of programmers who are out there making improvements all the time.

- When you want a change made, you can hire a programmer to do it for you—someone who's working for you alone, delivering to your exact specifications. Try *that* with a closed-source operating system.

The free-flowing development model characterized by Linux has been christened the *bazaar* model, as contrasted with the *cathedral* model, in which source code is locked in a virtual vault, and releases are permitted only when the developers (or, more often, marketing) decide that the software is ready to go. The paper that introduced these terms is Eric S. Raymond's *The Cathedral and the Bazaar*, available at **http://www.tuxedo.org/~esr/writings/**. The bazaar development model creates better software by encouraging experimentation, soliciting early feedback, and leveraging enormous numbers of brains. (Linux is far from the first project to use a bazaar-type process, by the way, although it is the most visible.)

To ensure that all this chaotic development proceeds in an orderly way, Linux employs a two-tree system. One of the trees is the *stable* tree; the other is the *unstable*, or *development*, tree. New features, experimental improvements, and so forth are introduced in the development tree first. If the change is a bug fix that also applies to the stable tree, the same change is made to the stable tree after it has been tested in the development tree. Once the development tree has progressed far enough, in Linus's opinion, the development tree becomes the new stable tree, and the process continues.

Version numbering for the source trees follows the pattern $x.y.z$. For stable trees, y is even; for development trees, y is one greater than for the corresponding stable tree (and, consequently, it's odd). At the time of this writing, the latest stable kernel version is 2.4.5 and the new development tree hasn't started yet; when it does, it will start with 2.5.0. A bug fix in the 2.5 tree might be back-propagated to the 2.4 tree, and when the 2.5 tree is sufficiently mature, it will become 2.6.0 (or maybe 3.0.0).

The latest kernel releases, stable and development alike, are always made available at **www.kernel.org** and its mirror sites. Before too long, if you'd like them to, they might start including some of your code.

Chapter 2

A First Look at the Code

This chapter begins with a high-level overview of the Linux kernel source code, including some general features of interest. It then covers some actual code. The chapter concludes with a discussion of how to compile the kernel so you can experiment with your own changes.

Some Characteristics of the Linux Source Code

The Linux kernel is implemented in C and assembler—period. The usual tradeoffs between these languages apply: The C code is more portable and easier to maintain, but the assembler is faster. The kernel generally uses assembler only where speed is crucial or when some naturally platform-specific feature, such as talking directly to the memory-management hardware, demands it.

As it happens, parts of the kernel will compile under g++ (the GNU C++ compiler), though it doesn't use C++'s object features. As object-oriented programming languages go, C++ has comparatively low overhead, but even this low overhead is too much for the kernel's developers.

The kernel's developers have evolved a programming style that gives Linux code its own flavor. The next few sections discuss some of those issues.

Use of gcc-Specific Features

The Linux kernel is designed to be compiled with the GNU C compiler, gcc. Not just any C compiler will do: The kernel code sometimes uses gcc-specific features, several of which I note as the book progresses.

Some of the gcc-specific code simply uses gcc's language extensions, such as allowing the **inline** keyword in C (not just in C++) to designate an inline function. An inline function is one whose code should be expanded

every time the function is called, thus saving the expense of the actual function call (though generally at the cost of a larger executable).

Even more commonly, code is written in a seemingly convoluted way, because gcc happens to generate more efficient code from some inputs than from others. Theoretically, a compiler could take any two equivalent ways of doing the same thing and optimize them to the same result, so that it wouldn't matter how you wrote the code. In practice, some ways of writing the code produce a faster executable than others. The kernel developers know which ways are the faster ways, and the code they write reflects this knowledge.

For example, consider the kernel's frequent use of **goto**, an ordinarily shunned feature that the kernel often resorts to in the name of speed. There are more than 500 uses of **goto** in the less than 50,000 lines of code included in this book, a first-approximation density of around 1 **goto** per 100 lines of code. Excluding assembler files and using exact figures, the actual rate is closer to 1 **goto** per 91 lines. In all fairness, this is partly a selection effect: One reason this rate is so high is that this book covers the core kernel code, in which speed is an even greater consideration than normal for the kernel. The density for the whole kernel is about 1 **goto** per 282 lines. Still, this is the highest concentration of **goto**s I've seen in one place since I stopped writing code in Basic.

The practice of tying code to a specific compiler is in sharp contrast not only to most application development efforts, but also to most other kernel development efforts. Most developers writing code in C try to stay within the bounds of portable behavior, even when writing operating systems. The advantages are obvious, the main one being that you can change compilers at any time if a better one comes along.

The kernel's blithe reliance on gcc-specific features makes the kernel harder to port to new compilers. Linus once summed up his position on this on the kernel mailing list: "Remember: a compiler is a TOOL." That's a good statement of the philosophy underlying the reliance on gcc-specific features: The point of a compiler is to get a

job done. If the job's criteria can't be met by sticking within the standard, the compliance to the standard should suffer, not the criteria.

In most cases, such a view would be unacceptable. It often is better to sacrifice features, speed, or convenience in the name of compliance to the language standards. Any other choice comes back to haunt you.

But in this case, Linus is right. The Linux kernel is a special case, in which the speed of the resulting executable is prized above its portability to other compilers. If the goal were to write a portable kernel that didn't have to be fast, or a kernel that anyone could compile with his favorite compiler, the decision would be different. That's just not the goal for Linux. In practice, gcc can generate code for nearly any CPU capable of running Linux anyway, so relying on gcc is not much of a barrier to portability.

Chapter 3 has more to say about the kernel's design goals.

Other gcc-specific features frequently used in the code include the following:

- *Code in header files*—Other compilers let you do this, too, but gcc's support for inline functions lets you put **static inline** functions in the header file. **static inline** functions are like macros in that they're expanded every time they're used, but with the advantages of argument type checking; also, the arguments are evaluated exactly once, yielding more intuitive behavior. The file include/linux/list.h (which begins at line 19862 and is explored later in the chapter) contains a number of examples.

- *Mixed C and assembler code*—gcc lets you include assembler code in the middle of your C code, using the **asm** or **__asm__** constructs. The latter is preferable, since gcc won't complain if you compile with -ansi, but they're identical in other respects. The **asm/__asm__** construct is usually accompanied by **volatile** or **__volatile__**, either of which instructs gcc to make fewer changes to the resulting assembler code when optimizing—very useful for those occasions when you know better than the compiler exactly what the resulting code must be. I won't try to do full justice to this construct here; the gcc documentation can tell you more about it. One file included in the book that uses inline assembler code extensively is arch/i386/lib/usercopy.c (starting at line 7772).

- *Named* **struct** *member initialization*—When you initialize a variable of **struct** type, gcc lets you name the specific **struct** members you're initializing, and it lets you initialize them in a different order than they appear in the **struct**'s definition. This is useful when the **struct** is large and you want to initialize only a few of its members. It's also useful when **struct** members might be added or reordered over time: You don't want to have to change every initializer, and you don't want to silently break code (as might happen, without named member initialization, if you swap the positions of two **struct** members with the same type). Finally, named member initialization makes the code much more readable. One good example of named member initialization occurs at line 31922; the **struct module** being filled out at this line names only a few of the many members of **struct module**, whose definition you can find at line 20842. With a glance at the initialization, you can see which members of the **struct** are being set.

Kernel Code Idioms

The kernel code exhibits some prominent idioms, and this section explores a few of the most frequently used ones. As you read through the code, what's really important is not the particular idioms themselves, but that you know that such idioms exist and that they are consistently applied. If you write code for the kernel, you should be aware of what idioms the kernel uses and you should apply them to your own code. As you read through the book (and the code), see how many other idioms you can discover for yourself.

I have to name the idioms so that I can talk about them, but I made up these names, just for the sake of this discussion. Nobody refers explicitly to these practices; they're just the way the kernel does things.

One common idiom is one that I call the *resource acquisition idiom*. In this idiom, a function must acquire a series of resources—memory, locks, and so on. (They need not all be the same kind of resource.) The function should progress to acquiring each resource only if every preceding resource is successfully acquired. At the end, the function must release all the resources it acquired, without trying to release resources it failed to acquire.

I've chosen to show the resource acquisition idiom in the company of another idiom, the *error variable idiom*, which uses a temporary variable to record a function's intended return value. Of course, lots of functions do that; what distinguishes the error variable idiom is that the error variable usually is used to cope with flow control that has been complicated for the sake of speed. The error variable's value is typically either 0 (to indicate success) or a negative value (to indicate an error). These two idioms go hand in hand, leading naturally to code that follows the pattern shown here:

```
int f(void)
{
    int err;
    resource * r1, * r2;
    err = -ERR1;            /* Assume failure. */
    r1 = acquire_resource1();
    if (!r1)                /* Not acquired. */
        goto out;           /* Returns -ERR1. */
    /* Got resource r1; try for r2. */
    err = -ERR2;            /* Assume failure. */
    r2 = acquire_resource2();
    if (!r2)                /* Not acquired. */
        goto out1;          /* Returns -ERR2. */
    /* Have both r1 and r2. */
    err = 0;                /* No error. */
    /* ... Use r1 and r2 .... */
out2:
    release_resource(r2);
out1:
    release_resource(r1);
out:
    return err;
}
```

Whenever the **out2** label is reached, both **r1** and **r2** have been acquired, and both are freed. Whenever the **out1** label is reached (either by falling through or because of the **goto**), **r2** is not valid (it might have just been freed), but **r1** is valid, and it must be freed. Similarly, whenever the **out** label is reached, neither **r1** nor **r2** is valid, and **err** is the error or success code to return.

In this stripped-down example, some of the assignments to **err** are unnecessary. The real code follows this pattern, however, because there are often several tests in a row, all of which should return the same error value, and it's simpler to assign the error value once rather than multiple times. I've chosen to preserve that property here, even though the reason for it is less compelling in the example. For a real case, see **sys_shmctl** (line 28586), which I discuss in Chapter 9.

Note that the existence of a variable named **err** is a dead giveaway that the error variable idiom is in use. Similarly, label names such as **out** point to the resource acquisition idiom.

You'll also occasionally find another idiom that I call the *goto/back idiom*, which is used most prominently in the process scheduler code I present in Chapter 7. The idea is that modern CPUs execute code fastest if they can drop straight through it, taking no branches. gcc can generate code that a CPU can drop straight through at maximum speed if you structure your C code correctly. You just take code that looks like this:

```
if (condition) {
    /* This is the uncommon case. */
    statement1;
    statement2;
}
statement3;
statement4;
return expression;
```

And make it look like this:

```
if (condition)
  goto foo;
foo_back:
  statement3;
  statement4;
  return expression;
foo:
  /* This is the uncommon case. */
  statement1;
  statement2;
  goto foo_back;
```

Pairs of **goto** labels with names like **foo** and **foo_back** are a good clue that the goto/back idiom is in use. The process scheduler function, **schedule** (line 34237), does this several times. It's important that the uncommon case is the one you move out of the main flow of execution; otherwise, the code ends up executing the jumps in the common case, which makes it slower than before.

Because it tends to obfuscate the code's control flow, the goto/back idiom is not used very frequently. There is a related, more common idiom, though, which I call *fast-path/slow-path*. This is much like the goto/back idiom, but the uncommon case is generally moved into a separate function. In Chapter 10 I show several examples of the fast-path/slow-path idiom, one of which is the function **down** (line 15351). **down**'s fast path is just two assembler instructions; its much larger slow path is moved into separate functions. The fast-path/slow-path idiom is especially useful when using **static inline** functions (such as **down**) or macros. The code would be much larger if both the fast path and the slow path had to be expanded every time the function was called. Moving the slow path into a separate function lets the compiler create only one copy of the non-inlined slow path, while still making the inlined fast path go as fast as possible.

The final idiom I'll discuss here is the *just do it idiom* (my apologies to Nike). You'll sometimes see the kernel do harmless but unnecessary work; commonly, it will initially look as if you could speed up the code by wrapping it in a simple **if** that would cause it to be skipped when not needed. But the **if** doesn't come free, especially when you consider that it might introduce the need for a (hidden) jump. So when doing the work is faster than checking whether it needs to be done, the kernel developers choose the lesser of the two evils—they just do it. Line 38984 (part of **sysctl_string**, examined in Chapter 11) is one example: The assignment at this line is nearly always superfluous, but the machine can do the assignment faster than it can check whether it needs to do the assignment, so the code just does the assignment all the time.

The tradeoff behind the "just do it" idiom isn't as simple as I've made it sound. The true tradeoff is subtle: It's a function of the cost of the check, the cost of the possibly avoidable work, and the probability that the work is indeed avoidable. Let's say C_c is the cost of the check, C_w the cost of the possibly avoidable work, and P_w the fraction of the time that the work is unavoidable (that is, the probability you'll have to do the work, on average). You have to compare C_w to $C_c + P_w C_w$ to decide whether to code the check or "just do it." Accurately comparing the two sides of that equation can be very complex, because different CPUs (even within the same CPU family) can have wildly different values for C_c and C_w, and P_w can depend on the workload, which can vary by user and by time. (Worse yet, C_c and C_w can depend on many aspects of your system's configuration, not just the CPU.) But that's what makes hacking the kernel so fun.

Reduced Use of #if and #ifdef

The Linux kernel has been ported to a wide variety of platforms and has had to solve the related portability problems. Most code that supports many different platforms ends up with a lot of ugly preprocessor crud, like this:

```
#if defined(SOLARIS)
/* ... do things the Solaris way .... */
#elif defined(HPUX)
/* ... do things the HP-UX way .... */
#elif defined(LINUX)
/* ... do things the right way .... */
```

```
#else
#error Unsupported platform.
#endif
```

This example is based on making code portable across operating systems, whereas Linux's concern obviously is with making its code portable across CPUs, but the principle is the same. The preprocessor is the wrong solution for this kind of problem. All the clutter makes the code hard to read. Worse, adding support for a new platform can require revisiting every one of these blocks of junk (you can only hope that you find them all), scattering bits of code here and there.

Instead, Linux usually abstracts away the platform difference behind a simple function (or macro) call. The kernel ports are expected to implement the function (or macro) in an appropriate way for each platform. Not only does this make the main body of the code far easier to read, it also tends to catch automatically anything that you forgot to do when implementing a new port: You get a link error that complains about an unresolved reference to a function. The preprocessor still is sometimes used to support different architectures, but it's uncommon.

By the way, note the strong analogy between this solution and the approach of using objects (or **struct**s full of function pointers, in C) rather than scattered **switch** statements to implement different types. At some level, the problems and solutions are the same.

Portability issues aren't limited to platforms and CPUs; compilers get into the act, too. This is one place where it helps that Linux simply assumes it will be compiled with gcc. There's no need to have **#if** blocks (or **#ifdef** blocks) selecting code for this or that compiler, because, as Linux sees it, there's only one compiler in the world.

The kernel code's principal use of **#if** and **#ifdef** is to support constructs that might or might not be compiled in—for example, the code often tests whether the **CONFIG_SMP** macro is defined, to decide whether to support SMP machines.

Automatically Generated Documentation

The kernel developers are slowly improving the documentation in the kernel itself, using a Javadoc-like documentation format called gdoc. This format uses structured comments to embed the documentation, which can then be automatically extracted into DocBook format (an application of SGML, the Standard Generalized Markup Language); from there, you can generate the documentation in Hypertext Markup Language (HTML), Portable Document Format (PDF), PostScript, and other formats.

An excellent example of one of these comments starts at line 45521. If they keep this up, I'll have to find something else to write books about.

Some Sample Code

The preceding sections are all just talk. There's no better way to give you the flavor of the Linux code than by showing you some of it. It's okay if you don't understand all of the nuances of the code discussed here—understanding the code fully is not the primary goal of this section, and some readers might want to just skim it. The goal is to get you started looking at the code, getting a sense of what kinds of things to expect. This discussion covers a few widely used pieces of the kernel.

printk

printk (line 33517) is the kernel's internal message-logging function. When an event of interest happens, such as when the kernel detects an internal inconsistency in its data structures, it uses **printk** to print some information to the system console. Calls to **printk** generally fall into one of the following categories:

- *Emergencies*—For example, the function **panic** (line 33207) uses **printk** several times. **panic** is called when the kernel has detected an unrecoverable internal error; it does its best to shut down the machine safely. The **printk**s in this function alert the user that the system is going down.

- *Debugging*—Line 10097 uses **printk** to print some information about the core file it's about to write—but only when the code is compiled with the **DEBUG** flag.

- *General information*—For example, when the machine is booting, the kernel must estimate the speed of the system so that device drivers can accurately busy-wait for very short periods. The function that computes this estimate is named **calibrate_delay** (line 25640), and it uses **printk** both to announce that it's about to compute the estimate (line 25647) and to report the result (line 25676). Incidentally, I explore the **calibrate_delay** function in detail in Chapter 4.

If you already looked up those line references, you probably noticed that **printk**'s arguments are like **printf**'s: a format string, followed by zero or more arguments to interpolate into the string. The format string itself may begin with a sequence of the form "*<N>*", where *N* is a digit from 0 to 7, inclusive. The digit specifies the message's log level, and the message is printed only if its log level number is below the level currently defined for the console (**console_loglevel**, line 33308). Root can thus lower the console log level to filter out less urgent messages. If no log-level sequence is detected in the format string, the message is always printed. (To be precise, the log-level sequence doesn't need to be in the format string; the code looks for it in the formatted text.)

The block of **#defines** starting at line 19632 names these special sequences to help callers clarify their calls to **printk**. Loosely, log levels 0 through 4 are what I call "emergencies," levels 5 and 6 are what I call "general information," and level 7 is obviously what I call "debugging." (I don't mean to imply by my categorizations that the finer distinctions are never useful, it's just that they aren't important right now.)

With that as background, let's take a look at the code itself.

printk

33517: The **fmt** argument is the **printf**-style format string. If you're not familiar with the "..." part, you might want to consult a good C book (look for "variadic functions" in its index). Also, the *stdarg* man page,

which should be installed on your GNU/Linux box, contains a good, concise description of variadic functions—just type "man stdarg".

Briefly, the "..." part alerts the compiler that any number and type of arguments can follow **fmt**. Because these arguments have no types or names at compile time, they're manipulated with a special trio of macros—**va_start**, **va_arg**, and **va_end**—and a type, **va_list**.

33523: **msg_level** records the log level of the current message. It might seem odd that it's **static**—why would the next call to **printk** need to remember this message's log level? The answer is that the "current message" doesn't end until a newline (\n) is printed or until a new log-level sequence is given. This lets the caller print a single long message in several shorter bursts, with only the last **printk** call including the message-ending newline.

33526: In an SMP box, the kernel might be trying to print to the console literally simultaneously from several different CPUs. (Something similar can happen on a uniprocessor [UP] box, but because I haven't covered interrupts yet, it won't yet be obvious how.) Without any coordination, the result would be a hopeless jumble—parts of each message intertwined with parts of every other message.

Instead, the kernel uses a spinlock to guard access to the console. I cover spinlocks in more depth in Chapter 10.

In case you're wondering why **flags** isn't initialized before it's passed to **spin_lock_irqsave**, don't worry: **spin_lock_irqsave** (see lines 23348 and 16969) is a macro, not a function. The macro actually writes to **flags**, rather than reading from it. The information stored in **flags** is read back at line 33571, by **spin_unlock_irqrestore**—see lines 23369, 16972, and 16957.

33527: Initializes the **args** variable, which represents the "..." part of **printk**'s arguments.

33529: Calls the kernel's own implementation of **vsprintf** (omitted for space). This acts just like the regular **vsprintf**, writing the formatted text to **buf** (line 33291) and returning the number of characters written (excluding the string-terminating 0 byte). In a moment, you'll see why this skips the first three characters of **buf**.

Observe that nothing strictly prevents a buffer overrun here (as admitted in the comment at line 33528). It is simply hoped that the 1,024-character size of **buf** is sufficient. It would be better if the kernel had a **vsnprintf** to use here, instead—**vsnprintf** takes an additional argument that limits the number of characters it will write to the buffer.

33530: Computes the last-used element in **buf**, then terminates the walk over the "..." arguments with a call to **va_end**.

33532: Begins iterating over the formatted message. There's an inner loop that does more processing (as you'll see shortly), so every time this loop iterates, it is at the start of a line to print. Because **printk** is normally used to print only one line, the loop normally iterates only once per call.

33534: If this message's log level is not already known, **printk** checks whether the line appears to begin with a log-level sequence.

33537: If the line does not begin with a log-level sequence, those first three unused characters of **buf** are now used. (On iterations after the first, this code overwrites part of the message text—but that's okay, because that text was part of a previous line that has already been printed and will not be needed again.) A log-level sequence is inserted into **buf**.

33543: At this point, the following properties hold: **p** points to the log-level sequence (which is followed by the message text) and **msg** points to the message text—note the assignments to **msg** at lines 33533 and 33542.

Because **p** is known to point to the beginning of a log-level sequence—possibly one that was constructed by the function itself—the log level can be extracted from **p** and saved in **msg_level**.

33545: Clears the **line_feed** flag; no newline has yet been seen.

33546: Here's the inner loop promised earlier; this one runs to the end of the line (that is, until it finds a newline character) or to the end of the buffer.

33547: In addition to printing messages to the console, **printk** can remember the last **LOG_BUF_LEN** characters it has printed. (**LOG_BUF_LEN** is 16,384—see line 33288.) If the kernel calls **printk** before a console is opened, the message clearly can't be printed on the console right away, but as much as possible is saved in **log_buf** (line 33316). When the console is later opened, the data waiting in **log_buf** is dumped to it—see line 33677.

log_buf is maintained as a circular buffer, with the **log_start** and **log_size** variables (lines 33317 and 33304) tracking the current beginning of this buffer and its length. The bitwise AND on this line is really doing a fast modulo (%) operation; its correctness depends on the fact that **LOG_BUF_LEN** is a power of 2.

33549: Maintains the variables that track the circular log. The log's size obviously can grow only until it reaches **LOG_BUF_LEN**. After that, **log_size** stays the same, and inserting additional characters causes **log_start** to advance.

33554: Note that **logged_chars** (line 33318), the total number of characters written by **printk** since the machine was booted, is updated on every loop iteration, rather than just once when the loop is over. For that matter, the same is true of **log_start** and **log_size**. This looks like an opportunity for an optimization—but I'll delay that discussion until I finish covering the function.

33555: Messages are broken into lines—separated by newline characters, of course. When a newline character is found, a complete line can be written, so the inner loop terminates early.

33560: Regardless of whether the inner loop exited early, at this point the characters from **msg** to **p** are intended for the console. (I call this sequence of characters the line, but bear in mind that the line might not be newline-terminated—because **buf** might not be.) The line will be printed if its log level is below the level currently defined for the system console, if there are currently any consoles to print it to. (Remember that **printk** can be called before any consoles have been opened.)

If no log-level sequence was found in this chunk of the message and **msg_level** wasn't already set from a previous call to **printk**, then **msg_level** will be –1 for this line. Because **console_loglevel** is always at least 1 (unless root screws it up using the sysctl interface), such lines will always be printed.

33562: This line should be printed. **printk** walks over the linked list of open console drivers, telling each to write the line. (Because device drivers are beyond the scope of this book, the console driver code is not included.)

33564: Note that the message is written without the log-level sequence—**msg** is used as the start of the message text, not **p**. However, the log-level sequence was saved in the **log_buf** buffer. This enables code that later reads **log_buf** to extract the log level of messages (see line 33687), without cluttering the display with the sequences.

33568: If the inner **for** loop found a newline, any remaining characters of **buf** are considered to begin a new message, so **msg_level** is reset. The outer loop continues until **buf** is exhausted.

33571: Releases the console lock, which was acquired at line 33526.

33572: Wakes up any processes that were waiting for the console log to be written to. Note that this happens even if no text was written to any consoles. That's okay, because the waiting processes are actually waiting to read from **log_buf**, which gets written to whether or not text is also written to a console. Line 33410 is where processes are put to sleep waiting for **log_buf** activity. I cover the mechanism used for this sleeping and waking, wait queues, in the next section.

33573: Returns the number of characters written to the log.

The **for** loop starting at line 33546 could be faster if it did less work per character. It's possible to get a small speedup by updating **logged_chars** just once, when the loop exits. But we can try for more. The message size is known in advance, so **log_size** and **log_start** need not be incremented until the end. Let's see whether we can make it faster. Here's the naive approach:

```
do {
  static int wrapped = 0;
  const int x = wrapped
    ? log_start
    : log_size;
  const int lim = LOG_BUF_LEN - x;
  int n = buf_end - p;
  if (n >= lim)
    n = lim;
  memcpy(log_buf + x, p, n);
  p += n;
  if (log_size < LOG_BUF_LEN)
    log_size += n;
  else {
    wrapped = 1;
    log_start += n;
    log_start &= LOG_BUF_LEN - 1;
  }
} while (p < buf_end);
```

Note that the loop typically iterates only once; it will iterate more than once only if the write must wrap around the end of **log_buf**. Consequently, **log_size** and **log_buf** will be updated only once (or twice, if the write wraps).

This is now faster—but we can't do it that way for two reasons. First, the kernel has its own version of **memcpy**, and we'd have to ensure that the call to **memcpy** would never call back into **printk**. (Some kernel ports define their own, faster versions of **memcpy**, so all the ports would have to agree on this point.) If **memcpy** called **printk** to report a failure, you could potentially end up in an infinite loop.

But that's not the killer. The big problem with the naive approach is that the kernel's version of the loop also watches for newline characters, so **memcpy**ing the whole message into **log_buf** is incorrect: If there's a newline in there, we'll rush past it.

We can try to kill both of those birds with one stone. This replacement attempt is slower than the naive one, but it preserves the semantics of the kernel's version:

```
/* In declarations section: */
int n;
char * start;
static char * log = log_buf;
/* ... */
for (start = p; p < buf_end; p++) {
  *log++ = *p;
  if (log >= (log_buf + LOG_BUF_LEN))
    log = log_buf;  /* Wrap. */
  if (*p == '\n') {
    line_feed = 1;
    break;
  }
}
/* p - start is number of chars copied. */
n = p - start;
logged_chars += n;
/*
 * Exercise for the reader:
 * Also use n to update log_size and log_start.
 * (It's not as simple as it might look.)
 */
```

Note that gcc's optimizer is smart enough to notice that the expression **log_buf + LOG_BUF_LEN** doesn't change within the loop, so we wouldn't gain anything by manually hoisting the computation above the loop.

Unfortunately, this is no longer much faster than the kernel's version, and it has become harder to understand (as you'll see if you write the code to update **log_size** and **log_start**). You can make your own decision about whether the tradeoffs are worth it. Either way, you learn something, and this is a common outcome: Succeed or fail, trying to improve the kernel's code deepens your understanding of why it is the way it is.

Wait Queues

The previous section briefly mentioned that processes (that is, running programs) can be put to sleep waiting for some event and wakened again when the event occurs. The kernel's technique for this is to associate a wait queue with each event. A process that must wait for the event is put to sleep and placed on the queue. When the event occurs, the kernel walks down the queue, waking the sleeping tasks as it goes. The awakened tasks are responsible for removing themselves from the queue.

Wait queues are surprisingly powerful and are widely used throughout the kernel. What's more, not much code is needed to implement them.

struct __wait_queue

25119: This simple data structure, **typedef**ed to **wait_queue_t** at line 25129, is a wait queue node. It has just three members:

- **flags**—A set of flags that modifies how the wait queue code will act on this node. The only currently defined flag is **WQ_FLAG_EXCLUSIVE** (line 25121); if set, this flag asks the wait queue code not to wake any nodes after this one.

- **task**—A pointer to the **struct task_struct** representing the waiting process. **struct task_struct** starts at line 21931 and I discuss it in Chapter 7.

- **task_list**—Maintains the list of nodes in the wait queue, using the generic list code covered later in the chapter. Wait queues, therefore, are represented as doubly linked lists.

A wait queue is represented by a variable of type **struct __wait_queue_head** (line 25167). Variables of this type are normally declared using the macro **DECLARE_WAIT_QUEUE_HEAD** (line 25197). For an example, see **log_wait** (line 33305), the wait queue used by **printk**. Individual wait queue nodes are typically declared with **DECLARE_WAITQUEUE** (line 25189) or initialized with **init_waitqueue_entry** (line 25216).

wait_event

22483: With this macro, kernel code causes the currently executing process to wait in the wait queue **wq** for the given **condition** (which can be an arbitrary expression) to be satisfied.

22485: If the condition is already true, the process clearly doesn't need to wait.

22487: Otherwise, the process must wait for the condition to become true. This is done by a call to __wait_event (line 22467), which I explore in the next section. Because __wait_event is separated from **wait_event**, pieces of the kernel code that already know that the wait condition is false can call **__wait_event** directly, rather than through a macro that will do a redundant (in those cases) test—although the code virtually never does this. More importantly, if the condition is already true, **wait_event** skips the code that places the process in the wait queue.

Note that **wait_event**'s body is enclosed in an unusual construct:

```
do {
  /* ... */
} while (0)
```

This little trick, I've been surprised to discover, is not nearly as well known as it deserves to be. The idea is to cause the enclosed code to act like a single statement.

Consider the following macro, whose intent is to call **free** if **p** is a non-**NULL** pointer:

```
#define FREE1(p)  if (p) free(p)
```

All well and good, until you use **FREE1** in a situation like this one:

```
if (expression)
  FREE1(p);
else
  printf("expression was false.\n");
```

After **FREE1** is expanded, the **else** is associated with the wrong **if**—**FREE1**'s **if**. I've seen programmers try to work around that problem with the following approaches:

```
#define FREE2(p)  if (p) { free(p); }
#define FREE3(p)  { if (p) { free(p); } }
```

Neither of these gives a satisfactory solution; the semicolon that a programmer naturally places after the macro call messes up the expanded text. Take **FREE2** as an example. After the macro expansion, and after adjusting the indentation to more accurately convey what the compiler sees, the code looks like this:

```
if (expression)
  if (p) { free(p); }
;
else
  printf("expression was false.\n");
```

This gives a syntax error: The **else** is not associated with any **if**. **FREE3** has essentially the same problem, and considering why it has the same problem will show you why it doesn't matter whether there's an **if** inside the macro body. You get into the same trouble just by wrapping the macro body in a set of braces, no matter what's inside.

This is where the **do/while (0)** trick comes in. We can now write **FREE4**, which has none of its predecessors' failings:

```
#define FREE4(p)  \
do {              \
```

```
  if (p)          \
    free(p);      \
} while (0)
```

After plugging **FREE4** into the same code as the others, the macro-expanded code looks like this (again adjusting indentation for clarity):

```
if (expression)
  do {
    if (p)
      free(p);
  } while (0); /* ";" following macro. */
else
  printf("expression was false.\n");
```

This, of course, executes correctly. The compiler optimizes away the loop-control overhead for the bogus loop, so there's no speed penalty, and we get a macro that acts the way we want.

I shouldn't leave this subject without mentioning that, even though this is an acceptable solution, writing a function is even better than writing a macro. When you just can't afford the expense of a function call—frequently the case in the kernel, although much less common in the rest of the world—use inline functions. (Admittedly, that's an option only when using C++, gcc, or a compiler that implements the recently revised ISO C standard, which at last adds inline functions to C.)

__wait_event

22467: **__wait_event** makes the current process wait in the wait queue **wq** until **condition** becomes true.

22472: The local variable **__wait** is linked into the queue through a call to **add_wait_queue** (see lines 30485 and 25241). Note that **__wait** is allocated on the stack, not on the kernel's heap—a common trick in the kernel. **__wait** is removed from the wait queue before the macro finishes, so the wait queue's pointer to it is always valid.

22473: Repeatedly yields the CPU to another process until the condition is met, as described in the following paragraphs.

22474: The process is put into the **TASK_UNINTERRUPTIBLE** state (line 21740), which means that it's sleeping and must not be awakened, even by a signal, until the condition it's waiting for occurs. Signals are covered in Chapter 6, and process states are covered in Chapter 7.

22475: If the condition has been met, the loop exits.

Observe that if the condition is satisfied on the first loop iteration, the assignment on the preceding line is a waste (because the process's state is set again immediately after the loop exits). **__wait_event** assumes that its condition is not met when the macro begins execution, however. Still, it would be harmless to delay the assignment to the process's **state** variable. It might be a gain in some very rare cases, such as when the condition is false when **__wait_event** begins, but is true by the time line 22475 is reached. The change would cause a problem only if **condition** evaluated to code that cared about what state the process was in, which doesn't happen for any of the existing kernel code.

22477: Calls **schedule** (line 34237, and discussed in Chapter 7) to hand off the CPU to another process. The call to **schedule** will not return until the process is given the CPU again; this happens only when processes on the wait queue are being awakened.

22479: The loop has exited, so the condition has been met. The process is placed back into the **TASK_RUNNING** state (line 21738), making it eligible for the CPU.

22480: The process is removed from the wait queue by a call to **remove_wait_queue** (see lines 30507 and 25272).

wait_event_interruptible and **__wait_event_interruptible** (lines 22511 and 22490, respectively) are just like **wait_event** and **__wait_event**, except that they allow the waiting process to be interrupted by a signal.

Signals, as previously mentioned, are covered in Chapter 6.

Note also that **wait_event_interruptible** is enclosed in

```
({
  /* ... */
})
```

Like the **do/while (0)** trick, this causes the enclosed code to act as a single unit. Here, the enclosed code is a single expression, not a single statement—that is, it evaluates to a value and can be used in a larger expression. This happens because of some nonportable gcc magic that makes the last expression computed in such a block be the value for the whole block. When **wait_event_interruptible** is used in an expression, the macro's body is executed and **__ret**'s value is the macro's value (see line 22517). This is a familiar concept to programmers with a background in Lisp, who can think of this construct as a C version of Lisp's **progn**, but it might seem strange if you know only C and related procedural languages.

__wake_up_common

34414: This is the function that wakes up processes that are waiting in a wait queue. It's called by **wake_up** and **wake_up_interruptible** (lines 22228 and 22243), among others. (Actually, these macros call **__wake_up**, line 34465, which immediately calls **__wake_up_common**.) These macros supply the **mode** argument; a process should be awakened only if it's in one of the states implied by **mode**.

34424: As I detail more fully in Chapter 10, locks are used to protect access to a resource. Locks are especially important on an SMP box, where one CPU might be modifying a data structure while another is reading it, or two CPUs might be modifying the same data structure simultaneously, and so on. In this case, the guarded resource is

clearly a wait queue. As you can see, each wait queue has its own lock, allowing two CPUs to modify different wait queues simultaneously. If both CPUs want to modify the same wait queue, one will have to wait for the other to finish.

34436: Walks over the nonempty queue, calling **wake_up_process** (line 34067) or **wake_up_process_synchronous** (line 34084) for each process in the queue that's in the right state. As I noted earlier, processes (queue nodes) are not removed from the queue here, mostly because a process might want to stay in the wait queue even though processes on the queue are being awakened—as you saw in **__wait_event**.

34456: Sometimes the kernel wants to limit the number of enqueued processes that can be awakened at once. This happens when all the enqueued processes are waiting for an inherently limited resource. For example, all of the enqueued processes might be waiting to grab the same lock; since only one of them can succeed anyway, it's wasteful to wake them all. (I show you an example of exactly this situation in Chapter 10.) Enforcing this limit is a simple matter of setting the **WQ_FLAG_EXCLUSIVE** flag in a wait queue node's **flags** member, which is commonly done by calling **add_wait_queue_exclusive** (line 30496). At the current line, the kernel honors the **WQ_FLAG_EXCLUSIVE** flag by refusing to wake more than **nr_exclusive** enqueued processes with that flag set. **nr_exclusive** is almost always 1.

Generic Linked Lists

The kernel frequently needs to build and traverse dynamic lists of objects, so its developers have created a simple, yet fast and flexible, implementation of doubly linked lists. Strictly speaking, these lists are really rings—that is, circular lists—but the kernel just refers to them as lists, so I'll do the same. It's an unusual implementation, but it minimizes special-case code. Most linked-list code would need special cases for adding nodes to the head or tail of the list and for adding a node to an empty list, but this code doesn't (partly due to its use of sentinels, which I'll discuss shortly).

List nodes are composed of type **struct list_head** (line 19878). Don't let the name throw you—**struct list_head** is used for all list nodes, not just the first. **struct list_heads** are usually initialized with one of the macros on lines 19882 through 19889.

A **struct list_head** is either the list's sentinel node—that is, the node that acts as the externally accessible pointers to the head and tail of the list—or it's part of an internal list node. Internal nodes are members of a larger **struct** type—for example, the **task_list** member of **struct __wait_queue** (see line 25123). This lets the kernel code create lists of many different types, just by embedding a **struct list_head** in whatever type the kernel wants to create a list of. In general, the kernel also needs a separate variable to act as the list's sentinel. Sometimes, the sentinel is also part of some larger type, as at line 25169.

The next few sections briefly describe the basic list operations you'll see used in this book.

__list_add

19896:   **__list_add** is the most general of the functions that add a node to a list. It adds **new** between **prev** and **next**. Since either **prev** or **next** can be the list's sentinel node, **__list_add** can be used to add a node to the head of the list (see line 19915) or to the tail of the list (see line 19929). It can also be called directly to add a node between any two internal nodes—although the banner comment above the function (and the __ prefix) discourage calling the function directly.

__list_del

19937:   Similarly, **__list_del** is the most general node-deletion function; it's called from lines 19951 and 19961. Note, however, that it just unlinks the list node; it doesn't free the unlinked node's memory. That's partly because the node might have been allocated on the stack, as you saw earlier in the discussion of **__wait_event**.

list_entry

20001:   Because **struct list_head**s for internal nodes are just members of a larger type, code that's walking along a list usually needs to get to the containing object. The **list_entry** macro lets it do that. It's not as complex as it might look. The second part of the macro looks like this:

```
(unsigned long)(&((type *)0)->member)
```

That part figures out the offset in bytes of **member** (the name of the **struct list_head** member) within **type** (the type of the enclosing **struct**), by asking what **member**'s address would be if an instance of **type** were at address 0, then casting that result to an integer type. The first part of the macro subtracts that offset from **ptr**, the pointer to the **struct list_head**. This returns a pointer to the base of the enclosing data structure, which the macro then casts appropriately.

ISO C includes a macro—**offsetof**—that would simplify **list_entry**'s implementation:

```
#define list_entry(ptr, type, member)  \
  ((type *) ((char *)(ptr) -            \
             offsetof(type, member)))
```

Line 34439—in **__wake_up_common**, discussed earlier—is a typical use of this macro. The surrounding code is walking over a list of **wait_queue_t**s (**struct __wait_queue**s) and needs to convert the **struct list_head**s into **wait_queue_t**s so it can do the real work.

list_for_each

20009:   The **list_for_each** macro simplifies walking over a list of objects chained together by their **struct list_head** members. Note that the list walk does not include the sentinel node, which makes sense, because by definition the sentinel node is conceptually external to the list.

Line 34294, in the process scheduler, uses this macro to walk over all processes ready to use the CPU.

Kernel Modules

The entire kernel doesn't need to be in memory simultaneously. Granted, a certain amount of the kernel must be loaded into memory all the time for the system to function at all—for example, the process scheduling code must always be resident. However, other pieces, such as most device drivers, are not needed all the time; these parts can be absent when the kernel doesn't need them.

For instance, the code that enables the kernel to talk to your CD-ROM drive needs to be in memory only when the kernel is actually talking to the drive, so the kernel can be configured to load that code just before it talks to the drive. When the kernel is finished talking to the drive, it can forget about it again—that is, the code can be removed when it is no longer needed. Sections of the kernel that can be added or removed while the system is running are called kernel modules.

One benefit of kernel modules is that they make developing the kernel itself easier. Suppose you just bought a new CD-ROM drive with a special high-speed mode that's not supported by the existing CD-ROM driver, and you want to add support for the new mode to improve the drive's performance on your system. If you compile the driver as a kernel module, you're in great shape: You can compile the driver, load it into the kernel, test it, remove it, make modifications, load it back into the kernel, test it, and so on. If the driver were compiled into the kernel, you'd have to recompile the kernel and reboot your machine every time you wanted to modify the driver. Much slower!

Naturally, you have to be careful with kernel modules. You must not remove the module that knows how to talk to the disk where the kernel modules reside; otherwise, the kernel will have to talk to that disk to find out how to talk to that disk—bad news. This is another reason why you get to choose whether to compile a section of the kernel as a module or to compile it into the kernel so that it is always resident. You know how your system will be set up, and it's up to you to make the right choices. (If you want to stay on the safe side, you can simply ignore the availability of the kernel module system and compile everything into the kernel.)

There's a small speed cost associated with kernel modules, because the needed code must be read in from the disk rather than already being resident in RAM. However, overall system performance is normally improved, because the extra RAM freed up by discarding unused modules is made available to applications. If that RAM were reserved by the kernel, applications would have to swap more frequently, and swapping slows down applications tremendously. (Swapping is covered in Chapter 8.)

Kernel modules also introduce a complexity cost, because adding or removing pieces of the kernel while it's running takes extra code. The complexity cost is manageable, however, as you'll see in this section. The complexity cost is lowered further by delegating some of the needed work to an external program. (To be more precise, this redistributes the complexity rather than reducing it.) This is a neat extension of the philosophy of kernel modules: Even support for kernel modules is partly external to the kernel and is loaded only when needed.

The program normally used for this purpose is named modprobe. The code for modprobe is outside the scope of this book, but it's included with all GNU/Linux distributions. The next few sections examine the kernel code that interacts with modprobe to load kernel modules.

request_module

31660: As the comment preceding the function states, **request_module** is the function that the rest of the kernel calls when it discovers the need to load a kernel module. As with nearly everything else the kernel does, this request is made on behalf of the currently running process. From the process's point of view, the request is usually implicit—the kernel is carrying out some other request on behalf of the process and discovers that it needs to load a module to succeed. For example, see line 11815, which is in some code I cover in Chapter 7.

31673: **request_module** refuses to attempt to load a module before the root file system is mounted—which makes perfect sense, since in that case there's nowhere to load the module from.

31692: Loading some modules might require loading other modules first. For example, loading a driver for a USB device might require first loading low-level USB modules. This opens up the possibility of an infinite loop, which the code guards against here.

31704: Executes the function **exec_modprobe** (line 31627, and discussed shortly) as a separate process within the kernel.

This is much like using **fork** to prepare for an **exec**—you can think of **kernel_thread** as a lightweight version of **fork** for the kernel. However, it has two important differences from **fork**: The new process begins execution at the named function, not at the same location as the caller, and it shares the kernel's entire memory space rather than getting its own copy. Just as with **fork**, the return value of **kernel_thread** is the process ID of the new process.

31706: Also like **fork**, a negative return value from **kernel_thread** is an error.

31715: As documented in the function, most signals are temporarily blocked for the current process.

31722: Waits for **exec_modprobe** to complete, indicating either that the requested module has been loaded or that the attempt failed.

31726: Finishes up, restoring signals and printing an error message if **exec_modprobe** returned an error code.

exec_modprobe

31627: **exec_modprobe** runs the program that attaches a kernel module to the kernel. The module name is a **void** * rather than a **char** * here for the simple reason that functions spawned by **kernel_thread** always take a single **void** * argument.

31629: Sets up modprobe's argument list and environment. **modprobe_path** (line 31625), which locates the modprobe program, can be changed while the kernel is running, using features I explore in Chapter 11 (see line 38002). This means that root can dynamically choose a different program to run instead of /sbin/modprobe—for example, if modprobe is installed in a different location, or to use an improved modprobe replacement.

31637: **exec_modprobe** actually runs modprobe using **exec_usermodehelper**, described next. If that function fails, **exec_modprobe** prints an error message and returns nonzero; if **exec_usermodehelper** succeeds, it does not return.

exec_usermodehelper

31569: This function executes a user-mode process that does some work at the kernel's behest. As you've seen, it's used to execute modprobe when loading kernel modules; it's also used to handle so-called hotplug buses, such as USB, which can deal with devices being physically connected and disconnected while the system is running (see line 31742 for more information).

31586: Gets rid of all pending signals and signal handlers, for security reasons (as described in the code). The most important part of this is the call to **flush_signal_handlers** (line 35100), which replaces any user-defined signal handlers with the kernel's defaults. If any signals arrive after this point, they'll get the default response, which is usually either to ignore the signal or to kill the process—either way, there's no security risk.

31593: Closes any files the calling process had open. Most importantly, this means that the modprobe program will not inherit standard input, standard output, or standard error from the calling process; inheriting these file descriptors could introduce security holes. (This might matter to a program that replaced modprobe, but modprobe itself doesn't actually care.)

31600: The modprobe program executes as root, with all of root's privileges. (See line 21929 for the definition of **INIT_USER**.)

31617: Tries to execute the given program (modprobe, hotplug, or whatever), returning an error code if this fails.

31619: When **execve** succeeds, it never returns, so this point is not reached. The compiler doesn't know that, though, so a **return** statement appears here to silence gcc.

Covering the kernel module system in greater depth would take us too far afield for this chapter, so I'll leave the topic at this point. However, the rest of the necessary code is included in the book, and you might want to peruse it after you read Chapters 4 and 5. The three main files involved are include/linux/module.h (which starts at line 20791), include/asm-i386/module.h (line 13339), and kernel/module.c (which starts at line 31869). In particular, note **struct module** (line 20842), as well as the functions **sys_create_module** (line 32175), **sys_init_module** (line 32223), **sys_delete_module** (line 32516), and **sys_query_module** (line 32812). These functions implement the system calls (see Chapter 5) used by modprobe, and the related programs insmod, lsmod, and rmmod, to install, locate, and remove modules.

It might seem odd for the kernel to invoke a program that simply calls right back into the kernel. There's more than that going on, though. modprobe has to go out to the disk and actually find the module files that are to be loaded, for one thing. Also, and more importantly, this method gives root more control over the kernel module system, because root can run modprobe and the related programs, too. Hence, root can manually load, query, and remove modules, or the kernel can do it automatically.

Configuring and Building the Kernel

You can study and appreciate the Linux kernel's source code without ever touching it. However, in the likely event that you're seized by the urge to implement and test an improvement to the kernel code, you need to know how to rebuild the kernel. This section shows you how to do that and wraps up with a discussion of how to distribute your changes to others so that everyone can benefit from your work.

Configuring the Kernel

The first step in compiling the kernel is configuring it. This is where you add or remove support for kernel features. You can also change the way some features behave—for example, you can instruct the kernel to use a different direct memory access (DMA) channel for your sound card. If the kernel is already configured to your liking, you can skip this step. Otherwise, read on.

To configure the kernel, become root and go to the kernel source directory:

```
cd /usr/src/linux
```

Then, type one of the following commands:

```
make config
make menuconfig
make xconfig
```

All of these commands allow you to configure the kernel, but they do it in different ways:

- **make config**—The simplest and least pleasant of the three methods. But, as the lowest common denominator, it works under all circumstances. This method simply asks you which features you would like to include in the kernel, querying you about every supported kernel feature. Most of the questions expect you to respond with y (yes, compile this feature into the kernel), m (compile as a module), or n (no, don't support this feature at all). Think before you answer, because you can't go back—if you make a mistake, you must press

Ctrl+C and start over. You can also press ? for help. Figure 2.1 shows this method running in an xterm.

Fortunately, this method does have some smarts—for instance, if you say no to SCSI support, it knows not to ask you any more detailed SCSI-related questions. In addition, you can just press Enter to give the default answer, which is the current setting (so if SCSI support is currently compiled into the kernel, pressing Enter in response to that question means to keep compiling it into the kernel). Even so, most users prefer one of the other two methods.

- **make menuconfig**—A terminal-based configuration mechanism; you can move around with the cursor keys, and so on. It even supports color if your terminal does. Figure 2.2 shows an xterm running **make menuconfig**. You need the ncurses library to be able to use menuconfig.

- **make xconfig**—My favorite. It works only if you're running an X server, and if you're willing to run X applications as root. (Real paranoids don't.) You must also have the Tcl windowing shell, wish, installed, which further implies that you need Tcl, Tk, and a working X installation. In exchange, you get a prettier, X-based equivalent to menuconfig. Figure 2.3 shows this method in action, with the Loadable Module Support subwindow opened.

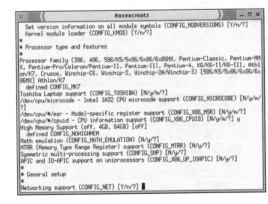

Figure 2.1   make config in action.

As stated, all three of these methods have the same effect: They write a .config file used when building the kernel. They differ only in how easy they make it to create this file.

Building the Kernel

Building the kernel is less work than configuring it. There are several ways to do it, though, and which one you choose depends on how you want your system set up. Over time, I've evolved the following routine. It's a little more than I strictly need to do, but it covers all the bases. First, if you're not already there, go to the kernel source directory again:

```
cd /usr/src/linux
```

Now, as root, make the kernel as shown next. Note that the **make** command is broken into two lines for space; this is all one command, on one line, when you type it into the shell:

```
make dep clean zlilo boot
    modules modules_install
```

(For speed, you can omit the **dep** and **clean** targets if you know it's safe.) When given multiple targets, make knows not to try the second and following targets unless all the preceding targets succeed. So if the make runs to completion and exits successfully, all the targets were correctly built. You can reboot your machine and play with your new kernel.

The Importance of Backups

When you're fooling with the kernel, you should always have a backup kernel to boot from. One way to do this is by configuring the Linux Loader (LILO) to allow you to select a kernel image to boot, one of which is the backup that you never touch (that's the way I do it).

If you have a little more patience, you can use the zdisk target instead of the zlilo target; this writes a bootable kernel image to a floppy diskette. You can then boot your experimental kernel simply by inserting the diskette at boot time; if you don't insert the diskette, you're booting from your normal kernel.

But watch out: The kernel modules aren't installed on the diskette—they're installed on your hard disk (unless you go to extra trouble). Consequently, even the zdisk target doesn't save you if you mess up the kernel modules. In fact, both methods I've outlined suffer from this problem. Although more elegant solutions are available, the simplest (and the one I use) is to compile the backup kernel as a strict monolithic kernel, without loadable module support. That way, if I mess up and have to fall back to my backup kernel, it won't matter whether the problem I'm recovering from was in my experimental kernel proper or in the kernel modules. Either way, everything I need is in the backup kernel itself.

Because the changes you make can damage your system—corrupting data on the disk and so on, and not only when you're messing with device drivers or file systems—it's also a good idea to have a recent backup of your system's data before you test a new kernel. (Device driver development is not a topic of this book, but I do want to point out that a device driver bug can cause physical damage to your system. Your monitor is impossible to back up and expensive to replace.) As a potential kernel hacker, your best investment (after this book, of course) is a tape drive and plenty of tapes. Or you can dedicate an entire separate machine to kernel hacking—either by buying one for the purpose (which is what I've done) or by creating a virtual system using a product such as VMware.

Distributing Your Changes

The following are some basic etiquette issues involved in distributing your changes:

- Check the latest kernel release to ensure that you aren't solving an already-solved problem.

- Follow the Linux kernel coding style. In brief, this means an eight-character indentation level and K&R brace style (the open brace goes on the same line as the **if**, **else**, **for**, **while**, **switch**, or **do**). The file

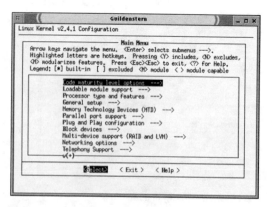

Figure 2.2   make menuconfig in action.

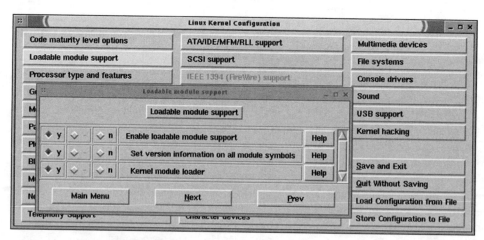

Figure 2.3   make xconfig in action.

Documentation/CodingStyle, under the kernel source directory, spells out the rules completely, but I've mentioned the most important parts. Note that the source code included in this book has been extensively edited to save space; in the process, I broke some of these rules.

- Distribute unrelated changes independently. That way, someone who wants to try only one of your changes can get it easily without having to try them all at once.

- Let everyone to whom you distribute your changes know what the changes are supposed to do. Similarly, you should give some indication of your level of confidence in them. Did you hack them out 15 minutes ago and haven't had time to compile them yet, or have they been running stably on your system and a friend's system since last March?

Now that you're ready to distribute your changes, the first step is to generate a file describing the changes you've made. You generate this file automatically, with the diff program. The output is referred to either as diffs or, more commonly in the Linux community, as a patch.

The procedure is actually quite simple. Assuming that the original, untouched source code is in the directory linux-2.4.1, that your changed source code is in the directory linux-my, and that there's not already a file or directory named linux (if there is, just temporarily rename it), you can simply do the following (run the ln only if the link doesn't already exist):

```
ln -s linux-my linux
make -C linux-2.4.1 distclean
make -C linux distclean
diff -urN linux-2.4.1 linux >my.patch
```

The output file my.patch now contains everything another user needs to apply the patch. (Warning: As shown, *all* the differences between the two source trees will end up in the patch file. diff can't tell which changes are related to which other changes, so it takes them all.) If the resulting patch is relatively small, you can simply post it directly to the kernel mailing list. If it's large, you should make it available via FTP or the Web, and post a URL to the mailing list.

The FAQ file for the Linux kernel mailing list is at **http:// www.ececs.uc.edu/~rreilova/linux/lkml-faq.html**. The FAQ includes instructions for subscribing to the list, posting to the list, what to expect when reading the list, and so on.

By the way, if you're interested in keeping up with the kernel's ongoing development, I highly recommend the invaluable Kernel Traffic site, **http://kt.zork.net**.

Chapter 3

Kernel Architecture Overview

This chapter explores the kernel at a high level. It begins with a look at the kernel's design goals, examines the kernel's architecture, and concludes by exploring the kernel's source directory structure.

Kernel Design Goals

The Linux kernel exhibits several intertwined design goals: clarity, compatibility, portability, robustness, security, and speed. Sometimes these goals complement each other, and sometimes they conflict. Still, as far as possible, they are consistently applied, and features of the kernel's design and implementation can always be traced back to them. The next few sections examine these design goals and sketch out some of the tradeoffs between them.

Clarity

To oversimplify a bit, the kernel's top goals are to be fast and correct; clarity of code is a secondary goal. Contrast this with most modern application development, in which the primary goals are usually to be clear and correct, and speed is secondary. Inside the kernel, then, the normal relative importance of speed and clarity is reversed.

To some extent, clarity complements correctness: An implementation that can easily be understood can more easily be proved correct or more easily be debugged when it is incorrect. These two goals, therefore, rarely clash.

However, clarity and speed are often in conflict. An algorithm that has been heavily hand-optimized, often in a way that reflects intimate knowledge of the compiler's code-generation techniques, is rarely the clearest of all implementations. When the goals of clarity and speed

conflict in the kernel, speed almost always wins. Even so, the kernel's developers plainly recognize the importance of clarity, and they do a consistently superb job of choosing the clearest way to be blindingly fast.

Compatibility

As I said in Chapter 1, the Linux kernel was originally written to form the nucleus of a complete, Unix-compatible operating system. Along the way, it picked up the goal of being a POSIX-compliant kernel, as well. As far as the kernel is concerned, there's not much difference between being Unix-compatible (in the sense of being compatible with a modern Unix implementation, at least) and being POSIX-compliant, so you might as well go for the brass ring.

The kernel offers another kind of compatibility. A Linux-based system provides optional support for running Java .class files as if they were native executables. (Indeed, Linux reportedly was the first operating system to provide such support.) Although actually interpreting the Java executables is the responsibility of a separate process—there's no Java Virtual Machine (JVM) built into the kernel itself—the kernel provides the mechanisms that let you make this support transparent to the user. Support for other executable formats can be plugged into the kernel in the same way, with varying amounts of the support provided by the kernel itself (as opposed to delegating most of the work to an external process, as is done with Java). This subject is explored in some detail in Chapter 7.

As a side note, the GNU/Linux system as a whole offers support for DOS executables through the DOSEMU emulator, and it offers some support for Windows executables through the Wine project. In a similar way, Windows-compatible file and print services are provided by Samba. These are not kernel issues, however, so I don't cover them in the book.

Another aspect of compatibility is compatibility with "foreign" file systems, which is explored in a bit more depth later in the chapter, but is generally outside the

scope of this book. Linux supports a wide variety of file systems—ext2 (the "native" file system), ISO-9660 (used on CD-ROMs), MS-DOS, Sun's Network File System (NFS), the Amiga Fast File System (AFFS), and many others. If you have a disk in another operating system's favorite format, or a network disk server, the chances are good that Linux knows how to work with it.

Still another aspect of compatibility is networking, which is ever more important in these Internet-aware days. Linux, being a Unix variant, has naturally had TCP/IP support since very early in its history. The kernel also includes code for the AppleTalk protocol, which enables a Linux box to play nicely with Macintoshes; Novell's protocols, namely Internetwork Packet Exchange (IPX), Sequenced Packet Exchange (SPX), and NetWare Core Protocol (NCP); the new version of the IP protocol, IPv6; and a large number of less well-known protocols.

The final aspect of compatibility that is considered here is compatibility with hardware devices. It seems that almost every weird video card, niche-market network card, nonstandard CD-ROM interface, and proprietary tape drive has a Linux driver out there somewhere. (As long as it's not crippled hardware that has deliberately been made dependent on a specific OS—and Linux even supports some of that junk.) The kernel's hardware support is only getting better, as more and more manufacturers see the light and open their source code for easier porting to Linux.

All this compatibility is achieved through an important secondary goal: modularity. Where possible, the kernel defines an abstract interface to a subsystem so that the abstract interface can be implemented in any number of ways. Kernel support for a new file system, for example, reduces to writing a new implementation for the Virtual File System (VFS) interface. Another example, this one explored in Chapter 7, is the kernel's abstract support for binary handlers—its method of supporting new executable formats, such as Java's. Adding support for a new executable format is mainly a matter of implementing the binary handler interface for that format.

Portability

A design goal somewhat related to hardware compatibility is *portability*, the ability to run the Linux kernel on a variety of hardware platforms. The system was originally developed for Intel x86 CPUs running in a standard IBM PC-compatible box, with no thought given to portability. Things have changed since then. The official kernel ports now include ports to systems based on Alpha, ARM, Hitachi SuperH, IA-64, MIPS, MIPS-64, Motorola 680x0, PA-RISC, PowerPC, SPARC, and SPARC-64 CPUs, plus IBM's S/390 mainframes. Therefore, you can run Linux on Amigas, old or new Macintoshes, workstations from Sun and SGI, NeXT machines, and more—and those are just the ports in the standard kernel distribution. Work is also progressing on unofficial ports to everything from old DEC VAXes to 3Com's Palm series of handhelds (such as the Palm III). Successful unofficial ports tend to become official later, so some of these will end up in the main development tree.

The wide variety of supported platforms is enabled, in part, by the kernel's clean separation of the source code into architecture-dependent and architecture-independent sections. I delve into this more deeply later in the chapter.

Robustness and Security

Linux is intended to be robust and secure. It should not have any bugs of its own, and it must protect processes (and users) from one another, as well as protecting the system as a whole from other systems. The last consideration is largely the domain of trusted user-space applications, but the kernel must, at least, provide the primitives upon which security can be based. Robustness and security generally trump any other considerations, including speed. (What good is it to crash fast?) You can think of robustness and security as aspects of another goal: correctness.

The single most important factor guaranteeing Linux's correctness is its open development process, which can be seen as massive peer review. Every line of code in the kernel, and every change, will be examined minutely

by countless developers around the world. One of them is bound to spot any bug that might be lurking therein—and it's in their self-interest to look for those bugs, because they want their own Linux systems to be robust and secure, too. Bugs that aren't caught by inspection can be isolated and fixed by whoever finds them, and the fixes are then merged back into the main development tree for everyone's benefit. Both security alerts and bug reports are generally fixed within days or even hours.

Linux might not be absolutely the most secure operating system available (many feel that title belongs to OpenBSD, a Unix variant that made security a principal goal), but it's a contender—and its robustness is hard to top.

Speed

This one mostly speaks for itself. Speed is a highly important design goal, although it ranks below robustness, security, and (sometimes) compatibility. It is one of the most visible aspects of the code, however. The Linux kernel code is thoroughly optimized, with the most-used pieces—the scheduler, for instance—optimized the most. Almost any time something in the code looks weird, it's because it was faster that way. (This is not always obvious, however, and frequently, you must try the alternatives yourself to find out for sure.) Sometimes there is a more straightforward implementation that is also faster, although I can count on one hand the number of times I've seen that.

In a few cases, this text recommends a more readable alternative to some code that was deliberately contorted in the name of speed. Because I know that speed was a design goal, however, I generally do this only when a) speed is not obviously crucial in the case under consideration, and b) I couldn't help myself.

A First Look at the Kernel's Architecture

Figure 3.1 is a fairly standard view of a Unix-like operating system—indeed, given its low detail, it could be

just about any operating system that cared about platform independence. It's intended to emphasize two properties of the kernel:

- The kernel separates applications from hardware.

- Part of the kernel is architecture- and hardware-specific, and part of it is portable.

The first point was made in earlier chapters, so the discussion need not be repeated here. The related second point, about architecture-independent vs. architecture-dependent code, is of more interest to this discussion. The kernel achieves portability, in part, by pulling the same trick with itself that it pulls with user applications. That is, just as the kernel separates user applications from hardware, part of the kernel separates the rest of the kernel from the hardware. Both user applications and portions of the kernel are rendered portable—at least in part—by this separation.

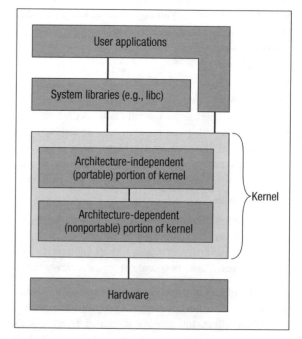

Figure 3.1 An initial view of the kernel's architecture.

Although this is not always made explicit in the code itself, the architecture-independent portion of the source code generally defines (or assumes) an interface to the lower-level, architecture-dependent portion. As a simple example, architecture-independent sections of the memory-management code assume that by including a certain header file, they'll pick up (among other things) a suitable definition of the **PAGE_SIZE** macro (see line 13386), which defines the size of the chunks into which the system's memory-management hardware likes to break the system's address space (see Chapter 8). The architecture-independent code doesn't care about the macro's exact definition, leaving that to the architecture-specific code. (By the way, this is much cleaner and more pleasant to read than an **#ifdef/#endif** block everywhere there's a platform-dependent line of code.) Porting the kernel to a new architecture thus becomes a matter of identifying such features and implementing them as needed by the new platform.

By the way, the portability of user applications is further assisted by a layer between them and the kernel, the standard C library (libc). Applications virtually never talk to the kernel directly, only by way of libc. The only reason Figure 3.1 shows applications talking directly to the kernel is because they could. In real life, however, they don't—there's no point. Anything applications can say directly to the kernel, they can say more easily by way of libc.

The way libc talks to the kernel is architecture-dependent (slightly contradicting what is shown in the figure), and libc takes responsibility for shielding user code from the details. Interestingly, most of libc doesn't need to know these details. A large fraction of libc, such as the implementations of **atoi** or **rand**, has no need to interact with the kernel at all. Much of the rest of libc, functions such as **printf**, do significant amounts of work before and/or after involving the kernel. (**printf** must first interpret the format string, extract the corresponding arguments, figure out how to print them, and record its intended output in a temporary internal buffer. Only then does it call the underlying system call, **write**, to

print this buffer.) Other pieces of libc are just the thinnest possible layers over the corresponding system calls; a call to one of these functions is translated immediately into a call to the kernel, which does the majority of the work. At the lowest level, most of libc funnels through a single "channel" to the kernel, through a mechanism detailed in Chapter 5.

Because of this design, all user applications, and even most of the C library, talk to the kernel in a mostly architecture-independent way.

A Closer Look at the Kernel's Architecture

Figure 3.2 shows an alternate way of conceptualizing the kernel. This view dispenses with the distinction between architecture-dependent and architecture-independent portions of the kernel in favor of a more informative view. Within the "Kernel" box, portions of the kernel that are covered in this book have their chapter numbers shown in parentheses. Symmetric multiprocessing (SMP) support is covered in this book, but it isn't shown in the figure, partly because much of the SMP code is distributed throughout the kernel, so it's hard to associate it with just one module. Likewise, kernel initialization support is covered in this book, but it isn't shown in the figure, either, simply because it's not very interesting from a design point of view. Finally, although the figure associates Chapter 6 with the "Interprocess Communication" box, that chapter is only partly about interprocess communication.

A process's interaction with the kernel usually goes as follows:

1. A user application invokes a system call, normally via libc.

2. This call is trapped by the kernel function **system_call** (line 898, Chapter 5), which forwards the request to another kernel function that will carry out the request.

3. That function then communicates with the relevant internal code modules, which in turn might communicate with other code modules and/or with the underlying hardware.

4. Results then flow back up the same path.

Not all interaction between the kernel and a process is initiated by the process, however. The kernel sometimes decides on its own to interact with a process, such as by suspending its execution to give another process a chance to run, by delivering a signal, or simply by killing the process outright (for example, because the process used up all the CPU time it's allowed). These

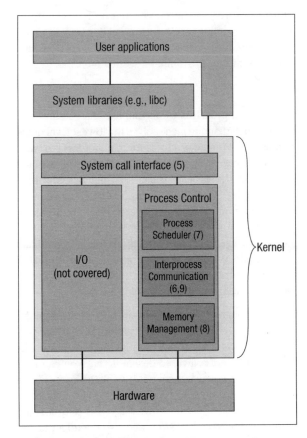

Figure 3.2   A more detailed view of the kernel's architecture.

interactions are not captured by the figure, mainly because they generally reduce to the kernel's modification of its own internal data structures (signal delivery being the exception to the rule).

So, Is It Layered, Modular, or What?

All methods for combating complexity are based on one principle: divide and conquer. That is, the methods are all variations on the theme of breaking a large, hard-to-solve problem (or system) into a number of subproblems (or subsystems) of lesser complexity, repeating the process as necessary until each piece is small enough to handle.

Here are three of the classic methods invented or adopted by computer science for building large systems: layers, modules, and objects. (I'll admit up front that these definitions are deliberate straw men.)

Layers

The layer approach is to decompose the solution into pieces, such that one piece solves the lowest level of the problem and provides a basis for a higher level to work at a higher level of abstraction. Still-higher levels are built on top of the levels below them. The Open Systems Interconnection (OSI) and TCP/IP protocol stacks are famous and successful examples of layered software design. A layered approach to operating system design might include one level that talks directly to the hardware and provides a level of abstraction over it, so that a higher level can talk about disks, network cards, and so on, without knowing any of the details of those devices.

One characteristic of layered design is that you gradually build up a vocabulary, with greater and greater expressive power as you rise through the layers. Another characteristic of a layered design is that you can usually swap out layers transparently to all the layers above and below. In the best case, porting a layered OS requires rewriting only the lowest layer. A pure layered implementation can be slow, because the upper layers must (indirectly) do all of their work through a series of successively lower layers—layer N talks to layer $N-1$,

which talks to layer $N-2$, and so on, until the real work is done at layer 0. Then, of course, the results have to be passed all the way back up. Consequently, layered designs usually include some provision for some higher layers to talk directly to some lower layers. This improves speed, at the cost of making it harder to swap out some layers (because more than one higher layer can directly depend on the one you want to replace).

Modules

A module hides some well-defined chunk of functionality behind an abstract interface. The big point of modules is to separate an interface from an implementation. Modules are allowed to depend only on each other's interfaces, so one module's implementation can be changed without affecting other modules. The scope of a module is intended to reflect the natural conceptual boundaries of some aspect of the solution domain. A purely modular OS, then, might have a module for the disk subsystem, a module for the memory subsystem, and so on. The main difference between a purely modular and a purely layered system is that a module can freely be used by any other module—there's no notion of "above" or "below" in a modular design. (In this sense, modules are a generalization of layers—in the pure view, a layer is like a module that can be used by at most one other module, the one directly above it.)

Objects

Objects are different from modules, because, for starters, they imply a different way of thinking and can have independent behavior. However, for our present purposes, an object is little more than a structured way of using a module. *Components*, a further refinement of the idea of objects, haven't really made a big splash in the world of operating system design yet. Even components, however, are not (from our point of view) sufficiently different from modules to be worth a separate category.

Figure 3.1 emphasizes a layered view of the kernel, with an architecture-independent layer above an architecture-dependent layer. (A more accurate view would have

included an additional architecture-dependent layer at the top, because the system call interface sits between applications and the kernel, and that interface is architecture-dependent.) Figure 3.2 emphasizes a more modular view of the kernel.

At some level of description, either of these views is right. Alternatively, they're both wrong. I could draw pictures all day to convince you that the kernel followed just about any set of design principles you can name, because it draws from many ideas at once. The truth is, simply, that the Linux kernel is neither strictly layered nor strictly modular, nor strictly anything but pragmatic. (In fact, if one word sums up everything about Linux, from design through implementation, "pragmatic" is it.) Perhaps the most easily defended point of view is that the kernel implementation is modular, although its modules sometimes deliberately cross module boundaries in pursuit of speed.

Linux's design, then, reflects both theory and pragmatism. Linux doesn't ignore design methodologies; rather, in the Linux development philosophy, design methodologies are like compilers—tools to get a job done. Choosing a single design principle (for example, objects) and applying it exhaustively, admitting no exceptions, might be a fine way to test the limits of the principle or to build a teaching system whose purpose is to illustrate the methodology. But it's a lousy way to design a kernel that meets Linux's design goals, which don't include being "pure" anything. The Linux developers are quite willing to violate a design principle that gets in the way of their goals.

Indeed, what is true of Linux is true of most successful designs. In general, successful, widely used, non-toy systems are essentially pragmatic. Some developers try to find *the* magic bullet, *the* design principle or methodology that cures all ills. They discover hammers, and suddenly everything looks like a nail. Successful designs, such as the Linux kernel's design, generally draw on multiple methodologies for different pieces of the system or at different levels of description. The result might not be clean and pure, but the hybrid is stronger and better than a comparable pure system would be.

The Linux Kernel Is Monolithic—Mostly

Operating system kernels can be either *microkernels* or *monolithic kernels* (the latter are sometimes called *macrokernels*).

Microkernels

In a microkernel, most of the kernel is implemented as separate processes that run in a privileged mode and communicate with one another by passing messages. Typically, the design has one such process per conceptual module—so if the design has a system call module, for example, there's a corresponding process that accepts requests for system calls and communicates with the other processes (modules) as needed to implement the system call.

In these designs, the microkernel proper is often little more than a message hub: When the system call module wants to send a message to the file system module, the message passes through the microkernel. This helps to insulate the modules from each other. (Sometimes, the modules can also pass messages directly to one another.) In some microkernel designs, more functionality, such as I/O, is in the microkernel. But the basic idea is to keep the microkernel as small as possible, partly so that you need to port only the microkernel itself when porting the kernel as a whole to a new platform. The other modules depend only on each other and on the microkernel, not directly on the hardware.

One advantage of a microkernel design is that it is easy to replace the file system module (for instance) with a more efficient implementation, without affecting the rest of the system in any way. It might even be possible to develop new system modules, or replacements for existing system modules, and add them on the fly, while the system is running. Another advantage is that unneeded modules don't need to be loaded, so microkernels can make more efficient use of memory.

Monolithic Kernels

A monolithic kernel is one big process. It might be subdivided into modules (or layers, or whatever) internally, but at runtime, it's a single, large binary image. Rather than pass messages, its modules communicate by directly calling functions in other modules.

Supporters of monolithic kernels claim that the efficiency of a microkernel suffers because of its message-passing overhead. Microkernel supporters claim that the increased flexibility, portability, and maintainability of a microkernel design more than make up for any loss—and that the difference is negligible anyway.

I won't get into all that, except to note, with some amusement, that the debate is reminiscent of the RISC vs. CISC argument that was all the rage in the CPU world a few years ago. Modern, successful CPU designs are a blend of both techniques, just as the Linux kernel incorporates both monolithic and microkernel ideas. The Linux kernel is basically monolithic, but it is not a pure monolithic kernel. The kernel module system, which I explored in the previous chapter, is a way of bringing some of the advantages of microkernels to Linux's otherwise monolithic design. (By the way, I think you could make an interesting case that Linux's kernel module system makes it a microkernel design that simply doesn't do message passing. I don't agree, but it's an interesting thought.)

Why is Linux essentially monolithic? One reason is historical: By Linus's own account, it was just plain easier to get the Linux kernel up and running in the first place by making it monolithic. That decision avoided the need to invent a message-passing architecture, to figure out how the modules would be loaded, and so on. (The kernel module system was retrofitted years later.)

Another reason is the effect of plentiful developer time. Linux has neither a shortage of developer time nor marketing-imposed release schedules, so the difficulty of making changes to the kernel is only a moderate constraint. The kernel's monolithic design is sufficiently modular internally that making changes or additions is not usually difficult anyway, but the real point is that there's no need to rewrite the Linux kernel to be a microkernel, just for the sake of a small and unproven increase in maintainability. (Linus, in particular, has repeatedly expressed the view that the purported benefits are not worth the costs in speed.) Later chapters occasionally reconsider the effects of plentiful developer time, in smaller, more concrete contexts.

If Linux were a pure microkernel design, it would be easier to port it to other architectures. Indeed, some microkernels, such as the Mach microkernel, have successfully demonstrated the portability benefits of the approach. As it is, porting the Linux kernel is nontrivial, but not daunting: In round numbers, a typical port to a completely new architecture requires anywhere from 30,000 to 60,000 lines of code, plus up to about 20,000 lines of code for drivers. (New driver code is not required for every port.) At a glance, I estimate 50,000 lines of code is a typical total for an average port. This is comfortably in the range of what a single programmer—or, at worst, a small team—can accomplish within a year. It's more code than one would likely have to write to port a microkernel, but Linux advocates would argue that the Linux kernel ports exploit the underlying hardware more efficiently than a microkernel can, so that the increased porting effort is balanced by improved system efficiency.

This particular design tradeoff is not to be taken lightly. The decision to implement a monolithic kernel flies in the face of conventional wisdom, which dictates that microkernels are the wave of the future. However, being (mostly) monolithic has worked out fine for Linux. The relative difficulty of porting the kernel hasn't noticeably discouraged the developer community, which has enthusiastically and successfully ported the kernel to most of the "real" architectures in existence, not to mention some unlikely targets, such as the Palm handhelds. As long as Linux's many benefits continue to make the effort worthwhile, new ports will continue to appear.

The Relationship between Design and Implementation

The remaining sections explore some useful correspondences between the kernel's design and its implementation. The most important of these is an overview of the kernel source directory structure. The chapter concludes with a brief examination of the relative sizes of architecture-dependent and architecture-independent code in the implementation.

Kernel Source Directory Structure

The kernel's source code is conventionally installed under the directory /usr/src/linux. Within this directory are several other directories, each dedicated to a certain subset of the kernel's functionality (or, very roughly, to a high-level code module).

Documentation

There's no kernel code under this directory, but it does include a collection of useful—if spotty—documentation. Some pieces of the kernel, such as file systems, have fairly good and fairly complete documentation in this directory; other pieces of the kernel, such as the process scheduler, have nothing. But now and then, you can find exactly what you need under here.

arch

All of the subdirectories under the arch directory contain architecture-specific code. The following subdirectories appear under the arch directory:

- *arch/alpha/*—The Linux kernel port to workstations based on the DEC Alpha CPU.

- *arch/arm/*—The Linux kernel port to the ARM line of CPUs, which are used in such machines as Corel's NetWinder and the Acorn RiscPC.

- *arch/i386/*—The closest thing the Linux kernel has to a "native" or "reference" platform. This is for Intel's 80386 architecture, which, of course, includes later CPUs in the same family (the 80486, Pentium, and so on), as well as clones from companies such as AMD, Cyrix, IDT, and Transmeta.

  This book generally refers to this architecture as the "x86," even though, strictly speaking, the term "x86" is too broad. Earlier Intel CPUs, such as the 80286, do not include all the CPU features Linux requires in order to run, and there's no official support for such

machines. (As a side note, however, there is an independent port of Linux to such CPUs, with reduced functionality.) When this book refers to the "x86 platform," it always means the 80386 or later CPUs. The x86 architecture is sometimes called "IA-32."

- *arch/ia64/*—The port to Intel's and Hewlett-Packard's new 64-bit architecture, the IA-64. This is the endlessly delayed CPU formerly known as Merced and now named Itanium.

- *arch/m68k/*—The port to Motorola's 680x0 line of CPUs. This supports machines based on everything from a 68020 (as long as it's coupled with a 68851 memory management unit, or MMU) up to the 68060. Many companies used the 680x0 line in their products—the Commodore Amiga, the Apple Macintosh, the Atari ST, and others. Many of these old machines are being turned into credible Linux workstations. In addition, ports are under way to NeXT workstations, Sinclair's Q40 and Q80, and various VME boards.

- *arch/mips/ and arch/mips64/*—The port to the 32-bit and 64-bit versions of the MIPS line of CPUs. The best-known machines based on these CPUs are Silicon Graphics (SGI) workstations, although several other manufacturers also built systems around the MIPS.

- *arch/parisc/*—The Linux kernel port to HP's Precision Architecture (PA-RISC) CPUs used in HP's workstations and servers.

- *arch/ppc/*—The port to the Motorola/IBM PowerPC line of CPUs. This includes support for PowerPC-based Macintoshes and Amigas, as well as the BeBox, IBM's RS/6000, and others.

- *arch/s390/*—The port to IBM's S/390 mainframes.

- *arch/sh/*—The port to systems based on Hitachi's SuperH microcontrollers.

- *arch/sparc/*—The port to 32-bit SPARC CPUs. This includes everything from the Sun SPARC 1 to the SPARC 20.

- *arch/sparc64/*—The port to systems based on 64-bit SPARC CPUs (the UltraSPARC line). This includes such machines as Sun's Ultra 1, Ultra 2, and higher-end machines, up to and including the jewel in Sun's crown, the Enterprise 10000.

Unfortunately, this book must remain x86-focused, so only code from the arch/i386 directory is included.

Each of these architecture-specific subdirectories includes at least these three further subdirectories:

- *kernel*—For architecture-specific implementations of such general kernel features as signal handling and SMP support

- *lib*—For fast, architecture-specific implementations of such generally useful functions as **strlen** and **memcpy**

- *mm*—For architecture-specific memory-management routines

In addition to those three subdirectories, most architectures also have a boot subdirectory, which contains part or all of the platform-specific code for booting the kernel on that platform. In some cases, some or all of the boot code is located in the platform-specific kernel directory instead.

Finally, most of the architecture-specific directories include additional subdirectories, as needed, for any additional features or for improved organization. For example, the i386 directory includes a math-emu subdirectory, which contains code to fake the existence of a math coprocessor (FPU) on CPUs that lack it. As another example, the m68k port includes a subdirectory for each of the 680x0-based machines supported by the port, so that code specific to each of those machines has a natural home.

drivers

This directory is a rather large chunk of the kernel; indeed, the code contained under the drivers directory is more than half of the total distributed kernel code. It contains the software drivers for video cards, network cards, SCSI adapters, floppy tape drives, PCI devices, and any other Linux-supported peripheral you can name.

Some of the subdirectories under the drivers directory are platform-specific—for example, the zorro subdirectory contains code for talking to the Zorro bus. Only the Amiga ever used the Zorro bus, so the code is essentially Amiga-specific. Other subdirectories, such as the pci subdirectory, are at least partly platform-independent.

fs

The fs directory contains subdirectories corresponding to all the file systems supported by Linux. A *file system* is code that mediates between a storage device and processes that want to access the storage device; it's a layer above the device driver.

A file system can represent a local, physically attached storage device, such as a hard disk or a CD-ROM drive; file systems such as ext2 and isofs are used in these cases. Other file systems represent storage devices accessed across the network; one example is the Network File System (NFS).

There are also pseudo-file systems, such as the /proc file system, that present other information (in /proc's case, internal kernel variables and data structures) as if they were files. There's no underlying storage device in this case, but processes can pretend that there is. (NFS can also be abused to act as a pseudo-file system.)

include

This directory contains most of the include (.h) files in the Linux source tree. The files are grouped into the following subdirectories:

- *include/asm-*/*—Several of these directories exist, one corresponding to each arch subdirectory, such as include/asm-alpha, include/asm-arm, include/asm-i386, and so on. The files in each of these directories contain preprocessor macros and short inline functions needed to support a given architecture. Many of the inline functions are implemented in assembler, in whole or in part, and it is intended that many of the files may be included from either C or assembler files.

When the kernel is being compiled, a symbolic link is set up from include/asm to the target architecture-specific directory. As a result, architecture-independent kernel source code can do something like this:

```
#include <asm/some-file.h>
```

This will **#include** the appropriate architecture-specific file.

- *include/linux/*—This directory is for header files that define constants and data structures that are needed both in the kernel and by user applications requesting certain kernel services. They are mostly platform-independent. This directory is copied (or, more commonly, linked), in its entirety, to /usr/include/linux, so that user applications can **#include** these header files and be guaranteed that the contents of the files they **#include** are the same as seen by the kernel. (Chapter 9 shows an example.)

Portions of these files that are needed by the kernel only, not by user applications, are wrapped as follows:

```
/* ... Stuff for user apps and kernel ... */
#ifdef __KERNEL__
/* ... Stuff for kernel only ... */
#endif /* __KERNEL__ */
```

- *include/math-emu/*—This directory is for header files related to the kernel's FPU emulator.

- *include/net/*—This directory is for header files related to the networking subsystem.

- *include/pcmcia/*—This directory is for header files related to PCMCIA devices. (No, PCMCIA doesn't stand for "People Can't Memorize Computer Industry Acronyms." It stands for "Personal Computer Memory Card International Association," the name of the organization that defined the PCMCIA standard.)

- *include/scsi/*—This directory is for header files related to Small Computer System Interface (SCSI) controllers and devices.

- *include/video/*—This directory is for header files related to video cards and frame buffers.

init

The more important of the two files in the init directory is main.c, which includes the lion's share of the code needed to coordinate the kernel's initialization. I explore this code in detail in Chapter 4.

ipc

The files in the ipc directory implement System V interprocess communication (IPC). Chapter 9 explores them in detail.

kernel

This directory contains the innermost core of Linux: the platform-independent, basic functionality. It includes such pieces as the process scheduler (kernel/sched.c) and the code for creating and destroying processes (kernel/fork.c and kernel/exit.c). I cover these particular pieces, and more besides, in Chapter 7. I don't want to leave you with the impression that everything you need to know is in this directory—there are other critical pieces in other directories. However, line for line, the most important code resides here.

lib

The lib directory contains two pieces. The functions in lib/inflate.c decompress a compressed kernel when the system is booting (see Chapter 4). Most of the remaining files in the lib directory implement a useful subset of the standard C library. The main focus is on string and memory functions (**strlen**, **memcpy**, and the like), along with functions in the vein of **sprintf** and **atoi**.

These files are written in C, so they're immediately usable by any new kernel port. As noted earlier in the chapter, some ports provide their own, faster versions of these functions, generally in handcrafted assembler, which they use instead of the generic ones.

mm

This directory contains architecture-independent memory-management code. As mentioned earlier, the architecture-specific memory-management routines, which implement the lowest-level primitives for each platform, are in arch/*platform*/mm. I cover much of the platform-independent and x86-specific code for memory management in Chapter 8.

net

This directory contains the code for Linux's recognized network protocols—AppleTalk, TCP/IP, IPX, and so on.

scripts

The scripts directory does not contain kernel code. It contains scripts used to configure the kernel. When you run a command such as **make menuconfig** or **make xconfig** to configure the kernel, you interact with the scripts in this directory.

Architecture-Dependent and Architecture-Independent Code

We're now in a position to estimate the relative sizes of the architecture-dependent and architecture-independent code. First, some quick numbers. The entire 2.4.1 kernel totals 3,190,024 lines of code. (Incidentally, note that this book includes under 50,000 lines of code, yet it still manages to cover a decent fraction of the core functionality.) Of this, a total of 816,717 lines are in the architecture-specific directories—both arch/* and include/asm-*. I estimate that a further 250,000 lines of code, total, are dedicated to drivers used by only a single architecture. This means that about 34 percent of the distribution is dedicated to architecture-dependent code.

However, for a *single* architecture, the fraction of architecture-dependent code is smaller. Naively, if the amount of code required for a single architecture is around 50,000 lines, and there are around 2,000,000 lines of architecture-independent code, the architecture-dependent code is as little as 2.5 percent of the whole. Of course, not all of the architecture-independent code is likely to be used in a given kernel, so the actual fraction of architecture-dependent code in a given kernel depends on how the kernel is configured. Nevertheless, it should be evident that the bulk of the kernel's code is platform-independent.

Chapter 4

System Initialization

When you want to run a program, you type its name into the shell—or, increasingly, you click on its icon from a desktop environment, such as GNOME or KDE—and the kernel loads and runs it. However, some other software first must load and run the kernel; this is typically a kernel loader, such as LOADLIN or LILO. Furthermore, other software must load and run the kernel loader—call it a "kernel loader loader"—and it would seem that running the kernel loader loader requires a "kernel loader loader loader," and so on, ad infinitum.

Something must eventually terminate this infinite regression, and that something is *hardware*. So, at the lowest level, the first step in booting the system requires help from the hardware. This hardware typically runs some short, built-in program—software, but software that's burned into read-only memory and stored at a known address, so it doesn't require a software loader. This software then runs something larger and more sophisticated, which in turn runs something even larger and more sophisticated, until the kernel itself can be loaded. In this manner, the system pulls itself up by its own bootstraps, which, of course, is the metaphor behind the term "booting." The details vary greatly among architectures, but the principles are the same everywhere.

After the kernel has been loaded, the kernel can initialize both itself and the rest of the system.

This chapter takes a short tour of how a typical x86-based PC boots itself, then reviews what happens when, at last, the kernel proper gets involved.

Booting the PC

This section looks briefly at how an x86 PC boots itself. The goal of this section is not to make you an expert on

how PCs boot—that's outside the scope of this book—but rather to show you the broad outlines of how a specific architecture boots, as a way to place the kernel's own initialization in context.

To begin, each CPU in the box must initialize itself, and it may then execute a self-test for a fraction of a second. In a multiprocessor system, the picture becomes more complicated right away—but not much, really. In a dual-processor Pentium system, one of the CPUs is always the primary CPU and the other is always the secondary CPU; the primary CPU carries out all the remaining work of booting, and the kernel activates the secondary CPU later. In a multiprocessor Pentium Pro or later system, the CPUs must "race for the flag"—dynamically deciding which of them will boot the system—according to an algorithm defined by Intel. The winner boots the system, and the kernel activates all the others later. In either case, there's only one CPU to worry about for the rest of the boot procedure. Thus, for the moment, you can pretend that only one CPU is present, heedless of any others that might be temporarily dormant. On the other hand, the kernel needs to explicitly activate any additional CPUs—you'll see it do this later in the chapter.

Next, the CPU fetches and executes the instruction at address 0xfffffff0, very nearly the last possible address on a 32-bit CPU. Because most PCs don't have 4GB RAM installed, they have no normal memory at this address; the memory hardware fakes it. Those few machines that do have 4GB of RAM simply lose a little memory at the upper end of the address space to the Basic Input/Output System (BIOS). The BIOS actually reserves a total of 64KB up there—a negligible loss in a 4GB machine.

The instruction at this address is a jump into the start of the code for the BIOS, which is built into the motherboard and controls the next stage of booting. Note that the CPU doesn't really care whether a BIOS exists, which makes it possible to use Intel CPUs in non-PC architectures, such as custom-built embedded systems. The CPU blithely executes whatever instruction it finds at the target address, and it's just part of the PC architecture to make

this a jump to the BIOS. (Strictly speaking, the jump instruction itself is part of the BIOS, but this is not the most convenient way to think about it.)

The BIOS begins by choosing a boot device, using built-in rules. Often, you can modify these rules by hitting a key during startup (on my system, for example, it's the Delete key) and navigating through some menu options. However, the normal process is that the BIOS first tries to boot from a floppy and, upon failure, attempts to boot from the primary hard disk. If even that fails, it might then try to boot from the CD-ROM drive. For concreteness, this discussion assumes the most common case, in which the boot device is a hard disk.

From this boot device, the BIOS reads the first sector—the first 512 bytes—which is called the *Master Boot Record (MBR)*. What happens next depends on how Linux was installed on the system. To keep the discussion concrete, I'll assume that LILO is the kernel loader. On a typical setup, the BIOS checks for some magic numbers in the MBR (to increase its confidence that it really is an MBR) and then inspects the MBR for the location of the boot sector. The BIOS then loads this sector, which contains the beginning of LILO, into memory and jumps to its start.

Note that the system has now made the transition from the realm of hardware and built-in software to the realm of "real" software, from the tangible to the intangible—that is, from the parts you can kick to the parts you can't.

Now LILO is in charge. It loads the rest of itself and finds its configuration data on the disk, which tells it, among other things, where to find the kernel and what options to pass to it on startup. LILO then loads the kernel into memory and jumps to it.

Usually, kernels are stored as compressed files that contain just enough uncompressed instructions at the beginning to decompress the rest—a self-extracting executable. So, the next step is for the kernel to decompress itself and then to jump to the beginning of the uncompressed kernel image. The kernel has now finished loading.

Here is a summary of the steps described so far:

1. The CPU initializes itself and then executes a single instruction at a fixed location.

2. This instruction jumps into the BIOS.

3. The BIOS finds a boot device and fetches its MBR, which points to LILO.

4. The BIOS loads and transfers control to LILO.

5. LILO loads the compressed kernel.

6. The compressed kernel decompresses itself and transfers control to the uncompressed kernel.

Just as you would expect from a bootstrapping process, each step takes you to a larger and more sophisticated piece of code, until at last you have a running kernel.

Depending on how you count the levels, this makes the CPU a kernel loader loader loader loader (the CPU loads the BIOS, which loads LILO, which loads the compressed kernel, which loads the uncompressed kernel). However, you can reasonably argue about whether some of these steps satisfy the definition of a "loader."

Initializing the Linux Kernel

After the kernel is loaded into memory (and decompressed, if necessary) and some of the crucial hardware, such as the memory management unit (MMU; see Chapter 8), has been set up at a low level, the kernel jumps to **start_kernel** (line 25815). This function does the remaining system initialization—which, indeed, is nearly all of it. Thus, **start_kernel** is the focus of this section.

start_kernel

25815: The **__init** tag (line 19051) expands to gcc compiler magic that places this function in a special section of the kernel. After the kernel has finished initializing itself, it can attempt to free up this special section. Actually, there are four such sections, .text.init, .initcall.init, .data.init, and .setup.init—the first two for code, the others for data. ("Text" is a term for "pure" sections of an executable, such as code and

constant literal strings, which may be shared among processes.) You'll learn more about how these work as the chapter progresses.

25823: Prints the kernel banner message (line 26114), which shows some information about how the kernel was compiled—on what machine, at what time, with what version of the compiler, and so on. If all else fails, knowing where the kernel came from can be a useful clue in figuring out why it won't boot on your machine.

25824: Initializes some of the components of the kernel itself—memory, hardware interrupts, the scheduler, and the like. In particular, the function **setup_arch** does architecture-dependent setup, returning a value in **command_line** (the options passed to the kernel, discussed shortly).

25827: Parses any options passed to the kernel. The **parse_options** function (line 25727, and discussed later, in the section "Parsing Kernel Options") also sets up init's **argv** and **envp** (that is, its arguments and environment).

25842: The kernel can profile itself as it's running, periodically sampling what instruction it's executing and updating a table with the answer. This is done by calling **x86_do_profile** (line 13054) during the timer interrupt, which I cover in Chapter 6.

The table divides the kernel into regions of equal size, as illustrated in Figure 4.1, and simply tracks how many times the instruction executing at the time of the interrupt was in each region. This profiling is necessarily somewhat crude—it's not even broken down by function or line number, just by approximate address—but it's also cheap, fast, and small, and it can certainly help an expert identify the worst hot spots. Also, the number of addresses covered by each table entry—and, therefore, the uncertainty about where a "hit" occurred—can be tuned simply by changing **prof_shift** (line 39665). **profile_setup**

(line 25427 and discussed later in the chapter) enables you to set **prof_shift**'s value at boot time, which is much cleaner and more convenient than having to recompile the kernel just to change this number.

A **prof_shift** value of 2, for example, allocates an amount of memory equal to 25 percent of the kernel's code size to profile the kernel. That would allocate 300KB for a kernel with a 1.2MB-sized code region (a number drawn from one of my test kernels). That's a lot of memory by

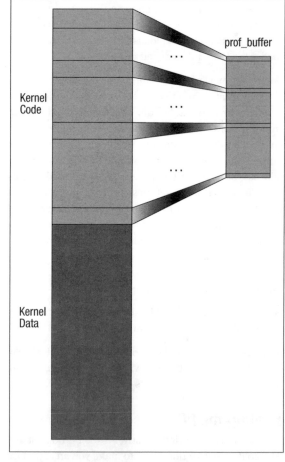

Figure 4.1   The profiling buffer.

kernel standards, and it can't be freed while the kernel is running, either; if you turn on kernel profiling at boot time, you can't turn it off without rebooting. However, the memory is allocated only when profiling is explicitly requested. In addition, using that much memory helps to identify hot spots with pretty good precision—leaving only a few instructions' worth of uncertainty, which should tend to constrain a hit to a line or two of source code. Finally, if you want to profile your kernel but really can't afford to use so much memory, you can just choose a larger **prof_shift** value to trade memory for precision.

This **if** block sets aside memory for the profile table and zeroes its entries. Note that if **prof_shift** is 0 (the default), profiling is off, the **if** block is not executed, and no room is set aside for the table.

25855: Starts paying attention to hardware interrupts by calling **sti** (line 16962 for the UP version). (I cover interrupts in much more detail in Chapter 6.) The immediate need is for the timer interrupt to be active, so that the subsequent call to **calibrate_delay** (line 25640) can compute this machine's BogoMIPS (described in the next section, "BogoMIPS"). The BogoMIPS value is needed by some device drivers, so the kernel must compute it before initializing most of the hardware, the file systems, and so on.

25892: Tests this CPU for various bugs, such as the Pentium f00f bug (see Chapter 8), and remembers which bugs were detected so that other parts of the kernel can work around them later. (The **check_bugs** function was omitted for space.)

25898: As described earlier, even in a multiprocessor system, only one CPU is used while booting. Intel calls this the *bootstrap processor (BSP)*, which, incidentally, is also called *BP* at various points in the kernel code. The BSP, therefore, must wake the other CPUs, and here is where it does so. It calls **smp_init** (line 25803), which calls the other functions that activate the additional CPUs on an SMP system. On the x86 platform, **smp_boot_cpus** initializes some kernel data structures that track the additional CPUs and then briefly puts the CPUs into a holding pattern; **smp_commence** at last lets them proceed.

In an SMP system, by the way, the BSP is the only CPU that ever invokes **start_kernel**; the others are routed to a function named **initialize_secondary** (omitted for space).

25899: Fires off the **init** function as a kernel thread. This is complex; see the discussion of **init** later in this chapter.

25902: Raises the idle process's **need_resched** flag, for reasons that, for the moment, might be obscure. This might not make complete sense until after you read Chapters 5, 6, and 7, but, no later than the next timer interrupt (discussed in Chapter 6), **ret_from_intr** (line 976, Chapters 5 and 6) will notice that the idle process's **need_resched** flag is raised and call **schedule** (line 34237, Chapter 7) to hand off the CPU to a more deserving process.

25903: Having completed the kernel's initialization—or, anyway, having transferred to **init** the responsibility for what is left—all that remains is to enter an idle loop to suck up any unused CPU time. So, this line calls **cpu_idle** (line 3117)—the idle loop. As you can see from looking at **cpu_idle**, the function never returns. However, it will be preempted when any real work needs to be done.

The **idle** function called by **cpu_idle** is always either **default_idle** (line 3080) or **poll_idle** (line 3095). The basic operation in **default_idle** is to execute the **hlt** (for "halt") instruction, putting the CPU into a low-power "sleep" mode. (See the definition of **safe_halt** at line 16965.) It follows that the CPU will be put into this mode when there is no real work for it to do. For reasons documented in the comment beginning at line 3091, **poll_idle** takes a different approach. The **rep/nop** combination used there reduces power consumption, but not as much as **hlt**.

Because the **pm_idle** function pointer has **extern** (non-**static**) linkage and **cpu_idle**'s outer loop periodically reinitializes **idle** from **pm_idle**, you could write a loadable kernel module that did whatever you wanted during the system's idle loop—just point **pm_idle** at your own function instead.

BogoMIPS

The BogoMIPS figure is computed by the kernel and printed during the system's initialization. It tells you approximately how many times per second the CPU can execute a short delay loop. Within the kernel, the answer is used mainly by device drivers that need to busy-wait for very short periods—for example, to wait a few microseconds to see whether some information has become available from a device.

The BogoMIPS figure is widely misused because, to the untutored, it appears to fulfill one of the deepest and most ancient of human needs: the need to reduce all the information about a computer's performance to a single number. The "Bogo" part of "BogoMIPS" derives from "bogus," precisely to discourage such usage. Even more than most benchmarking numbers, the BogoMIPS figure is inaccurate, misleading, useless, deceptive, entirely unsuitable for purposes of comparison between machines, and also fascinating, which is why I explore it here. (The "MIPS" part of the name, by the way, is short for "millions of instructions per second," a common unit in CPU benchmarking.)

calibrate_delay

25640: **calibrate_delay** is the kernel function that computes the approximate BogoMIPS number.

25648: As a first approximation, **calibrate_delay** works out how many loops per second **__delay** (line 7605), the delay loop, can execute within a single timer tick—that is, within a hundredth of a second.

25650: Counting how many loops can execute within a single tick requires starting the count at the beginning of a tick, or as close to it as possible. A global variable, **jiffies** (line 39661), counts how many timer ticks have elapsed since the kernel started keeping track of time; Chapter 6 reveals how it does this. **jiffies** is updated asynchronously, in an interrupt: A hundred times per second, the kernel suspends whatever it's doing, updates the variable, and then picks up where it left off. If it didn't do this, the loop beginning on the next line could never exit. At that, if **jiffies** were not declared to be **volatile**— meaning, loosely, that its value is subject to change for reasons not visible to the compiler— gcc still might optimize the loop so that it would never end. gcc is not currently that smart, but its maintainers would be entirely within their rights to make it so.

25655: The timer has just clicked ahead one tick, so a new tick has just begun. The next step is to delay for **loops_per_jiffy** iterations of the timer loop and then see whether that caused at least another whole tick to elapse. If so, the first-approximation loop exits; if not, it restarts with twice the value for **loops_per_jiffy**.

The correctness of this loop depends partly on the fact that existing machines can't execute the delay loop anywhere near 2^{32} times per jiffy— much less 2^{64} times per jiffy, for 64-bit machines—although that would be a nice problem to have.

25663: The kernel now knows that **loops_per_jiffy** iterations of the delay loop take this machine longer than a hundredth of a second to complete,

so it begins to refine the estimate. Effectively, it binary-searches for the true value of **loops_per_jiffy**, assuming, to start with, that the true value lies between the current estimate and half of the current estimate. The true value can't be larger than the current estimate, but it might be (and probably is) smaller.

25669: In the same way as before, **calibrate_delay** sees whether this reduced value of **loops_per_jiffy** is still large enough to consume an entire timer tick. If it is still large enough, the right value lies at or below the current estimate, so the search continues with a smaller value; if not large enough, the search continues with a larger value.

25676: The kernel has a good enough estimate of how many delay loop iterations it takes to consume one timer tick. Using **HZ** (line 13523), the number of timer ticks per second, it can now readily compute the number of delay loop iterations that can be performed per second. To thrill the user, the kernel prints this number. Note the conspicuous absence of the **%f** format specifier—the kernel avoids floating-point math whenever possible.

The magic constants in this computation are based on 500,000. This, in turn, comes from 1 million, for millions of instructions per second, divided by 2, the number of instructions in the heart of the delay loop (a **decl** and a jump, as you can see from the version of the delay loop at line 7601; the version for newer CPUs begins at line 7587).

Parsing Kernel Options

The **parse_options** function parses boot-time options sent to the kernel by the kernel loader, acting on some of them itself and passing others along to the init process (covered later in the chapter). These options might have been stored in a configuration file or typed by the user as the system was booting—the kernel doesn't care. Such details are entirely the kernel loader's concern.

parse_options

25727: The arguments have been collected into a single long command line, to whose beginning the kernel is given a pointer.

25738: Breaks out the next argument (which may be quoted), keeping a pointer to it for the next loop iteration. Notice that kernel arguments are separated by spaces, not by arbitrary white space; a tab wouldn't separate one argument from the next. If an argument-separating space is found, line 25751 overwrites it with a 0 byte, so that **line** can be treated as a normal C string that contains a single kernel option. If no space is found, the same property holds as far as the rest of the function is concerned—this just happens to be the last option in **line**, and the loop will terminate on the next iteration.

Observe that this code doesn't skip multiple spaces. Suppose **line** had the following value (two spaces):

```
rw  debug
```

This would be considered three options: "rw", "" (the empty string), and "debug". Because the empty string is not a valid kernel option, it gets passed on to init (as you'll see shortly)—almost certainly not what the user wanted! Therefore, the kernel loader is responsible for squeezing multiple spaces. LILO does this elegantly, by ignoring redundant spaces as they're typed.

25752: The kernel recognizes options of the form **option=value**. This line is a special case, in which the kernel loader has specified a command to run instead of init; it would take the form **init=/some/other/program**. This code discards the **init=** part, preserving the rest in **execute_command** for later use by **init** (line 26059, and discussed later). Unlike most of the other argument processing, this can't be done in **checksetup** (line 25613, and discussed in the next section), because it modifies variables local to this function.

The kernel also recognizes some options that are simple flags; these take no parameters and therefore do not include an = sign. You can find four examples just above **parse_options**, at lines 25713 through 25716. The first two of these options—**ro** and **rw**—tell the kernel to mount the root file system, the one where the / directory lives, in read-only or read/write mode. The third and fourth, **debug** and **quiet**, affect the default amount of debugging information that will be printed through calls to **printk** (line 33517).

25764: The bulk of the kernel's options are parsed by the **checksetup** function. If **checksetup** recognizes the option, it returns true and the loop is continued.

25769: Otherwise, **line** doesn't hold a recognized kernel option. In this case, it's treated as an option or environment variable for the init process—as an environment variable if it's of the form *envar=value*; otherwise, as an option. If enough room remains in the **argv_init** and **envp_init** arrays (lines 25422 and 25424, respectively), the option or environment variable is stored for later use by the **init** function.

That explains the comment starting at line 25755. The string **auto** is not a kernel option, so it's normally considered an argument to init and placed in the **argv_init** array—which is okay in most cases, because **auto** is an option that init recognizes. But when the **init=** option is given, it's normally used to execute a shell instead of init, and **auto** would confuse the shell. To be on the safe side, **parse_options** erases any init arguments seen to that point.

Curiously, the whole loop is terminated when either the **argv_init** or **envp_init** array fills up. Just because **argv_init** has filled up doesn't

mean **line** contains no more environment variables intended for init, and vice versa. In addition, there might be more kernel options left. This behavior looks even stranger when you consider that **MAX_INIT_ARGS** (line 25405) and **MAX_INIT_ENVS** (line 25406) are both **#define**d to 8, which is quite a low limit and thus easy to exceed. If the **break**s at lines 25771 and 25775 were changed to **continue**s, the loop would continue to process options without writing past the end of the **argv_init** and **envp_init** arrays. This could be very useful if **line** still contained more kernel options not destined for init.

25780: All kernel options have been processed. The last step is to **NULL**-terminate the **argv_init** and **envp_init** arrays, so that **init** will know where to stop reading from them.

checksetup

25613: The **checksetup** function handles most of the kernel's option processing, helped by some assembler and linker magic.

25618: **checksetup** scans through an array whose elements are of type **struct kernel_param** (line 19034), which associates an option prefix with a function that should be invoked when the option is located. If the **str** member of some entry in the array prefixes **line**, the corresponding function is invoked with the rest of **line** (that is, with the part following the prefix) and **checksetup** returns nonzero to indicate that it handled the option. If it runs off the end of the array without finding a match, the function returns 0.

This loop illustrates a point: In stark contrast to most of the kernel, initialization need not be as fast as possible. If the kernel takes a few microseconds longer to start than it might have, there's no real loss—user applications aren't running yet, so nothing is being taken away from them.

As a result, this code is uncharacteristically inefficient, leaving open the possibility of several optimizations. For instance, the lengths of the strings in the array could be cached in the array itself, instead of being repeatedly recomputed at line 25619. For an even bigger win, the entries in the array could be arranged alphabetically, so that **checksetup** could binary-search it.

There's no obstacle to such an arrangement, but there's probably no huge benefit, either, because binary search pays off only for large arrays that are searched frequently (where the precise values of "large" and "frequently" vary by circumstance). There are fewer than 200 kernel options defined in the entire kernel distribution and not all of these would be compiled into a single kernel (for example, because some of them are related to device drivers that might not be compiled in). Even so, there would probably be enough options included in a single kernel for a binary search to beat a linear search. However, it's rare that more than a handful of options are passed to the kernel, so lookups would not be frequent enough to make a binary search worthwhile. In addition, because the algorithm searches for prefixes rather than complete matches, it can be sensitive to the order in which it traverses the array's entries, so its exact properties would be difficult to retain in the face of a different search order. Still, these problems are hardly insuperable (the developers could statically build a prefix tree, for starters), and the effort might be justified if performance mattered here. But it doesn't, so simplicity won the day.

checksetup illustrates another, even more interesting feature of the code. You might have noticed that I didn't name the array the function iterates over. That's because there isn't one in the conventional sense. Instead, the array is built up using some special features of the GNU assembler and linker.

Every kernel option is declared using the **__setup** macro (line 19041). You can find a representative use of this macro just above **checksetup** itself, at line 25611. The macro expands to code that looks like this:

```
static char
__setup_str_root_dev_setup[]
__initdata = "root=";
static struct kernel_param
__setup_root_dev_setup
__attribute__((unused)) __initsetup =
{
  __setup_str_root_dev_setup,
  root_dev_setup
}
```

This creates a **struct kernel_param** that associates the string **root=** with the function **root_dev_setup** (line 25593). (As it happens, this function lets the user choose where the root directory should be mounted.) The tricky parts are the **__initdata** and **__initsetup** macros (lines 19055 and 19059), which cause the tagged data to be placed in dedicated sections of the kernel. **__initdata** places the tagged data in a section of the kernel named .data.init, and **__initsetup** places the tagged data (the **struct kernel_param**) in a section of the kernel named .setup.init. Similarly, the **__init** tag on the **root_dev_setup** function puts it in the .text.init section. The memory allocated for these sections is freed when the kernel's initialization is complete, helping the kernel reduce its memory footprint.

More important at the moment is the effect of putting all of the **struct kernel_param**s in their own section. As shown in Figure 4.2, all those **struct**s packed together look an awful lot like an array. If only there were some way to find the start and end of that array, we could write code to walk over it. . . .

True to form, the kernel's developers found a way to do precisely that. The file arch/i386/vmlinux.lds—a GNU linker script—tells the GNU linker to bracket the .setup.init section with two symbols, **__setup_start** and **__setup_end**. Now **checksetup** knows the array's bounds, so it can step through the array quite naturally.

This is a truly amazing solution. It has the following properties:

- *The array is exactly as large as it needs to be, yet the array's size need not be manually maintained.* Instead, developers can use **__setup** whenever they need to install a setup function, without explicitly increasing the array's size; the compiler toolchain does the dirty work. Similarly, if compiling out a feature causes its associated **__setup** to be compiled out, there's no need to manually reduce the array's size. A related point is that kernel developers don't need to create the **struct**

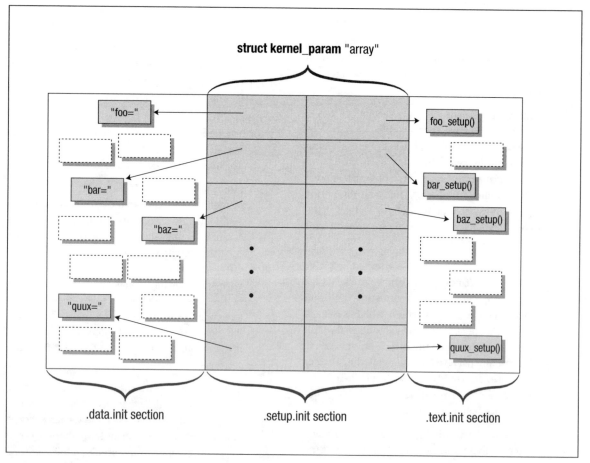

Figure 4.2   The .data.init, .setup.init, and .text.init sections.

kernel_param and then install it in an array as a separate step; with **__setup**, the act of creating the **struct kernel_param** installs it in the array.

- *The array's initialization is scattered throughout the kernel code.* This might not seem at first blush to be an advantage, but it is. It permits the setup functions and associated data to be **static**, reducing the danger of symbol collisions. It also encourages developers to put the setup code close to the code it sets up (as opposed to putting all setup functions in a single module, which would tend to make quite a mess). gcc would normally complain that the **static struct kernel_params** were unused, since that's how it looks to gcc at the compilation stage, but the **structs** are marked with **__attribute__((unused))** to silence this warning.

- *The array can be discarded when it's no longer needed.* As I said earlier, the entire array is jettisoned along with other initialization-only code and data when initialization is complete.

profile_setup

25427: **profile_setup** is the perfect example of the setup functions called by **checksetup**: It's short, it does something with its **str** argument, and you already have some notion of what it's for. I mentioned previously that the user can set **prof_shift** at boot time—well, this is how. **profile_setup** is called when the **profile=** option is supplied at kernel boot time. The prefix string and the function are associated by line 25435.

25431: Uses the first number supplied after **profile=**, if any, as **prof_shift**'s new value. Any additional parameters given for the option are summarily ignored. The **prof_shift** value is parsed using **get_option** (line 40597), one of a small family

of functions frequently used in parsing kernel options. The other two members of this family—**get_options** and **memparse** (lines 40629 and 40659)—aren't used by any code included in the book.

25432: **profile_setup** returns 1 to indicate that it recognized the kernel option. Note that it returns the same value whether or not it was given a valid integer value for **prof_shift**; this keeps an invalid **profile=** string from being passed to init as a bogus environment variable.

init

init is a special process in a number of ways. It's the first user process run by the kernel, and it is responsible for firing off all the other processes that are needed to put the system as a whole into a really usable state. This work is controlled by the file /etc/inittab and normally includes setting up getty processes, which allow users to log in; establishing network services, such as FTP and HTTP daemons; and much more. Without all of these processes, users couldn't do much, which would render the success of booting the kernel somewhat hollow.

An important side effect of this design is that init is the ancestor of every subsequent process on the system. init spawns a getty process, the getty process spawns a login process, the login process spawns your shell, and, with your shell, you spawn every other process that you run. Among other outcomes, this helps to ensure that all entries in the kernel's process table are eventually accounted for. Cleaning up after ("reaping") a process that has exited is first the responsibility of the process's parent; if its parent exits, init, which never exits, becomes responsible for reaping it.

So, to ensure that all of these important jobs get done, the last act of the kernel initialization process is to create init, described next.

init

26059: The **unused** argument comes from the unusual way in which this function is called. The **init** function—not to be confused with the init

process, which it goes on to create—begins life as a *kernel thread*, a process that runs as part of the kernel. (This might be different from the meaning of "kernel thread" that you've heard if you've done any multithreaded programming—it's not a kernel thread in that sense.) Effectively, the function **init** is like a stripped-down **main** for a new process, and the **unused** argument is a single pointer's worth of information that is given to this process—much less than is passed to a normal process through its **argc**, **argv**, and **envp** arguments. The **init** function happens not to need any extra information (the **argv** and **envp** for the process it goes on to create are stored in kernel-space variables that **init** can read directly), so its argument is named **unused**, to reinforce this fact.

To ensure that you aren't confused on this point, here's a recap: The **init** *function* is part of the kernel; it runs within the kernel, as an independently executing portion of the kernel; it is, in every respect, kernel code. The init *process*, however, is none of these things. It is, in some respects, a special, distinguished process, but it is not part of the kernel itself; its code resides in a distinct executable image stored on the disk, just like any other program. This gets confusing because the **init** function, which later begets the init process, just happens to be run as a process itself.

Because the idle process is already occupying process ID (PID) 0, the init process is assigned the next available PID, which is 1. (I discuss process IDs in Chapter 7.) The kernel repeatedly assumes that the process with PID 1 is init, so this property can't be changed without significant repercussions.

26061: Calls **lock_kernel** (line 23328 for the UP version; line 16424 for the SMP version) to execute the next several lines without any interference from other parts of the kernel that might be affected by what is about to be done here. The kernel lock is released soon after, at line 26068.

26062: Calls **do_basic_setup** (line 25946) to initialize the buses and spawn some other kernel threads, among other work. One of the functions called by **do_basic_setup** is **do_initcalls** (line 25925), which works much like **checksetup**: It walks through an array of function pointers (created by the same mechanism that created **checksetup**'s array), calling each of the registered initialization functions in turn.

26067: The kernel is now completely initialized, so **free_initmem** (line 8999) gets rid of the functions in the .text.init and .initcall.init sections of the kernel and the data in the .data.init and .setup.init sections. Any functions marked with __**init** or __**init_call**, or any data marked with __**initdata** or __**initsetup**, no longer are accessible, and the memory they once occupied can be reused for other purposes.

26070: Opens the console device, if possible, so that the init process will have a console to which it can write messages and from which it can read input. The init process doesn't use the console, except to write error messages, but if a shell or some other interactive process is invoked instead of init, it will need a source of interactive input. If the **open** succeeds, /dev/console becomes init's source of standard input (file descriptor 0).

26074: **dups** the /dev/console file descriptor twice, so that init will also use it for standard output and standard error (file descriptors 1 and 2). Assuming the **open** at line 26070 succeeded (the normal case), **init** now has the first three file descriptors—standard input, standard output, and standard error—all attached to the system console.

26082: If an explicit path to init (or some stand-in program) was given on the kernel's command line, **init** tries to execute it now.

Because **execve** doesn't return when it successfully executes the target program, each of the subsequent statements will be reached only if all of those preceding it fail. The next several lines try to find init in several places, in increasing order of desperation: first, /sbin/init, init's standard location, followed by two other reasonable candidates, /etc/init and /bin/init.

26087: Those are all the places init is likely to be. If it hasn't turned up by now, **init** has no idea where else to seek its namesake, and the machine is probably broken, anyway. So it tries to create an interactive shell (/bin/sh) instead. **init**'s best hope at this point is that root will repair the damage and reboot. (Root, you may be sure, is hoping the same.)

26088: **init** couldn't even create a shell—something must be really wrong! Well, as they say, when all else fails, **panic** (line 33207). This tries to sync the disks, ensuring that they're in a consistent state, and suspends any further processing. It can also reboot the machine after a timeout specified as a kernel option.

Chapter 5

System Calls

Most books about the internal workings of Unix seem to give short shrift to system calls, which I think is a shame. True, we already have pretty much all the system calls we need, so in a way, examining their implementation is a dead end. If you want to contribute to the Linux kernel, there are more rewarding areas in which to do so.

However, for our purposes, scrutinizing a few system calls will be time well spent. It's an opportunity to introduce some of the concepts that the book explores in greater detail as it progresses, such as process handling and memory. Looking at system calls also enables you to learn a lot about the nature of Linux kernel programming, including some of the ways in which it differs from what you probably were taught in school or on the job. Even more than most other programming tasks, Linux kernel programming is an ongoing battle among three obsessions—speed, correctness, and clarity—and they can't all win . . . or not always.

What Is a System Call?

A system call occurs when a user process (such as EMACS) requests a service the kernel provides (such as opening a file) by calling a special function (such as **open**). At this point, the user process is put on hold. The kernel examines the request, attempts to carry it out, and passes the result back to the user process, which is then restarted. I'll go into more detail about these mechanisms shortly.

System calls generally guard access to resources that the kernel manages, the largest categories of system calls being those dealing with I/O (**open**, **close**, **read**, **write**, and **poll**, among others), processes (**fork**, **execve**, **kill**, and so forth), time (**time**, **settimeofday**,

and so on), and memory (**mmap**, **brk**, and the like). Nearly all system calls fall into one of these categories. (There are some very interesting exceptions, though: Red Hat's Ingo Molnar developed a screamingly fast Web server, TUX, that is implemented as a set of kernel modules and provides a user-space API accessed through a special-purpose system call. Alas, this fascinating project is not part of the default kernel distribution and is not included in this book, but it does go to show that system calls need not be limited by traditional boundaries.)

Behind the scenes, however, a system call might not be what it seems. First, on GNU/Linux, the C library implements some system calls entirely in terms of other system calls. For instance, **waitpid** is implemented simply as a call to **wait4**, but both are documented separately as system calls. Other traditional system calls, such as **sigmask** and **ftime**, are implemented mostly, if not completely, in the C library rather than in the Linux kernel itself.

This sleight of hand is, of course, harmless—from the application's point of view, a system call looks just like any other function call; the application can't tell whether or not the kernel really got involved, or in what way, as long as the results are as expected. (It even has a nonobvious benefit: The less kernel code users are able to invoke, the fewer the opportunities for security holes.) However, the confusion introduced by such legerdemain can complicate discussion. In practice, the term *system call* often means whatever a system call was on the first version of Unix used by the speaker! In this chapter, though, we're interested only in "true" system calls—those that, at least in part, involve a user process invoking some code in the kernel.

A system call must return **long** or **int**. By convention, the returned value is zero or positive to indicate success; a negative return value indicates an error. As any veteran C programmer well knows, when a function in the standard C library fails, it sets the global integer **errno** to indicate the nature of the error—the same is true for system calls. The means by which this happens for system calls cannot be divined by studying the kernel's source code alone, however. On failure, the sys-

tem calls simply return the negative of the error number that they wish to raise, and the standard C library implementation is responsible for the rest. (The kernel's system functions normally are not invoked directly from user code, but rather via a thin layer of code in the standard C library that is responsible for exactly this translation.) To take an example at random, line 40389 (part of **sys_nanosleep**) returns -**EINVAL** to indicate that a supplied value was out of range. The code in the standard C library that actually invoked **sys_nanosleep** notices the negative return value, sets **errno** to **EINVAL**, and itself returns -1 to the original caller.

In recent kernels, it's no longer true that just any negative return value from a system call indicates an error. A few system calls (such as **lseek**) can return large negative values even on success; currently, only values in the range -1 to -4,095 are considered errors (but this includes ample room for future expansion: only the values -1 through -125 are currently used). The C standard library implementation is now responsible for interpreting the system call's return value in a more sophisticated way; the kernel itself does not do anything special when a return value is negative.

Interrupts, Kernel Space, and User Space

You'll refine your understanding of these concepts in Chapter 6, when I explore interrupts, and in Chapter 8, when I explore memory. But in this chapter, you need a rough-and-ready understanding of a few terms.

The first term is *interrupts*. Interrupts come in two flavors: *hardware interrupts*, such as when the disk indicates that it has some data (these are not relevant to this chapter), and *software interrupts*, an equivalent software mechanism. On the x86 CPU, software interrupts are how a user process signals the kernel that it wants to make a system call. (The interrupt used for this purpose is number 0x80, better known to Intel hackers as INT 80h.) The kernel responds to the interrupt with the **system_call** function (line 898), which we explore in a moment.

The other two terms are *kernel space* and *user space*, which refer to the memory reserved for the kernel and the memory reserved for a user process, respectively. Of course, there are usually many user processes running simultaneously and they normally don't share their memory; nonetheless, the memory used by any user process is generically referred to as "user space." The kernel normally is interacting with only one user process at a time anyway, so no confusion arises in practice.

Because these memory areas are separate, user processes can't directly access kernel space at all and the kernel accesses user space only through the **put_user** (line 17146) and **get_user** (line 17121) macros and their kin. Because system calls are the interface between a process and the operating system on which it runs, system calls have a frequent need to interact with user space, so these macros appear in system calls all the time. The macros aren't needed for passing arguments by value, but they are needed when the user passes the system call a pointer through which the kernel needs to read or write. The user process's pointer points into user space and the kernel code is running in kernel space, so the kernel must do extra work to cross the boundary between the two.

How System Calls Are Invoked

On x86 platforms, system calls are invoked in one of three ways: the **system_call** function, and the closely related **lcall7** and **lcall27** call gates (see lines 839 and 860). This section explores all three mechanisms in some detail.

As you read, observe that the system calls don't care whether they're being invoked by **system_call**, **lcall7**, or **lcall27**. This separation of the system call from the mechanisms that make the call possible is really quite elegant. If, for some reason, you had to add another method for invoking system calls, you wouldn't have to change the system calls themselves to support it.

Before you look at this assembler code, note that the order of the operands for machine instructions is reversed from the normal Intel ordering. Some other syntactic differences exist, but the reversed ordering of operands is the most disorienting. If you keep in mind that the Intel syntax

```
mov eax, 0
```

(which moves the literal constant value 0 into the EAX register) is written here as

```
movl $0, %eax
```

you should get along all right. (The kernel uses AT&T assembler syntax, because that's the syntax used by the GNU compiler toolchain—specifically, the GNU assembler—used to compile the kernel. The GNU assembler documentation has more information.)

system_call

system_call (line 898) is the entry point for all system calls (for native code, that is; **lcall7** is used for iBCS2 support and **lcall27** is used for Solaris/x86 support, as discussed later in this chapter). As noted in the banner comment above it, the goal is for the normal case simply to drop straight through, taking no jumps, so the pieces of the function are scattered hither and yon—overall flow control has been complicated for the sake of avoiding branches in the normal case. (Branches are worth avoiding, because they can be expensive. They can clear the CPU's pipeline, discarding the internal parallelism that gives modern CPUs much of their speed.)

Figure 5.1 shows the branch target labels that are part of **system_call**, as well as the direction of flow control between them, which might help orient you as you read through this discussion. The **system_call** and **restore_all** labels in this figure are bigger than the rest, because they're the normal entry and exit points to the function, although a couple of the other labels are also entry points, as you'll see later in the chapter.

system_call is invoked by the standard C library, which loads the CPU registers with the arguments that it wants to pass and then raises the software interrupt 0x80. (**system_call** is therefore an interrupt handler.) The kernel registers the association between that software interrupt and the **system_call** function at line 7498 (**SYSCALL_VECTOR** is **#define**d to 0x80 at line 12898).

system_call

899:     **system_call**'s first argument is the number of the system call to invoke; it's in the EAX register. **system_call** also allows up to six more arguments that will be passed along to the

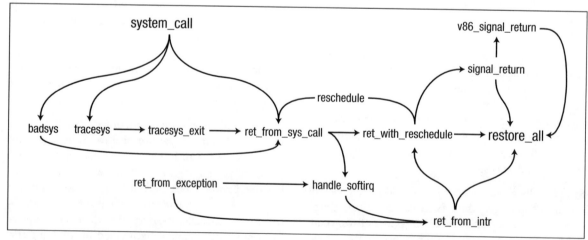

Figure 5.1 Flow control for **system_call**.

system call. In the rare cases in which the six-argument limit is burdensome, you can circumvent it by making one of the arguments a pointer to a structure, which then can contain as much additional information as you need.

An extra copy of EAX's value might be needed later, so it's saved now by pushing it onto the stack; this will become the value of the **ORIG_EAX(%esp)** expression that we'll see at line 950.

900: The macro **SAVE_ALL** is defined at line 789; it pushes copies of all the registers onto the CPU's stack. Later, just before **system_call** returns, these copies will be popped off the stack with **RESTORE_ALL** (line 804). In between, **system_call** is free to use the registers for whatever purpose it likes. More importantly, any C function that it calls will find its arguments on the stack—where it expects them—because **SAVE_ALL** put them there.

The resulting stack layout is documented starting at line 727. The expressions that look like **0(%esp)** and **4(%esp)** denote a displacement from the stack pointer (the ESP register)—0 bytes above ESP, 4 bytes above ESP, and so forth. In particular, note that the copy of EAX that was pushed onto the stack in the previous line has indeed become what this banner comment documents as **orig_eax**. It's on the stack above the registers saved by **SAVE_ALL** (the registers above **orig_eax** were there already).

This might be confusing—because the EAX copy we're calling **orig_eax** was pushed onto the stack first, wouldn't it be below the other registers, not above them? Yes and no. The x86's stack pointer register, ESP, *decrements* as you push items onto the stack—the stack grows downward in memory. So, **orig_eax** is logically below the other values, but is physically above them.

A set of macros starting at line 753 helps to make these displacements more readable. **EAX(%esp)**, for instance, will be the same as **18(%esp)**—but the first way makes it easier to determine that the expression refers to a copy of the EAX register that was saved on the stack.

901: Gets a pointer to the current task in the EBX register. The macro that does this, **GET_CURRENT** (line 835), is equivalent to the C function **get_current** (line 12522) used in most of the code.

When you see expressions like **foo(%ebx)** or **foo(%esp)** after this point, it means that the code is accessing fields in the **struct** representing the current process—**struct task_struct**, at line 21931—which is covered in greater detail in Chapter 7. (To be more precise, displacements from **%ebx** are in the **struct task_struct** and displacements from **%esp** are in the **struct pt_regs** associated with the **struct task_struct**. But the distinction is not really important here.)

902: Sees whether the system call number (in EAX) exceeds the maximum number of system calls. This instruction treats EAX as an unsigned integer, so negative numbers are simply treated as large positive numbers. As a result, this single instruction tests for both too-large and too-small (negative) values at the same time. Very efficient!

You might wonder why EAX needs to be checked at all. After all, **system_call** is being called from the system's C library (glibc on GNU/Linux systems), and surely the C library can be trusted, right? Well, no, it can't—the C library could be buggy or it could have been modified. What's more, although the normal path to **system_call** goes through the C library, there's no guarantee that that's what happened: User code can simply raise software interrupt 0x80 itself, with any value it wants in EAX. The kernel must always

be suspicious of values that come to it from user space, and here, that means range-checking the system call number in EAX.

If the system call number is out of range, it jumps ahead to **badsys** (line 958).

904: Checks whether the system call is being traced. Programs such as strace provide system call tracing as a tool for the curious or as extra debugging information: You can tell a lot about what a program is doing if you can spy on the system calls it's making. If system calls are being traced, control jumps ahead to **tracesys** (line 947).

906: Calls the system function. Several things are going on here. First, the macro **SYMBOL_NAME** is a do-nothing macro that is replaced by the text of its argument, so you can ignore it. **sys_call_table** is defined at the bottom of the current file (arch/i386/kernel/entry.S), starting at line 1128. It's a table of function pointers to the kernel functions that implement various system calls.

The second set of parentheses on the line contains three comma-separated arguments (the first argument is empty); this is what does the array indexing. The array it's indexing into is **sys_call_table**, of course; this is called the *displacement*. The three arguments are the array base address, the index (EAX, the system call number), and the scale, or the number of bytes in each array element—here, simply 4. Because the array base address is empty, it's treated as 0; however, this is added to the displacement address, **sys_call_table**, which simply means **sys_call_table** is treated as the array base. This line is basically equivalent to this C expression:

```
/* Call a function in an array of
# * #functions.*/
(sys_call_table[eax])();
```

But, of course, C handles the dirty work, such as remembering the array element size, for you. The system call's arguments are already on the stack, by the way, because they were supplied to **system_call** by its caller and pushed onto the stack by **SAVE_ALL**.

907: The system call has returned. Its return value, which is in the EAX register and which is to be **system_call**'s return value as well, is saved. The return value is stored in the EAX position on the stack so that **RESTORE_ALL** can restore the real EAX register from it, along with all the other registers.

908: The following code, although still part of **system_call**, is a separate entry point known by the name **ret_from_sys_call**. This is occasionally called directly from C, as well as being jumped to from other points in **system_call** itself (including, notably, from **lcall7** and **lcall27**).

909: The next few lines test whether a "softirq" is active and, if so, control jumps to the **handle_softirq** label (line 985) to handle it now. Softirqs are part of interrupt processing and are discussed thoroughly in the next chapter.

Although it might not look like it, the UP version of the code (lines 915 and 916) is just a simplified version of the SMP version (lines 910 through 913). The SMP version must index into an array of per-CPU structures, whereas the UP code always knows there's just one CPU and therefore just one array element. The array in question is **irq_stat**, which you can find at line 36276. It's an array of **irq_cpustat_t**, which in turn is defined at line 12662. Note that the SMP code accounts for the array element size at line 911; the array elements are marked ____**cacheline_aligned**, making them the size of an L1 cacheline.

921: Sees whether the process has been marked for rescheduling (recall that the expression $0 is simply the literal constant 0). If so, control jumps to the **reschedule** label (line 990).

923: Checks whether a signal is pending and, if so, the next line jumps ahead to **signal_return** (line 929).

925: The **restore_all** label is the exit point for **system_call**. Its body is simply that of the **RESTORE_ALL** macro (line 804), which restores the arguments saved earlier by **SAVE_ALL** and returns to **system_call**'s caller.

929: **signal_return** is reached when **system_call** notices, upon returning from the system call, that it has a signal to deliver to the current process. It begins by re-enabling interrupts, as explained in Chapter 6.

931: If returning to virtual-8086 mode (not a topic of this book), control jumps ahead to **v86_signal_return** (line 939).

934: **system_call** is about to call the C function **do_signal** (line 4822 and discussed in Chapter 6) to deliver the signal. **do_signal** expects two arguments, both passed in registers; the first is in the EAX register and the second is in the EDX register. **system_call** already (on line 932) set EAX to the value it wants for the first argument; here, it XORs the EDX register with itself, setting it to 0, so that **do_signal** sees it as a **NULL** pointer.

935: Calls **do_signal** to deliver the signal and then jumps back to **restore_all** (line 925) to finish up.

939: Because virtual-8086 mode is not a topic of this book, we'll mostly ignore **v86_signal_return**. It is, however, similar to the **signal_return** case.

947: The **tracesys** label is reached if the current process's system calls are being traced by its parent, as is done by the strace program. The basic idea of this portion of the code is to call

the system function through **syscall_table**, as at line 906, but to bracket the call with calls to the function **syscall_trace**. This latter function, not included in this book, stops the current process and signals its parent to alert it that the current process is about to invoke a system call.

The EAX manipulation interlaced with this code is puzzling at first. **system_call** sets the copy of EAX saved on the stack to the value -**ENOSYS**, calls **syscall_trace**, restores EAX's value from the copy it made way back at line 899, range-checks this value (seemingly redundantly, but we'll get to that in a minute), calls the real system call, and then puts the system call's return value in EAX's place on the stack and calls **syscall_trace** again.

The reason behind all of this is that **syscall_trace** (or, more accurately, the tracing program it forwards to) needs to know whether it's being called before or after the real system call. The -**ENOSYS** value can be used to indicate that it's being called before the real system call, because no actual, implemented system call would return -**ENOSYS**. Hence, the stack-based copy of EAX will be -**ENOSYS** before the first call to **syscall_trace**, but not before the second (except when calling **sys_ni_syscall**, which we don't care about tracing anyway). The middle use of EAX, lines 950 through 953, is simply to find the system call to invoke, as in the untraced case.

So far, so good. But what about that seemingly redundant range-check of the EAX copy? It looks just like the one at line 902 and the two values of EAX appear, at first blush, to be the same. **NR_syscalls** (the maximum number of system calls, currently 256) is a constant, so it can't have changed. It must be the EAX copy that changed, but this code hasn't changed it. So what could have made the change? The tracing program, that's what. It has access to the entire memory space of the process it's tracing, so it can really mess with that process if it wants to. In particular, it can cause a different system call to be invoked from the one the traced process meant to call. strace, for example, converts **vfork** into **fork** as a workaround for its inability to follow **vfork**. So, because the value might have changed, it must be checked.

957: The traced system call has returned; control jumps back to **ret_from_sys_call** (line 908) to finish up the same way as in the normal, untraced path.

958: The **badsys** label is reached when the supplied system call number is out of range. In this case, **system_call** must return -**ENOSYS** (**ENOSYS** is set to 38 at line 786). As mentioned before, the caller knows this is an error, because the return value is between –1 and –4,095.

963: The **ret_from_exception** label is reached following CPU exception interrupts, such as a divide-by-zero error (see line 1024). This label is not reached from any code within **system_call** itself. If a softirq is active, it's serviced now.

976: The **ret_from_intr** label is reached after handling a softirq or by simply falling through from the previous case (a CPU exception was raised but no softirqs were active). **ret_from_intr** is a globally accessible symbol, so it's also called from a few other places in the kernel.

980: The saved CPU EFLAGS and CS registers have been combined in EAX so that the upper 24 bits (which happen to include one bit of interest, **VM_MASK**, defined at line 772) are from EFLAGS and the lower 8 bits are from CS. This line obscurely tests pieces of both at the same time to see whether the process is returning to virtual-8086 mode (that's the **VM_MASK** part) or to user mode (that's the "3" part; user mode is privilege level 3). The following is approximately equivalent C code:

```
/* Mix eflags and cs in eax. */
eax = eflags & ~0xff;
eax |= cs & 0xff;
/* Simultaneously test lower 2 bits
 * and VM_MASK bit. */
if (eax & (VM_MASK | 3))
  goto ret_with_reschedule;
goto restore_all;
```

981: If either of these conditions is true, control jumps to the **ret_with_reschedule** (line 920) label to test whether the process needs rescheduling before **system_call** returns. Otherwise, the caller is a kernel task, so **system_call** skips the rescheduling part by jumping to **restore_all** (line 925).

985: The **handle_softirq** label is reached whenever **system_call** has a softirq to service. It simply calls the C function **do_softirq** (line 36282, covered in Chapter 6) and then jumps back to **ret_from_intr** (line 976).

991: The final component of **system_call** is under the **reschedule** label. This label is reached when the process that made the system call has been marked for rescheduling. Typically, this is because the process's timeslice has expired— that is, it has had the CPU as long as it's allowed for now and another process should be given a chance to run. So the C function **schedule** (line 34237) is called to hand off the CPU, if necessary, and control then jumps back to line 908. CPU scheduling is a major topic of Chapter 7.

lcall7

Linux supports the Intel Binary Compatibility Specification, version 2 (iBCS2). (The lowercase *i* in iBCS2 is apparently intentional, but unexplained; it does seem to be consistent with the practice of referring to Intel's CPUs as the i386, i486, and so on.) The iBCS2 specification lays out a standard kernel interface for applications across all x86-based Unix systems, including not only

Linux, but also the other free x86 Unix flavors (such as FreeBSD), as well as SCO Unix, Xenix, and the like. The standard interface makes it possible to run binary-only commercial software developed for those other Unix systems on your Linux box, or vice versa (these days, it's increasingly vice versa). The SCO Unix binary of Corel's WordPerfect, for instance, ran fine on Linux using iBCS2 even before there was a native Linux version.

If iBCS2 is the standard, why isn't it also the default system call interface? Why does Linux use the 0x80 software interrupt discussed earlier? The simple answer is speed: The **int** instruction used for software interrupts is faster than the **lcall** instruction used when invoking **lcall7** and **lcall27**. So Linux gets the twin benefits of speed (when executing native code) and compatibility (when executing binaries from other x86 Unix versions).

The iBCS2 standard has several components, but the one that we're currently interested in is how system calls are handled consistently across these disparate Unix types. This consistency is made possible by the **lcall7** call gate, a fairly simple assembler function (especially compared to **system_call**) that just locates and delegates to a C function that handles the details. (A *call gate* is an x86 CPU feature that enables user tasks to call kernel code in a safe, controlled manner.) This call gate is set up at line 7503. The closely related **lcall27** call gate, set up at the following line, is used for Solaris/x86 support. The two functions are virtually identical, as you'll see below.

lcall7

839: The first several lines adjust the processor stack so that it will be the same as expected by **system_call**. Some code within **system_call** is going to handle the cleanup, so everything must be in a consistent state.

849: In the same spirit, **lcall7** gets a pointer to the current task into the EBX register, the same situation as in **system_call**. It doesn't do this the same way that **system_call** does, though, which is odd. These three lines could be written, equivalently, as follows:

```
pushl %esp
GET_CURRENT(%ebx)
```

Although the resulting instruction sequence would be slightly different, it computes the same result and is more consistent with the rest of the code in the file—entry.S uses the **GET_CURRENT** macro everywhere else. It would also be clearer, and it might even be faster—my tests show a slight speedup for the rewritten version, although the difference is small and difficult to measure. (Also, to be fair, the rewritten version might be faster only on an Athlon, the CPU on which I did my testing. It might be slower on, say, a Pentium. Still, it's strange that the code does the job differently in different places.)

852: Gets a pointer to the current task's **exec_domain** field, uses that field to find a pointer to its **lcall7** handler, and then calls the handler, passing 7 as its first argument. This is the only difference between **lcall7** and **lcall27**: **lcall27** passes the handler 39 (0x27) instead of 7. Hence, the same handler function can be used to service both **lcall7** and **lcall27**. The handler's first argument tells it which one it's being called for. If it doesn't care, it can simply ignore this argument.

Execution domains are not covered in detail in this book, but, briefly, the kernel uses execution domains to implement part of the iBCS2 standard. You can find **struct exec_domain** at line 21500. The default execution domain, **default_exec_domain** (line 29699), has a default **lcall7/lcall27** handler. This is **no_lcall7** (line 29713), which basically tries to act like the SVR4 flavor of Unix, sending a segmentation violation signal to the calling process if it is unsuccessful.

858: Jumps to the **ret_from_sys_call** label (line 908—note that this is inside **system_call**) to clean up and return as if this had been a normal system call.

Some Example System Calls

Now that you've seen how system calls are invoked, it's time to take a look at a few sample system calls to give you the flavor of how they work. Note that a system call **foo** is nearly always implemented by a kernel function named **sys_foo**, although sometimes the guts of the function are moved into a helper function named **do_foo**.

sys_ni_syscall

36710: **sys_ni_syscall** is surely the simplest system call; it simply returns the **ENOSYS** error. Initially, this might not seem to be useful, but it is. Indeed, **sys_ni_syscall** occupies several positions in **sys_call_table**—and for more than one reason. To begin with, **sys_ni_syscall** is at position 0 (line 1129) because if buggy code calls **system_call** in some mistaken way—for example, without initializing the variable it passes to **system_call** as an argument—0 is the most likely value for this accidental argument. We wouldn't want to do something as drastic as killing a process if this happened—if we can avoid it. (Of course, you can't prevent *all* mistakes without preventing all useful work as well.) This habit of using element 0 of a table as a guard against such bugs is a pretty common practice in the kernel.

In addition, you can find **sys_ni_syscall** explicitly entered in a dozen more table positions. These entries represent system calls that have been removed from the kernel—such as at line 1173, where it takes the place of the obsolete **prof** system call. We can't just put a different "real" system call there, because some old binaries might still be using the obsolete system call's number. It would be very surprising if a program that tried to invoke one of these old system calls ended up, say, opening a file instead.

Finally, **sys_ni_syscall** occupies any unused positions at the end of the table; this is established by lines 1360 through 1362, which repeat the entry

as many times as necessary to fill out the table. Because **sys_ni_syscall** simply returns the **ENOSYS** error number, calling it has the same effect as jumping to the **badsys** label in **system_call**. That is, the effect when given a system call number that references one of these table entries is the same as it would be if the number indexed entirely outside the table. Consequently, system calls can be added to the table (or removed) without changing **NR_syscalls**, but the effect is exactly the same as if **NR_syscalls** had been changed (up to the limit established by **NR_syscalls**, anyway—recall that this is 256).

As you have probably guessed by now, the "ni" in **sys_ni_syscall**'s name is not for Monty Python's "Knights Who Say 'Ni'"; it stands for the somewhat less humorous phrase "not implemented."

The **asmlinkage** tag is one other thing that we should observe about this simple function. This is a **#define** at line 19809 for some gcc magic that tells the compiler that the function should not expect to find any of its arguments in registers (a common optimization), but only on the CPU's stack. Recall our earlier assertion that **system_call** consumes its first argument, the system call number, and allows up to six more arguments that are passed along to the real system call. **system_call** achieves this feat simply by leaving its other arguments (which were passed to it in registers) on the stack. All system calls are marked with the **asmlinkage** tag, so they all look to the stack for arguments. Of course, in **sys_ni_syscall**'s case, this doesn't make any difference, because **sys_ni_syscall** doesn't take any arguments, but it's an issue for most other system calls. And because you'll be seeing **asmlinkage** in front of many other functions, I thought you should know what it was about.

sys_time

39213: **sys_time** is a simple system call that illustrates a few important concepts. It implements the **time** system call, which returns the number of seconds that have elapsed since the epoch (midnight UTC, January 1, 1970). This number is held as a member of the global variable **xtime** (see line 39624; it's declared **volatile** because it's modified from an interrupt, as we'll see in Chapter 6) and is accessed through the **CURRENT_TIME** macro (see line 22211). If **xtime** weren't marked **volatile**, the compiler would be allowed to hold its value in a register, so code that accessed **xtime** might not notice changes to the value in memory. Marking it **volatile** forces the compiler to fetch **xtime**'s value from memory every time it is read. This is slower than using a register, but it guarantees that the code gets the right value every time.

39219: The function follows its simple definition quite straightforwardly. The current time is first stored into the local variable **i**.

39221: If the supplied pointer, **tloc**, is non-**NULL**, the returned value should also be copied to the pointed-to location. The one subtlety in the function occurs here; it copies **i** into user space rather than reevaluate the **CURRENT_TIME** macro, for two reasons:

- The **CURRENT_TIME** macro's definition might change in the future and its new implementation might be slower for some reason, but accessing **i** will always be at least as fast as anything **CURRENT_TIME** might expand to.

- Doing it this way guarantees consistent results: If the time happened to roll over between lines 39219 and 39221, **sys_time** could end up copying one value to *tloc** and returning another.

As a quick side note, it's a bit surprising that this portion of the code wasn't written with **&&** instead of two **if**s. The usual reason for unusual-looking code in the kernel is speed, but gcc generates identical code for both the **&&** version and the two-**if** version, so that can't be the reason here—unless it mattered to the earlier gcc version under which this code was developed.

39222: If **sys_time** can't access the supplied location (generally because **tloc** was invalid), it puts -**EFAULT** in **i** so that it will return an error code at line 39224.

39224: Returning **i** to the caller returns either the current time or -**EFAULT**.

sys_reboot

36811: Perhaps nowhere in the kernel is paranoia so advanced as in the implementation of **sys_reboot**—and with good reason: As its name makes plain, the **reboot** system call can be used to reboot the machine. It can also, depending on the supplied arguments, halt the machine, turn its power off, or allow or disallow the use of the Ctrl+Alt+Del keyboard sequence to reboot. If you're going to write code to use this function, you should take careful note of the warning in the banner comment above it: Sync the disks first, or data still in the disk cache might be lost!

Because of its potential consequences for the system, **sys_reboot** requires a few magic arguments, as discussed shortly.

36818: If the calling user lacks the **CAP_SYS_BOOT** (line 17969) capability, the **EPERM** error is returned. Capabilities are discussed in detail in Chapter 7; for now, the term's plain meaning will suffice: Capabilities are a method of checking whether a user has a certain privilege.

36822: Here, the paranoia goes into full force. **sys_reboot** checks the **magic1** and **magic2** arguments against magic numbers defined at lines 21533 through 21536. The idea is that if **sys_reboot** is somehow invoked accidentally, it's unlikely to also accidentally have values drawn from this small set in both the **magic1** and **magic2** parameters. Note that this is not meant to be a security measure as such, just protection against carelessness.

Incidentally, these magic numbers weren't chosen at random. The first (0xfee1dead) is relatively obvious, a sort of pun on "feel dead." The next three must be viewed in hex for full effect: They're 0x28121969, 0x5121996, and 0x16041998. These represent Linus's birthdate and the birthdates of his two daughters. Accordingly, as Linus and his wife have more children, the odds of an accidental reboot must, in some sense, increase. But I think his wife will stop him before they exhaust the 32-bit space of possibilities.

36828: Acquires the kernel lock, so that only one processor can be executing this code at a time. Any other code protected by a **lock_kernel/ unlock_kernel** pair will be similarly unavailable to other CPUs. On uniprocessor machines, this is a no-op (it does nothing); detailing its effect on SMP machines is a subject of Chapter 10.

36830: In the **LINUX_REBOOT_CMD_RESTART** case, **sys_reboot** calls a list of functions on the **reboot_notifier_list** to inform them that the system is restarting. No functions are placed on this list by any code in the book, but several device drivers use it to shut down hardware devices cleanly.

LINUX_REBOOT_CMD_RESTART and the other recognized values of **cmd** are #**defined** starting at line 21553. These values have no hidden significance; they're chosen simply because they're unlikely to occur by accident and are different from one another. (Interestingly, **LINUX_REBOOT_ CMD_CAD_OFF** is zero, which is the likeliest accidental value. However, because **LINUX_ REBOOT_CMD_CAD_OFF** simply disables the use of Ctrl+Alt+Del to reboot the machine, it's a "safe" accident.)

36834: After printing a warning message, **sys_reboot** calls **machine_restart** (line 3353) to restart the machine. As you can see from line 3348, the **machine_restart** function never returns, yet the call to **machine_restart** is followed by a **break** anyway.

Is this merely classic good programming style? Well, it is that, but there's more to it. This file, kernel/sys.c, is in an architecture-independent part of the code. However, **machine_restart**, being obviously architecture-specific, is in an architecture-specific part of the code (arch/i386/ kernel/process.c). It's therefore different for different ports. We don't know that the implementation of **machine_restart** in every future port of the kernel will be nonreturning— for instance, it might schedule a reboot with the underlying hardware but still continue to operate for a few minutes, returning from the function first. Or, more plausibly, it might not always be able to reboot for some reason; perhaps it is not even possible to reboot that hardware under software control. Finally, a port's **machine_ restart** function could be inadequately tested or buggy. On such platforms, **machine_restart** *could* return, so the architecture-independent code should be prepared for the possibility.

Indeed, the kernel used to include at least one version of **machine_restart** that could return, but I can no longer find any examples of that behavior in the 2.4 kernel. (In several cases, **machine_ restart** simply enters an infinite loop—not rebooting the machine, but not returning, either. However, only a **machine_restart** that could return would worry us here.)

So, we do need the **break** after all. What appears at first to be mere habit or even paranoia turns out to be necessary for the kernel's portability.

36837: The next two cases allow or disallow rebooting using the infamous Ctrl+Alt+Del key sequence (also known as the "Vulcan nerve pinch," the

"hacker's claw," or, my favorite, the "three-fingered salute"). These simply set the state of the global **C_A_D** flag (defined at line 36586 and checked at line 36891).

36845: This case is similar to the **LINUX_ REBOOT_CMD_RESTART** case, but halts the system rather than restarting it. One difference is that it calls **machine_halt** (line 3384)—a no-op on the x86, although on other platforms it does the real work of shutting down the machine—instead of **machine_restart**. Also, it has a fallback plan for machines on which **machine_halt** doesn't halt the machine: It uses **do_exit** (line 30262) to kill the kernel itself.

36853: By now, this is a familiar pattern. Here, **sys_reboot** powers off the machine, essentially the same as halting it except that it calls **machine_power_off** (line 3388) for systems capable of shutting off their own power from software.

36861: The **LINUX_REBOOT_CMD_RESTART2** case is a variation on the established theme. It accepts a command, passed as an ASCII string, that expresses how the machine should be shut down. The string is not interpreted by **sys_reboot** itself, but rather by the **machine_restart** function. Its meaning, if any, is therefore platform-dependent. (I say "if any" because commonly—and on the x86, in particular—there is only one way to restart the machine, so **machine_restart** ignores this extra information.)

36878: The caller passed an unrecognized command. **sys_reboot** does nothing and returns an error. Consequently, even if **sys_reboot** was passed the right magic numbers in **magic1** and **magic2**, it doesn't necessarily do anything.

36881: **sys_reboot** was given a recognized command. If control reaches this point, it was probably one of the two **C_A_D**-setting commands, because

the others normally stop or restart the machine. In any event, **sys_reboot** simply unlocks the kernel and returns 0 for success.

sys_sysinfo

31248: A system call can return only a single **long** or **int**. If it needs to return more information than that, it simply pulls a trick similar to the one for passing more than six arguments into a system call: The information is returned through a pointer to a **struct**. The **sysinfo** system call, which collects statistics on the system's resource usage, is an example of such a function.

31250: Allocates and zeroes a **struct sysinfo** (line 19722), to temporarily store the values to return. **sys_sysinfo** could instead copy out each field of the **struct** individually, but that would be slower, less convenient, and certainly harder to read.

31254: Disables interrupts. This is covered in more detail in Chapter 6; for now, suffice it to say that this keeps the values that **sys_sysinfo** is about to use from changing while it's using them.

31255: The **uptime** field of **struct sysinfo** is used to indicate how many seconds the system has been up and running. This is computed from **jiffies** (line 39661), which counts internal timer ticks while the system is running, and **HZ** (line 13523), a system-dependent parameter that is simply the number of internal timer ticks per second.

31257: The **avenrun** array (line 40208) records the average length of the run queue—that is, the average number of processes ready for the CPU—over the last 1 second, 5 seconds, and 15 seconds. It's periodically recomputed by **calc_load** (line 40210). Because floating-point math is essentially verboten in the kernel, these computations are performed in fixed-point, which accounts for the shifting.

31261: Also records the total number of processes currently in the system.

31264: **si_meminfo** (line 9031) fills in the **struct**'s memory-related members, while **si_swapinfo** (line 47155) fills in the pieces related to virtual memory usage.

31275: Statistics on total memory and available memory are computed and stored in the **struct**.

31306: The **struct** is now completely filled out. **sys_sysinfo** tries to copy it back into user space, returning the **EFAULT** error if it fails or 0 if it succeeds.

Chapter 6

Signals, Interrupts, and Time

Signals are a form of interprocess communication (IPC), a way for one process to send information to another. But not very much information—all you get is the fact that the signal was sent. No elaborate message can be sent along with a signal, not even the identity of the sender. (Not with classic signals, anyway; POSIX realtime signals let you send a little more information.) Signals are practically useless for bidirectional communication. Furthermore, within limits, the receiver of a signal is not obligated to respond in any way and can even entirely ignore most signals.

Even with these limitations, signals are a powerful and useful mechanism—indeed, they are undoubtedly the most frequently used Unix IPC mechanism. Every time a process exits or dereferences a **NULL** pointer, every time you hit Ctrl+C or use the kill program, a signal is sent.

Chapter 9 covers Linux's more sophisticated IPC mechanisms. Signals are plenty to talk about for this chapter.

Interrupts are, as a comment in the Linux code itself notes, like signals for the kernel. Interrupts are normally sent to the kernel from a hardware device, such as a disk, to alert the kernel that the device requires some attention. The timer device, which periodically alerts the kernel to the passage of time, is an important source of hardware interrupts. Interrupts can also be generated in software by a user process, as you saw in Chapter 5.

In this chapter, I look at Linux's implementation of signals and interrupts, and finish by investigating how Linux keeps time. The code covered in this chapter is exceptionally clear and well-written, even by the kernel's high standards. The general approach used in this chapter is to begin with the relevant data structures and their relationships to one another, then to look at the functions that manipulate and interrogate them.

A Brief Note about Locks

The general idea of a lock is to protect access to a shared resource, such as a file, a piece of memory, or a section of code that should be executed by only one CPU at a time. The Linux kernel's locking code is greatly simplified when running under UP, because it's written with the goal of avoiding the kinds of situations that require locking. However, on SMP machines, one processor sometimes needs to guard against unwanted interference from another.

Rather than wrap all the calls to the lock functions in unsightly **#ifdef**s, the file include/asm-i386/spinlock.h (which starts at line 16477) contains a set of mostly empty macros for UP machines; the macros expand to real code for SMP. Accordingly, the rest of the kernel's code looks the same for UP and SMP (with respect to this feature, that is), but the effect is quite different for each.

Chapter 10's coverage of SMP explores locks in depth. However, because you'll see calls to the locking macros all over the place, especially in the code examined in this chapter, you need some sense of what the macros are for—and why you can, for the most part, safely ignore them for now (important exceptions are noted along the way).

Signals

The Linux kernel divides signals into two categories:

- *Nonrealtime*—Mostly the traditional Unix signals, such as **SIGSEGV**, **SIGHUP**, and **SIGKILL**.

- *Realtime*—Mandated by the POSIX 1003.1b standard, these have slightly different characteristics from their nonrealtime counterparts. Specifically, realtime signals have process-configurable meanings—like the nonrealtime signals **SIGUSR1** and **SIGUSR2**—and extra information is delivered with them. They also are queued, so that if multiple instances of the signal arrive before the first instance has been handled, all the instances are delivered. This is not true for nonrealtime signals.

Chapter 7 provides more information about what realtime means to the Linux kernel and, in particular, what realtime does not mean.

The **#defines** for signal numbers begin at line 16086. Realtime signal numbers lie in the range **SIGRTMIN** to **SIGRTMAX** (lines 16126 and 16127, respectively).

Data Structures

This section looks at the most important data structures used by the signal code.

sigset_t

16073: **sigset_t** represents a set of signals. For example, it records the set of signals a process has requested to be blocked (as in **struct task_struct**'s **blocked** member—line 22040). Another **sigset_t** is contained in the same **struct**'s **pending** member, which tracks the signals that are waiting to be delivered to it. (**pending**'s type is **struct sigpending**, line 22929.) You'll see other similar uses as we go along.

16074: The sole component of a **sigset_t** is an array of **unsigned long**s, each bit in which corresponds to one signal. Observe that the type **unsigned long** is referred to throughout the signal code as a "word," which might not be what you expect—even when discussing recent x86 CPUs, "word" is sometimes used to mean a 16-bit type. Because Linux is a true 32-bit operating system, considering 32 bits a word is most definitely correct. (It's slightly inaccurate to call Linux a "true 32-bit operating system," because it's also a true 64-bit operating system on 64-bit CPUs.)

The size of this array, **_NSIG_WORDS**, is calculated straightforwardly at line 16069. (The "BPW" in **_NSIG_BPW** is an abbreviation of "bits per word.") On different platforms, **_NSIG_WORDS** varies from 1 (on the Alpha) to 4 (on the MIPS). On the x86, as you can see, its value happens to be 2, meaning that 2 **unsigned long**s contain enough bits to represent all signals Linux uses on the x86 platform.

struct sigaction

16204: **struct sigaction** represents the action that a process wants to take when a signal is received. This is wrapped in **struct k_sigaction** (line 16211), which in turn is wrapped in a **struct signal_struct**, an instance of which is pointed to by **struct task_struct**'s **sig** member (line 22038). If this pointer is **NULL**, the process is exiting and should not receive any signals. Otherwise, every process has **_NSIG struct sigactions**, one **struct sigaction** per signal number.

16205: **sa_handler** (of type **__sighandler_t**—a function pointer type defined at line 16188) states how the process wants to handle the signal. It can have one of the following values:

- **SIG_DFL** (line 16190) requests the default action for the signal, whatever that is—it depends on the signal. Note that this is equal to **NULL**.

- **SIG_IGN** (line 16192) means the signal should be ignored. Not all signals can be ignored, however.

- Any other value is the address of a user-space function to call when the signal arrives.

Curiously, the **SIG_ERR** macro (line 16193), defined in the same set as **SIG_DFL** and **SIG_IGN**, is never used.

16206: **sa_flags** further tailors the action of the signal-handling code. The set of possible flags is **#define**d starting at line 16148. These flags enable the user code to request that the default action be restored after one instance of the signal has been delivered (or that the custom action be retained), and so forth, as explained in the banner comment above the **#define** block.

16207: **sa_restorer** is used by some details of the signal-handling code that I don't cover in this book.

16208: **sa_mask** is the set of other signals that the process would like to be blocked while it's

handling this signal. For example, if a process wants **SIGHUP** and **SIGINT** to be blocked while it is handling **SIGCHLD**, then the **SIGCHLD**th **sa_mask** for the process sets the bits corresponding to **SIGHUP** and **SIGINT**.

siginfo_t

15805: **struct siginfo** (also known as **siginfo_t**) is the extra information sent along with a signal, particularly with a realtime signal.

15806: **si_signo** is, unsurprisingly, the signal number.

15807: **si_errno** lets the kernel include some information about the reason why a signal was generated; its only interesting uses are in driver code not included in this book. The kernel itself doesn't care about this value. In the code included in this book, in the few cases when it sets the member, it sets it to 0.

15808: **si_code** records the signal's source (not the sender's process ID [PID]—that's recorded elsewhere). The valid signal sources are **#define**d at lines 15891 and following.

15810: The last component of the **struct** is a **union** type; which of the **union**ed types is used depends on **si_code**'s value.

15811: The **union**'s first component is **_pad**, which pads the size of the **siginfo_t** to 128 bytes. Note that the size of this array, **SI_PAD_SIZE** (line 15803), accounts for the first three members of the **struct**. If more members were added, **SI_PAD_SIZE** would have to change accordingly. The **union**'s other members carry auxiliary signal-specific data.

struct sigqueue

22924: **struct sigqueue** is used to ensure that all realtime signals are delivered, if possible, along with the supplemental information (**siginfo_t**) for each. As you'll see later, the kernel maintains a queue of pending realtime signals per process. The queue also contains nodes for nonrealtime signals, but at most one such node for each signal number.

The queue type itself is minimal, consisting only of a pointer to the next node and the **siginfo_t** itself.

Utility Functions

One of the most important signal-related data structures, **sigset_t**, is manipulated with a set of simple functions defined in the file include/linux/signal.h, which begins at line 22915. On the x86, the same functions can be—and are—implemented more efficiently in assembler. These more efficient versions start at line 16245. (The m68k port is the only other port with an architecture-specific implementation.) Because both the platform-independent and the x86-specific versions are important, I'll look at both.

Platform-Independent **sigset_t** Functions

The platform-independent functions for working with **sigset_t**s live in include/linux/signal.h, which starts at line 22915. The so-called "bitops" (bit-level operations) functions are described next.

sigaddset

22941: **sigaddset** adds one signal to the set—that is, it turns on one bit in the set.

22943: Converts the signal from one-based to zero-based, as appropriate for the bit-level operations.

22945: If signals fit into a single **unsigned long**, the appropriate bit is set in it.

22947: Otherwise, **sigaddset** must go through a few more contortions, first locating the appropriate array element and then setting the right bit within it.

Line 22944, like similar code later in the file, is puzzling at first glance. In kernel code, speed is of the essence. Thus, you might expect that instead of runtime decisions such as this one:

```
if (_NSIG_WORDS == 1)
  set->sig[0] |= 1UL << sig;
else
  set->sig[sig / _NSIG_BPW] |=
        1UL << (sig % _NSIG_BPW);
```

you would see compile-time decisions such as this:

```
#if (_NSIG_WORDS == 1)
  set->sig[0] |= 1UL << sig;
#else
  set->sig[sig / _NSIG_BPW] |=
              1UL << (sig %
_NSIG_BPW);
#endif
```

Wouldn't this run faster? After all, the **if** condition is computable at compile time, so the preprocessor can remove the need for any runtime check.

The mystery disappears when you realize that the optimizer can do this, too. gcc's optimizer is smart enough to notice that the **if** statement can work out only one way, so it removes the unnecessary code. The resulting object code for the kernel's runtime version is identical to that for the proposed compile-time version.

But wouldn't the preprocessor-based version be better anyway, in case you're using a compiler with a poor optimizer? Not necessarily. For one thing, the preprocessor-based (compile-time) version is a little harder to read. The difference in readability is striking when the code becomes even slightly more complex than the preceding simple example. Consider, for instance, the **switch** in **sigemptyset**, starting at line 23056. The **switch** currently looks like this:

```
switch (_NSIG_WORDS) {
default:
  memset(set, 0, sizeof(sigset_t));
  break;
case 2: set->sig[1] = 0;
case 1: set->sig[0] = 0;
  break;
}
```

(Notice the deliberate fall-through from case 2 to case 1.) Rewritten to exploit the preprocessor, it might look like this:

```
#if ((_NSIG_WORDS != 2) && \
     (_NSIG_WORDS != 1))
  memset(set, 0, sizeof(sigset_t));
#else /* _NSIG_WORDS is 2 or 1. */
#if (_NSIG_WORDS == 2)
  set->sig[1] = 0;
#endif
  set->sig[0] = 0;
#endif /* _NSIG_WORDS test. */
```

gcc's optimizer produces the same object code for both. Which version of the source code would you rather read?

In addition, if a compiler's optimizer isn't even this good—this optimization is a fairly simple one—then the compiler probably isn't generating very good code anyway. Any help you offer it is doomed to be insufficient, so you might as well write code that's easier to read and maintain—another engineering tradeoff. Finally, as we've observed before and will again, compiling the kernel with a compiler other than gcc is a challenge already—one more gcc-specific bit of code won't matter that much.

sigdelset

22951: This code is very similar to **sigaddset**; the difference is that, here, a bit is being deleted from the set—it's being turned off.

sigismember

22961: Again, this code is similar to **sigaddset**; here, it's testing whether a bit is set. Note that line 22965 could equally well have been written as follows:

```
return set->sig[0] & (1UL << sig);
```

Much the same is true for line 22967. This wouldn't be an improvement, although it would be marginally more consistent with the way the other functions are written.

The change would alter the function's behavior slightly: It currently returns 0 or 1, and with this change, it could return other nonzero values when a bit is set. However, the change would break no existing code, because its callers only care whether the return value is 0 or not (they don't care about 1 particularly).

sigfindinword

22971: This function returns the position of the first bit set in **word**. The **ffz** function (line 12450) returns the position of the first 0 bit in its argument. The position of the first 0 bit in the bitwise-inverted **word**—which is what this function finds—is clearly the same as the position of the first 1 bit in the original. It starts counting at 0 from the least-significant bit.

sigmask

22976: Last of all, the useful **sigmask** macro simply converts a signal number into a bitmask with only one of the corresponding bits set.

Platform-Dependent sigset_t Functions

Though simple and efficient C code, the platform-independent versions can be implemented even more efficiently on the x86 platform, using the x86 CPU family's convenient and powerful bit-set instructions. Most of these reduce to a single machine instruction, so this discussion will be brief.

On the x86 (as on the m68k), the platform-independent functions are never even seen by the compiler. Line 22918 **#include**s the file asm/signal.h, which on the x86 resolves to include/asm-i386/signal.h, thanks to a symbolic link set up by the makefile. Line 16243 **#define**s the preprocessor symbol **__HAVE_ARCH_SIG_BITOPS**, which suppresses the definitions of the platform-independent versions of these functions (see line 22936).

sigaddset

16245: The x86-specific implementation of **sigaddset** uses the **btsl** instruction, which sets a single bit in its operand.

sigdelset

16251: Similarly, the x86-specific implementation of **sigdelset** uses the **btrl** instruction, which resets (clears) a single bit in its operand.

sigismember

16276: **sigismember** chooses an implementation based on whether its **sig** argument is a compile-time constant expression. The undocumented gcc compiler magic **__builtin_constant_p** is a compile-time operator (like **sizeof**) that reports whether the value of its argument can be computed at compile time.

If it can, **sigismember** uses the **__const_sigismember** function (line 16257) to do its work, because most of the expressions in it can be computed at compile time. Otherwise, the generalized version, **__gen_sigismember** (line 16265), is used instead. The more general version uses the x86's **btl** instruction, which tests a single bit in its operand.

Note that compile-time constant folding and dead-code elimination imply that this entire test will be executed only at compile time—in essence, **sigismember** will simply be replaced by either **__const_sigismember** or **__gen_sigismember**, as appropriate, with no hint in the resulting object code that the other was even considered. Pretty neat, eh?

sigmask

16281: The x86-specific implementation of **sigmask** is identical to the platform-independent version.

sigfindinword

16283: Finally, the x86-specific **sigfindinword** implementation just uses the x86's **bsfl** instruction, which searches for a set bit in its operand.

Set Functions

In addition to the preceding group, another group of macros and functions performs set-type operations on **sigset_t**s. Similarly to the previous group, these functions are protected by the **__HAVE_ARCH_**

SIG_SETOPS preprocessor symbol. No architecture currently provides its own architecture-specific implementations of these functions, however, so the architecture-independent versions are the only versions that exist.

_SIG_SET_BINOP

22983: All three of the binary operators we want to define—**sigorsets**, **sigandsets**, and **signandsets**—have essentially the same implementation. This macro simply factors out the code common to all three of them, so that only a name and an operator must be supplied.

22990: Begins by looping over all the complete quartets of **unsigned longs** in the **sigset_t**s, applying the operators as it goes. The loop is unrolled for speed—a well-known technique for increasing speed by reducing the loop-control overhead. Mostly, however, the loop never executes. On the x86, for instance, the compiler can prove at compile time that the loop's body will never be executed, because the truncated integer division **_NSIG_WORDS** / 4 is 0. (Recall that **_NSIG_WORDS** is 2 on the x86.)

23000: The **switch** starting at this line handles any leftovers at the end of the loop. If **_NSIG_WORDS** happened to be 6 on some platform, then the **for** loop would execute once and case 2 of this **switch** would also execute. On the x86, the loop never executes; only case 2 of the **switch** does.

By the way, I don't see any reason why the **switch** wasn't written to exploit fall-through, as its cousin **_SIG_SET_OP** (described next) does. The existing version might, in general, make marginally better use of the cache (as you'll see if you try to rewrite it)—but if that's the reason, then the same argument would surely apply to **_SIG_SET_OP**.

_SIG_SET_OP

23033: **_SIG_SET_OP** is similar to **_SIG_SET_BINOP**, just for unary operators instead of binary operators, so I don't need to explore it in detail. You should note, though, that it's used only

once—to generate **signotset** at line 23051—unlike **_SIG_SET_BINOP**. Consequently, in a sense, it's not needed—its implementer could have written **signotset** directly, not bothering to write **_SIG_SET_OP**, without duplicating any code. However, the object code comes out the same either way, and this way makes it trivial to add another unary operator later, if you so choose.

sigemptyset

23054: **sigemptyset** empties the supplied set—clearing all the bits in it. (The next function, **sigfillset**, is identical to this one, except that it sets all the bits instead of clearing them, so I need not explore it in detail.)

23057: The general case uses **memset** to zero all the bits in **set**.

23061: For small values of **_NSIG_WORDS**, it's faster simply to set one or two elements of the **sigset_t** directly. That is done here, exploiting fall-through.

sigaddsetmask

23088: This and the following few functions are one-liners that make reading and setting the lowest 32 (or whatever the word size is) signals easier and faster. **sigaddsetmask** simply sets bits as indicated by **mask**, leaving any existing bits alone—it's a set union.

siginitset

23106: Sets the lowest 32 (or whatever) bits from the supplied mask, and zeroes any other bits. The next function, **siginitsetinv** (line 23121), does the inverse: It sets the lowest 32 (or whatever) bits according to the bitwise-inverted mask, and then sets the remaining bits.

Sending Signals

From the user's point of view, sending a signal is quite simple: Invoke the system call **kill**, which takes a process ID and a signal to send. But the implementation is more involved, as this section shows.

sys_kill

35945: **sys_kill** is the deceptively simple implementation of the **kill** system call; the real work is hidden in **kill_something_info**, which I investigate next. The arguments to **sys_kill** are a signal to send, **sig**, and a destination for the signal, **pid**. The **pid** argument might not be just a process ID, as you'll see. (PIDs and other basic concepts of processes are detailed in Chapter 7.)

35947: Declares and fills out a **struct siginfo** based on the information supplied to **sys_kill**. In particular, note that **si_code** is **SI_USER** (because only a user process invokes this system call; the kernel itself never does, preferring lower-level functions instead).

35955: Passes this information on to **kill_something_info**, which does the real work.

kill_something_info

35630: The arguments to this function are similar to those of **sys_kill**, but with a pointer to a **struct siginfo** thrown in.

35633: If **pid** is 0, the current process wants to send the signal to its entire process group, which is done with **kill_pg_info** (line 35564).

35635: If **pid** is –1, the signal is sent to (nearly) every process on the system, as described in the following paragraphs.

35640: Uses the **for_each_task** macro (**#define**d at line 22542 and detailed in Chapter 7) to begin iterating over the list of all existing processes.

35642: If this is not the idle process, init, or the calling process, it is sent the signal, using **send_sig_info** (line 35480, and discussed later). **count** is incremented every time a suitable task is found, although **kill_something_info** really isn't interested in the count, but rather in whether any suitable process was found. If any attempt to send the signal fails, the failure is remembered so that **kill_something_info** can return a failure code at line 35649; if multiple failures occur, it returns the last failure.

35649: If any suitable candidates were found, **kill_something_info** returns the result of the most recent call to **send_sig_info** (barring -EPERM). If no suitable candidates were found, it returns the **ESRCH** error.

35650: Other negative **pids** (negative, but not –1) specify a process group to receive the signal; the absolute value of **pid** is the process group number. As before, **kill_pg_info** is used for this purpose.

35652: All other possibilities have been accounted for; **pid** must be positive. In this case, it's the PID of a single process to which to send the signal. This is accomplished with **kill_proc_info** (line 35609, and discussed soon).

kill_pg_info

35564: This function sends a signal and a **struct siginfo** to every process in a process group. The body of the function is similar to some of the code shown earlier in **kill_something_info**, so I cover it lightly.

35572: Begins iterating over all the processes in the system.

35573: If the process is in the right process group, it is sent the signal.

35576: If the signal was successfully sent to any process, **retval** is set to 0, so that success is returned at line 35581. If the signal could not be sent to any process, then either no process was in the given process group, in which case **retval** will still be -**ESRCH** from line 35570, or **kill_pg_info** tried sending the signal to one or more processes but failed every time, in which case **retval** is the value of the most recent error code from **send_sig_info**. Note the slight difference from **kill_something_info**, which generally returns the result of its last attempt to deliver the signal. Here, **kill_pg_info** returns success if the signal was successfully delivered to any process, even if later attempts failed.

35581: **retval** is now either set as just described, or it is -**EINVAL**, from line 35566, if the process group number was invalid.

kill_proc_info

35609: **kill_proc_info** is a quite simple function that sends a signal and a **struct siginfo** to a single process identified by its PID.

35615: Looks up a single process by the supplied PID; **find_task_by_pid** (line 22184) returns a pointer to this process, or **NULL** if no such process is found.

35618: If a match is found, the signal is sent to the target process by using **send_sig_info**.

35620: Returns the error indication, which is either -**ESRCH**, from line 35616, if no matching process was found, or the return value from **send_sig_info** otherwise.

send_sig_info

35480: The workhorse function for the last several functions you've looked at has clearly been **send_sig_info**. The functions have been locating processes in various ways and delegating the real work. Now it's time to see how the real work is done. **send_sig_info** sends the signal **sig**, using extra information pointed to by **info** (which can be **NULL**), to the process pointed to by **t** (**t** is assumed never to be **NULL**, a property the caller must enforce).

35492: Ensures that **sig** is in range. Notice that this tests

```
sig > _NSIG
```

rather than, as you might have expected,

```
sig >= _NSIG
```

because signal numbering is one-based, not zero-based. Hence, **_NSIG**, the number of valid signals, is itself a valid signal number, although no **#define** exists for this signal number.

35496: Calls **bad_signal** (line 35271, and covered in the next section) to perform additional sanity and permissions checks.

35503: Ignores signal 0 and refuses to deliver signals to zombie processes (processes that have exited but have not been removed from the system's data structures yet; see Chapter 7's "Process States" section and its discussion of the function **exit**).

35507: For some signals, a little extra work must be done before actually sending the signal. That work is done here, through a call to **handle_stop_signal** (line 35352, and discussed later on this page).

35513: If the target process wants to and is allowed to ignore delivery of the signal, delivery is skipped.

35519: Nonrealtime signals are not queued, meaning that if a second instance of the same signal arrives before the process can handle the first, the second is ignored. That's enforced here (recall that **struct task_struct**'s **pending** member holds the set of currently pending signals for a process).

35523: To send the signal, **send_sig_info** uses **deliver_signal** (line 35468), discussed later in this chapter.

35526: If the process was waiting for a signal to arrive and a signal is now waiting for it—either because **send_sig_info** just delivered one or because one was waiting already—then the process should be notified of the pending signal's existence. Accordingly, it's awakened now, with **wake_up_process** (line 34067).

bad_signal

35271: This function performs sanity and permissions checks for **send_sig_info**. The general idea is to check whether signals are being sent illegally. The kernel itself is allowed to send signals to any process, but users other than root can't send signals to processes owned by other users,

except for an obscure case involving **SIGCONT**. Altogether, this function's long Boolean expression says the following:

(Line 35275) If no supplemental information exists, or if it does but the signal is from the user rather than from the kernel, and . . .

(Line 35277) . . . the signal isn't **SIGCONT**, or it is **SIGCONT** but it isn't being sent to another process in the same session, and . . .

(Lines 35279 and 35280) . . . the effective user ID of the sender is neither the saved user ID of the target process nor the current user ID of the target process, and . . .

(Lines 35281 and 35282) . . . the current user ID of the sender is neither the saved user ID nor the current user ID of the target process, and . . .

(Line 35283) . . . the user isn't allowed to exceed normal permissions on this point (for example, because the user is root) . . .

. . . then the signal should not be sent; **bad_signal** returns true so that **send_sig_info** will jump over the signal-sending code.

Two points must be made about the preceding Boolean expression. First, if **info** is 1 when cast to **unsigned long**, it's not a real pointer to a **struct siginfo**. Instead, it's a special value indicating that the signal is from the kernel, but that no further supplemental information is available. The kernel never allocates memory for itself in the lowest page (memory pages are discussed in Chapter 8), so any address below 4,096 (except for 0, **NULL**) could be used as this special value.

Second, the bitwise XOR operator (^) takes the place of the more common logical inequality operator (!=) in several of the condition's terms. The two operators have the same meaning in this case, because if any bits are different

between two compared integer values, then at least one bit will be on in XOR's result, so that the result will be nonzero and therefore logically true. Presumably, an older version of gcc generated more efficient code for ^ than for !=, but both operators yield the same code in current versions of the compiler.

handle_stop_signal

35352: On behalf of **send_sig_info**, **handle_stop_signal** performs additional setup work before certain signals are delivered.

35359: If sending **SIGKILL** or **SIGCONT**, **handle_stop_signal** wakes up the process (that is, it allows it to run again if currently stopped). In the case of **SIGKILL**, the process will quickly notice the signal and exit.

35361: Sets the process's exit code to 0. If the process was stopped with **SIGSTOP**, the exit code field was used to communicate the stopping signal to the parent.

35362: Cancels any pending **SIGSTOP** (stopped as by a debugger), **SIGTSTP** (stopped from the keyboard, as by typing Ctrl+Z), **SIGTTOU** (a process running in the background tried to write to a TTY), or **SIGTTIN** (a process running in the background tried to read from the TTY). These are all conditions that normally stop the process but are rendered irrelevant by the more recent arrival of a **SIGCONT** or **SIGKILL** signal. **rm_from_queue** (line 35236) does the real work of canceling these pending signals.

35373: In the previous case, these four signals were canceled if **SIGCONT** or **SIGKILL** arrived. In a partial symmetry, if one of these four signals arrived, any pending **SIGCONT** is canceled. **SIGKILL** isn't canceled, however, following the principle that **SIGKILL** must never be blocked or canceled.

deliver_signal

35468: This simple function begins by using **send_signal** (discussed next) to actually deliver the signal, waking the receiving process as appropriate.

35473: If the signal was successfully sent and is not blocked, the target process is awakened with **signal_wake_up** (line 35443), which sets the process's **sigpending** flag and wakes it if it was sleeping.

send_signal

35378: To help orient you, the call chain that led here was **send_sig_info** to **deliver_signal** to **send_signal**.

35392: Realtime signals are queued—within limits. The most important limit is a configurable limit on the total number of realtime signals that can be queued simultaneously. This limit is **max_queued_signals**, which is defined at line 35007 and modified through Linux's /proc file system (explored in Chapter 11). If there is room to queue more signals, a **struct sigqueue** is allocated to hold the queued info.

Why limit the number of queued signals in the first place? To prevent denial-of-service attacks: Without this limit, a user could keep sending realtime signals until the kernel ran out of memory, which would prevent the kernel from providing this and other services to other processes.

35397: If a queue node was allocated, **send_signal** must now enqueue information about this signal.

35398: Adding the information to the queue is straightforward: **send_signal** increments the global number of pending signals, and then it appends the new node to the target process's queue of signals.

35402: Fills in the queue node's **info** member based on the **info** argument supplied to **send_signal**.

35403: 0 (**NULL**) means that the signal was sent from the user and probably came by way of one of the backward-compatible signal-sending

functions defined at lines 35660 through 35687. The target **siginfo_t** is filled with relatively obvious values.

35410: A value of 1 is a special value that indicates the signal came from the kernel—again, via the backward-compatible functions. As in the previous case, the target **siginfo_t** is filled with relatively obvious values.

35418: In the normal case, **send_signal** gets a real **siginfo_t** that it can simply copy into the queue node.

35421: No queue node was allocated—either **kmem_cache_alloc** returned **NULL** at line 35394, because the system is out of memory, or **send_signal** didn't even try to allocate a node, because the maximum number of queued signals had already been reached. In either case, **send_signal** does the same thing: Unless this signal was sent by the kernel or by the old-style signal functions (for example, **kill**), **send_signal** returns the **EAGAIN** error to tell the caller that the signal can't be enqueued now, but that the caller might succeed by retrying with the same arguments later. Otherwise, **send_signal** delivers the signal but doesn't enqueue it.

35430: At last, **send_signal** is actually ready to deliver the signal. The signal is entered into the process's set of pending signals. Note that this is done even if the signal is blocked, which might be surprising. But there's a reason for doing this: The kernel must provide **sys_sigpending** (line 36094; its workhorse function, **do_sigpending**, is discussed later in the chapter), which allows processes to ask what signals were delivered while blocked.

force_sig_info

35541: This function is used by the kernel to ensure that a process receives a signal, whether it wants it or not. This is used, for instance, to force the process to receive a **SIGSEGV** when it dereferences a wild pointer (see line 8231).

force_sig_info's arguments are the same as **send_sig_info**'s and have the same meaning.

35547: If the target process is a zombie, not even the kernel should be sending it any signals; the attempt is rejected.

35552: If the process thinks it's going to ignore this signal, **force_sig_info** disabuses it of that notion by forcing it to take the default action instead. This isn't as innocuous as it might seem: For the cases in which the kernel uses this function, the default response to the signal is to kill the process.

35554: Removes the signal from **t**'s **blocked** set.

35555: Because **t**'s **blocked** set changed, a pending signal can no longer be blocked. **recalc_sigpending** (line 22329; see the discussion of **has_pending_signals** in the next section) recalculates **t**'s **pending** flag accordingly.

35558: **force_sig_info** has now set up conditions so that **t** must accept the signal, so the signal is delivered with **send_sig_info**. This still might not deliver the signal if **send_sig_info**'s implementation were changed, so the two functions must be kept in sync.

has_pending_signals

22295: This function is the guts of **recalc_sigpending** (line 22329), which recalculates a process's **sigpending** flag; it's called when the process's **signal** or **blocked** set changes.

22320: In the simplest case, **has_pending_signals** bitwise-ANDs the **signal** set with the inverse of the **blocked** set. (Inverting the **blocked** set gives you the allowed set.) The other cases are merely generalizations of this one.

22322: If any of the preceding operations left any bits on in **ready**, then at least one signal in the pending set was not blocked; **has_pending_signals** therefore returns nonzero so that its caller, **recalc_sigpending**, raises the process's **sigpending** flag.

All **has_pending_signals** really needs to know is whether at least one signal is pending. It doesn't, for example, need to know how many are pending. Therefore, the code for the nontrivial cases could stop modifying **ready** (for example, by breaking the loop at line 22303 early) as soon as it's set to a nonzero value. However, any savings that might be derived from that optimization must be weighed against the expense of the additional tests. Because of this, and because **_NSIG_WORDS** is small (in practice, anyway), it's certainly faster as it stands.

ignored_signal

35338: **ignored_signal** helps **send_sig_info** decide whether to send a signal to a process.

35341: If its parent (probably a debugger) is tracing the process, or the signal is in the process's blocked set, it shouldn't be ignored. The second part might be unexpected; if the signal is blocked, shouldn't **send_sig_info** (and **ignored_signal**) ignore it? As it happens, no. What this function means by whether a signal should be ignored is whether the corresponding bit in the process's **signal** set should be set. As you've already seen, supporting the **sigpending** system call requires the kernel to set that bit if a signal arrives while blocked. Hence, blocked signals can't just be ignored.

35345: The rest of **ignored_signal**'s work is done by **signal_type**, explored next.

signal_type

35291: This function is more general than it needs to be—all that matters is whether it returns 0 to its sole caller, **ignored_signal**.

35296: If the process is a zombie, the signal should be ignored. This test seems unnecessary at first, because this situation was also checked at line 35503, before **signal_type** is even called. However, it's just possible the process would be killed (by another CPU in an SMP system) between then and now.

35299: If the process has a user-defined signal handler for the signal, the signal should not be ignored.

35306: A **handler** of 1 is **SIG_IGN**—the process wants to ignore the signal. Processes are allowed to ignore most signals, but not **SIGCHLD**. For **SIGCHLD**, POSIX gives **SIG_IGN** a special meaning, as documented at line 35999. The "automatic child reaping" mentioned there is carried out at line 4885.

35313: The handler isn't a user-defined handler and isn't the special **SIG_IGN** value. The only remaining possibility is the **SIG_DFL** (default) action. In most cases, the default behavior is to handle the signal rather than ignore it; the exceptions, as you can see, are **SIGCONT**, **SIGWINCH**, **SIGCHLD**, and **SIGURG**.

Receiving Signals

So far, you've seen about half of the story for signals—how the kernel records that a signal has arrived for a process. The other half of the story is how the process actually receives and handles the signal. Naturally, the kernel takes an active role in this part of the story as well, as you'll see.

do_signal

4822: **do_signal** is where a signal is delivered to a process. It's invoked from several points in the kernel—from lines 935 and 943, as you saw in Chapter 5, as well as from lines 4301 and 4331. What all of these cases have in common is that they want the current process to handle a pending signal (if any).

4833: **oldset**, if non-**NULL**, is used to return the current process's set of blocked signals. Because **do_signal** won't alter the blocked set, it can simply return a pointer to the existing blocked set.

4836: Enters a loop that extends nearly to the end of the function (line 4953). There are only two ways to exit the loop: by running out of possible signals to handle, or by handling a single signal.

4840: Dequeues a signal with **dequeue_signal** (line 35200, covered later). **dequeue_signal** returns either 0 or the number of a signal to handle, and it fills in any supplemental information in **info**.

4843: If no signal was waiting, the loop terminates now. This wouldn't normally happen on the first loop iteration.

4846: If its parent (probably a debugger) is tracing the current process, and the signal is not the unblockable **SIGKILL**, the process's parent must be alerted to the arrival of the signal.

4849: The signal number that arrived for the child is communicated to the parent in the child's **exit_code** field; the parent will collect it by using **sys_wait4** (line 30330, and covered in Chapter 7). **do_signal** stops the child, uses **notify_parent** (line 35753) to send the parent the **SIGCHLD** signal, and then calls the scheduler function, **schedule** (line 34237, Chapter 7), to give other processes—in particular, the parent—a chance to run. **schedule** will yield the CPU to another process, so it won't return until the kernel switches back to this process.

4855: If the debugger cancels the signal, **do_signal** shouldn't handle it here; the loop continues.

4860: A **SIGSTOP** probably occurred just because the process was being traced. There's no need to handle it; the loop continues.

4864: If the debugger changed the signal number that **do_signal** is to handle, **do_signal** fills in **info** according to the new information.

4874: As the comment says, if the new signal is blocked, it's requeued and the loop continues. Otherwise, control falls through to the following code.

4880: At this point, either the process isn't being traced, it is being traced but it got a **SIGKILL**, or control fell through from the previous block. In any of these cases, **do_signal** has a signal that it should handle now. It starts by getting the **struct k_sigaction** that tells it how to handle this signal number.

4882: If the process is trying to ignore the signal, then **do_signal** ignores it by continuing the loop, unless the signal is **SIGCHLD**. Why doesn't this test also ensure that the process is not trying to ignore **SIGKILL**, which is supposed to be unblockable and unignorable? The answer is that the action corresponding to **SIGKILL** can never be **SIG_IGN**, nor indeed anything but **SIG_DFL**—this is guaranteed by line 35984 (in **do_sigaction**). Thus, if the action is **SIG_IGN**, the signal number can't be **SIGKILL**.

4885: As documented at the banner comment starting at line 35999, the POSIX standard specifies that the "ignore" action for **SIGCHLD** really means to reap children automatically. The children are reaped with **sys_wait4**, after which the loop continues.

4894: The process is taking the default action for this signal. The default action for all signals received by the special process init is to ignore the signal entirely.

4898: The default action for the **SIGCONT**, **SIGCHLD**, and **SIGWINCH** signals is to do nothing, simply continuing the loop.

4903: For **SIGTSTP**, **SIGTTIN**, and **SIGTTOU**, the default action varies. If the process group to which this process belongs is orphaned—which simply means that it's no longer attached to a TTY—then POSIX says that the default action for these terminal-based signals is to ignore them. If the process's process group is not orphaned, then the default response to these signals is to stop the process—the same as the **SIGSTOP** case, to which control falls through.

4910: In response to **SIGSTOP** (or by falling through from the previous case), **do_signal** stops the process. In addition, unless its parent has asked not to be notified when one of its children stops, the parent is notified of this occurrence. As at line 4852, **schedule** is called to hand off the CPU to some other process. When the kernel gives the current process the CPU again, the loop continues in order to dequeue another signal.

This is unexpected—I would have thought that when **schedule** returned, the loop would exit, because a signal has been processed. The reason is that if the process was stopped, it woke up because it got a signal (probably **SIGCONT**) so it might as well check for and handle the signal now.

4920: The default reaction to other signals is to exit the process. Some of them cause the process to try to dump core first (see Chapter 8 for details). If this binary format (see Chapter 7 for details) knows how to dump core and the core dump succeeds, a bit is set in the process's exit code to indicate that the process dumped core before exiting. Then, control falls through to the **default** case, which will terminate the process. Note that **do_exit** (line 30262, another one that's covered in Chapter 7) never returns—hence the "NOTREACHED" comment at line 4939.

4951: At this point, **do_signal** has dequeued a signal that was associated with neither the **SIG_IGN** nor the **SIG_DFL** actions. The only other possibility is that it's a user-defined signal handler function. **do_signal** calls **handle_signal** (line 4776, and discussed a bit later in the chapter) to invoke this signal handler, and then returns 1 to indicate to the caller that the signal was handled.

4956: At this point, **do_signal** was unable to dequeue a signal for the current process. (This line is reached only from the **break** at line 4844). If the process was interrupted in the middle of a system call, **do_signal** adjusts the registers so that the system call will be restarted.

4965: Returns 0 to inform the caller that **do_signal** didn't handle any signals.

dequeue_signal

35200: **dequeue_signal** removes a signal from the process's signal queue, ignoring those specified by **mask**. It returns the signal number, and it returns the associated **siginfo_t** through the pointer argument **info**.

35209: Calls **next_signal**, discussed next, to get the number of the next nonblocked signal waiting for the current process. If the return value is 0, no such signal exists.

35210: A driver is allowed to intercept signals for a process (using **block_all_signals**, line 35123); this is rarely needed, but can help to ensure that a process that has temporarily locked a device gets a chance to unlock it before exiting. When this happens, the driver registers a notifier function that should be allowed to veto some or all signals sent to the process. If such a notifier function has been registered for this process, it is invoked now.

35220: If a signal is pending, **dequeue_signal** should try to dequeue it; it does this using **collect_signal** (line 35147, and discussed a little later in the chapter). If **collect_signal** doesn't collect a signal, **sig** is zeroed so that **dequeue_signal** will return failure at line 35233.

35227: The process's **pending** set might have changed, so **dequeue_signal** must recalculate the process's **sigpending** flag.

35233: Returns the number of the signal dequeued, or 0 if no signal was dequeued.

next_signal

35025: **next_signal** returns the number of the next signal that **dequeue_signal** should try to dequeue.

35030: Sets up a few aliases to avoid repeated dereferencing: **s** is the set of pending signals for the process (perhaps including some that are blocked, remember), and **m** is the masked set. In particular, note that the expression *s, which appears in the function a few times, is just a faster version of **tsk->pending.signal.sig[0]**.

35032: Inside this **switch**, **sig** is set to the first pending signal. It's easiest to understand by starting with the simplest case; the other cases are generalizations of this one.

35052: The simplest case is this one: It bitwise-ANDs the set of pending signals against the bitwise-inverted mask, storing the result in the temporary variable **x**; **x** is now the set of pending signals not ignored by **mask**. If **x** is not 0, then such a pending signal exists (at least one of **x**'s bits is set); **next_signal** gets the corresponding signal number using **ffz** (line 12450) and converts it to one-based signal numbering, storing the result in **sig**. As mentioned, the other cases just generalize this one; the important result is that **sig** gets set, if possible, in each of them. If **sig** is 0 after the **switch**, no pending signal passed through the mask.

collect_signal

35147: **collect_signal** attempts to dequeue a signal with the given number and fill in **info** accordingly; it returns a flag indicating whether it found the indicated signal.

35154: **collect_signal** scans the queue of signals waiting to be delivered to this process. If it finds a match, control jumps ahead to the **found_it** label.

35162: The signal was pending for this process (which we know from line 35150), but it was not in the queue. Normally, the queue contains a node for every realtime signal that has been sent; if the same realtime signal was sent more than once, then the queue would have more than one node with that signal number. If a nonrealtime signal was sent, the queue should contain exactly one node with that signal number, no matter how many times the signal was sent—but if the nonrealtime signal had already been collected, the corresponding bit would have been cleared

in the process's pending set, so control wouldn't have reached this point. Either way, we expect the loop to find the queue node. Failure to find the node can only mean—as documented here—that the queue was full. If that happened, **collect_signal** deduces that the queue contains no more instances of this signal; it deletes the signal from the process's pending set, fills out **info** as best it can, and returns success to indicate that a signal was collected.

35171: This is the expected case: The queue node was found. **q** points to this node, and **pp** points to the previous node's pointer to **q**. **q** is unlinked and the queue's tail is updated if **q** was the last node.

35182: As stated above, a realtime signal might be duplicated in the queue. If it is, the signal is still pending for the process and should not be deleted from the process's pending set. The loop starting at this line checks the queue for such a duplicate, skipping over the **sigdelset** call if one is found.

35189: Either the signal was a nonrealtime signal, or it was the only occurrence of a realtime signal. Either way, the process's pending set is updated and the function returns success.

do_notify_parent

35702: **do_notify_parent** does all the real work for **notify_parent**, locating a process's parent and informing it of a status change in the child—normally, the child has either been stopped or killed.

35707: Fills in the local variable **info** with information about the context in which the signal occurred.

35723: If the process was stopped by a signal, **why** is set to indicate that's what happened.

35730: If the child has exited, **why** is set to values indicating that it dumped core, was killed by a signal, or exited of its own volition, as appropriate.

35739: The preceding cases are supposed to cover all of the possibilities. If they didn't, **why** will still

be **SI_KERNEL** from line 35718. You can see, through inspection of the function's control flow, that this can never happen in the code as written.

35743: Sends the signal to the process's parent. The next line wakes up any processes waiting on this child, including its parent, offering them the CPU.

handle_signal

4776: **handle_signal** is invoked from **do_signal** when a user-defined signal handler is to be called.

4801: Sets up a stack frame in which the user's signal handler will run. If the process has asked for any supplemental information that the kernel might have about the signal's origin and context, the stack frame is set up with **setup_rt_frame** (line 4690); otherwise, it's done with **setup_frame** (line 4613). Both of these functions adjust the CPU registers and stack so that control will "return" to the user-mode signal handler, and when the signal handler returns, it'll return to the code that was executing when the signal arrived.

4806: If the **SA_ONESHOT** flag is set, the signal handler should be used only once. (Note that **sys_signal**, the implementation of the **signal** system call, uses **SA_ONESHOT**-type signal handlers—see line 36221.) In this case, the default action is restored now.

4809: **SA_NODEFER** means no extra signals should be blocked while executing this signal's handler. If the bit isn't set, extra bits are now added to the process's blocked set.

Other Signal-Related Functions

A few other representative signal-handling functions remain.

do_sigpending

35842: This short system call, which implements the guts of **sys_sigpending** (line 36094), lets the process ask whether any nonrealtime signals arrived while they were blocked. Through the supplied pointer, the function returns a bit-set indicating which signals they were.

35851: The heart of this function is a simple bitwise AND of the process's **blocked** and **signal** sets. It's only interested in the lowest 32 bits, which are all the nonrealtime signals.

35856: Copies the pending set back to user space through the supplied pointer. **-EFAULT** is returned if this fails, and 0 is returned if it succeeds. Notice that whether any signals were pending—that is, whether or not the returned set is empty—is not a criterion for success.

do_sigaction

35978: **do_sigaction** implements the interesting part of the **sigaction** system call. (The remainder is in **sys_sigaction**, line 4337.) **sigaction** is the POSIX equivalent of the ISO C function **signal**— it associates an action with a signal, so that the action is performed when the process receives the signal. Unlike handlers set up by **signal**, however, handlers set up by **sigaction** are not the **SA_ONESHOT** type, so they don't need to be reinstalled every time the handler is invoked.

35983: Sanity checks: Ensures that **sig** is in range and that the process is not trying to associate an action with **SIGKILL** or **SIGCONT**. Processes are simply not allowed to override the default behavior for these two signals.

35987: Gets a pointer to the **struct k_sigaction** associated with this signal.

35991: **sigaction** can return the old action through one of the supplied pointers. This is useful for "stacking" handlers, where a handler is temporarily overridden and later restored. If the **oact** pointer is non-**NULL**, the old action is copied to it. (This doesn't copy the information back to user space, though; the caller must do that.)

35994: If **do_sigaction** was given an action to associate with the signal, the two are associated now. **SIGKILL** and **SIGSTOP** must also be deleted from the action's mask, to ensure that these signals are not blocked or overridden.

36016: As stated by the banner comment starting at line 35999, the next several lines must go through a few contortions to comply with the POSIX standard, discarding some pending signals if necessary. You won't lose much by skipping the details.

sys_rt_sigtimedwait

35869: **sys_rt_sigtimedwait** waits for a signal to arrive, optionally timing out after a specified interval. Not just any signals will be accepted; the **sigset_t** pointed to by **uthese** says which signals the caller's interested in.

35891: **uthese** (which has been copied into the local variable **these**) is the set of signals to allow, but the kernel's primitives only know how to block signals. But that's okay: Inverting the set of allowed signals gives the set of signals to block, which can then be used directly.

35893: If the caller supplied a timeout, it's copied in from user space and its value is sanity-checked.

35902: Sees whether a signal is pending already—if one is, there's no need to wait for one. Otherwise, the caller must wait.

35904: If the user supplied no timeout, the timeout defaults to **MAX_SCHEDULE_TIMEOUT** (**#defin**ed to **LONG_MAX**, or $2^{31}-1$ on a 32-bit machine, at line 21798). This isn't forever—the timeout is in *jiffies*, ticks of the system clock that occur at a rate of 100 per second, so the timeout works out to about 248 days on a 32-bit machine. By contrast, on a 64-bit machine, **MAX_SCHEDULE_TIMEOUT** is about 3 billion years.

35906: If the user did supply a timeout, it's copied in from user space and converted to jiffies. The part of this expression following the "+" is a clever way to round up to the next jiffy—the idea is that **timespec_to_jiffies** (line 24675) might have rounded down, but the kernel must round up instead, because it must wait at least as many

jiffies as the user requested. It could check whether **timespec_to_jiffies** rounded down, but this way is cheaper and easier: It adds one jiffy if the user-supplied timeout wasn't zero, and says to heck with it. Linux isn't a true realtime operating system anyway—when you ask for a timeout, you're guaranteed only that Linux will wait at least that long.

35913: Saves the old **blocked** set, and unblocks any other signals defined by **these** so that, as desired, the arrival of these signals will allow the caller to proceed.

35919: Sets the current process's state to **TASK_INTERRUPTIBLE** (see Chapter 7). **schedule_timeout** (line 34106) is used to yield the CPU; execution will continue after either the specified time has elapsed or some other event occurs to wake the process up (such as receiving a signal).

35923: The process hopes it was awakened by a signal. **sys_rt_sigtimedwait** tries again to pull a signal off the queue of signals waiting for this process, and restores the old blocked set.

35930: At this point, the function still doesn't know whether a signal has arrived—it might have gotten one without needing to wait, one might have arrived while waiting, or the function might have waited and no signal arrived.

35931: If a signal arrived, the function delivers the information to the user process and returns the signal number.

35937: Otherwise, no signal arrived, despite waiting for one if so requested. In this case, the function returns either **-EAGAIN** (to indicate that the user process can try again with the same arguments) or **-EINTR** (to indicate that its wait was interrupted by a signal that could not be delivered for some reason).

How Code Differs for Realtime and Nonrealtime Signals

The short answer is, not much. I've mostly been glossing over the differences, and for good reason: there aren't many. Now, to make the point lucidly, I'll look at the two versions of the **sigprocmask** system call, which allows a process to manipulate its set of blocked signals—adding, deleting, or simply setting the set of signals.

sys_sigprocmask

36103: **sys_sigprocmask** is the original version of this function, the one that doesn't know or care about realtime signals. The **how** argument indicates the operation to perform; **set**, if non-**NULL**, is the operand for that operation; and the old blocked set is returned through **oset**, if **oset** is non-**NULL**.

36109: If **set** is **NULL**, the value of **how** is irrelevant: The operator won't have an operand, so the function can't do anything about it. Otherwise, it goes on to carry out the operator.

36111: Copies in the new blocked set, deleting **SIGKILL** and **SIGSTOP**, which are not blockable.

36116: Stores a copy of the current blocked set in **old_set**, in case it has to be copied back to user space later. The current blocked set will probably be modified in the following code, so its value must be saved before it changes.

36120: Ignores invalid operators, of course.

36123: The **SIG_BLOCK** operator indicates **new_set** should be interpreted as a set of additional signals to block. The signals are added to the blocked set.

36126: The **SIG_UNBLOCK** operator indicates that **new_set** should be interpreted as a set of signals to remove from the blocked set. They are removed now.

36129: The **SIG_SETMASK** operator indicates that **new_set** should be interpreted as the new blocked set, simply overwriting its previous value. So, **sys_sigprocmask** does exactly that. Note that it sets only the lowest element of the **blocked.sig** array—this element contains the low 32 bits, the nonrealtime signals, which is all this function cares about.

36138: If the caller has asked for the blocked set's previous value, execution jumps ahead to the **set_old** label (line 36142).

36140: If **set** was **NULL**, the caller is not asking to modify the blocked set, but the caller might still want to know about the blocked set's current value.

36144: **oset** was non-**NULL** (and **set** might have been, too). Either way, **old_set** contains a copy of the old blocked set, which **sys_sigprocmask** attempts to copy back to user space before returning.

sys_rt_sigprocmask

35784: **sys_rt_sigprocmask** is just like **sys_sigprocmask**, but it also takes account of the new realtime signals. Although the implementation details differ slightly, the overall logic is almost identical. There is, however, one subtle difference in the overall structure. Taking the **SIG_BLOCK** case as an example, **sys_sigprocmask**'s algorithm (simplified, obviously) looks like this:

```
/* How sys_sigprocmask does
SIG_BLOCK. */

new_set = *set;      /* Line 36111 */
blocked |= new_set;  /* Line 36124 */
```

By contrast, **sys_rt_sigprocmask**'s algorithm (simplified, again) looks like this:

```
/* How sys_rt_sigprocmask does
SIG_BLOCK. */

new_set = *set;        /* Line 35797 */
new_set |= blocked;    /* Line 35811 */
blocked = new_set;     /* Line 35820 */
```

I don't see any reason why **sys_rt_sigprocmask** can't be implemented the same way as **sys_sigprocmask**, and with a slight gain in efficiency.

Interrupts

Interrupts are well named, because they interrupt the system's normal processing. You've seen an example of an interrupt before, in Chapter 5: the software interrupt that provided the principal mechanism for system calls. In this chapter, I look at hardware interrupts.

As with system call interrupts, hardware interrupts might cause a transition to kernel mode and back. When an interrupt occurs while a user process is running, the system transitions to kernel mode, and the kernel responds to the interrupt. Then, the kernel returns control to the user process, which picks up exactly where it left off.

One difference from system call interrupts is that hardware interrupts can occur while the kernel is already running in kernel mode. This rarely happens with system calls—the kernel doesn't usually bother triggering the system call interrupt, because it can just call the target kernel function directly. If an interrupt occurs while the system is in kernel mode, the result is pretty much the same as if it had happened in user mode—the difference is simply that the kernel's own execution is temporarily interrupted rather than a user process's execution.

When the kernel doesn't want to be interrupted for a time, it turns interrupts off and on with the **cli** and **sti** macros (lines 16989 and 16990 are the UP versions; lines 16982 and 16983 are the SMP versions). These functions are named after the underlying x86 instructions: **cli** represents "CLear the Interrupts flag," and **sti** represents "SeT the Interrupts flag." This works the way it sounds: The CPU has an "interrupts allowed" flag, which allows interrupts if set and disallows them if clear. Hence, you disable interrupts by clearing the flag with **cli**, and then enable them later by setting it again with **sti**. In UP code, you can alternatively call the equivalent macros __cli and __sti—lines 16961 and 16962, respectively. In SMP code, the corresponding functions are __global_cli and __global_sti—lines 2205 and 2218.

Naturally, ports of the kernel to non-x86 platforms will use different underlying instructions—the **cli** and **sti** functions are simply implemented differently on those architectures.

IRQs

An *IRQ*, or interrupt request, is an interrupt notification sent from a hardware device to the CPU. In response to the IRQ, the CPU jumps to an address—an interrupt service routine (ISR), more commonly called an interrupt handler—that was previously registered with it by the kernel. The interrupt handler is a function that the kernel executes to service the interrupt; returning from the interrupt handler continues execution wherever it was before the interrupt.

IRQs are numbered, and each hardware device on the system is associated with an IRQ number. On the IBM PC architecture, for instance, IRQ 0 is associated with a hardware timer that generates 100 interrupts per second. Linking an IRQ number with a device enables the CPU to tell which device generated each interrupt, and therefore enables it to jump to the right interrupt handler. (In some cases, an IRQ number can be shared among multiple devices in a system, although this is not very common.)

The Linux kernel defines two kinds of interrupts, fast and slow, and one of the distinctions between them is that slow interrupts can themselves be interrupted, but fast interrupts can't. Therefore, while a fast interrupt is being handled, all other incoming interrupts—be they slow or fast—must simply wait. This places some pressure on fast interrupt handlers to run as fast as possible, and it has led to the creation of special kernel facilities, which you'll see later in the chapter, to partially defer interrupt processing.

Data Structures

As I did with signals, I'll begin with a tour of the important data structures for interrupts. Figure 6.1 illustrates the relationship among some of these data types.

To begin with, the architecture-independent header file include/linux/interrupt.h defines **struct irqaction** (line

19133), which represents an action the kernel should take upon receiving a certain IRQ (you'll see how **struct irqactions** are associated with IRQs later in the chapter). These are its members:

- **handler**—A pointer to a function that takes some action in response to the interrupt.

- **flags**—Drawn from the same set as **sa_flags**, shown earlier; it's the set starting at line 16148.

- **mask**—Not used by any of the x86 or architecture-independent code (except to set it to 0); it appears to be used only by the SPARC-64 port to track some information related to the floppy disk.

- **name**—A name associated with the device generating the interrupt. Because more than one device can share an IRQ, this can help distinguish them when printing a list for a human reader.

- **dev_id**—A unique ID for the device type—every model of every hardware device supported by Linux has a device ID assigned by the manufacturer and recorded in this member. Its possible values are drawn from a huge set that is omitted from the book because its inclusion would be boring and repetitious—it's just huge blocks of **#defines** that look like these:

```
#define PCI_DEVICE_ID_S3_868    0x8880
#define PCI_DEVICE_ID_S3_928    0x88b0
#define PCI_DEVICE_ID_S3_864_1  0x88c0
#define PCI_DEVICE_ID_S3_864_2  0x88c1
```

After you've seen a few of these, you've essentially seen them all. This excerpt, as you might have inferred, was selected from a section of the file containing device IDs for S3-based PCI video cards.

Although **dev_id** is a pointer, it doesn't point to anything, and dereferencing it would be a mistake. All that matters is its bit pattern.

- **next**—A pointer to the next **struct irqaction** in the queue, if the IRQ is shared. Normally, the IRQ is not shared and, therefore, this member is **NULL**.

The next two data structures of interest are in an architecture-dependent file, arch/i386/kernel/irq.h. The first, **struct hw_interrupt_type** (line 19560), abstracts an interrupt controller. It's mainly a set of pointers to functions that handle the controller-specific operations:

- **typename**—A human-readable name for the controller.

- **startup**—Allows events from the given IRQ on this controller.

- **shutdown**—Disallows events from the given IRQ on this controller.

- **enable** and **disable**—Basically, the same as **startup** and **shutdown**; the differences that exist aren't important for any code examined in this book. (In fact, the **enable/disable** functions and the **startup/shutdown** functions are identical for all the code included in the book.)

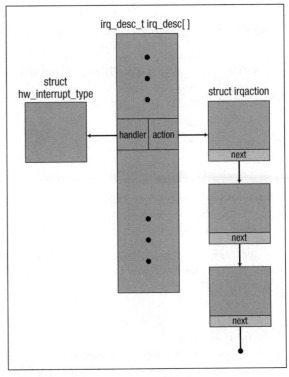

Figure 6.1 Interrupt-related data structures.

- **ack**—Sends the interrupt controller an acknowledgement for the interrupt; this is invoked as quickly as possible after the interrupt is detected.

- **end**—Called when interrupt handling is almost complete, this function tells the interrupt controller to re-enable an interrupt that had been temporarily disabled.

- **set_affinity**—Does any needed work to ensure that the interrupt handler will be run only on a given set of CPUs; the code for this is not covered in this book.

The other data structure of interest in this file, **irq_desc_t** (line 19581), has the following members:

- **status**—An **unsigned int** whose bits are for zero or more flags drawn from the set defined on lines 19542 through 19556. Together, they represent the state of the IRQ—whether the IRQ is disabled, whether devices on the IRQ are currently being autodetected, and so on.

- **handler**—A pointer to a **struct hw_interrupt_type**.

- **action**—Points to the head of a queue of **struct irqactions**. Normally, as previously mentioned, there's just one action per IRQ, so the linked list is normally of length 1 (or 0). But, if two or more devices share an IRQ, that many actions will be in the queue.

- **depth**—The number of current users of this **irq_desc_t**. It's mainly used to ensure that the IRQ isn't disabled while an event is being serviced.

- **lock**—Protects against unwanted interference when more than one CPU in an SMP system wants to use this **irq_desc_t** simultaneously.

irq_desc_ts are aggregated in the array **irq_desc** (line 1931). There is one array entry for each IRQ, so the array maps each IRQ number to its corresponding handler and other information in the **irq_desc_t**.

Actions and IRQs

A small, well-chosen set of functions handles linking and unlinking actions and IRQs. This section looks at those functions, along with the functions that initialize the IRQ system as a whole.

init_IRQ

1769: **init_IRQ** initializes IRQ handling.

1773: The symbol **CONFIG_X86_VISWS_APIC** is set for SGI Visual Workstations, SGI's x86-based workstation line. Although based on the x86 CPU, the Visual Workstations don't share many other features with the IBM-based PC architecture—in particular, as shown, their interrupt handling differs somewhat. I'll ignore the code specific to Visual Workstations.

1781: Sets up the interrupt descriptor table, giving default values for entries 32 through 255 (decimal, inclusive). This makes use of **set_intr_gate** (line 7313), which is explored soon.

1825: Sets up IRQ 2 (the cascade interrupt) and, a few lines later, IRQ 13 (for the FPU—see the note at line 1715). The **struct irqaction**s associated with these IRQs are **irq2** (line 1743) and **irq13** (line 1737), respectively.

init_ISA_irqs

1748: This function fills in the **irq_desc** array, initializing IRQs for ISA-bus machines (that is, for all standard PCs).

1755: For each element of **irq_desc**, fairly unobjectionable and unsurprising default values are supplied for the **status**, **action**, and **depth** members.

1761: Old (pre-PCI) IRQs are handled by **i8259A_irq_type** (line 1500).

1764: The higher-numbered IRQs are initialized to **no_irq_type** (line 1982), essentially a do-nothing handler. They might be changed later—indeed, they are if you have any PCI cards, as any modern PC does.

set_intr_gate

7313: **set_intr_gate** sets up an entry in the x86 CPU's interrupt descriptor table (IDT). Every hardware or software interrupt that occurs on an x86-based system has a number, which is used by the CPU as an index into this table. (Including the system call interrupt—number 0x80—which I explored in Chapter 5.) The corresponding entries in the table are the addresses of kernel functions to jump to when the interrupt occurs. The assembler code used to create entries in CPU tables such as the IDT is in the **_set_gate** macro (line 7294).

setup_irq

2787: **setup_irq** adds an action (a **struct irqaction**) for the given IRQ. This is used at line 6472 to register the timer interrupt, for example. It's also used by way of **request_irq** (line 2506), which is examined in the next section.

2797: Linux uses several sources of physical randomness—for example, interrupts—to supply an unpredictable stream of values to the devices /dev/random, a limited but highly random data source, and /dev/urandom, /dev/random's unlimited but less random counterpart. The randomness system as a whole is not covered in this book, but if you don't know of its existence, this chunk of code appears awfully mysterious.

2811: If the existing list of actions is not empty, **setup_irq** must ensure that the existing actions and the new one are all willing to share the IRQ.

2813: Verifies that the IRQ can be shared with all existing **struct irqaction**s already on this IRQ. This test is very efficient, based partly on the observation that there's no need to loop over all the actions in the queue and check that each of them will share. Any action after the first action wouldn't have been allowed to enter the queue unless both that action and the first action agreed to share the IRQ. So, if the first action will share, then any other actions in the queue will also share; and if the first action won't share, then no other actions are in the queue anyway.

2819: The IRQ is being shared. **setup_irq** walks **p** forward to the end of the queue of actions, leaving it pointing at the last queue element's **next** field. It also raises the **shared** flag, for use in line 2828.

2826: **p** now points to the last queue element's **next** field, if the IRQ is to be shared, or to **irq_desc[irq].action**—the pointer to the head of the queue—if not sharing. Either way, the pointer is set to the new element.

2828: If no actions were associated with this IRQ already, the rest of **irq_desc[irq]** isn't set up yet, so it needs to be initialized here. In particular, note line 2832, at which the **startup** function for this IRQ is called.

request_irq

2506: **request_irq** creates a **struct irqaction** from the supplied values and adds it to the list of **struct irqactions** for the given IRQ. (If you're familiar with an object-oriented language, such as C++ or Java, think of this as a constructor for actions.) Its implementation is quite straightforward.

2519: As noted in the code, this sanity-checks the **dev_id** argument when the interrupt is to be shared. Note, interestingly, that the function only prints a warning when the sanity check fails—it doesn't return an error.

2526: Sanity-checks a couple of the input values. Note that there's no need to test whether **irq** is less than 0, because it has an unsigned type.

2531: Dynamically allocates a new **struct irqaction**. The function used for this purpose, **kmalloc**, is covered in Chapter 8.

2536: Fills out the new action and attempts to add it to the list of actions with **setup_irq**.

free_irq

2566: **free_irq** is the inverse of **request_irq**. If **request_irq** is like a constructor for actions, this is the closest thing to a destructor.

2578: After ensuring that **irq** is in range, **free_irq** finds the corresponding **irq_desc** entry and begins iterating over its list of actions.

2583: Ignores this queue element unless it has the right device ID.

2588: Detaches this element from the queue and releases its memory.

2589: If the queue of actions is now empty—that is, if the queue's sole element was just unlinked—the device is shut down.

2604: If control reaches this point, **free_irq** walked over the entire list of actions without finding a matching **dev_id**. If it had found a match, the function would have returned at line 2602. Therefore, this was an erroneous attempt to free an IRQ action; **free_irq** prints a warning to this effect.

probe_irq_on

2625: **probe_irq_on** implements a significant part of the kernel's IRQ autoprobing. Read the banner comment that starts at line 19372 for a description of the whole process. The job here is to implement step three (only) in that description: to temporarily enable any unassigned IRQs, so that **probe_irq_on**'s caller can probe them.

2636: For each IRQ except IRQ 0 (the timer's IRQ), this and the following loop erase any record of any interrupts that might have occurred before **probe_irq_on** was called, allowing **probe_irq_on** to start its real work with the system in a known state.

2654: For each IRQ except the timer's, if the IRQ has no actions associated with it already, **probe_irq_on** records the fact that this IRQ is being autodetected and starts the associated device. Incidentally, I don't think there's any special reason why this loop iterates backward.

2667: Busy-waits for about a tenth of a second, to allow any devices that generate bogus interrupts to betray themselves. Of course, the kernel can't

predict the future any better than you or I, so it's always possible that some spurious interrupt doesn't show up within that tenth of a second, but it would have shown up if the kernel had waited just a little longer. The kernel can do no more than draw an arbitrary line and hope for the best, so that's what it does.

2674: Loops over all the IRQs again, this time to filter out any devices that generated bogus interrupts. This loop could start iterating at 1 rather than at 0, because IRQs that aren't being autodetected are ignored, and IRQ 0 is never autodetected. Not that speed matters here; next to that tenth of a second delay—an eternity, even from the perspective of a slow CPU—one loop iteration, more or less, is inconsequential.

2683: If the device triggered an interrupt during the delay at line 2667 (in which case its **IRQ_WAITING** bit was cleared at line 2424—see also line 2435), the interrupt probably is bogus: The system shouldn't have been talking to the device during that delay, so the device shouldn't have been talking to the system, either. The autodetect bit is cleared and the handler is shut down again.

2687: If no spurious interrupt was triggered, the interrupt line is probably reliable—we can expect that it will generate an interrupt only if a genuine hardware interrupt occurs. If it's a sufficiently low-numbered interrupt, the corresponding bit is set in **val**, which will later be returned.

2692: Returns **val**, a bitmask indicating the apparently reliable unassigned interrupt lines.

probe_irq_off

2755: **probe_irq_off** implements another significant part of IRQ autoprobing. Here, the job is to decide which IRQs responded to the probe, and to return the IRQ number of one of these. Its argument, as just described, tells which IRQ lines can be assumed to have generated an interrupt as a genuine response to the probe. Surprisingly, however, **val** is not used in the function (it is used in the corresponding implementation on other platforms—namely, on the MIPS).

2761: Loops over all IRQs, searching for any devices that responded to the caller's probe. This loop, too, could start iterating at 1, for the same reasons as given in the preceding discussion of **probe_irq_on**.

2768: If the kernel is not trying to autodetect anything on this IRQ, it skips to the next one.

2769: The **IRQ_WAITING** flag is cleared when an interrupt arrives for this IRQ. Because **probe_irq_on** presumably caught any bogus interrupts, this is assumed to be a genuine response to the probe. The count of IRQs successfully autoprobed is incremented, saving the number of the first.

2774: Whether or not this IRQ is successfully autoprobed, the autodetect flag is dropped and the handler is shut down again.

2781: If more than one IRQ was successfully autoprobed, this is communicated to the caller by negating **irq_found**.

2783: Returns **irq_found**—0, or the (possibly negated) number of the first IRQ successfully autoprobed. Observe that this is never 0 if a device was found, because the kernel never tries to autodetect IRQ 0. Therefore, **probe_irq_off** returns 0 exactly when no IRQs were autodetected.

Hardware Interrupt Handlers

The actual interrupt handlers for the x86 port are trivial; at the lowest level, they're built by repeatedly using the **BUILD_IRQ** macro (line 13040) to build a series of small assembler functions. **BUILD_IRQ** itself is used by the **BI** macro (line 1398), which in turn is used by the

BUILD_16_IRQS macro (line 1400), which is used at lines 1408 through 1424 to create the assembler routines. This chain of macro calls is simply intended to reduce the amount and the redundancy of the actual code that must be written—instead of 16 uses of **BUILD_16_IRQS**, we could have had 256 calls to **BUILD_IRQ**.

The assembler routines look like this:

```
IRQ0x00_interrupt:
  pushl 0x00-256
  jmp common_interrupt
```

That is, each one simply pushes its IRQ number (minus 256, for reasons documented at line 13030) onto the stack and then jumps to the common interrupt routine.

The common interrupt routine is called **common_interrupt**, and it's also short. It's built by the **BUILD_COMMON_IRQ** macro (line 13021), and it simply calls **do_IRQ** after arranging for **do_IRQ** to return to **ret_from_intr** (line 976)—part of the **system_call** routine explored in Chapter 5. **do_IRQ** (line 2401), which is explored shortly, takes responsibility for seeing that the interrupts are serviced.

Before exploring all the code, it will help to have the following high-level overview of how the pieces fit together when servicing a single interrupt:

1. The CPU jumps to the **IRQ0x*NN*_interrupt** routine (where *NN* is the interrupt number), which pushes its unique number onto the stack and then jumps to **common_interrupt**.

2. **common_interrupt** calls **do_IRQ** and sees to it that when **do_IRQ** returns, control will pass to **ret_from_intr**.

3. **do_IRQ** calls code that is specific to the interrupt controller chip—code that talks directly to the chip, as necessary, and that acknowledges the interrupt. For the 8259A controller chip prevalent on PC architectures, the **ack** function is **mask_and_ack_8259A** (line 1608); this function also temporarily disables the IRQ being serviced.

4. **do_IRQ** calls **handle_IRQ_event**. **handle_IRQ_event** enables interrupts for slow IRQs, or leaves them disabled for fast IRQs. It then walks over a queue of functions that have been associated with this IRQ, calling each in turn. Because interrupts are enabled for slow IRQs, this is where the handler for a slow IRQ might be interrupted by another interrupt.

5. **do_IRQ** calls the controller-specific **end** function; for the 8259A, this is **end_8259A_irq**, which calls **enable_8259A_irq** to re-enable the IRQ.

6. **do_IRQ** services any pending softirqs, and then returns. As you know, this returns to **ret_from_intr**. Chapter 5 covers the path from that point forward.

do_IRQ

2418: Updates kernel statistics and calls the **ack** function associated with this IRQ. For low-numbered IRQs on an off-the-shelf PC, this handler will be **mask_and_ack_8259A** (line 1608).

2424: The **status** field of the **irq_desc_t** associated with this interrupt is updated, and the action function to call, if any, is located.

2454: **handle_IRQ_event** (discussed next) is called to perform the IRQ-specific action. The enclosing loop exits when the action was successfully carried out.

2465: The controller-specific **end** function is invoked. As mentioned earlier, on the 8259A, this is **end_8259A_irq** (line 1483), which calls **enable_8259A_irq** (line 1545) to re-enable the IRQ.

2468: If any softirqs are active, they are handled now with **do_softirq** (line 36282, discussed later in the chapter).

handle_IRQ_event

2282: On behalf of **do_IRQ**, **handle_IRQ_event** calls the action function associated with an IRQ. It's also called from some other code that isn't covered in this book.

2292: Its documentation (line 16158) to the contrary, the **SA_INTERRUPT** flag is not a no-op. If the flag is not set, interrupts are allowed during the code that is to follow. This is what's left of the kernel's historical distinction between fast and slow interrupts, which was discussed earlier. (The code handling the two kinds of interrupts used to have many more differences, but the result was about the same—the code has been rendered much more elegant.) Appropriately, this flag seems to be used mostly for very slow devices—mainly, floppy disk drives.

2295: Iterates over the queue of actions for this IRQ (the head of the queue was supplied by the caller), calling the handler function for each.

2300: Here, the occurrence of an interrupt is used to add some randomness information for use by /dev/random and /dev/urandom—presumably, most interrupts occur randomly for devices whose **SA_SAMPLE_RANDOM** flag is set. Setting this flag for devices designed to generate interrupts at regular intervals—say, the timer device—would be a poor choice.

2302: Disallows interrupts (the caller will allow them again when ready).

Softirqs, Tasklets, and Bottom Halves

The *bottom half* of an interrupt handler is the part that you don't need to do right away. After some interrupts, you might not need to do it at all. Notionally, a given interrupt handler is divided into a top half and a bottom half; the top half of the processing is done immediately when an interrupt occurs, while the bottom half (if there is one) is deferred. This is done by making the top and bottom halves separate functions and treating them differently. In general, the top half decides whether its corresponding bottom half needs to be run. Anything that can't be deferred obviously doesn't belong in the bottom half, but everything that can be deferred is a candidate for inclusion in it.

You might well wonder why Linux bothers with this separation—why procrastinate? One reason is to minimize overall interrupt latency. Recall that most interrupts are so-called fast interrupts, during whose execution no other interrupts can be serviced. To handle these other interrupts as soon as possible, the kernel defers as much processing as it can to the bottom halves.

Another reason is that, at the lowest level, the interrupt controller chip is told to disable the specific IRQ being serviced while the kernel is executing the top half (this differs from the CPU-level disabling that distinguishes fast interrupts from slow interrupts). You don't want this situation to last longer than necessary, so only the most time-critical portion is done in the top half and everything else is deferred to the bottom half.

Still another reason to separate top from bottom halves is that the handler's bottom half consists of things that don't need to be done on every single interrupt, just as long as the kernel gets to them at some point after every batch of interrupts from the device. In such a case, doing the bottom-half processing on every interrupt, when it might have been deferred a while and then done only once, is sheer waste.

One implication of that last paragraph is worth spelling out: A bottom half is not necessarily called once per interrupt. Instead, the top half (or, occasionally, some other piece of code) simply "marks" the bottom half, setting a bit indicating that the bottom half must be performed. If the bottom half is marked again while already marked, it merely stays marked; the kernel services it when it can. If 100 interrupts occur for a given device before the kernel gets a chance to run its bottom half, the top half will be run 100 times, the bottom half once.

Bottom half handling is taken care of by a more general kernel facility, softirqs. Softirqs give the kernel a way to mark a piece of code and ensure that it will be run in the near future. A couple of softirqs in particular are dedicated to executing tasklets, and one of these is for executing bottom halves. Taken as a whole, it's a somewhat complicated system, but the individual pieces are easy enough to understand. In the next few sections, I

look at softirqs, tasklets, and bottom halves, and how they fit together.

For a while, the notion of bottom halves will necessarily remain abstract. The next section explores the timer interrupt in some depth, including its bottom-half handling, and shows an interesting abuse—I mean, an interesting generalization—of the notion of bottom halves.

Softirqs

At bottom, a softirq is just a function pointer and an argument to pass to that function. (If you're familiar with these terms, you can think of a softirq as a "thunk" or a "weak closure.") For each softirq, there is a one-bit flag that indicates whether it should be run; these flags are packed together in a single **unsigned int**. The kernel polls the flags regularly, so a piece of code that wants a softirq to be run has an easy job: It just sets the bit corresponding to that softirq, and a short time later, the kernel, in its normal processing, will notice the set bit and invoke the corresponding softirq.

There is just one exception: Even if a softirq is marked to be run, it can be temporarily disabled by a mask. If the corresponding bit is clear (0) in the mask, a marked softirq will simply stay marked until its mask bit is set. The next time the kernel checks, it will see that the softirq is marked and no longer masked out, and the softirq will be invoked then.

With all that in mind, let's take a look at the data structures and code that implement softirqs.

Softirq Data Structures

The main data structure related to softirqs is **struct softirq_action**; softirqs also rely on a couple of members in **irq_cpustat_t**. I'll look at each of these below.

struct softirq_action

19182: This **struct** represents the action to take for a particular softirq. These **structs** are aggregated in an array, **softirq_vec** (line 36279), which represents all available softirqs. As you can see, it's very simple, with only two members:

- **action**—A pointer to the function that does the work of this softirq. The kernel passes this function a pointer to the **struct softirq_action** to which it belongs, so that the function can access the **struct's data** member if it needs to.

- **data**—A pointer to any additional information, of any type, that might be needed by **action**. This can, of course, be a pointer to a **struct**, which can supply **action** with an arbitrary amount of context data. None of the existing softirqs uses this field, however—they always set it to **NULL**.

irq_cpustat_t

12662: Only two fields in this **struct** type are relevant to softirq handling, so I'll skip the others for now. The currently relevant fields are these:

- **__softirq_active**—Each bit in this **unsigned int** records whether the corresponding **softirq** is marked for later execution.

- **__softirq_mask**—Similarly, each bit in this **unsigned int** records whether the corresponding **softirq** is enabled. Normally, each bit is 1 if the corresponding softirq exists, but it's 0 if the softirq doesn't exist or is temporarily disabled.

There's one **irq_cpustat_t** for each CPU in the system. (As a result, on SMP systems, a softirq might be marked for execution on more than one CPU, or it might be temporarily disabled on one CPU but not on another, etc.) The central array of these **struct**s, **irq_stat**, is at line 36276.

Softirq Code

Next, let's have a look at how the kernel manipulates and uses the softirq data structures to implement softirqs. There are four basic operations:

- *Initializing the softirq data structures*—This is handled by **softirq_init** (line 36515).

- *Installing a softirq*—This is handled by **open_softirq** (line 36337).

- *Marking softirqs for later execution*—This is the province of **raise_softirq**. Also, the softirq's active bit is checked using the **softirq_active** macro (line 19515), which I don't explore separately due to its simplicity.

- *Running any marked softirqs*—This is the job of **do_softirq** (line 36282).

You might have noticed that this list omits setting and clearing a softirq's mask bit. That's because there isn't a separate function or macro dedicated to this job; the code just inspects and manipulates bits using the **softirq_mask** macro (line 19517) and bitwise operations. Also, in the current code, a softirq's mask bit is never cleared; it's set when the softirq is installed and then left alone.

softirq_init

36515: This simple function sets up a couple of widely used softirqs.

36519: Initializes the bottom half code. I'll return to this in my discussion of bottom halves later in the chapter.

36522: Uses **open_softirq** (discussed next) to set up two softirqs. Softirqs are identified by their position in the **softirq_vec** array, using integer values drawn from the unnamed **enum** that begins at line 19173. The same integer values define the bits corresponding to the softirq in **__softirq_active** and **__softirq_mask**.

open_softirq

36337: **open_softirq** initializes an element of **softirq_vec**.

36344: After protecting against interference, the indicated array element is filled in using the function's arguments.

36347: By default, a new softirq is eligible to be run—masked in, though not immediately marked active. Consequently, its mask bit is set. The

softirq_mask macro (line 19517) used here evaluates to the **__softirq_mask** member of the given CPU's **irq_cpustat_t**.

Note that there's no corresponding **close_softirq** function. You could get the effect of **close_softirq**, if you needed it, by simply clearing the softirq's mask bit and never setting it again. If you really wanted to erase all traces of the softirq, you could also call **open_softirq** with **NULL** for both the **action** and **data** arguments.

do_softirq

36282: **do_softirq** is called at four points in the kernel's processing:

- *When deciding which process should get the CPU next*—Line 34257, part of **schedule** (explored in Chapter 7)

- *When returning from a system call*—Lines 913 and 916

- *When returning from servicing a CPU exception*—Lines 969 and 972

- *After servicing hardware interrupts*—Line 2469, just before returning from **do_IRQ**

Three of those points, you'll notice, are in architecture-specific files; the function is also called at the corresponding points in the architecture-specific files for non-x86 ports.

36294: Stores the current set of active—that is, marked—softirqs in the local variable **active**, subtracting any that are temporarily masked out.

36301: This loop is about to service the softirqs whose bits are set in **active**, so the corresponding bits are cleared in the CPU-private field.

36306: The same bits are cleared in the local variable **mask**, so that **do_softirq** won't get stuck in a loop, handling the same softirq over and over—if the softirq is re-marked active while it's being serviced here, **do_softirq** won't notice because it will be masked out. Thus, the enclosing loop—which began at line 36299—can iterate at most 32 times.

36308: Simultaneously walks over the **softirq_vec** array and the bits in **active**. If the lowest bit in **active** is set, the corresponding softirq is invoked; then, the loop moves on to the next **softirq_vec** entry and the next bit in **active**.

Because this is a **do/while** loop, it executes at least once. In order to reach this point, execution must pass through line 36296 or line 36318, both of which ensure that **active** has at least one bit set. Anyway, it's easy to see that the loop would execute correctly even if no softirqs needed to run; this would waste time, but would not otherwise be harmful.

36313: The loop terminates when **active** has no bits set. Because **active** is shifted over as the loop progresses, this tests all remaining bits simultaneously, without necessarily cycling through all of them.

36317: If any softirqs were marked while the preceding loop was executing, they might be serviced now—but only if they can pass through the newly adjusted **mask**. If so, control jumps ahead to the **retry** label (line 36330), which simply jumps back to the **restart** label (line 36299). (This jump-to-a-jump seems circuitous, but it results in better assembler code.) Any active softirqs that can't pass through the mask now will get another chance soon—at the latest, the next time the timer interrupt fires, within a hundredth of a second or so.

Tasklets

A tasklet is little more than a glorified function pointer, not all that different from a softirq. The differences between tasklets and softirqs are documented in the banner comment starting at line 19213. The most significant difference is that a given tasklet can be scheduled for execution on at most one CPU at a time. Unlike plain softirqs, which can be marked for future execution on more than one CPU at a time (and might, indeed, be actively running on more than one CPU at a time), at most one instance of a given tasklet will be running at once, no matter how many CPUs are in the machine.

Two softirqs—**HI_SOFTIRQ** and **TASKLET_SOFTIRQ**—are devoted to running tasklets. As you'll see, the tasklet code currently defines two sets of tasklets. One set, the **HI_SOFTIRQ** set, is devoted to running bottom halves. The other set, the **TASKLET_SOFTIRQ** set, is used by several drivers, but not by any code included in the book. The code for executing both sets of tasklets is virtually identical, and because I'm currently interested in following the path that leads to bottom halves, I'll explore only the bottom-half-related tasklet code in the following sections. But first I'll present the tasklet-related data structures.

Tasklet Data Structures

There is only one important tasklet-related data structure, **struct tasklet_struct**. It's nice and simple.

struct tasklet_struct

19236: **struct tasklet_struct**, of course, represents a single tasklet. It has the following members:

- **next**—The next tasklet in a linked list attached to an element of the **tasklet_hi_vec** or **tasklet_vec** arrays (lines 36400 and 36355). Each of these arrays has one element—more precisely, one linked list—per CPU, each list representing the tasklets scheduled for execution on that CPU.

- **state**—Not, as you might think, an integer indicating the tasklet's state. Instead, the bits of this integer are independent flags, and the tasklet's state is derived from the combination of these bits. Currently, only two bits matter; they're the bits numbered by the unnamed **enum** that begins at line 19253.

  If **state**'s bit 0 (**TASKLET_STATE_SCHED**) is set, the tasklet should be executed in the future. If **state**'s bit 1 (**TASKLET_STATE_RUN**) is on, the tasklet is already running on a CPU. Both bits can be set; if so, the tasklet is already running and should be run again at the next opportunity.

- **count**—A tasklet can be temporarily disabled and later re-enabled by calling the **tasklet_enable** and **tasklet_disable** functions (lines

19327 and 19320; also see **tasklet_disable_nosync**, at line 19314). Each call to **tasklet_disable** increments **count**, and each call to **tasklet_enable** decrements **count**; when **count** is 0, the tasklet is enabled. This allows an individual function to disable and later re-enable a tasklet without worrying about whether the tasklet was already disabled by the function's caller. The disabling and re-enabling will simply nest properly.

- **func**—A pointer to the function that carries out the work of this tasklet.

- **data**—As in **struct softirq_action**, this is an argument for **func**. Unlike **struct softirq_action**, with tasklets, **data** is passed directly to the function—**func** is not passed the **struct tasklet_struct** to which it belongs.

Tasklet Code

Now that you've seen the principal tasklet-related data structure, it's time to take a look at the code that uses it to implement tasklets.

tasklet_init

36437: The function that initializes a **struct tasklet_struct** is the simplest in this group. The only features worth noting are that a tasklet is initially not scheduled for execution (line 36442) and that it's initially enabled (line 36443).

tasklet_hi_schedule

19297: **tasklet_hi_schedule** schedules a tasklet for later execution on the current CPU if it's not already scheduled.

19300: I'll defer complete coverage of the **test_and_set_bit** function (line 12306) until Chapter 10, when I can discuss it in a more informative context. Until then, suffice it to say that it sets the indicated bit to 1 and returns the bit's former value. For now, you can think of it as equivalent to this C fragment:

```
int temp = t->state &
           TASKLET_STATE_SCHED;
t->state |= TASKLET_STATE_SCHED;
return temp;
```

Hence, the **if** condition at this line will be true exactly when the **TASKLET_STATE_SCHED** bit is not already set in **t->state**.

19306: The tasklet's **TASKLET_STATE_SCHED** bit was not already set, so the tasklet is newly scheduled for execution. The tasklet is linked into the list of tasklets awaiting execution on the current CPU. Tasklets aren't executed in the order in which they were scheduled. This list is kept in LIFO (Last-In, First-Out) order—like a stack—not in FIFO (First-In, First-Out) order. This is in keeping with the conceptual model for tasklets: The kernel promises only that a scheduled tasklet will be run at some time in the future; it makes no guarantees as to their relative order of execution.

19308: Last, the appropriate softirq is marked active. Notice that three actions must all occur together to ensure that a tasklet will be run: setting its **TASKLET_STATE_SCHED** bit, linking the tasklet into the list, and marking the right softirq.

tasklet_kill

36446: **tasklet_kill** is a little less severe than its name makes it sound: It doesn't delete the tasklet from existence or prevent it from being run. The function takes its name from the fact that it's called when a hardware device associated with the given tasklet is being shut down—as a result, the tasklet won't be scheduled or invoked any more. If the tasklet is already scheduled for execution or actively running, the caller wants to wait until the tasklet has finished. If the tasklet is being killed in any sense, it's the caller that is doing the killing, not this function.

36451: While this tasklet is still scheduled for execution . . .

36454: . . . the current process is put to sleep and **schedule** (line 34237) is invoked. As a side

effect, **schedule** runs **do_softirq**, which will indirectly cause the given tasklet, **t**, to be run. **schedule** is repeatedly invoked until **t** is no longer scheduled for execution.

36459: At this point, **t** is no longer marked for execution, but, in an SMP system, it might still be running on another CPU. Accordingly, **tasklet_unlock_wait** (line 19270) is used to wait until the tasklet is no longer running.

36460: Finally, **t**'s **TASKLET_STATE_SCHED** bit is cleared and the function exits. It is the caller's responsibility to ensure that **t** won't be rescheduled, either by itself or by some other code.

tasklet_hi_action

36403: **tasklet_hi_action** is the action associated with the **HI_SOFTIRQ** softirq. It tries to run all tasklets slated for execution by the current CPU.

36409: **tasklet_hi_action** begins by detaching the list of tasklets awaiting execution by the CPU, keeping a local pointer to the head of the list in **list**.

36418: In order to run a tasklet, **tasklet_hi_action** must first ensure that it can acquire exclusive access to the tasklet and that the tasklet has not been temporarily disabled.

36420: If these conditions are met, the tasklet's **TASKLET_STATE_SCHED** bit is cleared so that the tasklet can be scheduled again. Note in particular that clearing the bit now, before the tasklet has been run, ensures that the tasklet can schedule itself for later execution, if it needs to.

36422: At long last, the tasklet is run. When it completes, **tasklet_hi_action** relinquishes exclusive access to the tasklet and continues to the next tasklet in the list, if any. The tasklet remains detached from this CPU's list of tasklets—unless it rescheduled itself, of course.

36426: If **tasklet_hi_action** got exclusive access to the tasklet but found that the tasklet was

temporarily disabled, the exclusive access must still be relinquished. That's done here.

36429: This point is reached whenever the conditions at lines 36418 and 36419 are not both met. The tasklet should still be run later, so it is reinserted into the list of tasklets waiting for this CPU and the loop proceeds to try the next tasklet from the original list.

Bottom Halves

As mentioned earlier, the bottom half of an interrupt is the part that doesn't have to be done right away. The bottom half code itself is simple, though of course that's thanks to all the support it gets from the softirq and tasklet code.

Bottom-Half Data Structures

There aren't any important bottom-half–related data structures per se, but there are a couple of important variables I should briefly touch on before proceeding to look at the bottom-half code. They're noted here.

bh_base

36467: This is an array of 32 pointers to functions that take no arguments and return nothing—the bottom-half handlers themselves.

bh_task_vec

36468: This array glues the tasklet code to the bottom-half code—its elements are tasklets that run bottom halves when executed, as you'll see momentarily.

Bottom-Half Code

There's very little bottom-half–specific code in the kernel. Indeed, there are only four such functions, and three of those—**init_bh** (line 36503), **remove_bh** (line 36509), and **mark_bh** (line 19363)—are too simple to merit detailed coverage. The fourth bottom-half–related function, **bh_action**, is covered next.

bh_action

36480: **bh_action** is a tasklet action function whose job is to invoke a bottom-half handler. The number of the bottom-half handler to invoke—an integer in the range 0 through 31 (inclusive)—is passed to this function as its argument. The loop at line 36519 (part of **softirq_init**) initializes the tasklets in **bh_task_vec**, setting them up so they'll all call **bh_action** with a different number when run.

36490: The essence of **bh_action** is in this and the following line: If there's a bottom-half handler at the supplied index, it invokes it.

36500: If the requisite locks couldn't be acquired, the bottom half is marked again for later execution; the kernel will try to run the bottom half at its next opportunity.

Putting It All Together

Okay: I've exhaustively covered the code and data structures for softirqs, tasklets, and bottom halves. By now, you are in a maze of twisty C statements, all alike. What you probably need now, in other words, is a recap that covers how all those pieces fit together to get a bottom-half handler to run. This section does exactly that. To make the recap easier to follow, I'll repeat line references here, even for functions I've already covered in detail.

Let's take a particular bottom half as an example—say, the timer interrupt's bottom half. This is the whole story, starting from the very beginning:

1. The timer bottom half is bottom half number 0, which is established at line 19146. The bottom half corresponding to this tasklet is therefore **bh_base[0]** (line 36467), which is **NULL** at the moment the kernel boots.

2. At line 34965—part of **sched_init**, called during kernel initialization—the **timer_bh** function (line 40251) is associated with this bottom half, through a call to **init_bh** (line 36503).

3. Later, the timer device fires and the timer interrupt's top half (**timer_interrupt**, line 6223) is run. This, in turn, calls **do_timer_interrupt** (line 6148), which calls **do_timer** (line 40257), and that calls **mark_bh** (line 19363) to mark the timer bottom half for later execution.

4. **mark_bh** calls **tasklet_hi_schedule** (line 19297), passing it the address of **bh_task_vec[0]**—the tasklet that bridges the gap between the timer interrupt and the timer bottom half. This specific tasklet will call **bh_action** (line 36480) with an argument of 0 (**TIMER_BH**), as established by line 36520.

5. Assuming the tasklet corresponding to the timer's bottom half isn't already scheduled for execution, **tasklet_hi_schedule** schedules it, setting its **TASKLET_STATE_SCHED** bit, linking it into the list at **tasklet_hi_vec[cpu]** (line 36400), and marking the corresponding softirq (the **HI_SOFTIRQ** softirq) with **__cpu_raise_softirq** (line 19192).

6. The timer interrupt handler was invoked by **do_IRQ**, so line 2468 notices that the softirq for bottom halves is active. As noted earlier in the chapter, the same check is performed when returning from system calls or CPU exceptions, or after process scheduling. Because the softirq is active, **do_IRQ** calls **do_softirq** (line 36282).

7. **do_softirq** walks over the set of active softirqs—a set that includes, at least, the **HI_SOFTIRQ** softirq—and invokes the corresponding action function.

8. In this case, the action function in question is **tasklet_hi_action** (line 36403), as established previously by a call to **open_softirq** (line 36337) from line 36523.

9. **tasklet_hi_action** walks the list of scheduled tasklets, calling their functions with their saved arguments—in this case, that means calling **bh_action** (line 36480) with an argument of 0 (**TIMER_BH**).

10. At line 36491, **bh_action** calls the function pointed to by **bh_base[0]**—namely, **timer_bh**, as set up in Step 2. And that's it—the timer bottom half was set up, marked, and run.

By now, you must be thinking that this is the most complicated way of calling a function that you've ever seen. In a sense, you're right: If the only point of softirqs were to run bottom halves, a much simpler system would suf-

fice. You wouldn't need softirqs or tasklets at all; you could just mark and call bottom halves. Indeed, earlier versions of the kernel did exactly that. In 2.4, the bottom-half facility was generalized (in part for the sake of networking code not included in this book), and this generalization is the reason behind the complexity you now see.

In any case, bottom halves are now considered a legacy feature. In future Linux kernels, some or all bottom halves will become "regular" tasklets, so the bottom-half code might eventually disappear altogether; that will dramatically simplify the above chain of events.

Time

This section ties together your knowledge of interrupts and bottom halves by looking at how a sample interrupt, the timer interrupt, works. The timer interrupt function, **timer_interrupt**, is associated with IRQ 0 at line 6472. The **irq0** variable used here is defined at line 6313. Line 34965 registers the **timer_bh** function as the timer bottom half, using **init_bh** (line 36503).

When IRQ 0 is triggered, **timer_interrupt** reads some values out of the CPU's timestamp counter, if the CPU has one (this is used by some code not examined in this book), and then calls **do_timer_interrupt** (line 6148). In addition to some other work, this calls **do_timer**, which is the interesting part of the timer interrupt.

do_timer

40257: This is, for our purposes, the interesting part of the timer top half.

40259: Updates the global variable **jiffies**, which tracks the number of system clock ticks since boot. (Obviously, this really counts the number of timer ticks that have elapsed since the installation of the timer interrupt, which doesn't happen at the instant the system boots.)

40263: Uses **update_process_times** (line 40166) to increment the system or user time charged to this process. I'll skip the details, but if you want to look at the code, **update_process_times** calls **update_one_process** (line 40153), which, in turn, uses **do_process_times** (line 40108). In keeping with the theme of this chapter, **do_process_times** sends the signals **SIGXCPU** and **SIGKILL** to processes that exceed their lifetime CPU time allocation.

The statistics kept by these functions are reported by such commonplace programs as time, top, and ps. You can see now that these statistics are not necessarily accurate: If a process managed never to be running when the timer interrupt fired, it could conceivably consume most of the CPU's time without being "charged" for any CPU usage. However, it's hard to imagine why (or how) a malicious process would try to carry this out, and for better-intentioned processes, the statistics should average out naturally—they'll get charged for some timer ticks in which they hardly held the CPU, but they won't get charged for others in which they held the CPU almost the whole tick, so it all washes out in the end.

40265: The top half has been run, so its bottom half is marked to be run as soon as possible.

40266: If any tasks are waiting in the timer queue, the timer queue bottom half is marked as ready to run (the timer queue bottom half is discussed shortly). That's it—that's the whole timer interrupt. It seems simple, but that's largely because much of the work was properly deferred to the bottom half.

timer_bh

40251: This is the timer's bottom half. It calls functions to update time-related statistics for the process and the kernel itself, and to service both old-style and new-style kernel timers.

update_times

40232: This function mainly updates statistics: It computes the system's load average, updates the global variable that tracks the current time, and updates the kernel's estimate of the amount of CPU time that has been used by the current process.

40242: Gets the number of timer ticks that occurred since the last time the bottom half ran.

40245: If that number was nonzero—as it normally is— **update_times** calls **update_wall_time** (line 40093, and discussed next) to update **xtime**, which tracks the current wall-clock time.

40248: Calls **calc_load** (line 40210, and explored momentarily) to update the kernel's estimate of the system's load factor.

update_wall_time

40097: Calls **update_wall_time_one_tick** (line 40054) for each tick that has yet to be processed. This updates the global **xtime** variable, trying to keep it in sync with the true time.

40100: Normalizes **xtime**, so that the number of microseconds is in the range 0 through 999,999. In the extremely unlikely event that more than a second's worth of timer ticks are lost, the **tv_usec** component of **xtime** could exceed 2 million, and this code could fail to normalize **xtime**. **xtime** would be fully normalized by subsequent calls, however.

calc_load

40210: **calc_load** is called from the timer bottom half to update the kernel's estimate of the current system load. Although exploring this is a bit of a digression, the function is of interest to anyone who's ever wondered how this omnipresent number gets calculated, so it's worth a quick look.

40213: A **static** variable, **count**, remembers how long it's been since the load average was last calculated. This is initialized to **LOAD_FREQ**, which is **#define**d at line 21713 to represent five seconds' worth of timer ticks. Each call to this function decrements the number of timer ticks that remain until the next load calculation.

40217: When the number of remaining ticks drops below 0, it's time to recalculate. (I'd expect this to test for less than or equal to 0, rather than

merely less than 0, but the difference can't amount to much in practice.)

40218: After reinitializing **count** so that it will trigger again in another five seconds, **count_active_tasks** (line 40188) is used to see how many tasks are currently in the system. The implementation of **count_active_tasks** probably won't be mysterious even now, but any questions that you have about it should be resolved by Chapter 7.

40219: The **CALC_LOAD** macro, **#define**d at line 21719, is used to update the three entries of the **avenrun** array (line 40208), whose three elements track the system's load over the last 5, 10, and 15 seconds. As stated in the previous chapter, floating-point math is all but banished from the kernel, so these computations are done in fixed-point, instead.

Task Queues and the Timer Queue

The initially startling idea behind the timer queue is that the bottom half associated with a top half doesn't have to have anything to do with servicing the interrupt. Instead, it might simply be anything at all that you want to do periodically. Making a function part of the bottom-half handler for the timer interrupt would ensure that the function was invoked about 100 times per second. (If running 100 times per second is too frequent, the function could keep a counter and simply return immediately 9 of every 10 times, for instance— you saw that **calc_load** does something like this.) The effect would be much like creating a new process whose **main** called the function in an infinite loop, but without the overhead normally associated with a process.

Bottom halves, however, are a limited resource—only 32 exist. You could expand the number of bottom halves by using a system similar to that implemented for signals, but that would simply increase the statically available number of bottom halves—it wouldn't let us expand the list of bottom halves dynamically.

In essence, that is what the timer queue provides: a dynamically extensible list of bottom halves, all tied to the timer interrupt. There's a separate bottom half for this—

TQUEUE_BH—which, as you've seen, is marked along with **TIMER_BH** if any tasks are in the timer queue. Hence, the timer interrupt has two bottom halves.

The timer queue actually is merely an instance of a more general kernel feature, task queues. Task queues are documented quite liberally in the kernel itself—see the file include/linux/tqueue.h, starting at line 24868. Consequently, I won't explore them in the text. However, they are an important kernel service, and the short file is well worth reading through.

Chapter 7

Processes and Threads

Ultimately, an operating system exists to provide a place to run programs. In Unix parlance, a running program is called a *process*. The Linux kernel, like that of all Unix variants, is *multitasking*; it can distribute time among many processes so that they all appear to be running simultaneously. Here, as always, the kernel arbitrates access to resources; in this case, the resource is CPU time.

A process traditionally has a *single context of execution*—a fancy way of saying that it's doing one thing at a time. At any given moment, you can determine precisely which portion of its code is executing. But sometimes you want a single process to do more than one thing at a time. For instance, you might want a Web browser to fetch and display a Web page while still monitoring whether the user clicks the Stop button. Launching a whole new program just to monitor the Stop button is clearly overkill. On the other hand, it isn't always convenient for the Web browser to divide its own time—to fetch just a bit of the page, check the Stop button, fetch a bit more of the page, recheck the Stop button, and so on.

A popular solution to this problem is the *thread*. Conceptually, threads are separate contexts of execution within the same process. Put more simply, they provide a way for a single process to do more than one thing simultaneously, as if the process were a miniature multitasking operating system in its own right. The threads within a thread group share all their global variables and have the same heap, so that memory allocated by **malloc** to one thread within the group is readable and writable by another. But the threads have different stacks (they don't share local variables) and can be running simultaneously at different places within the process's code. Thus, your Web browser can have one thread working on fetching and displaying the page while another thread watches the Stop button and interrupts the first thread if the button is clicked.

An equivalent view of a thread—and the view taken by the Linux kernel—is that threads are processes that happen to share the same global memory space. This means that the kernel doesn't have to invent for threads a whole new mechanism that would essentially duplicate the code already written to handle processes. It also means that this chapter's discussion of processes largely applies to threads as well.

Of course, those statements apply only to kernel-space threads. There are also user-space threads, which achieve the same effect but are implemented at the application level. User-space threads have advantages and disadvantages compared to kernel-space threads, but such a discussion is outside the scope of this book. Just to confuse matters further, there's a kernel function called **kernel_thread** (line 3443), which has nothing to do with kernel-space threads as the term is normally used.

Partly for historical reasons and partly because the Linux kernel does not really distinguish between the concepts of processes and threads, processes and threads are referred to in the kernel code by a more generic name, *task*. Along the same lines, this book tends to use "task" and "process" interchangeably.

Scheduling and Timeslices

Arbitrating access to the CPU is called *scheduling*. Good scheduling choices respect the priorities assigned by the user and create the believable illusion that all processes are running at the same time. Bad scheduling choices make an operating system appear clunky and slow. This is one reason the Linux scheduler is highly optimized. Conceptually, scheduling divides time into "slices" and allocates the slices to processes according to some algorithm. These slices of time are called—you guessed it—*timeslices*.

Realtime Processes

Linux offers three scheduling algorithms: a traditional Unix scheduler and two "realtime" schedulers mandated by the POSIX.1b (formerly known as POSIX.4)

operating system standard. Consequently, this text sometimes refers to realtime processes (as opposed to nonrealtime processes, technically, although I prefer "unreal time"). Don't get hung up on the term realtime, though—if you're coming from the hardware world, realtime means that you get certain guarantees about the operating system's performance, such as promises about interrupt latency, which Linux's realtime scheduling algorithms don't pretend to provide. Instead, Linux's scheduling algorithms are "soft realtime," meaning only that they give the CPU to a realtime process if any realtime process wants it, and otherwise they let CPU time trickle down to nonrealtime processes.

Some Linux variants promise "hard realtime," if that's a feature you really need. But, in the present Linux kernel—and, consequently, in this chapter—"realtime" always means "soft realtime."

Priorities

Priorities are simply integers expressing the relative weight that should be assigned to a process when deciding which process should be allowed to spend some time on the CPU—the higher its priority, the better its chances. Nonrealtime processes have two different kinds of priorities, a *static priority* and a *dynamic priority*. Realtime processes add a third kind of priority, the *realtime priority*:

- *Static priority*—Called static because it doesn't change with time, only when explicitly modified by the user. It indicates the maximum size of the timeslice a process should be allowed before being forced to allow other processes to compete for the CPU. (The process can be forced to yield the CPU for other reasons, too.)

- *Dynamic priority*—Declines with time as long as the process has the CPU; when its dynamic priority falls to 0, the process is marked for rescheduling. Hence, the dynamic priority indicates the amount of time remaining in this timeslice.

- *Realtime priority*—Indicates which other processes this process automatically beats out for the CPU. Higher realtime priority values always beat lower values. Because a process's realtime priority is 0 if it isn't a realtime process, any realtime process always beats any nonrealtime process if both are contending for the CPU. (A nonrealtime process can beat a realtime process under some circumstances, though. Realtime processes can explicitly yield the CPU, and they can be forced to yield it when waiting for I/O.)

Process IDs (PIDs)

Traditionally, every Unix process has a unique identifier, an integer in the range 0 through 32,767, which is called its *process identifier (PID)*. The PIDs 0 and 1 have special meaning to the system; all the rest are assigned to "normal" processes. In the discussion of **get_pid** later in the chapter, you'll see how PIDs are generated and assigned.

Reference Counting

Reference counting is a widely used technique for sharing common information among multiple objects. In general terms, one or more "holder" objects carry a pointer to a shared data object that includes an integer called its *reference count*. The value of this reference count equals the number of holder objects sharing the data. New holder objects that want to share the data are given a pointer to the same structure and must increment the structure's reference count.

When a holder object goes away, it decrements the reference count of the shared data and "the last one out turns off the lights." That is, when the reference count is reduced to 0, the holder object deallocates the shared object. Figure 7.1 illustrates the technique.

As you shall see, Linux uses reference counting to share common data among threads.

Capabilities

In the early days of Unix, either you were root or you weren't. If you were root, you could do nearly anything

you wanted, such as deleting every file on the system's boot disk, even if it was probably a really bad idea. If you weren't root—well, you couldn't hurt the system much, but you couldn't do any significant system administration tasks, either.

Unfortunately, a lot of applications' needs fall somewhere in between these two extremes of security. Changing the system's time, for instance, was something only root could do, so programs that did it had to be run as root. However, because it ran as root, the process that changed the system's time could do any of the other things that root could do, too. Well-written programs weren't a problem, but other programs could still mess up the system accidentally or maliciously. (Innumerable computer attacks were based on tricking root into running some seemingly trustworthy executable that then performed dirty tricks.)

Some of these problems could be worked around with the correct use of groups or with programs such as sudo, but some of them couldn't. For some important operations, you still had to give processes general root access, even when you really wanted to allow them to perform just one or two privileged operations. Linux addresses this problem with an idea plucked from a now-defunct POSIX draft standard: capabilities.

Capabilities enable you to dictate more specifically what a privileged process is allowed to do. You can grant a process the ability to change the system's time, for instance, without granting it the ability to kill every other process on the system, destroy all your files, and generally run amok. And, to help guard against accidental misuse of its privileges, a long-running process can (if allowed) acquire a capability temporarily, just long enough to do a specific chore, and then drop the capability when it's finished with that chore.

Capabilities are still being developed as of this writing. Some new features still must be implemented to fully realize the promise of capabilities—for instance, no kernel support exists yet for attaching a program's desired capabilities to the file itself. One result is that Linux still sometimes checks whether a process is running as

root rather than checking for the specific capability the process needs. Nonetheless, what has been done so far is quite useful.

Representing Processes in the Kernel

The kernel uses several data structures to track processes; they are interwoven with the representation of the process itself. These data structures are illustrated in Figure 7.2 and explained in detail next.

struct task_struct

21931: The kernel data structure that represents a process is **struct task_struct**. Go ahead and at least skim this structure's definition. It's rather large, but it's logically organized into pieces that

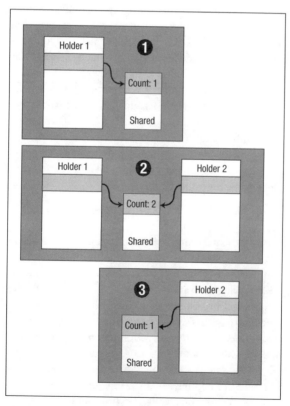

Figure 7.1 Reference counting.

will come to make sense individually over the course of this chapter. While you're at it, observe that many pieces of this structure are pointers to other structures. This comes in handy when a child and parent wish to share the pointed-to information—many of the pointers indicate information that's being reference-counted, as described earlier in the chapter.

21963: The tasks themselves form a circular, doubly linked list called the *task list*, using the **next_task** and **prev_task** members of **struct task_struct**. This permits kernel code to readily iterate over all existing tasks. Indeed, this iteration is so commonly required that a macro is available for it: **for_each_task**, at line 22542.

Although a one-liner, the **for_each_task** macro has a few noteworthy features. First, observe that it uses **init_task** as the start and end of the iteration. This is safe, because **init_task** never exits; hence, it's always available to use as a marker. However, note that **init_task** itself is not visited as part of the iteration—which happens to be what you want when using the macro. Also, as a minor point of interest, observe that you always walk forward through the list, using the **next_task** member. There's no corresponding macro to walk backward—and there's no need for one. The **prev_task** member is needed only to disengage a task from the list efficiently.

21960: Linux keeps another circular, doubly linked list of tasks, similar to the task list. This list uses the **run_list** member of **struct task_struct** and is generally thought of as a queue (Gesundheit). For this reason, this list is normally called the *run queue*. As with **prev_task**, **run_list**'s **prev** member is needed only to remove an entry from the queue efficiently; the queue is always traversed in the forward direction.

Tasks are added to the queue using **add_to_runqueue** (line 34041) and are removed with **del_from_runqueue** (line 22549). (As you can see, unlike a classic queue, new elements are added to the front of the run queue.) Sometimes, they are also shoved to the front or back of the queue, using **move_first_runqueue** (line 34055) and **move_last_runqueue** (line 34048), respectively. There is also an efficient way to tell whether a task is in the run queue: **task_on_runqueue** (line 22558). Note that nearly all of these functions are local to kernel/sched.c and the **run_list** field is used in no other file (except during process creation—in kernel/fork.c—and briefly while booting SMP machines, in code not included in the book). This is quite appropriate, because the run queue is needed only for scheduling.

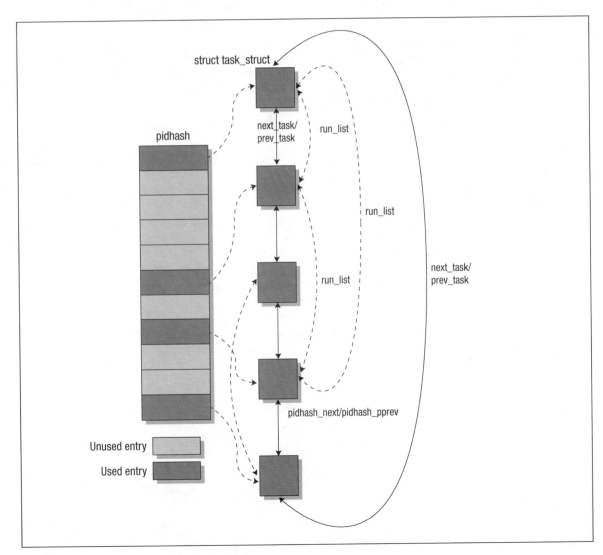

Figure 7.2 Kernel data structures for managing tasks.

21985: On top of that, tasks form a graph whose structure expresses the family relationships among the tasks. Because I don't know of any generally accepted term for this graph, I call it the *process graph*. This is quite independent of the **next_task/prev_task** linkage, in which a task's position is all but meaningless—an accident of history. Each **struct task_struct** maintains five pointers to position itself within the process graph. These five pointers are declared at lines 21985 through 21986:

- **p_opptr** points to the process's original parent, the process that spawned this one. When the process's original parent dies, this becomes a pointer to the system's child reaper process—normally, init.

- **p_pptr** points to the process's logical parent. When a process is being traced or debugged, its logical parent is set to the tracing or debugging process so that signal notifications will be delivered there. Under normal circumstances, the process's logical parent is the same as its real, or original, parent.

- **p_cptr** points to the process's youngest (most recent) child.

- **p_ysptr** points to the process's next-youngest (next most recent) sibling.

- **p_osptr** points to the process's next-oldest (next least recent) sibling.

Figure 7.3 illustrates these relationships. (The complete set of links is shown only for the node labeled "Me.") This set of pointers provides yet another way to navigate through the set of processes on the system. Obviously, the pointers are most useful for such jobs as finding a process's parent or walking through the list of a process's children. The pointers are maintained by two macros:

- **REMOVE_LINKS** (line 22520) removes a process from the graph.

- **SET_LINKS** (line 22531) inserts a process into the graph.

Both of these also adjust the **next_task/prev_task** links. If you examine the macros carefully, you'll see that they can add or remove only leaf processes—never processes with children.

30483: The **pidhash** array helps map PIDs to pointers to **struct task_struct**s. **pidhash** is initialized at lines 34960 and 34961, after which it is manipulated with a set of macros and inline functions defined in lines 22159 through 22193. These simply implement an unsurprising hash table. Note that the functions that maintain **pidhash** use two members in the **struct task_struct** itself—**pidhash_next** (line 21990) and **pidhash_pprev** (line 21991)—to maintain the hash buckets. With **pidhash**, the kernel can efficiently find a task by its PID.

The kernel could find a task by its PID even more efficiently if there were an array of 32,768 **struct task_struct**s, one for every possible PID—call it **task**. However, that would vastly increase the kernel's memory requirements. A single **struct task_struct** is 1,424 bytes under UP and 1,664 bytes under SMP—in round numbers, approximately 1.5KB. To hold 32,768 of these, **task** would balloon to 45,568KB, or 44.5MB—and remember, all this is without actually running any of those tasks. Besides, the maximum number of active tasks is usually set much lower than 32,768, so most of the room in such an array would be wasted, anyway.

Alternatively, the **task** array could merely store 32,768 pointers to **struct task_struct**s. At 4 bytes per pointer, this would still consume 128KB of valuable kernel memory, and again, most of this would be wasted. Still, on systems with memory to burn, this would conceivably be an improvement: It would eliminate the need for the **pidhash** array and the code and pointers

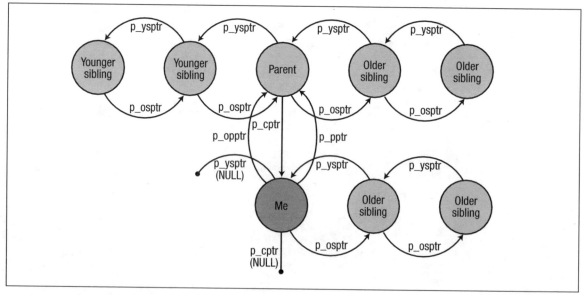

Figure 7.3 The process graph.

required to maintain it. More importantly, looking up a task by its PID would become maximally fast. Even so, any difference would be felt only on systems that typically had tens of thousands of processes running at a time, and it is much more common for systems to have only a few dozen or a few hundred processes running. With only a few hundred processes running, **pidhash**'s hash buckets typically contain at most one or two elements, so there's very little to be gained from this change. For nearly all real systems, the kernel's version is about as fast as it can be, and its memory requirements are minimal.

Just for fun, prove to yourself that the hash function—**pid_hashfn**, at line 22162—provides a uniform distribution over its domain, 0 to 32,767 (all valid PIDs). Of course, your idea of fun might differ from mine.

All these data structures provide a wealth of information about the running system, but at a cost: They must all be correctly maintained whenever adding or removing a process, or the system will go haywire. Partly because it's so hard to get this right, processes are created in only one place (by **do_fork**, discussed later) and deleted in only one place (by **release_task**, also discussed later).

Process States

At any given time, a process is in one of five states, as described in the following commentary. The process's current state is tracked in **struct task_struct**'s **state** member (line 21934).

Process State Constants

21738: **TASK_RUNNING** means the process is ready to run. Even on a UP system, more than one task might be in the **TASK_RUNNING** state at the same time—**TASK_RUNNING** doesn't mean the process is on the CPU right now (though it might well be), only that it's ready for the CPU whenever it becomes available.

21739: **TASK_INTERRUPTIBLE** is one of two waiting states. This state means that the process is waiting for an event, but it's okay to interrupt it with a signal.

21740: **TASK_UNINTERRUPTIBLE** is the other waiting state. This state means that the process is waiting for a hardware condition and must not be interrupted by a signal.

21741: **TASK_ZOMBIE** means the process has exited (or has been killed), but the **struct task_struct** that represents it has not yet been deleted. This is to allow a parent process to inquire after its dead child's status even after the child has exited. We'll cover this in much more detail later in this chapter.

21742: **TASK_STOPPED** means the process has been stopped. Generally, this means that it received one of the **SIGSTOP**, **SIGTSTP**, **SIGTTIN**, or **SIGTTOU** signals, but it could also mean that the process is being traced. (For example, it's being run under a debugger, and the user is single-stepping through the code.)

Where Processes Come From: **fork**, **vfork**, and **__clone**

Traditional Unix implementations offer exactly one way to create new processes after the system is running: the system call **fork**. (If you're wondering where the first process comes from, it's init, discussed in Chapter 4.) When a process calls **fork**, it conceptually divides in two—like a fork in the road—and the parent and the child are then free to pursue different paths. The parent and child are nearly identical just after the **fork**—all their variables have the same values, they have the same files open, and so on. However, if the parent changes the value of a variable, the child won't see the change, and vice versa. The child is a copy of the parent (at least at first), but they don't share.

Linux retains the traditional **fork** and adds a more general **__clone** function. (The two leading underscores help to emphasize that normal application code should

not call **__clone** directly, but instead should call functions from thread libraries built on top of **__clone**.) Whereas **fork** creates a new child process that is a copy of its parent but shares nothing with it, **__clone** lets you specify what the parent and child should share. If you give **__clone** one combination of flags, the child shares nothing with the parent, so it's just like **fork**. If you supply another combination of flags, the child shares everything with its parent, just like a traditional thread. Other combinations of flags land you somewhere in between.

One of the innovations introduced by the BSD strain of Unix is a related system call, **vfork**. **vfork** has strange semantics: The parent is suspended until the child process exits or **exec**s, and there are severe limitations on what the child can safely do. What's more, unlike **fork**, **vfork** doesn't copy the caller's memory space, so if the child changes a variable, the parent sees the change.

All of this seeming strangeness is by design. At the time **vfork** was introduced, **fork** was a very expensive system call, and the greatest expense was in copying the caller's memory space. BSD's implementers noticed that this copying often was wasted effort, because a child process often would immediately **exec** some other program, replacing the just-copied memory space with one set up for the new program. So **vfork** gave application programmers a way to avoid these unnecessary copies: If the child was just going to do an **exec** anyway, application programmers could call **vfork** instead of **fork**. Despite its advantages, **vfork** was only lackadaisically supported by Unix standardization efforts and has generally fallen into disfavor, partly because **fork** was eventually made much more efficient. (In the next chapter, you'll see how a technique called copy-on-write greatly reduces the expense of copying the **fork**er's memory space while providing additional benefits as well.) Still, because **vfork** is widely used—especially in older applications—Linux supports **vfork** as a **fork** variant.

As a side note, the kernel creates a few tasks for its own use with the function **kernel_thread** (line 3443). Users never call this function—indeed, they can't; it's solely for creating special processes, such as kswapd, which effectively are pieces of the kernel that are treated as tasks for the sake of convenience. Tasks created by **kernel_thread** have some unusual properties, which we won't go into in any detail (for example, they can't be preempted), but the main thing to note at present is that **kernel_thread** uses **do_fork** for most of its dirty work. So, even these special processes are, ultimately, created in practically the same way as the ordinary ones that you and I use.

do_fork

31014: **do_fork** is the kernel routine that implements **fork**, **vfork**, and **__clone**.

31030: Allocates a **struct task_struct** to represent the new process.

31034: Gives the new **struct task_struct** its initial values, copied straight from the current process. The rest of **do_fork**'s work consists mainly of making new copies of whatever information the parent and child won't share. (**current**, which you see at this line and throughout the kernel, is a macro that evaluates to a pointer to the **struct task_struct** representing the currently executing process. It's defined at line 12529, but that's just a call to the **get_current** function, which is at line 12522.)

31059: The new task is assigned a PID (the details underlying this will be explored shortly).

31061: Initially, the new process is not placed in the run queue. It's still possible that **do_fork** will fail, and it would be wasteful to put the new process in the run queue, only to take it right back out if something goes wrong. More seriously, the new task is not completely initialized yet, and we wouldn't want another CPU (in an SMP system) to hand control to this process prematurely. If everything else succeeds, then just before **do_fork** returns, at line 31159, a call to **wake_up_process** (line 34067) will put the process on the run queue.

31064: Normally, **do_fork**'s caller should be registered as the parent of the process it created. The only exception is when the **CLONE_PARENT** flag (line 21691) is set. This flag means that the new process should have the same parent as **do_fork**'s caller. At this point in the code, the two processes already have the same parent—thanks to the blanket copy at line 31034—so the normal assignment is simply skipped in the **CLONE_PARENT** case. Observe that **CLONE_VFORK** (line 21687) will override **CLONE_PARENT** if both are set.

31067: If the calling process is not being traced (by a debugger, for example), the caller is also made the new process's logical parent—the one to which signal notifications are sent. However, if the caller is being traced, the child's logical parent will remain the same as its parent's logical parent, the debugger process. This helps the debugger accurately trace child processes.

31105: This and the following several lines, using helper functions defined elsewhere in the file, create for the child its own private copies of selected portions of the parent's structure, based on the value of the supplied **clone_flags** argument. If **clone_flags** indicates that the relevant piece should be shared instead of copied, the helper function simply increments a reference count and returns; otherwise, it creates a new copy to be owned by the new process.

31113: **copy_thread** (line 3529) is architecture-specific code to handle low-level details of setting up the new process's register state. On the x86, this function also guarantees (at line 3544) that when **fork** returns, the child's execution will jump to **ret_from_fork** (line 882). On UP systems, **ret_from_fork** simply clears the process's **SCHED_YIELD** bit (at line 34218, ultimately), arranges for tracing the new process if need be, and then jumps to **ret_from_sys_call** (line 908) to clean up the same way as after any system call.

31151: By now, all the process's own data structures have been set up, but most of the kernel data structures that track processes have not. The first step in setting up the kernel structures is to add the process to the process graph.

31152: Enters the new process into the **pidhash** table by calling **hash_pid** (line 22165).

31159: Puts the new process in the **TASK_RUNNING** state and enters it into the run queue via a call to **wake_up_process** (line 34067).

31164: If **vfork**ing, the parent process waits for the child to release a special flag variable (called a *semaphore*; semaphores are discussed fully in Chapters 9 and 10). This special flag variable was declared at line 31020 and stored in the parent process's **struct task_struct** at line 31028. The child process will do its part, releasing the semaphore, at line 30728, which is reached during either an **exit** or an **exec**. Only then will the parent's execution proceed.

Note that not only is the **struct task_struct** now filled out, but all the relevant data structures—the process graph, run queue, and PID hash—have all been correctly modified to account for the new arrival. Congratulations, it's a bouncing baby task!

PID Allocation

PIDs are generated by the **get_pid** function (line 30533), which returns a PID not already in use. It uses **last_pid** (line 30481)—the most recently allocated PID—as its starting point.

The version of **get_pid** used in the kernel is an example of the kernel's frequent tradeoffs between simplicity and speed; here, speed won handily. **get_pid** is highly optimized. It's much more complex than a straightforward implementation would be, but it's also much faster. The most straightforward implementation would walk through the entire task list—typically dozens of entries long, and sometimes hundreds—for every candidate PID until a suitable value was found. The version of the kernel we see must do this walk sometimes, but can skip it in most cases. The net result is to help speed up process creation, a notoriously slow operation on Unix.

If all we need is to quickly compute an integer that's different for every running process, there are simpler and faster ways to do it. If we had the array of 32,768 **struct task_struct** pointers proposed earlier, we could simply take the process's index in that array. That might seem to do little more than create a new, equivalent problem—namely, how to efficiently find an empty slot in that array. Earlier versions of the Linux kernel had a clever solution for a similar problem: They made the available slots point to one another, forming a linked list (treated as a stack) of empty positions.

We already rejected that array because it's such a memory hog, but there's an alternative PID allocation strategy that would use about half as much memory. Consider the notion of a *PID pool*, a repository of available PIDs. The simplest and fastest implementation would be an array of 32,768 **unsigned short**s, organized as a stack, with a separate integer tracking the top of the stack. To allocate a PID, you would simply decrement the top-of-stack index and take the PID at the newly freed position. When a process exited, it would push its PID onto the stack and increment the top-of-stack index.

Both of these alternative PID allocation strategies share an advantage: They never need to walk the entire task list. Unfortunately, they also share an obvious flaw: They consume, by the kernel's standards, an awful lot of memory—128KB for the first strategy, 64KB for the second. This alone is probably enough reason to nix both ideas, but it's interesting to note that they also share a less obvious drawback. Because they organize available PIDs in a stack, the most recently released PIDs will be the first reallocated. The reason this is a problem is that many existing applications assume that it will be a while before a PID is reused. That's an unsafe assumption in

any case, but it's probably a bad idea to get the kernel into the business of arguing with those programs. The existing PID allocation strategy is still very fast (especially in the most common case, when there's no need to walk the task list), uses almost no memory, and has the advantage of rarely, if ever, exposing latent bugs in such applications (if you consider that an advantage).

get_pid

30535: The **next_safe** variable is a speed hack; it keeps track of the next-lowest candidate PID that might be reserved. (It could be more accurately renamed **next_unsafe**.) When **last_pid** is incremented above this boundary, the entire task list must be inspected to see whether the candidate PID is still reserved (the process that originally reserved it might have gone away since). Because walking through the task list can be very slow, it should be avoided when possible. So, while doing the walk, **get_pid** recalculates **next_safe**. If some processes have died, **next_safe** could be higher now, so **get_pid** might be able to avoid some future walks through the task list. (**next_safe** is **static**, so its value will be remembered next time **get_pid** needs to allocate a PID.)

30538: If the new process is to share a PID with its parent, the parent's PID is returned.

30542: Starts searching through candidate PIDs for an unused value. The bitwise AND just tests whether the new value of **last_pid** exceeds 32,767 (the largest allowed PID), by testing whether any but the low-order 15 bits are on. I doubt the kernel developers really needed this ounce of speed, but you never know. At the time of this writing, at least, gcc isn't smart enough to notice the equivalence and choose the slightly faster form used in the code.

30543: If **last_pid** has exceeded its maximum allowed value, it's rolled over to 300. There's nothing magical about the number 300—it has no

particular significance to the system—it's just another speed hack. The idea is that low-numbered PIDs tend to belong to long-running daemons that are created at startup time and never exit. Because they're always occupying the low-numbered PIDs, an unused PID will be found more quickly if the first few hundred values aren't even considered for reuse. In addition, because the space of PIDs is typically many times larger than the maximum number of tasks allowed at once, wasting a few PIDs in the name of speed is a good trade. (The maximum number of processes allowed at one time is held in **max_threads**, line 30478. It's initialized at line 30522 and can be changed through the /proc file system.)

30544: Because **last_pid** exceeded the maximum allowed PID, it must also have exceeded **next_safe**; hence, the subsequent **if** test can be skipped.

30546: If **last_pid** is still less than **next_safe**, its new value is available for use. Otherwise, the task list must be inspected.

30555: If the current value for **last_pid** is taken, it's simply incremented, rolling over to 300 if necessary, and the loop restarts. This loop might never exit. Suppose the maximum number of tasks is set to 32,768, the same as the number of possible PIDs, and suppose further that 32,700 tasks are running. If a new task is being created and the only available PIDs are below 300, this loop will simply continue until some process with a higher-numbered PID exits. On a UP system, the kernel will never exit this loop, so it will never hand the CPU to any such process. Consequently, no processes can exit and the system will freeze. Even an SMP system will freeze. If a task tries to exit on another CPU—an action that would normally free its PID—the kernel will become blocked on that CPU as well, because **get_pid** holds the **tasklist_lock** lock, which the exiting process needs to acquire before it can release its PID. Thus, even on a machine with gobs of memory, the maximum number of tasks should be kept below 32,468.

30574: **get_pid** has found an unclaimed PID, which is returned.

Running a New Program

If all you could do is **fork** (or **__clone**), you could only make copies of the same process over and over. Our Linux system could run only copies of the first user process ever created on the system, init. Init is useful, but it's not *that* useful; we'd like to be able to do other things, as well.

After we have a new process, it becomes something else by calling **exec**. (There's not really a single function named **exec**; rather, **exec** often is used as a generic term to refer to a family of functions, all of which do basically the same thing, but take slightly different arguments.)

So, creating a "really" new process—one that's the running image of a different program from its parent—takes two steps, one to **fork** and one to **exec**, leading to the familiar pattern of C code shown here:

```
/* Ignore the possibility of error below. */
if (fork()) {
  /* I'm the parent; continue normally. */
} else {
  /* I'm the child. */
  /* Become /some/other/program. */
  execl("/some/other/program",
      "/some/other/program", NULL);
}
```

execl is one of several functions in the **exec** family.

The underlying kernel function that implements all the functions in the **exec** family is **do_execve**, lines 11824 through 11897. **do_execve** has three jobs:

• *Read some identifying information from the executable file into memory.* **do_execve** farms this work out to **prepare_binprm**.

• *Prepare the new arguments and environment.* This is what C applications will see as **argc**, **argv**, and **envp**.

• *Locate a binary handler that agrees to parse the executable.* **exec** lets the handler do the rest of the work of modifying the kernel data structures. (I discuss binary handlers later in this chapter.)

With these tasks in mind, let's begin to look at **do_execve** in detail.

do_execve

11827: The type that represents all the information that needs to be tracked while **exec**ing a process is **struct linux_binprm** (see line 17650)—I believe **binprm** is an abbreviation for "binary format parameters." **do_execve** does its work, and communicates to the other functions to which it delegates some of its work, in terms of a variable of this type, **bprm**. Observe that **bprm** is discarded when **do_execve** returns; it's needed only while doing the **exec**, not over the whole lifetime of the process.

11832: **do_execve** begins by opening the executable file. It isn't read from just yet. The present concern is to ensure that the file exists, so **do_execve** knows whether to bother proceeding.

11838: The next step is to initialize a miniature page table (see Chapter 8) that tracks the memory pages allocated for the new process's arguments and environment. It allocates **MAX_ARG_PAGES** (**#define**d to 32 at line 17641) pages for this purpose; pages are 4KB on the x86 platform, so the total available space for arguments plus environment is $32 \times 4KB = 128KB$. Personally, I was happy to learn this, because I've occasionally exceeded this limit, usually when running something like **cat * > /tmp/joined** in a directory with thousands of files. All of those file names, concatenated, can exceed 128KB. I normally work around this by using the xargs program, but maybe I'll just recompile my kernel with a higher limit for

MAX_ARG_PAGES. At least now I know how to raise this limit if it really starts to annoy me again—and perhaps some eager reader will arrange to remove the hard-coded limit altogether. I love having the source code.

11842: Continues filling out **bprm**, particularly its **argc** and **envc** members. To fill out these members, **do_execve** uses the function **count** (line 11129), which steps through the passed-in **argv** and **envp** arrays, counting non-**NULL** pointers. The first **NULL** pointer terminates the list, so the number of non-**NULL** pointers found to that point is returned. This initially appears to be another possible point of slight inefficiency: **do_execve**'s caller sometimes knows the length of the **argv** and **envp** arrays already. So **do_execve** could be extended to accept integer **argc** and **envc** arguments, which, if not negative, would be taken to indicate the length of the respective arrays. But it's not so simple: **count** also checks along the way to see whether an error occurs in accessing the memory in the array that it's scanning. Forcing (and, more to the point, trusting) **do_execve**'s caller to check this would be a mistake. It's better as it stands.

11865: Copies the arguments and environment into the new process, mainly using **copy_strings** (line 11155). **copy_strings** looks very complicated, but its mission is simple enough: Copy the strings into the new process's memory space, allocating pages if necessary. The complexity arises from the need to manage the page table and to cross kernel/user space boundaries, as I discuss more fully in Chapter 8.

11878: If all went well up to this point, the last step is to find a binary handler for the new executable. If **search_binary_handler** locates one and it completes successfully, a non-negative value is returned to indicate success.

11886: If this point is reached, something went wrong in one of the preceding steps. Any pages allocated for the new program's arguments and environment must be freed, and a negative value must be returned to signal failure to the caller.

prepare_binprm

11579: **prepare_binprm** fills out significant pieces of **do_execve**'s **bprm**.

11587: This line begins a number of sanity checks, such as ensuring that the caller is trying to execute a file rather than a directory, and that the file's executable bit is set.

11598: Respects the setuid and setgid bits if they're set, making a note that the new process should treat the executing user as a different user (if setuid) and/or as a member of a different group (if setgid).

11632: Finally, **prepare_binprm** reads the first 128 bytes (**BINPRM_BUF_SIZE**, line 17644) of the file into **bprm**'s **buf** member.

Binary Handlers

A *binary handler* is the Linux kernel's mechanism for treating a variety of binary formats in a consistent way, which is necessary because not all programs are stored in the same file format. A good example is Java .class files. Java defines a platform-independent binary executable format—the files themselves are the same, no matter what platform they're running on—so the files clearly aren't going to be structured the same as Linux's native executables. Even so, Linux can treat them as if they were native executables, through the use of an appropriate binary handler.

I'll go into detail about binary handlers later, but you now know enough about them to find out how **do_execve** finds a suitable one. It delegates the work to **search_binary_handler** (line 11734).

search_binary_handler

11773: Begins to iterate over the kernel's linked list of binary handlers, passing **bprm** to each in turn. (The **regs** argument doesn't concern us now.) More precisely, each element of the linked list of binary handlers includes a set of pointers to functions that together provide support for a single binary format. (The definition of **struct linux_binfmt**, at line 17666, shows what's included: The interesting components are the ones to load a binary, **load_binary**; to load a shared library, **load_shlib**; and to create a core dump, **core_dump**.) **search_binary_handler** simply calls each **load_binary** function until one of them returns a non-negative value, indicating that it recognized and successfully loaded the file. **search_binary_handler** returns a negative value to indicate an error, including the error of being unable to find a suitable binary handler.

11815: If the loop that started at line 11773 fails to find a suitable binary handler, this line tries to load a new binary format that should result in the attempt's succeeding on the second try. Hence, the whole handler-seeking loop is included in another two-iteration loop that starts at line 11771. This is simple and it gets the job done, but the second iteration can waste work by presenting the file to binary handlers that already rejected it on the first iteration. However, it's not as bad as it looks: The newly loaded binary format is prepended to the list of binary formats (see line 11043), so it will be checked first. Therefore, work is wasted only in the unlikely event that the newly loaded binary format does not accept the file after all.

Executable Formats

As I mentioned in the previous section, not all programs are stored in the same file format, and Linux uses binary handlers to abstract away the differences.

Linux's current "native" executable format (if "native" means anything in a system with equally good support for so many formats) is the Executable and Linking Format (ELF). ELF has all but entirely replaced the older, so-called a.out format. a.out was not nearly as flexible—among other drawbacks, it is poorly suited to dynamic linking, making shared libraries difficult to implement. Linux still includes a binary handler for a.out, but ELF is preferred.

Binary handlers typically recognize files by some kind of "magic sequence" (a special byte sequence) embedded at the start of the file, and sometimes also by some property of the file name. For example, Java .class files are recognized by the fact that their first four bytes are (in hex) 0xcafebabe, as specified by the Java standard. Naturally, this sort of recognition falls short of proof—a random data file might just happen to have the same first four bytes as a valid Java .class file. The result in that case will be an error during execution of the file, but the kernel won't care.

The following binary handlers are supplied by the 2.4 kernel (on my x86-based system; ports of Linux to other platforms, such as the IA-64, MIPS, and SPARC CPUs, provide additional handlers):

- *a.out (in the file fs/binfmt_aout.c)*—For old-style Linux binaries. Still required for backward compatibility on some systems, but in general, a.out is rapidly dying an honorable death.

- *ELF (in the file fs/binfmt_elf.c)*—For new-style Linux binaries. Widely used, both for executables and for shared libraries. Most modern GNU/Linux systems (for example, Red Hat 7.1) ship with only ELF binaries, although they typically also support loading a.out binaries just in case you decide to install one. Note that even though ELF is conventionally considered Linux's native format, it uses a binary handler just like the other formats—the kernel doesn't play favorites. Avoiding special cases simplifies the kernel code.

- *EM86 (in the file fs/binfmt_em86.c)*—Helps you to run Intel Linux binaries on an Alpha machine as if they were native Alpha binaries.

- *Misc (in the file fs/binfmt_misc.c)*—By far the cleverest use of binary handlers, this handler can recognize a variety of binary formats by embedded magic numbers or by file name suffixes—but the best part is that it's configurable at runtime, not merely at compile time. Hence, within broad limits, you can add support for new binary file formats on the fly, without recompiling the kernel and rebooting. (A really great idea!) Comments in the source file suggest that the EM86 binary handler will be replaced by this one eventually.

- *Scripts (in the file fs/binfmt_script.c)*—For shell scripts, Perl scripts, and so on. Speaking somewhat loosely, any executable file whose first two characters are **#!** is taken care of by this binary handler.

Of these binary handlers, only the misc, ELF, and script handlers are included in this book (starting at lines 10349, 9042, and 10866, respectively). Our principal concern is more with how the kernel deals with the differences between various formats than with the details of each of the individual binary formats (although that's an interesting topic in its own right).

An Example: The Misc Binary Handler

As you saw earlier, **do_execve** steps through a linked list of **struct linux_binfmt**s representing binary handlers, calling the function pointed to by the **load_binary** member of each **struct** until one succeeds (or until it runs out of formats to try, of course). But where do these structures come from, and how are the **load_binary** functions implemented? For answers, we turn to the file fs/binfmt_misc.c.

misc_format

10419: By comparing the initialization of **misc_format** with the definition of **struct linux_binfmt** (line 17666), you can see that this module doesn't provide support for shared libraries or core dumps, only for loading executables. The **load_misc_binary** function provides this support.

init_misc_binfmt

10817: The entry point to this module is **init_misc_binfmt**. **init_misc_binfmt** is called during kernel initialization if miscellaneous binary support is compiled into the kernel, or by the kmod task or **sys_init_module** (line 32223) if miscellaneous binary support is compiled as a kernel module.

10828: This module is controlled with a couple of entries in the /proc file system, the subject of Chapter 11. This line creates the file /proc/sys/fs/binfmt_misc/status. Reading from or writing to this file triggers the functions **proc_read_status** and **proc_write_status** (lines 10696 and 10767).

10836: New entries are registered with this binary handler using the file /proc/sys/fs/binfmt_misc/register, which is created at this line. This file cannot be read, but writing to it triggers the function **proc_write_register** (line 10621).

10842: Pushes the address of **misc_format** onto the front of the system's list of binary formats, using **register_binfmt** (line 11027).

load_misc_binary

10523: This function is responsible for choosing and loading an appropriate interpreter for the file that the kernel is attempting to **exec**.

10539: Locates a structure representing an interpreter that accepts the file, using **check_file** (line 10494, and explored in the next section).

10554: Arranges to **exec** the interpreter and pass it the file to interpret, followed by the original arguments. For example, this might turn a command line of

```
Foo.class arg1 arg2
```

into

```
/usr/bin/java Foo.class arg1 arg2
```

The **copy_strings_kernel** function (line 11219) used here does most of its work with **copy_strings** (line 11155); as used here, each call simply prepends one string to the process's **argv** array.

10565: The interpreter is executed, using much the same procedure as you saw in **do_execve**. In particular, the function searches for a binary handler for the interpreter, using **search_binary_handler**, exactly the way **load_misc_binary** itself was found. (In practice, the interpreter will probably be an ELF binary, although it doesn't have to be.)

Remember that the other handler will not allocate a new **struct task_struct**—that already happened during the preceding **fork**. The other handler is just modifying the existing process's **struct task_struct**. If you want to look through all the gory details of how this is done, the place to start is **load_elf_binary** (line 9443). The interesting parts start at line 9641.

check_file

10494: **check_file** scans the list of registered miscellaneous binary formats, seeking one that will interpret the file the kernel was trying to **exec**. It returns a pointer to a structure representing the matching format, or **NULL** if no match is found.

10502: Begins looping over the list. List entries are of type **struct binfmt_entry** (line 10398); they are added to the list by **proc_write_register** (see line 10680) and removed by **clear_entry** (line 10434). While in the list, they can be disabled or re-enabled by **proc_write_status** (see lines 10775 through 10779).

10505: If the **ENTRY_MAGIC** flag (line 10412) is clear, then this list entry matches on file name extensions instead of magic byte sequences. The extension was located back at line 10498 and is checked here. If the original file name did not contain a period, **p** will be **NULL** here and the string comparisons are skipped.

10508: If the **ENTRY_MAGIC** flag is set, this list entry matches on magic byte sequences and ignores file names. The **while** loop iterates as long as any bits that differ between the file's contents and the expected magic byte sequence are only those that are allowed to differ by the entry's bitmask (if any). If the entire magic sequence matches, the corresponding entry pointer is returned.

Scheduling: See How They Run!

After an application is loaded, it must be given access to the CPU. This is the realm of the scheduler. Operating system schedulers generally fall into two basic categories:

- *Complex schedulers*—Take a relatively long time to run, but hope to repay that investment by improved overall system performance.

- *Quick-and-dirty schedulers*—Just try to do a reasonably good job and get out of the way fast so that the processes themselves can have the CPU as long as possible.

Linux's scheduler is the latter kind. Don't interpret "quick-and-dirty" as a pejorative, though. Linux's scheduler generally trounces its competition, commercial and free alike, in benchmarks.

The Scheduling Function and Scheduling Policies

The kernel's main scheduling function has the well-chosen name **schedule**, and it starts at line 34237. It's really a simple function, simpler than it looks, although its meaning is slightly obscured because it is three scheduling algorithms in one. It also picks up a small amount of complexity from its SMP support, which I defer examining until Chapter 10. Finally, its control flow is obfuscated in a way reminiscent of **system_call**'s (see Chapter 5), and for the same reason—for maximum speed, we want control to drop straight through, taking

no branches, in the normal case. Figure 7.4 shows an overview of **schedule**'s control flow. The **schedule**, **scheduling_in_interrupt**, and **same_process** labels in this figure are larger than the rest because they're the entry and exit points to the function.

The scheduling algorithm to use in a particular case depends on the process. The scheduling algorithm used for a given process is called its *scheduling policy* and it's reflected in the process's **struct task_struct**'s **policy** member. Normally, **policy** has just one of the **SCHED_OTHER**, **SCHED_FIFO**, or **SCHED_RR** bits set. But it can also have the **SCHED_YIELD** bit set, if the process decided to yield the CPU—for example, by calling the **sched_yield** system call (see **sys_sched_yield**, at line 34713).

The **SCHED_XXX** constants are **#define**d at lines 21765 through 21771.

Scheduling Policy Constants

21765: **SCHED_OTHER** means that traditional Unix scheduling applies—this is not a realtime process.

21766: **SCHED_FIFO** means that this is a realtime process, subject to POSIX.1b's FIFO (first-in, first-out) scheduler. It should run until it either blocks on I/O, explicitly yields the CPU, or is preempted by another realtime process with a higher **rt_priority**. **SCHED_FIFO** processes have a timeslice in Linux's implementation; they just aren't forced to give up the CPU when their timeslice is over. Hence, as mandated by POSIX.1b, such a process acts as if it has no timeslice. The fact that it keeps track of its timeslice anyway is merely an implementation convenience, so that we don't have to litter the code with **if (!(current->policy & SCHED_FIFO)) { ... }**. Also, it's probably faster this way—the other policies really do need to track the timeslice, and continually checking whether we need to track the timeslice would be slower than simply tracking it. This is a splendid example of the "just do it" idiom mentioned in Chapter 2.

21767: **SCHED_RR** means that this is a realtime process, subject to POSIX.1b's RR (round-robin) scheduler. It's the same as **SCHED_FIFO**, except that timeslices do matter. When a **SCHED_RR** process's timeslice expires, it goes to the back of the list of **SCHED_FIFO** and **SCHED_RR** processes with the same **rt_priority**.

21771: **SCHED_YIELD** is not a scheduling policy, but an extra bit that cuts across scheduling policies. As I previously stated, this tells the scheduler to yield the CPU if anyone else wants it. Note in particular that this will even cause a realtime process to yield to a nonrealtime process.

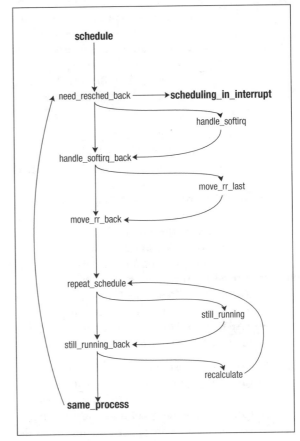

Figure 7.4   Flow control for **schedule**.

schedule

34240: **prev** and **next** will be set to the two processes of greatest interest to **schedule**: the one that was running when **schedule** was called (**prev**) and the one that should be given the CPU next (**next**). Keep in mind that **prev** and **next** can be the same; **schedule** can reschedule the process that already had the CPU.

34257: As I mention in Chapter 6, this is where softirqs—and hence the "bottom halves" of interrupt handlers—are run.

34268: Implements part of the kernel's realtime, round-robin scheduler (**SCHED_RR**) by moving an "exhausted" RR process—one that has used up its timeslice—to the end of the queue, so that other RR processes with the same priority have their shot. At the same time, this replenishes the exhausted process's timeslice. It's important that it does not do this for **SCHED_FIFO**, so that, as intended, the **SCHED_FIFO** processes won't yield when their timeslices happen to run out.

34272: **schedule** is often in use because some other piece of code has decided the process must be moved into or out of the **TASK_RUNNING** state—for example, if the hardware condition for which a process was waiting has occurred—so this **switch** changes the process's state, if necessary. If the process is already in the **TASK_RUNNING** state, it's left alone. If it was interruptible (waiting for a signal) and a signal arrived for the process, it is returned to the **TASK_RUNNING** state. In all other cases (for example, the process has entered the **TASK_UNINTERRUPTIBLE** state), the process should be removed from the run queue.

34289: **c** tracks the best "goodness" of all processes in the run queue—the process with the best goodness is the one with the best claim to the CPU. (I examine **goodness** shortly.) Higher goodness values are better—the reverse of the

weird situation Unix users are used to seeing, in which a higher priority (usually called a higher "niceness" level) means a process gets less CPU time. (At least things make sense inside the kernel.)

34290: If the process that holds the CPU now is still in the **TASK_RUNNING** state, the default values for **next** and **c** are computed differently: **prev** is the process to beat, not the idle task, and execution temporarily jumps ahead to line 34392 to arrange this. You'll see why in just a moment.

On the face of it, it would seem more efficient to move lines 34290 and 34291 before line 34288, so that **next** and **c** would be initialized only once. However, the resulting assembler is not obviously better or worse, and the difference, if any, is hard to measure.

34294: Begins to walk the run queue, tracking the runnable process with the best goodness. **tmp** is technically the loop iterator, but the point of this loop is really to walk **p** over each process in the run queue. Note that this code changes its notion of the best process only when the current record is broken, not when it's merely tied. Hence, ties are broken in favor of the first process in the queue.

You can also see now why **prev** is preferred to the idle task at line 34290 when **prev** is still contending for the CPU. Not only does this minimize swaps at line 34300, it also avoids some inexpedient context switches. If the best process other than **prev** is merely tied with **prev**, the tie will be broken in **prev**'s favor, even if **prev** appears later in the run queue.

34296: Only processes that can be scheduled are considered in this loop. The SMP version of the **can_schedule** macro is at line 33860. Its definition causes an SMP kernel to consider scheduling a task on this CPU only if the task is not already running on a CPU. (Which makes

perfect sense—it's wasteful to shuffle the tasks around unnecessarily.) The UP version is at line 33866 and is always true. In other words, in the UP case, every process in the run queue contends for the system's only CPU.

34305: A goodness of 0 means that the process has used up its timeslice. If **c** is 0 at the end of the loop, at least one process was contending for the CPU and every process contending for the CPU has used up its timeslice. (A process can be in the run queue but not contending for the CPU if its **SCHED_YIELD** flag was set; in this case, its goodness is negative. The idle task, which also has a negative goodness, is not contending for the CPU in this sense.) **schedule** jumps ahead to line 34378 to recalculate the processes' counters; the new counter value is half the old value plus the process's static priority—and because the old value is usually 0, **schedule** is usually just reinitializing the counters to their static priority values.

34334: Increments the kernel's internal context-switch count. This is one of several such statistics tracked by the kernel; see lines 19761 through 19778 for others. These statistics are useful for system tuning or monitoring.

34346: If **schedule** has chosen to schedule a different process from the one that was running before, it must switch to the new process's memory space, then suspend the old process and allow the new one to run. Switching control to the new process is handled by **switch_to**, which I explore in the next section. One important result of **switch_to** might seem very odd to application developers: The call to **schedule** doesn't return. Not right away, that is; it returns when the system switches back to the current task. As a special case, when **schedule** is being called because a task exited, that call to **schedule** never returns because the kernel never switches back to the task that exited. As another special case, if **schedule** didn't schedule a different process—that is, if **next** and **prev** are the same at the end of **schedule**—the context switch is not performed, and **schedule** does indeed return right away.

34369: The **__schedule_tail** and **reacquire_kernel_lock** functions at the (logical) end of **schedule** are no-ops on UP systems (except for clearing the task's **SCHED_YIELD** bit at line 34218), so this ends our examination of the core of the scheduler. Incidentally, to help ensure that you understand the code, try proving the following property to yourself: If the run queue is empty, the idle task will be scheduled next.

Context Switching

switch_to handles switching from one process to the next, which is called *context switching*; it's a very low-level feature that's handled differently on different processors.

In the classic picture of x86-based multitasking operating systems—and certainly in the picture Intel's designers had in mind—the OS uses a single hardware-supported TSS for each process in the system. (TSS stands for *task-state segment*, Intel's term for a CPU feature that supports hardware context switching.) However, because the CPU table normally used to store TSS pointers is a limited resource, Linux takes a different approach. Linux uses only one hardware-backed TSS per CPU, each TSS tracking the currently active process on that CPU. All of the information that classically would be stored in the CPU (using TSSs representing inactive processes) is instead tracked by the kernel, using two structures, **struct tss_struct** (line 14855) and **struct thread_struct** (line 14885).

Additional reasons for the kernel's nontraditional approach are documented in the banner comment above the function **__switch_to** (line 3632), which, along with the macro **switch_to** (line 16673), handles context switching.

Because so much of context switching depends on understanding how the kernel handles memory, which I don't address in detail until the next chapter, this chapter covers the topic superficially. The basic idea behind context switching is remembering where you were and what you were doing—that's the current context you must save—and then switching to another context that you saved previously. Using a little assembler, the **switch_to** macro saves two important pieces of the context, described next.

switch_to

16678: First, the **switch_to** macro saves the ESP register, which points to the process's current stack. The stack is discussed in depth in the next chapter; for now, you simply need to know that the stack holds local variables and function-call information. The next line restores the switched-to process's saved ESP register.

16680: The **switch_to** macro also saves the EIP register, which is the process's current instruction pointer—the address of the next instruction it would execute if it were going to be allowed to continue to run. The saved value for the instruction pointer is the address of the **popl** instruction at line 16684, which—when control switches back to this process—will restore the registers pushed onto the stack at the beginning of this macro, then proceed as if nothing had happened.

16681: Pushes **next->thread.eip**—the switched-to process's saved instruction pointer—onto the stack, making that the address returned to when the immediately subsequent **jmp** to **__switch_to** returns. The net effect is that when **__switch_to** returns, execution continues as the new process.

16682: Calls **__switch_to** (line 3632), which carries on the work of saving and restoring segment registers and page tables. Those magic words will make more sense after you read Chapter 8.

Computing the **goodness** Value

A process's goodness is evaluated by the function **goodness** (line 33886). **goodness** returns a value in one of

two classes: under 1,000 and over 1,000. Values over 1,000 are assigned only to realtime processes, and values from 0 through 999 are assigned only to nonrealtime processes. Indeed, the goodness values for nonrealtime processes occupy only the very bottom of this range, from 0 to 52 (or 0 to 67 for SMP, because SMP mode gives a process a bonus for staying on the same processor). The goodness values for realtime processes range from 1,001 to 1,099 on either SMP or UP.

What's important about these two classes is simply that the realtime range of values lies entirely above the nonrealtime range (so the offset could be, for example, 100 instead of 1,000). POSIX.1b makes the kernel responsible for ensuring that realtime processes are always preferred to nonrealtime processes when both are contending for the CPU. Because the scheduler always selects the process with the best goodness value—and because the goodness value of any realtime process that hasn't yielded the CPU always exceeds that of any nonrealtime process—Linux's compliance on this point is easy to demonstrate.

Despite the banner comment above **goodness**, the function never returns –1,000, although it can return values as low as –99 (for the idle process).

goodness is quite a simple function, yet it's a crucial part of the Linux scheduler. It's called for every process in the run queue every time **schedule** executes, so it has to be quick—but if it makes a bad decision, the whole system suffers. Considering these conflicting pressures, I think it would be hard to improve on what's here.

goodness

33895: Returns –1 if the process has yielded the CPU (the **SCHED_YIELD** bit will be cleared later through a call to **__schedule_tail**). Earlier kernels returned 0 in this case, but that caused unnecessary counter recalculations in **schedule** when, for example, the only user process in the run queue yielded the CPU.

33906: At this point, the code knows that this is a nonrealtime process. It initializes its goodness (called **weight** within the function) to its current counter value, so the process is less likely to get the CPU if it's already had it for a while or if it had a low priority to begin with.

33907: If **weight** is 0, the process's counter is used up, so **goodness** doesn't add in any more weighting factors. Other processes should get their chance. Otherwise, **weight** is in the range 1 through 11 on the x86, because counters are initialized using **NICE_TO_TICKS** (line 33814). (Note that **HZ** [line 13523] is 100 on the x86, so **NICE_TO_TICKS** uses the **TICK_SCALE** at line 33803, which divides by 4.)

33915: Adds in a largish bonus for staying on the same processor (SMP only—by the way, think about the implications of this for three processes running on a two-processor system). Since this bonus is 15 (see line 16384), **weight** is now in the range 1 through 26 (on SMP systems only).

33920: Adds a small bonus for sticking with the current process or within the current thread, which helps to exploit the cache and avoid expensive MMU context switches. **weight** is now in the range 1 through 12 on UP, or 1 through 27 on SMP.

33922: Adds in the process's priority, as calculated from its **nice** value. This way, **goodness** (and thus the scheduler) will tend to favor higher-priority processes over lower-priority processes, even when the former have partially used up their timeslices. **weight** now lies in the range 2 through 52 on UP systems, or 2 through 67 on SMP systems, and this is where the calculation ends for nonrealtime processes.

33929: If it's a realtime process, **goodness** returns a value placing it in the higher class; precisely where depends on its **rt_priority** value.

33931: Returns the computed goodness.

As a final note, **goodness** is called from one place other than the scheduler: It's also called from the function **preemption_goodness** (line 33938). Loosely speaking, this function measures the relative goodness of two processes. That, in turn, helps other code decide whether to raise a process's **need_resched** flag in order to allow a more deserving process to have a shot at the CPU—see line 34031, for example.

Nonrealtime Priorities

Every Linux process has a niceness value, an integer from –20 to 19, whose value is stored in the **struct task_struct**'s **nice** member. (For realtime processes, an additional member in **struct task_struct**—the **rt_priority** member—also applies. Further discussion follows shortly.) The extent of this range is bounded by **PRIO_MIN** (**#defin**ed to –20 at line 21627) and **PRIO_MAX** (**#defin**ed to 20 one line after)—theoretically, that is. Irritatingly, the functions that control priority—**sys_setpriority** and **sys_nice**—don't actually pay any attention to these manifest constants, preferring hard-coded values instead. (They also correctly use a maximum niceness value of 19, not 20.) For that matter, the **PRIO_MIN** and **PRIO_MAX** constants aren't used anywhere. Well, that's another opportunity for an enterprising reader to improve the code.

Because **sys_nice** (line 34542) is documented to be obsolescent—presumably to be reimplemented in terms of **sys_setpriority**—let's ignore it and explore **sys_setpriority**.

sys_setpriority

36737: **sys_setpriority** takes three arguments—**which**, **who**, and **niceval**. The **which** and **who** arguments provide a way to specify either a single process, a process group, or all processes owned by a given user. **who** is interpreted differently depending on the value of **which**; it will be read as a process ID, a process group ID, or a user ID.

36743: This is a sanity check, ensuring that **which** is valid. I think it's unnecessarily obscure. Instead of

```
if (which > 2 || which < 0)
```

it should probably read more like

```
if (which != PRIO_PROCESS &&
    which != PRIO_PGRP &&
    which != PRIO_USER)
```

or at least

```
if (which > PRIO_USER || which <
PRIO_PGRP)
```

36749: **niceval**, as the variable name indicates, is a niceness value, not a priority, and it must lie in the range –20 through 19. So, **sys_setpriority** must jump through a few hoops to truncate **niceval** values outside the allowed range.

36755: Loops through all the tasks in the system's list of tasks, making the changes it's permitted to make. **proc_sel** (line 36715) tells whether the given process satisfies the **which** and **who** values that are used to select a process; it's factored out of **sys_setpriority** because it's also used by **sys_getpriority**.

Both **sys_setpriority** and **sys_getpriority** (which has a similar inner loop, starting at line 36789) could be sped up a bit for the common case of getting or setting the priority of a single process. (This can be done by breaking the **for_each_task** loop early, if nothing else, although it would be faster to use **find_task_by_pid** to jump directly to the desired process.) **sys_setpriority** isn't called very often, but **sys_getpriority** might be common enough to repay the effort.

Default Timeslices and update_process_times

sys_setpriority affects only the process's **nice** member—that is, its static priority. Recall that processes also have dynamic priorities, represented by the **counter**

member, which you saw in the discussions of **schedule** and **goodness**. You already saw that **schedule** periodically replenishes each process's dynamic priority, based on its static priority, when the scheduler sees that **counter** is 0. But you haven't yet seen the other piece of the puzzle: Where is **counter** decremented? *How* does it reach 0? The answers determine the *default timeslice*—that is, the maximum amount of time a process with normal priority may run before the kernel considers preempting it. Choosing a good timeslice is as much art as science; up to a point, shorter timeslices can slow processing down (because of context-switching overhead) while seeming to speed the system up (because it responds more quickly to user input).

So what is the default timeslice? For UP, the answer lies in **update_process_times** (line 40166). (Again, I defer discussing SMP issues until Chapter 10.) **update_process_times** is called as part of **do_timer** (line 40257), which in turn is part of the timer interrupt, discussed in Chapter 6. As a result, it's invoked quite frequently—100 times per second. (That's frequent on the human scale only, of course—it's a glacial pace for a CPU.) On each invocation, it decrements the current process's **counter** by one "tick" (one hundredth of a second, or 10 milliseconds—see Chapter 6). When the counter drops to or below 0, **update_process_times** raises the process's **need_resched** flag, indicating that this process needs to be rescheduled.

Now, because a process's default niceness value is 0, it gets by default a six-tick timeslice: 60 milliseconds, pretty close to the target documented at line 33800. (Recall that **NICE_TO_TICKS**, line 33814, does this translation.) Interestingly, a different default is suggested by line 22094.

Even 60 milliseconds might seem like a long timeslice, but it's not so bad. After all, processes frequently don't use up their entire timeslice, because they often must block for I/O. And when several processes are CPU-bound, switching between them too frequently serves no purpose. (Especially on an architecture such as the x86, where context switches are relatively expensive.) Finally, I have to confess that I never noticed any slug-

gishness in my GNU Linux box's response times, so I suppose the 60-millisecond timeslice is a good choice.

If for some reason you need timeslices even longer than the current maximum (110 milliseconds, as **counter** ranges up to 11 on the x86), you can simply use the **SCHED_FIFO** scheduling policy and yield the CPU when you're good and ready—or rewrite **sys_setpriority** and **sys_nice**.

Realtime Priorities

Linux's realtime processes add a level to the priority scheme. The realtime priority is held in the **rt_priority** member of **struct task_struct** and it's an integer ranging from 0 through 99. (A value of 0 means the process is not a realtime process, in which case its **policy** member must be **SCHED_OTHER**.)

Realtime tasks still use the same **counter** member as their nonrealtime counterparts, so their dynamic priorities are handled the same way. Realtime tasks even use the **nice** member for the same purpose as nonrealtime tasks, as the value with which to replenish **counter** when it's used up. To clarify, **rt_priority** is used only to rank realtime processes against one another—they're otherwise handled exactly the same way as nonrealtime processes.

A process's **rt_priority** is set as part of setting its scheduling policy with the POSIX.1b-mandated functions **sched_setscheduler** and **sched_setparam** (which only root is normally allowed to call, as you'll see when I discuss capabilities). Note that this means that a process's scheduling policy can change over its lifetime, assuming that it has permission to make the change.

The system calls implementing these POSIX functions, **sys_sched_setscheduler** (line 34648) and **sys_sched_setparam** (line 34654), both delegate all the real work to **setscheduler** (line 34579).

setscheduler

34579: The three arguments to this function are **pid**, the target process (0 means the current process); **policy**, the new scheduling policy; and **param**, a **struct** containing additional information—the new value for **rt_priority**.

34591: Following some sanity checks, **setscheduler** copies the supplied **struct sched_param** from user space. **struct sched_param**, defined at line 21773, has just one member, **sched_priority**, which is the caller's desired **rt_priority** for the target process.

34599: Finds the target process using **find_process_by_pid** (line 34570), which returns either a pointer to the current task, if **pid** is 0; a pointer to the process with the given PID, if one exists; or **NULL**, if no process has that PID.

34605: If the **policy** argument was negative, the current scheduling policy is retained. Otherwise, it is accepted for now, if it's a valid value.

34617: Ensures that the priority is in range. This is enforced in a somewhat tricky way. This line is just the first step, ensuring that the supplied value is not wildly out of range.

34619: The new realtime priority is now known to lie between 0 and 99, inclusive. This test will fail if **policy** is **SCHED_OTHER** but the new realtime priority is not 0. The test also fails if **policy** denotes one of the realtime schedulers but the new realtime priority is 0 (if it's not 0 here, it's 1 through 99, which is what it should be). Otherwise, the test succeeds. This is not very readable, but it's correct, minimal, and (I imagine) fast. I'm not sure that speed is critical here, though—how often does a process set its scheduler, after all? The following would be more readable and surely not much slower:

```
if (policy == SCHED_OTHER) {
  if (lp.sched_priority != 0)
    goto out_unlock;
} else {  /* SCHED_FIFO or SCHED_RR */
  if ((lp.sched_priority < 1) ||
      (lp.sched_priority > 99))
    goto out_unlock;
}
```

34624: Not just any process should be allowed to set its own scheduling policy or that of another process. If this were the case, any process could usurp the CPU, effectively locking up the system, simply by setting its scheduling policy to **SCHED_FIFO** and entering an infinite loop. Clearly, that mustn't be allowed. For this reason, **setscheduler** allows a process to set its own scheduling policy to a realtime policy only if it has the capability to do so. I cover capabilities in more detail in the next section.

34627: Along the same lines, you don't want just anyone to be able to change the scheduling policy of any other user's processes; normally, you should be allowed to change the scheduling policy of your own processes only. Therefore, **setscheduler** ensures that the user either is setting his own process's scheduler or has the capability to set anyone's scheduling policy.

34633: Here's where **setscheduler** gets down to business at last, setting the **policy** and **rt_priority** fields in the target process's **struct task_struct**. If it's in the run queue (elegantly tested, at line 22560, by checking that its **next_run** member is non-**NULL**), the process is moved to the front of the run queue. This helps a new **SCHED_FIFO** or **SCHED_RR** process, which presumably has urgent business, get its shot at the CPU, and it doesn't hurt in the nonrealtime case. The process is marked for rescheduling and **setscheduler** cleans up and exits.

Respecting Limits

The kernel frequently must decide whether to allow a process to perform an operation. The process simply isn't allowed to do some operations, and is allowed to do some other operations only in restricted circumstances. These operations generally are expressed by capabilities and/or deduced from user and group IDs. Other times, a process is allowed to do something, but only up to a limit—for example, its CPU usage might be bounded.

Capabilities

In the preceding section, you saw an example of checking capabilities—the same capability twice, in fact. This was the **CAP_SYS_NICE** capability (line 17976), which controls whether a process should be allowed to set priorities (niceness levels) or scheduling policies. Because it applies to more than just niceness levels, **CAP_SYS_NICE** is a bit of a misnomer—although it's easy to see that setting a scheduler is a closely related concept and you likely won't want one capability without the other.

Every process has three sets of capabilities, stored in the process's **struct task_struct** (and located at lines 22013 through 22014):

- **cap_effective**—The effective set

- **cap_permitted**—The permitted set

- **cap_inheritable**—The inheritable set

A process's effective set of capabilities is the set of things it's currently allowed to do. This is the set checked by the widely used **capable** function, which is defined at line 22393.

The permitted set limits the capabilities a process normally can be granted. This set usually doesn't grow, with one exception: If a process has the **CAP_SETPCAP** capability, it can give other processes any capability in its own permitted set, even if the target process doesn't already have it.

If a capability is in the permitted set and not in the effective set, the process doesn't have the capability right now, but it can acquire the capability by asking for it. Why bother with this distinction? Well, when first discussing capabilities at the beginning of the chapter, I briefly considered the example of a long-running process that needed a capability only occasionally. To ensure that the process doesn't accidentally abuse the capability, the process can wait until it needs the capability, ask for it, carry out the privileged operation, and then drop the capability again. It's safer that way.

The inheritable set isn't quite what you might expect. It's not the set of capabilities that a parent process passes along to its child when it **forks**—indeed, at the moment of creation (that is, immediately following the **fork**), all three of the child's capability sets are the same as its parent's. Instead, the inheritable set comes into play during **exec**. The process's inheritable set before calling **exec** helps to determine the permitted and inheritable sets that it will retain after the **exec**—see **compute_creds** (line 11650) for the details. Note that whether a capability is retained following **exec** depends only partly on the process's inheritable set; it also depends partly on capability bits set in the file itself. (That's the plan, anyway—this feature is not completely implemented yet.)

Given these definitions, here are some of the relationships among the three sets. To begin with, the permitted set must always be a superset of, or the same set as, the effective set and the inheritable set. (Well, that's not quite true. Strictly speaking, the permitted set might not be a superset of the inheritable set. One process might expand another process's inheritable set so that it no longer is a subset of its permitted set, but this would be pointless as far as I can tell, so you can ignore the possibility from now on.) However, contrary to what you might expect, the effective set need not be a superset of, or the same set as, the inheritable set. That is, after an **exec**, the process might have a capability that it didn't have before, although the capability must have been in its permitted set—that is, a capability that the original *could have* acquired for itself. This is so that the process doesn't need to temporarily acquire a capability it has no use for, just so that it can **exec** a program that needs it.

Figure 7.5 illustrates the possibilities. It shows the three capability sets for a hypothetical process, with the bits numbered right to left. The process is permitted to obtain the **CAP_KILL** capability, which allows it to kill any other process regardless of owner, but it doesn't have that capability right now and won't gain it automatically upon **exec**. It currently has the capability to insert and remove kernel modules (using **CAP_SYS_MODULE**), but it won't gain that capability upon **exec**, either. It could obtain the **CAP_SYS_NICE** capability and will obtain it upon **exec** (assuming the file's capability bits agree). Finally, it can change the system's time right now (**CAP_SYS_TIME**) and it will retain this ability across an **exec** (again, assuming the file's capability bits agree). Neither this process, nor any that it might **exec**, can acquire any other capabilities unless the capability is supplied by some other process that has the **CAP_SETPCAP** capability.

The code for enforcing these various properties mostly lives in kernel/capability.c, which starts at line 29457. The two main functions are **sys_capget** (line 29479), which reads capabilities, and **sys_capset** (line 29588), which sets them. I discuss these later in this section. Inheriting capabilities across an **exec** is handled by fs/exec.c's **compute_creds** (line 11650), as I already mentioned.

Root, of course, typically has all capabilities. The kernel capabilities feature provides root a structured way to selectively grant only needed capabilities to a given process, regardless of whether the process is running as root.

An interesting property of capabilities is that they can be used to change the "flavor" of the system. As a simple example, setting the **CAP_SYS_NICE** capability for all processes would enable all processes to raise their own priorities (and set their schedulers, and so forth). If you change the way every process experiences the system, you change the system itself. I'll leave it to you to imagine inventing new kernel capabilities that allow tailoring the system in more exciting ways.

One perhaps under-recognized benefit of capabilities is that they clarify the source code. When the code is checking whether the current process should be allowed to set the system's time, being forced to ask instead whether the current process is being run by root isn't very intuitive. Capabilities enable you to say what you mean. The existence of capabilities even helps to clarify code that inquires about a process's user or group ID, because code that does so, presumably, is interested in the answer to that question, not in something else that can be deduced from it. Otherwise, that code would have asked specifically what it wanted to know, using capabilities. This property will become more reliable as capabilities are further integrated into the Linux kernel code.

Capability Constants and Macros

17807: The kernel's recognized capabilities start here. Because these **#defines** are liberally commented, I won't go into detail about each one in the text.

18030: The numbers assigned to each capability are simply consecutive integers, but because they're used to address bits within an **unsigned int**, they're converted to powers of two by the **CAP_TO_MASK** macro.

18031: The heart of setting and checking capabilities is just a set of simple bit manipulations; some macros and inline functions to clarify the bit manipulations are defined from here to the end of include/linux/capability.h.

sys_capget

29479: **sys_capget** takes two arguments: **header**, of type **cap_user_header_t** (line 17770), is a pointer to a **struct** defining the version of capabilities in use and supplying the target process's PID. **dataptr**, of type **cap_user_data_t** (line 17776), is also a pointer to a **struct** type—this **struct** contains the effective, permitted, and inheritable sets. **sys_capget** returns information through **dataptr**.

29491: In case of a version mismatch, **sys_capget** returns the version in use through the **header** pointer and then returns the **EINVAL** error (or the **EFAULT** error, if it was unable to copy the version information into the caller's space).

29508: Identifies the process whose capabilities the caller wants to know about. If **pid** is not 0 or the current process's PID, **sys_capget** searches for it.

29519: If **sys_capget** was able to locate the target process, it copies its capabilities into a temporary variable, **data**.

29529: If everything has gone well so far, **sys_capget** copies the capabilities back into the user's space, to the address supplied by the **dataptr** argument. Afterward, it returns the **error** variable. As usual, this is 0 if everything was okay and an error number otherwise.

sys_capset

29588: The arguments for **sys_capset** are almost the same as for **sys_capget**. The difference is that **data** (no longer named **dataptr**) is **const**. I suspect that this is intended to restrict us from modifying what **data** points to, but it actually restricts us from modifying **data** itself, so that it can't be made to point anywhere else.

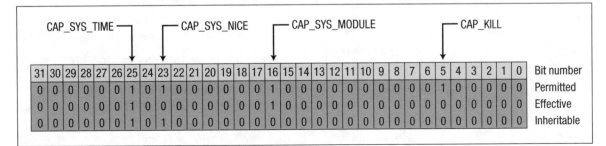

Figure 7.5   Capability sets.

29596: As with **sys_capget**, **sys_capset** ensures that the kernel and the calling process are using compatible versions of the capability system. If not, it rejects the attempt.

29609: If **pid** is nonzero, indicating that the caller wants to set the capabilities of another process, the attempt should be rejected in most cases. **sys_capset** allows the attempt anyway if the caller has the **CAP_SETPCAP** capability, which means that it's allowed to set the capabilities of any process. The first part of this test is a little too restrictive: It should also accept **pid** if it equals the caller's **pid**.

29612: Copies the new capabilities from user space and returns an error if this fails.

29623: Similar to the **sys_capget** code starting at line 29508, **sys_capset** identifies the process whose capabilities the caller wants to know about. The difference is that, here, it also allows negative values for **pid**, to specify process groups (or –1 specifies all processes). In such a case, **target** is still set to **current**, so the caller's capabilities are used in the subsequent calculations.

29638: **sys_capset** now must ensure that the new capability sets are taking on legitimate, and internally consistent, values. This test verifies that the new process's inheritable set doesn't include anything new, unless the new feature is in the caller's permitted set. Therefore, it's not giving away any capabilities the caller doesn't already have.

29645: Similarly, **sys_capset** ensures that the target's permitted set doesn't include anything that it didn't already have, unless the caller has it, too. So, again, it's not giving away any capabilities the caller doesn't already have.

29653: Recall that the process's effective set must be a subset of its permitted set. That property is enforced here.

29661: **sys_capset** is now ready to make the requested changes. A negative **pid** means it's changing capabilities for more than one process: all processes, if **pid** is –1, or all processes in a process group, if **pid** is any other negative value. In these cases, the work is done by **cap_set_all** (line 29558) or by **cap_set_pg** (line 29538), respectively; these simply loop through the appropriate set of processes, overwriting the capability sets for each in much the same way as for a single process.

29671: If **pid** is positive (or 0, which means the current process), the capability sets are assigned for the target process only.

User and Group IDs

As useful and powerful as capabilities are, they're not the only access-control weapon in the kernel's armory. In some circumstances, you need to know who's running a process, or whom the process is running as. Users are identified with integer user IDs, and a user also belongs to one or more groups, each of which has its own integer ID.

There are two flavors of user and group IDs: real and effective. Loosely, the *real* user (or group) ID tells you who created the process, and the *effective* user (or group) ID tells you whom the process is running as, in case that has changed. Because access control decisions depend more on whom the process is running as than on who created the process, the kernel checks effective user (or group) IDs more often than the real ones—in the code we're concerned with at the moment, anyway. The corresponding members of **struct task_struct** are **uid**, **euid**, **gid**, and **egid** (lines 22009 through 22010). Note that the user ID is different from the username; the former is an integer, the latter is a text string. The /etc/passwd file correlates the two.

Let's return once more to **sys_setpriority** and have a closer look at some code that I glossed over before, in lines 36758 and 36759. The intended behavior of **sys_setpriority** is to let any user lower the priority of

his own processes, but not the priority of anyone else's processes—unless the user has the **CAP_SYS_NICE** capability, that is. So, the first two terms of the **if** expression check whether the target process's user ID matches either the real or effective user ID of **sys_setpriority**'s caller. If neither is the case, and if **CAP_SYS_NICE** is not set, **sys_setpriority** correctly rejects the attempt.

Processes can change their own user and group IDs— if allowed—with **sys_setuid** and **sys_setgid** (lines 37112 and 36954), among other functions. User and group IDs can also be changed by **exec**ing a setuid or setgid executable.

Resource Limits

The kernel can be instructed to limit a process's use of various resources, including memory and CPU time. This is done with **sys_setrlimit** (line 37615). You can get an idea of the supported limits by looking at **struct rusage** (line 21598). Process-specific limits are tracked in— where else?—**struct task_struct**; see the **rlim** array member at line 22018.

The result of violating a limit is different for different limits. For example, for **RLIMIT_NPROC** (line 15090)—the limit on the number of processes a user can have—the result is simply that **fork** fails, as you can see in line 31037. The consequences of exceeding other limits can be more serious for the process. Exceeding the CPU time limit, for example, gets a process killed (see line 40115), as I mention briefly in Chapter 6. A process can ask about a specific limit by using **sys_getrlimit** (line 37582) or about its resource usage so far by using **sys_getrusage** (line 37707).

At line 37627, notice that a process can decrease its own resource limits at will, but it can increase its own limits only up to a maximum value that can be set independently for each limit. Hence, the current and maximum resource limits are tracked independently (using the **rlim_cur** and **rlim_max** members of **struct rlimit**, defined at line 21622). Processes with the **CAP_SYS_RESOURCE** capability, however, can override the maximum.

Contrast that with the rules for priorities: A process is allowed to lower its own priority, but it needs special permission to raise its priority, even in cases where it lowers its own priority and then wants to raise it again immediately. The twin notions of a current and maximum resource limit are not mirrored in the kernel's scheme for priorities. Also, observe that one process can change the priority of another (assuming it has permission, of course), but a process can change only its own resource limits.

All Good Things Must Come to an End—Here's How They Do It

You've seen how processes are born and how they're given their respective slices of life. Now, it's time to contemplate how they die.

exit

You can kill a process against its wish by sending it signal 9 (**SIGKILL**), as discussed in Chapter 6, but a voluntary exit is more common. Processes exit voluntarily by invoking the system call **exit**, which is implemented in the kernel with **sys_exit** (line 30325). (Incidentally, when a C program returns from **main**, it implicitly calls **exit**.) When a process exits, the kernel must free up all resources allocated to the process—memory, files, and so on—and, of course, stop giving it the CPU.

The kernel doesn't immediately deallocate the **struct task_struct** that represents the process, however, because the process's parent must be able to query for the child's exit status with the **wait** system call. **wait** returns the PID of the child whose death it reports, so applications could get confused if the dead child's PID were reallocated before the parent had **wait**ed on it. Among other problems, the same parent could end up with two children—one alive, one dead—with the same PID, and the parent wouldn't know which had exited. Consequently, the kernel must reserve the dead child's PID until the **wait** occurs. This is done automatically just by keeping its **struct task_struct** around; the code for allocating PIDs simply doesn't ask whether the processes it finds in the task list are alive.

Processes in this in-between state—no longer alive, yet not truly dead—are called *zombies*. **sys_exit**'s job, then, is to turn a living process into a zombie.

sys_exit itself is trivial; it simply converts the exit code into the format that **do_exit** expects, and then calls **do_exit**, which handles the real work. (**do_exit** is also called as part of sending signals, as I discuss in Chapter 6.)

do_exit

30262: **do_exit** takes the exit code as an argument and has the unusual symbol **NORET_TYPE** before its return type. Although **NORET_TYPE** (line 19643) is currently defined to be an empty comment—so it has no effect—it used to be **#define**d to **__volatile__**, which indicated to gcc that the function did not return. In light of this knowledge, gcc performed some additional optimizations and suppressed a warning about the function's failure to return. With its new definition, **NORET_TYPE** no longer has any effect on the compiler, but it is retained because it still conveys useful information to human readers.

30279: Frees its allocated memory, which I cover in Chapter 8.

30282: Frees its semaphores and other System V IPC structures, which I cover in Chapter 9.

30283: Releases its allocated files, as I discuss shortly.

30284: Releases its file system data, which is beyond the scope of this book.

30285: Releases its signal handler table, which I cover in Chapter 6.

30295: The exiting task's exit code is remembered for future use by its parent.

30296: Calls the liberally commented function **exit_notify** (line 30173), which puts the process in the **TASK_ZOMBIE** state and then alerts the exiting task's parent and the members of its process group to their compatriot's demise.

30297: Calls **schedule** (line 34237) to give away the CPU. This call to **schedule** never returns, because it switches context to another process and never switches back, so this is the last time the exiting process ever has the CPU.

Reference Counting and put_files_struct

How processes interact with files is not a major topic of this book. But we should take a quick look at **put_files_struct** (line 30051), because it will help complement our picture of **__clone**. Earlier, I discussed the **__clone** function, which let the parent and child processes share certain information. One of the components that the parent and child can share is their list of open files. As mentioned earlier, Linux uses a reference-counting scheme to ensure that processes can correctly clean up after themselves. Well, here's a good example of some of that cleanup.

put_files_struct

30051: Assuming the process had any open files (it nearly always will), **__exit_files** (line 30067), which is called by **do_exit**, calls **put_files_struct** to drop the current process's reference to its associated **struct files_struct**.

30053: The first step is to decrement the reference count that was originally held in **tsk->files->count**. Atomic operations, such as **atomic_dec_and_test**, are covered completely in Chapter 10; for now, suffice it to say that **atomic_dec_and_test** (line 12202) decrements its argument and returns true when the argument's new value is 0. Hence, it's true when **tsk**'s reference to the **struct files_struct** in question was the last. (If this was a private copy, not shared by any other process, then the reference count was initially 1, and it was certainly decremented to 0.)

30054: Before freeing the memory that is tracking the process's open files, all the files must be closed, which is done by calling **close_files** (line 30027).

30057: Frees the memory that holds the process's file descriptor array, **fd**, which is a subfield of **files**. When the number of open files is relatively small, the file descriptor data is held in **struct files_struct**'s **fd_array** member (line 21825). This avoids the expense of a separate allocation as well as the expense of freeing the memory here.

30059: Similarly, the process's heap-allocated file descriptor sets are freed.

30063: Last of all, **put_files_struct** frees **files** itself.

The concept behind the other **__exit_*x.x.x*** functions (and their helpers, such as **put_files_struct**) is similar: They decrement the task's own reference count to the potentially shared information, and if it was the last reference, they do whatever they need to do to free it all up.

wait

Like **exec**, **wait** is a family of functions rather than a single function. (Unlike **exec**, however, the **wait** family of functions actually includes a member named **wait**.) All the functions in the **wait** family are ultimately implemented in the kernel by a single system call, **sys_wait4** (line 30330), whose name reflects the fact that it's implementing the most general function in the **wait** family, **wait4**. Implementations of libc, the standard C library, must rearrange the arguments of calls to other **wait** functions and invoke **sys_wait4** instead. (Well, that's not the whole story: On most platforms, the kernel also provides **sys_waitpid**, for historical reasons. However, even **sys_waitpid** turns around and calls **sys_wait4**.)

Among other things, **sys_wait4**—and only **sys_wait4**—sends a zombie to the grave at last. From an application's point of view, however, **wait** and friends are for checking on the status of a child process: seeing whether any died and, if so, which ones died and how.

sys_wait4

30330: As befits a highly general function, **sys_wait4** has lots of parameters, some of which are optional:

- **pid**—As always, the target process's PID; zero and negative values are special, as you'll see.

- **stat_addr**—If non-**NULL**, the address to which the reaped child's exit status should be copied.

- **options**—A set of flags that can modify **sys_wait4**'s behavior.

- **ru**—If non-**NULL**, the address to which the reaped child's resource usage information should be copied.

30338: If given any invalid options, **sys_wait4** returns a failure code. This decision seems a bit harsh; we might consider just ignoring the irrelevant flags. The argument for doing it this way, of course, is that if the caller turned on bits that it didn't mean to, it might be expecting behavior that it's not going to get. In any case, it means that the caller is confused, and it's better to signal a failure in this case than to silently ignore the caller's confusion.

30350: Loops over all the process's immediate children (but not its grandchildren, great-grandchildren, and so on). As I mentioned earlier in the chapter, the process's youngest (most recently created) child is accessible through the **p_cptr** member of **struct task_struct**, and this youngest child's list of older siblings is available through its **p_osptr** member. Therefore, **sys_wait4** walks over all the parent's children by beginning with the youngest child and iterating over progressively older siblings.

30351: Filters out unsuitable PIDs, based on the value of the **pid** argument. Note how a **pid** argument of –1 will potentially select any process, as desired: That **pid** value fails the tests at lines 30351, 30354, and 30357, so it's never rejected. Therefore, it causes every child to be considered.

30389: This is the case we're currently interested in—the parent is waiting on a terminated child. Here

is where the zombie is truly reaped at last. It begins by updating the parent's notion of the user and system time used by its child processes (which is accessed through the **sys_times** system call, line 37294), because the child won't be around to participate in the calculation anymore.

30395: Other resource usage information is gathered (if it was requested) and the child's exit status is transferred to the specified address (again, if it was requested).

30400: Sets **retval** to the PID of the dead child being reaped. This is final; **retval** will not change again.

30401: If the moribund process's current parent is not its original parent—recall that this means that the process is being traced or debugged—the process disengages itself from its current location in the process graph (via **REMOVE_LINKS**, line 22520), reinstalls itself under its original parent (via **SET_LINKS**, line 22531), and then sends its parent the **SIGCHLD** signal, so that the parent knows that its child exited. The notification is delivered via **do_notify_parent** (line 35702, covered in Chapter 6).

30409: Otherwise—the normal case—**release_task** (line 29880) can at last be called to release the reaped child's **struct task_struct**. (I'll look at **release_task** in a moment, after finishing up with **sys_wait4**.)

30410: The child has now been successfully reaped, so **sys_wait4** pretty much just needs to return success; it jumps to line 30431, where it returns **retval** (the reaped child's PID).

30412: Note the unusual flow control; the **default** case **continues** the **for** loop that began at line 30350. Because the **default** case is reached only for processes that are neither stopped nor zombies, this flow control is correct, but easy to miss on a first reading. It's superfluous anyway, though; the loop would behave identically (and generate the same code) without it.

30417: The preceding loop is repeated for every thread in the calling process's thread group. (A thread is added to a thread group only by supplying the **CLONE_THREAD** flag to **do_fork**—see line 31147.)

30420: If this point is reached, the **for** loop ran to completion—the calling process iterated over its entire list of children without finding one to reap. The computation is now in one of three states: no child has yet exited, none of the task's children was matched by the supplied **pid** argument, or (a special case of the preceding) the task had no children at all.

30422: If **flag** is nonzero, line 30371 was reached during the **for** loop, indicating that at least one child process matched the supplied **pid** argument— it just wasn't a zombie or stopped, so it couldn't be reaped. In this case, if the **WNOHANG** option was supplied—meaning that the caller doesn't want to wait if no children could be reaped— this jumps ahead to the end, returning zero.

30425: If a signal was received, the function exits with an error. This signal probably was not **SIGCHLD**—if it were, a dead child would have been found, so this point wouldn't have been reached. However, in an SMP system, it's possible for the child to exit on another CPU after this CPU had iterated past it. This would lead to a strange result: **sys_wait4**'s exiting with an error because it received a signal indicating a child task's death.

30427: Otherwise, everything's okay; the caller just needs to wait for a child to exit. So the process's state is set to **TASK_INTERRUPTIBLE** (see line 30345) and **schedule** is invoked to hand off the CPU to another process. **schedule** won't return until the waiting process has another shot at the CPU, at which time it checks again for a dead child (by jumping back to the **repeat** label at line 30343). Recall that in the **TASK_INTERRUPTIBLE**

state, a process is waiting to be awakened by a signal—in this case, it's specifically hoping for a **SIGCHLD**, indicating that a child process has exited, but any signal could arrive.

30430: **flag** was 0, because either the process has no children or the supplied **pid** argument doesn't match any of its children—either way, **sys_wait4** returns the **ECHILD** error to the caller.

release_task

29880: **release_task**'s sole argument is a pointer to the **struct task_struct** to release.

29882: Ensures that the task is not trying to **release_task** itself—a nonsensical situation that would indicate a logic error in the kernel.

29898: The UP code really gets started by calling **free_uid** (line 40500), which frees the potentially shared **struct user_struct** that, among other things, helps **fork** ensure that a single user doesn't hog all the processes.

29899: Through a call to **unhash_process** (line 22563), **release_task** reduces the system's count of the total number of running tasks, releases the dying process's PID, and unlinks it from the process graph and the task list with **REMOVE_LINKS** (line 22520).

29902: The dying process's counts of minor page faults, major page faults, and the number of times that it was swapped out are added to the corresponding "child counts" of the current process. This is correct; **release_task** is called only by **sys_wait4**, which allows processes to release only their own children. Hence, the current process must be the parent of the dying one.

29916: Last of all, it's time to reclaim the moribund process's **struct task_struct**, which is accomplished by a call to **free_task_struct** (line 14982). This macro simply reclaims the pages that store the **struct**. And now, at last, the process is well and truly dead.

As a final note, who says programmers are Philistines? The quote at line 29952 is from Gilbert and Sullivan's comic opera *The Pirates of Penzance*. It comes shortly after the song "Model of a Modern Major-General"; the General asks it of the King. Line 29972 is the King's reply.

Chapter 8

Memory

Memory is one of the most important resources that the kernel manages. One characteristic that distinguishes one process from another is that two processes live in logically separate memory spaces (threads, by contrast, share most of their memory). Even if the processes are both instances of the same program—for example, two xterm or two Emacs processes—the kernel arranges for each process to see memory as if it were the only process running on the system. System security and stability are improved when one process cannot, accidentally or maliciously, scribble over another's working space.

The kernel, too, lives in its own memory space. This is known as *kernel space*, as opposed to *user space*, a general term for any nonkernel task's memory space.

Virtual Memory

Computer systems are built with several levels of storage. Figure 8.1 illustrates the most important of these, with approximate numbers drawn from my own original GNU/Linux box. The levels get larger but slower (and cheaper, per byte) as you progress to the right of the figure. Specifically, you can see that access speeds span six orders of magnitude—a factor of 1,000,000— but capacity spans more than eight orders of magnitude—a factor of 312,500,000. (The speed difference can be masked somewhat in practice, but these figures are good enough for purposes of this discussion.) The largest gap is the last one, the gap between RAM (or primary storage) and disk (or secondary storage).

All that additional storage capacity is awfully tempting, even if it's also awfully slow. It would be nice if you could make the disk stand in for RAM when RAM runs out, temporarily moving unused code and data to disk to make room for more. As you probably already know, Linux can do exactly this—it's called *virtual memory*.

Virtual memory, then, is the technique of seamlessly blending access to RAM and disk, primary and secondary storage. Applications see all of this memory as if it were really there. We know it's not—which is why we call it "virtual"—but, thanks to the kernel, applications can't tell the difference. To an application, it's as if there were huge amounts of RAM that's really slow sometimes.

The term "virtual memory" has another meaning, which, in a strict sense, is unrelated to the first meaning. Virtual memory also refers to the practice of lying to processes about the addresses at which they reside. Each process is permitted the delusion that its addresses begin at 0 and extend on up from there. Clearly, this can't really be true for all processes at the same time, but the fiction is convenient when generating code. Processes don't have to know that they don't really live at address 0, and they don't have to care, either.

These two meanings are not necessarily related, because an operating system theoretically could give each process its own logical address space without also conflating primary and secondary storage. All of the real systems that I'm aware of, though, do both or neither, which is probably what led to the confusion in the first place.

To avoid this polysemy, some purists prefer to reserve the term "virtual memory" to refer to the logical-address-space meaning only, and to use either "paging" or "swapping" for the disk-as-memory meaning (I'll define those terms in a moment). Although the purists have a good point, I accept the more common usage that conflates the two meanings, rarely bothering with the distinction unless it's necessary in context.

Swapping and Paging

Early virtual memory (VM) systems could move only an entire application's code and data—a whole process— to or from the disk. This technique is called *swapping*, because it swaps one process for another. For this reason, a section of disk set aside for VM is often called *swap space* (or simply *swap*), even though modern systems no longer swap in the original sense, as you'll see. Similarly, you'll often see the terms *swap device* and *swap partition*—synonymous terms for a disk partition dedicated as swap space—and *swap file*, a regular, fixed-length file used for swapping.

Swapping is useful, and much better than no VM at all, but it has its limitations. First, it requires an entire process to fit into memory at once, so it can't help when you want to run a process that requires more storage than there is RAM installed on the system—even if there's plenty of disk space ready to compensate.

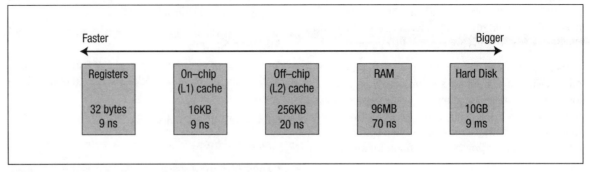

Figure 8.1 Storage levels, with their speeds and capacities.

Furthermore, swapping can be inefficient because you must swap out an entire process, even if this means swapping out an entire 8MB process just because you need another 2KB. Similarly, you must swap in an entire process, even if you are going to execute only a small portion of the swapped-in application's code.

Enter *paging*, which divides the system's memory into smallish chunks—pages—that can be moved to and from disk independently. Paging is like swapping, but with much smaller granularity. Paging has more bookkeeping overhead than swapping, because the number of pages far exceeds the number of processes, but you gain a lot of flexibility. Paging is faster, too, for several reasons—one is that you usually don't need to move a whole process to or from the disk, just enough of its pages to satisfy the request. Always remember that factor-of-1,000,000 speed difference—you want to avoid touching the disk whenever possible.

Pages traditionally are a fixed size on a particular platform—4KB on the x86, for example—which simplifies paging implementations. However, most CPUs now provide hardware support for variable-sized pages, often up to 4MB or even larger. Variable-sized pages can support faster and more memory-efficient paging implementations, but at a cost in complexity. The standard distribution of the Linux kernel doesn't support variable-sized pages, so I'll stick to assuming that pages are 4KB. (Patches that support the Cyrix variable-sized paging mechanism [VSPM] are available, but they aren't part of the official distribution as of this writing. Also, the performance gains are reportedly marginal.)

Because paging can do everything swapping can do, but more efficiently, modern systems such as Linux no longer swap; strictly speaking, they only page. However, the term "swap" is so well enshrined in common usage that the terms "swap" and "page" have become nearly interchangeable in practice. This book follows that usage, because the kernel does.

Linux can swap to a dedicated disk partition, to a file, or to both partitions and files in various combinations.

It even allows you to add and remove swap space while the system is running—very useful if you're going to need lots of extra swap space, but only temporarily, or if you discover a need for extra swap space, but don't want to reboot just to provide it. And, unlike some flavors of Unix, Linux can get along just fine without any swap space at all.

Although paging is faster than swapping, it's still relatively slow (as anything that accesses the disk must be), so the kernel must allocate memory wisely. Injudiciously permitting one process to hog the system's RAM will bring the whole system to a crawl, as the little RAM available to other processes must be constantly paged in and out. To help distribute memory well, Linux implements simple rules of thumb that require minimal bookkeeping but have a big payoff.

However, these rules apply only to managing memory allocated for user processes, never for the kernel itself. Neither the kernel's code nor its data can ever be swapped out. This makes life a lot simpler for kernel programmers, since you never have to worry about what will happen if your code must be interrupted in order to swap a page in or out, but it also puts additional pressure on the kernel to stay small. If the kernel greedily consumes most of the system's RAM, the effect on overall system performance will be as disastrous as if the memory hog were a user process—indeed, it's even worse, since the user has no hope of simply killing the kernel.

Address Spaces

An *address space* is simply a range of addresses representing memory locations. Address spaces come in three flavors:

- Physical address space

- Linear address space

- Logical address space, also known as the virtual address space

(Arguably, I/O addresses are a fourth kind of address space, but they're outside the scope of this book anyway.)

Physical addresses are the real, hardware addresses available on a system. If a system has 64MB of memory, its valid physical addresses range from 0 to (in hex) 0x3ffffff. Each address corresponds to a single set of transistors in those SIMMs that you (or the manufacturer) installed and to a distinct set of signals on the processor's address bus.

Paging can move a process, or just pieces of a process, into and out of different regions of physical memory—different physical addresses—over its lifetime. This is one reason processes are given a logical address space. As far as any given process is concerned, the address space it's using starts at 0 and extends (on Linux) to the hex address 0xbfffffff—a 3GB address space, which is quite enough for everyday needs. Even though every process has the same logical address space, the corresponding physical addresses are different for each process, so they can't actually step on one another.

Both logical and physical addresses are, for the kernel's purposes, divided into pages. Hence, just as you can speak of logical and physical addresses, you can speak of logical and physical pages. Every valid logical address lies in exactly one logical page and the same goes for physical addresses.

Linear addresses, by contrast, are not normally thought of as paged. The CPU (actually, the MMU, covered next) converts the logical address used by a process to a linear address in an architecture-specific way. On the x86, this conversion involves simply adding the virtual address to another address, the base address of the process's segment. Because this base address is set to 0 for every task, logical addresses and linear addresses are the same on this architecture. The resulting linear address is then converted to a physical address, to interact with the system's RAM.

The Memory Management Unit

Translating logical addresses to physical addresses is the shared responsibility of the kernel and the hardware *memory management unit (MMU)*. The MMU is integrated into modern CPUs—it's all part of the same chip—but it's still useful to speak of the MMU as a distinct component. The kernel tells the MMU which logical pages map to which physical pages for each process, and the MMU carries out the actual translation when the process makes a memory request.

When an address translation is not possible—for instance, because the supplied logical address was invalid or because the logical page no longer has a physical counterpart and must be paged in—the MMU signals the kernel. This is called a *page fault*, and I explore it in detail later in the chapter.

The MMU is also responsible for enforcing memory protection, such as by notifying the OS when an application attempts to write to a page of its memory that has been designated read-only.

The main advantage of an MMU is speed. To get the same effect without an MMU, an OS would have to validate every single memory reference for every process—every fetch and every store, for both data and instructions—in software, probably by creating a virtual machine for processes to live in. (Java does something like this.) The resulting system would be unbearably slow. But an MMU is integrated into the computer's hardware in such a way that legitimate memory accesses are not slowed down at all. After the MMU is set up for a process, the kernel has to get involved only occasionally—such as when a page fault occurs, which is very rare compared to the total number of memory references.

Also, an MMU can help to protect the kernel from itself. Without an MMU, the kernel might be able to protect a process from illegally stomping on its own memory space, or on that of other processes, but what would protect the kernel from doing the same? On Intel's 80486 and later CPUs (not the 80386), the MMU's memory-protection features apply to the kernel, too.

Page Directories and Page Tables

On the x86 architecture, resolving a linear address (or logical address—remember that on Linux, these have the same values) to a physical address is a two-level process that looks like the process shown in Figure 8.2. The linear address supplied by the process is broken into three pieces: a page directory index, a page table index, and an offset. A page directory is an array of pointers to page tables, and a page table is an array of pointers to pages, so resolving an address involves chasing a chain of pointers. A page directory gets you to a page table, which gets you to a page, and the offset gets you to an address within the page.

To put it more verbosely, but more precisely: The page directory entry at the given page directory index holds the address of a page table stored in physical memory. The page table entry at the given page table index holds the base address in physical memory of the corresponding physical page, and the linear address's offset is added to this physical address to find the final target address within the physical page.

Other CPUs use a three-level approach, as shown in Figure 8.3. This is particularly useful on 64-bit architectures, such as the Alpha, whose larger, 64-bit address space means that an x86-like address resolution would demand enormous page directories, enormous page tables, enormous offsets, or all three. Accordingly, the Alpha's designers introduced another level to the linear address scheme, which Linux refers to as a *page middle directory*; this sits between the page directory and the page table.

So, this really is the same thing as before, just with one more level. The three-level approach also has a page directory, but now each of its entries contains the address of a page middle directory. Each entry in the page middle directory contains the address of a page table and each page table entry, as in the two-level scheme, contains the address of a page in physical memory, to which the offset is added for the final address.

Just to make things even more confusing, observe that the first scheme, which has three-part addresses, is associated with two-level address resolution, but the second scheme, which has four-part addresses, is associated with three-level address resolution. This is because the "levels" I'm speaking of conventionally do not include the first step of indexing into the page directory (because this is not a translation, I suppose).

Is it any wonder that the kernel developers decided to deal with just one of these schemes? Most of the kernel code treats all MMUs uniformly, as if they all used the three-level procedure (that is, four-part addresses). On the x86, the page-related macros convert the three-level resolution to two-level resolution elegantly, by defining the size of the page middle directory to be one. The page middle directory is treated almost interchangeably with the page directory behind these macros, so that the main kernel code remains free to speak of addresses as if they had four parts.

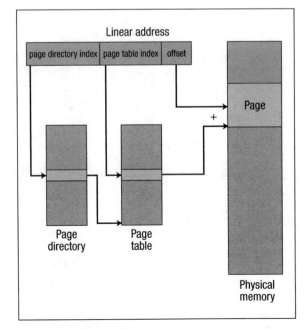

Figure 8.2   Paging on the x86.

On the x86, 10 bits of each 32-bit address are devoted to the page directory index, 10 more bits are devoted to the page table index, and the remaining 12 bits are devoted to the offset. This is what makes pages 4KB—2^{12} equals 4,096 offsets.

The functions and macros for creating and manipulating entries at each level are defined in several files:

- include/asm-i386/page.h (line 13381)

- include/asm-i386/pgtable.h (line 14084)

- include/asm-i386/pgtable-2level.h (line 13882)

- include/asm-i386/pgtable-3level.h (line 13954)

- include/asm-i386/pgalloc.h (line 13641)

- include/asm-i386/pgalloc-2level.h (line 13544)

- include/asm-i386/pgalloc-3level.h (line 13571)

- include/linux/mm.h (line 20015)

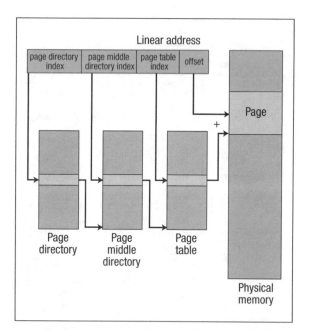

Figure 8.3   The kernel's generic view of paging.

The three-level variants of these files are used only on recent Intel chips that support Page Address Extension-mode (PAE) addressing. PAE allows 36-bit addresses, for a total of 64GB of addressable RAM, and requires three-level address resolution.

Page directories, page middle directories, and page tables are represented by arrays of **pgd_t**, **pmd_t**, and **pte_t** (see lines 13432 through 13440). Since the underlying representation of each of these types is simply an **unsigned long**, each type is wrapped up in a simple **struct**, thus enlisting the compiler's help in keeping them separate. Also note that, C being C, a pointer to one of these types (say, a **pgd_t ***) sometimes represents the base address of a whole array and sometimes just a pointer to one of the array's elements. Keep this in mind as you look through the functions and macros defined in the above files. Unfortunately, discussing all of these routines in detail would consume more of the chapter than is warranted. I'll discuss some of them later, though.

Page table entries record not only a page's base address, but also its *protections*, a set of flags designating the page as readable, writable, and/or executable (this is reminiscent of file protection bits, as you can see). The page table entry includes several other page-specific flags, as you'll see when I cover page protections in more detail.

Finally, a memory page is represented by **struct page** (line 20164), also known as **mem_map_t**. The kernel allocates an array of these, **mem_map** (line 40752), with one element for each page of memory in the system.

Translation Lookaside Buffers (TLBs)

If executed naively, translating a linear address to a physical address would require several memory references as the system chased the chain of pointers. RAM isn't as slow as the disk, but it's still much slower than the CPU, so this could easily become a performance bottleneck. To reduce this overhead, the results of the most recently executed address translations are stored in the MMU's *translation lookaside buffers (TLBs)*.

Linux doesn't need to manage the TLBs explicitly, except to occasionally inform the CPU that the TLBs have become invalid through some action by the kernel.

Of the functions and macros that work with the TLB, I'll present only **__flush_tlb**, which, on the x86, is the basis for most of the others anyway.

__flush_tlb

14124: CR3 (Control Register 3) is the x86 CPU register that holds the base address of the page directory. Loading a value into this register makes the CPU think that the TLBs have become invalid—even if the CPU is loading the same value that CR3 already had. Consequently, **__flush_tlb** is just two assembler instructions: It saves CR3's value to the temporary variable **tmpreg**, and then copies **tmpreg** right back into CR3. That's the whole thing!

Note that the x86 also allows invalidating a single TLB entry rather than the whole thing. This method uses the **invlpg** instruction—see line 14166 for its use.

Segments

The architecture-independent part of the Linux kernel doesn't know about segments, because segments aren't available on all CPUs. Just as important, how segments are handled—where available—differs greatly from CPU architecture to CPU architecture. Consequently, I won't spend too much time on the topic, but the way in which the kernel uses segments on the x86 is worth a quick look.

Segments can be viewed simply as another mechanism for defining regions of memory, a bit like pages. The two mechanisms can overlap: An address is always within a page and it might also lie within a segment. Unlike pages, segments can vary in size and can even grow and shrink over their lifetimes. Like pages, segments can be protected and the protections are enforced in hardware. When there's a conflict between the x86's segment-level protections and the page-level protections for the same address, the segment wins.

The x86 tracks segments with a few registers and a couple of types of tables: the global descriptor table (GDT) and local descriptor tables (LDTs). The *descriptors* are segment descriptors—8-byte objects that hold the base address and size of the segment and describe its protections. There is only one GDT, but Linux sets up an LDT for each user task.

The comment starting at line 12560 briefly describes the kernel's GDT layout. The kernel itself has separate code and data segments, which are described in entries 2 and 3 of the GDT. User tasks also have separate code and data segments, which are described in entries 4 and 5 of the GDT. In addition, each CPU uses two entries in the GDT, one to locate the LDT of the current process on that CPU and one to locate that process's TSS (task-state segment, covered briefly in the previous chapter).

Experienced x86 programmers might have already noted that Linux's use of the x86 segmentation mechanisms is minimalist; the main use of segments is simply to keep user code out of the kernel segment. Linux prefers the CPU's paging mechanisms. In large part, this is because paging is more or less the same across processors—or, anyway, the work has already been done to make it appear that way—so the more of the kernel that works in terms of paging, the more of it is portable.

As a final note, if you're deeply interested in the x86 segment mechanism, you cannot do better than to read the *Intel Architecture Software Developer's Manual Volume 3*, available for free from Intel's Web site (**http://developer.intel.com/design/pentiumii/manuals/243192.htm**).

The Memory Layout of a Process

Three data structures are important in representing a process's usage of its memory: **struct vm_area_struct** (line 20052), **struct vm_operations_struct** (line 20149), and **struct mm_struct** (line 21851). This section covers each of these data structures in turn.

struct vm_area_struct

The kernel tracks the memory areas used by a process with a set of zero or more **struct vm_area_struct**s, commonly abbreviated as VMAs. Each VMA represents a single contiguous region of the process's address space. Two VMAs never overlap: For a given process, an address is covered by at most one VMA; an address the process has never referred to in any way will not be in any VMA.

Note, importantly, that an address can be covered by a VMA even though the kernel hasn't allocated a page in which to store it yet. Indeed, one of the principal uses of VMAs is to decide how to react when a page fault occurs. Think of VMAs as high-level views of what memory areas a process knows about and how these areas are protected. The kernel could repeatedly recompute most of the information in the VMAs from the page tables, but that would be a much slower process.

In general, two characteristics distinguish one VMA from another:

- *Two VMAs might be discontiguous*—That is, the end of one doesn't have to be the beginning of the other.

- *Two VMAs might have different protections*—For example, one might be writable and the other nonwritable. Even if two such VMAs are contiguous, they must be managed separately because of the different protections.

However, that's not the whole story. The same process can have two contiguous VMAs with identical protections. Earlier versions of the kernel aggressively merged adjacent VMAs, in order to keep the total number of VMAs small (thereby reducing the cost of all code that iterates over a process's VMAs), but the 2.4 kernel does not. Empirically, the cost of merging adjacent VMAs outweighed the hoped-for savings. As a result, even two contiguous, otherwise identical VMAs are now managed separately by the kernel.

A process's VMAs are stored as a sorted, linked list, using pointers in the VMAs themselves to manage the list.

When a process has more than **AVL_MIN_MAP_COUNT** VMAs (**#define**d to 32 at line 21849), the kernel also creates an AVL tree to store them—again, using pointers in the VMAs themselves to manage the tree. An AVL tree is a balanced binary tree structure, so this approach makes lookups considerably more efficient when the number of VMAs is large. (Formally, AVL-tree lookups have logarithmic rather than linear cost. This is one reason it's not worth trying too hard to minimize the total number of VMAs attached to a process; the AVL tree makes lookups cheap even for the rare process with thousands of VMAs.) However, even after the AVL tree is built, the linear list is still maintained so that the kernel can loop over all of a process's VMAs easily and without recursion.

Two of the most important elements of **struct vm_area_struct** are its **vm_start** and **vm_end** members (lines 20054 and 20055, respectively), which define the beginning and end of the range the VMA covers. **vm_start** is the lowest address within the VMA and **vm_end** is one greater than the highest address. I'll be referring to these members repeatedly in this chapter.

Note that **vm_start** and **vm_end** are of type **unsigned long**, not, as you might have expected, **void ***. For that matter, the kernel uses **unsigned long** instead of **void *** all over the place when representing addresses. This is partly to avoid compiler warnings when performing some computations the kernel needs to perform on these addresses (such as bit-level operations) and also, perhaps, partly to avoid accidental indirection through them. When referring to the address of a data structure that exists in kernel space, the kernel code uses a pointer variable. When manipulating addresses in user space, it frequently uses **unsigned long**—indeed, it does so almost exclusively in the code covered in this chapter.

Observe that this places a requirement on the compiler that you use to compile the kernel. Using **unsigned long**s as addresses means that the compiler must use the same size type for **unsigned long** as it does for **void ***. This is not much of a constraint in practice, though. Using gcc on an x86 box, both of these types are naturally 32 bits. On architectures with 64-bit pointers, such as the

Alpha, gcc's **unsigned long** is also normally 64 bits. Still, a port of gcc could give **unsigned long** a different size from **void *** on a future architecture, which is something for kernel porters to be aware of.

Note, incidentally, that you don't have to worry much about the behavior of compilers other than gcc, because plenty of other gcc-specific features are in the code already. If you try to compile the kernel with some other compiler, the relative sizes of **unsigned long** and **void *** will have plenty of company on your list of problems.

struct vm_operations_struct

A VMA might represent an ordinary region of memory, such as that returned by **malloc**. But it might also be an area of memory that's been set up to correspond to a file, to shared memory, to a swap device, or to some other special object; such a correspondence is established by the system call **mmap**, covered later in the chapter.

However, you don't want to litter the kernel code with special knowledge about each of the objects that a VMA might be mapped to; having to decide repeatedly whether to close a file, detach from shared memory, and so on would be a monumental pain. Instead, an object of type **struct vm_operations_struct** abstracts the available operations—open, close, and so on—that the mapped-to object provides. A **struct vm_operations_struct** is just a set of function pointers, some of which may be **NULL** to indicate that an operation is unavailable for the mapped object type. For example, if a device driver doesn't need to do anything special when its memory-mapped device is attached to or detached from a memory page, the **open** and **close** members would be **NULL** for the **struct vm_operations_struct** that represents operations on that device.

All this means that if a VMA is mapped to an object, the VMA's **vm_ops** member is a non-**NULL** pointer to a **struct vm_operations_struct** representing the operations that the mapped object provides. For each object

type that can be mapped by a VMA, there's a single **static struct vm_operations_struct** somewhere that VMAs can point to. See line 28373 for an example.

struct mm_struct

The VMAs reserved by a process are all managed by **struct mm_struct**. A pointer to a **struct** of this type is in **struct task_struct**—specifically, it's the latter's **mm** member. This was the member used by **goodness** (line 33886) in the last chapter to decide whether two tasks shared the same memory space. Two tasks that have the same **mm** member (you can now see) are managing the same areas of global memory, which is a characteristic of threads.

struct mm_struct's **mmap** member (line 21852) is the linked list of VMAs mentioned earlier, and its **mmap_avl** member, if non-**NULL**, is the AVL tree of VMAs. As you can see from glancing through its definition, **struct mm_struct** includes quite a few other members, several of which I cover in this chapter.

struct task_struct keeps another **struct mm_struct** pointer—**active_mm**, at line 21964—whose use I'll show you now, even though it's a bit of a digression. As mentioned in Chapter 7, the kernel internally spawns a number of tasks for its own use. Since these tasks run as part of the kernel itself, they do not have their own user-space memory areas; the **mm** member of the **struct task_struct** for these tasks is always **NULL**. As a result, the kernel is sometimes able to avoid flushing TLB mappings when switching to or from these special kernel tasks. If, for example, the kernel switches control from an ordinary user task to one of these kernel tasks and then back to the same user task, the TLB will not be needlessly flushed and then (when the user task regains control) reloaded with the same mappings it had before.

This feature is called *lazy TLB switching*, and it works like this. For most tasks, the value of **active_mm** is identical to the task's **mm**; however, for kernel tasks with a **NULL mm**, **active_mm** points to an **mm** borrowed from a regular user task. The magic begins at line 34346, part of **schedule**:

34346:   To refresh your memory, **prev** and **next** are pointers to the tasks involved in the task switch: The kernel is transferring the CPU from **prev** to **next**.

34351:   If **next** has no **mm** of its own, it's one of those special kernel tasks. It borrows **prev**'s **active_mm** (which **prev** itself might have borrowed from some other task, if **prev** is also a kernel task) and increments this **struct mm_struct**'s reference count.

34353:   SMP kernels require a little additional bookkeeping in this case; the bookkeeping is handled by **enter_lazy_tlb** (line 13279). UP kernels give this function an empty definition at line 13286.

34357:   Otherwise, **next** has a real memory space of its own. **switch_mm** (line 13293) handles switching the active memory space; if the kernel is simply switching back to the process whose memory space was borrowed earlier, the test at line 13297 will fail and the expensive switch will be avoided.

34360:   If **prev** has no **mm** of its own, it must have borrowed one from another process. It drops its reference count to the other process's memory space. Though unlikely, it's possible that this is the last reference to that memory space (its original owner could have already exited on another CPU); in this case, **mmdrop** (see lines 22418 and 30686) will simply delete the **struct mm_struct** now.

Operating on VMAs

This section looks at a function used later in the chapter, **find_vma**; the next section will briefly inspect its cousin, **find_vma_prev**. This illuminates some of the aspects of VMA handling and prepares you for some code to come.

find_vma

42356: Loosely speaking, **find_vma**'s job is to find the first VMA containing the given address. More precisely, its job is to find the first VMA whose **vm_end** is greater than the given address—the address might still lie outside the VMA, because it might lie below this VMA's **vm_start**. The function returns a pointer to that VMA, returning **NULL** if no VMA could satisfy the request.

42364: First, the same VMA that satisfied the last request for this process is checked, using the **mmap_cache** member of **mm**, which exists specifically for that purpose. I haven't tested this myself, but the documentation for the function says the cache hit rate is 35 percent, which is pretty good, considering that the cache consists of only one VMA. Of course, it's helped along by the well-known property referred to as "locality of reference"—the principle that software tends to access data (and instructions) that are near the most recently used data (and instructions). Because a VMA contains a contiguous set of addresses, locality of reference makes it likely that the needed addresses will be in the same VMA that satisfied the previous request.

Elsewhere, when modifying the VMA list, this cache value is set to **NULL** to indicate that the changes to the VMA list might have invalidated the cache. In at least one of these cases, line 42683, nullifying the cache might not always be necessary; making this code a little smarter might materially improve the cache hit rate.

42367: The little cache missed. If no AVL tree exists, **find_vma** simply walks through all the VMAs in the list, returning the first that satisfies the condition. Recall that this list of VMAs is kept in sorted order, so the first VMA that satisfies the condition is the lowest-addressed VMA that does so. If it walks off the end of the list without finding a match, **vma** is set to **NULL**, and that's what will be returned.

42372: There are enough VMAs to make walking through the tree faster than walking through the linked list; because AVL trees are balanced, this is a logarithmic operation rather than a linear-time operation.

The iterative tree walk is not terribly unusual, but a few features are not immediately obvious. First, note the assignment at line 42380; this tracks the best node found so far, so it's what is returned if nothing better is found. The **if** test on the next line is an optimization, checking whether **addr** lies wholly within the VMA (we already know at this point that **addr** is less than the VMA's **vm_end**). Because VMAs never overlap, no other VMA will be a closer match, so the tree walk can be terminated early.

42388: If a VMA was found during the tree walk or list scan, the found value is saved in the cache for the next lookup.

42392: In any case, **vma** is returned; it will be either **NULL** or the first VMA that satisfied the search condition.

find_vma_prev

As stated in the preceding discussion, this function (which begins at line 42397) is the same as **find_vma**, but it additionally returns a pointer to the VMA before the one bounding **addr** (if any). This function is interesting not so much for its own sake as for something that its presence tells us about kernel programming in general and about Linux kernel programming in particular.

Most likely, an application programmer would have written **find_vma** as a layer over the more general **find_vma_prev**, simply discarding the pointer to the previous VMA, as follows:

```
struct vm_area_struct *
find_vma(struct mm_struct * mm,
         unsigned long addr)
{
    struct vm_area_struct * notused;
    return find_vma_prev(mm, addr, &notused);
}
```

An application programmer would have done this because applications typically are not constrained much by speed. Not to excuse mere extravagance, but the steady increase in CPU speeds has brought other concerns to the fore—we can now well afford an extra function call here or there, in the name of maintainability.

By contrast, a kernel programmer might not have the luxury of making an extra function call. Taking on the responsibility of maintaining a near-duplicate of some function might well be judged preferable to losing even a few CPU cycles. If nothing else, the fact that kernel developers take this attitude in the kernel is part of what enables application programmers to be comparatively profligate.

However, there's a deeper reason why such duplication is less important in the Linux kernel than in, say, a comparable closed-source operating system. Although the Linux kernel must constrain its use of CPU time, the Linux kernel development effort *is not constrained by programmer time*. Even most large commercial development efforts muster nowhere near the number of programmers who contribute to Linux. (And, just to be snide, I can't help pointing out that Linux's developers don't have to waste their time in meetings, nor are they bound by artificial timetables.) The existence of this enormous team, this massive mind, enables entirely different approaches to software development.

The Linux kernel's source code is available to anyone, and Linus himself famously said that ". . . given enough eyeballs, all bugs are shallow." If some important discrepancy were to arise between the implementations of **find_vma** and **find_vma_prev**, some Linux kernel developer somewhere would find it and fix it faster than you can say "recompile." In practice, Linux kernel development is faster than its commercial counterparts, and the resulting code runs faster and exhibits fewer bugs, despite the occasional presence of constructs that, in any other circumstance, would be considered unmaintainable.

Of course, I'll feel plenty foolish if the explanation turns out to be just that nobody *bothered* consolidating these functions, and the next kernel release merges them. However, I doubt this will happen, and even if I'm wrong in this particular case, I stand by the point in general. Something different is going on here, and that something different is part of what makes Linux, *Linux*.

Paging

A general overview of paging was given earlier in this chapter. Now, I'll show you in more detail how Linux does paging.

A Detailed View of Page Protections

As mentioned earlier, page table entries hold not only a page's base address but also flags indicating, among other information, what operations can be performed on the page. It's time to examine these flags more closely.

Because the page table entry holds only the base address of the page, and a page is obviously page-aligned, the lower 12 bits (on the x86) of this address—the offset part—normally would always be 0. However, instead of leaving these bits as 0, they are used to encode the extra page-related flags and are simply masked out to get the page's address. The following are the flags encoded in those 12 bits:

- The **_PAGE_PRESENT** bit (line 14246), if set, means that the page is physically present in RAM.

- The **_PAGE_RW** bit (line 14247) is 0 if the page is read-only, 1 if both readable and writable; there's no such thing as a write-only page.

- The **_PAGE_USER** bit (line 14248) is set for user-space pages, clear for kernel-space pages.

- The **_PAGE_PWT** bit (line 14249) is 1 to indicate that the cache policy for the page should be writethrough, 0 to indicate that the policy should be writeback (the default). *Writethrough* immediately copies any data written to the cache to main memory as well, although it's still kept in the cache for read

accesses. *Writeback*, by contrast, is more efficient, writing any changes back to main memory only when the cache line is being removed from the cache to make room for something else. (All of this is handled by the hardware, not by Linux.)

- The **_PAGE_PCD** bit (line 14250) turns off caching for the page; it's not used by any code covered in this book. (The "CD" stands for "caching disabled.") This could be more efficient if you happen to know that a page will not be used often enough to make caching it worthwhile. The bit seems to be more useful for memory-mapped I/O devices, though, for which you want to ensure that a write to memory representing the device is not buffered by the cache, but instead is copied through to the device immediately.

- The **_PAGE_ACCESSED** bit (line 14251), if set, means the page has been accessed recently. Linux is able to set or clear this bit itself, but normally this is done by the hardware. Because pages with this bit cleared haven't been used recently, they're preferred when swapping pages out.

- The **_PAGE_DIRTY** bit (line 14252), if set, means the page's contents have changed since the last time the bit was cleared. This means that the page cannot simply be discarded without saving its contents to swap. It's set by the MMU or by Linux when a page is first written to and it's read by Linux when removing the page from memory.

- The **_PAGE_PROTNONE** bit (line 14259) helps track whether a page is present in RAM (as opposed to being swapped out).

- **_PAGE_PSE** and **_PAGE_GLOBAL** are present in the same block of **#define**s, but they're not used for page-level protections, as the others are, so I'll ignore them here.

These flags are combined into higher-level macros later in the file.

Copy-on-Write

One way to be efficient is to be lazy—doing only the minimum work necessary, and then only when it needs to be done. This is sometimes a bad habit in the real world, at least when it leads to procrastination. In the world of computers, though, it is more often a virtue. *Copy-on-write* is one way the Linux kernel achieves efficiency through laziness. The basic idea is to mark a page as read-only, but to tag its enclosing VMA as writable. Any write to the page violates the page-level protections, triggering a page fault. The page-fault handler notices the contradiction between the page's and the VMA's protections, and then creates a writable copy of the page to use instead.

Copy-on-write is quite useful. Processes often **fork** and then immediately **exec**, making it wasteful for **fork** to copy their pages—the pages just have to be discarded after the **exec** anyway. During the **fork**, the kernel calls **dup_mmap** (line 30577) to duplicate the parent's memory map in the child; this function, in turn, calls **copy_page_range** (line 40833) to copy the parent's page table mappings corresponding to each of the parent's VMAs. Most of the time, **copy_page_range** just sets up a copy-on-write mapping for the parent's pages. The first write to the page triggers a page fault and a copy of the empty page is made then. In this way, pages are allocated only when their allocation cannot be postponed any longer.

Over the next few sections, you'll see how copy-on-write is actually implemented in the kernel.

Page Faults

Several times, I've mentioned the possibility that a page might not be present in RAM—after all, if the page were always present, virtual memory wouldn't have much of a purpose. However, I haven't yet described in any detail what happens when a page isn't in RAM. When a process tries to access a page that's not present in RAM, the MMU raises a page fault, which the kernel attempts to resolve. Page faults also occur when a process violates page-level protections, such as when a process tries to write to a read-only address.

Because page faults result from *any* invalid memory access, the same mechanism supports demand paging. *Demand paging* means reading pages from disk only when they're referred to—that is, on demand—another case of efficiency through laziness.

In particular, demand paging is used to implement demand-paged executables. To do this, only a small part of an executable image is read into physical memory when a program is first loaded. The kernel then relies on page faults to bring in other executable pages as they're needed (for example, when the process jumps to a subroutine for the first time). Except in pathological cases, this is always faster than reading in the whole thing at once—the disk is slow, and all of a program might not be needed anyway. In fact, the whole thing usually isn't needed, because most of a large program's features aren't used in any single run (indeed, the same is true for most small-to-medium-sized programs). This isn't the whole story for demand-paged executables—if you think about it, you'll realize that demand paging requires help from the binary handler, too—but it's a crucial component.

do_page_fault

8109: **do_page_fault** is the kernel function called back when a page fault occurs (this is set up at line 7491; the **page_fault** routine mentioned there forwards to **do_page_fault** at line 1114). When a page fault occurs, the CPU adjusts the process's registers so that, when the page fault has been resolved, the process restarts at the instruction that triggered the fault. This way, the offending memory access is automatically retried after the kernel makes it possible to complete it. Alternatively, if the fault is really a mistake and cannot be resolved, the kernel signals the offending process. The strategy is similar, but not identical, when the page fault is caused by the kernel itself, as you'll see.

8122: Control Register 2 (CR2) is the Intel CPU register containing the linear address that caused the page fault. The address is read directly from this register into the local variable **address**.

8147: The **find_vma** function (line 42356) returns the first VMA whose address range ends after **address**. As you know, this alone does not guarantee that the address is covered by the VMA—the address is known to be below the VMA's end, but it could also be below the VMA's start. Hence, this is checked, too. If it passes this test, meaning that **address** is within a VMA, control skips ahead to the **good_area** label (line 8166); I'll get to that soon.

8148: If the return value from **find_vma** was **NULL**, then **address** lies after every VMA for the process—in other words, above all memory referenced by the process. Control jumps ahead to the **bad_area** label (line 8218), which you'll see shortly.

8152: Both the start and the end of **vma** lie strictly above **address**; therefore, **address** is below the VMA. But all is not yet lost. If this VMA is the type that grows downward—in other words, if it's the stack—the stack might simply be able to grow downward to accommodate it.

8154: Tests bit 2 of the CPU-supplied **error_code**. This bit is set if the page fault occurred while in user mode rather than supervisor (kernel) mode. If in user mode, **do_page_fault** ensures that the given address was within the stack region set up for the process, as defined by the ESP register. (This can happen if, for instance, the code runs off the end of a stack-allocated array.) If in supervisor (kernel) mode, the latter test is skipped and it is simply assumed that the kernel is acting correctly.

8162: Expands the VMA to contain the new address, using **expand_stack** (line 20606), if possible. If this succeeds, the VMA's **vm_start** member will be adjusted to include **address**.

8166: When the **good_area** label is reached, it means that the VMA includes **address**, because either it already included **address** or the stack was expanded to include it.

Either way, the two lowest bits of **error_code**, which include more information about why the fault occurred, can now be tested. Bit 0 is the present/protection bit: If 0, the page simply wasn't present; if 1, the page was present, but the attempted access violated page-level protection bits. Bit 1 is the read/write bit: 0 for a read, 1 for a write.

8169: The **switch** methodically works through the four possibilities represented by those two bits:

- *Case 2 or 3*—Checks whether the enclosing VMA was writable. If so, this was a write to a copy-on-write page; the **write** variable is incremented (setting it to 1) so that the following call to **handle_mm_fault** will attempt to do the copy-on-write processing.

- *Case 1*—This means the page fault occurred when trying to read from a page that was present but unreadable; the attempt is rejected.

- *Case 0*—This means the page fault occurred when trying to read from a page that wasn't present. If the enclosing VMA's protections say the region is neither readable nor executable, reading in the page is only a waste of time—if the attempt were retried, another page fault would occur and **do_page_fault** would end up in case 1, so the attempt is rejected. Otherwise, **do_page_fault** goes on and tries to read in the page from disk.

8191: Asks **handle_mm_fault** (discussed next) to try to make the page present. If this fails, a **SIGBUS** error is issued (or **SIGKILL**, if the attempt failed because the system is out of memory). If **handle_mm_fault** succeeds, the faulting process's page fault counters are incremented. If **handle_mm_fault** was able to resolve the page fault without accessing the disk after all, the page fault is considered "minor." (This can happen when the page was stored in the kernel's page cache or swap cache, features I don't explore in this book.) Otherwise, **handle_mm_fault** really did have to involve the disk, so the page fault is considered "major."

8218:   The cleanup code for most kernel functions isn't all that noteworthy. **do_page_fault** is an exception; I'll describe its cleanup code in some detail. This label, **bad_area**, is reached in any of the following circumstances:

- The referenced address lies above all memory allocated (or reserved) for the process.

- The referenced address lies outside of any VMA and the stack couldn't be expanded to accommodate it, possibly because the VMA the address lies below is not the stack.

- A page's read/write protections were violated and the page was not designated copy-on-write.

8223:   If user code made any of the preceding mistakes, it is sent the dreaded **SIGSEGV**—a segmentation violation. (Note that the term "segmentation" here is historical, not literal—as far as the CPU is concerned, this is technically a paging violation, not necessarily a segmentation violation.) This signal normally kills a process, as discussed in Chapter 6.

8236:   The Intel Pentium CPU (and some of its clones) had the so-called f00f bug, which allowed any process to freeze the CPU by executing the invalid instruction 0xf00fc7c8. The Intel-proposed workaround is implemented here.

Part of the interrupt descriptor table (see Chapter 6) was previously marked as read-only, because that makes the CPU generate a page fault instead of freezing the CPU if the invalid instruction is executed. Here, **do_page_fault** checks whether the address that led to the page fault is at the location in the IDT that would result from executing the invalid instruction. If it is, the processor is trying to service the "Invalid Opcode" interrupt—the CPU bug makes it fail to do this part correctly, but the code makes the

right thing happen by calling **do_invalid_op** directly. The CPU otherwise never tries to write to the IDT (not while it's marked read-only, that is), so if the test at line 8241 fails, an invalid instruction wasn't being executed after all.

8247:   The **no_context** label is reached in one of the following cases:

- **bad_area** was reached in kernel (not user) mode and the CPU wasn't executing the invalid instruction that triggers the f00f bug.

- The page fault occurred while in an interrupt or when there was no user context (a user task wasn't executing); see line 8142.

- **handle_mm_fault** failed and the system was in kernel mode (we haven't seen this case yet).

Any of these situations is the kernel's problem (often caused by a driver, specifically), not a page fault generated by any user code. If the kernel (or driver) prepared for this possibility by setting up error-handling code in advance, the error-handling code will be located and jumped to with **search_exception_table** (line 7981).

8260:   Otherwise, the kernel tried to access a bad page, and **do_page_fault** doesn't know what to do about it. **do_page_fault** prints some information describing the problem and, at line 8279, terminates the kernel itself. (The **die** function used here is at line 6677.) This stops the whole system, so it's clearly not an action to be taken lightly. However, if the kernel reaches this point, it's out of options.

8292:   The next label to consider is **do_sigbus**, which is reached only when **handle_mm_fault** is unable to handle the fault. This case is relatively simple; mainly, it sends a **SIGBUS** error to the offending task, jumping back to **no_context** if this happened while in kernel mode.

8311:   The last label in this function is reached (from line 8135) when the faulting memory access occurred while accessing memory that might have been allocated by the kernel's **vmalloc** memory allocator, which is examined later in the chapter. The faulting process's page tables are adjusted to include the allocated memory if the access is valid; if the access was invalid, it's handled like any other invalid access, by jumping back to line 8221.

handle_mm_fault

41895:   The caller has detected the need for a page to be made available. The page is the one containing **address**, and this address belongs in **vma**. **handle_mm_fault** itself is fairly straightforward, but only because it's built atop several other macros and functions that handle the ugly details. I'll present those lower-level functions in turn after this one.

41903:   Finds the relevant page directory and page middle directory entries (this being the x86 platform, the two are actually the same, as previously described).

41907:   Gets or allocates (if possible) the page table for the page middle directory entry.

41909:   Calls **handle_pte_fault** to read the page into the page table entry.

41912:   Returns the result of calling **handle_pte_fault**, or –1 (from line 41899) if the function failed to get that far.

pgd_offset

14485:   Using **pgd_index** (line 14480), this macro simply divides **address** by $2^{\text{PGDIR\_SHIFT}}$ (**#define**d to 22 at line 13887), rounding down, and takes the result—the upper 10 bits before the shift—as an index into the supplied **struct mm_struct**'s **pgd** array. Therefore, its value is the page directory entry in whose corresponding page table **address** is located.

This is equivalent to

```
&((mm)->pgd[(address) >> PGDIR_SHIFT]);
```

although possibly more efficient. (However, the mask in the kernel's version is demonstrably unnecessary.)

pmd_alloc

13562: Because page middle directories are defined away on the x86 platform, this one is embarrassingly simple: It just returns the **pgd** pointer it was given, cast to a different type. On other platforms, it must do more work, similar to **pte_alloc**.

pte_alloc

13765: **pte_alloc** takes two arguments: a pointer to the page middle directory entry in which the desired address is located, and the address itself. The contorted logic of this function will be easier to explain if I jump around a bit, so watch the following line numbers.

13768: Converts **address** into an offset within the PMD, by extracting just the bits corresponding to the PMD index. After this calculation, adding **address** to the base address of its PMD—which happens at line 13774 and elsewhere—yields the entry for the pointer to the PTE associated with **address**'s original value.

13770: If this PMD entry doesn't point to any page table, the function jumps ahead to **getnew** to allocate one.

13777: Tries to grab a page table out of the **pte_quicklist** with a call to **get_pte_fast** (line 13715). This is a cache of page tables—the idea is that allocating page tables (which themselves are just single pages) is slow, but it's faster to allocate from a list of recently freed page tables. So, the code often frees page tables with **free_pte_fast** (line 13727), which puts page tables onto **pte_quicklist** rather than actually freeing them up.

13781: **pte_quicklist** was able to supply a page table page. The page table is entered into the page middle directory, and the function returns the offset of this page within the page table.

13780: No pages were left in the **pte_quicklist** cache, so **pte_alloc** needs to allocate one the slow way, by calling **get_pte_slow** (line 8476). This allocates a page with **__get_free_page** and performs much the same processing as when a page was found.

13772: If the PMD entry is not **NULL** but is invalid, **pte_alloc** prints a warning (through a call to **__handle_bad_pmd**, line 8437) and rejects the attempt.

13774: The normal, hoped-for case: **pte_alloc** returns a pointer to the PTE that contains **address**.

handle_pte_fault

41858: **handle_pte_fault** tries to fetch or create a missing page corresponding to a PTE.

41874: The given page table entry wasn't associated with any page in physical memory (line 41868), and indeed wasn't even set (line 41873). So, **do_no_page** (line 41790) is called to create a new page mapping and to increment the process's *resident set size (RSS)*, its count of the number of pages it has in physical memory.

41876: The page wasn't present in memory, but it has a non-empty entry in the page table, so it must be in swap space. **do_swap_page** (line 41716) is called to read it back in and to increment the process's RSS.

41883: The page was present in memory, so the problem was probably that the kernel is servicing a page protection violation. First, if this was a write access and the page is not writable, **handle_pte_fault** calls **do_wp_page** (line 41520). This is the copy-on-write case, so I'll cover it shortly.

41885: This was a write access to a writable page. **handle_pte_fault** sets the page's "dirty" bit, to indicate that it must be copied back to swap space before it's discarded.

41887: **handle_pte_fault** marks the page as recently accessed with **pte_mkyoung** (line 14427). Since the page has been recently accessed, it will probably be needed again soon; marking it young reduces the chance that the page will be swapped out.

41890: The requested page is now available for the caller's use, so **handle_pte_fault** returns 1 to indicate success.

do_wp_page

41520: As mentioned before, **do_wp_page** is reached when **handle_pte_fault** discovers that it's handling a copy-on-write fault. A task with the given **mm** was trying to write to **address**, which was within the given **vma** and controlled by the supplied **page_table**. Whenever **do_wp_page** succeeds, it does so without accessing the disk, so it returns 1 to signal its caller (**do_page_fault**, ultimately) that the page fault was minor.

41537: The first step is to see how many references to the shared page there are. If the faulting process had the only remaining reference to the page, it can skip the "copy" part of copy-on-write.

41543: Even when there are two references to the page, there is still some hope of skipping the copy. The faulting process has one of those two references, so there's only one left to worry about. If the other reference is held by the *swap cache*, the system's special-purpose disk cache for swap pages, it's safe to simply assign the page to the faulting process. (The swap cache never reads or writes to the pages it holds; it just stores them.) The **is_page_shared** function, which helps make this decision, is at line 23762.

41552: Either the page's only other user was the swap cache or it had only one user to start with. The page is marked writable and dirty (because it's being written to) as well as young (because it has been recently accessed and therefore should not be avoidably swapped out), and **do_wp_page** calls **establish_pte** (line 41477) to install the page in the faulting process's page table.

41562: Either the target page had more than two users, or it had exactly two users and the other one wasn't the page cache. In either case, there's no more hope of avoiding the copy. A new page is allocated with **page_cache_alloc** (line 21378), which acquires the page using the kernel's low-level page-allocation functions.

41571: Uses **break_cow** (line 41486) to copy the old page's contents to the new page and install the new page in the faulting process's page table.

41578: Releases either the new page (if the **if** at line 41568 was not satisfied) or the old one (see line 41575).

Paging Out

Now that you've looked a bit at determining when you need to swap pages in, take a look at the other end, swapping pages out.

try_to_swap_out

47936: Just about the lowest-level swap-out function is **try_to_swap_out**, which is periodically invoked (via a chain of other function calls) from the kernel task kswapd (see the **kswapd** function at line 48772). This function swaps out the page controlled by a single page table entry located in the given VMA. (More precisely, it adds this page to the swap cache. The page is ultimately written to disk by **rw_swap_page**—see lines 43924, 43944, and 43851.)

47945: If the page was accessed recently, writing it out is probably a bad idea—locality of reference makes it likely that the page will be needed again

soon. The page is marked "old" now (using **ptep_test_and_clear_young**, which has a generic version at line 11968 and an x86-specific version at line 14442) so that a future attempt to swap out the same page—which might occur very soon, if the kernel is desperate—can succeed. However, the page isn't written out yet.

47946: In addition to the young/old bit, the kernel implements a more sophisticated page-aging strategy using the **age** member of the **struct page** corresponding to each physical page. When accessed, the page's **age** is incremented, up to a limit (the increment and limit constants are at lines 23778 and 23779). Another function, **refill_inactive_scan** (line 48530), periodically halves pages' **ages** (using helper functions defined at lines 46157 through 46195). When a page's **age** drops to 0, it becomes eligible for reassignment when the system runs short of space.

Counterintuitively, a higher-numbered page **age** implies a younger page. It's like that for implementation convenience: Pages' **ages** decay exponentially—they're repeatedly halved—making them naturally converge on 0.

47952: If another process has the page locked, the page must be in use and should not be swapped out.

47959: The function simultaneously saves a copy of the page table entry corresponding to the victim page and clears that entry. It then clears the TLB entry for the page's virtual address.

47965: If the victim page is already in the swap cache, it was originally shared with another process that has already swapped it out. **try_to_swap_out** need do little more than increment a reference count to the swap cache entry and store a reference to that entry in the process's page table.

47992: The rest of the function is commented quite clearly and extensively, so I won't try to improve

on perfection. Do note, however, that **flush_cache_page** (line 14114), invoked at this line, is a no-op on the x86.

Swap Devices

Linux keeps a priority-sorted list of valid swap devices (and files, but for simplicity, I often use "devices" for both). When it needs to allocate a swap page, Linux allocates it on the highest-priority swap device that's not already full.

Linux also rotates among nonfull swap devices with equal priority, round-robin fashion, which can improve swapping performance by distributing paging requests among multiple disks. While waiting for one disk to satisfy the first request, another request is dispatched to the next disk. The fastest setup, then, distributes swap partitions among multiple similar disks, giving each the same priority; any slower disks would have a lower priority.

Rotation can slow down swapping, too. If multiple swap devices on the same disk have the same priority, the disk's read/write heads have to travel repeatedly back and forth across the disk to access both. This kind of situation is where that infamous factor-of-1,000,000 speed difference becomes almost impossible to disguise. Fortunately, the system administrator can avoid this problem by correctly allocating swap priorities. True to its Unix heritage, Linux gives you enough rope to hang yourself—but it also gives you the power to triumph. The simplest scheme is to give each swap device a different priority; this helps to avoid the worst cases, but it probably won't be the best case, either. Still, because it's simple and it helps to avoid the worst case, it is the default behavior if you don't specify priorities.

Swap devices are represented by the type **struct swap_info_struct** (line 23631). An array of these **struct**s, **swap_info**, is defined at line 46363. Functions in several files manipulate and use **swap_info** for swap management; I'll begin to examine them in a moment. These functions are much clearer, however, if you first examine some of **struct swap_info_struct**'s members:

- **flags**—Helps track the state of the swap device; the two valid flags are at lines 23623 and 23624.

- **swap_device**—The device number on which the swapping will take place; it's 0 if the **struct** represents a file rather than a partition.

- **swap_file**—The swap file or partition this **struct** represents.

- **swap_map**—An array that counts the number of users of each swap page within the swap space; if 0, the page is free.

- **lowest_bit** and **highest_bit**—Track the positions of the first and last available pages in the swap device. This helps to speed up loops that scan for a free element. The device's first page is a header that must not be used for swapping, so **lowest_bit** is never 0 (except briefly during initialization).

- **cluster_next** and **cluster_nr**—Used to group swap pages on the disk more efficiently.

- **prio**—This swap device's priority.

- **pages**—The number of pages available on the device.

- **max**—The maximum number of pages the kernel is allowed to use in this device.

- **next**—Helps to implement a singly linked list (kept in priority order, remember) of these **structs** within the **swap_info** array. Thus, the array is logically sorted, not physically sorted. **next**'s value is the index of the logically next element of the list, or –1 if the list is at an end.

swap_list, defined at line 46361, includes the index of the list's head (that's its **head** member—see the definition of **struct swap_list_t** at line 23740); this index is –1 if the list is empty. It also includes the confusingly named **next** member, which tracks the next swap device from which the kernel should try to allocate a page. This **next** is therefore an iteration cursor. It's –1 if either the list is empty or the kernel is currently out of swap.

__get_swap_page

46422: **__get_swap_page** gets a page from the highest-priority nonfull swap device available and marks the page as having **count** users; it returns a nonzero code describing the entry if one is found, or 0 if the system is out of swap. It is sometimes called through the **get_swap_page** macro at line 23737, which simply calls **__get_swap_page** with an argument of 1.

46433: Picks up the iteration where it left off the last time. If the list is empty or no swap remains, the function returns now.

46439: Otherwise, there is reason to believe swap space is available somewhere, and **__get_swap_page** just needs to find it. This loop iterates until the function either finds an entry (likely) or scans every swap device and concludes that none of them has any room left (unlikely).

46443: Scans the current swap device's **swap_map** for a free element, using **scan_swap_map** (line 46367), which also updates the **lowest_bit** and **highest_bit** members if an entry is found. **offset** will either be 0 or the entry to return.

46447: The current swap device was able to allocate a page. **__get_swap_page** now advances **swap_list**'s iteration cursor so that requests are correctly distributed among swap devices.

If either the end of the swap device list is reached or the next swap device has a lower priority than the current one, the iteration restarts at the head of the list. This has two important effects:

If some swap space has become available on a higher-priority device, **__get_swap_page** begins allocating swap from that device on the next iteration. Looking at this code in isolation, you might think the function can potentially allocate a few pages from lower-priority devices when a higher-priority device is available. But that's not true, as you'll see when you look at how swap pages are freed.

If no swap is available at a higher priority, then the next time the kernel allocates a swap entry, **__get_swap_page** will iterate through the list until it finds the first device at the current priority, and tries to allocate swap from that device. Therefore, the kernel continues to consider all devices at the higher priorities until they are all exhausted, before it moves on to devices at lower priorities. This implements the rotation discussed earlier.

46456: No swap was available on the current device or the current device was not writable (which amounts to the same thing for our purposes). So it skips to the next device, wrapping back to the beginning if it reaches the end and hasn't already wrapped.

46462: If **__get_swap_page** reached the end of the list and has already wrapped once, it has considered all swap devices and none had any free space. Therefore, it must conclude that no more swap is available, and return 0.

__swap_free

46479: **__swap_free** is the counterpart of **__get_swap_page**; it frees a single swap entry. As with **__get_swap_page**, the **count** argument says how many references to drop, and there's a **swap_free** macro (line 23739) that calls the function with a **count** of 1.

46499: Following a number of simple sanity checks, **__swap_free** checks whether the device on which it's freeing the swap page has a higher swap priority than the device that will be considered next. If so, it takes this as a cue to reset **swap_list**'s iterator to the head of the list. The next call to **__get_swap_page**, starting from the head of the list, will detect the newly freed higher-priority space.

46502: The usage count in each element of **swap_map** is maintained only up to a maximum, **SWAP_MAP_MAX** (**#define**d to 32,767 at line

23628). After it reaches this maximum, the kernel doesn't know how much higher the true count might be; therefore, it can't safely decrease its value. Otherwise, **__swap_free** decrements the usage count (at line 46505) and increments the total number of free pages (at line 46510).

46506: Adjusts the **lowest_bit** and/or **highest_bit** members if the newly freed page lies outside the range they define. You can see that if **__swap_free** is freeing a page in a previously exhausted device, this adjusts either **lowest_bit** or **highest_bit**, but not both. This makes the range wider than it needs to be, and swap page allocation can therefore be a bit slower than it needs to be. However, this happens only rarely. Anyway, the range tends to fix itself as more swap pages are allocated and freed.

sys_swapoff

46740: **sys_swapoff** removes the named swap device or file from the list of swap devices, if possible.

46755: Scans through the list of **swap_info_struct**s for the matching entry, setting **p** to point to this item, **type** to the index of this item, and **prev** to the index of the preceding item. **prev** will be –1 if the first element is removed.

46774: If **sys_swapoff** scanned through the entire list without finding a match, it was obviously given an invalid name. It returns an error.

46779: If **prev** is negative, **sys_swapoff** is removing the first element of the list; it updates **swap_list.head** appropriately. This is provably equivalent to

```
swap_list.head =
  swap_info[swap_list.head].next
```

but faster, because it involves fewer indirections.

46784: If the device being removed is the next one the kernel would otherwise have tried to swap on, the iteration cursor is reset to the head of the

list. This might slow the next allocation slightly, but not too much; anyway, this case must be quite rare in practice.

46792: If the device couldn't be freed because it's still in use, it is restored to its proper place in the list. If this was one of several swap devices with the same priority, it might not end up in the same relative position as before—it will be the first device with its priority even if it was previously the last—but it will still be in priority-sorted order.

It seems like wasted motion to delete an element from the swap device list when it's still possible that you will put it right back—shouldn't the code wait until it's sure the element will be removed?

The answer is that the call to **try_to_unuse** (line 46674) on the preceding line can end up, through a chain of function calls, handing off the CPU to another process (through a call to **schedule**) while waiting for a swap page to be read from disk. Anything at all might happen during that time—including other manipulations of the swap list and the devices in it—so the target swap device should be removed from the list in the meantime.

46809: If swapping on a partition, **sys_swapoff** releases its reference to it.

46820: **sys_swapoff** is finishing up, nullifying fields and freeing allocated memory. In particular, this line clears the **SWP_USED** bit, so the kernel will know the swap device is not available for use if it should attempt to swap on it again. Next, **sys_swapoff** clears the **err** indicator and goes on to return success.

sys_swapon

46892: **sys_swapon**, the counterpart of **sys_swapoff**, adds a swap device or file to the system's list.

46913: Finds an unused entry. This is a bit subtle. You might infer from **nr_swapfiles**'s name that it's

the number of swap files (or devices) in use. It's not. Instead, **nr_swapfiles** is one more than the maximum index value of **swap_info** that has ever been used; it's never decremented. (It tracks the high-water mark of this array.) Therefore, looping over this many entries in **swap_info** must either discover an unused entry or leave **p**, after the final loop increment, pointing after the **nr_swapfiles**th entry. In the latter case, if **nr_swapfiles** is less than **MAX_SWAPFILES**, then all the used entries happen to be packed to the left of the array and the loop leaves **p** pointing to a free slot to their right. When this happens, **nr_swapfiles** is updated.

Interestingly, this loop would still be correct even if **nr_swapfiles** were the count of the active swap devices rather than the high-water mark. Code elsewhere in the file (such as at line 46842) would break if you changed **nr_swapfiles**'s meaning, though.

46921: An unused entry was found in **swap_info**; **sys_swapon** starts filling it out. Some of the values supplied here will change.

46932: If the **SWAP_FLAG_PREFER** bit is set, then the desired priority is encoded in the lower 15 bits of **swap_flags**. (The constants used in this and the next few lines are defined starting at line 23589.) Otherwise, no priority was specified. As mentioned earlier, the default action in this case is simply to assign each new device a progressively lower priority, hoping to get decent swap performance without any help from a human.

46938: Ensures that the file or device that the kernel is supposed to swap on can be opened.

46947: Checks whether **sys_swapon** was given a file or a partition. If **S_ISBLK** returns true, it's a block device—a disk partition. In this case, **sys_swapon** goes on to ensure that the block device can be opened and that the kernel is not already swapping on it.

46980: Similarly, if not given a partition, **sys_swapon** must ensure that it has a regular file. If so, it goes on to ensure that the kernel is not already swapping on this file.

46990: If both tests fail, **sys_swapon** is not being asked to swap on either a disk partition or a file; it rejects the attempt.

47001: Reads the header page from the swap device into **swap_header**; this is of type **union swap_header**, defined at line 23597.

47004: Checks for a magic byte-sequence that tells which version of the swap header this is. The mkswap program writes this byte-sequence.

47017: Version 1–type swapping. Here, the header page is treated as a big bitmap, each bit representing a usable page in the rest of the device. Like all pages, the header page has 4,096 bytes, or 32,768 bits. Because each bit represents one page, the device may hold 32,768 pages, for a total of 128MB per swap device. (Actually, slightly less, because the last 10 bytes of the header are dedicated to the signature, and thus the kernel can't assume that the corresponding 80 pages are available; nor can the header page be used for swapping.) If the device is smaller than this, some of the bits in the header will simply be off. At line 47023, the function enters a loop to test which pages are usable, setting the **lowest_bit**, **highest_bit**, and **max** members of the **swap_info_struct** it's creating.

Note that the header bitmap is not maintained forever—indeed, it's freed when **sys_swapon** exits. The kernel uses the swap map to track which pages are in use; this header bitmap is used only to set **lowest_bit** and the other members of the **swap_info_struct**.

47033: Allocates the swap map and sets all of its usage counts to 0.

47046: Version 2–type swapping allows considerably more swap space per device, and it stores the header information in a somewhat more natural and efficient way. In this case, **swap_header**'s **info** member contains the information **sys_swapon** needs.

47057: The new swap header version doesn't require **sys_swapon** to treat the header as a bitmap to compute the **lowest_bit**, **highest_bit**, and **max** values. **lowest_bit** is always 1 (indicating that swapping may begin on the page after the header page), and the other two values can be computed in constant time from information stored explicitly in the header. This is both faster and simpler than a loop that does 32,768 bit tests and more than twice as many assignments! Still, this and the rest of the work is conceptually pretty much the same as before; **sys_swapon** just obtains most of the values it needs directly from the swap header, rather than needing to compute them.

Storing the total number of swap pages per device in an **unsigned int** theoretically means there can be about 2^{32} swap pages per device, or about 16TB of swap on the x86. (That's 16 terabytes, or about 16,384GB.) Other factors limit the actual size of a single swap device to 2GB, but you can have up to **MAX_SWAPFILES** (8; see line 23595) of them.

47104: **sys_swapon** is past reading the headers. It sets the first element of the device's swap map to **SWAP_MAP_BAD** (line 23629) to help keep the kernel from trying to swap on the header page.

47108: Updates the total count of swap pages available, and prints a message to this effect. (It subtracts 10 from the shift-count in line 47111 so that the output will be in kilobytes, 2^{10} being 1KB.)

47114: Inserts the new element into the logical list of swap devices—in priority-sorted order, as always. This code is functionally identical to the corresponding code in **sys_swapoff**, and there is no good reason to keep them separate. A simple inline function could replace both.

47129: Cleans up and exits.

Memory Mapping with **mmap**

mmap is an important system call that allows arbitrary regions of memory to be set aside for various purposes. The memory can be a proxy for a file or some other special object, in which case the kernel will keep the memory region and the underlying object coherent, or it can simply be plain old memory that an application wants to use. (Applications don't commonly use **mmap** just to allocate plain memory, however, because **malloc** is better suited to the purpose.)

One of the most common uses of **mmap** is for the kernel itself to memory-map an executable file (see line 9259 for an example). This is how binary handlers work with the paging mechanism to provide demand-paged executables, as hinted at earlier in the chapter. The executable is **mmap**ped into the appropriate region of the process's memory space, and **do_page_fault** brings in the rest of the executable's pages as needed.

Memory allocated by **mmap** may be marked executable, filled with instructions, and then jumped to; this is how Java Just-In-Time (JIT) compilers work. More simply, executable files can be mapped directly into a process's memory space while it is running; this technique is used to implement dynamically linked libraries.

The kernel function that implements **mmap**'s functionality is **do_mmap_pgoff**.

do_mmap_pgoff

42127: **do_mmap_pgoff** takes several arguments; together, they define the file or device that should be mapped into memory, if any, and the preferred address and characteristics of the memory region to be created. **do_mmap_pgoff** is commonly called by way of **do_mmap** (line 20535), which ensures that the requested address is page-aligned.

42143: **TASK_SIZE** (line 14785) is the same as **PAGE_OFFSET**, which is defined at line 13508, and this in turn is just **__PAGE_OFFSET** (line 13477)—it's 0xc0000000, or 3GB. This is the most memory that any user process may occupy, which makes the code make sense: Clearly, if **do_mmap_pgoff** is being asked to allocate more than 3GB, or if not enough room remains in the 3GB address space following **addr**, the request must be rejected.

42166: If **file** is **NULL**, **do_mmap_pgoff** is being asked to perform an *anonymous mapping*, which is a mapping that's not keyed to any file or other special object. Otherwise, the mapping is associated with a file and **do_mmap_pgoff** must go on to check that the flags it's supposed to set up for the memory area are compatible with the operations the user is allowed to perform on the file. For instance, at line 42169, the function ensures that if the memory area is writable, the file has been opened for writing. Omitting these checks would make it possible to subvert the checks that were done when opening the file.

42198: The caller is allowed to insist that **do_mmap_pgoff** either supply the mapping at the requested address or none at all. If the caller does insist, **do_mmap_pgoff** merely ensures that the supplied address begins on a page boundary. Otherwise, it obtains the first available address at or after **addr** (via a call to **get_unmapped_area**, which begins at line 42327) and uses that.

42211: Creates a VMA and starts filling it out.

42224: If **mmap**ping a readable file, the memory area is made readable, writable, and executable. (**do_mmap_pgoff** might revoke the write permission shortly—it's just an assumption.) In addition, if asked to make this memory area shared, it does so.

42239: If the file is not writable, the memory area must not be writable, either.

42243: In this case, there's no file whose open-modes and permissions **do_mmap_pgoff** must be compatible with—it's allowed to run free. Therefore, it makes the memory area readable, writable, and executable.

42257: Clears any old memory mapping at the address range being set up, using **do_munmap** (to be examined shortly). Because the new VMA hasn't been inserted into the process's list (only **do_mmap_pgoff** currently knows about it), the new VMA is not affected by this call.

42261: If the newly allocated memory would push the process over its currently defined address space limit (**RLIMIT_AS**, line 15096), the attempt is rejected with an **ENOMEM** error. Resource limits are covered in Chapter 7.

42272: If this is not an anonymous mapping, the newly created VMA is attached to the mapped object using its **mmap** method.

42294: Nothing more can go wrong. **do_mmap_pgoff** inserts the VMA into the process's list (and possibly its AVL tree) of VMAs with **insert_vm_struct** (line 42933), updates some statistics, and returns the address of the new mapping.

do_munmap

42633: **do_munmap** is the inverse of **do_mmap_pgoff**; it discards virtual memory mappings from a process's memory space.

42639: If the address that **do_munmap** has been told to unmap is not page-aligned or the region lies outside the process's memory space, it's clearly invalid, so the attempt is rejected here.

42643: Freeing 0 bytes would be an error. Otherwise, **len** is rounded up so that entire pages will be freed.

42651: Finds the VMA that includes the given address. Curiously, **do_munmap** returns 0—a nonerror— if the address is not in any VMA. In a sense, this is correct; **do_munmap** was asked to ensure

that the process no longer has a mapping for the given region of memory, and that's easy to do if it didn't have such a mapping to begin with. But it's still surprising; it would seem that this is an error on the caller's part and that **do_munmap** should report it somehow. However, some callers expect it to be this way— see line 42257, for example.

42660: If the supplied memory range lies entirely within a single VMA but doesn't lie at one end of the VMA containing it, then removing it will create a hole in the enclosing VMA. The kernel can't tolerate the hole, because VMAs, by definition, are contiguous regions of memory. Therefore, **do_munmap** needs to create another VMA in this case, so that it can have one for each side of the hole. However, if the kernel already created as many VMAs as allowed for this process, it can't do that, so **do_munmap** can't satisfy the request.

42675: Identifies all VMAs overlapping with or inside the region to free, putting each one on the local stack **free**. Along the way, **do_munmap** removes the VMAs from their AVL tree, if there is one.

42692: **do_munmap** has built the stack of VMAs to free; now it can free them.

42698: Calculates the exact range to free, bearing in mind that it may not span this entire VMA. Given suitable definitions for **min** and **max**, these three lines could be written as follows:

```
st  = max(mpnt->vm_start, addr);
end = min(mpnt->vm_end,   addr + len);
```

Hence, **st** is the start of the region that **do_munmap** actually starts freeing up, and **end** is this region's end.

42708: If this VMA was part of a shared mapping, **do_munmap** unlinks **mpnt** from the list of shared VMAs through a call to **remove_shared_vm_struct** (see lines 42022 and 42006).

42711: Updates the MMU data structures corresponding to the current subregion that is being freed up within this VMA.

42717: Fixes up the mapping with a call to **unmap_fixup**, which I present next.

42726: **do_munmap** has freed all the mappings represented by the VMAs in the range; the last important step is to free the page tables for the same range, which is done through a call to **free_pgtables** (line 42581).

unmap_fixup

42498: **unmap_fixup** fixes up the supplied VMA's mapping, either by adjusting one of the ends, by making a hole in the middle, or by deleting the VMA altogether.

42511: This first case is a simple one: unmapping the whole area. **unmap_fixup** simply needs to close the underlying file or other object, if any. As you can see, this doesn't remove the VMA itself from **mm**; it's already been removed by the caller. Because the VMA's whole range is being unmapped, there is nothing to put back, so **unmap_fixup** simply returns.

42521: The next two cases handle removing a range from the start or end of the VMA. These, too, are fairly simple; mainly, both cases need to adjust the VMA's **vm_start** or **vm_end** members.

42535: This is the most interesting of the four cases— removing a region from the middle of a VMA, thereby creating a hole. It begins by making a local copy of the extra VMA passed in, and then setting *extra to **NULL**, to signal to the caller that the extra VMA was used.

42538: Figure 8.4 represents the process of splitting the VMA. Most of the information is simply copied from the old VMA to the new one, after which **unmap_fixup** adjusts both VMAs' ranges to account for the hole. The original VMA, **area**, is

shrunk to represent the subrange below the new hole, and **mpnt** becomes the subrange above.

42559: Inserts the wholly new subrange into **current->mm**.

42562: In any but the first case (which returned), **unmap_fixup** kept the old VMA around. It has been shrunk, but it's not empty, so it is inserted back into **current->mm**'s set of VMAs.

User-Space Dynamic Memory

User tasks, like the kernel itself, often need to allocate memory on the fly. C programs generally do this with the well-known functions **malloc** and **free**; the kernel has its own similar mechanism. The kernel, of course, must provide at least the low-level operations that make C's **malloc** and **free** possible.

On Linux, as with other strains of Unix, a process's data area is divided into two usable parts, the stack and the heap. To keep these two parts from colliding, the stack begins at (actually, near) the top of the available address space and grows downward, whereas the heap begins just above the code segment and grows upward. Between the heap and stack is a no man's land of normally unused memory, although memory can be allocated in this space with **mmap**.

You can get a pretty good idea of where these address regions are, even without inspecting the relevant kernel code (although, of course, we'll go on to do that). The following short program shows the addresses of a few selected objects in the three different areas. For various reasons, it's not guaranteed to be portable to all platforms, but it will work under any version of Linux and should work on most other platforms that you try:

```
#include <stdio.h>       /* printf(). */
#include <stdlib.h>      /* malloc(). */


static void
one(void * p, const char * description)
{
```

```
    printf("%10p: %s\n", p, description);
}

int
main(void)
{
    int i;
    int j;
    one(&i, "A stack variable, \"i\"");
    one(&j, "Next stack variable, \"j\"");
    one((void *) one, "The function \"one\"");
    one((void *) main, "The function \"main\"");
    one(malloc(1), "First heap allocation");
    one(malloc(1), "Second heap allocation");
    return 0;
}
```

On my system, I got the following numbers. You might get slightly different results, depending on your versions of the kernel and gcc, as well as on which compiler flags you use. Still, they'll be pretty close to these results, if not identical:

```
0xbffff7b4: A stack variable, "i"
0xbffff7b0: Next stack variable, "j"
 0x8048400: The function "one"
 0x804841c: The function "main"
 0x8049698: First heap allocation
 0x80496a8: Second heap allocation
```

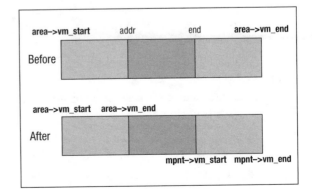

Figure 8.4 Splitting the VMA.

You can see that, in round numbers, the stack starts near 0xc0000000 and grows downward, code starts around 0x8000000, and the heap, as claimed, begins not far above the code and grows upward.

brk

The system call **brk** is the primitive operation underlying the C library functions **malloc** and **free**. A process's **brk** value is the breaking point between the process's heap space and the usually unmapped region between its heap and stack. Looked at another way, it bounds the process's highest legal heap address.

The heap lies between the top of the code region and **brk**. The C library function **malloc**, then, raises **brk** if sufficient free space isn't already available below **brk** to satisfy the request; **free** can lower **brk** if the freed space lies just below **brk**. Linux, incidentally, is the only Unix variant I know of that actually reduces the process's memory space upon **free**; the commercial Unix versions I have experience with keep that space reserved in the process—"just in case," apparently. (Other free Unix versions probably do the same as Linux, but I have no experience with them.) By the way, for large allocations, GNU's C library (glibc) uses the **mmap** and **munmap** system calls to implement **malloc** and **free**.

The relationship between the code region, the heap, and the stack is shown in Figure 8.5.

sys_brk

42058:   The function that implements the **brk** system call is **sys_brk**. It may change the process's **brk** value, and it returns the new value. The returned **brk** value is equal to the old value if the **brk** value could not be changed.

42066:   If the new value for **brk** lies in the code region, it is clearly too low and must be rejected.

42068:   Rounds up the **brk** argument to the next-higher page, using the macro **PAGE_ALIGN** (line 13462).

42069:   Page-aligns the process's old **brk** value. This seems to be a bit wasteful, because if the process's **brk** is set only here, it must already

be page-aligned. However, its **brk** can be set elsewhere, when initializing the process, and that code doesn't page-align it. It might be a little faster to page-align the process's **brk** wherever else it's set; that would allow the kernel to skip a page-align here, and because a process's **brk** is set here more frequently than anywhere else, it shouldn't slow execution at all and could be a marginal improvement.

42074:   **brk** is shrinking, but not into the code region, so the attempt is allowed.

42081:   If the size of the heap has a limit, it is respected. As Figure 8.5 makes clear, **brk - mm->start_data** is the size of the heap. (The stack and the heap, collectively, are the process's data region.)

42087:   If the region **brk** is expanding into is already **mmap**ped by a VMA, it's not available for use, so the new **brk** value is rejected.

42092:   The final sanity check is to see whether there are enough free pages to hold the to-be-allocated space.

42096:   Uses **do_brk** (line 42746) to allocate the space for the new region. Finally, **sys_brk** updates the process's notion of **brk**'s location and returns the new value.

As the comment above it states, **do_brk** is just a simplified version of **mmap**, so I won't cover it in detail. However, note particularly lines 42791 through 42798, which simply extend an existing VMA to cover the new **brk** address if possible. This code efficiently handles the most common case in which earlier kernel versions would have needed to merge adjacent VMAs, and it does so without creating a new VMA at all.

Low-Level Page Allocation: The Buddy System

Inside the kernel, the fundamental unit of allocation is the page. At the lowest level, the kernel allocates and frees blocks of pages. Any requests for a memory block

smaller than a page must either be rounded up or passed to a higher-level allocator, such as the slab allocator covered later in the chapter.

Not only does the kernel allocate memory only in page-sized chunks, it can't even allocate an arbitrary number of pages—the number of pages allocated or freed must always be a power of 2. This is an artifact of the kernel's low-level allocation algorithm, which works by iteratively splitting large areas of free memory in half until they're just the right size to satisfy the request. When the memory is later freed, the previously split areas will be merged if they have not themselves been allocated since. This algorithm is called *the buddy system*, because the two halves of a free region are "buddies" of each other: When either is freed, it checks to see if it can merge with its buddy. The algorithm is elegant, fast, and conceptually simple, though its implementation gets a little hairy.

Linux's buddy system always allocates memory from one of a set of disjoint *zones* (each represented by a **struct zone_struct**, line 20682); each zone covers a portion of physical memory. Within each zone, the kernel maintains several lists of free regions; each list tracks regions

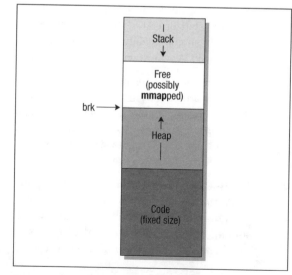

Figure 8.5   Code, the heap, and the stack.

that are 2^N pages long for some N. If possible, the buddy system allocates pages from a region of exactly the right size—if the caller is asking for eight pages and an eight-page free region is available, that region will be allocated. This saves the kernel the expense of splitting larger regions and implicitly avoids fragmentation, helping to ensure that the kernel will have large free regions available to satisfy large requests. The buddy system also ensures that a free region of N bytes begins on an N-byte boundary, which simplifies its code a little.

There are three kinds of zones, each represented by one of the manifest constants starting at line 20705:

- **ZONE_DMA** (line 20705)—Memory suitable for Direct Memory Access (DMA). DMA lets peripherals read directly from memory, or write directly to memory, without CPU involvement. This can be much faster than reading or writing a single byte at a time, so DMAable memory is preferred (indeed, it may be required) when communicating with devices capable of DMA. However, most memory on a typical system can't be used for DMA. It's up to the kernel to manage this limited resource wisely.

- **ZONE_NORMAL** (line 20706)—All the memory that doesn't fit into one of the other two categories. On most systems, nearly all memory belongs to this zone.

- **ZONE_HIGHMEM** (line 20707)—Memory that lies outside the normal addressing range. On Intel systems capable of PAE-mode addressing, memory above the 32-bit boundary (that is, memory after the first 4GB) would belong to this zone.

These constants are used as indexes into the **node_zones** member of a **struct pglist_data** (line 20728; this data type is also known as **pg_data_t**).

Within a zone, each set of free regions is represented by a **struct free_area_struct** (line 20675), also known as **free_area_t**. Each **free_area_t** consists of a list of **struct pages** (line 20164) and a dynamically allocated bitmap that helps track whether both members of a pair

of buddies are free. A zone contains an array of these **free_area_ts**—that's its **free_area** member, at line 20693. Each **free_area[i]** tracks all 2^i-sized free regions within that zone. As you can see, the array is bounded by **MAX_ORDER**, which is **#define**d to 10 at line 20673. Consequently, no single free region—and therefore no single kernel memory allocation—can consist of more than 2^9 pages. Still, this is a generous limit. On an architecture with 4KB pages (such as the x86), a single free region can be $512 \times 4\text{KB} = 2\text{MB}$; many architectures have 8KB pages, doubling the limit. The kernel never likes to allocate that much memory anyway.

With that as background, let's take a look at the code for the buddy system.

__alloc_pages

43223: This function implements the kernel's memory allocation strategy. Its job is not the low-level work of finding and splitting free regions; rather, it makes a series of attempts to allocate memory with the lower-level functions. When any of those attempts succeeds, the function returns the allocated memory. If an allocation attempt fails, **__alloc_pages** takes increasingly desperate measures to free up some memory before trying again.

__alloc_pages typically is not called directly. It's more commonly called through a helper function or macro, such as **__get_free_pages** (line 43445), **get_zeroed_page** (line 43456), **alloc_page** (line 20443), or **alloc_pages** (line 20429).

__alloc_pages tries to allocate 2^{order} pages from one of the zones in the supplied zone list. **zonelist** is of type **zonelist_t**; it represents a set of zones suitable for allocating memory that respects a certain **gfp_mask** (see **alloc_pages** for the relationship between a **gfp_mask** and a **zonelist_t**, and see the **#defines** starting at line 20571 for the legal values of **gfp_mask**). Since a given zone can satisfy more than one **gfp_mask**, it can be represented in more than one **zonelist_t**.

The function is copiously documented already, so I'll comment on it lightly.

43243: Within each zone, the kernel maintains a list of pages that have not been accessed recently and that don't need to be written to swap space before being reassigned (this is its **inactive_clean_list**; see line 20692). If necessary, it can allocate a single page from the pages on this list. (It can't reliably allocate larger regions from this list, because pages on the list are not guaranteed to be contiguous.) The function that ultimately allocates from this list is **reclaim_page** (line 48218), which also verifies that the page it's about to allocate has not become active or dirty since being placed on the list. At this line, the kernel merely sets a flag that will later indicate to lower-level functions that they may try allocating with **reclaim_page** if they please.

Since 2^0 is 1, an **order** argument of 0 instructs the function to allocate only one page, which explains the first test at this line.

43275: For each zone in the given zone list, **__alloc_pages** tries allocating pages from the zone using the buddy system (with **rmqueue**, line 43122, and discussed later)—if the zone isn't running low on memory. The function isn't desperate yet, so this part of the function tries to distribute allocations across equally good zones.

43290: **__alloc_pages_limit** (line 43173) tries allocating a page on behalf of **__alloc_pages**, with a customizable degree of desperation. On this call, **__alloc_pages** passes it the **PAGES_HIGH** (line 43167) limit, indicating that **__alloc_pages** is not very desperate yet. Lower limits are used at lines 43301 and 43334, as **__alloc_pages**'s desperation increases. **__alloc_pages_limit** allocates pages from the selected zone using **reclaim_page**, already discussed, or **rmqueue**.

The remainder of the function is sufficiently well documented that I doubt I can improve on it here. Instead, I'll move down a level and discuss the guts of the buddy system.

rmqueue

43122: Allocating a block of pages with the buddy system can be broken into two basic steps: Finding a large enough free region, and splitting the free region if it's too large. Not at all coincidentally, the code is split into exactly those two steps. This function, **rmqueue**, does the first step; it uses a helper, **expand** (covered in the next section), for the second step.

43132: This loop iterates over all of **zone**'s free-region lists that track free regions at least as large as the allocation request. **area** initially (at line 43125) points to the list that tracks free regions of exactly the right size. On subsequent iterations, it points to the list of free regions twice as large as the request, then four times as large as the request, and so on. **curr_order** tracks the size of the free regions in the current list. Naturally, it's initialized to **order** at line 43126.

43133: **rmqueue** tries to pop a free region off of the front of the list.

43136: If the current list is empty, control skips ahead to line 43157 to try the next-larger list.

43139: If the current list contained at least one free region, nothing better will be found. So **rmqueue** allocates this one, finding the **struct page** corresponding to the first page in the newly allocated region and calling **expand** to split the region into smaller regions if necessary. **rmqueue** also toggles the single bit corresponding to the chosen region and its buddy (using **MARK_USED**, line 43095). This last action is not easy to understand at first. Just note it for now, and I'll explain it when I discuss how regions are freed (under the discussion of **__free_pages_ok**).

43155: The newly allocated region is returned.

43162: The zone contained no free regions large enough to satisfy the original allocation request, so **rmqueue** returns **NULL** to indicate failure.

expand

43098: If the region allocated by **rmqueue** was larger than the caller's request, **expand** splits the allocated region and returns a pointer to a region of just the right size. Bear in mind that both memory requests and free regions are always some 2^N pages long, so if the allocated region is larger than the caller's requested size, it must be at least twice as large. If the allocated region is even larger than that, **expand** simply splits it iteratively, leading to the pattern of splitting shown in Figure 8.6.

In Figure 8.6, the caller wanted 16 pages, but the smallest free region available in the chosen zone was 128 pages. For the sake of concreteness, this discussion traces **expand**'s operation for this case.

Initially, in this case, **high** would be 7 (**rmqueue**'s **curr_order**), **low** would be 4 (**rmqueue**'s **order**), and **area** would point to **zone**'s list of 128-page free regions. That last phrase is awkward enough that it's worth inventing a notation for it: I'll say "the 128-list," "the 64-list," and so on, where the number indicates the number of pages in each element of the current free-region list.

43104: The loop iterates as long as the current region is larger than the request. For the example I'm tracing, the loop obviously iterates at least once (three times, specifically), but this is not true in general. If **rmqueue** allocates a free region of exactly the right size, **high** will equal **low** initially, so the loop's body will not execute.

43107: **expand** must split the current region, so it obtains a pointer to the next-smaller list. On the first iteration, that means the 64-list; on the second, the 32-list; on the third and last, the 16-

list. Similarly, it decrements **high** to track the order of this region (so on the first iteration, **high** is now 6). Also, **size**, which tracks the size of the current region in pages, is halved.

43110: **page** is added to the current list (on the first iteration, the 64-list). This effectively adds the lower half of the region to the appropriately sized free-region list. (The size of the free region is implied by the list its first page is on, so putting the base address of what happens to be a 128-page region in the 64-list effectively puts only the lower half of the region in the list.)

43111: Toggles the bit corresponding to the split region and its buddy. On the first iteration in our example, this would be the bit corresponding to the two 64-page regions formed by splitting the original region. (The bit corresponding to the parent 128-page region was already toggled at line 43144. Note that the bits being toggled are at different levels—that is, they're in the bitmaps attached to different **area**s.) When the

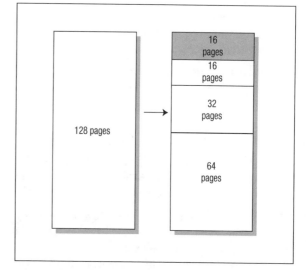

Figure 8.6 Splitting a free region.

upper 64-page region is split, the bit for its component 32-page regions is also toggled, and so on. I'll discuss the reason for all this toggling in the next section.

43113: **expand** makes **page** point to the upper half of the just-split region. (More precisely, **page** points to the **struct page** representing that address, not the address itself.) On the first iteration, **page** thus points to the first of the upper 64 pages. On subsequent iterations, the values it takes on (relative to the original value of **page**) will be **page** + 64 + 32, then **page** + 64 + 32 + 16. At that point, **page** will point to the uppermost 16 pages in the original block of 128 pages, and that's the value that will be returned at line 43117.

__free_pages_ok

43015: **__free_pages_ok** frees a 2^{order}-page region starting at the given **page**; if possible, it merges the freed region with its buddy, then merges that larger region with *its* buddy, and so on.

This function is where the buddy system's code really gets tricky. Indeed, the banner comment above this function says, in so many words, "You really aren't expected to understand this." Interestingly, this comment itself is an oblique allusion to a venerable bit of Unix folklore. In ancient times, the context-switch code in the V6 Unix kernel contained a comment—written by none other than Dennis Ritchie himself—that read, "You are not expected to understand this." (These days, Ritchie adds: "The real problem is that we didn't understand what was going on either." You can read his full explanation of that famous comment at **http://cm.bell-labs.com/cm/cs/who/dmr/odd.html**.)

43042: After some sanity checks designed to ensure that the page is not currently in use elsewhere in the kernel, **__free_pages_ok** resets the page's state, turning off its "referenced" and "dirty" bits and making it young again.

43048: **mask** serves two purposes in this function, only one of which is implied by its name. It initially has all zeroes in its low **order** bits and ones in all the upper bits, making it suitable for rounding down or (when inverted) extracting the lower bits of another **unsigned long**. You'll see its other use in a moment.

43049: Computes the base address of the zone to which the freed region belongs (or, more precisely, the **struct page** representing this address). The next line computes **page**'s zero-based index within that zone.

43051: If you think about the way they're allocated, you'll see that the freed region must begin at a 2^{order}-page boundary within its zone. The function tests for that property at this line.

43053: Each **area** maintains a bitmap with one bit for each pair of buddies covered by the area. **index** tracks the index of the bit in this bitmap that corresponds to the region to be freed and its buddy.

43055: Gets a pointer to the free-region list to which the region to be freed belongs. The region is not placed on the list yet, though—it might shortly be merged with its buddy, in which case it (and its buddy) would have to be removed from the list again and the merged region placed on the next-higher list. The function waits until the last possible moment (line 43083)—after any possible merging is complete—to add the region to the appropriate free-region list.

43059: **__free_pages_ok** adds the region's size back to the zone's count of free pages. "Since when does –= do addition?" I can hear you ask. Since they invented two's-complement arithmetic, which is used by all modern computers and in which—as the hint at line 43011 reminds us—negating an integer is the same as adding 1 to its bitwise complement.

Now, as we all learned in grade school, subtracting an integer is the same as adding the integer's negated value, so line 43059 is equivalent to this:

```
fp += -mask;
```

(I've replaced **zone->free_pages** with **fp** for convenience.) The property documented at line 43011 turns that into this:

```
fp += 1 + ~mask;
```

Recalling that **mask** is the bitwise complement of $2^{order} - 1$ (from line 43048), simple substitution provides the next step:

```
fp += 1 + ~(~(2^order - 1));
```

The two bitwise complements cancel each other out, of course:

```
fp += 1 + 2^order - 1;
```

And that's obviously just

```
fp += 2^order;
```

No wonder they say we're not expected to understand this code.

43061: This loop merges the newly freed region with its buddy, and that region with its buddy, and so on, as far as possible. In this loop, **area** tracks the list from which the final, merged region should be freed.

The loop condition might warrant a short explanation. Since **MAX_ORDER** is 10, the right-hand side of the addition is 1 << 9, or just 512—in hex, 0x200. Therefore, the sum is 0, terminating the loop, when **mask** reaches 0xfffffe00. At that point, the low-order 9 bits (only) of **mask** are off, indicating that the loop has iterated through all legal sizes of free areas.

Naturally, if a maximum-size (512-page) region is being freed, the loop will not iterate at all.

43066: Once more, the code toggles the bit corresponding to the current region and its buddy (using the **test_and_change_bit** function at line 12354). If the bit is 1 after this toggling (or, equivalently— and this is what the kernel tests— if the bit is 0 before the toggling), then the loop terminates because the region's buddy is allocated.

To understand what's going on here, first consider a restricted case: Suppose a parent region, P, was split into two children, H and L, which represent the high and low halves of P. By definition, H and L are buddies of each other. A single bit tracks the state of H and L; because the split allocates H, that bit is toggled at line 43111, making it 1. After that, allocating either buddy toggles the bit (at line 43144), and freeing either buddy also toggles the bit (at the current line). (For simplicity, assume for now that H and L themselves are never split.)

Diagramming the possible states and transitions leads to the state machine shown in Figure 8.7. Because H is allocated as part of the split, the state machine immediately transitions from state 1 to state 2 as part of the split. By following the arrows, you can see that the only way the map bit can be 0 after a free is when both H and L are free—the bit is 1 if exactly one of the two buddies is allocated. (This has exactly the flavor of an XOR; the bit is 1 if the buddies have different allocation statuses, 0 if their statuses are the same.) Consequently, if toggling the bit at the current line—which is part of the freeing code—leaves the bit 0, then the buddy of the region being freed must already be free. When that happens, H and L can be merged, and that's exactly what the code goes on to do.

The code is more complex than this example in only one respect: If H and L represent more than one page apiece, they can be further split. If any part of H or L is allocated, they must not be merged back into P. Hence, **rmqueue** and **expand** toggle the map bit at each level as they allocate and split regions, indicating that some part of one of the buddies at each level has been allocated. The bit will be toggled back after a merge at the lower level, and the buddy's children are merged only if both are free, making the buddy itself free.

43070: The region's buddy is free, so the two can be merged. Once again, this line takes advantage of the negation property documented at line 43011. As previously shown, **-mask** just works out to 2^N when **mask** is the bitwise inverse of $2^N - 1$, as it always is in this function (for varying N). Therefore, the right-hand side of the bitwise-XOR ($\char`\^$) operator is just a power of 2, and that means it has exactly one bit on. Specifically, **-mask** is the size of the region to be freed, and the bitwise-XOR expression inverts that bit in **page_idx**. This subtracts or adds the size of the region to be freed, depending on whether that region is in the upper or lower half of its parent region (the region it shares with its buddy). Thus, it locates the region's buddy. The region to be freed is now in **buddy2**, and its buddy is in **buddy1**.

43077: The buddy is removed from the free region in which it resides, and the loop variables are updated to try to merge the newly merged region with its buddy.

43083: No more merging is possible. Either some region's buddy was still allocated; the loop merged all regions with their buddies, all the way up to the top; or the freed region was already the maximum size (512 pages). In all cases, **page_idx** is the index of the first page in the (possibly merged) free region, and **area** corresponds to the free-region list for regions of that region's size. The free region is placed on the list, and the function cleans up and exits.

Because two buddies are merged immediately when both are free, Linux's buddy system is a *greedy algorithm,* as opposed to the lazy algorithms commonly found in the kernel. The worst case for the buddy system arises when some part of the kernel allocates and then frees a single page from a zone of maximum size. **rmqueue** and **expand** must split the parent regions until they end up with a one-page region to allocate, and then **__free_pages_ok** must merge all of the split regions when the page is freed. Worse yet, suppose that the caller decides to do this inside of a loop.

There are variations on the buddy system that are lazy, and these have reportedly shown significant performance improvements in other Unix kernels. (The basic idea underlying the algorithm's lazy variants is simply to delay merging. The clever part is figuring out when and for how long to delay merging, but that's outside the scope of this book.) Linux tends to sidestep the issue by employing various caching strategies. Rather than repeatedly allocate and

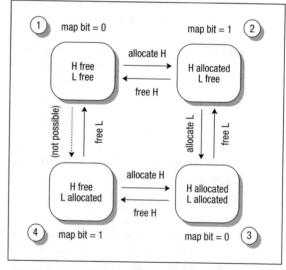

Figure 8.7 Tracking the allocation status of buddies.

free a single page inside of a loop, the kernel will simply allocate the page before the loop and free it afterwards. (Hoisting work out of a loop is faster anyway.) In addition, the slab allocator, explored later in the chapter, caches memory pages it allocates from the buddy system, further reducing pressure on the buddy system to be fast. Finally, the kernel is often able to satisfy memory allocation requests by reclaiming inactive pages with **reclaim_page**, bypassing the buddy system proper.

And that's the end of the buddy system. Maybe you aren't *expected* to understand this code, but there's nothing wrong with exceeding expectations.

vmalloc and vfree

One of the interesting aspects of kernel programming is getting along without many of the services that application programmers normally take for granted. Take **malloc** and **free**, for instance, C library functions that are built on top of the kernel's **brk** and **mmap** primitive.

I suppose the kernel could be revised to link with the standard C library and use its **malloc** and **free**, but the end result would be both clumsy and slow. These functions expect to be called from user mode, so the kernel would have to switch into user mode to call them. They'd then have to turn around and call back into the kernel, which would somehow have to keep track of the fact that this was going on, and so forth. To sidestep all of this, the kernel includes its own versions of many familiar functions, including **malloc** and **free**.

Indeed, the kernel provides two separate pairs of **malloc**- and **free**-like functions (in addition to the functions that talk directly to the buddy system). The first pair, **kmalloc** and **kfree**, manage memory that's allocated in the kernel's address space—chunks of memory whose actual addresses are known. The second pair, **vmalloc** and **vfree**, allocate and free virtual memory for the kernel's use. This memory is not swappable (kernel memory can never be swapped out), but it is addressed virtually, through the kernel's page tables.

Memory returned by **kmalloc** is better for purposes such as device drivers, because it's always physically contiguous. (DMA-capable devices require physically contiguous memory.) **kmalloc** is also faster, both because it doesn't require the kernel to adjust its page tables and because it implements a faster algorithm, the slab allocator. On the other hand, **vmalloc** is useful precisely because it doesn't require physically contiguous memory; it can satisfy memory requests using a page here and a page there. Therefore, allocating memory with **vmalloc** when possible helps leave large, physically contiguous chunks of memory for the code that really needs it.

vmalloc and **vfree** use **kmalloc** and **kfree** to allocate and free a bookkeeping structure, because the latter functions waste less memory for small allocations. (The smallest amount of memory **vmalloc** can allocate is a full page, and its bookkeeping structure is much smaller than that.) **kmalloc** and **kfree**, in turn, are implemented atop the buddy system.

Later in the chapter, I'll cover **kmalloc** and **kfree** in great detail. First, let's look at the much simpler **vmalloc** and **vfree** functions.

vmalloc

25042: **vmalloc** takes one argument, the size of the memory area to allocate. It returns a pointer to the allocated region, or **NULL** if the memory could not be allocated. As you can see, it does all of its work in terms of __**vmalloc**, covered next.

__vmalloc

47837: In addition to its **size** argument, __**vmalloc** takes two arguments describing desired characteristics of the returned memory. The first of these, **gfp_mask**, means the same as it does to the buddy system—indeed, it is passed to the buddy system eventually. The second, **prot**, specifies the desired page-level protections for the allocated memory.

The range of virtual addresses within which __**vmalloc** may allocate memory is bounded by the constants **VMALLOC_START** (line 14217) and **VMALLOC_END** (lines 14222 and 14224).

VMALLOC_START begins at least 8MB above the end of physical memory, to trap any mistaken kernel memory accesses in the region between, and **VMALLOC_END** lies not far below the maximum possible 32-bit address of 4GB. Unless your system has a lot more physical memory than mine, this means that most of the CPU address space is potentially available for __**vmalloc**'s use.

47843: __**vmalloc** begins by rounding up the requested size to the next-higher page boundary, if it's not on a page boundary already. (The **PAGE_ALIGN** macro is defined at line 13462.) The request is rejected if the resulting size is either too small (0) or obviously too large.

47848: Tries to locate an area big enough for a **size**-sized block with **get_vm_area**, which is covered next.

47852: Ensures that page-table mappings can be set up, through a call to **vmalloc_area_pages** (line 47739).

47857: Returns the allocated area.

get_vm_area

47772: **get_vm_area** tries to return a free region in the range **VMALLOC_START** to **VMALLOC_END**. Normally, this is on behalf of **vmalloc**; it's also used in a few other cases, in code not included in the book. The caller is responsible for ensuring that the **size** argument is a nonzero multiple of the page size.

vmalloc implements a *first-fit algorithm*, so called because it returns a pointer to the first block it locates that can satisfy the request. There are also *best-fit algorithms*, which allocate from the smallest available free region that's large enough to satisfy the request, and *worst-fit algorithms*, which always allocate from the largest available free region. Each type of allocator has advantages and disadvantages, but the first-fit algorithm implemented here is simple, fast, and sufficient for the purpose.

47778: Allocates a **struct vm_struct** to represent the new region. The allocated regions are tracked with a sorted, linked list, **vmlist** (line 47612), of **struct vm_struct**s (line 25022).

Each list element is associated with a single allocated block of memory, as shown in Figure 8.8. Visually, **get_vm_area**'s job is to find a sufficiently wide gap, either between the allocated regions or before or after all allocated regions.

47782: Adds a page (4KB on the x86) to the size of the reserved block, to catch memory overruns by the kernel—and, possibly, memory underruns from the next-higher block. Because the kernel doesn't set up a page mapping for this extra memory, an erroneous attempt to access it will cause an unresolvable page fault (which is almost unheard of in modern versions of Linux!). This will bring the kernel to a grinding halt, but that's better than allowing the kernel to silently trash its own data structures. At least you know about the grinding halt right away, which helps you to diagnose the problem. If the kernel didn't halt, you might not know there was a problem until after it had trashed your disk. Of course, memory overruns of more than a page can run into the next region, but memory overruns of less than a page will not.

47785: Starts looping through the list. The loop will either find a large enough free region or prove that no such region exists. It first tries **VMALLOC_START**, and then the address immediately following each allocated region. Observe that the test at line 47791 fails for perfect matches (because it tests < instead of <=), which is a mistake, and that the tests at lines 47786 and 47794 guard against wrapping around the top of the address space.

47800: The list was empty or the loop found a large enough region for the new block; either way, **addr** is now the lowest available address. The new **struct vm_struct** is filled out and will be returned.

vfree

47809: **vfree** is rather simpler than **vmalloc** (at least if you include **get_vm_area** with **vmalloc**), but let's examine **vfree** briefly, for the sake of completeness. **addr**, of course, is the start of the **vmalloc**ed region to free.

47821: Following a few simple sanity checks, the function loops through **vmlist**, seeking the region to free. This linear scan makes me think that it would be interesting to see whether a balanced tree structure, such as the AVL trees used to manage VMAs, would improve the performance of **vmalloc** and **vfree**.

47822: When the **struct vm_struct** matching **addr** is found, **vfree** detaches it from the list, frees the **struct** and its associated pages, and returns. Each **struct vm_struct** remembers not only its beginning address but also its size; that was handy for **get_vm_area**, and it's handy here, too, so that **vfree** knows how much to free.

47832: If **vfree** had found a match in the list, it would have returned already, so no match was found. This is probably a bad thing, but not bad enough to panic over. So **vfree** contents itself with printing a warning.

Kernel-Space Dynamic Memory with kmalloc and kfree: The Slab Allocator

In addition to the memory allocator implemented by **vmalloc** and **vfree**, the kernel provides a much faster allocator whose code is more complex and interesting. This is the slab allocator, and it's the topic of the following sections.

Overview and Design Objectives

In general, there are several features you want from a kernel memory allocator:

- *It should be fast.* Speed is always good, but it's especially important in a memory allocator. The kernel memory allocator is a widely used facility, so if it's slow, it will make many other parts of the kernel slow. In particular, device drivers sometimes need to be able to allocate memory very rapidly.

- *It should minimize wasted space.* This becomes even more urgent when the memory cannot be swapped out, as kernel memory can never be.

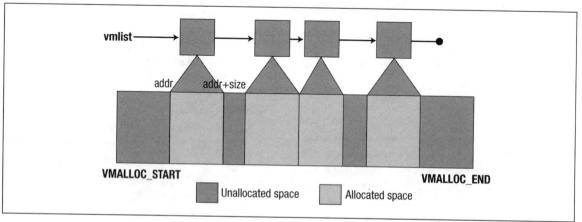

Figure 8.8   The list **vmlist**.

- *It should make good use of the hardware cache.* For example, it should distribute the addresses of allocated objects in a way that tends to distribute the objects throughout the cache. In addition, it should prefer to allocate a new object in the space vacated by a recently freed object, on the theory that the recently freed object's address will be in the cache already.

- *It should be able to allocate memory suitable for direct memory access (DMA).* DMAable memory is required by some device drivers—for the sake of speed, some devices expect to be able to read and write system memory without constant driver intervention.

- *It should be able to release unused memory for other purposes.* In particular, this means that the allocator should minimize fragmentation; if all the unused memory is packed together, it is more likely that some of it can be freed.

- *It should provide private spaces.* For example, a kernel module should be able to create its own memory pool, so that the pool can be entirely released when the module is unloaded.

A memory allocator that does a good job of meeting all these needs is the slab allocator, invented at Sun Microsystems for use in their Unix version, Solaris. This and the following several sections explore the slab allocator variant implemented in the Linux kernel.

Linux's slab allocator has the following characteristics:

- It allows any number of discrete memory pools, called *caches* or *slab caches* in the implementation. (Although accurate, this terminology is unfortunate because of the possible confusion with the CPU's own cache. When discussing the slab allocator, I'll stick to the terms "CPU cache" and "slab cache," never just "cache.") Each slab cache consists of a distinct, possibly empty set of memory slabs; each slab is a contiguous range of pages. When an object is allocated within a slab cache, it is placed on one of the slab cache's slabs if possible; if all of the slab cache's slabs are full, a new slab is first added to the slab cache. Multiple objects can be crammed into the same slab

if there's room, and an individual object might span pages but can never span slabs. The allocator provides a number of general-purpose slab caches, and any part of the kernel—including a module, of course—can create its own slab cache at any time.

Beware of one point of possible confusion. The slab allocator is named after what it does internally, not what it's used for. It allocates memory slabs to place objects on, but from the point of view of the rest of the kernel— "outside" the slab allocator itself—the point is simply to allocate space for arbitrary objects. The kernel as a whole doesn't care about slabs as such; slabs are merely an implementation detail. At line 47778, for example, the function **get_vm_area** doesn't care about allocating a slab, it cares about allocating a **struct vm_struct**.

- All objects allocated from a given slab cache have the same size, commonly 2^N bytes, which greatly speeds both allocating and freeing objects. **kmalloc** will round up the size of an allocation request; this wastes some space, but the speedup is worth it.

- In addition to the general-purpose slab caches underlying **kmalloc**, the kernel defines a number of special-purpose slab caches, typically allocating objects of a different **struct** type from each. These are declared at lines 23230 through 23238, and defined at various points in the kernel (for example, see lines 31186 through 31198).

- It can "color" the slabs, slightly offsetting their contained objects in memory in order to distribute pressure on the CPU cache.

- It separates DMAable memory from memory that might not be DMAable.

- Each slab has associated metadata. This metadata can be kept in the slab itself, or in a separately allocated block of memory, whichever wastes the least space in the slab. When the slab metadata is stored off-slab, the space for it is simply allocated from a slab cache dedicated to that purpose. (Naturally, *that* slab cache's slab metadata is kept on-slab.)

- It partially orders the list of slabs within a slab cache: The completely full slabs are kept in one group, the partly empty slabs are kept in another group, and the completely empty slabs are kept in a third group. To minimize fragmentation, objects are allocated from partly empty slabs rather than from completely empty slabs whenever possible. This grouping also makes it easy to find the slabs that can safely be released when the system is low on memory: They're the completely empty ones, and they're all together. (A slab is not immediately released when it becomes completely empty because the kernel might have to allocate another slab shortly anyway. In that case, reusing the recently emptied slab is faster than freeing and reallocating it with the low-level page allocation functions, and it makes better use of the hardware cache.)

- On SMP systems, Linux's slab allocator maintains a per-CPU stack of the addresses of recently freed objects. To minimize locking, the freed objects are released in a batch when the stack exceeds a certain size. What's more, when allocating an object, an address is simply popped off of this stack if the stack is not empty; again, this is faster than going through the low-level page allocation functions, and it makes better use of the hardware cache.

Indeed, this optimization alone can be much more efficient than it looks. Most systems spend most of their time in a steady state, with kernel memory neither increasing nor decreasing drastically. During such periods, the kernel may avoid locking altogether.

Phew! That's a tall order. But the kernel manages to do all this and more in only about 2,000 lines of code. The next several sections are devoted to studying the details.

Initializing the Slab Allocator

As befits such a widely used kernel facility, the slab allocator is initialized as part of the overall kernel initialization. During its initialization, the slab allocator creates a slab cache for its own later use. I'll defer exploring that code until the following, more general section on object allocation. For now, let's look briefly at the slab allocator initialization functions, in the same order as they're invoked by the kernel.

kmem_cache_init

44390: **kmem_cache_init** is the starting point for initializing the slab allocator.

44397: The kernel manages slab caches with objects of type **kmem_cache_t** (which is just a **typedef** for **struct kmem_cache_s**, defined at line 44158). And it has a slab cache to keep track of all the other slab caches: **cache_cache** (line 44331), which it begins to initialize here. It uses **kmem_cache_estimate**, covered shortly, to find a slab size that will help minimize wasted memory for this slab cache. (Naturally, the optimal size differs for different object sizes.)

44399: If **kmem_cache_init** fails to find a suitable slab size, something is wrong; the kernel reports the bug.

44402: Computes a suitable coloring for the initial slab cache; object coloring will be discussed later in the chapter.

kmem_cache_sizes_init

44411: This function creates the system's general-purpose slab caches, creating a slab cache for every power of 2 bytes from 32 bytes to 128KB. The slab caches it creates are held in the **cache_sizes** array at line 44311.

The array elements are of type **cache_sizes_t** (line 44305). Consequently, each array element maintains two slab caches—one for DMAable memory, and one for memory that may not be DMAable—and knows the size of the objects held in these two slab caches. The array's last element is a dummy that marks the end of the array. Since the array's length is known at compile time, the dummy element is unnecessary.

44420: Begins looping over the elements of **cache_sizes**.

44428: The kernel creates a pseudo-file, /proc/slabinfo, that contains information about all slab caches on the system. Each slab is uniquely named, and information about it appears as a line in this pseudo-file. Names for the general-purpose slab caches are created at this line (for non-DMAable slab caches) and at line 44442 (for DMAable slab caches). As you can see, the names will look like "size-32" and "size-32(DMA)". The Z in the **sprintf** format string is a gcc extension used for arguments of type **size_t**, since the definition of this type can vary from platform to platform.

44429: Creates a slab cache for non-DMAable objects through a call to **kmem_cache_create** (line 44608, and discussed later). Line 44443 does the same for DMAable memory, but its approach is slightly different—it separates the assignment from the **if** statement. There's no reason for this difference; the effect is the same.

44438: As it goes, **kmem_cache_sizes_init** also computes a limit on the number of objects in slabs whose management information is kept off the slab (see line 44723).

kmem_cpucache_init

44454: On SMP kernels only, the slab initialization code also calls **enable_all_cpucaches** (line 45700) to enable the per-CPU stacks of recently freed objects.

kmem_cache_estimate

44360: Though it's not solely an initialization function, it will be useful to cover **kmem_cache_estimate** here. The function computes the number of objects that will fit in a slab and the amount of wasted room in the slab, returning both values through pointers (**num** and **left_over**, respectively). The proposed slab would be $2^{gfporder}$ pages long, and the objects in it would each be **size** bytes long.

44374: The function begins by computing the number of objects that would fit in the slab. **base** and **extra** account for whether the slab management information is held on-slab or off-slab. **base** is 0 or the size of the **slab_t** that will be allocated in the slab. Similarly, because the slab allocator also allocates a **kmem_bufctl_t** for each object on the slab, **extra** is the size of a **kmem_bufctl_t** if the slab management information is held on-slab, 0 otherwise. At line 44383, the answer is stored through the supplied **num** pointer.

44384: Having computed the number of objects that will fit in the slab, it's easy for the function to compute how much room is left over. The total amount of occupied space is subtracted from **wastage** (initialized, at line 44365, to the total amount of space in the slab), and the result is returned through the **left_over** pointer.

Creating Slab Caches and Allocating Objects

The slab allocator would be of little use indeed if you couldn't use it to allocate memory. In this section, I'll show how the slab allocator does exactly that. Since you must create a slab cache before you can allocate memory from one, I'll begin by describing how slab caches are created.

kmem_cache_create

44608: **kmem_cache_create** creates a new slab cache. Among the parameters to this function are two function pointers, **ctor** and **dtor** (common abbreviations for "constructor" and "destructor"), which are invoked when slabs are created and destroyed. When a new slab is added to a slab cache, the slab cache's **ctor**, if non-**NULL**, is invoked for each object pointer within the slab; similarly, **dtor** is invoked for each object pointer just before the slab is released. These functions are used to help guarantee that objects are in a certain state just after allocation: **ctor** establishes the desired conditions before any objects are allocated from the new slab, and **dtor** can perform any associated cleanup. (For example, if the objects allocated from a slab cache are of some **struct** type, **ctor** might point to a function that gives some of the **struct**'s members desired default values.)

It would seem that **dtor** would be more useful if it were invoked each time an *object* is freed, not just when the slab itself is about to be freed.

It could reestablish the conditions initially established by the **ctor**, so that whenever an object was allocated from the slab cache—whether allocated from a given position for the first time, or reallocated following a free—the initial conditions would hold. Instead, the kernel requires the caller to reestablish any needed initial conditions before freeing the object, if that's what the caller wants. (When debugging is turned on, line 45394, called when freeing a single object, gives the **ctor** a chance to verify that the initial conditions were correctly restored.) Perhaps because this model makes **dtor** nearly useless, **dtor** is **NULL** for every call to **kmem_cache_create** in the standard kernel distribution.

44658: Following the extensive sanity checks, **kmem_cache_create** allocates a **kmem_cache_t** (supplied from the **cache_cache** slab cache set up during initialization) to describe the new slab cache. Most of the rest of this function is devoted to filling out this **kmem_cache_t**.

44668: Rounds up the object size to the next word boundary, for the reasons explained in the comment above this line.

44675: When debugging is turned on, the slab allocator is capable of a feature it calls "red zoning." This involves placing magic byte sequences before and after the allocated objects within a slab in order to help catch out-of-bounds writes to the objects. The slab allocator later checks these byte sequences to ensure they were not disturbed. Indeed, there are two such magic byte sequences, marking different points in the allocation process. Here's a brief overview of how red zoning works:

1. **kmem_cache_init_objs** (line 45029), called when adding a new slab to the slab cache, writes **RED_MAGIC1** (line 44268) before and after each object's position in the slab, calls the constructor function for each object, and then ensures that **RED_MAGIC1** is still there.

2. **kmem_cache_alloc_one_tail** (line 45220), called when allocating a single object in the slab, first checks that **RED_MAGIC1** is still where it was written by **kmem_cache_init_objs** or **kmem_cache_free_one**. It then writes **RED_MAGIC2** (line 44270) in the same locations.

3. **kmem_cache_free_one**, called when freeing a single object from a slab, checks that **RED_MAGIC2** is still where **kmem_cache_alloc_one_tail** wrote it, then writes **RED_MAGIC1** in its place.

4. Finally, **kmem_slab_destroy** (line 44538), called when detaching a slab from its slab cache, checks that **RED_MAGIC1** is still where **kmem_cache_free_one** placed it. (If not all objects within the slab were allocated—that is, if the slab never became completely full—then some of those occurrences of **RED_MAGIC1** were placed there by **kmem_cache_init_objs**.)

At the current line, the allocator merely increases the object size to make room for the **RED_MAGIC1** and **RED_MAGIC2** constants.

44682: On most architectures, word-aligned accesses are faster than unaligned accesses; on some, unaligned accesses are illegal. (Recall that, in the Linux kernel, a "word" is 32 or 64 bits, depending on the CPU; "word" sometimes means 16 bits, but not in the kernel.) In both cases, aligned accesses are better, so the slab allocator always ensures, at a minimum, word alignment for allocated objects. If the **SLAB_HWCACHE_ALIGN** flag was set in **kmem_cache_create**'s **flags** argument, then an even stricter alignment is required—each object will begin on its own L1 cache line, making more efficient use of the hardware cache.

44688: The caller is permitted to request that a slab's slab management structure (**slab_t**, line 44123) be kept outside the slab itself. Even if the caller

didn't request this, off-slab management is forced for large objects. The rule implemented here is that an object is "large" if eight or fewer of them will fit onto a single memory page. On the x86, this means that a "large" object is 512 bytes or bigger.

44694: This really belongs back at line 44685; it ensures that objects smaller than an L1 cache line are packed efficiently into a single cache line. If, for instance, **size** is 50 and the L1 cache lines are 128 bytes long, **size** is rounded up to 64 so that two objects will be packed into each cache line.

44711: Begins seeking a slab size that minimizes wasted memory. A slab's size is always $2^N *$ **PAGE_SIZE** for some N, since that's all the underlying page allocation functions are capable of. Using **kmem_cache_estimate** to compute the wasted space (in **left_over**) for each candidate slab size, the loop iterates until one of the following conditions is met:

- *Line 44718*—The loop discovers that the desired **size** is so large that the underlying page allocation functions cannot allocate enough memory for a slab that will hold even one object.

- *Line 44722*—It reaches the previously computed **offslab_limit** (line 44114).

- *Line 44732*—It exceeds the limit recorded in **slab_break_gfp_order** (line 44286). This limit is **BREAK_GFP_ORDER_LO** (**#define**d to 1 at line 44285) by default, but on machines with more than 32MB of memory, line 44419 raises the limit to **BREAK_GFP_ORDER_HI** (**#define**d to 2 at line 44284). As you can see, this is a pretty low limit on the number of loop iterations, and taken alone, it would imply a low limit on the maximum size of objects that can be created—four times **PAGE_SIZE**, even on a large-memory machine. However, line 44721 skips this test when the candidate slab size would not allow even one object to fit, thus permitting much larger object sizes. This code is therefore not particularly aggressive about minimizing memory overhead for large object sizes, though a comment suggests that this will change in the future.

- *Line 44735*—It finds an acceptably low level of wasted memory.

44743: When the loop exits, **cachep->gfporder** is the desired *N*, and **cachep->num** is the number of objects that will fit onto each slab. If the loop exited before finding a legal slab size that would allow even one object to fit on each slab, the function prints an error message, cleans up, and returns **NULL** to signal failure.

44750: The misleadingly named **slab_size** is computed. This is not the size of the whole slab, only of the associated slab management information. As previously stated, the kernel uses a **slab_t** to track information about each slab in a slab cache; it also keeps a stack of free positions within the slab, using a **kmem_bufctl_t** (line 44109) for each object on the slab. Each **kmem_bufctl_t** is just the index of the next free position within the slab, and the slab's **slab_t** includes a member, **free**, to locate the top of this stack. For efficiency, the total size of the slab management information is rounded up to the size of an L1 cache line using the **L1_CACHE_ALIGN** macro (line 17708).

44757: Even if the original plan was to keep the slab management information off-slab, the slab management information is kept on-slab if there's enough room in the slab for it. The idea is that this function knows better than its caller which way is more efficient, and it's more important to make good use of memory than to honor the caller's request on this point.

44763: Despite its best efforts, the slab allocator may end up with unusable room in a slab. Indeed, this is fairly common; it happens whenever

objects do not completely fill the slab they're packed into. So the slab allocator makes use of this extra room in another way: It uses the space to distribute pressure on the CPU cache.

The technique is called *object coloring*; it involves shifting the starting address of the data within each slab—moving some unused space from one end of the slab to the other. Distributing the offsets of the objects within the slab's pages distributes them throughout the CPU cache as well. The slab allocator figures out how many different positions it can use within the unused space while still respecting the caller's alignment requirements, then rotates through the possible starting positions as it allocates slabs.

44771: If the slab is the size of a single page (2^0 is 1) and the slab management data is on the slab itself, the following line turns on a flag that allows other code to find the slab containing an object faster than usual. This code (at line 45383) is currently commented out, however, so the flag has no effect in this release of the kernel.

44780: Each slab cache keeps a list of the slabs that belong to it (this is **kmem_cache_t**'s **slabs** member, at line 44161). As mentioned previously, this list is partially ordered: All of the completely full slabs are at the beginning of the list, all of the completely empty slabs are at the end, and the partly empty slabs are in between. To help it find the first slab with room for a new object, the slab cache also keeps a separate pointer into this list—**firstnotfull**, at line 44162. (More precisely, **firstnotfull** points to the **list** member of the first nonfull slab's **slab_t**, not to the slab itself.) Those two members are initialized here. Figure 8.9 shows a slab cache with its attached slabs. Note that the new slab cache is initially empty—that is, its list initially contains no slabs. Upcoming sections will explore how slabs are added to a slab cache.

44807: Prints an error message if another slab cache in the allocator's list of slab caches has the same name as the new one.

44813: Adds the new slab cache to the list of slab caches, then goes on to return the newly allocated slab cache.

__kmem_cache_alloc

45301: Once a slab cache has been created, its creator will probably want to allocate some objects in it. The function used for this purpose is **kmem_cache_alloc** (line 45516), which is implemented as a call to **__kmem_cache_alloc**.

__kmem_cache_alloc is also the function underlying **kmalloc** (line 45545), the kernel's general-purpose memory allocator. **kmalloc** simply finds the first general-purpose slab cache whose object size is large enough to satisfy its caller's request, then calls **__kmem_cache_alloc** to allocate memory from that slab cache. (Indeed, you could allocate objects from the same pool as **kmalloc** by using **kmem_find_general_cachep** [line 45602] to find the right general-purpose slab cache, then passing that slab cache to **kmem_cache_alloc**. If you were allocating many objects of the same size, this would bypass the minor **kmalloc**-imposed expense of repeatedly finding the same general-purpose slab cache. None of the kernel code bothers with this optimization, though; it's more common to simply create a special-purpose slab cache in such cases.) Hence, exploring this function is tantamount to exploring **kmalloc** itself.

45307: Calls **kmem_cache_alloc_head** to print error messages if the caller is asking to allocate DMAable memory from a slab cache whose contained memory is not guaranteed to be DMAable—or, conversely, if the caller is asking for non-DMAable memory from a DMA-only slab cache. (The second condition is less serious than the first, since DMAable memory can be used anywhere non-DMAable memory is expected.

However, since the reverse is not true, and since DMAable memory is a limited resource, the case is worth detecting.) **kmem_cache_alloc_head**'s body is empty when debugging is turned off, so the call is optimized away to nothing in that case.

45311: This is where SMP kernels allocate objects from the per-CPU object stacks if possible. If the per-CPU object stack exists but is empty, a whole batch of new objects is allocated using **kmem_cache_alloc_batch** (line 45275). This latter function delegates the dirty work to **kmem_cache_alloc_one_tail**, which is also ultimately used by **__kmem_cache_alloc**, as you'll see.

45331: UP kernels allocate new slabs using **kmem_cache_alloc_one** (line 45260). Since this is a **#define** whose control flow is tied to the function in which it's expanded, I'll break from my normal practice and trace the execution path into the macro now.

45267: If the slab cache contains no partly or completely empty slabs (perhaps because it includes no slabs at all), control jumps ahead to **alloc_new_slab** (line 45335) to allocate one and retry the object allocation. Note that the **goto**'s target label is within **__kmem_cache_alloc**, which is why **kmem_cache_alloc_one** must be a macro instead of a function.

45269: Otherwise, the function chooses the first slab with room for at least one object—the one found through the slab cache's **firstnotfull** pointer—to allocate a new object from.

45271: Allocates space for an object within the chosen slab, using **kmem_alloc_cache_one_tail**, covered next. Because the macro is enclosed in the **({ ... })** construct mentioned in Chapter 2, the value of the last expression evaluated within it behaves as the "return value" of the macro. It's as if the macro were a real function and this line read

```
return kmem_cache_alloc_one_tail(cachep,
                                 slabp);
```

instead. But again, if this macro were a function, the cute **goto** trick at line 45268 wouldn't work. The macro's body could simply be copied into **__kmem_cache_alloc** if this were its only use, but **__kmem_cache_alloc** uses the macro twice—the other use is at line 45326, which is reached (on SMP kernels only) when the per-CPU freed-object stacks haven't been allocated for the slab cache. A **goto** within a macro is a little weird, but at least it keeps us from having to maintain two copies of the same code.

45334: Returns a pointer into the chosen slab where the new object will reside. Since this line is reached only after line 45267 found a nonempty slab, it always returns a non-**NULL** pointer.

45341: This line is reached when the slab cache contains only full slabs or no slabs at all. If **kmem_cache_grow** (covered a little later in the chapter) is able to add a new (empty) slab to the slab cache, the object allocation is retried. Otherwise, the function has no choice but to return **NULL**.

kmem_cache_alloc_one_tail

45220: This function implements the last step in the process of allocating an object within a slab cache; it's called when its caller (either line 45271 or line 45291) has found a slab with space for at least one new object. Its arguments are the **slab_t** (slab management information) for that slab and the slab cache to which the slab belongs.

Note that this function does very little work when the slab allocator was compiled without debugging support. In the normal case, allocating an object within a slab is a remarkably cheap operation.

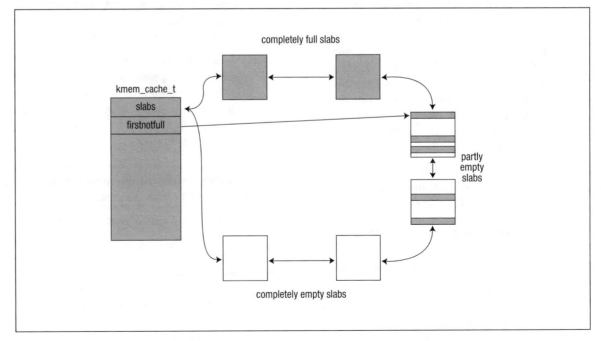

Figure 8.9 A slab cache and its list of slabs.

45230: The target slab's count of allocated objects is incremented and an address for the object is popped off of the stack of free addresses. (More precisely, the address is computed from a stack of free indexes, but the principle is the same.) Note that the **slab_t** contains a pointer, **s_mem**, to the first address in the slab where an object could be allocated. This neatly frees **kmem_cache_alloc_one_tail** (and most other slab functions) from having to worry about whether the **slab_t** is allocated in the slab it describes (on-slab) or in a separate slab (off-slab). If it's on-slab, the **slab_t**'s **s_mem** member will simply point elsewhere in the same slab that the **slab_t** itself belongs to; if the **slab_t** is stored off-slab, the **s_mem** pointer will simply point to some other slab in memory.

45234: The special index **BUFCTL_END** (line 44107) is used to signal the end of the stack of free positions within the slab. If the stack of free positions is now empty, the slab must be newly full. Accordingly, its containing slab cache's **firstnotfull** pointer is advanced to the next slab in the list, if any. (We know this is correct because the kernel groups the nonfull slabs together and always allocates from the first nonfull slab; therefore, if this slab is now full, the next slab in the list must be the list's first nonfull slab.)

45239: In addition to the "red zoning" described earlier in the chapter, the slab allocator can optionally "poison" objects, filling the object with copies of **POISON_BYTE**, line 44274 (except for the object's last byte, in which the poisoning code stores **POISON_END**, line 44275). Like red zoning, poisoning is supported only when the slab allocator has been compiled with debugging turned on.

Object poisoning helps the caller ensure that it's not reading from uninitialized memory within the allocated objects. For instance, suppose a kernel programmer is using a slab cache to allocate **struct**s that include pointer members, and sometimes—unpredictably—his code is going haywire. It may be that the caller inadvertently assumed that the **struct**s' pointer members would initially be **NULL**, and, indeed, the allocated **struct**s usually happen to contain all 0 bytes (and hence their pointer members are all **NULL**). However, when the allocated memory happens not to be filled with 0 bytes, the pointers are not **NULL**, exposing the calling code's bug. If the programmer suspects that this is going on, he can ask the slab allocator to poison the allocated objects; this will guarantee that the pointers are not **NULL** and help the programmer track down the bug.

The objects are poisoned by **kmem_poison_obj** (line 44506), called at line 45057 (when a new slab is being initialized) and at line 45410 (just after an object has been freed). The poison bytes are checked by **kmem_check_poison_obj** (line 44518), called at line 44566 (when a slab is being destroyed) and at line 45239—this line.

45241: This is part of the red zoning code discussed earlier in the chapter. Note that the **xchg** macro used here (see lines 16788 and 16851) stands for "exchange"—it simultaneously reads the old value from an address and writes a new one, returning the old value.

45251: If red zoning is turned on, the object really begins after the preceding red zone marker; the returned address is adjusted to account for this marker.

45254: Returns the address of the new object within the slab.

kmem_cache_grow

45076: Called from line 45341 (in **__kmem_cache_alloc**) when no nonfull slabs were available in the slab cache, **kmem_cache_grow** adds a new slab to a slab cache so that more objects can be allocated there.

45093: If **__kmem_cache_alloc**'s caller (which passed its **flags** argument along to this function) passed the **SLAB_NO_GROW** flag (line 23176), no new slab is allocated after all. It's hard to imagine why anyone would use that flag—the only reason I can think of is that the caller might want to ensure that the low-level page allocation functions are not invoked. In any event, no code in the standard kernel distribution uses it.

45116: Assigns a color to objects in this slab, wrapping around to 0 if necessary.

45135: Calls **kmem_getpages** (line 44467) to allocate enough pages for a new slab. **kmem_getpages** just turns around and calls the low-level page-allocation function **__get_free_pages**, part of the buddy system code covered earlier in the chapter.

45139: Similarly, **kmem_cache_grow** calls **kmem_cache_slabmgmt** (line 45003) to allocate a **slab_t** to describe the object. **kmem_cache_slabmgmt** allocates this **slab_t** either in the slab itself or in a separate slab cache dedicated to holding **slab_t**s for this slab cache.

45144: For each **struct page** associated with a memory page allocated for this slab, the following loop marks the **struct page** as belonging to a slab.

45153: Uses **kmem_cache_init_objs** (line 45029, and discussed in the following section) to initialize the objects in the new slab.

45159: The function's remaining work is simple. It mainly consists of adding the freshly allocated slab to the tail of its owning slab cache's list of slabs (recall that all empty slabs are placed at the end of the slab cache's list) and updating the slab cache's **firstnotfull** pointer accordingly.

After a slab has been created, it looks like Figure 8.10 if the slab management data is held on-slab, or like Figure 8.11 if the slab management data is held off-slab. Figure 8.10 also shows the effect of slab coloring: The contents of slabs A, B, and C have been offset by different amounts within each slab.

kmem_cache_init_objs

45029: **kmem_cache_init_objs** is called from line 45153 to initialize the objects in a new slab. As with **kmem_cache_alloc_one_tail**, this function's non-debug code is quite simple.

45035: Begins looping over all objects in the new slab. The following line obtains a pointer to each object in turn. Because it eliminates a multiplication, the following rewrite might run slightly faster:

```
void *objp = slabp->s_mem;
for (i = 0;
     i < cachep->num;
     i++, objp += cachep->objsize) {
```

However, since this version would perform one extra assignment (the one at the end of the last loop iteration), whether this is a win depends on the average number of times the loop iterates.

45050: If the slab cache has an associated constructor function (its **ctor** member), the constructor is invoked here.

45067: The stack of free positions is mostly built up here: Initially, the stack simply consists of increasing array indexes.

45069: After the loop completes, the stack of free positions is finalized: The last element of the stack names the special end-of-stack marker value as its next member, and the **slab_t**'s top-of-stack index (its **free** member) is set to the slab's first element.

Destroying Slab Caches and Freeing Objects

From the kernel's point of view, freeing memory is almost as important as allocating it. A regular user task with a memory leak isn't normally a terrible problem; if all else fails, you can force the task to free all its memory by simply killing it. But if the kernel leaked memory, you'd have to reboot the machine in order to reclaim any of the memory it had allocated. In this section, I'll present the kernel code for freeing allocated objects, slabs, and slab caches.

__kmem_cache_free

45479: Freeing an object allocated from the general-purpose memory allocator (**kmalloc**) is the job of **kfree** (line 45588); freeing an object from a specified slab cache is the job of **kmem_cache_free** (line 45568). Both functions delegate all of the real work to **__kmem_cache_free**, the natural inverse of **__kmem_cache_alloc** (covered earlier).

45486: An SMP kernel frees objects by pushing them onto the per-CPU stacks; if the test at line 45488 fails, the stack is full and a batch of objects should be freed. This is done through a call to **free_block** (line 45467), which simply acquires a lock and frees the batched objects using **kmem_cache_free_one** (discussed next).

45501: Even when the per-CPU stacks have not been created for an individual slab cache (normally because the objects are large—see line 45684), an SMP kernel still frees slabs using **free_block** (instead of calling **kmem_cache_free_one** directly) because **free_block** acquires the lock.

45504: UP kernels just call **kmem_cache_free_one** directly in order to free the object.

kmem_cache_free_one

45387: Cleverly works backward from the address of the object to be freed, to the slab in which the object resides. Line 45148 stored the slab's pointer in the **list** member of the **struct page** (line 20165) corresponding to the page in which the object resides, so the **GET_PAGE_SLAB** macro used here need only extract that saved pointer.

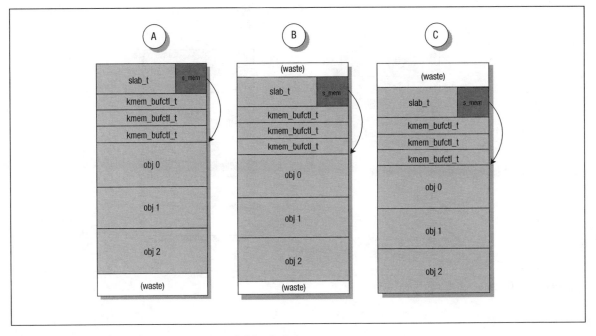

Figure 8.10 On-slab slab management data and slab coloring.

45411: I've already touched on most of this debugging code. Line 45394 lets the slab cache's **ctor** check that the freed object's initial state has been restored, lines 45397 through 45408 handle red zoning, and lines 45409 and 45410 poison the object's memory so that a later allocation at this address will return a poisoned object. This line calls **kmem_extra_free_checks** (line 45182), which performs some additional sanity checks. Although I won't cover the function in detail, I must say that the scan of the slab cache's free list (beginning at line 45195) is a clever way to detect attempts to free already-freed memory. It takes advantage of the observation that, if this object has already been freed and not yet allocated, it must be on the slab's free stack; consequently, scanning the free stack for its index would detect it.

45414: Computes the object's index from its offset within the slab, then pushes this index onto the slab's free stack.

45424: If the slab was full before this object was freed, the slab needs to be moved to the partly empty region of the slab cache's list of slabs. Execution jumps ahead to line 45430 to perform the required list manipulations. (The slab is placed at the beginning of the list of nonfull slabs and **firstnotfull** is updated accordingly.)

45426: Otherwise, if freeing this object made the slab empty, execution jumps ahead to line 45444 to place the slab at the end of the slab cache's slab list. Note that this line is never reached for slab caches that place only one object on each slab; the **if** condition at line 45424—the "partly empty" case—would be satisfied first. It's worth thinking about why the code is correct in that case anyway. (Cheaters can just read the comment at line 45431.)

kmem_cache_destroy

44966: Destroying an entire slab cache is the province of **kmem_cache_destroy**.

44978: The slab cache is tentatively removed from the allocator's list of slab caches (it may be replaced in a moment, as you'll see).

44981: **__kmem_cache_shrink** (covered next) frees all of the completely empty slabs in the slab cache, returning zero if all of the slabs were freed. If any of the slabs was not freed, then some objects must be in use elsewhere in the kernel. In this case, destroying the slab would be dangerous. Consequently, the slab cache and its contained objects are not freed; instead, the kernel prints a warning, replaces the slab cache in the global list, and returns nonzero to indicate failure.

44991: All slabs were removed from the slab cache, which is now empty. On an SMP kernel only, the per-CPU object caches are also freed.

44997: Last of all, **kmem_cache_destroy** frees the slab cache itself using **kmem_cache_free**, then returns 0 to indicate success.

__kmem_cache_shrink

44900: As you've just seen, **__kmem_cache_shrink** is called when destroying an entire slab cache. It is also called via **kmem_cache_shrink** (see line 44946) when the kernel is low on memory. Its job is to remove all empty slabs from a slab cache; it returns 0 if this makes the slab cache itself empty.

There is another function that also discards empty slabs—**kmem_cache_reap** (line 45725). That function is both more complex and less drastic than this one; it frees a few slabs from each member of a rotating list of victims on successive calls. It is periodically called from the kernel task kswapd,

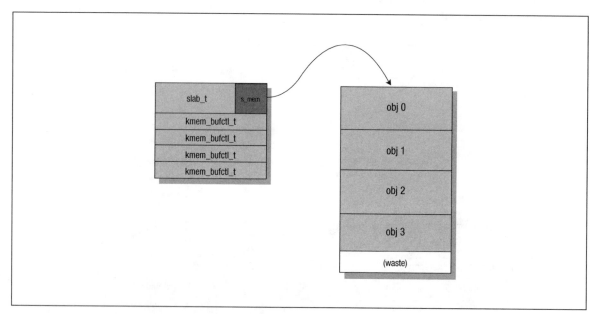

Figure 8.11   Off-slab slab management data.

among other places. Ultimately—at line 45834—it frees the slabs using **kmem_slab_destroy** (line 44538, and discussed in the next section), just as **__kmem_cache_shrink** does (as you'll see shortly).

44905: Frees all objects in the per-CPU object stacks through a call to **drain_cpu_caches** (line 44869 for the SMP version; the do-nothing UP version is at line 44897).

44913: As you know, all of the empty slabs are at the end of the slab cache's slab list. Consequently, each iteration of the enclosing loop tries to free the last slab in the list, stopping when the list is empty or (at line 44918) when it finds a nonempty slab.

44921: The slab is unlinked from the slab cache's list, and the slab cache's **firstnotfull** pointer is updated if the removed slab was the slab cache's first nonfull slab.

44926: The slab's memory pages are deleted by a call to **kmem_slab_destroy**.

44929: If the slab cache's list of slabs is now empty, **__kmem_cache_shrink** returns 0; otherwise, it returns 1.

kmem_slab_destroy

44538: **kmem_slab_destroy**, which releases the memory pages allocated to an empty slab, is another of those functions that's very simple once you ignore the debugging code interspersed through it.

44559: As discussed earlier in the chapter, the slab cache's **dtor** function is called for each object in the slab. Since the current kernel distribution never uses **dtor**s, this loop is never even executed (unless the slab allocator is compiled with debugging turned on; see line 44543).

44572: Frees the slab's own memory through a call to **kmem_freepages** (line 44488), which does little more than call the lower-level page-freeing function **free_pages** (line 43475).

44575: If the slab's associated **slab_t** was allocated separately from the slab itself (off-slab), the **slab_t** must also be freed separately.

The Kernel Stack

The kernel memory allocators I've shown you so far are like heap allocators for the kernel (that is, they're analogous to C's **malloc** and **free**). In addition to a heap, a user process has a stack. So does the kernel—indeed, the kernel has many stacks, one for each process. Unlike a user process's stack, whose growth is practically unbounded, the kernel's stack size is sharply limited.

Recall from Chapter 7 that the kernel allocates a **struct task_struct** for a new process using the macro **alloc_task_struct** (line 14980). As you can see, this macro allocates $2^1 = 2$ pages, or 8KB, to hold the **struct task_struct**. (This macro's definition is platform-specific, but platforms generally allocate either 8KB or 16KB.) However, as you might also recall from Chapter 7, a **struct task_struct** is only about 1,500 bytes, so the upper 6,700 bytes or so are not used by the **struct**. Instead, the kernel uses that extra space as its stack when it's running on behalf of that process. What's more, the top 60 bytes of this two-page allocation are used to store another **struct**, the **struct pt_regs** (line 15038) describing the process's registers. The resulting arrangement is shown in Figure 8.12.

Several mechanisms must work together in order to make all this happen. First, as described earlier in the chapter, the kernel installs in the global descriptor table (GDT) a task-state segment (TSS) describing the current process. Most of this TSS is effectively unused by the kernel, but one entry in particular is very important. It's the **esp0** field of the TSS, which points to the kernel stack that should be used for the process. (You can find the **esp0** field at line 14857; this is in **struct tss_struct**, a kernel-defined structure that exactly mirrors the layout of the CPU-defined TSS. This lets the kernel write to the real TSS more easily and more clearly.) If the process causes a transition to kernel mode, the CPU will load the stack pointer from the TSS's **esp0** field. The

esp0 value that should be used for each process is stored in the process's associated **struct thread_struct** at line 3542 (called during **fork**) and is loaded into the TSS at line 3642, during a context switch.

Next, think back to Chapter 5's discussion of the **system_call** function (line 898), which is the normal kernel entry point for system calls. **system_call** begins by pushing a bunch of registers onto the stack. (Most of this work is done by the **SAVE_ALL** macro, line 789.) Since **system_call** executes in kernel mode, the stack it's pushing the registers onto is the kernel stack—and since the kernel stack begins at the top of the 8KB allocation, where the process's **struct pt_regs** lives, **system_call** is effectively filling out that **struct pt_regs**. (The **struct pt_regs** members from lines 15049 through 15053 are placed on the stack by the **int** instruction that triggered the system call.)

From that point on, the kernel stack works much the same way as for a user process, except that it's important for the kernel to respect the 6,700-byte limit or it will overwrite the process's **struct task_struct**. The stack is used to hold function call information and local (in C terms, **auto**) variables, so the kernel must avoid deep chains of function calls (as might be produced by excessive recursion), and it must not allocate large data structures as local variables. This is another reason why **find_vma**, covered earlier in the chapter, traverses the AVL tree of a process's VMAs iteratively rather than recursively: Not only is an iterative traversal faster, it uses less stack space.

The kernel can use the kernel-mode stack pointer to obtain a pointer to the **struct task_struct** of the process on whose behalf the kernel is running. The kernel-mode stack pointer always points within a contiguous 8KB region allocated directly from the buddy system (not by way of **kmalloc** or **vmalloc**), and the buddy system ensures that a request for N bytes always begins on an N-byte boundary. The process's **struct task_struct** resides at the bottom of this 8KB region, so rounding the stack pointer down to the next-lower 8KB boundary must yield the address of the current process's **struct task_struct**. And that's exactly what the kernel does—see line 12525, the implementation of the widely used **current** macro, for example. (The same insight is applied elsewhere as well—see lines 12983, 835, 851, and 872.)

When the kernel returns to user mode, it restores the CPU registers from their saved positions in the process's **struct pt_regs**. When returning from a system call, for example, line 926—using **RESTORE_ALL**, line 804—pops the registers off the very end of the stack, in the **struct pt_regs**, again.

Dumping Core

Under some circumstances, such as when a buggy program tries to access memory outside of its allowed memory space, the process may dump core. To "dump core" is to write an image of a process's memory space—along with some identifying information about the application itself and its state—to a file for later perusal under a debugger such as gdb. ("Core" is an otherwise-obsolete term for memory.)

Of course, *your* code never makes a mistake like this, but it might happen to the less talented programmer in the cubicle next to you, who might ask you about it some day, so I'll cover the topic here.

Different binary handlers dump core differently. (Binary handlers are covered in Chapter 7.) The most common Linux binary format is ELF, so let's see how the ELF binary handler dumps core.

elf_core_dump

10075: **elf_core_dump** begins here. Because a process dumps core as a result of receiving a signal (which it may have sent to itself, as through a call to **abort**), the signal number is supplied in **signr**. **signr** doesn't affect how or whether the process dumps core, but the user looking at the core file in a debugger will want to know which signal caused the core dump, as a hint about what went wrong. The **regs** argument points to a **struct pt_regs** (see line 15038), which contains a description of the CPU's registers. Among other reasons, **regs** is important because

it contains the contents of the EIP register—the instruction pointer, which defines what instruction was being executed when the signal was received.

10094: Gets the number of VMAs attached to the dumping process. Although **elf_core_dump** keeps the count in a variable named **segs**, what it's counting are not memory segments in the strict sense of the term (that is, they're not the hardware-enforced segments described earlier in the chapter). Don't read anything special into this variable's name.

10102: The ELF core file format is defined according to an official specification. Its first component is a header that describes the file. The type **struct elfhdr** (see lines 18841 and 18646) mirrors this header format, and **elf_core_dump** fills out a local variable, **elf**, of this type.

10126: Sets the **PF_DUMPCORE** flag (line 22069), signaling that the process is dumping core. This flag isn't used by any code explored in this book, but just so you'll know, it's used by process accounting. *Process accounting* keeps track of a process's resource usage and other related information—including whether it dumped core upon exit—which is information that was originally used by computing centers to help figure out how much to charge each department or user for resource usage. Aren't we all glad *those* days are pretty well behind us?

10128: Writes the ELF core file header that was set up earlier. Some hidden flow control is involved here: The **DUMP_WRITE** macro, whose definition begins at line 10063, causes **elf_core_dump** to return if the write fails or if the attempted write would exceed the process's core file size limit (which was set up back at line 10086).

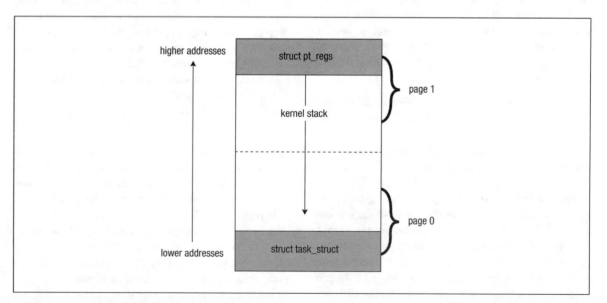

Figure 8.12 The kernel stack.

10135: The ELF core file header is followed by a series of notes; each of these has a specific purpose, recording certain information about the process. A note (type **struct memelfnote**, line 9989) includes a pointer to auxiliary data (its **data** member) and the length of the data (its **datasz** member). Most of the work of filling out a note is really a matter of filling out the auxiliary data structure and making the note point to it.

Some information is stored in more than one note. This repetition is not explained in the code, though at least some of the reason seems to be to copy behavior from other Unix variants. Keeping the file format consistent with other platforms helps in porting programs such as gdb to Linux; a bit of repetition is better than delaying the port and complicating the maintenance of such crucial tools.

10138: Note 0 records the process's heritage, signals, and CPU usage in the auxiliary data structure **prstatus** (type **struct elf_prstatus**; see line 18156). Observe in particular that line 10142 is where **elf_core_dump** stores the signal number that caused the process to dump core. So when you (or, rather, the inferior programmer in the cubicle next to you) run gdb on a core file and it says "Program terminated with signal 11, Segmentation fault," you'll know just where the information came from.

10187: Note 1 records general process information— its owner, state, priority, and so on—in the auxiliary data structure **psinfo** (of type **struct elf_prpsinfo**; see line 18197). Line 10193 contains a highly unusual, albeit correct, array index into a literal constant string; the selected character is a mnemonic for the process's state. These are the same state letters reported by the ps program's STAT field (except when the index is out of range, of course). More interesting is line 10216, which copies the executable name

(up to 16 characters, as discussed before) into the note. Both gdb and the program "file" use this field to report which program generated the core dump. In addition, lines 10199 through 10215 copy the process's **argv** into the note.

10219: Note 2 records the dumping process's **struct task_struct**, which clearly stores a great deal of essential information about the process. Because some of the information in the **struct task_struct** consists of pointers that will no longer be valid when a debugger looks at the code, **elf_core_dump** will later dump some of the pointed-to information—most critically, the process's memory space—separately.

10225: If this system has an FPU (floating-point unit, or math coprocessor), a note is written with its state. Otherwise, line 10227 decrements the number of notes to be stored.

10240: For each note that has been created, a header is written describing the note; the note itself will come later. The header is of type **struct elf_phdr**; see lines 18842 and 18688 for its definition.

10260: This is the first pass of writing the process's memory space. In this pass, the function writes header information (**phdrs** again) describing all the VMAs that it will proceed to write.

10284: At last, **elf_core_dump** actually writes the notes it so laboriously set up earlier.

10290: Skips ahead in the file to the next 4KB boundary, where the actual core file data should begin. The **DUMP_SEEK** macro used for this purpose is defined at line 10067 and, like **DUMP_WRITE**, it causes **elf_core_dump** to return if the seek fails.

10292: After all that setup, this almost seems anticlimactic. But this is the main part of a core dump: The function writes each of the process's VMAs. A little cleanup follows, and **elf_core_dump** is done.

Chapter 9

System V IPC

Unix has had pipes from its earliest days, and pipes work beautifully for unidirectional communication between two processes on the same machine (or bidirectional communication, using two pipes). Later, BSD's (Berkeley Software Distribution's) versions of Unix gave the world sockets, used for communication between two processes on the same or different machines.

The System V strain of Unix added a trio of services that collectively are now known as *System V IPC*. Like pipes, all of these services can be used only for communication between processes on the same machine. However, unlike both pipes and sockets, System V's IPC (interprocess communication) features enable communication among many processes on the same machine, not just two processes. Also, pipes—but not sockets—have the further restriction that the two communicating processes must be related. They must have a common ancestor process that sets up the pipe—usually, either one process is the parent of the other, or the two are siblings whose parent set up the pipe for both. System V IPC, like sockets, enables communication among processes that have no common heritage, only an agreement to communicate. (To be fair, a variant of pipes—named pipes—can be used to sidestep the relatedness requirement.)

The three IPC services that make up System V IPC are message queues, semaphores, and shared memory. The rest of the chapter is devoted to studying this code.

All three System V IPC services have certain architectural features in common. In earlier kernels, these similarities were implicit: If you read the code, you'd see what they had in common, but that's about as far as it went; they didn't share any data structure definitions or code. In the 2.4 kernel, the System V IPC subsystem was largely

rewritten, and now most of the architectural similarities are explicit. The method used for this rewrite was the obvious one: A new pair of files, ipc/util.h and ipc/util.c, encapsulate common definitions, data structures, and code. This will slightly complicate the discussion of message queues (which I explore first), because I can't really discuss the message queue code without simultaneously discussing the underlying, more general layer. (I could look at the lower layer alone before proceeding to any of the IPC services built on top of it, but that code looks pretty abstract and pointless unless you examine it in the context of the upper layers.) This all pays off handsomely later in the chapter, when I cover semaphores and shared memory, so the little bit of extra effort we invest up front will be well worth it.

Message Queues

System V's message queues are a way for processes to send messages to each other asynchronously. In this case, that means both that the sender doesn't have to wait for the receiver to check its messages—having sent the message, the sender can go on to do other things—and that the receiver doesn't have to go to sleep if no messages are waiting. Encoding and decoding the messages is the job of the sender and receiver processes; the message queue implementation gives them no particular help. This results in a general mechanism that's easy to implement, although that simplicity is achieved at the cost of some added complexity in the applications.

Here's a simple usage scenario that might occur on an SMP (symmetric multiprocessing) machine. A single dispatcher process running on one CPU sends requests for work to a certain message queue. Requests for work might take the form of a set of passwords to try in a code cracker, a range of pixels to calculate in a fractal drawer, a portion of a space to update in a particle system, or the like. Meanwhile, worker processes running on the other CPUs retrieve messages from the message queue whenever they're idle and send result messages to another message queue.

This architecture is easy to implement and, assuming good choices are made about the granularity of the work requested per message, makes highly efficient use of the CPUs in the machine. (And note that because the dispatcher probably wouldn't be doing all that much work, a worker process can run on the dispatcher's CPU most of the time.) In this way, message queues could be used as a low-level form of remote procedure call (RPC).

New messages are always added to the end of a queue, but they're not always removed from the front; they can be removed from anywhere in the queue, as you'll see later in the chapter. In some ways, a message queue is similar to voice mail: New messages are always at the end, but the message receiver can receive (and delete) messages from the middle of the list.

Message Queue Data Structures

There are three important data structures that participate in the kernel's message queue implementation: **struct msg_msg**, **struct msg_queue**, and **struct ipc_ids** (which is actually part of the generic layer of IPC code). I'll look at each of these in turn.

struct msg_msg

26176: **struct msg_msg** describes a message and holds its contents—it's the envelope and the letter all in one. If a message is too large to fit into a **struct msg_msg**, the part that won't fit is broken into one or more chunks and the chunks form a linked list of **struct msg_msgseg**s (line 26170) attached to the **struct msg_msg**. This situation is illustrated in Figure 9.1.

struct msg_msg has the following members:

- **m_list**—Maintains a list of the linked messages in a single queue.

- **m_type**—A user-assigned type code; its use is examined later in the chapter in the "Message Queue Code" section, in a discussion of how messages are received.

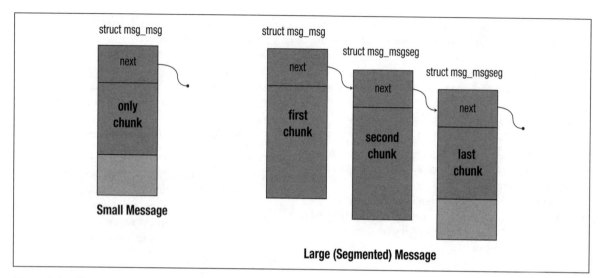

Figure 9.1 The structure of small and large messages.

- **m_ts**—Records the message's size ("ts" abbreviates "text size," although the message need not be human-readable text). The maximum size of a message is **MSGMAX**, which is **#defined** to 8,192 bytes at line 21235.

- **next**—This field points to the next chunk of the message—a **struct msg_msgseg**— if the message is too large to fit in this **struct**. It's usually **NULL**.

struct msg_queue

26189: **struct msg_queue**, of course, represents a single message queue. It has the following members:

- **q_perm**—Records who is allowed to read and write messages in this queue. All of the System V IPC services have such a member in their respective **structs**. It's of type **struct kern_ipc_perm**, which is defined at line 19472. As you can see, this **struct** contains a user ID, a group ID, a permissions mode—everything you'd need to implement a file permissions scheme—as well as some other members we'll cover later in the chapter.

- **q_stime** and **q_rtime**—Record the last time that a message was sent to the queue and the last time a message was read from the queue, respectively.

- **q_ctime**—Last queue change time—the time it was created or the time certain of its parameters were last set using the **msgctl** system call.

- **q_cbytes**—The total number of bytes currently in all messages in the queue.

- **q_qnum**—The number of messages in the queue.

- **q_qbytes**—The maximum number of bytes allowed for storing all messages in the queue; **q_cbytes** is compared to **q_qbytes** to see whether there's room for a new message. **q_qbytes** defaults to **MSGMNB**, although this limit can be raised dynamically by a user with the right capabilities.

MSGMNB is **#defined** to 16,384 bytes at line 21238. There are four reasons why this limit

is so low. First, in practice, you usually don't need to include much information in a given message anyway, so the limit is not too restrictive. Second, if the message senders have gotten very far ahead of the message receivers, there's probably no sense in their doing much more work—they might as well block for a while to let the receivers catch up. Third, this 16KB limit per queue can potentially be multiplied by the maximum number of queues in the system, and that can add up. The hard limit on the number of message queues in the system is **IPCMNI** (line 19467), or 32,768. With that many message queues in use, messages would consume a whopping 512MB of kernel memory, none of it pageable! However, the default limit on the number of message queues is a much more reasonable 16 (**MSGMNI**, at line 21232); with that setting, all the message queues together could use only about 256KB of kernel memory—not too bad.

However, the major reason for this limit is to prevent a denial-of-service attack: If there were no limits, a process could repeatedly send messages to a queue from which no one was reading, forcing the kernel to allocate memory for the messages until it ran out. Limiting the number of bytes in a queue's messages helps protect against this attack, but there is still a problem: Nothing prevents applications from sending zero-length (that is, empty) messages. (Empty messages can't simply be disallowed, because that would break compatibility.) **q_qbytes** isn't affected by such messages, and memory still must be allocated for the message headers, so a mean-spirited (or sloppy, or curious) programmer might try sending an infinite stream of zero-length messages. Consequently, as you'll see, the queue is protected both by checking the number of bytes in the queue and the number of messages in the queue.

- **q_lspid** and **q_lrpid**—The PIDs of the last message sender and the last message receiver.

- **q_messages**—A list of the messages (**struct msg_msg**s) waiting in this queue.

- **q_receivers**—Messages can normally be read from a message queue immediately. But what if no messages are waiting? In that case, processes get their choice: They can either regain control immediately (with an error code signaling the failure to read a message) or go to sleep, waiting for a message to arrive. This list holds the processes that decide to wait. The elements in this list are of type **struct msg_receiver** (line 26153).

- **q_senders**—Similarly, messages can normally be sent to the queue immediately. But, as I discussed before, the kernel limits how much data can be placed in a queue, in order to defend against denial-of-service attacks. In this case, again, processes get their choice: They can either regain control immediately (with an error code) or go to sleep, waiting in this list until there's room in the queue. The elements in this list are of type **struct msg_sender** (line 26165).

struct ipc_ids

29355: So far, we've seen a single message, and we've seen a message queue, but we haven't seen where the kernel keeps its message queues. It keeps them here, in a **struct ipc_ids**—part of the lower layer mentioned earlier. Most of **struct ipc_ids** is dedicated to tracking a dynamically resizable array of the message queues (or semaphores, or shared memory regions) in the system. It has the following members (for clarity of exposition, the order here does not match the order in the code):

- **entries**—This is the array of message queues, but it doesn't look that way at first. As far as the compiler is concerned, **entries** is an

array of type **struct ipc_id** (line 29366)—which, at first blush, doesn't seem to have much in common with **struct msg_queue**. Surely we want an array of **struct msg_queue**s, or perhaps pointers to them?

Once you realize that a **struct ipc_id**'s sole member is a pointer to the same type (**struct kern_ipc_perm**) that forms the first member of a **struct msg_queue**, however, the picture comes into focus: Each **struct ipc_id** in **entries** thinks it's pointing to a **struct kern_ipc_perm**—and it is. What it doesn't know is that there's more stuff after the **struct kern_ipc_perm** it's pointing to. In the **struct ipc_ids** that holds all of the system's message queues, each **struct ipc_id** in **entries** really points to a **struct msg_queue**. The message queue code allocates a whole **struct msg_queue**, passing the lower level only a pointer to the new **struct msg_queue**'s first element, and this pointer is installed in the **entries** array. The corresponding structures in the semaphore and shared memory code start with a **struct kern_ipc_perm**, too, so they pull the same trick.

The generic layer knows all it needs to know—it can store a pointer to the **kern_ipc_perm** part of these various structures and it returns this pointer when a higher layer asks it to look up an entry. The higher layer simply casts this pointer to and from the real type (**struct msg_queue** or whatever) as needed. ANSI C guarantees that a pointer to the first member of a **struct** equates to a pointer to the **struct** itself, so we're sure that the casts will have the desired effect.

- **size**—The number of elements currently allocated in **entries**.

- **in_use**—The number of elements of **entries** that are in use. Elements not in use are set to **NULL**.

- **max_id**—A high-water mark for the array—the largest index currently in use. The generic layer sometimes must loop over the entire **entries** array, but it's common for only a few array elements to be in use. By tracking the high-water mark, we can avoid looping over elements that could not possibly be in use.

It's possible to fool this simple optimization, of course: If an entry is installed in the last element of **entries** (which happens only when all entries have been allocated, as you'll see) and that last entry is never released, then **max_id** doesn't save us anything. Indeed, the work involved in maintaining **max_id** is simply wasted in this case. However, in practice, this situation is very unlikely, and it's far more common for **max_id** to speed things up considerably.

- **seq**—Tracks a "sequence number" associated with the message queues; you'll see its use shortly.

- **seq_max**—Imposes a limit on the sequence number, **seq**; **seq** ranges from 0 to **seq_max**, inclusive. You'll see the necessity for this limit later.

- **sem** and **ary**—Protect this **ipc_ids** from simultaneous modification; mostly needed on SMP systems.

That completes our tour of the message queue data structures. The relationship between these data structures is shown in Figure 9.2.

Message Queue Code

Processes are given four message-queue–related system calls:

- **msgget**—An unfortunate name: You'd think this gets a waiting message. It doesn't. The caller supplies a message queue key—an integer that uniquely identifies the queue—and **msgget** returns an identifier either for the existing queue with that key, if there is one, or for a new message queue with that key. What

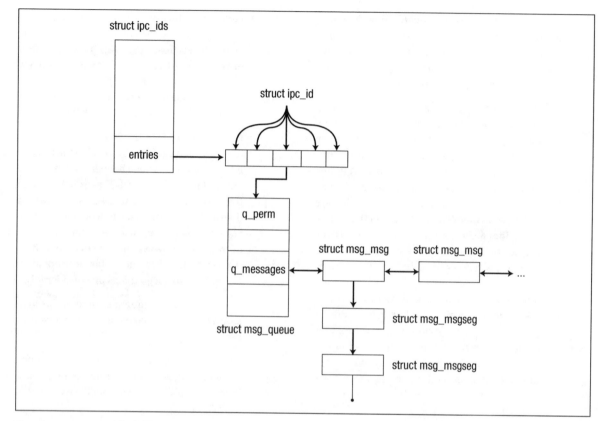

Figure 9.2   Message queue data structures.

msgget gets, therefore, is not a message, but rather an identifier that uniquely identifies a message queue.

- **msgsnd**—Sends a message to a message queue.

- **msgrcv**—Receives a message from a message queue.

- **msgctl**—Performs a set of administrative operations on a message queue—retrieving information about its limits (such as the maximum amount of message data allowed in the queue), deleting the queue, and so on.

I'll look at the code that implements these system calls shortly. Before any of these system calls can be invoked, however, the message queue code must be initialized. Since the required initialization is simple, I'll start exploring the message queue code by looking at **msg_init**.

msg_init

26236: **msg_init** is invoked by **ipc_init** (line 28968) during kernel initialization to initialize the message queue data structures.

26238: **msg_init**'s main job is to initialize the **struct ipc_ids** that tracks message queues—this is **msg_ids**, defined at line 26216. As you can see, the real work is handled by **ipc_init_ids** (line 28984)—part of the generic IPC layer—so we'll explore that code next.

26241: If support for the /proc file system (discussed in Chapter 11) is being compiled into this kernel, the pseudo-file /proc/sysvipc/msg is created.

When this pseudo-file is read, the function **sysvipc_msg_read_proc** (line 26990) is invoked to return information about the message queues in use. Basically, this function simply dumps the **struct msg_queue** for each active message queue to an ASCII string that will appear to the user to be the contents of that pseudo-file.

ipc_init_ids

28984: This simple function initializes the **struct ipc_ids** used for tracking one of the System V IPC services. Most of the assignments to the **struct**'s members are pretty obvious, so I'll skip ahead a bit.

28996: The sequence numbers and array indices will be encoded into an **int**, and there must be room for both. The maximum sequence number that will fit is computed and stored in **ids->seq_max**.

29003: Here, the underlying array is allocated using **ipc_alloc** (line 29145). As you can see, this simple utility function allocates memory using one of the facilities described in Chapter 8: either **vmalloc** or **kmalloc**, depending on the size of the allocation. The only downside is that you need to remember (or recompute) the original size of the request, so that the memory can be returned to the correct memory allocator (see **ipc_free**, line 29162).

29005: If the allocation failed, an error message is printed and the array's size is set to 0. Contrary to what the error message suggests, however, the IPC service is not necessarily disabled. You'll see why not later on.

29011: All the entries of the array are set to **NULL**. Note that since this loop depends on **size**, not **ids->size**, there will be a problem if the array allocation fails: This loop will try to dereference a **NULL** pointer and the kernel will panic.

sys_msgget

26438: **ret**, which tracks the function's desired return value, is needlessly initialized to -**EPERM**. **ret** is given a value on every path through the function, so the assignment at this line is redundant. However, gcc's optimizer is smart enough to eliminate the dead assignment, so this is a moot point.

26444: The special key **IPC_PRIVATE** (**#define**d to 0 at line 19416) says that the caller wants a new queue, whether or not there are any other message queues with the same key. In this case, the queue is simply created immediately, using **newque** (line 26246), which I cover later.

26446: Otherwise, **key** uniquely identifies the message queue the caller wants to work with. Generally, a developer chooses a key more or less at random (or gives the user a way to choose one) and hopes that it doesn't conflict with any other running application's key.

This might sound alarming, but temporary file names present much the same problem—you simply have to hope no other application chose the same naming scheme. In practice, there's rarely a problem—**key_t** is just a **typedef** for **int**, so there are over 4 billion possible values. (The size of the key space is the same on 64-bit machines: gcc uses 32-bit **int**s for those architectures, too.) The sheer size of this key space helps to reduce the chances of an accidental collision. And with message queue keys, as with files, a permissions scheme further reduces the likelihood of problems even if an accidental collision does occur.

Still, couldn't we make this better? Standard C library functions such as **tmpnam** help tremendously with generating temporary file names that are guaranteed to be unique systemwide, but there's no equivalent way to generate a message queue key that's guaranteed to be unique.

On closer inspection, these turn out to be two different problems. An application generally doesn't care what its temporary file name will

be, as long as it's something that's not already in use. However, an application generally needs to know in advance what its message queue key will be, so that other applications that want to send messages to it will know what queue to send them to. If an application chooses its message queue key dynamically, then it somehow needs to tell other applications about the chosen key. And if the applications involved already have a way to send messages like that to each other, what do they need message queues for? Consequently, it's probably not a problem worth solving. An application that wants a unique key for a nonprivate queue, but doesn't care too much what the key is, can get one simply by trying a **key** of 1 (remember that 0 is **IPC_PRIVATE**) and working up from there until it succeeds. That's a little more work, but it's not too likely to be necessary.

Anyway, this line uses **ipc_findkey** (line 29021, and discussed later) to search for an existing message queue with the given key. If such a queue is found, the corresponding array index is returned (or –1 is returned if no such queue is found).

26448: If the key is not in use, **sys_msgget** can create it. If the **IPC_CREAT** bit is not set, then the **ENOENT** error is returned; otherwise, **newque** (line 26246) creates the queue.

26452: The key is in use. If the caller set both the **IPC_CREAT** and **IPC_EXCL** bits, then the caller wanted an error in this case, and it gets one. (This is deliberately an exact parallel to **open**'s **O_CREAT** and **O_EXCL** bits.)

Offhand, it's hard to tell whether the **if** test is faster as written or in this equivalent form:

```
} else if (msgflg &
        (IPC_CREAT |IPC_EXCL) ==
        (IPC_CREAT | IPC_EXCL)) {
```

Both ways test whether both bits are set, but, for various reasons, you might expect either one to be faster than the other. However, it turns out that gcc generates identical code for both, at least when compiling with optimization. (If you're curious, the version it chooses is the straightforward translation of my suggested alternative—it converts the version that appears in the kernel into code that tests both bits simultaneously.) This is a pretty cool optimization, and one I didn't expect.

26455: Otherwise, the key is in use and the caller will accept using an existing queue with that key. (This is the most common case.) An error is returned if there's no message queue at the expected location (which should never happen, given that **ipc_findkey** found one back at line 26446 and **sys_msgget** protected **msg_ids** from other CPUs' changes at line 26443) or if the caller lacks permission to access it.

26461: The sequence number and array index are encoded in the return value, using **msg_buildid** (line 26225; this is just a wrapper for **ipc_buildid**, line 29431). This will become the **msqid** argument that the caller will pass to **sys_msgsnd**, **sys_msgrcv**, and **sys_msgctl**.

This encoding scheme has two important features. The more obvious feature is how the sequence-number part and the array-index part are kept separate: Because **id** is an array index into **msg_ids.entries**, it can take on values only up to (but not including) **IPCMNI**, the maximum number of elements in the array. Multiplying the sequence number by this value therefore leaves the lower bits free for storing **id**—it's kind of like base-**IPCMNI** arithmetic. (The multiplication step in **ipc_buildid** works in terms of **SEQ_MULTIPLIER**, but that's just **#define**d to **IPCMNI** at line 29349.)

Also notice that the return value can never be negative. This is important, because the C library implementation might interpret a negative return value as an error. Because **IPCMNI** is currently 32,768 (see line 19467), the array index occupies the low 15 bits of the return value. Sequence numbers are 16 bits, so only the low 31 bits of **ret** might be set to 1 by this assignment. The remaining bit—the sign bit—is 0, so **ret** is 0 or positive.

Interestingly, the comment beside **IPCMNI**'s definition is accurate. **IPCMNI** really could be set to **INT_MAX**, the largest possible value of **int**, and all of the code would work correctly. (Some memory allocations might fail, especially considering that this number is multiplied by the size of the allocated structures, but the basic logic is correct.) **IPCMNI** could also be set as low as 1. Keep these extreme values in mind as you read through the code, and think about how the code would adjust to them.

26465: However it was computed, **ret** is now returned.

ipc_findkey

29021: **ipc_findkey** locates the message queue with the given **key**, on behalf of **sys_msgget**. Since this is part of the generic layer, it performs the corresponding role for semaphores and shared memory as well.

29026: Begins looping over all possibly occupied slots in the **entries** array. As mentioned earlier, **ids->max_id** is the high-water mark for this array—it tracks the highest occupied array element. It's used here and maintained by **ipc_addid** and **ipc_rmid** (lines 29077 and 29114, respectively), which you'll see shortly. Without **ids->max_id**, this loop would need to iterate over the entire array—potentially as many as 32,768 elements—even though only, say, the first five were in use.

29027: The rest of this function is not very noteworthy: If a non-**NULL** entry with a matching key is found, its array index is returned; otherwise, the function returns –1.

newque

26246: With the help of the generic layer, **newque** locates an unused array entry and attempts to create a new message queue there.

26251: Optimistically allocates memory for a new message queue.

26255: Using **ipc_addid** (line 29077, and discussed next), **newque** locates an unused element of **msg_ids.entries**. As you'll see, the new queue is installed in the underlying array as a side effect. If the array is full, the allocated memory must be freed before returning.

26260: The rest of the function is devoted to filling out the allocated message queue. Since the assignments here are fairly straightforward given the data structure's definition, I won't cover them in detail.

ipc_addid

29077: **ipc_addid**, part of the generic layer, installs a new entry in an **entries** array if there's room.

29082: The array is first expanded to the requested size using **grow_ary** (line 29036, and discussed next). The array's size doesn't change very often, but it can be set using the **msgctl** system call, as you'll see later.

29083: The next step is a simple scanning loop that looks for an unused entry. Note that limiting the loop with **ids->max_id** would be inappropriate here: **ids->max_id** tracks the last-used array element, but of course there might be unused elements between that point and the end of the array. Control jumps ahead to the **found** label if an unused entry is found; otherwise, –1 is returned.

29089: Because it's certain at this point that a new entry will be installed in the array, it's time to update the **ids->in_use** count.

29090: If no elements were free below **ids->max_id** (a desirable situation, as it means **ipc_findkey** is doing no avoidable work), the **ids->max_id** limit

must be updated. If everything is working correctly, this just adds 1 to **ids->max_id**—as a result, the assignment could be turned into **ids->max_id++** instead. However, if there's a bug somewhere else that has caused **ids->max_id** to take on the wrong value, the assignment here will tend to fix it. It could still have the wrong value after the assignment, depending on the state of the array, but the result is never worse than a simple increment and might be better.

29096: This queue's sequence number is established and the sequence number is incremented for next time, wrapping around to 0 if the sequence number has exceeded its limit. (This is one of the places where it's interesting to consider the effects of the extreme redefinitions of **IPCMNI** mentioned earlier. What values of **seq_max** would result from these redefinitions, and what would happen here as a result?)

Although incrementing (and wrapping) the sequence number here is the obvious way to do it, it turns out that it's possible to delay that work until an array element is removed. You don't need a unique sequence number for every message queue (and likewise for the other services). You just need a different sequence number each time an array element is reused, so that the combination of an array index and a sequence number is unlikely to recur. An array index can't be reused until the object installed there is freed, so incrementing the sequence number can be delayed until that point.

29101: The new value is installed in the **entries** array and the array index of the new entry is returned. Observe again that the code doesn't know the real type being installed in the array—this is the generic layer.

grow_ary

29036: **grow_ary** ensures that **ids->entries** has at least **newsize** elements. It returns the array's new size.

29042: If the requested size exceeds the maximum allowed size, it's silently reduced.

29044: If the array is already at least the requested size, no more work needs to be done. Note that **ids->size** is not updated in this case. Needlessly reducing **ids->size** could result in wasteful reallocations later, if the array were "grown" again to the size it actually already had.

29047: The array really is growing. Since the kernel has no equivalent of **realloc**, the reallocation must be done manually here.

Incidentally, this is why the calling IPC subsystem isn't necessarily disabled even if the initial allocation in **ipc_init_ids**, at line 29003, fails: On the first call to **grow_ary**, **newsize** will be greater than the array's size (0) and the allocation is effectively retried. It's even possible that it would work now, since, unlike **ipc_init_ids**, **grow_ary** is called after the kernel frees up initialization-time memory.

In any case, **grow_ary** attempts to allocate memory for the larger array, returning its old size (unchanged) if the attempt fails. A single failure doesn't mean the array will never be expanded, though. The next call to **ipc_addid** will simply call **grow_ary** with the same **newsize**, and **grow_ary** will gamely try again.

29050: In the more likely case that the allocation succeeds, the old array's elements are copied into it and the new elements are all set to **NULL**. A **memset** would clear the new elements just as well, maybe a little faster.

29057: The rest is trivial: The new array is installed, the old array is freed, and the array's new size is returned. The **return** statement could return **newsize** instead; this would be equivalent and just a touch faster. You'd expect gcc to notice this equivalence itself and make the change for you, but you'd be wrong.

sys_msgsnd

26770: Begins a sequence of sanity checks. The second of the three tests on this line is unnecessary, given the first test—any message size that would fail the second test would fail the first, too.

26785: The message being sent to the queue is read from user space and a **struct msg_msg** is filled with the contents. The work is done by **load_msg**, which I'll explore in the next section. Because **load_msg** returns a pointer to the message structure, it uses special pointer values to encode error returns. The **IS_ERR** macro reports whether the pointer is one of these special values, and the **PTR_ERR** macro extracts the integer error code if it is. (These macros were omitted for space.) On success, the type and size of the new message are also filled in.

26792: **msg_lock** is called to provide a pointer to the underlying message queue and to begin protecting against simultaneous access by other CPUs. If the returned pointer is **NULL**, then there was no queue at the indicated index—the caller is asking to send messages to a queue that no longer exists, and maybe never did. In this case, the **EINVAL** (invalid argument) error is returned.

26798: The stored sequence number in the message queue must match the one encoded in the **msqid** argument. The idea is that just because there is a message queue at the right array index doesn't mean it's the message queue the caller wants. Since the time the caller got its reference to the queue, the message queue originally at that index might have been removed and a new one created at the same index. As we've seen, the sequence number is periodically incremented, so the new queue at the same index will have a different sequence number from the original. (Unless exactly 65,535 other new queues were created first, which is quite unlikely—or 131,071 other new queues, which is even more unlikely, and so on. Those numbers will vary, however, depending

on the value of **msg_ids.seq_max**, which in turn depends on **IPCMNI**—again, consider the effects of extreme legal redefinitions of **IPCMNI**.) Anyway, if the sequence numbers don't match, **sys_msgsnd** returns the **EIDRM** error to indicate that the message queue the caller wanted has been removed.

26802: Ensures that the caller has permission to write to the message queue. A similar system is covered in more detail in Chapter 11; for now, it's enough to say that a system just like Unix file permissions applies.

26805: Checks whether the maximum allowed queue size would be exceeded if the supplied message were written to the queue. As stated earlier, the number of messages in the queue also participates in computing this limit, in order to avoid accepting an infinite stream of empty messages.

26809: There's no space in the queue. If the **IPC_NOWAIT** bit is set in **msgflg**, the caller doesn't want to wait when this happens, so the **EAGAIN** error is returned.

26813: The calling process is about to be put to sleep. First, **ss_add** (line 26370) adds it to the queue of sleeping processes associated with this queue. The message queue code wakes the process when a message is removed from the queue; in addition, **ss_add** sets the process's state to **TASK_INTERRUPTIBLE** so that, as covered in Chapter 7, the process is awakened when a signal arrives for it. When the process awakes, it tries writing to the queue again.

Note that this is placing a local variable in the list of sleeping senders—very unusual; in application code, such data structures usually have heap-allocated nodes. It's safe in this case, because the node will be removed from the list before the function returns; context switching takes care of the rest.

26814: Releases the message queue lock. Without this step, there would be no way for messages to be removed from the queue while the current process was sleeping. As a result, the process could never succeed in writing its message to the queue. Even worse, no other processes could read or write any message queue.

26815: Calls **schedule** (line 34237, and covered in Chapter 7) to hand off the CPU to another process.

26818: The process has reawakened, either as the result of a signal or because the queue's status has changed. Anything at all might have happened while the process was sleeping, including the removal of the message queue to which it was trying to write. Therefore, the first step is to reacquire the message queue lock and make sure that the message queue still exists and looks like it's the right one.

26822: The process removes itself from the list of processes sleeping on the queue. It's important to wait to do this until after we're sure it's the right queue. If the queue was removed, its list was already cleared.

26824: If the process was awakened by a signal, honoring the signal is more urgent than sending the message. The process dutifully exits with the **EINTR** error. The signal will be delivered nanoseconds later, when the system call returns and **system_call** (line 898, Chapter 5) notices that the process has a pending signal.

26828: The message queue still exists, and no signal is pending. The process can now try sending its message again, and it does so, jumping back to line 26796.

26831: Control reaches this point when line 26805 decides that the queue has room for this process's message. (The process might have slept and reawakened any number of times—including zero—before reaching this point,

naturally.) **pipelined_send** (line 26743, and covered later) delivers the message to a suitable blocked receiver, if there is one.

26833: If there is no blocked receiver interested in this message, the message is simply enqueued for later delivery and the appropriate message queue statistics are updated.

26840: The caller's message was successfully sent or enqueued. More queue statistics are updated, **msg** is set to **NULL** (so that it won't be prematurely freed at line 26848), and **sys_msgsnd** returns 0.

load_msg

26288: **load_msg** is used by **sys_msgsnd** to read a message from user space and build up a **struct msg_msg** to hold its contents. If need be, the message is split into segments (**struct msg_msgseg**s) attached to the returned **struct msg_msg**.

26295: **alen** is set to the number of bytes of this message that will fit into the **struct msg_msg** itself, exclusive of any additional attached segments. The maximum value of **alen** is **DATALEN_MSG** (line 26184), which, as you can see, constrains the whole allocation to the size of one page.

26299: Memory is allocated for the control structure and the message. Because this is all performed in a single allocation, the message's contents will immediately follow the **struct msg_msg** in memory (exactly as depicted earlier in Figure 9.1).

26304: **next** (the pointer to the first attached segment) is set to **NULL**. This is unremarkable in itself, but note that it's important for **msg** to be in this state in case the following step fails and **msg** is passed to **free_msg** (line 26276).

26306: The message's contents—or as much as will fit in **msg**, anyway—are now copied in from user space. Note the use of the expression **msg + 1** to obtain a pointer immediately after **msg**.

26311: In case the message won't fit in **msg**, **len** and **src** are now updated to reflect the amount of data read in for this chunk. This work (and the following assignment to **pseg**) is wasted most of the time, because a message normally fits in a single **struct msg_msg**. Even when the work must be done, it doesn't need to be written twice—if you look ahead to lines 26332 and 26333, at the end of the **while** loop, you'll see the same logic repeated. On the last loop iteration, this work, too, is wasted. The following approach is both smaller and faster:

```
if (len > DATALEN_MSG) {
  /* Need additional segments. */
  pseg = &msg->next;
  while (len > alen) {
    struct msg_msgseg *seg;
    /* Delay this work until needed. */
    len -= alen;
    src = ((char *) src) + alen;
    /* Continue as before: */
    alen = len;
    /* ... Unchanged ... */
    pseg = &seg->next;
    /* len and src assigns removed. */
  }
}
```

Exactly the same kind of restructuring is possible at line 26354 (part of **load_msg**'s counterpart, **store_msg**).

26314: If there is still more to this message, the following loop allocates **struct msg_msgseg**s for the rest, building a linked list of these **struct**s attached to **msg**.

26316: The body of this loop looks very similar to the code that precedes it. The main differences are the **struct** type (**struct msg_msgseg** instead of **struct msg_msg**, of course) and the length limit per **struct**. Since **struct msg_msgseg**s are a little smaller than **struct msg_msg**s, they can store a little more message data. The limit is **DATALEN_SEG**, which is **#define**d at line 26185.

The only other feature worth mentioning is how the linked list of message chunks is updated. Notice that this uses **pseg**, a pointer to the previous link's **next** pointer. **pseg** doesn't care whether it points to a **struct msg_msg**'s **next** pointer or to a **struct msg_msgseg**'s **next** pointer, because they have the same type (**struct msg_msgseg ***).

26335: On success, **load_msg** returns a pointer to the successfully constructed **struct msg_msg**.

26337: On error, the allocated memory must be freed and an encoded error number is returned.

pipelined_send

26743: **pipelined_send** tries to deliver a message, **msg**, to a single blocked receiver waiting on **msq**.

26753: Everything up to this point is just loop setup. Here **pipelined_send** checks whether the message would satisfy the current recipient. The function that decides whether to deliver the message to the current receiver, **testmsg**, is defined at line 26721 and will be discussed in the next section.

26755: The current receiver is deleted from the list of waiting receivers if the message satisfied its criteria, but there's still one more reason why **pipelined_send** might not deliver: The receiver's buffer might not be large enough to hold the entire message body. In that case, the receiver is awakened with an error code instead of a real message, and the loop continues to seek a recipient. I presume that this behavior is why the send is called "pipelined."

26759: The message met the caller's criteria and will fit in this buffer. The lucky receiver is awakened and the message is delivered to it (by setting its **r_msg** pointer). The message queue's statistics are updated, and the function returns nonzero

for success. Notice the bug in the code that updates the queue's statistics. Because it's tracking the most recent message receiver here, it should be updating **msq->q_lrpid**. Instead, it sets **msq->q_lspid**, which tracks the most recent message sender. **msq->q_lspid** is correctly set at line 26842, but **msq->q_lrpid** will not be correctly updated in this case.

26767: If the loop exits without successfully delivering a message (possibly after waking any number of potential recipients with too-small buffers), **pipelined_send** returns 0 to indicate failure.

testmsg

26721: This simple utility function is used both by the message-sending and message-receiving code, in both cases for the same purpose: to test whether a message meets a potential recipient's criteria.

26725: In the simplest case, **SEARCH_ANY**, the caller will accept any message sent to the right queue, so **testmsg** always succeeds in this case.

26727: In the **SEARCH_LESSEQUAL** case, the caller is implementing a simple message priority scheme and wants the pending message with the smallest **m_type** value. In the only use of this function so far (when it was called from **pipelined_send**), there was only one candidate message in the queue (otherwise, there would have been no blocked receivers). Therefore, any message with a small enough type code must be the message with the smallest type code. **testmsg** is also used by **sys_msgrcv**, where—in the **SEARCH_LESSEQUAL** case—each call is just one step in a process. You'll see that later.

26731: The remaining cases, **SEARCH_EQUAL** and **SEARCH_NOTEQUAL**, are equally simple: They test whether a message has, or does not have, the specified type.

26740: If the designated test failed, or if **mode** had an invalid value (which never happens, of course), **testmsg** simply returns 0.

gcc generates slightly better code for this function if the non-**SEARCH_ANY** cases are modified slightly. The **SEARCH_LESSEQUAL** case, for example, currently looks like this:

```
case SEARCH_LESSEQUAL:
  if (msg->m_type <= type)
    return 1;
  break;
```

If the **if** condition fails, control falls through and **testmsg** returns 0. **testmsg** would do the same thing if the case looked like this:

```
case SEARCH_LESSEQUAL:
  return msg->m_type <= type;
```

With the same change applied to the **SEARCH_EQUAL** and **SEARCH_NOTEQUAL** cases, **testmsg** computes the same result, just faster—while still trapping invalid **modes** at line 26740. However, this change is no longer faster in the most recent versions of gcc (as of this writing, still unreleased), so there's probably no point in altering the code.

sys_msgrcv

26872: **sys_msgrcv**, of course, implements the **msgrcv** system call, invoked by a process that wants to receive a message from a message queue—checking its voice mail, as it were. This is where **struct msgmsg**'s **m_type** field comes into play. It's compared to **msgtyp** (whose meaning can be modified by **msgflg**) to select a waiting message, if any.

26885: Following a quick sanity check, **msgtyp** and **msgflg** are converted to a **mode** value that will make sense to **testmsg**. The **convert_mode** function used for this purpose is at line 26853; because it's simple and liberally documented, I won't cover it here. Do note, however, that in the **SEARCH_LESSEQUAL** case—the priority scheme case—the **msgtyp** value is negated.

26887: The array entry indicated by the low bits of **msqid** is located and the array is protected against unwanted interference. If there's no entry at the indicated position, the **EINVAL** error is returned.

26892: Checks whether the caller has permission to read from the message queue, returning the **EACCES** error if not.

26899: For each message in the queue, **testmsg** is consulted—as it was from **pipelined_send**—to see if this message would interest the caller. (Note, however, that **pipelined_send** was looping over processes, but this loop is looping over messages.) If so, **found_msg** is made to point to this message.

26901: Things are a little different here than they were in **pipelined_send**: Because the queue can contain more than one message that meets this recipient's criteria, **testmsg** alone can't decide whether the current message is the best one for this recipient. If the search mode is **SEARCH_LESSEQUAL** and it's still possible that a smaller **msg->m_type** is lurking in the queue, the loop simply updates its notion of the smallest **msgtyp** found so far and continues. (Note that the new value of **msgtyp** is one less than the current message's type value, so that the current message will beat out any later messages with an equal type.)

26905: In all other cases, the current message will be the best one for this recipient. The exact same assignment was done at line 26900, so the assignment at this line is redundant—only the **break** is needed. The same redundant assignment occurs in the previous branch of the **if**, at line 26902, too.

26909: If no message has been selected for delivery, the loop iterator is advanced to the next message.

26913: The preceding loop found a suitable candidate message for this recipient, but, as in **pipelined_send**, this message still might not be delivered if the caller's buffer is too small. However, here—unlike in **pipelined_send**—the **MSG_NOERROR** flag allows the code to proceed with delivering the message even if there is insufficient room. This does not indicate a bug in **pipelined_send**, though, as surprising as that might seem. You'll see why not in a moment. (I can't think of any reason an application would ever set the **MSG_NOERROR** flag, by the way, nor could I find any applications that use it.)

26917: Now nothing can stop **sys_msgrcv** from trying to deliver this message. The message is removed from the queue and the queue's statistics are updated.

26924: Because removing this message might have made room in the queue, any sleeping senders are awakened using **ss_wakeup** (line 26384) so that they can try again.

26925: **sys_msgrcv** has no further need for the queue or the underlying array at this point; they're unlocked so that other processes can send or receive messages.

26927: It's time to deliver the message. **msgsz** is set to the number of bytes to deliver, decreasing it to the number of bytes in the message if necessary. If the message is larger than the caller's buffer, **msgsz** won't change and the function simply copies whatever will fit. Either way, after this point, **msgsz** is the number of bytes that should be copied to the caller's buffer.

The more conventional way of writing this would probably also be a little more efficient:

```
if (msgsz > msg->m_ts)
  msgsz = msg->m_ts;
```

26928: At last, the message is copied out to user space. The bulk of the work is performed by **store_msg** (line 26342, and too similar to **load_msg** to be worth detailed discussion). If this copy fails, the **EFAULT** error will be returned.

26932: Either the message was successfully delivered or an error was encountered in the attempt. In either case, memory for the message is freed. Just to make this explicit, this means that if the delivery attempt failed, the message is not re-enqueued for later delivery. (What do you think this is, FedEx?) This decision might seem a little harsh, but it keeps the code simple, avoids endless failures, and makes room in the queue for messages that might do better. The code is also, at least, consistent: Along all paths that lead to some kind of delivery attempt, the message is either copied to the caller or discarded; it is never re-enqueued.

26933: System calls commonly return 0 on success. The **msgrcv** system call is an exception: It returns the number of bytes copied (or a small negative number on failure, of course).

26938: This line is reached when no message with a satisfactory **msgtyp** was in the queue (so **found_msg** was **NULL** at line 26911). If the caller does not want to wait for a message to arrive, the **ENOMSG** error is returned and the system call exits immediately.

26942: Otherwise, the caller is willing to go to sleep in the hope that a suitable message will arrive eventually. **sys_msgsnd** used **ss_add** for a similar purpose, but there's no corresponding **rr_add**; instead, the work is all done right here. A node describing the current process is added to the message queue's **q_receivers** list and is then initialized. This might seem backwards, but the order doesn't matter. The queue is still protected against interference, so the function just has to do both steps before releasing the lock.

26946: This is why **pipelined_send** doesn't need to check the **MSG_NOERROR** flag: It's accounted for here, before **pipelined_send** can even consider the waiting receiver. A process with the **MSG_NOERROR** flag doesn't discriminate on the basis of message size, so **pipelined_send** should effectively ignore the message size when deciding whether to wake the process. The most clever way to achieve that effect is to tell **pipelined_send** that this process will accept messages up to the maximum possible size— and that's exactly what happens. When the process is reawakened, it will be in the context of **sys_msgrcv**, which remembers the **MSG_NOERROR** flag (along with all the other information stored on the kernel stack) and accounts for it when copying the message out to user space.

26950: The process should awaken when either a message or a signal arrives; on the pessimistic assumption that a signal will be the trigger, the **EAGAIN** error is encoded as the reason the process was awakened. If it's awakened for some other reason, this value will simply be overwritten.

26951: To ensure that the process will respond to signals, it is placed in the **TASK_INTERRUPTIBLE** state.

26952: Because this process is about to go to sleep, it no longer requires exclusive access to the system's message queues. (Besides, if it went to sleep while it had exclusive access to the queues, nobody else could send a message to wake it up.) Accordingly, the queues are unlocked.

26954: Calls **schedule** (line 34237, and covered in Chapter 7), to allow other processes to run. This call will return upon arrival of a message or signal, and when it does, the calling process will be returned to the **TASK_RUNNING** state.

26957: If the caller was awakened with a real message, control jumps back to the **out_success** label— line 26926—so that delivery can proceed as if the caller had never slept. Note that **sys_msgrcv** doesn't update the message queue's statistics in this case. The necessary updating is performed by **pipelined_send** before the process is awakened.

26961: Otherwise, the caller was awakened with some kind of error. **sys_msgrcv** next tries to determine the error condition so that it can respond appropriately. The first step is to reacquire the message queue lock.

26964: In the unlikely event that a message arrives for the process between the return from **schedule** and this point, the earlier error is irrelevant and the lucky caller is sent its message. If the caller was awakened by a signal, the signal won't be ignored for long. The caller will get its message, but the signal will be noticed and delivered when the system call returns.

26972: More likely, the error condition will persist. (Because the message queues are now locked, there is no further hope of a last-minute rescue by the arrival of a message.) If so, the integer error code is extracted from the **msg** pointer.

26973: If the error code is the **EAGAIN** error, then either the call to **schedule** returned because a signal was delivered, or the process is being awakened by **sys_msgctl** (which we haven't seen yet). If it's any other error, control will simply drop through and return the error code at line 26986.

26977: If the process has a signal pending, **sys_msgrcv** returns the **EINTR** error and the signal will be delivered as the system call exits. Otherwise, the instigator was **sys_msgctl**, which might have changed the queue's permissions so that the caller no longer can read from this queue; in that case, the read is retried. Strictly speaking, it's possible for the process to be awakened by **sys_msgctl** *and* to have a signal pending at this point; this could happen if the signal arrived after **schedule** returned. If that happens, the signal wins.

26983: The **out_unlock** label is reached in a variety of cases, all of them returning an error code (the only point where success is ever returned is line 26933) and usually holding a lock on the message queues. The queues are unlocked if necessary and the error code is returned.

sys_msgctl

26563: **sys_msgctl** is easily the largest function in the message queue implementation. This is partly because it does a variety of different things— similar to **ioctl**, it's a grab bag of loosely related functionality. (Don't blame the Linux developers for this mess, by the way; they're just providing compatibility with System V's ugly design.)

The **msqid** argument names a message queue, and **cmd** says what **sys_msgctl** should do with it. As you'll see shortly, **buf** might or might not be needed, depending on **cmd**, and its meaning differs from case to case even when it is used.

26574: When the System V IPC subsystem was rewritten for 2.4, some of the user-visible data structures and constants were changed. To provide support for old binaries that are unaware of the change, the **ipc_parse_version** function (line 29254, with a special IA-64-only macro version at line 29453) checks **cmd** to see whether the caller is explicitly requesting the new approach. You'll see the effects of this at line 26649.

26577: In the **IPC_INFO** and **MSG_INFO** cases, the caller wants information about the properties of the message queue implementation. It might use this information to choose a message size, for example—on machines with large maximum message sizes, the calling process might raise its own limit on the amount of information it sends per message.

All of the variables and manifest constants that define the limits on the message queue implementation are copied back through an object of type **struct msginfo** (line 21221).

Slightly different values are copied out if **cmd** was **MSG_INFO** rather than **IPC_INFO**, as you can see from line 26594. The **MSG_INFO** case returns current settings for some values, whereas the **IPC_INFO** case returns default limits for the same values; the two cases are otherwise identical.

Notice that the caller's buffer, **buf**, was declared as a pointer to a different type, **struct msqid_ds** (line 21189). It doesn't matter. The copying is performed by **copy_to_user** (line 17589), which doesn't care about the types of its arguments, although it will raise an error if it's asked to write to inaccessible memory. If the caller supplies a pointer to a large enough space, **sys_msgctl** copies the requested data there; it's up to the caller to get the type (or at least the size) right.

26608: If the copy succeeded, **sys_msgctl** returns one additional piece of information, **max_id** (copied from **msg_ids.max_id** at line 26603). Note that this case entirely ignored the **msqid** argument. This makes perfect sense, because it's returning information about the message queue implementation as a whole, not about any message queue in particular. However, it's a matter of opinion whether a negative **msqid** should be rejected by the sanity checks at line 26571 in this case. Admittedly, rejecting invalid **msqids**, even when **msqid** won't be used, certainly simplifies the code.

26610: **MSG_STAT** and **IPC_STAT** request the statistical information that the kernel has kept on a specific message queue identified by the caller—the queue's current and maximum size, the PIDs (process IDs) of its most recent reader and writer, and so on. The difference between these two cases is that **MSG_STAT** assumes that **msqid** is the array index only, not including the sequence number; by contrast, **IPC_STAT** expects (indeed, insists on) the sequence number as well. This makes **MSG_STAT** useful for gathering statistical information about all queues

in the system, for example, whether or not the caller had earlier used **msgget** to acquire the queues' identifiers. **IPC_STAT** would probably be used by a process that was actually reading from the message queue it's asking about.

26617: Even without the sequence number, it's possible to check whether the array index is out of range. The call to **msg_lock** at line 26622 ends up checking the same thing, so the test here probably slows things down negligibly in the common case that the input is valid.

26620: Clears the stack object, **tbuf**, that will be copied back to user space if everything goes well. See line 26584 (where a similar **memset** was done) for the reason **tbuf** must be cleared even if all its members are assigned to. This **memset** could be delayed as late as line 26638, marginally speeding up the error cases.

26631: In the **IPC_STAT** case, the sequence number is verified; the **EIDRM** error is returned in case of a mismatch.

26636: Returns an error if the caller lacks permission to read the queue. Read permission on the queue, therefore, means permission not only to read the enqueued messages, but also to read metadata about the queue itself.

26639: The caller passed the tests. **sys_msgctl** copies the requested information to **tbuf**, and then copies **tbuf** back through the caller's buffer. The function used for this copy, **copy_msqid_to_user** (line 26468), is what makes use of the **version** variable. It either copies out the new-style **struct msqid64_ds** (line 13360) used internally, or it translates the new-style **struct msqid64_ds** to an old-style **struct msqid_ds** (line 21189) and copies that out instead.

26651: Returns the "complete" identifier, in the **MSG_STAT** case, or 0, in the **IPC_STAT** case. (It's pointless to return the complete identifier

in the **IPC_STAT** case, because the caller already has it.) These return codes were prepared at lines 26627 and 26633.

26653: There are two cases left: **IPC_SET** and **IPC_RMID**. Unlike the cases you've seen so far, which were completely handled within this **switch**, the remaining two are only partly handled here. The first of these, **IPC_SET**, simply ensures that the user-supplied buffer is non-**NULL** and then copies it into **setbuf** for further processing later in the function. The function used for copying in the buffer, **copy_msqid_from_user** (line 26521), does a translation similar to that done by **copy_msqid_to_user**, then extracts the few fields it cares about and installs them in the supplied **struct msq_setbuf** (line 26514).

26659: The last case, **IPC_RMID**, does no work in this **switch**; all of its work is deferred to later in the function.

26661: **cmd** wasn't one of the recognized commands after all, so the caller gets the **EINVAL** error.

26665: This code is common to both of the remaining cases and it should look familiar by now: It obtains a pointer to the indicated array index, ensures that a valid message queue exists at the indicated index, and validates the sequence number.

26676: Since both **IPC_SET** and **IPC_RMID** are performing administrative tasks on the queue— **IPC_SET** changes ownership, size, and permissions, and **IPC_RMID** deletes the queue—it's important to ensure that the calling process should be allowed to do these things. To fool with the message queue in this way, the caller either must own the queue or have the **CAP_SYS_ADMIN** (line 17966) capability. (Capabilities are discussed in Chapter 7.) Otherwise, the attempt is rejected with an **EPERM** error.

26686: Raising the limit on the maximum number of bytes in the message queue beyond the normal maximum is much like raising any other resource beyond its hard limit, so it requires the same capability, **CAP_SYS_RESOURCE** (line 17989). (Resource limits are discussed in Chapter 7.)

26689: The caller should be allowed to perform the operation, so selected parameters are set as specified by the caller.

26698: As discussed earlier and noted in the code here, tighter permissions might deny some blocked receivers the ability to read any further messages from the queue. The code could conceivably analyze both the old permissions and the new permissions and inspect each blocked receiver to see if it would be affected, but it's a lot easier—and still pretty fast—just to wake them all up and let them figure it out. So that's what the code does, waking the processes with **expunge_all** (line 26400). As you saw with **sys_msgrcv**, waking the sleeping processes with the **EAGAIN** error (as happens here) causes them to retry reading, and they'll return with an **EPERM** error if the permissions are too tight.

26701: As noted in the code, some or all of the sleeping senders might now succeed if they try again. Again, **sys_msgctl** could analyze the queue's former size, its new size, and the sleeping senders, and carefully wake just the right ones— or it could wake them all and let them sort it out themselves. You won't be surprised to learn that it does the latter.

26705: **IPC_RMID** means to delete the specified queue—not just the messages in it, but the queue itself. The work is done by **freeque** (line 26415), which is discussed in the next section.

26709: All of the function's interesting work has been done. All that's left is to clean up, returning 0 in the normal case.

freeque

26415: **freeque** does the work of the **IPC_RMID** case of **sys_msgctl**, entirely removing a message queue from the system and freeing all of its associated data.

26420: The queue is actually removed by **msg_rmid** (line 26221), which is just a simple wrapper for **ipc_rmid** (line 29114, and discussed in the next section).

26422: Much as in the **IPC_SET** case of **sys_msgctl**, any sleeping receivers are expunged and any sleeping senders are awakened. There are minor differences here, though. First, the sleeping receivers are awakened with the **EIDRM** error, not **EAGAIN**, so the receivers will know the queue has been removed and return **EIDRM** to their respective callers. And second, **ss_wakeup** is given a nonzero **kill** argument, causing it to destroy the list of sleeping senders as it wakes them.

26426: **freeque** frees any remaining messages in the queue, using **free_msg** (line 26276), which frees a message and any attached extra segments.

26434: Finally, global message queue statistics are updated and the queue structure itself is freed.

ipc_rmid

29114: **ipc_rmid** is the generic-layer function that removes an array entry (such as a single message queue) for a System V IPC service.

29118: The array index corresponding to **id** is extracted and sanity-checked.

29121: The indicated array element is marked unused by setting it to **NULL**, although the element hasn't been freed yet.

29127: After updating the count of in-use array elements, **ipc_rmid** checks whether the entry being freed is the highest used entry. If so, **ipc_rmid** lowers the high-water mark, **ids->max_id**, as far as possible. After the loop, **ids->max_id** is again the index of the highest used array entry, or –1 if all entries are unused.

Semaphores

Semaphores are a way of guarding access to a resource. The usual conceptual model for a semaphore is that of a signaling flag (hence the name), but I think a key is a better metaphor. Don't confuse this with the integer keys I've been talking about—for the sake of this analogy, I mean your front door key.

In the simplest case, a semaphore is simply a single key hanging on a hook by a locked door. To pass through the door, you must take the key from the hook; you replace the key on the hook when you come out. If the key isn't there when you arrive, you have to wait for its possessor to replace it—if you're determined to get through the door, that is. Alternately, you might impatiently give up if you can't get the key right away.

That describes waiting for a resource that only one entity can use at a time; in this case, where there's just one key, the semaphore is referred to as a *binary semaphore*. For resources that can be used by more than one entity at a time, the semaphores are referred to as *counted semaphores*. These work the same as binary semaphores, just with more keys hanging on the hook. If the resource can support four users at a time (or if four equivalent resources are available, which is basically the same thing), there are four keys. The generalization is natural.

Processes use semaphores to coordinate their activities. For example, suppose you're writing a program and want to ensure that at most one instance of the program is running on a given machine at a time. A good example is a sound file player—you probably don't want to play more than one sound at a time, because the result would be a confusing mishmash. Another example is an X server. There are occasionally good reasons to run more than one X server simultaneously on the same machine, but it is reasonable for an X server to disallow this, at least by default.

Semaphores provide a way to solve this problem. Your sound player, X server, or whatever, can define a semaphore, check whether the semaphore is in use, and proceed if it isn't. If the semaphore is already in use, another instance of the program is running. In this case, your program can either wait for the semaphore to be released (likely behavior for the sound player), just give up and exit (likely behavior for the X server), or go on and do something else for now, trying for the semaphore again later. By the way, such a use of semaphores is often called *mutual exclusion*, for obvious reasons; its common abbreviation, *mutex*, appears repeatedly in the kernel source.

Lock files are a more common way to get the same effect as binary semaphores, at least in some circumstances. Lock files are a bit simpler to use, and some implementations of lock files work across the network; semaphores don't. On the other hand, lock files are slow and don't generalize well beyond the binary case. In any event, lock files are beyond the scope of this book.

The semaphore and message queue code are so alike that there's no need to discuss **sem_init** or **sys_semget**, because they are almost exactly like their message queue counterparts. I can also almost entirely skip **newary**, the counterpart of **newque**, except for one small note: Observe that the memory allocation at line 27185 includes space for the semaphores immediately following the **struct sem** that describes them.

Semaphore Data Structures

There are five important data structures that participate in the kernel's System V semaphore implementation: **struct sem**, **struct sem_array**, **struct sem_queue**, **struct sembuf**, and **struct sem_undo**. (**struct ipc_ids**, covered in the discussion of message queues, plays an equally important role in the semaphore code.) I'll look at each of these in turn.

struct sem

22745: **struct sem** represents a single semaphore. It has two members:

- **semval**—If 0 or positive, **semval + 1** is the number of keys still hanging on this semaphore's hook. If negative, its absolute value is one more than the number of processes waiting to access it. Semaphores are

binary by default, but they can be made counted by using **sys_semctl** (line 27832); the maximum semaphore value is **SEMVMX** (**#define**d to 32,767 at line 22725).

- **sempid**—Stores the PID of the last process to operate on the semaphore.

struct sem_array

22753: **struct sem_array** is the counterpart of **struct msg_queue**: It tracks all the information about a single semaphore set and a queue of operations to be performed on it. It has the following members:

- **sem_perm**—Records who is allowed to inspect and modify semaphores in this set; it fills exactly the same role as **struct msg_queue**'s **q_perm** member. Note, importantly, that it's the first member of this **struct**, so that the generic layer of the IPC code will treat this **struct** interchangeably with a **struct msg_queue**.

- **sem_otime**—This is like **struct msg_queue**'s **q_stime** and **q_rtime** members rolled into one. It tracks the last time an operation was performed on a semaphore.

- **sem_ctime**—Just like **struct msg_queue**'s **q_ctime**, **sem_ctime** tracks when the semaphore set was created or when certain of its parameters were last set using the **semctl** system call.

- **sem_base**—Points to an array of **struct sem**s—in other words, to an array of semaphores. Just as a single **struct msg_queue** can contain multiple messages, so a **struct sem_array** can contain multiple semaphores—collectively, the semaphores in the array are typically referred to as a *semaphore set*. Unlike message queues, however, the number of semaphores tracked by a single **struct sem_array** doesn't change over its lifetime. The array's size is fixed.

The maximum length of one of these arrays is controlled by the first element in the **sem_ctls** array (line 27153), for which there is a handy alias,

sc_semmsl, at line 27155. The default maximum is **SEMMSL**, which is **#define**d to 250 at line 22719. However, this maximum can be raised using the /proc interface covered in Chapter 11. The array's actual length is recorded in **struct sem_array**'s **sem_nsems** member.

- **sem_pending**—Tracks a queue of groups of pending semaphore operations. Semaphore operations are completed immediately, when possible, as you'd expect, so nodes are added to this queue only when an operation must wait. This is the rough equivalent of **struct msg_queue**'s **q_receivers** and **q_senders** members.

- **sem_pending_last**—Tracks the tail of the same queue. Note that it doesn't point directly to the last node—it points to a pointer to the last node, which results in slightly faster (if slightly harder to understand) code later on.

- **sem_undo**—A queue of operations that should be performed when various processes exit. This is discussed later in the chapter.

struct sem_queue

22771: **struct sem_queue** is a node in the queue of sleeping operations on a single **struct sem_array**. It has the following members:

- **next** and **prev**—The next and previous nodes in the queue. As with **sem_pending_last**, **prev** is a pointer to a pointer to the previous node. You'll see why later in this chapter. **prev** never becomes **NULL**; in the degenerate case, when the queue is empty, **prev** points to **next**.

- **sleeper**—A pointer to the process for which this queue node was allocated. The process sleeps until the operations can complete, hence the name.

- **undo**—An array of operations that will undo the operations implied by **sops**—stated another way, it's the inverse of **sops**.

- **pid**—The PID of the process that's trying to carry out the operations represented in this queue node.

- **status**—Records how the sleeping process was awakened.

- **sma**—Points back to the **struct sem_array** in whose **sem_pending** queue this **struct** resides.

- **id**—The unique ID of the **struct sem_array** to which this **struct** belongs.

- **sops**—Points to an array of one or more operations this queue node represents; it's never **NULL**. The goal of the work represented by this queue node is to carry out all the operations in **sops**.

- **nsops**—The length of the **sops** array.

- **alter**—Says whether the operations will affect any of the semaphores in the set. It might seem that this would always be true, but bear in mind that waiting for a semaphore to reach 0 (that is, to become available) doesn't affect the semaphore itself.

struct sembuf

22685:   **struct sembuf** represents a single operation to perform on a semaphore. It has the following members:

- **sem_num**—The array index, in a **struct sem_array**'s **sem_base** array, of the semaphore to which this operation applies. There's never any confusion about which **struct sem_array**'s semaphore array the operation is intended for; it's always clear from context, so this **struct** keeps no explicit reference to a **struct sem_array**.

- **sem_op**—The semaphore operation to perform. Normally, it has the value –1, 0, or 1. –1 means to procure the semaphore (take the key from the hook), 1 means to vacate the semaphore (replace the key on the hook), and 0 means to wait for the semaphore's value to become 0. Values other than these are useful, however, and they simply translate to procuring or vacating more values of the semaphore—that is, taking or replacing more keys on the hook. (The words "procure" and "vacate" might look a little weird in this context. Don't worry about it; it's common semaphore terminology.)

- **sem_flg**—One or more flags (each a single bit in this **short**) that might modify how the operation is performed.

Figure 9.3 illustrates the relationships among these data structures.

struct sem_undo

22795:   **struct sem_undo** contains enough information to undo a single semaphore operation. When a process performs a semaphore operation with the **SEM_UNDO** flag set, a **struct sem_undo** is created that will undo the operation. All the undo operations implied by a process's list of **struct sem_undo**s are performed when the process exits. Readers familiar with design patterns might recognize an instance of the Command pattern here.

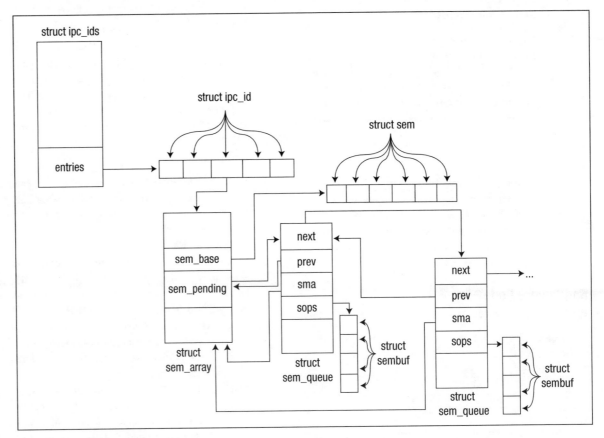

Figure 9.3   Semaphore data structures.

This feature allows a process to guarantee that, however it exits, it will automatically clean up after itself. That way, it won't accidentally leave other processes waiting around for a semaphore release that can never happen. (Unless it acquires the semaphore and then enters an infinite loop, but it's not the kernel's job to protect against that. In this case, the intent is to offer processes a way to do the right thing, not to force them to do it.)

struct sem_undo has the following members:

- **proc_next**—Points to the next **struct sem_undo** in the owning process's list of **struct sem_undo**s.

- **id_next**—Points to the next **struct sem_undo** in the list of **struct sem_undo**s associated with a semaphore set. You read that right: The same **struct sem_undo** is in two different lists simultaneously. As the chapter progresses, you'll see how both are used.

- **semid**—Identifies the semaphore set to which this **struct sem_undo** belongs.

- **semadj**—An array of adjustments to be performed on each of the semaphores in the semaphore set associated with this **struct sem_undo**. Semaphores about which this structure has no opinion have a 0 in this array—no adjustment.

Semaphore Code

Processes are given three semaphore-related system calls:

- **semget**—The counterpart of **msgget**, **semget** creates a semaphore set.

- **semop**—Performs an operation on one or more semaphores in a set—taking or releasing semaphores, or waiting for them to become available.

- **semctl**—Like **msgctl**, **semctl** performs administrative operations on a semaphore set.

As I noted before, the implementation for **semget** (see **sys_semget**, line 27211) virtually duplicates that for **msgget**, so it won't be covered. I will, however, look at the code for the **semop** and **semctl** system calls.

sys_semop

27924: **sys_semop** implements the **semop** system call. There's no exact equivalent to **sys_semop** in the message queue code; it's the counterpart of **sys_msgsnd**, **sys_msgrcv**, or both, depending on how you look at it. In any case, its job is to carry out one or more operations on one or more semaphores. It tries to carry out all the operations atomically (that is, without interruption). If it can't do them all, it won't do any of them.

27935: Sanity-checks the arguments. Note in particular that **nsops** is constrained to **sc_semopm** (line 27157), the maximum number of semaphore operations that can be attempted at once. This defaults to **SEMOPM**, which is **#define**d to 32 at line 22723, but, as with **sc_semmsl**, the limit can be raised dynamically through the /proc interface.

27944: Copies the description of the requested operations from user space into a temporary buffer, **sops**. This buffer is the stack-allocated **fast_sops** (line 27929) if the number of operations is below a certain limit (**SEMOPM_FAST**, **#define**d to 64 at line 27144; consequently, with the default value of **sc_semopm**, the fast buffer is always used). Otherwise, the buffer was allocated from the heap at line 27940. The point of **SEMOPM_FAST**, of course, is precisely to avoid the heap allocation when possible. **kmalloc** may be fast, but allocating space on the stack is even faster. However, since the kernel stack is a severely limited resource, **SEMOPM_FAST** must be carefully chosen to avoid using too much of it. As documented at its definition, the current value of **SEMOPM_FAST** causes **fast_sops** to occupy about 372 bytes.

27949: The following few lines should look familiar from the discussion of message queues. An entry in the underlying array of semaphore sets is located and its sequence number is checked. Behind the scenes, the macros involved—**sem_lock** (line 27124) and **sem_checkid** (line 27129)—are using the same generic IPC functions as their counterparts in the message queue code.

27957: Begins a loop over all the specified operations. It first checks whether the semaphore number given in the operation is out of range, rejecting it if it is. Curiously, a failure here returns the **EFBIG** (file too big) error rather than the **EINVAL** (invalid argument) error. This matches the documentation, though.

27960: Counts the number of operations whose **SEM_UNDO** flag is set. **undos** is just used as a flag—all that matters is whether it's 0—so assigning 1 (or any other nonzero value) to it when the condition is satisfied would have the same effect. However, the kernel's version is slightly faster. And because the containing loop iterates at most **sc_semopm** times—and **sc_semopm**, like **undos**, is just an **int**—**undos** can't be incremented so many times that it wraps around and becomes 0 again.

27962: The next few tests update two local flags: **decrease** and **alter**. These track whether any operation in the set will decrease a semaphore's value and whether any operation will alter a semaphore's value, respectively. **alter** is not fully computed until after the loop, at line 27967—inside the loop, it only tracks whether any operation increases a semaphore's value; this is later combined with the information in **decrease** to decide whether any alteration will occur.

Note that the code does not attempt to see whether any combinations of operations would cancel each other out—maybe one operation will decrease some semaphore's value by 1 and another operation will increase its value by 1. If these are the only operations, then, in a sense, the values of the **decrease** and **alter** flags will be misleading. The kernel could try to optimize this (and more elaborate versions of the same thing), but it can't possibly be worth the time and effort: An application that's stupid enough to perform such a circuitous no-op deserves what it gets, and smarter applications shouldn't be punished for its stupidity.

27970: Ensures that the process has permission to carry out the specified operations on the semaphores. If **alter** is true, the process is modifying the semaphores and therefore needs write permission; otherwise, it's only waiting for one or more semaphore values to reach 0, so it merely needs read permission. Again, this check is implemented in terms of the same underlying generic layer already covered in the message queue discussion.

27976: The set of operations included some undo operations. If the current process already has a set of undo operations to be performed for this semaphore set at exit, the data from the new set of undo operations should be merged into that one. This loop finds the existing undo set, if one exists, leaving **un** pointing to it if so, or **NULL** if not.

27980: Along the way, the loop watches for undo sets corresponding to semaphore sets already freed by **freeary** (line 27452, and discussed later); these sets are marked by a **semid** value of –1. At this point, the obsolete undo set is simply freed, one **struct sem_undo** at a time, by **freeundos** (line 27871, and discussed later), and the loop continues normally to the next undo set.

27986: The process doesn't already have an undo set for this semaphore set, so a new one is allocated, using **alloc_undo** (line 27892, and discussed later).

27991: No operations in the supplied set of operations will need to be undone by the kernel, so **un** is simply set to **NULL**.

27993: Calls **try_atomic_semop** (line 27307, discussed later) to attempt to perform all the operations in a single shot. If there are any mutating operations, **un** is non-**NULL**; on failure, it is used to undo any partially completed operations before the function returns.

27995: **try_atomic_semop** returns 0 on success, negative on error. In either of these cases, control jumps ahead to line 28050.

28001: Otherwise, **try_atomic_semop** returned a positive value. This is neither success nor failure; it merely indicates that the operations couldn't all be performed right now, but the process wants to wait and try again later. To begin with, a local **struct sem_queue** is filled out.

28008: Nodes representing operations that will modify semaphores are placed at the end of the queue; nodes representing operations that are all waiting for semaphore values to reach 0 are placed at the front. You'll see why when **update_queue** (line 27368) is investigated later in the chapter.

28014: Begins a loop that repeatedly tries to perform the operations, exiting only when all the requested operations were successfully performed or when an error occurred.

28021: Sleeps until interrupted by a signal or until there's some point in trying again.

28034: If the process was awakened by **update_queue** because it now has a chance of succeeding, it retries the operations.

28040: Alternately, **queue.status** might be 0 (if the **try_atomic_semop** call in **update_queue** succeeded), -**ERANGE** (if the semaphore would

be adjusted out of the allowed range by that same call), or -**EINTR** (if the sleeping process was interrupted by a signal).

In general, **update_queue**'s call to **try_atomic_semop** can also set **queue.status** to -**EAGAIN**. That can't happen here, though, because it only happens when the calling process has the **IPC_NOWAIT** flag set, and if the calling process had the **IPC_NOWAIT** flag set, then it wouldn't be sleeping.

28048: This and the following line remove the calling process from the queue of processes waiting to modify the semaphore set.

28051: If this set of operations altered the queue, it might have established the conditions some other process was waiting for. **sys_semop** calls **update_queue** to find and wake any such processes.

28056: If the requested number of operations was so large that **sops** had to be allocated from the kernel's heap, the allocated buffer is freed before exit.

freeundos

27871: This function is not as complicated as it looks. Maybe it doesn't look complicated at all to you, but something about the similarities among the important variable names (**u**, **un**, and **up**) makes my eyes cross when I look at it. In case it does the same to you, it's all sorted out here.

Just to refresh your memory, **freeundos** is called from **sys_semop** when it discovers an obsolete undo set attached to a process, which can happen when the corresponding semaphore set was previously deleted. The job of **freeundos** is to free the obsolete **struct sem_undo** and return a pointer to the **struct sem_undo** following it.

freeundos has the following parameters and local variables (**sma**, passed as a parameter, is not used in the function):

- **un**—Points to the obsolete **struct sem_undo** discovered by **sys_semop**. As you'll see in a moment, once that **struct sem_undo** is found, **un**'s role changes: It becomes a temporary.

- **u**—Iterates over the **struct sem_undo**s attached to the current process.

- **up**—Points to a pointer that points to **u** (think "**u** pointer"). **up** is like **u** with an additional level of indirection: It walks along the pointers to the pointers to each **struct sem_undo** attached to the current process.

27877: Begins iterating **u** and **up**. (**u** isn't actually initialized until the following line. Incidentally, note the seemingly unnecessary parentheses on that line—they silence a gcc compiler warning about an assignment's being used where an equality comparison might have been intended.)

27881: If the sought-after **struct sem_undo** has been found, the next two lines use **un** as a temporary to help unlink the **struct sem_undo** from the list.

27883: Last, the **struct sem_undo** is freed and **un**— which now points to the **struct sem_undo** after the one it initially pointed to—is returned.

alloc_undo

27892: **alloc_undo** allocates space to track undo operations for all semaphores in a semaphore set; it's a utility function for **sys_semop**.

27899: The size for the array to be allocated is computed—following a practice that should look familiar by now, the space for the adjustment array is allocated in the same memory block as the **struct sem_undo** it belongs to. Since this computation doesn't depend on any elements of the semaphore set or the underlying array, it could be swapped with the following line, narrowing the lock's scope a bit.

27907: The semaphore lock is dropped during the allocation, in case the allocation puts the process to sleep. The lock must be reacquired now, but

only if the semaphore set still exists—it might have disappeared while the process slept. This is the job of **sem_revalidate** (line 27249), whose body should look familiar to you by now: It acquires the lock and checks the semaphore set's sequence number and permissions.

27914: If the semaphore set was still valid, the rest is a cakewalk: The **struct sem_undo** is filled in, and it's linked into the process's **semundo** list and the **struct sem_array**'s **undo** list.

update_queue

27368: **update_queue** is an important function. We've already seen that it's called from **sys_semop** and it's also called from **semctl_main** and **sem_exit**, both of which you'll see later. Called when a semaphore's value has changed, **update_queue** completes any pending operations that can now succeed (or that will fail), removing them from the pending queue. Consequently, its dominant feature is a loop over the supplied **struct sem_array**'s **sem_pending** list.

27375: If this node's **status** flag was already raised on a previous call to **update_queue**, the process associated with the node hasn't had a chance to remove itself from the **sem_pending** list yet. When the function returns, the other process gets a chance to perform its pending operations and disengage itself from the list; for now, **update_queue** simply moves on.

27378: Checks whether the current set of pending operations can now complete. **q->alter** is passed as the last argument, so mutating operations are automatically undone if they would succeed. This is because the process will go on to attempt the operations itself and they should not be performed twice.

27384: In case of error or success (as opposed to a need to continue to wait), this node's associated process is awakened. Otherwise, the node is left in **sem_pending**, to be tried again at some future point.

27387: If the set of operations includes some mutating operations, the **q->status** flag is raised so that the process will know that it awoke because it can succeed now; it will try the operations and remove itself from the **sem_pending** list. The flag is checked at line 28034, as previously discussed.

Observe that here the node is deliberately not removed from **sem_pending**. By the time the associated process has a chance to try its operations, it might be unable to succeed—if, say, another process sneaked in and grabbed the semaphore this process was about to acquire. In that case, the process simply stays on the list (going back to sleep) and the work of redundantly dequeuing and re-enqueuing it is avoided. We pay for that, though, in occasionally having to skip nodes that represent already-awakened processes—as at line 27375—so it's not clear to me whether trying to be lazy here is a gain or a loss.

27388: The function returns now so that multiple mutating processes won't all try their possibly incompatible changes at the same time. Recall that the nonmutating operations are kept at the front of the queue, and the mutating operations are kept at the end. As a result, all the nonmutating processes (which won't interfere with each other) are awakened first, and at most one mutating process is awakened afterwards.

27390: Otherwise, an error occurred. The error code is saved in **q->status** and the queue node is immediately removed from **sem_pending**.

try_atomic_semop

27307: The banner comment above this function mentions that it tests whether all operations in the given set can be performed. It neglects to mention that if they can all be performed, they normally are.

27315: Begins looping over all the passed-in operations, trying each in turn.

27319: A **sem_op** of 0 means that the caller wants to wait for **curr->semval** to reach 0. Consequently, if **curr->semval** is not already 0, the caller has to block, which means the operations can't be performed atomically (because other work will be done while this process is blocked).

27322: The caller's PID is provisionally stored in the low 16 bits of **curr->sempid**; the previous PID is moved into the upper 16 bits for now.

27323: **curr->semval** is adjusted as requested by **sem_op**—again, provisionally. Neither here nor in its callers is **sem_op** range-checked, although the result of the operation is range-checked at lines 27327 through 27330. This can lead to some surprising consequences for values of **sem_op** that are either so large or so small that they cause the **semval** to wrap around.

27324: If this operation's **SEM_UNDO** flag is set, indicating that the operation should be automatically undone when the process exits, the corresponding undo structure is updated. Note that this assumes **un** is non-**NULL**; it's the caller's responsibility to see to it that this is so.

27327: Range-checks the new **curr->semval**.

27333: The loop ran to completion, so all the operations would succeed. If the caller just wants to know whether the operations will succeed, but doesn't want to perform them now, the operations are immediately undone. Otherwise, the operations have already been performed, and **try_atomic_semop** proceeds to return success.

27342: The **out_of_range** label is reached when an operation would have incremented **semval** too far. It simply arranges to return the **ERANGE** error, and then jumps ahead to the undo code.

27346: The **would_block** label is reached when the process would have to wait on the semaphore, either because it would have to wait for the semaphore to reach 0 or because the operation would be unable to acquire the semaphore immediately. If the caller doesn't want to wait in this case, the **EAGAIN** error is returned. Otherwise, the function returns 1 to indicate that the caller would need to sleep.

27352: The code following the **undo** label undoes all the work that's been done so far in the **for** loop starting at line 27315.

sys_semctl

27832: **sys_semctl**, which implements the **semctl** system call, is the counterpart of **sys_msgctl**. However, it is considerably more complex—so much so, that it is broken into several helper functions: **semctl_nolock**, **semctl_main**, and **semctl_down**. (By the way, I don't mean to accuse this **semctl** implementation of being unnecessarily complex. I actually think this is a good implementation; it's just that the original System V design, with which Linux tries to be compatible, crams a lot of responsibility into this system call.) Since **sys_semctl** does almost no interesting work of its own, I'll proceed immediately to discussing those helper functions.

semctl_nolock

27507: **semctl_nolock** implements **sys_semctl**'s **IPC_INFO**, **SEM_INFO**, and **SEM_STAT** cases. Its name derives from the fact that it's called with no locks held, although it acquires locks itself when it needs them.

27513: The **IPC_INFO** and **SEM_INFO** cases are very similar to each other. They are also quite similar to the **IPC_INFO** and **MSG_INFO** cases of **sys_msgctl** (see lines 26577 through 26609), so they need not be covered in detail here.

27543: Similarly, the **SEM_STAT** case is much like **sys_msgctl**'s **MSG_STAT** and **IPC_STAT** cases (see lines 26610 through 26652).

semctl_main

27582: Like **semctl_nolock**, **semctl_main** is called with no locks held (though it freely acquires locks as it needs them). It handles most of the cases of the main **switch** in **sys_semctl**: **GETALL**, **GETVAL**, **GETPID**, **GETNCNT**, **GETZCNT**, **IPC_STAT**, **SETVAL**, and **SETALL**. The setup work for this function is all stuff you've seen before—acquiring the semaphore array lock, then checking the sequence number and read/write permissions.

27609: The **GETALL** command is a request for all the values of all the semaphores in a semaphore set.

27614: Pulling the same trick we saw with **fast_sops** in **sys_semop**, a stack variable (**fast_sem_io**, line 27588) is used for temporary storage if the number of semaphores in question is small enough. In this case, "small enough" is 256—that's **SEMMSL_FAST**, **#define**d at line 27143. As documented there, the resulting kernel stack usage is 512 bytes. If **nsems** exceeds this limit, a larger buffer is dynamically allocated and **semid** is revalidated afterwards, just as in **sys_semop**.

27624: Whether the buffer was allocated on the stack or on the heap, **sem_io** now points to it. The semaphore set's values are copied to the temporary buffer, the lock is released, and the temporary buffer is copied out to user space.

27633: The **SETALL** command sets the values of all the semaphores in the set.

27640: The new semaphore values must be copied in from user space. As before, temporary space is allocated from the heap if these values will not fit in the stack-resident **fast_sem_io** buffer. Note that the logic is slightly different here: The semaphore lock is dropped even if the stack-resident buffer is going to be used. The lock won't be needed again until it's time to set the values, so other processes can be allowed to use the System V semaphores until then.

27652: After copying the suggested new values in from user space, the values are range-checked; if any value lies outside the allowed range, the entire attempt is rejected with an **ERANGE** error.

27658: All of the new semaphore values are legal, but the lock must be reacquired before installing them. As usual, that's done here with **sem_revalidate**.

27662: A simple loop copies the new values into the semaphore set.

27664: All the undo adjustments related to all the semaphores in the set are zeroed. This does nothing special when the semaphore is being set to the value it already had—as well it shouldn't. If the caller wants every semaphore except one set to a new value, it can't cheat by setting that semaphore to the value it already has. Instead, it must use the **SETVAL** command (covered shortly) on all the semaphores in the set except the one that shouldn't change.

27670: As always, changing a semaphore's value might allow some sleeping process to proceed, so **update_queue** gives them their shot.

27674: The **IPC_STAT** case is a simplified version of the corresponding case in **sys_msgctl**, so we need not explore it in depth here.

27691: The preceding cases all returned, one way or another, so we're done with them. The remaining cases are all fairly simple, and they all deal with a single semaphore. To begin with, the supplied semaphore number is range-checked; if it's in range, **curr** is made to point to this semaphore.

27697: The **GETVAL** command returns the value of a single semaphore, so the value is simply read and returned.

27700: The **GETPID** command returns the PID of the last process that changed the semaphore. The mask might seem unnecessary, but it is definitely

needed: Recall the **sempid** assignment in **try_atomic_semop**, back at line 27322. In the success case, the old PID, which was stored in the upper 16 bits of **sempid**, was never erased— so it's still there. Since semaphore values are changed in **try_atomic_semop** much more often than they are read using semctl's GETPID command, clearing the upper 16 bits of **sempid** every time **try_atomic_semop** succeeds would be less efficient than simply masking off the upper 16 bits here.

27703: The next two cases, **GETNCNT** and **GETZCNT**, delegate their work to simple helper functions we explore in the next two sections.

27709: The final case in **semctl_main**, **SETVAL**, is just a simplified version of **SETALL**—it sets the value of a single semaphore only. Notice that the last statement in this case, the **goto** at line 27725, is unnecessary.

count_semncnt

27411: **count_semncnt** is called from line 27704 to implement the **GETNCNT** command in **semctl_main**. Its job is to count the number of tasks that are blocked waiting to acquire the semaphore.

27418: This loop executes for every pending operation in every task waiting in **sma**'s pending queue. It increments **semncnt** every time it finds a satisfying operation—one that's trying to procure the specified semaphore and that doesn't have the **IPC_NOWAIT** flag set.

count_semzcnt

27431: **count_semzcnt** is called from line 27707 to implement the **GETZCNT** command in **semctl_main**. It's almost exactly like **count_semncnt**, except that it counts tasks waiting for the semaphore to reach 0 (that is, tasks waiting for the semaphore to become available). The only difference, therefore, is at line 27444, where it tests for equality with 0 instead of testing for less than 0.

semctl_down

27777: The last **semctl** helper function is **semctl_down**. Called with the semaphore lock held, it implements the **IPC_RMID** and **IPC_SET** cases. Most of the work here is already familiar to you, especially after seeing similar code in **sys_msgctl**, so a couple of short notes here will suffice.

27807: The work done here to implement **IPC_RMID** is trivial; the real work is delegated to **freeary**, which I explore in the next section.

27811: **semctl_down**'s **IPC_SET** is just a simplified version of **sys_msgctl**'s. The message queue code needed to deal with the possibility that a relaxed limit on the message queue's size might have enabled some blocked message senders to proceed; there's no corresponding situation for semaphores. The message queue code also considered the possibility that stricter permissions would deny some sleeping message sender or receiver the chance to ever succeed, and it woke them all to let them sort it out. The corresponding operation is not performed here, and there doesn't seem to be any good reason why not.

freeary

27452: **freeary** is, of course, the counterpart of **freeque**. Although the two functions are almost identical in concept—one frees a semaphore set, the other frees a message queue—they are not entirely similar in implementation, so a few brief notes are in order.

27459: The common work for these two functions is properly factored out, using **sem_rmid** (line 27127), a simple wrapper for **ipc_rmid**. This, as you'll recall, is the same generic-layer function used to implement part of **freeque**.

27465: As discussed before, when a semaphore set is removed, the corresponding undo structures become obsolete. They are flagged here and will be removed later during a **sys_semop** call—or, as the comment here says, they'll be removed during **sem_exit**, discussed in the next section.

27470: Obviously, any processes waiting to perform operations on this queue are now out of luck. They are awakened with an **EIDRM** error.

27478: Recall that **ipc_free** needs to know the size of the memory allocation it's undoing, in order to free memory from the right allocator. Interestingly, in this case, the size is not stored—it's simply recomputed now.

sem_exit

28073: **sem_exit** has no counterpart in the message queue code. It performs any undo operations the process asked to have automatically performed when it exited. Consequently, it's called when a process is exiting (at line 30282).

28082: If the process's **semsleeping** member is non-**NULL**, then one of two things is true: Either the process was sleeping on some **sem_queue** queue, or it had just been removed from the queue but **semsleeping** hadn't been updated yet. If the former, the process is removed from the queue in which it was sleeping.

28096: Begins walking over the current process's list of **struct sem_undo**s. Each will be processed in turn, and they're freed in the loop's update part (line 28098).

28100: If the semaphores corresponding to this undo structure have been freed, no undo adjustments should (or can) be performed; the loop is simply continued.

28103: Similarly, if the corresponding semaphore set no longer exists, the loop is continued. Line 28109 is conceptually the other half of this check.

28106: The semaphore set could possibly have been removed between line 28100 and when the lock was acquired at line 28102. That's caught here.

28113: Loops over **sma**'s list of **struct sem_undo**s to find the one preceding the one that's about to be removed (this is very similar to the loop in

freeundos, discussed earlier). When this is found, **sem_exit** jumps ahead to the **found** label at line 28121.

28119: If the undo structure wasn't found in **sma**'s list, something is wrong. **sem_exit** prints a warning message and moves on to the next undo structure.

28122: The undo structure was found in **sma**'s list, and **unp** points to a pointer to its predecessor. **un** is removed from the queue.

28125: All the semaphore adjustments in this undo structure are carried out.

28135: The operations performed by this function might have established the conditions for some sleeping process to awaken. As always, this requires a call to **update_queue**.

28139: All the still-valid **struct sem_undo**s have been acted on, so the current process's **semundo** queue is set to **NULL** and the function returns.

append_to_queue

27273: Appends **q** to **sma**'s **sem_pending** queue. This is a compact implementation; it would normally look something like this:

```
q->prev = sma->last;
if (sma->sem_pending) /* Not empty? */
  sma->sem_pending_last->next = q;
else
  sma->sem_pending = q;
sma->sem_pending_last = q;
q->next = NULL;
```

The real advantage is that the kernel's implementation avoids the potentially expensive branch. The more efficient implementation is made possible partly by making **sem_pending_last** a pointer to a pointer to a queue node, rather than simply a pointer to a queue node.

prepend_to_queue

27281: Prepends **q** to **sma**'s **sem_pending** queue. Because **sem_pending** is not a pointer to a pointer, this implementation has essentially the same form as the naive implementation previously considered.

remove_from_queue

27293: The last primitive operation on **struct sem_queue** queues is this one, which removes a node from a queue.

27296: Partially unlinks **q** from the queue by modifying the previous queue node's **next** pointer.

27297: Also updates the next node's **prev** pointer, if there is a next node, or **sma->sem_pending_last**, if this is the last node in the queue. Note that there's no explicit code for removing the queue's only node—it's worth your while to work through why this case works, if you don't see why already.

27301: Sets the removed node's **prev** pointer to **NULL**, so that lines 28041 and 28087 can efficiently discover whether the node is still enqueued.

Shared Memory

Shared memory is exactly what it sounds like: A region of memory is set aside, and a set of processes is given access to it. Because it touches on both IPC and memory-management issues, this discussion pulls together material from earlier in this chapter and also from Chapter 8.

Shared memory is, by far, the fastest of the three IPC services explored in this chapter, and it's the easiest to use. To the process, it looks just like any other memory after it's been acquired. Changes written to the shared memory by one process are immediately visible to all the other processes—they can simply read through a pointer that points into the shared memory space and, bingo, there's the new value. However, System V shared memory has no built-in way to ensure mutual exclusion: One process might be writing to a given address in the shared memory region at the same time that another process reads from the same address, resulting in the reader's seeing inconsistent data. This is most obviously a problem on SMP machines, but it can happen on UP machines, too—for example, if the writer is context-switched out while in the middle of writing some large structure into the shared memory space and the reader reads from the shared memory before the writer gets a chance to finish.

As a result, processes using shared memory must do something to ensure that reads are carefully separated from writes (and writes from each other, if you think about it). Locks, and the related concept of atomic operations, are explored thoroughly in the next chapter. But you already know a way to guarantee that accesses to the shared memory region are mutually exclusive: Use a semaphore. The idea is to acquire the semaphore, access the memory region at full speed, and then release the semaphore when done.

Shared memory could be used for some of the same purposes for which message queues are used—a dispatcher process could write a request for work into one portion of the shared memory region, and the worker processes could write results into another portion. This means that the total space for requests and results must be bounded in advance by the application, but the dispatching and result writing are faster than with message queues.

A more common use of shared memory is to expose an application's internal state. This gives other applications a way to read and report on that state, or possibly even to modify it, without perceptibly slowing processing. One popular application that uses shared memory for this purpose is the SETI@home project's GNU/Linux client. This program, setiathome, can optionally expose its internal state through a shared memory region. A separate program, xsetiathome, periodically reads setiathome's state from the shared memory region and displays that state in an X window, generating all kinds of impressive-looking graphs at blinding speed. When I get tired of the graphics, I just kill xsetiathome; setiathome neither notices nor cares.

A shared memory region need not appear at the same address for each process. If process A and process B are both using the same shared memory region, process A might see it at one address, and process B might see it at another address. Of course, a given page from the shared memory region will be mapped to at most one physical page. The virtual memory mechanisms covered in the previous chapter simply apply different translations for each process's logical addresses.

In the kernel code, shared memory regions are referred to as *segments*, the same terminology that is sometimes misleadingly applied to virtual memory areas (VMAs). Just to forestall any confusion, this is an informal use of the word; it's not related to hardware-enforced (MMU) segments, which are discussed in Chapter 8. I'll continue to use the term *regions* to avoid this confusion.

Shared Memory Data Structures

In addition to the generic layer's **struct ipc_ids** and memory-related data structures you saw in Chapter 8, there is only one important data structure for the shared memory code: **struct shmid_kernel**, examined next.

struct shmid_kernel

28228:   **struct shmid_kernel** has the following members:

- **shm_perm**—Exactly as in the message queue and semaphore code, the main shared memory data structure has a **struct kern_ipc_perm** as its first argument so that the generic IPC layer can treat it interchangeably with the others.

- **shm_file**—The shared memory implementation is based on the concept of **mmap**ping a file in memory, a concept already familiar to you from Chapter 8. Indeed, the implementation actually uses the **mmap** code to do the heavy lifting. All the kernel really needs is a fake file for the processes to **mmap**. **shm_file** is that file, as established starting at line 28400. Among the many other salutary consequences of this elegant implementation, **fork** and **exit**

will automatically attach new child processes or detach exiting processes as part of their normal processing—they already open or close files as needed, and **shm_file** looks just like any other file to them.

- **id**—The unique ID of the shared memory region represented by this **struct**.

- **shm_nattch**—The number of tasks "attached" to this region, to use the typical terminology—in other words, the number of tasks using the shared memory region. This member is a reference count.

- **shm_segsz**—The size of this shared memory region, in bytes (not pages).

- **shm_atim**—The time a process last attached to this shared memory region.

- **shm_dtim**—The time a process last detached from this shared memory region.

- **shm_ctim**—This is documented in the man page as "last change time," but that's a little imprecise—it's the time the shared memory region was created, or the time **IPC_SET** was last used on it.

- **shm_cprid**—The PID of this shared memory region's creator.

- **shm_lprid**—The PID of the last process that attached to or detached from this shared memory region.

Shared Memory Code

Processes are given four shared-memory–related system calls. You'll notice that there are no system calls for reading from or writing to a shared memory region. There's no need—by design, user processes can simply use normal pointer operations on the shared memory region once it has been attached, with no further kernel involvement. Consequently, these system calls suffice:

- **shmget**—As with **msgget** and **semget**, **shmget** returns a unique identifier for a shared memory region, creating a new shared memory region if necessary. **shmget**, again, is so much like its counterparts that its implementation (**sys_shmget**, line 28433) need not be covered here.

- **shmat**—Attaches the calling process to a shared memory region.

- **shmdt**—Detaches the calling process from a shared memory region.

- **shmctl**—Like **msgctl** and **semctl**, **shmctl** performs administrative operations on a shared memory region.

Except for the already-familiar **shmget**, I'll explore each of these system calls in turn. (I also won't cover **shm_init**, line 28274, except to note that—unlike its counterparts for the other IPC services—it incorrectly lacks an **#ifdef** around its call to **create_proc_read_entry**.)

sys_shmat

28775: **sys_shmat** is invoked with a shared memory region identifier, a suggested address at which the caller would like the shared memory region to appear in its address space (usually **NULL**, so that **sys_shmat** is free to choose its own), and a set of flags to modify **sys_shmat**'s behavior. Its final argument is needed internally by the kernel but does not come from the user: On success, **raddr** is used to return the user-space address at which the shared memory region was mapped.

28791: Following a simple sanity check, **sys_shmat** begins to work out the address at which the shared memory region should appear in the calling process's memory space.

28792: In general, a non-**NULL** address is always honored, except that it might be rounded first. Addresses are rounded to **SHMLBA**-sized boundaries. As you can see from line 15698, **SHMLBA** is simply **#define**d to **PAGE_SIZE** (line 13386).

If **SHMLBA** and **PAGE_SIZE** are the same, why have both? The answer is that **SHMLBA** is **PAGE_SIZE** on most—but not all—platforms. On the MIPS and MIPS-64 CPUs—which have a **PAGE_SIZE** of 4KB—Linux **#defines SHMLBA** to a whopping 0x40000 (256KB). A comment in older versions of the kernel suggested that this large value was chosen to conform to SGI's Application Binary Interface (ABI) for MIPS-based machines. The MIPS ABI versions 2 and 3, however, explicitly state that **SHMLBA**'s value "is allowed to differ between conforming implementations," so it's not clear why the kernel developers thought that the 256KB value was mandated. Maybe that value was required by a very early ABI version, but I checked ABI versions going back to 1.2 and still couldn't find any such requirement. In the 2.4 kernel, the explanatory comment has disappeared, but **SHMLBA**'s definition is unchanged.

On other platforms, non-**PAGE_SIZE** values are employed for **SHMLBA** for simple efficiency reasons, exploiting the peculiar properties of those architectures. On the IA-64, for example, **SHMLBA** is 1MB because that helps avoid performance degradation on that platform. On older SPARC architectures, **SHMLBA** appears to be related to the cache size, presumably to improve cache performance.

Finally, on the SPARC-64, **SHMLBA** is twice the **PAGE_SIZE** (which in turn is 8KB, in case you're curious); unfortunately, this difference is not explained in the code.

28796: If the supplied non-**NULL** address did not already lie on a suitable boundary and the caller did not supply the **SHM_RND** (line 22863) flag to allow rounding, **sys_shmat** has no choice but to return an error.

28798: The caller supplied a suitable non-**NULL** address or one was obtained through rounding. The **MAP_SHARED** flag (line 13223) will be passed

to **do_mmap** (naturally), as will the **MAP_FIXED** flag (line 13227)—**sys_shmat** will not allow **do_mmap** to choose a different address.

28800: A **NULL** address means that **sys_shmat** should choose an address in the process's memory space (although it allows **do_mmap** to do the choosing). Only the **MAP_SHARED** flag will accompany the address.

28802: If the **SHM_RDONLY** (read-only) flag is supplied, the caller needs only read permission; otherwise, the caller needs both read and write permissions. The next step is to translate the caller's request into terms that **ipcperms** and **do_mmap** can understand. This is just a question of choosing analogous page-level protections (**prot**) and file-style access modes (**acc_mode**) that will be passed to those functions below. **o_flags**, which is also computed here, is not used.

28814: The usual: Acquires a pointer to the **struct shmid_kernel** implied by the **shmid** argument and verifies permissions.

28821: The caller has identified the shared memory region and appears to have the requisite permissions. The region's **shm_nattch** count is incremented, and **sys_shmat** attempts to map the fake file representing the shared memory region into the calling process's memory space, using **do_mmap**.

28835: The region's **shm_nattch** count is decremented again, and the shared memory region is freed if the count is 0. This might look like a bug: Why increment the attach count, only to decrement it almost immediately, possibly destroying the very region to which the process just attached?

The root of the answer lies in **do_mmap**, which, at line 42281, calls the **mmap** member of the **struct file_operations** associated with the shared memory region's fake file. This member, as you can see from line 28370, leads to the function **shm_mmap** (line 28360). **shm_mmap**, in turn, calls **shm_inc** (line 28302), which increments the attach count. The end result is that if the **mmap** attempt succeeds, the attach count was incremented twice—once at line 28822, and again at line 28310. So decrementing **shm_nattch** will leave it 0 here only in the event of an error.

Observe that the region is not necessarily freed even if this decrement drops the last reference to the region; the region must also be marked with the **SHM_DEST** flag (line 22897). The **SHM_DEST** flag can be among the flags set by the caller; it can also be set later by the **IPC_RMID** case of **sys_shmctl**—see line 28719. In this way, a shared memory region might outlive all of its attached processes. This can be useful for the same kinds of reasons that leaving a checkpoint file lying around sometimes can be useful: You might have a long-term process that runs for a few hours each night, leaving its results in a shared memory region that persists even after the process's current chunk of work is done. Simply by attaching to the leftover shared memory region, it can pick up the next night exactly where it left off. (Of course, because shared memory regions—unlike files—disappear when the computer is turned off, this approach is unsuitable for work you can't risk losing.)

28841: Returns (through **raddr**) the address actually chosen for the shared memory region in the caller's space, and then returns a value based on the chosen address—if the chosen address was actually an encoded error, the error number is returned; otherwise, **sys_shmat** returns 0 to indicate success.

sys_shmdt

28851: The inverse of **sys_shmat**, **sys_shmdt** detaches a shared memory region from the caller's memory space, possibly freeing the region as well.

28857: Begins iterating over all the VMAs representing the process's memory.

28859: If the VMA represents a shared memory region (which is elegantly tested by inspecting its **vm_ops** member), and the VMA starts at the target address, then the VMA should be unmapped.

28862: **do_munmap** (line 42633) calls **unmap_fixup** (line 42498), which (indirectly) calls **shm_close** (covered next) at line 42513. Both **do_munmap** and **unmap_fixup** are covered in Chapter 8.

shm_close

28339: This function, called when a process is detaching from a shared memory region, should be pretty easy to understand by now. It has just one potentially confusing feature.

28348: While reading through this function, you might note that it locks the underlying array element without validating the sequence number. This doesn't match the pattern you see elsewhere, but it's not a bug. **shm_close** is called with at least one process still attached: The one on whose behalf **sys_shmdt** is (indirectly) calling this function. Since the array slot will not be reused until the attach count reaches 0, the array element must have the right sequence number if it exists at all. The same reasoning explains why a **NULL** return from **shm_lock** is considered serious enough to cause a kernel panic here.

sys_shmctl

28586: **sys_shmctl** bears many similarities to its counterparts in the message queue and semaphore code. Consequently, there's no need to cover the **IPC_INFO**, **SHM_INFO**, **SHM_STAT**, **IPC_STAT**, **IPC_RMID**, or **IPC_SET** cases.

28674: **SHM_LOCK** allows a process with sufficient capabilities to lock an entire region in physical memory, preventing it from being swapped out. **SHM_UNLOCK**, its inverse, unlocks a locked region, making the pages in it eligible for swapping once more.

The work in these two cases doesn't look like much: It's just making sure that the caller has the right capabilities, and that the region to be unlocked is currently locked (or vice versa), and then setting or clearing the appropriate **shm_flags** bit. But this is all that needs to be done—the effect shows up in the swapping code, though the affected code was omitted for space.

Note that there's a separate capability for locking and unlocking shared memory, **CAP_IPC_LOCK** (line 17900).

The System V IPC Demultiplexer

Before we leave this topic, it's time I confessed to a little white lie. Throughout the chapter, I've been referring to various System V IPC system calls. The truth is, in a strict sense, none of the functions we've covered so far in this chapter is a system call. Go ahead and search **sys_call_table** (line 1128) for them—they're not there.

However, what you will find, at line 1246, is an entry for the function **sys_ipc**. This function, defined at line 5623, is the so-called "System V IPC demultiplexer." Its first argument is an integer identifying the system call that the caller is trying to invoke—this integer should be drawn from the set starting at line 13129. Based on this argument, **sys_ipc** turns around and invokes one of the functions covered in this chapter, passing along any other arguments supplied by the caller, as needed.

This seems like an oddly inelegant design, and, indeed, nobody claims that it's pretty. (Not even its own author, as you can see from line 5622.) It's like this for historical reasons. Older kernel versions provided System V IPC services through a loadable kernel module, and **sys_ipc** was used as the single entry point to that module.

sys_ipc doesn't do any interesting processing of its own, so I won't walk you through it here. But I do want to alert you to its existence, if only for the sake of completeness.

Chapter 10

Symmetric Multiprocessing (SMP)

Throughout this book, I've generally skipped over symmetric multiprocessing (SMP) code, preferring to concentrate on the relatively simple cases in which only one processor is involved. Now, it's time to revisit some of what you've learned, looking at it from a new angle: What happens when the kernel must support machines with more than one CPU?

Generally, using more than one CPU to do a job is called *parallel processing*. You can think of parallel processing as a spectrum, with distributed computing at one end and SMP at the other end. Generally, a system becomes more tightly coupled—sharing more resources between CPUs—and more homogeneous as you move along the spectrum from distributed computing to SMP. In a typical distributed system, each CPU usually has at least its own cache and its own RAM. Frequently, each CPU has its own disk(s) as well, and each might have its own graphics subsystem, sound card, monitor, and so on.

In the extreme case, distributed systems are often nothing more than a bunch of ordinary computers, possibly of completely different architectures, working together over a network—they need not even be on the same LAN. Some interesting distributed systems that you might have heard of include Beowulf, a generic term for fairly conventional but extremely powerful distributed Linux systems; SETI@home, which harnesses millions of computers across the Internet to assist in the search for evidence of extraterrestrial life; and distributed.net, another implementation of a similar idea, which tends to focus on cracking codes developed here on Earth.

SMP is a special case of parallel processing in which all CPUs in the system are identical. You yoke together two 80486s or two Pentiums (with the same clock speed), for example, but not an 80486 and a Pentium, or a Pentium and a PowerPC. In normal usage, SMP also means that all the CPUs are "under the same hood"—that is, they're all inside the same computer, communicating with one another through special-purpose hardware.

An SMP system is usually an otherwise ordinary single computer; it just has two or more CPUs inside. Therefore, an SMP system has one of everything except CPUs—one graphics card, one sound card, and so on. These and similar resources, such as RAM and the disk, are shared by the system's CPUs. (Each CPU normally has its own cache memory, though.)

Distributed configurations require little or no special support from the kernel; coordination among the nodes is handled by user-space software and by unmodified kernel components such as the networking subsystem. But SMP creates a different hardware configuration inside the computer and therefore requires special-purpose kernel support. For example, the kernel must ensure that the CPUs cooperate when accessing their shared resources—a problem you don't have to face in the UP world.

SMP is becoming common primarily because it offers increased performance that's cheaper and simpler than buying several separate machines and hooking them together. In addition, you get the speedup much sooner than if you wait for the next generation of CPUs to be released.

Asymmetric multi-CPU configurations are not widely supported, because both the hardware and software support required for symmetric configurations are usually simpler. However, the architecture-independent portion of the kernel code actually doesn't particularly care whether the CPUs are identical—that is, whether the configuration is truly symmetric—although it doesn't do anything special to support asymmetric configurations, either. For instance, in an asymmetric multiprocessing system, the scheduler should prefer to run processes on the faster CPUs rather than on the slower ones, but the Linux kernel makes no such distinctions.

As the saying goes, "There ain't no such thing as a free lunch." With SMP, the price you pay for increased performance is increased complexity in the kernel and increased coordination overhead. The CPUs must arrange not to interfere with each other's work, but they must not spend so much time on this coordination that they significantly eat into the extra CPU power.

The SMP-specific portions of the code are compiled out for UP, so UP boxes aren't slowed down just because SMP boxes exist in the world. This satisfies two time-tested principles: "Optimize for the common case" (UP machines are far more common than SMP machines) and "You don't pay for what you don't use."

Parallel Programming Concepts and Primitives

An SMP machine with two CPUs is the simplest possible parallel configuration, but even the simplest configuration opens a whole new realm of problems—getting even two identical CPUs to work together harmoniously seems, at times, like trying to herd cats. Fortunately, there's a large and well-understood body of research on the subject, going back at least 30 years. (That's a surprisingly long time, considering that the first electronic digital computers were built less than 60 years ago.) Before examining how SMP support affects the kernel code, it will greatly simplify matters to take a tour of some of the theoretical concepts on which the support is based.

Note that not all of this information is specific to SMP kernels. Some of the issues raised by parallel programming occur even on a UP kernel, both to support interrupts and to handle interactions between processes. So this discussion should be worthwhile even if you have no particular interest in SMP issues.

Atomic Operations

In a parallel environment, certain activities must be performed atomically—that is, without possibility of interruption. Such operations must be indivisible, just as atoms were once thought to be.

Consider reference counting, for example. If you want to release your hold on a shared resource and see whether any others are still using it, you decrement the shared resource's count and test it against 0. A typical sequence of actions might start off as follows:

1. The CPU loads the current count (say, 2) into one of its registers.

2. The CPU decrements the value in its register; now it's 1.

3. The CPU writes the new value (1) back to memory.

4. The CPU decides that, because the value is 1, some other process is using the shared object, so it won't free the object.

For UP, you don't have much to worry about here. But for SMP, the picture is quite different: What if another CPU just happens to be doing the same thing at the same time? The worst case, which is illustrated in Figure 10.1, goes something like this:

1. CPU A loads the current count (2) into one of its registers.

2. CPU B loads the current count (2) into one of its registers.

3. CPU A decrements the value in its register; now it's 1.

4. CPU B decrements the value in its register; now it's 1.

5. CPU A writes the new value (1) back to memory.

6. CPU B writes the new value (1) back to memory.

7. CPU A decides that, because the value is 1, some other process is using the shared object, so it won't free it.

8. CPU B decides that, because the value is 1, some other process is using the shared object, so it won't free it.

The reference count in memory should now be 0, but instead it's 1. Both processes dropped their references to the shared object, but nobody freed it.

This is an interesting failure, because each CPU did exactly what it was supposed to do, yet the wrong result occurred anyway. The problem, of course, is that the CPUs didn't coordinate their activities—the right hand didn't know what the left hand was doing. What makes it even worse is that the problem might not occur every time the kernel decrements the protected reference count. If CPU A and CPU B don't try to decrement the protected reference count simultaneously, the code will work. It is very hard to debug problems that occur only, say, 1 time in 100.

How can you try to solve this problem in software? Take it from the point of view of either CPU—say, CPU A. To signal CPU B that it should leave the reference count alone because you want to decrement it, you have to somehow change some information that CPU B can see—that is, update a shared variable somewhere in memory. For example, you could set aside some variable for this purpose and agree that it would contain a 1 if either CPU was trying to decrement the reference count, and 0 if not. The special variable (which I'll call the "guard") would be used like this, as illustrated in Figure 10.2:

1. CPU A loads the value from the guard into one of its registers.

2. CPU A checks the value in its register and sees that it's 0. (If not, it tries Step 1 again, repeating until the register is 0.)

3. CPU A writes a 1 back to the guard.

4. CPU A accesses the protected reference count.

5. CPU A writes a 0 back to the guard.

Uh-oh, that looks disturbingly familiar. Nothing prevents this from happening:

1. CPU A loads the value from the guard into one of its registers.

2. CPU B loads the value from the guard into one of its registers.

3. CPU A checks the value in its register and sees that it's 0.

4. CPU B checks the value in its register and sees that it's 0.

5. CPU A writes a 1 back to the guard.

6. CPU B writes a 1 back to the guard.

7. CPU A accesses the "protected" reference count.

8. CPU B accesses the "protected" reference count.

9. CPU A writes a 0 back to the guard.

10. CPU B writes a 0 back to the guard.

Well, maybe a guard could be used to protect the guard that was supposed to protect the original variable. . . .

Face it: We're doomed. This approach can only push the problem back another level, it can't solve it. Ultimately, atomicity simply can't be guaranteed by software—not without special help from the hardware.

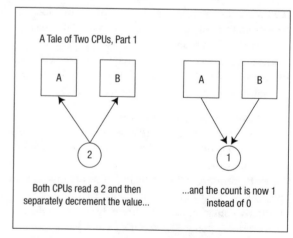

Figure 10.1 Unprotected reference counts under SMP.

On the x86 platform, the **lock** instruction provides exactly this help. (To be precise, **lock** is a prefix rather than a separate instruction, but the distinction is irrelevant for our purposes.) The **lock** instruction locks the memory bus—at least for the destination memory address—during the execution of the instruction that follows it. Because the x86 can decrement a value directly in memory, without first needing to read it explicitly into a register, you have all you need to implement an atomic decrement: **lock** the memory bus and then immediately **decl** the memory location.

The function **atomic_dec** (line 12195) does exactly this for the x86 platform. The SMP version of the **LOCK** macro, **#define**d at line 12143, expands to the **lock** instruction. (The UP version, **#define**d two lines later, is simply empty—a lone CPU doesn't need to protect itself from other CPUs, so locking the memory bus would be a complete waste of time.) By prefixing inline assembler

code with the **LOCK** macro, the instruction that follows it is locked for SMP kernels. If CPU B executes **atomic_dec** while CPU A's lock is in effect, CPU B automatically waits for CPU A to remove the lock. Success!

Well, almost. The original problem still hasn't quite been solved. The goal is not only to decrement the reference count atomically, but also to know whether the resulting value is 0. The atomic decrement can now be done, but what if another processor sneaks in between the decrement and the test of the result?

Fortunately, solving this part of the problem requires no special-purpose help from the CPU. Locked or not, the x86's **decl** instruction always sets the CPU's Zero flag if the result is 0, and this flag is CPU-private, so nothing another CPU does can affect the flag between the decrement part and the test part. Accordingly, **atomic_dec_and_test** (line 12202) does a locked dec-

rement, as before, and then sets the local variable **c** from the CPU's Zero flag. The function returns nonzero (true) if the result after the decrement was 0.

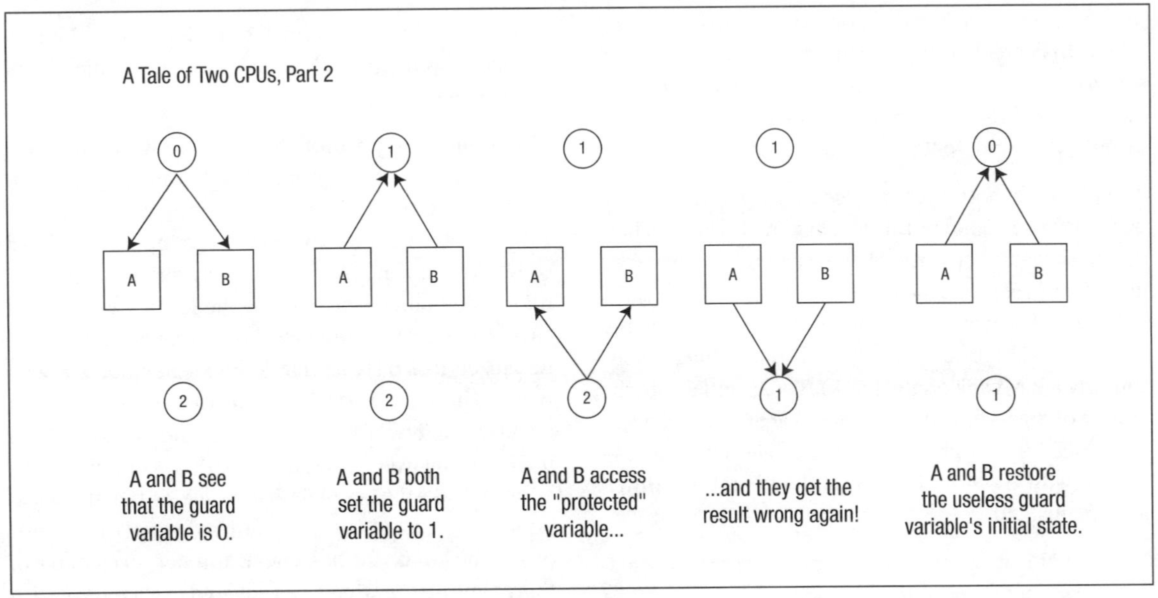

Both **atomic_dec** and **atomic_dec_and_test**, like the other functions defined in the same file, operate on an object of type **atomic_t** (line 12152). Like **LOCK**, **atomic_t** has different definitions for UP and SMP—the difference being the introduction, in the SMP case, of a **volatile** qualifier, which instructs gcc not to make certain assumptions about the marked variable (for example, not to assume that it can be safely held in a register).

Test-and-Set

The classic parallel primitive is test-and-set. A test-and-set operation atomically reads a value from a memory location and writes a new value into it, returning the old value. Typically, the location can hold either 0 or 1 and the new value that test-and-set writes is a 1—hence, the "set." Test-and-set's counterpart is test-and-clear, which is the same thing except that it writes a 0 instead of a 1. Some variants of test-and-set can write either 1 or 0, so that test-and-set and test-and-clear become the same thing, just with different operands.

A test-and-set primitive is sufficient to implement any other parallel-safe operations. (In fact, test-and-set is the only such primitive provided on some CPUs.) For example, test-and-set could have been used to protect the reference count in the previous example. The originally proposed solution was similar—read a value from a guard variable, see whether it's 0, and, if so, write a 1 and proceed to access the protected value. This attempt failed not because it was logically unsound, but because no way was available to accomplish it atomically. Given an atomic test-and-set, you can get by without using **lock** to make the **decl** atomic.

There are downsides to test-and-set, however:

- *It's a low-level primitive.* When it's all you have to work with, you have to implement all the other primitives on top of it.

A Tale of Two CPUs, Part 2

| A and B see that the guard variable is 0. | A and B both set the guard variable to 1. | A and B access the "protected" variable... | ...and they get the result wrong again! | A and B restore the useless guard variable's initial state. |

Figure 10.2 **The simple fix doesn't work.**

- *It's wasteful.* What happens when the machine tests the value and finds that it's already 1? The value wasn't messed up in memory, because the same value was simply written over it. But the fact that it was already set means that someone else is already accessing the protected object, so execution can't proceed yet. Additional logic is needed—a test and a loop—which wastes CPU cycles and makes the program slightly larger (which, in turn, wastes room in the cache).

The x86's **lock** instruction makes higher-level primitives easier to implement, but you can do an atomic test-and-set on the x86, too. The most straightforward way is to use **lock** in conjunction with the **btsl** (bit test-and-set) instruction.

Another way to implement test-and-set on the x86 is with its **xchg** (exchange) instruction, which is automatically treated by the x86 as if it were preceded by a **lock**—when one of its operands is in memory, anyway. **xchg** is more general than the **lock/btsl** combination, because it can exchange 8, 16, or 32 bits at a time rather than just one bit. Except for one use at line 16545 (in architecture-specific code), the kernel's uses of the **xchg** instruction are hidden behind the **xchg** macro (line 16788), which in turn is implemented on top of the **__xchg** function (line 16851). This is so that the kernel code can use the **xchg** macro in the architecture-independent code; each platform provides its own equivalent implementation of the macro.

Interestingly, the **xchg** macro is the basis of another macro, **tas** (test-and-set; line 16792). However, this macro isn't used anywhere in the kernel code.

The kernel sometimes uses the **xchg** macro to do a simple test-and-set (although not necessarily looping until the lock becomes available, such as at line 4169), and uses it for other purposes (such as at line 45399).

The kernel also provides a **test_and_set_bit** function (line 12306), which uses the **btsl** instruction to save the bit's old value in the CPU's Carry flag (setting the bit as a side effect) and the **sbbl** instruction to copy the Carry flag to the result variable. Related kernel functions include **test_and_clear_bit**, at line 12329, and several others in the same file.

Semaphores

Chapter 9 discusses the general notion of semaphores and demonstrates their use for interprocess communication. The kernel has its own semaphore implementation for its own purposes, and these are typically called "kernel semaphores." (In this chapter, the unmodified word "semaphores" should be understood to mean "kernel semaphores.") Exactly the same basic semaphore concept discussed in Chapter 9 applies to kernel semaphores: Allow a maximum number of users of a resource (a certain number of keys are initially placed on the hook), and establish the rule that each applicant for the resource must acquire a key before proceeding to use the resource.

By now, you probably perceive how semaphores could be built atop either test-and-set, for binary ("one-key") semaphores, or a function such as **atomic_dec_and_test**, for counted semaphores. This is precisely what the kernel does: It represents the semaphores with integers and uses the functions **down** (line 15351) and **up** (line 15424), among others, to decrement and increment the integer. As you'll see soon, the underlying code for decrementing and incrementing the integers is the same as that used by **atomic_dec_and_test** and similar functions.

As a historical note, the first researcher to formalize the notion of a semaphore, Edsger Dijkstra, is Dutch. Thus, the fundamental operations on semaphores are named in Dutch: *Proberen* and *Verhogen*, usually abbreviated to P and V. The words translate to "test" (seeing whether a key is available, and taking it if so) and "increment" (putting a key back on the hook). Those initials are the source of the terms "procure" and "vacate," which were introduced in the previous chapter. The Linux kernel breaks with tradition by calling the operations **down** and **up**, instead.

The kernel uses a very simple type to represent semaphores: **struct semaphore**, defined at line 15271. It has just three members (when the code is compiled without debugging):

- **count**—Tracks the number of keys still available. If 0, the key is taken; if negative, the key is taken and additional applicants are waiting for it. (The rule isn't really that simple, as you'll see.) Incidentally, there's nothing magical about using a positive number for the initial **count** and decrementing it to signal that you want the semaphore. You can just as well use a negative (or 0) initial count and increment, or follow some other scheme. Decrementing an initially positive number is simply the way kernel semaphores do it, and it happens to fit nicely with the mental model of keys on a hook. Indeed, read/write semaphores, which I cover later in the chapter, employ a more complex strategy.

- **sleepers**—Used during the **down** operation when the semaphore was unavailable. It's initially 0; when not 0, it is either 1 or 2, no matter how many processes are waiting to acquire the semaphore. You'll see it in operation shortly.

- **wait**—The queue of processes that had to be suspended, waiting for this semaphore to become available once more.

The **sema_init** function (line 15304) allows a semaphore's **count** to be initialized to any value, so kernel semaphores can be binary (by initializing **count** to 1) or counted (by giving it some larger initial value). All of the kernel semaphore code fully supports both binary and counted semaphores, the former as a special case of the latter. In practice, however, **count** is always initialized to 1 or 0, so that kernel semaphores are always binary. (Initializing **count** to 0 might be counterintuitive. What's the good of a hook with no keys on it? The answer is that it's a handy way to create the hook and take the key at the same time, so that the semaphore is locked at the moment it's created; its creator places the key on the hook later. You saw an example of this at line 31020, which was covered in Chapter 7's discussion of **do_fork**.) As a point of interest, there's exactly one exception to the general rule that kernel semaphores are binary. The driver code for IEEE 1394 (FireWire) devices initializes a semaphore with a **count** of 64, apparently to support up to 64 simultaneous asynchronous transactions over the IEEE 1394 bus. In all other cases—in particular, in all cases included in the book—the rule holds.

Semaphores can also be declared using the __DECLARE_SEMAPHORE_GENERIC macro (line 15295)—which, like **sema_init**, allows **count** to be initialized to any value—or the __MUTEX_INITIALIZER macro (line 15292), which uses an initial **count** of 1. There are also **DECLARE_MUTEX** and **DECLARE_MUTEX_LOCKED** (lines 15299 and 15301), which declare binary semaphores in the unlocked or locked state, respectively. **init_MUTEX** and **init_MUTEX_LOCKED** (lines 15321 and 15326) are similar. (Recall from Chapter 9 that "mutex"—which derives from "mutual exclusion"—is a common term for binary semaphores.)

down

15351: The **down** operation decrements the semaphore count. You might expect it to be as simple in implementation as it is in concept, but alas, life is not so easy.

15359: Decrements the semaphore's **count**—ensuring, for SMP, that this is done atomically. For SMP (and, indeed, for UP), essentially the same thing is being done as in **atomic_dec_and_test**, except that the integer being accessed is inside a different kind of **struct**.

You might wonder whether **count** can underflow. It can't: A process always sleeps after decrementing **count** if it fails to acquire the semaphore. Thus, a given process can grab for only one semaphore at a time, and there are many more negative values of **int** than there are processes.

15360: If the sign bit is set, the semaphore is negative. This means that it was 0 or negative even before it was decremented, so the process failed to get the semaphore and thus should sleep until it becomes available. Accomplishing this involves packing a lot of magic into the next few lines.

The **js** jumps if the sign bit is set (that is, it jumps if **decl**'s result was negative), and **2f** names the jump target. **2f** is not a hex value—it's special GNU assembler syntax. **2** means jump to the local symbol "2," and **f** means to scan forward for this symbol. (**2b** would mean to scan backward for the most recent local symbol "2".) This local symbol is at line 15363.

15361: The branch was not taken, so the process got the semaphore. Consequently, when the semaphore is available, acquiring it is dirt cheap—it's just two instructions, a decrement and an untaken jump. This is actually at the end of **down**, even though it doesn't look like it. This is explained in the next couple of paragraphs.

15362: The tricky part of **down** is the **.section** directive immediately before the jump target, which tells the assembler to assemble the following code into a separate section of the kernel—a section named **.text.lock**. The section will be allocated in memory and treated as executable. That's specified by the **ax** flag-string following the section name—note that this **ax** has nothing to do with the x86's AX register.

As a result, the assembler moves the instructions at lines 15363 and 15364 to a different section of the executable kernel from the section **down** is in, so the object code produced from these lines is not physically contiguous with the code produced from the preceding lines. This is why line 15361 is the end of **down**.

15363: This is the jump target reached when the semaphore was not obtained. It immediately jumps off to __**down_failed** (line 3942). This function saves a few registers on the stack (see line 3933 for why) and calls __**down** (line 3830), which I'll present later, to do the work of waiting for the semaphore. When __**down** returns, __**down_failed** returns to **down**, which also returns. __**down** doesn't return until the process

has acquired the semaphore; as a result, whenever **down** returns, the process has the semaphore, whether it got it immediately or had to wait for it.

15364: The **jmp 1b** does not jump to the hex address 0x1b. Instead, this **1b** is the same GNU assembler syntax previously seen in the **2f** at line 15360—it refers to an instruction address; in this case, it's the address of the first local label "1" encountered while scanning backward. So this jumps backward to the end of **down**—line 15361.

15365: The effect of the **.previous** assembler directive is undocumented, but it means to revert to the previous section, terminating the effect of the **.section** directive on line 15362.

down_interruptible

15371: **down_interruptible** is used when the kernel wants to acquire a semaphore but is willing to be interrupted by a signal while waiting for it. (Strictly speaking, it is not the kernel that would be the target of the signal, but rather the process on whose behalf the kernel is calling **down_interruptible**.) The function's implementation is very similar to **down**'s, but with two differences, explained in the next two paragraphs.

15374: The first difference is that **down_interruptible** returns an **int** to indicate whether it got the semaphore or was stopped by a signal. The return value (in **result**) is 0 in the former case, negative in the latter case. This is partly accomplished by line 15384, which zeroes **result** if the function got the semaphore without waiting.

15387: The second difference is that **down_interruptible** jumps away to __**down_failed_interruptible** (line 3954) rather than to __**down_failed**. Following the pattern established by __**down_failed**, __**down_failed_interruptible** simply adjusts a couple of registers and invokes __**down_interruptible** (line 3862), which I'll present later.

Note that the line that **down** will jump back to after **__down_failed_interruptible** returns, line 15385, follows the **xorl** that zeroes **result** in the case where the semaphore was acquired immediately. When **down_interruptible** can't get the semaphore immediately, it ends up returning whatever **__down_interruptible** returns.

down_trylock

15396: Sometimes, if the semaphore can't be obtained immediately, the kernel just wants to move on. That's what **down_trylock** is for. **down_trylock** is identical to **down_interruptible**, except that its failure case calls **__down_failed_trylock** (line 3964, which, of course, calls **__down_trylock**, line 3914, which I'll discuss later). Consequently, there's no need to cover **down_trylock** here. Like **down_interruptible**, **down_trylock** returns 0 on success and nonzero on failure.

__down

3830: This function is the "slow path" of **down**. Called when **down** could not acquire the semaphore immediately, its job is to wait for the semaphore to become available, then acquire it.

3834: The current process should not proceed until it acquires the semaphore, even if a signal arrives for it—otherwise, the kernel would have called **down_interruptible** instead. Consequently, the task is placed in the **TASK_UNINTERRUPTIBLE** state. (Task states are covered in Chapter 7.)

3835: Using the wait queue code examined in Chapter 2, the process is entered into the queue of processes waiting to acquire this semaphore. Because the process is enqueued with **add_wait_queue_exclusive** (line 30496), at most one enqueued process is awakened when the semaphore is released. The alternative (plain old **add_wait_queue**, line 30485) would permit all enqueued processes to race for the flag simultaneously, which would be inefficient (because only one of them can win).

3839: Begins a loop that the process will not exit until it acquires the semaphore.

3844: This line effectively tests whether the semaphore is available, partially accounting for other processes that might be waiting on it. In the simplest case, in which some other process (process A) already owned the semaphore and the current process (process B) is the only one waiting for it, **sem->count** was –1 on entry to the function and **sem->sleepers** was 0. Process B incremented **sem->sleepers** to 1 at line 3838, so this line is equivalent to the following:

```
if (!((sem->count -= 0) < 0)) {
```

See the definition of **atomic_add_negative**, line 12223, for why this is so. Or, more simply:

```
if (sem->count >= 0) {
```

This probably seems unduly complicated and, indeed, it's overkill for the simplest of all possible cases. After I've finished my initial presentation of this function, I'll show you a more complex scenario that justifies the complexity of this code. For now, the important point is that this code does work for the simplest case: The loop waits for **sem->count** to become 0, indicating that the semaphore's owner has incremented its **count**.

3852: The semaphore was not available, so the process can do nothing more for now. It hands off the CPU to any other process that wants it. The waiting process will be reawakened (and the call to **schedule** will return) when the semaphore's current owner releases the semaphore. At that point, the loop will continue and the process will grab for the semaphore again. Note that even though **schedule** returns only when the semaphore's owner releases the semaphore, the sleeping process can't simply assume that the semaphore is available. If another process tries

to grab for the semaphore, that process might acquire the semaphore before this one gets a chance. The loop will iterate as often as needed, although usually not more than once.

By the way, observe that **__down** tries to grab for the semaphore before calling **schedule**. Why not do it the other way around, if **sem->count** is known to be negative on entry to the function? It won't matter for any loop iterations after the first, but removing an unnecessary check might speed that first iteration just slightly. The reason is that the semaphore could have been released (maybe on another processor) in the few nanoseconds since it was first checked, and the cost of an extra grab attempt is much less than the cost of an extra reschedule. So **__down** might as well make one last quick check before rescheduling.

3857: The process acquired the semaphore it was waiting for. It removes itself from the queue of processes waiting to acquire the semaphore, transitions back to the **TASK_RUNNING** state, and wakes up the next process waiting on the semaphore, if any. This last step might strike you as surprising—if the current process has the semaphore, isn't it just a waste of time to wake some other process that's waiting for the same semaphore? Won't that process just discover that the semaphore is still held and have to go right back to sleep? The answer is no, as you'll see in the following scenario.

Suppose you have a four-CPU system (lucky dog) and four processes contend for the same semaphore simultaneously on different CPUs. Call these processes A, B, C, and D. One of these—let's say A—acquires the semaphore immediately (at line 15359) and proceeds to do its work. The other three processes all end up in **__down**.

Of these three, one (let's say B) gets the spinlock at line 3837, guaranteeing it exclusive access to the code that follows until it drops the spinlock. (I discuss spinlocks later in the chapter.) B increments **sem->sleepers** to 1 at line 3838, then discovers the semaphore is still in use at line 3844. (Because **sem->count** was initially 1 and four processes decremented it, its value is currently –3.) So B sets **sem->sleepers** to 1 (redundantly, in this case), releases the spinlock, and hands off its CPU to another process. **sem->sleepers** is now 1 and **sem->count** is now –3.

As soon as B releases the spinlock, one of the other waiting processes grabs it—let's say C. C increments **sem->sleepers** to 2 at line 3838 and then, like B before it, discovers at line 3844 that the semaphore is still in use. However, because **sem->sleepers** is 2, line 3844 does something slightly different this time: As a side effect, it increments **sem->count**, making it –2. However, **sem->count** is still negative, so C sets **sem->sleepers** to 1, releases the spinlock, and gives up its CPU.

Next, the last of the four processes, D, does the same as C: It increments **sem->count** at line 3844 but finds that it's still negative, so it gives up its CPU. **sem->sleepers** is now 1 and **sem->count** is now –1. A has the semaphore, and B, C, and D are all waiting for it.

Assuming no other processes try to grab the semaphore, that's how things will stay until A releases it. At that point, A increments **sem->count** to 0 and discovers (at line 15432) that **sem->count** was previously negative, indicating that other processes are waiting on it. At line 3825, it wakes the first of these waiting processes (B), then continues with other work.

At line 3844, B discovers that **sem->count** is no longer negative. From that and the fact that it was awakened, B can correctly deduce that the

semaphore's owner released the semaphore. B is now the owner of the semaphore. It sets **sem->sleepers** to 0, exits the loop, and awakens the next waiting process (C). **sem->count** and **sem->sleepers** are now both 0.

While B proceeds to do other work, C ends up at line 3844 again. Because **sem->sleepers** is now 0, C decrements **sem->count** to –1. This value is negative, so C realizes that some other process has the CPU. C sets **sem->sleepers** to 1 and goes back to sleep. D does not get involved.

When B releases the semaphore, it does the same as A did before it, incrementing **sem->count** and waking C. This time, C acquires the semaphore at line 3844; it zeroes **sem->sleepers**, wakes D, and proceeds with other work. **sem->count** and **sem->sleepers** are now both 0 again.

At this point, D could do the same as C did when B woke it, setting **sem->count** to –1 and **sem->sleepers** to 1, then going back to sleep. But let's make the story a little more interesting: Suppose that C releases the semaphore almost immediately, before D reaches line 3844. That means that when C increments **sem->count** at line 15431, **sem->count** becomes positive (1). C, therefore, does not take the branch at line 15432, so it doesn't end up waking a process in **__up**. That's okay, because D was already awakened, it was just a little slow to react. When D does reach line 3844 (with **sem->sleepers** 0 and **sem->count** 1), it decrements **sem->count** to 0. Since this value is not negative, D knows that it has acquired the semaphore. When D later releases the semaphore, it will increment **sem->count** to 1 and not attempt to wake any processes. Note that this series of actions has restored the initial conditions: **sem->count** is 1 and **sem->sleepers** is 0.

Naturally, this example could have been complicated in any number of ways. For instance, other readers could have come along

and grabbed for the lock at various points. Sometimes, the other reader would simply have enqueued itself; at other points, the other reader would have rudely stolen the semaphore before some process that had patiently waited its turn got a chance at it (this can happen to D). However, the code reacts correctly in all cases.

One of the really interesting features of this code is that it seeks equilibrium states. **sem->count** can be less than –1, but only briefly; the code pushes **sem->count**'s value back up to –1 as the waiting processes check **sem->count** at line 3844. Similarly, **sem->count** can briefly be 0 when the semaphore is taken but there are queued sleepers; the queued sleepers will push it back down to –1. Under the stress of many processes contending for the same semaphore, the code reacts flexibly, temporarily tolerating unusual states and then automatically drifting back to normalcy. Like the reed in Jean de la Fontaine's poem, "Le Chêne et le Roseau" ("The Oak and the Reed"), the code bends but it does not break. (Or, since I grew up in the Seventies: Like a Weeble, the code wobbles but it doesn't fall down.)

This code has another useful property: It keeps the risk of starvation low. Starvation occurs whenever a process is perpetually unable to get a resource that it must have in order to continue. Starvation could occur here if one process is waiting in the queue and another process always happens to grab the semaphore (without waiting in the queue) just before the first process reaches line 3844. The first process would never acquire the CPU. This scenario isn't quite as implausible as it sounds—suppose one process is running with a niceness of 20 and the other is a realtime process. Still, it's unlikely to happen once, and it's even less likely to happen repeatedly. In practice, both processes will end up in the queue, and both will get a shot at the semaphore (and thus the CPU) in turn.

I didn't discuss it previously, but Linux's scheduler can also completely starve a process of the CPU under the right circumstances. This isn't necessarily a bad thing—just a design decision—and at least the principle is consistently applied throughout the kernel code, which is good. Also note that starvation can occur equally well with the other mechanisms previously discussed. The test-and-set primitive, for example, is just as much (if not more) a potential source of starvation as kernel semaphores. Practically speaking, starvation is rare—but it is an interesting theoretical case.

__down_interruptible

3862:   **__down_interruptible** is essentially the same as **__down**, except that it allows interruptions by a signal.

3867:   Consequently, the task is placed in the **TASK_INTERRUPTIBLE** state instead of the **TASK_UNINTERRUPTIBLE** state, both here and at line 3898.

3879:   In addition, each iteration of the loop checks for the arrival of a signal before it attempts to acquire the lock, returning **-EINTR** ("interrupted by signal") if a signal shows up. If the signal arrives at the same instant the semaphore becomes available, the process responds to the signal and leaves the semaphore for someone else. That's probably a wise decision: The signal might well kill the process anyway, in which case some other process waiting for the semaphore might have been denied it a little longer for no good reason.

__down_trylock

3914:   **__down_trylock** is reached when a semaphore isn't available and the kernel doesn't want to wait for it. Consequently, **__down_trylock** doesn't place the process on the **sem->wait** queue and doesn't sit in a loop. The process already tried to grab the semaphore and failed (at line 15406), decrementing **sem->count** as a side effect, so **__down_trylock** must undo the decrement with an increment.

3925:   The increment is done here, using logic similar to that in **__down** and **__down_interruptible**. If the semaphore becomes available as a result of this action, **__down_trylock** wakes a process waiting for the semaphore (if any) before returning. This is a little surprising—I'd have expected **__down_trylock** to keep the lock for itself in this case, kind of like catching a ball on the first bounce.

up

15424:   I've exhaustively narrated what happens when the kernel tries to acquire a semaphore, as well as what happens when it fails. It's time for the other end: what happens when releasing a semaphore. This part is comparatively simple.

15431:   Atomically increments the semaphore's **count**.

15432:   When nobody is waiting for the semaphore, semaphore's **count** is 0 and incrementing it makes it 1. If the result after the increment is less than or equal to 0, someone was waiting to be awakened. **up** jumps ahead to line 15435.

15434:   **up** is pulling the same trick as in **down**: This code goes into a separate section of the kernel, not in **up** itself. **up** jumps to **__up_wakeup** (line 3974), which does the same register manipulation as **__down_failed** and calls **__up**, discussed next. When **__up_wakeup** returns, **up** jumps backward to line 15433, the true end of **up**.

__up

3823:   **__up** is responsible for waking all the processes waiting for the semaphore. The wait queue code discussed in Chapter 2 makes this as simple as a single call to **wake_up** (line 22228), which ends up in **__wake_up_common** (line 34414). Because processes add themselves to the **sem->wait** queue with **add_wait_queue_exclusive**, at most one enqueued process will be awakened.

Spinlocks

The last parallel-programming primitive that is important for this chapter is the spinlock. The idea of a spinlock is to sit in a tight loop, trying over and over to grab a resource (a lock) until you succeed. This is often implemented by looping—that is, spinning—over something such as test-and-set until you get the lock.

If this sounds a lot like a binary semaphore, that's because it is. The only conceptual difference between a spinlock and a binary semaphore is that you don't necessarily spin waiting for a semaphore—you can grab for a semaphore and just give up if you don't get it immediately. As a result, spinlocks could be implemented by wrapping loops around the semaphore code. However, because spinlocks are a restricted case of semaphores, they have a more efficient implementation.

The spinlock variable is always of type **spinlock_t** (line 16495), whose **lock** member tracks the lock's state. Only the lowest byte of a **spinlock_t**'s **lock** field is used. The byte is 1 if the lock is available, 0 if it's taken and no processes have tried to acquire it recently, or any other value (usually a small negative number, if you consider the byte signed) if the spinlock is taken and additional processes contended for the spinlock after the last time it was released. (I phrased the last part carefully. Even if 10 processes are contending for the same spinlock, the spinlock's **lock** member is reset to 1 when the spinlock is released, so its value does not reliably indicate the number of waiting processes.)

In a declaration, a spinlock is initialized to the value **SPIN_LOCK_UNLOCKED** (line 16510); it can otherwise be initialized with **spin_lock_init** (line 16513). Both of these simply set the **spinlock_t**'s **lock** member to 1—unlocked. The code also includes various alternate definitions of the spinlock macros and functions, which are used for UP and various levels of debugging.

One highly important spinlock is **kernel_flag** (line 5081), which is used by the **lock_kernel** and **unlock_kernel** functions. At most one CPU can be within a **lock_kernel/unlock_kernel** pair. (The generic versions of these functions are at lines 12042 and 12048; for historical reasons, there are effectively identical x86-specific versions at lines 16424 and 16440. Since the kernel doesn't need to defend against interference from other CPUs on a UP system, there are empty UP versions at lines 23328 and 23329.) **lock_kernel** and **unlock_kernel** are a sort of "generic lock" currently used in the following cases:

- *Process creation and destruction, memory allocation, and core dumps*—See lines 11667, 11703, 11916, 11955, 11962, 30281, 47748, and 47767.

- *Kernel initialization and shutdown*—See lines 25822, 25901, 26061, 26068, 36828, 36864, 36878, and 36881.

- *Module creation and queries*—See lines 32183, 32217, 32234, 32496, 32526, 32589, 32818, 32863, 32880, and 32925.

- *Dynamic kernel configuration*—See lines 38174 and 38177.

- *Swapping, and adding and removing swap space*—See lines 41725, 41728, 46754, 46824, 46911, and 47151.

Linux's original SMP support consisted mainly of acquiring this spinlock upon entry to kernel mode and releasing it upon return to user mode. This meant that at most one CPU could be executing in kernel mode at a time, which was a severe restriction that caused comparatively poor SMP performance. As Linux's SMP support has matured, the kernel programmers have defined more and more locks, specifying more and more precisely which sections of the kernel need to be protected from which other sections, and narrowing the scope of these locks as much as possible. (Every locked region is a place where an SMP system potentially turns into a UP system, as the processors that don't own the lock might need to wait for it. Therefore, the less locking the kernel can get away with while still being correct, the better its performance on SMP systems.) It will be interesting to see how much less widely used **kernel_flag** becomes as Linux's developers continue to refine the kernel's SMP support.

Note that line 16519 tersely considers and rejects fairness—fairness is the flip side of starvation (starving a CPU, or a process, is "unfair").

The spinlock locking and unlocking code is built on top of the assembler code in **spin_lock_string** and **spin_unlock_string**, so this section covers only **spin_lock_string** and **spin_unlock_string** in detail. The other macros simply add interrupt disabling and enabling, if anything.

spin_lock_string

16526: This macro is at the heart of **spin_lock** (line 16552), the function that acquires a spinlock.

16528: Decrements the lowest byte of some **spinlock_t**'s **lock** member, with the memory bus locked so that this action is atomic with respect to any other accesses to the same spinlock.

16529: If that succeeded in acquiring the spinlock, control drops through; otherwise, the result is negative, so **spin_lock_string** jumps ahead to line 16531. This is the same trick you've seen several times already: The jump target is in a separate section of the kernel.

16532: Begins a loop, waiting for the spinlock's **lock** member to become positive.

16533: As suggested by Intel, the kernel uses a **rep/nop** combination to pause briefly while waiting for the spinlock's owner to release it. This approach reduces power consumption, among other advantages. Intel's complete rationale is spelled out in the following document: **ftp://download.intel.com/design/perftool/cbts/appnotes/sse2/w_spinlock.pdf**. Intel's documentation speaks in terms of a "PAUSE" instruction, not **rep/nop**, but they're exactly the same thing as far as the CPU is concerned.

16534: If the spinlock's **lock** member is not yet positive, the code jumps back to line 16531 to wait for another opportunity.

16535: The byte was positive, so **spin_lock_string** should make another grab for it. It jumps back to line 16527, the beginning of **spin_lock_string**, to start over. Several processes on different processors might all see a positive **lock** at the same time, but only one of them will be the first to execute the locked decrement at line 16528; the others will reenter the loop.

This code could be simplified to just two instructions plus the **lock** prefix:

```
1: lock ; btsl $0, %0
   jc 1b
```

(This uses a test-and-set instruction, a different approach than currently used in the kernel. The unlocking code would have to do a test-and-clear, of course.) However, with this simpler version, system performance would suffer noticeably, because the memory bus would be locked on every loop iteration. The version used in the kernel is longer, but it allows other CPUs to run more efficiently, because it locks the memory bus only when it has reason to believe it might be able to grab the lock.

On the Linux kernel mailing list, Manfred Spraul pointed out a flaw in the kernel's implementation: The **rep/nop** should precede the **cmpb** (that is, lines 16532 and 16533 should be swapped). As it is, when the spinlock is released, the kernel will notice the release at line 16532, pause, and then jump back to grab for the spinlock. By swapping lines 16532 and 16533, the kernel would no longer pause between the test and the jump.

spin_unlock_string

16539: Trivial: Just writes a 1 into the **spinlock_t**'s **lock** member.

Read/Write Spinlocks

A special case of spinlocks are read/write spinlocks. The idea here is that, in some cases, you want to allow multiple readers of some object but permit no other readers or writers while the object has a writer.

The reason for read/write spinlocks is efficiency. There's no reason why two processes shouldn't be allowed to inspect the same linked list at the same time. As long as neither process changes the list, no harm can result. However, if a third process wants to modify the list while the first two are reading it, it had better wait until they finish. With read/write spinlocks, the two readers can proceed in parallel; if regular spinlocks were the only tool in your toolbox, you'd have to force one reader to wait until the other had finished.

Following the same pattern as for **spinlock_t**-based spinlocks, read/write spinlocks are represented by **rwlock_t** (line 16588), which can be initialized in a declaration with **RW_LOCK_UNLOCKED** (line 16603; also see line 15145). The lowest-level functions and macros for working with **rwlock_t** are **read_lock**, **read_unlock**, **write_lock**, and **write_unlock**, which are covered in this section. The macros that are built on top of them (see lines 23355 through 23391 for several examples) are all fairly obvious after you understand these initial four functions and macros.

The **lock** member of **rwlock_t** is 0 or negative when someone is holding the write lock. It's **RW_LOCK_BIAS** (line 15145; see also line 15146) when there are neither readers nor writers, and it's positive but less than **RW_LOCK_BIAS** when there are readers but no writers—in this case, there are **RW_LOCK_BIAS** – **lock** readers. This implementation therefore permits **RW_LOCK_BIAS** simultaneous readers and (with the particular value of **RW_LOCK_BIAS** used in the code) up to 128 simultaneous pending writers.

read_lock

16620: When compiling without debugging, the body of this function is generated using the **__build_read_lock** macro (line 15172). Depending on whether the compiler can determine the address of the **rwlock_t** at compile time, this macro uses either **__build_read_lock_ptr** or **__build_read_lock_const** (lines 15148 and 15158). The compiler usually doesn't know the value of a

function's argument at compile time, but **read_lock** is a **static inline** function declared in a header file, so the compiler expands the function's code wherever the function is used. As a result, when the function is called with a global variable as its argument, the compiler knows exactly where that variable will reside in memory, so it can use the **__build_read_lock_const** macro to generate the function's body. Naturally, this results in slightly faster code.

I'll cover only **__build_read_lock_ptr**; **__build_read_lock_const** is identical in concept.

__build_read_lock_ptr

15149: The first step is to decrement the **lock** field of the **rwlock_t** passed to **read_lock**. The correctness of this instruction relies on the fact that a pointer to a **struct** (which is technically what the macro is working with) is guaranteed identical to a pointer to the **struct**'s first member.

15150: If the result of the subtraction is negative, some process is already holding the write lock; control jumps ahead to line 15153 to wait for the writer to finish.

15153: Calls a helper function that waits for the writer. In **read_lock**'s case, the helper function is **__read_lock_failed** (line 4199), explored next. The helper returns only after acquiring the read lock.

__read_lock_failed

4199: This assembler function implements the slow path of waiting for the read lock.

4200: It begins by atomically incrementing the **rwlock_t**'s **lock** member. This undoes the effect of the speculative decrement at line 15149.

4201: Begins a two-instruction loop that exits only when the **rwlock_t**'s **lock** becomes positive. Transliterated into C, the loop looks like this:

```
while ((rw->lock - 1) < 0)  {}
```

4204: The loop exited, so the target **lock** must have become positive (meaning that the last writer must have gone away). **__read_lock_failed** decrements it.

4205: If another writer sneaked in and grabbed the write lock between lines 4201 and 4204, **__read_lock_failed** jumps back to its own beginning to wait for the new writer to finish.

4206: Otherwise, the process has acquired the read lock, so **__read_lock_failed** returns.

read_unlock

16638: Trivial: Just increments the count.

write_lock

16629: Like **read_lock**, the body of **write_lock** is generated by a macro that can expand to either a constant or a non-constant version. I'll cover only the non-constant version, **__build_write_lock_ptr**.

__build_write_lock_ptr

15181: Atomically decrements the **rwlock_t**'s **lock** member by **RW_LOCK_BIAS**.

15183: When there are no readers or writers—the only case in which a write lock can be immediately acquired—the lock's **lock** member is **RW_LOCK_BIAS**, so the subtraction yields 0. In that case, the process acquires the write lock and proceeds. Otherwise, it jumps ahead to line 15186 to wait out the other readers or writers.

15186: As with **__build_read_lock_ptr**, **__build_write_lock_ptr** uses a helper function to wait for the write lock; the helper function returns only when it acquires the write lock. **write_lock**'s helper function is **__write_lock_failed**, explored next.

__write_lock_failed

4187: This assembler function implements the slow path of waiting for the write lock.

4188: The body of this function is very similar to its counterpart, **__read_lock_failed**. The differences are that this function adds or subtracts

RW_LOCK_BIAS instead of 1, and that it spins until its subtraction yields 0. Consequently, I won't cover it in detail.

write_unlock

16641: Trivial: Just adds **RW_LOCK_BIAS** to the **rwlock_t**'s **lock** member.

The kernel also defines read/write semaphores, a cross between read/write spinlocks and semaphores. Read/write semaphores are very similar to read/write spinlocks—indeed, they are constructed partly from the **__build_read_lock** and **__build_write_lock** macros (see lines 15530 and 15546), but with different helper functions.

APICs and CPU-to-CPU Communication

Central to the Intel multiprocessing specification is the use of Advanced Programmable Interrupt Controllers (APICs). CPUs communicate with each other by sending each other interrupts. By attaching actions to the interrupts, the CPUs can control one another to some extent. Each CPU has its own APIC (called the local APIC for that CPU) and there is also a single I/O APIC that handles interrupts generated by I/O devices. In a normal Intel multiprocessor system, the I/O APIC takes the place of the interrupt controller chips mentioned in passing in Chapter 6.

The following are a few example functions to give you the flavor of how this works.

smp_send_reschedule

5374: This one-line function simply sends an interrupt to the target CPU whose ID is given as an argument. It calls **send_IPI_mask** (line 5145) with the CPU ID and the **RESCHEDULE_VECTOR** vector. **RESCHEDULE_VECTOR**, along with the other SMP interrupt vectors, is **#define**d in a block beginning at line 12912.

Line 1433 associates **RESCHEDULE_VECTOR** with the function **smp_reschedule_interrupt** (line 5471; also see lines 12992 through 13003 for the definition of **BUILD_SMP_**

INTERRUPT). As a result, when one CPU in the system sends another CPU the **RESCHEDULE_VECTOR** interprocessor interrupt (IPI), the target CPU handles the interrupt by jumping to **smp_reschedule_interrupt**.

As you'll see when I present the SMP version of the scheduler later in this chapter, **smp_send_reschedule** is invoked after the scheduler raises the **need_resched** flag of a process executing on another CPU. When the target CPU returns from handling the interrupt, it finds itself at line 977 (the beginning of the **ret_from_intr** code discussed in Chapter 5). Generally, this jumps off to line 921, which notices the process's newly set **need_resched** flag and (at line 991) calls **schedule**.

send_IPI_mask

5145: **send_IPI_mask** sends a single IPI (specified by its **vector** argument) to the CPUs whose corresponding bits are set in its **mask** argument. In this code, the kernel is talking to the sending CPU's local APIC, at a fairly low level.

5154: Calls **apic_wait_icr_idle** (line 12090) to wait for the APIC to become idle. The APIC will be busy if it has not finished sending a previous IPI.

5157: Gets the contents of the upper half of the Interrupt Command Register (ICR)—the register through which the local APIC is programmed—but with its destination field set to mask. Despite the use of "2" in **__prepare_ICR2** (line 5099), the CPU actually has one ICR, not two. But it's a 64-bit register, which the kernel prefers to treat as two 32-bit registers—in the kernel code, "ICR" means the lower 32 bits of this register, whereas "ICR2" is the upper 32 bits. The ICR's destination-CPU field, which is what you want to set, is in the upper 32 bits—in ICR2.

5158: Writes the modified information back to the ICR. The ICR now knows the destination CPUs.

5161: Calls **__prepare_ICR** (line 5092) to set the interrupt vector that the caller wants to send to the destination CPUs. (Note that nothing prevents the set of destination CPUs from including the current CPU—the APIC is perfectly capable of sending an IPI to its own CPU. I can't think of any reason you'd do this, though, and the kernel doesn't do it.)

5165: Sends the interrupt by writing the new configuration to the ICR. The kernel sends IPIs other than the **RESCHEDULE_VECTOR** IPI. For example, it establishes one very general IPI, the **CALL_FUNCTION_VECTOR** IPI, which is serviced by the function **smp_call_function_interrupt** (line 5476). This IPI lets one CPU in the system tell all the other CPUs to call a given function with a given argument, which helps cut down on the number of special-purpose IPIs the kernel needs to define. The **CALL_FUNCTION_VECTOR** IPI is sent using **smp_call_function** (line 5396). One of the places it's used is by the slab code (covered in Chapter 8) when one CPU wants to alert the others that the user has resized the per-CPU free-object stacks—see lines 46040, 45659, and 44849.

How SMP Support Affects the Kernel

Now that you've studied the primitives that make SMP support possible, let's look through the kernel's SMP support. The remainder of the chapter is devoted to looking at a representative set of SMP-specific code distributed through the kernel.

Effects on Scheduling

schedule (line 34237), of course, is the kernel's scheduler function, which is covered quite thoroughly in Chapter 7. The SMP version of **schedule** has two main differences from the UP version:

- A block of code from lines 34311 through 34314 and a related line shortly after (line 34326), in **schedule** itself, that compute some information needed elsewhere.

- The call to **__schedule_tail** (line 34158), which happens on both SMP and UP, executes only one line of code (line 34218) on UP kernels. The function does considerably more work for SMP kernels.

In addition, the function **reschedule_idle** (line 33952) operates very differently for UP and SMP kernels. The function is not called by the UP scheduler, but it is called by the SMP scheduler, so I cover it a little later in the chapter.

schedule

34312: **schedule** has decided to run **next** on the current CPU (that is, the CPU executing **schedule**). So it records the fact that **next** is getting a CPU, and which CPU it's getting. This information is used by the **can_schedule** macro (whose SMP version is at line 33860), **reschedule_idle** (line 33952, and discussed below), **goodness** (line 33886), and **schedule** itself.

34326: Gets the current time, as the number of cycles that have elapsed since the machine was turned on. This is a lot like checking **jiffies**, but with a granularity measured in CPU cycles rather than timer ticks—obviously, this is much more precise. This information helps **reschedule_idle** decide which CPU has been idle the longest, as you'll see. Contrary to the comment above it, this line is not reached when rescheduling to the same process (see line 34317).

__schedule_tail

34158: Called from the scheduler at line 34369, the SMP version of **__schedule_tail** is simpler than it looks. Essentially, the function does two things:

- Clears **prev**'s **has_cpu** flag.

- Finds another CPU for **prev** to run on, if appropriate. Delegating this work to **reschedule_idle** keeps **__schedule_tail** lean and mean.

Doing these two things as fast as possible just makes it a little complicated.

34182: **prev** lost the CPU to **next**, so **__schedule_tail** clears **prev**'s **has_cpu** flag.

34184: If **prev** is still in the **TASK_RUNNING** state, then it would be happy to continue using the CPU. For whatever reason—because **next** had a better goodness value or because **prev** yielded the CPU—**prev** shouldn't have the current CPU, but maybe it would be worthwhile to find it another home. Control jumps ahead to line 34201 to see.

34207: The idle process shouldn't be moved to another CPU, and a process that yielded the CPU shouldn't be reinstalled on another CPU immediately. Those cases cause control to jump back to line 34187, which exits the function.

34213: Otherwise, it is probably a good idea to try to find **prev** a new home. If **prev** is still in the **TASK_RUNNING** state (another CPU might have changed its state since the check at line 34184), **__schedule_tail** calls **reschedule_idle** to relocate **prev** if possible.

reschedule_idle

33952: You've just seen one of the two calls to **reschedule_idle**. The other is at line 34078 (in **wake_up_process**), which is reached when the process being awakened—which is passed to **reschedule_idle** as **p**—is not already in the run queue. In either case, **reschedule_idle** tries to schedule **p** on a different CPU, preferably an idle one.

Of course, it's always possible that the apparently idle CPU that gets chosen is just temporarily idle and is about to be swamped by a dozen high-priority, CPU-bound processes that are going to wake up on it a nanosecond from now. So this function isn't perfect, but it's pretty good in a statistical sense—and remember, choices like these are in perfect keeping with the scheduler's quick-and-dirty attitude.

reschedule_idle finds a destination CPU for **p** with the following algorithm:

- Run **p** on whatever CPU it ran on last, if that CPU is now idle.

- Otherwise, if another CPU is idle, run **p** on it. If more than one CPU is idle, run **p** on the one that has been idle for the longest time.

- Otherwise, if **p** has a higher goodness (recall Chapter 7's discussion of this term) than some other currently running process, allow **p** to preempt the process with the lowest goodness.

- Otherwise, all CPUs are running processes that have a higher goodness than **p**, so **reschedule_idle** just gives up.

33962: This is the first step of the algorithm. **best_cpu** is the CPU that **p** was just running on; it's the "best" CPU because leaving **p** there involves the least overhead. For instance, if **p** was formerly running on the CPU that is now executing **reschedule_idle**, **reschedule_idle** can run **p** on this CPU without sending the **RESCHEDULE_VECTOR** IPI, which incurs a cost for both the sending and the receiving CPU.

33965: If **p** is allowed to run on the currently executing CPU and the current CPU is now idle, then **p** can be run on its "best" CPU. A CPU is idle if it's executing its idle process; there's one of these for each CPU, and the **idle_task** macro (line 33859) returns it.

33972: Sets the target CPU's idle process's **need_resched** flag, so that it will notice that it should give away the CPU. If **p**'s "best" CPU is not the current CPU, then **reschedule_idle** sends the other CPU a **RESCHEDULE_VECTOR** IPI with **smp_send_reschedule**.

33985: This begins the second and third steps of the algorithm (they're interwoven so that the code doesn't have to walk through all CPUs twice). **oldest_idle** helps track the "most idle" CPU by recording the most recent schedule time of the CPU that has been idle the longest. It is the maximum possible value of a **cycles_t** (an **unsigned long long**) if no idle CPU has been found.

33986: **target_tsk** points to the task that **p** should replace, or **NULL** if no such task has been selected.

33987: **max_prio** helps decide whether **p** should preempt a non-idle process, if no CPUs are idle.

33989: The loop beginning at this line walks over all CPUs in the system, checking to see whether any of them is idle or, if not, whether **p** should preempt the non-idle process already running there.

33991: If **p** has been barred from running on this CPU, the loop continues to the next CPU.

33998: This CPU is idle. If this is the first idle CPU found, or if this CPU has been idle longer than all previously found idle CPUs, **p** should be run on this one (unless a better choice is found later, of course). **target_tsk** is made to point to this CPU's idle process.

34003: This CPU is not idle. If an idle CPU has been found, then **oldest_idle** will be less than its initial value (the maximum possible **cycles_t**), so the **if** condition at this line fails. Note that this line says **-1ULL** where line 33985 said (**cycles_t**) **-1**; since **cycles_t** is just a **typedef** for **unsigned long long**, they're the same value. The code is saying the same thing in both places; it would be better if both lines said it in the same way.

If no idle CPU has been found yet, then line 34004 uses **preemption_goodness** (line 33938) to find out how much better **p** is than the process running on this CPU. If the difference in the two processes' goodness values exceeds the initial value of **max_prio** (1) or if the difference exceeds all such previous differences computed in the loop, then **p** should preempt this process (unless, again, a better choice is found later). **target_tsk** is updated accordingly.

The converse of the problem mentioned earlier arises here: Just because the CPU isn't idle now doesn't mean that all of its processes aren't about to die and make it idle. However, **reschedule_idle** has no way to know this, so it might as well assume the target CPU is going to be occupied for a while. That's probably true anyway, and when it's not true, some process will be scheduled on the newly idle CPU soon enough.

34015: If **target_tsk** (whose value has now been copied into **tsk** for no apparent reason) is not **NULL**, then the loop found a process that **p** should preempt. If **p** is preempting one of the idle processes, the code jumps back to line 33967 to do this. Otherwise, the target task's **need_resched** flag is raised, and (if necessary) the task's CPU is sent the **RESCHEDULE_VECTOR** IPI using **smp_send_reschedule**.

As you can see, **reschedule_idle** is a beautiful example of inter-CPU coordination that is simply unnecessary in a UP system. For a UP box, asking which CPU a process should have is equivalent to asking whether it should be given the system's one CPU or no CPU at all. An SMP box must also put some effort into deciding which of the CPUs in the system would be the best home for the process. Of course, the enormous speed gains achieved in exchange make this extra effort quite a bargain.

You might not expect SMP support to be an issue when a process is exiting. But it is, as you'll see in the following discussion of **release_task**.

release_task

29880: The non-SMP-specific part of **release_task** is covered in Chapter 7—this is where a zombie is being sent to its grave and its **struct task_struct** is being freed.

29888: Sees whether the process is running on a CPU. (The CPU that owns it might not have gotten around to clearing this flag just yet; it will shortly.) If not, **release_task** exits the loop and goes on to free the **struct task_struct** as usual.

29891: Otherwise, **release_task** waits for the process's **has_cpu** flag to be cleared. When it is, **release_task** tries again. This seemingly odd situation—a process is being killed, yet it has the CPU—is indeed rare, but not impossible. The process might have been killed on one CPU, which hasn't had time to clear the **has_cpu** flag yet, but its parent is reaping it from another CPU.

SMP Timer Interrupts

SMP kernels have what amount to two different timer interrupts. The first works the same way as in UP kernels: As covered in Chapter 6, the function **timer_interrupt** (line 6223) is invoked 100 times per second and **timer_interrupt** calls **do_timer_interrupt** (line 6148). SMP kernels can also take advantage of the fact that each CPU's local APIC can be programmed to interrupt that CPU more frequently than 100 times per second, enabling SMP kernels to perform finer-grained kernel profiling.

The function **smp_apic_timer_interrupt** (line 642) is the APIC timer interrupt for SMP kernels. This is set up at line 1447, using the **BUILD_SMP_TIMER_INTERRUPT** macro #defined at line 13005. The interesting part of **smp_apic_timer_interrupt** is in **smp_local_timer_interrupt**.

Despite its name, **smp_apic_timer_interrupt** (and, therefore, **smp_local_timer_interrupt**) can also be invoked on single-CPU machines running UP kernels. The deciding factor is not whether the kernel was compiled with SMP support but whether the system contains a local APIC (which some single-CPU systems do). The kernel will automatically detect a local APIC if present on a single-CPU system and enable the **smp_apic_timer_interrupt** handler.

smp_local_timer_interrupt is also called from line 6181, which is in the normal UP timer interrupt, **do_timer_interrupt**. This happens only when running an SMP kernel on a UP machine.

smp_local_timer_interrupt

599: If the system was running in kernel mode (not user mode) when the APIC timer fired, the kernel calls **x86_do_profile** (line 13054, described in Chapter 4) to perform kernel profiling.

602: Even if the APIC timer is firing more frequently than the normal timer interrupt, the kernel should call **update_process_times** (line 40166, described in Chapter 6) only at the normal rate. So each CPU knows how many APIC timer interrupts will occur per normal timer interrupt and it counts down from that number on every APIC timer interrupt. When the counter reaches 0, the APIC timer interrupt invokes **update_process_times**.

The number of APIC timer interrupts per normal timer interrupt is stored in the **prof_multiplier** array (line 31), one of a set of three parallel arrays. The other two arrays are **prof_old_multiplier** (line 32), which helps the kernel detect when the multiplier has changed, and **prof_counter** (line 33), which records each CPU's current countdown value.

609: This CPU's countdown has reached 0. It reinitializes its counter from the multiplier.

610: If the multiplier has changed, the CPU should tell its local APIC to call it back at the new rate. It calls **__setup_APIC_LVTT** (line 406) to reconfigure its local APIC, then records the new multiplier so it can detect the next change.

By the way, the root can change the multiplier on the fly, using the /proc interface covered in Chapter 11. When the multiplier changes, the kernel invokes **setup_profiling_timer** (line 556) to install the new value in the **prof_multiplier** array. As you can see, the same multiplier value is used for each CPU.

616: On SMP kernels only (remember that this code can be invoked by some UP kernels), this CPU calls **update_process_times** to update process timing statistics and to kill processes that have exceeded their CPU-time resource limits.

cli and sti

As I explained in Chapter 6, **cli** and **sti** are used to disable and enable interrupts, respectively. For UP, these reduced to a single **cli** or **sti** instruction each. That's not sufficient for the SMP case, in which you need to not only disable interrupts for the local CPU, but also temporarily shut out all other CPUs from handling IRQs. So, for SMP, the **cli** and **sti** macros become calls to the functions **__global_cli** and **__global_sti**.

__global_cli

2209: Copies the CPU's EFLAGS register into the local variable **flags**.

2210: The x86's Interrupts Enabled flag is in bit nine of the EFLAGS register—explaining the definition of **EFLAGS_IF_SHIFT** at line 2194. This is used to see whether interrupts are already disabled, in which case nothing further needs to be done to disable them.

2212: Disables interrupts on this CPU.

2213: If the CPU is not already handling an interrupt, **__global_cli** calls **get_irqlock** (line 2175) to acquire the global IRQ lock. This is not done when the CPU is already handling an interrupt, for reasons explained in the comment above the function.

__global_sti

2222: If the CPU is not already handling an interrupt, **__global_sti** calls **release_irqlock** (line 12713) to drop the global IRQ lock, which was acquired in **__global_cli**.

2224: Allows interrupts on this CPU once more.

irq_enter and irq_exit

A region of code enclosed in an **irq_enter/irq_exit** pair is atomic with respect to every other such region; it's also atomic with respect to **cli/sti** pairs. Among other places, these functions are used in **handle_IRQ_event** (line 2282), discussed in Chapter 6. UP kernels use the simple macros **#define**d at lines 12689 and 12690; the SMP versions are explored next.

irq_enter

12724: Records that this CPU is now handling an interrupt. The **local_irq_count** macro used here is **#define**d at line 19519; it simply indexes into the per-CPU **irq_stat** array described in Chapter 6.

12726: This loop simply spins while any other CPU has the global IRQ lock. This is how **__global_cli**, discussed in the previous section, prevents other CPUs from handling interrupts. If CPU A grabs

global_irq_lock using **__global_cli**, CPU B will reach the current line as part of its interrupt handling and wait for CPU A to release the lock.

You can be sure that CPU A won't also end up spinning in this loop, by the way: Before acquiring the global IRQ lock, CPU A disabled local interrupts. Therefore, it can't reach this line while holding the global interrupt lock (unless the code does something stupid, such as calling **irq_enter** outside of interrupt-handling code). If CPU A did end up in this loop while holding the lock, the system would quickly freeze. CPU A would be waiting for itself to release the global IRQ lock—which can never happen, since it would be stuck in this loop. As the system's other CPUs attempted to service interrupts, they'd also end up waiting forever for CPU A to release the lock.

irq_exit

12733: The SMP version of **irq_exit** is as simple as its UP counterpart: It simply records that it has exited an **irq_enter/irq_exit** pair.

You might wonder why **irq_enter** and **irq_exit** increment and decrement a counter, rather than treat the counter as a simple flag and just set it to 1 or 0. When you recall (from Chapter 6) that some interrupts can themselves be interrupted, the reason becomes obvious: If the code just used a one-bit flag for this purpose, then when interrupt 2 interrupted interrupt 1, the kernel would prematurely (when finished with interrupt 2) think that it was no longer servicing an interrupt. Using a counter ensures that the kernel accurately records when it has finished with all interrupts, even interrupts that were themselves interrupted.

By the way, notice that for both **irq_enter** and **irq_exit**, current versions of the kernel always ignore the **irq** argument (and not just on the x86; the same goes for all other platforms as of the 2.4 kernel).

Chapter 11

Tunable Kernel Parameters

Following the lead of the BSD 4.4 flavor of Unix, Linux provides the **sysctl** system call for inspecting and reconfiguring certain features of the system on the fly, without requiring you to edit the kernel's source code, recompile, and reboot. This is a vast improvement on earlier Unix versions that made tuning the system an often painful chore. Linux organizes the system features that may be inspected and reconfigured in this way into several categories: general kernel parameters, virtual memory parameters, network parameters, and so on.

The same features are also accessible through a different interface: the /proc file system. (Because it's really a window onto the system rather than a container of real files, /proc is a "pseudo file system"; however, that's a clumsy term and the distinction isn't important here.) The categories of tunable kernel parameters appear as subdirectories under /proc/sys and each individual tunable kernel parameter is represented by a file in one of the subdirectories. The subdirectories can, in turn, include further subdirectories, which contain still more files representing tunable kernel parameters and perhaps still more subdirectories, and so on, although in practice the nesting level never gets very deep.

/proc/sys bypasses the usual **sysctl** interface. The value of a tunable kernel parameter can be read simply by reading from the corresponding file and its value can be set by writing to the file. Normal Unix file system permissions apply to these files, so that not just any user can read or write them. Most of the files are readable by any user but writable only by root, although there are a few exceptions. For example, the file /proc/sys/kernel/cap-bound can be read and written to by root only. Without /proc/sys, inspecting and tuning the system would require writing a program to call **sysctl** with

the desired parameters—not a Herculean task, but not nearly as convenient as using /proc/sys, either.

When you've finished reading this chapter, you might want to take a look at the code from lines 45843 through 46052. This code makes slab-related information visible through the /proc file system and provides a good example of how various kernel subsystems can expose their data through this interface.

struct ctl_table

24589: This is the central data structure used by the code covered in this chapter. **struct ctl_table**s normally are conglomerated in arrays, each such array corresponding to the entries in a single directory somewhere under /proc/sys. (In my opinion, it would be a bit better to name it **struct ctl_table_entry**.) **root_table** (line 37944) and the arrays that follow it form a tree of arrays, using **struct ctl_table**'s **child** pointers to join the tree nodes (**child** is covered in the upcoming list). Note that these are all arrays of **ctl_table**, which is just a **typedef** for **struct ctl_table**; this is established at line 24508.

The tree-of-arrays relationship is illustrated in Figure 11.1. This figure shows a small part of the tree formed by **root_table** and the tables that it points to.

struct ctl_table has the following members:

- **ctl_name**—An integer that uniquely identifies the table entry—uniquely within the array in which it resides, anyway; the numbers can be reused in different arrays. Such a unique number already exists for any array entry—its array index—but array indexes shouldn't be used to identify **struct ctl_table**s through the **sysctl** interface, because we want to maintain binary compatibility across kernel releases. The tunable kernel parameter associated with an array entry in one kernel version might disappear in a future kernel version, so if parameters were identified by their array indexes, reusing the obsolete item's position in the array could confuse programs that haven't been recompiled under the new kernel. Over time, the arrays would become cluttered with unusable entries

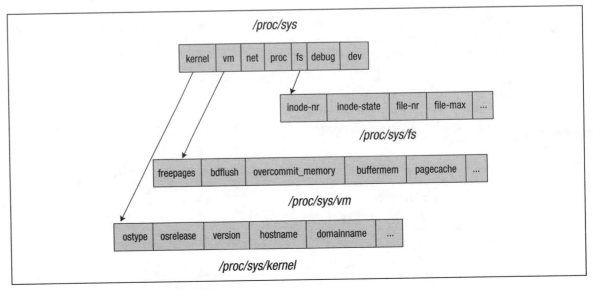

Figure 11.1   A partial tree of **struct ctl_table** s.

that were just wasting space for the sake of backward compatibility. Instead, this approach merely "wastes" integers, which are plentiful. On the other hand, lookups are slower, because a simple array index won't suffice with this method.

This might remind you of the system call table from Chapter 5: Just as each **struct ctl_table** entry is identified by a unique integer, so is each system call. But the system call table takes another approach to dealing with change, keeping array indexes the same across kernel versions and allowing the system call table to become cluttered with obsolete entries. The reason for the difference in approaches is simple: With system calls, speed is critical; system calls are invoked all the time and must go as quickly as possible. Where **struct ctl_tables** are used, speed is less important, so the kernel developers decided to optimize for space instead.

- **procname**—A short, human-readable file name for the corresponding entry under /proc/sys.

- **data**—A pointer to the data associated with this table entry. This usually points to either an **int** or a **char** (and, of course, a pointer to **char** is a string).

- **maxlen**—The maximum number of bytes that can be read from or written to **data**. If **data** points to a single **int**, for example, **maxlen** should be **sizeof(int)**.

- **mode**—The Unix-style file permission bits for the /proc file (or directory) corresponding to this entry. Explaining this requires a very short detour into the world of file systems. Like other Unix implementations, Linux uses three sets of three bits each to record a file's permissions. These are displayed as the three groups of r(readable), w(writable), and

x(executable), characters in a listing produced by **ls -l** (see Figure 11.2; note that the kernel generally uses 16-bit types to represent permissions). These occupy the lower nine bits of **mode**. A file system dedicates the remaining bits in the file's **mode** to other purposes, such as tracking whether the file is a regular file (bit 15, as it happens), a directory (bit 14), a setuid or setgid executable (bits 11 and 10), and so on. For the purposes of this chapter, however, those other bits are of no concern.

Where the kernel inspects these bits, you'll often see the octal constants 4, 2, and 1 used in conjunction with **mode**—these are checking the r, w, and x bits, respectively, possibly after shifting **mode** over to get to the right set of three bits. This shifting and checking is ultimately done in **test_perm**, line 38185.

Note that if a table entry has a **maxlen** of 0, it's effectively neither readable nor writable, no matter what its **mode**.

- **child**—A pointer to the child table, if this is a directory-type entry. In this case, because no data is associated with the entry itself, **data** will be **NULL** and **maxlen** will be 0.

- **proc_handler**—A pointer to a function that actually reads from or writes to the **data** member. **proc_handler** is used when reading or

writing data through the /proc file system. This allows any type of data to be pointed to by **data** and the **proc_handler** function correctly handles working with it. **proc_handler** is normally either **proc_dostring** (line 38461) or **proc_dointvec** (line 38645). I discuss these and the other commonly used functions later in the chapter. (Any function with the right prototype can be used.) For directory-type entries, **proc_handler** is **NULL**.

- **strategy**—A pointer to another function that actually reads from or writes to the **data** member. **strategy** is used when reading or writing through the **sysctl** system call. It's usually **sysctl_string** (line 38950), but can also be **sysctl_intvec** (line 38993). I discuss both these functions later in the chapter.

Linus hates the **sysctl** interface and it shows here. Most of the tunable kernel parameters can be modified through the /proc interface but not through the **sysctl** system call, so this pointer is **NULL** more often than not.

- **de**—A pointer to the **struct proc_dir_entry** used by the /proc file system code to track a file or directory in the file system. If non-**NULL**, the **struct ctl_table** has been registered under /proc somewhere.

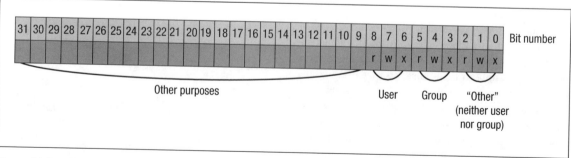

Figure 11.2   File mode bits.

- **extra1** and **extra2**—Pointers to any extra data needed when processing this table element. These are currently used only to specify the minimum and maximum values for certain integer parameters.

/proc/sys Support

Not all of the code that implements the /proc/sys interface to tunable kernel parameters is included in this book. Indeed, most of the code isn't included, because it mostly belongs to the /proc file system. Still, if you don't worry about how the rest of /proc works, it's not hard to understand the code in kernel/sysctl.c, which works with the /proc file system to make tunable kernel parameters visible under /proc.

register_proc_table

38329: **register_proc_table** registers a **ctl_table** under /proc/sys, causing one or more new subdirectories to appear there. Note that nothing requires the supplied table to be a root-level node (that is, a **ctl_table** without a parent). It should be one, but that's up to the caller to enforce.

The table is installed directly under **root**, which should correspond to /proc/sys or one of the subdirectories under it. (On the initial call, **root** always points to **proc_sys_root**, but its value changes on recursive calls.)

38336: Begins iterating over all the elements of the **table** array; the iteration terminates when the current element's **ctl_name** member is 0, signaling the end of the array.

38338: If the **ctl_table**'s **procname** field is **NULL**, then it shouldn't be visible under /proc/sys (even though other elements of the same array may be), so it's skipped. Currently, there are no such **ctl_tables**: Every **ctl_table** in this file, as well as all others I can find in the 2.4 kernel, has a non-**NULL** **procname** and therefore appears under /proc/sys.

38341: If the table entry has a **procname**, meaning it should be registered under /proc/sys, it must also have either a **proc_handler** (if a leaf, or file-like, node) or a **child** (if a directory-like node). If a table entry has neither, a warning is printed and the loop is continued.

38351: If the table entry has a **proc_handler**, it's marked as a regular file.

38353: Otherwise, as can be deduced from line 38341, the entry must have a non-**NULL child**, so it will be treated as a directory. Note that nothing prevents a **ctl_table** from having both non-**NULL proc_handler** and **child** members. All of the code must agree to do the same thing in this case; either it should treat the entry as a file, or it should treat the entry as a directory. However, in the current code, no **ctl_table** has both fields non-**NULL**, so this is a moot point.

38355: Scans for an existing subdirectory with the given name, leaving **de** pointing to the existing entry if one is found, or leaving **de NULL** if one is not found. Why no similar check is done for files is hard to understand. The answer doubtless lies in some detail of the /proc file system that I haven't yet grasped.

38363: If the named subdirectory doesn't already exist or if **table** corresponds to a file rather than a directory, the new file or directory is created through a call to **create_proc_entry** (not included in this book).

38369: If the table entry is a leaf node, **register_proc_table** tells the /proc file system code to use the file and inode operations defined by **proc_sys_file_operations** and **proc_sys_inode_operations** (lines 37921 and 37926). **proc_sys_file_operations** defines only two operations, reading and writing (not seeking, memory mapping, or any of the others). These operations are carried out with the **proc_readsys** and **proc_writesys** functions (lines 38443 and 38449), which are discussed later in the chapter. **proc_sys_inode_operations** is

even more Spartan, defining only **proc_sys_permissions** (line 38455), which checks whether the user should be permitted to access a /proc entry.

38373: At this point, **de** is known to be not **NULL**; either it was non-**NULL** already or it was initialized at line 38363.

38375: If the entry being added is a directory-type entry, **register_proc_table** is recursively invoked to add all of the entry's children as well. This is a rare use of recursion in the kernel. Recursion is acceptable here because the recursion depth (and therefore the kernel stack usage) can be bounded in advance: It's proportional to the tree depth. Since the tree passed to this function always comes from kernel code, never from user code (not even indirectly), it's reasonably safe to assume that the caller will be aware of the limitation and structure the tree accordingly. If this were to change—for example, if a new system call allowed user code to supply the data for this function—**register_proc_table** would have to check its input more carefully.

unregister_proc_table

38381: **unregister_proc_table** deletes the association between a tree of **ctl_table** arrays and the /proc file system. The entries in the **ctl_table**—and all the entries in any "subdirectories" below them—will disappear from /proc/sys.

38385: As at line 38336, this begins an iteration over the supplied array of table entries.

38386: Table entries not associated with an entry under /proc/sys have a **NULL de** member; these obviously can be skipped.

38390: If the /proc file system thinks this is a directory, but the table entry is a leaf (non-directory), the two structures are inconsistent. **unregister_proc_table** prints a warning and continues the loop without trying to remove this entry.

38394: Directories are freed recursively—another rare use of recursion in the kernel.

38398: After the recursive call returns, **unregister_proc_table** checks that all the subdirectories and files were recursively removed. If they weren't, the current element can't safely be removed and the loop is continued.

38404: Here's why some of the subdirectories (and the files in them) might not have been removed: They might currently be in use. If this one is in use, the loop is simply continued, so the element will not be removed.

38408: The node is removed from the file system via **remove_proc_entry** (not included in this book). If successful, this function also frees the memory associated with the removed node.

do_rw_proc

38412: **do_rw_proc** implements the guts of both **proc_readsys** (line 38443) and **proc_writesys** (line 38449), the functions used by the /proc file system code to read from and write to **ctl_tables**.

38423: Ensures that a table is associated with this entry under /proc/sys.

38426: Note that the first test on this line is redundant with the second test on line 38423 because **table** is initialized from **de->data**.

38429: Ensures the calling process has permission to read or write, as appropriate.

38436: Calls the table entry's **proc_handler** to do the actual read or write. (Note that line 38426 proved that the **proc_handler** member is non-**NULL**.) As mentioned before, the **proc_handler** member is usually either **proc_dostring** or **proc_dointvec** (lines 38461 and 38645), which are discussed in the next few sections.

38440: **do_rw_proc** returns the number of bytes actually read or written. Notice that the local

variable **res** is entirely superfluous; it could be replaced by the **count** argument.

proc_dostring

38461: **proc_dostring** is the function that the /proc file system code calls to read or write a kernel parameter that is a C string.

Note that the **write** flag means the caller is writing to the table element, but this mainly involves reading from the input buffer. Consequently, the code for writing is dominated by reading. Similarly, if the **write** flag is not set, the caller is reading from the table entry, which mainly involves writing to the supplied buffer.

There's also a stub implementation of this function at line 38894. This stub is used when the /proc file system is compiled out of the kernel. Similar stubs for most of the other functions that will be covered follow that one.

38476: Characters are read from the input buffer until a terminating ASCII NUL (0) byte or a newline is found, or until the maximum allowed amount of data (as specified by **lenp**) has been read from the input buffer. (To forestall confusion on this point, bear in mind that **NULL** is a C pointer constant, whereas NUL—one *L*—is ASCII's term for character number 0).

38483: If the number of bytes read from the buffer exceeds what can be stored in the table entry, the number is reduced. It probably would be more efficient to constrain the maximum input length (**lenp**) before the loop instead, because reading more than **table->maxlen** bytes from **buffer** is pointless. As it is, the loop might read, say, 1,024 bytes, and then reduce the count to 64 because that's all that can be stored in the table entry.

38485: The string is read from the input buffer and then NUL-terminated.

38488: The kernel maintains a "current position" variable for each file owned by each process;

this is **struct file**'s **f_pos** member, the value returned by the **tell** system call and set by the **seek** system call. Here, the file's current position is advanced by the number of bytes written.

38490: The reading case begins by checking the length of the data already in the table entry. The amount of data returned will be the largest of this length, the **maxlen** value for the table entry, and the length supplied by the caller. (Note that the length of the table's data should never exceed **maxlen**, making that test theoretically unnecessary.)

38495: If those checks left anything to write (by leaving **len** positive), the data is copied out to user space now. If there's room left over, a newline is copied out as well.

38503: The amount of data returned to the caller is stored through **lenp**. (The caller can't depend on **strlen** to compute this length, because **proc_dostring** may not have copied a NUL to the caller-supplied buffer.)

38504: As in the writing case, the **struct file**'s **f_pos** member is advanced by the number of bytes the caller read.

proc_doutsstring

38512: **proc_doutsstring** simply calls **proc_dostring**, after acquiring the **uts_sem** semaphore (line 37511)—note that this is a read/write semaphore, so whether it's locked for reading or writing depends on the **write** flag. This function is used by several of the entries in **kern_table** (line 37957) to set various components of the **system_utsname** structure (line 26109).

do_proc_dointvec

38535: **proc_dointvec** (line 38645) delegates its work to this function. **do_proc_dointvec** reads or writes an array of **int**s pointed to by **table**'s **data** member. The number of **int**s to read or write is passed through **lenp**; it's normally 1, so the function normally is used to read or write only a single **int**.

The values for the **ints** are specified by **buffer**. The **ints** aren't passed as a raw array of **ints**, though; instead, they're given as ASCII text, which the user is writing into the associated /proc file.

38553: Begins iterating over all the **ints** to read or write. **left** tracks the remaining number of **ints** the caller wants to read or write, whereas **vleft** tracks the number of valid elements remaining in **table->data**. The loop terminates when either of these reaches 0 or when it exits from the middle.

Note that the whole loop could be made very slightly more efficient, though harder to maintain, if the **if** at line 38554 were hoisted out of the loop. That is, instead of code structured like this:

```
for (; left && vleft--; i++, first=0) {
  if (write) {
    /* Write stuff. */
  } else {
    /* Read stuff. */
  }
}
```

It could be structured like this:

```
if (write) {
  for (; left && vleft--; i++, first=0){
    /* Write stuff. */
  }
} else {
  for (;left && vleft--; i++, first=0){
    /* Read stuff. */
  }
}
```

This way, the value of **write**, which doesn't change within the loop, would be checked only once, not on every loop iteration.

38555: Scans forward for a nonspace character, the beginning of the next number in the input.

38568: Copies a chunk of data from user space into the local buffer **buf** and then NUL-terminates **buf**. **buf** now contains all the remaining ASCII text from the input—or as much of this text as it can hold.

This approach looks a little inefficient, because it might read more than it needs to. However, because **buf**'s size is only 20 (**TMPBUFLEN**, line 38540), it can't read *that* much more than it needs to. The idea is probably that it's cheaper just to read a little extra than to check each byte to see whether the read should terminate.

The values read from **buf** are **ints**, so they're 32 bits on both 32-bit platforms and 64-bit platforms. **buf** only needs to be large enough to hold the largest possible 32-bit number (11 characters, if you count the leading - sign).

38574: Handles a leading minus (-) sign, skipping past the minus sign and setting a flag if one is found.

38578: Ensures the text that was read from **buffer** (possibly after the leading minus sign) at least begins with a digit, so that it can be successfully converted to an integer. Without this check, it would be impossible to tell whether the call to **simple_strtoul** at line 38580 returned 0 because the input was "0" or because it was unable to convert any text.

38580: Converts the text to an integer, scaling the result by the **conv** argument. This scaling step is useful for functions such as **proc_dointvec_jiffies** (line 38885), which converts its input from seconds to jiffies by the simple expedient of multiplying by the constant **HZ** (line 13523). Generally, however, the scale factor is 1—no scaling.

38582: If more text remains to be read from the buffer and the next character that would be read isn't an argument-separating space, then the whole

argument wouldn't fit into **buf**. Such input is invalid, so the loop is terminated early. However, no error code is returned, so the caller might be falsely led to believe that everything was okay. Well, that's not quite true: An error code will be returned at line 38639, but only if the invalid argument is detected on the first loop iteration. If detected on a subsequent loop iteration, no error will be noticed.

38584: The argument has been read successfully. The leading minus sign is now honored if it was present, and the other local variables are adjusted to move on to the next argument.

38588: What happens next depends on the value of **op**; this should be one of the **OP_XXX** constants that are #**define**d at lines 38529 through 38533.

38589: In the most common case, **op** is **OP_SET**, and the argument is simply stored in the table entry through the pointer **i**.

38592: Alternately, the value already in the table can be bitwise-ANDed or bitwise-ORed with the argument (**OP_AND** and **OP_OR**).

38598: Finally, the table value may be set to the maximum or minimum (**OP_MAX** and **OP_MIN**) of the current value and the value supplied by the caller.

The **op** parameter clearly makes **do_proc_dointvec**'s behavior quite flexible, but most of that flexibility currently goes to waste: As you can see from examining the only calls to this function (lines 38648, 38660, and 38888), only the **OP_SET** and **OP_AND** values are used.

38608: The caller is reading values from the table entry—a much simpler case, because no parsing of ASCII text is required. The output is tab-separated, so a tab is written into the temporary buffer on any loop iteration but the first. (It's not written after the last argument, either; only between arguments.)

38611: Next, the current integer is scaled down by a factor of **conv** and printed into the temporary buffer.

38612: Copies the textual representation of the current **int** to the output buffer—or as much of it as will fit, anyway—and updates the local variables to move along to the table entry's next array element.

38622: Newline terminates the output, if the caller was reading. The **if** condition also ensures that the loop wasn't terminated on its first iteration and that there's room to write the newline. Note that the output buffer is not terminated with an ASCII NUL byte (as you might have expected), because it doesn't need to be: The caller can deduce the length of the returned string from the new value written through **lenp**.

38627: Skips over any white space following the last argument that was read from the input buffer, if the caller was writing values into the table entry.

38640: Updates the file's current position and **lenp**, and then returns 0 for success.

proc_dointvec_minmax

38664: **proc_dointvec_minmax** is just like **do_proc_dointvec**, except that it also treats the table entry's **extra1** and **extra2** members as arrays of constraints on the values that may be written into the table entry. The values in **extra1** are minima, and the values in **extra2** are maxima. The other difference is that **proc_dointvec_minmax** doesn't take a **conv** argument.

Because of the similarities between these two functions, only the differences are covered in this section.

38720: Here's the biggest difference: When writing, values that are out of the range defined by **min** and **max** (which loop over the **extra1** and **extra2** arrays) are silently skipped. The intent of this code, apparently, is for **min** and **max** to proceed along with **val**. As a value is read from

the input, it should be checked against the next **min** and the next **max**, and then either accepted or skipped. But that isn't quite what happens.

Suppose the current value from **buffer**, which has been parsed and is in **val**, is lower than the minimum; further suppose, for the sake of concreteness, that it's the third loop iteration, so that **min** and **max** each point to the third elements of their corresponding arrays. Then **val** will be checked against **min** and found to be out of range (too small), so the loop will be continued. But **min** is updated as a side effect of the check, and **max** isn't. Now, **min** points to the fourth element of its corresponding array, but **max** still points to the third element of its array. The two are out of sync, and they'll stay that way, so the next value (indeed, all subsequent values) read from **buffer** may be tested against the wrong limit. The following is the easiest fix:

```
if (min && val < *min++) {
    /* Keep max & min in sync. */
    if (max) max++;
    continue;
}
if (max && val < *max++)
    continue;
```

The sysctl System Call

The other interface to tunable kernel parameters is the **sysctl** system call, along with its associated functions. This interface is in some disfavor. And why not? For most real-life purposes, **sysctl**—however great an advance it may have been over the older method, tuning the kernel by hacking the source code—is simply clumsier than accessing files through /proc. Reading and writing through **sysctl** requires a C program (or something similar), whereas /proc is readily accessible through shell commands (or, equally, through shell scripts).

On the other hand, if you're working in C already, calling **sysctl** is much more convenient than opening a file, reading from it and/or writing to it, and then closing the file again, so **sysctl** will have its uses for some time to come. In the meantime, let's have a look at its implementation.

do_sysctl

38135: **do_sysctl** implements the guts of **sys_sysctl** (line 38165), the **sysctl** system call. Note that **sys_sysctl** also appears at line 39059—that version is a simple stub function that is used when the **sysctl** system call is compiled out.

The kernel parameter's old value is returned through **oldval** if **oldval** is not **NULL**, and its new value is set from **newval** if **newval** is not **NULL**. **oldlenp** and **newlen** indicate how many bytes should be written to **oldval** and read from **newval**, respectively, when the corresponding pointers aren't **NULL**; they're ignored when the pointers are **NULL**.

Note the asymmetry: The function takes a pointer to the old length, but not a pointer to the new length. This is because the old length is both an input and an output parameter. Its input value is the maximum number of bytes that can be returned through **oldval** and its output value is the number of bytes that actually were returned. By contrast, the new length is an input parameter only.

38142: Sets **old_len** from **oldlenp**, if the caller wants the kernel parameter's old value.

38147: Begins walking over the circular list of trees of tables. (See the discussion of **register_sysctl_table**, later in the chapter.)

38153: Uses **parse_table** (line 38201, discussed in the next section) to locate the tunable kernel parameter and to read and/or write its value.

38156: If **parse_table** allocated any context information, it's freed. It's hard to tell exactly what this context information is meant for. It's not used by any code covered in the book—indeed, as far as I can tell, it's not currently used by any code anywhere in the kernel.

38158: The **ENOTDIR** error simply means that the named kernel parameter was not found in this tree of tables, although it might still be in another table tree not yet searched. Otherwise, **error** is some other error code or 0 for success; in either case, it should be (and is) returned.

38160: Advances the loop iterator.

38162: Returns the **ENOTDIR** error, to report that the named kernel parameter wasn't found in any table.

parse_table

38201: **parse_table** looks up an entry in a tree of tables, analogous to the way a fully qualified file name is resolved in a directory tree. The idea is as follows: The lookup proceeds along an array of **ints** (the array name), looking for each **int** in a **ctl_table** array. When a match is found, the corresponding **child** table is recursively consulted (if the matching entry is a directory-type entry) or the entry is read and/or written (if it's a file-type entry).

38207: This, somewhat surprisingly, is the start of a loop that iterates for all elements of the integer array **name**. It would have been more conventional to wrap everything from here to line 38234 inside of a **for** loop, which might begin like this:

```
for ( ; nlen;
     ++name, --nlen,
     table = table->child)
```

(This would also require deleting lines 38208 and 38209, and replacing lines 38225 through 38228 with a **break**.) However, as you might expect, the version actually used generates better object code—much better, shaving 96 instructions to 82, with much of the gain coming where it does the most good, inside the inner loop. What's

more, where the naive version generates a normally taken branch in the inner loop, the kernel's version generates a normally untaken branch. (Recall that taken branches are expensive, so eliminating them from inner loops can yield significant speedups.) None of these differences between the naive version and the kernel's version is obvious from a casual perusal of the source code; finding them requires a careful analysis of the gcc-generated assembler code, showing that somebody lovingly refined this code.

38210: Reads the "name" (actually an integer) into **n**, so that it can be checked against the **ctl_name** of each table entry.

38212: Begins looping over all table entries, looking for one with the current name; the loop ends when the table is exhausted (**table->ctl_name** is 0) or when the named table entry has been found and processed.

38213: Checks whether the current **ctl_table**'s name matches the name being sought, or whether it has the special "wildcard" value, **CTL_ANY** (line 23930), which will match anything. **CTL_ANY** isn't currently used anywhere in the kernel source. It may be for future plans—I don't think it's a leftover from the past, because **CTL_ANY** wasn't used in the 2.0 or 2.2 kernels, either, and the whole **sysctl** interface only goes back to the development tree that preceded 2.0.

38216: If this table element has a **child**, it's a "directory."

38217: Following standard Unix behavior, checks the x (executable) bit of the directory to see whether the current process should be allowed to enter it. Observe that this is doing something very much like a file system, even though this is not the file system (/proc) interface. This is so that the two interfaces onto tunable kernel parameters will give consistent results. It would

be very surprising if the same user had permission to modify a kernel parameter through one interface but not the other.

38219: If the table entry has a **strategy** function, it might want to override the decision to allow the process to enter the directory. The **strategy** function is consulted and if it returns nonzero, the entire lookup is aborted.

38225: The directory has been entered. This effectively continues the outer loop, moving on to the next component of the name.

38230: This table node is a leaf node, so the kernel parameter has been found. Note that this doesn't bother checking whether the **name** array is on its final element (that is, whether **nlen** is now 1), although it's arguably some kind of error if it is not. Either way, **do_sysctl_strategy** (line 38240, covered in the next section) is given the responsibility of reading and/or writing the current table element.

38235: The **name** array was not empty, but its elements were exhausted before a leaf node was found. **parse_table** returns the **ENOTDIR** error, to signal a failure to find the named node.

do_sysctl_strategy

38240: **do_sysctl_strategy** reads and/or writes the data in a single **ctl_table**. The plan is to use the **strategy** member of the table element, if present, to do the read/write. If the table element doesn't have its own **strategy** routine, some generic read/write code is used instead. As you'll see, it doesn't work exactly as planned.

38247: If **oldval** is non-**NULL**, the caller is trying to read the old value, so the r bit is set in **op**. Similarly, the w bit is set if **newval** is non-**NULL**. Then line 38251 checks the permissions, and returns the **EPERM** error if the current process lacks the requisite permissions.

38254: If the table entry has its own **strategy** routine, the routine is given a chance to handle the read/write request. If it returns negative—an error—the error is passed up to the caller. If it returns positive, 0 (success) is passed up to the caller. If 0, the **strategy** routine declined to handle the request itself, and the default behavior will be used instead. (You can imagine a **strategy** routine that never returns anything but 0, which would still be useful if it does some other work, such as collecting statistics on how often it has been called.)

38267: This is the beginning of the generic read code. Observe that the return value of **get_user** (line 17121) is not checked. (Line 39016 also calls **get_user** without checking its return value, but it's okay in that case, as we'll see.)

38269: Ensures that no more data will be returned than is specified by the table entry's **maxlen** field.

38271: Copies the requested data from the table through **oldval**, and stores the amount of data actually written through **oldlenp**.

38279: Similarly to **oldlenp**, ensures that no more data may be written into the table entry than allowed by its **maxlen** member. Note that **table->data** might end up only partially updated if the **copy_from_user** call at line 38281 detects an error partway through.

38285: Returns 0 for success. This point is reached in any of three cases:

- The caller was trying neither to read nor write this table entry.

- The caller was trying to read and/or write this table entry, and all steps along the way were successful.

- The table entry has no associated data, or it's effectively read-only because its **maxlen** is 0.

The first of these cases is moderately surprising, and the last is more so. The first case is mildly surprising because calling **sysctl** without a

request to either read or write the named table entry doesn't make much sense, so that might legitimately be treated as an error. Still, it's generally consistent with the kernel's implementation of other system calls to treat a no-op request as no error. For example, **sys_brk** (line 42058), covered in Chapter 8, doesn't signal an error when the new **brk** value specified by the caller is the same as the old value.

The third case is more surprising than the first, because it really might reflect an error. Calling code might try to write to a parameter whose **maxlen** is 0, for instance, and think that the attempt succeeded, because the system call returns a success value. It would seem that this doesn't really matter, because a **maxlen** of 0 makes the entry useless anyway, but there is a table entry with a **maxlen** of 0—see line 37994. (Admittedly, this is the only such entry and it has a **NULL strategy**, so this case doesn't arise in the current kernel code.) Ultimately, it all comes down to how **sysctl** is documented and the man page is silent on this point. Still, I think **do_sysctl_strategy** should return the **EPERM** error in this case.

register_sysctl_table

38288: Inserts a new tree of **ctl_tables**, whose root is supplied, in the circularly linked list of trees.

38293: Allocates a **struct ctl_table_header** to manage the information about the new tree.

38297: If the allocation was successful, the new header is initialized.

38299: Inserts the new header (which tracks the new tree of arrays of **ctl_tables**) into the linked list of headers.

38306: Calls **register_proc_table** (line 38329, discussed earlier in the chapter) to register the new tree of tables under the /proc/sys directory. This is compiled out if the kernel is being compiled without support for the /proc file system.

38308: The newly allocated header is returned to the caller, so that the caller can later remove the tree by passing the header to **unregister_sysctl_table** (line 38312).

unregister_sysctl_table

38312: As previously stated, this simple function just removes a tree of **ctl_tables** from the kernel's circular list of such trees. It also removes the corresponding data from the /proc file system, if the kernel is being compiled with /proc support.

From glancing back at lines 38147 and 38161, you can see that **root_table_header** (line 37896)—the list node corresponding to **root_table**—is used as the beginning and end node when walking over the circular list of trees. You can see now that nothing in **unregister_sysctl_table** actually prevents **root_table_header** from being deleted from the table header list—it just isn't done.

sysctl_string

38950: **sysctl_string** is one of **ctl_table**'s strategy routines. As you'll recall, strategy routines may be called from line 38255 (in **do_sysctl_strategy**) to optionally override the default read/write code for a table entry. (Strategy routines can also be invoked from line 38220.)

38956: If the table has no associated data, or if the length of the accessible part is 0, the **ENOTDIR** error is returned. This is inconsistent with the behavior of **do_sysctl_strategy**, which returned success in the same case.

38968: The current string value is copied out to user space, and the result is NUL-terminated (this means that one more byte than specified by **lenp** can be copied out—which is possibly a bug, depending on the documentation). Because the current value is already NUL-terminated, these four lines of code could easily be reduced to two:

```
if (copy_to_user(oldval, table->data,
    len + 1))
    return -EFAULT;
```

The correctness of this change relies partly on three properties that the rest of the code observes when writing to **table->data**:

- The rest of the code won't copy more than **table->maxlen chars** into **table->data**. (This also makes the test at line 38966 unnecessary. Even if the test were necessary, it would need to check only **>**, not **>=**.)

- **table->data** is then NUL-terminated, overwriting the last copied-in byte, if necessary, so that the total length, including the NUL, is no more than **table->maxlen**.

- **table->maxlen** never changes.

Because all three of these properties hold, **len** will always be strictly less than **table->maxlen** at line 38968, and a terminating NUL byte must appear at or before **table->data[len + 1]**.

38976: Next, the new value is copied in from user space and the result is NUL-terminated. In this case, however, not copying the NUL byte from user space is the right thing to do, because it would be less efficient to copy it from user space than simply to assign the NUL to the appropriate byte of **data**. Also, this way, **table->data** is NUL-terminated even if the input wasn't. Of course, the string read from **newval** may be NUL-terminated already, in which case the assignment at line 38984 is superfluous. This is yet another case in which just doing the work is faster than checking whether it needs to be done.

38986: Returns 0 to indicate success. The return value should be positive, instead, so that line 38259 would interpret the result as a success. Instead, the calling code thinks **sysctl_string** wants default processing to occur and it proceeds to redundantly copy the data from user space again. On the other hand, returning nonzero here would make line 38222 think there had been an error when there really hadn't. This could be fixed, though.

sysctl_intvec

38993: **sysctl_intvec** is the other strategy routine defined in kernel/sysctl.c. (**sysctl_jiffies**, defined in this file at line 39027, is not used by any code included in the book, so it doesn't count. It's used by the networking subsystem, though.) **sysctl_intvec** ensures that if the caller is writing to the table entry, all **ints** being written lie within certain minimum and maximum values.

39000: If the new amount of data to write doesn't end on an **int**-sized boundary, it's invalid, so the attempt is rejected.

39003: If the table entry doesn't specify a set of maximum or minimum values, the input values can never be out of range, so the generic writing code in the caller (in **do_sysctl_strategy**, starting at line 38265) is good enough. In this case, **sysctl_intvec** returns 0.

39014: Begins a loop that ensures that all the values from the input array lie in the proper range.

39016: As I have already mentioned, this code doesn't check the return value of **get_user**—there's no compelling need to do so. If **sysctl_intvec** returns 0 (success) when an input memory location can't be read, **do_sysctl_strategy** will notice the problem when it tries to read the whole array. Alternately, if **get_user** can't read the memory location, garbage may end up in **value** and the value may be incorrectly rejected. In this latter case, the caller will get an **EINVAL** error rather than an **EFAULT** error, which is a minor bug.

39017: Note that this doesn't suffer from the bug that afflicts similar code at line 38720, where the parallel iteration over the minimum and maximum arrays could get out of sync.

39023: Returns 0 for success. This is not a mistake, as it was at line 38986, because **sysctl_intvec** doesn't write into **table->data**. The values read from user space are simply read into a temporary variable, range-checked, and then discarded; **do_sysctl_strategy** will do the one and only write to **table->data**.

Appendix A

GNU General Public License

Version 2, June 1991
Copyright (C) 1989, 1991 Free Software Foundation, Inc.
59 Temple Place, Suite 330, Boston, MA 02111-1307 USA

Everyone is permitted to copy and distribute verbatim copies of this license document, but changing it is not allowed.

Preamble

The licenses for most software are designed to take away your freedom to share and change it. By contrast, the GNU General Public License is intended to guarantee your freedom to share and change free software—to make sure the software is free for all its users. This General Public License applies to most of the Free Software Foundation's software and to any other program whose authors commit to using it. (Some other Free Software Foundation software is covered by the GNU Library General Public License instead.) You can apply it to your programs, too.

When we speak of free software, we are referring to freedom, not price. Our General Public Licenses are designed to make sure that you have the freedom to distribute copies of free software (and charge for this service if you wish), that you receive source code or can get it if you want it, that you can change the software or use pieces of it in new free programs; and that you know you can do these things.

To protect your rights, we need to make restrictions that forbid anyone to deny you these rights or to ask you to surrender the rights. These restrictions translate to certain responsibilities for you if you distribute copies of the software, or if you modify it.

For example, if you distribute copies of such a program, whether gratis or for a fee, you must give the recipients all the rights that you have. You must make sure that they, too, receive or can get the source code. And you must show them these terms so they know their rights.

We protect your rights with two steps: (1) copyright the software, and (2) offer you this license which gives you legal permission to copy, distribute and/or modify the software.

Also, for each author's protection and ours, we want to make certain that everyone understands that there is no warranty for this free software. If the software is modified by someone else and passed on, we want its recipients to know that what they have is not the original, so that any problems introduced by others will not reflect on the original authors' reputations.

Finally, any free program is threatened constantly by software patents. We wish to avoid the danger that redistributors of a free program will individually obtain patent licenses, in effect making the program proprietary. To prevent this, we have made it clear that any patent must be licensed for everyone's free use or not licensed at all.

The precise terms and conditions for copying, distribution and modification follow.

Terms and Conditions for Copying, Distribution and Modification

This License applies to any program or other work which contains a notice placed by the copyright holder saying it may be distributed under the terms of this General Public License. The "Program", below, refers to any such program or work, and a "work based on the Program" means either the Program or any derivative work under copyright law: that is to say, a work containing the Program or a portion of it, either verbatim or with modifications and/or translated into another language. (Hereinafter, translation is included without limitation in the term "modification".) Each licensee is addressed as "you".

Activities other than copying, distribution and modification are not covered by this License; they are outside its scope. The act of running the Program is not restricted, and the output from the Program is covered only if its contents constitute a work based on the Program (independent of having been made by running the Program). Whether that is true depends on what the Program does.

1. You may copy and distribute verbatim copies of the Program's source code as you receive it, in any medium, provided that you conspicuously and appropriately publish on each copy an appropriate copyright notice and disclaimer of warranty; keep intact all the notices that refer to this License and to the absence of any warranty; and give any other recipients of the Program a copy of this License along with the Program.

   You may charge a fee for the physical act of transferring a copy, and you may at your option offer warranty protection in exchange for a fee.

2. You may modify your copy or copies of the Program or any portion of it, thus forming a work based on the Program, and copy and distribute such modifications or work under the terms of Section 1 above, provided that you also meet all of these conditions:

   a) You must cause the modified files to carry prominent notices stating that you changed the files and the date of any change.

   b) You must cause any work that you distribute or publish, that in whole or in part contains or is derived from the Program or any part thereof, to be licensed as a whole at no charge to all third parties under the terms of this License.

   c) If the modified program normally reads commands interactively when run, you must cause it, when started running for such interactive use in the most ordinary way, to print or display an announcement including an appropriate copyright notice and a notice that there is no warranty (or else, saying that you provide a warranty) and that users may redistribute the program under these conditions, and telling the user how to view a copy of this License. (Exception: if the Program itself is interactive but does not normally print such an announcement, your work based on the Program is not required to print an announcement.)

These requirements apply to the modified work as a whole. If identifiable sections of that work are not derived from the Program, and can be reasonably considered independent and separate works in themselves, then this License, and its terms, do not apply to those sections when you distribute them as separate works. But when you distribute the same sections as part of a whole which is a work based on the Program, the distribution of the whole must be on the terms of this License, whose permissions for other licensees extend to the entire whole, and thus to each and every part regardless of who wrote it.

Thus, it is not the intent of this section to claim rights or contest your rights to work written entirely by you; rather, the intent is to exercise the right to control the distribution of derivative or collective works based on the Program.

In addition, mere aggregation of another work not based on the Program with the Program (or with a work based on the Program) on a volume of a storage or distribution medium does not bring the other work under the scope of this License.

3. You may copy and distribute the Program (or a work based on it, under Section 2) in object code or executable form under the terms of Sections 1 and 2 above provided that you also do one of the following:

a) Accompany it with the complete corresponding machine-readable source code, which must be distributed under the terms of Sections 1 and 2 above on a medium customarily used for software interchange; or,

b) Accompany it with a written offer, valid for at least three years, to give any third party, for a charge no more than your cost of physically performing source distribution, a complete machine-readable copy of the corresponding source code, to be distributed under the terms of Sections 1 and 2 above on a medium customarily used for software interchange; or,

c) Accompany it with the information you received as to the offer to distribute corresponding source code. (This alternative is allowed only for non-commercial distribution and only if you received the program in object code or executable form with such an offer, in accord with Subsection b above.)

The source code for a work means the preferred form of the work for making modifications to it. For an executable work, complete source code means all the source code for all modules it contains, plus any associated interface definition files, plus the scripts used to control compilation and installation of the executable. However, as a special exception, the source code distributed need not include anything that is normally distributed (in either source or binary form) with the major components (compiler, kernel, and so on) of the operating system on which the executable runs, unless that component itself accompanies the executable.

If distribution of executable or object code is made by offering access to copy from a designated place, then offering equivalent access to copy the source code from the same place counts as distribution of the source code, even though third parties are not compelled to copy the source along with the object code.

4. You may not copy, modify, sublicense, or distribute the Program except as expressly provided under this License. Any attempt otherwise to copy, modify, sublicense or distribute the Program is void, and will automatically terminate your rights under this License. However, parties who have received copies, or rights, from you under this License will not have their licenses terminated so long as such parties remain in full compliance.

5. You are not required to accept this License, since you have not signed it. However, nothing else grants you permission to modify or distribute the Program or its derivative works. These actions are prohibited by law if you do not accept this License. Therefore, by modifying or distributing the Program (or any work based on the Program), you indicate your acceptance of this License to do so, and all its terms and conditions for copying, distributing or modifying the Program or works based on it.

6. Each time you redistribute the Program (or any work based on the Program), the recipient automatically receives a license from the original licensor to copy, distribute or modify the Program subject to these terms and conditions. You may not impose any further restrictions on the recipients' exercise of the rights granted herein. You are not responsible for enforcing compliance by third parties to this License.

7. If, as a consequence of a court judgment or allegation of patent infringement or for any other reason (not limited to patent issues), conditions are imposed on you (whether by court order, agreement or otherwise) that contradict the conditions of this License, they do not excuse you from the conditions of this License. If you cannot distribute so as to satisfy simultaneously your obligations under this License and any other pertinent obligations, then as a consequence you may not distribute the Program at all. For example, if a patent license would not permit royalty-free redistribution of the Program by all those who receive copies directly or indirectly through you, then the only way you could satisfy both it and this License would be to refrain entirely from distribution of the Program.

If any portion of this section is held invalid or unenforceable under any particular circumstance, the balance of the section is intended to apply and the section as a whole is intended to apply in other circumstances.

It is not the purpose of this section to induce you to infringe any patents or other property right claims or to contest validity of any such claims; this section has the sole purpose of protecting the integrity of the free software distribution system, which is implemented by public license practices. Many people have made generous contributions to the wide range of software distributed through that system in reliance on consistent application of that system; it is up to the author/donor to decide if he or she is willing to distribute software through any other system and a licensee cannot impose that choice.

This section is intended to make thoroughly clear what is believed to be a consequence of the rest of this License.

8. If the distribution and/or use of the Program is restricted in certain countries either by patents or by copyrighted interfaces, the original copyright holder who places the Program under this License may add an explicit geographical distribution limitation excluding those countries, so that distribution is permitted only in or among countries not thus excluded. In such case, this License incorporates the limitation as if written in the body of this License.

9. The Free Software Foundation may publish revised and/or new versions of the General Public License from time to time. Such new versions will be similar in spirit to the present version, but may differ in detail to address new problems or concerns.

Each version is given a distinguishing version number. If the Program specifies a version number of this License which applies to it and "any later version", you have the option of following the terms and conditions either of that version or of any later version published by the Free Software Foundation.

If the Program does not specify a version number of this License, you may choose any version ever published by the Free Software Foundation.

10. If you wish to incorporate parts of the Program into other free programs whose distribution conditions are different, write to the author to ask for permission. For software which is copyrighted by the Free Software Foundation, write to the Free Software Foundation; we sometimes make exceptions for this. Our decision will be guided by the two goals of preserving the free status of all derivatives of our free software and of promoting the sharing and reuse of software generally.

No Warranty

11. BECAUSE THE PROGRAM IS LICENSED FREE OF CHARGE, THERE IS NO WARRANTY FOR THE PROGRAM, TO THE EXTENT PERMITTED BY APPLICABLE LAW. EXCEPT WHEN OTHERWISE STATED IN WRITING THE COPYRIGHT HOLDERS AND/OR OTHER PARTIES PROVIDE THE PROGRAM "AS IS" WITHOUT WARRANTY OF ANY KIND, EITHER EXPRESSED OR IMPLIED, INCLUDING, BUT NOT LIMITED TO, THE IMPLIED WARRANTIES OF MERCHANTABILITY AND FITNESS FOR A PARTICULAR PURPOSE. THE ENTIRE RISK AS TO THE QUALITY AND PERFORMANCE OF THE PROGRAM IS WITH YOU. SHOULD THE PROGRAM PROVE DEFECTIVE, YOU ASSUME THE COST OF ALL NECESSARY SERVICING, REPAIR OR CORRECTION.

12. IN NO EVENT UNLESS REQUIRED BY APPLICABLE LAW OR AGREED TO IN WRITING WILL ANY COPYRIGHT HOLDER, OR ANY OTHER PARTY WHO MAY MODIFY AND/OR REDISTRIBUTE THE PROGRAM AS PERMITTED ABOVE, BE LIABLE TO YOU FOR DAMAGES, INCLUDING ANY GENERAL, SPECIAL, INCIDENTAL OR CONSEQUENTIAL DAMAGES ARISING OUT OF THE USE OR INABILITY TO USE THE PROGRAM (INCLUDING BUT NOT LIMITED TO LOSS OF DATA OR DATA BEING RENDERED INACCURATE OR LOSSES SUSTAINED BY YOU OR THIRD PARTIES OR A FAILURE OF THE PROGRAM TO OPERATE WITH ANY OTHER PROGRAMS), EVEN IF SUCH HOLDER OR OTHER PARTY HAS BEEN ADVISED OF THE POSSIBILITY OF SUCH DAMAGES.

How to Apply These Terms to Your New Programs

If you develop a new program, and you want it to be of the greatest possible use to the public, the best way to achieve this is to make it free software which everyone can redistribute and change under these terms.

To do so, attach the following notices to the program. It is safest to attach them to the start of each source file to most effectively convey the exclusion of warranty; and each file should have at least the "copyright" line and a pointer to where the full notice is found.

```
<one line to give the program's name and
 a brief idea of what it does.>
Copyright (C) 19yy <name of author>

This program is free software; you can
redistribute it and/or modify it under the
terms of the GNU General Public License as
published by the Free Software Foundation;
either version 2 of the License, or
(at your option) any later version.

This program is distributed in the hope that
it will be useful, but WITHOUT ANY WARRANTY;
without even the implied warranty of
MERCHANTABILITY or FITNESS FOR A PARTICULAR
PURPOSE. See the GNU General Public License
for more details.

You should have received a copy of the GNU
General Public License along with this
program; if not, write to the Free Software
Foundation, Inc., 59 Temple Place, Suite
330, Boston, MA  02111-1307   USA
```

Also add information on how to contact you by electronic and paper mail.

If the program is interactive, make it output a short notice like this when it starts in an interactive mode:

```
Gnomovision version 69, Copyright (C) 19yy
name of author Gnomovision comes with
ABSOLUTELY NO WARRANTY; for details type
'show w'. This is free software, and you are
welcome to redistribute it under certain
conditions; type 'show c' for details.
```

The hypothetical commands 'show w' and 'show c' should show the appropriate parts of the General Public License. Of course, the commands you use may be called something other than 'show w' and 'show c'; they could even be mouse-clicks or menu items—whatever suits your program.

You should also get your employer (if you work as a programmer) or your school, if any, to sign a "copyright disclaimer" for the program, if necessary. Here is a sample; alter the names:

```
Yoyodyne, Inc., hereby disclaims all copy-
right interest in the program 'Gnomovision'
(which makes passes at compilers) written
by James Hacker.

<signature of Ty Coon>, 1 April 1989
Ty Coon, President of Vice
```

This General Public License does not permit incorporating your program into proprietary programs. If your program is a subroutine library, you may consider it more useful to permit linking proprietary applications with the library. If this is what you want to do, use the GNU Library General Public License instead of this License.

Index

What's on the CD-ROM

The companion CD-ROM for the *Linux Core Kernel Commentary, 2nd Edition* contains elements specifically selected to enhance the usefulness of this book, including:

- *linux-0.01*—The original Linux kernel distribution, dating from 1991—for historical interest.

- *linux-2.4.1*—The complete distribution of the version of the kernel code used in this book.

- *linux-2.4.5*—The latest stable kernel at the time the CD-ROM was prepared.

- Tags files for all of the included kernel distributions.

- *lckc_code*—All of the code included in this book, in a single large file with the lines numbered—exactly as it appears in the first part of this book.

- *lckc-find-line.el*—A short Emacs Lisp file that makes it easier to navigate lckc_code.

- A cross-reference listing for lckc_code, in a variety of formats:

  - *xref.pdf*—The cross-reference in Adobe's Portable Document Format (PDF).

  - *xref.ps*—The cross-reference in PostScript format.

  - *xref2.ps*—The cross-reference in 2-up PostScript format (two logical pages per physical page, to save paper when printing).

  - *xref.html*—The cross-reference in HTML format, usable directly from your favorite Web browser.

All of the above software is covered by the GNU General Public License (GPL), meaning that you're free to use, copy, or modify it to your heart's content.

System Requirements

Software

- To view the code, you can use any operating system capable of reading files from a CD-ROM. GNU/Linux, of course, will do nicely. However, compiling the code is easiest under GNU/Linux, so if you want to do that, you should have a functioning GNU/Linux system with gcc installed.

- Emacs, vi, or another tags-aware text editor will make it easier to browse the source code. (No text editor is included on this CD-ROM.)

Hardware

- There are no special CPU or RAM requirements to view the kernel code. (However, a CD-ROM drive is strongly recommended. It is hard to read the files on the CD using only your naked eye.)

- The code can be compiled on any system capable of running GNU/Linux. For compiling, an Intel (or equivalent) Pentium 133MHz processor is recommended, along with at least 16MB of RAM. Of course, another platform will do, but it should be of similar speed.

- If you just want to inspect the code, you can use all files directly from the CD-ROM, so no additional hard disk space is required. To compile a kernel, however, you will want to copy the source code to your hard disk, which takes approximately 130MB per kernel distribution (for the 2.4.x kernels). After compilation, this figure can rise to 150MB or more, depending on how the kernel was configured. If you also copy all of the tags files, those figures will rise to 290MB and 320MB, respectively.